THE [ ] E

GERMANY

OTHER AVAILABLE REAL GUIDES
**NEW YORK, MEXICO, PERU, FRANCE, SPAIN,
PORTUGAL, GREECE, KENYA, PARIS,
CALIFORNIA AND THE WEST COAST,
AMSTERDAM, AND MOROCCO**
FORTHCOMING
**ITALY, IRELAND, SCANDINAVIA,
YUGOSLAVIA, BRAZIL, AND HUNGARY**

REAL GUIDE CREDITS

Series Editor: Mark Ellingham
U.S. Text Editor: Marc Dubin
Editorial: Martin Dunford, John Fisher, Jack Holland
Production: Susanne Hillen
Typesetting: Greg Ward
Design: Andrew Oliver

Many **thanks** to all the regional and local offices of the **German Tourist Board** who helped with the research for this book: in particular Herr Stopperich and Frau Aschauer (Bavaria); Erhard Schlieter, Marianne Esch and Maria Antoinette Ritter (Cologne); Jürgen Mensendiek (Westphalia); Brigitte Kraft (Wuppertal); Isolde Engel (Darmstadt), Hans Wanger (Hameln); Sabine Mass (Rottweil); Peter Brodersen (Berlin) and Gunter Nischwitz (London).

For their invaluable help, encouragement and advice: Janet Barrie, Karin Patzelt, Claire Farrar, Claudia Köhn, Captain David Bartlett, Christoph Blacka, the Hohenleutner family, Helena Uren, Frau M. Meier-Ewert, Pam, Gianni Lancellotti, Victor, Erika Brettschneider-Bass, Colin Bass, Michael Prellberg, Helen McLachlan, Toby Morrhall, Ann Holland, Mary Foley, and Martin Dunford. Special editorial thanks must go to John Gawthrop, Jonathan Buckley, and (for input beyond the call of duty) Gordon McLachlan.

Thanks also to those who helped **produce** this book: Mick Sinclair, Wendy Ferguson, Marc Dubin, Wendy Reed, Andy Hilliard, Jamie Jensen, Rosie Ayliffe, Lou Mallard, Kate Berens, Greg Ward, and particularly Susanne Hillen for suffering the headaches and late nights. And three cheers for Jack Holland, who pulled it all together.

Published in the United States by Prentice Hall Trade Division, A Division of Simon & Schuster Inc., 15 Columbus Circle, New York NY 10023.

Typeset in Linotron Univers and Century Old Style.
Printed in the United States by R.R. Donnelley & Sons.
Illustrations in Part One and Part Three by Ed Briant; Basics illustration by Simon Fell;
Contexts illustration by David Loftus.

Includes index.

Library of Congress Cataloging-in-Publication Data

McLachlan, Gordon W.
The real guide: Germany / written and researched by Gordon W. McLachlan and Natascha Norton, with additional accounts by Jack Holland, John Gawthrop, Jackie Jones, Phil Lee, Janet Barry, and Claire Terry.
Edited by Jack Holland.
768p.
ISBN 0-13-783556-6
1. Germany (West)—Description and travel—1981—Guidebooks
2. Berlin (Germany)—Description—Guidebooks. I. Natascha Norton. II. Gordon W. McLachlan. III. Title.
DD258.42.M35 1989
914.304'878—dc20
89-37538
CIP

THE REAL GUIDE

GERMANY

WRITTEN AND RESEARCHED BY

GORDON McLACHLAN and NATASCHA NORTON

With additional accounts by
Jack Holland, John Gawthrop, Jackie Jones,
Phil Lee, Janet Barry, and Claire Terry.

Edited by
JACK HOLLAND

PRENTICE HALL ■ NEW YORK

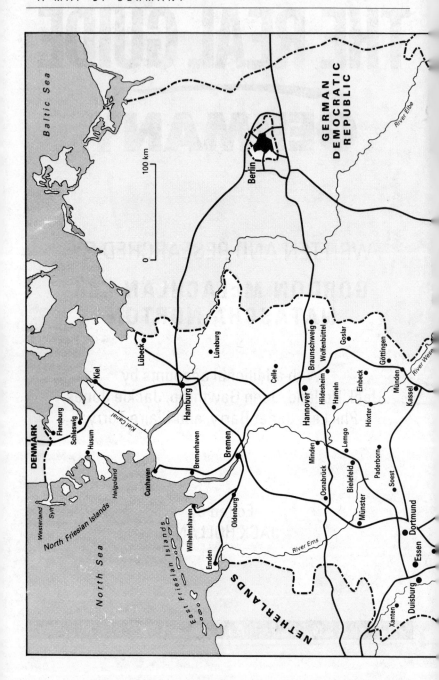

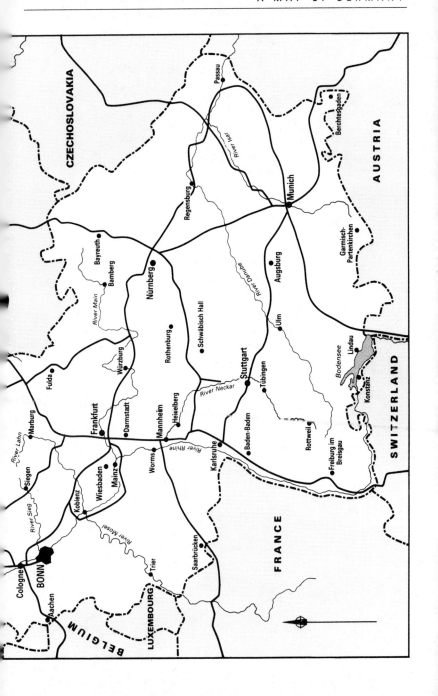

CONTENTS

Introduction viii

INTRODUCTION

Germany has always been the problem child of Europe. For over a thousand years the region was divided up into hundreds of separate states, kingdoms, and conquered territories, whose shifting alliances caused constant upheaval. When unification belatedly came about in 1871, the new nation was consumed by thirst for power and expansion abroad, which ended almost inevitably in World War I. The harsh reparations exacted by the victorious nations caused Germany years of economic hardship and social discontent which was ruthlessly exploited by the fervent nationalism and hypnotic rhetoric of the Nazi Party in their rise to power. After World War II the victors quarreled over how best to prevent Germany ever again becoming dominant, and ended up dividing the country in two. The western powers took control of the western parts, now the Federal Republic (the FDR or West Germany); the Soviet Union retained control over the eastern section, which is now the German Democratic Republic (the GDR or East Germany).

Traveling through the Federal Republic today, it's hard to believe that in 1945 Germany stood literally and metaphorically in ruins. Yet, within not much more than a decade, the western part—which was seen as the natural successor to the old Reich, if only on account of its size—had not only picked itself up by the bootstraps, but developed into what many outsiders regarded as a **model modern society**. A nation with little in the way of a liberal tradition, and even less of a democratic one, quickly developed a degree of political maturity that put other countries to shame. In atonement for past sins, the new state committed itself to providing a haven for foreign refugees and dissidents. It also quickly became a multiracial and multicultural society—even if the reason for this was less one of penance than the self-interested need to acquire extra cheap labor to fuel the economic boom. A delicate balance has been struck between the old and the new. Historic town centers have been immaculately restored, while the corporate skyscrapers and well-stocked department stores represent a commitment to a modern consumer society. Vast sums of money are lavished on preserving the best of the country's cultural legacy, yet equally generous budgets are allocated to encouraging all kinds of contemporary expression in the arts. In all, West Germany represents an uncanny mix of European tradition and American vitality.

For all its successes, the Federal Republic has had to face many crises, not least the building of the **Berlin Wall** in 1961 which provided a shocking manifestation of the division of the nation, as well as an embarrassing reminder of the moral brutality of the not-so-distant past. A wave of anarchist violence a decade later rocked the society to its roots, and necessitated unpleasant retaliatory measures which still leave a scar. Nonetheless, the country has proved remarkably resilient, demonstrating that its postwar "miracle" was by no means an aberration.

Yet the Federal Republic has never quite shaken off its identity crisis. Officially, it's a "provisional" state, biding its time before national re-unification occurs. Yet by now there's a realization that nobody outside Germany is really much in favor of this. "I love Germany so much I'm glad there are two of them", scoffed the French novelist François Mauriac, articulating the unspoken gut reactions of the powers on both sides of the Iron Curtain. German division may be cruel, but at least it has provided a lasting solution to the German "problem". The time will certainly come—perhaps sooner rather than later, given the lightning developments in super-power relations—when German re-unification is a feasible option. Even so, this can be no more than the nineteenth-century concept of a *Kleines Deutschland* ("little Germany"): Austria, for centuries the dominant force in the nation's affairs, would not be included in the equation, far less the "lost" Eastern Territories, which are now firmly part of Poland, Czechoslovakia, and the Soviet Union.

In total contrast to all this is Germany's **romantic image**. This is the land of fairy-tale castles, of thick dark forests, of the legends collected by the Brothers Grimm, of perfectly preserved timber-framed medieval towns, and of jovial locals swilling from huge foaming mugs of beer. As always, there *is* some truth in these stereotypes, though most of them are conditioned by the southern part of the country, particularly **Bavaria**, which, as a predominantly rural and Catholic area, stands apart from the urbanized Protestant northern part of the country which engineered the unity of the nation and thereafter dominated its affairs.

Regional characteristics, indeed, are a strong feature of German life, and there are many hangovers from the days when the country was a political patchwork, even though some historical provinces have vanished from the map, and others have merged. More detail on each of the current Länder, as the constituent states are now known, can be found in the chapter introductions. **Hamburg** and **Bremen**, for example, retain their age-old status as free cities. The imperial capital, **Berlin**, also stands apart, not only physically as an island in the midst of the GDR, but also in terms of its continued status as an occupied city, which has still not been integrated into the Federal Republic. In polar opposition to it, and as a corrective to the normal view of the Germans as an essentially moribund race, is the **Rhineland**, where the great river's majestic sweep has spawned a particularly rich fund of legends and folklore, and where the locals are imbued with a Mediterranean sense of fun.

Where And When To Go

There's enough variety within all but the smallest Länder to fill several weeks of travel, and you may prefer to confine your trip to just one or two regions. Among the **scenic highlights** are the Bavarian Alps, the Bodensee, the Black Forest, and the valleys of the Rhine and Mosel. There are also many areas of less spectacular natural beauty, which can be found in every province—these are the places the Germans themselves love the most, and where so many spend their holidays and weekends. Several of the cities have the air of capitals, though **Bonn**, the actual seat of government, barely fills the role, being a deliberately crass choice for the role in line with the "temporary" nature of the state. Nearby **Cologne**, on the other hand, is one of the most characterful cities in the country, and the richest in historic monuments. Bavaria's capital, **Munich**, is another obvious star, boasting of having the best the country has to offer—whether in museums, beer, fashion or sport. **Berlin** has an atmosphere at times electrifying, at times disturbing, while **Nürnberg** reflects on its bygone years. **Frankfurt** looks on itself as the "real" capital of the country; **Stuttgart** and **Düsseldorf** compete for the title of champion of German postwar success. However, as all these cities have suffered to a considerable extent from bomb damage and ugly postwar redevelopment, the smaller places in many respects offer a richer experience. There's nowhere in Germany as well-loved as the university city of **Heidelberg**, star and guiding light of the Romantic movement. Bamberg, Regensburg, Rothenburg, and Marburg are among the many towns which deserve to be regarded among the most outstanding in Europe.

The best **times to come** are between April and October. Germany has a fairly volatile climate, not so very different from New England's. Summers are usually warm, but not overpoweringly so; good weather may come at an unexpected time, while it's not uncommon to have several abrupt changes in temperature within a single day. Rain occurs fairly regularly throughout the year. Unless you're intending to go skiing, winter travel can't really be recommended, other than for seeing the cities stripped of tourist hordes. Otherwise, there's a chance of snow at any time from November onwards. In the really popular areas, the claustrophobic effect of masses of organized tour groups is a factor to be taken into account between mid-June and mid-September: best avoid such places altogether then, and head for the many less spoiled alternatives. All things considered, however, the ideal times for visiting Germany are late spring and early autumn.

AVERAGE TEMPERATURES (F)

		Berlin	Frankfurt	Hamburg	Munich
January	Max.	48	50	36	35
	Min.	10	14	28	23
February	Max.	52	54	37	38
	Min.	10	16	28	23
March	Max.	63	66	44	48
	Min.	19	25	31	30
April	Max.	72	75	55	56
	Min.	28	32	38	38
May	Max.	82	84	64	64
	Min.	36	37	46	45
June	Max.	86	88	69	70
	Min.	43	45	51	51
July	Max.	90	91	73	74
	Min.	48	50	55	36
August	Max.	88	90	72	73
	Min.	46	48	54	55
September	Max.	82	82	66	67
	Min.	39	41	49	54
October	Max.	70	70	55	62
	Min.	30	32	43	48
November	Max.	55	59	45	56
	Min.	25	27	37	40
December	Max.	50	52	39	44
	Min.	16	19	31	33

To convert °Fahrenheit to °Centigrade subtract 32 and multiply by 5/9

Rainfall is consistent throughout the year for all the above cities, at 2–3 inches per month; only Munich exceeds this, with an average 4–6 inches per month in summer.

PART ONE

THE

BASICS

GETTING THERE

West Germany is the destination of many airlines from North America, not least because of the large, continued U.S. military presence there. Prices are accordingly competitive, and unless you're coming from Canada there's no financial advantage to stopping off in London first. Frankfurt is Europe's second largest airport after London's Heathrow, and most international flights will arrive there. Munich, Hamburg, Berlin, Stuttgart, and Düsseldorf are the alternate gateways, in roughly that order.

DIRECT FROM THE USA

There is direct service from various U.S. cities, usually without the necessity of hubbing through New York. Discounters advertising in the Sunday travel sections have the most competitive fares, often for consolidated seats on major airlines rather than on charter companies. Student/youth agencies can also be worth contacting if you can meet their conditions. Given the wealth of budget options, the APEX offerings of the major carriers will probably be of only passing interest.

EASTERN AND CENTRAL STATES

Seat consolidator prices begin at around $180 one-way, $340 round-trip on the **New York-Frankfurt** route; come summer you should count on paying well over $250 one-way, and almost $600 round-trip to the same port of entry. Special offers to Munich, Stuttgart, Berlin, and Hamburg are also commonly available and only marginally

more expensive (if at all). Among the more consistent outlets to be found in the *New York Times* Sunday travel supplement are *Access International*, 250 W. 57th St., Suite 511, New York, NY 10107, ☎212/333-7280 or ☎800/333-7280, and *TFI*, 34 W. 32nd St., New York, NY 10001, ☎212/736-1140 or ☎800/223-6363. Fares from **Chicago** or **Washington, D.C.** through the same or similar agencies are little different; check the travel pages of the *Chicago Tribune* and the *Washington Post* respectively. You can even find quotes of $450 round-trip (low-season) in the *Miami Herald*.

Among the **student/youth agencies**, *STN* offers one-way fares to Frankfurt, Berlin, Munich, Nuremberg, and Stuttgart from New York for between $220 and $325 depending on the season; these tend to be on scheduled airlines with some flexibility in ticket conditions. *CIEE* tends to be more restrictive about whom they sell to but price-wise they have a slight edge on high-season round-trips: roughly $550 out of New York, $590 from Boston, $630 leaving Washington, D.C., and $798 out of Atlanta.

All of the major carriers flying into Germany offer **APEX** fares, but bedeviled as these are with the usual restrictions they will not be too attractive to non-business customers. One company worth checking out is **LTU** (☎800/888-0200), which bills itself as "Germany's other airline"; they quote low-season round-trip fares of $399 from New York to Frankfurt, Munich, or Düsseldorf.

Lufthansa (☎800/645-3880) flies from more than a half-dozen cities east of the Mississippi to Frankfurt, with immediate connection to other German cities (no stopover allowed) for only a few dollars more, but even so the fare structure is hardly tempting. Youth (under 25) and Super-APEX (7-to-21 days) round-trips out of New York run $480 to $600 depending on the season, with weekend surcharges applicable. Ninety-day APEX tickets cost $600 (low) to $850 (high).

Many other airlines link the eastern USA with the Federal Republic; in terms of direct service between **less busy parts** of each country, *Delta* (☎800/221-1212) is probably the most useful, with their flights hubbing through **Atlanta** en route to Munich, Hamburg, and Stuttgart. The low-to-high-season fare spread is $570 to $940.

CIEE ADDRESSES IN THE U.S.

Head Office: 205 E. 42nd St., New York, NY 10017; ☎800/223-7401

CALIFORNIA
2511 Channing Way, Berkeley, CA 94704; ☎415/848-8604
UCSD Student Center, B-023, La Jolla, CA 92093; ☎619/452-0630
5500 Atherton St., Suite 212, Long Beach, CA 90815; ☎213/598-3338
1093 Broxton Ave., Los Angeles, CA 90024; ☎213/208-3551
4429 Cass St., San Diego, CA 92109; ☎619/270-6401
312 Sutter St., San Francisco, CA 94108; ☎415/421-3473
919 Irving St., San Francisco, CA 94122; ☎415/566-6222
14515 Ventura Blvd., Suite 250, Sherman Oaks, CA 91403; ☎818/905-5777

GEORGIA
12 Park Place South, Atlanta, GA 30303; ☎404/577-1678

ILLINOIS
29 E. Delaware Place, Chicago, IL 60611; ☎312/951-0585

MASSACHUSETTS
79 South Pleasant St., 2nd Floor, Amherst, MA 01002; ☎413/256-1261

729 Boylston St., Suite 201, Boston, MA 02116; ☎617/266-1926
1384 Massachusetts Ave., Suite 206, Cambridge, MA 02138; ☎617/497-1497

MINNESOTA
1501 University Ave. SE, Room 300, Minneapolis, MN 55414; ☎612/379-2323

NEW YORK
35 W. 8th St., New York, NY 10011; ☎212/254-2525
Student Center, 356 West 34th St., New York, NY 10001; ☎212/661-1450

OREGON
715SW Morrison, Suite 1020, Portland, OR 97205; ☎503/228-1900

RHODE ISLAND
171 Angell St., Suite 212, Providence, RI 02906; ☎401/331-5810

TEXAS
1904 Guadalupe St., Suite 6, Austin, TX 78705; ☎512/472-4931
The Executive Tower, 3300 W. Mockingbird, Suite 101, Dallas,TX 75235; ☎214/350-6166

WASHINGTON
1314Northeast 43rd St., Suite 210, Seattle, WA 98105; ☎206/632-2448

WEST COAST

A scan of the Sunday travel pages of either the *Los Angeles Times* or the *San Francisco Examiner/Chronicle* will reveal any number of consolidator deals out of the respective cities. Rock-bottom one-way to **Frankfurt** from California will set you back $310, perhaps $470 round-trip; a pairing of $340/$640 would seem more realistic. For somewhat more, i.e. $380 one-way/$660 round-trip, you can fly to Munich, Hamburg, or Stuttgart with the consolidators. The most conspicuous franchise seems to be *Airkit* 16 California St., San Francisco, CA 94111 (☎415/362-1106), or 1125 W. 6th St., Los Angeles, CA 90017 (☎213/482-8778).

Offerings of the two major **student/youth** agencies are fairly similar, but *STN*, in addition to the usual add-on program (roughly $100 each way) to the basic fare out of New York, offer **direct polar flights** to Frankfurt from Seattle, San Francisco, or Los Angeles for $300–375 each way depending on the time of year.

Lufthansa has flights hubbing through Frankfurt from Los Angeles, San Francisco, Dallas, Houston, and Anchorage, but again the youth/Super-APEX fares ($680 low season, over $800 high season) and the normal APEX ($850/$1050 low/high) are fairly steep and none of the other scheduled airlines are likely to significantly undercut these figures.

DIRECT FROM CANADA

The news is mostly bad, and you may be better off flying to London or making your way to New York and jumping off from there.

Many flights offered through the student/youth agency *Travel Cuts* may in fact involve a mandatory change in London. Best selection is out of **Toronto**, with one-ways to Frankfurt starting at CDN$400, round-trips at CDN$500; from Montreal count on CDN$625 to CDN$825 round-trip depending on the season, and from **Vancouver** budget CDN$750 to CDN$1100 (one-ways exist from B.C. for about CDN$500).

The lure of *Lufthansa's* extensive route network out of Canada—flights from Vancouver, Calgary, Toronto, and Montreal—is dulled somewhat by the absence of youth fares and the usual weekend surcharges. Still, they are not that much more than the nominally discounted *CUTS* prices. Expect to pay CDN$660 for a low-season APEX out of Montreal, CDN$930 high-season; from Vancouver, CDN$880 versus CDN$1180. *Air Canada's* fares are likely to be indistinguishable.

VIA GREAT BRITAIN

FLIGHTS

There's not much cost advantage for U.S.-based individuals to break their journey in Britain. Many of the air-fare deals available tend to be on scheduled airlines plying long-haul routes between the USA and the Gulf States which happen to stop in London. In London try the *German Travel Centre* (8 Earlham St., London WC2 ☎01/379-5212); recent sample round-trip fares, with little seasonal variation, included Düsseldorf for £69; Frankfurt for £63; Hamburg for £79; Munich for £105; and Berlin for £104.

Other flights are with charter or quasicharter companies such as *Dan Air*, *Air Europe*, and *Monarch*. For current outlets, consult—if you've arrived in London—the travel ads in the Sunday newspapers, weekly magazines such as *Time Out* or the many freebie streetcorner publications. Count on saving up to twenty percent off of the prices cited above, but with a corresponding decrease in flexibility.

TRAINS

Unless you qualify for one of the discounts cited below, there's no financial advantage in traveling to Germany by train; a plane or bus is always cheaper compared to full fare. The only exceptions to this are the **European Saver** round-trips offered to Hamburg (£54); Bonn, Cologne, and Düsseldorf (£59 each), and Dortmund (£65), but these limit you to just four days at your destination.

Rail travel is more economically feasible if you're a **student**, **under 26**, or **over 60**. Those in the first two categories qualify for the discounted tickets offered by **Eurotrain** (52 Grosvenor Gardens, London SW1 ☎01/730-3402). You can realize savings of up to 25 percent of the full round-trip fare, but even then you will still probably pay slightly more than for a discounted flight.

Another cash-saving possibility for those under 26 (and resident in Europe at least six months) is the **InterRail** pass, currently sold for £145 at any major London train station. This entitles the bearer to one month's travel on most European (and Moroccan) railways, and allows half off on British trains and some cross-channel ferries. Obviously this will pay for itself most by its use on Germany's extensive domestic train system (see "Getting Around" below).If you're 60 or over, the **Rail Europ Senior Card** is your entree to a program very similar to InterRail; details from any British Rail Travel Centre.

Note that **EurRail**, the North American answer to InterRail, is nowhere near as good a bargain unless you plan to virtually live on German (and other European) trains during the month or two of its validity.

Routes from London Victoria are served at least daily and cross the channel to Belgian Ostend or to the Hook of Holland. Once on the other side, connections are simple and quick.

BUSES

Once again, you can pay the same as for a flight, with considerably less comfort. Depending on the destination city, services are run three to seven times a week, winter and summer, with no seasonal fare variation. All vehicles are run by **Eurolines** (52 Grosvenor Gardens, London SW1 ☎01/730-0202) from the Victoria Coach Station. Student, youth, or other discount bus fares are advertised but with small savings.

DRIVING OR HITCHING

If you intend to set out from Britain to Europe with your own vehicle, the first step is to choose a channel crossing. There is only one direct UK-Germany ferry, linking Harwich and Hamburg from mid-March to the end of September (*Scandinavian Seaways*, 15 Hanover St., London W1 ☎01/493-6696). It's a 21-hour trip costing a minimum of £55—far more in high season, on weekends, or with a car. This route makes most sense if you're heading for northern Germany or Berlin.

If your interest lies in the Rhineland and the south, it's better to take one of the **shorter channel crossings** by boat or hovercraft from Dover, Folkestone, or Ramsgate to Boulogne, Calais, or Dunkerque in France, or to Ostend/Zeebrugge in Belgium, or from Harwich/Hull to the Hook of Holland/Rotterdam. Costs work out at about £13 per person and £53 for a motor vehicle

in summer, or about £170 for two people and a car on the hovercraft. In general, however, what you save on the shorter crossings will be neutralized by the extra gasoline costs.

Sealink has services from Dover (☎0304/210-755) and Folkestone (☎0303/42954); *P & O* from Dover (☎0304/203388); *Hoverspeed* from Dover (☎0304/214-514 and in London ☎01/554-7061); *Sally Lines* from Ramsgate (☎0843/595-5222 or in London ☎01/409-2240); and *North Sea Ferries* from Hull (☎0492/795-141).

Once across, expressways, especially through Holland or Belgium, allow speedy transit to points in the Federal Republic: three hours to Cologne, seven to Frankfurt, twelve to Munich.

Hitchhikers who start thumbing in the UK will almost certainly have to pay their ferry passage anyway, so they may as well buy a bus or boat ticket to Ostend or the Hook of Holland and begin hitching there. Then again, if you have some money but not a lot, you'd possibly be best off **ridesharing**. The German *Mitfahrzentrale* (Ridesharing Centers — see "Getting Around") organization has an office near London, at 50-60 Grant Place, Croydon CR0 6PJ (☎01/654-3210), and numerous branches throughout Germany. For a small fee the staff puts drivers and riders together and stipulates the latters' contribution for gas; the total outlay for a London–Munich ride, for instance, would be DM88.

RED TAPE AND VISAS

U.S. and Canadian citizens need only a valid passport to enter the Federal Republic of Germany. For a touristic visit no visa in advance is required; you'll merely be given a ninety-day date stamp in your passport on arrival (and guards at many land crossings tend to be lax about this).

If you know that your stay will be longer than this, apply for an extension visa from the nearest West German embassy or consulate *before* you go. In order to extend a stay once in the country,

all visitors should contract the *Ausländeramt* (Alien's Bureau) in the nearest large town; addresses are in the phone book.

To **work in Germany**, North Americans must obtain a guarantee of a job from a German employer *before* arrival in order to get a **work permit**, which must be applied for at the nearest German embassy or consulate. For casual labor during harvests or in the hotel and catering trades, nobody will ask too many questions, but wages are accordingly low and the work tough.

GERMAN EMBASSIES AND CONSULATES

USA
Embassy: 4645 Reservoir Rd. NW, Washington, D.C. 20007-1998, ☎202/298-4000
Consulates: Atlanta, Boston, Chicago, Detroit, Houston, Los Angeles, Miami, New Orleans, New York, San Francisco, and Seattle.

CANADA
Embassy: P.O.B. 379, Post Station A, Ottawa, Ont. K1N 8V4, ☎613/232-1101
Consulates: Edmonton, Montreal, Toronto, Vancouver

COSTS, MONEY AND BANKS

Germany is one of the most industrialized and wealthiest consumer societies in the world, and its currency, the Deutchsmark, is one by which international financial standards are set. It's also a cash society— people carry money with them, rather than rely on credit cards. In the face of these facts, it's surprising that this is a country that's affordable to travel in, with the reasonable price of food and accommodation helping keep costs down.

COSTS

If you're prepared to cut corners by staying in youth hotels or campgrounds, and never eating out, you could get by on a minimum of DM30 ($17) per day, though DM50–60 is a much more realistic budget on which to enjoy yourself properly. If you have the means to spend a bit more than that, you should be able to live really well.

Accommodation costs can be confined to an average of about DM15 per day for youth hostels, around DM25 for rooms in private houses, and around DM25–35 for basic guest houses and hotels: there's rarely anything saved by taking a double room.

Though **food** prices in shops are similar to those in North America, eating out is markedly cheaper at every level. Snack bars abound, and for around DM8 you can put together a very filling meal. DM20 should buy a hearty German meal plus drink in a pub-restaurant, while a decent dinner in a classy restaurant can often be had for DM30, or not much more. **Drink** is

marginally more expensive than in North America, but the quality, especially of the beer, is significantly higher.

Public transit is the one area where prices are likely to present a problem. A single fare within a city is often as high as DM2.50, while a sample single train fare from Munich to Frankfurt would be DM85. The only ways in which you can soften these costs are to utilize rail and other passes or make use of the organized alternative, the *Mitfahrzentralen* (see Getting Around).

MONEY

West German currency is the *Deutschmark*, which comes in **notes** of DM10, DM20, DM50, DM100, DM500, and DM1000; **coins** of DM0.01 (one *Pfennig*), DM0.02, DM0.05, DM0.10, DM0.20, DM0.50, DM1, DM2 and DM5. You can bring as much currency as you wish into Germany.

TRAVELER'S CHECKS AND CREDIT CARDS

Traveler's checks are the safest way of carrying the majority of your money. They can be cashed in banks or exchange offices, and used in flasher shops in larger cities. Unusually, for such a consumer-oriented society, **credit cards** are little used: only the major cards will be known and accepted, and then only in department stores or upscale restaurants in the larger cities.

Should you need **cash** on your plastic, the *Deutsches Verkehrsbank* (see below) will give a cash advance against *Visa* and *Master Card* cards, subject to a DM100 minimum. Various other banks offer cash advance facilities—look for stickers in their windows to find out which credit card they're associated with. *American Express* card holders can use that company's facilities in the major cities.

BANKS

Banking hours are Monday to Friday 9am–noon and 1:30–3:30pm, though these are often extended. If you're on a tight budget, it may be worth shopping around several banks, (including the savings banks or *Sparkasse*), as the rates of exchange offered can vary, as can the amount of commission deducted. The latter tends to be a flat rate, meaning that small-scale transactions should be avoided whenever possible.

Exchange facilities for cash and traveler's cheques can be found in virtually all banks as well as in commercial exchange shops called *Wechselstuben*, usually located near stations and airports, though often also in city centers, on the main shopping street. The *Deutsches Verkehrsbank* has branches in railroad stations of most main cities; these are generally (but not invariably) open seven days a week, and until quite late in the evening.

HEALTH AND INSURANCE

For minor complaints, or to just get a prescription filled, you need to go to an *Apotheke*; German pharmacists are well-trained and often speak English. *Apotheken* (pl) able to fill **overseas prescriptions** can be found in most large cities—and very likely in any community near an American military installations. A list of **after-hours** or **all-night Apotheken** in larger towns is posted on the door of each *Apotheke*.

German **doctors** are likely to be English-speaking, and to provide care of at least the level you are accustomed to, but if you want to be certain, your consulate can provide a list of English-speaking doctors in the major cities. In the event of an **emergency** anywhere in the country, phone ☎110 for the police, who will then summon an ambulance.

INSURANCE

The Federal Republic of Germany has no recipro-cal health care agreements with either the USA or Canada, and with cost of care equalling or exceeding that at home, it would be wise to look into medical coverage beforehand. Before you purchase special **travel insurance**, whether for medical or property mishaps, check that you won't duplicate any **existing plans** which you may have. For example, **Canadians** are usually covered for medical expenses by their provincial

health plans (but may only be reimbursed after the fact). Holders of **ISIC** cards are entitled to $2000 worth of accident coverage and sixty days ($100 per diem) of hospital in-patient benefits for the period during which the card is valid. **Students** will often find that their student health coverage extends for one term beyond the date of last enrollment. Bank and charge **accounts** (particularly American Express) often have certain levels of medical or other insurance included. One item which tends to be excluded by home-based insurance, however, is transportation by ambulance—this can get very expensive if you're not specifically covered. **Homeowners' or rent-ers'** insurance often covers theft or loss of docu-ments, money, and valuables while overseas though exact conditions and maximum amounts vary from company to company.

Only after exhausting the possibilities above might you want to contact a specialist travel insurance company; your travel agent can usually recommend one. Travel insurance offerings are quite comprehensive, anticipating everything from charter companies going bankrupt to delayed or lost baggage, by way of sundry illnesses and accidents. If you've purchased any sort of discounted air ticket, whether APEX, char-ter, or a consolidated seat, these tend to be non-refundable and often date-inflexible; thus it would be wise to consider a trip cancellation policy if nothing else; this will entitle you to compensation should you be unable to use your ticket(s) on the specified dates.

Premiums vary widely, from the very reason-able ones offered primarily through student/youth agencies (though available to anyone), to those so expensive that the price tag for anything more than two months of coverage will probably equal the cost of the worst possible combination of disasters. Note also that very few insurers will arrange on-the-spot payments in the event of a major expense or loss; you will usually be reim-bursed only after going home.

A most important thing to keep in mind—and a source of major disappointment to would-be claimants—is that *none* of the policies currently available insure against **theft** of *anything* while overseas. (Americans have been easy pickings for foreign thieves—naivete on the part of the former, an all-Americans-are-rich attitude among the latter led to companies going broke paying robbery/burglary claims.) North American travel policies apply only to items **lost** from, or

damaged in, the custody of an identifiable, responsible third party, i.e. hotel porter, airline, luggage consignment, etc. Even then, you will still have to contact the local police to have a complete report made out so that your insurer can process the claim. In addition, time limits for submitting claims often apply, so promptness in getting back to your insurer is essential.

INFORMATION AND MAPS

Before you leave, it's worth contacting the nearest branch of the German National Tourist Office, which has extensive information on campgrounds, youth hostels, hotels, train timetables, and many glossy brochures besides. Branches in North America include:

747 Third Avenue West, **New York**, NY 10017; ☎212/308-3300

44 S. Flower St., Suite 220, **Los Angeles**, CA 90017; ☎213/668-7332

Place Bonaventure, **Montréal**, Québec H5A 1B8; ☎514/8778-9885

ON-THE-SPOT INFORMATION

This is rarely a problem in Germany. You'll find **tourist offices** everywhere, even in tiny villages, and they're almost universally friendly and very efficient, providing large amounts of maps, useful literature, and glossy brochures in various languages. A few places charge for these, but the majority provide them free. The German word for a tourist office is *Fremden-verkehrsamt* (or just

Verkehrsamt) though many sport a sign saying *Tourist Information*. Another useful facility is that they can book a room for you, for which there's normally a small fee (see "Sleeping"). Addresses of relevant offices are listed in the guide. The **German National Travel Agency** is universally represented by the *DER* offices, generally to be found near train stations or next to tourist offices. They'll reserve your national and international train tickets, as well as provide general information about travel onwards from Germany. It's worth knowing that there's a *DER* office in London at 18 Conduit St., W1R 9TD (☎01 499 0577).

MAPS

German **maps** set international standards, and there's no shortage of excellent regional, car touring and hiking maps in most bookshops, newsstands and tourist offices. The best general maps are those printed by *RV* or *Kümmerly and Frey*, whose 1:500,000 map is the most detailed single sheet of the country available.

Specialist maps marking cycling routes or Alpine hikes can be bought in the relevant regions, and addresses for written or personal inquiries are listed in the guide. Information on German **Alpine climbs and hikes** can be obtained from the *Deutscher Alpenverein*, Prater Insel 5, 8000 München 22. Other useful reference guides available are: *Fahrrad-Atlas* (DM14.95), the best for bike routes in Germany; and *Mitfahrzentralen in Europa* (DM6), which is in three languages and lists all hiking agencies, their fees, and regional accommodation options. If you'd like to order these books before commencing on your journey write to *DJH-Hauptverband*, Postfach 220, 4930 Detmold. In the USA, the best selections of maps are at *Pacific Travellers Supply* 529 State St., Santa Barbara CA. 93101 (☎805/963-4438) or at any branch of *Rand McNally*.

GETTING AROUND

While it may not be cheap, getting around Germany is spectacularly quick and easy. Barely a square inch of the country is untouched by an unfailingly reliable public transit system and driving, too, is a painless, straightforward affair (once you've adapted to the high speeds) on what's probably the best road network on the continent. Other forms of travel are equally well-organized and it's a simple matter to jump from train to bus on the integrated network. Costs can be offset by the special summer discounts available to visitors, and it's worth studying all the options outlined below before committing yourself.

TRAINS

By far the best form of public transit in Germany are trains: the **rail network**, operated by the national company *Deutsche Bundesbahn (DB)*, covers most of the country and where natural obstacles or a sparse population make rail routes unrealistic, *DB's* buses (*Bahnbusse*, see below) take over. North–south travel is particularly straightforward, while east–west journeys are likely to be less direct and require a change of train (or bus) along the way. Everywhere services are fairly punctual (except on Sunday, when slight delays are commonplace) and very efficient, although generally as expensive as their equivalents in the North America, averaging about DM20 per 100km.

There are several **types of train**: the fastest and most comfortable, and therefore the best option between major cities, are the **InterCity (IC)** and **EuroCity (EC)** trains (identical except that the *ECs* cross international borders). With these you can travel from one end of the country

to the other—Hamburg to Munich, for example, takes 6½ hours. The only drawback is the supplement (*Zuschlag*) of DM7 (or DM6 if you buy it at the station before boarding the train), which is compulsory unless you've already invested in a *DB-Tourist Card* (see below).

Slightly downscale from the *IC*s and *ECs* are the new *InterRegio (IR)* trains offering a swift service between smaller centers—and charging a DM4 supplement for journeys of under 50km. As yet, however, only a few *IR*'s are up and running and you're more likely to be traveling on the rolling stock they're designed to replace—the relatively cumbersome *D-Zug*. Slowest of the lot are the ambling *E-Zug* trains, which seem to stop at every milk churn. Around major cities, the *S-Bahn* is a commuter network on which **InterRail** cards and the *DB-Tourist Card* are valid, but neither can be used on the underground U-Bahn system, or on municipally-owned trams and buses.

Plan your route using the free national time-table (*Städteverbindungen*) which the German National Tourist Office, the DER Travel Service or any North American travel agent specializing in Germany will give you, or which you pick up at the information counter at any big German railroad station.

TICKET TYPES

Regular tickets (*Fahrkarten*) are valid for two months and permit you to break the journey as often as you wish. Prices are based on distance traveled and therefore a round-trip fare will cost the same as two one-ways. If you're making a lot of rail journeys, it's extremely sensible to buy one of the two **discount passes** exclusively for foreigners, and available from a number of agents around the country, or at most large German railroad stations.

The most flexible pass is the **DB Tourist Card** (*Touristenkarte*) which entitles the holder to unlimited travel on all trains and *Bahnbusse* in the country, on the buses which ply the tourist-orientated "scenic routes" such as *Burgenstrasse* ("Castle Road"), *Rhein-Mosel*, *Romantische Strasse* ("Romantic Road") and *Schwarzwald Hochstrasse* ("Black Forest Highway"), and the K-D Line steamers on the Mosel and on the Rhine between Cologne and Mainz (see "By Boat", below). For return visits to Berlin with this ticket you need to pay a DM50 supplement *before* commencing your journey.

Valid for four, nine or sixteen days and costing approximately DM180, DM270, and DM360 respectively respectively, the *DB-Tourist Card* can be excellent value. There is a slightly cheaper version for those **under 26**, rather demeaningly known as the **DB Junior Tourist Card** (*Juniortouristenkarte*), which offers the same benefits but is only available in nine or sixteen day form, for DM 180 and DM 240 respectively.

More localized but still temptingly priced, the **DB Regional Rail Rover** (*Tourenkarten*) gives unlimited travel on trains and *Bahnbusse* for any 10 days out of 21 in a specific area of Germany— all the major holiday spots, in fact. To qualify for one of these you need a round-trip rail ticket into your chosen area that totals over 250km in *each* direction. The pass costs DM57, or DM81 for two people sharing. Ask at your travel agent for exact details or at any *DER* office once in Germany.

Two other cost-saving possibilities for several people traveling together are the *Sparpreis* and *Super Sparpreis* fares, whereby one person pays the full round-trip fare, and those accompanying (up to five people) pay just half the same fare, although this only applies to trips of over 435km and 311km respectively.

BUSES

At such rare times as you *have* to forsake the trains for buses, you'll find no decline in the standard of efficiency, many buses being the *DB*-run *Bahnbusse* although there are a few **privately operated routes** on which rail passes cannot be used. You're most likely to need buses in remote rural areas—or along the designated "scenic routes" mentioned on the facing page. On these routes scheduled buses take the form of luxury-class coaches, often packed with tourists, and pause long enough at the major points of scenic or historic interest for passengers to hop out and take photographs. Although expensive to use without a railcard (*DB Tourist Card* holders travel free and *InterRail* cards merit a 50% reduction), these coaches are usually the only way to visit certain locales if you don't have your own transportation or the patience to zigzag around with the slow local buses (trains sometimes whizz through the same areas but seldom is there a convenient station to get off at or a chance to see much of the landscape through the windows).

BOATS

Traveling by **boat** is another option, though more for relaxation than as a way of covering large distances. All along the **Rhine** and **Mosel** rivers, and various Bavarian lakes, there are innumerable local boats waiting to ferry you across or around the waters for a small sum. For a longer trip, *K-D Line* steamers sail on the Rhine between Cologne and Mainz, and on the Mosel between Koblenz and Cochem, every day from April to October inclusive. On this vessel, possession of a *DB Tourist Card* gets you free passage—although with any other railcard you'll need to pay the full fare.

The steamer calls at many riverside hamlets and you can get on or off wherever you want. The fare, as you'd expect, depends on how far you travel; Cologne to Koblenz, for example, costs DM60.61, although you can make savings by making a round-trip journey along a shortish section, such as Koblenz to Lorelei and back for DM24.50. Several smaller companies also operate short-haul services along both the Rhine and Mosel.

Germany's biggest lake, an enormous bulge in the Rhine called the **Bodensee**, is also a prime spot for water-borne travel, either for a lazy cruise or to explore the nooks and crannies of its shoreline, which spans Austria and Switzerland, as well as Germany; full details are in Chapter Two, *Baden-Württemberg*.

PLANES

While **domestic flights** are numerous and quick between the major cities, they are also expensive: Frankfurt–Hamburg DM260, Frankfurt–Berlin DM209, both one-way, for example— clearly only worthwhile if you're in a desperate rush. If you are, it's worth looking out for any special reductions on return flights since it may save money just to use the return ticket for one-way travel. There are a few **student fares**, though these are only applicable to those living and studying in Germany. Any tourist office or *Lufthansa* agent will be able to provide full details of the current offers. If you definitely want to fly between German cities and are starting and finishing your journey in North America, it may be cheaper to book all the flights together, although this usually means that dates of travel cannot be changed.

PUBLIC TRANSIT IN CITIES

Municipal transportation in most German cities is still centered on **trams**. More often than not, these are sleek modern numbers capable of moving at a fair speed between stops; nowadays, they also often have an underground stretch in the city center, where they're known as the **U-Bahn**. This is often a source of confusion; it's important to remember that cities such as Berlin and Munich have a much more extensive U-Bahn system using tube trains as distinct from trams, while in cities with trams only you may have to look both above and below ground in the central area to find the stop for the service you want. **Buses** are also much in use, particularly in servicing suburbs and outlying areas.

Tickets are valid on all the different forms of transportation (which include the S-Bahn and mainline trains as well as in conurbations such as Frankfurt, Stuttgart, Cologne-Bonn and the Ruhrgebiet) and you can change from one to another, with no supplement for transfers. **Single** fares are expensive—DM2.50 is the minimum rate in many cities. It's therefore advisable either to buy in **batches** (usually offering a total saving of around 30%), or investing in a **fixed time period** (generally 24 hours). The latter can be a tremendous bargain—in some cities, up to two adults and two children are covered by the ticket, for an outlay of around DM9.

CARS

German traffic moves *fast*, and if you're used to the 55-mph pace of U.S. interstates you'll soon be reduced to a bundle of nerves. Once you get used to it, though, driving on Germany's excellent road system is an unadulterated pleasure. Most of the Gerhard Berger impersonating is done on the motorways, or *Autobahnen*—the most extensive and efficient such network in Europe. Gas stations, roadside restaurants, and motels are located every 30–40km, and virtually every city and town is within simple striking distance, using equally high-quality secondary roads to link them to the *Autobahnen*. High-octave **gas** currently costs around DM1.25 per liter.

There are no legally enforced **speed limits** on the *Autobahnen*, although there is a *recommended* limit of 100–130km/hr. There is an official speed limits on country roads of 80–100km/hr, and in built-up areas of 50km/hr.

The main **driving rules** to bear in mind are quite simple: traffic coming from the right normally has **right of way**; **seatbelts** are compulsory for those riding in the front seats; and **children under 12 years** must sit at the back. There are on **the spot fines** for speeding and other offenses: for speeding these are charged on a sliding scale from about DM20–DM50; after a cutoff point of roughly 25km above the limit, you're charged and taken to court.

Foreigners may drive for one year with a North American or international driving licence (for more than a year you must have a German driving licence). Third party **insurance** is mandatory (third party insurance in the USA may not cover foreign travel, although more extensive polices do—check with your insurers to be sure).

If you **break down**, the *A.D.AC (Allgemmeiner Deutscher Automobileclub*—the German equivalent of the *AA* A) will fix your car free of charge if it's a minor problem, but for jobs taking over half an hour you'll have to pay for labor and parts in full (so make sure your insurance covers this). On an *Autobahn*, the *A.D.AC* can be contacted with one of the **orange emergency telephones**, indicated by yellow luminous markers along the shoulder. On the phone, ask specifically for *Stassenwachthilfe*(road patrol assistance).

CAR RENTAL

Car rental (*Autovermietung*) is available at most airports and major train stations, and regional tourist offices will always be able to inform you of the nearest car rental firm. Although the major companies like *Avis*, *Budget*, or *Hertz* are easy to find, smaller local companies often offer better rates. Rates tend to be higher than in the USA (around DM350 for a small hatchback for a week), but you can save quite a bit by booking a week or more in advance through a North American office and picking up (and paying for) the car when you arrive. With these major firms there are no **drop-off charges** (i.e. you can collect a car, say, from Hamburg and drive it to Munich, and return it to the company's office there for no additional fee) although you'll be expected to leave a deposit.

TAXIS

Taking into account the high cost of local public transit, several people sharing a city cab may actually save money over using a local bus or train. Most taxis are comfortable Mercedes with a sign on the roof which is illuminated if they are free. Hail one from the street, or wait at the taxi stands; alternatively there are always plenty hovering around railroad stations and big hotels.

HITCHING

Hitching is common practice all over Germany, and with the excellent *Autobahn* network it's usually quite easy to cover long distances in a short time—provided you get a lift *before* you reach the motorway, since hitching (like walking and cycling) on them, or their access roads, is illegal. You're likely to have just as much luck using the secondary roads, or *Bundestrassen*, anyway. The crisscrossing nature of the road system means the drivers will have no idea where you're going unless you remember to make a **sign** stating your destination.

If you don't want to face the uncertainty of traditional hitching, the Germans have developed an institutionalized form called **Mitfahrzentralen**, located in most large cities (and listed in the *Guide* where applicable). These are agencies that put drivers and hitchers in touch with each other for a nominal fee, and then it's up to the participants to work out an agreeable petrol contribution, usually a simple two-way split, although the agency does suggest a reasonable sum. There's a valuable safety factor in this system, since all drivers have to notify the agencies of their addresses and car registration numbers. There are also a few **women-only** hitching agencies, known as *Frauenmitfahrzentralen*—again, these are listed in the *Guide*.

CYCLING

Cyclists are well catered to in Germany: though (sensibly) they're banned from the *Autobahnen*, many smaller roads have marked bike-paths, and bike-only lanes are a common sight in cities and towns. Fairly hassle-free **long distance bicycling** is possible all over the country, but obviously you'll need a strong pair of legs and a sturdy, reliable machine to get much joy out of

the Bavarian Alps (a good map is essential too— see "Information and Maps"). To take your own **bike on a train** (not permitted on *ICs*, *ECs* or small local trains), you need to purchase a "bicycle ticket" or **Fahrrad-Karte** which costs DM7.60 (reduced to DM4.20 if covering a distance of less than 100km)—and you have to take the bike to the luggage van yourself.

Between April and October, the best place to **rent a bike** is from a railroad station participating in the **Fahrrad am Bahnhof** scheme (most of them, in fact), whereby a bike costs just DM10 per day.You can return it to any other participating station and *DB-Tourist Card* or *InterRail* card holders get a 50% discount. This is obviously perfect for splitting train travel with pedaling as and when the mood, terrain, or weather, takes you. During the rest of the year, or in an area where there's no suitable station, simply look in the phone book under *Fahrradverleih* to find the address of a local bike rental outlet. Renting this way, however, means you'll have to leave a deposit, usually around DM50.

WALKING AND HIKING

The German countryside is laced with **hiking trails**, most of which are no more arduous than a Sunday afternoon stroll (for a large number of locals, in fact, they *are* Sunday afternoon strolls), though many trails are actually sections of much longer hikes. Virtually none of the hikes pass through romoto or isolated areas and thoro's always a village, campground, or youth hostel fairly close by (or even on the route) so you can make a trek of just a few hours or of several days' duration without much trouble. We've listed the best of the trails in the *Guide* and the local tourist office will have masses of information and maps relating to the walks in their area.

Because the hikes are so easy, you won't need any specialist equipment, but make sure you're wearing well-worn-in shoes and have a comfortable daypack for carrying picnic provisions. A first aid kit is also a good idea for treating scrapes and cuts.

SLEEPING

Be it high-rise city hotels or half-timbered guest houses in the country, accommodation of all types is easy to find in Germany and it often can be good value—especially in the growing number of rooms available in private houses. For those on a really tight budget, the youth hostels and campgrounds which proliferate over the entire country are a sound, cost-cutting alternative.

HOTELS AND PRIVATE ROOMS

An immensely complicated grading system applies to German **hotels**, with no fewer than eighty classifications according to price and services provided. Despite this, and perhaps ironically, they're all more or less the same: clean, comfortable, and functional with conveniences like TV, phone, and attached bathroom usually taken for granted in the medium-range establishments upwards. The listings in the *Guide* concentrate on the best options from the points of view of convenience and economy. However, you should always stop at the nearest tourist office to check any special deals which they may have with local establishments; this can result in you spending less than the figures quoted on the official **hotel lists** which every tourist office provides. Many tourist offices charge DM3 for finding you a room, but others perform the service gratis. You should take care *not* to turn up in a large town or city when there's a trade fair, or *Messe*, taking place—at such time hotels often double their rates, and still manage to get booked solid.

Rarely is there any great saving to be made by two people sharing as opposed to one person traveling alone. In country areas, the least you'll have to spend is about DM30 for a single, DM50 for a double—at least DM10 or DM15 extra for something similar in a city. Remember that any accommodation costs cut by staying on the outskirts of a city will be offset by the high cost of public transit into the center.

To escape the formality of a hotel, look for one of the plentiful **pensions**, which may be rooms above a bar or restaurant or simply space in a private house; in urban areas these cost about the same as a hotel but in the countryside are usually a bit cheaper. An increasingly prevalent budget option (especially in busy holiday areas) is **bed-and-breakfast** accommodation in a private house (look for signs saying *Fremdenzimmer* or *Zimmer frei*). These are seldom other than a really good deal; prices vary but are usually around DM25 for a single, DM40 for a double. You'll also find bed and breakfast available in some cities but this will cost more—up to DM75 for a double. Also in the more rural areas, and particularly plentiful along the main touring routes, are **country inns** or **guest houses** (*Gasthäuser*). These charge around DM45 per night for a double (much more in really popular areas), in what's usually an atmospheric old building, and the cost includes a wholesome country breakfast.

Farmhouse holidays are increasingly popular in Germany, and in many ways are the best bargains of all, with full board rates from as little as DM30 per day. Full lists are available from local tourist offices; the major snag is that this option is really only feasible if you have your own transportation.

YOUTH HOSTELS

In Germany, you're never far away from a **youth hostel** (*Jugendherberge*)—the YH movement was born here, in fact, in 1909—and these are likely to form the backbone of genuine budget traveling. Note, however, that at any time of the year they're liable to be reserved en masse by school groups—this is particularly prevalent on weekdays during the summer, and on weekends out of season. It's therefore advisable to make a reservation by phoning or writing to the hostel as far in advance as possible to be sure of a place—and be prepared to put up with the marauding adolescents. Though most **wardens** and their staff are courteous and helpful, there's an unfortunate minority who seem to be leftovers from the leadership of the Hitler Youth, insisting on rigid regimentation and pedantic enforcement of the rules. You should be wary, too, of **age restrictions** (see below) and the fact that prices are slightly cheaper if you're under 27 years of age.

All hostels are run by the German Youth Hostel Association (*Deustchejugendherberge*) and indicated by signs reading 'DJH.' The hostels divide into a number of **categories** according to facilities and size of room, which determines their price per night: **Grade I** hostels (charging DM9) are basic affairs with large dormitories, sometimes even lacking heating and hot water; **Grade II** (DM11) hostels are slightly better-equipped and usually have eight-bedded rooms; **Grade III** (DM11.50) hostels have four- and six-bedded rooms, more communal leisure rooms and washing facilities; **Grade IV** (DM12.50) hostels are another step up and generally in busier regions, with leisure and sports facilities, while **Grade V** hostels (DM13) are essentially the same as those in Grade IV but located in cities. **Grade VI** (DM14.80–26) hostels are also known as **youth guest houses**, and contain two and four-bedded rooms, and the fee includes breakfast and full bed-linen.

All these prices are for International Youth Hostel Federation (*IYHA*) members **over 27** (those **under 27** pay DM2–3 less per night); non-members will be charged an extra DM4 per night. If you're not a member and intend to use hostels for more than a couple of nights, it's wise to buy a year's *IYHF* **membership** for about $20 from your local branch of **American Youth Hostels Inc**. before leaving. You can buy the same thing at larger hostels in Germany but it's slightly more expensive.

Only **sheet sleeping bags** or sheets are permitted (you may be asked to show them to the warden): and if you don't have either, you can **rent a sleeping bag** for up to 10 days for DM2.

German youth hostels do carry a number of other **rules and restrictions**. **Reservations** will only be held until 6pm unless you've informed the warden that you'll be arriving late. When things are busy, **priority** is given to people under 18, or hiking families traveling with children. Those **over 27**, if they've not made a reservation, are only supposed to get a place if the hostel is not fully booked at 6pm—though this is by no means strictly applied. A more serious restriction for this age group is that they can't use the hostels in **Bavaria** at all, unless accompanying children. All hostels have a **curfew**, which can be as early as 10pm (and usually is in rural areas) but may be later, as is the case in all the big cities. **Length of stay** is officially limited to three days unless a longer period has been booked in advance. You can, however, stay longer—provided you're not going to deprive new arrivals from getting in. In **winter** many hostels close altogether; many more shut every other weekend.

Most hostels have **kitchens** where you can prepare your own food, and all but the most basic also provide **meals**—some hostels, particularly those in major cities, make a compulsory charge for breakfast (around DM4) although, of course, you don't have to eat it.

The location of many of the country's youth hostels, plus directions for reaching them by public transit, can be found in the *Guide*. If you need a complete list (there are some 550 in all), it can be found in the German Youth Hostels Association's handbook, called *Deutsches Jugenendherbergsverzeichnis*, available at most German hostels and tourist offices for DM6.

The **Naturfreundehaus** association offers a variant on the hostel theme. Its establishments, often located in rural countryside close to towns and cities, are designed more for older people, with accommodation in singles, doubles, or very small dorms.

CAMPING

Big, well-managed **campgrounds** are a feature of Germany, and they're located almost anywhere anybody could even think about wanting to camp. It's significant that sites are officially graded on a scale beginning at "good" and working up to "excellent." Even the lowest grade has toilet and washing facilities and a shop nearby on the grounds, while the grandest are virtually open-air hotels with swimming pools, supermarkets, and various other comforts—though it must be said that camping purists find German grounds rather too regimented. **Prices** are based on facilities and location, comprising a fee per person (DM3–5) and per tent (DM3–4). There are extra fees for cars, trailers, etc, so you could easily spend quite a bit more than you might in other countries if there are several of you traveling in a car.

Bear in mind, too, that many sites, especially those in popular holiday areas, are nearly always full from June to September, and you should arrive early in the afternoon for a good chance of getting in. Most campgrounds close down in the winter, but those in popular skiing areas remain open all year.

We've listed the most useful sites in the *Guide*, and you can also pick up the highly condensed **list** which is available free from the German National Tourist Office and other German travel specialists in North America, or, for DM19.80, you can get the complete official guide from the German Camping Club, the *DDC*, directly from them at Mandlestr. 28 D 8000, Munich 23. The German auto club, *A.D.AC* also produces a similarly priced guide which includes Germany and much of northern and central Europe.

Rough camping has recently been made illegal in the interests of protecting the environment.

EATING

German food is, as a rule, both good value and of high quality. However, it does help if you share the national penchant for solid, fatty food accompanied by compensatingly healthy fresh vegetables and salad. The pig is the staple element of the German menu— it's prepared in umpteen different ways, and just about every part of it is eaten. It also forms the main ingredient for sausages, which are not only the most popular snack, but are regarded as serious culinary fare— in Bavaria, there are even specialized *Wurstkuchen* (Sausage Kitchens) which have gained Michelin ratings.

BREAKFAST

The vast majority of German hotels and guest houses include breakfast in the price of the room; in many youth hostels, you also have to pay for this meal on top of the regular accommodation charges. Although some places go in for the spartan French affair of rolls, jam, and coffee, the normal German breakfast lies midway betweeen this and the elaborate Scandinavian cold table. Typically, you'll be offered a small platter of **cold meats** (usually sausage-based) and **cheeses**, along with a selection of marmalades, jams, and honey. Granola or another cereal is sometimes included as well, or as an alternative to the meats and cheeses. You're generally given a variety of **breads**, one of the most distinctive features of German cuisine. Both brown and white rolls are popular; these are often given a bit of zap by the addition of a condiment, such as caraway, coriander, poppy, or sesame seeds. The rich-tasting black rye bread, known as *Pumpernickel*, is a particular national favorite, as is the salted *Bretzel*, which tastes nothing like any foreign imitation. Coffee (which is normally freshly brewed) is the normal accompaniment, but tea—whether plain or herbal—is now far more popular in Germany than was the case even a few years ago, while drinking chocolate is another common alternative. A glass of fruit juice—almost invariably orange—is sometimes included as well.

If breakfast isn't included in your accommodation costs, you can usually do quite well by going to a local **baker's shop**, which generally open at 7am, if not before. Most chain bakeries have an area set aside for breakfast, a practice taken up by some family establishments as well. The coffee and chocolate available tend to be of high quality, and there's the added bonus of being able to choose from the freshly-made bakery on display; DM2 or DM3 should cover an adequate breakfast. More filling fare can be obtained from cafés and snack bars.

SNACKS AND FAST FOOD

Just as the English have their morning and afternoon tea, so the Germans have *Kaffee und Kuchen* (coffee and cakes). Though the elegant type of **café** serving a choice of espresso, capuccino, and mocha to the accompaniment of cream cakes, pastries, or handmade chocolates is indelibly associated with Austria, it's every bit as popular an institution in West Germany. This hardly constitutes a cheap snack, but is unlikely to be a rip-off—except in the most obvious tourist traps.

More substantial food is available from **butcher's shops**; even in rural areas, you can generally choose from a variety of freshly roasted meats to make up a hot sandwich. It's also worth going to the open-air **markets** which are held anything from once to six times a week in the central square of most towns. With a bit of judicious shopping round the stalls, you should be able to make up an irresistible picnic for an outlay of a few Deutschmarks. Larger cities tend to have a daily indoor version of this, known as the *Markthalle*.

The easiest option for a quick snack, however, is to head for the ubiquitous **Imbiss** stands and shops. In the latter you have the option of eating in or taking out; the price is the same. The indigenous type of snack bar tends to serve a range of sausages, plus meat balls, hamburgers and french fries; the better ones have soups, schnitzels, chops, and salads as well. Spit-roasted chicken is usually recommendable, and often very cheap, at around DM3.50 for half a bird. Mustard is usually available at no extra cost with all dishes, whereas small supplements are levied for mayonnaise or ketchup. Most Imbiss places sell beer, but as many are unlicensed you may be forbidden to consume it on the premises.

Among the fast-food **chains**, *Kochlöffel* stands out for cleanliness and good food. The specialty here is spit-roast chicken; prices compare very favorably with the American-owned hamburger joints, whose popularity is wholly undeserved. Another chain with acceptable food is *Weinerwald*, but its menu, set-up, and price structure are more comparable to a restaurant than a snack bar. The butcher's chain *Vincent Murr* sells full main courses to be eaten on your feet, costing DM5–10. Virtually the only places outside northern Germany where you can eat saltwater fish are in the shops of the *Nordsee* chain. These vary a lot in quality, but unfortunately the standard of the fish prepared for

consumption on the premises is seldom equal to that sold for home cooking.

Ethnic snack bars are predominantly Italian or Greek/Turkish. The **pizzerias** are a major boon if you're on a tight budget. Either taking out or eating standing up, prices start at around DM3.50 for a simple tomato and cheese pizza, rising sharply according to the topping chosen. Look out for the ones using a coal-fire oven; these are likely to produce a tastier (and not necessarily more expensive) product than those tied to electricity. Most pizzerias also serve pasta dishes, though these are usually less of a bargain. As always, the **kebab** houses adapt their technique do suit the national taste. What in Britain would be called a "Donner kebab" is more like New York-style *Gyros*, and is based much more on real lamb meat and fat. It's served in a fluffy type of bread, generally with *tsatziki* as a sauce, and costs DM4–5.

MAIN MEALS

All **restaurants** display their menus and prices by the door, as well as which day is their *Ruhetag*, when they're closed. Hot meals are usually served throughout the day, but certainly where it says *durchgehend warme Küche*. The *Gaststätte*, *Gasthaus*, *Gasthof*, *Brauhaus* and *Wirtschaft* establishments, the nearest equivalents to an old-fashioned English inn, mostly belong to a brewery and function as a social meeting point, drinking haven, and cheap restaurant. Their style of cuisine is known as **Gutbürgerliche Kuche**; this resembles hearty German home cooking (hence the comparatively low prices), and portions are almost invariably generous. Most such places have a hard core of regular customers who sit at tables marked *Stammtisch*; unless invited to do so, it's not the done thing to sit there. The bulk of the menu is the same all day, though some establishments offer two- or three- course lunches at bargain prices.

Choice for **soup** is fairly restricted, and tends to be based on an adaptation of foreign fare; prices are usually in the range of DM3 to DM6. Among the most popular are *Gulaschsuppe*, a liquified version of the staple Magyar dish (despite often being dignified as *Ungarische*, it's not something a Hungarian would recognize); *Bohnensuppe*, which is often quite spicy, and derived from the Serbian model; and *Zwiebelsuppe*, which is a direct copy of the famous French brown onion soup, usually with

A LIST OF FOODS AND DISHES

Basics

Frühstück	breakfast	*Brötchen*	bread roll	*Zucker*	sugar
Mittagessen	lunch	*Butter*	butter	*Pfeffer*	pepper
Abendessen	supper, dinner	*Butterbrot*	sandwich	*Salz*	salt
Messer	knife	*Belegtes Brot*	open sand-	*Öl*	oil
Gabel	fork		wich	*Essig*	vinegar
Löffel	spoon	*Marmelade*	jam	*Senf*	mustard
Speisekarte	menu	*Honig*	honey	*Sosse*	sauce
Teller	plate	*Käse*	cheese	*Reis*	rice
Tasse	cup	*Fleisch*	meat	*Spätzle*	a kind of
Glas	glass	*Fisch*	fish		shredded
Vorspeise	starter	*Eier*	eggs		pasta
Hauptspeise	main course	*Gemüse*	vegetables	*Maultaschen*	form of ravioli
Nachspeise	dessert	*Obst*	fruit	*Rechnung*	bill
Brot	bread	*Joghurt*	yogurt	*Trinkgeld*	tip

Soups and Starters

Suppe	soup	*Ochsenschwanzsuppe*	oxtail soup
Erbsensuppe	pea soup	*Flädlesuppe,*	clear soup with pancake
Linsensuppe	lentil soup	*Pfannkuchensuppe*	strips
Bohnensuppe	bean soup	*Leber Pastete*	liver paté
Zwiebelsuppe	onion soup	*Lachsbrot*	smoked salmon on bread
Hühnersuppe	chicken soup	*Melone mit Schinken*	melon and ham
Gulaschsuppe	thick soup in imitation	*Grüner Salat*	mixed green salad
	of goulash	*Gurkensalat*	cucumber salad
Leberknödelsuppe	clear soup with liver	*Fleischsalat*	cut sausage salad with
	dumplings		onions
Fleischsuppe	clear soup with meat	*Schnittlauchbrot*	chives on bread
	dumplings	*Sülze*	jellied meat loaf

Meat and Poultry

Aufschnitt	mixed slices of cold sausage	*Gyros*	kebab
		Hackbraten	mincemeat roast
Bockwurst	chunky boiled sausage	*Hackfleisch*	mincemeat
Bratwurst	grilled sausage	*Hammelfleisch*	mutton
Currywurst	sausage served with spicy sauce	*Hase*	hare
		Herz	heart
Eisbein	pig's knuckles	*Hirn*	brains
Ente	duck	*Hirsch, Reh*	venison
Fasan	pheasant	*Huhn, Hähnchen*	chicken
Fleischpflanzerl	meatball (in Bavaria)	*Innereien*	innards
Frikadelle	meatball	*Jägerschnitzel*	cutlet in wine and mush-room sauce
Froschschenkel	frogs' legs		
Gans	goose	*Kaninchen*	rabbit
Geschnetzeltes	shredded meat, usually served with rice	*Kassler Rippen*	smoked and pickled pork chops

Meat and Poultry (continued)

Kotelett	cutlet (cheapest cut)	Schnitzel Natur	uncoated cutlet (usually pork)
Krautwickerl	cabbage leaves filled with mincemeat	Schweinebraten	roast pork
Lamm	lamb	Schweinefleisch	pork
Leber	liver	Schweinehaxen	pig's knuckle
Leberkäse	baked meatloaf served hot or cold	Speck	bacon
		Truthahn	turkey
Lunge	lungs	Weisswurst	white herb sausage made with veal and pork
Nieren	kidneys		
Ochsenschwanz	oxtail	Wiener Schnitzel	thin cutlet in breadcumbs
Rahmschnitzel	cutlet in cream sauce	Wienerwurst	standard boiled pork sausage
Rindfleisch	beef		
Schaschlik	diced meat with spicy sauce	Wild	wild game
		Wurst	sausage
Schinken	ham	Wildschwein	wild boar
Schlachtplatte	mix of cured meats, including blood sausage, liver sausage, and boiled meat	Zigeunerschnitzel	cutlet in paprika sauce
		Saure Lunge	pickled lungs
		Sauerbraten	braised pickled beef
Schnecke	snail	Zunge	tongue

Fish

Aal	eel	Muscheln	mussels
Forelle	trout	Sardinen	sardines
Hering, Matjes	herring	Schellfisch	haddock
Hummer	lobster	Scholle	plaice
Kabeljau	cod	Schwertfish	swordfish
Karpfen	carp	Seezunge	sole
Kaviar	caviar	Skampi	scampi
Krabben	crab	Tintenfisch	squid
Lachs	salmon	Thunfisch	tuna
Makrele	mackerel	Zander	pike-perch

Vegetables

Bohnen	beans	Pellkartoffeln	jacket potatoes
Bratkartoffeln	fried potatoes	Pilze, Champignons	mushrooms
Brokkoli	broccoli	Pommes frites	chips
Erbsen	peas	Salzkartoffeln	boiled potatoes
Grüne Bohnen	green beans	Reibekuchen	potato cake
Gurke	cucumber	Rosenkohnl	brussels sprouts
Karotten, Möhren	carrots	Rote Rübe	beetroot
Kartoffelbrei	mashed potatoes	Rotkohl	red cabbage
Kartoffelpuree	creamed potatoes	Rübe	turnip
Kartoffelsalat	potato salad	Salat	salad
Knoblauch	garlic	Sauerkraut	pickled cabbage
Knödel, Kloss	dumpling	Spargel	asparagus
Lauch	leeks	Tomaten	tomatoes
Maiskolben	corn on the cob	Weisskohl	white cabbage
Paprika	green or red peppers	Zwiebeln	onions

Fruits

Obstsalat	fruit salad	*Mandarine*	tangerine
Ananas	pineapple	*Melone*	melon
Apfel	apple	*Orange*	orange
Banane	banana	*Pampelmuse*	grapefruit
Birne	pear	*Pfirsich*	peach
Datteln	dates	*Pflaumen*	plums
Erdbeeren	strawberries	*Rosinen*	raisins
Feigen	figs	*Schwarze*	black currants
Himbeeren	raspberries	*Johannisbeeren*	
Johannisbeeren	red currants	*Trauben*	grapes
Kirschen	cherries	*Zitrone*	lemon
Kompott	stewed fruit or mousse		

Cheeses and Desserts

Emmentaler	Emmental Swissl	*Kaiserschmarrn*	shredded pancake served
Käseplatte	mixed selection of cheeses		with powdered sugar,
Schafskäse	sheep's cheese		jam and raisins
Weichkäse	cream cheese	*Kasekuchen*	cheesecake
Ziegenkäse	goat's cheese	*Keks*	biscuit
		Krapfen	doughnut
Apfelstrudel mit	apple strudel with fresh	*Nüsse*	nuts
Sahne	cream	*Nusskuchen*	nut cake
Berliner	jam doughnut	*Obstkuchen*	fruitcake
Dampfnudeln	large yeast dumplings	*Pfannkuchen*	pancake
	served hot with vanilla	*Schokolade*	chocolate
	sauce	*Schwarzwälder*	Black Forest pastry
Eis	ice cream	*Kirschtorte*	
Gebäck	pastries	*Torte*	gateau, tart

Common Terms

Art	style of	*Geräuchert*	smoked
Eingelegte	pickled	*Gutbürgerliche*	traditional German
Frisch	fresh	*Küche*	cooking
Gebacken	baked	*Hausgemacht*	home-made
Gebraten	fried, roasted	*Heiss*	hot
Gebraten . . "blau"	cooked rare	*Kalt*	cold
Gedämpft	steamed	*Spiess*	skewered
Gefüllt	stuffed	*Topf (Eintopf)*	stew, casserole
Gegrillt	grilled	*Vom heissen Stein*	raw meats you cook your-
Gekocht	cooked		self on a red hot stone

floating cheese and croutons. More authentically German are the clear soups with dumplings, of which the Bavarian *Leberknödelsuppe* is the best known. Other **starters** tend to be fairly unsophisticated—either a salad, paté or cold meat dish; prices are similar to those for soups.

Main courses in all German restaurants are overwhelmingly based on **pork**. As a rule, this is of noticeably higher quality than in North America, and the variety in taste wrought by using different sauces (it's quite common to find a choice of up to twenty different types), and unexpected parts of the animal, mean that the predominance of the pig is far less tedious than might be supposed. As an alternative to the ubiquitous *Schnitzel*, try *Schweinehaxe* (knuckle) or

Eisbein (knuckles), both particularly delicious when roasted. **Sausages** regularly feature on the menu, and can be surprisingly tasty, with distinct regional varieties. Whereas a main course pork-based dish is likely to cost DM15 or less, one with **beef** will cost a fair bit more. As is the case with snack bars, **chicken** dishes are comparatively cheap. Many restaurants have a **game** menu, with more exotic poultry such as duck or goose, along with venison, rabbit, and hare; prices then tend to be DM20 or more. Outside northern Germany, where a wide variety of newly caught saltwater **fish** is readily available, you'll probably have to be content with freshwater varieties; trout is by far the most popular, though there's obviously a greater choice in places close to lakes and rivers.

The main course price invariably includes **vegetables**. Potatoes are usually roasted, chipped, fried in slices or made into a cold salad, but rarely baked, boiled, or mashed. Dumplings made from potatoes and flour are a common alternative. Cabbage is the other popular accompaniment—the green variety is pickled as *Sauerkraut*, whereas the red is normally cooked with apple as *Apfelrotkohl*. Salads of lettuce, cucumber, beetroot, carrots and gherkins are often included as a side-dish. The noodles known as *Spätzle* and *Maultaschen* are a distinctive component of Swabian cuisine, occasionally adopted elsewhere.

Desserts in restaurants are an anti-climax, where they exist at all. The Bavarian *Dampfnudel* is one of the few distinctive dishes; otherwise there's just the usual selection of fresh and stewed fruits, cheeses and ice creams. Sweet tooths are obviously far better catered for in cafés.

Germany now being a multicultural society, there's a wide variety of **ethnic** eateries. The density of these is very much in line with the general *Gastarbeiter* influx, and hence there's a heavy southern European bias. Of these, the Italian are generally the safest recommendations; there's also plenty offering Balkan and Graeco-Turkish cuisines. All of these are worth heading for if you're on a tight budget. **Vegetarians** may at times have a tough time finding anything other than salads, omelets and pancakes, though major cities and towns do tend to have innovative specialist restaurants (listed in the guide whenever possible), and even small communities often have a simple wholefood place.

DRINKING

The division between eating and drinking in Germany is less demarcated than it is in North America. Despite the connotations of beer and wine, the *Brauhäuser* and *Weinstuben* inevitably double as restaurants, though there are some purely drinking dens, generally known as *Kneipen*.

Beer and wine apart, there's nothing very distinctive about German beverages, save for *Apfelwein*, a variant of cider. The most popular **spirits** are the fiery *Korn* and after-dinner liqueurs, which are mostly fruit-based. Both **hot** and **soft** drinks are broadly the same as in North America.

DRINKS GLOSSARY			
Wasser	water	*Orangensaft*	orange juice
Sprüdel	sparkling mineral water	*Tomatensaft*	tomato juice
Milch	milk	*Zitronenlimonade*	lemonade
Milchshake	milk shake	*Bier*	beer
Kaffee	coffee	*Weisswein*	white wine
Kaffee Komplett	coffee with milk	*Rotwein*	red wine
Tee	tea	*Roséwein*	rosé wine
Zitronentee	lemon tea	*Sekt*	sparkling wine
Kräutertee, Pflanzentee	herbal tea	*Glühwein*	hot mulled wine
Kakao	cocoa	*Apfelwein*	apple wine
Schockolade	drinking chocolate	*Weinbrand*	brandy
Apfelsaft	apple juice	*Korn*	rye spirit
Traubensaft	grape juice	*Likör*	liqueur
		Grog	hot rum

BEER

For serious beer drinkers, West Germany is the ultimate paradise. Wherever you go, you can be sure of getting a product made locally, often brewed in a distinctive style. The country has over a third of the world's breweries, with some 800 (more than half the total) in Bavaria alone. It was in this province in 1516 that the *Reinheitsgebot* (Purity Law) was formulated, laying down stringent standards of production, including a ban on chemical substitutes. This has been rigorously adhered to ever since (even in products made for export), and was also taken up by the rest of the country, but only for beers made for the domestic market. Unfortunately, it has run afoul of the EC bureaucrats, who deem it a restriction on trade (very few foreign beers meet the criteria laid down, and therefore could not be imported). Only time will tell whether or not German brewers will heed this invitation to lower their standards, but the current outlook is still rosy. Although the odd brewery bites the dust each year, there has been a revival of long-forgotten techniques, often put into practice in new small *Hausbrauereien*.

More generally, there's an encouraging continuation of old-fashioned **top-fermented** brewing styles. Until last century, all beers were made this way, but the interaction of the yeasts with a hot atmosphere meant that brewing had to be suspended during the summer. It was the Germans who discovered that the yeast sank to the foot of the container when stored under icy conditions; thereafter, brewing took on a more scientific nature, and yeast strains were bred so that beer could be **bottom-fermented**, thus allowing its production all year round. While the *Reinheitsgebot* has ensured that bottom-fermented German brews are of a high standard, the technique has been a major factor in the insipidity of so much beer in other countries, including Britain. The top-fermentation process, on the other hand, allows for a far greater individuality in the taste (often characterized by a distinct fruitiness), and can, of course, now be used throughout the year, thanks to modern temperature controls. All wheat beers use this process.

A quick beer tour of Germany would inevitably begin in **Munich**, which occupies third place in world production statistics. The city's beer gardens and beer halls are the most famous drinking dens in the country, offering a wide variety of premier products, from dark lagers through tart *Weizens* to powerful *Bocks*. Nearby **Freizing** boasts the oldest brewery in the world,

dating back to the eleventh century. In Franconia, distinctive traditions are found in **Bamberg** (national champion for beer consumption per resident), **Kulmbach**, **Coburg**, and **Bayreuth**.

In Baden-Württemberg, the local brews are sweeter and softer, in order to appeal to palates accustomed to wine; **Stuttgart** and **Mannheim** are the main production centers. Central Germany is even more strongly wedded to wine, though there are odd pockets of resistance. Indeed, **Frankfurt**, the German cider metropolis, also has the largest brewery in the country, Binding.

Farther north, where it's too cold to grow grapes, the beer tradition returns with a vengeance. **Cologne** holds the world record for the number of separate breweries within a city, all of which produce the jealously-guarded *Kölsch*. **Düsseldorf** again has its own distinctive brew, the dark *Alt*. **Dortmund** even manages to beat Munich for the title of European capital of beer production, and is particularly associated with *Export*. Less well known, but equally good, are the delicate brews of the **Sauerland** and **Siegerland**, using the soft local spring water.

Hannover, **Bremen**, and **Hamburg** all have long brewing pedigrees, with many of their products widely available abroad. The most distinctive beers of the northernmost Länder, however, are those of **Einbeck** (the original home of *Bock*) and **Jever**. In contrast to these heady brews is the acidic *Weisse* of **Berlin**, which is completely transformed into a refreshing summer thirst-quencher by the addition of a dash of syrup.

WINE

Most people's knowledge of German wine starts and ends with *Liebfraumilch*, the medium-sweet easy-drinking wine that for the last few years has monopolized ad campaigns in North America. Sadly, its success has obscured the quality of other German wines, especially those made from the Riesling grape, which many consider one of the world's great white grape varieties; and it's worth noting that the *Liebfraumilch* drunk in Germany tastes nothing like the exported bilge.

The vast majority of German wine is white, since the northern climate doesn't ripen red grapes regularly. If after a week or so you're pining for a glass of red, try a *Spätburgunder* (the Pinot Noir of Burgundy).

First step in any exploration of German wine should be to understand what's on the label: the predilection for Gothic script and gloomy martial crests make this an uninviting prospect, but the

BEER GLOSSARY

Alt	literally, any beer made according to an old formula; particularly associated with the dark brown top-fermented barley malt beer of Düsseldorf (also made in Mönchengladbach and Münster)	*Klosterbräu*	brewery attached to a monastery
		Kölsch	top-fermented, pale colored beer peculiar to Cologne, invariably served in small glasses
Altbierbowl	glass of *Alt* with addition of a fresh fruit punch	*Kristall-Weizen*	sparkling brew made from wheat: the beer answer to champagne
Berliner Weisse	wheat beer from Berlin, usually served in a bowl-shaped glass, and with addition of woodruff (*mit Grün*) or raspberry essence (*mit Schuss*).	*Maibock*	pale, high premium *Bock*, specially made to celebrate spring
		Malz	unfermented black malt beer, similar to sweet stout
Bock	light or dark strong beer, originally from Einbeck, but particularly popular in Bavaria, containing at least 6.25% alcohol	*Märzenbier*	strong beer made in March, but stored for later consumption; particularly associated with Munich's *Oktoberfest*
Dampfbier	"steam beer" from Bayreuth, a fruity brew top-fermented in its own yeast.	*Münchener*	brown colored lager, a style pioneered in Munich
Doppelbock	extra-strong *Bock*, usually made specially for festivals	*Pils*	bottom-fermented golden colored beer; very high hop content.
Dunkel	generic name for any dark beer	*Radler*	shandy
Eisbock	"ice beer," particularly associated with Kulmbach; the freezing process increases and concentrates the alcohol	*Rauchbier*	aromatic beer from Bamberg made from smoked malt
		Spezial	name given by breweries to their premium product, or to that made for special events
Export	originally, beers made to be exported; Now used to describe a premium beer, or in association with the brewing style of Dortmund, stronger than a Pils and lying midway between dry and sweet in taste	*Starkbier*	generic name for strong beers
		Steinbier	beer made with the help of hot stones, an old technique recently revived in Coburg
		Urquell	name used to identify the original of a particular brewing style
Hausbrauerei	"house brewery," or pub where beer is brewed on the premises	*Vollbier*	standard (as opposed to premium) type of beer
		Weihnachts-bier	special strong beer made for Christmas
Hefe-Weizen	wheat beer given strong yeast boost		
Hell, Helles	generic names for light beers	*Weisse*	pale colored wheat beer
Hofbräu	brewery formerly belonging to a court; that in Munich is the most famous	*Weizen*	light or dark wheat beer
		Zwickelbier	unfiltered beer

division of categories is intelligent and helpful—if at first a little complex.

Like most EC wine, German wine is divided into two broad categories: *Tafelwein* ("table wine," for which read "cheap swill") and *Qualitätswein* ("quality wine"), equivalent to the French *Apellation Controllée*.

TAFELWEIN

Tafelwein can be a blend of wines from any EC country; *Deutscher Tafelwein* must be 100% German. *Landwein* is a superior *Tafelwein*, equivalent to the French *Vin de Pays* and medium dry. Like all German wines, *Tafelwein* can be *trocken* (dry) or *halb-trocken* (medium dry).

QUALITÄTSWEIN

There are two basic subdivisions of *Qualitätswein*: **Qba** (*Qualitätswein eines bestimmten Anbaugebietes*) and **Qmp** (*Qualitätswein mit Präedikat*). "Qba" wines come from eleven delimited regions and must pass an official tasting and analysis. "Qmp" wines are farther divided into six grades:

Kabinett The first and lightest style.

Spätlese Must come from late-picked grapes, which results in riper flavors.

Auslese Made from a selected bunch of grapes, making a concentrated, medium-sweet wine. If labeled as a *Trocken*, the wine will have lots of body and weight.

Beerenauslese Wine made from late-harvested, individually picked grapes. A rare wine, made only in the very best years, and extremely sweet.

Trockenbeerenauslese Trocken here means dry in the sense that the grapes have been left on the vine until some of the water content has evaporated. As with *Beerenauslese*, each grape will be individually picked. This is a very rare wine which is intensely sweet and concentrated.

Eiswein Literally "ice wine," this is made from *Beerenauslese* grapes—hard frost freezes the water content of the grape, concentrating the juice. The flavor of an *Eiswein* is remarkably fresh tasting, due to its high acidity.

GRAPE VARIETIES

These often appear on wine labels and are a handy guide to judging a wine's flavor.

Riesling Germany's best grape variety. It can have a floral aroma when young, is often "honeyed" when ripe, and develops interesting bouquets after five to seven years in the bottle.

Gewürztraminer Gewürz means spicy, and the wine has an intense aromatic nose, likened by some to lichi nuts, and by others to Turkish delight.

Müller-Thurgau The most widely planted grape in Germany. Its flavor is less distinguished than Riesling but is generally fruity, has less acidity, and a grapey, Muscat taste.

Silvaner A fairly neutral wine, quite full-bodied and often blended with more aromatic varieties.

WINE REGIONS

Particularly at the *Qualitätswein* level, regional variations in climate produce markedly differing styles of wine.

Mosel-Saar-Ruhr The steep banks of the winding river Mosel and two of its tributaries enable the vines to catch long hours of sun, thus allowing grapes to ripen in one of the most northerly plantations in the world. Much Riesling is grown in the slatey soil, producing elegant wines in the best years.

Rheingau On the sloping northern bank of the Rhine as it flows between Hochheim and Assmanshausen, this is a small, prestigious region that produces wines slightly fuller than those from the Mosel region. They're considered to be among the country's finest.

Nahe Both geographically and stylistically between the Mosel-Saar-Ruhr and the Rheingau, this is a relatively small region whose wines are often underrated.

Rhein-Hessen Germany's main producer of *Liebfraumilch* from large plantations of Müller-Thurgau and Silvaner grapes.

Rheinpfalz A southern wine region that produces full-bodied, ripe wines, chiefly *Liebfraumilch* and *Riesling*.

Baden The most southerly wine-growing region, extending as far as the Bodensee. The warm climate allows French grape varieties to be grown here, and the majority of the wines are dry in flavor.

COMMUNICATIONS

POST OFFICES

Post offices (*Postamt*) are normally open Monday to Saturday from 8am to 6pm. In the major cities, there's a separate **parcels office** (marked *Pakete*), usually a block or so away, where you have to go to send bulky items.

    General Delivery (post restante) services are available at the main post offices in any given town (see listings in the guide for addresses in the major cities): collect it from the counter marked *Postlagernde Sendungen* (always remember to take your passport). It's worth asking anyone writing to you to use this designation as well as, or instead of, *poste restante*. Incredible as it may seem in view of the country's reputation for super-efficiency, many German post offices don't understand the international term, and are likely to return a letter to the sender marked "address unknown." Bear in mind also that mail is usually only held for a couple of weeks. **Telegrams** can be sent either by phoning ☎1131, or from any post office.

TELEPHONES

Another facility of the main post offices (*Hauptpost*) is the **direct phone service**. A phone booth will be allocated to you from the counter marked *Fremdgespräche*, which is where you pay once you're finished. This is much more convenient than battling with a pay phone and saves a lot of hassle if you don't have the right change. However, you can dial directly abroad from all kiosks, except those clearly marked *National* only. Main international direct dialling codes are: **USA and Canada** 00 1; **Britain** 00 44; **Irish Republic** 00 353; **Australia** 00 61; **New Zealand** 00 64. For international directory phone ☎400 118. Calling rates are slightly cheaper after 8pm and on weekends. In the guide, local codes are included with each telephone number, except in major cities, where you'll find it included in the "Listings" section at the end of the account.

MEDIA

Germany is well supplied with British newspapers, much less so with North American ones (except for the ubiquitous *USA Today*). In the larger cities it's relatively easy to pick up most of the London-printed editions on the same day.

With a few exceptions, **German newspapers** tend to be highly regionalized, mixing local and international news. Only the liberal *Frankfurter Rundschau* and Munich's *Süddeutsche Zeitung* are distributed much outside their own areas. Berlin produces two reputable organs: *Tagespiegel*, a good left-wing read, and the Green-ish/alternative *Tageszeitung*, universally known as the *Taz*. Of the national daily papers, the two best sellers come from the presses of the late and unlamented Axel Springer: *Die Welt* is a right-wing heavyweight, and the tabloid *Bild* a reactionary, sleazy, and sensationalist rag that even Rupert Murdoch would be ashamed to publish. The *Frankfurter Allgemeine* is again conservative, appealing particularly to the business community, but unusual in following a politically independent line.

Germany has more **magazines** than any other country in Europe. The leftish weekly news and current-affair magazine *Der Spiegel* is best for in-depth political analysis and investigative journalism, but unless your German is fluent it's a heavy and often difficult read. Though farther to the right, *Die Zeit*, the weekly magazine of the newspaper of the same name, is a wider-ranging (and to learners of the language, easier-to-read) alternative. *Stern* is the most popular current affairs magazine, though no longer in the same league as *Die Zeit* or *Der Spiegel* since its prestige took a tumble following its publication of the forged Hitler diaries a few years ago. In order to bolster a flagging circulation it has resorted to a broader-based, populist low-brow content. Of the style magazines, *Tempo* is a rip-off of *The Face* but less fashion-obsessed and more likely to come up with interesting articles. *Wiener* is similar, but more iconoclastic and acerbic.

German **television** can't hold a candle to North American TV, its ads and presentation style generally still stuck in the modes used in the 1960s and early 1970s. But satellite TV is bringing a new impetus to the industry, and it being a very rich enterprise, a great deal of change is undoubtedly on the horizon. Whether it will improve quality is another story. There are two main national channels, *ARD* and *ZDF*, and then there's the *Drittes Programm*, which features separate regional and educational programs. Austrian and Swiss channels are sometimes available, and each state also has its local channels. The only **English-speaking radio** channels are the *BBC World Service*, the British Forces station *BFBS* and the dire American Armed Forces radio station *AFN*, which combines American music charts with military news.

BUSINESS HOURS AND HOLIDAYS

Shopping hours in Germany were strictly curtailed by a law passed in the 1950s in a bid to counter national workaholic tendencies, a measure which has defied numerous attempts at reform. All shops must close promptly at 6:30pm on weekdays, at 2pm on Saturday (or at 6pm on the first Saturday of the month, known as *Langer Samstag*, and in the four weeks before Christmas), and all day Sunday (except for bakers, who may open between 11am and 3pm).

Pharmacists can extend their opening hours on a strict basis of rotation. The only other exceptions are shops in and around railroad stations, which generally do stay open late and on weekends. These are for *bona fide* travelers only, and you could theoretically be asked to show a ticket, though in practice you're most unlikely to find this absurd restriction applied.

Museums and **historic monuments** such as castles and palaces are, with very few exceptions, closed all day Monday. Otherwise, opening times (which are always detailed in the guide) are noticeably more generous than in other countries, with lunchtime closures rare. Most major civic museums are additionally open on at least one evening per week.

In range and diversity, German museums far surpass those of most other European countries, a legacy of the nation's long division into a plethora of separate states, and of the Romantic movement, which led to a passion for collecting. **Admission charges** of the museums vary enormously, and tend to reflect whether the relevant authority regards them as a social service or an exploitable asset, rather than their intrinsic quality. All the museums in Stuttgart, for example, are free, whereas those in comparably wealthy Düsseldorf (which arguably are not as good) average DM5 each. Historic monuments tend to charge around DM2 or DM3, comparing favorably with similar places in the USA. A **student card** nearly always brings a reduction in admission costs.

There's rarely any difficulty gaining access to **churches**; hence opening times are only listed in the guide for ancillary attractions such as treasuries or towers, or when set times are rigidly enforced. One point to look out for is that churches used for Protestant worship (predominantly in Swabia, Hessen, and northern Germany) tend to keep office hours, whereas those in Catholic areas usually open earlier and close later. At lunchtimes, many churches leave the vestibule open, but have the body of the building closed off by a grille.

PUBLIC HOLIDAYS

New Year's Day (Jan. 1); Epiphany (Jan. 6); Good Friday (changes annually); Easter Monday (changes annually); May Day (May 1); Ascension Day (changes annually); Pentecost Monday (changes annually); Corpus Christi (changes annually, and is honored only in Baden-Württemberg, Bavaria, Hessen, Rhineland-Palatinate, North Rhineland–Westphalia and Saarland); Day of German Unity (June 17), Feast of the Assumption (Aug. 15; honored only in Bavaria and Saarland); All Saints Day (Nov. 1, honored only in Bavaria, Rhineland-Palatinate, North Rhineland–Westphalia and Saarland); Day of Prayer and National Repentance (variable date in Nov.); Christmas Day (Dec. 25), Boxing Day (Dec. 26).

FESTIVALS AND ANNUAL HOLIDAYS

West Germany probably has more annual festivals than any other European country, with almost every village having its own summer fair, as well as a rich mixture of religious and pagan festivals that have merged over the ages to fill the whole calendar.

The most famous German festival is undoubtedly the **Oktoberfest** in Munich, but **Carnival** and the **Christmas fairs** are other annual highlights, and take place all over the country. There's also a wealth of **music festivals**, ranging from opera seasons to open-air jazz and rock concerts. Main events are listed in the guide (with the most important described in detail), but here's a general overview.

GERMANY'S MUSEUMS—A TOP TWENTY

Berlin (West) *Dahlem Museum* (p.656). One of the most comprehensive collections of old masters in the world; particular strengths are the early Netherlandish, German, Dutch, and Italian schools. Fabulous displays of sculpture and ethnology are also featured.

Berlin (West) *Resistance Museum* (p.653). Comprehensive and moving account of the history of the struggle against the Nazi regime within wartime Germany.

Berlin (East) *Pergamon Museum* (p.681). Archaeology museum full of blockbuster exhibits from all the great classical civilizations.

Braunschweig *Herzog Anton Ulrich Museum* (p.568). Choice display of old master paintings (especially Flemish, Dutch, and German) and decorative arts.

Cologne *Roman-Germanic Museum* (p.425). Wide-ranging archaeology museum specially constructed around a giant Roman mosaic.

Cologne *Wallraf-Richartz/Ludwig Museum* (p.424). Works by the most distinctive school of German fifteenth-century painters rub shoulders with a staggering cross section of international twentieth-century art.

Darmstadt *Landesmuseum* (p.311). An absorbing and eclectic mix of German Primitives, old masters, Jugendstil decorative art, avant-garde sculpture, archaeology, and natural history.

Düsseldorf *Kunstsammlung Nordrhein-Westfalen* (p.445). The ritziest, most extravagantly funded gallery of modern art in the country.

Frankfurt *Städel* (p.300). One of Europe's most comprehensive art galleries, where the whole course of German painting can be compared to trends elsewhere in Europe.

Hamburg *Kunsthalle* (p.600). Wide-ranging art gallery—the best place to see the diversity of nineteenth-century German painting.

Hannover *Landesmuseum* (p.550). Varied mix of European art down the centuries, plus archaeological and natural history departments.

Karlsruhe *Kunsthalle* (p.190). 19th C. period-piece art gallery; the most off-beat collection of old master paintings in the country.

Kassel *Gemäldegalerie* (p.330). A collection of seventeenth-century Dutch and Flemish paintings equal to any in the Low Countries, along with classical sculptures and other old masters.

Munich *Alte Pinakothek* (p.50). One of the greatest art galleries in the world. Along with by far the best collection of old German masters in existence, there's an outstanding representation of the early Netherlandish, Flemish, Dutch, Italian, French, and Spanish schools.

Munich *Bayerisches Nationalmuseum* (p.54). Works by most of the great late Gothic/early Renaissance woodcarvers, plus European decorative art and Bavarian folklore displays.

Munich *Deutsches Museum* (p.55). Compendious and spectacular celebration of technology in all its forms; its hands-on displays are equally fascinating for kids and graduate engineers.

Nürnberg *Germanisches Nationalmuseum* (p.123). A monument to the best of German civilization down the centuries—medieval statuary, Renaissance globes, historic musical instruments, and paintings from all periods.

Stuttgart *Daimler-Benz Museum* (p.201). A glittering and diverse array of historic vehicles, all designed and manufactured by this merged company or its two predecessors.

Stuttgart *Staatsgalerie* (p.198). Excellent collection of (particularly German) old master paintings, plus the country's answer to the Pompidou Center.

Trier *Landesmuseum* (p.358). Startlingly fresh interpretation of classical civilizations that's a world away from the usual dry-as-dust style of presentation.

JANUARY is a quiet month, though there are various events associated with the **Carnival season**, particularly the proclamation of the "Carnival King." Climax of the season comes in FEBRUARY or MARCH, seven weeks before the date nominated for Easter. The Rhenish *Karneval* tends to have rather more gusto than its Bavarian counterpart, known as *Fasching*. Cologne has the most spectacular celebrations (see description under "Cologne" in the *Guide*), followed by those of Mainz and Düsseldorf; the *Rosenmontag* parades are the highlight. Baden-Württemberg's *Fastnet* is a distinctive, very pagan, Carnival tradition, best experienced in the town of Rottweil. Another old pagan rite is the *Schäfertanz* held in Rothenburg in March. This time of year sees things gearing up for **Easter**, and colorful church services are held throughout the country, particularly in rural Catholic areas. Another important APRIL festival is the witches' sabbath of *Walpurgisnacht*, celebrated throughout the Harz region on the 30th of the month.

MAY marks the start of many **summer festival seasons**. Costume plays such as the *Rattenfänger Spiele* in Hameln begin regular weekend performances, while there are classical concerts in historic buildings, notably the Schlosstheater in Schwetzingen. Every ten years (next in 1990), the famous *Passionspiele* in Oberammergau begins its run. On a lighter note, there's the *Stabenfest* in Nördlingen. **Pentecost**, which usually falls towards the end of the month, sees distinctive religious festivals in the small Bavarian towns of Kötzting and Bogen. On the same weekend, there are two celebrated reconstructions of historic events—the *Meistertrunk* drama in Rothenburg and the *Kuchen und Bunnen Fest* in Schwäbisch Hall. Shortly afterwards, *Corpus Christi* is celebrated in Catholic areas, and is best experienced in Cologne. JUNE sees important **classical music** festivals, with the *Bach-Woche* during the second weekend of the month in Lüneburg, the *Händel-Festspiele* in Göttingen, and the *Europäische Wochen* in Passau, while there's a big festival of all kinds of music held under canvas in Freiburg. Throughout northern Germany, the shooting season is marked by *Schützenfeste*, the largest being Hannover's. Bad Wimpfen's *Talmarkt*, which begins at the end of the month, is a fair which can trace its history back a thousand years.

JULY is a particularly busy festival month, with summer fairs and both **wine** and **beer** festivals opening up every week; pick of the latter is that in Kulmbach. Dinkelsbühl's *Kinderzeche* and Ulm's *Schwörmontag* are the most famous folklore events at this time. The Bayreuth *Opernfest*, exclusively devoted to Wagner, is held during late July, but note that all tickets are put on sale a year in advance, and immediately snapped up. AUGUST is the main month for colorful displays of fireworks and illuminations, such as the *Schlossfest* in Heidelberg and *Der Rhein in Flammen* in Koblenz. There are a host of *Weinfeste* during the month in the Rhine-Mosel area, notably those in Rüdesheim and Mainz, while Straubing's *Gäubodenfest* is one of the country's largest beer festivals. Other important events at this time are the *Plärrer* city fair in Augsburg, the *Mainfest* in Frankfurt, and the *Zissel* folk festival in Kassel.

Paradoxically, Munich's renowned *Oktoberfest* actually begins on the last Saturday in SEPTEMBER. This month sees many of the most bacchanalian festivals, such as Heilbronn's *Weindorf* and Bad Cannstatt's *Volksfest*. OCTOBER sees things quieting down, though there's still the odd *Weinfest* in the Rhineland, along with the *Freimarkt* folk festival in Bremen. In NOVEMBER, there's the month-long *Hamburger Dom* fair in Hamburg, while the *Martinsfest* on the 10th/11th of the month is celebrated in Northern Baden and the Rhineland, most notably in Düsseldorf. Finally, DECEMBER is the month of Christmas markets (variably known as *Christkindelsmarkt* or *Weihnachtsmarkt*), and, if you were to choose just one, it should be Nürnberg's, which swells with traditional stalls selling everything from toys and trinkets to delicious sweets and biscuits.

SPORT

SKIING

The German Alps offer some very attractive ski resorts, often overlooked in the rush to get to Austria, Switzerland, and France. Everyone has heard of **Garmisch-Partenkirchen** (720m–2966m), if only because of the Olympic runs that are still used by many of the professionals today. As a resort it has all the winter sporting facilities you could wish for, as well as an extensive après-ski scene. But it's also one of the most expensive German resorts, with a strong emphasis on commerciality, which has sadly diminished its charm for the visitor. For equally excellent facilities, plenty of runs and lifts, affordable prices, and a beautiful setting, **Oberstdorf** (700m–2224m) is undoubtedly the all-round winner. Other, smaller resorts, which are high on picturesque views and ideally suited to novice and medium skiers, are **Reit im Winkel** (700m–1850m), **Bayrischzell** (800m–1724m), **Mittenwald** (750m–2385m), **Berchtesgaden** (550m–1800m) and **Schliersee** (800m–1693m). These are all traditional resorts, each with quite a few runs, good accommodation, and plenty of activities other than skiing available. Families are especially well catered for, with resident ski schools to take care of the kids. **Travel** to the German resorts is normally by plane to Munich, where trains connect with most ski areas, the journey taking less than two hours in all cases. If you go on a package tour, a coach will normally pick you up from the airport, but check with your travel agent. The largest expense apart from your flight ticket will be the ski pass, and the following is a guide to the kind of prices to be expected.

> **Average prices for six-day ski passes**:
> **Garmisch-Partenkirchen** DM176, DM117 kids, (50 lifts)
> **Oberstdorf** DM172, DM129 kids, (35 lifts)
> **Reit im Winkel** DM137, DM90 kids, (13 lifts)
> **Bayrischzell** DM131, DM98 kids, (25 lifts)
> **Mittenwald** DM115, DM75 kids, (7 lifts)
> **Berchtesgaden** DM115, DM75 kids, (10 lifts)
> **Schliersee** DM120, DM75, (20 lifts)

SOCCER

Soccer is the nearest Germany comes to having a national sport. The *Bundesliga* (the elite division) is as fiercely competitive a league as any in Europe; it has only 18 teams, so even some of the better-known clubs are liable to find themselves in relegation difficulties if they are in indifferent form. The German style of play, mirroring the national character, tends to be based on well-organized, methodical teamwork, rather than on the individual brilliance favored in Latin countries. League matches are held on Saturday afternoons; European cup games are usually on Wednesday evenings. By far the most famous **team** is *Bayern München*, whose record down the years entitles them to be ranked among the world's top clubs. Given the game's blue-collar roots, it's not surprising that many of the other leading clubs are based in industrial towns— *Borussia Mönchengladbach*, *Borussia Dortmund*, and the two company teams of the country's main chemical conglomerate, *Bayer Leverkusen* and *Bayer Uerdingen*. Others who have enjoyed success are *Hamburger SV*, *FC Köln* and *VfB Stuttgart*. The national team has rather a reputation for being the bridesmaid in major events— the only World Cup tournament victory was achieved in 1974, when there was the distinct advantage of being host nation—but has a record of consistency equal to any.

TENNIS

Tennis is the current German obsession: in just a few years, the country has jumped from being a long-term backwater for this sport to a position of international pre eminence. The big breakthrough came in 1985 when the 17 year-old Boris Becker blasted all his opponents off the court to become the first unseeded and youngest-ever men's singles champion at Wimbledon, and has ranked in the top handful of players ever since. Even more significant has been the steamrolling success of Steffi Graf, the most ferocious hitter women's tennis has ever seen, who won the Grand Slam (all four major international tournaments) at the age of 19 in 1988. She has built up an such an aura of invincibility (apparently only losing when ill) that many have worried that the women's game is being killed off, though this same characteristic has made her a national idol, her photo adorning billboards all over the country. Germany does not have a major international championship; the most important **events** are in Hamburg in May and July, and in Stuttgart in November.

OTHER SPORTS

Table tennis is taken very seriously in Germany, with players from all over Europe competing for club teams in a professional league. The same is true of **handball** and **volleyball**, which are both far more popular than they are in any English-speaking country; **hockey** is also well-established. Main venues for **motor sports** are Hockenheim near Heidelberg (where the Formula 1 Grand Prix is held each July) and the venerable Nürburgring. The leading **equestrian** events are held consecutively in Hamburg and Aachen in June, while the celebrated dressage displays in Celle take place in September and October. Germany's **horse-racing** calendar is dominated by the spring and autumn season at Iffezheim near Baden-Baden, and by the Derby week in Hamburg in late June.

From December to February, **winter sports** competitions, many associated with the skiing World Cup, are held in the southern part of the country. The main venues are Garmisch-Partenkirchen and Oberstdorf in Bavaria, and the Black Forest resorts of Todtmoos, Todtnau, Furtwangen, and Schonach.

POLICE, TROUBLE AND SEXUAL HARASSMENT

The German police (*Polizei*) are not renowned for their friendliness, but they usually treat foreigners with courtesy. It's important to remember that you are expected to carry **ID** (your passport, or at least a student card or driving licence) at all times. Failure to do so could turn a routine police check into a drawn-out and unpleasant process. **Traffic offences** or any other misdemeanors will result in a rigorous checking of documentation, and on-the-spot fines are best paid without argument. The police are generally very correct, and shouldn't subject you to any unnecessary chicanery. **Reporting thefts** at local police stations is straigh forward, but inevitably there'll be a great deal of red tape to wade through. All **drugs** are illegal in Germany, and anyone caught with them will face either prison or deportation: consulates will not be sympathetic towards those on drug charges. Throughout Germany the number to ring for the police is ☎110.

The level of **sexual harassment** is fortunately very low in Germany, and single women in restaurants, bars, and cafés are nothing unusual and don't generally get bothered. People will come and sit at your table if there's limited space, but that doesn't automatically mean you're about to get chatted up. Even hitch hiking is relatively safe here, and although men in Germany can be just as macho as anywhere else, they don't often show it in public. Large cities increase the likelihood of problems, as do long train journeys, but common sense and a firm manner should be enough to evade most unpleasant encounters. (see also the following section).

WOMEN'S GERMANY

Women have traditionally been confined to a very subordinate role in German society, and this has improved only relatively amid the postwar prosperity of the Federal Republic. Few women reach senior positions in the main **political parties**; indeed, Chancellor Kohl has been chauvinistic enough to woo the female vote by referring to "our pretty women" as "one of Germany's natural resources." To some extent, the situation has changed with the arrival of the Greens as a credible political force, with the formidable Petra Kelly the best-known of several women in its corporate leadership. Many commentators, however, see this merely as a natural extension of the tendency for women to be at the forefront of German radicalism, continuing the tradition established by the early Communist leader Rosa Luxemburg, and continuing via the terrorist groups of the 1970s.

There are no effective laws against sex discrimination. Few women manage to get to the top in the **professions** and civil service, even although they now account for nearly half the total of university undergraduates. The situation has improved somewhat in medicine, with 20% of doctors being women, and in the Protestant churches, which now allow women to become pastors. It's similarly difficult for a woman to climb the corporate ladder, though it's now quite normal for a daughter to succeed her father as head of a **business**—a far cry from the days when the Kaiser had to intervene personally to find a suitable husband for Bertha Krupp, in order to ensure the continuing credibility of the famous armaments conglomerate.

If you want to find out about grass-roots feminism, the best bet is to contact the local **women's center** (*Frauenzentrum*). These are found in most cities, and are listed in the *Guide* whenever known. They're run with the usual

German sense of organization and efficiency; they usually have a café and discussion groups and workshops. Another distinctive feature of the feminist scene is the provision of **Women's houses** (*Frauenhäuser*) to cater to rape victims and battered wives. There's at least one in every major city; addresses obviously have to be kept secret, but the telephone numbers can be found in the appropriate local directory. To end on a brighter note, there are plenty of **women's bookshops** (the best of which are listed in the *Guide*), as well as women-only *Mitfahrzentralen* (See Getting Around). The *Frauen Adressbuch Berlin :Courage)* gives full feminist listings.

GAY GERMANY

West Germany is one of the best countries in Europe in which to be gay (in German, *schwul*). The only real legal restriction is that the male age of consent is 18, and on the whole it's a tolerant place as far as attitudes go.

However to this rosy picture it's necessary to add a serious **caveat**. In rural areas people are often hostile towards gays and this intensifies in the Catholic southern part of the country, particularly in ultra conservative **Bavaria**. Here small-town prejudice was given a judicial edge by the local parliament which, in 1987 under the late and fairly unlamented Franz-Josef Strauss, introduced mandatory AIDS testing for people who were suspected of being HIV-positive. Not content with this draconian measure they also formulated a law whereby HIV-positive people who don't follow official guidelines on "proper behavior" could be arrested and held indefinitely. Both these measures remain firmly in force

.Fortunately saner attitudes prevail in the rest of Germany, particularly in the **big cities**, all of which have thriving gay scenes, as do many medium-sized and even relatively small towns. The listings sections in this book usually give a run-down of the gay scene in the larger cities and towns, giving some kind of gay group contact address and telephone number wherever possible.

The main gay meccas are West Berlin, Hamburg, Cologne, Munich, and Frankfurt. Berlin in particular has, despite the horrors of the past, a good record for tolerating an open and energetic gay and lesbian scene; as far back as the 1920s Christopher Isherwood and W.H. Auden both came here, drawn to a city where, in sharp contrast with oppressive London, there was a gay community that did not live in fear of harassment and legal persecution.

The national gay organization is the *Bundesverband Homosexualität*, PO Box 120 630, 5300 Bonn 12 and there's a also a national AIDS help organization; the *Deutsche AIDS-Hilfe e.V (D.A.H.)* at Nestorstrasse 8–9, 1000 Berlin 31 (☎030 896 9060). The most widely read gay magazine is *Männer* which comes out bi-monthly and costs DM16.80.

Many of the attitudes described above apply equally to **lesbians**. Outside of major cities, Germany's lesbian community is perforce more muted; being openly out in rural areas is impossible. Most of the women's centers listed in the *Guide* have details of local bars and meeting places. Alternatively, *GAIA's Guide*, available from bookstores in Britain and Germany, lists lesbian bars and contact addresses throughout the country. Worth scanning while you're in Germany is *UKZ-Unsere Zeitung*, the monthly lesbian magazine.

DIRECTORY

ADDRESSES The street name is always written before the number. *Strasse* (street) is commonly abbreviated as *Str.*, and often joined on to the end of the previous word. Other terms include Gasse (alley), Ufer (quay), Platz (square), Allee (avenue) and Ring (beltway).

AIRPORT TAX does not apply in Germany.

BOOKS The Germans are voracious readers, and all large cities have a superb choice of bookshops, many of which also stock a range of English-language publications.

CONTRACEPTIVES From pharmacists, though you have to see a doctor for the pill or IUDs.

DISABLED TRAVELERS The **Touristik Union International** (TUI), Postfach 610280, 3000 Hannover 61, (☎ 0511-5670) has a centralized information bank on many German hotels, pensions, and resorts that cater to the needs of disabled travelers or those with specific dietary requirements—not in specially designed and separate establishments, but within the mainstream of German tourist facilities. The TUI can book you on to a package tour or organize rooms according to individual itineraries, taking into account each customer's needs, which are gauged from a questionnaire filled out before reservation arrangements commence. Their services also include such details as providing suitable wheelchairs for train travel, the transportation of travelers' own wheelchairs, and the provision of conveyances at airports and stations.

EMBASSIES AND CONSULATES are listed under the relevant cities. Bear in mind that the level of help, other than in Bonn, is likely to be variable—some cities keep up a fantasy diplomatic life, in which the honorary consul is a local businessman who has bought the title for the kudos it confers on him.

JAYWALKING is illegal in Germany, and you can be fined if caught. Except in the irreverent atmosphere of West Berlin, locals stand rigidly to attention until the green light comes on—even when there isn't a vehicle in sight.

KIDS Traveling with youngsters shouldn't be a problem. Kids under 4 travel free on the railroads; those between 4 and 11 qualify for half-fare. On many municipal public transit tickets, kids travel free if accompanied by an adult. Similarly reduced rates are offered by hotels and guest houses. Most towns and cities have daycare facilities: contact tourist offices for details. The most suitable entertainments for kids are listed in the *Guide*.

LAUNDRY A laundromat (*Wäscherei*) is not a very common sight in Germany, but they do exist and have been listed in the guide. Dry cleaners (*Reinigung*) are more frequent, but also quite expensive. Many youth hostels have washing machines in their basements; otherwise you'll have to make do with a sink.

LUGGAGE CONSIGNMENT main stations have numerous luggage storage lockers. The smallest and cheapest are large enough to hold all but the bulkiest backpack or suitcase, and at DM1 for 24 hours they make carrying heavy luggage around town a false economy. Leaving bags with the station attendants costs about twice as much, but may be the only option in small towns, where the hours of service are often very restricted.

RACISM Thanks to the massive influx of *Gastarbeiter*, mainly from southern Europe, Germany is now firmly multicultural. However, there's no effective law against racial discrimination, and it's far from unknown for cranky pub owners or nightclub proprietors to refuse entry on simple color grounds.

STUDENT CARDS are worth carrying for the substantial reductions on admission fees they bring.

PART TWO

THE

GUIDE

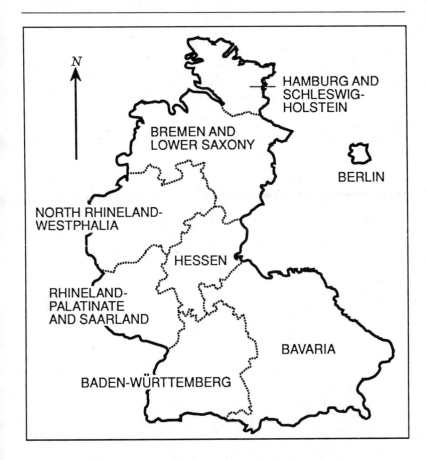

N

HAMBURG AND
SCHLESWIG-
HOLSTEIN

BREMEN AND
LOWER SAXONY

BERLIN

NORTH RHINELAND-
WESTPHALIA

HESSEN

RHINELAND-
PALATINATE
AND SAARLAND

BAVARIA

BADEN-WÜRTTEMBERG

CHAPTER ONE

BAVARIA

B AVARIA or *BAYERN* is the home of German clichés: beer-swilling Lederhosen-clad men, dachshunds, cowbells and Alpine villages, sauerkraut and *Wurst*, and Neuschwanstein Castle. But that's only one small part of the Bavarian picture, and almost entirely restricted to the region south of the state capital **Munich**, which is also where the classic picture-book landscapes of snow-capped Alps and sparkling lakes are to be found. Heading towards the state's western region, **Bavarian Swabia** and its pristine capital **Augsburg** offer quite a different experience. The food is less pork and sausages and more pasta and sauces, the landscape tends to be gentle farming country

ideal for camping and cycling vacations, and the only set attractions outside Augsburg are the medieval towns along the **Romantic Road** and the River Danube. To the north lies **Franconia**, whose main city is **Nürnberg**. The land here is mostly characterized by vineyards and nature parks, and there's hardly any traditional Bavarian culture. People sometimes even take offense at being called Bavarian, the reasons for which are historical: the region has only been part of Bavaria since 1803, and Franconians still like to cultivate their own heritage—which they consider more refined than that of their southern cousins. One of the most obvious contradictions is the wine-drinking culture in the northwest around **Würzburg**, while in the northeast the most striking difference is the elegantly plain baroque architecture unique to the Lutheran strongholds of **Ansbach** and **Bayreuth**. The contrasting influences of Lutherism and Catholicism are most apparent in Franconia because, in the aftermath of the Reformation, the region was more or less split down the middle in terms of dominant faith: the legacy of that division remains much in evidence today. **Eastern Bavaria**, on the other hand, is less refined and more rustic, a relatively poor region where life in the highland forests revolves around logging and workshop industries such as traditional glass production. Except for the regional capital of **Regensburg**, it's still quite a remote area; the Upper Palatinate and the Bavarian Forest to the east are off the beaten tourist trail and excellent for hiking without crowds.

The countryside and outdoor pursuits provide the main experience when exploring this state, since there are only four large towns other than Munich. Having said that, the state capital is certainly one of the star attractions of any trip to Germany, and definitely shouldn't be omitted from anyone's itinerary. The other urban centers of Augsburg, Regensburg, Nürnberg, and Würzburg are also some of the most interesting in the country. Augsburg and Regensburg both started life as Roman forts and evidence of their 2000-year heritage can be seen in some excellent museums as well as in the architecture of the towns themselves. Augsburg is predominantly characterized by its grand Renaissance buildings, while Regensburg has the most complete medieval townscape in Germany. Nürnberg and Würzburg were both extensively destroyed during World War II, but Nürnberg's ancient city center has been carefully restored, and the place retains at least some of its historic flavor. Attempts to rebuild Würzburg have been less successful, but it is still a major artistic center. Among Bavaria's smaller towns, **Bamberg**, with its magnificently varied architectural legacy, ranks as the most outstanding, while **Passau** is notable for its harmonious baroque layout.

Historically and **politically**, Bavaria has always been a moving force. A kingdom from 1806 and a Free State after the 1918 Revolution, it was one of the few German states to retain its traditional borders when the Allies redrew the map in 1945. As a result, Bavarians have a highly developed sense of cultural identity. The traditional and deeply Catholic south dominates the entire state—a fact most clearly apparent in local architecture and politics. With the exception of Franconia, Bavaria is dominated architecturally by the baroque style, a legacy of the Catholic resurgence during the Counter-Reformation. On the political front, Minister-President Franz-Joseph Strauss, the uncrowned king of Bavaria, did his best to assert his state party's interests, not just in Bavaria but in national politics as well, until his death in 1988. Certainly he was the political bogeyman of the nation, and it remains to be seen whether this notoriously right-wing state will now relax a little, though it seems there are plenty of people eager to step into the dead man's shoes. The rest of the country tends to be rather wary of Bavarians, seeing them as loud bullies always intent on getting their own way. However, that's just another stereotype. They're famous for being loud, rude, and bad-tempered—but also for warmth, humor and having a good time. No half-measures here.

Travel is made easy by a good network of train connections and regional buses, though public transportation in Bavarian Swabia and Eastern Bavaria is a little scanty. Here either a car or cycle is handier. Cycling is an excellent and very popular way to see more of the countryside, and is facilitated by a great many marked bike paths throughout the state. An unfortunate restriction for travelers **over 27** is that they're barred from using the youth hostels, but reasonable alternatives can usually be found, and you'll only be handicapped if you're on the tightest of budgets.

MUNICH

Founded in 1158, **MUNICH** (*MÜNCHEN*) has been the capital of Upper Bavaria since 1255, and of the united province since 1503—and as far as the locals are concerned, it may as well be the center of the universe. *Münchener* pride themselves on their special status and have strong views on who exactly qualifies to be counted as one of them. Even people who have made Munich their home for most of their lives are still called *Zugereiste* ("newcomers"), meaning they are accepted city residents, but are by no means considered equals. It's the sort of stubborn pride that is both endearing and extremely irritating.

Next to Berlin, Munich is Germany's most popular city. Everyone wants to study here, the rich and jet-set like to live here, as do writers, painters, musicians, and film-makers, all creating a vibrant cultural life that's hard to beat. The city has everything you'd expect to find in a cosmopolitan capital, but it's small enough to be digestible in one visit, and it's got the added bonus of a great setting, with snow-dusted mountains and Alpine lakes just an hour's drive away. A day or two here would be long enough to see the sights as well as a bit more, and get to know the city a little. The best time of year to do this is from June to early October, when all the beer gardens, street cafés, and bars are in full swing. Find out what's going on in the magazines *Münchener Stadtzeitung* or *Im München* available at any kiosk.

Staying here will cost you, but it's worth every penny and if you're not fussy about accommodation, money can be saved. For visits of over a week, buying a travel pass will save a great deal, and cheap meals aren't difficult to find. The university mensas are rock-bottom, and open to anyone with a student card.

Föhn

If people seem even more bad-tempered than usual, and especially if car-drivers are being particularly aggressive, look up—if you see a picture-book blue sky without a cloud in sight, and there's a warm wind, you'll probably find it's **Föhn**.

Föhn is a type of weather peculiar to the alpine region of Southern Germany, but it's also found around the Rocky Mountains, the Andes, and in Japan. No one is quite sure exactly why it occurs, but here it has something to do with high pressure zones over the mountains which results in clear skies and warm weather in southern Germany, while on the Italian side it's cloudy and often raining. Usually visitors and new residents don't have any problems with Föhn. It's only after five to ten years that people become sensitive and suffer various combinations of migraine, fainting spells, irritability, and sleeplessness. So while you're enjoying the fantastic views, don't be too surprised if all around you are in a foul mood.

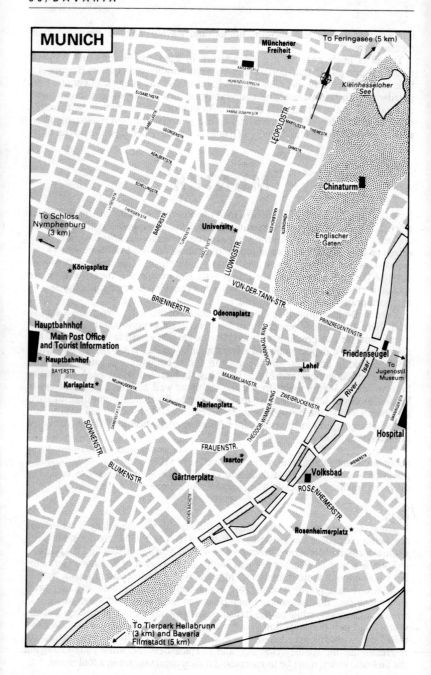

MUNICH

To Feringasee (5 km)

Münchener Freiheit ★

KAISERPLATZ

HOHENZOLLERNSTR

Kleinhesseloher See

ELISABETHSTR

GABELSTR

GEORGENSTR

FRANZ-JOSEPH-STR

L E O P O L D S T R.

MARTIUSSTR. · THIEMESTR

ONMSTR.

ADALBERTSTR

Chinaturm ■

SCHELLINGSTR

To Schloss Nymphenburg (3 km)

B A R E R S T R.

THERESIENSTR

GIRELSTR

KAULBACHSTR.

University ★

VEIERINARSTR.

L U D W I G S T R.

Englischer Gaten

★ Königsplatz

VON-DER-TANN-STR.

PRINZREGENTENSTR

BRIENNERSTR.

Odeonsplatz ★

SCHÖNFELD RING

Hauptbahnhof
**Main Post Office
and Tourist Information**

★ **Hauptbahnhof**

BAYERSTR

NEUHAUSERSTR.

Karlsplatz ★

MAXIMILIANSTR.

Lehel ★

Friedenseugel ■

To Jugenostil Museum

River Isar

SMARINGERSTR

S O N N E N S T R.

DAMENSTIFTSTR

KAUFINGERSTR

★ Marienplatz

THEODOR-WIMMER-RING

ZWEIBRÜCKENSTR.

Hospital

FRAUENSTR.

BLUMENSTR.

Isartor ★

WIENERSTR

Volksbad ■

Gärtnerplatz

REICHENBACHSTR

ROSENHEIMERSTR.

Rosenheimerplatz ★

To Tierpark Hellabrunn
(3 km) and Bavaria
Filmstadt (5 km)

The City

Heart of the city is **the Marienplatz**; the pedestrian center fans out from here in an approximate circle of one square kilometer. This is tourist- and shopping-land, with all the city's major department stores, the central market, the royal palace, and the most important churches. North of the Marienplatz, Ludwigstrasse and Leopoldstrasse run straight through the heart of **Schwabing**, the entertainments quarter full of Schickies (German yuppies) who frequent the many bars and pose in the street cafés. It's also close to the city's main park, known as the **Englischer Garten**, and the best-known beer garden around the Chinese Tower. To the west of the axis between the Marienplatz and Schwabing is the **museum quarter**, with the superb Alte Pinakothek and the most important of Munich's 36 museums. Running the length of the eastern sector is the Isar River, and under the heading *Along the Isar*, you'll find a description of a side of Munich not usually seen by visitors.

Arriving and Getting Around

Arriving by plane at the tiny old airport of **Riem** just outside the city, the quickest way into town is the *Flughafen-City* bus, which goes to the **Hauptbahnhof** every twenty minutes between 6:40am and 9pm for DM5. The bus stop is directly in front of the airport terminal. Failing this, take a #139 or #37 bus to the Riem S-Bahn stop and change on to a fast train to the Hauptbahnhof. Taxis are prohibitively expensive and a waste of money. If you arrive when no buses are running, it's only a twenty-minute walk to the S-Bahn stop: as you come out of the airport, follow the road to your right, which goes over the expressway. Immediately after crossing the expressway, a footpath goes off to the left. Follow this to the village and the main road called Riemerstrasse. Turn right off the main road and walk to the end of Leibergerstrasse and the S-Bahn stop. **Arriving by bus**, the Hauptbahnhof is a stone's throw away.

There's a **tourist information desk** in the "arrivals" area of the airport for general information plus free maps and lists of hotels, but they can't reserve rooms. At the Hauptbahnhof, the main **tourist office** (Mon.–Sat. 8am–11pm, Sun. 1–9:30pm;☎239 1256/57) is opposite platform 11. They will reserve rooms for a fee of DM3, and provide free brochures about the city and what's on. Other useful items in the vicinity are a **bank**, **luggage lockers**, and a **24-hour post office**, just across the street from the tourist office.

Public Transit

Your best bet is to buy a **travel pass** on arrival from the ticket office at the Hauptbahnhof—go down to the U-Bahn level and follow signs to the Starnberger Bahnhof and then to the *Zeitkartenstelle*. Prices vary according to how many zones are required, but zones 0000 and 1200 cover the city center and most of Schwabing, and cost DM10.50 for a week or DM41.60 for a month. One drawback is that passes are only valid from Monday to Sunday, so buying mid-week means losing out. A weekly pass for the entire city transit system, including places like the Ammersee or Dachau, costs DM45.50. Just the city without the regional S-Bahn routes costs DM28.50 per week or DM106.50 per month. There are also *Zeitkarten* offices at the Ostbahnhof and at the Poccistrasse U-Bahn station. You'll need your passport and a couple of **photos** to buy any of these passes.

Otherwise, tickets for city transport are available from ticket machines in all U-Bahn stations, at some bus and tram stops, and inside trams. This is where it gets a bit complicated . . . If you're going longer distances across the city you will need to buy a **blue ticket** (DM9.50 or DM15), and then cancel two strips for every zone crossed. To find out how many strips you need to delete, either ask the conductor or at a ticket office. Alternatively, look at the route maps at any station, tram or bus stop, which show the number of zones between any two points. **Red tickets** (DM6.50) are only for children aged 4 to 15 or short trips for adults. **Twenty-four-hour tickets** for the entire city cost DM7, or DM12.50 for the city and S-Bahn region. Tickets must be stamped before any journey, though it's not necessary to stamp every strip, just the last one needs to be deleted. Those freeloading without a canceled ticket face an on-the-spot DM40 fine, which is frequently enforced. Plain-clothes ticket controlers turn up regularly, and anyone without ready cash or ID is taken to the nearest police station.

Finding a Place to Stay

Cheap accommodation can be hard to find, especially during the summer high season, though prices are usually constant throughout the year. The least expensive option for those under 23 is the *Kapuzinerhölzl* mega-tent, run by the city council during the summer, where up to 500 people sleep *en masse* for DM5 each. Those under 27 can use one of the city's three **hostels**, which begin at around DM10; for those over 27 the cheapest option is the very central *Haus International*, which charges DM25.50 a night. But for just a little more money, considerably greater comfort can be found at the city's **pensions** and **hotels**. Prices start in the region of DM35 per person and average around DM50. The tourist office at the Hauptbahnhof will reserve rooms for you for a fee of DM3, and whatever your choice, it would be sensible to phone ahead. There are also four main **campgrounds** in and around the city.

Hostels

If you're under 27 or a parent traveling with children under 18, there's a choice of three youth hostels. Most central is at *Wendl-Dietrich-Strasse 20*, München (☎131156): U-Bahn to Rotkreuzplatz, then walk down the Wendl-Dietrich-Strasse. This is the largest and most basic hostel, with 535 beds in assorted dormitories. Prices start at DM10.70 for bed and breakfast, plus DM2.50 extra for sheets if you don't have a sleeping bag. Hot meals are available from DM5.50. Check-in time noon–1am. Smaller, though more luxurious, is the *Youth Guesthouse Thalkirchen* at Miesingstr. 4, München (☎723 6550/60): U-Bahn to Harras, then tram #16 to Boschetsriederstrasse. Prices (including breakfast) range from DM15 for a bed in a large dormitory, to DM22 for a single room. Check-in time 7am–11pm. Not very central, but in an old castle right next to the Isar River, is *Burg Schwaneck*, Burgweg 4–6, 8023 Pullach (☎793 0643): S-Bahn #7 to Pullach and then follow the signs to the *Jugendherberge*. Prices range from DM10 in six- to eight-bed rooms, to DM11.20 in four-bed rooms, all including breakfast. Check-in time 5pm–1am.

A further choice for which you don't need a youth-hostel card, and for which there's no age limit, is the *Haus International*, Elisabethstr. 87, München (☎185081/2/3): U-Bahn to Hohenzollernplatz, then bus #33 or tram #12, and get off two stops later at Barbarastrasse. Centrally located in Schwabing, room sizes range from five beds (DM25.50 per person) to singles (DM38). Phone first. There's a Youth Hostel for **women only**, with an age limit of 25, very near the

Hauptbahnhof at Goethestr. 9, München (☎555891). Prices are around DM25–27, and again it's advisable to phone ahead.

Camping

Among the camping options, the cheapest for under-23s is the *Kapuzinerhölzl* youth camp, open from the end of June to the end of August: U-Bahn to Rotkreuzplatz, then tram #12 to the Botanischer Garten, walk down Franz-Schrank-Strasse and turn left at the end of the road. Apart from the sleeping tent, there are showers, a canteen and an information bureau. Price per person is DM5, which includes blankets, an air mattress, and tea in the morning. Check-in time 5pm–9am. If you don't mind the lack of privacy and the imperfect security for personal belongings, this is a cheap and fun place to be, and although its officially reserved for travelers under 23 and for a maximum of three nights, the people in charge are very flexible, and older girlfriends or boyfriends won't usually be turned away. For more information, call ☎141 43000.

The best "proper" campground is *Thalkirchen* at Zentralländerstr. 49, München (15 March–31 Oct.; ☎723 1707): U-Bahn to Implerstrasse, then bus #57 to its final stop. (Once the new U-Bahn routes are finished, take the underground to Thalkirchen.) It's the most central grounds to downtown and in an attractive part of the Isar River valley. Be warned that it's very popular during the Oktoberfest period because of its proximity to the fairground. Second choice would be the *Obermenzing* grounds, at Lochhausenerstr. 59, München (15 March–31 Oct.; ☎811 2235): S-Bahn to Obermenzing, then bus #75 to Lochhausenerstrasse about five stops later. This campground is in a wealthy suburb and close to the magnificent Nymphenburg palace and parks.

The campground at *Dachauerstr. 571*, München, (☎150 6936) is open all year, but awkward to reach: S-Bahn to Moosach, then bus #709 or #710 to the site. The *Langwieder See* campground at Eschenriederstr. 119, München (April–Oct.; ☎814 1566) is even worse, since it's not only right next to the Augsburg–Stuttgart expressway, but also only accessible by car and a way out of town.

Hotels and Pensions

Reckon on an absolute minimum of DM35 for a single room; most often you'll pay around DM45. Usually the shower will be shared and breakfast is always included in the price. Many pensions offer rooms with three to six beds, and these are a very good way to cut costs if you're traveling in a group, and much more pleasant than hostel-type accommodation. Almost all the places listed here are in Schwabing or the university district, and all are within close range of where you'll want to be.

Singles from DM35–55 and Doubles DM60–100

Am Kaiserplatz, Kaiserplatz 12 (☎349190). Singles DM35–37, doubles DM65–69, three-to-six-bed rooms for DM87, DM110, DM130, and DM150 respectively. Very friendly, good location and big rooms. Wacky decor, with each room done in a different style—ranging from red satin to Bavarian rustic.

Clara, Wilhelmstr. 25 (☎348374). Six doubles at DM80. Close to the Leopoldstrasse.

Excelsior, Kaulbachstr. 85 (☎348213). Only has doubles at DM74–86. Opposite the Irish pub and close to the Leopoldstrasse.

Frank, Schellingstr. 24 (☎281451). Singles DM45, doubles DM70–80, three-to-four-bed rooms for DM35 per person. Best place in town in terms of prices and atmosphere. Mainly frequented by young travelers. Nice big rooms, and there's a fridge available to keep food in.

Isabella, Isabellastr. 35 (☎271 3503). Singles DM25–35, doubles DM58–60. Only has 12 beds with one bathroom on the landing. Run by a quirky old lady.

Steinberger, Ohmstr. 9 (☎331011). Singles DM45–69, doubles DM85–115. Friendly and good location.

Strigl, Elisabethstr. 117 (☎271 3444). Singles DM40–50, doubles DM70. Rather gruff management, but good location and reasonable prices.

Wilhelmy, Amalienstr. 71. Singles DM42.50, doubles DM85, three-to-four-bed rooms at DM37.50 per person. Very quiet and well situated.

Singles from DM55–85 and Doubles DM80–145

Adria, Liebigstr. 8a (☎293081/83). Singles DM75–85, doubles DM125–145. Quiet residential area, but close to Schwabing. Hotel standard rather than pension.

Hauser, Schellingstr. 11 (☎281006). Singles DM75–85, doubles DM100–140. Nothing special, but good location.

Hotel Eder, Zweigstr. 8 (☎554560). Singles DM55–80, doubles DM80–140, three-bed rooms DM165–185. Quiet road, but very central between the Hauptbahnhof and the Marienplatz.

Lettl, Amalienstr. 53 (☎283026). Singles DM84–125, doubles DM130–150. Friendly hotel.

Münchener Kindl, Damenstiftstr. 16 (☎264349). Singles DM55, doubles DM80–95, 3-bed rooms DM110. Couldn't really get closer to the Marienplatz and yet the street is very peaceful, out of the maelstrom of busy shoppers.

Stephanie, Türkenstr. 35 (☎284031). Singles DM 55–81, doubles DM100–130. Useful only if everywhere else is full.

The City Center

Almost nothing is left of Munich's original medieval city, but three of the gates remain to mark today's downtown. Bounded by the Odeonsplatz and the Sendlinger Tor to the north and south, and the Isar Tor and Karlstor to the east and west, it's only a fifteen-minute walk from one end to the other. But don't think this means you can see everything in one day—the place is densely packed with attractions and realistically needs two or three days to explore thoroughly.

Around the Marienplatz

The **Marienplatz** marks the hub of the city and the heart of the U-Bahn system below. About a fourth of the size of London's Trafalgar Square, there's something almost cozy about the Marienplatz. Street musicians and artists entertain the crowds and local youths lounge around the central fountain. At 11am and noon, the square fills with gaping tourists and the noise of clicking shutters as the desperately tuneless **carillon** in the Rathaus tower jingles into action, displaying two events that happened on this spot: the marriage of Wilhelm V to Renata von Lothringen in 1568, and the first *Schäfflertanz* ("coopers' dance") of 1517, intended to cheer people up during the plague. The dance is held every seven years, next in 1991.

The **Rathaus** itself is an ugly neo-Gothic monstrosity built in the late nineteenth century, whose only redeeming feature is the open-air café in the cool and breezy courtyard, perfect for having a drink in away from the crowds. To the right is the plain Gothic tower of the **Altes Rathaus**, which was rebuilt in the fifteenth century after being destroyed by lightning; today it houses a toy museum (see below). Following the traffic on the right, the slightly elevated **Peterskirche** looks out across the hubbub of the central market, or the *Viktualienmarkt*. It's the oldest church in Munich and most notable for one of the

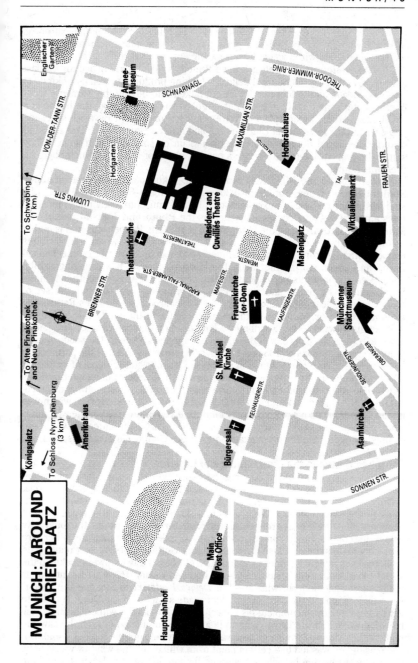

MUNICH: AROUND MARIENPLATZ

Englischer Garten

Armee-Museum

SCHNARNAGL

THEODOR-WIMMER-RING

MAXIMILIAN STR.

Hofbräuhaus

AM KOSTTOR

Hofgarten

VON-DER-TANN STR.

To Schwabing (1 km)

LUDWIG STR.

Residenz and Cuvilliés Theatre

Viktualienmarkt

TAL

FRAUEN STR.

Theatinerkirche

THEATINERSTR.

WEINSTR.

Marienplatz

BRIENNER STR.

KARDINAL-FAULHABER-STR.

MAFFEISTR.

Frauenkirche (or Dom)

Münchener Stadtmuseum

To Alte Pinakothek and Neue Pinakothek

KAUFINGERSTR.

OBERANGER

St. Michael Kirche

SCHDLINGERSTR.

Königsplatz

Amerika Haus

NEUHAUSERSTR.

Asamkirche

To Schloss Nymphenburg (3 km)

Bürgersaal

SONNEN STR.

Main Post Office

Hauptbahnhof

grisliest shrines you're likely to see. The skeletal relics of St. Munditia, patroness of single women, are poised in a glass box on a side altar, including the skull wrapped in netting with two glass eyes gazing out from a deathly face.

The **Viktualienmarkt** itself has been the city's main marketplace for the last 200 years, and bossy women sell delicious-looking produce, as well as all kinds of cheeses, meats, and deli items. If you get talked into buying, be warned it's not cheap, though the quality is excellent. Right in the middle of all the bustle is a small beer garden, a good place to have a snack. For a sweet Bavarian specialty, pop over to *Café Frischhut* at Blumenstr. 8 and order a *Dampfnudel*. This is a kind of large deep-fried doughnut, eaten either plain or sprinkled with sugar. They start baking at 5am here, so it's also a popular place for hungry nightclubbers on their way home.

Almost next to the Viktualienmarkt, on St. Jakobsplatz, is the **Münchener Stadtmuseum** (Tues.–Sat. 9am–4:30pm, Sun. 10am–6pm; DM3, DM1.50 students). This is the city's excellent local history museum, which also incorporates a number of other collections such as the **Photo and Film Museum**, the **Museum of Brewing**, and the **Puppet Museum**. The Puppet Museum is highly recommended; it's one of the largest collections in the world and includes puppets ranging from Indian and Chinese paper dolls to the large mechanical European variety. On the first floor, the History Museum has changing exhibitions to complement its permanent display of city models, eighteenth- and nineteenth-century furniture, and a collection of graphics. Look out for the set of *Morris Dancers*, carved as adornments for the ballroom of the Altes Rathaus by **Erasmus Grasser**, Munich's leading sculptor in the fertile late Gothic period.

Heading towards the Sendlinger Tor on Sendlinger Strasse, the small **Asamkirche** at no. 62 is one of the most enchanting examples of a rococo church in Bavaria. Built between 1733 and 1746, it's the crowning effort of the partnership of the two Asam brothers, who here successfully achieved their goal of a building whose architecture was completely integrated with all aspects of its interior decoration. The younger brother, Egid Quirin Asam (who was the sculptor and stuccoist), bought the land and underwrote the cost of the whole enterprise, which was intended to serve as his private family church. If you're not used to the wild interplay of color and gold, and countless plaster curls, the interior will seem completely excessive. But as an example of rococo design, it's a perfect specimen.

Churches Between the Marienplatz and Karlstor

Following the pedestrianized Kaufingerstrasse south from the Marienplatz, you pass most of the major department stores and the focus of the city's commercial activity. (Across the Karlsplatz, more department stores line an almost straight route to the Hauptbahnhof.) Only a stone's throw away from the mainstream of shoppers, the double-towered **Frauenkirche** (or **Dom**) dwarfs the busy city below. Its copper, onion-domed towers, one a little shorter than the other, are Munich's main symbol. Close up, the redbrick Gothic cathedral isn't really seen to its best advantage; it's finer from a distance, when the twin towers make up the visual focus of the city's skyline. Badly bombed during the war, its interior is today stark and modern, with just the *Devil's Footprint* to intrigue the visitor. According to legend the cathedral builder made a pact with the Devil: in order to get enough money to complete his church, he had to build it without a single visible window. When the Devil came to inspect the completed church, he saw the high Gothic windows from a distance and thought he'd get the builder's soul. But once inside, he was led to a certain point from which not one window was visible, since all were hidden by pillars. Stamping his foot in rage the Devil stormed off, leaving his black footprint in the marble. Rebuilding has meant the trick no longer works, but the footprint is still there.

A little farther up Kaufingerstrasse, the Renaissance facade of **St. Michael** stands unassumingly in line with the street's other buildings. Built between 1583 and 1597 under the auspices of Wilhelm V, the church was intended to symbolize the victory of Catholicism over Lutherism. The large bronze statue between the two entrances shows the Archangel Michael fighting for the Faith and killing Evil in the shape of a satyr. The interior, with its barrel vault second only in size to Rome's St. Peter's, is decorated in elegant white stucco in the ordered fashion of the German Renaissance. In the crypt below (Mon.–Fri. 10am–1pm and 2–4pm, Sat. 10am–3pm; DM1) you'll find the coffins of the Wittelsbach dynasty, who gained control of Bavaria in 1180, and retained power right up to 1918. Famous castle-builder Ludwig II is down here too, a candle permanently burning at the foot of his coffin and flowers on its lid.

Not far from the Karlstor stands the **Bürgersaal** at Neuhauserstr. 48. As its name implies, it was originally built as a civic meeting hall, but it has been a consecrated church since 1778. The actual shrine is upstairs (Mon.–Fri. 11am–3pm), but it's the crypt at entrance level that is most visited, since **Father Mayer**, one of the city's main anti-Nazis, is buried here and his grave has become something of a pilgrims' shrine. Father Mayer was the parish priest during the war and became such a nuisance to the authorities that he was shipped off to a concentration camp. But because of his immense popularity, and the bad press his death would have caused, he was transferred to house arrest in the Alpine Ettal monastery, and survived to return to the Bürgersaal after the war. He died shortly afterwards, in 1945.

North of the Marienplatz

This is the chic end of downtown, where ritzy shops and expensive cafés line streets like Theatinerstrasse, Maffeistrasse, and Maximilianstrasse. Today the palaces of Munich's earlier rich have all been turned into banks and insurance houses, but their ostentatious facades are still worth seeing and the grandest of the lot are along Kardinal Faulhaber-Strasse. Nearby is one of Munich's most regal churches—the **Theatinerkirche**. Its golden yellow towers and the green copper dome add a splash of color to the city skyline, and its baroque facade by François Cuvilliés stands proud on the Odeonsplatz. The church was designed by Agostino Barelli after the Roman St. Andrea della Valle in the late seventeenth century, but it wasn't completed until 1768—hence its baroque rather than rococo finish.

The **Maximilianstrasse** is the Champs-Elysées of the city. In between the Opera House, Cuvilliés Theater and Schauspielhaus, the exclusive fashion houses have their shops, and the *Hotel Vierjahreszeiten* is one of the best addresses in town. When the refinement gets too much, the little Kosttor road leads straight to the Platzl and a perfect antidote: the **Hofbräuhaus**. Everyone has heard of it, no local would be caught dead in it. But if you don't mind getting ripped off for a *Mass* ("measure") of beer, go ahead. Munich's largest and most famous drinking hall resounds with the cheers of tourists from all over the world, while professional Bavarians entertain them with traditional oompah music.

Best left for a fresh day, the **Residenz** (Tues.–Sat. 10am–4:30pm, Sun. 10am–1pm; DM2.50) at the beginning of the Maximilianstrasse was the palace of the former Wittelsbach rulers. Regarded as one of the finest examples of Renaissance architecture, it was modified and expanded down the centuries, before being extensively destroyed in the last war and almost totally rebuilt in the 1950s and

1960s. It's so large that to see the whole thing you have to go on two consecutive tours—one in the morning and one in the afternoon—though if this sounds too tedious you're at liberty to wander around by yourself. In that case, though, you'd be well-advised to buy the *Residenz Guidebook*, which covers everything in clear and exhaustive detail.

On the morning tour you see the **Antiquarium**, the oldest and most original part of the palace. This long, cavernous chamber was built in 1571 to house the family's famous collection of antiquities. A generation later, its austere architecture was sharply modified in accordance with the Mannerist taste of the time to serve as a banquet hall, and its tunnel vault covered with humanist-inspired frescoes of grotesques, illustrations of the Virtues, and views of Bavaria. As a prelude to this transformation, the adjoining **Grotto Court** was created, its centerpiece of tufa, crystal, and colored shells framing a statue of Mercury by Giambologna. The **Ancestors' Gallery** is decorated in the richest rococo style, and looks for all the world like a Hall of Mirrors, except that the glass is replaced by 121 (mostly imaginary) portraits of the Wittelsbachs, who tried to give their line the most prestigious roots possible by including such dubious ancestors as Charlemagne. In the **Rooms of the Elector**, look out for three paintings by Bernardo Bellotto, who here applied to Munich (as he did to a number of other European cities) the technique his uncle Canaletto had used so successfully to immortalize the Venice of his day. Other highlights of the morning circuit include a passageway hung with a cycle of 25 views of Italy by the Munich Romantic painter Carl Rottmann, and a suite of rooms containing extensive collections of eighteenth- and nineteenth-century European porcelain, along with fourteenth-to-eighteenth-century Chinese and Japanese examples.

The last stage of the morning tour can also be seen in the afternoon. This includes the eight appropriately named **Rich Rooms** in the sumptuous rococo style of François Cuvilliés, and the five **Halls of the Nibelungs**, in which medieval Germany's most famous epic is depicted in a series of paintings by Julius Schnorr von Carolsfeld. A former member of the Nazarene Brotherhood in Rome (see *Contexts*), the artist worked for forty years on this project, painting in the highly detailed, glossy style later taken up in England by the Pre-Raphaelites. Other rooms can be seen in the afternoon only, and include further displays of ceramics, along with the silverware collection and the baroque **Golden Hall**. You can also see the two **chapels**, which were both built in the early years of the seventeenth century. The larger one was for general use, while the more lavish "Secret Chapel" was built for the private meditations of one of the most famous of the Wittlesbachs, Maximilian I. Another memento of Maximilian comes with the **Steinzimmer**, a suite of profusely furnished rooms with a complicated set of allegories illustrating the Elector's personal vision of the world and the afterlife.

A separate ticket is necessary to see the fabulous treasures of the **Schatzkammer** (same times; DM2.50), which is the nearest secular equivalent to the matchless treasury of the Dom in Aachen. Among the early items, look out for the late ninth century **miniature ciborium** belonging to King Arnulf of Carinthia, adorned with embossed golden reliefs of Christ's ministry, and the **cross** of Queen Gisela of Hungary, made for the grave of her mother, the Duchess of Bavaria. There's a spectacular array of **crowns**, including one allegedly worn by the Empress Kunegunde, another which was formerly on the head-reliquary of her husband Henry II in the Bamberg Dom, plus one which belonged to Princess Blanche of England. Star piece of the whole display, kept in a room of its own, is the **statuette of St. George**, made in Munich around 1590 for Wilhelm V. This has a base of gold, silver, and enamel, and is encrusted with diamonds, rubies, sapphires, emeralds, chalcedony, agate, and rock crystal to create a truly dazzling effect. The outstanding German Renaissance tradition in the decorative arts can be seen in a host of chalices, tankards, caskets, pendants, clocks and portable altars. Famous artists were often commissioned to provide plans for these, as in the **rock crystal dish**, whose gold mount is known to have been designed by Holbein the Younger. Faced with such competition, the Bavarian **crown jewels**, made in the early nineteenth century soon after the duchy was promoted to a kingdom, seem rather tame. However, the **ceremonial swords** from Turkey and Persia which end the display are worthy rivals to their German counterparts.

Yet another ticket has to be bought for the **Cuvilliés Theater** (Mon.–Sat. 2–5pm, Sun. 10am–5pm; DM1.50), which is a very special treat worth making time for. Formally part of the Residenz and the Wittelsbachs' private theater, it's a perfectly intact rococo gem, dripping in gold and bristling with intricate carvings and delicate stucco. Nowadays, it's deservedly named after the tenacious little Walloon who built it. **François Cuvilliés** began his career in the debilitating role of court dwarf to the Elector Max Emanuel, but proved that he was capable of greater things by designing defensive systems for the army he was precluded from joining; as a result, he was sent to Paris to study the latest architectural theories. On his return, he developed the new rococo style to its most extravagant limits in a series of stunningly original buildings, of which this is one of the finest.

Also worth popping into for a stroll and a civilized drink is the **Hofgarten**, a former royal park whose entrance is just off the Odeonsplatz. At the far end, the bombed **Armeemuseum** was until recently left as an anti-war memorial. Now it's being rebuilt to house a museum of Bavarian history, but it's already known as the "Straussoleum," after the man whose pet project it was.

Schwabing

The Marienplatz might be the physical center of town but **Schwabing** is its hub. Munich must be one of the most cliquish cities around, and there's nowhere better to observe its different tribes than around the **Leopoldstrasse**. Only three stops by U-Bahn from the Marienplatz, Schwabing encompasses a large part of Munich's northern sector, with the Leopoldstrasse forming a more or less straight axis through the middle. A much larger area than downtown, Schwabing spreads untidily to the left and right of its central line, the Englischer Garten making up one pleasant border. The rest of the quarter reaches as far north as Studentenstadt, and to the Olympiapark and Josephsplatz in the west. If you intend to venture any farther than the bars and cafés of the Leopoldstrasse, renting a bicycle is the best solution (see *Listings*, below).

Schwabing actually divides into three distinct areas. Around the university and west of Leopoldstrasse, residential streets mix with wacky shops, student bars, and restaurants. In the center and to the east, trendy shops and café-bars ensure permanent crowds, day and night. Nightclubs are thick on the ground here too, especially around the Wedekindplatz near Münchener Freiheit. The far north of Schwabing is a tidily bourgeois residential area, uninteresting for visitors apart from the Olympiapark, which is way out at the end of a U-Bahn line.

A disproportionate number of wealthy people live in Munich, and the worst kind are the Schickies, who can be found posing in Schwabing cafés. Favored spots are the *Reitschule, Palmengarten*, or *Munich*. The trendy rather than wealthy tend to prefer places like *Capri* or *Drugstore*, and those who simply enjoy a friendly atmosphere go to *Café an der Uni, Oase*, or *Studiotheater*. Of course there are loads more places and they've only been divided here in the most general terms. The whole quarter is very fluid and it's impossible to make hard and fast rules (for full listings see "Eating and Drinking" below).

The one diversion that unites everyone is beer drinking, which seemingly takes place all the time, especially in the summer when all the beer gardens are open. One of the most famous is around the **Chinesischer Turm** (known locally as the **Chinaturm**) in the **Englischer Garten**, though its days as the best beer garden in town are long gone. What used to be *the* place to meet in Munich has sadly been overcommercialized, with expensive food on sale and uniformed guards to watch over propriety. But it's still worth seeing at least once, and it remains one of the city's most famous landmarks, at it's best (or worst) on Sunday afternoons, when a Bavarian band blares across the crowd from the heights of the Chinaturm itself. Two more peaceful beer gardens are not far off by the **Kleinhesseloher See**. The lakeside one is the more attractive and especially good for mellow summer evenings, while the **Hirschau** beer garden tends to have a local crowd rather than tourists, and is found by following the small road as you turn right out of the parking lot.

When you've had enough of the city, the Eisbach meadow opposite the Monopteros in the Englischer Garten is a good place to relax. People come here to sunbathe, picnic, swim in the aptly named *Eisbach* (Ice River), or ride horses in the city's main playground. Visitors often find the large-scale nudity a little unnerving—and it certainly wouldn't be acceptable in any other German city. Even "respectable" businessmen will pop over at lunch hour, fold their suits in a neat pile, and read the paper stark naked. There are rules on exactly where nude sunbathing is allowed, but the police have given up trying to face the inevitable protest and bare bottoms.

During the summer months of July and August the **Olympiapark** hosts open-air rock and pop concerts every weekend. Usually it's local bands of varying standards, but it doesn't cost anything and is worth checking out. The venue is a modern-day Greek theater construction known as the **Theatron**, right next to the park's lake. The Olympic stadia all around were built for the **1972 Olympics** and still have a somewhat futuristic look about them. In particular, the main stadium is a strange construction of steel poles and fiberglass, looking rather like an overgrown tent.

The Olympic village nearby is where the Arab "Black September" group launched one of the most horrific terrorist attacks in recent decades. On the morning of September 5, the terrorists stormed the Israeli quarters, killing two athletes and taking nine hostages, with demands that 200 Palestinians in Israeli jails should be released. The Olympic Games were suspended while 12,000 police moved into action around the Israeli quarter, and Chancellor Willy Brandt flew in to conduct negotiations with the terrorists. It was agreed that they would be flown with their hostages to a friendly Arab country, but as the terrorists and their captives crossed the tarmac to board a waiting jet, the police cut the airport lights and began shooting. The result was a bloodbath: all nine hostages were killed along with four Arabs and one policeman; three Arabs survived. This severely tarnished the ideal of the "Olympic spirit," and the subsequent games have taken place under a shadow of fear and massive security.

Along the River Isar

If the Marienplatz and Schwabing are the stuff of tourist brochures, then the environs of the **River Isar** are the private face of Munich. The northern reaches offer a peaceful contrast to the city and the Eisbach crowds, with a couple of good places to go swimming. Heading south, the river swings past Haidhausen, an old Turkish quarter now a trendy alternative to Schwabing, and as the river valley widens, the city's zoo and film studios are conveniently close in the southernmost suburbs.

Taking the Chinaturm as a starting point, the northern stretch is about five kilometers long and the southern one about nine kilometers. There are S-Bahns and buses heading back to downtown from both ends of the river, but renting a bike is really the best way to explore since the valley widens out to about a kilometer in places.

North from the Chinaturm

The Englischer Garten takes its name from the eighteenth-century landscaping convention, which tried to create parks resembling untouched nature; heading north past the Kleinhesseloher See, you get the feeling of being in the countryside rather than in a city park. Paths criss-cross the flat wooded valley, and the *Aumeister* beer garden by the Föhringer Ring overpass is just the place to have a leisurely drink and some good food. Just beyond, along Sondermeierstrasse, you come to an outdoor swimming pool known as the *Floriansmühle*. Set in some fields, the pool is a little on the dilapidated side, but its small scale makes it a much better place than the teeming city pools.

For swimming in more natural surroundings, head for the **Unterföhringer See**, on the other side of the Isar. To get there, cross over the river by the *Aumeister* at Leinthaler Brücke and follow the main road through the village of Unterföhring, then left down Am Poschinger Weiher. The little lake itself is almost totally obscured by trees, providing plenty of shade on hot summer days. Try to avoid weekends when space gets very tight.

In exactly the opposite direction of the Unterföringer See, the **Feringasee** is a much larger artificial lake at the end of Aschheimerstrasse. Since it was a byproduct of building the Nürnberg expressway it's not exactly beautiful, and there isn't a spot of shade to be found. But it is one of the largest lakes near the city, and its exposed position makes it good for windsurfing.

Back towards town, there's a bike path on the east side of the Isar from Leinthaler Brücke, and only a short way along, the *St. Emmeram's Mühle*, up on St. Emmeramstrasse is a rather posh little beer garden with prices to match. It's pretty and worth stopping off for a quick drink, if not to eat. The quarter along this part of the river is known as the **Herzogpark**, and some of the city's more exclusive villas line its leafy streets. Cross back over the river at Max-Joseph-Brücke, and the road will lead straight on to the Englischer Garten and the Chinaturm.

South from the Chinaturm

Past the Eisbach meadow, busy Prinzregentenstrasse soon marks the end of the Englischer Garten. To the east, the **Friedensengel**, a nineteenth-century monument to peace, stands high above the city, shining in its newly restored gold splendor. There's a good view of Munich from up here, and on New Year's Eve people come up to watch the fireworks across the city. Past the Europaplatz at

Prinzregentenstr. 60, the Villa Stuck houses the **Jugendstil Museum** (Tues.–Sun. 10am–5pm; DM3). A rather patchy collection of unrelated objects is kept here, and the museum also has changing exhibitions of twentieth-century art.

South along the Ismaningerstrasse, the Wienerplatz marks the beginning of **Haidhausen**. Around here it's still more or less the working-class quarter that it always was, with its own market and the large and shady beer garden of the Hofbräukeller. Until the early 1980s, the rest of Haidhausen was a run-down part of town that had become something of a Turkish ghetto. The peeling squares and prewar houses have since been rediscovered, and now trendy little health-food stores, alternative craftshops, and hip bars have sprouted like mushrooms. It's become *the* place to live, and, as you might expect, spiraling rents have forced out most of the original inhabitants.

Down towards the Isar on Rosenheimerstrasse is hidden one of Munich's real gems: the **Volksbad** (Tues.–Thurs. 8am–7:30pm, Fri. 8am–8:45pm; Sat. 8am–5pm; Sun. 7:30am–12:30pm; DM5) is a beautifully restored Jugendstil indoor pool. High, stuccoed ceilings arch over two separate pools, with mahogany changing cubicles surrounding each, and the sound of splashing water issuing from sculptured fountains completes the atmosphere. There's also a traditional Turkish bath and a couple of saunas. Across the Isar, the area around Gärtnerplatz is the focus of Munich's gay scene, though you'd hardly know it looking around, and Fassbinder's favorite Gasthaus, *Deutsche Eiche* on Reichenbachstrasse, is indistiguishable from any other establishment.

From the Reichenbachbrücke onwards, paths follow the course of the Isar all the way to the city's zoo, **Tierpark Hellabrunn**, and the suburb of Menterschwaige. The east bank rises steeply here and the river and canals are completely hidden by thick woodland. Finally, if you want to see Bavaria's equivalent to Hollywood, and Europe's largest film-making studio, there are guided tours through **Bavaria Filmstadt** (April–Oct. daily 9am–4pm; DM10). It's about two kilometers farther south of the zoo, by Bavariafilmplatz.

The Museum Quarter

Sandwiched between the western sectors of the city center and Schwabing, the museum quarter is bounded by Briennerstrasse (originally the royal road connecting the five-kilometer stretch between the Residenz and Schloss Nymphenburg) and Theresienstrasse. Though covering only two blocks, the area is still quite expansive because the streets are built in the grandiose proportions of the nineteenth century, while the museums have enough treasures to keep you absorbed for days on end. All the state-owned museums are free on Sundays and National Holidays.

Alte Pinakothek, *Barer Str. 27. Tues.–Sun. 9am–4:30pm, Tues. and Thurs. 7–9pm as well; DM4, DM1 students.*

Munich's best and most celebrated museum, the Alte Pinakothek is one of the largest galleries in Europe, housing an outstanding collection of fourteenth-to-eighteenth-century paintings, including the finest representation of the German School to be found anywhere in the world (for more information on these artists, see *Contexts*). Yet, in spite of its size, it's still possible to come to grips with the whole. The ground floor covers fifteenth-century German painting in the left wing, and sixteenth- and seventeenth-century German and Dutch painting in the right, while the upper floor begins with fifteenth-century Netherlandish painting in the left wing, and then proceeds to German, Italian, Flemish, Dutch, French and Spanish art.

German painting of the fifteenth century has predominantly religious themes, and, in keeping with an age that believed art was for the greater glory of God, the names of many of the artists have not survived. Look, however, for the beautifully observed narrative cycle which has provided the nickname of **Master of the Life of the Virgin** for an unknown Cologne painter, and the idiosyncratic *trompe l'oeil* scenes of a Bavarian contemporary, **Master of the Tegernsee Altar**, whose panels are executed as if in imitation of a carved retable. From the following generation, the works of the Tyrolean **Michael Pacher** (the only major Austrian artist of the period) stand out. Though better known as a sculptor, his luxuriant *Altarpiece of the Four Fathers of the Church*, an early attempt at fusing the rich late Gothic style of southern Germany with the new approach of the Italian Renaissance, shows he was no less talented with the brush than with the chisel. Among Netherlandish works of the same period, **Rogier van der Weyden**'s *Adoration of the Magi*, which was commissioned by a church in Cologne, is regarded as one of the best portrayals of this classic, Christmas-card subject. It makes a fascinating contrast with the tiny house altar of the same scene (known as "The Pearl of Brabant" because of its highly polished sheen), which seems to be the only surviving painting by **Dieric Bouts the Younger**. Equally outstanding is **Memling**'s lyrical *Seven Joys of the Virgin*, which integrates all the scenes into a single dream-like fantasy of architecture and landscape.

Under the impact of the Renaissance, portraiture was also becoming popular, and **Dürer**'s *Self-Portrait* is one of the most famous paintings from this time, the artist looking out with a self-assured poise, his face framed by shoulder-length golden locks and his torso clad in a regal fur coat. The inscription on the painting reads: "Thus I, Albrecht Dürer from Nürnberg, painted myself in imperishable colors at the age of 28." He certainly achieved everlasting fame, but his self-portrait as a Christ-like figure, together with the inscription, is just a touch Dorian Grayish. The famous panels of *The Four Apostles* (actually an inaccurate title, as Saint Mark is an outsider in the group which also includes Saints John the Evangelist, Peter and Paul) come from the very end of Dürer's career, and are generally held to be his greatest achievement. Originally, they were meant as wings of an altarpiece dedicated to the Virgin, but the project was scrapped when the city of Nürnberg—with the artist himself an enthusiastic supporter—went over to Protestantism.

Another painting with a fascinating Reformation connection is **Grünewald**'s *Disputation of Saints Erasmus and Maurice*. This was commissioned by the leading member of the conciliatory Catholic party, Cardinal Albrecht von Brandenburg, Archbishop-Elector of Mainz. The gorgeously attired Saint Erasmus, who is shown arguing for the peaceful conversion of the world against the armed struggle favored by the Negro warrior St. Maurice, represents a double allusion to the contemporary approach favored by the Cardinal and his great friend, Erasmus of Rotterdam. Ironically, Grünewald himself was of a far more impassioned nature—as can be seen in his early *Mocking of Christ*—and he shortly afterwards became a supporter of the extreme wing of Protestantism. Strange as it seems, the cardinal also patronized Luther's very own propagandist, **Lucas Cranach the Elder**, who took advantage of the new liberties of the age to introduce sensually explicit nudes—such as the full-lengths of *Lucretia* and *Venus and Cupid*—into German art for the first time. This approach was soon taken up and developed by **Hans Baldung**, as in the pair of allegorical female figures, perhaps representing *Prudence* and *Music*.

Albrecht Altdorfer's *Battle of Alexander* is a masterpiece of another new genre, that of historical painting, depicting the victorious battle of Alexander the Great over the Persian king Darius III in 333 B.C. It's a large work, packed with action. Literally hundreds of soldiers are individually painted in minute detail, but at the same time represented as a heaving mass, dramatically giving the sense of a momentous battle between two great powers. This artist often used identifiable landscapes in the Danube valley as background for his paintings; indeed, in *St. George and the Dragon* the ostensible subject is an excuse for a masterly nature study of the lush foliage of the beech trees which are a feature of the region.

From later in the sixteenth century are some particularly distinguished works from the Low Countries. **Jan Sanders van Hemessen's** *Mocking of Christ* goes even further than Grünewald's in its graphic depiction of hateful human expressions, featuring an old woman pulling her mouth apart with her fingers. Such detailed characterizations are the most striking feature of these Dutch painters, and **Marinus van Reymerswaele's** *Taxman and his Wife* is an excellent example. An important idea behind Dutch art of the time was to express some kind of moral, and the close attention with which the subjects are painted draws attention to the couple's greedy faces and the hands counting the money, while an extinguished candle in the backround reminds that all worldly life must end. **Pieter Bruegel the Elder's** *Land of Cockaigne* is the most famous of these didactic paintings, depicting a seemingly utopian scene of plenty, where food cooks itself and pigs come ready-roasted. A little boiled egg on legs, with its top already off, is just one of many entertaining details—but however funny, the purpose of the work was actually to condemn gluttony and idleness.

The Italian section begins with three little panels from a dispersed altarpiece by **Giotto**; other highlights include **Fra Filippo Lippi's** classically inspired *The Annunciation*, **Botticelli's** theatrical *Pietà*, **Raphael's** tender *Holy Family*, and a rare authenticated example of the young **Leonardo da Vinci**, *Madonna of the Carnation*. However, works by **Titian** steal the show here, notably the *Seated Portrait of Charles V*, which perfectly captures the self-confident poise of a man of destiny, and *Christ Crowned with Thorns*, dating from the end of the artist's very long life, and executed with an amazingly Impressionistic sense of freedom. From a couple of centuries later comes a sumptuous altarpiece by **Tiepolo**, *The Adoration of the Magi*. The French display includes **Poussin's** *Lamentation over the Dead Christ*, several classical landscapes by **Claude**, and a number of frilly eighteenth-century works, most notably **Boucher's** *Mme. de Pompadour* (Louis XV's mistress for twenty years). There's also a room of seventeenth-century Spanish painting, including a *Portrait of a Young Man* by **Velázquez**, and several genre pictures by **Murillo**; the latter were to have an enormous influence on French and English art of the following century.

Highlight of the entire museum, and the main consideration in the architectural design of the building, is the collection of works by the seventeenth-century Flemish painter **Rubens**. Sixty-two paintings display a wide range of the artist's prodigious output, including everything from the *modellos* (study sketches) the master made for the guidance of his large workshop to such massive finished altarpieces as *The Fall of the Rebel Angels* and *The Last Judgment*; from intimate portraits such as *Rubens and Isabella Brandt in the Honeysuckle Bower* (painted to celebrate his first marriage) to such boisterous public occasions as *The Lion Hunt*; and from the quiet beauty of *Landscape with a Rainbow* to the horrors of *The Massacre of the Innocents*. The paintings with mythological subjects invariably show the artist in top form, and *Drunken Silenus* is one of the finest of these. Silenus was the teacher of Dionysus, the god of wine, and in this scene he's represented as an inebriated flabby old man. For all his drunkenness, he retains some dignity, which is in cruel contrast to the woman lying at his feet, who stares blankly at the ground while her two children suck at her breasts. The painting is full of humorous detail too, such as the Negro squeezing a handful of Silenus's chubby thigh.

Van Dyck, Rubens's most distinguished pupil, is also extensively represented, with portraits and religious works drawn from the main phases of his career. The small cabinet rooms beyond contain the largest collection of works in existence by **Adriaen Brouwer**, the most trenchant observer of the seemier side of life in seventeenth-century Flanders. There's also a haunting *Passion Cycle* by **Rembrandt**, commissioned by the House of Orange as Reformed Protestant visions of Holy Week. In both *The Raising of the Cross* and *The Deposition*, the familiar figure of Rembrandt himself appears as a leading witness to the events.

Neue Pinakothek, *Barer Str. 29. Tues.–Sun. 9am–4:30pm, Tues. 7–9pm as well; DM3.50, DM1 students.*

Just across the road from the Alte Pinakothek, the Neue Pinakothek houses collections of eighteenth- and nineteenth-century European painting and sculpture. After the wealth and variety of its neighbor, this museum can't help but seem a little thin on the ground. However, it does have some good examples of neoclassical, Romantic, Realist and Impressionist art, and is well worth an hour or so.

After the French Revolution, baroque and rococo art seemed singularly inappropriate to the new spirit of the age. An art form was required that better reflected the new rationalism, and it was found in the style broadly defined by the term neoclassicism. Sober and clear, the portrait of the *Marquise de Sourcy de Thélusson* by the French painter **David** is a beautiful example of this marmorial style of shiny white skins and glossy canvases.

Of all the works from the mid-nineteenth-century Romantic period, those by the German painter **Carl Spitzweg** are among the best. He painted scenes from everyday life, depicting human emotions and frailties with a wry sense of humor and cartoon-like execution. *The Poor Poet, The Bookworm*, and *The Childhood Friend* cover just some of his themes, which are always subtly observed and with a dig against pretension. In the second half of the nineteenth century, artists were drawn back to the themes of classical antiquity, but rather than portraying events they tried to communicate moods or sentiments—*Pan in the Reeds* by **Böcklin** is a good example.

Of the works by French Impressionists, **Manet's** *Breakfast in the Studio* is probably the most famous, but other than that, there's not much to choose from in this section. Turn-of-the-century art is represented by a few paintings by **Cézanne, van Gogh**, and **Gauguin**, highlights of which are one of van Gogh's *Sunflowers* and Gauguin's *Breton Farmwomen*. The main German exponent of this phase is **Liebermann**, whose *Boys by the Beach* beautifully captures a scene from turn-of-the-century life. The museum rounds off with a small selection of art nouveau. **Von Stuck's** *Sin* is the most striking piece, the vice rather unfairly represented as a lascivious-looking woman exposing herself. Much more romantic and stylized is **Gustav Klimt's** portrait of *Margarethe Stonborough-Wittgenstein*.

Glypothek, *Königsplatz 3. Tues., Wed. and Fri.–Sun. 10am–4:30pm, Thurs. noon–8:30pm; DM3.*

Staatliche Antikensammlungen, *Königsplatz 1. Tues. and Thurs.–Sun. 10am–4:30pm, Wed. noon–8:30pm; DM3.50 or joint ticket DM6.*

Designed as a Greek temple square, the large neoclassical Königsplatz houses two suitably classical collections. The Glyptothek contains Ludwig I's collection of ancient Greek and Roman sculptures plundered from the Aphaia temple on Aegina. Among the exhibits in the Antikensammlungen are Greek vases from the fifth and sixth centuries B.C., as well as beautiful jewelry and small statues from Greek, Etruscan, and Roman antiquity. Not one of the city's most fascinating museums, it's tomb-like atmosphere is very apt for these ancient artifacts.

Lenbachhaus, *Luisenstr. 30. Tues.–Sun. 10am–6pm; DM3, DM1.50 students.* Situated just off Königsplatz, the nineteenth-century villa of the Bavarian painter **Franz von Lenbach** is set in a picturesquely manicured garden. The house itself provides a pleasant setting for some of German art's most interesting painters, housing collections from the nineteenth century, as well as from the early twentieth-century Munich School. The highlight is provided by paintings from the group known as the *Blaue Reiter* (see *Contexts*), whose members included **Kandinsky**, **Klee**, **Marc**, and **Macke**. In recent years the museum has also concentrated on collecting important contemporary German art, and of all Munich's galleries, this is one that's always worth checking.

Munich's Other Museums

Bayerisches Nationalmuseum, *Prinzregentenstr. 3. Tues.–Sun. 9:30am–5pm; DM3, DM1 students.* Most of the items of general interest in this huge, rambling decorative-arts museum are on the first floor. Alongside arms and armor, ivories, and sacred objects, there's a superb display of German wood sculpture at its fifteenth- and sixteenth-century peak. In particular, there are examples of **Tilman Riemenschneider**'s art drawn from all phases of his career, ranging from the early *St. Mary Magdalene Surrounded by Angels* to the serene late *St. Barbara*. A complete set of *Apostles* originally made to adorn the Marienkapelle in Würzburg date from his middle period. Some of these are carved in the round, others in shallow relief; each is given a distinct characterization. Many of Riemenschneider's most talented contemporaries—Hans Multscher, Michel and Gregor Erhart, Hans Leinberger and Erasmus Grasser—are also well represented. From the following generation is a statuette of *Judith with the Head of Holofernes* by **Conrad Meit**, the only major German sculptor to work in an Italianate style. There's also a miniature *Portrait of Harry Meynert* by **Hans Holbein the Younger**; this depicts a painter-colleague at the English court of Henry VIII. It's one of only a baker's dozen of miniatures by Holbein to have survived, and is the only one left in Germany.

Despite the focus on Bavarian art, there's also a decent Italian Renaissance section, which includes six magnificent bronze reliefs of *The Passion* by **Giambologna**, plus sculptures by Luca della Robbia and Antonio Rossellino. The museum's entrance level features Bavarian folk art and a collection of Christmas cribs, while the second floor has stained glass, crystal, ceramics, clocks, and models of Bavarian towns as they appeared in the sixteenth century.

BMW-Museum, *Petuelring 130. Daily 9am–5pm; DM4.30, DM3 students.* High-tech museum of BMW cars and motorbikes of today rather than the past; disappointingly, there are hardly any vintage cars and the museum is more a flash advert for the BMW company than a source of illumination on its products.

Deutsches Jagd und Fischereimuseum, *Neuhauserstr. 53. Daily 9:30am–5pm; plus Mon. 7–9pm; DM4, DM2 students.* Hunting and fishing museum not quite in line with mainstream attitudes to blood sports, but if you like looking at heads nailed to walls, this is the place.

Deutsches Museum, *Isarinsel (by the Ludwigsbrücke on the island). Daily 9am–5pm; DM5, DM2 students and kids.* Covering every conceivable aspect of technical endeavor, from the first flint tools to the research labs of modern industry, this is the most comprehensive collection of its type in Germany—which amounts to saying it's the best in Europe. The sheer scale of the place is in itself impressive and some of the examples of innovative engineering—biplanes, cars, boats, and so forth—are ranged in rooms the size of hangars. But the Deutsches Museum is more than a conventional science and technology museum writ large; it's the consistent clarity and imagination of its presentations that make a visit so enjoyable. One part of the building has been converted into a replica of the Lascaux caves, while elsewhere there's a convincingly gloomy mock-up of a coal mine. Meticulously constructed large-scale models are featured, and the use of interactive displays makes them as absorbing for kids as adults. It's best to go there in the morning; come later on and you'll regret leaving too little time.

Erstes Nachttopfmuseum der Welt, *Böcklinstr. 30. Sun. 10am–1pm, Thurs. 3–7pm; DM2, DM1 students.* An assortment of chamberpots for those potty enough to be into that sort of thing.

Prähistorische Staatssammlung, *Lerchenfeldstr. 2. Tues.–Sun. 9am–4pm, Thurs. until 8pm; DM2.50.* A good attempt has been made here to bring alive Bavarian prehistory, the Roman occupation and early medieval life. Lots of models, drawings, and artifacts presented in an accessible and interesting manner.

Schackgalerie, *Prinzregentenstr. 9. Wed.–Mon. 9am–4:30pm; DM2.50, DM1.50 students.* Count Schack was Munich's most important art patron during the nineteenth century, supporting struggling painters such as Franz von Lenbach, Marées, Böcklin, and others until they achieved public acclaim. The museum concentrates on the German Romantic period and contains a number of masterpieces by the those already mentioned, as well as by Feuerbach and Spitzweg. Very rewarding for fans of this distinctive painting era, and certainly one of the largest and most representative collections of the period.

Siemens Museum, *Prannerstr. 10. Mon.–Fri. 9am–4pm, Sun. 10am–2pm; free.* History of electricity and its application. All plugs and fuses and precious little zap.

Spielzeugmuseum, *in the Altes Rathaus. Mon.–Sat. 10am–5:30pm, Sun. 10am–6pm; DM3, DM1 kids.* Relive your childhood wandering around this toy collection, and see many marvelous toys long out of fashion.

Staatliche Graphische Sammlung, *Meiserstr. 10. Mon.–Fri. 9am–1pm and 2–4:30pm; free.* Graphics from the late Gothic to the present day, which hold little interest for any but enthusiasts of this particular art genre.

Staatliche Sammlung Ägyptischer Kunst, *Hofgartenstr. 1. Tues–Sun 9:30am–4pm, Tues 7–9pm as well; DM3, DM1.50 students.* As well as objects from all periods of Egyptian antiquity, the museum has displays of Coptic art and monumental reliefs from Assyria.

Staatliches Museum für Völkerkunde, *Maximilianstr. 42. Tues.–Sun. 9:30am–4:30pm; DM3, reduction for students.* Art and history of non-European cultures, plus changing anthropological exhibitions from exotic lands, always excellently presented.

Staatsgalerie Moderner Kunst, *Prinzregentenstr. 1. Tues.–Sun. 9am–4:30pm, Thurs. 7–9pm as well; DM3.50, reduction for students*. Museum of twentieth-century European painting and sculpture, which picks up where the Neue Pinakothek leaves off. Picasso, Braque, Matisse, Dalí, Magritte, Mondrian, and de Chirico head the international lineup, while there are examples of all the main German artists of the century. It's always worth looking out for the regular special exhibitions.

Nymphenburg

Schloss Nymphenburg (Tues.–Sun. 10am–12:30pm and 1:30–4pm; DM2.50, or DM5 including the pavilions; take the U-Bahn to Rotkreuzplatz and then tram #12) was the summer residence of the Wittelsbach rulers of Bavaria. Its kernel is a small Italianate palace begun in 1664 for the frivolous Electress Adelaide, who dedicated it to the pastoral pleasures of the goddess Flora and her nymphs (hence the name). Her son Max Emmanuel commissioned an ingenious extension, whereby four pavilions were built to the side of the palace, and connected to it by arcaded passages. Later, the palace itself was modified and more buildings added, resulting in a remarkably unified whole, despite having been nearly a century in the making. By this time, an extensive French-style park had been laid out as an appropriate backdrop. In 1761 the famous porcelain factory was transferred to the site, but plans to establish a planned town on the model of Ludwigsburg in Württemberg came to nothing.

The approach to the palace is along either side of a tree-lined canal stretching nearly a kilometer, and in the winter it sometimes freezes over to become a mecca for ice-skaters. Once through the palace gates, the first hundred meters continue the strict symmetry of the palace with manicured lawns and straight paths lined with marble statues. The park then opens up into a country landscape, with two lakes and a number of small royal lodges. As you'd expect, the interior of the palace is high baroque, with rich, gold-plated stucco ornamentation and ceiling frescos. The most famous room is King Ludwig I's gallery of women, known as the *Schönheitsgallerie*: a collection of 36 portraits of Munich beauties who caught the King's eye between 1827 and 1850. In the south wing you can visit the **Carriage Museum** (same times; DM2) containing the incredibly elaborate coaches and sleighs of the Wittelsbachs, including several made for the ill-fated Ludwig II.

More enticing than the palace itself are the walks in the wonderful park. Three of the four pavilions, which are all of a markedly different character, were designed by **Joseph Effner**, the innovative court architect who was also responsible for the harmonization of the palace. Immediately behind the northern wing sits the **Magdalenenklause**, deliberately built to resemble a ruined hermitage, with a grotto and four simple cell-like rooms within. It's a very early example of the historicism which was later to become a German obsession, borrowing elements from the vocabulary of Roman, Gothic and even Moorish architecture. The Electors would come here when they wished to meditate—and he hadn't far to go if he tired of its peace and asceticism. Westwards through the park is the **Pagodenburg**, which was used for the most exclusive parties thrown by the court. It's typical of the passion for all things Chinese which was a feature of European courtly life of the period, but a certain amount of cheating was necessary—because the Wittelsbachs owned no original china, the walls had to be faced with Dutch tiles. Effner's third building, the **Badenburg**, lies on the opposite side of the canal. Again, it reflects the interest in chinoiserie, though both the bathing room and the two-story banqueting hall are in the richest tradition of European baroque.

For all their charm, Effner's pavilions are overshadowed by the stunning **Amalienburg**, the hunting lodge built behind the south wing of the Schloss by his successor as court architect, **François Cuvilliés**. This is arguably the supreme expression of the rococo style, marrying a cunningly thought-out design—which makes the little building seem like a full-scale palace—with the most extravagant decoration imaginable. The entrance chamber, with its niches for the hunting dogs, must be the most tasteful kennel ever built. However, the showpiece is the circular **Hall of Mirrors**, best seen on a bright day when the shimmering light casts magical reflections on the silvery-blue walls, the inlaid console tables, the paneled garlands, and the rich stucco nymphs and putti.

To the north of the Schloss, the **Botanical Gardens** (daily 9am–7pm, greenhouses closed 11:45am–1pm; DM2, students free) hide all manner of plants in their steamy greenhouses, and the landscaped herbarium and other plant collections make up a very fragrant whole.

Eating and Drinking

Mensas are the cheapest places to get a good basic meal; you're supposed to have a valid student card to eat in one, but no one seems to check. Standard opening times: Mon–Thurs 9am–4:45pm, Fri 9am–3:30pm in the snack bar; lunch 11:30am–1:30pm only; the most central mensa is at Leopoldstr. 15, in the back courtyard. Two more are in the main building at Schellingstrasse, and at the Technical University, Arcisstr. 17. If you're really hard up, most **butchers' shops** sell bread rolls with various hot and cold fillings from as little as DM1.80. Excellent places for this type of snack are the *Vinzenz Murr* butchers, which usually have an area within the shop to eat snacks, and serve larger meals too. In Schwabing, there are branches at Münchener Freiheit and Schellingstr. 21. Otherwise it's not difficult to eat well for little money in Munich. **Italian restaurants** are especially cheap and do excellent pasta dishes for around DM8.50, and in the Bavarian *Gaststätten*, filling soups, salads, and sandwich-type dishes can be found for around DM5. Even more substantial Bavarian meals like *Weisswürste*, *Leberkäse*, *Schweinebraten*, and *Knödel* or *Hacksteak* are normally between DM8 and DM12. Not surprisingly, drinking is never a problem in this city, and beverages of any kind are available all day and almost all night. Apart from the *Gaststätten* and beer gardens, Munich also has a very lively café-bar culture, which carries on well into the early hours.

Restaurants

Worth trying while you're here are the **Balkan** restaurants, of which there are quite a few, and usually not too expensive. The *Dalmatiner Grill*, Geibelstr. 10, *Makarska Grill*, Schleissheimerstr. 182, and *Zadar Grill*, Theresienstr. 54 offer good food and service at medium prices. And the *Isabellahof*, Isabellastr. 4, is a very popular, cheap restaurant in Schwabing, with excellent cooking.

French restaurants are often expensive gourmet havens, but a few offer meals at sensible prices. Try *Alter Ego*, Artilleriestr. 5, *Le Fleuron de Isar*, Erhardstr. 27, *Stengelhof*, Stengelstr. 2, or the brasserie *Le Zig Zag*, Andreestr. 10. A great place to go for crêpes is *Bernard & Bernard*, Innere Wienerstr. 32, closed Saturday, right next to the Wienerplatz in Haidhausen.

Greek restaurants are widespread, reflecting the large Greek community. Loosely they divide between "proper" restaurants with tacky decor and music wafting across the tables, and more down-to-earth bar-restaurants where you'll find most of the local Greeks. Of the former variety, places worth trying are: *Lyra*, Bazeillestr. 5; *Mouses*, Keller/Metzstrassen; *Rembetiko*, Dreimühlenstr. 2; and *Symposium*, Ligsalzstr. 38. Of rougher places, *Anti*, Jahnstr. 36, and *Entaxi*, Bergmannstr. 46, are both good value and fun.

There's an **Italian** restaurant on virtually every street corner in Munich, so there's an enormous range to choose from. The best chain is the *Bella Italia* restaurants, of which there are six, with the one at Weissenburgerstr. 2 being a long-standing institution. The *Adria*, Leopoldstr. 19, is a popular late-night joint, with good food at reasonable prices. For something a little bit more special try *Taverna Ischitana*, Pündterplatz 2.

In spite of the large Turkish immigrant population, there aren't many **Turkish** restaurants. The following offer predominantly kebab dishes: *Istanbul*, Landwehrstr. 42; *Marmara*, Goethestr. 7a; and *Saray*, Schwanthalerstr. 119.

Vegetarian restaurants are scarce: best option downtown is the *Vierjahreszeiten*, Sebastianplatz 9, which is a light and airy restaurant with reasonable prices. The only other place that isn't ridiculously expensive is the unappetizingly named *Vitamin-Büffet*, Herzog-Wilhelmstr. 25. Vegetarian *Imbiss*-type places are the *Kornstadl*, Frauenstr. 18, and *Kornkammer*, Haimhauserstr. 8.

Gaststätten and Beer Gardens

For traditional **Bavarian cooking**, the following places are cheap and friendly, often with music, providing meals to a predominantly student clientele: *Atzinger*, Schellingstr. 98, is one of the best places to pop in for a cheap lunch; the *Schelling Salon*, Schellingstr. 54, is excellent for large cheap breakfasts and playing pool. For a bit of theater with your beer, head for the *Frauenhofer*, Frauenhoferstr. 9, which usually gets packed early in the evening. Also good for a relaxed evening of socializing are: *Baal*, Kreittmayrstr. 26; *Alter Ofen*, Zieblandstr. 41; or *Burg Pappenheim*, Baaderstr. 46.

For a more formal setting in which to try the local cuisine at a medium price range, try: *Braunauer Hof*, Frauenstr. 40; *Bürgerheim*, Bergmannstr. 33; *Kaiser Friedrich*, Friedrichstr. 27; *Weisses Brauhaus*, Tal 10. An excellent and unpretentious place in the middle of Schwabing, but still cheap, is the *Weinbauer* at Fendstr. 5.

Of the hundreds of assorted **beer gardens**, nine stand out by reason of their size and popularity. The *Augustiner Keller*, Arnulfstr. 52, is near the S-Bahn stop Hackerbrücke, in one of Munich's shabbier quarters. But don't let that put you off, because the large garden is a shady island of green, with hardly a tourist in sight. The *Aumeister*, Sondermeierstr. 1, at the far northern end of the Englisher Garten is a good place for daytime breaks. The *Chinesischer Turm* on the other hand, while worth a passing visit, is a tourist trap. Away from the city crowds, the *Hirschgarten* at Hirschgartenallee 1, near the Nymphenburg palace, is rather civilized—which is not necessarily a recommendation in a beer garden. The *Hofbräukeller* at Innere Wienerstr. 19, nestling under ancient chestnut trees, is very popular in the evenings as well, while the *Hirschau*, Gysslingstr. 7, is all right when you're not being deafened by oompah bands. The nearby *Kleinhesseloher See*, has a far better setting. High up on the Nockerberg, and venue for the spring strong-beer festival, the *Salvator-Keller* at Hochstr. 77 is one of the oldest havens for serious beerdrinkers. Favorite of the lot though, in spite of being way out in the southern suburbs, is the *Menterschwaige*, Harthauserstr. 70: a large beer garden on the edge of the Isar valley, this is the place to bring a picnic to go with your beer.

Bars

The city's social life revolves around its bars. Coffee and snacks are served in most places, and while the list of "in" and "out" bars is ever-changing, these are top of the heap for the moment. In **Schwabing**, typical haunts of the Schickies are the *Reitschule*, Königinstr. 34; *Palmengarten*, Herzogstr. 93; *Munich*, Leopoldstr. 9 and *Extrablatt*, Leopoldstr. 7. Trendies tend to prefer *Drugstore*, Feilitzschstr. 12; *Studiotheater*, Ungererstr. 19, and *Café an der Uni*, Ludwigstr. 24, although *really* trendy people don't bother with Schwabing any more, and hang out in **Haidhausen**. Places to go for here include: *Casino*, Kellerstr. 21; *Grössenwahn*, Lothringerstr. 11; and *Sedan*, Gravelottestr. 7.

For those free spirits who like to think they're not fashion victims, there's plenty of places with a more changeable crowd, such as *Evi's*, Kurfürstenstr. 2; *Franci's*, Franziskanerstr. 2a; *Café Giesing*, Bergstr. 5, which also usually has live music; *Kairo*, Breisacherstr. 30; *Oase*, Amalienpassage; and *Ruffini*, Orffstr. 22.

For health food fans, the *Hinterhof Café*, Sedanstr. 29, and *Stöpsel*, Preysingstr. 18 are the places to be. For good cocktails check out the "happy hour" at *Julep's*, Breisacherstr. 18. Night owls have only a choice of two late-late spots: Bolshevik chic reigns supreme at *Iwan's*, Josephspitalstr. 18 (11am–3am); and the *Nachtcafé*, Maximiliansplatz 5 (7pm–5am) is the place to be and be seen in the early hours of the morning.

Traditional Cafés

Those of coffee-and-cake fame, with the classic characters and their lap-dogs... Best and most expensive is *Café Kreuzkamm*, Maffeistr. 4, which has a delicious array of cakes and sweets. Equally ritzy but less special places are: *Café Feldherrnhalle*, Theatinerstr. 38; *Café Hag*, Residenzstr. 25 and *Café Luitpold*, Briennerstr. 11. For a more basic kind of café with a plainer clientele, try the cozy little *Café Schneller*, Amalienstr. 59. All these cafés are only open during normal shopping hours, which usually means from 8:30am to 6pm.

Wine Bars

Not a great deal of choice in this beer haven: the *Pfälzer Weinprobierstuben*, Residenzstr. 1, and the *Weinstadl*, Burgstr. 6 are unpretentious places serving excellent wines. Friendly venues for an evening's wine-drinking are *Le Bordeaux*, Erich-Kästner-Strasse 14; *Clochemerle*, Rablstr. 37; *St. Georg Weinstuben*, Lamontstr. 11 and *Südtiroler Weinstadl*, Amalienstr. 53. For late-night wine-drinking check out the *Weintrödler*, Briennerstr. 10 (5pm–6am), which is the last boozer to close in town.

Music and Nightlife

Munich has a great deal to offer musically, whether you're into classical concerts or more modern stuff. There's everything you'd expect to find in a cosmopolitan capital, and during the summer a glut of open-air music festivals takes place in or around the city. Three orchestras of international repute are based here, and the annual opera festival in July is as much on the classical music calendar as the Salzburg and Bayreuth festivals. But it's not all highbrow. There's plenty of trash and tinsel too, though perhaps the bars are more interesting than the discos. Best source for what's on are the *Münchener Stadtzeitung* or *Im München*, available at any kiosk.

Rock and Pop

During the summer the **free rock concerts** by the lake in the Olympiapark, at the *Theatron*, usually get going around 2pm. Several **venues** have regular music programs throughout the year: *Café Giesing*, Bergstr. 5, is run by the singer Konstantin Wecker and usually features small bands or solo artists; *Crash*, Lindwurmstr. 88, is a club that tends to have heavy metal; *Domicile*, Leopoldstr. 19, has mostly jazz bands with some rock; and *Jukebox*, Feilitzschstr. 13, and *Mariandl*, Goethestr. 51, have a mix of everything.

Jazz

Munich has a monthly jazz magazine called *Münchener Jazz-Zeitung*, available in music shops and jazz venues. The city is corportate headquarters of *ECM*, an avant-garde jazz record label, and club dates are accordingly more exciting than the German norm, with name acts touring. The following venues play predominantly jazz, but check programs: *Allotria*, Türkenstr. 33; *Domicile*, Leopoldstr. 19; *Drehleier*, Balanstr. 19; *Jam*, Rosenheimer Str. 4; *Jenny's Place*, Georgenstr. 50; *Max-Emanuel*, Adalbertstr. 33; *Schwabinger Podium*, Wagnerstr. 1 and *Unterfahrt*, Kirchenstr. 96, closed Monday .

Discos and Nightclubs

For your normal run-of-the-mill disco, with the usual Top-40 sounds try *Cadillac*, Theklastr. 1 (9pm–4am); *East Side*, Rosenheimerstr. 30 (10pm–3am); *Sugar Shack*, Herzogspitalstr. 6 (11pm–4am); *Ten to Three*, Hohenzollernstrasse (10pm–3am); *Tanzlokal Grössenwahn*, Klenzestr. 43 (9pm–1am); and *Wolkenkratzer*, Leopoldstrasse (in the *Hertie* tower, 10pm–4am). Wherever you go, entrance prices tend to be around DM10, and drinks cost about the same.

For more **exclusive nightclubs** check out: *Charly M*, Maximilianstr. 5 (10pm–4am); *Jackie O*, Rosenkavalierplatz 12 (10pm–4am); *Maximilian's*, Maximilianstr. 16 (10pm–4am); *Park Café*, Sophienstr. 7 (10pm–3am); and *P1*, Prinzregentenstr. 1 (10pm–4am). This last place is the coolest place to be—if you can get past the door. Dress up in your best rags and bring tons of money.

In a country where **heavy metal** and early Seventies music are still wearily popular, it's not surprising that several discos specialize in head-banging sounds. Try *Blue Box*, Trautenwolfstr. 6 (10pm–1am); *Crash*, Lindwurmstr. 88 (8pm–1am, Fri.–Sat. 8pm–3am); *Mandy's*, Baaderstr. 11 (8pm–1am); *Romy's Finest*, Zweigstr. 6 (9pm–1am, Fri.–Sat. 9pm–6am) and *Round Up*, Leopoldstr. 23 (10pm–4am). Prices are the same as at the other discos.

Classical

A number of resident orchestras and two opera houses cater to a very spoiled audience. The *Münchener Philharmonie* is conducted by Sergiu Celibidache, one of the great conductors working today, who has developed a mystique by his stubborn refusal to make records. The *Bayrisches Rundfunk Sinfonie Orchester* is conducted by the Englishman Sir Colin Davis, and the *Staatsorchester* plays for the opera under the direction of Wolfgang Sawallisch. Of the subsidized orchestras, the *Münchener Kammerorchester* and the *Kurt Graunke Orchester* are perfectly respectable, but their subsidies mean that they have to play to their sponsors' tastes, which aren't always sensational. Main venues for concerts are the spanking new *Gasteig Kulturzentrum* on Kellerstrasse (☎418614) and the plush *Herkulessaal* in the Residenz. The *Nationaltheater* (☎221316) on Max-Joseph-Platz is Munich's answer to London's Covent Garden, with grand opera and ballet, whereas the *Staatstheater* on Gärtnerplatz (☎2016767) has a varied schedule of operetta, musicals and the more popular operas.

The best way to find out what's on, and for how much, is to buy the city's **official monthly program** (*Monatsmagazin*) from the tourist office. Advance tickets for concerts can be bought at the relevant box offices or commercial ticket shops, such as the one located in the Marienplatz U-Bahn station. Opera tickets can be bought at the advance sales office at Maximilianstr. 11, Mon.–Fri. 10am–12:30pm and 3:30–5:30pm, Sat. 10am–12:30pm. On the night of a show, you could try the box office in the opera house, which opens one hour before performances. The city's annual **Opera Festival** takes place from the middle of July to early August.

Theater and Film

Munich has a very lively arts scene with eleven major **theaters** and around 28 fringe theaters, plus eight cabaret venues, all listed in the official programs and the local press. Almost all productions are exclusively in German, though with a smattering of the language things aren't too incomprehensible. Check the *Münchener Stadtzeitung, Im München*, or the *Monatsmagazin* for what's currently showing. One place always worth checking out is the *Theaterfabrik Unterföhring* on Föhringer Allee (☎950 5666), which is used for pop concerts as well as cabaret shows. The star venue for drama is, of course, the *Cuvilliéstheater* (☎296836); traditional dramatic fare is also performed at the nearby *Residenztheater* (☎225754) on Max-Joseph-Platz, *Münchener Kammerspiele* (☎237210) on Maximilianstrasse, and *Deutsches Theater* on Schwanthalerstrasse—the last-named is also used for visiting spectaculars. Kids will enjoy productions at the *Marionettentheater* (☎265 1712) at the corner of Blumenstrasse and Sendlinger-Tor-Platz; once a week, the puppets are put to more serious use in the performance of an opera or drama classic.

Non-German **films** are usually dubbed into German, but if you're in need of hearing some English, *Im München* will specify original-language soundtracks. Also check out the following places, which specialize in showing films with the original soundtrack: *Cinema*, Nymphenburger Str. 31 (☎555255); *Europa im Atlantik*, Schwanthalerstr. 2-6 (☎555670) and *Türkendolch*, Türkenstr. 74 (☎271 8844). Entrance prices vary according to where you sit, but range between DM8 and DM12.

The Oktoberfest and Other Annual Events

The **Oktoberfest** hardly needs introducing. It's the world-famous, combination beer festival and amusement park that takes place from the last Saturday in September until the first Sunday in October. Held on the *Theresienwiese* fairground, this is quite simply an orgy of beer-drinking, while the midway offers some great rides to churn your guts, some so hairy that they're banned in countries like the US. For information on the opening ceremonies and pageants, read the *Monatsmagazin* or contact the tourist office. Even though entrance to the grounds is free, expect to spend lots of money. Accommodation during this time is not usually hiked up price-wise, but you'll have trouble finding anything at all if you haven't reserved in advance.

The festival has its origins in the marriage between the Bavarian Crown Prince Ludwig and Princess Therese von Sachsen-Hildburghausen on October 17 1810. On that occasion, a massive fair was held on the fields now named after the

Princess, and everyone was invited to take part in horse-racing, jousting, and shooting competitions. It was such a popular event that it's been repeated annually ever since, growing larger with every year. The traditional opening ceremonies revolve around the great horse-drawn brewery wagons arriving at the fairground to the sound of brass bands and much pomp and speech-making. The first of the massive beer barrels is set flowing by the mayor, and the world's largest beer festival begins—a period during which thousands of gallons of beer will be consumed, not to mention the roast chickens, fish, oxen, and pigs. It's a ritual from which all other Bavarian festivals take their cue.

On the second day, another procession leaves from the middle of town, this time made up of hundreds of traditional folklore groups, marching bands, musicians, jesters, commercial floats, and decorated horsemen that slowly converge on the fairground, watched by the thousands of spectators who've come to enjoy Germany's most important *Volksfest*. And although this is undoubtedly a time of *very* heavy drinking, it's also most definitely a family affair, with rides and stalls of every description jostling for customers. The proportions of the fair are so massive that the grounds are divided along four main avenues, creating a boisterous city of its own, crawling with revelers from morning til night for sixteen consecutive days.

Each brewery has its own huge tent where, in addition to beer, pretzels of the season and chicken halves are sold. One sits amicably ten to a bench with acquaintances and strangers alike, and after a few steins half the hall is dancing and belting out numbers on the tables.

Fasching is Munich's **carnival**, which exists more in tourist brochures than in reality, though there are large fancy-dress balls from mid-January until the beginning of Lent. Read the monthly city programs for details.

An annual **Christmas market** known as the *Christkindlmarkt* is held on the Marienplatz during the month of December, though for less commercialized markets with more hand-made crafts, go to the ones at the Münchener Freiheit, and around the Pariser Platz in Haidhausen.

The **Auer Dult** is a traditional market that takes place on the Mariahilfplatz during the last weeks of April, July and October each year. It has a combination of hardware, crafts and antiques, as well as a fairground for the kids.

The **Münchener Opern Fest** has a very high reputation, and runs from the middle of July to the beginning of August. Classical concerts are also held at Schloss Nymphenburg, Schloss Schleissheim, and in the courtyard of the Residenz at this time of year.

The Gay Scene

In 1987 the Bavarian State Government passed a law mandating AIDS testing on people suspected of being carriers. Furthermore, those testing positive who don't follow the authority's guidelines on "proper behavior" can be arrested and held indefinitely. The terrifying implications of these draconian laws have obviously had a serious effect on the gay community, and openly gay lifestyles have experienced a serious setback. Vigorous campaigns have been mounted by the *Anti-Strauss-Komitee*, Waltherstr. 28 (☎533328) and others, but the outlook is certainly bleak at the moment. Strauss' demise has certainly not heralded a more humane approach.

There's no proper gay quarter here, even though there are a couple of gay bars around the Gärtnerplatz, and your best bet is probably to contact the **Gay**

Cultural Center, Auenstr. 31 (☎725 4533), which meets every fourth Thursday of the month at 8pm. Alternatively, take one of the gay guides with you.

Women

The Women's Center, *Frauenzentrum*, Güllstr. 3 (Mon.–Fri. 6–11pm; ☎725 4271) runs a series of workshops and a café for all women, not just lesbians. On Tuesday between 1pm and 8pm, women from 13 to 20 years meet in the café, with Friday evenings specifically for lesbians. Cafés that cater predominantly to lesbians are *Café am Gift*, St. Martinstr. 1; *Frauncafé im Kofra*, Baldestr. 8; and *Mädchenpower-Café*, Baldestr. 16. The only nightclub is *Mylord*, Ickstättstr. 2a (daily 6–9pm, 6pm–3am weekends), which gets mixed reviews.

Men

The male gay scene has become understandably cagey of late, and a lot of places don't advertise themselves at all. The following bars, however, are well known: *Bolt*, Blumenstr. 15; *Cock*, Augsbergerstr. 21; *Colibri*, Utzschneiderstr. 8; *Die Spinne*, Ringseissestr. 1; *Juice*, Baaderstr. 13; and *Klimperkasten*, Maistr. 28. The *Ochsengarten*, Müllerstr. 47, is a leather bar, and the *Deutsche Eiche*, Reichenbachstr. 13, a Gasthaus with a mainly (though by no means exclusively) gay clientele.

Listings

Airlines *British Airways*, Promenadeplatz 10 (☎292121); *Lufthansa*, Lenbachplatz 1 (☎51130); *Pan-Am*, Promenadeplatz 9 (☎598686); *TWA*, Landwehrstr. 31 (☎597643)

Airport information (☎921 12127).

American Express Promenadeplatz 6 (☎21990), Mon.–Fri. 9am–5:30pm, Sat. 9am–noon.

Area code (☎089)

Babysitter service (☎229291 or ☎394607).

Banks Outside normal banking hours, you'll find the bank at the Hauptbahnhof is open daily 6am–11:30pm.

Bike rental *Aktiv-Rad*, Hans-Sachs-Str. 7. DM10 per day; DM50 per week. The *bicycle stand* by the entrance to the Englischer Garten on the corner of Königinstrasse and Veterinärstrasse charges DM15 per day, DM50 per week. *Bayern Bike Tours*, Hauptbahnhof, exit Arnulfstrasse, daily 9am–6:30pm, rents out bikes complete with maps and commentary to guide you around the sights via the city's bike paths. DM22 per day, DM30 overnight; DM150 or passport as deposit. You can also rent bikes at many of the outlying *S-Bahn stations*, such as Aying, Dachau, Freizing, Herrsching, Holzkirchen, Starnberg and Tutzing— useful when exploring the city's environs.

Books *The Anglia English Bookshop*, Schellingstr. 3, has a good selection of paperbacks and English-language newspapers.

Car rental *Europcar*, Schwanthalerstr. 10a (☎594723). Also offices at the airport.

Car repairs Phone the *ADAC* on (☎767676) any time.

Consulates *American*, Königinstr. 5 (☎23011); *Canadian*, Maximiliansplatz 9 (☎558531); *British*, Amalienstr. 62 (☎394015).

Cultural institutes The following have film shows and run various social functions advertised in the local press: *Amerika-Haus*, Karolinenplatz 3 (☎595367) has a useful library and recent newspapers; *British Council*, Bruderstr. 7/III (☎223326) offers the same services; *Deutsch-Englische Gesellschaft*, 8 München 33, Postfach 328 (☎362815); *Deutsch-Kanadische Gesellschaft*, Lohensteinstr. 33 (☎566843); *Munich Scottish Association*, Waldsaumstr. 19 (☎714 6990).

Emergencies Police (☎110); Doctor (☎558661); Dentist (☎723 3093); Pharmacist (☎594475); Gynecological (☎218 02611). At the *Internationale Apotheke* (Neuhauserstr. 8), you can get your prescription filled no matter which country it comes from.

Guided tours If you can stand them, these are the quickest and easiest introduction to the city. They leave outside the Hauptbahnhof in front of the *Hertie* department store. A one-hour tour costs DM13, starting at 10am, 11:30am and 2:30pm between May and October; 10am and 2:30pm in the winter. The guides all speak English. An extended version, including a trip up the Olympic Tower costs DM20. Or there's a 2½–hour **cultural tour** covering the Frauenkirche and Alte Pinakothek in the morning, and Schloss Nymphenburg and the Residenz in the afternoon. The morning trip starts at 10am, the afternoon part at 2:30pm, every day except Monday. Price DM23. There's also an interesting "Alternative Munich tour" in German only, which is run by the city's trade unions. Primarily aimed at schools and colleges, they always keep a few seats for tourists as well. If you're interested in the city's political history, particularly during the Third Reich, then this is the tour for you. It's free and leaves from the Schwanthalerstr. 64 at 10am on the first Saturday of every month. Nearest U-Bahn station is Theresienwiese.

Hospital Ismaningerstr. 22 (☎41401).

Laundromats Pestalozzistr. 16; Lilienstr. 73; Lindwurmstr. 38; Amalienstr. 61; Münchener Freiheit 26; Belgradstr. 11a; Herzogstr. 32 and 67; Kurfürstenstr. 10, 14, and 37; Wendl-Dietrich-Str. 23; Schleissheimer Str. 117.

Mitfahrzentrale Amalienstr. 87 (☎280124); also a women-only branch at Güllstr. 3 (☎725 1700).

Peace movement *Deutsche Friedens-Union* (*DFU*), Hess Str. 51, 10am–5pm.

Police Ettstr. 2 (☎2141).

Poste Restante at the main post office: Bahnhofsplatz 1, (☎538 82732). Open 24 hr. a day; take your passport.

Sports *FC Bayern München*, Germany's best soccer club, winners of many European trophies down the years, play at the *Olympiastadion* in the Olympiapark, which is also the venue for major athletics meetings.

Taxis (☎21611).

Travel firms *Studiosus Reisen*, Luisenstr. 43 and Amalienstr. 73.

Views Good vantage points from which to see the city are the *Rathaus tower* on the Marienplatz (May–Oct. Mon.–Fri. 9am–4pm, Sat. and Sun. 10am–7pm; DM2). Much less crowded than the touristy Rathaus, the tower of the nearby *Peterskirche* offers a good view for the same price (Mon.–Fri. 9am–8pm, Sat. 8:30am–7pm, Sun. 10am–7pm). DM3 will take you to the top of the 190-meter *Olympic Tower*, with views of the Alps as well as the city.

Women's bookshop Arccistr. 57 (☎272 1205).

Women's center Güllstr. 3 (☎725 4271).

Around Munich

Munich offers so much that most people probably won't have time for day trips. But if you are staying a little longer, it's a pity not to explore the city's environs. The most obvious destinations are the southern lakes, of which the **Ammersee** and **Starnberger See** are the two largest, both on the city's S-Bahn network. To the east, the small medieval towns of **Wasserburg** and **Burghausen** are highlights of an otherwise featureless region. The north has quite a few day trips to offer: just a couple of stops out of the city, **Dachau** concentration camp is a harrowing but valuable experience, and, farther afield, **Freizing**, **Landshut**, and

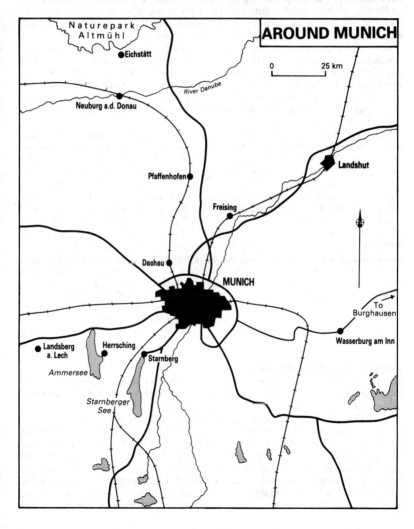

Neuburg an der Donau are attractive old towns offering a varied architectural legacy. Not far away, **Eichstätt** is an important episcopal see, and the gateway to the **Altmühltal**, with its tumbledown castles and quiet bike paths. The **Holledau** is also a good region to explore by bike; the world's largest hop-growing area, its main town is Pfaffenhofen, only half an hour by train from Munich.

Ammersee and Starnberger See

At the end of the S-5 line, the resort of **HERRSCHING** on the **AMMERSEE** is a favorite place to go swimming and sailing. There's a footpath along the water's edge to the left of Herrsching, where a few public beaches are slotted in between stretches of private property. It gets crowded during the summer, especially on weekends, so for a quieter time take the ferry to the other side of the lake and visit the old Augustine convent of **St. Maria**, which has impressive baroque architecture by J. M. Fischer and a high altar by Cuvilliés.

One of Bavaria's most popular beer-drinking havens is near Herrsching: **Andechs** is a Benedictine monastery and pilgrim center beautifully situated on top of a wooded hill. The walk up here from Herrsching winds through attractive woodland paths, but be warned that it's quite strenuous towards the end—the lazy alternatives are buses #951 and #956 that go from outside the S-Bahn stop. The monks of Andechs brew their own delicious beer, which they serve in the *Gasthaus* attached to the monastery.

The **STARNBERGER SEE** is the largest lake around Munich and predominantly the domain of the city's rich and their weekend villas. The main resort on the lake is **STARNBERG**, but the #6 S-Bahn continues to smaller places like POSSENHOFEN and TUTZING. The bracing alternative is to take a round trip on one of the lake's ferries for DM16.50, with trips from one stop to the next costing only DM4.50. On the eastern shore, the lake is mainly lined with private properties and it's not always possible to get at the water, though there are some small public stretches between the villages of BERG, LEONI, and AMMERLAND. The western shore is more commercial, developed for public use with cafés and restaurants vying for your money. **Possenhofen** is the main public beach here, which also happens to be where the ill-starred King Ludwig II mysteriously drowned in 1886. He'd recently been deposed for spending too much state money on building his fairytale castles, and rumor has it that he might have been murdered because he was a political embarrassment. Others say he was simply mad, and drove his coach into the waves on purpose. Perhaps it was a genuine accident, but the ex-king was a brilliant swimmer and had often swum the whole width of the lake. The mystery remains and it seems a fitting end to the sad melodrama of Ludwig's life.

Wasserburg and Burghausen

East of Munich, the landscape can't compete with the beauty and variety of the southern lakes. Here the countryside is rich farmland, but it's a back-water and public transit connections are uncharacteristically awkward. The small town of **WASSERBURG** is easy enough to reach by train though, and worth a day trip if you've got the time. The medieval town is situated on a peninsula on the River Inn, and during the fifteenth and sixteenth centuries it gained importance with salt trading. Today it's a sleepy little place with narrow streets and crooked medieval houses, attractive in an untouristy sort of way, whose best views are found by crossing the Inn and turning left up the Kellerbergweg. Another medieval river-town is **BURGHAUSEN**, which is named after the castle it surrounds. This is actually the longest castle in Europe, being 1030m from end to end, but that's about its only claim to fame. Connections from Munich are very infrequent, and you certainly couldn't make it a day trip.

Dachau

Not far from Munich, on the S-2 line, **DACHAU** is a picturesque provincial town. But whatever its charms may be, the place, the word itself, has associations with horrors that have been indelibly stamped on the consciousness of the twentieth century. Dachau was Germany's first **concentration camp**, built in 1933, and the model for all others. Though not expressly an extermination camp, many thousands were murdered here, and the motto that greeted new arrivals at the gates—*Arbeit Macht Frei* (Work Brings Freedom)—has taken its own chilling place in the history of Third Reich brutality. The camp was mainly for political prisoners, and numbered among its inmates Pastor Martin Niemöller, the former French premier Léon Blum, and Johann Elser, who tried to assassinate Hitler in 1939.

The rows of huts where prisoners lived were all torched by the Allies after the war, and neat, windswept patches of rectangular gravel mark their former outlines. A replica of one of these huts gives some idea of the cramped conditions prisoners were cooped up in, but the only original buildings still standing are the gas chambers, never used, since the war ended before they could be set to work. Open ovens gape at the shuddering visitor, and bright whitewashed walls almost distract from the ominous gas outlets set in the ceilings of the shower rooms. The stark wire perimeter fencing and watchtowers also remain.

There's no entrance fee and no guided tour; instead, a permanent **exhibition** with photographs and accompanying text in several languages including English, speaks for itself. Turn up at 11:30am or 3:30pm and you can also view the short, deeply disturbing, documentary *KZ-Dachau* in English. In recent years there have been repeated arguments about whether or not to open a center for visitors to attend discussion forums on the issues raised by visiting the camp. In 1987 an international youth center was to be opened for German and foreign schoolchildren to meet, but it was blocked by the right-wing town council—an important opportunity lost. The camp and exhibition are open Tuesday through Sunday from 9am to 5pm; get there by taking bus #722 from Dachau S-Bahn station.

Schloss Schleissheim

Close to Munich, at the S-Bahnhof Oberschleissheim, the city's third major palace, **Schloss Schleissheim** (Tues.–Sun. 10am–12:30pm and 1–5pm; DM2), stands in its enormous park, and that's really the best part. The palace itself was extensively destroyed during the war, and although it's been impressively restored, its rooms are echoingly empty, and it can't compete with Nymphenburg. Calling it Munich's "Versailles," as is the wont of the local tourist board, is raising expectations impossible to fulfil these days. A collection of some 300 baroque paintings in the *Neues Schloss* is only interesting to enthusiasts, and otherwise not worth the trip.

Freising

FREISING is some 35km north of Munich, and makes an easy day trip. It's one of Bavaria's oldest towns, and, as an important episcopal see from 739 to 1803, it used to be the spiritual capital of southern Bavaria; its title is still retained by the archbishop, who now resides solely in Munich. The **Dom**, situated on a hill above the picturesque town center, retains its Romanesque shell, but the interior was transformed into the grand baroque style by the Asam brothers. They didn't, however, tamper with the crypt, whose vault is supported by the amazing *Bestiensäule*, a column covered with carvings of fantastic animals. A secular claim to fame here is the **Weihenstephan Brewery**, which has been operating since 1040 and claims to be the oldest brewery in the world. Today it's all very modern and part of Munich's Technical University, but its traditional beers are still served in the adjoining beer garden.

Landshut

A further 35km northeast lies **LANDSHUT**. The Wittelsbachs established a base here in the early thirteenth century, and the town became capital of Lower Bavaria. For a while, Landshut outshone Munich, but when the local dukes died out in the sixteenth century and Bavaria became a united province, it went into decline, never to recover. It still preserves an unusually intact and photogenic town center dating from the high point of prosperity in the fifteenth and early sixteenth centuries.

The main street, somewhat oddly named the **Altstadt**, is lined with a resplendent series of high-gabled buildings of widely varying design. Two very different hall churches stand at either end; both were designed by Hans von Burghausen, one of the most brilliant late Gothic architects. The tower of **St. Martin** is extraordinary: it begins as a square design, then narrows and changes into an octagonal one. With a height of 133 meters, it's said to be the tallest brick structure in the world. Its interior, with slender pillars sweeping up to the lofty latticework vault, is hardly less impressive. In the south aisle is a larger-than-life, polychromed wood *Madonna and Child*, carved around 1520 by a local sculptor Hans Leinberger. Deliberately made to be admired from different angles (and thus not seen to good effect in photographs), it's a work which attracts glowing reviews from cognoscenti.

At the opposite end of the street, the **Spitalkirche** uses the same architectural methods as St. Martin, but each detail is cleverly modified: the tower, for example, is stumpy but still retains an idiosyncratic shape. The hospital buildings it served are across the road; they were rebuilt during the baroque period, a style also featured extensively on the parallel street, appropriately named Neustadt. Back on Altstadt stands another remarkable building, the **Stadtresidenz** (daily 9am–noon and 1–5pm in summer, Tues.–Sun. 9am–noon and 1–4pm in winter; DM3, DM2 students). Modeled on Giulio Romano's famous *Palazzo del Tè* in Mantua, this was begun in 1537 as the first palace in the Italian Renaissance style to be built north of the Alps. Though the wing facing the street is still German in spirit, the rest of the building (in particular the magnificent courtyard) immediately evokes a sunny Mediterranean atmosphere.

To the southeast of the center looms a romantically dilapidated castle, **Burg Trausnitz** (same times; DM1.50, DM1 students), which is worth the long haul up hundreds of steep steps, if only for the motley view of the town's red-tiled roofs and church steeples. Parts of the old fortress remain, including a double Romanesque chapel and a Gothic hall, but the bulk of the surviving complex results from the Renaissance rebuilding, which is a generation later than the Stadtresidenz. A highlight is the *Narrentreppe* ("Buffoons' Staircase"), decorated with vivacious portrayals of characters from the *commedia dell'arte*.

The Holledau

Directly north of Munich lies the **HOLLEDAU**, a region of gently rolling hop-growing country, with forests of hop-poles interspersed with natural woodland areas and rustic villages where Bavarian cooking can often be sampled at its best.

Bikes are ideal for exploring this region, and an interesting route would be to take country roads from the S-Bahn stop at Petershausen via JETZENDORF and SCHEYERN to PFAFFENHOFEN, where trains go back to Munich. (Unfortunately there's no bicycle rental at Petershausen S-Bahn station.) Alternatively, the roads from Pfaffenhofen to the villages of ENTRISCHENBRUNN, PAUNZHAUSEN, and down to REICHERTSHAUSEN also run through typical hop-growing country.

Neuburg an der Donau

NEUBURG AN DER DONAU, about one and a half hours by train from Munich, doesn't seem to be on any tourist trail or in many guidebooks, and yet the place is a rarity for Bavaria: medieval towns are two a penny, but Neuburg is characterized by Renaissance architecture and dreamy cobbled streets that almost give it the feeling of a forgotten realm. Perched on a chalk promontory overlooking the Danube, the town was a strategic trading post in Roman times, but its real moment of glory was in 1505, when it became the capital of the duchy of Pfalz-Neuburg. Over the next century it was redesigned and built up into an elegant place with an imposing castle and beautiful Renaissance and baroque buildings on leafy squares. The **Karlsplatz** in particular is a perfect picture of stylish sixteenth-century design, and the baroque facade of the **Hofkirche** forms a fine base to the square's symmetry. The interior of the church is wonderfully plain white stucco, with just a lick of gold and sparing use of black veined marble-effect to create a light and harmonious whole.

Neuburg's most significant building is the **Residenzschloss**, built between 1530 and 1545 by order of Ottheinrich, the future Elector of the Palatinate, who was later to transform the great Schloss in Heidelberg. Today it houses the **Schlossmuseum** (Tues.–Sun. 10am–5pm, DM3, DM2 students), which concentrates on presenting the history of the duchy of Pfalz-Neuburg, the region's palaeolithic origins, and its religious art and garments—a bit of a strange combination, but interesting nevertheless. Major highlights of the collection are the embroidered **altar cloths** and **ceremonial vestments**, each delicately embroidered in a particular range of colors depending on the ceremony they were used for.

Eichstätt and the Altmühltal

About 20km north of Neuburg lies the respectable small town of **EICHSTÄTT**. The main reason for coming here is to set off along the valley of the river Altmühl, but the **Dom** certainly merits a visit. Essentially a fourteenth-century Gothic church incorporating parts of its Romanesque predecessor, along with a number of baroque accretions, it's especially notable for a number of outstanding works of art. Prominent among these is the **Pappenheimer altar** in the north aisle, which was chiseled out of limestone by Veit Wirsperger in 1495. The scene is of Christ at the cross, with the masses below, crowding around for the grue-some spectacle. What's amazing is the execution of the work, rather than the scene portrayed: the stone has been worked with infinite skill to create individual characters, each with a different expression on their face, and together forming an incredibly varied portrait of medieval humanity. In the chancel, there's a seated statue of St. Willibald (one of the Dom's patrons) by a local sculptor, Loy Hering; though dating from just a couple of decades after the altar, it shows a marked move towards the Renaissance style. Off the west side of the cloisters is the **Mortuarium**, which is anything but the grim chamber its name suggests. It's a superb Gothic hall divided by a row of columns, one of which is deservedly known as the *Schöne Säule* (Beautiful Pillar) from its profuse carvings; there's also a brilliantly colored stained-glass window of *The Last Judgment*, designed by Holbein the Elder. South of the Dom is the **Residenzplatz**, lined with magnificent baroque and rococo palaces, along with the cheerful *Marienbrunnen*.

The **Altmühltal** winds its way in both directions from Eichstätt, and is part of a larger area designated as a nature park. You can follow the river along bike paths and small roads all the way to KEHLHEIM, about 80km to the east. But after BEILNGRIES, the river is steadily being ruined by the Rhein-Main-Donau canal, which is turning its meandering, picturesque route into a straight shipping lane; it's not really worth going past Beilngries. Heading west along the river is a better idea if you plan to make your way back to Munich, since the train more or less follows the valley, making return journeys a quick and easy option.

THE SOUTH: MOUNTAINS AND LAKES

The **Alps** and the **Upper Bavarian lakes** make up the southeast of Germany, forming some of the most gloriously beautiful countryside in Europe. The Alps extend about 250km along the Austrian border, and the lakes cover the lower reaches of the glacial valleys of Upper or Old Bavaria, the rich farming country dotted with villages and towns. It's here among the classic picture-book scenery that you'll find the Bavarian folklore and customs that are the subject of so many tourist brochures: men still wear leather *Lederhosen* and checked shirts, and women the traditional *Dirndl* dresses with frilly blouses and embroidered aprons. On a superficial level it can all seem very kitschy, but look beyond the packaged culture and you'll find life here steeped in a fascinating mixture of Catholic and pagan rites that dominate the annual calendar—events usually accompanied by large amounts of eating and drinking.

The Upper Bavarian pre-Alpine region, with its mild climate and beautiful scenery, is a popular place to retire to or have a vacation home, and during the summer the area is full of pensioners and German vacationers, as well as thousands of foreign tourists. As a rule you can expect any place with the prefix *Bad* ("Spa") to be absolutely chock-full of the elderly, particularly **Bad Wiessee** and **Bad Tölz**, where every other house is either a spa hotel or a sanatorium. You'll get the distinct feeling of being on someone else's turf in these places, and they don't cater to the independent traveler either. Prices are exorbitant, and there's absolutely nothing going on in the evenings. That said, Bavaria's lakes and mountains are hardly the place to look for nightclubs.

In general, the **western reaches** of the Alpine region are cheaper and less touristy—first, because they're not so easily accessible to Munich's weekend crowds, and second because the western Alps, called the **Allgäu**, are still home to a working agricultural community. Much of the eastern region from the **Tegernsee** to **Berchtesgaden** is heavily geared to the tourist trade. Places like Rottach-Egern and Berchtesgaden ooze with wealth and the villages have a manicured orderliness about them, which can feel unreal. But if you time your trip outside the high season of July and August, you should have a good chance of avoiding the crowds and not straining your finances. The best time of year for **skiing** is from January to early April.

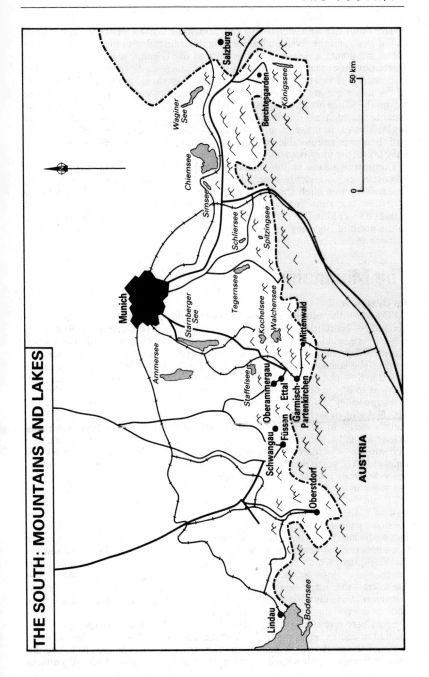

THE SOUTH: MOUNTAINS AND LAKES

Salzburg

Berchtesgaden

Königssee

Waginer See

Chiemsee

Simsee

Schliersee

Spitzingsee

Munich

Tegernsee

Kochelsee

Walchensee

Mittenwald

Starnberger See

Ammersee

Staffelsee

Oberammergau

Ettal

Schwangau

Füssen

Garmisch-Partenkirchen

Oberstdorf

AUSTRIA

Lindau

Bodensee

50 km

0

The **mountains** are defined by the **Bodensee** (*Lake Constance*) and **Lindau** to the west, and the Austrian border near Berchtesgaden to the east. In between these two points are famous places such as the Olympic ski-resort **Garmisch-Partenkirchen**, and **Schwangau** with its fantasy castle Neuschwanstein, but also many less well-known towns and villages that shouldn't be overlooked. Most of the **lakes** are just to the north of the mountains' eastern range, and spread across the whole area between here and Munich, though some are actually in the mountains, such as the **Walchensee** and fabulous **Königssee**. The largest lowland lakes, in order of size, are the **Chiemsee**, **Tegernsee** and **Staffelsee**, and there are innumerable smaller ones. Among them, the **Schliersee** is scenically one of the most rewarding.

Communications in the Alpine areas aren't as bad as you might expect. Almost every place can be reached by public transportation; the only snag being that bus services often only operate once or twice a day. There's a long-distance bus route that runs from Lindau via Oberstdorf and Füssen to Garmisch, and trains connect from there to destinations farther east. Train connections heading to the north of Germany are very efficient, and roads from Munich fan out to all sections of the Alps.

The Mountains

An Overview

To the west, the **mountains** rise up sharply almost as soon as you get to the outskirts of **Lindau**, on the shores of the Bodensee. The **German Alpine Road** begins here, winding its way in a wriggly pattern through mountain passes and across valleys until it arrives at the other end of the chain and the Austrian border. The landscapes are straight out of *The Sound of Music*, even on this side, and the first place worth spending some time in is **Oberstdorf**, which also happens to be the ultimate Alpine resort of the entire region. Nestling at the end of a large valley system designated as a national park, the village lies at the foot of **Mt. Nebelhorn** and a couple of other peaks, collectively offering a cheaper but equally excellent alternative to the better-known places. From here, the roads detour around a bulge of Austrian territory to reach the towns of **Füssen** and **Schwangau**, which aren't particularly memorable in themselves, but get a lot of mileage out of being next door to the fairytale **castles**. Continuing east, the landscape becomes gentler for a while, with rich mixed forests rather than pines filling the slopes. The Alpine Road follows a wide valley forged by one of the mountain rivers, passing the small settlements of **Oberammergau** and **Ettal**, as well as **Linderhof Castle** nearby, of which the first is the best-known for the Passion Play performed there every ten years. From here it's only a few kilometers to the international ski-resort of **Garmisch-Partenkirchen**, and the dividing point between the western and eastern mountain ranges. Towering above town is the **Zugspitze**, which at 2962m is Germany's highest and most famous peak. Another one close by, which is a popular day tour for sporty types, is the **Alpspitze**—get maps and advice or hire a guide via the tourist office in Garmisch. Virtually next door to Garmisch is **Mittenwald**, which often gets unfairly skipped due to its prestigious neighbor.

From here onwards, virtually nothing of the entire eastern range of the Alps rises to dramatic heights until the *Berchtesgadener Land*, which is the collective name for the most easterly point of the German mountains, an area including the town of **Berchtesgaden** itself as well as the marvelous peaks of **Mt. Watzmann** and the high ridges that form the border with Austria and Salzburg, just on the other side. This certainly doesn't mean that the area along the chain until Berchtesgaden is uninteresting—in places, it's stunning. Much of it can also be explored while visiting the lakes that lie among the foothills of the eastern range.

To the east, the gentle forested slopes are perfect walking country. If you're looking to get away from it all, the **Sudelfeld** hills above the village of BAYRISCHZELL are usually quiet since no public transit goes up there. They also have the advantage of a hill-top youth hostel, which is an excellent base for summer tours or winter skiing. At the far eastern end of the Alps, you're back to grandiose, snow-capped peaks and the icy **Königsee**. An interesting underground attraction here are the **saltmines**, and the famous café culture of Austrian SALZBURG is only 1½ hours on the train from Berchtesgaden.

Lindau

At their most westerly point the Alps descend to the waters of the **Bodensee** and the tiny island town of **LINDAU**. In the Middle Ages this was a bustling trading post, and rich merchants built grand gabled houses on town squares that have a distinct Italian flavor. The half-timbered buildings lean over like stacks of dominoes, and narrow streets like the Zitronengasse lead to quiet nooks and crannies.

Stone-hewn Bavarian lions look out defiantly across the lake from the former royal port, and large hotels front the tiny port left over from an age when nineteenth-century travelers resided here in luxury. As soon as the summer sun comes out, the harbor promenade fills with coffee tables, giving a Mediterranean feeling to the bustling waterfront. The ferries operate on the lake between June 1 and September 6, or if you prefer a bit more independence, all sorts of boats, canoes and windsurfers can be hired from the yacht marina next to the main harbor. Year-round access is provided by the less romantic Neue Seebrücke.

On the **Reichsplatz** nearby, the recently restored Rathaus and its elaborate frescoes seems rather overdressed compared with the buildings around it. In much better taste is the **Haus zum Cavazzen** on the Marktplatz, whose three-story baroque facade is painted in subtle sandy-red tones, and which contains one of the most attractive local history museums of any town in Bavaria (Tues.–Sat. 9am–noon and 2–5pm, Sun. 10am–noon; DM2). There's an intriguing collection of seventeenth-century family trees painted on wooden panels that open up like a photo-album, to reveal little portraits and dates for each member. A particular rarity among the other items are the seventeenth- and eighteenth-century paintings mocking Luther, known as *Spottbilder*. On the second and third floors there's a good collection of eighteenth and nineteenth century middle- and working-class furniture, ranging from items from the workshops of Lindau's former artisan guilds to the beautifully inlaid *Biedermeier* furniture of polite society. Other sections of this tightly packed museum include gruesome sixteenth-century torture instruments and weaponry, etchings of Lindau, and clocks through the ages.

Should you only have time for one trip outside Lindau, take bus #7 to the suburb of HOYREN, and walk up **Mt. Hoyrenberg** for a stunning view of the lake and the Austrian and Swiss Alps. The villages and apple orchards around Mt. Hoyrenberg seem very quiet after Lindau, and OBERREITNAU, UNTERREITNAU, and BODOLZ are especially pretty villages. The very friendly **youth hostel**, Herbergsweg 11, (☎08382 5813; buses #1, #3, and #6 from the Bahnhof) on mainland Lindau, can give you plenty of advice on worthwhile excursions, and they also organize mountain tours.

If the hostel is full, cheapish places on the island costing DM28 to DM40 per person are the *Inselgraben*, Hintere Metzgergasse 4–6 (☎08382 5481); *Gästehaus Ladine*, In der Grub 25 (☎08382 5326); and *Gästehaus Limmer*, In der Grub 16 (☎08382 5877). The **campground** *Lindau-Zech* by the lake is open from April to September. The **tourist office** (Mon.–Fri. 8am–noon and 2–6pm, Sat. 9am–12:30pm) opposite the **Bahnhof** supplies free maps of Lindau and endless amounts of other publicity. You'll find that the cheapest **restaurants** are in the road suitably named "In der Grub", and there's also a friendly bar here called the *Schalldämpfer*. Don't expect too much in the way of nightlife, though it's worth checking out the purpose-built entertainments area of bars and discos on Von-Behring-Strasse in the mainland suburb of REUTIN.

The main annual festival around here is the **Bregenz Operatic and Music Festival**, which takes place from mid-July to mid-August, and although Bregenz is on the Austrian side of the Bodenzee, many people stay in Lindau because it's cheaper. Performances are held on an enormous stage in the water, with the audience watching from an open-air amphitheater on shore.

Oberstdorf

About 70km east of Lindau, **OBERSTDORF** is tucked away in valleys that are classic "Sound-of-Music" countryside. The **Alpine Road** that winds its way up and around from Lindau is one of the most beautiful drives in the south. Pastures are full of the sound of tinkling cowbells, and villages are ablaze with geraniums on every balcony and window ledge. The air is exhilaratingly fresh and clean, the aromatic pine forests are still alive with deer, and on the mountain crags you might even catch a glimpse of chamois.

Imagine your ideal mountain resort and Oberstdorf will almost certainly fit the picture: the old village has grown discreetly, without the high-rise aberrations found elsewhere, but with excellent sports facilities, including swimming pools, a skating rink and an Olympic ski-jump. The streets around the market square have lots of friendly bars to explore, yet if you walk a little farther, the roads soon lead to open fields. The agricultural life of the place makes itself felt too, especially during the summer, when the clanking of cowbells wakes you at daybreak.

The higher mountain valleys beyond Oberstdorf take you to lonely Alpine huts and the sort of views that give a surge of energy. Most of the mountain roads are restricted to agricultural traffic, but they're fine for bicycles, and that way you can cover a very good distance before setting off on foot. A quicker way, of course, is to take one of the cable cars. Serious mountaineers will find **Mt. Nebelhorn** the most challenging, while for hiking and less strenuous Alpine walking the **Fellhorn** and **Söllereck** mountains are a good idea—the Söllereck is especially gentle. During the winter, Mts. Nebelhorn, Fellhorn and Söllereck form the heart of an excellent skiing range, with 35 cable cars and lifts covering over 42km of pistes. A six-day ski pass costs around DM172 (DM129 kids), and for cross-country skiers there are also 85km of prepared routes in the surrounding valleys.

For **bars and restaurants** your best bet is the area around the Pfarrstrasse. Try the *Ungewitter* bar in Freiherr-von-Brutscherstrasse or the *Intermezzo* on the corner of Pfarr- and Oststrassen. You'll soon see which places are kitschy tourist traps and which aren't—if there's a band playing "traditional" music, carry on walking.

What makes Oberstdorf just about perfect is abundant cheap **accommodation**. In the neighboring village of KORNAU you'll find the nearest **youth hostel** (bus connection from Oberstdorf Bahnhof), but there are also a number of reasonably priced guest houses from DM18 to DM34 per person near the town center: for example, the *Alpenglühn*, Wittelsbacherstr. 4 (☎08322 4692); the *Amman*, Weststr. 23 (☎08322 2961); or the *Buchenberg*, Lorettostr. 6 (☎08322 2315). The **tourist office** (Mon.–Sat., 8am–noon and 2–6pm) on the Marktplatz can reserve you a room when you arrive. They also provide free maps of the whole region, with all the hiking routes marked on them, as well as helping to arrange guided mountain tours. The **campground** is open all year, at Rublingerstr. 10 (☎08322 4022).

Füssen and Schwangau

Forty kilometers further east along the Alpine Road, between the **Forggensee** reservoir and the **Ammer** mountains, the adjacent towns of **FÜSSEN** and **SCHWANGAU** are in a great setting. If you happen to be in Schwangau on October 13, you'll see the unique **Colomansfest** at the Coloman church, a kilometer out of town. So many people come for this event that the church service is held in the fields outside: it's to give thanks for the cows' safe return from the Alpine pastures, and to bless the horses that used to perform the dangerous work of bringing logs from the mountain forests. When it comes to blessing the horses, they're ridden around the church three times for good luck. The priest and honorary guests lead the procession in beautifully decorated horse-drawn carriages, and a hundred or so riders follow behind. After the ceremony, the whole procession slowly makes its way to the village to the sounds of a brass band, and of course there's beer and food as well.

But what people usually come here to see are the royal castles of **Hohenschwangau** and **Neuschwanstein**. Highly commercialized and very expensive, these are nonetheless worth the trip, if only for the surrounding scenery. Hohenschwangau (daily 10am–4pm; DM6, DM3 students) is the older of the two and used to belong to the parents of **King Ludwig II**. It's a "genuine" royal castle, originally built in the twelfth century, but heavily damaged by Napoleon in 1800 and 1806. It was restored a few decades later when Crown Prince Maximilian II bought it, and his son Ludwig II spent his youth here. A mark of his individualism remains in the bedroom, where he had the ceiling painted with stars that were spotlit in the evenings. The music room testifies to one of Ludwig's main passions, and in particular to his special friendship with the composer Richard Wagner, who used to come and stay. Nearby is the quiet **Alpsee**, great for quiet walks and very cold swims.

Neuschwanstein (same times and prices) was built by Ludwig II between 1869 and 1896. A little higher up the mountain, it has since become famous in countless posters and cards as the ultimate story-book castle, all fairy-tale pinnacles, swirled in a dream-like mist. It really looks far better from a distance than close up or inside: the architecture is a hotchpotch of styles, ranging from the Byzantine throne-hall to the Romanesque study, to an artificial grotto next to the living room. The castle was never completed because King Ludwig was dethroned in 1886 for incompetence and wasting the state's money. It's a bizarre monument to a very sad and lonely man.

A path behind the castle leads to the dramatic **Poellat Gorge** and the **Marienbrücke**, a steel bridge built across the gorge in the last century and quite a feat of engineering for the time. Continue steeply past the bridge for about another three hours and you reach the top of **Mt. Tegelberg** and views stretching as far as Munich on a good day. Another way to get up here is to take the cable car (daily 8:30am–5pm, DM8 one way), which can be reached by bus #9713 or #9715 from Schwangau. The *Gasthaus* just below the castle isn't as expensive as you might expect. Otherwise you'll find that there's more choice in Füssen than around Schwangau.

Apart from the royal castles, this is a very good region to explore by bicycle or car. The countryside around the village of **STEINGADEN** (20km northeast of Füssen) and the Wieskirche has very little traffic, but lots of quiet country roads. In Steingaden there's a romantically dilapidated Romanesque abbey, whose natural sandstone architecture is a welcome change to the plethora of baroque. In contrast, the **Wieskirche** is one of the most famous rococo churches in Germany. Unassumingly tucked into the countryside, its plain exterior belies the almost indecent extravagance inside. Light streams in from the high windows of the oval nave, creating an inviting and joyful atmosphere; plain white pillars sparkle like the snow-capped mountains, but at the same time form a modest contrast to the stuccoed and gold-plated ornamentation of the arches above, and the vast fresco by Johann Baptist Zimmermann in the cupola. The contrast is intended to symbolise earth below and the glorious heavens above, with the blue base of the central fresco representing God's pity and forgiveness spreading over mankind. **Dominikus Zimmermann** (brother of J. B.) built the Wieskirche between 1746 and 1754, and was so proud of it that he lived nearby for the rest of his life. Unfortunately, extensive restoration work will be in progress until 1990, blocking the view of the whole interior.

The nearest **youth hostel**, Mariahilferstr. 5 (☎08362 7754) is in Füssen. Two **guest houses** near the castles are the *Haus Schwansee*, Parkstr. 9 (☎08362 8353), and *Pension Weiher*, Hofwiesenweg 11 (☎08362 81161): both have rooms from DM22 to DM40. There are **campgrounds** by the BANNWALDSEE and the FORGGENSEE, and the **tourist office** (Mon.–Sat. 9am–5:30pm; ☎08362 81051) on the main road in Schwangau will reserve accommodation and provide brochures on the area.

Oberammergau, Ettal, and Schloss Linderhof

About 50km farther on from Schwangau, the Alpine Road winds along the Ammer river valley, passing the mountains of the same name. These constitute a national park covered by an ancient forest which in autumn turns into a magnificent red-gold sea. On the main road itself, you pass the villages of **Oberammergau** and **Ettal**, while Schloss Linderhof is hidden away in the lonely GRASWANG VALLEY that leads to Austria.

OBERAMMERGAU is world famous for the **Passion Play** that the local villagers have been performing since 1633. Originally the play was written and performed in thanks for being spared by the plague epidemic, and the play was fittingly staged in the cemetery. These days a more agreeable setting is used, and over the centuries thousands of people have crammed into the little village to watch the all-day open-air performance. The show takes place every ten years and the next Passion Play is in 1990 between May and September. The cast is always exclusively made up of local villagers, who vie for the honor of a role, but with up to 200 players on stage in some scenes, most get a chance to participate. Even the props have to be made locally, displaying a shrewd sense for combining piety with business. More than a touch of controversy surrounds the forthcoming production—for the first time ever, a Protestant has been given a key part, while, in defiance of the hitherto strictly enforced convention that Mary can only be played by a virgin, one of the actresses who will alternate in the role is mother of two children. Cynics scoff that these decisions were made to attract media attention; defenders argue that Oberammergau doesn't need any more publicity than it already receives.

Many of the houses in the village have the traditional outside **frescoes** of religious or Alpine scenes, which you can see as either quaint or kitsch, and that goes for the numerous wood carvings in the souvenir shops as well. If the place sounds like a bit of a tourist trap, that's just what it unfortunately is: in summer the tourist coaches and exhaust fumes are positively choking. On the other hand the surrounding area is excellent hiking country, so the local **youth hostel**, Mahlensteinweg 10 (☎08822 4114), would be a good base for walking tours.

ETTAL, down the road, is a little less touristy and mainly interesting for a Benedictine **Kloster**, with its church remarkable for the rare twelve-cornered nave design, based on the Church of the Holy Sepulcher in Jerusalem. The original fourteenth-century interior was extensively changed to suit baroque tastes in the eighteenth century by Enrico Zucalli, and the rich stucco decorations were molded by the same team who decorated the Wieskirche near Steingaden.

Schloss Linderhof (April–Sept. 9am–12:15pm and 12:45–5pm; DM6 including grotto and Moorish pavilion) is one of King Ludwig's more restrained fantasies. About 5km off the main road near Ettal, it was built as a private residence rather than a statement in royal architecture, and from the garden terraces its creamy white walls and square shape make it look like a sparkling wedding cake. As you enter, it's impossible to miss a large bronze statue of one of Ludwig's heroes, the French Sun King Louis XIV. In spite of this being a private retreat, the King still had a royal reception room built with intricate gold-painted carvings, stucco ornamentation, and a throne canopy draped in ermine curtains, said to be from the coronation gown of the Greek King Otto. The bedroom too is daftly luxurious: the large bed is cordoned off by a richly carved balustrade, and royal-blue velvet extends to a great canopy overhead, no doubt creating the reassuring feeling of sleeping on the throne.

But the real attraction is the delightful **park**. The castle forms the axis of a cross design, which is built on the Italian Renaissance model of terraces, cascades and pools rising up in front and behind, while the shorter gardens to the right and left have strictly manicured lawns, hedges and flowerbeds. Initially, it's hard to tell that the surrounding "wild" scenery is actually a clever English garden design that gradually blends into the forests of the mountain beyond. A number of romantic little buildings are dotted around the park, the most remarkable of which is the **Venus Grotto**. It's supposed to be based on the set from the first act of Wagner's opera *Tannhäuser*. The grotto has an illuminated lake, with an enormous golden conch floating on it in which the king would sometimes take rides.

Garmisch-Partenkirchen

Twelve kilometers down the road, **GARMISCH**, as it's commonly known, is the most famous town in the German Alps, partly because it's at the foot of the highest mountain—the **Zugspitze** (2962m)—and also because it hosted the Winter Olympics over fifty years ago. The location is marvelous, placed between the gentle Ammer mountains and the imposing peaks of the Zugspitz chain. During the winter months Garmisch is a premier skiing resort, and it has excellent facilities for skating and other winter sports too. In summer, mountaineers and hiking enthusiasts come to explore the craggy heights or follow the gentler routes on the unfortunately named **Wank** mountain, or walk down the dramatic **Partnachklamm Gorge**.

What were once two separate villages, Garmisch and Partenkirchen, have merged over the years to form one town, but there are still two distinct identities, with the Garmisch side aspiring to ritzy shops and trendy brasseries, while Partenkirchen still retains its Alpine-village feel. Its attractive Ludwigstrasse, lined with traditional painted houses, also has some friendly inns and cafés that aren't overly expensive. In the Garmisch end of town, you're likely to be asked to make room for someone else if you don't spend enough money.

Once the darling of the tourist brochures, Garmisch-Partenkirchen has become a very expensive commercial business, selling itself on the tainted, dusty laurels of the 1936 Games. Vast numbers of tourists are herded through on coach tours that pack them off up the Zugspitze for DM47, an expensive meal, and then away. The result is a complacent and manifestly unfriendly **tourist office**, Bahnhofstr. 34 (Mon.–Sat. 8am–6pm, Sun. 10am–noon; ☎08821 1800). Free maps of the area are available, and there's also info on guided tours and hiking routes. If you plan on spending some time hiking here, it might be worth buying a special seven-day pass that allows use of most cable cars. The passes are available from the *Zugspitzbahn* office from June 1 to October 31, for DM62 or DM37 for kids under 16. Winter ski passes for the region are valid six days and cost about DM176 and DM117 respectively.

The **youth hostel**, Jochstr. 10 (☎08821 2980; bus #6 or #7 from the Bahnhof) isn't that great—for one thing they insist on turning the lights out at 11pm, and it's not very central either. A much friendlier place in the same price range and without an age restriction is the *Naturfreundehaus*, Schalmeiweg 21 (☎08821 4322). Otherwise the *Ohlsenhof*, Von-Brug-Strasse 18 (☎08821 2168) comes highly recommended by other travelers, and has singles around DM29 and doubles around DM28–DM34. The *Mirabell*, Hindenburg Strasse 20 (☎08821 4826) is good too, and charges around DM25–DM28 for singles and DM24–DM28 for doubles. Nearest **campground** is in the outlying village of REUTTE.

Mittenwald

It's absurd that Garmisch gets the lion's share of tourism when, just 15km down the road, **MITTENWALD** has the best of everything but on a smaller and friendlier scale. Goethe said of Mittenwald in 1786 that it was like a "living picture book." It remains so to this day. A large village with traditional frescoes on many houses, Mittenwald still has the feel of being a community and not just a resort. This is reflected in the local **church** of St. Peter and St. Paul, which has beautifully carved seats, and each family's nameplate attached to their special section on the benches. The statue outside is in honor of **Mathias Klotz** who brought the highly specialized craft of violin-making to Mittenwald in the seventeenth century, saving the village from becoming an impoverished backwater. In the preceding two centuries, Venetian merchants had located their main market here for trading Italian and German goods, making Mittenwald rich in the process. But that source of wealth was destroyed when the merchants returned their market to its original location in Italy, and the village went into decline until the new "industry" was founded. Since then the local violin makers have achieved international fame, with musicians paying up to DM15,000 for a violin that will last for generations. Examples from some of the finest violin makers can be seen in the dollhouse-like museum, the **Geigenbaumuseum** (May–Oct. Mon.–Fri. 10–11:45am and 2–4:45pm; DM2) in the Ballenhausgasse.

Not far away, in the road called Im Gries, stand the oldest Mittenwald houses, with old frescoes decorating their frontages, the kitsch effect pleasantly diminished by faded colors. This style, known as *Lüftlmalerei*, originates from the baroque era, when Catholics used architecture and fresco painting to decorate their churches and illustrate the glory of their religion during the Counter-Reformation; thus the frescoes on so many homes in southern Bavaria are a secular expression of a sacred art form, unique to the regions that remained Catholic. That's also why the scenes depicted are usually based on biblical stories.

The **Karwendl** mountain towering above Mittenwald is one of the most popular climbing destinations in Germany, and the local **mountaineering school** (Dekan-Karl-Platz 29) runs tours and courses throughout the summer, as well as supplying guides for small groups. The view from the top of Mt. Karwendel is one of the most exhilarating and dramatic to be found, and a cable car goes there for DM22 round trip.

When it comes to bars and looking for something to eat, you're most likely to end up in a traditional inn. **Accommodation** in the youth hostel is not very practical in Mittenwald as it's an hour's walk from the Bahnhof. But there are plenty of good places to stay in the village, such as the *Haus Alpenruh*, Schillerweg 2 (☎08823 1375); *Gästehaus Bergfrühling*, Dammkarstr. 12 (☎08823 8089); or *Haus Berghof*, Grobelweg 37 (☎08823 1556). They all charge around DM16.50–DM26 for singles and doubles. The nearest **campground** is 3km north, on the road to Garmisch and open all year. The **tourist office**, Dammkarrstr. 3 (Mon.–Sat. 9am–5pm ☎08823 1051) will reserve rooms and provide free maps and brochures of the area.

Berchtesgaden

Between Mittenwald and **BERCHTESGADEN** the Alps drop to the highlands and glacial valleys of the lakes, creating a gap of about 125km as the crow flies, before the mountains rise up to majestic heights again at Bavaria's most southeasterly point. Almost entirely surrounded by mountains, *Berchtesgadener Land* gives the impression of being a separate little country, and there's a magical atmosphere here—especially in the mornings—when mists rise from the lakes and curl around lush valleys and rocky mountainsides. Not surprisingly the area is steeped in legends, which usually feature the spiky peaks of **Mt. Watzmann**. The most popular one has it that they're really the family of a tyrant king, who ruled the area so mercilessly that God punished its members by turning them to stone.

Star attraction of the region is **KÖNIGSSEE**: Germany's highest lake bends around the foot of the Watzmann for nearly five kilometers, like a Norwegian fjord. However, that's where the similarity ends, since this is anything but a lonely place, and it's sometimes difficult to appreciate the stunning beauty when blanketed by hordes of tourists. It really is worth getting up early to catch the atmosphere of the place before everyone else arrives. Ferries make round trips to the far end of the lake, and although they're not cheap at DM13.50, it's worth the money and there are some great mountain trails to follow from **St. Bartholomä** and the **Obersee**. The commercial boats have been electrified since 1909, so the deep, green waters are refreshingly clean and healthy. Another lake well worth the bus fare is the smaller and less crowded **Hintersee** by the little village of

RAMSAU. The whole area is wonderful hiking country, but take your own food to avoid the expensive mountain restaurants. Useful maps with suggested walking routes can be bought at the **tourist office**, Königsseer Strasse (opposite the Bahnhof, Mon.–Fri. 8:30am–5:30pm) in Berchtesgaden, which also organizes guides or special tours.

One of the best mountain excursions involves taking a cable car from Königssee (daily 8am–5:30pm; DM16 single, DM21 round trip) or walking up **Mt. Jenner**, from which you get a spectacular view of the Königssee and surrounding peaks. It gets very busy, but it's better than the expensive bus tour up to **Mt. Hehlstein**, and swarming onto the summit terrace and restaurant. Undoubtedly the view is marvelous, but the area's main claim to fame is in its connection with **Adolf Hitler**. Hitler rented a house in the nearby village of OBERSALZBERG, which he later had enlarged into the **Berghoff**, a stately retreat where he could meet foreign dignitaries. Approached by a long winding road, and with a final dramatic sweep of steps, it was expressly designed to awe visitors. Here, in 1938, British Prime Minister Neville Chamberlain journeyed to dissuade Hitler from attacking Czechoslovakia, the first in a series of meetings that ended with Chamberlain returning from Munich clutching the infamous piece of paper that would ensure "peace in our time." In putting his name to this agreement the Führer had bided his time, and the Czech people's sovereignty was treacherously sacrificed for the sake of Britain and France's vanity. "He seemed a nice old man," smirked Hitler of the agreement, "so I thought I would give him my autograph." Today the remains of the Berghoff are almost entirely overgrown and vanished, the building having been blown up by U.S. troops in 1952.

An experience you certainly shouldn't miss here is going down the **saltmine** (May 1–Oct. 15 daily 8:30am–5pm, Oct. 16–April 30 Mon.–Fri. 12:30–3:30pm), which has been the region's source of wealth since 1515. There'll be long lines and it costs DM 11.50, but this is one time when it really is worth it. Wearing the traditional protective clothing (don't wear a skirt), you're taken deep into the mountain astride a wooden train, rather like those that kids ride on, except bigger. Once underground the one-hour tour passes all the machinery and processes of salt-mining in disused shafts connected by wooden chutes, which everyone descends in groups of three. It's great fun, so don't let the commercial trappings of the tour spoil it for you.

The town of **Berchtesgaden** itself has an attractive square in front of the royal **Schloss** (Oct.–April Mon.–Fri. 10am–1pm and 2–5pm, May–Sept. Sun.–Fri. 10am–1pm and 2–5pm; DM4.50, DM3 students), which used to be a monks' priory before it was secularized and taken over by the Bavarian kings in 1810. It's the former residence of Crown Prince Rupert, but there are no royal furnishings left here. Instead it houses the Prince's collections of medieval religious wood carvings, sixteenth- and seventeenth-century Italian furniture, and a fearsome collection of weaponry. It's not the most fascinating museum you'll ever visit, but the thirteenth-century Romanesque cloister before the entrance has some beautiful columns to stroll past. Apart from the Schloss and the church nearby, the main pleasure in Berchtesgaden is to wander around the winding streets and enjoy the lovely views of the valley and surrounding mountains.

Restaurants are, unfortunately, not particularly cheap because as a resort, Berchtesgaden caters almost exclusively for the wealthy elderly and families. It's a respectable place, and the nearest **youth hostel** is in the village of STRUB (Gebirgsjägerstr. 52; ☎08652 2190; bus from Berchtesgaden's Bahnhof). There's also a privately run hostel (Seestr. 29; bus from Berchtesgaden) right next to the Königssee, in the village of the same name. Apart from those, the following guest houses charge between DM17 and DM28 per person: *Hansererhäusl*, Hansererweg 8 (☎08652 2523); *Haus Bergwald*, Duftbachweg 3–5 (☎08652 2586); and *Berlerlehen*, Rennweg 19 (☎08652 1590). The tourist office can help with reserving rooms or directing you to any of the five **campgrounds** in the valley.

The Lakes

An Overview

Receding glaciers left a great many lakes in Upper Bavaria, which together with the region's moor lakes and reservoirs, combine to form a large "lake district," stretching below the eastern Alps in a wide band beginning roughly south of Munich, and continuing beyond the Austrian border. There are at least forty lakes in the region, and the main ones tend to be situated in clusters, though that doesn't necessarily imply any similarity among them. For example the **Staffelsee**, a little north of Garmisch is a warm and shallow moor lake, encompassed by thickets of reeds. But the nearby **Kochelsee** is a deep glacial lake, largely surrounded by a flat, bare landscape, save for the mountains rising up on the southern side. A road winds steeply up these mountains, climbing over a high pass to come out suddenly by the windswept **Walchensee**, an Alpine lake with a dramatic backdrop of rugged mountains and long stretches of uninhabited, sheer rock.

About 30km east, the Tegernsee, Schliersee and Spitzingsee lakes form another approximate group, different again from the first three and very different to each other. The **Tegernsee** is beautifully set in the green rolling hills of the Alpine lowlands, which accounts for its popularity and the numerous private residences along its shore. The much smaller **Schliersee** on the other hand, only five minutes' drive from its neighbor, is picturesquely rustic in its environment. Here, farms and a small town are still home to a working community rather than cosmopolitan weekenders, and prices are noticeably more reasonable. The **Spitzingsee** is another Alpine lake, but this time tiny, only meriting a dot on the map. It's almost exclusively associated with winter sports, when the surrounding slopes make for good weekend skiing. But in the summer, the mountainside here is bare and uninspiring, with few visitors.

Continuing east for about another 35km, you soon come to Bavaria's largest lake, the **Chiemsee**. Covering about 180 square kilometers, it's also known as the "Bavarian Sea," and on one of its islands King Ludwig II built yet another of his fantasy constructions. Unfortunately, a expressway follows the lake's southern shore, but beyond it lies some marvelous hiking country, in particular the **Kampenwand** mountains, which shouldn't be missed if you're in this region and enjoy Alpine walks. The nearby **Simsee** and **Waginger See**, to the west and east respectively, are both about an eighth of the size, and the latter is again a moor lake. It's especially popular with campers, and there are no less than seven lakeside campgrounds. Being close to the Austrian border, and a mere 25km from Salzburg, makes it a cheap base for Austrian excursions as well.

The key to this region, then, is variety. And if the geography is fascinating, a further pleasure in the form of wonderful old *Gaststätten*, often with beer gardens, where traditional Bavarian menus and innumerable regional beers are a welcome surprise. "Bavarian" means Upper Bavarian in this context, so don't expect to find the same things in Swabia or Franconia. You'll find that certain dishes are only supposed to be eaten at certain times: the famous *Weisswürstl*, for example, are strictly speaking meant for brunch around 11am, to go with the first *Weissbier* of the day. Then there are delicious snacks such as *Obatzter*, which is a paste made of Camembert, butter, caraway seed, paprika, pickles and onions, to be eaten with bread. Another favorite is *Leberkäs*, which is a baked meatloaf made of pork, onions, marjoram and nutmeg, usually eaten hot in a roll or as a main meal with fried eggs and salad. This last can be bought as a cheap take-out snack in most butchers' shops too. Vegetarians will have a bit of a tough time unfortunately, since most dishes are slanted firmly toward carnivores. But there are loads of freshwater fish from the lakes, if you're not too strict.

Accommodation around or near the lakes is no problem. Private rooms are usually advertised by a sign outside saying *Zimmer frei*; if they're full it will say something like *Zimmer belegt*. You'll also find **youth hostels** throughout the area. **Local travel** is mainly by bus, and though services aren't necessarily frequent, all places mentioned here can be reached by public transportation. If you're coming from Munich, there are fast and frequent services to Kochel, Tegernsee, Schliersee, and Chiemsee, with connecting lines to most of the others.

The Staffelsee, Kochelsee, and Walchensee

The dark waters of the **STAFFELSEE**, near the village of MURNAU, 50km south of Munich, get agreeably warm in the summer and make it ideal for swimming. On the western shore, only accessible by boat, there's a nudist beach, though you'll find that topless sunbathing is pretty much standard practice in most places. The countryside around the lake is flat marshland—don't forget the mosquito repellent. If you want a quieter but colder experience, the RIEGSEE is not far to the east of the Staffelsee. For brochures and hiking maps see the **tourist office** (Kohlgruberstr. 1, Murnau).

About 10km southeast of Murnau lies the **KOCHELSEE** at the foot of the Benediktenwand mountains. A large lake, it combines lowland and highland attractions, with the Benediktenwand virtually rising out of its southern shore. The village of **KOCHEL** is the largest settlement on the lake, and there are a couple of smaller villages dotted around to the north. The lakeside has an agreeably empty feel compared with many others, with hardly any private property around the edges. That said, the lake and immediate surrounding area are a bit boring in themselves, being completely flat and without memorable views. The **tourist office** (Kalmbachstr. 11) supplies free maps and brochures, and helps with accommodation. There's a **youth hostel** at Badstr. 2 and a bus will take you to another one in the nearby village of URFELD at Mittenwalder Str. 17.

Kochel is interesting mainly for two of its former inhabitants: Balthasar Mayer, the celebrated **Blacksmith of Kochel**; and **Franz Marc**, perhaps the greatest Bavarian painter of the twentieth century. The "Blacksmith of Kochel" led the 1705 rebellion of Upper Bavarian farmers against the Austrian occupation. Bavaria had fought against the Austrian Habsburg rulers in the War of the Spanish Succession and lost, so Austrian troops had occupied the region. Their brutal rule led to the farmers' rebellion, which has since become a symbol of Bavarian *Heimatliebe* or patriotism. The plotters of the uprising were betrayed, and they and their leader died in the battle at Sendling near Munich. Their graves are still to be found in Sendling churchyard, now a part of the capital.

Marc was a member of the *Blaue Reiter* group of German abstract painters that included Kandinsky, Macke and Klee. Marc lived around here from 1908 until 1916, when he died in World War I at the age of 36. Unlike his friends, he preferred country life, and his pictures of horses and other animals are his most famous works. A **Franz Marc Museum** (Herzogstandweg 43, Tues.–Sun. 2–6pm; DM3, DM2 students) has a highly representative collection of his work, comprizing about a hundred paintings as well as works by other members of the *Blaue Reiter* group.

The nearby **WALCHENSEE** is far more dramatic and beautiful than the Kochelsee, and the Kesselberg road winds steeply up from the valley, twisting and turning until it reaches its windswept waters. Nobody knows just how deep the Walchensee is. The water is so cold in the lower reaches that the many trees fallen from the steep shores haven't been able to sink completely. Instead they've formed a sort of false bottom to the lake, which is quite impenetrable. The mysteries surrounding the lake aren't just about its physical nature either—many people believe that it was here that the Nazis dumped their hoarded treasures in the last few days of the war, because truck after truck is said to have driven up here and emptied its contents into the lake. Perhaps it's true, but there's no way of finding out because of the trees below. Plenty of divers have tried their luck and many have died, tangled up in the branches or with their lifelines ripped: it can be sinister up here when the sun has gone.

But on a sunny day the lake is beautiful and boats cut through the green waves, their sails full with the mountain breeze. If you're into boats and windsurfing, this is a good place to come, especially since it's never as crowded as the lowland lakes and is cheaper too. Rowing boats can be rented for the day from the *Hotel Schwaigerhof* for DM14 or DM8 to DM12 per hour, depending on the number of people. Surfboards cost DM15 per hour, DM28 for two hours, DM35 for three hours, and DM50 per day. A very popular tour around here is to walk about two hours from URFELD to the HERZOGSTAND summit. From the top you can see both the Kochelsee and the Walchensee, as well as snow-capped Austrian peaks to the south, and the Bavarian plateau to the north. Alternatively, take the *Herzogstandbahn* cable car from the village of Walchensee (8:45am–4:45pm; DM10 round trip, DM6.50 one way).

The Tegernsee, Schliersee, and Spitzingsee

The **TEGERNSEE**, about 45km south of Munich, is perhaps the most beautiful lake in Bavaria. For this reason it's long been a haven of the rich, who built their weekend homes along its privately owned sections, and in the southern village of ROTTACH-EGERN you'll find one of the most expensive hotels in Bavaria, complete with high-fashion boutique and piano-bar. The *haute couture* in Rottach-Egern is pretty incongruous in this rural setting, and the neo-locals take themselves ever so seriously.

A perfect antidote to these designer Bavarians is the *Bräustüberl* in the village of **Tegernsee**, where the local farmers go to drink each other under the table and play cards. Things get quite rowdy sometimes when fists start hammering the tables, but there's also a large beer garden, so you needn't upset the regulars sitting around the *Stammtisch* inside. The *Bräustüberl* is in the north wing of the **Kloster**, which is one of the oldest in Bavaria and was a major cultural center for many centuries. In 1500 its library was more extensive than the Vatican's, but the valuable archives and books were largely destroyed during secularization, and the rest were taken to Munich. The village is also the best place from which to take **boat trips** on the lake. The nearest **youth hostel** is only a few kilometers away by bus, in the village of SCHARLING at Nördliche Hauptstr. 91.

Surrounded by wooded mountains and lush farmland, the **SCHLIERSEE** has more of an Alpine feel about it, and its pretty town of the same name hasn't yet been annexed by the Porsche-driving set. Traditional life is still strong here, and one of those traditions is poaching game. Of course it's illegal and the foresters don't hesitate to shoot poachers on sight, even nowadays. But it still goes on, and one of the most famous poachers in all the Alps is buried just outside Schliersee. His name was **Jennerwein**, and just to make a point, the local poachers yearly put a freshly killed mountain buck on his grave on the anniversary of his death.

There's a sailing school in Schliersee where you can hire boats and surfboards, but for swimming you're better off at the southern end of the lake, past the village of FISCHHAUSEN. A special tip for some brilliant cake and coffee is the *Winkelstüberl Café* on the road between FISCHBACHAU and ELBACH, which is open in the evenings as well: the size of the cake portions is famous throughout the valley. During the summer months, a good day trip involves taking a bus from SCHLIERSEE or BAYRISCHZELL to the **Thiersee** in Austria. It's in a beautiful valley and a great place to spend the day. (Don't forget your passport.) An alternative to taking the bus would be to rent a bike at either Schliersee or Bayrischzell Bahnhöfe, which is a good idea anyway around here, because public transportation isn't that frequent and doesn't go to the out-of-the-way places either. The **Sudelfeld** hills above Bayrischzell are one of those places, and it's a great area to go walking away from the crowds. If you like crowds, you could go and watch the hang gliders on the bare hilltops of the Sudelfeld; for a fee you can have yourself strapped in with a professional and take off.

The **SPITZINGSEE** above the JOSEFSTHAL valley is a little lake mostly associated with winter sports. During the summer there's nothing particularly attractive about the lake or village, and it wouldn't be worth a special trip to see it. But snow and ice magically transform the place, and the surrounding slopes are one of the busiest skiing resorts near Munich. While the skiing is much better here than on the Sudelfeld, both get hopelessly crowded at weekends. There are two **youth hostels** in the area: one in the Josephsthal valley (Josephstalerstr. 19; ☎08026 71068; nearest Bahnhof is FISCHHHAUSEN-NEUHAUS), and another up on the Sudelfeld hills (☎08023 675) above Bayrischzell, which can be reached by walking from the Bahnhof to the chair lift on the other side of the village, and then taking a ride to the top. It's advisable to phone before making the trek up there.

The Chiemsee, Simssee, and Waginger See

The **CHIEMSEE** is Bavaria's largest lake, and arriving by train in PRIEN you're at the hub of commercial attractions such as water sports or ferry connections to each of the islands. The larger island is called the **Herreninsel** and is the site of King Ludwig's final monument to glorious absolutism and isolation: **Schloss Herrenchiemsee** (daily 9am–5pm; DM4, DM2 students). After saving the island from deforestation, Ludwig II began building a complete replica of Versailles, but the money ran out in 1885 and only the central body of the palace was ever built. The king had only lived there one week when he died in the Starnberger See. The island is a great place to go for walks, and you can imagine Ludwig galloping through the mists on his morning ride. By the landing jetty there's a beer garden, with a good view of the lake. The **Fraueninsel** is a much smaller island, built up with holiday homes, restaurants, cafés and an ancient Benedictine nunnery, hence the name of the island. There used to be a monastery on the Herreninsel and they say quite a lot of midnight traffic used to pass between the two islands . .

The northeastern shoreline is much quieter than the west, and on a clear day the view of the Alps is wonderful. If you want to get to know the glorious countryside around the lake, rent a bicycle at PRIEN Bahnhof and visit places like STEIN, with its legendary cave hideout and castle brewery, or the island monastery of SEEON; in the south, the region around MT. KAMPENWAND is definitly worth checking out, quite apart from the mountain itself being one of the most popular hiking areas in the Alps.

The **SIMSSEE**, a little to the west of the Chiemsee, is less touristy, though by no means quiet, because it's so close to ROSENHEIM, an unattractive industrial town. There's an adequate beer garden by the water's edge in PIETZING, where there's also a public beach; alternatively KROTTENMÜHL on the other side of the lake is a good place for swimming. The nearest **youth hostel** for the Chiemsee and Simsee is in the village of Prien (Carl-Braun-Str. 46), and there's also one by the moor lakes in the nature reserve to the north, in the hamlet of HEMHOF (Haus 84); take a bus from Prien or Endorf.

Lastly, to the far east of southern Bavaria the **WAGINGER SEE** and **ABTSDORFER SEE** are very close to the Austrian border, and although they can be reached by train, are still out of the way and off the main tourist trail. The area around here is known by the rather comical name of *Rupertiwinkel*: The shallow moor lakes are popular with campers, who use them as a cheap base for day trips to Salzburg. Other places worth visiting in the region are TEISENDORF, which has excellent beer at the *Weininger* brewery in the Poststrasse; and the monasterial brewery in HÖGLWÖRTH a few kilometers south, which has a charming lakeside setting—actually it's more of a fishpond than a lake, but still very picturesque.

BAVARIAN SWABIA

Approximately bordered by the Rivers Iller and Lech, the central southwestern part of Bavaria has a small-scale landscape of rolling farmland dotted with quiet villages and medieval towns. The region is known as **Bavarian Swabia** (*Bayerisch-Schwaben*) to differentiate it from a larger area stretching into neighboring Baden-Württemberg, which collectively used to be the medieval Duchy of Swabia. To the north, the Danube winds its way eastwards, washing past the ancient settlements of **Günzburg**, **Lauingen**, and **Dillingen**, towns that grew from Roman military camps and medieval trading posts, and are now picturesquely provincial. Heading south, the gentle farming plateau gradually becomes more hilly and forested until you come to the Alpine region known as the **Allgäu**, where everything is played against the dramatic backdrop of snow-capped mountains and sparkling lakes. Regional capital of Swabia is **Augsburg**, an elegant city with fine Renaissance architecture, by and large unspoiled by later building.

Quite a stretch of the **Romantic Road** runs through Swabia, passing through countryside which is pleasant enough, but chiefly interesting for its medieval towns steeped in turbulent history. The Thirty Years' War laid waste to much of Swabia, so much so that the area was badly depopulated until this century. **Nördlingen** is one of the few towns to have retained its medieval fortifications and much of its original character. In the south, the little town of **Kaufbeuren** is worth a stroll through the cobblestoned center, and a little to the east, the

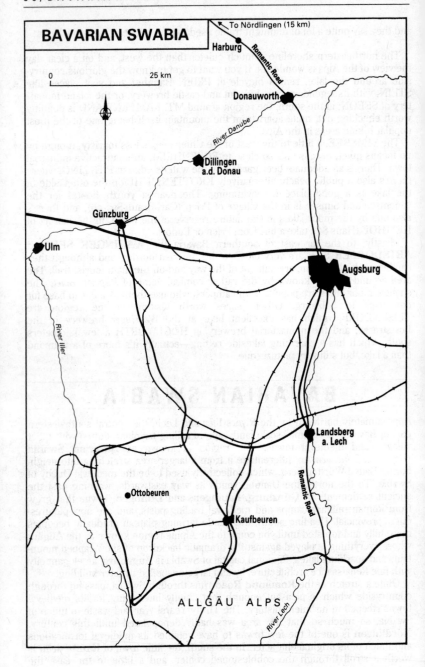

BAVARIAN SWABIA

To Nördlingen (15 km)

Harburg

Romantic Road

0   25 km

Donauwörth

River Danube

Dillingen
a.d. Donau

Günzburg

Ulm

Augsburg

River Iller

Landsberg
a. Lech

Ottobeuren

Romantic Road

Kaufbeuren

ALLGÄU ALPS

River Lech

Benedictine abbey at **Ottobeuren** should stun even the most jaded visitor of baroque churches. An added pleasure of traveling through this part of Bavaria is the distinctive and excellent food: delicate handmade pasta and rich sauces quite different from the Italian kind, followed by sweets with irreverent names like *Nonnenfürzle* (Nun's Fart) and *Versoffene Jungfern* (Drunken Virgins).

Travel along the Romantic Road is made easy by the *Europabus*, which goes twice daily between FÜSSEN in the Alps and WÜRZBURG in the far north of Bavaria. Train routes also follow the old highway, as well as branching off along the Danube. Away from these main routes things get very slow and quiet, with occasional buses being the only public transportation available. But most of Swabia is very gentle countryside and traveling by bicycle provides a painless chance to explore some of the less well-trodden paths, such as the **marked cycle route** along the Danube that goes all the way from Ulm to Regensburg. You'll find **youth hostels** in Donauwörth, Günzburg, and Nördlingen, and most villages offer private rooms at reasonable prices.

Augsburg

Only 60km northwest of Munich, and a quarter of the size, **AUGSBURG** certainly doesn't have to suffer any inferiority complexes. The Romans founded the city in 15 B.C., which makes it one of the oldest in Germany. A Free Imperial City from the thirteenth century onward, and a seat of the Diet, Augsburg had its heyday in the Middle Ages, when the Welser and Fugger dynasties made it one of the most important centers of high finance in Europe, and enabled the city to employ **Elias Holl**, whose stylish Renaissance architecture still dominates the cityscape today.

Local people seem genuinely proud of the town, and they've gone to vast expense to restore the numerous palaces and civic buildings to their original splendor. In fact civilian municipal life is the key to the town's history. It was ordinary, working people who created the wealth here, principally linen weavers. With related trade and banking came further riches, and a social conscience—in 1514 Augsburg built the world's first housing project for the poor, the **Fuggerei**, an institution still in use today. Here too the revolutionary reforms of Martin Luther found their earliest support. Innovations, religious or secular, have usually found fertile ground here.

Despite these associations, Augsburg isn't just a museum piece. There's a lively cultural scene ranging from Mozart festivals to jazz and cabaret, and the local university means that plenty of student bars and a thriving "alternative" culture keep the place on its toes.

Getting Around and Finding Somewhere to Stay

Everything you'll want to see in Augsburg is within easy walking distance of the middle of town, and the **tourist office** (Mon.–Fri. 9am–6pm, Sat. 9am–1pm; ☎36026/7) is just a couple of minutes from the Hauptbahnhof at Bahnhofstr. 7. They supply free brochures on the city and also help with accommodation and arranging guided tours. There's a choice of bus or walking tours, and considering the compact street plan, the latter are better value at half the price: DM6, DM3 students. The **youth hostel** is centrally located, three minutes' walk from the Dom, at Beim Pfaffenkeller 3 (☎33909); if you're coming from the Bahnhof, take tram #2 to Stadtwerke. Good **pensions** in the region of DM27 for singles and DM46 for doubles are to be found in the suburb of LECHHAUSEN, 1.5 km from downtown and well connected by three bus routes. Try the following for good value: *Bayerische Löwe*, Linke Brandstr. 2 (☎702870); *Linderhof*, Aspernstr. 38 (☎73216); and *Märkl*, Schillerstr. 20 (☎791499). The nearest **campground** is at expressway exit *Augsburg-Ost*, next to the Autobahnsee (☎714121).

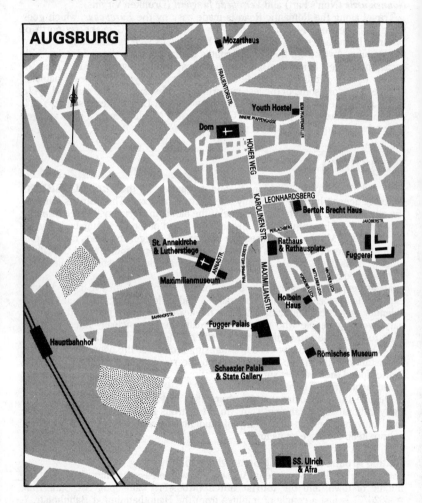

The Center

Heart of the city is the spacious cobbled **Rathausplatz**, which turns into a massive open-air café during the summer and a glittering Christmas market in December. At the baseline of this great semicircle stands the massive **Rathaus**, built by Elias Holl between 1615 and 1620, and regarded by many as Germany's finest example of a secular Renaissance building. The proportions and style of the elegantly plain exterior topped by two octagonal towers recall a Florentine palace rather than a town hall, a likeably overstated symbol of Augsburg's wealth and influence. As with so many of its kind, what stands today is a replica of the one bombed out in World War II, and the interior is taken up by municipal offices. Only the building's shell is original, not that you'd know it from the facelift it's recently received. Take a look inside to see the spick-and-span restoration of the **Goldener Saal**, whose gold-leaf pillars and marble floor recall its ostentatious history. Augsburg's wealth was mainly created by the banking and merchant successes of the Welser and Fugger families. The Fuggers were to Germany what the Medici were to Italy, and if it hadn't been for their financial support, Emperor Charles V would certainly never have gained the crown of the Holy Roman Empire. Next to the Rathaus stands the **Perlachturm** (daily 10am–6pm); originally the town's watchtower, it was remodeled by Holl to its present height of 78m. The top offers a good vantage point from which to take in the whole town and get your bearings on Augsburg's main axis, neatly formed between the Dom to the north and the church of Saints Ulrich und Afra at the far end of Maximilianstrasse to the south.

The **Maximilianstrasse** itself was built to be seen—a showpiece lined by the palaces of the rich merchant families, punctuated by early seventeenth-century fountains as it widens and sweeps up to the above-named church. Soon after the Mercury fountain, the **Fugger Palais** stands proudly to the right. Built in 1515 by Jacob Fugger "the Rich," it still belongs to his wealthy descendants, but you can walk through the main door to see its luxurious arcaded courtyard, designed in Italian Renaissance style and often used for putting on plays in the summer. In 1518 the courtyard was the venue for the meeting between Martin Luther and Cardinal Cajetan, the great reformer attempting to justify his 95 theses against the Catholic faith. If you're a fan of Elias Holl's buildings, walk down the Apothekergasse to the **Zeughaus** for one of his earliest works.

Strategically placed opposite the Hercules fountain, the **Schaezler Palais** (Tues.–Sun. 10am–4pm; free) is the town's foremost rococo building, and contains a sumptuous ballroom, one of the very few that exist in original condition—right down to the candlelit chandeliers that are still used during the annual Mozart concerts held in June and July. There's also a collection of sixteenth- to eighteenth-century art, fine if you like mainly landscape and still-life painting, but essentially an acquired taste. Through the courtyard is the old Dominican nunnery of St. Catherine, and the **State Gallery** (times as above), containing a collection of fifteenth- and sixteenth-century Renaissance paintings by the "Augsburg Masters" such as Hans Holbein the Elder and Hans Burgkmair, as well as Dürer's famous portrait of Jacob Fugger, looking every bit the king-maker that he was.

At the far end of the Maximilianstrasse the Catholic basilica of **Saints Ulrich und Afra** towers over the adjoining, smaller Lutheran **St. Ulrich**. Inside the late Gothic basilica are gold baroque high altars by Hans Degler, and the tomb of St. Ulrich, the city's patron saint. In contrast, the Lutheran St. Ulrich is baroque, its gabled front creating a cheerful contrast to its sober neighbor.

At the other end of the town's axis, the (Catholic) **Dom** stands in the grounds of the former episcopal palace, now the seat of the regional government. Founded by St. Ulrich in the tenth century, the most interesting remains of its Romanesque origins are the enormous **bronze doors** at the southern entrance and the **stained-glass windows**, which are the oldest of their kind still in position. The doors are decorated with endearingly simple designs on their 32 panels, each portraying events from the story of Adam and Eve. Five stained-glass windows on the south side show the Old Testament figures of Moses, David, Hosea, Daniel, and Jonah, and the freshness of color makes it hard to believe they were made in the eleventh century. There are also a number of **altarpieces** by Hans Holbein the Elder, which were commissioned when the original Romanesque basilica was Gothic in the fourteenth and early fifteenth century. The four panels, fixed on to the left-hand pillars and depicting scenes from the life of the Virgin Mother, are among the few Holbein works that remain outside of a museum.

Apart from its money-makers, Augsburg was also home to Holbein, Mozart and (most recently), Bertolt Brecht. Each of their homes has been turned into a **museum**, and what's more they're all free. The **Mozart Haus** (Wed.–Mon. 10am–noon and 2–5pm, Fri. 2–4pm) isn't far from the Dom, at Frauentorstr. 30. It documents the lives of Leopold and Wolfgang Amadeus, together with a number of bits and pieces from the original furnishings of their house. The Mozarts left Augsburg when Wolfgang Amadeus was very young, since the real opportunities (and hard cash) for a musical prodigy were in Vienna. It also conveniently removed the love-struck youth from his cousin Bäsle, but you can't really blame Augsburg for wanting to claim a place in the Mozart biography.

The city's relationship with **Bertolt Brecht** was a little more clouded: the embarrassing truth is that the people of Augsburg couldn't stand Brecht while he was alive; but then neither could Brecht stomach bourgeois little Augsburg. Today, however, all is forgotten, and the city has turned his family home at Auf dem Rain 7 (Tues.–Sun. 10am–5pm) into a memorial museum. Not surprisingly this concentrates on the artist's Augsburg period, using mainly photographic material of the playwright and his contemporaries, as well as of early theatrical productions of his works.

Brecht was born in Augsburg in 1898, the son of a sales assistant, and to all appearances destined for a conventional, middle-class life. He went to the local grammar school, was confirmed in the Lutheran church, and was just trying his hand on the school paper when World War I broke out in 1914. He remained in Augsburg for the duration of the war, emerging as a staunch pacifist and becoming a porter in the local hospital. When he left the town in 1919, it was to enroll as a medical student in Munich, though it was soon apparent where his ambitions really lay, and he became a regular contributor to the literary and theatrical events at the University.

Turn right at the bottom of the Leonhardsberg here, and you can wander through the old artisans' quarter along the narrow canals of the Vorderer, Mittlerer and Unterer Lech. The backstreets here must have looked very similar a few hundred years ago, when they were populated with the tradesfolk and craftspeople who serviced the grand houses up on the Maximilianstrasse. At Vorderer Lech 20 the **Holbein Haus** (Tues.–Sun. 10am–5pm) stands on the site of the original, which was destroyed in 1944. Documents on the artist's life are complemented by changing exhibitions.

The town's historical museum, known as the **Maximilianmuseum** (Philippine-Welser-Str. 24; Tues.–Sun. 10am–4pm; free) is housed in the former town house of the Welser merchants. If you're interested in the town's architectural and cultural development, then this is the place to see Holl's models and building plans, as well as exhibits from the town's artisan and trade guilds from the tenth to the eighteenth centuries—look for the exquisite book illustrations. Prehistoric and Roman remains are shown separately in the **Römisches Museum** (Dominikanergasse 15; Tues.–Sun. 10am–4pm; free) housed in the old Dominican church. The light and whitewashed interior makes an excellent setting for the Roman masonry and bronze artifacts, and the uncluttered layout is a real pleasure after the usually warehouse-like museums. One of the highlights is a life-sized, second-century A.D. bronze horse's head, which was probably part of a statue honoring Emperor Marcus Aurelius.

One "Our Father," one "Hail Mary," and one "Creed" daily, plus DM1.72 per annum, and good Catholic paupers can retire to the **Fuggerei** at the age of 55. It's the world's oldest housing project for the poor and must be one of the cleverest and most generous ploys ever devised for a place in Heaven. With an entrance on Jacoberstrasse, it's a town within a town, and compared with modern housing projects is idyllic: two-story houses overgrown with ivy line six car-less streets, the cloister-like atmosphere disturbed only by the odd ringing doorbell. Admittedly it all seems like walking through a giant doll's house, though the inhabitants are used to having hordes of tourists peering through their windows. But for the price and the odd prayer it still seems like a pretty good deal; the rent, the equivalent of one Rhenish guilder, has been frozen since the scheme started in 1514. **Number 13** in the Mittleren Gasse is one of only two houses from the original foundation; today it's a museum piece full of furnishings that show how people lived here from the sixteenth to the eighteenth centuries. **Number 14** is the other original, where Mozart's great-grandfather lived in the late seventeenth century.

Exactly the other side of town, on Annastrasse, stands the unassuming **St. Anna-Kirche**; judging from its outside appearance, you'd never guess that it's one of the most important monuments in Augsburg. In 1509, Ulrich and Jacob Fugger endowed a memorial chapel for themselves and their deceased brother Georg. The clout they wielded is shown by the fact that, against all convention, this formed an extension of the nave, instead of the humbler normal position off an aisle. It seems there was a certain amount of skulduggery on both sides of this agreement—the prior thereby hoped to increase the capacity of his church without having to dip into ecclesiastical funds, while the brothers did their utmost to seal off public access from the word go. The sumptuous **Fuggerkapelle** which resulted marks the belated German debut of the full-blooded Italian Renaissance style, a spin-off of the family's extensive business interests in Italy. An integrated, no-expenses-spared decorative scheme—marble pavement, stained glass, choir stalls, balustrade with putti, a monumental sculptural group of *The Lamentation over the Dead Christ*, and memorial relief tablets honoring the brothers made after woodcuts designed by Dürer—creates an effect of overwhelming richness, now sadly somewhat diminished as a result of wartime destruction. Curiously, nobody knows for sure whether the chapel was created by German or Italian craftsmen, but its influence on Augsburg was profound and long-lasting—it became the only major German city which took the Renaissance style to its heart.

The architectural innovations aren't the only reason for St. Anna's importance; it's also celebrated because of its historical role during the Reformation. Augsburg is inextricably linked with that era in German history, not least because it was here that the final confrontation between the papal court and Luther took place in 1518, as well as the signing of the Augsburg Peace in 1555, which finally sanctioned religious parity. Luther found refuge with the Carmelites of St. Anna during the time he was summoned to see the Pope's legate Cardinal Cajetan, and today his room has, along with several others in the old monastery, been turned into the **Lutherstiege** (Tues.–Sun. 10am–noon and 2:30–4pm; free), a museum of the reformer's life and times. Unfortunately the commentary is in German only and the exhibits mean little without it, but the exhibition is logically and clearly laid out in six consecutive rooms, the steps (*Stiege*) being counted as number one.

The *Karmeliten Zimmer* (2) records the first arrival of the Carmelites in 1270. A mendicant order, they lived off begging and donations, but with money rolling in from wills and the beneficence of wealthy locals, they soon had more money than they knew what to do with—and so built themselves this monastery. The *Cajetan Flur* (3) has various exhibits relating to events leading up to Luther's heresy hearing with Cardinal Cajetan. The straw that broke the camel's back for the Pope was Luther's 95 theses against the Catholic church, and exhibit 306 is a copy of the original. Once the author had fled Augsburg, the points were nailed to the cathedral doors by his supporters, entitled "From one poorly informed, to Pope Leo X for his better instruction." Contrary to popular belief, it wasn't the 95 theses that caused the rift between Luther and the Catholic church: they were just one of a series of writings and events, though perhaps the most critical.

The essential bone of contention was the practice of selling **indulgences** to absolve sins and ensure salvation. The Church used them to finance building programs and living costs, and they were open to much abuse, both by church commissioners and by parishioners, who thought they could conveniently buy salvation. Exhibit 304 is a portrait of Johann Tetzel, who is said to have preached, "As long as there's money in the (collection) box, your soul is safe from hellfire." The largest indulgence ever issued to the general public was one from Pope Julius II, in order to finance the building of St. Peter's in Rome. Commissioners all over Europe were nominated to flog this one, and to Luther it seemed the height of cynicism: he campaigned against it vigorously until being called before Cajetan (Portrait 318) to answer heresy charges. Of the remaining rooms, the *Confessio Zimmer* (4) deals with the political crisis provoked by the Reformation; the *Luther Kammer* (5) is the actual room where Luther stayed in 1518; the *Empore* (6) is the old gallery for the Carmelite monks and shows Luther's excommunication document.

Eating, Drinking, and Festivals

The cheapest place for on-your-feet **snacks** is the market and meat halls off Annastrasse, where you'll find a couple of good *Imbiss* stands. A cheap **Italian** restaurant is *Don Giovanni*, Schmiedberg 15a. More up-scale, but really excellent Swabian food is served at the *7-Schwaben Stuben*, Am Königsplatz. Read up on "Drunken Virgins" and "Stone Men" in the newspaper-type menu. The easiest thing is probably to order a set meal—just make sure you're pretty hungry. The only **vegetarian** restaurant is the *3-Rosen* at Blücherstr. 27, which closes on Wednesdays.

For evening **drinking** student bars are the best bet, and considering Augsburg's size, there are quite a few: *Grauer Adler*, Mittlerer Lech 7 is one of the city's main cabaret venues; *Kresslesmühle*, Barfüsserstr. 4 is similar but has the feel of a community center rather than nightspot, since that's exactly what it is; *Riegele*, Herman-Köhlstr. 5 is spacious and serves small meals as well as drinks. *Striese*, Kirchgasse 1 is another theater and music venue; while *Thing*, Vorderer Lech 45 is a youth meeting place, mainly frequented by teenage boys. A **jazz** bar with unimaginative music but a good atmosphere and late opening hours is *Underground*, Kapuzinergasse 1. Augsburg's only **gay** bar seems to be the *Alte Münz*, on Mittlerer Lech. **Discos** and nightclubs are a bit scarce, but try the *Alexis*, Ulmerstr. 121 (Sun.–Thurs. 9pm–2am, Fri.–Sat. 9pm–3am). Rock fans should check out the *Rockpalast* in Riedinger Strasse, north of the city center on tram route #26 from the Königsplatz.

Annual festivals are the *Mozartfest* in June and July; the *Bierfest* at the end of July; the *Friedenfest* on August 8; the *Sommerfest* at the end of August; and the *Weihnachtsmarkt* from November 23 to December 24, which ranks as one of the country's most colorful markets next to those of Nürnberg and Munich. First mentioned in 1653, the spectacular market opening is accompanied by a pageant and live Christmas music, and each weekend until Christmas musicians play by the stalls.

Listings

American Express Arras-Barraks, building 24 (☎402024) in the US military compound.

Area code (☎0821).

Bike rental Available at the Hauptbahnhof.

Books *Probuch*, Göggingerstr. 34, specializes in contemporary German literature and alternative books.

Community Arts Center *Kresslesmühle*, Barfüsserstr. 4 (☎37170). A meeting place for action groups, with live music and cabaret in the evenings (see above).

Laundromats *Karkosch*, Vorderer Lech 27; *Kraus*, Bismarckstr. 11; *Poloczek*, Katharinengasse 22; *Steidle*, Ulmer Str. 143.

Student cultural center *Asta Kulturzentrum*, Reitmayrgasse 4 (☎519610). Basically offers the same services as a student union building.

Women's center *Frauenzentrum*, Mauerbergstr. 31 (Mon.–Tues. 10:15am–12:15pm, Thurs. 1–6pm; ☎153307). Runs a café and advice bureau at these times.

The Romantic Road and the Danube Valley

Glibly named, but with many treasures along it, the *Romantische Strasse* or **Romantic Road** runs for 350km from Würzburg in northern Bavaria to Füssen in the Alps; its central section crosses Bavarian Swabia, going from **Nördlingen** in the north to **Landsberg** in the south. The road gets its name from the fact that it passes gently rolling countryside, which is never very dramatic but instead pleasantly unspoiled and tranquil—the kind of region where nature lovers and romantics feel most at home . . . according to the tourist board, at least.

If you're pressed for time, taking *Europabus* (daily at 9am from the bus station next to Munich Hauptbahnhof) along the whole or part of the route is a good way to get a quick impression. But this only covers the well-trodden tourist trail of medieval showpiece towns. It's essential to detour from the main drag to get a full impression of the area and to escape the tourists. Exploring the regions alongside the road becomes much more rewarding with your own vehicle, and presents an ideally peaceful holiday tour. For the northern Bavarian section of the road, see *Franconia*. For the route south of Landsberg, where the road merges with the *Alpine Road* (another tourist board label), see *The South: Mountains and Lakes*. There's also a section in Baden-Württemberg (see *Chapter Two*).

The **Danube** flows through Swabia from west to east, between Ulm and Donauwörth respectively, and the best way to explore the river's environs is without doubt by bicycle. There's a well-marked bike path (240km) all the way from Ulm to Regensburg in Eastern Bavaria, passing great countryside and quaint medieval towns. If you're into easy cycling vacations, with few hills to tackle, this is an ideal route. Most convenient places for **bike rental** are the Bahnhöfe, and you can return your bike to another Bahnhof almost anywhere in West Germany.

Heading North from Augsburg

Coming out of Augsburg, the Romantic Road follows the flat and featureless Lech valley. But the countryside to the west is attractive enough, and heading to Donauwörth via the little town of WERTINGEN is an enjoyable detour. **DONAUWÖRTH** is a busy, workaday market town at the confluence of the Danube and the river Wörnitz. Its history spans over a thousand years, but as with so many places, the town reached its peak in the Middle Ages, when it was a strategic point on the important trade route between Augsburg and Nürnberg, and grand houses along the main road and central market square give testimony to that time. About 10km farther north, the town of **HARBURG** is dominated by a fortified castle that stands high above the banks of the River Wörnitz. Never taken in battle, its fortifications and the castle itself are still in pretty good condition. The Harburg **museum** holds one of the most extensive collections of work outside Würzburg by the great woodcarver Tilman Riemenschneider.

From here another detour via WEMDING to Nördlingen would be in order, though from now on the Romantic Road itself passes more interesting country. **NÖRDLINGEN** lies in an enormous old crater, known as the *Ries*, formed by a meteor over 15 million years ago. The crater, which has a diameter of about 25km, is one of the largest on earth, and provides one of the main locations for scientists to study stone formations similar to those on the moon. It also served as ideal terrain for the Apollo 14 team to prepare for their lunar mission.

Nördlingen is one of three towns along this route that have almost completely retained their fortified medieval character, and it's still possible to walk along parts of the wall which surrounds the town in an almost perfect circle. Of the three, it's probably the least dreamy, the historic ambience diluted by a couple of modern eyesores; but looking out from vantage points such as the sentry walk or the church spire, the illusion remains near. Symbol of the town is the 90-meter **Danielturm** (9am–sundown; DM2), the highest building and also the bull's-eye of the town's circle. Halfway up the stairs is what looks like a huge wooden hamster wheel: built for convicts, whose job it was to keep the wheel that operated the elevator turning, it was used until the last century. The tower forms part of the **Georgenkirche**, a light and airy late Gothic hall church. At the high altar, there's an emotional polychrome wood *Crucifixion* group which has recently been recognized as the work of the Dutchman Nicolaus Gerhaert (see Baden-Baden, *Chapter Two*), one of the greatest sculptors of the fifteenth century. Originally, this was grouped with a colorful cycle of paintings (*The Legend of St. George*) by the local master Friedrich Herlin, but the latter have been moved to the museum.

The best thing to do in town is simply to wander the quiet streets, where many areas have remained almost unchanged for centuries. Near the Marktplatz, the **Rathaus** has an entertaining little detail by its outdoor stairway: the space underneath the steps used to hold the town's prisoners, and just by the wooden entrance is a medieval fool carved into the wall with an inscription underneath saying *Nun sind unser zwei*—"Now there are two of us." (Him, and you looking at him.) In the **museum** (Vordere Gerbergasse 1; Tues.–Sun. 10am–noon and 2–4pm; DM2, DM1 students) there's the usual local history section, with terrible exhibits from the torture chambers that were used throughout the Middle Ages, but especially during the sixteenth-century witch-hunts. In Nördlingen alone 35 women were killed during that time. There's also a detailed exhibition on the Ries crater's formation and geological history.

If you're around town in mid-May, it's worth looking out for the *Stabenfest*, an annual **festival** which celebrates the arrival of spring with a children's procession. On the appointed day, usually a Monday, trumpets sound the beginning of the festival from the heights of the Danielturm. Boys gather holding flags and poles decorated with flowers, while the girls wear special costumes and crowns of flowers around their heads. At around 9am, the procession moves off accompanied by music and song until it reaches the Kaiserwiese, where the usual trappings of a Bavarian fair are set up around the beer tent. Check with the tourist office for exact times and dates.

The **youth hostel** is just outside the old town walls at Kaiserwiese 1 (☎09081 84109). Otherwise the cheapest accommodation, at DM20 per person, is in the Gasthaus *Neue Welt*, Brettermarkt 9 (☎09081 4336). If that's full, try *Zum Goldenen Lamm*, Schäfflesmarkt 3 (☎09081 4206) or *Zinke*, Münzgasse 10 (☎09081 3645) for prices between DM25 and DM35 per person. The **tourist office**, Marktplatz 2 (☎09081 4380 or ☎84116) will help with finding rooms as well as supplying free brochures and organizing guided tours.

Heading South from Augsburg

Twenty kilometers south of Augsburg the Romantic Road passes out of Swabia, and strictly speaking **LANDSBERG** is already beyond the regional border. Its full name is Landsberg am Lech, being on the banks of the River Lech, and emblem of the town is the fifteenth-century Gothic **Bayertor**, which is one of the old town gates that defended the city in medieval times. In those days Landsberg was a fortified border town between Swabia and Bavaria, and made its money on levies and trade passing on the salt road from Salzburg to Memmingen. From these rich pickings, Landsberg's burghers built themselves a flashy **Rathaus**, which today forms the showpiece of the main square. Originally built in the fifteenth century, its fancy stuccoed baroque facade is from the eighteenth century, when the great churchbuilder and artist Dominikus Zimmerman lived here. Another famous resident, if only for nine months, was Hitler, who was locked up in the local fortress for trying to mount the Munich *Putsch* in 1923. He used the time to write his infamous treatise *Mein Kampf*.

There's no youth hostel here, but an excellent **campground** just a few minutes walk from the middle of town, at the far end of the Pössingerstrasse, which turns into the Pössinger Weg. It's right next to a forest and near the river Lech. The cheapest **hotel**, at DM27 per person, is the *Hotel Zederbräu*, Hauptplatz 155, (☎08191 2241), and there are also rooms in private houses for approximately DM20 per person. Try *Ferienhaus Kander*, Aggensteinstr. 14, (☎08191 2517) or *Erna Rabe*, Johann-Festl-Str. 4 (☎08191 46931). The **tourist office** in the Rathaus on Hauptplatz (☎08191 128246) hands out brochures and offers guided tours.

The Swabian countryside in the south gradually becomes hillier as it approaches the Alps, and it's one of the most peaceful and attractive rural landscapes in Bavaria. The region is very much left to its own devices because, until the Alps, there's little in the way of specific tourist attractions—just enjoyable countryside interspersed with a few pleasantly forgettable towns. One place worth stopping off at, however, is **KAUFBEUREN**, about 25km south of Landsberg, which is a sweet cobblestoned town with picturesque medieval houses.

Another 25km due west from there lies **OTTOBEUREN**. Situated on a gentle incline, the **Kloster** stands alone above the village, which gathers at a suitably respectful lower level. This monastery is one of the most imposing and grandiose places of worship north of the Alps. Among the oldest Benedictine monasteries, it was founded in 764, and its patron Charlemagne gave the abbot and his monks important rights to ensure its prosperity, such as elevating the abbot to the rank of a prince who could make levies on the locals.

Architecturally the Kloster has undergone many changes since its foundation, but its present baroque interior was created by the Munich master Johann Michael Fischer in the eighteenth century. It's huge—physical details such as the 90-meter nave and 60-meter transept hardly convey the bombastic impression you get on entering. The wealth of altars, frescoes, paintings and stuccoed embellishments takes time to be appreciated fully, and yet there's nothing busy about the whole effect. Among the many treasures, a twelfth-century Roman-esque *Crucifixion* is the most valuable, but also special are the three organs, built by the master Karl Joseph Riepp and considered among the most beautiful church organs in the world.

Apart from the abbey, there's also a monasterial **museum** (Mon.–Sat. 10am–noon and 2–5pm; Sun. 10am–noon and 1–5pm; DM2), which is housed in a part of the abbot's palace. Highlights are the amazingly delicate seventeenth- and eighteenth-century inlaid furniture pieces and the beautiful baroque library, which looks more like a ballroom than a place for contemplation, so rich is the decor of marble pillars and frescoed ceiling. Note also the theater, which was an important element of arts teaching in any eighteenth-century Benedictine monastery.

The Danube Valley

The stretch from Ulm to Donauwörth is only about 80km of a river that runs all the way from southwestern Germany to the Black Sea, and at this stage the Danube is not yet a great river. But the landscape of the wide river valley, with its flat marshland interspersed by chalky promontories, makes for good walking and cycling country, and the small towns lining the bank are welcome stopping points.

Coming from Ulm, the first large town is **GÜNZBURG**, which is a likable small market town, with gabled houses characteristic of the late Middle Ages. Two annual **festivals** liven up the place in the summer: the two-day *Guntia-Fest* at the end of June, and the *Sommerfest* in August. For information on exact dates, contact the **tourist office** (Rathaus, Schlossplatz 1; ☎08221 903111), which also provide brochures and help with accommodation. Cheapest place in town is the *Gasthof Rose* (Augsburger Str. 23; ☎08221 5802), which charges between DM18 and DM23 per person. There's also a **youth hostel** at Schillerstr. 12 (☎08221 95525).

After Günzburg, two towns worth stopping off at are LAUINGEN and DILLINGEN, but again, it's really the countryside that draws people to the area, and it's best explored via the many paths and country roads throughout the river valley. For a decent map of the area, contact the **tourist office** in the Rathaus in Donauwörth and ask for the *Donau Radwander-Karte* (DM6). Alternatively try the offices of the larger towns in the region.

EASTERN BAVARIA

Eastern Bavaria is the least well-known region of the whole state, and that goes for Germans as well as foreigners. Part of the reason for this is that the Bavarian Forest and the Upper Palatinate run along the Czechoslovakian border, which is a dead end unless you've obtained a visa to travel on beforehand. For the rest, few main roads and a misconception of the region as remote forests and bumpkin inhabitants have kept almost everyone except hiking enthusiasts away. So while tourists crowd each other out in the southern and Alpine regions, the east remains an insider's tip even during the busy months of July and August.

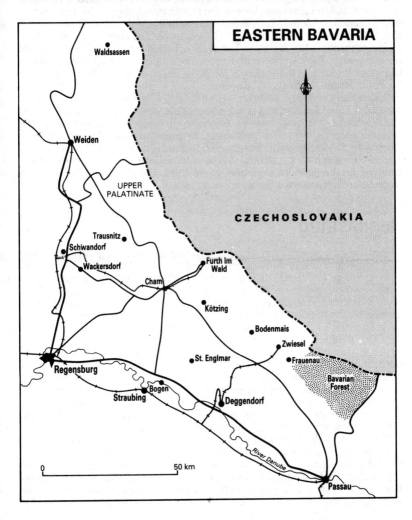

In the Middle Ages, trading along the route from Nürnberg to Prague brought wealth to the people here. But the Thirty Years' War completely ruined the economy, and it wasn't until the seventeenth century that people began to move back into the forests to form woodcutting and glass-making communities. The **northeast** is known as the **Upper Palatinate** (*Oberpfalz*), which is confusing since the Palatinate proper (*Pfalz*) is in the Rhineland. It's a historical rather than geographical link, and a reminder that both areas used to belong to the same duchy of Pfalz-Neuburg. The **southeast** mostly consists of the **Bavarian Forest**, the largest forested area in central Europe and one that still retains much of its primeval character, especially in the **National Park** between Frauenau and Mauth. Traditionally a poor and remote region, a couple of train routes make it relatively accessible, and campgrounds, hostels and private rooms abound. It's more mountainous here than further north, though the highest peaks such as Grosser Arber and Grosser Rachel barely reach the 1500m mark. Yet, apart from the obvious hiking attractions, the Bavarian Forest is culturally one of the most vibrant regions you're likely to encounter, especially during summer, when **festivals** take place throughout the region. Some of the best to watch out for are in **Furth im Wald, Bogen, Kötzing**, and **Regen**.

Regensburg, Eastern Bavaria's regional capital, managed to escape almost unscathed in the last war, and stands today as the most complete and one of the most beautiful medieval cities in Germany. Heading downstream along the Danube, ancient towns like **Straubing, Deggendorf**, and **Passau** are easy targets, the last in particular, with enough to detain you for at least a day or two. The stretch south of the Danube tends to be flat and uninspiring agricultural land, but on the northern side, hills, castle ruins, and forests enliven the landscape before it reaches the Bavarian Forest.

Regensburg

"Regensburg surpasses every German city with its outstanding and vast buildings," drooled Emperor Maximilian I in 1517. The center of **REGENSBURG** (also known as *RATISBON*) has changed remarkably little since then; its undisturbed medieval panorama still beats all other cities in the country hands down, while its history and sights, beer gardens, and *Gaststätten*, along with its stunning location on the banks of the Danube, make it a great place to spend a couple of days. Founded as the military camp *Castra Regina* by the Romans, most of the surviving architecture originates from the glory days between the thirteenth and sixteenth centuries. Regensburg was then a free imperial city, independently ruled, and rich from trade with Europe, the Balkan states and the Orient. Goods sailed into town on the Danube and ships still ply the route to the Black Sea today. Although other cities may have a more spectacular cathedral or town hall as a focal point, none can match the satisfyingly integrated nature of the Regensburg townscape, which gives a unique insight into the size, shape, and feel of a prosperous community of the Middle Ages.

One of the city's other main attractions is undoubtedly the presence of bars and beer gardens, mostly populated by and priced for the large student population. The best time of year to visit is from early summer to autumn, when the city's considerable sights, such as the **Dom**, the **Altes Rathaus**, and **Schloss Thurn und Taxis**, can be complemented by the leisurely attractions of the open-air haunts. There's a lively summer cultural program as well, highlights being the

Bach Week at the beginning of July, and the **Bavarian Jazz Weekend** two weeks later.

Regensburg is also an excellent base from which to discover the idyllic countryside along the northern reaches of the Danube, and surrounding river valleys such as the Naab Valley and the Regen Valley. Train connections into the Bavarian Forest and south to Passau, are fast and efficient from here.

Getting Around and Finding Somewhere to Stay

The **Bahnhof** is at the southern end of the city. From there, follow Maximilianstrasse straight ahead to reach the center. The **tourist office** in the Altes Rathaus (Mon.–Fri. 8:30am-6pm, Sat. 9am–4pm, Sun. 9am–noon; ☎507 2141) is smack in the middle of town, and provides all the brochures and info you might want, as well as reserving rooms or arranging English-speaking guided tours. Everything of interest is within easy walking distance around downtown, and the **youth hostel** at Wöhrdstr. 60 (☎26839) is about five minutes' walk from the heart of things, on an island in the Danube. Cheapest hotel in the city center is the *Weisse Lilie*, Fröhliche-Türkenstr. 4 (☎57515), which charges around DM30 for singles and DM48 for doubles. Two more very central hotels, in the region of DM28–60 for singles and DM52–DM95 for doubles, are *Peterhof*, Fröhliche-Türkenstr. 12 (☎57514/58874) and *Roter Hahn*, Rote-Hahnen-Gasse 10 (☎560907/52599). On the other hand, the *Spitalgarten*, St. Katharinen-Platz 1 (☎84774) and the *Stadlerbräu*, Stadtamhof 15 (☎85682), just the other side of the Steinerne Brücke, charge around DM20–25 for singles and DM40–50 for doubles, and are also next to the town's best beer garden. The local **campground** (March–mid-Nov. only) is about twenty minutes' walk from the center of town, pleasantly situated next to the Danube by Weinweg 40 (☎26839).

The Center

The best view of Regensburg's medieval skyline is from the twelfth-century **Steinerne Brücke** (*Stone Bridge*). Legend has it that the builder made a pact with the Devil to give him the first soul that crossed the finished bridge. In return the builder was able to complete his project in just eleven years and so beat the cathedral builder, who'd bet him he'd be finished first. But the bridge builder not only fooled his competitor, he also tricked the Devil, because the first living thing that was sent across the bridge was a donkey.

At the time the bridge was built, it was the only safe and fortified crossing along the entire length of the Danube and had tremendous value for the city as a major international trading center. Of the three original watchtowers, the one above the bridge's town gate is the only survivor. On the left, just past the medieval salt depot, the **Historische Wurstküche** (7am–7pm) originally functioned as the bridge workers' kitchen. It's been run by the same family for generations and serves nothing but delicious Regensburger sausages with sweet mustard and sauerkraut. Have a look at the watermark on the outside wall, and you'll see that the whole place was almost washed away during the 1988 floods.

Along the road known as Unter den Schibbögen, remains of the original Roman fort are still visible at the corner of one of the houses. **Porta Praetoria** was once the northern watchtower and was discovered during restoration work in 1887. The medieval core of Regensburg is only about twice the size of the old fort, so exploration on foot is an easy business. Just around the next block, the Dom comes into full view. Before you cross over, take a look inside **Haus**

Heuport for a little fourteenth-century curiosity. The building itself was once a fortified merchant house, and at the left-hand corner of the courtyard staircase there's a stone relief: the two figures represent the seduction of a careless virgin. The seducer's bad intentions are symbolized by the snake coming out of his back and the apple held out to the young woman, while she's lost her grip on a cup of oil, symbolizing loss of wisdom. Perhaps it was to warn the daughter of the house. . .

The **Dom**, begun around 1250, is Bavaria's most magnificent example of the Gothic building period. It replaced an earlier Romanesque church, of which the **Eselsturm** (*Donkey Tower*) is the only remaining part above ground; this takes

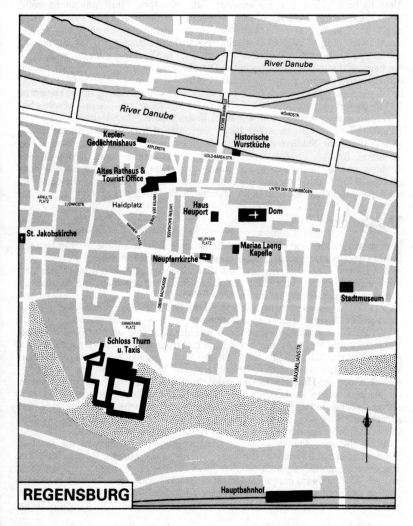

REGENSBURG

its name from the thirteenth-century building period when donkeys were used to carry building materials up a ramp inside. If you look up to the top from the cathedral's back courtyard, a man holding a jug sticking out from the upper ledge becomes visible; he's supposed to be the original architect, who threw himself off the tower when he lost his bet with the bridge builder.

Two points of interest on the cathedral's exterior relate to the medieval Jewish community. Directly opposite the Haus Heuport, a relief on the left main pillar shows small figures dancing around a calf—an architectural expression of an old prejudice that Jews are only interested in money, symbolized by the golden calf. Pure malice, on the other hand, prompted the little relief on the left-hand pillar of the cathedral's entrance, where Jewish figures are suckling a great sow, a calculated insult to the Jewish community, considering that pigs are unclean animals according to their faith.

The cathedral took almost 300 years to build, from 1250 to 1525, and the two spires weren't erected until 1859. Main reason for the delay in completion was the Reformation, during which the bishop remained Catholic, while the secular leadership went Lutheran. At the time it was unthinkable to contribute financially to a Catholic cathedral and so building was stopped for a hundred years. Once work was resumed in the seventeenth century, the interior was decorated and adapted to the baroque fashion, which unfortunately meant throwing out many of the medieval stained-glass windows. In their stead, plain white glass was put up to give the maximum amount of light for the baroque altars. Over the centuries, architectural fashions and tastes changed a few more times, and the last forty years have been spent trying to combine restoration with recovering the original Gothic character of the interior. The only baroque element now left is the beautiful silver altar.

Highlights include the expressive late thirteenth-century statues of *The Annunciation* and the last remaining fourteenth-century **stained-glass windows** in the south transept. The nine windows also contain parts from the original Romanesque cathedral, which were removed in 1273. On the wall below, the wooden **crucifix** is from the late sixteenth century and there is real human hair on the Christ figure, which according to local legend will augur Judgment Day when it grows to knee-length. Another quirky feature is the pair of fourteenth-century figures in the niches either side of the western nave entrance: on the left is the **Devil's grandmother** and on the right the **Devil** himself, who were to remind the congregation that as soon as they left the safety of the church, evil and temptation awaited.

The **cloisters**, only accessible during **guided tours** (Mon.–Sat. 10am, 11am, and 2pm, Sun. 11:30am, and 2pm; DM2.50, DM1.50 students), have two interesting chapels, of which the **Allerheiligen Kapelle** is a Romanesque treasure, with many of the original twelfth-century frescoes surviving. Nearby, the eleventh-century **St. Stephanskapelle** was the bishop's private chapel, and though the frescoes have been lost, the altar is from the original building period. The hollowed-out section of the altar indicates that it used to contain the relics of a martyr, generally believed to have been Saint Florian, and the openings at the base were for the faithful to insert notes to their saint. For a collection of eleventh- to twentieth-century ecclesiastical vestments and gold and silver ceremonial ware, see the **Domschatzmuseum** (Tues.–Sat. 10am–5pm, Sun. 11:30am–5pm), whose entrance is in the cathedral. Finally, it's worth trying to hear a concert or service featuring the *Domspatzen* (Cathedral Sparrows). The most famous choir in the country, they're the nearest West German equivalent to the likes of Vienna Boys Choir.

On the corner of the Pfauengasse leading off the Domplatz, there's a very nondescript door just past the corner shop which leads to an interesting place of folkloric worship. Dedicated to the Virgin Mary, it's the town's smallest chapel, known as the **Mariae Laeng Kapelle**. The name goes back to the seventeenth-century belief that the best way to get one's prayers heard was to write out prayer notes the same length (*laeng*) as the statue of Mary herself. The church never accepted this idea, but people have come here ever since to pray to Mary and leave notes and gifts. Occasions when help has appeared are recorded by the faithful in little framed cards or pictures, crowding the back of the chapel.

The area between Kohlenmarkt and Haidplatz has many of Regensburg's rich merchant and patrician houses, and **Haidplatz** in particular was built to be seen. The largest building on the square is the **Haus zum Goldenen Kreuz**, which was the town's main hotel between the sixteenth and nineteenth centuries, and the site of one of Regensburg's biggest scandals, when Emperor Charles V fell in love with a local girl called Barbara Blomberg. They used to meet in this house, and their son Juan de Austria was born here in 1547. In the grand tradition of royal illegitimates, he went on to become a great soldier and died Governor of the Netherlands in 1578. Less scandalous, but fun in passing, is the little stone mouse hidden in the right-hand corner outside the shop window on the ground floor. The locals say that if you rub it your purse will never be empty.

The **Thon-Dittmer Palais**, also on the Haidplatz, is one of the main cultural venues these days; during the summer concerts and plays are held out in its courtyard. Only a few minutes' walk away, the Neupfarrplatz is the focus of Regensburg's commercial life and the site of modern-day town planners' only botch-up, in the box-like *Kaufhaus* superstore. The **Neupfarrkirche** stands rather forlorn in the middle of the parking lot, occupying the site of the old syna-gogue, which was wrecked during the 1519 expulsion of the Jews. Originally, it was intended to be a vast pilgrimage church dedicated to the Virgin as thanksgiv-ing for deliverance from the Jewish "peril"; the model for this ambitious design can be seen in the Stadtmuseum. However, the city council's cynical attempts to foster the bogus cult met with such apathy on the part of the faithful that it was hastily dropped. When the council decided to adopt the Reformation a few years later, the church was completed in a much reduced form to serve as the city's Protestant flagship. Notwithstanding its unfortunate history and situation, the interior is very dapper, with an unusual little hexagonal nave. In the courtyard of Neupfarrplatz 7 (Mon.–Fri.) you'll see a pilfered Jewish tombstone—the ultimate status symbol for medieval Christians—set into the wall.

Unique for a German medieval town are the many towers built in the style of Italian fortified palaces. The higher the tower, the richer and more prestigious the occupant, and there are about twenty of these left around the middle of town. Walking around the bumpy cobbled streets, it's not uncommon to see fortified towers with high balconies, and one of the most beautiful is the **Baumburgerturm** in Watmarkt, off the Kohlenmarkt. The **Goldener Turm** on Wahlenstrasse is the town's highest remaining tower, and on its top floor there's a very cozy wine bar (see "Eating and Drinking" below).

Apart from the Dom, the town's most important Gothic structure is the **Altes Rathaus** on the Kohlenmarkt. From the outside, it's difficult to get an idea of its grand scale. To appreciate this, you need to take a guided tour of the **Reichstags-museum** within (Mon.–Sat. 9:30am, 10:30am, 11:30am, 2pm, 3pm, and 4pm, Sun. 10am, 11am, and noon; tickets from the tourist information next door; DM2, DM1 students), which is worth it to see, among other things, the beautiful Renaissance paneling and fittings in the Elector's Ante-Chamber and the Blue Hall, with its glittering star-studded ceiling. All the original furnishings remain, including the torture chamber in the basement with some pretty gruesome instruments. But the largest and most significant room in the Rathaus is the **Imperial Diet Chamber**, where the Perpetual Imperial Diet met from 1663 to 1806. A kind of parliamentary forum for the Empire, it was where representatives from the ruling orders came together to debate the country's imperial policies. The seating order was strictly defined by status, and the different coloring of the benches indicates individual groups—red for Electors, green for princes.

Outside, on the right of the Rathaus entrance, a little alleyway twists around the back, known as *Zum Roten Herzfleck* (Red Heart Patch), a polite name that barely admits its origin, since for many years the house in the corner here was the town's brothel. Meanwhile, on the left of the Rathaus steps, the town's official measurements cast in iron and mounted on the wall are medieval relics, used to sort out disputes between merchants and customers. People who felt they'd been cheated would take their cloth or shoe, for example, and compare it to the fixed measures on the Rathaus. The public nature of these settlements functioned as a good deterrent to would-be crooks, since all could witness the proceedings.

On nearby Keplerstrasse, the **Kepler-Gedächtnishaus** (guided tours Tues.–Sat. 10am, 11am, 2pm, and 3pm, Sun. 10am, and 11am; DM2) is dedicated to the famous astronomer who lived and worked in Regensburg during the early seventeenth century. Famous for expanding the Copernican theory of the solar system, he was also a notable figure in local politics in the days when this was a free imperial city. His family actually lived at Keplerstr. 2, but he died at no. 5 while visiting a merchant friend, and it's this house that's been turned into a museum of the astronomer's life and times.

Another museum worth looking into is the **Stadtmuseum** on Dachauplatz (Tues.–Sat. 10am–4pm, Sun. 10am–1pm; DM2, DM1 students). This encompasses over 100 rooms spread out on four floors of the former Minorite monastery, and charts the town's cultural and artistic history over the past 2000 years. Not surprisingly the wealth of exhibits and information is rather overwhelming, but the layout is clear, with each floor related to a different subject or era. Of particular interest is the section on **Albrecht Altdorfer**, who, apart from being one of Germany's greatest artists, was also a leading local politician, being involved in the decisions which saw the expulsion of the Jews and the introduction of the Reformation. Among his etchings shown here are two of the beautiful Romanesque–Gothic synagogues he helped destroy, which make a fascinating documentary record. The remains of the frescoes he painted for the *Kaiserbad* are also here, along with a panel showing *The Two St. Johns*, which is set in a typically luxuriant Danube landscape.

Schloss Thurn und Taxis (guided tours Mon.–Fri. 2pm and 3:15pm, Sun. 10am and 11:15am; DM3, DM1.50 students), home of the local Prince of Thurn and Taxis, who owns most of Regensburg and much more besides, is situated on Emmeramsplatz in the city's eastern quarter. This used to be the St. Emmeram monastery, which, until secularization, was one of the most important centers of learning in Europe. In the early twentieth century it was largely redesigned into the most modern residence of the day, with hot and cold running water, flushing toilets, central heating, and electricity. The palace isn't open to the public when the present Prince is at home, but at all other times a guide will show you the **state rooms**, still regularly in use, with some wonderful Brussels tapestries on the walls recording the family's illustrious history.

The former **cloisters**, now partly the library, represent some of the finest Gothic architecture to be found, with each wing showing stylistic development from early Gothic in the twelfth century, to late Gothic in the fourteenth century. It's easy to tell how far each abbot progressed with the building program by the number of arches along the ceiling before his portrait is hewn into the stone at the crossover. Highlight of this section is the **Normannisches Portal**, its zigzag patterns around the arch indicating the Norman origins of the first monks to settle here. Also included in the tour is the **Marstallmuseum**, which holds an enormous collection of Thurn and Taxis coaches down the ages, ranging from coaches the family used during the centuries when they held the imperial postal franchise, to ceremonial carriages, traveling coaches, and winter sleighs. All this bears witness to the immense wealth of the family, which continues undiminished via many enterprises, including the Thurn und Taxis brewery, though locally its beer is known as *Tod und Teufel* ("Death and the Devil").

One of the most important examples of Romanesque architecture in Regensburg is the **St. Jacobskirche**, also known as the *Schottenkirche* because of the Scottish monks who used to live here. The first monks were actually Irish, but it became a Scottish Catholic monastery in the sixteenth century, and remained one until its dissolution in 1878, when the monks returned to Fort Augustus on Loch Ness. Pollution from the busy road in front of the church has blackened the exterior, and the profusion of sandstone figures is badly eroded, but the **main portal** is still as intriguing as ever, with its mixture of pagan and Christian images and delicate patterns carved on the pillars. The meaning of these images and patterns has been lost over the ages, and researchers are still puzzling over the many animal figures—mythical and real—that decorate the portal and walls.

Trips and Guided Tours in and Around the City

A short **city tour** (May–Sept. hourly 10am–4pm; Oct.–April 11am and hourly 1–4pm; minimum of ten people; DM7), which includes going through the rapids under the Steinerne Brücke (Stone Bridge), is the standard tourist attraction, with highlights of the Regensburg skyline pointed out as the trip progresses. Considering the same view can be had for free from the bridge, and the sights are best explored on foot, it hardly seems worth the money, but if it's your cup of tea, tickets can be bought right next to the Steinerne Brücke where the ferries leave.

More interesting is the boat trip to Ludwig I's **Walhalla** monument (April–Sept. 9am–6pm; DM 1.50). Built like a Greek temple in 1842, the Walhalla stands high above the Danube on its steep southern banks and seems ridiculously out of place. But the view across the Danube valley is magnificent from up here, and the surrounding park and forests would be a good place for a picnic. The monument itself is named after the Nordic mythological resting place for warriors' souls, and contains busts of 118 famous Germans, along with 64 plaques for older celebrities whose likenesses are unknown. Ferries go from the island UNTERER WÖHRD, just past the Eiserne Brücke (April–15 Oct., 2pm from Regensburg, arriving at Walhalla 2:30pm, returning 4pm; additional ferry 11am 14 July–15 Sept.; DM9 round trip; DM7 one way).

When you've had enough of sightseeing, one of the touristy but nevertheless enjoyable things to do is to go on a Danube **river trip**. There are basically four different trips to choose from. The **all-day tour** down to PASSAU and the Austrian border 125km southeast is a very long journey only worth taking if you really enjoy spending all day on a boat as there's no time to stop off anywhere. There are restaurants and bars on all the ferries, and the route itself is certainly very attractive, but it's definitely a passive experience. On the other hand it would be a very relaxing way to travel onwards, if you were heading for towns farther downriver, or Austria.

Another short trip going from KEHLHEIM—a brief bus or train journey from Regensburg—passes through the famous **Donaudurchbruch** gorge to the Weltenburg monastery (May 16–Sept. 13, 9:15am, 10am, 10:30am, and then every 30 min until 5:10pm; DM4.50 one way, DM6.50 round trip; bicycles carried for DM3:30). It's one of the most popular tours, since the Danube washes past some very attractive wooded hillsides, and then dramatically cuts through white cliffs, becoming a fast current only 80m wide. It took the Danube an estimated 4000 years to cut through these rocks, and once past the obstacle, the river widens out into a generous sweep to flow more peacefully past the monastery on its banks. Situated on a bend of the river, **Weltenburg** is Bavaria's oldest monastery, founded in the seventh century by Benedictine monks. Its church is notable for the baroque interior design by the famous Asam brothers, but these days the monastery is best known for its dark beer, brewed on the premises and served in its own *Gaststätte*.

Eating and Drinking

You're spoiled for places **to eat** in Regensburg. Probably some of the best and cheapest *Schnitzel* in the world are to be eaten in *Zur Goldenen Krone*, Kepplerstr. 3. These aren't your standard ham and cheese either: there's a choice (ranging from straight ones, Camembert and redcurrant sauce, asparagus and bacon, and many more) all in the region of DM8.50 to DM12. As an added attraction there's a beer garden in a quaint medieval courtyard, overgrown with vines. Two more *Gaststätten* with good traditional and cheap Bavarian fare are *Kneitinger*, Arnulfsplatz 3, and the *Kreuz Schenke*, Kreuzgasse 25. A recommendable **fish restaurant** is the *Fischer Haus*, Untere Regenstr. 7; for **vegetarian** fare try the *Antagon*, Rote Hahnengasse 2. The university **mensa** is a cheap place to eat, but in this case, its location outside the center of town makes it a rather unrealistic prospect. If you're still interested, take bus #4, which goes via the Haidplatz. A more worthwhile bus trip (#12 heading to HEITZENHOFEN), is to the *Adlersberg Gasthaus* in the village of the same name. Perched on top of a small hill, it is how a country *Gasthaus* should be, with a large shady beer garden and good, sensibly priced food. You can also go for very peaceful walks around here.

Going out in the evenings, there's a wide range of relaxed and friendly places to choose from, beginning with the above-mentioned *Zur Goldenen Krone*. For more of a **bar** type of atmosphere, usually with good music, try *Namenlos*, Rote Löwengasse 10; *Jensiets*, Am Römling 1; and *Unterholz*, Silberne Fischgasse 17. Popular student hang-outs include *Schwedenkugel*, Haaggasse 15, and also the *Goldene Ente*, Badstr. 32. For **discos**, the most enduringly popular place is the *Sudhaus*, Untere Bachgasse (9pm–2am). Try also *Scala*, Gesandtenstr. 6, Pustet Passage (9pm–3am) and *Why Not*, Obermünsterstr. 14 (8pm–4am), which are pretty provincial musically.

The coziest **wine bar** in town is *Türmchen*, Wahlenstr. 14, at the top of Regensburg's highest medieval tower. During the summer it's usually much more pleasant to sit outside, and in that case the wine bars by the Fischmark are best, although at DM4.50 per glass they're not cheap. For traditional **beer gardens**, *Kneitinger Garten*, Unterer Wöhrd, Müllerstr. 1 (Thurs.–Tue. 10am–11pm) has a great location, being on one of the Danube islands. A favorite with many is the *Spitalgarten*, Stadtamhof, Katharinenplatz 1, right by the river at the far side of the Steinerne Brücke. The largest beer garden, with 1200 seats, is *Kneitinger Keller*, Galgenbergstr. 18, up by the University.

There are also quite a few **cafés** in Regensburg, although they tend to be patronized by the local Schickie element. Best breakfasts are served in *Ambrosius*, Brückstr. 5 (10am–1am), but if you want to be with the "in crowd," go to *Palletti*, Gesandtenstr. 9, Pustet Passage. *Orphée*, Untere Bachgasse 8 (6pm–12:30am), aspires to the same crowd, but has been overtaken by *Paletti*. *Altstadt Café*, Hinter der Grieb 8 (9am–8pm) is probably the nearest to a "normal" café, and it also happens to be in one of medieval Regensburg's most characteristic streets.

Listings

Area code (☎0941)

Bike rental from the tourist office.

Car rental *Avis*, Friedenstr. 6 (☎97001); *Inter-Rent*, Hermann-Geib-Str. 5 (☎75094/95).

Laundromats *Martin*, Malergasse 9; *Potempka*, Heiliggeistgasse 1; and *Self-Service*, Ostengasse, near the Donaumarkt.

Medical emergencies (☎73073 or ☎560066).

Mitfahrzentrale Jakobstr. 12 (☎57400/58267), Mon.–Wed. noon–6pm, Thurs.–Fri. 10am–6pm, Sat. 10am–2pm. They also function as a normal travel office.

Women's center *Frauenzentrum* (☎57404).

South Along the Danube

Between Regensburg and Passau, the Danube flows through some of the most fertile land in Bavaria. Lined by the highlands of the Bavarian Forest to the north and the Bavarian Lowlands to the south, the *Gäuboden*, as it's known, is one of the country's main granaries. Its flatlands have been cultivated for centuries, and archaeological finds go back as far as the Neolithic Age. But for the visitor the agricultural land south of the Danube holds little interest, though the larger towns along the river itself, such as **Straubing**, **Deggendorf**, and **Passau** are certainly worth a visit. The first two are small market towns, with enough together to fill a day trip, while the latter is a rarely visited beauty perched on a peninsula at the confluence of the Danube, Inn, and Ilz. Formerly a Free Imperial City, Passau was the seat of one of the most powerful bishoprics next to Salzburg, and its imposing cathedral stands at the heart of a photogenic medieval and baroque town center.

Although excellent road and train connections exist along the Danube's course, traveling this stretch without exploring the **highlands** north of the river would mean missing out on the first glorious reaches of the Bavarian Forest region. Heading north the wooded countryside soon rises up, quickly becoming a landscape of hillside villages and dozens of medieval castles. It's probably too hilly for all but the fittest cyclists, so motorbikes or cars are the only solution for country day tours. Straubing, Deggendorf, and Passau are each good towns to use as a base, Passau being the liveliest. Budget accommodation needs are served by **youth hostels** in Straubing and Passau.

Straubing and Deggendorf

About 30km downriver from Regensburg, **STRAUBING** is the main market town of the *Gäuboden*, and each year in August, Bavaria's second largest **fair** takes place here. It began in the early nineteenth century as an occasion for the farmers of the region to meet, do business, and celebrate. These days it has expanded into a streamlined Oktoberfest—though one that still attracts over a million visitors. Check ahead with the tourist office (see below) for exact dates of the festival, and don't expect to find cheap accommodation available during this time.

The pedestrianized heart of Straubing is dominated by the town's symbol, the five-pointed Gothic tower next to the Rathaus, and lined by the medieval and baroque facades characteristic of Bavaria's rural towns. Visually Straubing is nothing out of the ordinary, but its wide central market on the main street makes for a pleasant stroll. Following Fraunhoferstrasse away from the main thoroughfare, you'll find the **Gäubodenmuseum** (Tues.–Sun. 10am–4pm; DM2, DM1 students), which holds a famous Roman treasure, the *Römerschatz*, discovered in the region in 1950. It's one of the most important archaeological finds from the Roman period in Northern Europe, and the highlight of the museum. An extensive collection, it includes everything from iron and bronze tools and domestic ware to beautifully crafted armor and masks. There are stylish bronze masks for both soldiers and horses, and their high quality indicates they were used for parades and exhibition games rather than war. Their decoration shows the diversity of influences on Roman art, which includes the distinctly different shapes and patterns of both Oriental and Hellenic styles.

Also worth a look is the **St. Jakob Münster** on the Jakobsgasse. A late Gothic church built during the fifteenth and sixteenth centuries, the profusion of baroque altars and chapels from a later age clashes with the more puritanical Gothic. There's an almost indecent profusion of side chapels, each sponsored by different wealthy families, and all trying to outshine each other. The **Schuster** chapel is the most prestigious, boasting an original painting by Holbein the Elder. But the fifteenth-century stained-glass windows behind the main altar (right-hand side) are the most valuable element in the church, though more impressive for sheer extravagance is the richly adorned rococo pulpit, all gold-leaf shells, leaves, and curls, like an overdressed Christmas tree.

A **theatrical festival** that takes place every four years (next in 1993), relates the death of a local girl called Agnes Bernauer. In the best tradition of tragedy, the story revolves around the love between two people from separate worlds destroyed by bigotry and self-interest. In the fifteenth century, the local duke's son fell in love with the beautiful commoner Agnes and they got married in secret. But when the old duke found out about this, he tricked his son into leaving town for a while, and then had Agnes tried for witchcraft and drowned in the Danube. She's been a favorite character in local songs and storytelling ever since, and the play about her life and death is taken from a ballad written in the last century. The guilty duke erected a chapel for Agnes in atonement in the **St. Peter** basilica, just east of the town center.

The **tourist office** in the Rathaus (Mon.–Fri. 8:30am–noon and 2–5pm; ☎09421 16307) hands out free brochures and also arranges accommodation. Cheapest hotel in town is the *Goldener Löwe*, Innere-Passauer-Strasse 20 (☎80160) at DM20–30 for singles and DM50–60 for doubles. Otherwise the choice is between the **youth hostel** at Friedhofstr. 12 (☎80436), and the **campground** at Dammweg 17, (near the Gstütt bridge; 1 May–15 Oct; (☎12912). Cheap places from which to **rent a car** are *Buchbinder*, Regensburgerstr. 60 (☎10954), and *Völkl*, Stadtgraben 46a (☎22035).

Twenty-five kilometers downriver from Straubing, **DEGGENDORF** doesn't merit an overnight stay in itself, but the nearby forests and countryside of the northern hills are a great area for hiking. If you're into beer festivals, try to time your visit for the end of July and first week of August, which is when the Deggendorfer *Volksfest* is on.

Around Straubing and Deggendorf

Of the smaller towns around Straubing, the most rewarding for a side trip are **BOGEN** and **ST. ENGLMAR**. A few kilometers farther along the Danube, **Bogen** is an old pilgrimage center on the banks of the river and at the foot of the Bogenberg hill. An uneventful place for most of the year, Bogen bursts into life on Pentecost each May, with a great pilgrimage and fair, when a 12.5-meter candle is carried up the steep Bogenberg and into the church at the top. The origins of this vaguely bizarre event are found in the fifteenth century, when a beetle plague around Holzkirchen near Passau ruined much of the forest. The people vowed that if the plague would end, they'd carry a pine pole wrapped in wax to the Bogenberg church as thanks—one of the dafter examples of faith on record. The plague did disappear, and the annual 75-kilometer pilgrimage from Holzkirchen to Bogen has taken place ever since.

Up in the hills 10km to the north of Bogen, **St. Englmar** is the venue for another religiously based festival each Whit Monday. Legend has it that a hermit named Englmar came to live here around the year 1086, and was murdered by a jealous companion, who hid the body under snow in the forest. But at Whitsunday the next year, the local priest found Englmar's perfectly preserved body and brought it to the village chapel to be buried. Ever since, the spot has been a pilgrimage center, and on Whit Monday the villagers re-enact the search for Englmar, riding festively decorated horses and wearing medieval-style clothes.

Around Deggendorf, villages like BERNRIED, KALTECK, BISCHOFSMAIS, and RUSEL are good places from which to go hiking, with plenty of clearly marked paths through the forests and connecting the peaks. Dedicated hikers tend to stay in **OBERBREITNAU** near Bischofsmais, which has a few simple guest houses as well as a **youth hostel** (☎09920 265), only accessible on foot or via the **Geisskopfbahn** chair lift service. The **tourist office**, on Oberer Stadtplatz, in the *Stadt-Café* building (Mon.–Fri. 8am–noon and 2–6pm; ☎0991 380169) in Deggendorf can advise you on the most interesting hiking routes, and also sells the appropriate maps.

Many of the local farmers rent out parts of their farms for residential holidays around here, something which is becoming increasingly popular, especially for people with young children. The tourist office in Straubing can advise you on booking and prices, or you can write to the head office for eastern Bavarian tourism: *Fremdenverkehrsverband Ostbayern* (Landshuter Str. 13, 8400 Regensburg (☎0941 57186), who'll send you brochures and prices.

Passau

Marauding Napoleon is supposed to have said, "In all of Germany I never saw a town more beautiful than **PASSAU**." Tucked away in the far southeast on the Austrian border, the town is often overlooked by visitors; usually people pass by en route to Austria and thus miss a place that the tourist brochures hail as the

"Bavarian Venice." While that's the standard exaggeration, the town does have a certain magic, and its character is indeed very much defined by water. The town in tightly packed on to a peninsula between the confluence of the Danube and Inn, and the river Ilz joins here as well, coming down from the hills of the Czech border. A day or two is probably enough time here, though the countryside to the north merits a similar length of time in its own right.

Virtually the whole place burned down in the seventeenth century, so the architectural picture features predominantly baroque, rococo and neoclassical facades, which give Passau a pleasingly elegant feel in spite of the unceremoniously tight squeeze of buildings. Space is at a premium on the peninsula, which is only a few meters wide at its tip and still only 300m wide by the time you come to the enormous **Dom** 1km inland. Not surprisingly, Passau spilt across the two rivers to form suburbs on the banks of the Danube and Inn. On the north side, across the Danube, the land rises up sharply to where the bishop's former palace, the **Veste Oberhaus** overlooks town. Contrary to what you might expect, the palace wasn't fortified to protect Passau's citizens in times of war, but to protect the bishop from the townspeople who resented his rule. They attacked the Veste on a number of occasions but never succeeded in breaking through. The bishop, on the other hand, had an excellent vantage point from which to bombard the town, his favorite hobby when his subjects got too rebellious.

Passau's history is closely linked to the Church, and from 739 to 1803 the town was the capital of one of the largest and most powerful German bishoprics—the bishops of Passau were prince-bishops, which meant they owned the town and ruled its subjects. Being placed at such a vital point of trade between Eastern and Western Europe however, Passau's merchants became wealthy and understandably wanted control over the municipal rule of the town: hence the battle with the bishops.

Heart of Passau's Altstadt is the Domplatz and the **Dom**. The original Gothic structure was almost completely destroyed in a great fire in 1662, and its replacement, designed by the Italian masters Lurago, Carlone and Tencalla, is suitably enthroned at the town's highest point, towering over everything else and dominating the skyline. Inside, white stucco ornamentation crowds into almost every available space, creating a heavy and overloaded impression. The most notable piece is the **organ**, which is the largest in the world with no less than 17,300 pipes and 231 separate registers. Turn up between noon and 12:30pm on a weekday and you can hear it being played during the lunchtime organ recitals (May–Oct.; DM3; also Thurs. at 7:30pm until Dec. 3; DM6). Guided tours of the Dom take place after the organ recitals from May to October and cost DM1. The **Residenzplatz**, round the back of the Dom, is one of the very few open spaces in this tightly packed town. Lined by the airy, pastel-colored eighteenth-century homes of former wealthy families as well as the bishop's residence, the small cobbled square still holds something of the atmosphere of a once-salubrious past.

Down towards the Danube, the **Rathaus** is an imposing Gothic building presenting a blank face to the Veste Oberhaus across the river. Originally a nobleman's home, the building became the town hall after one of the local rebellions in the thirteenth century. Look just under the Rathaus tower and you'll see the marks from the alarmingly high floods that have always plagued the town. From the Rathausplatz to the tip of the peninsula, alleys and lumpy streets intertwine in picturesque disorder, the original medieval townscape most visible here.

Of Passau's museums, that in the **Veste Oberhaus** (March 15–Oct. 31 Tues.–Sun. 9am–5pm; DM3, DM1.50 students) is the largest, covering local and regional history from Roman times to the present, with a mixed bag of collections including porcelain, baroque art, torture instruments, and plenty more. You also get a picture-postcard view of the island town from up here. If you don't fancy the steep walk up the hill, take a bus from the Rathausplatz, which leaves every thirty minutes from 10:30am to 11:30am and from 12:30pm to 4:30pm. For those interested in the art of handmade glass, the **Glasmuseum** (daily 9am–5pm; DM2.50) in the hotel *Wilder Mann* on Rathausplatz has a collection ranging from Biedermeier to Jugendstil styles, with an awful lot of kitsch in between. Finally there's the **Spielzeugmusem** on the Residenzplatz (daily 9am–6pm; DM3), with a small collection of nineteenth-century European and American toys, and a few reproductions of wooden toys and games on sale.

Nightlife in Passau is a livelier prospect than you might imagine in such a small place, since a new university founded in 1978 has spawned the *Scharfrichterhaus*, Milchgasse 2 (Tues.–Sun.; ☎35900), a venue for live music and cabaret with a movie theater and relaxed bar. Another youthful watering hole is the *Stadtschreiber* on the corner of Schustergasse and Schrottgasse. The *Altstadt Café* in the Schustergasse is best for a snack and coffee in the daytime, and at *Zum Passauer Tölpel*, Fritz-Schäffer Promenade, Höllgasse 22 (11am–11pm), you'll find a **vegetarian** restaurant. In the same area, the *Innstadt Bräustüberl*, Schmiedgasse/Löwengrube, is a cheap *Gasthaus* with main meals for less than DM10.

The **tourist office** (Mon.–Fri. 9am–6pm, Sat. 9am–noon; ☎33421) is near the Bahnhof, in the Nibelungenhalle just off Neuburgerstrasse. They provide the usual brochures, accommodation bookings, and also sell detailed hiking maps of the surrounding area. The **youth hostel** is located in the Veste Oberhaus (☎41351), and there's a **campground** for tents only, next to the river Ilz, at Halserstr. 34 (☎41457). Two affordable **hotels** in Passau's Altstadt, pleasantly located at the tip of the peninsula, are *Pension Rössner*, Bräugasse 19 (☎35218) and *Gasthof zum Hirschen*, Im Ort 6 (☎36238). Both charge around DM30–40 for singles, DM48–70 for doubles.

Listings

Area code (☎0851)

Bike rental at the Bahnhof. DM5 per day if you're also using the trains, DM10 per day if you're not.

Car rental *Plechinger Europcar*, Neuburgerstr. 93 (☎6033/51111).

Tour bus trips to Prague are run from May 9 to October 24 every Saturday, and there's a choice of day trips or overnight weekend stays. Phone ☎34262 or ask the tourist office for details. From Passau to Prague is only 190km, but car-drivers need to apply for their visa at least 10–14 days in advance so a bus trip is an easier option for most people since group visas are granted immediately.

Danube cruises *DDSG-Agentie Passau* (☎33035), for trips from Passau to Vienna and Budapest between May and October. *Donauschiffahrtgesellschaft Wurm & Köck*, Höllgasse 26 (☎2066/2065) for one-hour cruises around Passau, daily from the Rathausplatz, every thirty minutes; DM6.

Festivals During the *Europäische Wochen* in June, July, and August, concerts played by internationally renowned orchestras and musicians, and there's also ballet and opera. In May the *Maidult* is one of the largest and colorful annual markets and beer festivals.

Women's center Schustergasse 6 (☎34986). A café is run every Thursday from 5:30pm, a bar every second and fourth Sunday of the month from 7pm.

The Bavarian Forest

Rather uncharitably known as the "Bavarian Congo" because it's poor, provincial, and a bit out of the way, the **BAVARIAN FOREST** is not only one of the last wildernesses in Europe, it's also a region that's retained much of its traditional culture in an unpackaged form, by virtue of being less well-known and visited than the more obvious target of the Black Forest. The craggy earth here is full of rocks and barely fertile, and the people of the region had to develop means of survival other than farming. Easy availability of firewood made **glassblowing** a viable industry, and workers still tend to be employed in the traditional huts, working by hand and mouth in the heat of the furnaces. Except for one or two large factories, glass production is still more of a craft than an industry here, and going on a tour of one of the traditional glass-blowing huts is a treat you shouldn't miss.

Prices are relatively low, and even during the height of summer finding accommodation is never a problem. Transportation to the area is provided by train services from Regensburg, Straubing, and Deggendorf. There's also a good regional bus service, but don't expect buses to go more than once or twice a day. If you want to go on some of the longer hikes and take in the sights and scenery, reckon on staying around a week.

The Forest

The actual *Bayerischer Wald* (the forest, as opposed to the general area) is part of a much larger whole spreading across the Czech border into Bohemia, to form central Europe's largest forest region. On the German side, it's approximately defined by the Czechoslovakian border to the north and the Danube to the south, the Austrian border to the southeast and the town of KÖTZTING to the northeast. It's brilliant hiking country, with well-marked paths of varying length and difficulty throughout the region. Specialized maps pointing out routes are on sale in almost every village tourist office.

The most ancient part of the forest has been declared a **national park**, which is about 130 square kilometers roughly defined by the Czech border and the villages of MAUTH, GRAFENAU, SPIEGELAU, and FRAUENAU. The two highest mountains are the **Rachel** (1453m) and the **Lusen** (1373m), but the region isn't all mountainous, and stretches of moorland open up the forest, while the **Rachelsee** is an isolated splash of blue at the foot of Mt. Rachel. An excellent **information center** about the park and its facilities is located in NEUSCHÖNAU in the *Hans-Eisenmann Haus*, Böhmstr. 35 (Mon.–Sat. 9am–5pm; ☎08558 1300). They also run slide shows and tours of the National Park, and although they're all in German, you will undoubtedly find someone who can explain things in English if necessary. This would also be the place to find out a bit more about *Waldsterben*, the death of Europe's forests due to acid rain. The statistics are grim and the damage is increasing at an alarming rate: for example in 1983 forty percent of Germany's forests were diseased. By 1985 it had risen to 78 percent, and the problem shows little sign of improving in the near future.

Outside the national park, the **Grosser Arber** (1456m) is the highest mountain of the region, and together with the **Arbersee**, this is the most touristy area, and the only place where you're likely to encounter bus-loads of people touring the "sights." Much quieter, and with great views across to Bohemia, is **Mt. Grosser Osser** near LAM and the Czech border. For easy hiking, head for the central highlands and the **Kaitersberg** hills near Kötzting, which has what's considered the best hiking route of the whole area.

There's a **youth hostel**, Waldhäuser, Herbergsweg 2 (☎08553 300; bus from Grafenau Bahnhof) right in the middle of the National Park, which makes an ideal base for hiking. Other hostels are spread around the region generally, in Mauth, Frauenau, Zwiesel, on Mt. Arber, and in Lam. **Guest-house** prices are generally in the neighborhood of DM15–25 per person, and if you stay in a farm-house, prices can be as little as DM11–18 each.

Some Long-Distance Hikes

Special maps outlining these routes should be on sale in most regional tourist offices and local bookshops. You don't need a tent, as all routes are structured around mountain huts and villages with cheap accommodation. You do need suit-able hiking gear.

The *Nördliche Hauptwanderlinie* is a tough 180-kilometer tour that can be done in seven days in a crunch, but is much more rewarding at a more leisurely pace. Heading from **Furth im Wald** to the **Dreisesselberg** mountain, it passes through most of the natural highlights this part of the country has to offer.

The 105-kilometer *Südliche Hauptwanderlinie* is a much gentler tour for which you should budget on at least five days, covering the lower hills of the outer Bavarian Forest region, near the Danube valley. Less dramatic but just as beauti-ful, this route will take you from **Rattenberg** (a village on the train route between Straubing and Cham) to **Kalteneck** near Passau.

A favorite with many people is a 50km two-day tour from **Kötzting** to **Bayrisch Eisenstein**, via the Kaitersberg hills and Arber mountain. Accommodation is available in the *Kötztinger Hütte* (hut), the *Berggasthof Eck* (inn), and in the hamlet of SCHAREBEN.

Frauenau, Bodenmais, and Kötzting

The best place to see the living craft of glassblowing and cutting is in the village of FRAUENAU, to the northeast of the National Park.

Frauenau's **Freiherr von Poschinger Kristallglasfabrik** (tours Mon.–Sat., 9:45–11:30am and 12:45–1:30pm; DM1) is the oldest glassmaking factory in the world and an excellent place to watch workers transform red molten lumps into glasses, plates, and ornaments. The men have to work with temperatures around 2200°F, and it takes considerable care and skill to blow molten glass into shape as soon as it's on the end of the blowing tube. The time involved for the making of most objects is a matter of seconds, but then the glass has to lose its internal pressure in a long cooling process to prevent explosion.

For a more technical history of glass production and to see representative work of each age, the **Glasmuseum**, Am Museumspark (daily 9am–5pm; DM3, DM2.50 students) gives a very comprehensive illustration. Highlights of the collection are exquisite seventeenth- and eighteenth-century Venetian pieces, and some anarchic Jugendstil vases. Local specialties, such as heavy cut crystal and delicate snuff bottles, are also included.

The **tourist office** is in the Rathaus (Mon.–Fri. 8am–noon and 1–5pm, Sat. 9–11:30am; ☎09926 710) and supplies guest-house addresses and prices. Most charge about DM15–25 per person. If you want to stay in a farm, you'll have to go a couple of kilometers up the road to the village of FLANITZ, where prices hover around DM13–16 per person. The **youth hostel** (☎09926 543) is in *Haus Hermann* opposite the police station on the main road.

BODENMAIS is typical of small towns of the region, surrounded by picturesque countryside, and alive with colorful fairs during the summer and religious festivals throughout the year. The most interesting **hiking route** up the Arber goes from here, passing the waterfalls of the **Risslochschlucht** gorge on the way. For this reason Bodenmais is one of the most popular places to base a holiday, and during summer it gets very busy, though nothing like as crowded as the Alpine region.

Iron and silver were once mined in this region, and tours are guided through Bodenmais' *Erzbergwerk* mine on the Silberberg mountain (bus from Bodenmais) about two kilometers outside the village. The whole mountain is riddled with horizontal mineshafts, and the **Barbara-Stollen** shaft (daily 10am–5pm; DM5) halfway up, is open to the public. But unless your German is very good, you won't understand the guides, who speak a strong local dialect, and apart from the original fifteenth-century part of the shaft, it's not a particularly interesting tour.

A better use of time would be to keep your feet firmly above ground and head for **KÖTZTING**, at the foot of the Kaitersberg, right on the edge of the Bavarian Forest region. The most interesting time to come here is around the *Pfingstritt* festival on Pentecost. This is a religious festival, probably founded in an ancient Germanic fertility rite, which involves the menfolk riding their richly adorned horses to a nearby pilgrimage church, and a symbolic wedding of a young couple elected as Pentecost bride and groom. For the rest of the year, the surrounding hiking opportunities constitute the main attraction of this place. It's not wildly picturesque in itself, but rather a handy base for excursions, with plenty of inns and *Gasthäuser* to fill the evenings.

The Upper Palatinate

The **UPPER PALATINATE** is shaped like a tall triangle. The baseline is roughly defined by **Schwandorf**, **Furth im Wald**, and **Cham**, with the apex at **Waldsassen**. It's a lonely region, with few towns and a scant population. But it's also beautiful, especially between the hilly forested border and the B22 road connecting Weiden to Cham. The landscape is less dramatic than further southeast, so the area has had little tourism and continues to be a sleepy backwater of farms and villages, punctuated with the occasional dilapidated castle. As you might expect, public transportation is a problem here, and north–south travel is only practicable on the mainline train route that heads north from Regensburg, via the towns on the edge of the Upper Palatinate. Subsidiary routes make inroads to the east at various points, however, so Cham and Furth im Wald are connected, and routes lead east from Schwandorf, Schwarzenfeld and Neustadt. But to see the region thoroughly, which would only take a day or two, you really need your own wheels.

The South

The two small towns of **CHAM** and **FURTH IM WALD** are the best springboard into the region, and if you arrive on the second and third Sundays in August, you'll witness one of Bavaria's largest traditional **festivals**: the *Drachenstich* in Furth im Wald. Best time to go is on the second Sunday, when the festivities kick off with a great procession of some 200 horses and hundreds of people in traditional costume. The festival, which goes back as far as 1431, is based on the legend of St. George and the dragon, and the story is re-enacted in a show that's performed several times over the festival period. The whole spectacle lasts for about 75 minutes, ending in the grand and gory finale of the dragon's death, where the skewerd monster spews blood over the street during its death throes. Tickets for the show cost between DM4 for a standing position and then rise steadily to DM22, depending on where you want to sit. (Booking and information from *Drachenstichfestausschuss*, Furth im Wald, Stadtplatz 4; ☎09973 9308.) If you don't fancy the dragon spectacle, the beer tents and fair offer a lively alternative.

There's a **youth hostel** at Daberger Str. 50 (☎09973 9254) in Furth im Wald, but cheap alternatives are easy to find throughout the whole region. The **tourist office** in Cham is at Propsteistr. 46 (☎09971 4933), and as well as offering the usual services, they also offer a special service of transporting your backsack for you on certain hiking routes, an innovation called *Wandern ohne Gepäck*.

If you do have your own vehicle and you're interested in seeing one of Germany's most controversial nuclear projects, then head for the village of **WACKERSDORF** near SCHWANDORF. In fact the power plant is being erected in the middle of the forest, blazing a great hole into the green landscape, and the best vantage point from which to gauge its scale is to take the small country road that turns left off the B22 highway at RÖTZ, and goes to SCHWARZENFELD. Wackersdorf has seen some of the bitterest clashes in Germany between anti-nuclear protesters and the government, with the police using highly controversial strong-arm methods to put down demonstrations. It was thought that by situating this project in the middle of a remote forest, opposition would be minimal. Instead it's become a battleground, not just for demonstrators but also in the nearby law courts in NEUNBURG VORM WALD. In the summer of 1988 a public hearing was finally called, where state officials were to be accountable to concerned parties. But the whole thing ended in a farce, with the chairman closing the hearing after a few days, to prevent further embarrassing arguments being heard. The conflict remains and the station continues to be built—a great blot in an otherwise beautiful countryside.

The North

Heading north on the B22 road, you pass through a landscape of rolling hills, forest,s and little river valleys. About 25km north of Cham, a small road goes off to **TRAUSNITZ**, a village set in a bend of the river Preimd, with a **youth hostel** in the local medieval castle. It's pretty basic, but then staying in a castle isn't something you do every day, and if you wake early enough, you might see the forest deer out in the valley for their morning grazing. **WEIDEN**, another 10km north, is a busy market town with nothing in particular worth staying over for; from here on the best option is to take the smallest roads you can find, preferably near the border region if you enjoy remote empty landscapes.

WALDSASSEN, right on the northern edges of the Upper Palatinate, is best known for its huge **Stift**, built by Georg Dientzenhofer in the late seventeenth century, and ranking as one of the masterpieces of German baroque. The most impressive part of the complex is the monasterial **library** (summer, Tues.–Sun. 10–11:30am and 2–5pm; winter, Tues.–Sun. 10–11am and 2–4pm), whose wooden bookcases are embraced by idiosyncratic statues representing all the trades that go into the making and selling of books. Carved by local artists Karl Stilp and Andreas Witt, they include everyone who is even remotely connected with books, such as the shepherd (whose sheepskins are turned into book-binding), the pulp-maker, plus more obvious ones like the bookseller and the reader.

Though strictly speaking in Franconia, the **Kappel** pilgrimage church is so close to Waldsassen that the two should be mentioned together. Also by Dientzenhofer, this church is set in tranquil countryside a couple of kilometers up the road, and built in a rare circular design. It's made up of three apses and three little onion-domed towers, which neatly symbolize the Holy Trinity to which it's dedicated.

FRANCONIA

Geographically the largest part of Bavaria, **Franconia** (*Franken*) makes up the north of the state, with East Germany, Hessen and Baden-Württemberg forming the borders. About half the region is covered by four highland forest ranges (all designated as *Naturparks*), which reach down from north to south and span the whole width of Franconia. In the most northwesterly corner above **Würzburg**, the **Spessart** and **Rhön** regions are great hiking country, with ancient oak forests and highland moors. Closer to Franconia's center, the **Hass** highlands and the **Steigerwald** region are also covered by thick forests, mostly pine. Over to the northeast, separated by a vale and the small towns of **Bamberg** (a real artistic treasure-chest) and **Coburg**, the **Frankenalb** or "Franconian Switzerland" is a gentler landscape of hillside orchards and farming pastures, but also rocky with Jurassic stone and strange subterranean cave formations. Most northeasterly of all, the **Fichtelgebirge** are more mountainous and characterized by a great many streams, including the sources of the rivers Main, Saale, Eger, and Naab, which flow out from here in all directions. Tucked just between the Fichtelgebirge and the Frankenalb, you'll find Wagner's **Bayreuth**.

Towards southern Franconia the highlands peter out into the Bavarian plateau and a much flatter countryside, with only a few rivers to make any dents in the landscape. Right in the middle is the city of **Nürnberg** and close by, to the south-west, the regional capital **Ansbach**. Also not far from here, the **Romantic Road** continues its course up from the Alps, and the untouched medieval towns of **Dinkelsbühl** and **Rothenburg ob der Tauber** are star attractions on the tourist trail.

Franconia's **history** goes back a long way, taking its name from the Frankish tribes of whose territory it formed a major part. In the tenth century it was made into a duchy which stretched all the way to the Rhine, but this was later split into two, and the name retained only for the eastern half. Somehow the region could never establish itself as a coherent entity like Bavaria, and so rulership was always dominated by people from the outside. Even the mighty bishop of Würzburg's secular title of Duke of Eastern Franconia did little to unite the area, which was splintered into many different power bases. Emperor Maximilian I's decision to restructure the Empire into ten confederate regions in the sixteenth century did at least establish Franconia as a distinctive cultural entity. This lasted until 1803, when the Empire was dissolved and most of Franconia was absorbed into the new Bavarian kingdom.

Today, even after nearly 200 years of being part of Bavaria, the people still cling to their regional heritage and often only grudgingly see themselves as Bavarian. Certainly their dress, food, and dialect are quite different. No one wears *Lederhosen* here and Nürnberg, Bavaria's second largest city, is one of a very few to have a Socialist mayor in this conservative state. On the other hand, the border regions by East Germany harbor some of the most fanatically nationalist and right-wing people in the country, most notably in the town of Coburg.

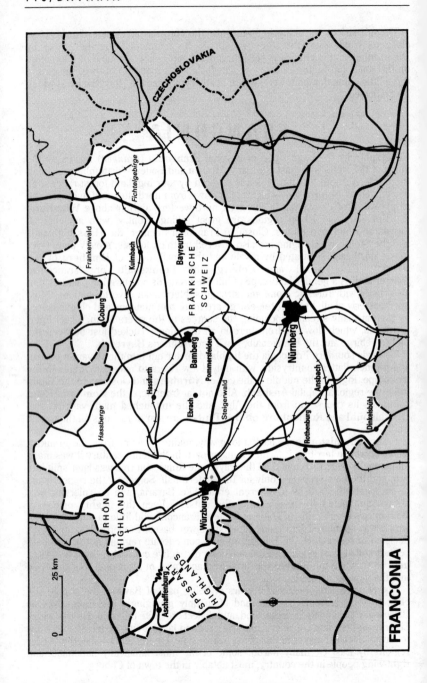

CZECHOSLOVAKIA

Fichtelgebirge

Frankenwald

Kulmbach

Bayreuth

Coburg

FRÄNKISCHE SCHWEIZ

Bamberg

Hassfurt

Pommersfelden

Ebrach

Steigerwald

Nürnberg

Ansbach

Rothenburg

Dinkelsbühl

Hassberge

RHÖN HIGHLANDS

Würzburg

Aschaffenburg

SPESSART HIGHLANDS

25 km

0

FRANCONIA

This political divide has been closely linked to the religious divide in Franconia, created by the adoption of the Reformation in the margraviates of Ansbach and Bayreuth—a divide noticeable not only in political leanings, but also in the architecture, which is far less theatrical and colorful in the Lutheran regions, though the plain lines and more somber colors of their baroque buildings are a welcome contrast to the sometimes overrich Catholic style. Interestingly, drinking habits are different as well, with central and western Franconia a staunch beer-drinking zone, while the region around Würzburg is very much a wine area.

Travel around Franconia is easy by rail between the larger towns and cities, but away from these in the *Naturparks* public transportation connections are much less comprehensive and frequent. However, cheap accommodation isn't hard to come by and there are plenty of youth hostels in villages around the highlands: **Lohr** and **Bischofsheim** are best for the Spessart and Rhön respectively. **Königsberg** and **Ebrach** are suitable bases for exploring the Hassberge and Steigerwald; for the Frankenalb the best base is **Streitberg** or **Gössweinstein**; and for the Fichtelgebirge head for **Oberwarmensteinach**. All towns covered in this section except Ansbach also have **youth hostels**.

Nürnberg

Nothing more magnificent or splendid is to be found in the whole of Europe. When one perceives this glorious city from afar, its splendor is truly dazzling. When one enters it, one's original impression is confirmed by the beauty of the streets and the comeliness of the houses. The burghers' dwellings seem to have been built for princes. In truth, the kings of Scotland would be glad to be housed so luxuriously as the ordinary citizen of Nürnberg.

This mid-fifteenth-century eulogy, written by the future Pope Pius II, shows the esteem in which medieval **NÜRNBERG** (*NUREMBERG* in its anglicized form) was held. As the favorite royal residence, and seat of the first Diet called by each new emperor, the city then functioned as the unofficial capital of Germany. It was a status which had been achieved with remarkable speed, since Nürnberg was only founded in the eleventh century; thereafter, its position at the intersection of the north–south and east–west trading routes led to economic prosperity, and, as a corollary, political power. The arts flourished, too, though the most brilliant period was not to come until the late fifteenth and early sixteenth centuries, when the roll-call of citizens was led by **Albrecht Dürer**, Germany's most complete personification of Renaissance Man.

Like other wealthy European cities, Nürnberg went into gradual economic and social decline once the maritime trading routes to the Americas and Far East had been established; moreover, the official civic adoption of the Reformation cost the city the patronage of the Catholic emperors. It made a comeback in the nineteenth century, when it became the focus for the Pan-German movement, and the **Germanisches Nationalmuseum**—the most important and extensive collection of the country's arts and crafts—was founded at this time. In 1835, the first German railroad was built there, linking the city to the neighboring town of FÜRTH.

Nürnberg's symbolic status for the German nation was given a horrifying twist during the Third Reich. Even today the city's image as the home of quaint markets and dreamy spires, and as the world's leading center for the production of children's toys, is marred by its indelible association with the Nazi regime and the war-crimes trial after the war. The site of the old mass rallies still stands, and in spite of all the picturesque views the medieval city center offers, the weather-beaten Nazi architecture outside town creates an equally telling impression.

Even though the historic area (or **Altstadt**) is quite small there's so much to see in Nürnberg that two or three days are probably the minimum amount of time necessary to get to know the place. It's especially enticing in the summer, when the Altstadt is alive with street theater and music, and when there are open-air pop concerts in the parks and stadiums; but there's always a wide and varied range of nightlife.

Getting Around and Finding Somewhere to Stay

Arriving at the **Hauptbahnhof**, you're just outside the medieval fortifications of the Altstadt. The **tourist office** (Mon.–Sat. 9am–8pm, Fri. until 9pm; ☎233632) is conveniently situated in the central hall of the Hauptbahnhof, and supplies free brochures of the city, sells maps and arranges accommodation. There's another office at Hauptmarkt 18 (☎233634) in the Altstadt itself. **Public transit**, though hardly neccessary for the compact city center, is provided by trams, U-Bahns, and buses, and the same tickets are valid on all three. Tickets can be bought at almost any station and the price of a journey is dependent on how many zones you cross. Maps next to ticket machines explain the zone system, and drivers will advise you if necessary.

A first-class **youth hostel** (☎241352; U-Bahn to Plärrer and then tram #4 to the Vestnertor) is located in part of the city's castle overlooking the Altstadt. There's another **youth hotel** (without age restrictions) to the north of the city, at Rathsbergstr. 300 (☎529092; the journey from the Hauptbahnhof by tram #2 and then bus #41 takes 20 minutes). The cheapest **guesthouses** charge DM30–40 for singles, DM60–70 for doubles. Those with a reasonably central location are: *Altstadt* (Hintere Ledergasse 2, ☎226102; nearest U-Bahn Lorenzkirche); *Humboldtklause* (Humboldtstr. 41, ☎413801; tram #8 from the Hauptbahnhof); and *Melanchthon* (Melanchthonplatz 1, ☎412626; tram #9 from the Hauptbahn-hof). The **campground** (May–Sept. only) is in the Volkspark near the Dutzendteich lakes (☎408416; tram #12 from the Marientunnel near the Hauptbahnhof).

The Altstadt

On January 2, 1945 a hailstorm of bombs reduced ninety percent of Nürnberg's city center to ash and rubble. Yet walking through the Altstadt today, you'd never guess this had ever happened, so loving and effective was the postwar rebuilding. Covering about four square kilometers, the reconstructed medieval core is surrounded by its ancient **city walls** (guarded by eighty towers and pierced by four massive gateways) and neatly sliced by the River Pegnitz. To walk from one end to the other takes about twenty minutes, but much of the center, especially the area around the castle (known as the **Burgviertel**) is on a steep hill, and speedy walking is impractical. It makes wandering around all the more interest-ing, the rise and fall of the streets creating lopsided views and houses squeezing together as if for comfort. The atmosphere is pleasantly relaxed as well; most of the area is pedestrianized, and there's little in the way of city rush within the forti-fications. It's not all medieval vistas though. Significant areas of modern architec-ture and open spaces are nearby, such as at the **Hauptmarkt** in the heart of the

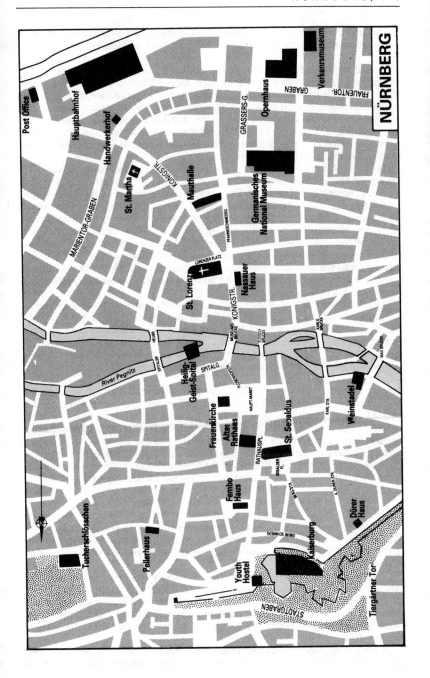

NÜRNBERG

Post Office
Hauptbahnhof
Handwerkerhof
St. Martha
KÖNIGSTR.
Mauthalle
MARIENTOR-GRABEN
GRASSERS-G.
Opernhaus
Verkersmuseum
FRAUENTOR-GRABEN
PFANNENSCHMIEDG.
Germanisches National Museum
LORENZER PLATZ
St. Lorenz
Nassauer Haus
KÖNIGSTR.
HELBR.
SPITALBR.
MUSEUMS-BRÜCKE
FLEISCH-BRÜCKE
KARLS-BRÜCKE
MAX-BRÜCKE
River Pegnitz
Heilig-Geist-Spital
SPITALG.
FLEISCHBRÜCKE
KARL-STR.
Weinstadel
KAR.-STR.
Frauenkirche
Altes Rathaus
HAUPT-MARKT
St. Sebaldus
RATHAUSPL.
SEBALDER PL.
Fembo Haus
BERGSTR.
A.-DÜRER-STR.
Tucherschlösschen
Pellerhaus
Dürer Haus
OBERE SCHMEDG.
Kaiserburg
Youth Hostel
STADTGRABEN
Tiergärtner Tor

city, around the University and down by the Germanisches Nationalmuseum near the Hauptbahnhof, which all ensure a refreshing (and deliberate) mix of old and new.

On one of the highest points of the city, and offering the best views, the **Kaiserburg** (guided tours of the interior daily 9:30am–noon and 12:45–4pm; DM3) sits chunkily above all else. Scene of many imperial meetings from the eleventh to the sixteenth centuries, this castle was the "treasure chest of the German Empire," and, despite innumerable modifications and war damage down the centuries, it remains a key feature of the city's silhouette. In fact, it's two fortresses rolled into one, and as such offers an unusually illuminating insight into the history and politics of medieval Germany.

The earliest surviving part of the castle is the **Fünfeckturm** (*Pentagonal Tower*) on the eastern side, which dates back to the eleventh-century Salian epoch. A century later, Frederick Barbarossa decided to extend the castle to the west, using the Salian buildings as the first line of defence. From this period there remain several examples of the smooth ashlar structures characteristic of the Hohenstaufens. The **Sinwellturm** (*Round Tower*), built directly on the rock, can be ascended for the best of all the views. Another survivor is the two-story **Kaiserkapelle**, whose high and airy upper level was reserved for the use of the emperor, with the courtiers confined to the squat and heavy lower tier. In a most unusual architectural arrangement, the bizarrely named **Heidenturm** (*Heathens' Tower*) was built over its chancel.

At the extreme east end of the complex is the only fourteenth-century addition, the **Luginslandturm**, which was erected by the city council. Its function, odd though it seems, was to protect Nürnberg against the ambitious Hohenzollern family, who had acquired the old Salian part of the fortress as a hereditary fief, and aimed to use it as their base for establishing control over local affairs. After a long war of attrition, the city emerged victorious, but most of the original castle was destroyed in the process.

Apart from the east wall, the Hohenstaufen residential quarters were demolished in the mid-fifteenth century and replaced by the late Gothic **Palas**, which retains its suite of halls. These now look rather plain and soulless, redeemed only by two eye-catching painted wooden ceilings, which were added the following century. One of these bears the 24 coats of arms of the European-wide possessions of Charles V, while the other has only a huge Double Eagle, the symbol of the Holy Roman Empire. At the end of the fifteenth century, the local authorities joined their Luginslandturm to the formerly hostile Fünfeckturm by building the vast **Kaiserstallung**. Originally, this was a cereal warehouse, but takes its name from the fact that the emperors' horses and carriages were kept here during their frequent visits. Now its newly renovated interior makes the perfect setting for a youth hostel. During the sixteenth century, the covered **Tiefer Brunnen** (*Deep Well*) was built, and the defenses strengthened by the erection of huge bastions on the north side, but by then the castle had begun to lose both its political and military significance.

The area around the **Tiergärtner Tor** next to the Kaiserburg is one of the most attractive parts of the old town center, and the open space inside the city gate is the main meeting point for summertime street vendors, artists and musicians. On warm evenings the surrounding pubs spill out onto the cobblestoned piazza and the half-timbered houses form a picturesque backdrop for relaxed summer drinking.

Virtually next door, the **Dürer Haus** (Tues.–Sun. 10am–5pm, Wed. to 9pm; DM3, DM1 students) is where the versatile painter, engraver, scientist, writer, traveler, and politician lived from 1509 to 1528, and is one of the very few original houses still standing in the Altstadt. Much of the furniture and decor dates back to the fifteenth century, giving a real sense of how people lived in the late Middle Ages, right down to their kitchen utensils. Don't come here looking for original Dürer paintings: there are only copies, plus works by other artists paying homage to the great man. However, there are examples of his prowess in the graphic arts, alongside original editions of his three treatises—on Geometry, Fortifications, and Human Proportions. A few minutes' walk away, beyond the city walls and along the Johannisstrasse, the artist is buried in the **St. Johannisfriedhof.** A medieval cemetery outside the old city, it's one of the country's most fascinating graveyards. The tombstones lie lengthwise above the graves, like so many coffins lined side by side, each simply decorated with a bowl of red-flowering plants. Look carefully on the "lids"—some show little scenes from the deceased person's life or trade chiseled into the stone.

Also in the Burgviertel at Burgstr. 15 is the **Fembohaus,** now containing the **Municipal Museum** (Tues.–Sun. 10am–5pm, Wed. to 9pm; DM3, DM1 students). Originally built for a rich merchant, the interior decor proves that bad taste isn't a twentieth-century invention: the upper rooms are painted in rich pastel pink, yellow, and green, with white stuccoed ceilings forming the icing on top. Of the exhibits, the most entertaining are in room 22: frivolous pictures of human passion, dreams, and bodily functions—for some reason bees and wasps crop up a lot.

Nürnberg's oldest and most important church, the twin-towered **Sebalduskirche,** is just down the road from the Fembohaus. The original structure, closely modeled on the Dom in Bamberg, was erected in the thirteenth century in the transitional style between Romanesque and Gothic, with a choir at both ends of the building. A century later, the eastern chancel was replaced by a soaring hall design. An astonishing array of works of art—enough to make any museum curator green with envy—can be found inside. Particularly striking is the bronze **shrine of St. Sebald,** an early sixteenth-century masterpiece which combines late Gothic and Renaissance decoration and is heavy with religious symbols: the snails and dolphins at the base represent the world of living creatures and are a reference to newer humanist ideas, whereas the Apostles belong to traditional Christian faith. **Peter Vischer the Elder,** aided by his two sons, took eleven years to complete this project; look out for the self-portrait of the master founder at work, dressed in skullcap and apron. On the pillar behind is an expressive *Crucifixion* scene (whose figures are taken from two separate groups, made two decades apart) by Nürnberg's most famous sculptor, **Veit Stoss.** The same artist also made the statue of Saint Andrew, and the three stone *Passion* reliefs on the end walls of the chancel; the latter were his first commission on his return to Nürnberg following a brilliantly successful twenty-year interlude in the service of the kings of Poland—ever since, Stoss has been rated by the Poles as their greatest-ever artist. Facing the church is the **Pfarrhof;** this otherwise plain fourteenth-century parish house is adorned with a magnificent carved oriel window, known as the *Chörlein* ("Little Choir").

Just to the east is the **Altes Rathaus,** a self-confident late Renaissance building in the style of a Venetian *palazzo* which incorporates two older houses. If you're into the gorier side of medieval times, visit the torture chambers in the **Lochgefängnisse** underneath (May–Sept. Mon.–Fri. 10am–4pm, Sat. and Sun. 10am–1pm; DM3, DM1 students).

Commercial heart of the city and main venue for weekly markets and the famous Christmas market, the **Hauptmarkt** is a couple of minutes' walk away. Its east side is bounded by the **Frauenkirche**, one of the first buildings by the Parler family (see Architectural Chronology, *Contexts*), commissioned by Emperor Charles IV as his court chapel. The facade was enlivened in the early sixteenth century by the addition of a gable, an oriel, and a clockwork mechanism known as the *Männleinlaufen*, which tinkles away for the tourists each day at noon. The rather recondite story it tells is of the seven Electors who honored the church's founder in 1356 on the occasion of his designating Nürnberg the city in which every new emperor had to hold his first Imperial Diet.

Also on the Hauptmarkt is a copy of the famous late fourteenth-century **Schöner Brunnen** (*Beautiful Fountain*). A tall stone pyramid chiseled out in fili-gree style and adorned with statues of the Electors accompanied by pagan, Jewish and Christian heroes, prophets, evangelists, and church fathers, it looks more like a lost church spire than a fountain. In Rathausgasse, a lighter note is struck by the Renaissance **Gänsemännchen Brunnen**, which shows a farmer carrying two water-spouting geese to market. Equally entertaining is the **Ehekarussell Brunnen**, on the Ludwigsplatz at the western end of the pedes-trian zone: based on a poem by the celebrated cobbler Hans Sachs (see below), it displays six scenes from marriage, humorously alternating between bliss and nightmare.

East of the Hauptmarkt is Egidienplatz, on the north side of which stands the **Pellerhaus**. Originally the finest patrician house in the city, it was almost totally destroyed in the war, but the arcaded late Renaissance courtyard has been pains-takingly reconstructed. Farther east, in the shadow of the modern University buildings, the earlier **Tucherschlösschen**, home of another (still prominent) Nürnberg dynasty, has survived in better shape (guided tours Mon.–Fri. 2pm, 3pm and 4pm, Sun. 10am and 11am; DM1.50).

Walking southwards from Hauptmarkt, you cross the River Pegnitz by Museumsbrücke, which gives you a good view of the **Fleischbrücke** to the right (modeled on the Rialto Bridge in Venice) and the **Heilig-Geist-Spital** on the left. The latter—one of the largest hospitals built in the Middle Ages—stands on an islet, with two graceful arches spanning the water. Now a restaurant, it has an old-world inner courtyard with wooden galleries.

Passing the oldest house in the city, the thirteenth-century **Nassauer Haus**, you shortly come to the **Lorenzkirche**. At first sight, it's remarkably similar in appearance to the Sebalduskirche. The reason for this goes back to the fact that Nürnberg grew out of two separate settlements on either side of the River Pegnitz, which competed with each other for the most imposing church. In fact, it soon becomes apparent that, notwithstanding nearly identical shapes and floor-plans, the churches are actually quite different, with the constituent parts of the Lorenzkirche built about fifty years after those of its counterpart. Thus the nave, complete with a resplendent rose window, is modeled on the High Gothic cathe-drals in France, while the hall chancel, lit by a gleaming set of stained-glass windows, is in the Flamboyant style. The interior is jam-packed with artistic masterpieces. Look out for the graceful late fifteenth-century **tabernacle** some 20m high, worked out of local sandstone by **Adam Kraft**, who depicted himself as a pensive figure crouching at the base. Equally spectacular is the larger-than-life polychrome wood *Annunciation* by **Veit Stoss** which is suspended from the ceiling above the high altar. It's set in a garland of roses and rosary beads; if you look closely you'll see seven small roundels depicting the mysteries of this cult.* Outside the church is another wonderful fountain, the Mannerist **Tugendbrunnen**, in which water gushes from the breasts of the Seven Virtues and from the trumpets of the putti.

Farther down Konigstrasse in the direction of the Hauptbahnhof sits the massive and austere Renaissance **Mauthalle**, whose sloping roof is pierced by six tiers of windows. Formerly a granary and later a customs house, it's now a restaurant. Beyond is the Gothic **Marthakirche**, whose main claim to fame is that it served as the hall of the *Meistersinger*. Nürnberg was only one of many homes of the distinctive form of lyric poetry known as *Meistergesang*, which flourished from the fourteenth century onwards, practiced mainly by members of the skilled artisan class. The rules were highly pedantic, with words having to be fitted to *Töne* composed by thirteenth-century minstrels, and by the sixteenth century it had become a rather moribund art, despite a relaxation of the restrictions placed on the introduction of new *Töne*. However, it had a glorious final fling in Nürnberg, thanks above all to **Hans Sachs**. For a man who had to fit his literary activities into his spare time away from his trade of shoemaking, Sachs was unbelievably prolific, producing some 6000 works, including well over 100 full-length plays which do not, however, show him at his best. Apart from some of the most accomplished *Meistergesänge*, Sachs wrote *Schwänke* (humorous stories told in doggerel verse) and *Fastnachtspiele* (dramatic interludes performed at Shrovetide). He was also a propagandist for the Reformation, coining Luther's proudly borne nickname of "the Nightingale of Wittenberg." That grandest of grand operas, Wagner's *Die Meistersinger von Nürnberg*, is a celebration of the art of Sachs and his cronies; though historically rather wayward, it ranks as the most spectacular of the many tributes paid to the city by the Romantic movement.

Finally, if you've time or inclination there's the **Handwerkerhof** (March 20–Dec. 23 daily 10am–6:30pm; restaurants open until 9pm) by the Königstor, an enclosed "medieval" village that brings to life historic Nürnberg trades such as handmade tin soldiers, dolls, brass objects, and the famed *Lebkuchen* spice-cakes. Hot *Apfelstrudel* or the local delicacy of *Nürnberger Bratwürste* for sale in old-style taverns are very tasty.

Nürnberg's Museums

The **Germanisches Nationalmuseum** on Kornmarkt (Tues.–Sun. 9am–5pm, Thurs also 8–9:30pm; DM4, DM1.50 students; free on Sun. and Thurs. evening), which concentrates almost exclusively on the German cultural tradition, is one of the largest and most varied collections in the country. It occupies the late fourteenth-century **Karthaus** (*Charterhouse*) which is itself of considerable interest, being the most complete example of this type of monastery in Germany, though the modern galleries which have been added to provide badly needed extra display space seriously mar the effect. That drawback apart, there's a great deal to enjoy in a museum which really does live up to the claim of having something for everyone. Several visits are necessary to see it thoroughly—and to figure out its rambling and confusing layout.

On the ground floor, the first rooms contain the earliest items, ranging from a golden cone from the Bronze Age to the tenth-century *Echternach* Gospels. Immediately following is the section devoted to medieval **stone sculptures** from some of Nürnberg's most famous buildings, brought here for conservation

---

* The reason the Protestant churches of Nürnberg retain an unusually large number of art treasures, including many with "idolatrous" subjects is that the oligarchic city council which adopted the Reformation consisted of the very same patrician families who had commissioned these works, sometimes only a few years before. Not surprisingly, they were reluctant to scrap what they had so recently paid for.

reasons, and replaced in situ with faithful copies. The two most impressive objects are the *Chörlein* from the Pfarrhof of the Sebalduskirche, and the remaining parts of the original *Schöner Brunnen*; there are also figures from the portals of the two great parish churches. You next enter the **Karthauskirche**, which still preserves the simple Gothic form favored by the silent Carthusian monks. The most important exhibits here are the reliefs of *The Seven Stations of the Cross* by **Adam Kraft**, which originally lined the road to the St. Johannisfriedhof.

In the adjoining cloister are carvings by **Veit Stoss**, including an anguished *Crucifixion*, a light-hearted pair of *Tobias and the Archangel Raphael*, and the *Rosenkranztafel*. The last-named is a large wooden panel graphically portraying the drama of Judgment Day and incorporating many smaller scenes within the whole, including one character cheerfully defecating into the mouth of another in hell. A few sculptures by the other great woodcarver of the day, **Tilman Riemenschneider**—notably a noble figure of *St. Elizabeth*— can be seen in the gallery beyond, which is chiefly devoted to fifteenth-century painting. There are examples of many of the Cologne masters, with **Stefan Lochner's** *Crucifixion and Saints* standing out. However, the most important work here is *The Annunciation*, one of the best of the few surviving works of **Conrad Witz**, who played a crucial role in moving German painting towards a greater sense of realism: the perspective attempted in this panel is a world away from the flat backgrounds found in most of the other paintings here. Next comes an outstanding collection of historical **musical instruments**, which occupies the whole of the south wing.

German painting at its Renaissance peak dominates the first floor. Here at last you can see some **Dürer** originals. *Hercules Slaying the Stymphalian Birds* is a fairly early work; curiously enough, in view of the popularity of classical subjects at the time, it's the only mythological painting by the artist to have survived. The pair of imaginary portraits of *The Emperor Charlemagne* and *The Emperor Sigismund* were commissioned to adorn the room in which the imperial treasury (now in Vienna) was kept during the years it was displayed in Nürnberg; the actual crown, orb, and scepter are accurately depicted in the paintings. In contrast, *Emperor Maximilian I* is a portrait made from life, though Dürer doesn't seem to have been as inspired by the sitter as he was by *Michael Wolgemut*. Dürer had served his apprenticeship in Wolgemut's studio, and this touching yet unsentimental portrayal of his former teacher, by then a wrinkled old man of 82, is proof of the depth of gratitude he felt for the quality of training he had received. Three panels from a dispersed series of *The Life of St. Florian* by **Altdorfer** use the landscapes of the Danube valley to impressive effect; this same backdrop also occurs in **Baldung's** *Rest on the Flight into Egypt*. Most interesting of several works by **Cranach** is *King Christian II of Denmark*; the monarch had by then been deposed and had fled to Wittenberg, where he stayed as the artist's house guest.

The following rooms focus on the diversity of Nürnberg's achievements during the Renaissance. There was a strong tradition of craftsmanship in gold and silver, shown to best effect in the superbly fashioned model of a three-masted ship. The city also played a leading role in the fast-developing science of geography, and you can see the first globe of the earth, made by **Martin Behaim** in 1491—just before the discovery of America. From three-quarters of a century later is a globe of the heavens by another local man, Wenzel Jamnitzer.

This floor's south wing is entirely devoted to German **folklore**, and in particular religious traditions which show the roots of customs still very much alive in rural areas. Exhibits concentrate mostly on Catholic worship, notably *Votivgaben* or votive offerings. These take weird forms: wax toads were offered for help with women's complaints, and hollow clay heads filled with grain, the symbol of fertility. It's also worth searching out the costume and textile collection, with its traditional Sunday-best clothes and headgear, some intricately designed and embroidered, some starkly black and white. The rooms showing domestic life are excellently presented in reconstructed sections of farms, each in a different regional style, and complete with all the utensils and furniture the country people of the eighteenth and nineteenth centuries would have had.

Nürnberg also has two important special-interest museums. The **Spielzeugmuseum** (in the process of moving—ask at the tourist office for venue) has a large collection of toys down the ages and from all over the world. It's a must for kids—but is just as enjoyable for adults, who can have a sentimental wallow in nostalgia. The **Verkehrsmuseum** (*Transport Museum*) at Lessingstr. 6 (April–Sept. daily 9am–5pm, Oct.–March Mon.–Fri. 10am–4pm, Sat. and Sun. 10am–5pm; DM4, DM2 students) concentrates on the history of German railroads and has many of the original locomotives, including the country's first train (named the *Adler* after Germany's symbol), parked in its showrooms. Most of them can be inspected from the inside as well. There's also an instructive section on the role of the railroads during the Third Reich.

Nürnberg under the Nazis

In virtually everyone's mind the word Nürnberg conjures up thoughts of Nazi rallies and the war-crime trials. And in most peoples' memories are the scratchy black-and-white newsreels of fanatical crowds roaring *"Sieg Heil,"* and of Göring, Ribbentrop, and other leaders standing in the dock a few years later. Nürnberg has the unenviable task of facing up to its historical role more closely and openly than other cities, and the local tourist board, to its credit, has made a positive move towards helping visitors get to grips with the events of that time. On the Zeppelin and Mars fields, the site of the rallies, Albert Speer's Stadium and Congress Hall lie derelict, used for the occasional pop concert or car race. The tourist board has put together a multi-media presentation called "Fascination and Force," but the atmosphere of the stadium, with the darkly remembered images of the massive, impersonal rallies, needs little explanation. Ask for the leaflet "Nürnberg 1933–1945" from the tourist office, and also for details of the film show (available May–Oct.) about the Nazis and their rallies.

As the present city council is eager to point out, the Nazis' choice of Nürnberg as the backdrop for their *Reichsparteitage* had little to do with local support of the "brown" ideology, and much more to do with what the medieval city represented in German history. Also, the local police made it very easy for the NSDAP to gain the upper hand here, since they resented centralized Bavarian control and hoped to gain more independence if the Nazis took over. The rallies themselves were held each year between 1933 and 1938, Hitler using the 1938 rally to raise world tension during the Munich crisis. The most important display of Nazi power at home and abroad, they were highly organized and ritualized mass demonstrations, with Hitler's speeches forming the climax of the show. Up to 250,000 people took part in these events—expertly stage-managed and totally hypnotic for the mass of participants. The best record of the week-long rallies is Leni Riefenstahl's film *Triumph of the Will*, a lyrical, often poetic hymn to Nazism.

The passing of the "Nürnberg Laws" in 1935 deprived Jews of their citizenship and forbade relations between Jews and Gentiles. It was through these laws that the Nazis justified their extermination of six million Jews, 10,000 of whom came from Nürnberg. Only ten remained here after the war. So it was highly significant that the war criminals of the Nazi regime were tried in the city formerly used for their proudest demonstrations of power. Ten of the most important Nazi officials were hanged here on October 16 1946: Keitel, Ribbentrop, Rosenburg, Kaltenbrunner, Frank, Frich, Streicher, Sauckel, Jodl, and Seyss-Inquart. Ex-Field Marshall Hermann Göring committed suicide by swallowing a concealed cyanide pill just hours before his appointed execution. Of the rest, 177 Nazi leaders were tried and sentenced.

Eating, Drinking, and Nightlife

Nürnberg is the liveliest Bavarian city next to Munich, with a wealth of *Studentenkneipen* catering to the large student population, and plenty of café-bars to assuage their not-inconsiderable thirst. So large is the selection of every kind of establishment that the following can only be an introduction into the jungle of the city's entertainments and culinary offerings. Best way to find out what's going on around town is either the *Monatsmagazin* (DM2) available from the tourist office, or the *Plärrer* magazine (DM3) available from any kiosk, packed with daily listings and contact addresses. The addresses and relevant public transit are listed for all places mentioned here, but many are in the Altstadt and quicker to reach on foot if you're staying downtown.

Eating

If the Bavarian's favorite snack is a *Weisswurst*, the Franconian's is the *Bratwurst*. These are slim pork sausages, roasted over wood fires and served with either sauerkraut or potato salad. Equally ubiquitous are Nürnberger *Lebkuchen*, delicious spice cakes made from flour, nuts, honey, eggs, and spices. Usually they're only eaten around Christmas; this is the only place you can buy them all year round.

The **cheapest meals** in town are to be found in the youth hostel where residents can eat a hot dinner for around DM6, and the University **mensa**, located in the concrete boxes that make up the University in the north-eastern corner of the Altstadt. Otherwise there are plenty of *Imbiss*-type snack-joints huddle in the pedestrian zone between St. Lorenz and the Ehekarussel, and most restaurants serve a plate of sausages plus side dish for around DM8.

If you want to combine reasonably priced food with a bit of socializing and a good atmosphere, head for the *Frankens U-Bahn* (Pilotystr. 73; tram #4 to Juvenellstrasse). Excellent meals and similar atmosphere can also be found in the following: *Zum Peter* (Regensburger Str. 51; tram #4 to Peterskirche) and *Palais Schaumburg* (Kernstr. 46; U-Bahn to Gostenhof). These two also have **beer gardens** attached and all three include vegetarian dishes on their menu, though the *Schaumburg* is best and cheapest for vegetarian food. For a choice of riverside beer garden or cool vaulted cellar, try *Pele-Mele* (Grossweidenmühlstr. 17; bus #34 to Grossweidenmühlstrasse). If you prefer a traditional *Gasthaus* and picturesque beer garden, also by the river Pegnitz, try the *Kettensteg* (Kettensteg; bus #36 to Hallertor). Excellent Spanish meals in a bar-type setting are served at the *Zig-Zag* (Rohledererstr. 6; tram #6 to Hallerstrasse).

Drinking

Nürnberg's bars aim to cater to the wealthy, so if that's not your scene you're better off sticking with places like the *Ruhestörung*.

For evening drinking, the *Starclub* (Maxtorgraben 33; bus #47 to Maxtor) is a combination of beer haven and music bar, with a tiny beer garden thrown in for good measure, while the café-bar *Ruhestörung* (Tetzelgasse 21; bus #47 to Rathaus) is one of the main young and trendy watering holes, always worth looking in at. If you like the idea of spare car parts for interior design and your beer served out of a gas pump, try the *Werkstatt* (Adam-Klein-Str. 87; U-Bahn to Maximilianstrasse). Outside the city center and a bit off the beaten track there's an Irish pub: *O'Neill's* (Bärenschanzstr. 121; U-Bahn to Bärenschanze). The *Zabo-Linde* (Zerzabelshofer Hauptstr. 28; bus #43 or #44 to Zerzabelshof/Mitte) combines a traditional *Gaststätte* and beer garden with regular live music, ranging from rock to disco. Worth making the trip out for, if the evening's music program happens to appeal to you. (Check in the *Plärrer*.) For **late-night** weekend drinking and occasional live music, the *Landwehr* (Schlotfegergasse 36; U-Bahn to Weisser Turm) is a good choice, and has the advantage of also serving late-night food.

For those with a more expansive wallet, the following are good starting points: the *Freudenpark* (Kilianstr. 125; bus #46 to Langer Steig) has a thirty-page drinks list that should keep you busy, and the *Cosmopolitan* (Johannisstr. 40; tram #6 to Hallerstrasse; Tues–Sun 6pm–1am) serves excellent cocktails and a few snacks. Art deco fans will appreciate the interior of the *Vogel-Bar* (Pirkheimerstr. 7; tram #9 to Friedrich-Ebert-Platz), which serves a choice of 160 cocktails to a very yuppie clientele. The excellent café-bar *Meisengeige* (Innere-Laufer-Gasse 37; bus #36 to Innerer-Laufer-Platz) is tiny, but caters to a mixed and less pretentious crowd. There's also a small **movie theater** attached that runs an off-beat selection of films you won't find in the first-run houses.

Something (thankfully) peculiar to Nürnberg is the inordinate number of **heavy metal bars**. If you want to give your ear drums a pounding the *Rock-Café Brown Sugar* (Marientorgraben 3; tram #13 to Marientor) is about the best, with pinball machines and videos among the heady attractions. Two more to try out are the *ON-U* (Rothenburger Str. 57; U-Bahn to Rothenburgerstrasse) and the *Metal-Mania* (Comeniusstr. 2; U-Bahn to Hauptbahnhof).

Slightly more amusing and certainly quieter are two **jazz bars**: *Schmelztiegel* (Bergstr. 21; tram #4 to Tiergärtnertor) plays predominantly Dixieland, and *Steps* (Johannisstr. 83; bus #34 to Brückenstrasse) plays anything but Dixieland.

Nürnberg has a shortage of good **cafés**, but *Balazzo Brozzi* (Hochstr. 2; tram #4 to Obere Turnstrasse) is a useful place to start the day if you want a choice of cheap and decent breakfast dishes. More traditional though far from cheap, the *Mohr* (Färberstr. 3; U-Bahn to Weisser Turm) serves excellent crêpes.

Nightclubs

Good nightclubs are hard to find in Nürnberg. The most unusual venue is *Das Boot* (Hafenstr. 500; bus #67 to Rotterdamer Strasse; Sun.–Thurs. 8pm–4am, Fri. 8pm–8am, Sat. 8pm–9am; DM3 weekdays, DM10 weekends). As you'd expect from the name, this was a ship whose three decks have been converted into a disco. In compensation for the weekend prices, your ticket entitles you to DM6 off your first drink.

However, the trendiest nightclub in Nürnberg at the moment is the *Mach 1* (Kaiserstr. 1–9; U-Bahn to Lorenzkirche; Wed.–Sun. 9pm–4am; budget on about DM10 to get in), which ensures variety with four different bars, and some good lighting effects. Rather cozier, and offering TV, video games, and pinball machines, is the *Dröhnland* (Humboldstr. 116; U-Bahn to Aufsessplatz; daily 7pm–1am; DM5). It's popular with people who like going to nightclubs without having to make too much of an effort, and also serves food. For **country-and-western** fans the *Lonestar* (Felsenstr. 5; bus #67 to Grosskraftwerk; daily 7pm–3am; charge for live gigs only) caters mainly to the American GIs from the nearby base in Fürth.

Only two of the **gay nightclubs** are marginally worth a visit: the *Amico* (Köhnstr. 53; tram #13 to Widhalmstrasse; Sun.–Wed. 9pm–2am, Fri.–Sat. 9pm–3am) has a tiny dance floor, and is more a place for drinking than dancing. The *Comeback* (Engelhardgasse 2/Ottostrasse; U-Bahn to Weisser Turm; daily 8pm–4am; DM5) is only a disco during the summer and otherwise it's a very expensive *Pilsbar*, a bit too respectable for most people's liking.

Culture, Festivals, and Annual Events

The main **theater** venue, with the *Opernhaus* and the *Schauspielhaus*, is at Richard-Wagner-Platz, just a few minutes' walk to the west of the Hauptbahnhof. **Concerts**, notably those by the *Nürnberger Symphoniker*, are held at the *Meistersingerhalle*, some 2km southeast of downtown. Nürnberg really comes alive in the summer when **open-air music festivals and concerts** abound. A special calendar entitled *Sommer in Nürnberg* is available from the tourist board, and tickets are available from *AZ-Kartenvorverkauf* (Winklerstr. 15); *Karstadt-Kartenvorverkauf* (An der Lorenzkirche 2); *Kartenvorverkauf Werner* (Bretie Gasse 47).

The **Bardentreffen** in the first week of August is a popular annual event where singers and songwriters from Europe come together in free open-air concerts all over the city. Ask at the tourist office for dates and venues. An **International Organ Festival** is held in late June. Concerts are held in the city's churches as well as the *Meistersingerhalle*. For information and tickets contact *Internationale Orgelwoche* (Bismarkstr. 46, ☎163528). An equally high status is enjoyed by the **East-West Jazz Festival**, which encompasses every jazz style and brings together musicians from both sides of the border. This festival takes place during the last week in April.

The **Norisring Car Races** in late June are held on Germany's most famous track, when the stars of the racing world slog it out for the International German Car Racing Championship. For information and tickets contact *MCN Motorsport-Club Nürnberg* (Spittlertorgraben 47, ☎267990). Towards the end of September, the **Altstadtfest** is a local fair celebrating Franconian culture, with lots of food and drink, as well as river tournaments and a procession in traditional costumes.

Finally, with a 400-year tradition, the Nürnberg **Christmas market** (*Christkindlesmarkt*) held on the Hauptmarkt is the largest and most popular in Germany, as well as being the founder of what has become very much a national institution, with derivatives found in every town of any size. It usually runs from November 25 until December 24, and is set apart from the others by the wealth of quality handmade goods on sale, such as toys, brass utensils and tin soldiers, glass objects of all kinds, and, of course, the delicious *Lebkuchen*.

Listings

Airport Nürnberg has an important regional airport, also with international connections. *Air France*, *Alitalia*, *Lufthansa*, *PanAm* and *Swissair* operate regular services from here. For airport information phone ☎3506 200.

Area code (☎0911)

Car rental *Avis Rent-a-Car* (airport, ☎49696 or ☎528966); *Hertz* (airport, Untere Grasergasse 25, ☎209086 or ☎527719); *ES Europa-Service*, Fürther Str. 31 (☎260308).

Guided tours The tour operator *Reba-Eno Reisen* (Hallplatz 2, ☎204033) runs city tours lasting 2½ hours, in English (May–Oct., daily at 9:30am, DM15, DM7.50 kids.

Hospital Flurstr. 17 (☎3980). U-Bahn to Ostenhof, then bus #34 heading towards Rathenauerplatz.

Laundromats On the corner of Obstmarkt and Bindergasse.

Mitfahrzentrale Allersbergerstr. 31a (☎446 9666).

Medical emergencies Kesslerplatz (☎533771).

Post Restante Bahnhofsplatz 1 (☎2171).

Taxis (☎20555).

Women's bookshop Innerer Kleinreuther Weg 28 (Mon.–Fri. 10am–6pm, Sat. 10am–1pm; ☎352403).

Women's center Saldorferstr. 6 (☎263309); U-Bahn to Gostenhof. Runs an evening bar on Tues., Fri., and Sat.

Ansbach

ANSBACH, 25km east of Nürnberg, is the former seat of the Margraves of Brandenburg-Ansbach, one of the offshoots of the Hohenzollern family. It wears a grand air which is quite disproportionate to its small size: having chosen the town as their home, the local nobility were keen to have a seat of suitable splendor, and over the centuries Ansbach became quite polished, its streets characterized by Renaissance and baroque buildings. Alongside its architecture, Ansbach has gone down in the annals of German history as the site of the unsolved murder of enigmatic **Kaspar Hauser**, Europe's most notorious foundling, and the local museum devotes itself to his life and times.

The Renaissance **Residenzschloss** (daily 9am–noon and 2–5pm; DM2.50) is situated just on the edge of the old town center, and is best known for its rococo interior. Highlights are the high-ceilinged ballroom, the "Cabinet of Mirrors," and the "Porcelain Gallery," which displays thousands of delicately designed tiles made in the local factory. Just across the road the **Hofgarten** and **Orangerie** form a pleasant setting for walks along paths lined by centuries-old trees. It's in this park that poor Kaspar Hauser was stabbed to death in 1833, and just next to the Orangerie is a stone memorial with the inscription: "Here died a man unknown by means unknown."

As the story goes, a young boy came wandering into Nürnberg one day in 1828, plainly dressed and carrying a letter for the local dignitary Friedrich von Wessenig. In it the anonymous sender wrote, "I hereby send you a boy who wants to serve his king." The boy's name was Kaspar Hauser, but he was unable to tell anyone where he came from or write anything except his name. His appearance caused a sensation in the local press and across Germany, with all kinds of wild speculation as to his origins. One particularly popular theory held that he was an illegitimate son of the noble house of Baden.

In due course Kaspar was educated and proved to be highly intelligent and creative, becoming a celebrated and notorious journalist and artist. But apparently he didn't enjoy being the constant subject of lurid articles and popular attention, so he moved to Ansbach in 1831 in the hope of a more peaceful life. This proved to be a false hope, however, since two years later he was stabbed to death in a local park. His murderer was never found, adding a final unsettling mystery to Kaspar's story. Much has been written about him since, little of it conclusive. The local **museum** (Schaitbergerstr. 10 and 14; Tues.–Sun. 10am–noon and 2–5pm; DM1) documents all this in a comprehensive fashion, though you'll need to know some German to get the most from the exhibition.

The **St. Gumbertus-Kirche**, right in the middle of the old town, is especially interesting architecturally. Being one of the places that embraced the Reformation, Ansbach rejected the extravagant baroque of Catholic regions. The style developed in its place is plainer and less vivid than its counterpart, but has a distinctive elegance of its own. St. Gumbertus was originally part of a Romanesque Benedictine monastery, but the only remainder from that period is the **crypt** (Fri.–Sun. 11am–noon and 3–5pm). Elsewhere, the interior ranks as the best example of Lutheran baroque to be found in Bavaria today, and is certainly a classic among German Protestant churches; all slate gray and cream, without paintings or side altars, it presents a cool clarity. The church's focus is the small marble altar, and above it the pulpit marks the only splash of gold in the whole interior. Encircling the church on three sides is a gallery, which is the best vantage point from which to get a good impression of the complete effect.

A number of **festivals** take place in Ansbach, of which the best known is the *Bach Week*, which occurs every two years at the end of July. Concerts are held in St. Gumbertus, which has excellent acoustics. The *Ansbacher Rokokospiele* are period plays performed in the Residenzschloss and the local parks at the beginning of July each year. Every four years, the *Heimatfest* (next in 1990) is a grand occasion where eighteenth-century music and dance play the most important part, but there's also a fair with plenty of regional delicacies. For inquiries about these as well as the usual tourist services, visit the **tourist office** in the Rathaus on Martin-Luther-Platz (Mon.–Fri. 8:30am–12:30pm and 2–5pm; ☎0981 51243).

Dinkelsbühl and Rothenburg ob der Tauber

The **Romantic Road**, which winds its way along the length of western Bavaria, enters the Franconian region just before **DINKELSBÜHL**, which lies some 40km southeast of Ansbach, and 30km north of the previous stop at NÖRDLINGEN. Most tourists break their journey here—usually for a twenty-minute stroll before returning to the bus laden with souvenirs. Then it's on, past picturesque villages such as FEUCHTWANGEN, to the unchallenged star of medieval views: ROTHENBURG OB DER TAUBER, 45km north. Both Dinkelsbühl and Rothenburg are almost completely closed to traffic, which makes wandering around much more pleasurable, and the impression of a medieval town more authentic. Half-timbered houses photogenically line the cobbled streets, and the old ramparts encircling everything offer wonderful bird's-eye views of pointed red-tiled roofs and church spires. Surprisingly, accommodation isn't that expensive, though the plethora of souvenir shops and cafés certainly are.

In Dinkelsbühl the best thing to do is just wander as the fancy takes you. The central building is the **Georgenkirche**, an airily light Gothic hall church with slender pillars and elaborate network vaults which is very similar to its Nördlingen counterpart, except for the tower that remains from the Romanesque church which formerly occupied the site. Most outstanding of the old houses is the fifteenth-century half-timbered **Deutsches Haus** on Weinmarkt. If you want to follow a guided route around the others, then the **tourist office** on Marktplatz (Mon.–Fri. 9am–noon and 2–6pm, Sat. and Sun. 10am–noon and 2–4pm; ☎09851 90240) provides a free brochure.

You can also reserve accommodation there, though the cheapest **guesthouse** is *Roter Hahn* (Lange Gasse 16, ☎09851 2225), which charges DM21–35 per person. Similar prices can be expected at *Goldenes Lamm* (Lange Gasse 26–28, ☎09851 2267); *Sonne und Palmengarten* (Weinmarkt 11 and Schmiedgasse 14, ☎09851 2330 and ☎09851 6044); *Zum Nördlinger Tor* (Nördlinger Str. 46, ☎09851 456); and *Pension Lutz* (Schäfergässlein 4, ☎09851 454). The **youth hostel** is at Kopengasse 10 (☎09851 509 or ☎09851 825).

For ten days in mid-July, Dinkelsbühl hosts a major **popular festival**, the *Kinderzeche*. This commemorates the occasion in the Thirty Years' War when the marauding Swedish troops intended to destroy the town, but were dissuaded by a deputation of local kids. The events are re-enacted in plays performed in the Kornhaus, while on each of the two Sundays there's a pageant through the streets. Music is provided by the *Knabenkapelle*; perhaps the best known boys' band in Germany, its members are gussied up (ominously or charmingly, depending on your point of view) like little soldiers in red-and-white eighteenth-century uniform.

ROTHENBURG OB DER TAUBER is the most famous and most visited medieval town in Germany, and although it's very beautiful, and completely preserved in its original form, it has been reduced to the ultimate museum-piece with little life of its own except that which revolves around the tourist trade. In spite of being a classic tourist-trap it should still merit at least one overnight stop: the only way to get this place to yourself is to stay the night and go out, either early in the morning or in the evening, when the crowds have gone.

Perched high above the River Tauber in its deep furrow of a valley, the location of Rothenburg is a good reason to use the town as a base, especially if you're in the mood for country walks. The highly efficient **tourist office** on Marktplatz (Mon.–Fri. 9am–noon and 2–6pm, Sat. 9am–noon; ☎09861 40492) has produced a small map with marked paths on it, as well as all the other brochures you'd expect to find.

Rothenburg's status as the only walled medieval town in Germany without a single modern building is due to a fortuitous series of circumstances. Its prosperous medieval period was followed by a spectacular slump in its fortunes as it found itself cut off from the new trading routes and reduced to the status of a very provincial market town. Without money to expand or erect new buildings, it vegetated until the nineteenth century, when its self-evident attraction for the Romantic movement led to the enforcement of strict preservation orders. Having already had a narrow escape from total destruction in the Thirty Years' War (see below), it was similarly fortunate to survive World War II, when it lay directly in the path of the American advance. Thankfully, a civilian working for the U.S. army, J. J. McCloy (later the High Commissioner to Germany), knew and loved Rothenburg, and persuaded the generals to spare it from saturation shelling.

It takes about half an hour to walk around the town via the **sentry walk** on the fourteenth-century wall and the old moat, and that's the best way to get your bearings and a first impression. Tightly packed within, the town's houses get larger towards the middle, where the local patricians and merchants lived. Nearer the wall, tradesfolk and peasants lived in crooked little dolls' houses, half-timbered and with steeply pointed roofs. A map of Rothenburg reveals a kind of question-mark shape, and its elongated southern stalk contains the old hospital quarter. The two **youth hostels** are located down here, one in the courtyard of the **Spital** itself, the other around the corner, in an old mill called **Rossmühle**.

To the western side of town, a small bulge sticks out on to a promontory formed by a twist in the Tauber below. In the early Middle Ages there used to be a castle here, but it was destroyed by a violent earthquake in 1356. The only parts remaining from that period are the **Burgtor** watchtower, which is the oldest of all the 24 towers, and the **Blasiuskapelle**, with murals dating from the fourteenth century. You get the best view of the Tauber valley from here as well. The nearby **Herrngasse** leads up to the town center, and is the widest street in Rothenburg, being where the local bigwigs lived. It's well worth taking time to look into the courtyards of these mansions, particularly that of the **Staudtsches Haus**, with its wrought iron gratings, galleries, oriel window and staircase tower. Also on this street is the severe early Gothic **Franziskanerkirche**, which still preserves its rood screen to divide the monks from the laity. Its walls and floor are covered with funerary monuments to local families, and there's a startlingly realistic fifteenth-century retable showing *The Stigmatization of St. Francis*.

The sloping **Marktplatz** is dominated by the arcaded front of the **Renaissance Rathaus**, which supplanted the Gothic building which stands behind it. Its sixty-meter-high **tower** (April–Oct. daily 9:30am–12:30pm and 1–5pm; DM 1.50) is the highest point in Rothenburg and provides the best view of the town and surrounding countryside. The original **Gothic Rathaus** (daily 8am-6pm; free) is separated from the newer one by a covered courtyard, which is where you'll find the crumbly old entrance, unchanged for centuries. Inside are sixteenth-century furnishings and a stark imperial hall dating from the thirteenth century; this was often used as the main law court, and prisoners were kept in dungeons just below, said to be more dreadful than any others of the day.

The other main tourist attractions on the Marktplatz are the figures that look out of the windows either side of the three clocks on the gable of the **Ratsherrntrinkstube**. Every day at 11am, noon, 1pm, 2pm, 3pm, 9pm, and 10pm, the two figures re-enact the most famous moment in Rothenburg's history. In 1631, during the Thirty Years' War, the imperial army, led by the fearsome Johann Tilly, captured the town and intended to destroy it as a punishment for its support of the Protestant cause. In a gesture of peace, the general was brought the huge civic tankard known as the *Meistertrunk*, filled with wine to its capacity of 3.25 liters, and was persuaded to accept the wager that Rothenburg should be spared if one of the councillors could chugalug the contents. The former burgomaster Georg Nusch duly obliged: it's supposed to have taken him ten minutes, after which he needed three days to sleep off the effects.

Nusch's home, now an inn called *Roter Hahn*, can be seen at Schmiedgasse 21, which leads off the southeastern corner of Marktplatz. Another of Rothenburg's most famous mayors, Heinrich Toppler, lived at no. 5 on the same street, now the *Gasthof zum Greifen*. He was council leader at the time of the town's greatest prosperity, but fell into disgrace and was imprisoned in the Rathaus dungeons, dying there after two months of starvation and torture. Next door is the *Bauermeisterhaus*, the finest mansion in town, built by Leonard Weidmann, the same architect who designed the Renaissance Rathaus. The first floor is adorned with statues of the Seven Virtues; on the next level, the Seven Deadly Sins sound their warning notes. All three of these houses are now four-star **restaurants**, and the first two both have bargain menus.

To the opposite side of the Marktplatz is Rothenburg's largest building, the Gothic **St. Jakob-Kirche** (daily 9am–5:30pm; DM1.50), whose main body and two towers rise above the sea of red roofs like a great ship, visible for miles around. The entrance fee is worth paying to see the work of the famed sculptor **Tilman Riemenschneider**. His early sixteenth-century *Heilig-Blut-Altar* is exquisitely carved in linden wood, and its centerpiece shows the Last Supper, just at the point when Jesus announces that one of the disciples will betray him. The scene is unusual in that the central standing figure isn't Christ, but Judas turning to his master with the thirty pieces of silver in his hand, while Christ in turn offers him bread. Also of note is the church's high altar, the *Zwölfbotenaltar*, by the Nördlingen artist Friedrich Herlin. The outer wings illustrate *The Legend of St. James*; the scene where the dead saint's body is carried to a medieval town features a depiction of fifteenth-century Rothenburg.

One other church worth seeing is the late Gothic **St. Wolfgang** at the extreme northwestern end of town, reached via Klingengasse. Traditionally the parish of the local shepherds, it forms a unit with the **Klingentor** as a key part of the town's fortifications. On one side, the traceried windows are replaced by a formidable row of casemates, yet the church's interior is spacious and pleasing, with many fine works of art.

Of the local **museums**, the most fascinating is the **Kriminalmuseum** at Burggasse 3 (daily 9:30am–6pm; DM3), which contains extensive collections attesting to medieval inhumanity in the shape of torture instruments and related objects—for example the beer barrels that drunks were forced to walk around in. An added attraction is that all exhibits are fully labeled and explained in English.

The **Reichstadtmuseum** on Klosterhof (daily 10am–5pm; DM2.50) is located in the former Dominican convent, and is most interesting for the building's original medieval workrooms such as the kitchen complete with its former utensils. Displays relate mainly to Rothenburg's history, art, and culture, and include a selection of furniture, sculpture, paintings, and arms. Interesting also is the collection relating to Jewish local history. In the thirteenth century Rothenburg had a large settlement of Jews, but their synagogue and ghetto were destroyed in the early fifteenth-century pogroms.

If you want to find out about how medieval tradesfolk lived, the **Handwerkerhaus** on Alter Stadtgraben (daily 9am–6pm and 8–9pm; DM3) is located in a workman's house, with all the original furnishings and tools remaining. Just a few steps away, the **Puppen und Spielzeugmuseum** at Hofbronnengasse 13 (daily 9:30am–6pm; DM3.50) holds Germany's largest private collection of toys and dolls, dating from 1780 to 1940. Dolls made from materials as diverse as papier-mâché, porcelain, wood, and wax are lovingly displayed in spacious surroundings. A highlight of the collection is the display of dolls' houses.

For sights which are (relatively speaking) off the beaten track, go down the path leading from the Burggarten to the River Tauber, and cross over to see the **Topplerschlösschen** (guided tours April–Oct. 1–5pm, Nov.–March 1–4pm; DM2.50). This late fourteenth-century tower house has a bizarre top-heavy effect, with the upper stories jutting out well over the stumpy base. It was built as a summer and weekend retreat for burgomaster Heinrich Toppler. The hill behind, the **Engelsburg**, was formerly covered with vineyards; from the summit there's a superb long-range view of Rothenburg. A quite different but almost equally good panorama can be had by following the S-bend in the Tauber upstream to the **Doppelbrücke**, a Gothic viaduct faithfully reconstructed following its destruction in the war.

If you can stand the crowds, and a cloying sense of cuteness, it's worth trying to coincide your visit with one of the many **festivals**. Each Pentecost, the *Meistertrunk* drama is re-enacted—albeit with no more than a pretence at matching Nusch's feat. The preceding day sees one of the renditions of the historic *Schäfertanz* ("Shepherds' Dance") in front of the Rathaus; this is repeated on selected Sundays in spring and summer. According to one tradition, the dance began as a thanksgiving for Rothenburg's deliverance from the plague; another theory asserts that it derives from the celebration of a discovery of hidden treasure by one of the shepherds. Also at Whit, and throughout July and August, there are costume performances of plays by Hans Sachs. The second weekend in September sees the *Freiereichstadtfest*, featuring pageants and a fireworks display.

Accommodation is a little more expensive than Dinkelsbühl, but still affordable if the cheaper places are available. As mentioned earlier, the two **youth hostels** are in beautifully restored half-timbered houses off the bottom of the Spitalgasse. One is the *Rossmühle* (☎09861 4510), the other the *Spitalhof* (☎09861 7889), and there's little to choose between them. Private homes renting out rooms are the next cheapest options, charging around DM18–30 per person. Two cheap places to try would be the *Blasi* family at Alter Stadtgraben 12 (☎09861 5198), or *Frau Angermeier* at Schrannenplatz 12 (☎09861 3456). Finally, two pensions in the region of DM28–35 for singles and DM50–70 for doubles are: *Pension Schmölzer* (Rosengasse 21, ☎09861 3371) and *Pension Hofmann* (Stollengasse 29, ☎09861 3371).

DETWANG, a village about 2km further down the Tauber, makes for an easy excursion by foot. It's the next stop on the Romantic Road and is now officially part of Rothenburg, but has an even longer history. The Romanesque **Pfarrkirche** (April–Oct daily 8:30am–noon and 1:30–5pm, Nov–March Tues–Sun 10am–noon and 2–4pm) contains another masterpiece by Riemenschneider, the *Kreuzaltar*, featuring a central *Crucifixion* by the master, with wing reliefs of *The Agony in the Garden* and *The Resurrection* by his assistants.

For the next stage of the Romantic Road, which crosses into Baden-Württemberg immediately after leaving Detwang.

Würzburg

Terminus of the Romantic Road, and capital of Franconian wine, **WÜRZBURG** lies on both banks of the River Main some 60km north of Rothenburg. During the night of March 16, 1945 it got the same treatment from Allied bombers that Nürnberg had received two months earlier. It was a senseless destruction of a 1200-year-old city, with no important war industries worth mentioning, but whose downfall was the local railroad junction. However, unlike Nürnberg, Würzburg has been less successful in rebuilding itself in the old character and suffers from some rather ugly twentieth-century architecture, which spoils the overall effect. Gone is the Altstadt, and instead there are individual surprises of baroque and Gothic beauty sandwiched between modern supermarkets and the new town. For all that, Würzburg's location on the banks of the River Main, the surrounding landscape of vineyards and a number of outstanding sights such as the palatial **Residenz**, the **Festung Marienberg** and **Mainfränkisches Museum**, and a couple of interesting churches, easily justify a visit of two or three days.

Würzburg has been one of Germany's most influential episcopal cities for many centuries, and thus some of the greatest architects and artists were hired by the Catholic prince-bishops. The Residenz, for example, was entrusted to Balthasar Neumann, who was then totally unknown and untried, but who duly developed into the most inventive and accomplished architect of eighteenth-century Europe. Another famous artist associated with this city is Tilman Riemenschneider, whose sculptures with their haunting characterization, executed in the heady years leading up to the Reformation, decorate so many of Franconia's churches. Many of his finest works are displayed in the Mainfränkisches Museum.

Getting Around and Finding Somewhere to Stay

Just outside the **Hauptbahnhof** at the northern end of the city center there's a **tourist office** (Mon.–Sat. 8am–8pm; ☎37436), which will provide all the maps and brochures you'll need, and can reserve rooms for DM3. Two other offices are near the middle of town, at the *Haus zum Falken* in the Eichhornstrasse (Mon.–Fri. 9am–6pm, Sat. 9am–2pm; ☎37398), and in the *Würtzburg-Palais am Congress Centrum* near the Friedensbrücke (Mon.–Thurs. 8am–5pm, Fri. 8am–noon; ☎37335). The heart of Würzburg is quite compact, and most of what you'll want to see is within easy walking distance. An exception is the Marienburg, which sits on a steep hill the other side of the Main, and for that your best option is a #9 bus, which goes from the Alte Mainbrücke.

The local **youth hostel** (Burkarderstr. 44, ☎42590; tram #3 to Ludwigsbrücke from the Hauptbahnhof) is situated below the Marienberg fortress. The nearest **campground** (Winterhäuserstrasse, ☎705598) is in the suburb of HEIDINGSFELD, about 4km south of Würzburg and best reached by taking the #16 bus from Barbarossaplatz. Two **pensions** in the region of DM35–55 for singles and DM65–100 for doubles are: *Groene* (Scheffelstr. 2, ☎74449) and *Wörther Hof* (Frankfurter Str. 9, ☎42051/2; bus #18 from the Hauptbahnhof). **Hotel** accommodation is not very cheap here, and the best you'll manage is the reasonably central *Ochsen* (Juliuspromenade 1, ☎53546; tram #2 from the Hauptbahnhof), which charges DM37–48 for singles, DM72–85 for doubles. Failing that, it's a question of staying a kilometer or two from the town center, if you don't want to spend too much.

The City

Heart of the old city is the area between the River Main and the Residenz, roughly encompassed by the Juliuspromenade to the north and Neubaustrasse to the south. With the exception of the Marienberg fortress you'll find all the sights within this area. The **Marktplatz** is the main square, and a daily fresh food market ensures that there's always a lively bustle around here. Just off the market square, the **Haus zum Falken** is the city's prize example of a rococo town house, bristling with white stucco decorations and perfectly restored to the very last curl. It now houses one of the city's tourist offices, and also the municipal library.

Overlooking the central Markt is the fourteenth-century Gothic **Marienkapelle**, whose most interesting feature is the arch above the northern portal, on the side facing away from the square. The scene represented is *The Annunciation*, and if you look closely, you'll see that the artist has chosen to be very literal in his interpretation. There's the usual archangel with his scripted band indicating speech to Mary, but another band leads from God the Father above to Mary's ear, and tucked away in the folds of this band, a little baby is sliding down towards her. Originally the church was adorned by some of Riemenschneider's most famous statues, such as *Adam and Eve*, but they were already so badly eroded by the 19C that copies were made, and the originals are now in the Mainfränkisches Museum. Inside, the burial place of Balthasar Neumann is marked on the first pillar to the right from the market portal, and another famous local artist, the fifteenth-century painter Mathis Grünewald, is commemorated by a copy of his *Isenheim Altar*.

The Kürschnerhof, leading off the Marktplatz, continues the pedestrian shopping zone and about halfway down, the **Neumünster's** baroque facade in dusky pink stands out among the postwar houses either side. It's said to be the work of Johann Dientzenhofer, and it certainly is very stylish, its perfect symmetry highlighted by a twin set of steps leading up to the elevated entrance from either side. The church was built over the graves of the three Franconian apostles Saints Kilian, Kolonat, and Totnan, who were Irish missionaries martyred in 689 for trying to Christianize the region. Today the **Kiliani festival** at the beginning of July is Franconia's most important religious festival, during which thousands of Catholic pilgrims come here to worship and celebrate.

Inside the church are sculptures by Riemenschneider and frescoes by Johann Zimmermann, of Wieskirche fame, but the most precious element is the **St. Kilian crypt**, where the apostles are buried. The busts of the three martyrs on the thirteenth-century altar are copies of the original Riemenschneider ones, which were destroyed in 1945. If you leave the Neumünster by its northern exit, you'll come to the tiny **Lusamgärtchen** and the remains of the twelfth-century cloister. These days it's a romantically overgrown square, and in the middle is a commemorative block to the famous medieval minstrel Walther von der Vogelheide. He was the most popular poet and singer of the early thirteenth century, but also a valued political commentator of the Staufen rulers, which is why he was given a pension from the estate of this church and is assumed to have been buried in the cloister in 1230. His popularity still holds, and local residents always ensure that fresh flowers decorate his memorial stone, over 750 years after his death.

The **Dom**, again consecrated to St. Kilian, is virtually next door, but it was completely burnt out in 1945, and only the exterior is true to the original Gothic, with Neumann's baroque chapel of the Schönborn bishops added on to the north side and the sacristy and vestry on the east side. Inside, the rich stucco embellishments of the eighteenth century have only been restored in the transept and chancel, and for the rest the walls are left plain white, with surviving **tombstones** of canons and prince-bishops lining the pillars. At the end of the northern transept, the **Schönbornkapelle** holds four bishops from the house of Schönborn, whose most notable legacy are the great episcopal palaces of Würzburg, Bamberg and Bruchsal, but who also left behind many other residences, of which Schloss Weissenstein near Bamberg is the greatest.

From the cathedral, the Domstrasse leads straight on to the **Alte Mainbrücke**, the oldest bridge spanning the Main. Built in 1133, it was often damaged over the centuries, most recently in 1945, when the Allies toppled the eighteenth-century statues of the town's bishops and saints off the bridge and into the river. Designed by the prince-bishop Friedrich Carl von Schönborn, copies and some originals now oversee the traffic once again. The view from here presents Würzburg from its best side, though the prize view only comes once you're up on the Marienberg and see not just the city but the vineyards too.

The **Festung Marienberg** (guided tours April–Sept. Tues.–Sun. 9am–noon and 1–5pm, Oct.–March 10am–noon and 1–4pm; DM1.50, DM1 students) was home to the ruling bishops from the 13C until 1750, when they moved to the new palace in town. What you see today is therefore the result of 500 years of building that was usually concerned with improving fortifications against possible attack from the mob across the river. Clashes between the bishops and the people weren't uncommom, especially since the town's loyalty tended to be to the emperor and not the bishop. Two of the most momentous attacks on the fortress were the farmers' rebellion in 1525 and the Swedish occupation in 1631. The former was unsuccessful, which was unfortunate for the local mayor and artist Tilman Riemenschneider. He found himself on the wrong side of a lost battle and was locked up in the Marienberg dungeons, where he was held and tortured for eight weeks before being sent off into obscurity, to die two years later.

The Swedish sacking of Würzburg and the Marienberg was successful, however, and they carried off most of the fortress' contents as well as the state coffers, which had been brought here for safe-keeping. Among the many treasures lost at that time was the valuable court library, which can now be found in the Swedish town of Uppsala. The fortress was twice more devastated: once by the Prussian army in 1866 and latterly in 1945. So although much of the original structure has been restored, the interiors are largely missing.

The fortress consists of a central medieval core, which contains in its courtyard the round **Marienkirche**, one of Germany's oldest churches, as well as the **Brunnenhaus**, whose unbelievable 105-meter well was chiseled through rock around the year 1200 to ensure self-sufficiency in water. Surrounding this are a number of other courts from different building periods, such as the great **Echterbastei**, which was built under Julius Echter after two devastating fires in 1572 and 1600, only to be sacked by the Swedes thirty years later. The massive fortifications encasing the Marienberg were built under Philipp von Schönborn after the Swedes had left. He also built the **Zeughaus** which now houses the large **Mainfränkisches Museum** (daily April–Oct. 10am–5pm, Nov.–March 10am–4pm; DM2.50, DM1 students). First place among the collections is taken by the Riemenschneider sculptures, but there are exhibits from all genres of art through the ages, as well as an interesting display of old winepresses and odds and ends connected with the making and drinking of Franconian wine. The restaurant up here serves excellent Franconian specialties, highly recommended if you can afford to splurge a bit.

Back down in Würzburg, the **Residenz** (April–Sept. Tues.–Sun. 9am–5pm, Oct.–March Tues.–Sun. 10am–4pm; DM3.50, DM2.50 students) on the eastern edge of the town center is a truly marvelous palace set in a park to match. It was intended to symbolize all the wealth and status of the Würzburg bishops, and to show they could hold their own among such great European courts as Versailles, and Schönbrunn in Vienna. The project, however, only became feasible when Johann Philipp von Schönborn won 600,000 florins in a lawsuit in 1719, the first year of his reign. Work began the following year; the skeleton of the building was complete by 1744, with the most important decorations finished a decade later. Several leading French, German, and Austrian architects were consulted about the designs, but the construction was left largely in the hands of the prolific **Balthasar Neumann**, who had started off as a humble craftsman of church bells and weapons before working his way into the fine art of architecture. The palace is built in a great U-shape made up of a central pavilion and four equally proportioned two-story courts. In themselves, the external proportions are impressive, with a length of 167m and a depth of 92m, but they're rather overshadowed by the overwhelming magnificence of the interior.

As you enter the palace via the central wing, you're almost immediately confronted with the famed **staircase**—one of the great sights of Germany—which is covered by a single unsupported vault of audacious design. In response to jealous rivals who claimed this was bound to collapse, Neumann offered to have a battery of artillery fired under it. This experiment was never carried out, but vindication of Neumann's faith in his design came in 1945, when the vault held firm against bombardment. Its **fresco**, the largest in the world, thus survived unscathed. An allegory extolling the fame of the prince-bishops in the vainest way imaginable, it was painted by the greatest decorator of the age, the Venetian **Giovanni Battista Tiepolo**, aided by his two youthful sons. The four continents then known are depicted paying their respects to the ruler of Würzburg, Carl Philipp von Greiffenklau, who ascends to Heaven in triumph in the center of the composition. Each continent is personified as a female character: Asia is a woman riding an elephant, America a red Indian on a crocodile, Africa a princess on a camel, and Europe is a Greek goddess enthroned above a globe to symbolize that continent's status as ruler of the world. To her right, sitting on an old cannon, a reference to his original trade, Balthasar Neumann surveys the scene; behind him are Tiepolo and his fellow decorators.

The guided **tour** of the palace will take you on to the **Weisser Saal**, whose plain white stucco is a tasteful contrast to the staircase, and gives the visitor a break before being hit by the opulence of the **Kaisersaal**, which is the building's highlight. Originally reserved for the use of the emperor whenever he happened to be in the area, it now provides a very glamorous setting for the annual **Mozart Festival** in June. The marble, the gold-leaf stucco, and the sparkling chandeliers combine to produce an effect of dazzling magnificence, but finest of all are more frescoes by Tiepolo, which dovetail perfectly with the architecture. This time, they glorify the concept of the Holy Roman Empire, and Würzburg's part within it. On the ceiling, Beatrix of Burgundy is brought to the city as Frederick Barbarossa's betrothed. On the southern wall, the couple are married by the prince-bishop, who is bestowed with the title of Duke of Franconia by the Emperor in the scene opposite. From here, the tour continues through an array of **state rooms**, painstakingly recreated from the ashes with the help of photographs and old etchings.

Built discreetly into the southwest corner of the palace in order not to spoil the symmetry, the **Hofkirche** (which you visit independently) is a brilliant early example of the spatial illusionism that was to become a Neumann specialty—the interior, based on a series of ovals, appears to be much larger than is actually the case. The decorative scheme, executed under the Austrian Lucas von Hildebrandt, is a good example of Viennese baroque, dripping with embellishments, and with a color scheme of purple, black, gray, red, and gold which is if anything too sumptuous. Both the side altars, representing *The Assumption* and *The Fall of the Rebel Angels*, are by Tiepolo.

During work on the Residenz, Neumann also took time to build the **Käppele**, a pilgrimage church imperiously perched on the heights at the southwestern end of the city. Its twin towers, crowned with onion domes, seem to beckon the faithful to make the ascent. Apart from the opportunity to see the interior, lavishly covered with frescoes and stucco, it's well worth visiting for the **view** from the terrace—the finest in Würzburg—which offers a frontal view of the Marienberg on the next hill, with the city nestling snugly in the valley below.

Eating and Drinking

Würzburg is a place for gourmets, or even for those who simply enjoy good food, for although meals aren't necessarily cheap, they're certainly worth it. The best places to sample Franconian cooking are in the great wine-drinking institutions *Bürgerspital* (on the corner of Theaterstrasse and Semmelstrasse; Wed.–Mon.) and *Juliusspital* (Juliuspromenade 19; Thurs.–Tues.). Both were originally founded as homes for the poor, old, and sick, in the fourteenth and sixteenth centuries respectively, and were set up to finance themselves by their vineyards. Today they still live off their wines, and in accordance with the wishes of the Bürgerspital founders, residents get a quarter of a liter of wine each day and double rations on Sundays. Another famous wine cellar and restaurant is the *Stachel* (Gressengasse 1; Mon.–Sat.), which is the city's oldest wine-drinking inn. It has a very picturesque courtyard too, but as you'd expect with such a place, it's pretty expensive. Unlike the first two mentioned here, which are neither expensive nor touristy, the *Stadt Mainz* (Semmelstr. 39; Wed.–Sun.), though excellent, is *the* tourist spot in town, so keen to cater to everybody that it not only prints its menu in five languages, but also in Braille. Much less pretentious is the *Paulaner Bräustüberl* (Bronnbachergasse 10) near the Marktplatz, which also has the advantage of serving food until midnight. For **student bars** head over to the Sanderstrasse in the southern part of town.

Listings

Area code (☎0931).

Bike rental At the Hauptbahnhof.

Car rental *Avis*, Schürerstr. 2 (☎50661).

Guided tours Leave from the Busbahnhof next to the Bahnhof, April 26–Oct. 18, Mon.–Sat. 2:30pm, Sun. 10:30am; DM8; duration 1 hr.

Main cruises Information and tickets by the *Alter Kranen* on the riverbank at the bottom of Juliuspromenade. Two different firms operate daily cruises 10am–4pm, Sun. until 5pm, to the rococo palace and gardens of VEITSHÖCHHEIM downstream, and OCHSENFURT and SULZFELD upstream for about DM10 round trip.

Mitfahrzentrale, Bahnhofsvorplatz-Ost (☎12904).

Aschaffenburg

In the nineteenth century King Ludwig I of Bavaria called **ASCHAFFENBURG** his "Bavarian Nice," and although the city has lost some of its charm since those days, the well-preserved historic quarter and pleasant parks make it an agreeable place to spend a day or two. Once the second residence of the archbishops of Mainz, Aschaffenburg is now mainly a dormitory town for Frankfurt and home to 8000 American soldiers—who have done a lot for local fast-food outlets and used car dealerships.

Aschaffenburg's center is compact and can easily be covered in a few hours. From the **Hauptbahnhof** walk down Frohsinnstrasse, turn right into Erthalstrasse, and you come to **Schloss Johanissburg**, the town's main attraction. This early baroque red sandstone palace served the bishops of Mainz as a palace rather than filling any defensive role. Today the first and second floors of the Schloss are home to the **Schlossmuseum** (April–Sept. daily 9am–noon and 1–5pm. Oct.–March daily 10am–noon and 1–4pm; DM3, DM2 students). The museum houses over 400 paintings from the fifteenth to the eighteenth centuries, with the emphasis on devotional works by Lucas Cranach the Elder and his contemporaries, along with Dutch and Flemish landscapes. The other thing to look out for is the **Schlosskirche**, which contains fine alabaster reliefs by the seventeenth-century sculptor Hans Juncker, and has a magnificent doorway with a sculpture depicting the baptism of Christ, also by Juncker.

A few minutes' walk along the river Main, downstream from Schloss Johannisburg, is **Das Pompejanum**, a replica of the house of Castor and Pollux in Pompeii, which was built between 1840 and 1848 by the Bavarian court architect Friedrich von Gärtner for King Ludwig I. Unfortunately only the exterior of this very Roman-looking villa has been restored following extensive war damage, but its gardens planted with Mediterranean trees and plants and its terraced vineyard sloping down to the Main make for an enjoyable stroll.

A walk down Pfaffengstrasse from Schloss Johannisburg takes you through the heart of the Altstadt, with its narrow streets of half-timbered houses, and leads to Stiftsplatz, and Aschaffenburg's other main sight—the **Stiftskirche St. Peter und Alexander** (weekdays 9am onwards; Sunday noon onwards. For guided tours inquire at Stiftsgasse 1). Founded in 957, the church combines Romanesque, Gothic, and baroque styles and it's this architectural identity crisis that gives it real visual impact. The church boasts late Romanesque cloisters, a crucifix dating from 1120, and a small panel of *The Lamentation* by Grünewald.

Also worth visiting are **Schöntal Park**, on the eastern edge of the old city center, with a lake, ruined monastery, and the **Fasanerie** (Pheasantery). It's reached by walking up Lindenallee, crossing the railroad bridge and going up Bismarckallee, which is itself a recreational hotspot in summer with restaurants and beer gardens. **Schönbusch Park**, on the western bank of the Main (best reached by bus #3 from Freihofplatz) is an "English"-style landscape garden, designed by eighteenth-century Germany's premier landscape gardener, Friedrich Ludwig von Sckell, and featuring a labyrinth of paths leading through woods and gardens past miniature temples and mazes.

Finally, on the southern edge of town at Obernnauer Str. 125, the **Rosso Bianco Collection** (Tues.–Fri. 10am–4pm, Sat. and Sun. 10am–6pm; DM10, DM6 students; bus #1 from Schweinheimer Strasse) has the biggest collection of racing cars in the world—some 200 gleaming Porsches, Ferraris, Alfa-Romeos, and the like which even non-enthusiasts will find themselves drooling over.

Practicalities

The **tourist office** is at Dalbergstrasse 6 (☎06021 30426). **Camping** is possible at Mainpark See (☎06021 278222), in the suburb of Mainaschaff (☎06021 278222), fifteen minutes away by a #44 bus from the Hauptbahnhof. The **youth hostel** is at Beckerstrasse 47 (☎06021 92763) and is best reached by #22 bus from Platanenallee, getting off at the third stop on Würzburger Strasse. A few cheap **hotels and pensions**: *Hotel Central*, Steingasse 5 (☎06021 23392) which is in the middle of town in the pedestrian zone and offers singles at DM32 and doubles at DM65; *Hotel Goldenes Fass*, Sandgasse 26 (☎06021 22801), which has four singles at between DM21 and DM50 and one double at DM55, is also centrally located and in the pedestrian zone; *Hotel Syndikus*, Loeherstr. 35 is a few minutes' walk from the Stiftskirche and has singles at DM40.

Eating and drinking are well provided for, with the best restaurants, cafés, and bars in the Altstadt, focussing on Rossmarkt and Dalbergstrasse, main centers of the Aschaffenburg social scene. *Klimperkasten* at Rossmarkt 21 is a lively, friendly pub with regular live music, and *Café Blech* at Rossmarkt 43 is trendy café-bar. *Engelsberg* at Dalbergstr. 66 is a traditional but arty pub and a good starting point for exploring Dalbergstrasse and the surrounding streets, which are full of of reasonable *Gaststätte* and *Weinstuben*. There's also a cluster of reasonably priced bars and eateries in Würzburger Strasse, not far from the town's youth hostel. Worth checking out in the summer are the *Hofgut Fasanerie*, Bismarckalle 1, whose beer garden is part of the Fasanerie, and the *Zeughaus*, Bismarckallee 5, where you can drink locally produced ciders in the shade of chestnut trees.

The Spessart and Rhön Highlands

A great many rivers flow through the western part of Franconia, their valleys lined by the vineyards of the famous *Bocksbeutel* wines; the flat oval bottles are their exclusive trademark. Fine dry white wines such as *Silvaner*, *Müller-Thurgau*, and *Gewürztraminer* are all served in the local wine cellars and on wine-tasting tours where vintners show you around the ancient cellars which often still hold bottles from centuries back.

From Würzburg, the River Main twists and turns in great slalom leaps through the countryside, firstly flowing northwards, but turning south again by GMÜNDEN, some 25km away. From here until ASCHAFFENBURG its course more or less defines the **SPESSART** highlands. This region is covered by one of Germany's largest remaining forests, and ranks alongside the Black and Bavarian Forests in terms of natural beauty. Like the latter, it has so far escaped becoming a commercial Disneyland. It also contains some of Germany's oldest oaks, many dating back well over 500 years; delicious wild mushrooms grow in abundance; and there's a rich wildlife. In the old days it was a haven for bandits and highway-men, who terrorized passing travelers and made journeys a hazardous business. The **RHÖN**, as the highlands are known after the river Sinn, continue the north-easterly direction of the range, but have a slightly different character. Here the range is made up by the remains of ancient volcanoes and the vegetation is more sparse, the forest tending to stay in the valleys, keeping the hilltops as windy moorlands which are very popular with hang gliders.

This is ideal hiking and touring country, and there are marked paths for both hikers and cyclists. Separate maps for the Spessart and Rhön called *Ravenstein-Wanderkarten* are available from the central **tourist offices** responsible for the region: either *Ferienland Main Spessart*, Würzburger Str. 25, 8782 Karlstadt (☎09353 501/793/344); or *Tourist-Information Rhön*, Landratsamt, 8740 Bad Neustadt an der Saale (☎09771 94216). As at Cham, *Wandern ohne Gepäck* service is available, free of charge. Ideal bases for exploring the central and northern Spessart would be GMÜNDEN or LOHR, and for the southern Spessart in the Main's loop, MILTENBERG and AMORBACH. For the Rhön region, BISCHOFSHEIM is the best base. All these towns have youth hostels and cheap alternatives aren't hard to find.

Bamberg

Bambergers are reputedly very bourgeois, ponderous and superstitious, and prone to drink too much beer. The last may well be true, but the rest doesn't seem to apply these days, and the local university helps to liven up what might otherwise be a rather staid little town. Admittedly this has a lot to do with drinking. The people of **BAMBERG**, which lies 60km north of Nürnberg and 95km east of Würzburg, knock back proportionately more **beer** than any other town in the entire country. There are no less than ten breweries which together produce

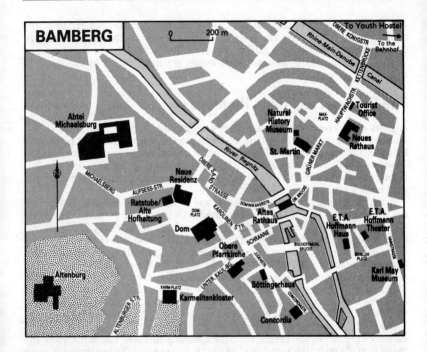

thirty different kinds of beer, most notably the appropriately named *Rauchbier* (smoky beer). Made from smoked malt according to a formula developed in the sixteenth century, it's as distinctive a local brew as you'll find in Germany, leaving its own very special lingering aftertaste.

An episcopal see since 1007, Bamberg has been an important religious and political center for many centuries. It was brought to prominence by the saintly eleventh-century Emperor Heinrich II, who wanted to turn it into a German metropolis of a scale and importance to rival Rome. Though the city has in fact never grown very big, it nonetheless has a sense of spacious grandeur which belies its actual size. Like the Italian capital, Bamberg is built on seven hills, with the Dom and related structures taking up the entire crown of the main hill and towering high above the town to form the **Domstadt**. Unique in Germany, it's still one of the most important Catholic bishoprics in the country. Clinging to the lower slopes of the valley of the River Regnitz are the districts inhabited by the burghers, thus constituting an unusually complete baroque townscape.

Bamberg's isolated geographical position has been a key factor in preserving its magnificent **architectural heritage** from the ravages of war. There can be no doubt of its status as one of the most beautiful small towns, not just in Germany, but anywhere in the world. More can be learned about architectural history in a couple of days here than from weeks of studying textbooks: every single European style from the Romanesque onwards has left its mark on Bamberg, each bequeathing at least one outstanding building. For art lovers, there's the added bonus of the most marvelous array of **sculpture** to be found in the country. As far as photography is concerned, there's a ready-made package of subject-matter. Toiling up and down the hills, you'll find any number of vantage points, each offering a quite different perspective on the city. Lower down, a myriad of cobbled alleyways lead to all sorts of picturesque corners, with the play of light on the river lending an extra sense of magic to the scene.

Around Town

Bamberg's **Bahnhof** is about fifteen minutes' walk to the northeast of the historic district. From there, follow Luitpoldstrasse straight ahead, before turning into the third street on the right, Obere Königstrasse. Then cross the bridge over the *Rhein-Main-Donau-Kanal* on to Hauptwachstrasse and you shortly come to the **tourist office** (Mon.–Fri. 8am–5/6pm according to season, Sat. 8am–12:30pm; ☎0951 21040), which occupies the eighteenth-century guard house that gives the street its name.

Heart of the lower town is the **Maxplatz**, dominated by Balthasar Neumann's **Neues Rathaus**, which was originally built as a seminary. Your best bet is to use this square as a focal point for wandering around the center, and gradually head towards the Domstadt across the river. A market is held every day on Maxplatz and the adjoining Grüner Markt, which stands in the shadow of **St. Martin**, a huge Jesuit church designed by the Dientzenhofer brothers, who were responsible for many of the best baroque buildings in the city.

On an islet anchoring the Obere Brücke and Untere Brücke together is the **Altes Rathaus**, which is almost too picturesque for its own good. Except for the half-timbered section overhanging the rapids, the original Gothic building was transformed into rococo, and its walls are busily tattooed with exuberant frescoes. The famous **Klein-Venedig** (*Little Venice*) of fishermen's houses is best seen from the Untere Brücke, and presents one of the very few medieval scenes you'll find in the lower parts of town.

Elsewhere, the architectural character is almost completely baroque. Walking around town the facades glow in rich ocher and russet tones, their elaborate stucco and intricate frescoes unashamedly exuding the wealth of their former residents. Grandest, but perhaps a little vulgar too, is the **Böttingerhaus** at no. 14 in the Judengasse, on the western side of the Regnitz. Built by the Franconian chargé d'affaires in the early eighteenth century, it now houses a very posh restaurant and hotel. The nearby **Concordia** water-palace on the banks of the river belonged to the same man. Best time to see it is in the evenings from the opposite river bank, when the effect is heightened by its glittering reflection in the water.

Uphill lies the Domstadt. The spacious, sloping **Domplatz** is lined with such a superb variety of buildings that it has no possible rival for the title of Germany's finest square. It unfolds like a great picture book of architecture: with no more than a turn of the head you can see how Romanesque evolved into Gothic; how the latter developed through various phases before giving way to the Renaissance, which in turn was supplanted by baroque.

The **Dom** (often dignified as the **Kaiserdom**) was consecrated in 1012, but in the following two centuries it burned down twice, and the present structure of golden sandstone is the result of a slow rebuilding process that continued throughout the thirteenth century. During this period architectural tastes were beginning to change, but the ground plan follows the precedent of the Romanesque imperial cathedrals of Mainz, Worms, and Speyer in having a choir at both ends of the building, each of which is flanked by twin towers. The east chancel is dedicated to the warrior St. George, symbolizing the empire, while its western counterpart bears a dedication to St. Peter, representing the papacy. These were the first and last parts of the Dom to be completed, and you can see that the rounded Romanesque arches and heavy vaults of the eastern choir had given way to the tall pointed windows and graceful ribs characteristic of early Gothic by the west end. In between, the nave was erected in the transitional style, offering a fascinating insight into the way the original masons were experimenting with the new techniques. Notwithstanding the addition of identical lead steeples during the baroque period, the **towers** are also very different. The eastern pair are massive and heavy, whereas those to the west have a lighter, almost ethereal feel; they're closely modeled on those of the French cathedral of Laon, which were then thought to be the most daring and magnificent that had ever been built.

What makes the Kaiserdom one of Europe's greatest cathedrals is the astonishing array of **sculptural decoration**; it's no exaggeration to say that this is an assemblage comparable in stature to any of the supreme masterpieces of the art, such as the Parthenon marbles or Michelangelo's Medici Tombs. As with the architecture, the sculpture was initially executed in an orthodox Romanesque style. The best example of this is the *Fürstenportal* on the north side of the nave, facing the main slope of the square; its tympanum warns of *The Last Judgment*, while the progressively receding arches are each adorned with the figure of an Apostle standing on the shoulders of an Old Testament prophet. The latter—a brilliant iconographical idea—implies that the Apostles had a broader vision, but that this was thanks to the groundwork prepared by the earlier men. Carvings in a similar style can be found on the *Marienportal* on the right-hand door to the east chancel, which shows the Madonna and Child adored by the Kaiserdom's patrons, founders, and builders; and on the panels of the choir screen, which again place Apostles and prophets in juxtaposition.

At some point, a sculptor of genius came to Bamberg. His name is unknown; he had certainly worked in a cathedral lodge in France, but was to move far away from the stock figures favored by the French. Combined with the work of his anonymous contemporaries in Naumburg and Magdeburg (both now in the GDR), his art represents a high point of German cultural history, one of the occasions when the country clearly led the rest of Europe. All the sculptures made by this artist and his school are now indoors, although they presumably once adorned the portals. The most famous of all is the enigmatic **Bamberger Reiter**, one of the few equestrian statues which had been made since the days of classical antiquity. Nobody knows for sure who this noble figure is; the Romantics imagined it was an idealized portrait of a German emperor of the Hohenstaufen line. This was eagerly seized on by the Nazis, and during the Third Reich the statue was the national symbol of Germanic perfection, adorning every public hall and classroom.

Two other statues to look out for are *Ecclesia* and *Synagogue*, the female personifications of the Christian and Jewish faiths, now placed at the southeast end of the nave. The victory of Christianity over Judaism is highlighted by the women's contrasting countenances: the Christian is a beautiful woman clad in rich cloth, while the Jewess stands blindfolded holding a broken rod, and wearing a plain tunic that emphasizes the outline of her sagging breasts. Even finer are the two figures of *The Visitation* directly opposite. The Virgin Mary is young and bright, draped in a swirling dress; Saint Elizabeth is an ancient, haggard old crone whose expression bespeaks an overwhelming sense of pathos.

As a perfect complement to the carvings associated with its construction, the Dom also contains a masterpiece by the each of the two most famous sculptors of another great period for German art, the early sixteenth century. Focus of the nave is the white limestone **tomb** of the canonized imperial couple Heinrich II and Kunigunde, which stands slightly elevated as a result of the crypt built below. **Tilman Riemenschneider** labored away for fourteen years on this sarcophagus, whose reliefs depict scenes taken from the life and times of the couple. At the base of the panels, snakes, frogs, and snails represent death and resurrection, and are supposed to remind the faithful that while humans have to die, their souls rise up and go to heaven. The south transept contains **Veit Stoss'** dark limewood *Nativity Altar*, made when the artist was about eighty years old, as a result of a commission from his son, who was a Carmelite prior in Nürnberg. It was meant as a sort of artistic testament, executed without the usual studio assistance. Unfortunately, it's unfinished—the younger Stoss, a virulent anti-Protestant, was kicked out of Nürnberg when the city council adopted the Reformation, and the sculptor received no payment for his retable, which was soon afterwards moved to Bamberg.

Though not accessible to the public, it's worth knowing that the western choir holds the only papal grave in Germany, that of Pope Clement II. He was the local bishop before becoming Pope, but died in 1047 after having ruled for a mere twelve months. Tomb slabs to the Dom's other bishops can be found scattered throughout the church. The most impressive, artistically speaking, is the *Monument to Friedrich von Hohenlohe* in the south aisle, just before the transept. Dating from the latter half of the fourteenth century, it conveniently represents the period midway between the Bamberger Reiter and the works of Riemenschneider and Stoss.

The **Diocesan Museum** (Easter–Oct. Tues.–Sun. 10am–5pm; DM2) is in the chapter house off the cloisters on the south side of the Dom, and is entered from the square. Highlight is the collection of **ecclesiastical vestments**, notably robes worn by the imperial couple Heinrich II and Kunigunde, as well as the shroud of the eleventh-century Bamberg bishop Gunther. The vibrant colors and intricate designs are amazingly well preserved. Also kept here are the six original statues from the *Adamportal*, the dogtooth doorway to the left of the east choir. Here the ubiquitous Emperor and his wife turn up in the company of the Dom's two patrons, plus Adam and Eve. The last two are unashamedly sensual; covered only by fig leaves, they come as near to erotic art as was ever dared in the prudish Middle Ages.

Opposite the cathedral, the **Ratstube** is a Renaissance gem, with elegantly tapering gables and an ornate oriel window. It now contains the **Historical Museum** (May–Oct. Tues.–Sat. 9am–noon and 2–5pm, Sun. 10am–1pm; DM1), which covers local and regional history from the Stone Age to the twentieth century, as well as Bamberg's rich art history. Adjoining it is the **Reiche Tor**, in which Heinrich and Kunigunde appear once more; in contrast to their figures in the Diocesan Museum, the model they carry is recognizably the Kaiserdom. This gate leads into the huge fifteenth-century courtyard of the **Alte Hofhaltung**, the former episcopal palace, which incorporates the remains of the eleventh-century hall of the Imperial Diet. The overhanging eaves of the huge sloping roof shelter two tiers of wooden galleries, and there's an unusual perspective on the towers of the Dom.

Across the street is the building which supplanted it, the **Neue Residenz** (daily 9am–noon and 1:30–5pm; DM2.50). Designed by Leonhard Dientzenhofer around the beginning of the eighteenth century, it's an early example of the passion for building huge new palaces in the baroque style that was to sweep across the German principalities. It's built in a massive L-shape and stands in sumptuous splendor overlooking the town below. Inside, the richly decorated state rooms culminate in the emperor's ballroom, complete with chandeliers, frescoes, and a surprisingly plain marble floor. Also housed in the palace is the **Staatsgalerie Bamberg**, with medieval and baroque paintings by German masters. Look for *The Great Flood*, a typically idiosyncratic work by **Hans Baldung Grien**, who here tackled with relish a subject most painters shied away from; there are also several examples of Lucas Cranach the Elder. While you're here, have a look into the reading room of the **Staatsbibliothek** too, for a glimpse of a delicate white and pink stucco ceiling in the best tradition of baroque interior design.

From the rose garden at the back of the Neue Residenz is a view of the **Michaelsburg**, which is crowned by a huge **Abtei**. Much of the original Romanesque shell of the church remains, though it was modified in the Gothic period and further transformed in baroque style by Leonhard Dientzenhofer, who added a new facade approached by a monumental flight of steps. The interior is an amazing hodgepodge: its ceiling depicts over 600 medicinal herbs; there are lavish rococo furnishings, of which the most eye-catching is the pulpit; and there are the tombs of many more Bamberg bishops. Housed in the cellars of the monastic buildings is the **Fränkisches Brauereimuseum** (Mon.–Fri. 1–4pm; DM2, DM1 students), which shows just how those famous local brews are made, and displays all the old gear that used to be necessary for traditional brewing. There are a couple of pretty impressive statistics too, such as the fact that the average Bamberg resident consumes 330 liters of beer annually, compared to the national average of "only" 146 liters. Even if you're not interested in brewing, it's worth coming up here for the wonderful panorama of Bamberg's skyline and surrounding hills.

Yet another place for a great view is the **Altenburg**, a ruined castle at the end of the very steep Altenburger Strasse. Walk up the Untere Kaulberg and past Karmeliten-Platz, and you'll find the **Karmelitenkloster**. The church is again by Dientzenhofer, but the Romanesque **cloister** (daily 8–11am and 2–5:30pm; free), the largest in Germany, has been preserved. Its sculptured thirteenth-century columns each have their own individual patterns, revealing just how rich the imagination of early medieval craftsmen could be. Along with the depiction of biblical scenes, ingeniously worked round the confined space on the capitals, a fabulous bestiary, ranging from fearsome dragons to weird creepy-crawlies, is illustrated. Lower down the hill is the **Obere Pfarrkirche**, a fourteenth-century Gothic church in the style of the Parler family. Its *Brautportal*, through which wedding processions passed, bears, as if by way of warning, delicate carvings of the Wise and Foolish Virgins.

On Schillerplatz, a few minutes' walk away on the opposite side of the river, is the tiny **E.T.A. Hoffmann Haus** (May–Oct. Tues.–Fri. 4–6pm, Sat.–Sun. 10am–noon; DM1), which was the home of one of Germany's most famous nineteenth-century Romantic writers. A native of Königsberg (then a famous Prussian university city but now, under the name of Kaliningrad, part of the Soviet Union), Hoffmann was a man with prodigious talents in all the arts. For most of his life, he was employed by the civil service, but for the years he lived in Bamberg (1808-13) he tried to establish himself as a composer, conductor, and theater director. However, his real forte was to be as an author of short stories of a weird and fantastic character, reflecting his own rather schizophrenic nature; this is the side of him portrayed in Offenbach's opera *The Tales of Hoffmann*. His finest achievement, written some years after he left Bamberg, is *Mademoiselle de Scudéry*, which is now generally regarded as the first detective story ever written, predating Poe's *The Murders in the Rue Morgue* by two decades. Everything in the house is as it was during the writer's lifetime, with graphics, portraits, and excerpts relating to his times and work.

Of more passing interest is the **Karl May Museum** (Wed. 2–5pm, Thurs.–Sat. 9am–noon and 2–5pm, Sun. 9am–1pm; DM2) round the corner on Hainstrasse. This houses the works of the much-translated author of countless cowboy-and-Indian stories along with a collection of Native American weapons and tools. Also of specialized appeal is the **Naturkundemuseum** on Fleischstrasse (Mon.–Fri. 8am–noon and 1–5pm; DM1), though an added attraction here is that the collections of rare and exotic birds and other animals are displayed in beautiful exhibition rooms built in the neoclassical style of the early nineteenth century.

Food, Drink, and Practicalities

Eating cheaply in Bamberg isn't particularly easy, but apart from the usual *Imbiss* places downtown, at least two restaurants are worth trying. If you're in the mood for **Greek** food, the *Alt Nürnberg* (Obere Sandstr. 11) is the place to go for; or if you prefer **vegetarian** fare, try the *Bürgerbräu-Stübla* (Urbanstr. 18). Good **cafés** are much easier to find, and three of the best for excellent *Kaffee und Kuchen* are *Am Dom* (Ringleinsgasse 2), *Michaelsberg* (Michaelsberg 10e), and *Rosengarten* (Neue Residenz, open May—Oct.).

Drinking is never a problem: best places to try the **local beers** are Bamberg's three combination beer cellars/gardens, starting with *Spezial* on the Sternwartstrasse, known locally as *Zinser* after the ebullient character who runs it. Two more are the *Greiffenklau* (Laurenziplatz 20) and *Mahr* (Oberer Stephansberg 36). Alternatively, try the old beer halls *Hofbräu-Schänke* and *Das Schlenkerla*, both on Dominikanerstrasse, and both also offering *bürgerlich* cuisine. A predominantly young clientele is to be found in the so-called *Musikkneipen*, of which the *Café Abseits* (Pödeldorferstrasse) and the *Strandcafé* (Memmelsdorferstr. 82) are frequented by "alternative" types; there's also the *Fischerhof* (Gaustadter Hauptstr. 109).

If **wine** is more your tipple, check out *Zum Zwiebeltreter* (Promenadestr. 6a) or *Zur Drehorgel* (Obere Sandstr.), and also *Pizzini* (Obere Sandstrasse). A good **nightclub** is *Downstairs* (Langestr. 16; daily 10pm–3am; DM8 Fri. and Sat., of which DM5 goes towards the first order). If you're still raving at closing-time, head for the *Weinstadl* (Dominikanerstr. 5), which stays open until 4am.

Two **youth hostels** serve Bamberg: the *Stadion* (Pödeldorferstr. 178, ☎0951 12377/56002; bus #2 from the Bahnhof), is rather plain but with a handy situation, and the *Wolfsschlucht* (Oberer Leinritt 70, ☎0951 56002/54552; bus #1, #7, or #11 from the Bahnhof to ZOB Promenade, then change to bus #18 to Regnitzufer), is a first-class youth hostel, pleasantly situated on the banks of the river Regnitz, 2km south of downtown. Another 2km farther down the river you'll find the local **campground** (☎0951 56320).

Guesthouse accommodation is in the region of DM25–40 for singles and DM50–78 for doubles. Cheapest places in town are the *Wilder Mann* (Untere Sandstr. 9, ☎0951 56462) and *Zum Gabelmann* (Kesslerstr. 14, ☎0951 26676), but rates don't include breakfast. A very pleasant place to stay is the *Spezial* (Obere Königstr. 10, ☎0951 24304) which charges DM30–40 for singles and DM66–75 for doubles. Only fractionally more expensive, the *Anita* (Kleberstr. 39, ☎0951 23533) is conveniently central. It's also worth bearing in mind that the tourist office makes no charge for booking accommodation. Finally, if you're thinking of staying here for longer periods, it's worth consulting the **Studentenwerk** (Austr. 37, ☎0951 203283) for advice on renting rooms in student halls over the summer.

For its size, Bamberg is an amazingly vibrant cultural center, especially for **classical music**. Indeed, it's probably the smallest city in the world with a top-class symphony orchestra. The *Bamberger Symphoniker* was actually the old *Deutsches Orchester* of Prague, which fled over the border at the time the Iron Curtain was dropped. They're especially known for their candlelit concerts in the Neues Residenz. The main **theater**, not surprisingly, is the *E.T.A. Hoffmann Theater* on Schillerplatz; the resident company also holds an open-air season in June and July in the Alte Hofhaltung. Tickets for all musical and theatrical events are available from the *Bamberger Veranstaltungsdienst* at Lange Str. 24; you can also book there for **river cruises**. Main **festivals** are *Corpus Christi* (variable date in May/June) and the *Sandfest* in August, which features colorful church processions and fishermen's jousts. The **Women's Center** is at Untere Sandstr. 9 (☎0951 55440).

Around Bamberg

West of Bamberg, the heavily forested **Hassberge** mountain ranges and **Steigerwald** are both popular hiking regions. The area of **Frankenwald** to the east has some of the country's most pleasing landscapes, as well as a plethora of castles and palaces. Information and hiking maps are available from the following regional tourist offices: *Tourist Information Hassberge* (Rathaus, Obere Sennigstr. 10, Hofheim, ☎09523 267); *Tourist Information Steigerwald* (Rathaus, Ebrach, ☎09553 217); and *Tourismus-Zentrale Fränkische Schweiz* (Oberes Tor 1, Ebermannstadt, ☎09194 8101).

If you're not into long walks, however, there are still a number of places worth a day trip. In the case of the northwestern Hassberge, star attraction is the small town of **HASSFURT** and its fifteenth-century **Ritterkapelle**, a late Gothic church with a number of interesting features such as the stone tympanum depicting the journey of the three Magi to the newborn Christ. Apart from Hassfurt, many other little towns and villages still retain much of their old Franconian character, and more often than not there's a small castle nearby as well. Good examples are KÖNIGSBERG near Hassfurt, and WALTERSHAUSEN and IRMELSHAUSEN near the East German border to the north. The latter village sports a gorgeous moated castle, unfortunately not open to the public, but worth passing by if you happen to be up this end of Bavaria.

The southwestern Steigerwald area is more varied in its attractions, with marvelous scenery and some impressive sights. For those with their own vehicle, a trip along the *Steigerwald Höhenstrasse* from ELTMANN to **EBRACH** and down to SCHLÜSSELFELD, would be an ideal way to see the best of this region. Ebrach grew out of a twelfth-century Cistercian abbey, of which large parts still remain today. The church was considered one of the finest German examples of the order's distinctive early Gothic building style, but unfortunately the interior was radically changed in the eighteenth century, with pink stuccoed marble pillars and golden yellow ornamentations. The large monastery attached was only built in the seventeenth century, and is another important work by Leonhard Dientzenhofer; after his death, Balthasar Neumann is thought to have taken over the project.

In **POMMERSFELDEN**, about 10km south of Bamberg, stands **Schloss Weissenstein**, the jewel in the crown of Prince-Bishop Schönborn's enormous building legacy. Lothar Franz von Schönborn was elected Prince-Bishop of Bamberg when he was 38 years old, and by previously ensuring the election of Emperor Charles VI in 1711, he'd also assured himself a sizable fortune, which he proceeded to spend on a building program that ranged from the episcopal palace in Bamberg to this, his great private residence. Built around the same time as Germany's other great baroque palaces such as Nymphenburg and Würzburg, Weissenstein was designed by Johann Dientzenhofer in equally ostentatious proportions, but with the added feature of a double-sided **central staircase**, which is perhaps the ultimate in everything that's good about baroque design. The entrance hall of the central pavilion takes up the full height of the three-story palace, and the double staircase swings up to upper galleries that encase the hall rather like great Italian courtyards. The ceiling fresco by Johann Rudolph Byss uses clever perspective to give the impression of yet another gallery and elegantly rounds off a perfect whole.

The rest of the interior is much the same as others of its kind, with richly decorated mirror cabinets, state rooms, and the obligatory ballroom, known as the **Marmorsaal** because of the stuccoed marble pillars that line its walls. From mid-July to mid-August, it's used for the classical concerts of the *Collegium Musicum*, an international festival of young musicians. (For information and tickets contact *Schlossverwaltung Weissenstein*, 8602 Pommersfelden, ☎09548 203.)

The **Frankische Schweiz** (*Franconian Switzerland*, as tourist brochures like to call it) lies to the east of Bamberg, and encompasses a large area stretching from LICHTENFELS in the north to HERSBRUCK in the south. More sparsely forested than the western ranges due to the infertile Jurassic ground, the Frankische Schweiz holds other natural attractions such as strange rock formations, lonely high plateaux and, to the south around STREITBERG and POTTENSTEIN, quite a few interesting caves. While poor-quality soil also accounts for the low population, the region nevertheless has a plethora of castles, usually perched on conical hills above tightly packed villages such as GÖSSWEINSTEIN and Pottenstein, or overlooking picturesque valleys like the Wiesenttal by WIESENTFELS. The most famous peak, if you can call it that, is the **Walberla**, a flat-topped hill a few kilometers east of FORCHHEIM, traditionally dedicated to St. Walpurgis. On the first Sunday of May, Franconia's best festival takes place here, and thousands gather for the annual *Volksfest* and an orgy of beer and food. The villages around here, such as KIRCHEHRENBERG, LEUTENBERG, and HUNDSHAUPTEN are well known in their own right for having some of the best country *Gaststätten* in the region.

Coburg

COBURG lies about 25km north of Bamberg, and a stone's throw away from the East German border. Once an important royal residence, and birthplace of Queen Victoria's husband Albert, its proximity to **the Wall** has meant a losing battle against obscurity, in both the economic and touristic sense. There's little reason to come here unless you're especially interested in seeing where Albert was born, and being so close to a dead end, there are few casual passersby. On the face of it, the local fortress, palace, and surrounding countryside, rich in castles, would certainly be worth an overnight visit. But after Bamberg and its light-hearted atmosphere, Coburg has something uncomfortable about it. It looks nice but it feels bad, and when you find out that the town is a stronghold of right-wing extremists, who annually hold neo-Nazi parades, there seems at least some kind of tangible reason for the town's disquieting atmosphere. There are residents who feel equally bad about the town's blight, and at least some of the tension stems from the conflict between these different groups.

Known as the **Veste Coburg**, the great fortified castle that gives the town its name is one of the largest remaining in Germany. Towering high above the valley, the original fortress was probably built in the twelfth century, but the present massive structure of twin walls and inner courts was built in the sixteenth century, from which time it belonged to the Saxe-Coburg dynasty. The inner court is made up of four main buildings and the part known as the **Hohes Haus** (Tues.–Sun. 9:30am–1pm and 2–5pm; DM2.50, DM2 students) is home to a very extensive collection of art, glassware, weapons and an historical exhibition. Most famous is the 300,000-strong collection of graphics, which can only ever be partially displayed and includes work by Rembrandt, Dürer, and Cranach.

In 1530, the year of his heresy trial, Martin Luther took refuge in Coburg for a while, finding time to write no less than sixteen works on the issues arising from the Reformation. He stayed in the building known as the **Fürstenbau** (Tues.–Sun. 9:30am–noon and 2–4pm; DM3.50, DM2.50 students), where his room is preserved. Look out too for the portrait gallery of the illustrious Saxe-Coburgs, whose clever marriage policy during the nineteenth century resulted in family ties with many of Europe's royal courts, including Britain, Belgium, and Bulgaria.

The Saxe-Coburgs didn't actually live in the Veste. They chose, in common with the fashion of the sixteenth century, to live nearer their subjects in **Schloss Ehrenburg** (Tues.–Sun. 10am–noon and 1–5:30pm; DM2.50, DM1.50 students) in the town center. Considering that this wasn't a proper royal household, the palace is incredibly rich and sumptuous in its interior design, with precious tapestries lining walls and intricate parquet floors made to different designs in each room. The furnishings are also priceless pieces collected from all over Europe, and there are even "modern" gadgets such as Germany's first flushing toilet in the room Queen Victoria used to stay in. The **church** attached to the palace is worth a look too, since it's a fine example of Lutheran baroque, whose no-frills interior has been beautifully restored.

Albert Saxe-Coburg was born at tiny **Schloss Rosenau** (not open to the public) in 1819, and spent much of his youth playing around this romantic little castle set in a great park designed in the English fashion to imitate nature. If you've got the time, there's an attractive 14-kilometer path leading from the Veste to the park of Rosenau and back to Coburg. The oldest part of town is around the main **Marktplatz** and up towards the Ehrenburg palace, but other than that, turn-of-the-century architecture is most common. The **tourist office**, just off the Marktplatz, provide the usual town maps and any other information you may need. For a slightly more alternative view of Coburg, head for the **Bürgerhaus**, which runs a daily café-bar and also functions as a general meeting point for young people and local activists. The local **youth hostel** (Schloss Ketschendorf, Parkstr. 2, ☎09561 15330) is unfortunately one of the most draconian you're likely to encounter, so if at all possible you'd be better off staying in a guesthouse.

Banz and Vierzehnheiligen

Only about 10km south of Coburg, **Kloster Banz** is perched high above the valley of the River Main. This former Benedictine monastery was begun by Leonhard Dientzenhofer in 1695. After his death, his brother Johann took over, designing the elongated church, which is richly decorated with frescoes, altars and fancy woodwork. The monastic buildings now belong to the CSU, who've turned the place into a grand venue for conferences and training courses for their party faithful; unless you number yourself among them, you won't be going inside.

Much more rewarding to visit is the pilgrimage church known as **Vierzehn-heiligen** (*Fourteen Saints*), which faces Banz from the opposite bank. One of the most important and original baroque churches in the country, it's generally considered to be Balthasar Neumann's supreme accomplishment. It takes its name (Fourteen Saints) from the legend that a shepherd had recurring visions here of Christ with the fourteen Saints of Intercession. The focus of the basilica is an altar dedicated to the fourteen saints, known as the **Gnadenaltar**, around which the entire interior is designed. This gives it the unusual shape of an oval nave and short transept, with the altar taking up the central point of the transept crossing. The marble-and-stucco altar is built in a pyramid design, rich in rococo curls and cherubs as well as the white marble figures of the fourteen saints.

Bayreuth

About 25km east of Bamberg, polished and respectable **BAYREUTH** enjoys its reputation as one of the great cultural centers of Europe. Except for the festival period during late July and the first three weeks in August, it's a quiet, provincial town, and none of the creative spirits that have made Bayreuth famous were home-grown. It's all a bit of a fluke, beginning with the eighteenth-century Margrave's wife Wilhelmine. One of Frederick the Great's sisters, she was intended for the English royal throne, but her father was diplomatically inept and messed up his daughter's chances, so in the end she got stuck with the notoriously boring margrave Friedrich. Instead of settling down to obscurity, however, Wilhelmine set about creating a lively court, hiring Europe's best architects, artists and musicians to transform her surroundings into something more elegant and sophisticated. Hence the stylish palace, Eremitage, and opera house, all built to the distinctive Wilhelmine baroque taste.

A century later, **Wagner** decided to settle in Bayreuth because the town offered to build him a stage large enough to put on his grand-scale opera productions. The cultural impetus generated by this great composer was tremendous, and Bayreuth's opera festival has been rightly famous ever since. Wagner's music was tarnished by the fact that Hitler patronized the annual festival and used the Germanic legends of the operas to his own propagandist ends. But both music and festival have survived, and audiences annually come from all over the world. Such is the demand for tickets that the waiting lists are full for the next five years and the only way you'd have a chance of getting in is by being part of a special festival package tour from abroad.

Around Town

The attraction of Bayreuth lies in its proximity to beautiful countryside and the legacies of Wilhelmine and Wagner. The **tourist office**, Luitpoldplatz 9 (☎0921 22015) supplies brochures on all the buildings and museums relating to these two people, plus a free map of town, and they'll also help with accommodation.

Two major architectural contributions are the **Opernhaus** (Opernstrasse, Tues.–Sun., guided tours 9–11:30am and 1:30–4:30pm; DM2, DM1.50 students) and the **Neues Schloss** (Ludwigstrasse, Tues.–Sun., guided tours 10–11:30am and 1:30–4:30pm; DM2, DM1.50 students), both wonderful examples of Wilhelmine's sophisticated interpretation of the contemporary baroque style. The Opernhaus was built in 1748 and is one of the few baroque theaters in Germany still in its original state, without any changes or restorations. Designed by Guiseppe and Carlo Galli da Bibiena, the theater is unobtrusively built to blend in with the general contours of the street, keeping its glamor for the interior, which is all dusky greens, blues, browns, and gold. This subdued elegance makes for a fascinating contrast with the gaudy glitter of its Munich counterpart, the Cuvilliés Theater. Equally rich in shape and form, the very different execution of baroque style is not just a mark of Wilhelmine's influence, but also of the prevailing Lutheran taste that had established itself here since the sixteenth century.

In 1753 the unfortunate Margrave Friedrich accidentally burned down most of his palace with a misplaced candle. Due to inadequate financial resources the new palace had to be built and designed around a number of already existing buildings, which explains the somewhat unusual proportions of the present Neues Schloss. Wilhelmine succeeded in creating something all her own and each room is different, ranging from the Ballroom in white, gold and blue, to a Japanese Room, a Mirror Room, grottoes, and a striking wood-paneled dining-room. The Mirror Room, lined from top to bottom with broken and uneven shapes, as if put together from several broken mirrors, is after a personal design by Wilhelmine and is thought to be her comment on the false glamor of her age, too concerned with appearances. Her other personal stamp is the split-tailed dragon motif, which was her favorite emblem and appears throughout the palace in different sizes and materials.

A sort of curiosity just outside town is the **Eremitage** (Wieland-Wagner-Strasse, Tues.–Sun., guided tours 9–11:30am and 1–4:30pm; DM1.50, DM1 students; bus #2 from the Marktplatz). The place has its origins in the eighteenth-century fad of the nobility for playing at asceticism by occasionally staying in bare monks' cells and eating nothing but soup. But when the original hermitage was given to Wilhelmine as a birthday present, she proceeded to build a glamorous retreat set in landscaped gardens decorated by fountains and pools, with live peacocks adding the final touches to her quirky vision of retreat as perfect indulgence. The old hermitage still stands, and some of the excessively bare cells remain. Wilhelmine's **Sonnentempel** is built at a small distance at the highest point of its romantic park. Designed in a horseshoe shape and fronted by arcades lined with pillars, the whole thing is completely encrusted by glass mosaics that sparkle madly in the sun. It seems horribly gaudy by modern standards, and the only way to appreciate it at all seems to be to stand back slightly so that the multitude of glittery colors doesn't overwhelm. In accordance with the fashion of the times, there's also a small artificial ruin, which was used as an open-air theater, where even Wilhelmine took to the stage, often with her friend Voltaire.

Wagner's legacy is the **Festspielhaus** (Schulstrasse, Nov.–Sept. Tues.–Sun., guided tours 10–11:30am and 1:30–3pm; DM2), remarkable for its unique acoustics rather than its architecture, which is why people are prepared to pay silly prices to attend the annual summer festival. The opera house opened in 1876, and the festival has continued with very few interruptions ever since, performing nothing but Wagner's operas. After his death in 1882, his wife Cosima ensured that the festival continued in its success, and various family members have been in charge of this famous musical event ever since. It was during his English daughter-in-law Winifred's "reign" from 1931 to 1944 that the festival had the unfortunate honor of Hitler's patronage, and he stayed as her house guest whenever he came to Bayreuth. Wagner buffs still argue over the extent to which she should be blamed for the misappropriation of Wagner's music during the Nazi era. These days the arguments have lost some of their relevance, however, and the focus is back on the musical productions, now run by Wolfgang Wagner.

If you're interested in the life and times of the composer, his music and family, then the **Richard Wagner Museum** (Richard-Wagner-Str. 48, daily 9am–5pm; DM2.50, DM3.50 in July and Aug., DM1 students) is just the place. It's housed in the composer's home, which he had built according to his own designs, and enigmatically called *Haus Wahnfried*, which literally means "peace from delusion." A rather characterless box, built in the nineteenth-century villa fashion, the interior was perfectly tuned to cozy middle-class life, centered around a large salon-and-concert-room for the composer. This was the setting for Wagner's famed soirées, attended by intellectuals, musicians, and royalty alike. Wagner's wife Cosima was the daughter of another famous composer, Franz Liszt, and the combination of the couple's backgrounds and interests made the household an important focus of German cultural life. Theirs was also one of the most famous love stories of the nineteenth century, and they lie buried together in the villa's garden.

Two other museums worth visiting if you've got the time are the **Stadtmuseum** (Kanzleistr. 1, Tues.–Fri. 10am–5pm, July–Aug. Mon.–Fri. 10am–5pm; DM2) and the **Deutsches Freimaurer-Museum** (im Hofgarten, Tues.–Fri. 10am–noon and 2–4pm, Sat. 10am–noon; DM2). The former concentrates mainly on the eighteenth century, with collections of fine local porcelain and glazed beer mugs, rustic furniture and weapons, as well as exhibits relating to the Bayreuth Margraves. The latter is an intriguing museum dedicated to Freemasons, representing them as a collective peace movement rather than anything sinister, and its library of some 12,000 volumes is an important center for research. It's revealing to see just how many well-known people were Freemasons, including Harry S. Truman, Churchill, Frederick the Great, Dickens, Goethe, Haydn, and Mozart. The movement has its origins in seventeenth-century England and Scotland, where it was originally a society for stonemasons. Hence the grades of membership still relate to that trade, and a new member is called a "rough stone," who is to live by the motto of "introspection."

More practically, the **youth hostel** (Universitätsstr. 28, ☎0921 25262; bus #4 from the Bahnhof) isn't particularly central, but the bus service is regular since it's almost next door to the university. Otherwise the cheapest accommodation is in the region of DM25–45 for singles and DM50–80 for doubles. Most convenient (it's opposite the train station) is *Schindler* (Bahnhofstr. 9, ☎0921 26249), and not far away is *Zum Herzog* (Herzog 2, Kulmbacherstrasse, ☎0921 41334). In a quiet quarter near the middle of town, the *Gasthof Goldener Löwe* (Kulmbacherstr. 30, ☎0921 41046) is very cozy and serves great food and local beers in its *Gasthaus* section.

Around Bayreuth

The **FICHTELGEBIRGE** just east of Bayreuth are not really as mountainous as their name ("Spruce Mountains") would imply, but rather a craggy landscape of crumbling granite hills, wildly romantic and full of bubbling streams and highland paths. The highest of the "mountains" is the **Ochsenkopf** at 1053m, and the other peaks are of the same caliber, covered by large areas of forests interspersed with bare highland moors. The Ochsenkopf is unfortunately very touristy, with a great big television tower on it, and a *Schwebebahn* ("suspension railroad') plus attendant commercial trappings. But the region stretches from Bayreuth to the Czech border and there are plenty of places where hikers are undisturbed. The youth hostel in OBERWARMENSTEINACH would be a good base for hiking. Other accommodation in local farms and guesthouses in the region can be arranged by contacting the *Tourist Information Fichtelgebirge* (Bayreuthestr. 4, 8591 Fichtelberg, ☎09272 6255). The strangest landscape the Fichtelgebirge has to offer is what's known as the **Luisenburg** near WUNSIEDEL—again the name is misleading, as there's no castle here but instead a rocky sea of granite blocks, eroded over the years to look like some giant child's pebbles left strewn untidily across the countryside.

One of Franconia's largest fortified castles, the **Plassenburg** (1 April–30 Sept. Tues.–Sun. 10am–4:30pm; DM1) sits Colditz-like 116m above the town of **KULMBACH** just north of Bayreuth. In fact the comparison isn't that far-fetched, because it was used as a prison throughout the nineteenth century, and very little of the original interior remains. Some state rooms have been restored, but the castle's main function is to house the **Zinnfigurenmuseum** (April–Sept. Tues.–Sun. 10am–4:30pm, Oct.–March 10am–3:30pm; DM2, DM0.50 students). The collection of tin figurines includes 300,000 individual pieces and must be one of the largest anywhere. As you might expect, the main theme is battle formations, and various historic showdowns are meticulously recreated. To round off, there's also a gallery of seventeenth- and eighteenth-century paintings of hunting and battle scenes and a collection of traditional hunting paraphernalia that continue the blood-thirsty vein.

Back down in the town, the main attractions are the breweries. . .or rather their products. There are quite a few breweries here and their origin lies in the fact that in medieval times, anyone who became a citizen of Kulmbach automatically received the right to brew their own beer. The *Eisbock* of the *Reichelbräu* is a powerful ice beer; the *Schwarzbier* of the old monastic *Kloster* brewery is one of Germany's best dark beers; while *EKU's Kulminator 28* claims to be the strongest brew in the world. A major **beer festival** is held annually in late July/early August.

travel details

trains
From Munich to Augsburg (3 an hour; 30min), Regensburg (1; 2hr), Nürnberg (1; 1½hr), Würzburg (1; 2hr 20min).

From Nürnberg to Coburg (1; 1hr 35min), Bamberg (2; 45min), Passau (1; 2hr 20min), Ansbach (2; 45min), Bayreuth (2; 1hr 10min), Minden (1; 1½hr).

CHAPTER TWO

BADEN-WÜRTTEMBERG

B ADEN-WÜRTTEMBERG is the youngest of the German Länder, only coming into existence in 1952 as a result of the merger, approved by plebiscite, of three relatively small provinces established by the American and French occupying forces. Theodor Heuss, the first federal president, saw it as "the model of German possibilities," and it hasn't disappointed, maintaining its ranking as the most prosperous part of the country, as well as one of the few to go against the national trend of a diminishing population. Being weak in natural resources, the area has had to rely on ingenuity to provide a spur to its industrial development, and ever since the motor car was invented here last century, it has been at the forefront of the world technology scene.

Ethnically, culturally and historically, the Land has two separate roots. The people of **Baden**, the western part of the province, are predominantly Catholic, and are generally seen as being of a relaxed, almost carefree disposition. Their neighbors in **Württemberg** (or **Swabia**, as the locals still prefer to call it), on the other hand, are renowned for being hard-working, thrifty, and house-proud, values instilled in them since the Reformation they embraced so openly. This stark division, however, has been much modified by the extensive influx of refugees from the Eastern Territories after World War II: along with their descendants, they now account for about a quarter of the total population.

For variety of scenery, Baden-Württemberg is rivaled only by Bavaria. The western and southern boundaries of the province are defined by the river Rhine and its bulge into Germany's largest lake, the **Bodensee**. Immediately beyond lies the **Black Forest**, one of Europe's main holiday areas. Here rises another of the continent's principal waterways, the **Danube**, which later forms a grandly impressive gorge at the foot of the **Swabian Jura**, the range in which the Neckar begins its increasingly sedate northerly course. At the eastern end of the province, there's an even gentler valley, that of the **Tauber**.

Each of Baden-Württemberg's three largest cities—**Stuttgart**, **Mannheim**, and **Karlsruhe**—was formerly a state capital (of Württemberg, the Palatinate, and Baden respectively). All were extensively damaged in World War II and none could be called beautiful, though each has plenty of good points. Unfortunately, the historical centers of **Freiburg im Breisgau** and **Ulm** were also bombed, but both their Münsters, which rank among Germany's greatest buildings, were spared. Other than this, Baden-Württemberg's lack of a heavy industrial base meant that it escaped the war relatively lightly. Germany's two most famous university cities, **Heidelberg** and **Tübingen**, were hardly touched, enabling the former to maintain its cherished role as the most romantic and swooned-over place in the entire country.

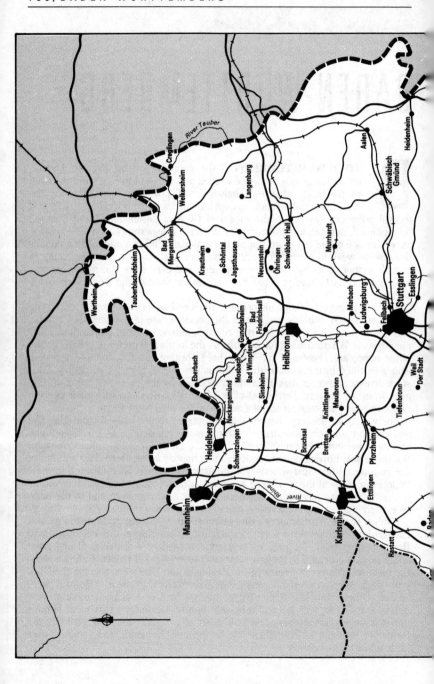

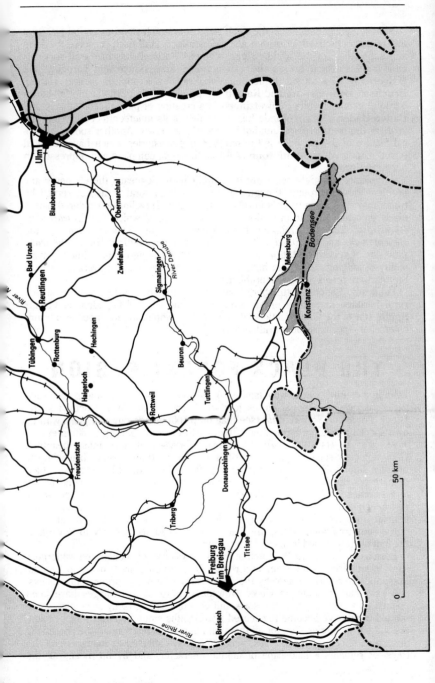

Almost equally enticing is the wealth of towns which stand as period pieces of different epochs. **Bad Wimpfen** and **Schwäbisch Hall** each preserve the form and appearance of the Middle Ages, whereas **Rottweil** has medieval survivals amid streets which bridge the gap between Renaissance and baroque, and **Haigerloch** is a varied confection enhanced by a superb natural setting. **Bruchsal**, **Ludwigsburg** and **Rastatt** are proud courtly towns in the full-blown baroque manner, while **Schwetzingen** is a creation of pure rococo fantasy and **Baden-Baden** remains wonderfully evocative of its nineteenth-century halcyon years as the favorite playground of European aristocracy. Another special histori-cal feature of the province is the number of monasteries which have survived intact, among which **Maulbronn** ranks as the most complete and impressive in northern Europe.

A typically comprehensive **public transit** network means there's never any problem moving around, though waiting periods in rural areas not served by trains may be longer than is normal in Germany. Traveling is rendered partic-ularly enjoyable by the profusion of scenic routes, of which the *Schwarzwald-Hochstrasse* and the railroad lines known as the *Schwarzwaldbahn*, the *Höllentalbahn* and the *Donautalbahn* are the most outstanding. There's the usual provision of **accommodation** in youth hostels and campgrounds, while the avail-ability of lodgings in private houses is well above the national average. Only in Stuttgart are prices a possible problem.

Politically, Baden-Württemberg leans well to the right, a legacy of its strong rural heritage and small urban proletariat. The Minister-President is **Lothar Späth**, star of the liberal faction within the CDU, who is widely tipped as a future chancellor—perhaps sooner rather than later.

THE BLACK FOREST REGION

Even in a country where woodland is so widespread as to exert a grip over such varied aspects of national life as folklore, literature and leisure activities, the **Black Forest** or *Schwarzwald* (see map on p.166) stands out as a place with its own special mystique. Stretching 170km north to south, and up to 60km east to west, it's by far the largest German forest—and the most beautiful. Geographically speaking, it's a massif in its own right, but forms a pair with the broadly similar French Jura on the opposite side of the Rhine valley, which demarcates the borders with both France and Switzerland. The name of the forest comes from the dark, densely packed fir trees on the upper slopes; oaks and beeches are characteristic of the lower ranges. With its houses sheltering beneath massive sloping straw roofs, its cuckoo clocks and its colorful, often outrageous traditional dress, the Black Forest ranks second only to Bavaria as the font of stereotyped images of the country.

Even as late as the 1920s, much of this area was a rarely penetrated wilderness sunk in an eerie gloom, forming a refuge for everything from boars to bandits. Romantics were drawn here by the wild beauty of watery gorges, dank valleys, and exhilarating mountain views. Nowadays, most of the villages have been opened up as spa and health resorts, full of shops selling tacky souvenirs, while the old trails have become manicured gravel paths smoothed down for pension-ers and baby buggies. Yet, for all that—and in spite of fears about the potentially disastrous effects of *Waldsterben*, which may have affected as many as half the trees—it remains a landscape of unique character, and by no means all the modernizations are drawbacks. **Railroad** fans, for example, will find several of the most spectacular lines in Europe, some of them brilliant feats of engineering. It should be noted, though, that the trains tend to stick closely to the valleys, that **bus services** are much reduced outside the tourist season, and that **walking** is undoubtedly the most satisfying way to travel.

Most of the Black Forest is associated with the Margraviate (later Grand Duchy) of **Baden**, whose old capital of **Baden-Baden**—the ultimate playground of the mega-rich—is at the northern fringe of the forest, in a fertile orchard and vineyard-growing area. This was later usurped by custom-built **Karlsruhe**, which is technically outside the Black Forest, but best visited in conjunction with it. The only city actually surrounded by the forest is **Freiburg im Breisgau**, one of the most distinctive and enticing in the country.

Freiburg im Breisgau

FREIBURG IM BREISGAU, "capital" of the Black Forest, basks in a laid-back atmosphere which seems completely un-German. As the seat of a university since 1457, the city has an animated, youthful presence which, unlike so many other academic centers, is kept up all year round, with the help of a varied program of festivals. It's a city of music, of street theater and buskers—and a haunt of color-fully-clad gypsies, who find here the one German city in which they can feel at home. Furthermore, the sun shines here more often, and there are more vine-yards within the municipal area, than in any other city in the country.

The locals explain Freiburg's singularity by the fact that they aren't Germans at all, but Austrians. Between 1368 and 1805, when it was allocated to the buffer state of Baden, the city was almost continuously under the protection of the House of Habsburg. It's often claimed that the Austrians brought a touch of humanity to the German character, and that it was their eventual exclusion from the country's affairs which led to the triumph of militarism. Yet the persistence here of the relaxed multicultural climate characteristic of Austria is living proof that there's more than a grain of truth in this cliché.

Freiburg makes the most obvious base for visiting the Black Forest, with fast and frequent public transit connections to all the famous beauty spots. In its own right, it well warrants a couple of days' exploration, and, even if you're only pass-ing through, you should make a point of visiting the lovely **Münster**. Even though the city was extensively destroyed in a single air raid in 1944, no modern building has been allowed to challenge the supremacy of its magisterial tower, which the doyen of art historians, Jacob Burckhardt, described as "the greatest in Christendom."

Arrival and practicalities

The **Hauptbahnhof**, which has the **bus station** on its southern side, is about ten minutes' walk from the city center. **Exchange facilities** are available within the former (Mon.–Sat. 7am–8pm, Sun. 9am–1pm). Following Eisenbahnstrasse straight ahead, you come to the **tourist office** on Rotteckring (May–Oct. Mon.–Weds. and Sat. 9am–6pm, Thurs. and Fri. 9am–9pm, Sun. and holidays 10am–noon, Nov.–April Mon.–Fri. 9am–6pm, Sat. 9am–3pm; ☎216 3286).

For DM3, the tourist office will find you a room; if you arrive after closing time, there's an electronic noticeboard equipped with a phone, telling you which places

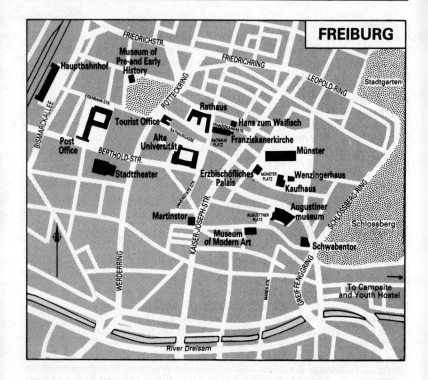

have vacancies, though this is not an exhaustive service. Prices start at around DM20 in **private houses**, but a stay of at least three nights may be required. Among **hotels** with a central location, the cheapest are *Stühlinger*, Klarastr. 65 (☎272522), charging DM25 per head, and *Schemmer*, Eschholzstr. 63 (☎272424), with singles upwards of DM30, doubles at DM60. Comparable options farther out include *Pension Gisela*, Am Vogelbach 27 (☎82472) at DM28 per person, *Hirschen*, Breisgauer Str. 47 (☎82118) at DM30; *Löwen*, Breisgauer Str. 62 (☎84661) and *Gihring*, Eggstr. 10 (☎74963).

The luxurious **youth hostel** is at Karthäuserstr. 151 (☎67656; take tram #1 to Hasemannstrasse) at the extreme western end of the city, ideally placed for walks in the hills or along the banks of the River Dreisam. Nearby, but slightly nearer town, is one of five **campgrounds**, *Hirzberg* (April–mid-Oct.; ☎35054); while *Möselpark* (mid-March–Oct.; ☎72938) is south of the houses on the opposite side of the river. Southwest of the center, and open all year, is *St. Georg*, Basler Landstr. 62 (☎43183). Cheapest place to camp is the all-year *Breisgau* (☎07665 2346), way to the north in the village of HOCHDORF; also here is the huge *Tunisee* site (April–Oct.; ☎07665 2249 or 1249).

If you're staying far out, it makes sense to invest in a **rover ticket** on the public transit system. Prices are DM5 for 24 hours, DM8 for 48 hours, and DM11 for 72 hours; single journeys are DM2.50, or DM10 for strips of five.

The city

Crafted out of a dark red sandstone quarried in one of the surrounding hills, the **Münster** (or **Dom**) is so magnificent and overpowering an edifice that it puts the rest of the city in the shade. Not the least remarkable fact about it is that, though it rivals any of the great European cathedrals, it was built as a mere parish church. No funds from the well-lined coffers of the ecclesiastical hierarchy were forthcoming for its construction—the costs were met entirely from the pockets of local citizens, to whom it was the ultimate symbol of municipal pride. In 1827, on the suppression of the prince-bishopric of Konstanz, the Münster's artistic standing was given due recognition when it became the seat of the Upper Rhenish archbishopric.

Work on the Münster began in about 1200, to replace a much simpler church dating from the time of the town's foundation eighty years before. The transepts were built first, in the picturesque late Romanesque style then still popular in Germany. However, there was an abrupt change when the masons became aware of the structural advantages of Gothic, which the French had already mastered. At first, the same masons began building in this unfamiliar idiom; later, one of the architects of Strasbourg Cathedral took over. He created a masterly **nave**, resplendent with flying buttresses, gargoyles, and statues, yet already diverging from French models in its sense of spatial unity.

Further originality is evident in the west **porch**, begun around 1270. Part of both the interior and exterior (it's fenced off these days, but you can enter it from inside), it had to accommodate the same sculptural program that the French were able to spread all over the facade and transept. The figures, which still bear traces of coloring, are much the most important German works of their time. A sweetly-carved *Madonna and Child* guards the door; above, the tympanum illustrates the entire New Testament, from the Incarnation to Judgment Day. On the end walls, the Wise and Foolish Virgins confront each other. Deliberately shrouded on the west wall, at the point where the natural light is weakest, are the most striking figures: Satan as Prince of Darkness, beguilingly disguised as a youthful knight, and Sensuality, who has toads and serpents writhing on her back.

The single **tower** (March–Nov. Tues.–Sat. 10am–5pm, Sun. 1–5pm; DM1) above the porch was a unique design for its time, but was subsequently much imitated, most notably at Ulm. In spite of its seemingly organic unity, it wasn't planned as a whole. The square plan of the lower stories was brilliantly converted into a soaring octagon, bearing animated statues of prophets and angels, which forms the stage above the bells. From the platform here, you're rewarded with a fine panorama over the city and the Black Forest. However, the best view is of the lacelike tracery of the **openwork spire**, which rounds off the tower with a bravura flourish. The first of its kind, it was inspired by the mystical spiritual exercises of the time, and symbolizes the human soul stretching out to receive divine knowledge. Many similar spires were planned for subsequent German churches, though most remained unbuilt until the nineteenth century. Exceptions are the two miniature versions which were immediately placed on Freiburg's own **Hahnentürme** (*Cock Towers*).

For the **chancel**, begun in the mid-fourteenth century (about 25 years after the completion of the spire), the authorities again struck lucky with their choice of architect, a man named Johannes of the famous Parler dynasty. His regular geometric layout marked a major advance on French models, and his two

portals, particularly the northern one dedicated to the Creation, are adorned with superbly expressive sculptures—look out for the unusual depiction of God resting on the seventh day. As it happened, there was a lull in building activity for nearly a century, and the chancel was only completed just before the Reformation.

Inside, the transept is lit by luminous **stained glass** windows of the early thirteenth century. Most of those in the nave date from a hundred years later, and were donated by the local trades and guilds, who incorporated their coats-of-arms. The miners' window is especially interesting for including a vignette of them at work. Other items to look out for are a delicate late thirteenth-century *Madonna* on the west wall, a poignant fourteenth-century *Holy Sepulcher* in the south aisle, and the pulpit, an archaic Gothic work of the mid-sixteenth century with depictions of Freiburg personalities of the day. At the entrance to the chancel is a fine *Adoration of the Magi* by the leading local woodcarver of the late Gothic period, Hans Wydyz. This artist sometimes collaborated with the mercurial **Hans Baldung**, Dürer's most talented follower, whose high altar triptych of *The Coronation of the Virgin*—arguably his masterpiece—can be glimpsed from this point.

Regrettably, the powers that be take a mercenary attitude to the wonderful **art treasures** housed in the ambulatory chapels. To see them, and to get a better view of the Baldung triptych, including a look at the nocturnal *Crucifixion* on its reverse side, you have to take a **guided tour** (daily departure times posted at the south transept entrance; DM1). In the Universitätskapelle, there are two wings of a curious **Holbein** retable. The portraits of the donor family are by Hans the Elder, but the main scenes of *The Nativity* and *Epiphany* are youthful works by his son, whose superior gifts are already in evidence. A *Rest on the Flight into Egypt* in the Kaiserkapelle has sculptures by Wydyz and a painted background by Baldung, who also designed many of the stained glass windows in the chapels, though many of these have been replaced by copies. Another talented local sculptor of the time, Hans Sixt von Staufen, carved the *Madonna of Mercy* in the Locherer Kapelle. In the Villinger Kapelle is a rare relic of the first Münster, a chased silver *Crucifix*.

Until the war, the spacious **Münsterplatz** formed a fitting setting for the great church in its midst. However, the north side was flattened by bombs (which miraculously hardly touched the Münster itself) and only the late fifteenth-century **Kornhaus**, the municipal granary, has been rebuilt. The rest of the square has survived in much better shape; the daily markets are one of the most enticing in Germany, with a mouth-watering selection of goodies on offer to make up a picnic. There are also a couple of pretty **fountains** directly in front of the Münster—the *Georgsbrunnen* and the *Fischbrunnen*, along with three tall columns bearing statues of the local patron saints.

The south side of the square is dominated by the blood-red **Kaufhaus**, a sixteenth-century merchants' hall. Its arcaded facade bears coats of arms and four statues by Sixt von Staufen of members of the House of Habsburg, while each end has an extravagant oriel with a sharply pointed roof. On either side of the Kaufhaus are handsome baroque palaces—to the west is the **Erzbischöfliches Palais** while the **Wenzingerhaus** stands to the east. The latter was named after the artist Christian Wenzinger, who built it as his own residence; an elaborate font designed by him can be seen in the Münster's *Stürzelkapelle*. Plans are afoot to convert the interior into a museum; this will be well worth visiting, if only to see the resplendent rococo staircase, complete with frescoed ceiling. The square is closed on the far side by another baroque building, the former **Hauptwache** (*Guard House*), and by the canons' residences.

A peculiarity of Freiburg is the continuous visible presence throughout the old part of the city of its **storm drain system**, known as the *Bächle*. These are rivulets, fed by the river Dreisam, which run in deep gulleys, serving as a continuous trap for the unwary pedestrian or motorist. Formerly used for watering animals, and as a sure precaution against the fire hazard which accounted for so many medieval towns, they have their purpose even today, by helping to keep the city agreeably cool.

Following the main channel of the *Bächle* southwards, you come to the **Schwaben Tor**, one of two surviving towers of the medieval fortifications. On Oberlinden, just in front, is **Zum Roten Bären**, which is generally considered to be Germany's oldest inn—a function it has held since 1311, although the building itself is two centuries older. The parallel Konviktstrasse has won conservation prizes for the restoration of its old houses.

Just to the west is Salzstrasse, which is lined with baroque and neoclassical mansions. Also here is the **Augustiner Museum** (Tues. and Thurs.–Sun. 10am–5pm, Weds. 10am–8pm; free), which takes its name from the former monastery whose buildings it occupies. One of the most pleasing smaller collections in Germany, it makes an essential supplement to a visit to the Münster, containing as it does many works of art, such as gargoyles, statues and stained glass, which have been replaced in situ by copies to prevent farther erosion. Also on show are examples of the religious art of the Upper Rhine, along with folklore displays on the Black Forest.

There are also a few top-class old masters. Three panels of a *Passion Altar*, including the central *Crucifixion*, constitute the most important surviving paintings by the great but mysterious draughtsman known as **Master of the Housebook**. *The Miracle of the Snow* by **Grünewald** is one of the wings of the altarpiece now in Stuppach. It depicts Pope Liberius laying the foundation-stone of Santa Maria Maggiore in Rome, following a miraculous fall of snow on Midsummer's Day. As well as his stained glass, **Baldung** is represented by three typically unorthodox paintings, notably a *Cupid in Flight*. A number of the artist's engravings are shown alongside, while there's also a brightly-colored *Risen Christ* by **Cranach**.

South of here, on Marienstrasse, a **Museum of Modern Art** (same times; free) has been set up in an old school building. Though it can't rival the richness of the parent collection, it does have good cross section of twentieth-century German painting. Beside it stands the baroque **Adelhauserkirche**, retaining important works of art from its predecessor, notably a fourteenth-century *Crucifix*. The former convent buildings now house an **Ethnographical Museum** (Tues.–Sun. 9:30am–5pm; free), with exhibits drawn from all non-European cultures. From here, follow Fischerau, the old fishermen's street, and you come to the other surviving thirteenth-century tower, the **Martinstor**, which now stands in the middle of Freiburg's central axis, Kaiser-Joseph-Strasse.

Immediately west of here is the **university quarter**. Alongside the inevitable modern buildings are several interesting older structures, including two rococo courtyards, and a large Jugendstil lecture hall. On Bertoldstrasse, to the north, are the Universitätskirche, formerly a Jesuit college, and the baroque Alte Universität.

The **Neues Rathaus**, formed out of two separate Renaissance houses, one of which has an oriel adorned with a noble relief of *The Lady and the Unicorn*, was an even earlier home of the University. It forms part of a shady chestnut tree-lined square, whose other buildings include the **Altes Rathaus**, itself a fusion of several older buildings, and the plain Gothic Franciscan monastery church of St. **Martin**. There's also a statue in honor of Bertold Schwarz, who, when a monk here in the mid-fourteenth century, supposedly invented gunpowder. A few minutes' walk to the west, in the Columbipark opposite the tourist office, is the **Museum of Pre- and Early History** (daily 9am–7pm; free), which has important archaeological collections on the Black Forest region, particularly of the times of the Alemanni and the Franks.

In the alley behind St. Martin is the cheerful late Gothic facade of the **Haus Zum Wallfisch**. For two years, this was the home of the great humanist Desiderius Erasmus, the most conciliatory and sympathetic of the leading figures of the Reformation period, who was forced to flee from his residence in Basel in the light of the turbulent religious struggles there. A late fifteenth-century palace nearby, on the main Kaiser-Joseph-Strasse, is known as the **Baseler Hof**, as it served for nearly a century as the residence of the exiled cathedral chapter of the Swiss city.

It's well worth climbing one of the hills surrounding the city for the sake of the wonderful views they offer. The **Schlossberg** immediately to the east of the city center makes for an easy ascent by a path from the Schwabentor; there's no need to take the cable car. This summit also has the benefit of including close-range views of the Münster. For photography, it's best to come in the morning. To the south, the **Lorettoburg** (where the stone for the Münster was quarried) makes a good afternoon or evening alternative. Far higher, and thus with more spectacular panoramas, than either of these is the **Schauinsland** (1284m), still within the city boundaries, but a good 15km southeast, reached by tram #2 to Günterstal, then bus #21. A series of marked nature trails comb the area, which is still inhabited by chamois, or you can ascend by a 15-minute cable car ride.

Eating, Drinking, and Nightlife

Freiburg is a superb place for food and drink, with **restaurants** to cater to all pockets. If you want to splurge, try the aforementioned *Zum Roten Bären* on Oberlinden, or the fifteenth-century *Markgräfler Hof* on Gerberau, which is renowned for its astonishing wine list. On Münsterplatz are two top-notch wine cellars which are rather less pricey—*Oberkirchs Weinstuben* and the *Ratskeller*—while *Zur Traube* on Schusterstrasse just behind is equally good. Hearty South German cooking can be sampled at *Kleiner Meyerhof* on Rathausgasse or *Grosser Meyerhof* on Grünwälderstrasse; the latter in particular is surprisingly reasonable, considering its quality. Best place for Italian cuisine is *Wolfshöhle* on Konviktstrasse; *Milano* on Schusterstrasse makes a good cheap alternative. *Tessiner Stuben* on Bertold Strasse is a combination vegetarian restaurant wine-bar, complete with garden. First choice for outdoor eating, however, is the terrace of *Greiffenegg-Schlössle* on Schlossbergring.

As you'd expect, the animated **student bars** are mostly clustered around the university quarter. Currently, the trendiest place to be seen is *Uni-Café* on Universitätsecke, which serves a wide selection of coffees, and has good snacks. Somewhat more expensive is *Café Journal* on Universitätsplatz, which is more of a disco-bar. Drinks at *Café Windlicht* on Filcherau are good value, and can be consumed at tables set out on the cobbled street outside, while *Damfross* on Löwenstrasse serves inexpensive meals. Somewhat out of the quarter, but with a large student clientele, is *Café Atlantik* on Schwabentorring, a run-down music pub serving very cheap food in the evenings. At the moment the "in" **disco** is

Unverschämt on Humboldstrasse; among its competitors is the Rajneeshi-run *Zorba the Buddha* on Löwenstrasse.

Freiburg now ranks as one of the leading German cities for **jazz**, thanks to the new *Jazzhaus* on Schwenlinstrasse, which has concerts every evening at 8:30pm. The list of those who have appeared here already includes many of the world's leading artists. **Classical music** can be heard in a variety of locations: orchestral concerts at the *Stadthalle* on Messplatz, chamber and instrumental recitals in the *Paulussaal* on Dreisamstrasse, the *Kaufhaus* on Münsterplatz, and the *Musikhochschule* on Schwarzwaldstrasse. All types of music are performed at the University's *Audimax*.

Main **theater** venue is the *Freiburger Theater* on Bertoldstrasse, which has three auditoriums plus the *Theatercafé*, where late-night cabaret and variety shows are held. The intimate *Wallgrabentheater* on Rathausgasse specializes in modern plays. Pick of the **movie houses** are *Cinemathek* on Bertoldstrasse and *Kommunales Kino*, Alter Wiehrebahnhof.

Listings

Area code (☎0761).

Bike rental *Zweirad Müller*, Klarastr. 80 (☎278320) or Friedrichring 27 (☎274244).

Car rental *Avis*, Moltekstr. 42 (☎42288); *Europcar*, Wilhelmstr. 3a (☎36446); *Hertz*, Eschholzstr. 42 (☎272020); *InterRent*, Wilhelmstr. 1a (☎31066).

Festivals The *Fastnet* celebrations are among the best in Baden-Württemberg; there are burning ceremonies on the evening of Shrove Tuesday, as well as parades of jesters the day before. Both the *Frühlingsfest* in May and the *Herbstsfest* in October last for ten days, and include spectacular fairground amusements. In June, the two-week *International Tent Music Festival* features all varieties of music, performed under canvas. Later in the month, five days are given over to a wine market known as the *Weintagen*. Mid-August has the nine-day-long *Weinkost*, a sampling session for wines produced in the Freiburg region.

Mitfahrzentrale Belfortstr. 55 (☎36749).

East of Freiburg

Some 20km east of Freiburg, and connected by regular bus services, is **ST. PETER**, a tiny health resort clustering round a Benedictine **Kloster**. This was founded in the eleventh century, but the present complex belongs to a rebuilding begun in 1724. Peter Thumb built the striking twin-towered church, a classically-inspired baroque design of unusual width and spaciousness. On the pillars are statues of members of the House of Zähringen by Josef Anton Feuchtmayer, in commemoration of the fact that this monastery was, like the city of Freiburg, one of their foundations. The monastic buildings, now used as a seminary, are rococo in style, dating from a generation later. Particularly eye-catching is the galleried **library**, gleaming with white stuccowork and frescoes. Colorful costumed **festivals** are held in the village on Corpus Christi and on the Sunday after the feast day of Saints Peter and Paul (June 29).

A few kilometers northwest is **GLOTTERTAL**, reached via the gentle wine-growing valley of the same name. This has gained national fame as a result of the clinic perched above the village, which forms the setting for Germany's answer to *Coronation Street* and *Dallas*.

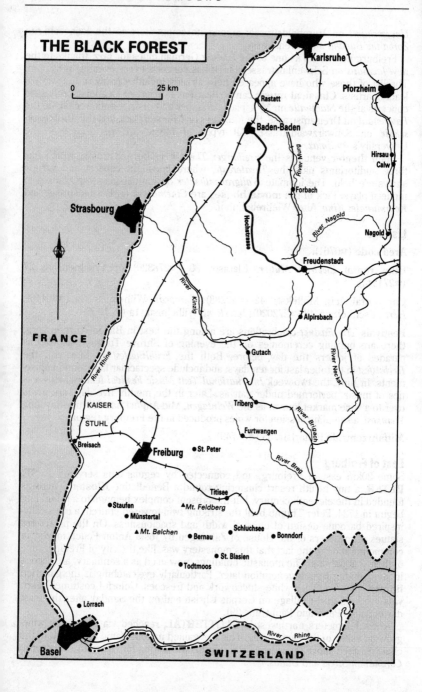

Breisach and the Kaiserstuhl

Whoever the war was between, and whatever it was about, Alt Breisach was bound to be in it. Everybody besieged it, most people captured it; the majority of them lost it again; nobody seemed able to keep it. Whom he belonged to, and what he was, the dweller in Alt Breisach could never have been quite sure. One day he would be a Frenchman, and then before he could learn enough French to pay his taxes he would be an Austrian. While trying to discover what you did in order to be a good Austrian, he would find he was no longer an Austrian, but a German, though what particular German out of a dozen must always have been doubtful to him.

Jerome K. Jerome, *Three Men on the Bummel.*

BREISACH, perched high above the Rhine on a promontory about 30km west of Freiburg, is an archteypal frontier post in what has been one of the most heavily-disputed parts of Europe. Even if the river is now firmly established as a natural border, and the town regarded as being indisputably German, the turbulent legacy of its past is still clearly visible.

As has been the case since at least the early thirteenth century, the upper town is surrounded by **ramparts**. The ones visible today bear the unmistakable stamp of the greatest of all military engineers, the Frenchman Sébastien Vauban, who was also responsible for laying out the town of NEUF BREISACH on the opposite bank. Indeed, the monumental **Rheintor** at the northwest end of Breisach itself is as purely French a building as can be seen in Germany, in the classically-influenced baroque style characteristic of the age of Louis XIV. Yet, just above it, the gabled medieval **Kapftor** could hardly be more German in feel, and the same applies to the earlier **Hagenbachtor** on the brow of the hill farther south. Just beyond the last-named is one of Breisach's many belvederes, offering grandstand views of France.

Looming high above all else in the spacious, half-deserted upper part of town is the **Münster**. From outside, it's no beauty, fashioned out of rough, diffuse stone-work, and truncated on the southern side in order to squeeze into an irregular, constricted space. It was originally built in the late Romanesque period on the foundations of a Roman fortress; the nave, transept and the two "Cock" towers survive from this time. The upper parts of the southern tower were re-fashioned in Gothic style in the early fourteenth century, a period which also saw the construction of a new chancel (under which is an open crypt—apparently the only one of its kind in the world) and the stumpy facade, which boasts a delicately carved tympanum illustrating scenes from the life of the Münster's patron, Saint Stephen. At the end of the fifteenth century, it was decided to commission spectacular new decorations for the interior of the Münster rather than rebuild it; as a result, it acquired some of the most impressive **works of art** of any church in Germany, all created at the transitional point between Gothic and Renaissance.

Filling the west end is a huge **fresco cycle** of *The Last Judgment* by **Martin Schongauer**, the father-figure of the golden age of German art. Sadly, it's in a very faded condition, but enough remains to suggest that it must have been nearly as remarkable as Michelangelo's famous depiction of the same subject in the Sistine Chapel, painted nearly half a century later. The facade has a hierachical representation of Judgment Day, with an all-powerful Christ surrounded by saints, patriarchs, and angels. On the north wall, the torments and tortures of Hell, strewn with abysses and populated by misshapen fiends, are depicted with relish, to serve as a warning to the congregation of the perils of a dissolute life-style. Directly opposite, the serene voyage of the Elect towards Eternal Paradise illustrates the prize the faithful should strive to attain.

Contemporary with the frescoes is the **rood screen**, which is in the ultimate filigree tradition of late Gothic. In the chapel beside it is a silver **shrine** containing the relics of the early martyrs Saints Gervase and Protase, which were pilfered from Milan at the same time as those of the Three Magi (which were taken to Cologne), and allegedly arrived in Breisach by miraculous means, whereupon they became the joint patrons of the town. The reliefs on the lid include an illustration of this journey, complete with an accurate depiction of fifteenth century Breisach.

Saints Gervase and Protase turn up again on the right wing of the main **retable**, while on the opposite side of the central *Coronation of the Virgin* are the martyred deacons, Saints Stephen and Lawrence. This altarpiece is an astonishing piece of wholly eccentric yet hyper-skilled woodcarving. It may be late Gothic, but the entwined mass of cherubs, not to mention the swirling hair and drapery folds of the figures, are uncannily anticipatory of the baroque style of over a century later. Many attempts have been made to unmask the identity of the mysterious sculptor, known as **Master HL** after his cryptic signature, but to no conclusive effect. The sinuous upper part of the retable is by a more orthodox carver, but is still remarkable for the fact that it's actually higher than the ceiling, a trick achieved by means of a subtle slant.

Breisach's **Bahnhof** is at the southern end of town; from there follow Neutorplatz and Rheinstrasse and you come to Werd, where you'll find the **tourist office** (Mon.–Fri. 8:30am–12:30pm and 1:30–5:30pm, Sat. 8:30am–noon; ☎07667 83227). Ask there about **Rhine cruises** and visits to **wine cellars**—the town is the headquarters of the largest winery in Europe, the *Zentralkellerei Badischer Winzergenossenschaften* (☎07667 82270). **Cafés** and **restaurants** are scattered all over the lower town, but are almost entirely absent in the upper part. The simple **youth hostel** has an ideal location at Münsterbergstr. 30 (☎07667 7665) right beside the Hagenbachtor. Cheapest **hotel** is *Kaiserstühler Hof*, Richard-Müller-Str. 2 (☎07667 236). Alternatively, there's a **campground**, *Münsterblick* (☎07667 285), in the village of HOCHSTETTEN 2km south.

Some 25km west of Breisach is the old Alsatian city of **COLMAR**, which makes an unmissable excursion; there are five buses per day. French since 1918, Colmar was German for much of its history, a fact abundantly clear from its general appearance. It was the home town of Martin Schongauer, and a good deal of his work can be seen there. Even more significantly, the city possesses Grünewald's titanic *Isenheim Altar*, generally regarded as the supreme masterpiece of German painting. For more details, see *The Real Guide:France*.

The Kaiserstuhl

Breisach stands in the shadow of the **KAISERSTUHL**, an isolated volcanic mass which appears much higher than its 559 meters courtesy of the flat landscape all around. Its name, meaning "Emperor's Seat," is tenuously associated with a legend similar to that of King Arthur and the Knights of the Round Table: it's said that Emperor Frederick Barabarossa, who died while on his way to the Holy Land to fight the Infidel, is resting in this mountain, waiting for his second coming.

The Kaiserstuhl was formerly a haunt of nature lovers, who came to admire its luxuriant orchids and butterflies. However, the 1970s saw a stepping-up of its status as a **wine** area, with the plantation of vineyards arranged in neat, regular terraces; this went so far that there have been worries that the ecological balance has been irretrievably spoiled. Whatever the case, the volcanic soils impart a sharp, distinctive taste to the local white wines, notably *Silvaner*, *Riesling*, *Gewürztraminer* and *Ruländer*; there's also a much-praised rosé, *Weissherbst*.

The cemetery church of St. Michael in **NIEDERROTTWEIL**, 8km north of Breisach, has another superb retable, again based on a *Coronation of the Virgin*, by Master HL. Just to the north is the old wine-growers' town of **BURKHEIM**, which preserves a number of seventeenth-century houses. Prettiest of all the towns in the area is **ENDINGEN** on the northern side of the mountain, built around a graceful Marktplatz, whose Rathaus and Kornhaus both date back to the sixteenth century.

Public transit in the area is sparse by German standards; the only service *Deutsche Bundesbahn* runs is between Breisach and Freiburg. However, there's a privately-owned line circling the Kaiserstuhl, with several trains per day; steam locomotives are occasionally run on this route in summer. Otherwise, it's ideal country for gentle walking.

The Southern Black Forest

The **SOUTHERN BLACK FOREST** is the mountainous region south of Freiburg, encompassed by the French border to the west and the Swiss border to the south, and gradually petering out towards the southeast, somewhat before the shores of the Bodensee. Its landscape of forested hills is especially wonderful around the two highest points, **Mt. Belchen** and **Mt. Feldberg**. At 1414m and 1493m respectively, they're hardly mountains in the alpine sense, but on clear days you get vast panoramas from their summits, reaching as far as the Swiss Alps and the western Rhine valley.

Unfortunately, almost everyone in Europe knows about the beauties of this region, and in the summer months it's not unusual to find yourself sharing the sights with half a dozen coachloads of other people. The only advantage of all this organized tourism is that facilities for vacationers are excellent. **Accommodation** of all types is plentiful, if not always cheap, and most of the resort villages have pools, tennis courts, and other sporting opportunities. In fact the region is ideal for people who want to combine a bit of nature with all of life's material comforts, which in this case usually means pensioners and families with young children.

While there are only two large highways heading from west to east (one following the Swiss border on the southern side of the region, and the road connecting Freiburg to KONSTANZ on the northern side), **travel** around the edges of the region is easy and efficient by train. As for the interior of forest and mountains, it may only be about 50km as the crow flies from Freiburg to the Swiss border and 100km from the French border to the Bodensee, but there are mountains to circumnavigate. Though there's a comprehensive bus network, routes are circuitous, frequencies low, and many connections may only be possible once daily. A **seven-day bus pass** is available for the Southern Black Forest area, valid from the Rhine to the Bodensee (DM35 single, DM50 for two, and DM65 for families), which you may find useful and can buy either on the bus or at larger train stations with *Deutsche Bundesbahn* bus stations attached.

Around Mt. Belchen

MT. BELCHEN, surrounded by deep gorges some 20km south of Freiburg, is the most beautiful of the southern peaks, with wonderful views and quiet little villages in the valleys. One of those valleys is the **Münstertal**, dotted with the characteristic low shingle roofs of traditional Black Forest farms, set among lush pastures clinging to the steep hillsides of the northern Belchen reaches. On the southwestern reaches, near the village of NEUENWEG, you'll find the **Nonnenmattweiher**, which is one of the oldest lakes of the region, formed during the receding Ice Age, and an excellent place to combine hiking with fishing or simply picnicking. Be prepared for a lot of steep paths and deep furrows, and take some strong hiking shoes.

Some time in the seventh century, Irish missionaries came to Christianize this area; the most famous, Saint Trudpert, was murdered in 607 after only three years of missionary work. The **St. Trudpert** monastery in the upper Münstertal was founded about 250 years later, and the large baroque complex you see today, designed by Peter Thumb in the early eighteenth century, is the visual center of the whole upper valley. It was a Benedictine monastery until secularization in 1806, but now it's home to the *Josephschwestern*. Worth seeing is the church, whose refreshingly plain baroque interior is considered Thumb's masterpiece. White stucco decorations predominate, with only the ceiling frescoes and side altars adding discreet color.

Following the Münstertal west, the foothills sink into the Rhine valley, the landscape quickly changing into gently rolling hills that make up some of Germany's most famous vineyards and provide a lucrative living to many small and ancient towns. Of these, **STAUFEN** is particularly attractive. Situated at the bottom of the Münstertal, and surrounded by its vineyards, its location is idyllic and makes a great base for relaxed hiking tours, while the cobbled streets and medieval houses mean it's worth a visit in its own right.

The place also harbors a murky past in the shape of **Doktor Faustus** (Johannes Faust—see also p.255), who is said to have resided at the *Gasthaus Zum Löwen* in 1539. No. 5 on the third floor was his room, and you can still stay there if you're not too worried about his ghost coming to haunt you. Dr. Faustus came to Staufen at the behest of the local Count Anton von Staufen, who was in serious debt and hoped to bail himself out if only the good doctor could successfully make gold for him. But the doctor accidentally killed himself when one of his experiments exploded in his hotel room, and because of the putrid smell emanating from the room, the legend of his being taken by the devil soon became fixed in local folklore, a theme taken up by writers ever since—most famously by Goethe.

The **tourist office** in the Rathaus (☎07633 6041) supplies brochures on the town and its famous past, and also provides accommodation lists. If you want to stay in the *Zum Löwen*, Hauptstr. 47, (☎07633 7078), a single will cost DM60 and a double DM120. Much cheaper is the attractive gabled *Bahnhof-Hotel* on Bahnhofstr., (☎07633 6190), which charges DM20 per person and also offers cooking facilities to guests. Two more alternatives in the region of DM30 to 45 per person are *Kreuz-Post*, Haupstr. 65, (☎07633 5240); and *Sonne*, Albert-Hugard-Str. 1, (☎07633 7012). The annual *Sommerfest* is held during the last week in June, while the local *Weinfest* takes place on the first weekend in August. Star vineyards of the area are on the **Batzenberg** just north of town, and wine connoisseurs come from all over for wine-tasting sessions in the surrounding cellars. An even bigger *Weinfest* is held in nearby SCHÖNBERG in late April and early May.

Youth hostels can be found throughout the region. The nearest to Mt. Belchen is in WIEDEN (train from Freiburg to Münstertal, then bus); and for the Feldberg there's a choice of two, either in the village of TODNAUBERG (bus from Freiburg) or actually on the mountain itself (train from Freiburg to Feldberg-Bähire, Germany's highest train station, and then bus to the *Hebelhof*).

There are also hostels in Altglasshütten, Bonndorf, Menzenschwand, Seebrugg (for Schluchsee), and Titisee. Accommodation in **guest houses** will cost in the region of DM20 to 40 for singles and DM30 to 60 for doubles.

At the most southern tip of the wine region, in the left-hand bottom corner of Germany and about 25km south of Staufen, lies the industrial town of **LÖRRACH**, not in itself particularly attractive, with its tall chimneys and pylons. The ruin of **Burg Rötteln** (Tues.–Sun. 10am–6pm, DM2) on the outskirts of the town is an impressive monument to the region's medieval rulers. It was here that the margraves of Hachberg-Sausenberg, followed by the margraves of Baden, resided until the castle was wrecked by the French in 1678. The oldest part is the *Grüner Turm* keep, which was probably built in the twelfth century and offers an excellent view of the Rhine valley and the foothills of the Black Forest. Large parts of the castle's basic structure remain, and wandering around you come to some interesting little places like the *Hexengewölbe*, which, as the name implies, is where suspected witches were locked up.

Around Mt. Feldberg

Once, **MT. FELDBERG** must have been a remote and wild place, far away from human habitation. In the eighteenth and nineteenth centuries, however, the rounded heights were denuded of forest and turned into highland pastures, so today the Feldberg stands treeless above a sea of forest and isn't in itself particularly attractive. The TV tower and radio dishes plus the chairlift (DM3 one-way, DM4 return) and gravel path to the top don't do the place any favors either, and the hotel and souvenir shop just about ruin it. But the area around the Feldberg is still one of the best hiking regions, with many beautiful trails through uninhabited forests and gorges laced with a couple of romantic waterfalls and streams along the way. Even near the Feldberg itself, you'll find unspoilt and quiet places like the **Feldbergsee**, only accessible on foot, and the **Windgfällweiher**, another lake near the village of ALTGLASSHÜTTEN a few kilometers southeast.

One of Germany's most dramatic **train rides** is in this region too. It's the route going from Freiburg to FELDBERG-BÄRENTAL, which winds its way steeply through the narrow **Höllental** (*Hell Valley*) gorge. The track was built in the early part of this century, and was certainly an amazing technical achievement for the time. Trains crawl up the mountainside towards the Feldberg, passing through numerous viaducts and tunnels, eventually coming out at the Lake Titisee, only to continue its climb until Feldberg-Bähire, by which time the train has reached 976m above sea level, and the country's highest station.

The **TITISEE** and **SCHLUCHSEE**, about 10km northwest and southwest of the Feldberg respectively, are the two largest lakes in the Southern Black Forest region, and their towns of the same name are popular summer resorts. Titisee is far more commercialized than Schluchsee and very much the domain of spa holiday-makers around retirement age. The Schluchsee seems preferable, especially if you stay in lakeside **SEEBRUGG**, which has a decent beach and also sailing and windsurfing facilities. (Boat hire costs about DM5–12 for half an hour and DM10–23 for a full hour, depending on how many want to use it.) Motorized boats aren't allowed on the lake, which makes for pleasantly peaceful (and clean) swimming. There's a **youth hostel** (☎07656 494) just minutes from Seebrugg's Bahnhof, along with *Pension Berger* (☎07656 238), which charges DM18 to 20 per person. Alternatively, the **campground** (☎0765 7739) at this end of the lake is at WOLFSGRUND.

For keen hikers, the best places to stay are higher up, in the village resorts of Bernau (5km south of Feldberg), Todtmoos (10km south of Feldberg), or Bondorf (25km east of Feldberg). **BERNAU** is actually a collection of small villages and farms, ideal for groups looking for farmhouse accommodation or private vacation flats. The surrounding countryside is marvelous, and if you've got a car, this would be a great base for a holiday. Contact the **tourist office** in the *Kurverwaltung* (☎07675 896) for accommodation lists and brochures.

The picturesque village of **TODTMOOS** is one of the main centers for hiking enthusiasts, offering all the facilities of Alpine villages. The **tourist office** in the *Kurpark* (Mon.–Sat. 8am–noon and 1–5pm; ☎07674 534), provides accommodation lists, local brochures and hiking maps. There's no youth hostel here, but instead the *Europäisches Jugendgästehaus* (☎07674 410), which has no age restriction or IYHA-members only policy, and charges DM16 per person. Todtmoos is also an ideal base from which to explore the rarely-visited **Hotzenwald**, which seamlessly extends south from the Black Forest, until dropping sharply towards the Rhine valley that marks the Swiss border.

BONNDORF, on the eastern edges of the Black Forest, is another excellent hiking base, set just below the forest among rich orchards. It's also very close to the so-called "Grand Canyon" of the Black forest, the **Wutachschlucht**, which is a small riverine gorge, very narrow in places, with gushing white water shooting over mossy rocks and lined by ancient forest. About 10km long, it has been declared a nature reserve. Guided hikes are organized between June and October, and information on this and all other matters is available from the **tourist office** (☎07703 7607) on Schloss Strasse, who also sell a map of the gorge for DM6. The local **youth hostel** is at Waldallee 19, (☎07703 359; bus from Titisee-Neustadt).

The most famous monastery of the Southern Black Forest is in **ST. BLASIEN**, about 12km southeast of Mt. Feldberg. Burned down a number of times, the church was given its present shape in 1768, when the local prince-abbot hired the Frenchman Michel d'Ixnard to design one of Germany's grandest classically-inspired churches. The great dome, carried by twenty Corinthian pillars, was modeled after St. Peter's in Rome, and is one of the most notable pieces of neoclassical architecture in the country. Inside, the great rotunda is a blaze of white marble, shining oppressively new and creating an atmosphere something akin to a cold, oversized bathroom. This is perhaps a rather unfair description for an architectual masterpiece, but the overwhelming white everywhere distracts from appreciating the beautiful symmetry and uncluttered space.

For brochures and accommodation lists contact the **tourist office**, Am Kurgarten (Mon.–Fri. 9:30am–noon and 2:30–5pm, Sat. 10am–noon; ☎07672 41430). The nearest **youth hostel** is in MENTZENSCHWAND, at Vorderdorferstr. 10 (☎07675 326; bus from Seebrugg). This is a particularly beautiful hostel, located in one of the all-wood traditional farmhouses, 8km up the road from St. Blasien.

The Central Black Forest

Heart of the central part of the Black Forest is the little town of **TRIBERG**, which lies at an altitude of 1000m on the main railroad line between Konstanz and the Rhine, and some 50km north of Titisee by road. It's a spa and health resort, with the forest acting as a dust filter, ensuring particularly pure air. Some of the most imposing scenery in the region is nearby, and Triberg itself makes a good base for a day or two's relaxation. Arriving at the **Bahnhof** is a strange experience, as there's nothing but cliffs on either side of the narrow tracks, and it's easy to understand the derivation of the town's name, a corruption of "three mountains," in honor of the peaks which surround it. From here, the center is a ten minute walk uphill.

Prime attraction of the town is the **Gutach Waterfall**. At 162m, it ranks as the highest in Germany, and is undeniably impressive, even though it plunges in seven separate stages, instead of a single dramatic dive. Unfortunately, there's something tacky and commercialized about this place, which, in a crass reverse of the normal German penchant for unrestricted access to nature, is sealed off, with a DM2 levy for admission.

Ample compensation, however, is provided by the **Heimat Museum** (mid-May–Sept. 8am–6pm, rest of year 10am–noon and 2–5pm; DM3) on Wallfahrtstrasse, which offers fascinating insights into the rural culture of the Black Forest as it was—and, to some extent, still is. There's a fine group of wood-carvings by the rustic local artist Karl Josef Fortwängler (nicknamed "Wood-carver Joe") who depicted the thick-set country bumpkins of the area in an idiosyncratic yet highly sympathetic manner. In addition, there's a large model of the *Schwarzwaldbahn*, one of the most dramatic railroad lines in Europe, which runs through the middle of the Black Forest via Triberg. Music boxes, clocks, and examples of the traditional dress for carnivals and everyday wear complete the display. The most colorful items are the outrageous woollen red or black pom-pom hats, which are worn over a silk cap. Contrary to popular belief, these are not a regional costume of the Black Forest—they're worn only by the unmarried women of the nearby villages of GUTACH, KIRNBACH, and REICHENBACH.

Triberg's other major sight is the baroque **Wallfahrtskirche St. Maria in den Tannen**. Pilgrims came here because of two miracles associated with a painting of *The Virgin of the Pines*—legend has it that a child discovered this picture and took it home with her. She then became fatally ill, whereupon her mother prayed to Mary for a cure, and was told in a dream that if she put the picture back into the hollow of the tree where it was found, the girl would be healed. Later the painting was discovered again by soldiers on a manoeuvre; as they drew closer, they were surrounded by brilliant white light and the sound of heavenly singing. The piece of wood with the picture inside was taken to this church and set into the altar, and from that time onwards it became a place of pilgrimage. Another painting inside the church also has a legendary history as it was carried from Villingen to Triberg by barefooted citizens, in homage to God who had rid them of the plague.

The **youth hostel** is high in the hills at Rohrbacher Str. 35 (☎07722 4110); a bus will take you as far as the waterfall, and then it's a very steep twenty-minute climb. If you can't face the walk, try one of the cheap **guest houses**, such as *Krone*, Schulstr. 37 (☎07722 4524), which also serves excellent food; *Haus Charlotte*, Schwerstr. 12h (☎07722 4394); or *Gasthaus Scwarzwaldstube*, Ober-Vogthuber-Str. 25a (☎07722 3324). Most of the **cafés** here are reasonable, especially those along Hauptstrasse, where you'll also find several restaurants.

If you want to buy, or find out about, that ultimate Black Forest cliché, the **cuckoo clock**, then the area around Triberg is the place to come, with a multiplicity of shops catering to all levels of taste and price, from cheap junk to beautiful items handmade to the customer's specification. The village of **SCHONACH**, just a couple of kilometers to the west, takes great pride in having the largest cuckoo clock in the world. It's a hideously kitsch sight (in full working order) with a giant grotesque cuckoo which appears every hour on the hour.

For a serious historical perspective on the craft—which has a perfectly legitimate tradition—head 15km south to **FURTWANGEN**, which is the leading center of production. This isn't one of the more appealing towns in the region, but it boasts the **German Clock Museum** (April–Nov. daily 9am–5pm, Dec.–March Mon.–Fri. 9am–noon and 2–4pm; DM2), with over 1000 timepieces of all weird and wonderful shapes and sizes on view, including many from overseas. Cuckoo clock-making began in the Black Forest in the eighteenth century as an adjunct to farming and forestry, and originally it was a cooperative venture involving several families, each of whom specialized in a different part of the business, such as woodcarving, painting, or making the mechanism. The products were sold by itinerant hawkers, who gradually began to expand their operations abroad; eventually, demand became so great that clock-making became a lucrative full-time trade for many families, a situation which persists to this day.

Among a number of recommendable excursions which can be made from Furtwangen, two stand out. The **Brend**, 6km to the northwest, is one of the best vantage-points in the central part of the Black Forest, standing at a height of 1148m. Another road leads in a roughly parallel direction just to the north along the side of the Breg to the river's source. This is known as the **Donauquelle** (*Danube Spring*), as the Breg is one of the two Black Forest rivers which meet at DONAUESCHINGEN (see p.225) to form the Danube, and thus has a good (if contentious) geological claim to be regarded as the ultimate source of the great river itself.

On either side of Triberg are the most impressive sections of the *Schwarzwaldbahn*—the narrow, deep and rocky stages to ST. GEORGEN to the east and to HORNBERG to the north; each stretch has an occasion when the train has to completely double back on itself in order to accomplish the climb. Before reaching St. Georgen, the railroad starts to follow Brigach, the other Danube headstream, and continues along its course all the way to Donaueschingen.

In the opposite direction, the railroad's path follows the river Gutach. Just after Hornberg, where the landscape becames light and airy again, is the town of **GUTACH** itself, outside which is an important **Open-Air Museum** (April–Oct. daily 8:30am–6pm; DM3). Centerpiece is what's probably the most famous house in the Black Forest, the late sixteenth-century *Vogtsbauernhof*. With its huge sloping roof and tiered facade, it's an outstanding example of the characteristic vernacular building style of the region. This was the original farmhouse on the site, whereas the various other exhibits have, of course, been removed from other locations. There are four more farmsteads, along with a wooden chapel, and all kinds of workshops—smithies, granaries, a bakehouse, a distillery, and various types of mills. Displays on the folklore and lifestyle of the region are also featured, and all the old crafts are demonstrated.

At the next stop, HAUSACH, the Gutach merges with the Kinzig; similarly, there's the junction of the *Scwarzwaldbahn* with the *Kinzigtalbahn*. The former line continues westwards along the Kinzig towards OFFENBURG, which lies on the express line between Freiburg and Baden-Baden. **HASLACH**, an old market town and health resort just 8km from Hausach, is the most striking place on this stretch. Its Rathaus is over-cutely painted with depictions of locals in traditional dress, while the former **Kapuzinerkloster** (April–Oct. Tues.–Sat. 9am–5pm, Sun. 10am–5pm, Nov.–March Tues.–Fri. 10am–5pm; DM2) has a huge collection of Black Forest costumes, along with other folklore displays.

WOLFACH, 5km west of Hausach at the point where the river after which the village is named joins the Kinzig, also has a museum worth seeing if you've developed a taste for the customs of the region. Housed in **Schloss Furstenberg**, its main subject is mining, in honor of the fact that there were once 500 pits in operation. The masks used at *Fastnet* are also on display, the celebrations here being rated among the best in Baden-Württemberg. **SCHILTACH**, a pretty, flower-lined place of half-timbered houses a farther 10km east, is again set at the confluence of its river with the Kinzig. From here, the railroad continues to ALPIRSBACH (see p.176).

The Northern Black Forest

To non-Germans, the northern stretch of the Black Forest is the least familiar part. Yet here are some of the most imposing of the landscapes—the forest really does look its blackest, and is cut by several deep, dark valleys which provide the strongest possible contrast to the long panoramic views obtained from the hills. There are three main **touring routes**, each offering a widely varying choice of scenery: the Black Forest Highway (*Schwarzwald-Hochstrasse*), the Black Forest Valley Road (*Schwarzwald-Tälerstrasse*) and the circuitous Black Forest Spa Road (*Schwarzwald-Bäderstrasse*). Walking or bicycling are undoubtedly the best ways for **getting around**, but superb scenic railroad lines, closely hugging the river valleys, enable all of the second and part of the third of these routes to be followed by even the most sedentary. Buses fill in the gaps, though the frequency of these varies considerably according to season, often drying up altogether in the winter months.

Freudenstadt

The hub of the transportation system of the Northern Black Forest is **FREUDENSTADT**, situated at high altitude on a plateau bordered by the rivers Murg and Kinzig. There's no more polished, spick-and-span town in the country; coupled to its extreme climate and arcaded streets, it has a feel reminiscent more of Switzerland than Germany. Its regularly built streets look gleamingly new, but it's new only in one sense, its history being dogged by ill-luck in complete contradiction of its name, which means "town of joy."

Freudenstadt was in fact founded in 1599 by **Duke Friedrich I of Württemberg**. He had three main aims in establishing the new community: to give a much-needed boost to his ever-empty state coffers by exploiting the silver mines in the nearby Christophstal; to provide a home, at a time of high religious rivalry, for Protestant refugees from Austria; and to have a new, "secret" capital for Württemberg, which he dreamed of building up as an effective counterweight to France on the one hand and the Habsburg-dominated Holy Roman Empire on the other.

A highly talented Italian-trained architect, Heinrich Schickhardt, was accordingly charged with designing the first planned town in the province. He laid it out in the manner of a vast Roman camp, centerd on a spaciously grandiose **Marktplatz**. In the middle, there was meant to be an even bigger Schloss than the one in Stuttgart, but it was never built—the silver mines proved to be a mirage, and the town was devastated by epidemic and fire within 35 years of its birth, whereupon it lost all sense of importance. Something of a comeback was made in the nineteenth century with its development into one of the leading spas in the Black Forest. Two weeks before the end of World War II, disaster struck again—French artillery bombarded the town, and when it fell, the victors ran amok; only two streets survived the blaze intact. Within five years, however, Freudenstadt had been completely rebuilt to the old plans. This was regarded as a stunning achievement, even by the miraculous standards of German post-war reconstruction, but it does leave the undeniable effect—generally avoided in more painstaking restoration projects—that the historic buildings look anachronistically modern.

Nonetheless, Freudenstadt is still sufficiently singular to justify a look around, even if you aren't attracted to the leisure facilities or the excellent hiking opportunities in the neighborhood. The Marktplatz must have seemed extraordinary when it was first built; it's an impressive sight even to the modern eye, which is far more attuned to the large-scale, and it still ranks as much the largest square in Germany. At diagonally opposite corners are the two main public buildings, the **Rathaus** and the **Stadtkirche**.

The latter is particularly intriguing, built in an L-shape in order that the men and women of the congregation could be segregated. Indeed, the arrangement meant they could not even see each other—the better to concentrate their minds on the sermon. The church houses a magnificent polychrome wood **lectern** made around 1150, which bears large statues of the Four Evangelists and their symbols; it's unique of its kind and one of the most important pieces of Romanesque church furniture to have survived. Along with the **font**, made about half a century earlier and adorned with carvings of symbolic fantastic animals, it presumably came from one of the Black Forest monasteries.

Freudenstadt has two railroad stations: the **Stadtbahnhof** is just a few minutes' walk from Marktplatz and has the **bus terminus** just outside, whereas the **Hauptbahnhof** is at the eastern edge of town, at a much lower altitude. The **tourist office** (April–Oct. Mon.–Fri. 9am–6pm, Sat. and Sun. 9am–noon, Nov.–Mar. Mon.–Fri. only 9am–noon and 2:30–5pm; ☎07441 8640) is in the *Kurverwaltung* on Promenadeplatz. **Hotels** and **pensions** are scattered all over town; for the lowest rates, at DM25 per head or less, try the concentration on Lauterbadstrasse. Alternatively, there's a **youth hostel** at Eugen-Nägele-Str. 69 (☎07441 7720), not far from the Stadtbahnhof, and a **campground**, *Langenwald* (☎07441 2862), 3km to the west. Plenty of elegant **cafés** and **restaurants** line Marktplatz; best food is at no. 12, *Jägerstüble*. A good alternative is *Gasthof See* on Forststrasse, near the Stadtbahnhof.

The Black Forest Valley Road

The *Tälerstrasse* is the only one of the three scenic routes which doesn't officially begin at Freudenstadt. Instead, the first stop is deemed to be **ALPIRSBACH**, 18km south, and reachable via the *Kinzigtalbahn*, a railroad line which thereafter continues through the central Black Forest region along the generally westerly course of the river after which it's named.

Alpirsbach is grouped round the former **Kloster**, now a Protestant parish church. Begun at the very end of the twelfth century, it preserves much of the simple, pure Romanesque form characteristic of the style of building championed at Hirsau (see below). The east end is especially notable—later Gothic masons ingeniously perched the chancel above the existing story. Only one of the towers was built, however, and it was not finished until the Renaissance period, when it received an unusual gabled top. Inside, some original wall paintings survive, as does a twelfth-century pew, the oldest in the country. The late Gothic cloisters are frequently used for open-air concerts in summer.

A number of handsome half-timbered buildings decorate the center of Alpirsbach, most notably the Rathaus; the town also makes a good center for walks in the Kinzig valley. If you want to stay, there's a **youth hostel** high on the Sulzberg at Reinerzauersteige 80 (☎07444 2477); there are also two **campgrounds** and plenty of reasonably priced pensions.

The stretch of the *Tälerstrasse* north of Freudenstadt is reached by arguably the most scenic of these railroads, the *Murgtalbahn* line to RASTATT, some 60km away. Though never more than a modest stretch of water, the river Murg cleaves an impressively grand valley in its downward journey towards its confluence with the Rhine. One of the recommendable hikes which can be made from **BAIERSBRONN** (the first stop, 6km north of Freudenstadt) is westwards along the course of the young river towards its source in the shadow of the 1055 meter-high **Schliffkopf**.

All the little towns along the Murg have impressive settings, and make a good base for exploring an underrated part of the Black Forest. Particularly worthy of mention is **FORBACH**, about halfway down the line, which has a wonderful sixteenth-century, single-span covered wooden bridge, the largest of its type in Europe. West of town is some fine countryside, with the artifical **Schwarzenbach Stausee**, a watersports center, and the tiny **Herrenwieser See**. The latter lies below the **Badener Höhe**, whose TV tower commands an extensive view of the region. There's a **youth hostel** just to the north of Forbach at Birket 1 (☎07228 2427) and another out in the sticks at Haus no. 33 in HERRENWIES (☎07226 257). **Campgrounds** are also to be found in both locations, as well as a good number of cheap pensions.

GERNSBACH, 13km farther north, is also very pretty, boasting a handsome gabled Renaissance Rathaus, along with historic ramparts, fountains and half-timbered houses. Though there's no hostel or campground here, accommodation in private houses starts from as little as DM16 per head.

The Black Forest Highway

The *Schwarzwald-Hochstrasse*, linking Freudenstadt with BADEN-BADEN, is one of Germany's most famous roads. Up to five buses run daily in each direction in summer along this sixty-kilometer stretch, whose settlements are nothing more than hamlets. However, there are plenty of **hotels**, many with spa facilities, though nearly all on the expensive side. In addition, there's a single **youth hostel**, *Zuflucht* (☎07804 811), located at a particularly scenic part just off the main road 19km north of Freudenstadt. It makes an excellent base for hiking in summer, and for skiing in winter. Hiking along the accompanying trail is really much the best way to see the area, which is pocked with belvederes offering vast panoramas towards the Rhine and the French Vosges.

Just beyond the hostel is the **Buhlbachsee**, the first of several tiny natural lakes along the highway. Before this, however, is a secondary road leading west to OPPENAU which joins with another fine scenic road running north to the canyon of **Allerheiligen**, rejoining the *Hochstrasse* at RUHESTEIN. Allerheiligen has the ruins of a former Premonstratensian **Kloster**, the first Gothic building in southwest Germany, probably built by the same team of masons as Strasbourg Cathedral. An impressive stepped **waterfall** can also be seen.

East of Ruhestein is the **Wildsee**, but the most celebrated of the lakes is the **Mummelsee** a farther 8km north. It stands at the foot of the Hornigsrinde (1164m), the highest point in the northern Black Forest, and one offering a particularly outstanding view. The Mummelsee itself, now a popular boating center, is allegedly haunted by water-sprites, and by the luckless King Ulmon, who was condemned by a sorceress to live for 1000 years, in spite of his continuous pleas to be released to join his friends in the afterlife. This legend has proved a potent inspiration for many German writers down the centuries, and formed the subject of one of Eduard Mörike's most evocative poems.

The Nagold valley

Between Bremen and Naples, between Vienna and Singapore, I have seen many pretty towns: towns by the sea, towns high on the mountains . . . . The most beautiful town of all that I know, however, is Calw on the Nagold, a little, old, Swabian Black Forest community.

Hermann Hesse

Much the most impressive stretch of the *Schwarzwald Bäderstrasse* is the wonderfully dark, secret **valley of the river Nagold**; this is the only part of the Black Forest generally considered to belong to the near-mythical province of Swabia. The *Nagoldtalbahn*, which runs most of the way alongside it, begins at the railroad junction of HORB, which has connections to Stuttgart, Tübingen, and Rottweil, but there's also a branch line to Freudenstadt which links up 6km farther north, at EUTINGEN.

CALW, an old textile town, is the focal point of this valley. **Hermann Hesse's** eulogy of it needn't be taken too seriously—his judgment was more than a little colored by the fact that he happened to have been born and bred there, though he eventually chose to reside in Switzerland. Fans of Hesse's novels—which have achieved a cult status far beyond the German-speaking world—will certainly want to come here, in order to see his birthplace on Marktplatz, and the collection of memorabilia which forms the centerpiece of the **Heimat Museum** (May–Oct. Mon.–Fri. 2–4pm, Sun. 10am–noon; free) on Bischofstrasse.

Other than this, Calw boasts an impressive array of half-timbered houses, mostly dating from the late seventeenth and early eighteenth centuries, just after a fire had destroyed the medieval town. One of the few older monuments is the **Nikolausbrücke** from around 1400, which incorporates a picturesque little votive chapel. Hesse, true to form, considered the bridge and the square on its west bank to form an assemblage superior to the Piazza del Duomo in Florence.

If you want to stay, there's a **youth hostel** right in the center of town at Im Zwinger 4 (☎07051 12614). **Campgrounds** are found at Eiselstätt (☎07051 12131 or 13437) in the eastern part of town, and in the outlying villages of STAMMHEIM (☎07051 4844) and ALTBURG (☎07051 50788). There are a couple of **pensions** on Bahnhofstrasse, and two more in the town center, all charging in the range of DM25 to 35 per head.

HIRSAU, 2km downstream, is now a small spa and officially part of Calw, but actually has a far longer history. Its Benedictine **Kloster**, indeed, was once the most powerful monastery in Germany, serving as mother-house to a host of dependent congregations, and initiating a highly influential reform movement whose main effect was to free religious houses from the clutches of secular patrons, placing them instead under the direct control of the Pope. The simple original monastic church is tucked away in among a number of much later buildings, not far from the bridge over the Nagold. A ninth-century Carolingian structure, it was rebuilt in the mid-eleventh century, and now serves as the Catholic parish church of **St. Aurelius**.

The reconstruction had not been fully completed when the great reformer, Abbot Wilhelm, arrived from Regensburg. A decade later, he ordered the erection of a magnificent new complex, directly modeled on the most famous and powerful monastery of the day—that of Cluny in Burgundy—on sloping ground above the west bank of the Nagold. Regrettably, the church was almost completely destroyed by the French in the War of the Palatinate Succession, and only the **Eulenturm** (*Owl Tower*), originally one of a pair, survives from this epoch: you have to go to Alpirsbach to get an impression of how it must once have looked. However, there are also fragments from later building periods, notably the late fifteenth-century **cloisters**, the early sixteenth-century **Marienkapelle** (now restored to serve as the Protestant church), and the Renaissance **Jagdschloss** of the dukes of Württemberg, who expelled the monks after the Reformation, taking the land over as pleasure and hunting grounds for their own exclusive use. In the light of the beautifully warm red sandstone used in the construction, not to mention the superb setting, there's little doubt that Kloster Hirsau ranks among the most evocative ruins in the country.

Most of the other places of concrete interest in the Nagold Valley are south of Calw. **BADTEINACH-ZAVELSTEIN**, just a few kilometers away, is a curious federation of disparate communities. Bad Teinach is an orthodox spa, Zavelstein is a fortified medieval township with a ruined castle, while the incorporated hamlet of **KENTHEIM** has the oldest church in southern Germany, the 9C Candiduskirche. From here, a detour 6km southwest brings you to **NEUBULACH**, where you can visit the historic **silver mine** *Hella-Glücksstollen* (guided tours April–Oct. Mon.–Sat. 10am–noon and 2–4pm, Sun. 9:30am–5pm; DM3).

WILDBERG, 10km up the Nagold from Bad Teinach, preserves part of its walls, including two towers, along with a thirteenth-century Dominican monastery, a late fifteenth-century Rathaus, an old stone bridge and a Renaissance fountain. Further south on the eastern side of the valley are two gentle peaks well worth climbing for their panoramic views—**Kühlen** and **Emmingen**. The latter is best reached from **NAGOLD**, the only town of any size in the area, other than Calw. Shaped like an ellipse at the point where the river Waldach flows in from the west, Nagold is surprisingly industrial, but also possesses plenty of handsome timber-framed houses. There's another fine view to be had from the ruined Burg perched high above the town.

None of these towns has a hostel, though Neubulach, Wildberg, and Nagold all have **campgrounds**. Plenty of cheap accommodation is also available in private houses and inns.

Pforzheim

The end of the Black Forest proper, some 30km north of Calw, comes at the large industrial town of **PFORZHEIM**. Here the river Nagold joins the Enz, which thereafter follows an easterly course to its confluence with the Neckar. Pforzheim often christens itself *Goldstadt*, in recognition of its continuing role, held since the Middle Ages, as a leading center of the jewelry trade. However, this is a good deal less promizing than might seem to be the case: the town was devastated at the end of the war, and its overall appearance is uncompromisingly modern.

There are a couple of fairly interesting Gothic churches in the town center. The **Schlosskirche**, immediately opposite the Hauptbahnhof, has a lofty chancel containing the grandiose Renaissance wall tombs of the Margraves of Baden, who lived for a spell in the now-vanished castle. On Altstädterstrasse, **St. Martin** retains a Romanesque portal, and has mid-fifteenth century wall paintings in the choir. Otherwise, the only attraction is the **Reuchlinhaus** (Tues. and Thurs.-Sun. 10am–5pm, Weds. 10am–8pm; DM1) on Jahnstrasse south of the center. Named in honor of the great humanist and Hebrew scholar (see p.213) who was a native of the town, this contains a museum illustrating the history of jewelry from ancient Egypt to the present day.

Pforzheim is the starting point for all three of the main Black Forest **long-distance hikes**. The *Westweg* follows the western course all the way down to the Swiss city of BASEL via Forbach, the Mummelsee, Hausach, and Titisee; it's the longest and most demanding of the three, with twelve days the normal walking time for its 280-kilometer stretch. Nine days is the average time needed to cover the *Mittelweg*, which is some 60km shorter, running via Wildbad, Freudenstadt, Schiltach and Titisee to WALDSHUT. The 240-kilometer *Ostweg* is again reckoned to take nine days, passing down the Nagold Valley via Calw to Freudenstadt, Alpirsbach and Villingen to SCHAFFHAUSEN in Switzerland.

The **tourist office** (Mon.–Fri. 9am–1pm and 2–6pm, Sat. 9am–noon; ☎07231 392190) on Marktplatz is the main center for information about the northern parts of the Black Forest. Pforzheim isn't the sort of place you're likely to want to hang around in for long, but the **youth hostel**, housed in the ruined Burg Rabeneck (☎07231 72604) in the village of DILLWEISSENSTEIN to the south, makes a good base for exploring the lower reaches of the Nagold Valley.

Tiefenbronn

TIEFENBRONN, an unassuming-looking village situated at the extreme edge of the Black Forest in the peaceful valley of the river Würm 12km southeast of Pforzheim, has two claims to fame. Firstly, it's a renowned gastronomic center; people come not only from Pforzheim, but also from Stuttgart and beyond, in order to eat at the *Ochsen-Post*, a hotel in a seventeenth-century timber-framed building. The main restaurant, one of the best in Southern Germany, is incredibly expensive, but the *Bauernstuben*, open evenings only, is just about affordable.

From the outside, there's little to suggest that there's anything remarkable about the steep-roofed fourteenth-century Gothic church of St. **Maria Magdalena**. Architecturally, it's very ordinary indeed, yet it contains a magnificent array of **works of art** which put to shame those in most cathedrals. Jewel-like stained glass windows, made in Strasbourg around 1370, illuminate the choir, and there are fifteenth-century wall-paintings throughout the church, including a depiction of *The Last Judgment*, a frieze of coats-of-arms, and portraits of the family who provided the endowments. The main retable, made in the 1460s by Hans Schüchlin of Ulm, tells the story of the Passion by a mixture of paintings and sculptures, and has panels of the Nativity on the reverse.

However, this and all the many other altarpieces in the church is outclassed by that dedicated to the local patron saint, which is housed in the southern aisle. One of the most beautiful of all European Gothic paintings, it bears a curious inscription: "Weep, Art, weep and lament loudly, nobody nowadays wants you, so alas, 1432. Lucas Moser, painter of Weil der Stadt, master of this work, pray God for him." Nothing is known about the embittered **Lucas Moser**, whose style is actually very modern for its day. The first German painting to try a realistic approach, including a sense of perspective, it still has all the grace and delicacy characteristic of the earlier "Soft Style." It shows Mary Magdalene washing Christ's feet, her miraculous journey in a ship without sail or rudder to Marseille, her stay there, and her last communion in the Cathedral of Aix-en-Provence. On the predella, Christ is depicted between the Wise and Foolish Virgins.

Baden-Baden

It is an inane town, full of sham, and petty fraud, and snobbery, but the baths are good ... I had had twinges of rheumatism unceasingly during three years, but the last one departed after a fortnight's bathing there, and I have never had one since. I fully believe I left my rheumatism in Baden-Baden. Baden-Baden is welcome to it. It was little, but it was all I had to give. I would have preferred to leave something that was catching, but it was not in my power.

Mark Twain, *A Tramp Abroad.*

Mark Twain's ambivalent reactions to **BADEN-BADEN**—he actually seems to have reveled in the snob aspect, delighting in the fact that the little old woman he sat behind in church, and had decided to give a ride home, turned out to be the empress of Germany—mirrors the contrasting reactions of late nineteenth-century visitors to this town, then the glittering rendezvous of the wealthy and famous.

In the present century, the idle rich classes who made Baden-Baden the "summer capital of Europe" have been almost entirely wiped out. The Bolshevik Revolution accounted for the Russian landowners, while World War II took care of their counterparts in Prussia and the Balkans. Yet, if Baden-Baden isn't quite what it was, it has still maintained its image remarkably well; like Bath in England, it has a sense of style which no other spa in the country can quite match. This is in large measure thanks to the German infatuation with the concept of the spa cure, which is underpinned by an incredibly lenient health insurance system. Buoyed by the postwar economic prosperity, people flock here to enjoy a taste of a lifestyle their parents could only have dreamed about. It remains a place you're likely to either love or hate, but is somewhere which definitely should be experienced at first-hand; decide for yourself whether it deserves the epithet "morally delicious" that Henry Adams bestowed on it.

In view of the fact that it was the train which brought most of the royal and aristocratic visitors to the town in its heyday, it's ironic that today's **Bahnhof**, on the fast Freiburg to Karlsruhe line, is 4km northwest of the center in the suburb of OOS. The branch-line has now closed, and the **Alter Bahnhof**, at the fringe of the spa quarter, is now a restaurant and arts center. Take bus #1 or #3 (services every 10 minutes); walking is a false economy, and the elliptical valley of the Oos River isn't at all scenic at this point.

The discovery of hot springs in the **Florintinerberg**, on the east side of the river, was due to the Romans, who found in them cures for arthritis and rheumatism. They established a settlement at this point, known simply as *Aquae* ("Waters"). The vernacular form of this was later used not only for the town, but also for the margraviate established by the Zähringen family, who moved here in the eleventh century, to rule their combined territories at the western frontiers of the Holy Roman Empire. In the sixteenth century, the Swiss alchemist and doctor Paracelsus utilized the springs to save the life of Margrave Philipp I. However, Baden-Baden's rise to international fame only came about as a result of

Napoleon's creation of the buffer state of Baden in 1806. The grand dukes promoted their ancestors' old seat as a modern resort, and began embellishing it with handsome new buildings, many designed by the neoclassical architect Friedrich Weinbrenner. As the focal point of the new spa quarter on the west side of the Oos, Weinbrenner built the **Kurhaus** in the early 1820s. Its solemn, stately facade of eight Corinthian columns, in front of which stand six gas candelabra, each of six branches, is now approached via an elegant shopping arcade of expensive shops, which was added four decades later. The **casino**, which formed an integral part of the Kurhaus facilities from the beginning, was revolutionized in 1836 with the arrival from Paris of the flamboyant impressario Jacques Bénazet, *Le Roi de Bade*. With gambling now outlawed in France, he devoted all his energies to building up Baden-Baden as the gambling capital of Europe. His son Edouard, *Le Duc de Zero*, added an opulent suite of gaming rooms to the Kurhaus, employing the same team of designers as had worked on the Paris Opéra; they married the contemporary style of *La Belle Epoque* to the extravagant type of decor found at Versailles.

The easiest way to see these is to take a **guided tour** (April–Sept. 9:30am–noon, Oct.–March 10am–noon; DM2). Highlight is the Winter Garden, with its glass cupola, Chinese vases, and pure gold roulette table, which is used only on Saturdays or for special guests. Particularly striking is the Red Hall, covered from top to bottom in red silk damask from Lyon, and with a glorious marbled fireplace and raised oval ceiling. Theatrical to the extreme, it's no surprise to learn that it, like the Winter Garden, was used for performances to a "selected public" before 1872. That was when Kaiser Wilhelm I—a faithful annual visitor to Baden-Baden over a period of forty years—abolished gambling throughout his newly-united Empire. The visitors' book hosts a vast array of famous names, notably Dostoyevsky, who was a compulsive addict, a theme treated in his novella *The Gambler*.

The **gaming tables** were licensed again by Hitler in 1933, and have remained in operation ever since, save for a break caused by World War II. A day-ticket costs DM5, with no obligation to participate. Formal dress is a precondition of entry; access is officially forbidden to residents of Baden-Baden, anyone under 21, and students, though the last barrier isn't unsurmountable. Roulette is played daily from 2pm to 2am (until 3am on Saturday), black jack from 5pm to 1am Monday to Thursday, 4pm to 1am Friday and Sunday, 4pm to 2am Saturday, while baccarat is for the real night owls, running daily from 3pm to 6am. Minimum stake is DM5; maximum (except for baccarat) is DM50,000.

South of the Kurhaus runs Baden-Baden's most famous thoroughfare, the **Lichtentaler Allee**. This was originally lined with oaks, but was transformed at the instigation of Edouard Bénazet into a landscape in the English style, with the addition of exotic trees and shrubs. It requires little effort of the imagination to visualize the procession of aristocratic carriages along this route; at Kettenbrücke, at the far end, an attempt was made on the life of Wilhelm I in 1861.

First of the buildings on Lichtentaler Allee is the Parisian-style **Theater**. This opened in 1862 with the premiere of Berlioz's opera *Béatrice et Bénédict*, and a high standard of both musical and theatrical performance is maintained there to this day. Next in line comes the **International Club**, built by Weinbrenner for a Swedish princess, but now the headquarters of the big flat races which are held in IFFEZHEIM, 12km northwest of Baden-Baden. There's a meeting in May, and a *Grosse Woche* in late August, which is the most important in the German calendar, and now ranks as the highpoint of the Baden-Baden season. Further along is the **Kunsthalle** (Tues. and Thurs.–Sun. 10am–6pm, Weds. 10am–8pm), which often hosts major loan exhibitions of twentieth-century art.

Immediately north of the Kurhaus is the **Trinkhalle** (*Pump Room*), built by a follower of Weinbrenner, Heinrich Hübsch. There are fourteen large frescoes by the Romantic painter Jakob Götzenberger, illustrating legends about the town and the nearby countryside. Different varieties of spring water are dispensed from a modern mosaic fountain, with grape juice offered as an alternative.

The Michaelsberg, which rises behind the spa quarter, is named after the last Romanian Boyar of Moldavia, Michael Stourdza, who settled in Baden-Baden after he had been expelled from his homeland. In 1863, his teenage son was murdered in Paris; as a memorial, he commissioned the **Stourdza Mausoleum** (daily 10am–6pm; DM1) to be built on the hill. Construction of this domed chapel, the most distinguished of the three nineteenth-century churches in Baden-Baden built for expatriate communities, was entrusted to the aged Leo von Klenze, who had created so much of nineteenth-century Munich, though he died before it was complete.

Little remains of the old town of Baden-Baden, which was almost completely destroyed in a single day in 1689, the result of a fire started by French troops. However, half-way up the Florintinerberg is the Marktplatz, where you'll find the **Rathaus**, formerly a Jesuit college, but was partially remodeled by Weinbrenner to serve as the original casino. Opposite is the **Stiftskirche**, a Gothic hall church whose tower is a curious amalgam of the Romanesque lower stories of the first church, a Gothic octagon, and a baroque cap.

It may seem out of keeping that Baden-Baden possesses one of the all-time masterpieces of European sculpture, but the Stiftkirche's 5.4-meter-high sandstone *Crucifixion*, depicting Christ as a noble giant triumphant over his suffering, certainly warrants such a rating. Carved in 1467, it stood for nearly five centuries in the Old Cemetery, before being moved inside for conservation reasons. The work is signed by **Nicolaus Gerhaert von Leyden**, a mysterious, peripatetic sculptor of Dutch origin who pioneered a realist approach to art which was to have a profound influence on the brilliant group of German carvers of the next generation. As with all his few other remaining works, this shows complete technical mastery allied to a wholly original form of expression. The tabernacle was made about twenty years later by a mason who had clearly come under Gerhaert's spell, while there are also several impressive **tombs** of the margraves of Baden lining the chancel; particularly eye-catching is the rococo monument to "Türkenlouis" (see p.185), replete with depictions of his trophies.

Hidden underneath the Stiftskirche are the remains of the Roman imperial baths; the more modest **Römerbad** (guided tours daily 10am–noon and 1–4pm; DM2) just to the east on Römerplatz was probably for the use of soldiers. If you don't pay the entrance fee, you can still see the ruins through the glass-fronted windows.

Above the ruins is what must rank as one of the most magnificent bathing halls in the world, the **Friedrichsbad** (Mon. and Weds.–Sat. 8am–10pm, Tues. 8am–4pm). Begun in 1869 to plans by Carl Dernfeld, it's as grandly sumptuous as a Renaissance palace. This elaborateness is at least partly due to the fact that, as gambling was outlawed while the building was under construction, the medicinal springs became even more crucial to local prosperity than they had been before. The red and white sandstone facade is crowned with sea-green cupolas, while inside the pools are surrounded by pillars, arches and classical-style tiles, giving a truly exotic atmosphere. Specialty of the house is a "Roman-Irish Bath," which consists of a two hour program of showers, hot air and steam baths, soap and brush massage, thermal bathing, and a half-hour snooze in a specially-designed rest room. The entire treatment is nude, with mixed bathing on Wednesday and

Friday from 4pm, and on Saturday from noon. It will set you back all of DM25, though there are cheaper options—and the really broke need only fork out DM0.10 for a glass of thermal water.

The **Caracalla Therme** (daily 8am–10pm) on the same square is a vast complex, completed in 1985, as a replacement for the former *Augustabad*. There are seven pools, both indoors and out, which are all at different temperatures, along with a sauna, solarium, and massage facility. In reality, it's no more than an upscale swimming hall with thermal water springs, and isn't remotely to be compared to the Friedrichsbad. This is reflected in the considerably cheaper prices: it costs DM13 for a two-hour swim, and DM6 for each subsequent hour.

From here you can climb the steep steps to the **Neues Schloss** (Tues.–Sun. 10am–6pm; DM2), a mixture of Renaissance and baroque buildings, with many subsequent interior modifications, which was the seat of the margraves of Baden from 1437, and of the Catholic line of Baden-Baden when the house divided in 1525.* It still belongs to the Zähringen family, who were demoted back to their old title after their heady period as grand dukes of an independent state. Inside are displays on the history of the town and dynasty. There's also the added attraction of the best view over Baden-Baden, a dramatic mixture of roof-tops, church spires and the Black Forest surroundings. From here, you can walk via Alter Schlossweg to **Hohenbaden**, the earlier castle of the margraves, situated on the wooded slopes of the Battert, some 3km away. It once boasted over a hundred rooms, but is now ruinous, albeit still worth visiting for the sake of the views.

The Südstadt, immediately south of the Florentinerberg, was traditionally the home of foreign nationals. Just off Bertholdsplatz is the onion-domed **Russian church**, while the neo-Norman **Johanneskirche** on Bertholdstrasse was built as the Anglican parish of All Saints, and was the place where Mark Twain had his encounter with the empress. Beyond the church, which was given to German Lutherans in 1938, is the **Gönneranlagen**, a fine floral park with pergolas, fountains, and a rose garden.

Still farther south is the old village of **LICHTENTAL**, which can be reached directly from the town center (or, indeed, the Bahnhof) by bus #1 or #3. The tranquil thirteenth-century **Kloster** (Mon.–Sat. 9am–noon and 2–5:30pm. Sun. 3–5pm, closed first Sun. in month; DM1:30) is still occupied by Cistercian nuns, who keep up a long tradition of handcrafts, and also make and sell several fiery liqueurs. There are two Gothic chapels: the larger one is used for services, while the other (the *Fürstenkapelle*) served as the pantheon of the margraves of Baden prior to the Stiftskirche. Particularly outstanding is the tomb of the foundress Irmengard, carved by a Strasbourg mason in the mid-fourteenth century.

Just up the road from here, at Maximilianstr. 85, is the **Brahms Haus** (Mon., Wed., and Fri. 3–5pm, Sun. 10am–1pm; DM1), a tiny attic crammed with memorabilia, left exactly as when the great composer lived in it during the years 1865 to 1874. This was the period when Brahms, ever-conscious of his mantle as Beethoven's successor, was struggling to establish himself as a symphonist, only publishing his first, tormented essay in this form after he had passed his fortieth birthday. Its elegaic successor was largely written during a later visit to Lichtental, while part of the massive *Ein Deutsches Requiem*, his most important choral work, was also composed here.

---

* The division of the House of Baden into the Baden-Baden and Baden-Durlach lines explains the town's double-barrelled name. Although in common usage since the sixteenth century, this was only officially adopted in 1931, more out of snobbery than anything else, in order to distinguish it from lesser spa towns named Baden in Austria and Switzerland.

Similarly absorbed by Baden-Baden are a number of wine villages to the south-west—VARNHALT, NEUWEIER, UMWEG and STEINBACH. Near the first two are the ruins of **Yburg**, a thirteenth-century knight's castle commanding a vast panorama over the Rhine plain. East of town, there's also a Burg at the edge of another wine-growing community, **EBERSTEINBURG**. Like Hohenbaden, which lies between it and the town center, this was formerly the property of the local margraves. Further south is the **Merkur**, the highest hill in the Baden-Baden range. There's a choice of trails along it, or you can ascend to the summit by an unusually steep rack railroad (daily 10am–6pm; DM6 return).

Practical Points

Baden has the reputation of being an expensive watering-place, and probably is so to those who live at the first-class hotels, attend all the numerous concerts, and liberally patronize the shops and bazaars; but many of the advantages of the place may be enjoyed without very serious inroad on the finances.

This advice, culled from last century's *Baedeker Guide*, is as sound now as it was then. The **tourist office** in the *Kurverwaltung* on Augustaplatz (Mon.–Sat. 9am–10pm, Sun. 10am–10pm; ☎07221 275200) has full accommodation lists, and will help you find somewhere to stay. Rooms are available in **private houses**, scattered all over town, for DM20 or even less. Main concentration of cheap **hotels** is in OOS, within easy reach of the Bahnhof. *Zum Engel*, Ooser Hauptstr. 20 (☎07221 61610) charges from DM22 per head, while *Zur Linde*, Sinzheimer Str. 3 (☎07221 61519) has singles at DM24, doubles at DM47; *Goldener Stern*, Ooser Hauptstr. 16 (☎07221 61509) charges DM34 for singles, DM66 for doubles. In LICHTENTAL, *Deutscher Kaiser*, Hauptstr. 35 (☎07221 72152) has singles from DM30, doubles from DM50. The town center is much more expensive, though *Zum Nest*, Rettigstr. 1 (☎07221 23076), has five rooms going for DM32 per head.

Baden-Baden's **youth hostel** is between the Bahnhof and the center at Hardbergstr. 34 (☎07221 52223); take bus #1 or #3 to Grosse-Dollen-Strasse, from where the way is signposted. **Camping** presents more of a problem, with no sites in the immediate vicinity. Nearest is in a large pleasure-park named Oberbruch (☎07223 23194) in the outskirts of BÜHL, three stops away by slow train.

Among places to **eat** and **drink**, the *Münchener Löwenbräu* on Gernsbacher Strasse makes a good choice; complete with beer garden, it's like a transported little corner of Bavaria, and serves excellent meals. The aforementioned *Zur Nest* is another of the town's best restaurants, as is *Badener Stuben* directly across the street. For a trendy atmosphere, try *Leo's* on Luisenstrasse, while for solid, low-cost German food, there's *Bratwurstglöckle* on Steinstrasse. If you are in the mood for something totally uncosmopolitan as an antidote to the town, there are plenty of cozy little wine taverns in the outlying vineyard-growing villages.

Rastatt

In 1698, Margrave Ludwig, nicknamed "Türkenlouis" on account of his victories over the Turks, decided to shift his seat from Baden-Baden to **RASTATT**, then an insignificant village 15km to the north, just before the point where the river Murg flows into the Rhine. This move was partly precipitated by the dilapidated condition of the Neues Schloss after the War of the Palatinate Succession. However, it was also conditioned by the courtly culture of the time, which had decided that hilltop fortresses were now redundant, and should be replaced by planned palatial towns on the model of Versailles.

In just ten years, the massive red sandstone **Schloss** was built, to plans by an Italian architect, Domenico Rossi. It's approached via a spacious U-shaped courtyard, guarded by a balustrade with writhing baroque statues, while the central wing is topped by a glistening figure of Jupiter, dubbed the *Goldenen Mann*. The main reception rooms of the interior have been inaccessible to the public for some years, but at the time of writing plans were afoot to institute guided tours round them. Until then, you have to be content with seeing the **Army Museum** (Tues.–Sun. 9:30am–5pm; free) and the **Museum of Liberation** (Tues.–Fri. 9:30am–5pm, Sat. and Sun. 9am–noon and 2–5:30pm; free) on the ground floor. The former shows weapons, uniforms and other military memorabilia from medieval times to the present day. It grew out of the collections of the former states of Baden and Württemberg (whose examples still predominate), but has now been designated as the national museum. The latter traces the history of German liberalism—a slender theme, alas. Rastatt was chosen as the venue for this museum because it was the last stronghold of the rebels in the revolutions of 1848–9—one of the few occasions when the authoritarian nature of German society was seriously challenged. In the north wing of the building, entered from Lyzeumstrasse, is the sumptuous **Schlosskirche**; it's generally kept locked, but a notice will tell you where to get the key.

The most imposing part of the Schloss' gardens is now unfortunately cut off by an arterial road to the south, though at least it does leave a peaceful corner at the edge of town. Here is the graceful **Einsiedelner Kapelle**, a miniaturized version of the great Swiss church of the same name. Türkenlouis' widow, Margravine Augusta Sibylla, went on pilgrimage there to pray for her son Ludwig Georg, who, at the age of six, was still unable to speak. Needless to say, her faith worked the trick, and she even had a copy of the miraculous Swiss *Black Madonna* made to adorn the chapel. Later, the **Pagodenburg** was made as a play-house for the prince and his brother. This was modeled on its counterpart in Nymphenburg on the outskirts of Munich; like the chapel, it was built by the new court architect, Johann Michael Ludwig Rohrer, who, along with the margravine herself, originally came from Bohemia. Behind is the Jugendstil **Wasserturm**, now a café.

Rastatt's town center was planned in conjunction with the Schloss, but only finished in the mid-eighteenth century by Rohrer's younger brother, Johann Peter Ernst. Focus is the elliptical Marktplatz, with several fountains, the **Rathaus** and the **Stadtkirche St. Alexander**, the last-named already showing neoclassical influence. Between here and the Schloss are a number of handsome courtiers' houses. One of these, Herrenstr. 11, houses the **Heimat Museum** (Wed., Fri. and Sun. 10am–noon and 3–5pm; free), which traces the history of the town, and includes displays of medieval art and souvenirs of Türkenlouis.

South of Rastatt, on the way to Baden-Baden, is **Schloss Favorite** (guided tours mid-March–Sept. at 9am, 10am, 11am, 2pm, 3pm, 4pm, and 5pm, Oct.–mid-Nov. 9am, 10am, 11am, 1pm, 2pm, 3pm, and 4pm; DM3), the summer residence of Augusta Sibylla in her years as regent. In it, J.M.L. Rohrer attempted to create the smaller-scale opulence characteristic of the Central European courts, which the margravine preferred to the French-inspired grandeur favored by her husband. The interiors are often riotously ornate, notably the *Spiegelkabinett* with its 330 mirrors, and the *Florentiner Zimmer*, lavishly adorned with colored marbles, stucco, rare woods, and semiprecious stones.

Rastatt's **Bahnhof** is at the eastern end of town; here the scenic *Murgtalbahn* from Freudenstadt connects with the express line down the Rhine. Cheapest

hotel, with singles DM28, doubles DM46, is *Nagel*, Schloss Str. 15 (☎07222 35262); most of the alternatives downtown charge around DM35 per head. As can be seen from the smoking chimneys, Rastatt is a **beer** town in the middle of a wine region. The *Braustübl* of *Hofbräu Hatz* is on Poststrasse; the food here is also reasonably priced. Products of the rival *Franz* brewery can be sampled at *Gastätte Türkenlouis* on Bahnhofstrasse.

Karlsruhe

KARLSRUHE is the baby of German cities. It didn't exist at all until 1715, when **Carl Wilhelm**, Margrave of Baden-Durlach, began the construction of a retreat at the edge of the Hardter Wald. There he could escape a wife who bored him, in order to pursue his cultural interests—and to enjoy the company of several mistresses. The planned town which subsequently grew up around the palace was given an appropriate appellation—"Carl's Rest." Initially modest in size, its growth was stimulated by its establishment as the capital of the reunited state of Baden in 1771, and by the subsequent elevation of its rulers to the title of grand dukes under Napoleon's reorganization of the European political map. Karlsruhe flourished throughout the nineteenth century, enjoying what was, by German standards, a remarkably liberal atmosphere, and becoming a major center for both science and art. In 1945, however, it finally lost its status as a regional capital; Baden was divided between the American and French occupation zones, and Stuttgart made the obvious choice as seat of government for the embryonic province of Baden-Württemberg. As if by way of compensation, Karlsruhe was nominated as the home of the two highest courts of the Federal Republic, a role which has saved it from sinking to the status of a provincial backwater.

By no means the central target of anyone's travels, Karlsruhe nonetheless has much to offer—to discerning eggheads at least. The city's own propaganda baldly proclaims that it occupies fifth place in the hierarchy of the country's cultural centers, carefully omitting to say which four surpass it. Whether or not this self estimation is accurate, the **museums** (which are among the oldest public collections in Germany) are undeniably first-rate, sufficient reason in themselves for a visit.

Around Town

Looking at a map or an aerial photograph, Karlsruhe appears as an extraordinarily handsome city, thanks to its superbly symmetrical **fan-shaped plan**. As in an earlier purpose-built princely town, Mannheim, the hub of the system is the **Schloss**, here placed in isolation to the extreme north. Again this building is U-shaped, but thereafter the geometric patterns become far more imaginative and complex. The Schloss gardens are circular, with the outer half left in a natural state, while the inner is closed by a crescent of regular buildings; this forms a triangle with the Schloss which takes up exactly a quarter of the grounds. From here radiate nine dead-straight avenues (representing each of the Muses); the central axis, Karl-Friedrich-Strasse, runs in a vertical line from the palace's central pavilion, while the two end ones shoot outwards at angles of 45 degrees from the wings, with the others placed at regular intervals in between.

At ground level, the streets are rather less impressive, due largely to the fact that most of the original buildings have been supplanted by undistinguished successors, something for which war damage is partly, but by no means entirely, responsible. Nonetheless, some outstanding architecture survives—including what are arguably the finest **neoclassical buildings** in Germany—even if the lack of venerability means they aren't usually accorded the status they deserve. Although the oldest surviving building, the Schloss is actually the second on the site, built in the French-influenced baroque style of the 1750s. Sadly, it was completely gutted in the last war; the interior has now been modernized to house the Landesmuseum (see below). Few buildings from the same generation as the Schloss remain; an exception is the sole place of worship the town then possessed, the **Kleine Kirche** on the main horizontal street, Kaiserstrasse.

The next phase of the building of Karlsruhe only occurred with Baden's promotion to an independent grand duchy. During the next 25 years, a remarkable local architect, **Friedrich Weinbrenner**, completely transformed the city into a worthy capital. As a young man, he had traveled to Rome; having assimilated the style of the ancient world, he employed its grand idioms in the creation of the great public buildings required by a modern city. Between the Schloss and the start of the central axis, he laid out the rectangular Marktplatz, at the far end of which is an austere red sandstone **Pyramid** containing the tomb of Carl Wilhelm. The western side of the square is dominated by the long pink range of the **Rathaus**. Opposite, the Corinthian facade of the **Stadtkirche** looks like an updated version of a Roman temple. Its present interior is modern and functional, the dignified galleried original having been a casualty of wartime bombs. Periodically it's open for exhibitions; otherwise the key is available on weekday mornings at the church offices at Erbprinzenstr. 5.

Immediately south is another square, Rondellplatz, this time circular in shape. It contains the **Palais** (now a bank), whose forms are almost identical to those of the Stadtkirche. In the center of the square rises an **Obelisk** in honor of the Grand Duke Carl, celebrating his granting of a constitution to the citizens of Baden. Further evidence of the enlightened, tolerant nature of this young state is provided by the Catholic church of **St. Stephan**, reached down Erbprinzenstrasse. This was built by Weinbrenner, himself a Protestant, at the same time as he was working on the Stadtkirche for members of his own faith. Just as the Rathaus forms a pair with the Stadtkirche, so does St. Stephan, but in a wholly different way—the main body of the church is circular while the portico is Doric, the whole being a conscious reinterpretation of the great Pantheon in Rome. Just opposite is the **Landesbibliothek** (Mon.–Fri. 9:30am–6pm, Sat. 9:30am–12:30pm, closed Sun.; free), which displays its treasures—including many wonderful medieval illuminated manuscripts—in a series of temporary exhibitions.

Down Ritterstrasse is a heavy, late nineteenth-century palace formerly used by the heir to the Grand Duchy; it now houses the **Federal Supreme Court** (*Bundesgerichthof*). This is where the most important postwar criminal trials have been held, including those of several of the Baader-Meinhof gang. Of even higher status is the **Federal Constitutional Court** (*Bundesverfassunsgericht*), housed in a building immediately to the left of the Schloss. This is, in theory, an essential bulwark against the rise of any would-be Hitler, whose accession to power was greatly facilitated by the excessively liberal constitution of the Weimar Republic, which gave full rights to groups pledged to its destruction. The West German "Basic Law" has been made much tougher; all political parties must now pledge themselves to the democratic process, or else be outlawed by this court. Karlsruhe's third Federal institution is the **Mint** (*Münze*) on Stephanienstrasse just to the west. Weinbrenner's last building, this is still serving its original purpose, albeit on a much larger scale.

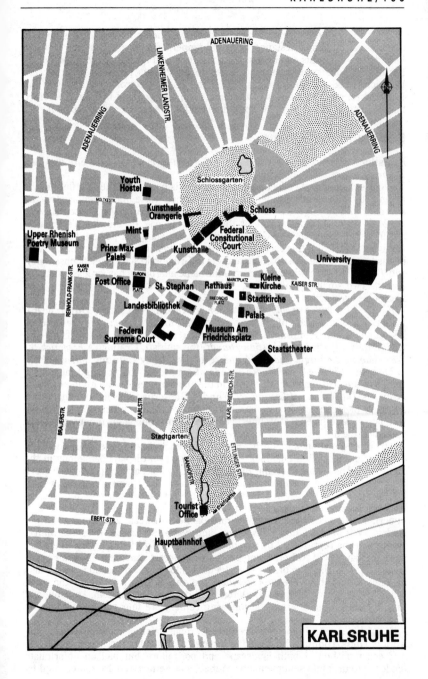

KARLSRUHE

The **University**, the *Fridericiana*, is located at the far end of Kaiserstrasse in neoclassical buildings designed by Weinbrenner's successor, Heinrich Hübsch. Founded in 1825, this has been a specialist technical institution from the outset. Its most famous professors (both lured to prestigious posts elsewhere) were Heinrich Hertz, the pioneer researcher in the field of electromagnetic waves, and Fritz Haber, whose synthesis of ammonia from nitrogen and hydrogen provided the solution which enabled the world demand for chemical fertilizers to be met.

Karlsruhe's museums

Kunsthalle, *Hans Thoma Str. 2. Tues.–Fri. 10am–1pm and 2–5pm, Sat. and Sun. 10am–6pm; free.*
The city's magnificent collection of old masters is housed on the first floor of the mid-nineteenth-century Academy of Art, reached via a monumental staircase adorned with a huge fresco by **Moritz von Schwind**, *The Consecration of Freiburg Münster*. Focal point of the gallery is one of the world's greatest pictures, *The Crucifixion* by **Grünewald**. The last and most powerful of his four surviving versions of this scene, it conveys an almost unbearable feeling of tragic intensity. One of the most baffling aspects of Grünewald's art is its inconsistency, and *The Fall of Jesus*, which came from the same altarpiece, has far less emotional impact. Two small monochromes, *Saint Elizabeth* and *Saint Lucy*, give a good idea of his early style.

A tiny *Christ with Symbols of the Passion* is a recently discovered **Dürer**; near it hangs a painted version of his famous woodcut *Knight, Death, and the Devil* by his pupil **Hans Hoffmann**. Other German paintings to look out for are **Burgkmair**'s *Portrait of Sebastian Brandt* (the satirist), **Cranach**'s *Frederick the Wise Adoring the Virgin and Child*, and several works by **Baldung**, among which is *Margrave Christoph I of Baden in Adoration*; Moritz von Schwind included a cameo of the artist painting this work in the stairway fresco. Among the gallery's rarities is *The Raising of Lazarus* by **Wendel Dietterlin**. This artist made a classic book of fantastical Mannerist engravings which was immensely influential with late sixteenth-century architects and decorators, but all his monuments have been destroyed.

The representation of Flemish, Dutch, and French painting is equally good, but the snag is that only a changing selection is kept on display; parsimony in the Land capital is blamed for the decade which has already elapsed since work began on a much-needed extension to the gallery. *Saint Jerome in the Desert* by **Patinir** is one of the few paintings definitely from the hand of this elusive Antwerp master of landscapes with fantastic rock formations. There are also important examples by three other rare painters—**Lucas van Leyden**'s *Saint Andrew*, **Wtewael**'s *Chicken Inspection*, and **Sweerts'** *Roman Wrestling Match*. **Rembrandt** is represented by a middle-period oval *Self-Portrait*, while there are several examples of **Rubens**. One of **Claude**'s largest canvases, *Adoration of the Golden Calf*, is the star of the seventeenth-century French section, which also includes a diptych of *The Annunciation*, the only known painting by the great Mannerist engraver **Jacques Bellange**, and canvases by Poussin, Le Brun, and the Le Nain brothers. From the following century are four superb still lifes by **Chardin**.

A notable array of nineteenth-century German painting is dominated by the work of **Hans Thoma**, who served as director of this gallery for twenty years. He was accomplished at both landscape and portraiture but had an unfortunate tendency to drift into sentimentality. **Menzel** and **Feuerbach** are represented by important works, but the gem of this section is **Friedrich**'s *Rocky Reef by a Beach* which, in spite of its tiny size, exudes a truly monumental sense of grandeur.

Kunsthalle Orangery, *Hans Thoma Str. 6. Tues.–Fri. 10am–5pm, Sat. and Sun. 10am–6pm; free.*
The Kunsthalle's annex houses paintings by many of the established names of twentieth-century European art, along with a cross section of nineteenth-century French schools, ranging from Delacroix and Courbet to the Impressionists and their followers. There's a good representation of the *Blaue Reiter* group, notably a couple of fine animal paintings by **Marc**. Another Expressionist masterpiece is **Kokoschka**'s *View of Mont Blanc from Chamonix*. **Beckmann**'s *Transport of the Sphinxes* is an allegorical canvas alluding to France's liberation from Nazism.

Landesmuseum, *Im Schloss. Tues., Wed., and Fri.–Sun. 10am–5:30pm, Thurs. 10am–9pm; free.*
The Schloss' interior has been completely modernized to house this excellent collection of antiquities and decorative arts. To the left of the entrance is the **archaeology** section. Highlights are a relief of two horsemen from Nineveh; a Sicilian statuette of the goddess Nike, and a carving of a gift bringer from Xerxes' palace in Persepolis. Farther on are some impressive pieces of Roman sculpture, notably *Hanging Marsyas* from a villa near Rome; *Mithras Killing the Bull*, which came from near Heidelberg; and a relief of two underwater gods from a settlement not far from Karlsruhe.

Many of the museum's finest pieces are in the Renaissance gallery upstairs, including four stunningly bold stained glass windows designed by **Baldung** for the Carthusian monastery in Freiburg; a polychromed limewood *Madonna and Child* by **Riemenschneider**; textiles made in the nearby monastery of Lichtental; a host of fancies created by Augsburg goldsmiths; and bronzes by Giambologna, Adrian de Vries, and others. At the far end of this wing is the **Turkish Booty** (*Türkenbeute*), captured by the margrave Ludwig of Baden-Baden in his campaigns against the Turks between 1683 and 1692. This array is unparalleled in Western Europe, and includes embroidery, illuminated books, cutlery, jewelry, leather, woodwork, saddles, harnesses and weapons of all types. The museum's dazzling art nouveau objets d'art are also particularly worth seeing.

Museum am Friedrichsplatz, *Friedrichsplatz. Tues. 10am–8pm, Weds.–Sat. 10am–4pm, Sun. 10am–5pm; free.*
The original late neoclassical home of the grand ducal collections is now entirely given over to natural history. It's mostly devoted to stuffed animals, but has a good prehistoric section, which includes the only complete skeleton of a Hipparion (a forerunner of the horse) yet discovered.

Prinz Max Palais, *Karlstr. 10. Tues.–Sun. 10am–1pm and 2–6pm, also Weds. 7–9pm; free.*
This stolid Wilhelmine mansion is now named after one of its former owners, who served a heady five-week stint in the autumn of 1918 as last chancellor of the Second Reich. In that time, he democratized the constitution, dismissed the military dictator Erich Ludendorff, began peace negotiations, and announced the abdication of the Kaiser before the latter had consented; whereupon he himself resigned and vanished from the national stage. The top floor of the building now contains the local history museum, with maps and prints, plus a model of how the city looked in 1834, when it was at its most splendid. Also exhibited is the *Draisienne*, first exhibited in Paris in 1818 by the Karlsruhe inventor **Karl von Drais**: decide for yourself whether or not it deserves its disputed title as the

world's first bicycle: the wheels are wooden, and the rider had to propel himself by paddling movements against the ground.

Practicalities and Nightlife

The **Hauptbahnhof** is situated well to the south of the city center; **exchange facilities** are available there (Mon.–Sat. 7am–8pm, Sun. 9am–1pm). Directly facing the entrance is the **tourist office** (Mon.–Fri. 8am–7pm, Sat. 8am–1pm; ☎0721 35530). Ask here if you're interested in a **Rhine cruise**; there's a varied choice of routes from Easter to November, departing from the port at the western extremity of the city. The 24-hour ticket on the **public transit** system is a bargain at DM5 for Karlsruhe itself, DM10 for the entire circuit. To reach the center, you can either go from the eastwards-pointing stop with tram #3 or #6 (the latter is circuitous) to Marktplatz, or from the westward-pointing stop with tram #3 or #4 to Europaplatz. **Mitfahrzentrale's** office is at Rankestr. 14 (☎0721 33666).

The **youth hostel** has a good location just five minutes' walk from the Schloss at Moltkestr. 2b (☎0721 28248). Centrally-situated **hotels** are plentiful, but cater overwhelmingly to the business market. Expect to pay at least DM40 per head; rooms at this price are available at *Pension am Zoo*, Ettlingerstr. 33 (☎0721 33678); *Pension Central*, Sophienstr. 6 (☎0721 27324); *Kolpinghaus*, Karlstr. 115 (☎0721 31434) and *Kaiser Barbarossa*, Luisenstr. 36 (☎0721 37250). You can stay for much less in the outlying villages, where there's also a campground (see below).

For a university city, Karlsruhe is surprisingly quiet come the evening; only a few scattered pockets seem to spring to life. Some animated student **bars** can, however, be found in and around Ludwigsplatz; *Das Krokodil* and *Café Salmen* both offer raucous music, while the latter serves a good selection of salads. In contrast, *Goldenes Kreuz*, just around the corner on Karlstrasse is a late eighteenth-century beer hall serving excellent food; it's also the flagship of the local *Hoepfner* brewery. Nearby on Erbprinzenstrasse is a small vegetarian restaurant, *Sonne*. The trendiest **cafés**, patronized by artists and art students, are *Rix* on Waldstrasse and *Stephanie*, farther north on the street of the same name. Others can be found on Akadamiestrasse, where there are also several pizzerias and an adventurous Arab snack bar, *Arafat Imbiss*. Round the corner in Kaiserpassage is *Restaurant Afrika*, featuring African food, often to the accompaniment of traditional music; there's also a rock pub, *Mad House*. Again this area also offers the alternative of a traditional tavern-restaurant, *Moninger*, named after Karlsruhe's largest brewery, which is particularly renowned for its dark Alt beer.

The main **theater** is the *Staatstheater* on Baumiesterstrasse, which presents opera, operetta, musicals, ballet, and concerts in its main auditorium, straight plays in the smaller hall. Other venues for drama include *Kammertheater*, Karl-Friedrich-Str. 24 and *Die Insel*, Wilhelmstr. 14, while *Marotte*, Kaiserallee 11, has puppet shows. Other concerts are held at the *Stadthalle* on Festplatz, while **live jazz** is performed at *Jubez*, Am Kronenplatz.

Around Karlsruhe

DURLACH, 5km east of the city center, can be reached by train, or by tram #1 or #2. It was the original residence of the local margraves, and is hence described as the "mother town" of Karlsruhe, of which it's now officially a part, though it retains its own quiet atmosphere. The **Karlsburg** palace was destroyed in the War of the Palatinate Succession, but was rebuilt in the eighteenth century. Part of it now houses the museum of the Pfinz district (Sat. 2–5pm, Sun. 10am–noon and 2–5pm; free), with displays on local history and on German communities in Slovakia. At the far end of town is the **Turmberg**, which can be ascended by a rack railroad. The summit commands great views over the surrounding countryside, and there are a couple of good **restaurants**, *Burghof* and *Schützenhaus*. In Durlach itself is a good old world inn, *Alte Schmiede* on Ochsentorstrasse, which serves a range of salads and specializes in a delicious ten year old plum brandy. At the northeastern end of town by the River Pfinz is a **campground** (☎0721 44060).

ETTLINGEN, 8km south of Karlsruhe and reached by train or tram #A, has avoided Durlach's fate of being incorporated into the city. It has quaint narrow streets with half-timbered houses and a handsome baroque Rathaus, but the overwhelmingly dominant monument is yet another **Schloss**, this time housing the museum of the Alb region (Sat. 3–5pm, Sun. 10:30am–noon; DM1.50). By far the most impressive part of the palace is the **chapel**, now converted for use as a concert hall. It was built by Cosmas Damian Asam, who also painted the frothy frescoes on the walls and dome. Good places to **eat** and **drink** can be found on Marktplatz, and there's an excellent café, *Arkaden*, on Klostergasse.

STUTTGART AND AROUND

Baden-Württemberg's capital, **Stuttgart**, stands somewhat apart from other Swabian cities. Whereas they enjoyed independent status for centuries, its development was closely tied to the fortunes of the House of Württemberg, which gradually established control over the rural parts of the province. Thus its dominance was achieved largely because of Napoleon, who promoted Württemberg to a kingdom, and placed the former free imperial cities under its control. Though Stuttgart's standing as a royal capital was only to last for a century, the city has never looked back.

Nearby are two towns that provide a potent contrast: **Esslingen** preserves a great deal of its heritage from its days of glory as headquarters of the Swabian League of Free Imperial Cities, while **Ludwigsburg** is a planned town which was built to supplant Stuttgart, but failed to find favor. Also on the conurbation's S-Bahn network are a number of smaller places well worth a visit, notably **Marbach**, **Schorndorf**, and **Weil der Stadt**.

Stuttgart

STUTTGART breathes of modern-day success. Düsseldorf may have more millionaires, but Stuttgart has the highest general standard of prosperity of any city in Germany, or, indeed, in Europe. Beaming out imperiously from its lofty station above the city center is the local trademark, the three-pointed white star of *Daimler-Benz*. The famous *Mercedes* vehicles produced by this company are cherished status symbols to which executives the world over aspire, while those of the rival *Porsche* factory are the high-performance playthings which have become an essential acquisition for those who feel the need to flaunt their wealth. Together they have made Stuttgart into a car production center to rival Detroit; along with the almost equally celebrated electronics giant *Robert Bosch* they have given the city a place at the world forefront of the high-tech industrial scene.

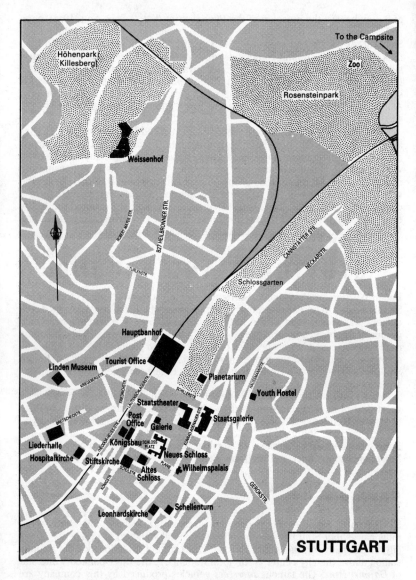

STUTTGART

These days, Stuttgart is the one sure-fire Christian Democratic stronghold in Germany; since 1974, its mayor has been the high-profile **Manfred Rommel** (son of the wartime general). Yet, for all the present self-confidence, it was initially slow to develop. Founded around 950 as a stud farm (*Stutengarten*—hence the city's name), it only became a town in the fourteenth century, and lay in the shadow of its more venerable neighbors right up to the early nineteenth century.

From the point of view of conventional sights, Stuttgart has relatively little to offer. On the other hand, it has a range of superb **museums** to appeal to all tastes, and a varied cultural and nightlife scene. It also has the advantage of an enviable **setting** in a hollow surrounded by hills, which enables the cultivation of vineyards within a stone's throw of the center, and means that unsightly industrial pockets can be tucked away out of sight. This is complemented by a liberal endowment of parks and gardens, which successfully soften what would otherwise be a drab and unappealing cityscape.

Arrival and Practicalities

The **Hauptbahnhof**—an impressive example of railroad architecture, built during the Weimar Republic—is smack in the middle of the city. **Exchange facilities** are available there (Mon.–Sat. 9am–8:30pm, Sun. 9am–8pm). Right behind is the **bus station**. Line #A departs every 20 minutes between 5am and midnight to the **airport** (☎790 1388 for flight information); the journey costs DM6.

In front of the Hauptbahnhof is the underground Klett-Passage, whose shops stay open until late at night. Here also is the **tourist office** (*i-Punkt*; Mon.–Sat. 8:30am–10pm, Sun. 11am–6pm or 1–6pm according to season; ☎222 8240). The integrated **public transit** network, which covers nearby towns as well as the Stuttgart metropolitan area, enables you to switch among buses, trams, the U-Bahn and mainline and S-Bahn trains. Given that the sights are rather scattered, it's worth investing in a DM8 24-hour ticket.

To some extent, the astronomical cost of rented accommodation in Stuttgart— even London prices are in an altogether lower league—is reflected in **hotel** rates. However, there are bargains going, often with a decent location to boot. Cheapest are *Pension Märklin*, Friedrichstr. 39 (☎291315), with singles from DM26, doubles from DM50, and *Pflugfelder*, Ostendstr. 20 (☎262 2731) with singles from DM25, doubles upwards of DM45; the latter is, however, some way from the center. Other budget options are *Pension Schilling*, Kernerstr. 63 (☎240860), which charges DM32 for singles, DM50 for doubles, *Schwarzwaldheim*, Fritz-Elsar-Str. 20 (☎296988), with singles at DM35, doubles DM60, and *Landhaus am Berg*, Pfizerstr. 12 (☎240115), with singles at DM38, doubles DM60. Alternatively, ask the tourist office to reserve you a room; there's no charge for this service.

The **youth hostel** is only about fifteen minutes' walk east of the Bahnhof at Haussmannstr. 27 (☎241583). Check the rates carefully before paying, as prices are sometimes mysteriously inflated. There's also an unofficial hostel, the *Jugendwohnheim*, at Richard-Wagner-Str. 2–4a (☎241132), which is a bit more expensive at DM20 per night. The **campground** is at Cannstatter Wasen (☎558696) on the banks of the River Neckar in BADCANNSTATT.

The City Center

From the Hauptbahnhof, follow Königstrasse straight ahead past the modern Dom (a strong contender for the title of the dullest cathedral in Europe), and you arrive at **Schlossplatz**. The vast open space here comes as a welcome relief after the hectic bustle of the neighboring streets, but it does mean that it's the favorite spot of the tramps and alcoholics who form a noticeable sub-class amid the prosperity all around them. On the eastern side of the square is the colossal baroque **Neues Schloss**, now used for various state purposes by the government of Baden-Württemberg, and otherwise out of bounds to visitors. Opposite is the **Königsbau**, lined with shops all along its 135-meter-long facade. It's in the late neoclassical style much favored in the city; another example of this is the **Jubileumssäule**, erected in the center of Schlossplatz to commemorate the 25th anniversary of the accession of King Wilhelm I of Württemberg.

The **Schlossgarten** stretches 4km northwards from the far corner of the square, all the way to the banks of the Neckar. On the right is the straggling complex of the Staatstheater, a mecca for the performing arts. Farther on, close to the Hauptbahnhof, is the **Planetarium** (sessions Tues. and Thurs. 10am and 3pm, Weds. and Fri. 10am, 3pm, and 8pm, Sat. and Sun. 2pm, 4pm, and 6pm; DM5), which ranks as one of the most modern in Europe. The equipment was made by *Carl Zeiss*, the famous Stuttgart optics company which was originally based in Jena (now in the GDR), but which now operates as two quite separate organizations in each of the Germanys.

Facing the Staatstheater from the other side of Konrad-Adenauer-Strasse is the **Staatsgalerie**. It's not often that an art gallery ranks as one of the most imposing buildings in a major city, but this is an exception. James Stirling—internationally regarded as Britain's most accomplished postwar architect—was commissioned to build an extension to the solid neoclassical home of the city's magnificent collection of paintings (see below), which was no longer big enough to accommodate the every-growing acquisition of modern works. His design, completed in 1984, has been much praised as an original masterpiece. In some ways it resembles another British design on foreign soil, the much larger Pompidou Center in Paris, but is wholly lacking in the deliberate perversities of that structure, while varying the surface textures to far better effect.

At the southern end of Schlossplatz is the **Altes Schloss**. A fortress was first built on this site in the tenth century to protect the stud farm; one wing survives of the fourteenth-century moated castle which succeeded it. In the 1550s, the rest of the building was replaced by a resplendent Renaissance palace with a majestic triple-tiered courtyard, designed by Aberlin Tresch. This forms the perfect setting for nominally-priced concerts of classical music throughout the summer. Badly damaged in the war, the Schloss' interior has been restored to house the Landesmuseum (see below). Ask at the porter's desk for the key to the **Schlosskapelle**, which is particularly intriguing in that it's very probably the earliest-ever example of Protestant religious architecture. The interior was specially designed in accordance with the tenets of the new faith, with its emphasis on preaching rather than the sacraments: it's a simple rectangular hall with galleries on three sides, and the elevated pulpit is given the same prominence as the altar.

To the west, the Altes Schloss overlooks **Schillerplatz**, Stuttgart's sole example of an old-world square. A pensive statue of Schiller himself, erected the year after his death by the Danish neoclassical sculptor Bertel Thorwaldsen, presides in the middle. Also here are two more Renaissance buildings—the **Alte Kanzlei** (*Old Chancellery*) and the gabled **Fruchkasten** (*Granary*). Behind its facade, the latter preserves its original fourteenth-century core; this has now been converted to house the **Lapidarium** (Tues. and Thurs.–Sun. 10am–5pm, Weds. 10am–7pm; free). It's well worth popping in to see its collection of stone fragments from Roman times; particularly impressive are the surviving parts from a massive Jupiter Column, erected around A.D. 200 in a settlement near Heilbronn.

At the back of Schillerplatz is the **Stiftskirche**. Its present form is due to the prolific late fifteenth-century Stuttgart architect Aberlin Jerg, whose special skill, shown here to good effect, lay in welding old and new parts of buildings into a coherent whole. The western tower, an octagon on a square base, is Jerg's own work; unfortunately, the planned openwork steeple has never been built. Inside the church, the choir is lined with one of the most important pieces of German

Renaissance sculpture, an **ancestral gallery** of the counts and dukes of Württemberg. Each of the eleven swarthy figures is brilliantly characterized—a considerable feat of the imagination on the part of the sculptor, Sem Schlör. Look out also for the gilded late Gothic pulpit, and the relief of *Christ Sheltering Humanity*.

South of the Staatsgalerie on Konrad-Adenauer-Allee is the neoclassical **Wilhelmspalais**, used by the last kings of Württemberg as their main residence; it's now the main municipal archive and library. Farther down the road is the **Leonhardskirche**, another church reworked by Aberlin Jerg, containing the funerary monument to the celebrated Renaissance humanist and Hebrew scholar, Johannes Reuchlin. At the high altar there's a copy of a poignant monumental *Crucifixion* by the Heilbronn sculptor Hans Syfer. The original has been moved to the **Hospitalkirche** at the opposite end of the city center. This church is a rare example of Jerg being allowed to design his own building from scratch, but unfortunately only the chancel has survived intact.

Outside the Center

In the hills to the east of the city, reached by tram #15, is the 217-meter-high **Television Tower** (daily 8am–10:30pm; DM4 including ascent by elevator). Completed in 1956, this was the first such structure ever built, and has been much imitated all round the world, most of all in Germany itself, where it often became a civic obsession to acquire such an amenity. The view from the observation platform is much the best Stuttgart can offer, stretching over the Swabian Jura to the Black Forest and the Odenwald, with the Alps visible on clear days.

Below the Killesberg hill to the northwest of the center, reached by bus #43, is the **Weissenhofsiedlung**. This settlement was laid out in 1927, in conjunction with an exhibition of the *Deutscher Werkbund*. Sixteen well-known architects contributed to this Bauhaus scheme, among them Le Corbusier, Gropius and Mies van der Rohe. Badly bombed in the war, the houses have been restored, but with variable success, and it's only worth making a special trip here if you're passionately keen on modern architecture. The **Höhenpark Killesberg** (May–Sept. DM1.50, free at other times) immediately behind is a large, remarkably peaceful recreation area. It's equipped with scented gardens, a flamingo park, and fields with donkeys, rabbits, and sheep, making it a good place to take kids.

More generally enticing is the **Rosensteinpark** at the far end of the Schlossgarten; take U-Bahn #1 or #2 to Mineralbader. At the bottom end of the park is an artificial lake; a little way up the hill is the ritzy **Schloss Rosenstein** (Tues., Thurs., and Fri. 9am–5pm, Weds. 9am–8pm, Sat. 9am–6pm, Sun. 10am–6pm; free), the former country house of the kings of Württemberg, complete with rose garden, fountains and heroic statues. The interior now houses a natural history museum; the fossil part of the collection is separately housed at the western end of the park in the **Museum am Löwentor** (same times; free). At the northern extremity is the superbly landscaped **Wilhelma** (daily 8am–4/5/6 according to season; DM7, kids DM2.50), originally laid out as a Moorish garden for King Wilhelm I. Nowadays, it has a zoo with some 8000 animals, along with hothouses and other botanical arrangements.

From here, it's just a hop across the Neckar to the old spa town of **BADCANNSTATT**, whose favorable situation at a bend in the river meant that it initially outstripped Stuttgart, only to lose importance down the centuries, to the extent that it was incorporated into its erstwhile rival in 1905. If you're coming from the city center, take either a mainline train, or S-Bahn #1, #2 or #3.

Nowadays, Cannstatt is best known as the home of a huge beer festival (see below), and as the main sports and recreation area of the Stuttgart megalopolis. However, it also preserves some of the faded elegance of a once-fashionable spa, and a great deal of self-confident turn-of-the-century architecture remains. There are a few older buildings, too, such as the **Stadtkirche**, another Aberlin Jerg confection, retaining parts of earlier Romanesque and Gothic structures. The **Kurpark**, with its mineral water springs and shady, willow paths, is the most restful spot in Stuttgart.

Overlooking the park at Taubenheimerstr. 13 is the **Gottlieb Daimler Memorial** (April–Oct. 11am–4pm; free). In 1882, Daimler, who was consumed by the dream of developing a new means of mechanical propulsion, gave up his highly successful corporate career, and acquired a villa in Cannstatt (destroyed during the war), and carried out his top-secret experiments in an expanded version of its greenhouse, which somehow managed to escape the bombs. This humble, unpromising setting is where Daimler toiled away in obscurity for four years, aided only by his protégé Wilhelm Maybach. In their quest to create a light, fast-moving internal combustion engine which could power a moving vehicle, Daimler and Maybach invented the motorbike by 1885; the following year, the motorboat and four-wheeled motor car had been added to the list. A year later, they established a factory in the town.

North of Cannstatt, reached by tram #14, is **MÜHLHAUSEN**, another old town which has been gobbled up by the state capital. The late fourteenth-century **Veitskapelle** ranks as the most notable medieval monument in the conurbation; unfortunately, unless you come around the time of the 9:30am Sunday service, you have to phone ahead for an appointment to see it (☎532313). It's a fascinating legacy of the period when Bohemia was not only part of the Holy Roman Empire, but provided its artistic leadership. A local man named Reinhard, who became a wealthy citizen of Prague, sent a team of masons and painters back to his home town to create this chapel in honor of his recently deceased brother. Inside, the walls are busy with frescoes forming a complete illustrated Bible. The original high altar can now be seen in the Staatsgalerie; it has been replaced here by three late Gothic retables made by Swabian carvers.

Another important historic monument some way from central Stuttgart is **Schloss Solitude** (April–Oct. Tues.–Sun. 9am–noon and 1:30–5pm, Nov.–March Tues.–Sun. 10am–noon and 1:30–4pm; DM2), high in the hills to the west, reached by bus #92. This exquisite oval pleasure palace, built in the 1760s, was the main summer residence of the Württemberg court. It's the masterpiece of Pierre Louis Philippe de la Guêpière, one of the prime movers behind the introduction of the Louis XVI style (which marks the transition from rococo to neoclassicism) into Germany. A bonus here is that you're free to wander round its marbled and paneled apartments without being forced onto a guided tour.

Stuttgart's Museums

Staatsgalerie, *Konrad-Adenauer-Strasse 30–32. Tues. and Thurs. 10am–8pm, Wed. and Fri.–Sun. 10am–5pm; free.*
The display of this gallery, Stuttgart's prime sightseeing attraction, begins upstairs in the old building. Of the medieval works, the earliest and most important is a **Bohemian School** altarpiece made in 1385 for the Veitskapelle in Mühlhausen. You'll either see the inner part, in which Good King Wenceslas is flanked by Saint Vitus and Emperor Sigismund, or else the Biblical scenes on the

wings; the position is changed every fortnight. Among many examples of the fifteenth-century Swabian School, those by **Master of the Sterzing Altar**—an artist who worked in the studio of the great Ulm sculptor Hans Multscher—stand out, particularly the courtly *Journey of the Magi*. Another fine painter from the same city, **Bartolomäus Zeitblom**, is represented by three dismembered retables.

The most startling work in the entire gallery is the huge, violently expressive *Herrenberg Altar* by **Jerg Ratgeb**, a man who knew all about violence himself in his other calling as a radical political leader. His reputation rests almost entirely on this single work, which cleverly compresses all the Passion scenes into four panels, and has an unusual reverse side, showing the Apostles going out to preach the Word to all the corners of the earth. By another idiosyncratic artist, **Hans Baldung**, are *Man of Sorrows* and *Portrait of Hans Jacob Freiherr*, while two other talented pupils of Dürer, Hans Leonard Schäuffelein, and Master of Messkirch, are represented by some of their best works. There are also some good examples of **Cranach**, notably a calm-looking, luxuriantly clad *Judith*, showing off the severed head of Holofernes.

The Italian section begins with two wonderfully stylized panels of *The Apocalypse* by a mid-fourteenth-century **Neapolitan** master, and continues with some excellent examples of the Venetian Renaissance, including works by Bellini, Carpaccio, and Tintoretto. Pick of the seventeenth-century canvases are *Christ and the Samaritan Woman* by **Preti** and a foreshortened *Dead Christ* by **Annibale Caracci**, which refines the famous work by Mantegna. However, the gems of the display are several sketches by **Tiepolo**, notably a superbly compressed study for the central section of the great staircase fresco in Würzburg's Residenz.

Memling's sensual *Bathsheba at her Toilet* kicks off the Low Countries section. The brilliant but rare Mannerist **Joachim Wtewael** is represented by an animated cycle of portraits of *The Four Evangelists* and by a highly-finished little *Adoration of the Shepherds*. There are two masterpieces by **Michael Sweerts**, another long-forgotten artist who has recently come to the fore: the pendants *Taste* and *Sight*, each characterized by an allegorical female figure. **Rembrandt** also treated the theme of sight—a subject particularly close to an artist's heart—in the tender *Tobit Healing his Father's Blindness*. It forms a sort of unofficial counterpart to the horrific *Blinding of Samson* in Frankfurt, which was painted the same year. One of Rembrandt's earliest works, *Saint Paul in Prison*, is also on show, along with important works by Hals, Rubens, and Terbrugghen.

Biggest surprise of the gallery is a whole room devoted to **Edward Burne-Jones**'s cycle of *The Legend of Perseus*. Commissioned by Arthur Balfour, who was later to become British prime minister, this constitutes one of the finest achievements of the Pre-Raphaelite movement. Three of the eight scenes were never completed, but the full-scale cartoons shown here make ample substitutes. Other nineteenth-century high points are *Bohemian Landscape* and *The Cross in the Woods* by **Friedrich**, an impressive group of works by local neoclassical sculptor **Johann Heinrich Dannecker**, and a decent cross section of French Impressionism.

The modern extension begins with the seven vibrant figures **Oskar Schlemmer** made for the kaleidoscopic *Triadschen Ballett* in 1922. Displayed high up on pedestals, they're arguably his most original creations. Alongside are monumental bronzes by **Matisse**, while examples of many of the century's leading sculptors can be found in the sculpture court downstairs, or scattered throughout the galleries.

A wooden group entitled *The Bathers* is one of the main items in what's regarded as the finest **Picasso** collection in Germany. **Modigliani** is represented by *Portrait of Chaim Soutine* (the Russian-born painter) and *Reclining Nude*. The entire progress of German art this century is copiously traced; particular outstanding are **Kirchner's** *Friedrichstrasse, Berlin*, **Dix's** *Matchstick Seller*, and **Beckmann's** *Self-Portrait with Red Scarf*. Avant-garde works occupy the end halls, while important temporary exhibitions are regularly featured downstairs.

Landesmuseum, *Altes Schloss, Schillerplatz 6. Tues. and Thurs.–Sun. 10am–5pm, Weds. 10am–7pm; free.*

Highlight of this richly varied museum is the **Kunstkammer** of the House of Württemberg, displayed in one of the corner towers. The first floor has small bronze sculptures of predominantly Italian origin, while the second is laid out in the manner of a Renaissance curio cabinet, with the star exhibit being a beautiful set of Gothic playing cards, arranged in suits of duck, falcon, hound, and stag. On the top story are the nineteenth-century crown jewels, the most notable being a necklace with the 22-carat *Harlequin*.

The baroque sleighs of the dukes can be seen on the ground floor of the main part of the building, along with a sparkling array of glass. Upstairs is a large and important collection of Swabian devotional wood sculptures, arranged themati- cally rather than chronologically, thus offering inviting comparisons. Many of these are in a folk idiom, others show a profound sense of artistic pathos, as in **Multscher's** *Muttergottes*, **Riemenschneider's** *Holy Women* and *Saint James*, **Syrlin the Younger's** *Passion* cycle (made for the original Münster in Zwiefalten) and the graceful *Talheim Altar*, with carvings by an anonymous Ulm craftsman and paintings by **Master of Messkirch**. Displayed alongside are fine examples of stained glass.

On the same floor, the **archaeology** section includes excavations from Troy, varied Roman antiquities (notably a stunning third-century cameo of Jupiter), the intact grave of a Celtic prince, and jewelry from the Frankish period. The top floor features historical musical instruments, predominantly of the keyboard variety, and a wonderful array of **clocks**, of which the most unusual is a sixteenth-century bear-and-ostrich automation timepiece from Augsburg.

Galerie der Stadt Stuttgart, *Kunstgebäude, Schlossplatz. Tues.–Fri. 10am–6pm, Sat. and Sun. 11am–5pm; free.*

The municipal art collection is understandably very much a poor relation of the Staatsgalerie, but it does contain some superb works by **Otto Dix**. The luridly- colored *Grosstadt* triptych, indeed, is one of his finest canvases, perfectly conjur- ing up the Weimar Republic's false sense of values and its smoky, decadent night- club scene. In *Unlikely Lovers* and *The Triumph of Death*, Dix returned to two subjects popular with painters of the German Renaissance, giving them a vicious modern twist; he also gave visual vent to the horrors of World War I in *Trench Warfare*. After this, the rest of the gallery is an anticlimax, but there are a number of small works by the three leading Stuttgart painters of this century—Adolf Hölzel, Oskar Schlemmer and Willi Baumeister.

Linden Museum, *Hegelplatz 1. Tues., Weds., and Fri.–Sun. 10am–5pm, Thurs. 10am–8pm; free.*

This well-presented ethnology museum has displays covering the full gamut of non-European cultures, with Peru, Melanesia, Benin, and the Congo being partic- ular strengths. A full-scale reproduction of an Islamic bazaar, using many original exhibits, is one of the most eye-catching features.

Daimler-Benz Museum, *Mercedestr. 136. Tues.–Sun. 9am–5pm; free.*
Unless you positively rue the day the car was invented, this museum, the best of
its kind in the world, is an absolute must. It was set up in 1986 to celebrate the
remarkable twin centenary of the invention of the motor car by **Gottlieb
Daimler** and **Carl Benz**, neither of whom was aware of the other's work, and
who both went on to run highly successful factories producing their inventions;
these were united in 1926 (long after Daimler's death and Benz's retirement).
Even entering here is an experience—take S-Bahn #1 to Neckarstadion, then
walk straight ahead at the exit to the works entrance, or else go by bus #56 to
Stadion. In accordance with the company's megalomaniacal obsession about
industrial espionage, you then have to wait for a special sealed minibus to take
you through the factory complex to the museum doors, which are opened only in
conjunction with these arrivals.

Over seventy **historical vehicles** are on display, all with their bodywork
restored to pristine condition and looking fully roadworthy. The earliest exhibit is
the *Daimler Reitwagen* of 1885, the first-ever motorbike, which was capable of
12km/h. Benz's patent *Motorwagen* (a tricycle whose engine and bodywork are
both his own design) from January the following year just beats the Daimler-
Maybach *Motorkusche* (which was fitted into a four-wheeled horse-carriage) for
the title of the world's first car. Both used one-cylinder engines, and had a maximum speed of 16km/hr. The Daimler company's first *Mercedes* dates from 1902.
This Spanish-sounding name was borrowed from the daughter of the firm's principal foreign agent, Emil Jellinek; it proved so successful a trademark that it
replaced the recently-deceased founder's name on all products. In the merged
conglomerate, it was firstly used in tandem with Benz, but has now completely
usurped him as well.

You'll doubtless find your own favorites among the exhibits, which include fire
engines, motor boats, airplanes and buses. However, the **luxury cars** steal the
show—look out for the elite, handmade *Grand Mercedes* models of the 1930s,
including one used by the Japanese royal family, the official *300d* limousine of
Konrad Adenauer, and the first of the "Popemobiles," the *Landaulet* of Paul VI.
Equally impressive are the space-age vehicles specially designed for world
record attempts; these look so futuristic it's hard to believe they were made
more than half a century ago. In 1938, the *W125* achieved 437.7km/hr on the
Frankfurt–Heidelberg autobahn, still the fastest speed ever registered on a public
road. The *T80* was designed for travel at 600km/hr—but World War II killed off
this project, which was never subsequently revived.

Porsche Museum, *Porschestr. 42. Mon.–Fri. 9am–noon and 1:30–4pm; free.*
In accordance with its carefully cultivated flash image, *Porsche* is considerably
more relaxed about prying visitors than *Daimler-Benz*. Not only can you wander
at will around the factory site—which is right beside the Neuwirtshaus station on
S-Bahn #6—there are free **guided tours of the production lines** every working
day. These are generally booked solid weeks in advance, but a few extra visitors
are allowed to tag on at short notice, though it's best to phone first (☎827 5685).

The Bohemian-born **Ferdinand Porsche** had already had a brilliant career
when he set up in Stuttgart after World War II. As Austrian director of *Daimler-
Benz*, he was responsible for the design of the handsome if underpowered
Pullman saloons, and led the technical team involved with the world record
attempts. His services had also been acquired by Hitler for the creation of the
original *Volkswagen*. For his own enterprise, Porsche concentrated on the opposite end of the market. The fifty vehicles on show illustrate all the company's

models from the *356 Roadster* of 1948 to those currently in production. They show that the basic formula of a sleek aerodynamic design coupled to a high-performance rear engine has in fact altered remarkably little, even if the "duck's tail" spoiler, first introduced in 1973, has definitely helped boost the macho image even farther.

Schwäbisches Brauerei Museum, *Robert-Kocj-Str. 12. Tues.–Sun. 10:30am–5:30pm; free.*
Recently established in the former ice cellar of the *Schwabenbräu* brewery in the suburb of VAIHINGEN (reached by S-Bahn #1, #2, or #3), this charts the history of beer-making from the third century B.C. right up to the present day. Exhibits include a complete experimental brewery from the 1930s, a collection of drinking vessels, and pieces of old equipment. Needless to add, there's an enticing selection of beers on sale at the bar.

Eating and Drinking

Stuttgart's expensive reputation thankfully doesn't entirely extend to food and drink; though fancy restaurants abound, there are also any number of places offering traditional Swabian dishes at low cost, with plenty of ethnic eateries to stimulate the most jaded palate. Local **wines** are almost equally divided between *Riesling* (white) and *Trollinger* (red) varieties. Demand for these within Stuttgart itself is often so high that they can't be obtained elsewhere. A wide variety of **beers** are produced here as well. The *Hofbräu's* gentle, sweetish *Herren-Pils* is probably the most popular brew locally; the rival *Schwaben-Bräu's Meister-Pils* has a far more bitter taste. Outside the city, *Dinkelacker's* products are the best-known: these include the classic *CD-Pils*, plus both light and dark varieties of *Weizen*.

The best and safest recommendations for good quality food and drink are the many **Weinstuben**. These cozy, homely establishments are archetypally German, and are as well known for their solid cooking as for wine. *Zur Kiste*, Kanalstr. 2, is generally agreed to rank as the best of these, though the city's bigwigs prefer *Kachelofen*, Ebehardstr. 10. Best choice of wines is at *Weinhaus Stetter*, housed in an old prison tower at Rosenstr. 32. *Bäckerschmiede*, Schurwaldstr. 42, is renowned for its *Gaisburger Marsch*, the apotheosis of Swabian cooking, a rich stew of beef, potatoes and *Spätzle*. Bad Cannstatt is ideal for a wine-bar hop; particularly notable are *Klösterle*, Marktstr. 71, occupying a former nunnery, and *Am Stadtgraben* at no. 6 in the street of the same name.

Back in the city center, the best restaurants in a **beer hall** set-up are *Zeppelin-Stüble*, directly opposite the Hauptbahnhof at Lautenschlager Str. 2, and *Ketterer*, Marienstr. 3b. The only pub in the city with an adjoining house-brewery is *Stuttgarter Lokalbrauerei*, Calwer Str. 3. *Movenpick* on Königstrasse is much the best **self-service** restaurant, with salads particularly good value. For **vegetarian** fare, *Iden*. Schwabenzentrum, Ebeharstr. 1, has the best range; alternatives are *Excelsior*, Kienestr. 35, and *Village*, Olgastr. 43. Among **ethnic restaurants**, the most popular student haunts include the Greek taverna *Olympic* on Bohnenviertelstrasse, and the pizzeria *Max und Moritz*, Geiss Str. 5. Italian food in a lively atmosphere with occasional live bands and regular art exhibitions can be had at *L'Aleph*, Eberhardstr. 22. The many other cuisines on offer in the city include Hungarian at *Gastätte Brendle*, Wangener Str. 74, Russian at *Russische Datscha*, Aachener Str. 23 in Bad Cannstatt, Thai at *Bangkok*, Hauptstsätter Str. 61, Indonesian at *Bali*, Bebelstr. 20, Mexican at *El Sombrero*, Talstr. 110, African at *Keyeh Bari*, Schloss Str. 28 and *Ebony*, Herzogstr. 11, Arab at *Aldar*, Marktplatz 6, and Israeli (kosher) at *Schalom*, Hospitalstr. 36.

Nightlife

Despite Stuttgart's status as a large university city, there's no single concentration of trendy nightspots. Instead, the action takes place in a variety of small pockets spread throughout the city; the following is a list of those currently "in."

Café Stella, Tubingen Strasse. One of the leading gay hangouts; less trendy than some, and never uncomfortably busy.

Casino, Mörikestr. 69. Crowded cellar bar with an underground, punkish feel to it.

Dixieland Hall, Marienstr. 3 (Tues.–Sat. 7:30pm–1am). Leading traditional jazz venue, though modern styles are also featured. Entrance upwards of DM6, but drinks and food are reasonably priced.

Exil, Filderstr. 61. A former punk paradise taken over by arty types; jazz and blues are played in a laid-back atmosphere.

Jenseitz-Schwulencafé, Bebelstr. 25. Stuttgart's main gay café; predominantly male, and prone to become very crowded.

Laboratorium, Wagenburgerstr. 147. Crowded jazz café popular with the alternative set, including a large Green Party contingent; occasionally features cabaret.

Life, Bolzstr. 10. Café with live rock and occasional reggae; looks far more rough than it actually is. Serves huge cheap pizzas and excellent beer.

Longhorn, Heiligen Wiesen 6. The place to go to hear country and western music.

Merlin, Furtbachstr. 14. Alternative café and arts center.

Oz, Kronprinzstr. Lively but musically run-of-the-mill disco.

Rock Café Soho, Schwabstr. 16a. Small bar with modern decor and predominantly young clientele.

Röhre, Wagenburgtunnel, Neckarstr. 34 (daily 8pm–2am). The celebrated "tunnel" nightclub occupies what was originally designed as a new railroad line. Live bands play everything from jazz to punk; it's also a disco patronized mainly by the most fashion-conscious locals.

Roxy, Hirschstr. Popular if conventional disco.

Treff Fröhlich, Liederhalle, Schloss Str. Best place for cocktails; expensive, but generally worth it.

Culture

Stuttgart's leading highbrow venue is the **Staatstheater**, Obere Schlossgarten 6 (☎221795), a complex of three separate houses. The resident **ballet** and **opera** companies alternate in the *Grosses Haus*; the former is one of the most famous in the world, with the great tradition established in the 1960s by the South African-born John Cranko (many of whose choreographies remain in the repertoire) ably carried on under his protégé, the Brazilian Marcia Haydée. Straight **drama** is featured in the *Kleines Haus*, while the James Stirling-designed *Kammertheater* is equipped with a movable stage and seating, and puts on more experimental work. The *Theater im Depot*, Landhausstr. 188 is an even more way-out subsidiary venue.

Among the city's **other theaters**, the Jugendstil *Altes Schauspielhaus*, Kleine Königstr. 9 (☎225505) specializes in nineteenth- and twentieth-century classics, while contemporary plays and forgotten older works are performed at *Theater der Altstadt* on Charlottenplatz (☎244332). Comedies of all kinds are put on by

Kömodie in Marquardt, Bolzstr. 4–6 (☎291484). *Renitenz-Theater*, Königstr. 17 (☎297075) is the place to go for satirical cabaret; good German is obviously needed for an appreciation. *Theaterhaus Stuttgart* (☎402070) is the big venue for alternative events, including feminist work and visiting foreign groups. At Höhenpark Killesberg between May and October, the *Varieté-Theater* presents circus-type shows between 4pm and 8pm daily. Other places suitable for taking **kids** are the *Puppen und Figuren Theater*, Eberhardstr. 61d (☎241541), home of several puppet companies, and the *Kruschteltunnel*, Möhringer Str. 56 (☎282543 or 473396), whose shows are meant for the under-12s. Mime is the predominant fare at the *Makai-City-Theater*, Marienstr. 12 (☎626208).

The three halls of the *Liederhalle* on Schloss Strasse (☎221795) serve for concerts of all kinds, but particularly **classical music**. Pick of the city's five orchestras is Karl Münchinger's *Stuttgarter Kammerorchester*; their style may now be a little old-fashioned, but they played a crucial role in dusting the cobwebs off baroque music, being primarily responsible for raizing Vivaldi from the oblivion of two centuries to his present status as one of the most genuinely popular of all composers. The smaller halls often feature performances by the local *Melos-Quartett*, currently one of Europe's finest string quartets. Stuttgart is, after Leipzig, the main center for research into Bach performance practice, so any concerts by Helmut Rilling's *Bach Collegium* are worth looking out for. The city has more top-class choirs than anywhere else in Germany, the most celebrated being the *Hymnus Chorknaben*. Free concerts are often held in the churches—the Stiftskirche has a series at 7pm during the winter months. Every three years (next in August/September 1991), Stuttgart is host to an international *Musikfest*, with guest orchestras from all over the world.

Leading **movie theater** is the *Kommunales Kino*, Neckarstr. 47 (☎221320), which shows a lot of British and American films. These are sometimes in the original, sometimes dubbed—the program always makes clear which. An even bigger, but more mainstream, selection of English-language films can be seen at *Corso*, Hauptstr. 6 (☎734916). Other worthwhile movie theaters are *Atelier*, Kronprinzstr. 6 and *Lupe*, Kriegsbergstr. 11.

Listings

Airlines *British Airways* Kriegsbergstr. 28 (☎299471); *Lufthansa*, Lautenschlagerstr. 20 (☎20441); *American Airlines*, Charlottenstr. 44 (☎2369412); *Pan-Am*, Flughafen (☎790 1314); *TWA*, Sophienstr. 38 (☎058183).

American Library Friedrichstr. 23a (☎229 8317).

Area code (☎0711)

Bookshops *Weises Hofbuchhandlung* and *Wittwer*, both on Obere Königstrasse, are the main general shops. A women's bookshop (*Frauenbuchladen*) is at Olgastr. 75.

Car rental *Autohansa*, Hegelstr. 25 (☎693322); *Avis*, 18 Katharinenstrasse (☎241441); *InterRent*, Friedrichstr. 28 (☎221749); *Hertz*, Hohenstaufenstr. 18 (☎643044).

Consulates *American*, Urbanstr. 7 (☎210221).

Duty Dentist (☎780 0266).

Duty Doctor (☎280211).

Festivals Main annual event is the sixteen-day *Cannstatter Volksfest*, held on the last week in September and the first in October. Founded in 1818 by King Wilhelm I of Württemberg, it's the second biggest beer festival in the world. In fact, most of the features—the huge beer tents, the spectacular amusement-park rides. The booths, and even the costumes worn—are direct imitations of the larger *Oktoberfest* in Munich, although the beers on tap are all Swabian. If wine is your tipple, the *Stuttgarter Weindorf*, held in the city center from the last Friday in August until the first Sunday in September, has over 300 varieties available for tasting. The *Weihnachtsmarkt*, beginning in late November, has existed since the seventeenth century and is thus one of the oldest in the country, but the harlequins and tightrope walkers have unfortunately long gone, to be replaced by the standard offerings. Other notable events are a *Lichtfest* on Killesberg in early July, and the *Frühlingsfest*, lasting for a fortnight in late April/early May.

Markets The daily markets in the *Markthalle* on Schillerplatz are ideal for putting a picnic together. On Saturday mornings, a *flower market* is held on Schillerplatz itself, while there's also a *flea market* on Schlossplatz.

Mitfahrzentrale Lerchenstr. 68 (☎221453).

Neckar cruises *Neckar-Personnen-Schiffahrt*, Anlegestelle Wilhelma, Bad Cannstatt (☎541 0473).

Pharmacies (☎224310) for information as to which one is open outside normal hours.

Post office Main office, with general delivery, is at the rear of the Königsbau on Schillerplatz. The branch in the Hauptbahnhof is open until 11pm.

Sports The *Neckarstadion* in Bad Cannstatt is the main stadium for outdoor events, including the matches of the leading local soccer team, *VfB Stuttgart*, one of the most consistent in Germany in recent seasons. Indoor events, including an international tennis tournament in November, are held at the Martin-Schleyer-Halle alongside (☎561565).

Taxis (☎566061).

What's happening The tourist office's well-filled monthly program of events, *Stuttgarter Monatsspiegel*, costs DM1.60. "Alternative" listings can be found in both *Stuttgart Live* and *Ketchup*, available from newsagents.

Women's center Kernerstrasse 31 (☎296432).

Schorndorf, Fellbach, and Weil der Stadt

If your interest in the motor car hasn't been exhausted in Stuttgart, head for **SCHORNDORF**, some 30km east, by S-Bahn #2, or by a mainline train going towards SCHWÄBISCH GMÜND. At Höllgasse 7 you can visit the house where Gottlieb Daimler was born in 1834; it's now designated as a small **museum** (Tues. and Thurs. 2–4:30pm; free) in his honor.

The nearby **Marktplatz** is neatly divided in two by the baroque **Rathaus**, where free leaflets (German only) on the town, including a guided walking tour, can be picked up. A superb set of half-timbered buildings, including two pharmacies, line the square and its continuation, Obere Marktplatz. These mostly date from just after Schorndorf's complete destruction by fire in 1634. On the next square, Kirchplatz, more fine buildings cluster around the late Gothic **Stadtkirche**, whose handsome tower, an octagon on a square base, completely dominates the town. Inside, the *Marienkapelle* has an extraordinary vault, whimsically crafted into the shape of a Tree of Jesse, which is attributed to the Bohemian master mason Anton Pilgram, architect of the Dom in Vienna. At the opposite end of the old town are the other main buildings, the sixteenth-century **Jagdschloss** and **Burgschloss** (the latter clearly showing the plan of its moated medieval predecessor) of the dukes of Württemberg, both of which are now used as municipal offices.

Closer to Stuttgart, and on the same S-Bahn line, is **FELLBACH**, occupying an agreeable location between the rivers Rems and Neckar at the foot of the vineyard-covered Kappelberg. The time to come here is on the second weekend in October, when one of the best **wine festivals** in southern Germany, the *Fellbacher Herbst*, is held. Booths for wine-tasting are set up on the Friday, while there's a procession through the streets the following afternoon. Needless to say, local vintages can be sampled all year round in the town's many *Weinstuben*.

WEIL DER STADT, 30km west of Stuttgart at the terminus of S-Bahn #6, is the conurbation's gateway to the Black Forest. From here, it's only a short bus journey either to CALW, or down the valley of the Würm to TIEFENBRONN. Not far from the Bahnhof is Aberlin Jerg's **St. Peter und Paul Kirche**, which, true to his inimitable manner, incorporates the Romanesque-Gothic towers of its predecessor. Overlooking the river at the foot of the town is the impressive half-timbered **Spital**, which served as an old folks' home for four centuries, only recently being displaced by a purpose-built modern structure.

The sloping **Marktplatz** has an arcaded seventeenth-century Rathaus, plus two Renaissance fountains—one with a statue of Emperor Charles V, the other with the Imperial Eagle. In addition, there's a monument to the town's most famous son, the astronomer **Johannes Kepler**, compiler of the *Rudolphine Tables* and author of *The Mystery of the Universe*, whose birthplace just off the square has been turned into a **museum** (Mon.–Fri. 9am–noon and 2–4pm, Sat. 10am–noon and 2–5pm, Sun. 11am–noon and 2–5pm; DM1). In spite of having to waste much of his life dabbling in astrology in order to earn his keep from the superstitious monarchs of his day, Kepler achieved major advances in the study of both astronomy (by proving the elliptical path of planetary movements) and optics (being the first to understand how the eye works).

Ludwigsburg and Marbach

The creation of **LUDWIGSBURG** can be said to have begun in 1697, when French troops destroyed an isolated hunting lodge of the House of Württemberg which lay some 15km north of Stuttgart and 35km south of Heilbronn. Although German petty princes often fought against France, they were ardent admirers of the absolutist form of government practiced there, and when Duke Eberhard Ludwig decided to rebuild the lodge, he soon found himself desiring something rather grander. By 1704, he hit on the idea of a planned town (named, needless to say, in his own honor); five years later, he had decided to make this his main residence, and the duchy's new capital. To entice people to come to live there, he provided free land and building materials, plus exemption from taxes for fifteen years—an offer which duly found plenty of takers.

The baroque **Schloss** (guided tours April–Oct. daily 9am–noon and 1–5pm, Nov.–March Mon.–Fri. at 10:30am and 3pm, Sat. and Sun. at 10:30am, 2pm, and 3:30pm; DM3.50) took thirty years to build under the direction of a whole team of architects, and was only completed in the year of the patron's death. By then, funds had completely dried up, and much of the lavish interior decoration, which is predominantly in the rococo and Empire styles, was only put in place by his successors, who rather nullified the initial concept of Ludwigsburg by preferring to reside in Stuttgart. There are 432 rooms in all, grouped in eighteen separate buildings arranged round three courtyards; some sixty of these are included in the compulsory tour. Among the highlights are two chapels, one each for the Protestants and Catholics, and a theater, which was the first in the world to be equipped with a revolving stage. The *Ordenshalle* serves as an opulent venue for the concerts which take place throughout the summer festival season. Also housed in the Schloss is a branch of the **Landesmuseum** (Tues.–Sun. 10am–5pm; free). Appropriately enough, this concentrates on the decorative arts produced in baroque courts, including plenty of examples of the local porcelain.

The **gardens** (daily 7:30am–8:30pm) are the scene of a huge floral festival, *Blühendes Barock*, held between April and October each year. In front of the Schloss, the formal baroque section has been re-created from old plans. To the east are various modern additions to the facilities, including a Japanese garden, an aviary, and the *Märchengarten*. The last-named is a kitsch folk-tale playground with huge model giants, witches, and other fairy-tale figures, complete with sound effects. Kids will love it, but otherwise it's not worth paying the inclusive DM9 entrance fee.

A better destination for a stroll is **Schloss Favorite** (guided tours Tues.–Sun. 10am–noon and 1:30–4pm; DM2) in the grounds immediately to the north, which was built as a resting place for Ludwig and his cronies on their hunting trips. Even if you don't want to see yet another baroque interior, it's still worth coming to enjoy the grounds, to which there's free access. Nowadays, the deer here are tame; red squirrels are also much in evidence.

It's then a walk of about 30 minutes to the third and last of Ludwig's palaces, **Monrepos** This has a tranquil lakeside setting which is perfect for a picnic, but the building itself is in private hands, and there's no admission. Within the grounds is the town's top luxury hotel; surprisingly, this has a reasonably priced (and excellent) restaurant.

In contrast to Mannheim and Karlsruhe, the Schloss is not the epicentre of the Ludwigsburg plan; that distinction belongs to the **Marktplatz**. As with the Schloss, there are churches for both the Catholic and Protestant faiths, facing each other across the square; from the tower of the latter, a brass band intones a chorale at midday from Tuesday to Friday inclusive. Markets are held each Tuesday, Thursday, and Saturday, in continuance of an uninterrupted tradition since the town's foundation.

One of Ludwigsburg's main claims to fame is that it has nurtured rather more than its fair share of literary celebrities, and an obelisk in **Holzmarkt** immediately to the north commemorates four nineteenth-century writers who were born in the town—the Romantic poets Eduard Mörike and Justinus Kerner, the realist philosophers Friedrich Theodor Vischer (who was also a notable liberal politician, and author of a skit on the Faust legend), and David Friedrich Strauss. Mörike was the most significant of this group; in spite of an uneventful life as a tutor and country pastor, he produced some of the greatest lyric poetry of the age, which was to be a major source of inspiration to all the leading songwriters in the German tradition, especially Hugo Wolf. Schiller went to school in the town, while the revolutionary writer Friedrich Schubart did a six-year stint as organist of the Protestant church.

Ludwigsburg's **Bahnhof** is just a short walk to the west of the town center. As well as being on the main line between Stuttgart and Heilbronn, it's linked to the state capital by S-Bahn #4 and #5. The **tourist office** (Mon.–Fri. 8:30am–noon and 2–5:30pm, Sat. 9–11:30am; ☎07141 910636) is at Wilhelmstr. 12. If you want to stay the night, rather than visit on a day trip, your best **hotel** bet is *Zum Hasen*, conveniently near the Bahnhof at Solitudestr. 43 (☎07141 23479), and charging DM25 per head. Other options tend to be expensive, or far out. Similarly distant is the rather luxurious **youth hostel** at Gemsenbergstr. 21 (☎07141 51564); take bus #423 from the Bahnhof to its terminus.

Most young inhabitants of Ludwigsburg confine their nightlife to Stuttgart, but the town has several good, inexpensive **restaurants**. Among the obvious choices are *Roter Ochsen* and *Margherita* on Holzmarkt, along with the pricier *Weinhaus Schnepple* on Marktplatz. Even better is *Württemberger Hof* on Bismarckstrasse, which offers a comprehensive vegetarian menu, alongside standard Swabian fare. For cheap Italian food, try *Café Roma* in the Marstallcenter.

A few kilometers northeast of Ludwigsburg, at the terminus of S-Bahn #4, is **MARBACH**. This small town of half-timbered houses is indelibly associated with **Friedrich Schiller**, who was born there in 1759. Considered in Germany to be one of the great lions of world literature, Schiller's fame elsewhere largely depends on a single poem, known in English as *Ode to Joy*, part of which was used by Beethoven for the choral finale of his titanic Ninth Symphony—the first time ever that words had been used in a symphonic composition. The strong liberal sentiments of this work are wholly characteristic of the output of Schiller, who was very much a product of the Age of Enlightenment. After his early *Sturm und Drang* period, he began to concentrate increasingly on large-scale historical problems, and was himself a practicing historian, holding a chair at the University of Jena (now in East Germany), and writing a mammoth, Protestant-inspired account of the Thirty Years' War. This research provided him with the raw material for his dramatic masterpiece, the *Wallenstein* trilogy. Like his other mature plays, which took Mary Stuart, Joan of Arc and William Tell as subjects, this addresses basic moral issues in the light of the vexed question of historical greatness.

The **house** at Niklastorstr. 20 where Schiller was born has been turned into a small museum (daily 9am–5pm; DM1). It's a modest building, entirely typical of Marbach—the writer's mother had also been born in the town, and the family moved back to this rented property when his father retired from the army. As space is obviously restricted here, a much grander memorial was created early this century in the shape of the **Schiller Nationalmuseum** (daily 9am–5pm; DM2), which is housed in a huge mock-baroque castle perched high above the Neckar Valley. If you're at all into literary memorabilia, this is a must, with mementoes not only of Schiller, but of all the other leading Swabian writers as well.

The *Stadthalle* near the museum is one of the best **restaurants** in town, offering the bonus of fine panoramic views from its terrace; *Goldener Löwe*, on the same street as Schiller's birthplace, is another good choice. There's no hostel or campground, but **rooms** at DM25 per head are available at *Zum Bären*, Marktstr. 21 (☎07144 5455) and *Pension Schmierer*, Marktstr. 7 (☎07144 15565).

Esslingen

If Stuttgart seems rather thin on historic monuments, ample compensation is provided by **ESSLINGEN**. Nowadays, this is virtually a southeastern suburb of the state capital, reached in 15 minutes by S-Bahn #1, but for centuries it was a free imperial city, and jealously guards its municipal independence. During the last century, it became an important center of machine tool manufacturing, and is still ringed by ugly factories which provide a sharp contrast to the vineyard-clad hills above. However, the old center has been preserved almost intact. With its winding streets, narrow alleys, spacious squares, and dramatic views, it's one of the most visually pleasing—and most unexpected—parts of this otherwise high-tech-dominated part of Baden-Württemberg.

From the Bahnhof, go straight up the street of the same name. To the left, the Neckar canal is crossed by an old footbridge. Two more bridges can be seen down to the right; the second of these, the fourteenth-century **Innere Brücke**, is outstanding, incorporating a graceful chapel, which now serves as a memorial to the victims of the Third Reich.

Heart of the town is the **Marktplatz**, scene of markets on Wednesday and Saturday mornings. To the left is the **tourist office** (Mon.–Fri. 8am–6pm, Sat. 9am–noon; ☎0711 3512 441 or 645). Dominating the square is the Romanesque-Gothic **Stadtkirche St. Dionys**, whose two towers are bizarrely linked by a covered passageway, which served as a defensive lookout post. The church preserves its late Gothic rood screen, along with a soaring tabernacle and a font from the same period. In the chancel are glittering stained glass windows, made during the late thirteenth and early fourteenth centuries. If you're keen on arch-aeology, it's well worth coming here on a Wednesday between 2pm and 5pm, to view the extensive underground **excavations** for DM1.50. These include Roman finds, plus the foundations of two previous churches on this spot, which date from periods where surviving buildings are extremely scarce—the first was erected around 720, the second throughout the first half of the following century.

On the south side of the Stadtkirche, next to the canal, is an old cemetery chapel of similar date which was converted in the Renaissance epoch to serve as the **Stadtarchiv**. Facing the back of the church is the **Speyrer Zehnthof**, a mid-sixteenth-century tithe barn. Since 1826, this has served as the headquarters of the oldest *Sekt* cellar in Germany; production of high-quality sparkling wines remains a local specialty. The **Spitalkelter**, a half-timbered structure on the north side of Marktplatz, is an earlier relic of the city's wine tradition, having been built as a winepressing factory, before later becoming a hospital.

Adjoining Marktplatz to the east is Rathausplatz. The **Altes Rathaus** began life in the early fifteenth century as a merchants' trading hall and tax collection point. When this large half-timbered building was taken over for municipal purposes at the end of the following century, the Renaissance architect Heinrich Schickhardt (later to come to prominence as the planner of Freudenstadt) was commissioned to provide a new facade overlooking the square. He responded with a cheerful pink frontispiece, much influenced by Dutch buildings of the time; this was immediately adorned with an astronomical clock. Opposite is the baroque **Neues Rathaus**, originally a patrician palace. Beyond are a number of picturesque old streets, along with the Hafenmarkt, where you'll find the thirteenth-century **Gelbes Haus** (*Yellow House*), probably Germany's oldest-surviving and most architecturally distinguished brothel. However, it hasn't served its original purpose since a fire devastated the town in 1701.

Just west of Marktplatz is **St. Paul**, a Dominican monastery consecrated by Albertus Magnus in 1268. It's of particular significance in marking the debut on German soil of the sober, unadorned Gothic architecture characteristic of the mendicant religious orders. In total contrast is the **Frauenkirche** on the brow of the hill behind, which represents the Gothic style at its most elaborate. The marked resemblance, albeit on a reduced scale, to the great Münster in Ulm is no coincidence: it shared the same master masons, members of the Ensinger and Böblinger families. There are two exquisite portals, showing the *Life of the Virgin* and *The Last Judgment*, while the hall church interior has lovely stained glass windows made a generation after those in the Stadtkirche. However, as at Ulm, it's the highly decorated **tower**, crowned with an openwork spire, which provides the most memorable feature.

At the east end of the Frauenkirche is the **Blaubeurer Pfleghof**, the most impressive of about a dozen such institutions in Esslingen, which served as town headquarters and charitable institutions of rural monasteries. From here, you can ascend to the **Burg** along its own covered ramparts. What was once a mighty thirteenth century defensive system, bolstered in the sixteenth century, has almost entirely disappeared, save for the walls themselves, the bulky *Hochwacht* (the corner tower where the fortifications stop climbing), and the *Dicker Turm* ("Fat Tower") at the summit. The last-named was restored last century in the Romantic manner, and is now an excellent, if pricey, restaurant. From here, there's a good **view** over the town and Neckar valley towards the Swabian Jura.

Esslingen makes an alternative base to Stuttgart, if you don't wish to pay the latter's prices. The **youth hostel**, however, is rather a long way to the north of town at Neuffenstr. 65 (☎0711 381848). A more viable commuting base would be *Gasthof Falken*, Bahnhofstr. 4 (☎0711 357288), with singles at DM30, doubles DM50. The town center abounds with places to **eat** and **drink**. *Palmscher Bau* on Innere Brücke has a beer garden, while *Zum Schwanen* on Franziskanergasse has a tiny house brewery, and specializes in *vom Heissen Stein* dishes. If you fancy a **hike**, the *Höhenweg* is a 27-kilometer-long circular marked path round the hills; a free leaflet on it is available from the tourist office.

SWABIA

Swabia (*Schwaben*) has long ceased to exist as any form of political entity, yet such is the emotional attachment to the name (which at times takes on a near-mystical significance), that it stubbornly refuses to vanish from the map, far less from local consciousness. The rugged plateaux cutting right through the middle of the province continue to be known as the **Swabian Jura**, and two of many former free imperial cities, **Schwäbisch Gmünd** and **Schwäbisch Hall**, have adopted their present forenames in order to show where their loyalties lie. Certainly, the name is far more popular than that of Württemberg, taken from the aristocratic family who established dominance over most of rural Swabia in the Middle Ages. It remains something of a sore point that the Land of Baden-Württemberg was not designated as Swabia, on the grounds that to do so would have offended the people of Baden, with their very different ethnic and historical background.

In many respects, the position of Swabia within Germany is analogous to that of Scotland within Great Britain, and it's the butt of broadly similar jokes: indeed one of these maintains that the *Schwobs* were originally Scots, but were booted out of their homeland for taking thriftiness just a bit too far. At the Reformation, the extreme wing of Protestantism—here known as **Pietism**—took firm root, bringing with it a firm commitment to the work ethic and a burning sense of individualism, tempered only by communal loyalties. Even today, the jingle *Schaffe, spare, Häusle baue* ("work, save, build a house") remains something of a Swabian motto. There's also no doubt that the intellectual rigor fostered in the province has led to its nurturing a gallery of inventors, philosophers and poets out of all proportion to its size.

If you despair of mastering the horrendous complexities of the German language, it's worth bearing in mind that the ingenious Swabians have developed a partial solution to the problem, put to everyday use in their own **dialect**. By adding *-le* to most nouns, they don't have to worry about genders (which immediately become neuter), while they omit the cumbersome *ge-* prefix from past participles, and regularize the declension of verbs. The local **cuisine** is no less distinctive, with noodles as ubiquitous as in Italian or Chinese cooking. Nearly every savory dish comes with either *Spätzle*, a shredded pasta made from eggs and flour, or *Maultaschen*, which, with the exception of the sauces used to cover it, is broadly similar to ravioli. Equally popular are *Flädle* (pancakes) which turn up in both soups and desserts.

Swabia's exact boundaries are a matter of controversy. The *echt* (real) *Schwob* lives in an area bounded by **Heilbronn**, **Tübingen**, and the two towns with *Schwäbisch* as their prefixes. However, the term has historically been used to describe all of southwestern Germany, other than the bulk of the Black Forest, all the way south to the **Bodensee**, and eastwards to **Ulm** and Augsburg which, horror of horrors, were allocated by Napoleon to Swabia's long-time rival Bavaria, although the former soon managed to escape from its clutches.

Tübingen

"We have a town on our campus" runs a local saying in **TÜBINGEN**. No irony is intended—the **university** dominates the life of this city to an extent unparalleled even in Germany's other world-famous centers of learning, such as Heidelberg, Marburg, and Göttingen. Over half the population of 70,000 is in some way connected with the University, and the current size of the town is due entirely to the twentieth-century boom in higher education—it was not until a hundred years ago that the number of inhabitants reached five figures, having remained static since the time of the university's foundation in 1477.

Tübingen's **setting**, on the gentle slopes above the willow-lined banks of the Neckar, some 30km south of Stuttgart, immediately sets the tone of the place. Upstream, the river follows a turbulent course, but here it's serene and placid, the perfect backdrop for the unhurried and unworldly groves of academe. For obvious reasons, the town is often described as a German counterpart of Oxford or Cambridge. Certainly, it's the nearest equivalent, and the sight of the students punting on the river on a balmy summer evening is strongly reminiscent of similar scenes on the Cam or Cherwell. However, there are important differences. Germany has a far more egalitarian higher education system than England or America—most students attend their local institution, and there's no trace of the Anglo-Saxon conception of an intellectual, social, and political elite being nurtured in a couple of historic universities. Indeed, Tübingen actually goes against the generally conservative grain of German higher education; it has one of the few left-wing councils in Baden-Württemberg, and the Greens have chalked up many successes, notably the dropping of plans for an urban ringway. Moreover, there's no collegiate system, and little in the way of student societies, other than the small and discredited duelling *Verbindungen* (see p.268). There are no impassioned student union debates, extravagant balls, or nostalgic wallowings in ancient traditions, while carefree displays of high jinks are kept firmly in check. Instead, study is treated as a serious business, and the prevailing atmosphere is that of the peace and quiet that's necessary for scholarly contemplation.

The old town, having been spared the ravages of war, is a visual treat, a mixture of brightly painted half-timbered and gabled houses ranging from the fifteenth to the eighteenth century, grouped into twisting and plunging alleys. There are few truly outstanding buildings, but the whole ensemble is much more than the sum of its parts, and two large squares provide an appropriate setting for communal activities. The first of these, **Holzmarkt**, is built around a fountain dedicated to Saint George. Here also is the *Buchhandlung Heckenhauer*, where Hermann Hesse, having dropped out of formal education, spent a four-year apprenticeship at the end of last century as a bookbinder and bookseller.

Dominating the square is the **Stiftskirche St. Georg**, an outwardly gaunt late Gothic church erected at the end of the fifteenth century, with a contrastingly stunning interior. Under the extravagant stellar vault of the nave, there's a Flamboyant pulpit adorned with reliefs of the Madonna and Four Doctors of the church, and crowned by a tapering canopy; more fine sculptured figures can be seen around the north windows. A triple-arched rood screen sheltering a painted retable by Hans Schäufelein, a pupil of Dürer, leads to the **chancel** (April–Sept. Mon.–Sat. 10am–noon and 2–5pm, Sun. noon–5pm, Oct.–March Fri. 2–4pm only; DM1). Here an outstanding series of stained glass lancet windows, dating from the same period as the church's construction, cast their reflections on the pantheon of the House of Württemberg. In 1342 this family bought Tübingen, then no more than a village, from the local grandee; on the promotion of their territory to a duchy in 1495, they made the town their second residence. The thirteen tombs show the development of Swabian sculpture in the Gothic and Renaissance periods; finest is that of Countess Mechthild, made in the workshop of Hans Multscher of Ulm. Look out also for the monument to Count Eberhard the Bearded, founder of the university. The **tower** (same times, summer only; DM1) can be ascended for a view over the red roofs of Tübingen to the Neckar and the Swabian Jura.

On the far corner of the square, which doubles as part of Munzgasse, is the original home of the university, the **Alte Aula**, rebuilt in baroque style for celebrations marking the 300th anniversary of its foundation. Also here, at no. 15, is **Cottahaus**, the former headquarters of the famous company, now based in Stuttgart, which marked the high-point of Tübingen's publishing tradition, begun soon after the foundation of the University. **Johann Friedrich Cotta**, who took over an ailing family company set up five generations previously, was one of the most astute publishers of all time; through friendship with Schiller, he came to know and publish all the leading figures of the German Enlightenment, and also set up the *Allgemeine Zeitung*, whose independence and liberal views came as a blast of fresh air in the context of the censored and despotically controlled press of the time. The **Studentenkarzer** (*Students' Prison*) at no. 20 in the same street is older than the one in Heidelberg and has more varied graffiti, but unfortunately isn't so accessible (guided tours Sat. at 2pm; DM1).

Overlooking the banks of the Neckar on Bursagasse, the street immediately below, is the **Hölderlinturm** (Tues.–Fri. 10am–noon and 3–5pm, Sat. and Sun. 2–

5pm, closed Mon.; DM2). Originally part of the medieval fortifications, it's now named after one of Tübingen's most famous alumni, **Friedrich Hölderlin**, who lived here in the care of a carpenter's family, hopelessly but harmlessly insane, from 1807 until his death 36 years later. There's a collection of memorabilia of the poet, largely ignored in his lifetime, but now regarded as one of the greatest Germany ever produced. Hölderlin's odes show complete mastery of the rhythms used by the bards of ancient Greece; he also saw their gods as symbolic of real forces whose presence was felt in everyday life alongside those of the Christian virtues. Just before the onset of his madness, he produced his most striking work, grandiose apocalyptic visions couched in complex language and highly original imagery, showing the anguished state of his own existence—"A son of earth I seem, born to love and suffer."

Further along the street is the **Bursa**, a former student residence and philosophy lecture hall from the earliest days of the university, rebuilt at the beginning of the nineteenth century in neoclassical style. There's a memorial to Philipp Melanchton, who lectured here for a time after his graduation at the age of seventeen. At no. 4b is the house of the Reformer's uncle, the humanist and Hebrew scholar **Johannes Reuchlin**, who was the star academic of the early years of the university. His research interests embroiled him in a major controversy when the Dominicans, backed by the emperor, tried to suppress all Jewish books on the grounds of blasphemy; a posse of distinguished scholars immediately leapt to his defense.

At the end of the street is the **Evangelisches Stift**, a Protestant seminary established in a former Augustinian monastery in 1547 as the theological faculty of the university. It has maintained a high academic reputation, but the nature of the courses, encouraging the questioning of traditional theology rather than its indoctrination, has led to the ironic if logical result that its most famous graduates have followed careers outside the church: it's been nicknamed the "Trojan Horse of intellectual giants." An early example of this trend was the great astronomer Johannes Kepler, who studied here at the end of the sixteenth century. Hölderlin, who never managed to find the sense of belief to accompany his essentially religious outlook was another; he was joined by his classmates, Hegel and Schelling, subsequently the dominant figures of German philosophy. From here you can continue down Neckarheide to **Theodor Haering Haus** (Tues.–Sun. 2:30–5:30pm; free) which contains collections on the history of the town, and on publishing and the book trade. En route, at no. 24, is the birthplace of **Christoph Uhland**, the lyric poet and chronicler of old German legends who gave up his professorship in order to enter politics, serving as the local deputy in the German National Assembly of 1848–9.

The **Markt**, heart of old Tübingen, is just a short walk uphill from the Stift. It preserves many of its Renaissance mansions, along with a fountain dedicated to Neptune, around which markets are held on Monday, Wednesday, and Friday. The **Rathaus**, originally fifteenth-century but much altered down the years, is covered with historical frescoes, though these are hardly more than a hundred years old; other eye-catching features are the pulpit-like balcony for public announcements, and the gabled pediment housing an astronomical clock made in 1511.

Burgsteige, one of the oldest and most handsome streets in town, climbs steeply from the corner of the Markt to **Schloss Hohentübingen**, the Renaissance successor to the original eleventh-century feudal castle. Entry is via a superb **gateway** in the form of a triumphal arch, made in 1604. It's adorned with the arms of the House of Württemberg and the riband of the Order of the Garter;

the latter had recently been bestowed on Duke Friedrich by Queen Elizabeth I. What comes afterwards is an anticlimax—there's a second, less ornate doorway leading to a drastically restored courtyard—but it's worth going up for the sake of the view. You can wander around the complex freely, but only by taking a **guided tour** (April–Sept. Sat. 5pm, Sun. 11am and 3pm; DM3) can you see the prison and the cellars with a great vat capable of holding 18,700 gallons.

The northwestern part of town, immediately below the Schloss, has traditionally been reserved for the nonacademic community. Here are some of the city's oldest and most spectacular half-timbered buildings, such as the municipal **Kornhaus** on the alley of the same name, and the **Fruchtschranne**, the storehouse for the yields of the ducal orchards, on Bachgasse. The quarter is especially associated with the *Gogen*, or vine-growers, who often doubled as farmers or agricultural laborers. They're renowned for their rich fund of predominantly earthy **humor**, mainly dating from the turn of the century when there was a lucrative trade in the contents of cesspools, which were then used as fertilizers. The pomposity of the academic world offered a ready-made target for the wit of the *Gogen*, as in the following exchange:

Gog: Do you read the *Tübinger Chronik*?

Student: Certainly not; I read the *Frankfurter Allgemeine*. The *Tübinger Chronik* is so worthless that I only use it to wipe my behind.

Gog: In that case you'd better watch out that your ass doesn't get cleverer than your head.

The corresponding quarter northeast of the Markt is once more dominated by the university. Down Collegiumsgasse is the **Wilhelmstift**, built in the late sixteenth century as the Collegium Illustre, an academy for members of the Protestant nobility, but since 1817 the site of the Catholic seminary. This building became the focus of worldwide media attention in the early 1970s when its leading theologian, the Swiss **Hans Küng**, published a series of articles and books attacking cherished doctrines, notably papal infallability. The upshot was that he was stripped of his sacral offices, but he has remained in Tübingen as a professor, a celebrity, an ecumenical leader—and a Catholic. (Interestingly enough, the majority of priests on the staff here cohabit and consort openly with their "housekeepers," but they run no risk of being sacked—unless they should wish to regularise their relationships in line with Biblical teaching.) Küng is one of a few cult figures on whom the university depends for such vitality as it has; another is the left-wing novelist Walter Jens, who teaches classics.

Crossing Langegasse, and continuing along Metgergasse, you come to the **Nonnenhaus**, most photogenic of the half-timbered houses, with its outside stairway and *Sprachhaus*. Two other buildings of note just off the Holzmarkt are the **Lateinschule** at Schulberg 10, and the enormous **Pfleghof** on the street named after it. The latter, now converted into student residences, was built in the fifteenth century as the tithe barn of the Bebenhausen monastery (see below).

Just outside the northeastern boundary of the old town are the former **Botanical Gardens**. These have been replaced by another complex (Mon.–Fri. 7:30am–4:45pm, Sat. and Sun. 10–11:45am and 1:30–4:30pm), complete with arboretum and hot houses, located, along with most of the modern buildings of the university, a kilometer or so north by the ring road. The gardens serve as a reminder that botany has long been one of Tübingen's strong subjects. One of the leading lights in the academic life of the sixteenth century was Leonhard Fuchs (after whom the fuchsia is named), who published an exhaustive and practical encyclopaedia on plants and their medicinal properties.

Practical points

The **Hauptbahnhof** and **bus station** are side by side just five minutes' walk from the old town—turn right and follow Karlstrasse straight ahead. At the edge of Eberhardsbrücke is the **tourist office** (Mon.–Fri. 8:30am–6:30pm, Sat. 8:30am–12:30/5pm according to season; ☎07071 35011); this is the only place you can change money outside the standard banking hours. The **youth hostel** is on the banks of the Neckar a short walk to the right on the far side of the bridge at Gartenstr. 22/2 (☎07071 23002). To reach the **campground**, also with a riverside setting at Rappenberghalde (☎07071 43145), it's quicker to turn left on leaving the Hauptbahnhof, and crossing at Alleenbrücke. **Hotels** aren't thick on the ground, and tend to be expensive, far out, or both. *Zum Ritter*, just outside the old quarter at Am Stadtgraben 25 (☎07071 22502) is the best bet, with singles at DM38, doubles DM65. *Am Schloss*, Burgsteige 18 (☎07071 21077) has an ideal location and rooms beginning at DM35, though the average price is much higher. Other budget options involve a long commute—*Kürner*, Weizsäckerstr. 1 (☎07071 22735) charges from DM38 per head; *Kreuzberg*, Vor dem Kreuzberg 23 (☎07071 4626) has singles at DM40, doubles at DM70. Otherwise, there are simple pensions in most of the outlying villages.

The best **restaurant** in the center of Tübingen is *Forelle*, an old-world wine bar at Kronenstr. 8; the town's other citadels of gourmet food are *Museum*, Wilhelmstr. 3, and *Landgasthof Rosenau* in the new botanical gardens. For cheaper eating, try *Café Pfuderer* on Marktplatz, which serves Swabian specialties in a tea-room atmosphere. Also on this square is *Marktschenke*, a lively student bar with jukebox. Nearby on Haaggasse are *Deutsche Weinstube*, with a good basic menu, and *Jazzkeller*, which features live music in the evenings.

For highbrow **culture**, there's a choice between the traditional fare of plays and concerts at *Landestheater*, Eberhardstr. 6, and the experimental productions of the tiny *Zimmertheater*, Bursagasse 16. Tübingen also boasts a number of good **bookshops**, notably on Munzgasse and Bursagasse. **Bikes** can be rented either at the Hauptbahnhof or the campground, with tandems available at the latter. **Rowing boats** are available at Neckarbrücke; if you want to try **punting**, ask at the tourist office, or take the DM6 piloted trip which leaves from the Hölderlinturm at 4pm on Saturdays.

Bebenhausen and Naturpark Schönbuch

Immediately to the north of Tübingen are the former hunting grounds of the dukes and kings of Württemberg, now restocked with deer and designated as the **Naturpark Schönbuch**. The main road to Stuttgart cuts right through this protected landscape, but its 150 square kilometers are virtually uninhabited—a welcome break from the urban area which encircles it. Several streams cut through this gently undulating countryside, which is largely covered with a coniferous forest of spruce, pine, larch, and fir; as usual, there's a network of marked hiking trails.

Within the park is the village of **BEBENHAUSEN**, just 5km north of Tübingen, of which it's now officially a part. It can be reached by bus, but it's far more fun to sample the park's scenery on foot. There's a choice of trails—you can either follow the course of the Goldersbach, parallel to the main road, or else set out from the botanical gardens, and continue via Heuberger Tor and the path beside the Bettelbach. In 1190, a group of Cistercian monks arrived in Bebenhausen, taking over from a Premonstratensian congregation who had settled there just a decade before. The **Abtei** (Tues.–Fri. 9am–noon and 2–5pm, 10am–noon and 2–5pm; DM2) is set in a walled enclosure with many half-timbered outbuildings matching those in the village; the superb main complex presents a cross section of medieval European architecture. That the buildings survive in remarkably complete condition is due to the fact that they were converted into a Protestant seminary (which is now defunct) after the Reformation.

Best place to begin your tour is with the **church**, in the Transitional style between Romanesque and Gothic characteristic of the Cistercians; it was completed in 1228, but modernized a century later with the addition of the huge, airy east window, still with the original stained glass in between the tracery. At the beginning of the fifteenth century an eccentric crown-shaped tower topped with a miniature openwork steeple was built over the crossing. Unfortunately, the nave was truncated to a third of its original size after the suppression of the monastery, so the dimensions are now more those of a chapel. A suite of rooms—the chapter house, parlatorium, and lay brothers' hall—was built along the east walk of the present cloister in a pure early Gothic style after work had finished on the church.

In the middle of the fourteenth century, the **summer refectory** was added to the southern side. Not only is this Bebenhausen's great glory, it's one of the finest Gothic buildings in Germany, a dining room like no other. Three central pillars stand like palm trees sprouting out their branches to form a vault of consummate grace and precision, which is painted with motifs of plants and birds. Two more refectories were built on the west wing in the late Gothic period, one for the lay brothers, the other for winter use, but they're very ordinary in comparison. In the same period, the outer walls of the cloister were built, including a pretty **well-house**. This isn't quite symmetrical, as the mason himself realized, playfully confessing his guilt by adding a corbel of a fool holding up a mirror to show him where he had gone wrong.

Also in the monastery grounds is the **Jagdschloss** of the Kings of Württemberg (guided tours, lasting 1 hr., Tues.–Fri. 9am, 10am, 11am, 2pm, 3pm, 4pm, Sat. and Sun. 10am, 11am, 2pm, 3pm, 4pm; DM2.50). This was adapted from the monastery's former guest house, and is luxuriantly furnished in nineteenth-century style, with many souvenirs of the chase. The building later did improbable service as a parliament, being the headquarters of the Land of Südwürttemberg-Hohenzollern, which was set up by the French in 1945, but merged into the more viable province of Baden-Württemberg seven years later. Be warned that the tours are heavy on detail, and that there's nothing very exciting to see—it certainly makes an anticlimax to a visit to the monastery.

Rottenburg

The old Roman town of **ROTTENBURG**, 14km up the Neckar from Tübingen, can be reached in a few minutes by either bus or train. It looks remarkably similar to its younger but more famous neighbor, though its setting is far less dramatic—the hills rise much farther away from the river—and there is, of course, no university.

However, because Rottenburg remained Catholic, it became an important episcopal center, and has been the seat of a bishop since 1828. The **Dom** is actually an upgraded Gothic parish church and is beaten for the title of Germany's least imposing cathedral only by the nondescript modern building in Stuttgart which serves as joint headquarters of this same diocese. Its one notable feature is the late fifteenth-century tower with its openwork spire; the interior of the building was re-decorated in baroque style following a fire. Far more imposing is the jolly **Marktbrunnen** directly in front, which is contemporary with the spire. One of the finest fountains in Germany, its shaft bears figures of members of the House of Habsburg, along with Biblical personages.

Both Marktplatz and Königstrasse, which runs from both ends of the square, are lined with handsome baroque mansions. Much the largest of these, at the far northern end of the street, is the **Bischöflisches Ordinariat**, which was formerly a Jesuit college. At the opposite end of Königstrasse is the **Spital**, part of whose Renaissance frontage survives. Just over the Neckar is the **Stiftskirche St. Moriz**, inside which are fragments of fourteenth- and fifteenth-century frescoes, along with the surviving original parts of the Marktbrunnen. The half-timbered **Nonnenhaus** immediately opposite dates from around 1440 and is the oldest house in town.

The Swabian Jura

The **SWABIAN JURA** (*SCHWÄBISCHE ALB*) is the name given to the series of limestone plateaus forming the watershed between the valleys of the rivers Rhine, Neckar and Danube. It's a harsh, craggy landscape, with poor soils and a severe climate, though its appearance has mellowed thanks to the plantation of forests. Geological faults have meant that individual mountains have become detached from the main mass; these formed ideal natural defensive fortresses for feudal overlords, and many are still crowned by castles.

The Jura has few towns, and even less in the way of major sights; the area is primarily of note for its **hiking** possibilities. As normal in Germany, marked trails cross the countryside, and the views on offer have a majestic sweep, even if they're often rather monotonous. It's an area rich in **flora**, with thistles, daphnes, anemones, and lady's slippers being particularly prominent.

The following section describes the western and central parts of the Jura. For the southern border (which has much the grandest scenery of all), see *The Upper Danube Valley*. At the eastern end of the range are the towns of HEIDENHEIM and AALEN (see p.243), while to the north the Jura merges with the STAUFERLAND (see p.243). **Public transit** in the area is slightly complicated. The railroad lines tend to run parallel to each other, involving circuitous connections, while some of the bus companies are entirely in private hands, meaning that (most unusually) rail/bus passes are not always valid.

Reutlingen

Just 10km east of Tübingen, reached in a few minutes by Stuttgart-bound trains, **REUTLINGEN** is generally considered to be the gateway to the Swabian Jura. Unfortunately, it isn't a very auspicious beginning, now being almost entirely given over to the high-tech engineering industries which have made this part of Germany so prosperous. In total contrast to Tübingen, which it must once have resembled, it was devastated during World War II, and only a few notable monuments remain.

Prominent among these is the Gothic **Marienkirche**, whose tall spires can be seen all over the town, making the sole challenge to the skyscrapers' monopoly.

The church was begun as a thanksgiving for the successful defense of Reutlingen in 1247 against the forces of the royal pretender Heinrich Raspe, an action which preserved its status as a free imperial city; it was completed a century later with the erection of the main **tower** (Tues.–Fri. 4–5:30pm, Sat. 10am–1pm, Sun. 8–11:30am). Inside the church are some surprisingly well-preserved frescoes, fifteenth century stained glass windows, and an octagonal font and Holy Sepulcher from around the turn of the sixteenth century.

The **Heimat Museum** (Weds. 3–5pm, Sat. 2–5pm, Sun. 10:30am–noon and 2–5pm; free) is in a converted convent on Oberamteistrasse. Entirely devoted to local history, it's especially informative on the old guilds of Reutlingen. Otherwise, there are some pretty **fountains**—the *Marktbrunnen* and the *Kirchbrunnen* are both sixteenth-century in date, and each bears a statue of an emperor. The list of sights just about ends there, and it's certainly not worth staying the night as Reutlingen is expensive (there's no hostel or campground), noisy, and for the most part very ugly.

The Swabian Jura Road

The *Schwäbische Alb Strasse*, a designated scenic route through the heart of the Jura between TUTTLINGEN and AALEN, can be picked up at **LICHTENSTEIN**, 12km south of Reutlingen. This village is famed for its **Schloss** (daily 8:30am–noon and 1–5:30pm; DM2), set on a high, narrow peak, and familiar through its appearance on the covers of all the tourist brochures to the region. Like many other castles in the area, it's a Romantic fantasy, erected in the 1840s as a replacement for one demolished in 1802. In the rebuilding, the architects were strongly influenced by the imaginary descriptions of its predecessor contained in the historical novel *Lichtenstein*, which was published in 1826. This was written by a remarkable author, Wilhelm Hauff, who died at the age of 25, but bequeathed a very considerable output, including many fairy stories which are still popular in Germany today. He was here closely imitating the approach pioneered by Sir Walter Scott, yet he often modified this romanticized view of the Middle Ages with a sharp sense of realism. It's a good thirty minutes' walk from the village to the castle, but worth doing for the fantastic views across the Jura.

Traveling eastwards, the next stop is **BADURACH**, some 20km on. This handsome old town now primarily devotes itself to serving as a health resort, and has the standard, predictable spa facilities. Nevertheless, it also has many half-timbered houses (otherwise a rarity in the Jura), with the most impressive being the sixteenth-century group on **Marktplatz**, which also boasts a Renaissance fountain with a statue of St. Christopher.

The **Residenzschloss** (Tues.–Sun. 10am–5pm; DM2) was begun in the mid-fifteenth century, around the time of the birth here of Duke Ebehard the Bearded, founder of the University of Tübingen. Its most impressive room is the *Goldenes Saal*, originally built by Ebehard, but transformed at the end of the Renaissance epoch. Landesmuseum's hunting and weapons collections can also be seen. Likewise associated with Ebehard is the **Stiftskirche**, erected in late Gothic style by his court architect, Peter von Koblenz; the octagonal tower was, however, only completed last century. Inside are marvelous furnishings contemporary with the architecture—two pulpits, choir stalls, Ebehard's own praying desk, a font and stained glass.

If you're traveling here by road, stop off at the **Uracher Wasserfall**, which is notable for its wonderful secluded setting, rather than for the volume of water it produces, which can be minimal in the summertime. Farther into the hills are more waterfalls, a nature reserve, and the eerie Guterstein stables. The last-named were originally built in the sixteenth century for Duke Wilhelm Ludwig, but now appear almost deserted with only the horses and the sound of the chiming, quarter-hourly bell. From here, it's a walk of about thirty minutes to Urach itself via a clearly signposted route.

There's a **youth hostel** at Burgstr. 45 (**☎**07125 8025) on the southwestern side of town, and a **campground**, *Pfahlhof*, (**☎**07125 8098), along with an abundant choice of **guesthouses**. The surrounding countryside is beautiful, particularly around the nearby tiny village of GLEMS in the foothills of the Jura. Here the scenery is luxuriant and verdant, brimming with wild flowers and foliage.

Hechingen and Burg Hohenzollern

HECHINGEN lies on and around a hill 25km southwest of Reutlingen, with regular rail connections from both there and Tübingen. In the lower part of town, close to the Bahnhof, a pilgrims' route, complete with wayside shrines, leads to the **Franziskanerkirche St. Luzen**. This late sixteenth-century church is advanced for its time, by German standards, showing the late Renaissance feeling its way towards baroque. Rather plain from outside, it's lusciously ornate within, containing richly decorated half-columns and pilasters, an elaborate vault with polychromed keystones, and shell-shaped niches with statues of the Apostles.

The upper town, which preserves a number of quaint, twisting streets, is entered via the bulky **Unterer Turm**. Built at the same time as St. Luzen, this is now the only surviving part of the fortifications. Crowning the highest point of the hill is the **Stiftskirche**, erected in the grandly sombre neoclassical Louis XVI style by the French architect Michel d'Inxard. Look out for the grave slab of Count Eitelfriedrich von Zollern, made by the doyen of bronze-casters, Peter Vischer of Nürnberg. In the nearby Goldschmiedstrasse, which plunges back down the hill, is a baroque **synagogue**, recently immaculately restored to serve as a cultural center.

There's no nearby hostel or campground, but **hotel** prices are reasonable. Best **restaurants** are *Schwanen* on Bahnhofstrasse and *Klaiber* on Obertorplatz.

Rearing high above Hechingen, some 4km south of town on the most prominent of all the isolated rocks of the Swabian Jura, is **Burg Hohenzollern** (daily April–Oct. 9am–5:30pm, Nov.–March 9am–4:30pm; DM4), the ancestral seat of what became the most powerful family in Germany. Even in a country whose entire history is dominated by the rise and fall of powerful dynasties, there's nothing quite comparable to the story of the Hohenzollerns. Their path to national leadership seems like a carefully hatched master-strategy which took centuries to achieve, yet which had a certain remorseless inevitability about it. The barren, windswept territories they ruled in their capacity as counts of Zollern from the thirteenth century hardly seemed an auspicious beginning, while their first attempt at aggrandizement, in their capacity as burgraves of Nürnberg—then the effective capital of the Holy Roman Empire—was soundly defeated by that city's independently-minded council.

Frustrated in their quest for power at the heart of the empire, the Hohenzollerns turned to its periphery. In 1415, they were put in charge of the March of Brandenburg, and were thus responsible for securing the country's eastern frontier; they also gained one of the seven seats on the imperial electoral college. The big breakthrough came in 1525, when they acquired the Polish

Duchy of Prussia; this gave them a power base beyond the jurisdiction of the Emperor. By 1701, the Hohenzollerns had wrested Prussia from dependency on Poland; they conferred royal status on themselves, and merged their territories. In time, they built up a centralized military state which, by skilful warfare and diplomacy, became one of the great powers of Europe. The nineteenth century saw the completion of the jigsaw—as the Habsburgs increasingly turned their attentions towards the Balkans, the Hohenzollerns ousted them from German leadership, eventually excluding them altogether from the unified nation they created by 1871. As if by a bitter irony, the family's reign was brief—Germany's defeat in World War I led to the collapse of the old aristocratic order, and the abolition of the monarchy.

From afar, the fortress, girded with intact battlements and bristling with a varied assortment of soaring towers, looks like the perfect incarnation of a vast medieval castle. Close up, however, it's soon apparent that the present complex is almost entirely a Romantic dreamland—not inappropriately so, given the fantastic nature of the family saga. It was commissioned by the most heritage-conscious of the clan, King Friedrich Wilhelm IV, and built by the military architect August Stüler, a pupil of the great Schinkel. Only the fifteenth-century **St. Michael Kapelle** survives from the previous fortress; it has been retained for the use of the Roman Catholic branch of the family, and preserves beautiful Gothic stained glass windows, along with Romanesque reliefs from its own predecessor.

The neo-Gothic **Schlosskapelle** contains the tombs of Friedrich Wilhelm I, the "Soldier King," and his son of the same name, Frederick the Great. These were formerly kept in Potsdam, but were moved for safety to a saltmine during World War II, where they were found by American soldiers and brought here at the request of the descendants. The **Schatzkammer** contains valuable heirlooms, notably the crown of Prussia, reconstructed in 1889 after the original was destroyed. There's also the snuffbox that saved the life of Frederick the Great at the Battle of Kunersdorf by absorbing a bullet, which is still embedded. Many of the portraits are of good artistic quality, notably one of *Young Fritz* (Frederick the Great as a youth) by Antoine Pesne.

Haigerloch

Unchallenged star of the heart of the Swabian Jura is **HAIGERLOCH**. Buses run from Hechingen, which is 17km west, and from Tübingen via Rottenburg, but the railroad line is now used only for occasional steam-train jaunts in the summer months. One of the most outstanding small towns in Germany, Haigerloch's isolation means it's considerably less self-conscious than most of its rivals. Here there's a perfect blend of landscape and architecture, with the unorthodox setting, on rocks high above an S-bend on the River Eyach, playing a crucial role. The surrounding countryside is at its most luxuriant in May, when the **lilac** is in full, riotous bloom, but the autumnal tints are almost equally beguiling, and it's hard to be disappointed by the picture at whatever time of year you choose to come.

The northern side of the river is dominated by the **Schloss**, a photogenic jumble of mostly Renaissance buildings, which replaced a medieval fortress. Until a few years ago, it was in the possession of the Hohenzollern family, which were probably based in Haigerloch in the eleventh and twelfth centuries—before they moved to what is considered their ancestral home. Nowadays, the Schloss serves as a hotel and arts center, so there's nothing to see inside. You can, however, enter the **Schlosskirche** lower down the hill, which has an outwardly Gothic appearance, in spite of being built at the turn of the seventeenth century. The interior was given the full rococo treatment 150 years later, with the addition of elaborate altars, frescoes and stuccowork. It's also worth walking eastward through the woods from the Schloss courtyard; after a few minutes, you come to the **Kapf**, a belvedere with a large cross, which commands a superb view over both parts of Haigerloch.

Underneath the Schloss' rock is the **Atom Museum** (May–Sept. daily 10am–noon and 2–5pm, March, April, Oct. and Nov. same times Sat. and Sun. only; DM1). Here, during March and April 1945, a distinguished group of German scientists carried out a series of experiments in nuclear fission. Throughout the war, the Allies had trembled at the prospect that Germany would be first to develop atomic weapons; thankfully, Hitler never took the project very seriously, while Himmler, who was nominally in charge of the scientists, constantly diverted the researchers into absurd pet projects of his own. When the Americans captured Haigerloch on April 23, they made a point of rounding up the scientists; the reactor was dismantled and shipped to the USA in order to help with the successful testing of the atomic bomb just three months later.

Ironically, the American victory in this particular race owed a lot to Albert Einstein, who, as a Jew, had been forced to leave Germany in 1933. Haigerloch itself had been something of a Jewish stronghold until 1941. The **ghetto** can be seen at the western edge of the upper town; the synagogue and the rabbi's house still survive, though neither is used for its original purpose. There's also a Jewish cemetery, which (most unusally) is located well inside the municipal boundaries.

Farther up is the pilgrimage church of **St. Anna**, erected between 1752 and 1755 as an integrated ensemble with the monumental garden enclosure and the facing curate's house. The interior of the church has a sense of spaciousness out of all proportion to its small size. It's filled with examples of rococo workmanship of the highest class—extravagant stucco work, vivacious sculptures, a ceiling fresco showing the dedication of the church, and a silvery-toned organ. This miniature masterpiece has traditionally been assumed to be the work of Johann Michael Fischer. However, it's now thought to have been built by Tiberius Moosbrugger, a member of an inventive family of Swiss architects who built extensively throughout central Europe.

Outside the church is a belvedere offering the directly opposite panorama to that from the Kapf. Another fine view can be had from the **Römerturm** (April–Oct. Sat. and Sun. 9am–6pm, variably on other days; DM1) which dominates the center of town. In spite of its name, it's of Romanesque, not Roman origin, and formed part of the citadel of the Counts of Zollern. The nineteenth-century Protestant **Pfarrkirche** contains a meticulously made copy of Leonardo da Vinci's *Last Supper*. If you see a busload of excited Italian tourists in town, the reason is that they've come specially to see this painting, which is, needless to say, in far better condition than the original.

Haigerloch, like so many places in the Jura, has no hostel or campground. There are, however, a couple of cheap **pensions**—*Nägele*, Hohenbergstr. 34 (☎07474 6162) charges DM25 for singles, DM44 for doubles, while *Krone*, Oberstadtstr. 47 (☎07474 411) has singles at DM32, doubles at DM60; the latter also has an excellent restaurant. The chimney of the *Schlossbräu* brewery on the banks of the Eyach is the only sign of industry for miles around. A surprisingly adventurous range of **beers** is made there: Pils, three varieties of Weizen, shandy, and *Spezial*. Best place to sample these is their own *Gaststätte Schlössle* on Hechinger Str., which also does good meals at reasonable prices.

Rottweil

When the Romans came on a road-building mission to Baden-Württemberg around 73 A.D., they brought with them dogs to drive the livestock and defend the camp; in time, these were successfully bred with local species. The resultant crossbreed has survived down the centuries, named after **ROTTWEIL**, the town which developed from the Roman settlement of *Arae Flaviae*, which stood at the intersection of the two main highways linking Strasbourg with Augsburg, and the Aargau region of Switzerland with the Middle Neckar. A familiar sight all over the world, the **Rottweiler**, with its characteristic mixture of black and tan markings, stocky frame and stubby tail, has built up a reputation as hard-working and (overly) loyal. Local butchers trained the Rottweiler to pull their carts—hence its alternative name of *Metzgerhund* ("butcher's dog")—but it's now best-known for its extensive use by the German police, army, customs, and mountain rescue services, and as a guide for the blind.

In spite of the fact that the dog has put Rottweil's name into many foreign languages, the town itself is relatively little known. Lying between the Black Forest and the Swabian Jura, it's way off the beaten tourist track, with nothing else of interest nearby, and no overwhelming set piece of its own to draw the crowds. Yet, in farther contrast with the Rottweiler (which, for all its intelligence, is rather an ugly brute), the town is a visual marvel. Its isolation spared it from the horrors of modern warfare, and it has changed little since the seventeenth century. Add to this highly original townscape a dramatic **setting** (Rottweil is ready-made for photography), a history as remarkable as that of any epic, one of the most impressive arrays of sculpture in Germany, and a rich tradition of festivals, and you have what deserves to be considered one of the most enticing small towns in the country.

There's actually no difficulty in reaching Rottweil—it lies on the main railroad line between Stuttgart and Tuttlingen, with onward connections to Switzerland; even international trains stop here. It can also be reached from various points in the Black Forest via the junction of HORB, 35km north. Arriving at the **Bahnhof**, turn right and walk uphill as far as the Hochbrücke. The site of Arae Flaviae lies just over 1km to the left down Königstrasse; extensive **Roman baths** have been excavated at the corner of what is now the cemetery. In the succeeding Alemannian period, the town became the royal seat of *Rotuvilla*; it was subsequently moved to its present position on a strategically secure spur high above the still-young Neckar River. This restricted area meant the buildings had to be packed tightly together, with no room for expansion.

The Hochbrücke spans a deep gully, and was formerly guarded by a tower, which gave its name to the street which forms the town's north–south axis. Here you immediately see the grouping of brilliantly colorful **old houses** characteristic of Rottweil. These are mostly late Renaissance or baroque in style, and are adorned with three-sided oriel windows, sometimes reaching up several stories. Each balcony tries to outdo its neighbor in the profusion of carvings. These often illustrate the coat-of-arms of the original family or the emblem of the guild to which they belonged; others bear the Imperial Eagle, proud symbol of a free imperial city (a status this little town held for nearly six centuries), while heraldic animals and purely decorative designs are also featured. At the end of Hochbrücktorstrasse is the slender red sandstone **Marktbrunnen**, the most elaborate of the town's four Renaissance fountains. Built in tiers like a wedding cake, it's decorated with delicate statuettes made after woodcuts by Hans

Burgkmair, and is crowned by a figure of a Swiss soldier, in commemoration of the "perpetual bond" between Rottweil and the Confederation of Switzerland.

Standing in a cramped square just behind is the **Kapellenkirche**, Gothic successor to an old pilgrimage chapel. It was begun in the early fourteenth century as a miniature version of the Münster in Freiburg, but money ran out with only the square lower part of the tower completed. This is built in a manner reminiscent of the English Decorated style, and was perhaps designed by one of the Parler family. Some 150 years later, the Duke of Württemberg's architect, Aberlin Jerg, added a double octagonal story to the tower, which is a surprisingly effective foil to the older section, providing Rottweil with the dominant central monument it needed. The church's outstanding **sculptural decoration** is by several identifiable masters, with the mystical and gentle style of the *Marienmeister* perfectly contrasting with the lively narrative approach of his successor, the *Christusmeister*. These works have been replaced in situ by copies; the originals are now in the Lorenzkapelle (see below).

From the northern side of the church, you pass into the resplendent main street, **Hauptstrasse**, which runs uphill by constantly changing gradients. It's lined by an even more impressive group of houses than those on the perpendicular Hochbrücktorstrasse. The oldest of these, no. 62, dates back to the thirteenth century, while the next two buildings are in late Gothic style. First of these is the historic inn *Gasthaus Zum Stern*, which has been restored into the sort of hotel traveling salesmen dream about staying in, with four-poster beds in wood-paneled rooms as well as all the modern amenities. To see the backs of these houses, whose half-timbering is uncharacteristic of Rottweil, go down to the massive viaduct, a notable piece of nineteenth-century engineering, which carries the road out of town high over the valley. From here, there's also a sweeping view over the Swabian Jura.

Among the houses in the upper half of Hauptstrasse is the home at no. 20 of the family of Bartholomäus Herder, founder of a publishing house whose interests include Europe's largest output of Catholic books. It now serves as the unusually absorbing **Stadtmuseum** (Mon.–Thurs. and Sat. 9am–noon and 2–5pm, Fri. 9am–noon, Sun. 10am–noon; free). On the ground floor are the most important excavations from Arae Flaviae, dominated by the second-century **Orpheus Mosaic**. Made of some 570,000 colored stones, this shows the god playing his lyre to the enchantment of the birds and beasts around him—among them a dog, who is doubtless an early Rottweiler. Upstairs, the extraordinary **Pürschgerichtskarte** of 1564—a tour-de-force of detail—proves how little Rottweil's overall appearance has altered. An adjoining room is devoted to the town's **Fastnet** celebrations (see below), with wooden masks of the principal characters and a painstakingly-executed cardboard cutout of the *Narrensprung*—which makes an acceptable substitute if you don't manage to see the real thing.

Directly across the street, the **Apostelbrunnen**, with its figures of SS. Peter, James and John, has been re-erected in front of the **Altes Rathaus**, whose simple Gothic architecture gives the street a rare touch of sobriety. Entered from Rathausgasse is the **tourist office** (Mon.–Fri. 9:30am–12:30pm and 2–6pm, May–Sept. also Sat. 9:30am–12:30pm; ☎0741 494280). Ask here to see the *Ratsaal*, the former council chamber of the city-state, which boasts a coffered ceiling, carved woodwork, stained glass windows, and an old oven.

The alley leads shortly to Münsterplatz, with the **Heilig-Kreuz-Münster**, a late Gothic basilica with a tall tower. Its most important work of art is an anguished *Crucifixion* at the high altar, which is attributed to Veit Stoss. Until recently the square outside was adorned with the **Georgsbrunnen**, which included statues of the Madonna, Saint Catherine and Saint George; at the time of writing this has been removed for restoration, and may be rebuilt in its original location by the Hochbrücke. Proceeding down Bruderschaftsgasse at the eastern side of the Münster, you pass the **Dominikanerkirche**, a Gothic church with a sumptuous baroque interior and the last of the Renaissance fountains, the **Christophorusbrunnen**, with a relief of the city's coat-of-arms as well as a statue of Saint Christopher carrying the Christ child.

At the end of Lorenzgasse is the **Lorenzkapelle** (Tues.–Sat. 10am–noon and 2–5pm, Sun. 2–5pm; DM1), a late Gothic funerary chapel which for over a century has housed a remarkable collection of Swabian **wood sculpture**. Among the early works, generally in a folk-art idiom, a refined early fourteenth-century series of apostles stands out. By the fifteenth century, sculptors had gained a more prestigious position in society, and showed a more definite artistic personality, as can be seen here in the work of the masters of Ulm, such as Hans Multscher, Michel Erhart, and Jörg Syrlin the Younger. Due to lack of space, only a fraction of the collection is on view, though that should change by the end of 1990, with the opening of a new museum.

When this is ready, it's planned to devote the chapel to **stone sculpture**, which is now displayed in the modern annex. Pride of place here is given to the original carvings from the Kapellenkirche. Look for the two reliefs by the *Marienmeister*, which rank among the most original and touching works of the Middle Ages: *The Opening of the Book* symbolizes Knowledge, while the tender *Betrothal of the Knight* is an allegory of the marriage of Jesus to the Christian soul. From the same church is the *Weckenmännle*, a humorous figure who probably served as the basis of the pulpit; it's thought to be a self-portrait of Anton Pilgram, who later became master mason at the Dom in Vienna.

Outside the Lorenzkapelle is the semicircular **Pulverturm** (*Powder Tower*), one of the remaining vestiges of the old fortifications. To see the other surviving parts, you have to go to the top of Hauptstrasse, which is closed off by the formidable **Schwarzes Tor** (*Black Tower*). The lower section, with its rough masonry, dates back to 1230; the upper stories were added around 1600 as a prison. Continuing uphill, you come to the **Hochturm** via the alley of the same name. This also belongs to the Staufian period, and is a watchtower guarding Rottweil's vulnerable western flank, the only one to lack a natural defensive barrier. In the late eighteenth century, an octagon was added to the top to serve as a lookout gallery; it commands a superb **view** of the town and surrounding countryside. A plaque on the door tells you which family currently holds the key; otherwise, ask for it at the tourist office.

For a sight with a difference, go to the southwestern corner of town, well beyond Arae Flaviae. On the banks of the Prim, a Neckar tributary, stand the **Saltworks** (*Salinenmuseum Unteres Bohrhaus*; May–Sept. Weds. and Sat. 2:30–5pm; DM1). Still in full working order, these half-timbered buildings were erected in the 1830s, and were one of the mainstays of the local economy until their closure in 1969. There are displays of the old equipment, along with illustrations of the methods used. Further south, at the extreme end of town, is the point where the peaceful **Eschach Valley** joins with the Neckar. Several nature trails are marked in this area, which offers a varied range of forest, along with a plentiful supply of waterfowl and butterflies. It's most notable, however, for wild flowers, including blue and white monkshood, Turk's head lily, narcissi, white hyacinths, thistles, and different varieties of orchids.

Festivals and Practicalities

Rottweil, which these days is normally an unhurried provincial market town, really comes to life during the Carnival season, and its **Fastnet** celebrations—which are fifteenth-century in origin and very different from those in the Rhineland—are arguably Baden-Württemberg's top popular festival. The action begins on the evening of the Thursday before Carnival Sunday (variable date Feb/March) with the *Schmotzige*, in which groups perform satirical revues of the previous year's events. On the Sunday, the mayor hands over control of the town for the duration of the festival, and the afternoon features a children's procession. The highpoint comes at 8am sharp the following morning with the *Narrensprung* ("Parade of Fools'), which is repeated on Shrove Tuesday at both 8am and 2pm. This features a galaxy of colorfully-dressed characters in wooden masks. Their names are untranslatable; among the most important are the friendly *Gschell*, who represents the promise of summer, the fiery *Biss* and the vampire-like *Federahannes*, who both appear to symbolize the winter months, and the haughty, aristocratic woman known as *Fransenkleid*. Other **festivals** include the week-long *Volksfest* in mid-August and the *Stadtfest* on the second weekend in September. On a more highbrow note, there's a series of concerts of Renaissance and baroque music in late April/early May, and of chamber recitals later in the month, while for a fortnight in October a mixed program of drama, movies, exhibitions, jazz and classical music takes place.

The **youth hostel** has an ideal location in the center of town at Lorenzgasse 8 (☎0741 7664), but there's no campground. Three cheap **pensions** lie on Hauptstrasse, all charging less than DM30 per head. *Hasen* at no. 69 (☎0741 7798), at the foot of the street by the viaduct, has a friendly management which offers good-value meals in the style of their countries of origin—Mexico and Greece. Across the road at no. 66 is *Löwen* (☎0741 7640), while farther up at no. 38 (☎0741 7412) is *Goldenes Rad*. If you want to splurge, there are two **historic inns** worth considering: *Lamm* at no. 45 on the same street (☎0741 45015) has singles at DM50, doubles from DM72, along with a good restaurant, while *Mohren* at Friedrichsplatz 11–13 (☎0741 6802) charges upwards of DM40 in singles, DM75 in doubles. Prices at the aforementioned *Zum Sternen* are way above normal, but it's possible to enjoy the superb cuisine in its *Weinstube* without making too outrageous a dent in the budget. There's also a wide choice of genteel **cafés** around the town center. The local *Pflug* brewery makes both Pils and Weizen.

Donaueschingen

DONAUESCHINGEN owes both its name and fame to its status as the source of one of the world's most celebrated rivers, the **Danube** (*Donau*). In the Schlosspark in the middle of town, a grandiose, early nineteenth-century fountain has been erected around the *Donauquelle*, a very unassuming spring. This flows eastwards through the grounds (at times invisibly), before joining the Brigach, a headstream which rises in the Black Forest, and which has become a substantial river by the time it reaches this point. At the edge of town a couple of kilometers farther on is the more substantial confluence with another Black Forest headstream, the Breg; from then on, the combined waters are known as the Danube. It's the longest river in Europe after the Volga, and the only important one to flow from west to east, following a course of some 2840 kilometers through seven different countries, eventually forming a labyrinth-like delta in Romania which feeds into the Black Sea. Whether or not the *Donauquelle* is really the ultimate source of this great river is a matter for dispute—the springs which feed the Brigach and the Breg both have a better geological claim. However, given that the crucial merger occurs at Donaueschingen, it's easy to see why the town has managed to be blessed with official recognition.

Lying on the exposed Baar Plateau, between the Black Forest and the Swabian Jura, Donaueschingen's harsh climate mitigated against its growth—it was no more than a hamlet until the 1720s, when Prince Joseph Wilhelm Ernst of the **Fürstenberg** dynasty descended from his feudal castle in the hills above to begin the planning of a new courtly town. In spite of their meagre and unpromizing holdings of land, the Fürstenbergs belonged to the first rank of German nobility, owing their promotion to having for long served as confidants and advisers of the hereditary emperors, the Habsburgs. They farther built up their power base by earmarking certain sons for careers in the church; by this means they gained the Bishopric of Strasbourg and control of several monasteries.

The **Schloss** (guided tours April–Sept. Mon. and Weds.–Sun. 9am–noon and 2–5pm; DM3) is actually a fairly unassuming baroque building at the far end of the park; much of the interior was modernized at the end of the nineteenth century. Its trappings are typical: Brussels tapestries, assorted *objets d'art*, and family portraits. Among the last-named, there's one surprise—*Max Egon* was painted by the English artist Graham Sutherland. The sitter kept up the family tradition of musical patronage (Mozart and Liszt had both been houseguests) by establishing in 1921 a **festival** now known as the *Donaueschinger Musiktage*. Held each October in the modern *Donauhalle* at the western end of town, this focuses on the work of contemporary composers. Many of the leading musicians of the century—Stravinsky, Hindemith, Boulez, and Stockhausen—have had works premiered there.

The main family treasures, known as the **Fürstenburg-Sammlungen** (March–Oct. Tues.–Sun. 9am–noon and 1:30–5pm, Dec.–Feb. Tues.–Sun. 9am–noon and 1:30–4pm; DM3), are housed in a building on Karlsplatz, a baroque square situated across the main road directly behind the Schloss. Here various zoological and mineralogical collections are set out in the old-fashioned manner of cabinets of curiosities. There's also a room devoted to the history of the Fürstenbergs, complete with their ceremonial coach and sleighs.

However, the main attraction is the outstanding second-floor display of South German and Swiss painting and sculpture of the fifteenth and sixteenth centuries. Highlight is **Hans Holbein the Elder**'s *Gray Passion*, an expressive cycle of twelve pictures formerly in St. Ulrich und Afra in Augsburg. It takes its name from the idiosyncratic device of showing all the participants dressed in grey—until half-way through, when they change into white. There's also an important array of works by the enigmatic **Master of Messkirch**, one of Dürer's most distinctive followers, including parts of his eponymous work and the jewel-like *Wildensteiner Altar*.

On a terrace to the side of the Schloss is the twin-towered **Johanniskirche**, whose restrained baroque style is reminiscent of the churches then being built in Bohemia, rather than elsewhere in southern Germany. In the nave there's a wooden *Madonna* by the eccentric **Master HL** (see p.168); though predating the building by over 200 years, it doesn't look at all out-of-place.

Other than these obvious attractions, all closely grouped together, Donaueschingen doesn't have much in the way of sights. However, several **streets** are good examples of period pieces. An example is Josefstrasse, linking the Bahnhof with the town center, which is lined by stately baroque and neoclassical mansions. The outbuildings of the court are found on Haldenstrasse; the library here possesses one of the three original thirteenth-century manuscript versions of *The Nibelungenlied*. Though this street is now tucked away between the town center and the Brigach, it's easily located by the chimneys of the *Fürstenberg* **brewery**, one of the most famous in Germany. In its present form, it dates back to 1705, but the family's initial beer-making rights were granted in the thirteenth century. Obvious place to sample the products is the *Bräustüble*, housed in a pink baroque palace on Postplatz.

Plenty more places to **eat** and **drink**, including several classy cafés, can be found on Karlstrasse, the town's main shopping street, which runs west from the Johanniskirche. At no. 58 is the **tourist office** (Mon.–Fri. 8am–noon and 2–5/6 according to season, Sat. 9am–noon; ☎0771 3834). They have a list of private houses with **rooms**, which cost from DM20 for singles, DM30 for doubles. Alternatively, *Pension Wölfle*, Mühlenstr. 25 (☎0771 2808) and *Bären*, Josefstr. 7–9 (☎0771 2518) both charge around DM25 per head. There's no hostel, while the **campground** (☎0771 5511) is 8km away on the banks of the RIEDSEE.

Konstanz and the Bodensee

The **BODENSEE** (also know as Lake Constance, or the *Schwäbischer Meer*—the "Swabian Sea") is really a bulge in the river Rhine, which enters it at the southeastern side near the Austrian town of BREGENZ, and leaves it in the northwest, at STEIN AM RHEIN.

KONSTANZ (*CONSTANCE* in its anglicized form) lies at the tip of a tongue of land sticking out into the lake; it's about 55km southeast of Donaueschingen, and is connected by regular international rail services. Never damaged by any wars, Konstanz retains much of its ancient layout and quite a few medieval houses. A small town by modern standards, it has a long history reaching back as far as the sixth century, when its bishopric was founded, and from then on it was an important center of European Christendom and culture. Its heyday of influence was in the early Middle Ages, and from 1414 to 1418 the conclave met here to resolve the schism that had been splitting the Church because of conflicting claims to the papacy.

The town itself is divided in two by the Rhine, which flows through the Untersee and into the main body of the Bodensee at this point. The **Altstadt** is actually on the southern mainland, a German enclave on the otherwise Swiss side of the lake, which is why it was never bombed by the Allies, who couldn't risk hitting neutral Switzerland. Small and compact, it doesn't take long to wander around the tangles of small streets and stroll along the lakeside promenade. It's a cozy little place, with a slightly Mediterranean atmosphere about it during the summer months, when street cafés invite long pauses and the water is a bustle of colorful sails. The **Konzilgebäude** (not open to the public) on the waterfront next to the Bahnhof, was originally a storehouse, but in 1417 was used as the venue for the conclave, which eventually elected Pope Martin V once other pretenders had been neutralized. In front of it, on the water's edge, a **memorial** stands to the famous flying Count Ferdinand von Zeppelin, who was born in the town in 1838. Inspired by flights in hot-air balloons while he was in America, he returned to Germany to build his first airship in 1900.

The most prominent church is the **Münster**, suitably set on the highest point of the Altstadt and built over the remains of the original eleventh-century Dom that collapsed in 1052. Begun during the Romanesque era, building continued for 600 years, so there are marked differences in style, particularly in the interior. The aisles and their chapels are Gothic, while the organ was built during the Renaissance, and the original ceiling was replaced by a vaulted baroque one. The church was home to the local bishopric for over one thousand years, and it was here in 1417 that the papal court tried **Johannes Hus**, the Bohemian reformer who was called before the council for attempting to institute changes in the rites of confession, and challenging apostolic primacies. He was burned at the stake as a heretic and the spot on which he is said to have stood during his trial is marked in the central aisle, by the 24th row. Once the Reformation had taken hold a little more than a hundred years later, the local bishop was driven out of town, and after the Konstanz bishopric was dissolved in 1821, the church sank into insignificance altogether. For a great view of the town however, climb up the **tower** (Mon.–Sat. 10am–5pm, Sun. 1–5pm; DM1).

If you'd like to find out more about the reformer Hus, then visit the **Hus-Haus** (Hussenstr. 64, viewed by appointment via the Rosgartenmuseum), which covers the life and death of the man. It's run by the Prague museum society, who bought this house in 1923 to turn it into a memorial to one of Czechoslovakia's most important national heroes. Born a farmer's son in 1371, he went on to become the first rector of the newly recognized Prague university in 1409. Apart from his importance as a religious thinker, Hus had a major influence on the Czechoslovakian sense of nationhood and almost single-handedly established national Czech literature. Being someone much too popular for the Catholic Church, it was political expediency as much as anything that led to his heresy trial and eventual execution.

Konstanz's most important museum is the **Rosgartenmuseum** on the street of the same name (Tues.–Sun. 10am–5pm; free), which has a fine collection of local archaeological finds, in particular from the paleolithic period, and also art and craft exhibits from the Middle Ages. The museum was designed in 1871, and everything, including the original display cabinets, is as it was then, creating a pleasantly musty atmosphere. You'd think from the name that the building must originally have had something to do with roses, but it's an old euphemism for the local horse abattoir. The German for horse was traditionally 'Ross,' but by omitting one letter people could say 'Rosgarten' and ignore its sorry purpose.

The usual maps, brochures, and accommodation lists are available from the **tourist office** in front of the Bahnhof at Konzilstr. 5, (Mon.–Fri. 8:45am–6pm, Sat. 9am–1pm and 4–6pm, Sun. 4–6pm; ☎07531 284376). Information on cruises and ferry timetables is available from the *Bodensee-Verkehrsdienst* at Hafenstr. 6 (☎07531 281398). Worth knowing is that cyclists can take bikes on the ferries, which is handy if you want to explore the various shores more extensively. The return fare to Meersburg is only DM6.80. Longer trips, such as to the picturesque **Rheinfall** in Switzerland cost DM36, but it's worth that much to travel up one of the Rhine's most scenic stretches and see Europe's largest waterfall.

The local **youth hostel** is at Zur Allmannshöhe 18, (☎07531 32260; bus #4 from the Bahnhof to *Jugendherberge*, or bus #1 to *Post Allmannsdorf*). A cheap **pension**, centrally located, is *Anker* at Sigismundstr. 8 (☎07531 23344), which charges from DM30 to 48 for singles and DM60 to 80 for doubles. If you fancy staying on the lake's shore, try the *Gasthaus Seeschau*, Zur Schiffslände 11 (☎07533 5190), or *Gasthaus Anker*, Zur Schiffslände 5 (☎07533 6220), both in the suburb of DINGELSDORF. They charge between DM25 and 35 for singles and DM50 to 70 for doubles.

Around the Bodensee

The hilly landscape of forests and orchards **around the Bodensee** bask in almost Mediterranean heat during the summer, and together with the Bodensee itself, this part of the country has plenty to warrant a couple of days' visit. Second largest of the Alpine lakes, the Bodensee is 14km across at its widest point and about 65km long, offering a wealth of opportunity for watersports and cruises. The two forks of water around the Konstanz peninsula are known as the **Überlinger See** on the north side and the **Untersee** or **Zeller See** on the south side. Ferries regularly leave Konstanz for destinations all over the lake, including the southern Swiss shore and the eastern Austrian shore at the far end.

The island of **REICHENAU** in the Zeller See can be reached by boat in about 20 minutes; it's also connected to the mainland by a small dam, with a regular bus service covering the 8km to Konstanz. Reichenau is virtually flat, and given over to intensive fruit and vegetable farming, with a character not dissimilar to the tulip-growing regions of Holland. Very quiet and sedate, the island is a popular resort with pensioners and families, who rent holiday apartments around its coast. At 1.5km wide and 5km long, it doesn't take long to get to know the place, and the chief draw, apart from the shoreline, is the presence of three **Romanesque churches**, which are among the oldest in Germany.

First to be built was the **Münster** in MITTELZELL, which was constructed around 816 under the abbot Heito I, a close ally of Charlemagne and responsible for establishing the island's monastery as one of the most important centers of Central European learning. His successor, Hatto III, was the most powerful German abbot ever, simultaneously holding the office of imperial chancellor under Emperor Arnulf. This period was the peak of the island's status, and thus this tiny place could afford to treat itself to two more churches: **St. Georg** in OBERZELL and **St. Peter und Paul** in NIEDERZELL. The former is distinguished by containing the relics (the head, no less) of St. George and also some well-preserved Ottonian frescos depicting Christ's miracles. The latter had its interior redesigned into the rococo style and is rather less significant.

MAINAU is a much smaller island of about 45 hectares, this time in the Überlinger See, and is famed for its extremely rich **botanical park** covering the whole island. Even palm trees, citrus trees and other Mediterranean plants grow here due to the unusually mild climate. Flower beds cover every possible bit of space, and, especially during spring and summer, the colors and scents are wonderful. It's up to you whether it's worth forking out DM8 (DM5 students), for the privilege of walking around Count Bernadotte's manicured park with hundreds of other tourists.

On the other hand, it's definitely worth enduring the crowds in order to see **MEERSBURG**. Clinging on to the steep bank of the northern shore, this ancient little settlement can be reached from Konstanz in 30 minutes by a ferry which also carries cars—a useful facility, as the drive round the lake otherwise takes an hour or more. Pride of the town is the **Altes Schloss** (March–Sept. daily 9am–6pm, Nov.–Feb. 10am–5pm; DM5, DM4 students, DM3 kids), which is the oldest one in Germany still inhabited and almost entirely in its original medieval state. The Bishops of Konstanz moved here when they were driven out during the Reformation. A few hundred years later, one of Germany's greatest female poets, Annette von Droste-Hülshoff, came to live here as well. During the 1840s she stayed as personal guest of her brother-in-law, Baron von Lassberg. Her rooms are still as they were in her day, and many of her most famous poems are exhibited on the walls. Also interesting are the castle's old kitchen and dungeons that still have their original utensils, and in the case of the dungeon, a collection of medieval armor and weapons.

The nearby **Neues Schloss** was built by the prince-bishops in the mid-eighteenth century under the direction of Balthasar Neumann, and today houses the town's (missable) cultural center and local history museum. Between the Neues and Altes Schloss, ancient half-timbered houses line steep streets around the upper part of the town, while, down on the waterfront, the lake-side promenade looks out across the waves to the southern Swiss Alps.

Meersburg's **tourist office** (Mon.–Fri. 8am–noon and 1:30–5pm, Sat. 10am–noon; ☎07532 82383) is on Schlossplatz. If you'd like to stay over, the cheapest hotel in the old upper part of town is the seventeenth century *Gasthof zum Bären*, Marktplatz 11 (☎07532 6044), which charges DM50 for singles and DM47 for doubles. Alternatively, there's the modern *Seehotel Zur Münz* at Seestr. 7 (☎07532 9090) on the shore, which charges DM46–72 for singles and DM46–64 per head in doubles. If you plan on staying during the high summer season, you'd be well advised to book accommodation in advance as this is a very popular place.

A corniche road runs southeastwards from Meersburg along the shore of the Bodensee towards the Bavarian town of LINDAU (see *Chapter One*), some 40km away. Traveling in the opposite direction, the superbly sited rococo monastery of **Birnau** is reached after 10km. It's a collaboration by some of the finest artists of the day—the architect Peter Thumb, the fresco painter Gottfried Bernard Götz and the sculptor Josef Anton Feuchtmayer—and the dazzling interior provides a fitting complement to the natural beauty of the setting. Look out for the famous statuette known as the *Honigschlecker* (a cherub sucking the finger that has just been inside a bee's nest); it's placed beside an altar dedicated to St. Bernard of Clairvaux, in honor of the claim that his words were as sweet as honey.

A farther 5km on is **ÜBERLINGEN**, another old lakeside resort frequently seething with visitors. The town preserves much of its original sandstone **fortifications**, including seven gates and towers, and it's well worth walking round them: the moated western section is especially impressive. Otherwise, the main monuments are grouped round Münsterplatz in the heart of town.

The **Münster** itself was built in the sixteenth century in an archaic late Gothic style; its sober exterior hardly prepares you for the majestic unfolding of the five-aisled nave, whose intricate vaults show Gothic bowing out with a bang. There are many eye-catching furnishings, most notably the tiered main **altarpiece**. Carved by Jörg Zürn in the early seventeenth century, it also marks the end of an era, being the last of the great series of wooden retables illustrating Biblical stories which adorn so many German churches. Behind the Münster are the Renaissance **Alte Kanzlei** and the Gothic **Rathaus** (Mon.–Fri. 9am–noon and 2:30–5pm, Sat. 9am–noon; free). On the first floor of the latter is the *Ratsaal*, a masterpiece of late fifteenth century civil architecture, complete with paneled walls with projecting arches, a ribbed ceiling, and statuettes representing the various powers in the Holy Roman Empire.

The Upper Danube valley

The river valley forms the centerpiece of the **Naturpark Obere Donau**, which stretches northwards to the Heuberg, the highest range of the Swabian Jura; about half the area is forest, though a large amount is used for farming. It's superb country for **hiking**, particularly above the valley, where there are any number of viewpoints offering wonderful views of the river's meandering course. If you've an interest in **flora**, note that springtime sees the countryside awash with snowdrops, narcissi and daphnes, while orchids and the tall Turk's cap lily blossom at the end of the season. Autumn is if anything even more beautiful; then the white limestone rocks of the valley are perfectly offset by the golden tones of the trees and shrubs lower down. Plenty of inexpensive accommodation makes this region ideal for a quiet break away from the crowds.

Tuttlingen and Around

The train doesn't stop between Immendingen and the district capital **TUTTLINGEN**, but between the two there's a geological curiosity, the *Donauversickerung* ("Disappearing Danube"). Here, a branch of the river vanishes from sight in the deep fissures, traveling underground for 12km in a southerly direction. It surfaces again as a spring of awesome force (which releases more water than any other in Europe) at the village of AACH, forming the source of the river of the same name.

Tuttlingen itself (where there's a railroad junction with the main line between Stuttgart and Switzerland), is an industrial community with little in the way of sights, unless you're particularly keen on Jugendstil architecture, in which case it's worth seeing the Stadtkirche, one of the finest churches in this style in the province. The simple **youth hostel** at Stockacherstr. 1 (☎07461 99299), conveniently placed in the middle of town, makes the cheapest of all bases for exploring the region, but hotels are pricier than in rural locations.

NEUHAUSEN OB ECK, 11km to the east and reachable by bus, has a more concrete attraction in the **Open-Air Museum** (April–Oct. Tues.–Sun. 9am–6pm; DM3). Though the buildings come from all over southern Baden-Württemberg, they've been reerected to form a self-contained village, complete with church, town hall, school, mill, workshops, and houses. As usual, practical demonstrations of the old crafts are featured.

Another possible bus excursion is to **MÜHLHEIM**, the next settlement on the Danube, but not served by the train. It's a quaint medieval village, built partly on the banks of the river, and partly on a rocky spur above. The latter preserves its fortified Stadttor, along with an early fifteenth-century Rathaus, numerous half-timbered houses, and an eighteenth-century Schloss with domed towers.

Beuron

In about a quarter of an hour the train reaches **BEURON**, right in the heart of the *Junge Donau* at the point where the scenery is at its most dramatic. It's immediately obvious that religion has loomed large in this place—one of the tall, seemingly impenetrable rocks on the opposite bank of the Danube is crowned by a large cross.

The village itself, laid out on a terrace above the river, clusters around the enormous **Kloster**. Originally founded by the Augustinians in the eleventh century, it was completely rebuilt in the baroque period, the size of the complex belying the fact that very few monks (sometimes no more than fifteen) ever actually lived there. Architecturally, the late seventeenth-century monastic buildings (by one of the most ubiquitous builders of the time, Franz Beer) are superior to the church, which dates from forty years later. By south German standards, it's fairly restrained, though the nave vaults are decorated with colorful frescos; the legend of the monastery's foundation is sandwiched between scenes from the lives of its patrons saints, Martin and Augustine.

Sixty years after the Napoleonic suppression, the Kloster was taken over by a Benedictine congregation who played a leading role in the revitalization of European monastic life, an ideal that by then seemed to be a thing of the past. They pioneered a new, simple style of architecture based on early Christian and Romanesque models; an example is the *Frauenkapelle* which they added to the north side of their own church to house a fifteenth-century Swabian sculpture of the *Pietà* alleged to possess miraculous powers. Even more significant was the revival of the use of **Gregorian chant**, and the monks remain among the world's leading practitioners of the art. Try to catch one of the main services (High Mass Mon.–Sat. 11:15am, Sun. 10am; Vespers Mon.–Sat. 6pm, Sun. 3pm) to hear the stark, ethereal beauty of this, the most elemental of all forms of music.

Among the many superb **hikes** which can be made around Beuron, two stand out. Back in the direction of Tuttlingen (but reached via the Holzbrücke, at the opposite side of town from the Bahnhof), you come after 6km to **Knopfmacherfelsen**, reckoned to be the finest of all the belvederes overlooking this stretch of the Danube. To the east, a similar distance away, is **Burg Wildenstein**, a feudal castle-stronghold dating back to the eleventh century in a stunningly precarious situation overlooking the Danube; part of it now houses a **youth hostel** (☎07466 411).

Information on these walks, and on the Naturpark as a whole, is available during normal working hours from the **tourist office** in Beuron's Rathaus. Here you can also obtain a list of private houses with **rooms** to rent from as little as DM17. Otherwise, the cheapest place to stay is the pilgrims' *St. Gregorius-Haus* (☎07466 202) opposite the Kloster at DM30 per head, while *Pension Wasch* beside the Bahnhof (☎07466 423) charges DM32. The **campground** (☎07579 559) is in HAUSEN IM TAL, the next village to the north.

Sigmaringen

Just beyond Hausen is the last stretch of high cliffs; between THIERGARTEN and GUTENSTEIN, these are replaced by jagged rock needles. Thereafter the landscape is tamer, though there are exceptions, notably at **SIGMARINGEN**, the train's next stop. This pint-sized princely capital came into the hands of the **Hohenzollern** dynasty in 1535, having at one time belonged to their great rivals, the Habsburgs. The branch of the family who lived here remained Catholic, and supplied the last ill-fated kings of Romania. They were very much junior relations of their Berlin cousins, but provided a useful south German foothold for the Prussians during their predatory takeover of the whole country last century.

There's no doubting the photogenic quality of the **Schloss** (Feb.–Nov. daily 8:30am–noon and 1–5pm; DM5). However, it's essentially a product of the final phase of the Romantic movement, a sort of Swabian counterpart to "Mad" Ludwig's castles in Bavaria, which moves abruptly from one pastiche style to another. Only the towers remain from the medieval fortress, which was sacked in the Thirty Years' War, then ravaged by fire in 1893. The *Waffenhalle*, with over 3000 pieces of arms and armor, is reckoned the best private collection in Europe; it's also a reminder of just how much the Hohenzollerns' rise to national leadership owed to their espousal of the military solution to problems. A dream-like neo-Gothic hall contains a good collection of south German paintings and sculptures of the fifteenth and sixteenth centuries, including works by the so-called **Master of Sigmaringen**, who was actually two people: the brothers Hans and Jacob Strüb. The entry ticket also covers admission to the **Museum of Coaches**, housed in the former stables.

Beside the Schloss is the rococo **Johanniskirche**, containing the shrine of Saint Fidelio, a local man who became the first Capuchin martyr in 1622 when he was murdered by the fiercely Calvinist inhabitants of the Grisons region of Switzerland. In the town itself, there's nothing much to see, other than the usual array of half-timbered houses, mostly dating from the baroque period.

If you want to use Sigmaringen as a base, there's a **youth hostel** at Hohenzollernstr. 31 (☎07571 13277) at the northeastern side of town, a **campground** (☎07571 5479) by the Danube, and a clutch of reasonably-priced hotels, with the lowest rates at *Pfauen*, Mühlbergstr. 1 (☎07571 13222), which charges from DM20 per person. The **tourist office** (Mon.–Fri. 9am–12:30pm and 2–5:30pm, Sat. 9am–noon; ☎07571 106233) is at Schwabstr. 1, between the Bahnhof and the Schloss. Main **festivals** are *Fastnet* and the *Donaufest*; the latter is held at the end of July, and features a small-scale version of the fishermen's jousts made famous in Ulm (see p.241). The local *Zoller* **beer** is widely available throughout the province.

Zwiefalten and Obermarchtal

Between the next two train stops, MENGEN and RIEDLINGEN, there's an extensive stretch of marshland on the right bank of the Danube, frequented by many species of waterfowl. Riedlingen is an agreeable if unremarkable town in the shadow of the Osterberg; from here, buses connect to two nearby villages clustered round grandiose baroque monasteries.

ZWIEFALTEN, 13km north, lies in a valley at the edge of the Swabian Jura. The name, meaning "duplicate waters," refers to the two streams which converge at this point. In the late eleventh century, a daughter church of Hirsau was established here. The huge Romanesque complex survived until 1738 when, in preparation for its change in status to an imperial abbey, subject only to the rule of the emperor, and in accordance with the passion for all things baroque, it was demolished to make way for an entirely new set of buildings. This arrangement lasted for only a few decades; after the Napoleonic suppression, the church was given to the local Catholic parish and the outbuildings were converted into an asylum—a situation which persists to this day.

The **Münster** has a strong claim to be regarded as the foremost eighteenth-century building in Baden-Württemberg, a worthy rival to the great pilgrimage churches of Bavaria. Its highly original design, largely the work of **Johann Michael Fischer**, is apparent from the outside, where the identical white towers with their green onion domes are placed over the transept, leaving room for a classically-inspired facade whose alternate use of concave and convex shapes imparts a feeling of movement. However, this is just a prelude to the lavishness of the interior, in which Fischer was aided by the best decorators of the day.

Standing by the entrance grille, your eye is drawn down the enormous length of the church, yet is also diverted to the wavy lines of the side chapels; to the grey and rose marble columns with their gold-leaf capitals which shine like jewels against the pristine white walls; to the huge vault paintings glorifying the Virgin; and to the confessionals shaped like fantastic grottoes. At the end of the nave, a statue of the fiery prophet Ezekiel set in an elaborate baldachin with depictions of the coming fall of Babylon, strikes a warning note; this theme is continued in the **pulpit** opposite, in which his visions of sin and death on the base are contrasted with the triumph of the Cross on the sounding board. The monks' choir is the most extravagantly sumptuous part of all, featuring a virtuoso set of walnut **stalls**, adorned with gilded limewood reliefs illustrating the life of the Virgin. Be warned that the entrance grille is generally closed between 11am and 1pm during the summer, and all day through the week in winter, leaving you only with the sweeping initial view.

If you want to use Zwiefalten as a base for exploring the Jura, **rooms** are available in five different pensions from around DM25 to 30 per head, or in private houses for a little less. *Gasthof Post*, Hauptstr. 44 (☎07373 302), has the largest capacity, as well as the best restaurant; it's also the obvious place to sample the excellent **beer** made in the adjacent *Klosterbräu*.

Unfortunately, there's no direct bus to **OBERMARCHTAL**, which lies on the right bank of the Danube about 8km away, between Riedlingen and the next train stop, Munderkingen; without your own transportation, you have to walk, or else connect via one of the stations. The former Premonstratensian **Kloster**, though superficially similar to Zwiefalten with its twin towers and extensive monastic buildings, actually belongs to an earlier age. It's a product of the late seventeenth-century Voralberg School of architects, led by Michael Thumb, who were the first to establish an authentically Germanic version of baroque, in opposition to the Italianate style which was then predominant. The overall effect of both the architecture and the furnishings is somewhat heavy, though it was jazzed up a bit by later craftsmen, who covered the interior with gleaming white stuccowork.

Blaubeuren

After EHINGEN, the stop following Munderkingen, the railroad leaves the Danube Valley and loops towards Ulm via **BLAUBEUREN**, which lies in a wonderful amphitheater-like setting in the Swabian Jura. With its mix of natural and artistic attractions, this ranks as one of the most enticing places in the region, and a good choice as a **hiking** base. The rocky hills above not only afford superb views over the red roofs of the spaciously laid-out little town and the wilder landscape beyond; they also offer constant surprises, such as labyrinths, caves, grottoes, and ruined castles.

At the opposite end of town to the Bahnhof is the **Blautopf**, a shady pool formed during the glacial period; it's the source of the Blau River, the Danube tributary from which the town derives its name. In spite of its small size, the Blautopf is 20m deep, while its waters have a constant temperature of 48° F. The best time to see it is on a sunny, showery day. In bright weather, the pool is a deep emerald blue, but the rain turns this successively to a lighter shade, then green, then a yellowish brown. Alongside is the **Hammerschmiede** (daily 9am–6pm; DM2), a remarkable piece of industrial archaeology. Built in the mid-eighteenth century as a water-mill, it was converted into a smithy at the beginning of the following century, before serving as a mechanical workshop up to 1956, when it was finally retired—though the clanking machinery is still in full working order.

To the side of the Blautopf is the extensive complex of the former **Kloster**. Like Zwiefalten, this was founded at the end of the eleventh century from funds provided by secular patrons, and first settled by Benedictines from Hirsau. It was also totally rebuilt, but this time at the end of the fifteenth century in the late Gothic style. Just 25 years after the monastery had been completed, Württemberg went over to the Reformation; the monastery was disbanded, and the buildings were put to use as a Protestant school.

As in Maulbronn (see p.252), with whose seminary Blaubeuren is now united, there's a remarkably complete picture of a monastic community, with a series of picturesque half-timbered workshops lining the courtyard. You can wander at leisure around here, and also in the cloister with its abutting lavabo and chapter house with tombs of the patrons. The **church** (Palm Sunday–1 Nov. daily 9am–6pm, rest of year Mon.–Fri. 2–4pm, Sat. and Sun. 10am–noon and 2–5pm; DM1.50) represents an ingenious piece of design by the architect, Peter von Koblenz. He left the tower of its Romanesque predecessor as a barrier separating the monks' choir from the nave. The latter, plain and unadorned, is now closed off and used as a concert hall, whereas the former bristles with flamboyant works of art. On high are characterful statues of the apostles, while the stalls were carved by Jörg Syrlin the Younger in imitation of the set his father had made for the Münster in Ulm.

However, what really catches the eye is the **high altar**, one of the finest in the country, and the only one of its kind to have escaped the iconoclasts. It's a co-operative work by at least two major Ulm studios—that of the sculptor **Michel Erhart** and his son **Gregor**, and of the painter **Bartholomäus Zeitblom**, who was assisted by **Bernhard Strigel** and at least one other pupil. When closed, it illustrates the Passion; the first opening shows scenes from the life of John the Evangelist, patron of the Kloster. The carved heart of the retable has figures of the Virgin and Saints flanked by reliefs of *The Adoration of the Shepherds* and *The Adoration of the Magi*. Two small panels above—a less than humble position—have portraits of the abbot and the hirsute count who had commissioned the work. Originally, this part was only shown on the major feast days of the church calendar. Nowadays, it can be seen any time a tour group is passing through, which means frequently during the summer months, though the only guaranteed times are Sunday at 2:30pm and 3:30pm.

Also within the monastery walls is another survivor which is unique of its kind, the **Badhaus**, which was added to the amenities in 1510. It now houses the local museum (daily 10am–5pm; DM1.50), but the main interest is in the building itself—on the ground floor, you can see the baths and heating system, while upstairs is a room decorated with hunting frescos. The archaeological part of the collection is housed in the **Spital** (April–Oct. Tues.–Sun. 10am–5pm, closed Mon.; DM1), the most imposing of the half-timbered houses in the town center.

There's a **youth hostel** at Auf dem Rucken 69 (☎07344 6444) on a hill at the eastern side of town, between the Bahnhof and the Blautopf. Alternatively, there are two **hotels** on Marktstrasse (*Zum Ochsen* has the best restaurant in town), and two more near the Kloster, all with a going rate of around DM30 per head. Tourist information is available at the Rathaus during office hours.

Ulm

When Hermann Hesse returned to **ULM**—"this extraordinarily beautiful and unusual city"—several decades after his only previous visit, he wrote: "I had not forgotten the city walls or the Metzgerturm, nor the Münster's choir and the Rathaus; all these images encountered those in my memory, and hardly differed from them; however, there were countless new images, that I saw as if for the first time: ancient fishermen's homes tilted at an angle in the water, tiny houses on the city ramparts, stately burghers' residences in the alleys, an unusual gable here, a majestic doorway there."

This description shows how much more there is to Ulm than the two reasons its name is so familiar to teacher's pets and TV quiz contestants—for having the highest church spire in the world, and for being the birthplace of one of the all-time giants of science, **Albert Einstein**. Regrettably, some tolerance is now necessary for enjoyment of Ulm; a single air-raid at the end of 1944 caused one of the worst devastations suffered by any German city, wiping out the vast majority of the historic quarter. Much of this had to be rebuilt quickly in a functional modern style. Try not to let this put you off; many of the finest streets escaped lightly, and are still the subject of painstaking restoration projects. Moreover, only superficial damage was inflicted on Ulm's magnificent centerpiece, one of the greatest buildings in Germany.

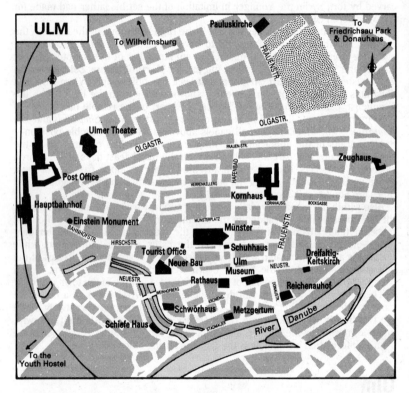

The City

From miles away, the massive west tower of the **Münster** acts as a beacon to the city. Even seeing it for the first time from the unprepossessing surroundings of the bland shopping precinct which leads to town from the **Hauptbahnhof**, you can hardly fail to be impressed—the openwork **steeple** soars so high above everything else it seems to be a real-life fulfilment of those old master paintings which depict an imaginary Tower of Babel shooting through the clouds. In fact, the spire and upper storey of the tower were for centuries no more than a seemingly impossible dream, and were only finished in 1890, faithfully following drawings made four hundred years before.

Apart from offering the satisfaction of seeing the Münster completed exactly according to the wishes of those who planned and funded it, there's the bonus of the stupendous **view** to be had by ascending to the viewing platform (daily June–Aug. 8am–6:45pm; times reduce seasonally as far as 9am–3:45pm; DM2). Most unusually, you're allowed to go as high as the top of the spire, which is only eighteen meters short of the 161-meter-high summit. A fair amount of stamina is needed to climb the 768 steps, but you're rewarded with a panorama which stretches over the city and the Danube to the Swabian Jura and Black Forest, with the Swiss Alps visible on a clear day. On the final stage, there's also the rare opportunity to see the filigree architecture of an openwork spire at close quarters.

Work on the Münster began in the last quarter of the fourteenth century under the direction of the most famous master mason of the day, **Heinrich Parler**, and was continued by his descendants. Credit for its ultimate appearance, however, must go to the head of the succeeding dynasty, **Ulrich von Ensingen**, who altered the plans to make the church wider and loftier, and designed the lower part of the great tower. Despite the Münster's huge size, it was built as, and remains, no more than a parish church. For all that it stands as an act of humility before God, this church was also an expression of a vain civic pride, its capacity of 20,000 was more than twice the population of the city at the time, then one of the largest in Germany.

At the end of the fifteenth century, when the structure was substantially complete, the architect **Matthäus Böblinger** made a drawing (which can be seen in the Ulm Museum) for the completion of the tower, reaching to a height that had never previously been attempted. When he tried to build it, however, cracks appeared in the masonry, and he fled in disgrace. As his successor's main problem was to repair the existing building, no more work was done on the tower, and the project was abandoned altogether when the city formally adopted the Reformation in 1530.

In accordance with Ulm's great sculptural tradition, there are no less than five superb **portals** to the Münster; that under the tower is appropriately the grandest. Above the doorway are depictions of the *Book of Genesis*, while the pillars have masterly statues of saints in the "Soft Style" of **Master Hartmann**, the first Ulm sculptor known by name. The ensemble is completed by a poignant *Man of Sorrows* (now replaced by a copy; the original can be seen inside), an early work by **Hans Multscher**, the founding father of the remarkable group of late Gothic and early Renaissance German sculptors, whose legacy is one of the peaks of the country's heritage. He sharply modified received traditions by experimenting with new poses and expressions, and also broke away from the lodge system by establishing his own independent studio, ending up as a prosperous local citizen.

The **interior's** sense of massive space is as overwhelming as the tower's great height; the impression is aided by the simplicity of the design, which comprises a wide nave of five aisles culminating in a single chancel, with no intervening transept. In 1944, it formed an appropriately grand setting for the notorious state funeral of Field Marshal Erwin Rommel, who accepted this consolation prize, along with a dose of poison, rather than face trial and certain public execution for his alleged involvement in the July Plot against Hitler.

The best time to come here is on a bright morning, when the sun's rays filter through the stained glass windows on to what might legitimately claim to be the greatest set of **choir stalls** ever made: "a bold oaken outburst of three dimensional humanism" was how Patrick Leigh Fermor described them. Made between

1469 and 1474 under the direction of two local men, **Jörg Syrlin the Elder** and **Michel Erhart**, the sheer profusion and originality of their carvings—particularly the vibrant life-sized busts—immediately grab your attention. They're a hymn of praise to the achievements of the ancient as well as to the Christian world, with women, for once, given the same recognition as men.

Ulm's obsession with the steeple motif can be seen in the huge canopy covering the **font**, and in the sounding board added to the **pulpit** which includes, high up above the column capitals, a second pulpit inaccessible to a human preacher—a symbol that the sermon was really delivered by the Holy Ghost. It's seen even more spectacularly in the slender, tapering **tabernacle**, a structure of gossamer delicacy for all its towering height. In spite of its figurines of popes and bishops, this somehow survived the iconoclasm which denuded the Münster following the introduction of the Reformation.

Over the triumphal arch leading to the chancel is a colossal crowded **fresco** of *The Last Judgment*, placed in such a position in order that every member of the congregation could see it. As an antidote to the massiveness that is the dominant characteristic of the Münster, there's the **Besserer-Kapelle** to the right of the chancel, a private family chapel retaining its beautifully drawn and colored fifteenth century stained glass windows.

The obvious place to begin your exploration of the rest of Ulm is at the **Rathaus**, that other self-conscious symbol of civic pride, situated just a block away from the Münster across Neuestrasse, the central arterial road. Even in a country as rich in picturesque town halls as Germany, there's none quite so aggressively photogenic as this disparate jumble of buildings, which has been restored to a pristine approximation of how it looked in 1540. That was when the northern front was rebuilt in the Renaissance style, and equipped with an arcaded passageway; the local painter **Martin Schaffner** was then let loose on the exterior walls, covering them with a series of brilliantly colored **frescos** of religious subjects, plus allegories of the Vices and Virtues. On the southern side of the building he painted battle scenes, along with a barge (symbolizing Ulm's dependence on the Danube), plus the coats-of-arms of the city's trading partners. Between the windows here are polychromed statues of six of the electors, carved the previous century by Master Harmann. Even more luxuriant is the eastern facade, with figures by Multscher of Charlemagne, the kings of Hungary and Bohemia, and two pages; there's also an elaborate astronomical clock made in 1520. Inside the Rathaus, you can see a replica of the equipment used in 1811 by **Albrecht Beblinger**, "The Tailor of Ulm," in an ill-fated attempt to fly across the Danube; widely regarded in his own day as an eccentric fool, he's since been elevated to the status of a local hero.

Behind the Rathaus is the Marktplatz, preserving a few old houses, but dominated by the brightly-colored **Fischkasten** (*Fish Crate*), finest of the many old fountains in the city. Made during the late fifteenth century in the workshop of Syrlin the Elder, it features statues of three saints attired as knights, bearing the coats-of-arms of city and Empire. In Taubenplätzle, just off the eastern end of the square, is the bronze **Dolphin Fountain**; almost exactly a century younger, it was formerly part of a water-tower.

Behind stands a Renaissance mansion which has been adapted to house the **Ulm Museum** (June–Sept. Tues., Weds., and Fri.–Sun. 10am–5pm, Thurs. 10am–8pm, Oct.–May Tues., Weds., Fri., and Sat. 10am–noon and 2–5pm, Thurs. 10am–noon and 2–8pm, Sun. 10am–1pm and 2–5pm; free). On the ground floor are choice examples of the city's artistic heritage; the **original figures** from the Rathaus and several of the fountains have been moved here. Alongside further works by Multscher and Erhart are carvings by **Daniel Mauch**, whose Italianate style represents the last flourish of Ulm's great sculptural tradition. The city's heritage in painting is far less rich, but Schaffner's *Eitel Besserer* (a descendant of the family who endowed the chapel in the Münster) is a masterpiece of Renaissance portraiture, and there are several works by an influential master of the previous generation, **Bartholomäus Zeitblom**. Highlight of the archaeology department is a weird *Statuette of a Woman with the Head of a Lioness*, which dates back to 30,000 B.C. Upstairs, Ulm's history is extensively documented; the section on the construction of the Münster is particularly illuminating, showing how the architects' ideas for the tower became increasingly ambitious.

Westwards down Neuestrasse is the vast bulk of the **Neuer Bau**, a municipal warehouse built in the sixteenth century; its pentagonal courtyard contains a graceful staircase tower and a fountain with a statue of Hildegard, one of Charlemagne's wives. Turning left into Sattlergasse, you come to Weinhof, whose main building is the early seventeenth century **Schwörhaus** (*Oath House*). Each year, the mayor addresses the citizens from the balcony, taking an oath according to the constitution of 1397, by which he must be "the same man to rich and poor alike in all common and honorable matters without discrimination or reservation." This was an advanced statement for its time, and is often taken as evidence that medieval Ulm was a democratic state. In fact, what the document signified was a passing of power from the patrician class to the guilds, who established an inbuilt majority for themselves on the council.

One of the most interesting features of Ulm is the way the old patterns of settlement can still be clearly discerned. Between here and the Danube is the celebrated **Fishermen's Quarter** (*Fischerviertel*), whose quaint scenes of half-timbered houses, waterways, courtyards and tiny bridges so delighted Hermann Hesse. This was actually the area where the artisan classes lived—the island on the Blau and the streets alongside were inhabited by tanners and millers, while on Fischergasse you can see a boatman's house at no. 18, a baker's at no. 22, as well as a fisherman's at no. 23. Look out for the **Schiefe Haus** (*Crooked House*), a hefty half-timbered building from about 1500 standing beside a remnant of the twelfth-century fortifications; it takes its name from its pronounced tilt over the river, into whose bed it's fastened by stilts. Another picturesque vista is on Fischerplätzle, which looks towards Häuslesbrücke and boasts the late fifteenth century **Zunfthaus** (the fishermen's guildhall) and the seventeenth-century **Schöne Haus**, adorned the following century with a scene of shipping on the Danube.

From here, you can walk high above the Danube along the medieval ramparts, now laid out as a shady promenade with a view over the backs of the Fishermen's Quarter. Parallel with the Rathaus is the most impressive surviving gate, the **Metzgerturm** (*Butchers' Tower*), locally dubbed "The Leaning Tower of Ulm" because it slants a good two meters from the vertical. Beyond Herdbrücke is the patrician **Reichenau Hof**, while Grünen Hof just to the north has the oldest intact buildings in Ulm—the Romanesque **Nikolauskapelle** (whose interior has Gothic frescos), and a stone house of similar date. Nearby is the **Dreifaltigkeitskirche**, a plain Lutheran preaching house in the late Renaissance style, incorporating the Gothic chancel of the monastery which previously stood on the site. For a really superb **view** of Ulm, with the Münster rearing high up behind the houses of the Fishermen's Quarter, cross over to the quays of NEUE-ULM, which to all intents and purposes is the city's southern extension, but which isn't even in the same province, the Danube marking the frontier with Bavaria.

The merchants and craftsmen of medieval Ulm tended to live in the streets north of Neuestrasse. These aren't nearly so well preserved, but some fine buildings remain. Just behind the Münster's east end is the sixteenth-century **Schuhhaus**, the guildhall of the shoemakers; it's now used for art exhibitions. Beyond is the Judenhof, the former ghetto; no. 10 seems to predate the pogrom of 1499. The streets immediately north of the Münster contain rows of simple houses once inhabited by skilled craft workers, along with several stores, finest of which is the **Kornhaus**. In spite of its self-confident look and its current function as a concert hall, this was built as a panic measure at the end of the sixteenth century in the belief that there would soon be a famine. Look out also for Herrenkellergasse 12, whose turret served as a lookout post for fathers trying to keep an eye on the evening jaunts of their eligible daughters.

Farther north on Frauengrabben and Seelengrabben are rows of soldiers' houses from the early seventeenth century, beyond which is the **Zeughaus** with a monumental Renaissance gateway, and other surviving parts of the medieval fortifications. Ulm's military role reached a peak in the mid-nineteenth century with its transformation into a fortress of the German Confederation. This citadel was seventeen years in the making, but never once had to withstand a siege; the crumbling buildings are dotted all around the outer perimeter of the city. Finest is the **Wilhelmsburg**, an intact fort crowning the commanding heights of the Michelsberg at the extreme north of the city; it's well worth climbing up for the superb **view** which provides a perfect counterpart to the one from the banks of the Danube. If you walk up via Frauenstrasse, you can see the **Pauluskirche**; built to serve the Protestant members of the garrison, it ranks as one of the finest Jugendstil churches in Germany.

Practicalities, Nightlife, and Festivals

The **tourist office** (Mon.–Fri. 9am–6pm, Sat. 9am–12:30pm; ☎0731 64161) is housed in an ugly modern pavilion in front of the Münster; be sure to pick up their free monthly program of events, *Wohin in Ulm*. Several **pensions** are conveniently located; the cheapest is *Fischkasten*, Marktplatz 16 (☎0731 64910), which charges DM26 per head. Alternatives include *Bauer*, Hafengasse 23 (☎0731 64471) and *Pühler*, Hartmannstr. 7 (☎0731 63489), which both have singles from DM28, doubles from DM55; *Hirschmann*, Syrlinstr. 1 (☎0731 64671), with singles from DM30, doubles from DM55; and *Anker*, Rabengasse 2 (☎0731 63297), from upwards of DM33 per person. The **youth hostel** is 4km southwest of the center at Grimmelfinger Weg 45 (☎0731 384455); take tram #1 to Ehinger Tor, then bus #4 or #9 to Königstrasse. However, there are no camping facilities in the surrounding area. **Motor boat trips** on the Danube (May–Sept.) depart from Metzgerturm.

Ulm has a wide range of places to **eat** and **drink**. The *Ratskeller* is a bit more adventurous than usual, featuring a good vegetarian supplement to the menu. Behind on Markplatz is *Kneipetrödler*, a lively tavern popular with local students which is a real mecca for lovers of the tart and refreshing Weizen beer—there are over twenty varieties to choose from. The Fisherman's Quarter is ideal for a bar hop. On Fischergasse are two traditional inns—*Allgäuer Hof*, which is the place to come for pancakes, and *Forelle*, arguably the city's best restaurant, especially for fish dishes. The old *Zunfthaus* on the same street has been converted into a beer hall serving Swabian dishes, while *Gerberhaus* on Weinhofberg is another good choice for this style of cuisine. For a wine bar atmosphere, try *Weinkrüger* on Weinhofberg. At the eastern end of Neuestrasse is the old-world *Café im*

Gindele; there's also a good choice of cafés in and around Münsterplatz. Three more inns with a long heritage can be found north of the Münster—*Herrenkeller* on the alley of the same name, *Goldener Bock* on Bockgasse, and *Drei Kannen* in a wonderful Renaissance building with a loggia front on Hafenbad. Local **beers** are *Münster* and *Gold Ochsen*; the *Braustüble* of the former is west of the center at Magirusstr. 44, on the route of tram #1.

In 1641, Ulm became the first city in Germany to establish a permanent civic **theater**; its modern successor, the *Ulmer Theater* on Olgastrasse, presents drama, opera, and operetta; it also has a small movie theater. For cabaret, there's *Theater im Fundus* on Deinselsgasse. **Concerts** (all kinds) and large-scale spectaculars are featured at the *Donauhalle* in Friedrichsau Park by the Danube; more intimate highbrow musical events are held in the *Kornhaus*. Choral music is performed in the Münster every other Saturday, while the five-manual organ can be heard daily between 11am and noon. There's jazz most evenings at *Sauschsdall*, Prittwitzstr. 36, while *Charivari*, Stuttgarter Str. 13, is a youth center featuring live bands and adventurous film programs.

The main annual **popular festival** is *Schwörmontag* on the penultimate Monday of July; this begins at 11am in the Weinhof with the mayor's taking of the oath, and continues in the afternoon with a barge procession down the Danube. On the preceding Saturday evening there's the *Lichterserenade*, with thousands of illuminations. Each June, the *Stadtfest* is held in Münsterplatz. However, the most spectacular local tradition, *Fischerstechen* ("Fishermen's Jousting"), a colorful tournament with boats in place of horses, is only held at four-year intervals (next on July 15 and 22, 1990). Prior to the competitions, there are processions and dances in the streets.

Wiblingen

WIBLINGEN, 5km south of Ulm and reached by bus #3 or #8, is now a large dormitory suburb, but for centuries was no more than a hamlet clustered around the Benedictine **Abtei**. The present extensive complex, which offers a rare opportunity to see the luxuriance of South German baroque in close proximity to a bastion of the Reformation, was erected in a leisurely fashion throughout the eighteenth century. Only twenty years after completion, the abbey was secularized; the monastic quarters are now used by the University of Ulm. The buildings are the fruit of the labors of a succession of architects—the initial plans were drawn up by Christian Wiedemann, while Johann Michael Fischer was the most distinguished of those later involved.

Left of the entrance is the **Library** (April–Oct. Tues.–Sun. 10am–noon and 2–5pm, Nov.–March Tues.–Fri. 2–4pm, Sat. and Sun. 10am–noon and 2–4pm; DM2). One of the most opulent designs of its kind, it's lavishly adorned with stuccowork of shells, leaves, and putti, columns painted pink and blue to resemble marble, large allegorical statues representing the Virtues (four secular, four monastic) and a colossal ceiling fresco glorifying wisdom, with subjects from the Bible and pagan mythology freely mixed together.

The **church**, which is later in date, shows a shift from rococo self-indulgence towards the solemnity of neoclassicism. On the flattened domes are masterly, highly theatrical trompe l'oeil frescos by **Januarius Zick**, with a foreshortened *Last Supper* and a cycle illustrating *The Legend of the Cross*. This latter subject was chosen to act as a stimulus to the meditations of the pilgrims who came here to see relics of the Crucifix; the powerful sculpture of the scene by Michel Erhart was acquired from the Münster for the same reason.

Heidenheim and Aalen

HEIDENHEIM, which lies 45km north of Ulm, is at the very edge of the Swabian Jura. It's the eastern terminus of the scenic *Schwäbische Alb Strasse*, which can be followed here from Bad Urach via the industrial town of GIESLINGEN. There's a fair amount of unsightly industry in the suburbs of Heidenheim itself, but downtown is a big improvement.

The dominant sight is the hilltop **Schloss Hellenstein**, whose jumble of buildings date mainly from the late Renaissance period, though some parts of the older medieval fortress also survive. In the deconsecrated church, there's a **museum** (April–Oct. Tues.–Sun. 10am–noon and 2–5pm; DM2), whose main strengths are its archaeological displays from the paleolithic, Roman and Alemannic periods. A vast nature reserve, complete with an open-air theater, has been laid out around the castle. The *Schlossgastätte* is renowned for its hearty and reasonably-priced Swabian dishes; there's also the bonus of fine panoramic views across the town. Heidenheim also claims to have the largest collection of Picasso posters in the world, over 500 in all. A selection from this is periodically shown in the airy **Villa Waldenmaier** (Tues.–Sun. 3–6pm; free) behind the Rathaus. Under the post office is the only other monument of note, a **Roman Bath** (Weds.–Sun. 10am–noon and 2–5pm; DM2) from the second century A.D.

If you want to stay, there's a **youth hostel** at Giengener Str. 88 (☎07321 51414) to the south of town, along with abundant cheap **guest house** accommodation. Nearest **campground** is in DISCHINGEN, 18km east.

Like Heidenheim, **AALEN**, which lies a farther 30km north, was originally a Roman site, built on the route of the Limes Wall, a fortified road linking the Rhine with the Danube. The **Limes Museum** (Tues.–Sun. 10am–noon and 1–5pm; DM2) on St. Johannstrasse occupies the site of one of the forts on this route. It charts the history of the Roman occupation of Baden-Württemberg, and has a good display of relics found locally, along with expert reconstructions and copies of more spectacular items.

Continuing the Roman theme are the superb **Limes Thermal Baths**, an exquisitely designed swimming pool complex in a mixture of modern and classical styles. You can swim to the soothing sight of blue marbled columns; the outdoor pool also has the benefit of stunning views across Aalen and the Swabian Jura. If you go on a weekday it's fairly empty and costs about DM9 for two hours. There are regular services from the bus station, with a journey time of around ten minutes.

Aalen's old town has picturesque cobbled streets lined with half-timbered houses. On Marktplatz you'll find the **Heimat und Schubart Museum** (Tues.–Sun. 10am–noon and 1–5pm; DM2), which is devoted chiefly to memorabilia of the eighteenth-century revolutionary writer, Christian Friedrich Daniel Schubart. Scourge of the petty tyrant, Duke Carl Eugen of Württemberg, Schubart was imprisoned for ten years because of his liberal views. He gained his freedom as a result of intervention from an unlikely source, namely Frederick the Great, who was an admirer of his work. The other local hero is the "spy from Aalen," who successfully duped Napoleon's army by pretending to be a double agent. In gratitude at the town having been saved by his actions, grateful citizens placed on top of the **Rathaus** a humorous statue of him puffing on his pipe. His head turns in all directions in order to show that he is watching over Aalen and its people.

The **tourist office** (Mon.–Fri. 9am–noon and 2–5pm; 07361 500301) is in the Rathaus. There's a **youth hostel** at Stadionweg 8 (☎07361 49203) to the west of the town center; farther out, on the road to ESSINGEN, is a **campground** (07361 296). Alternatively, the following **guest houses** have rooms at around DM30 per head: *Brauerei-Gasthof Fuchs*, Ulmer Str. 32 (☎07361 31949), *Zum Falken*, Schubartstr. 12 (☎07361 62780), *Zum Posthorn*, Bahnhofstr. 97 (☎07361 61541), and *Im Pelzwasen*, Eichendorfstr. 10 (☎07361 31761). The last-named has one of the best **restaurants** in town; otherwise, *Pizzeria Italia* on Friedhofstrasse is recommendable for Italian food, *Sasthof Waldhorn* on Beinstrasse for Greek. For coffee and cakes, try the tiny, antique *Reichstadter Café* on An der Stadtkirche, or the more modern *Café Schieber* on Spritzauchplatz.

The artificial lake of **Rainau Buch**, surrounded by pine trees and situated along the Limes Wall, lies 8km north of Aalen. You can swim, row and fish here in a delightful setting, particularly if you're prepared to walk some way around the lake, away from the parking lot where most of the tourists congregate.

Schwäbisch Gmünd and the Stauferland

SCHWÄBISCH GMÜND, which lies on the almost straight east–west railroad line between Aalen and Stuttgart, 25km from the former and 45km from the latter, is by far the most attractive of the towns of the **STAUFERLAND**. This stretch of countryside, with its gentle slopes, lush meadows, and juniper heathland, straddles the northern end of the Swabian Jura and the southern edge of the Swabian Forest, and is ideal for hiking if you prefer routes which aren't too strenuous. It's named after its former overlords, the **Hohenstaufen dynasty**, who were one of the dominant forces in the politics of early medieval Germany and Italy. Originally counts of Swabia, they captured the office of Holy Roman Emperor in 1133, and held on to it until 1254. Their leading member was the great crusader and champion of chivalry **Frederick Barbarossa**, later to become one of the heroes of the nineteenth-century Romantic movement.

Just south of Gmünd (whose forename is a modern addition to distinguish it from other German towns of the same name) the landscape is characterized by three conical wooded hills, the **Kaiserberge**, each commanding an extensive view, and each formerly crowned by a feudal castle; to walk around them makes for the best day trip in the region. Most westerly is **Hohenstaufen** (684m) itself, which lies midway between Gmünd and GÖPPINGEN. Unfortunately, the ancestral home of the family was completely destroyed in the Peasants' Revolt, leaving little more than the foundations. A few kilometers on is the vacation resort of RECHBERG, nestling below **Hohenrechberg** (707m), whose Romanesque Burg survived largely intact until being burned out during the last century. It's an impressive ruin nonetheless, and is definitely the one to visit if you haven't time to see all three. The area has been a place of pilgrimage since the fifteenth century; the present baroque church is approached uphill via a set of Stations of the Cross. Farther east is **Stuifen** (757m), the highest but least atmospheric of this group of hills.

Gmünd was founded by the first of the local emperors, Conrad III; after the Hohenstaufens fell from power, it became a free imperial city, a status it retained until the Napoleonic epoch. Today, it's a lively provincial town, which has neither grown too big for its own good, nor got stuck in a time-warp. Not that the latter has ever been an option, as Gmünd has had a large American military presence since the end of the war. The northern suburb of MUTLANGEN, indeed, is Germany's answer to Diablo Canyon, frequently hitting the national headlines through the protests which have erupted there. These began in 1983, with the decision to allow **Cruise and Pershing missiles** to be installed on the site, an act which inflamed particular passions in West Germany, as the country is expressly forbidden under the postwar treaties from holding nuclear weapons of her own. Many prominent intellectuals, including the world-famous novelists Günter Grass and Heinrich Böll, were at the forefront of the peace campaign, while another well-known writer, Walter Jens, was arrested and fined for blocking the road to the base when the missiles arrived the following year.

Medieval Gmünd's prosperity was based on the trade in the luxury goods produced by its goldsmiths, silversmiths, jewellers, glass-blowers, and watchmakers. Yet the higher forms of art also flourished. The two most eccentric painters of the German Renaissance, Jerg Ratgeb and Hans Baldung Grien, were born in the city; more significantly, it was the cradle of an extraordinary dynasty, the **Parler** family, whose impact on the world was certainly more felicitous than that of the Hohenstaufens. These masons revolutionized both architecture and sculpture, usurping France's long-standing leadership and making an indelible mark on a host of cities throughout *Mitteleuropa*. Their celebrity status is confirmed by the fact that, in contrast to the general anonymity of most of the masons who designed the great medieval cathedrals of Europe, they are relatively well-documented.

Around 1310, the citizens of Gmünd began the construction of the **Heiligkreuzmünster** as the centerpiece of their town. Some time later, Heinrich Parler arrived from Cologne and took charge of operations. He was later aided by his young son Peter, who was soon after called to Prague, where he developed into one of the most brilliant and imaginative architects Europe ever produced. In spite of the lack of a tower, the church, whose exterior bristles with highly elaborate pinnacles, gables, and gargoyles, floats high above the town. Its five entrance **portals** introduce the characteristic Parler style of sculpture, which aimed at a far greater sense of realism than had hitherto been in vogue. The figures are short and stocky, and are often placed in dramatic relationships to each other; they have life-like facial expressions, and wear contemporary dress, with heavy horizontal drapery folds.

However, there's no doubt that it's the **interior** which is the real show-stopper; it was the first hall church to be erected in southern Germany, and triumphantly gives the lie to the theory that this form of building is inherently dull and unvaried. Standing just inside the main western entrance, you're confronted by the majestic spectacle of 22 huge rounded pillars marching towards the choir. They support a spectacular colored vault which grows ever richer, moving from a fanciful pattern of ribs in the nave to a rich tapestry of network and star-shapes in the chancel which, contrary to normal practice, was the last part to be built. The ring of side chapels, cleverly placed between the buttresses so that their presence can't be gauged from outside, contain a wealth of late Gothic altarpieces, notably a *Tree of Jesse* in the baptistery. There's a wonderful set of Renaissance **stalls** by the Augsburg carver Adolf Daucher, who also made the pulpit. Above the seats stand animated figures of the apostles (on the left) and Old Testament prophets; a peculiarity is that each figure is carved twice and placed back-to-back, so that he faces the ambulatory as well as the choir. At the opposite end of the church, the flowery mid-seventeenth-century case of the organ presents a contrasting piece of virtuoso woodwork.

The original parish church, the octagonal-towered **Johanniskirche** on the central Bocksgasse, is overshadowed by the Münster, but is nevertheless a highly unusual building. It dates from the very end of the Romanesque period in the mid-thirteenth century, and is extravagantly adorned all around its exterior with delicate reliefs of fantastic animals, fables, hunting scenes, flowers, and foliage. The interior (May–Oct. Sun.–Fri. 10am–noon and 2–4pm, Sat. 2–4pm, Nov.–April Sat. 2–4pm, Sun. 10am–noon and 2–4pm only) has nineteenth-century pastel murals and also serves as a repository for original lapidary fragments from the Münster and elsewhere.

Facing the west end of the Johanniskirche is the **Prediger**, a former Dominican monastery which has been converted into a cultural center. Here you'll find the **tourist office** (Mon.–Fri. 9am–5:30pm, Sat. 9am–12:30pm, May–Oct. also Sun. 10am–1pm; ☎07171 66244) along with a **museum** (Tues.–Fri. 2–5pm, Sat. and Sun. 10am–noon and 2–5pm; free). The latter contains good collections of medieval and baroque sculpture, along with examples of the town's expertise in jewelry-making and the usual local history displays. On the opposite side of the Johanniskirche is the **Marktplatz**, now largely baroque in character, with several cheerful mansions and a rather saccharine fountain bearing a double-sided statue of the *Madonna and Child*. However, there are also a number of half-timbered houses from earlier periods, notably the **Amtshaus Spital** at the far end. A bit farther east are four of the five remaining towers of the fourteenth-century city wall, with the highest of the group, the **Königsturm**, a short walk to the south.

The **Hauptbahnhof** is just to the northeast of the center, which is reached by following Uferstrasse straight ahead, before turning into Bocksgasse. Just behind, there's a wonderful wooded uphill walk along Taubentalstrasse past shrines dating as far back as the fifteenth century, to the dark, secret **St. Salvator Kapelle** at the top. This former hermit's cave and its adjoining stone-walled rooms are bedecked with candles, icons, statues, and other religious paraphernalia.

The **youth hostel**, at Taubentalstr. 45 (☎07171 2260), shares this peaceful location. **Camping** is possible to the west of town at *Schurrenhof* (☎07165 8190). Among the centrally-placed **guesthouses**, cheapest are *Weisser Ochsen*, Parlerstr. 47 (☎07171 2812), with singles at DM25, plus a double at DM42; *Kronprinzen*, Hintere Schmiedgasse 41 (☎07171 2290), at DM26 per head; and *Goldener Stern*, Vordere Schmiedgasse 41 (☎07171 66337), which charges DM27 per person. If you want to coincide your visit with a **festival**, come on the second Saturday in June, when *Schwabenalter* celebrates those who have passed their fortieth birthday—the watershed year for the acquisition of true wisdom, according to Swabian custom. Otherwise, *Fastnet* is the main event, reaching a climax on Shrove Tuesday.

There are plenty of good places to **eat** and **drink** downtown; best for traditional Swabian fare is the historic *Fuggerei* on Münstergasse, though it's on the expensive side. Recommendable cafés include *Margrit* on Johannisplatz, which has delicious cakes, the long-established *Zieher* on Marktgässle, the candlelit *Eiscafé Piazetta* on Marktplatz, and *Spielplatz* on Münsterplatz, which often features exhibitions of contemporary international artists. Alternatively, try the restaurant in the *Stadtgarten* (between the Hauptbahnhof and the center) which offers quality dishes at low cost, with the bonus of views across the park; in the halls here **concerts** of all kinds take place. The local **beer** is *Aloisle*, made with the soft spring water of the Swabian Jura. For serious drinking, you should head for *Bierakademie* on Ledergasse, which serves what it claims to be the fifteen best brews in the world. *Taverne* on Kornhausstrasse is the main concession to the American community, fitted out to resemble a saloon bar of the Fifties.

Schwäbisch Hall

SCHWÄBISCH HALL, which lies 45km north of Schwäbisch Gmünd via the dense tracts of the Swabian Forest, likewise held the status of free imperial city for centuries, having previously belonged to the Hohenstaufens. It was during the reign of Frederick Barbarossa that the town became an important center of minting, making the silver *Häller* (or *Heller*), the smallest unit of currency used in the Holy Roman Empire. Though now long out of circulation, the *Heller*'s name lives on as a simile for worthlessness in many idiomatic expressions in modern German. Ultimately, the coin's name derives from the industry on which the local economy was originally based: *Hall* means "Place of Salt." Excavations show that the salt springs attracted Celtic tribes to establish a permanent settlement here; following the medieval revival, they served as the keystone of local prosperity, only going into decline during the nineteenth century with discoveries of richer deposits elsewhere. Subsequent attempts to develop a more modern industrial base failed, as did a bid to make Hall a bathing and health resort on the lines of so many other German spas. Coupled with the fact that bombing in World War II caused little more than superficial damage, this means that the town preserves an unusually intact reminder of its medieval self, complete with tantalizing insights into the social and political preoccupations of the time.

The central, steeply sloping **Marktplatz** is lined by a series of superb buildings which form an encyclopedia of German architecture. Its present character was largely determined during the late medieval period, at a time when the rampantly successful bourgeoisie had ousted the aristocracy from control of the council, forcing many of the latter to leave town. As a symbol of the self-confident spirit, it was decided to build a spectacular new church, to be approached by a monumental flight of 42 (now 54) steps. The dramatic possibilities of this backdrop were immediately evident, and the space was used for jousting and tournaments.

Today, the Marktplatz is put to triumphant use as an **open-air theater**. This is one of the most impressive you're ever likely to come across, with magical staging effects in a dense, rapt atmosphere. The season lasts from mid-June to early August, and usually features a play by Shakespeare, a European classic, and a twentieth-century work. Performances start at 8:30pm, but the scramble for the best seats begins as early as 6pm. Tickets cost around DM15, and are available from the theater headquarters at no. 8 on the square. Next door is the **tourist office** (April–Sept. Mon.–Fri. 9am–noon and 2–6pm, Sat. and Sun. 10am–2pm, Nov.–March Mon.–Fri. 9am–noon and 2–5pm; ☎0791 751246/751321). If you want to make a detailed visit of the old streets, ask for their *Walking Tour* brochure, which has a good map and extensive historical information in English.

The late Gothic **Münster** (mid-March–Oct. Mon.–Sat. 9am–noon and 2–5pm, Sun. 11am–noon and 2–5pm; DM1 including ascent of the tower) has a nave in the hall church style with slender pillars and wide vaults, that contrasts with the much higher choir, which was only completed in 1525, the year that the authorities of Hall decided to go over to Protestantism. Luther's youthful protégé **Johannes Brenz**—a far more tolerant figure than most of the leading lights of the time—came from Heidelberg to be the new preacher. His portrait can be seen on one of the epitaphs of the nave. Another particularly interesting memorial tablet is in the fourth chapel from the left in the ambulatory; this was made for his own tomb by the sixteenth-century artist and calligrapher Thomas Schweiker, who painted with his feet, having been born without hands or arms. The most striking work of art, however, is Michel Erhart's impassioned

Crucifixion, placed above the Netherlandish *Retable of the Passion* at the high altar.

Another embellishment to the square, erected at the same time as the Münster's chancel, is the **Marktbrunnen**, showing Saint Michael in the company of two other warriors against evil, Samson and Saint George. Rather bizarrely, the structure also incorporates the pillory, still preserving the manacles which bound the wrongdoers. The north side of the square is lined with a picturesque jumble of buildings, including what are now two of the best (and most expensive) hotel-restaurants in town, the graceful half-timbered *Goldener Adler*, an inn since the sixteenth century, and the gaunt stone *Ratskeller*. Opposite are a series of houses which traditionally belonged to various religious and charitable bodies. The west side of the square seems to be jinxed—the church which formerly stood there was destroyed by fire in the eighteenth century, to be replaced by the **Rathaus**, which was in turn a rare casualty of the last war. However, it's been successfully restored, its ritzy curved facade and stately belfry giving it the look of a sumptuous baroque palace.

South of Marktplatz run a series of alleys—Untere Herrngasse, Obere Herrngasse, and Pfargasse—which are all lined with superb old buildings, and are periodically linked to one another by stairways. They all lead to the **fortifications**, which survive in part all around the town, unfortunately shorn of most of the towers, which were demolished when Hall became part of the Kingdom of Württemberg in the early nineteenth century. Rizing high above the weakest part of the defensive system is the massive **Neubau**, which, in spite of its name, dates back to the time of the Reformation. It served as an arsenal and granary, and is now a concert hall. The other dominant building at this side of town is the eight-storey **Keckenburg**, a tower-house from the Staufer period. Along with a diverse series of historic buildings nearby, it houses the **Hällisch-Fränkisches Museum** (Tues. and Thurs.–Sun. 10am–5pm, Weds. 10am–8pm; free). Well above average for a regional collection, this has displays on local history and industry, archaeology, geology, crafts, and sacred sculpture.

A short walk from here brings you to the banks of the sedate Kocher River, lined with weeping willows, and with a picturesque group of stone and wooden bridges reaching out to three islets. From the quays on the opposite side, you have an outstanding **view** of the main part of the town, rising majestically in tiers. The left bank, which had its own set of walls and towers, was the artisans' district; it clusters around **St. Katharina**, a Gothic church with gorgeous fourteenth-century stained glass windows. At the northern end is a reproduction of the oldest of the bridges, **Henkersbrücke** (*Hangman's Bridge*), named after the house on it, in which the holder of the least-coveted municipal office was forced to live, as the stigma of the position meant he was forbidden to reside in town.

The northern quarter of Hall presents another characterful old quarter, beginning at the **Säumarkt** (*Pig Market*), which features a sixteenth-century tower and weigh-house, behind which is the late seventeenth-century tannery, whose arcades were used for drying skins until 1972. As a contrast, there's the neoclassical solemnity of the guard station of the Württemberg army. Leading off the square is Gelbinger Gasse, the longest and arguably the finest street in Hall, whose buildings cover the full gamut of styles from Gothic to Jugendstil. Look out in particular for no. 25, the **Engelhardbau**, the baroque mansion of a town councillor; and no. 47, the late Renaissance **Gräterhaus**, whose beam decoration includes the scraping tools of the tanners, an indication that the house was built by a prosperous member of that guild.

Practical Points

Schwäbisch Hall's **Bahnhof** is on the western bank of the Kocher; it's a fifteen-minute walk to the center straight ahead via Bahnhofstrasse, then over the river. The **bus station** is at the diametrically opposite end of town, by the bank of the Kocher just outside the northern quarter. There's a **youth hostel** at Langenfelderweg 5 (☎0791 2260); from the rear of Marktplatz, follow Crailsheimer Strasse (the beltway) in an easterly direction, then turn left into Blutsteige. The **campground** is south of town at *Steinbacher See* (April—mid-Oct. only; ☎0791 2984). Two **guest houses** on Bahnhofstrasse offer some of the most competitive rates in town. *Rose* at no. 9 (☎0791 6558) has singles from DM25, doubles from DM44, while *Kronprinz* at no. 17 (☎0791 6212) charges DM27 for singles, DM47 for doubles. *Bürgerstüble* at Hauffstr. 14 (☎0791 51807) is the cheapest of all at DM24 per head, but is rather remote. For a downtown location best value are *Krone*, Klosterstr. 1 (☎0791 6022) at upwards of DM27 per person, and *Dreikönig*, Neuestr. 25 (☎0791 7473) at DM28.50 per head.

Many of the best **restaurants** have their eyes on the well-heeled short-stay tourist, but homely Swabian cooking is available at low cost at *Zum Darle* on Blockgasse and *Salzsiedler* on Schulgasse. There's also a widely varied clutch of ethnic eateries along Gelbinger Gasse. The local *Haller Löwenbräu* **beer** (not to be confused with its Munich namesake) is available as both Pils and Weizen. Evening entertainment possibilities are headed by the open-air theater, but **kids** will prefer the *Marionettentheater* near the left bank quay at Im Lindbach 9, which has both historical and modern puppets.

Hall's salt heritage is celebrated each Pentecost weekend in one of Baden-Württemberg's most famous **festivals**, the *Kuchen und Brunnen Fest der Haller Salzsieder* ("Cake and Fountain Festival of the Salt-Simmerers of Hall"). This commemorates the occasion when the salt workers quenched a fire at the town mill. It features dancing and music on the Grasbödele (one of the islets) by the simmerers in their red, black, and white historical costume. There's also a simulation of the blaze and a tattoo, both held on the Marktplatz.

Outside Schwäbisch Hall

Perched magisterially on its hill a couple of kilometers south of Limpurg via the banks of the Kocher is one of the most outstanding sights of southern Germany, the awesome **Klosterburg Gross Comburg**. Fortress-monasteries are common enough in Spain and the Middle East, but such blatant expressions of the Church Militant are extremely rare in western Europe. In 1079 this collegiate foundation was endowed by the Count of Comburg, Burkhard II, who, as a cripple, felt unable to perform the normal aristocratic duties, and decided to retire to a monastic life. Much of the original Romanesque architecture survives intact, including the mighty ring wall with its defensive towers. The extensive additions to the complex made down the years included the progressive strengthening of the entrance, and you now pass through the baroque *Bastion* and the Renaissance *Zwingertor*, before arriving at the Romanesque **Michaelstor**, guarding a 12-meter-long tunnel which served as the last line of defense. As the baroque monastic buildings are now used as a college, there's normally unrestricted entry to the courtyard. Here you can see another Romanesque survival, the hexagonal **Ebehardskapelle**, which is ornamented with a graceful dwarf gallery. Its function is disputed, but it probably served as an ossuary.

The **Klosterkirche** (mid-March–mid-Nov. Tues.–Sat. 9am–noon and 1:30–5pm, Sun. 1:30–5pm; DM1) retains the three imperious towers of the first church, but was otherwise rebuilt in the Würzburg baroque style. Although the exterior retains much of the austerity of its predecessor, the interior, with its gleaming white stuccowork, comes in complete contrast. It still preserves, however, two stunning twelfth-century treasures made in the monastery's once-celebrated workshop: an enormous golden wheel-shaped **chandelier** (which is even larger and more impressive than those in Aachen and Hildesheim, the only others to have survived) and the gilded beaten copper **antependium** (altar front), which has engravings of Christ surrounded by his disciples. A number of masterly tombs, including that of the founder, can be seen in the **chapter house**, which still preserves its Romanesque form.

It's also worth crossing over to the hill directly opposite, crowned by the **Klein Comburg**. This was founded as a convent about thirty years after its big brother, and was also used for some time as a hospice. The church here was always very much the poor relation, but scores in the fact that it preserves its simple original form.

Also some distance from the center of Hall is the **Open-Air Museum** (April, May, and Oct. Tues.–Sun. 10am–5:30pm, June–Sept. Tues.–Sun. 9am–6pm; DM3), situated some 5km northwest at WACKERSHOFEN. This brings together redundant rural buildings from throughout the north of Baden-Württemberg, including the Tauber Valley and the eastern Jura, but concentrating on the Hohenlohe region. Ceramics, furniture-making, and textiles are among the crafts demonstrated, while there's a *Backofenfest* on the last weekend in September. A historic inn, *Roter Ochsen*, is among the reconstructed buildings, providing a handy stopping-off point for lunch.

The Swabian Forest

The **Swabian Forest** (*Schwäbischer Wald*) stretches over a neat, almost square geographical area between Schwäbisch Hall and Schwäbisch Gmünd in the east, and Heilbronn and Stuttgart to the west. To the north, it enters Franconia, where it gives way to the flat plain of Hohenlohe, while its southern extremity borders the Stauferland. Stretching over some 900 square kilometers, the whole area is designated a *Naturpark*. Thickly wooded, it consists of three separated forest areas, plus two ranges of hills. Though there's little that's tremendously dramatic, the region offers the opportunity of escaping from the crowds, on weekdays at least. The old Roman Limes Wall, some of whose towers have been restored to serve as vantage-points, traverses the forest from north to south; and there's a marked trail along the entire route.

At the heart of the forest is the town of **MURRHARDT**, which lies on the railroad line between Schwäbisch Hall and Ludwigsburg, and makes the obvious base from which to plan your explorations. The only **youth hostel** in the region is at Karnsberger Str. 1 (☎07192 7501) at the northern end of town, while there's a **campground**, *Am Waldsee*, in the neighboring village of FORNSBACH (☎07192 6436). Murrhardt also boasts an outstanding monument in the **Walterichskapelle**, a tiny, highly ornamented late Romanesque chapel adjoining the fifteenth-century Stadtkirche. A number of half-timbered houses and a section of the town walls also survive.

Heilbronn

"It cannot be a matter for surprise that a town which combines the charms of a beautiful and fertile region with so many refined customs attracts strangers and instils in them the desire to share these benefits for a time," wrote Schiller about **HEILBRONN**. Lying in the Neckar valley just to the east of the Stromberg region, this former free imperial city is deemed to mark the boundary of the mystical concept of Swabia—no true *Schwob* would live any farther north. Today, it still boasts one of the richest folklore traditions in Germany, and is also a leading center for **wine** production—some five million liters, mostly *Riesling* and *Trollinger* varieties, are produced each year by the surrounding vineyards. Sadly, however, the old streets were almost razed to the ground in an air raid at the end of 1944. The rebuilding program was unusual in that it concentrated on providing housing in the town center, with most commercial activity banished to the suburbs. Only a few first-class monuments now remain, and it's best to coincide your visit with one of the many **festivals** which dot the calendar.

Foremost of these is the *Heilbronner Herbst*, which begins with a procession through the streets on the first Saturday in September, and continues with a parade of lantern-bearing children and a fireworks display the next day. Later in the week, the *Weindorf* ("Wine Village") is set up for nine days downtown, with the inevitable oompah bands to enliven the atmosphere. Nearly 200 vintages are available at the various booths; in contrast to the inflated prices normally charged at German festivals, the rates are surprisingly reasonable—usually DM1 per glass. Heilbronn's other big event is the *Neckarfest*, featuring historical boat pageants, a flotilla of bizarre home-made "water transport" contraptions, aquatic tournaments, and a serenade of lights. This takes place during June, but in even-numbered years only, as it alternates with the more orthodox *Stadtfest*. Other festivals are the huge *Pferdemarkt* ("Horse Fair") in February and the *Unterländer Volksfest* in late July/early August; the latter sees beer take a rare leading role in this wine stronghold.

The surviving monuments are conveniently grouped closely together in the town center. By far the most imposing is the Gothic hall church of **St. Kilian**—or rather, its amazing later adjunct, the sixteenth-century belfry. One of the few examples of ecclesiastical architecture in Northern Europe directly inspired by the Italian High Renaissance, its lower parts are richly decorated, much in the manner of the late Gothic style then still popular elsewhere in Germany, while the upper stories are built in the manner of a miniature classical temple. At the summit, the *Männle* (a statue of an infantryman bearing the municipal coat-of-arms) lords over the town. Inside the church is a wonderful retable of *The Virgin and Child with Saints* by a local man, **Hans Syfer**, one of the seemingly endless number of virtuoso carvers active in late fifteenth-century Germany. Underneath the building is the *Heiliger Brunnen*, a well with supposedly miraculous properties, from which the town's name is derived.

Directly opposite St. Kilian is the **Rathaus**, another amalgam of Gothic and Renaissance, whose facade is enlivened by a graceful balcony used for making public pronouncements, and by an astronomical clock. The latter, which tells the day and the month as well as the time, was considered the ultimate municipal status symbol when it was installed in 1580. Its construction was entrusted to Isaak Habrecht, the finest horologist of the day, who had previously created what still ranks as one of Europe's most spectacular clocks, that inside Strasbourg Cathedral.

Also on Marktplatz is the **Käthchenhaus**, a Gothic patrician mansion embellished with a Renaissance oriel. It takes its name from the legend of Käthchen of Heilbronn, best known as a result of the play by Heinrich von Kleist. Käthchen was the product of a one-night stand between a German emperor and the wife of the blacksmith of Heilbronn. Her true identity was only revealed when, as a fifteen-year-old, she developed a mystical attraction to a count who had a premonition that he was going to marry an emperor's daughter. The town still gets a lot of mileage out of the story—every two years, a pretty local girl is designated as "Käthchen," to preside over all the festivals, and to adorn the front cover of all the glossy promotional brochures.

In the pedestrian precinct south of Marktplatz is the **Deutschhof**, formerly belonging to the Teutonic Knights, which contains a Gothic church and baroque administrative buildings. The **Städtisches Museum** (Tues. 10am–7pm, Weds.–Sun. 10am–noon and 2–5pm; free) is now housed in the latter, though its natural history and archaeology departments are in the Renaissance **Gerichtshaus** (*Law Courts*) across the street. There's also a third section, devoted to shipping on the Neckar, in its own building on Frankfurter Strasse, not far from the river itself. Up Obere Neckarstrasse from the Gerichtshaus is one of the rare surviving parts of the medieval fortifications, the tower known as the **Götzenturm**. It's so called as a result of the daring escape made from it by the great adventurer Götz von Berlichingen, who was held prisoner there in 1519.

The **Hauptbahnhof** is situated just to the west of the center, which is reached by following Bahnhofstrasse straight ahead. Most of the cheap **hotels** are near the station—*Beck*, Bahnhofstr. 31 (☎07131 86626 or 81589), *Schlachthof*, Frankfurter Str. 83 (☎07131 81413) and *Olga*, Olgastr. 55 (☎07131 86738) all charge around DM30 per head. Otherwise, the **tourist office** (Mon.–Fri. 9am–5:30pm, Sat. 9am–12:30pm; ☎07131 562270) on Marktplatz will find you a room at no extra cost. The **youth hostel** is at Schirrmannstr. 9 (☎07131 72961): take bus #1 to the Trappensee terminus.

Best **restaurant** for Swabian specialties is the *Ratskeller*; for something a bit cheaper, try *Kronprinz* on Bahnhofstrasse. *Sonnenstube* on Querschulgasse is a good vegetarian café, while *Rialto* on Innsbrucker Strasse is recommendable for Italian fare. *Dechpavilion*, on top of a row of shops on Kaiserstrasse, is the most enticing **bar** in Heilbronn, offering a fine view over the town by night. Youthful hangouts include *Freak* on Albert-Schaffler-Strasse (reached by bus #10), *Altstadt* on Happelstrasse (which runs musical theme nights), *Hard Rock Café* on Neckarsulmer Strasse, and *Bukowskis* on Hafenstrasse (which, come the weekend, never seems to close).

Classical music can be heard at the *Harmonie* concert hall on Allee; look out for performances by the *Württemberger Kammerorchester*, one of the best chamber orchestras in Europe. On the same street, the spanking new *Stadttheater* presents all forms of **drama**. The booking office for **Neckar cruises** is beside Friedrich-Ebert-Brücke. There are generally at least a couple of sailings each day in summer to GUNDELSHEIM; trips round the harbor are occasionally offered as an alternative.

Around Heilbronn

WEINSBERG, 6km east of Heilbronn, is, as its name suggests, a town surrounded by sloping vineyards. It's particularly associated with the nineteenth-century *Schwäbischer Dichterkreis* (Swabian School of Poets), which often held rendezvous in the home of one of their members, the Weinsberg doctor, Justinus

Kerner. This is now a **museum** of memorabilia (Tues.–Sun. 10am–noon and 2–5pm; DM1.50). Kerner was fascinated by the supernatural, and the **Geisterturm** in his own grounds is so named after the spirits who haunted it. The part-Hungarian, part-German Nikolaus Lenau stayed there when writing his unfinished *Faust*; this was to inspire the celebrated, demoniac *Mephisto Waltz* by a man of similarly mixed nationality, Franz Liszt.

Above Weinsberg are the scanty remains of the **Weibertreu** (*Faithful Wives*) fortress, named in honor of the curious legend with which it's associated. In the twelfth century, the castle was besieged by the brother of its owner, who had taken the opposing side in one of the frequent disputes between the emperor and the pope. Before moving in for the final massacre, the attackers decided to show clemency to the women of the castle, telling them they could go free, taking with them only what they were themselves able to carry. When the women came out, the besiegers were dumbfounded by what they saw—each had hoisted her husband on her shoulders, thus, by the terms of the agreement, saving his life.

NECKARSULM, a similar distance north of Heilbronn, has a heavily-restored castle formerly belonging to the Teutonic Knights, which now houses the **German Two-Wheeler Museum** (*Deutsches Zweirad Museum*; daily 9am–noon and 1:30–5:30pm; DM2.50), with some 250 bikes and motorcycles from the early nineteenth century to the present day. This also incorporates the collection of *NSU*, Germany's leading manufacturer in this field.

From here, it's only a short journey by train to BAD WIMPFEN and the route of the Neckar castles (see p.257). The countryside immediately to the southeast of Heilbronn is also attractive, marking the start of the Swabian Forest region.

Maulbronn and the Stromberg Region

'In the cells and halls of the monastery between the round arched windows and sturdy double columns made of red sandstone, monks lived, taught, studied, administered and ruled. The arts and sciences flourished, each succeeding generation passing on its skills. Books were written and dissected, systems were developed, classical writings collected, manuscripts illuminated, the faith of the common people nurtured, and their credulity smiled on. Here there was time for everything—belief and learning, profundity and simplicity, the wisdom of the Greeks and the Evangelists, black and white magic, repentance and solitude, high living and companionship.'

This evocative characterization of medieval monastic life occurs at the beginning of Hermann Hesse's picaresque novel *Narziss and Goldmund*. One of the highpoints of twentieth-century literature (and, in many eyes, the most beautiful piece of sustained prose writing in the German language), the story is set in and around the great Cistercian Kloster of **MAULBRONN**, thinly disguised as Mariabronn. The writer had direct experience of this, the best-preserved medieval monastery north of the Alps, having been a pupil in the Protestant school which was established there in 1557, just a couple of decades after the last monks had left. Thanks to its new function, under the protection of the Dukes of Württemberg, Maulbronn never suffered the normal fate of serving as a stone quarry, far less as a target for iconoclasts and revolutionaries, and stands today as a complete monastic complex which has few parallels anywhere in Europe, giving a unique insight into a way of life which exercised such enormous power and influence throughout the medieval period.

A characterless modern town has grown up on the slopes above the Kloster, but that is forgotten as soon as you enter the walled precincts of the monastery by the Romanesque **Klostertor**. Immediately to the right of the entrance is a ruinous chapel, in which early masses were said; facing it is the priest's house, now converted into a **museum** (April–Oct. daily 9:30–noon and 2–5pm; free). It's well worth popping in, if only to see the model explaining the whole layout.

Beyond here, you pass into the spacious main **courtyard**, the first part of which is taken up by a jumble of half-timbered buildings, generally late Gothic in style, though some were later rebuilt, and others date back as far as the thirteenth century. These served as the storerooms and workshops, which were the province of the lay brothers of the monastery. They're now put to a variety of uses: the forge has been converted into a restaurant; the stables serve as the Rathaus and **tourist office** (Mon. and Thurs. 8am–noon and 1–5:30pm, Tues. and Weds. 8am–noon and 1–4:30pm, Fri. 8am–1:30pm, Sat. and Sun. 11am–5pm; ☎07043 10317); while the stone-built mill, the oldest of the buildings, is a **youth hostel** (☎07043 6535). This is linked to the passageway along the ramparts, at the end of which is the thirteenth-century **Haspelturm** (*Witches' Tower*).

Facing the outbuildings is the **Kloster** proper (April–Oct. daily 8:30am–6:30pm, Nov.–March Tues.–Sun. 9:30am–1pm and 2–5pm; DM3), founded in 1147 in what was then the isolated valley of the river Salzach. This was exactly the sort of location favored by the reforming Cistercian order, whose rule stressed both spirituality and the importance of manual labor. Here they had access not only to water, but also to the wood and stone which were necessary for the extensive building works. According to legend, the site was chosen when the monks, who had established their monastery at an unsuitable place nearby a few years before, stopped to water their mules—hence the name Maulbronn, meaning "Mule Well."

The **church** was the first part to be built; it's in the severe, unadorned style laid down in the tenets of the order, with no tower and no decoration. Later generations were less enthusiastic about asceticism, whether in life or architecture; in order to enliven their church they replaced the wooden roof with a lofty net vault, added a row of chapels with elaborate traceried windows to the south side, and commissioned works of art. There's also a fascinating glimpse into the sense of worldly hierarchy practiced by the monks right from the time of the church's construction. The fathers reserved the eastern part of the church for their own exclusive use, confining the lay brothers to the nave by the erection of a stone screen; members of the public weren't allowed into the church at all.

Instead, a **porch** (or "Paradise"), enabling visitors to look in on the services, was built on to the facade of the church in 1220. This seems to be the earliest building in Germany to show awareness of the new Gothic style pioneered in France. The same anonymous mason then began building the cloister, completing the southern wing, plus the **monk's refectory** on the opposite side. His style shows all the sense of discovery characteristic of the beginning of an era; still influenced by the Romanesque penchant for mass, he introduced the ribbed vault and the pointed arch not only for their constructional advantages, but also for the decorative effect which could be obtained by varying the forms they took. The refectory is a masterpiece, which is all the more appropriate in view of the Cistercian custom of making the dining hall particularly splendid and luminous, in order to draw thoughts away from the frugality of the meals.

The rest of the cloister, including the graceful **chapter house** on the east side, dates from around a century later; the use of elaborate tracery is the first visible sign of the dilution of the early Cistercian ideal of austerity. As a culmination, a striking polygonal **well house** was added to house the fountain where the monks washed before each meal. Buildings continued to be added periodically—the long, narrow **parlatorium** beside the chapter house was built by a lay brother at the end of the fifteenth century, while the cloister was given a picturesque half-timbered upper story soon after.

In the early sixteenth century, as the original Cistercian ideal of plain and unadorned architecture held ever less appeal, the most violently expressive of German artists, **Jerg Ratgeb**, was commissioned to execute a series of fresco cycles. He made a series of preliminary red chalk drawings, which can still be seen; these include the depiction of the legend of the monastery's foundation in the well house, and a number of allegorical subjects (incorporating a stern self-portrait) in the refectory. Completion of the project was interrupted by the Reformation, when the painter abandoned art in favor of politics, serving as "War Councillor" and "Chancellor" of the Peasants' Revolt. The failure of this rebellion led to Ratgeb's arrest; he was quartered in the Markt in Pforzheim a decade before his erstwhile patrons became very different casualties of the Reformation.

A tour of the Kloster can be completed by walking around the outside of the main quarters. At the southeast corner is the **Faustturm**, so called from having been the residence of the original Dr. Faust (see below) whose claim to be able to manufacture gold gained him employment for a time by an unscrupulous abbot who was willing to try anything to bolster the monastery's sagging finances. Within the corresponding corner to the north the dukes of Württemberg built a Renaissance **Jagdschloss** with fairy-tale corner turrets; it now forms the girls' section of the school they founded.

Maulbronn is slightly tricky to reach by **public transit**. It's best to come by bus from MÜHLACKER, which is a regular stop for trains between Stuttgart and Karlsruhe; although there's a stop named "Maulbronn West" on the branch railroad line to Bruchsal, it's some 3km from the Kloster. As an alternative to the excellent but expensive **restaurant** *Klosterkeller*, go just outside the gates to *Scheffelhof*, which serves homely and hearty fare, including imaginative vegetarian dishes. A short walk to the east of the Kloster is the **Tiefer See**, an artificial lake created by the monks in order to give themselves a regular supply of fish; it's now a center for swimming and water sports. As an alternative to the hostel, there are five **guesthouses**. All are reasonably priced; cheapest are *Undi*, Südmährer Str. 6 (☎07043 7225), at DM23 per head, and *Ochsen*, Stuttgarter Str. 54 (☎07043 7314), whose rooms cost DM24.

Naturpark Stromberg-Heuchelberg

The **Naturpark Stromberg-Heuchelberg** stretches over an area of 330 square kilometers north and east of Maulbronn as far as the Neckar River. It's cut by two deep valleys, the Kirbach and the Metter, which provide fertile agricultural land. Grapes have been cultivated on the slopes since the eighth century, if not before. Red **wines**—*Trollinger*, *Lemberger*, *Schwarzriesling*, *Spätburgunder*, and *Portugieser*—make up the bulk of the current output; white varieties include the well-known *Riesling*, as well as *Müller-Thurgau*, *Kerner*, and *Ruhlander*. Much of the area, however, is taken up by the two separate mountain ranges after which the park is named. These are actually fairly gentle, with even the highest peaks being under 500 meters. A **footpath**, laid out in the seventeenth century for military use, crosses right through the middle of the park, linking Mühlacker with EPPINGEN directly to the north; it makes a good day's hike, offering a mixture of forest and upland scenery. There are also a couple of **bird sanctuaries** within easy reach of Maulbronn—*Rossweiher* is just beyond Tiefer See, while *Aalkistensee* is a couple of kilometers west of the town.

Knittlingen

KNITTLINGEN, 6km northwest of Maulbronn, is notable for only one reason—it was the birthplace of the notorious necromancer **Johannes Faust**. Inevitably, a **museum** charting his impact has been set up in the half-timbered house where he is believed to have been born (Tues.–Fri. 9:30am–noon and 1:30–5pm, Sat. and Sun. 10am–6pm; DM2). Surprisingly little is known about him, though he seems to have been a celebrity in his day, and the leading intellectuals of the time took him seriously, while regarding his practices as wholly evil. Unlike other leading practitioners of the occult, such as Nostradamus and Paracelsus, Faust left no tangible legacy, and his name would certainly have passed into oblivion had it not been for an unknown author who in 1587 published the *Faustbuch*, a potboiling collection of tales allegedly told by the magician, who had died nearly half a century before; this quickly became a bestseller, despite the crudity of the text. It was the English playwright Christopher Marlowe who, just a few years afterwards, first realised the dramatic possibilities of the story, endowing the hero with a tragic dignity.

Ever since, the Faust legend—with its themes of absolute knowledge, absolute power, and the relationship between the two—has ranked as one of the great subjects of the European literary tradition, one capable of a vast variety of interpretations, and a convenient backdrop for the discussion of all kinds of issues. Lessing provided a happy ending, a lead followed by **Goethe**, whose vast two-part drama is the unchallenged summit of all German literature. It took him the best part of sixty years to write; in it, he explored the entire European cultural heritage. In the present century, the Faust themes are equally relevant, and Thomas Mann provided an appropriately updated version of the story in his novel of 1950.

THE KRAICHGAU
AND THE PALATINATE

North of Karlsruhe are various territories which were only incorporated into Baden as a result of the Napoleonic redistribution of the map of Europe, and whose very different history means that they're best considered separately.

The fertile **Kraichgau** region, between the Rhine and the Neckar, was particularly associated with the prince-bishops of Speyer, who established their resplendent new palatial headquarters at **Bruchsal** in the eighteenth century. On the Neckar itself is the outstanding small town of **Bad Wimpfen**, for centuries a free imperial city, and one which defies classification—it's been considered Swabian, Franconian, and Hessian at various times.

Farther north is the heart of the **Palatinate** (*Pfalz*), which was ruled by the Count Palatine, the most senior official in the Holy Roman Empire, and one of the seven electors. The name of this old state lives on in the Land of Rhineland-Pfalz, but the original boundaries were very different. For five hundred years its capital was **Heidelberg**—now the best-loved of all German cities, and a place which definitely warrants several days' stay. The planned town of **Mannheim** was built as the new Palatine capital in the early eighteenth century, with **Schwetzingen**—whose fantastical gardens are unlike any other—used by the court in the summer months.

Bruchsal

It was the first time I had seen such architecture. The whole of next day I loitered about the building; hesitating half-way up shallow staircases balustraded by magnificent branching designs of wrought metal; wandering through double doors that led from state room to state room; and gazing with untutored and marveling eyes down perspectives crossed by the diminishing slants of winter sunbeams.

Patrick Leigh Fermor, *A Time of Gifts*

On his walk to Constantinople, Patrick Leigh Fermor struck it lucky at **BRUCHSAL**, staying as guest of the burgomaster in the resplendent baroque **Schloss**. His description reflects the fact that this is no ordinary palace; indeed, it's a complete courtly town, comprising over fifty different buildings, which stands as an oasis in the midst of the ugly modern community which now surrounds it.

Construction of the Schloss began in 1720 by order of the newly enthroned prince-bishop of Speyer, Cardinal Hugo Damian von Schönborn, who had fallen out with the local burghers, and so decided to move his seat across the Rhine to what was then no more than a hamlet in the heart of the Kraichgau region. A member of a dynasty which specialized in collecting bishoprics (six others were then in family hands), the cardinal was keen not to be outdone by his brother in Würzburg, who had also put the erection of a magnificent new residence for himself at the top of his list of priorities. Several talented architects were recruited to carry out the work, and the great **Bathasar Neumann** was occasionally seconded from his employment at Würzburg to supply the bravura touches needed to lift the project into the artistic first division.

The Schloss complex, whose cheerful yellow, red, and white buildings have been restored to pristine condition following their devastation in an air raid at the end of the war, stands on Schönbornstrasse, which leads north to Heidelberg. Along the eastern side of the street are a series of offices, with the chancellery center-stage; the army of lackeys lived in the large edifice to the south. At the northern end of the street is the **Damianstor** (a baroque reinterpretation of a fortified gateway), while a smaller triumphal arch gives access to the main courtyard. To the left is the **Hofkirche**, whose haughty onion-domed belfry towers over all the other buildings; the interior has unfortunately been modernized. On the opposite side is the **Kammerflügel**, where prestigious international **concerts** are often held.

However, the great reception rooms are all in the central **Corps de Logis** (Tues.–Sun. 9am–1pm and 2–6pm; DM2). Facing you on entry is Neumann's ingenious monumental **staircase**. This is very different from its Würzburg counterpart, being based on a great central cylinder. The lower section of this is laid out as a dark grotto, covered with antique-style frescos; you then ascend via walls richly covered with stucco to the airily bright oval landing. Here a brilliant *trompe l'oeil* fresco—an integral part of the overall design—apparently extends the height of the dome, extending a perspective into the open heavens. Painted by **Januarius Zick**, the most accomplished German decorative artist of the day, it eulogizes the history of the Speyer diocese. Neumann and Zick also collaborated on the two rooms off the staircase. The *Fürstensaal* is devoted to the supposedly wise government of the prince-bishops, while the *Marmorsaal*, which glitters with gold-leaf and colored marbles, pays tribute to the everlasting nature of the bishopric of Speyer by presenting it in the guise of Mount Olympus.

It's definitely worth paying the extra money to visit the **Museum of Mechanical Musical Instruments** (guided tours, lasting 1 hour, at 10am, 11am, noon, 2pm, 3pm, 4pm, and 5pm; DM5 including Schloss admission) which has recently been installed in some of the vacant rooms. Short demonstrations are given on a cross section of the 200-odd exhibits, which were regarded as scientific miracles in their own time. Earliest of these are the musical clocks which were much in favor in eighteenth-century courts such as Bruchsal itself, and for which even the greatest composers were forced to prostitute their talents— Haydn wrote a delightful set of miniatures, while Mozart created several profound masterpieces, which have to be played on a full-sized organ for maximum effect. From the turn of the present century are examples of the piano-roll system pioneered by the German *Firma Welte*, which enables the accurate playback of performances by famous pianists. This technique was later ambitiously adapted for the organ, and there's a marvelous instrument here which was formerly used to entertain guests in the *Hotel Excelsior* in Berlin.

Other than the Schloss, Bruchsal has very little to offer, the modern town center an illustration of how far standards in planning have slipped in recent years. However, it's worth crossing it (via Kaiserstrasse, then uphill over the stream) to see the oldest quarter, dominated by the twin onion towers of **St. Peter**, burial church of the prince-bishops. Designed by Neumann during one of his sorties to the town, its domed interior features elaborate altars and stucco work.

Bruchsal's **Bahnhof** is a junction on the railroad lines linking Stuttgart, Karlsruhe, and Heidelberg. To reach the Schloss from there, turn left and continue straight on; you'll reach the gardens within a few minutes. Alternatively, turn right on arriving at Kaiserstrasse; this soon brings you to the end of Scönbornstrasse. A **campground** and *Naturfreundehaus* are at Karlsruher Str. 215 (☎07251 15016) to the south of downtown. Cheapest **hotel** is *Graf Kuno*, Württemberger Str. 97 (☎07251 2013), charging from DM30 per head. For a meal or a drink, try *Zum Bären*, within the Schloss complex; it serves the best food in town and has a beer garden. The **tourist office** (Mon.–Weds. and Fri. 8am–noon and 2–4pm, Thurs. 8am–noon and 2–5pm; ☎07251 79301) is in a modern shopping center called *Bürgerzentrum*.

Bad Wimpfen

The prefix "Bad," used by hundreds of German towns as free publicity for the presence of spa facilities, immediately conjures up the image of geriatrics and hypochondriacs pottering around the manicured lawns of soulless white-walled sanitariums, with only the chirping of birds to disturb the deathly hush. **BAD WIMPFEN** has a spa quarter at its northern extremity which conforms to this stereotype, but is otherwise so totally different it seems strange the authorities want to use such a misleading designation. It certainly shouldn't be needed to draw visitors, as this pocket-sized town with a population of just a few thousand, built high above a bend in the Neckar marginally beyond the point where the Jagst flows in from the east, is a real visual treat, preserving a wonderful array of monuments as testament to its richly varied history. The site has been inhabited since prehistoric times; Romans, Frankish kings, and the bishops of Worms were later rulers, prior to its choice, from around 1200, as a favorite **residence of the Staufian emperors**. Some 150 years later Wimpfen was made a free imperial city, an independence it retained, courtesy of the lucrative salt trade, until the advent of Napoleon.

A century ago, Mark Twain found Wimpfen "very picturesque and tumble-down, and dirty and interesting." Only the first and last of these adjectives still hold good, an extensive program of restoration and scrubbing-up since having turned the town into a very desirable place to live. What's immediately impressive is the **skyline**, one of the most dramatic in Germany, equalled within Baden-Württemberg only by Heidelberg. It's best seen from the right bank of the Neckar, where its imperious towers give it the appearance of a miniature medieval Manhattan. This is particularly stunning when illuminated by night, giving you the sensation of being whisked back centuries in time. The very different vistas from the western approach roads are almost equally photogenic.

On leaving the **Bahnhof**, turn right and you're immediately on Hauptstrasse, the central street of the upper town, known as *Wimpfen am Berg*. About halfway up is the **Schwibbogen Tor**, which formerly gave access to the **Kaiserpfalz** (*Imperial Palace*). What isn't immediately obvious is that the medieval town grew up within the area formerly occupied by the court buildings, which were already in ruins. It's even more surprising that substantial portions of the palace remain to this day, ranking among the most important of the relatively few surviving examples of Romanesque civil architecture in Europe. The austere riverside wall, which had the advantage of a formidable natural barrier behind, survives largely intact. At its southern end, it's guarded by the **Nürnberger Türmchen**, named in honor of the relief offered by the citizens of Nürnberg to Wimpfen following the latter's sacking at the hands of Tilly in 1622, and by the **Roter Turm** (*Red Tower*), a gaunt box-like structure which was the last line of defence. From here, there's a fine view over the town and valley.

Further along is the **Kaiserkapelle** (April–Oct. daily 10am–noon and 2–4:30pm, closed Nov.–March; DM1), now containing a small museum of religious art. Photographs show how this building miraculously survived drastic conversions for use as a storeroom before being returned to its simple original form. The gallery was reserved for the emperor who could, if necessary, make a quick getaway through a passageway to the haven of the Roter Turm. Adjoining the chapel is the sole surviving part of the **Palast** itself—a weather-worn but still elegant row of arcades, each of whose paired columns is carved in a different manner.

Also from the Staufian epoch is the large **Steinhaus** (*Stone House*), which stands out among the later predominantly half-timbered buildings. Originally the home of the castle commandant, it was modernized in the sixteenth century by the addition of Gothic gables. It's currently fitted out as the local **museum** (April–Oct. Tues.–Sun. 10am–noon and 2–4pm; DM2), with exhibits from all periods of the town's history.

Diagonally opposite is the symbol of Wimpfen and the most potent reminder of its days of power and glory, the **Blauer Turm** (*Blue Tower*; April–Oct. Tues.–Sun. 9am–noon and 1:30–5pm; DM2). Named after the tints of the limestone used in its construction, this watchtower was all but destroyed in a fire in 1848, and was only made fully secure again in the 1970s. At noon on Sundays from April to September, the resounding live strains of a trumpeter playing chorales from the platform at the top can be heard throughout the streets.

The twin towers of the **Stadtkirche** are the last main features of the Romanesque part of Wimpfen's skyline; the rest of the building is a late Gothic hall church. Behind can be seen an emotional *Crucifixion* group, similar to the one its sculptor, Hans Backoffen, made for his own tomb in Mainz. Close by is the **Wormser Hof**, part of which is also Staufian; it was the residence of the administrator in the service of the bishop of Worms, with a barn to store the tithe of agricultural produce he collected. Nowadays, it's home to the 250 historic dolls of the **Puppenmuseum** (Wed, Sat., and Sun. 2–5pm; DM1).

It's worth sauntering round all the streets of the old town, which curve and plunge their way past half-timbered houses, baroque mansions and quiet squares with Renaissance fountains. Among the many surprising vistas, that from the **Adlerbrunnen** (*Eagle Fountain*) at the junction of Hauptstrasse and Salzgasse is particularly fine. The best-preserved street is **Klostergasse**, several of whose buildings have exterior galleries which formerly served as bath houses. Down Bollwerkgasse is the artillery bastion, built during the sixteenth century to designs by Dürer, no less. At the junction of Klostergasse and Langgasse is the **Konventhaus**; as a symbol of the concern shown by the citizens of Bad Wimpfen towards the displaced German-speaking peoples of Eastern Europe, part of this now houses a museum on "Ödenburg" (the Hungarian city of Sopron) and the area surrounding Lake "Neusiedl" (Fertö). For more information about these places as they are today, see *The Real Guide to Hungary*. Restoration work is being carried out on the monumental half-timbered fifteenth-century **Spital** on Hauptstrasse, in order that it can also become a museum in due course.

The lower town, known as *Wimpfen in Tal*, can be reached in ten minutes by foot from the Bahnhof by following the main road to the left. It's built around the great **Ritterstift St. Peter** (Mon.–Sat. 10am–noon and 3–5pm, Sun. 10:30am–noon and 3:30–5pm) which, after a break of five centuries, was repopulated in 1947 by Benedictine monks who had fled from Silesia. Come here during their services, which use the Gregorian chant, and Wimpfen's illusion of transporting you back in time will be complete.

The fortress-like facade of the **church**, with a huge porch and a pair of octagonal towers, dates from the tenth century; the rest of the building is a masterly French-inspired Gothic design. This is generally attributed to the near-legendary mason **Erwin von Steinbach** who built part of Strasbourg Cathedral; in Germany he's been regarded as a real celebrity among the largely obscure architects of the Middle Ages ever since Goethe penned a flowery prose-poem in his honor. Superb original sculptures can be seen on the south doorway and inside the chancel; the latter group includes then recently deceased Saint Francis of Asslsl. Access to the **cloister**, which has sections in each of the three phases of the Gothic style, is only allowed to groups who have booked in advance, but you can tag along with one of these (which are frequent during the summer) if you ask at the shop.

Wimpfen in Tal is the scene of one of Germany's oldest **popular festivals**: it's claimed the week-long *Talmarkt* in honor of Saints Peter and Paul (June 29 to July 5) has been celebrated every year since 965. Nowadays, the end is marked by a spectacular fireworks display. Two more fairs dating back to the Middle Ages are held in the center of *Wimpfen am Berg*—the *Hafenmarkt* for handicrafts at the end of August, and the *Weihnachtsmarkt* in December, which is a cut above the imitative versions found in practically every German town. *Fasching* also has a long tradition here; highlights are the Sunday parade and the evening celebrations on Ash Wednesday.

Provided you're not looking for a swinging nightlife, Bad Wimpfen makes a good place to stay, particularly as accommodation is cheap, with over twenty private houses—which are scattered all over town—offering **rooms** at DM25 per head or less; similar rates are available at *Pension Ute*, Erich-Sailer-Str. 23 (☎07063 222). The **youth hostel**, run by an exceptionally hospitable family, has an unbeatable location at Burgviertel 21–23 (☎07063 7069)—it's in an old half-timbered house built against the ramparts right beside the ruins of the Palast.

There's a clutch of **restaurants** serving hearty *bürgerlich* cuisine all down Hauptstrasse; *Klosterkeller* is the best and most expensive, whereas *Traube* at the end of the street is particularly good value. Alternatively, try *Kräuterweible* on Marktrain, well thought of by the locals for its chicken dishes. The **tourist office** (Mon.–Fri. 9am–noon and 2–4pm, also Sat. and Sun. April–Sept. 10am–noon and 2–4pm; ☎07063 7052) is in the Rathaus on Marktplatz, facing the Stadtkirche; they have free maps with English commentary. Ask here about **Neckar cruises**, which run both upstream and down throughout the summer months, departing from the jetty beside Neckarbrücke.

The route of the Neckar castles

Beyond Bad Wimpfen, the Neckar meanders through a gentle landscape of vineyards and market gardens; this later changes to one of thick craggy woodland as it cuts through central Germany's most extensive forest, the Odenwald. All of this is designated as a national park, the Baden-Württemberg section being known as the **Naturpark Neckartal-Odenwald**. A series of bleak castles on the heights above the river serve as a reminder of a feudal past, as well as a rich source of **legends**. Though this countryside is best seen from a boat, the train makes a good alternative, as it keeps close to the river most of the way to Heidelberg, a distance of some 70km.

On the right bank some 15km north of Bad Wimpfen is the small medieval town of **GUNDELSHEIM**, set in the shadow of **Schloss Horneck**, baroque successor to a fortress of the Teutonic Knights. The Bahnhof here is the nearest to the most interesting castle of the region, **Burg Guttenberg** (March–Nov. daily 9am–6pm; DM6); to reach it, you have to cross the bridge to the other side of the river. This building, with a tall narrow keep and an impressive curtain wall, dates back to the Staufian epoch, but has been much altered inside. Among its many curiosities are the wooden library, and a herbarium in which the plants were stored in a series of trick compartments. However, the castle's main claim to fame is for having Europe's largest collection of **birds of prey**—over a hundred in all. Each day at 11am and 3pm, there's an exhilarating demonstration of several of these birds in free flight under the control of Claus Fentzloff, reckoned to be a falconer without peer. Yet all this is not just for show—there has been a highly successful program for breeding endangered species, and an average of fifty birds per year are released back into the wild. If you'd like to hang around for a while, there's a good restaurant, set on a terrace commanding an extensive view over the valley.

The change in landscape to the Odenwald begins just before **NECKARZIMMERN**, 5km north of Gundelsheim. This village has the oldest of the Neckar castles, **Burg Hornberg** (April–Oct. daily 9am–5pm; DM2), home for 45 years of the great robber-baron, Götz von Berlichingen (see also p.280), whose armor is on display. Every so often, he would imperiously descend from his seat to confiscate the cargo of passing ships, distributing the profits to the poor; in his memoirs, he thanked to God for delivering particularly rich pickings at the times of greatest need. An earlier story associated with this castle is reminiscent of the Rhenish Lorelei legend—it tells of how the heiress fell in love with a poor crusader, but was forbidden to marry him, and escaped to live in a nearby cave, singing an anguished ballad written by her lover which the locals mistook for the cries of an evil specter. It was said that ill-luck befell anyone who heard the voice, but all the locals were too cowardly to try to kill the spirit. When the crusader returned from the Holy Land, he resolved to undertake the task, recognizing his own composition only after he had fired the fatal shot.

A few kilometers inland from Neckarzimmern, on the Elzbach tributary, is **MOSBACH**, which boasts an outstanding array of half-timbered houses. Its **youth hostel**, Am Sonnenrain 60 (☎06261 2940) on the hills overlooking the town to the south, makes a good cheap base for exploring the Odenwald.

North along the Neckar itself, a section of limestone cliffs presently gives way to the region's characteristic sandstone. Another 20km beyond is **ZWINGENBERG**, whose **Burg** (guided tours May–Sept. Tues., Fri., and Sun. 2–4:30pm, DM3) is the seat of the current holder of the now-meaningless title of Margrave of Baden. It occupies a picturesque setting above the village, and is impressively complete, with a thirteenth-century keep surrounded by a fifteenth-century defensive wall, along with various embellishments from later periods. Below is the **Wolfsschlucht** (*Wolf's Glen*), scene of the most famous Neckar legend. It was the haunt of the devil, disguised as Samiel, a wild huntsman. He would lure his victims by offering them seven of his magic bullets, which inevitably hit their target. The first six would do what the victims wanted; Samiel killed them with the seventh. Carl Maria von Weber, who visited the glen in 1810, made it the central scene scene of his opera *Der Freischütz* (the first full-blooded piece of Romanticism in musical history) a decade later.

At **EBERBACH**, 10km north, the Neckar deviates sharply from its hitherto northerly course, turning westwards towards the Rhine. This former free imperial city owed its growth and prosperity to sailing craft; its shipbuilders' guild is the second oldest in the country. The tradition lives on, albeit on a modest scale—most of the rowing boats used in the Olympic Games are made in Eberbach. Nowadays, the town's main function is as a health resort. For this reason, locals are especially proud of the thirteenth-century *Altes Badhaus* on Am Lindenplatz, the oldest intact public bath-house in Germany; it's now a hotel and restaurant. Other survivals from medieval times are the four corner towers of the fortifications, and a series of half-timbered buildings set in cobblestoned streets and squares. Eberbach also stakes a claim for its own footnote in British history, being the place where Queen Victoria was conceived—a fact commemorated by a plaque outside the *Haus Thalheim*, home of her parents. There's a **youth hostel** in the hills above at Richard-Schirrmann-Str. 6 (☎06271 2593), as well as a **campground** by the river (☎06271 1071), along with plenty of other cheap accommodation in private houses and inns.

A stretch of the northern bank which follows, including HIRSCHHORN, falls within Hessen. On the opposite bank 23km west of Eberbach is another former free imperial city, NECKARGEMÜND, now incorporating the quaint old village of **DILSBERG**. This is surrounded by walls, in one of whose towers is a **youth hostel** (☎06223 2133), which makes a possible base for visiting HEIDELBERG, just 15km away and connected by regular bus services. Dilsberg had a reputation for being able to withstand the most determined of besiegers (even managing to hold out against the much-feared Johann Tilly in the Thirty Years' War); tradition has it that this was thanks to a secret subterranean passage under the Neckar which led to a well-stocked storeroom. The ruined **Burg** (daily 9am–noon and 1–6pm; DM1) is associated with the legend of a practical joke which ended tragically. A young knight, betrothed to the niece of the lord of the castle, was utterly convinced that whoever slept in the "haunted chamber" would not wake up for fifty years. His mischievous friends gave him a sleeping draught, and put him to bed in a disused room hanging with cobwebs; they then dressed up as old folk, in order to fool him when he awoke shortly after. Having had their fun, they pulled off their disguises and subjected the shell-shocked youth to ridicule for his naivety. Alas, his mind had already snapped, and he was to spend the remaining years of his life in harmless insanity, comforted only by the girl who reminded him so much of what he believed to be his long-dead love.

Heidelberg

When the Romantic movement discovered **HEIDELBERG** in the late eighteenth century, the city was very much a fallen star. Capital of the Palatinate for 500 years, it had never fully recovered from two sackings at the hands of French troops in the previous century; its rulers had abandoned their magnificent, crumbling **Schloss** in favor of the creature comforts of their new palace in Mannheim. Yet this wistful feeling of decay only enhanced the charms of the city, majestically set on both banks of the swift-flowing Neckar between two ranges of wooded hills—a real-life fulfilment of the ideal German landscape, and a site known to be one of the earliest inhabited places in the world. Add to all this the fact that the city was home to the oldest **university** on German soil (which was the custodian of rich and bizarre traditions), and there was an intoxicatingly heady brew which not only stirred the Romantic imagination, but has seduced generations of travelers ever since, to an extent no other German city comes close to matching. To many of the rushed Grand Tour of Europe motorcoach parties of today, Heidelberg *is* Germany, the only place in the country they see.

For English-speaking visitors, the distinguished roll-call of predecessors gives Heidelberg special claims on the attention. Earliest of these was the Scots-born princess, **Elizabeth Stuart**, daughter of the first monarch of the United Kingdom, James VI and I. She arrived in 1613 as the seventeen-year-old bride of the Elector Palatine, and presided over a spectacular court life for five years, before leaving for Prague and her ill-fated spell as the "Winter Queen." Heidelberg's greatest painter is also Britain's greatest; **J.M.W. Turner** first came to the city in 1836, and, in a series of oils and watercolors, captured its changing moods and magical plays of light in his own inimitable way. Among Americans, **Mark Twain** deserves pride of place; he began the hilarious travels round Europe recounted in *A Tramp Abroad* in Heidelberg in 1878, and his descriptions of the city have never been surpassed. By this time, Heidelberg was already a popular sojourn for Americans visiting Europe, though the numbers were a trickle in comparison with the situation today. After World War II (in which, significantly, the city was spared from aerial bombardment), Heidelberg was chosen as the headquarters of the U.S. Army in Europe. Nowadays some 20,000 American nationals (about one in seven of the total population) live there, mostly in PATRICK HENRY VILLAGE, a purpose-built community to the south.

Practicalities and Orientation

Heidelberg is best avoided in high summer; the students, who make such an essential contribution to the life of the city, clear out then and are replaced by hordes of tourists. Surprisingly, it's possible to cover all the essential sights fairly quickly, but you should certainly plan on staying for at least several days, in order to soak up the city's atmosphere.

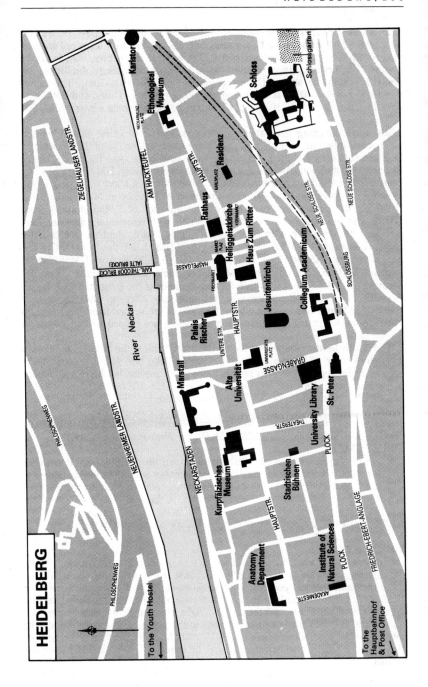

HEIDELBERG

Karlstor

Ethnological Museum

Schloss

Schlossgarten

NECKARMÜNZ PLATZ

ZIEGELHAUSER LANDSTR.

AM HACKTEUFEL

Residenz

HAUPTSTR.

KARLPLATZ

NEUE SCHLOSS STR.

Rathaus

Heiliggeistkirche

Haus Zum Ritter

KORNMARKT

NEUE SCHLOSS STR.

PHILOSOPHENWEG

KARL-THEODOR BRÜCKE
(ALTE BRÜCKE)

River Neckar

HASPELGASSE

FISCHMARKT

Collegium Academicum

SCHLOSSBURG

Jesuitenkirche

Palais Rischer

UNTERE STR.

HAUPTSTR.

Marstall

Alte Universität

UNIVERSITÄTS PLATZ

GRABENGASSE

St. Peter

NEUENHEIMER LANDSTR.

NECKARSTADEN

University Library

THEATERSTR.

PLÖCK

Kurpfälzisches Museum

Städtischen Bühnen

HAUPTSTR.

PLÖCK

Institute of Natural Sciences

FRIEDRICH-EBERT-ANLAGE

Anatomy Department

PLÖCK

AKADEMIESTR.

PHILOSOPHENWEG

To the Youth Hostel

To the Hauptbahnhof & Post Office

Be warned that first impressions of Heidelberg are likely to make you wonder what all the fuss is about; the **Hauptbahnhof** and intercity **bus terminal** are situated in an anonymous quarter some 1½km west of the center, with a dreary avenue, Kurfürsten-Anlage, leading towards town. **Exchange facilities** are available within the station (Mon.–Sat. 7am–8pm, Sun. 9am–1pm). The rather harrassed **tourist office** is on the square outside (Mon.–Thurs. and Sat. 9am–7pm, Fri. 9am–9pm, Sun. 10am–6pm in summer, 10am–3pm in winter; ☎21341 or 27735).

It's worth checking here about accommodation possibilities; although there are **hotels** dotted all over the city, these are often booked solid. If you want to look yourself, glance at the chart outside the tourist office, which tells you where vacancies exist. A couple of budget options, charging around DM20 for a bed in a small dorm, are *Krokodil*, Kleinschmidstr. 12 (☎24059), a short walk away in the direction of downtown, and *Jeske*, in the heart of the city at Mittelbadgasse 2 (☎23733); the former also has singles from upwards of DM35, doubles from DM55. The few other conveniently-sited hotels with reasonable rates are *Zum Weinberg*, Heliggeiststr. 1 (☎21792), with singles DM35, doubles DM55; *Roter Hahn*, Haupstr. 44 (☎24157), singles upwards of DM40, doubles from DM70; and *Elite*, Bunsenstr. 15 (☎25734), singles from DM40, doubles from DM55. *Frisch*, Jahnstr. 34 (☎400327), charging DM36 for a single, DM65 a double, is on the northern side of the Neckar, within walking distance of the Hauptbahnhof, but all the other cheaper options are well out, and may offer no advantages over commuting from another town. Otherwise, ask in the second-hand clothes shop *Flic-Flac* at Unterestr. 12, where young travelers are helped to find rooms in private houses.

The **youth hostel** is near the Zoo on the north bank of the Neckar, about 4km from the center at Tiergartenstr. 5 (☎412066); take bus #11. It's large, fairly luxurious and very liberal—not only is there a late curfew, but there's also a bar in the basement. If it's full, as is regularly the case, you'll find another hostel in DILSBERG, 15km down the Neckar (see p.261); the hostel in MANNHEIM (see p.278) is also close enough to make commuting cost-effective. Both **campgrounds** are east of the city by the river—*Heide* (☎06223 2111) is between ZIEGEL-HAUSEN and KLEINGEMÜND; *Neckertal* (☎802506) is in SCHLIERBACH.

If you're staying far out, the 36-hour ticket on the **public transit** network makes a good investment; it costs DM6 for journeys within the city boundaries, DM10 for the full circuit. The Altstadt is completely pedestrianized; tram #1 takes you from the Hauptbahnhof to Bismarckplatz, at the western end of the long, straight Hauptstrasse. Alternatively, bus #11 goes to Universitätsplatz on the southern side of the old city, bus #34 to Kornmarkt at the eastern end.

Viewpoints

Heidelberg is a ready-made subject for picture-postcard **photography**; with its hilly setting, there are plenty of angles to choose from. If you take the trouble to go to the same vantage point at different times of day, you'll see the reason for Heidelberg's hold on painters: the red sandstone buildings change their hue with the movement of the sun, and the shafts of light make magical effects as they illuminate and cast into shadow different parts of the scene. "One thinks Heidelberg by day the last possibility of the beautiful," wrote Mark Twain, "but when he sees Heidelberg by night, a fallen Milky Way. . . he requires time to consider upon the verdict."

The best-known view is from the northern quays of the Neckar, where you get a full-frontal panorama of the Altstadt nestling snugly below the Schloss, itself sharply etched against the background of the wooded Königstuhl. The spectacle from street level is surpassed by climbing up the slopes of the Heiligenberg via the celebrated **Philosophenweg** (*Philospopher's Walk*), so-called because of the stimulus it offered to the meditation of Heidelberg thinkers.

As an alternative, start from the town center, and follow Neue Schloss Strasse and Molkenkurweg to the *Molkenkur Hotel*, whose terrace gives a very different perspective. Farther up, the Königstuhl is crowned by a **Television Tower** (March–Oct. daily 10am–5pm; DM1), commanding a sweeping panorama over the Neckar valley and Odenwald.

The Schloss

Centerpiece of all the views of Heidelberg is the **Schloss**, one of the world's great castles ... "with empty window arches, ivy-molded battlements, moldering towers—the Lear of inanimate nature—deserted, discrowned, beaten by the storms, but royal still, and beautiful," to quote Mark Twain. A series of disparate yet consistently magnificent buildings of various dates, it somehow hasn't been diminished by its ruined condition; if anything, it has actually grown in stature. Enough remains (with the help of the plentiful pictorial records which exist) to give a clear idea of what it looked like in its prime, yet a new dimension has been added by the destruction, which reveals otherwise hidden architectural secrets, and magnifies its umbilical relationship with the surrounding landscape.

The Schloss originally dates back to the first quarter of the thirteenth century. It was then that the title of **Count Palatine**, the most senior office under the Holy Roman Emperor, and one carrying the status of an elector, was bestowed on a Wittelsbach, Duke Ludwig of Bavaria, whose family retained the dignatory right to the end of the Holy Roman Empire. The earliest significant portions of what can be seen today date from the following century, as the castle evolved into a sturdy medieval fortress capable of withstanding the most powerful siege weapons of the day. During the sixteenth century, the inner courtyard of the Schloss began to be embellished with sumptuous palatial buildings, as its role as a princely residence became of increasing importance; this gathered momentum in mid-century when the electors converted to Protestantism, and began the construction of the most splendid **Renaissance buildings** in Germany.

Lutheranism was later jettisoned in favor of Calvinism, and the **Heidelberg Cathecism** of 1562 remains the basic creed for many Reformed churches. This took on an increasingly militant aspect when Elizabeth Stuart's youthful husband, **Friedrich V**, became nominal leader of the Calvinist League, which aimed to establish the irreversible supremacy of Protestantism in Germany, and to topple the Habsburgs from their position of pre-eminence in the country's affairs. Friedrich's ham-fisted attempt to establish a Protestant, anti-Habsburg majority in the Electoral college by usurping the Bohemian throne in 1618 was not only a personal disaster (he was defeated, exiled, and stripped of his titles), but also it led to the Thirty Years' War, which devastated the country. However, it was French designs on the Palatinate in 1689 which led to the destruction of Heidelberg and its Schloss; although their claim on the territory was eventually withdrawn, the Electorship passed to a Catholic branch of the family. Unable to establish a rapport with the locals, they moved their seat; the planned rebuilding of the Schloss never occurred, and Heidelberg was left to vegetate for the next century.

The Schloss can be reached by funicular from the Kornmarkt for DM3.50 return, but it's more fun to walk up via the Burgweg; that way, you can make a complete circuit of the exterior before entering. At the northwest corner is the sixteenth century **Dicker Turm** (*Fat Tower*), now a semicircular shell, its outer wall, along with its top, having been blasted away. Behind the northern fortifications you get a glimpse of the Renaissance buildings, and pass the Arsenal, before coming to the **Redoute**, built just a few years before the Schloss was destroyed. Behind it stands the **Glockenturm** (*Bell Tower*), originally a single-story defense tower, to which six residential levels were later added. It's a very early skyscraper—pressure of space within the castle was the sole reason for the need to build upwards.

Continuing along the eastern side, you see the protruding **Apothekerturm**, an old defensive tower which was later converted into the apothecary plus residential quarters. Between it and the Glockenturm is a superb oriel window, part of a now-vanished banqueting hall. At the southeastern corner is the most romantic of the ruins, the **Pulver Turm** (*Powder Tower*), now generally know as the **Gesprengter Turm** (*Blown-up Tower*). Originally a gunpowder store, it was destroyed by miners who tunneled underneath and blew it up from the center. This left a clean break in the now-overgrown masonry; the collapsed section still lies intact in the moat, leaving a clear view into the chambers of the interior, with their once-elegant central column supports.

From here, it's best to proceed to the western side of the Schloss, an artificial plateau formerly used as a gun battery, but converted by Friedrich V into a pleasure garden. At its entrance is the graceful Roman-inspired **Elizabethpforte**, a gateway said to have been erected in a single night in 1615 as a surprise for the princess; the sober **Englischer Bau** adjoining the Dicker Turm was also built in her honor. At the western end of the garden is the semicircular **Rondell**, commanding a view over the rooftops of the city.

The **Schlosshof** (free access at all times; guided tours of interiors, some in English, daily 9am–5pm; DM4) is reached by a series of sixteenth-century defensive structures—the Brückenhaus, the bridge itself, and the severe **Thorturm** (*Gate Tower*), the only part of the Schloss not blown up. It's an immediately impressive sight, every bit the equal of Heidelberg's long-range views, where the famous palatial buildings are either half-hidden, or out of sight altogether. Immediately to the left of the entrance is the Gothic **Ruprechtsbau**, where you can see two restored chambers, one with an elaborate chimneypiece. After the ruined library comes the **Frauenzimmerbau**, where the women of the court resided; its colossal hall has been restored as a concert venue. Looking counter-clockwise from the entrance gate, you first of all see the Gothic **Brunnenhaus** (*Well House*), a loggia with a graceful star vault. Its marble columns were brought from Charlemagne's palace at Ingelheim (near Mainz), and had previously adorned a Roman building. This is followed by a series of functional buildings— the **Kaserne** (*Barracks*) and the **Oekonomiebau**, which housed offices and workshops; part of it has been converted to the *Weinstube Schloss Heidelberg*, one of the best restaurants in town, and surprisingly reasonable in price.

What really catches your eye in the courtyard, however, is the group of Renaissance palaces on the north and east sides. Next to the Oekonomiebau is the mid-sixteenth-century **Ottheinrichsbau**, now just a shell, but preserving its vigorous horizontal facade. The magnificent sculptural decoration by the Fleming Alexander Colin has successive tiers of allegorical figures representing Strength, the Christian Virtues, and the Planetary Deities. In the basement is the German **Apothecary Museum** (April–Oct. daily 10am–5pm, Nov.–March Sat. and Sun.

only 11am–5pm; DM2), an offbeat but thoroughly worthwhile collection. Among the displays are several complete baroque and rococo workshops from different parts of Germany, an early seventeenth-century traveling pharmacy, and an Herbarium. You can also descend to the bowels of the Apothekenturm, which has been rigged out with a furnace and distilling apparatus in an attempt to re-create its old appearance.

The triple loggia of the earlier **Saalbau** forms a link to the celebrated, late sixteenth-century **Friedrichsbau**. With its strong vertical emphasis, this is a perfect counterbalance to the Ottheinrichsbau. It's a swaggering Mannerist composition handled with superb aplomb by the Alsatian architect Johannes Schoch; he paid respect to the past by using the three great orders of classical antiquity, yet also anticipated the baroque in the intersecting pillars, with their dependency on the effects of light and shade. A series of bucolic, larger-than-life statues by the Swiss sculptor Sebastian Götz is a pantheon of the House of Wittelsbach, beginning with Charlemagne (the alleged founder of the dynasty) and continuing right up to the ruling elector. Those now on view are copies, but the originals can be seen inside, along with a number of restored rooms which have been decked out in period style. On the ground floor is the intact **Schlosskapelle**, which, in total contrast to the facade, harks back to the Gothic period; not surprisingly, in view of the photo opportunities outside, it's now a popular venue for weddings.

The **Fassbau** (daily April–Oct. 9am–7pm, Nov–March 9am–6pm; DM1, but included in price of guided tours) is down a passageway facing the Schlosshof. It contains the famous **Great Vat**, said to be the largest wine barrel in the world with a capacity of over 50,000 gallons; this is crowned with a platform which did service as a dance floor. Made in the late eighteenth century, the vat is the third in a spectacular line; though a folly and long out-of-service, it's reputed to have been filled on at least one occasion, when there was a particularly good grape harvest in the Palatinate (whose elector was entitled to claim a tithe). Facing the entrance, as a ploy to elicit a gasp from visitors when they turn the corner and see the real thing, is the so-called **Little Vat**, itself of ample proportions.

The University

In comparison with the Schloss, other Heidelberg monuments can seem prosaic; although the old layout of the medieval city survives, the French devastation means that nearly all the buildings are eighteenth-century or later, and are excessively sober in style. Nevertheless, an enjoyable idea for a stroll is to look around the places associated with the city's academic tradition. To many people, these are familiar from the Hollywood version of *The Student Prince* by the Hungarian-American composer Sigmund Romberg. Its lushest melodies were sung by the ringing golden tenor voice of Mario Lanza, and had to be dubbed on to the sound-track, as he was by then far too old and obese to play the dashing hero.

The **University** is officially known as the *Ruperto-Carola*, in honor of its two founders. It was established in 1386 by the Elector Ruprecht I; this makes it the oldest in what is now Germany. Thereafter, its future was closely tied to that of the Palatinate electors, becoming a great center of humanism and of the Reformation, but falling into decline during the eighteenth century. It was revived in 1803 by Grand Duke Karl Friedrich as the first state university of Baden. In spite of the vicissitudes of German history since then, it has managed to preserve its reputation, largely escaping the strictures so often leveled at what's normally regarded as the failure of the West German higher educational system. Heidelberg's is particularly renowned in the natural sciences, where it has nurtured a stream of Nobel Prize winners; it was also here, under Max Weber, that sociology was developed as an academic discipline.

One side of Universitätsplatz in the heart of the old town is occupied by the **Alte Universität**, dating back to the first quarter of the eighteenth century. The rest of the square, in the middle of which is the **Löwenbrunnen** (*Lion Fountain*), is occupied by the Neue Universität. This was erected in 1931 thanks to American munificence; Henry Ford was a prominent contributor. With the postwar boom in higher education, it has proved to be hopelessly small, and a new campus had to be laid out along the Neckar northwest of town. The **University Library** (Mon.–Fri. 8:30am–10pm, Sat. 9am–5pm; free) is down Grabengasse to the south of the square, with the entrance for temporary exhibitions round the corner on Plöck. These vary widely in appeal, but in summer there's generally a display centerd on some of the treasures of the collection. Particularly outstanding is the fourteenth-century *Codex Manesse*; apart from containing 137 beautiful miniatures, it ranks as the most important collection of Middle High German poetry. Across the road from the library is the Gothic university church of **St. Peter**, while diagonally opposite is the baroque **Collegium Academicum**, originally a seminary, now a student residence.

Following Plöck in a westerly direction, you come to the former **Institute of Natural Sciences** at the junction with Akadamiestrasse. Heidelberg's most famous scientist, **Robert Wilhelm Bunsen**, was based there for four decades. His name is familiar to school pupils all over the world for popularizing that staple gadget of the laboratory, the "Bunsen burner"; he was also the first to separate the colors of the spectrum. Facing you on Hauptstrasse at the end of Akadamiestrasse is the nineteenth-century building of the **Anatomy Department**, occupying the site of a Dominican monastery which had been hastily converted a few decades before, with its church used for dissections, and its sacristy as a morgue.

At no. 151 on Hauptstrasse, while still a student, **Clemens Brentano** and his brother-in-law **Achim von Arnim** put together the collection of folk-poetry known as *Des Knaben Wunderhorn* ("The Boy's Magic Horn") in the years 1805–8. This was to be a key influence on the future evolution of German Romanticism. It directly inspired the research of the Brothers Grimm, whose prose folk-tales (being more amenable to translation) have gained a far wider international fame. However, the work of Arnim and Brentano has been spread by the composer Gustav Mahler, who gave the verses idiomatic tunes and cloaked them in succulent orchestral colors. Several found their way into his symphonies, which are now among the most hip parts of the orchestral repertoire.

The oddest of Heidelberg's **traditions** was the fact that, until the present century, its students were not subject to civil jurisdiction. This meant that when a crime or breach of the peace was committed, the offender had to be dealt with by the university authorities. Moreover, when found guilty, the student did not need to serve his punishment immediately; he could do so at his leisure. Nor was there any stigma attached to imprisonment—indeed, it was seen as an essential component of the university experience. Nobody knows how this system came into being, but it presumably dates back to the times when most alumni were aristocratic, and subject to the mores of *noblesse oblige*. Now a protected monument, the **Students' Prison** (*Studentenkarzer*; Mon.–Sat. 9am–5pm; DM1) is at the back of the Alte Universität on Augustinergasse. This was used from 1712 to 1914, by which time every available square centimeter of the walls of the otherwise spartan cells had been covered with graffiti, with a black silhouette self-portrait of the prisoner the most popular motif.

The **Palais Rischer** on Unterestrasse was the most famous venue for a second Heidelberg tradition, and one which spread throughout Germany—the **Mensur**, or fencing match. Students were divided into fraternities according to the region of their birth; the members wore a distinguishing cap, and were forbidden from socializing with those belonging to other groups. At least three (in practice, far more) duels were held on two days of every week. Each bout lasted for fifteen minutes, excluding stoppages, unless it became dangerous to proceed; if the outcome was inconclusive, it had to be restaged at a later date. The combatants wore goggles, and every vital organ was padded, so that the risk of death was minimal. They were then placed at arm's length from each other, and fought by moving their wrists alone; to flinch or to step back were the ultimate disgraces. Wounds were frequent, particularly on the top of the head and left cheek; these were treated immediately by a surgeon or medical student. What was really bizarre was that the wounds became highly prized badges of courage; for optimum prestige, salt was rubbed into them, leaving scars which would remain for life. Foreign commentators have continuously poured scorn on this tradition—Patrick Leigh Fermor described it as "duelling which wasn't duelling at all, of course, but tribal sacrification. Those dashing scars were school ties that could never be taken off . . ." Mark Twain characteristically pilloried it for a very different reason, pointing out that the French concept of a duel to the death in reality led to no-one being hurt at all. The anachronistic ideal of chivalry that is the *Mensur* precariously staggers on, however, among right-wing toffs, while its effects can still be seen on elderly professorial brows.

Another tradition associated with the fencing corps was the **Kneipe**, a stag party where competition was confined within the group. The idea was to down as many mugs of beer as possible in a given space of time; the winner became the *Bierkönig*. As the rules were concerned solely with emptying the contents of the glass down the throat, and not about retaining the alcohol in the system, those who didn't mind the agony of consistently vomiting were able to accomplish prodigious totals of close to one hundred pints in an evening. Several **taverns** (see below) which were the scene of these bouts still exist; they're sights in themselves, with their faded photos and daguerrotypes, their trophies, swords, pads, helmets, and miscellaneous paraphernalia.

Other monuments

The finest surviving buildings in the Altstadt are grouped on Marktplatz. In the middle is the red sandstone **Heiliggeistkirche**, which was founded a decade after the University; its lofty tower, capped by a baroque dome, is one of the city's most prominent landmarks. Note the tiny shopping booths between its buttresses, a feature ever since the church was built—this was a common practice in medieval times, but has been frowned upon for so long that examples are now rare. Inside, it's light, airy, and uncluttered, but was not always so, as the church was built to house the mausoleum of the Palatinate electors. Only one tomb now remains—that of Ruprecht III, who became King of Germany, and his wife, Elizabeth von Hohenzollern. Furthermore, the triforium gallery once housed one of the great libraries of the world, the *Bibliotheca Palatina*; this was confiscated by Tilly as war booty, and presented to the Pope. Some items were returned last century, but the finest books remain in the Vatican.

Facing the church is the only mansion to survive the seventeenth-century devastations of the town, the **Haus zum Ritter**, so called from the statue of Saint George dressed as a knight which crowns the pediment. Built for a Huguenot refugee cloth merchant, it was clearly modeled on the Ottheinrichsbau in the Schloss to which, with its extravagant decoration of oriels, caryatids, scrollwork, and fancy gables, it stands as a worthy competitor. Now a hotel, it completely outclasses its baroque neighbors, among which is the **Rathaus** on the eastern side of the square. Plenty more baroque mansions can be found dotted all over the Altstadt; most notable is the **Residenz** of the grand dukes of Baden on Karlsplatz, which now houses the German Academy of Sciences and Letters. The most eye-catching baroque building, however, is the **Alte Brücke**, reached from the Marktplatz down Steingasse. Dating from the 1780s, it's at least the fifth on this site; in the last war, it suffered the inevitable fate of being blown up but has been painstakingly rebuilt. Particularly notable is its fairy-tale monumental gate-way—the twin towers and portcullis are reminiscent of medieval fortifications, but the ornamental bell-shaped roofs betray a lack of any defensive purpose. It's just the sort of building favored by the elector Carl Theodor, the creator of Schwetzingen. Near the next bridge upstream is the neoclassical **Karlstor**, a triumphal arch in his honor, designed by the court architect Nicolas de Pigage.

Housed in the **Palais Morass** at Hauptstr. 97, an early eighteenth-century mansion built for a law professor, is the **Kurpfälzisches Museum** (Tues., Weds., and Fri.–Sun. 10am–5pm, Thurs. 10am–9pm; DM1). It's best kept until the end of your stay, as it provides an effective summing-up of what you have seen. The archaeology section includes a cast of the jawbone of *Homo heidelbergiensis* (the original is owned by the university); this is estimated to come from the inter-glacial period 500,000 years ago, making it one of the oldest human bones ever discovered. On the first floor is a room devoted to the history of the Palatinate. The intact Schloss can be seen in a large documentary picture from the early seventeenth century; it also turns up in the background of Jan. Brueghel's exquisite *Allegory of Summer*. There are sensitive portraits of Elizabeth Stuart and her family by both the Honthorst brothers, dating from her exile in Holland when she was extolled as "The Queen of Hearts" by a whole generation of galants. From here, you pass through a suite of period rooms before seeing the museum's prize possession, the limewood *Altar of the Twelve Apostles* by **Tilman Riemenschneider**. For centuries masked under a thick coat of polychromy, it was only recognized as the work of the master about a generation ago; it has since been returned to its original unpainted state, revealing a wonderful sense of characterization and pathos in each of the figures.

The **Jesuitenkirche** on Schulgasse is, like the Palais Morass and the nearby Alte Universität, the work of Johann Adam Breunig. It's in the sombre style favored by this evangelizing order, who came here with the intention of recapturing Heidelberg for Catholicism, a mission which doesn't seem to have been particularly successful. Housed in its gallery and the adjoining monastery is a rather moderate **Museum of Sacred Art** (May–Oct. Tues.–Sat. 10am–5pm, Sun. 12:15–5pm, Nov.–Apr. Sat. 1–5pm and Sun. 12:15–5pm only; DM2.50).

Another baroque building, the **Palais Weimar** at Hauptstr. 235 contains the **Ethnological Museum** (Tues.–Sat. 3–5pm, Sun. noon–1pm; DM1), with good African collections. By now, there should be a museum in the birthplace in Pfaffengasse of **Friedrich Ebert**, a journeyman saddler who, in the traumatic period following defeat in World War I, simultaneously became the first social democrat to come to power in Germany, and the country's first freely-elected leader. Alas, this is one romantic Heidelberg story without a happy ending; Ebert was unequal to the superhuman task of curbing the reactionary vested interests that held a stranglehold over German society at the time, and a scurrilous hate campaign mounted by the press hounded him to an early grave.

Eating, Drinking, and Entertainments

Heading the list of nightlife attractions must be the **festivals** using the Schloss as a backdrop. On the first Saturdays of June and September, and the second in July, there are firework displays and historical pageants; these attract horrendously large crowds, but are highly enjoyable all the same. From late July until the end of August, there are open-air concerts and opera performances (inevitably, *The Student Prince* is included) in the Schlosshof at 8pm on most evenings (☎58976 for tickets and information); in bad weather, they're transferred indoors.

Hauptstrasse and the adjacent sidestreets are jammed with places of entertainment to suit all tastes; there's no better place for a bar hop in all of Germany. The much-ballyhooed **student taverns** are a must; they're perfectly genuine and are still patronized by the leftovers of the old fraternities, even if parties of tourists now make up the bulk of the clientele. All serve homely food, with basic dishes available at reasonable prices. At the eastern end of Hauptstrasse are the two most famous pubs—*Zum Sepp'l* at no. 213, which has been used by the student corps continuously since 1634; and *Roter Ochsen* at no. 217. Now an expensive hotel, *Hirschgasse* on the street of the same name (north of the Neckar) dates back to the fifteenth century; it has a hall still used for duelling. Less celebrated, and consequently less touristed, is the oldest of the taverns, founded only a couple of decades after the university, *Schnookeloch* at Haspelgasse 8 (on the northern bank of the Neckar).

Among other traditional **restaurants**, *Perkeo* at Hauptstr. 75 is particularly notable; it's named after one of Heidelberg's great characters, the dwarf Clementino Perkeo, custodian of the immediate predecessor of the Great Vat. At no. 115 on the same street is *Güldenes Schaf*, which features an excellent menu of game dishes. Across Bismarckplatz is Bergheimer Strasse at whose western end are two top-class places serving traditional fare—*Zieglerbräu* at no. 1b, again noted for game, and *Denner* at no. 8, which features fish specialties. For cheaper eating, try *Essighaus*, Plöck 97, or *Goldener Hecht*, Steingasse 2. There's a vegetarian restaurant at Kurfürsten-Anlage 9 (closed weekends).

The largest selection of local **wines** is available in *Brunn*, a shop at Bergheimerstr. 35; their own sparkling vintage is called *Perkeo-Sekt*. Oldest winebar in town is the eighteenth-century *Schnitzelbank* at Bauamtsgasse 7, while the one with the best food is in the cobbled courtyard setting of the *Kurpfälzisches Museum*. For a more relaxed atmosphere, try *Abel's* at Hauptstr. 133, where you can sit outside. If you prefer **beer**, *Biermuseum* at Hauptstr. 143 has 101 varieties to choose from, ten of them on tap. *Vetters*, Steingasse 9, has its own small house brewery which makes Pils, Bock, and Weizen. Most other pubs in the city serve the products of Heidelberg's main brewery, *Schlossquell*; these are made from spring water and have a soft, delicate flavor.

Cafés are similarly thick on the ground, though their tradition is much shorter. The mid-nineteenth-century *Knösel*, Haspelgasse 20, is the oldest; its specialty is *Heidelberger Studentenkuss*, a dark chocolate filled with praline and nougat. *Schaftheutele*, Hauptstr. 94, has its own garden, and is celebrated for its marzipan fancies. *Café 7* on Marktplatz is best-known for its ice creams; it also has a branch which forms part of *Perkeo*. There's a modern re-creation of palm-court days in

Palmbräuhaus at Hauptstr. 185, complete with resident pianist. Many other cafés have converted to a bistro set-up, and are popular with students and other young people. The crowded *Café Journal*, Hauptstr. 162, is the best of these; it also offers a wide selection of international newspapers. *Hard Rock Café*, Hauptstr. 142, is more American in feel; it has huge pop video screens, and serves delicious baguettes.

For the most sophisticated nightspots, there's again a wide choice. **Live jazz** is performed at *Cave 54*, Krämergasse 2, with full-scale concerts on Monday and Tuesday evenings. It also features, alternating with rock, at *Doctor Flotte*, Hauptstr. 130. **Cabaret** can be seen at *Alte Krone*, Brückenkopfstr. 1. **Discos** include *Time*, Fahrtgasse 18, and *Club 1900*, Hauptstr. 117. The most adventurous cocktails in Heidelberg are served at *Trinidad*, Friedrich-Ebert-Anlage 62.

Classical music concerts are held in the modern *Kongresshaus Stadthalle* overlooking the Neckar. The *Heidelberger Kammerorchester* is a Mozartian-sized orchestra of good standing, even if their programs tend to be conservative. At the main **theater**, the *Städtischen Bühnen* on Theaterstrasse (☎58279/20519), there's a varied mixture of plays, opera, operetta, and performances by an experimental *corps de ballet*. Straight drama is also offered at the tiny *Zimmertheater*, Hauptstr. 118, and the *Landfriedhaus*, Bergheimerstr. 147. Productions for **kids** are performed at the *Heidelberger Kinder und Jugendtheater*, Zwingerstr. 3–5. There are several **movie theaters** on Hauptstrasse.

Listings

Area code (☎06221).

Bike rental available at the Hauptbahnhof for DM10, or DM5 with rail ticket.

Bookshops try around Sofienstrasse and Universitätsplatz.

Car breakdown (☎19211) for 24-hr. service.

Car rental *Avis*, Bahnhofstr. 2 (☎22215); *Hertz*, Bergheimer Str. 144 (☎23434); *InterRent*, Bergheimer Str. 159 (☎20845).

Cultural institute *Amerika Haus*, Sophienstr. 12 (☎24771).

Festivals Apart from those in the Schloss (see above), there are various fairs held on Karlsplatz—*Heidelberger Frühling* (early June); *Weindorf* (mid-Sept.); *Heidelberger Herbst* (late Sept.). The climax of *Carnival* (variable date Feb./March) is the Rose Monday parade; there's another procession through the streets on the third Sunday before Easter.

Gardens *University Botanical Gardens*, Im Neuenheimer Feld (Mon.–Thurs. and Sun. 9am–noon and 1–4pm). *Zoo*, Tiergartenstrasse (April–Oct. daily 9am–7pm, Nov.–March daily 9am–5pm; DM6, kids DM3).

Kids *Märchenparadies* on top of the Königstuhl (mid-March–mid-Oct. daily 10am–6pm; DM3, kids DM2) is an adventure playground featuring fairy-tale characters and a miniature railroad.

Markets Weds. and Sat. on Marklplatz, Tues. and Fri. on Friedrich-Ebert-Platz.

Mitfahrzentrale Kurfürsten-Anlage 57 (☎24646).

Neckar cruises leave from the quay beside the Stadhalle mid-May to mid-Sept., run by *Rhein-Neckar-Fahrgastschiffahrt* (☎20181) and *Personenschiffahrt Hornung* (☎480064). A 45-minute local sail costs DM5; the round trip to Neckarsteinach, DM15.

Post office Main branch with general delivery is beside Hauptbahnhof; others are on Universitätsplatz and Sofienstrasse.

Shopping Untere Strasse is the trendiest street, featuring some amazing second-hand clothes shops, with quality ballgowns and hats available at knock-down prices. Apart from *Flic-Flac*, mentioned above, look out for *Py*, with an eye-swimming array of sunglasses from the Fifties.

Sports The main swimming pool is beside the Zoo. Tennis has recently become a Heidelberg mania, as the two German superstars Boris Becker and Steffi Graf, both come from villages just outside the city. Grand Prix motor racing takes place at nearby HOCKENHEIM.

Travel agencies *American Express*, Friedrich-Ebert-Anlage 16 (☎29001); *HS Reisebüro*, Bismarckplatz (☎27151) does student deals.

What's happening the tourist office publishes a weekly *Heidelberg diese Woche*, priced DM0.50.

Schwetzingen

There's nothing quite like the gardens of **SCHWETZINGEN**. This town, which lies 12km west of Heidelberg, was first associated with the counts Palatine in the fourteenth century, but was of very minor significance until the 1740s. There isn't even anything remarkable about the **Schloss**, a rather cut-price palace designed earlier in the eighteenth century by the Heidelberg architect Johann Adam Breunig, whose coat of pinkish-orange paint is a rather desperate attempt to make it appear more striking than it is.

Schwetzingen's stunning transformation from its long history of mediocrity was due to the new elector, **Carl Theodor**, who inherited the Palatinate from his childless uncle, and later became a somewhat reluctant Elector of Bavaria as well, when another branch of his family died out. His goal was to prevent the excessive dominance of Germany by either Prussia or Austria. This made him a thorn in the flesh of the ever-ambitious Frederick the Great, who derided him as "a lucky dog," commenting bitterly that "without drawing his sword even once that lazy fellow has gained more territory than I have been able to do in three wars, one of which lasted seven years." If Carl Theodor's political achievements were ultimately in vain (the Palatinate was carved up just two years after his death in 1799), his track record as a patron of the arts has proved far more enduring. The most important decision he took was to make Schwetzingen his summer residence, and to embellish it with the pleasure park he craved yet was unable to have in his fortified seat at Mannheim.

The **Schloss Gardens** (daily during official summertime 8am–8pm, rest of year 9am–5/6pm; DM2) are a supreme triumph of the art of landscaping and of the rococo style, representing a highly original escape into a world of pure fantasy. It took some thirty years to lay out the gardens and adorn them with a series of whimsical buildings. These aimed at capturing the atmosphere of various far-off civilizations; this fascination with the exotic marks out Schwetzingen as one of the precursors of the budding Romantic movement. Best time to see the gardens is late spring—the lilac, ivy, and chestnut trees are a riot of color in May, while the linden trees are at their most fragrant during June. High summer can be uncomfortably crowded; off-season, you might have the park to yourself, but, in addition to the absence of bloom, the pavilions are then kept locked.

The **Schlosstheater** (guided tours in summer at times listed on noticeboard; DM2) was added to the main building by **Nicolas de Pigage**, an ingenious architect from Lorraine who arrived in Schwetzingen in 1750, and spent much of the next three decades constructing its garden buildings. In an individual confection, mixing rococo with neoclassicism, Pigage built a triple-tiered auditorium in the shape of a lyre, facing a deep stage harboring complicated machinery underneath. It was originally intended for the performance of French comedies, and Voltaire, a personal friend of the elector, was a regular visitor.

With its grand dimensions, long vistas, straight avenues and symmetrical layout, the French-style **formal garden** is very much a product of the Age of Reason. It's richly endowed with fountains (which play daily in summer), mock-antique urns, and a host of mythological and allegorical statues, some of which are masterpieces. In a shady grove to the northwest of the circle is a sensuous nude *Galatea*, being eyeballed by a lustful old Triton, the work of Giovanni de Grupello; nearby is a gently mocking *Pan* carved by the Mannheim sculptor Simon Lamine. Just west of here is the **Grove of Apollo**, which served as an open-air auditorium. A sunken garden with sphinxes leads to an artificial mound crowned by a temple in the style of Classical Rome housing a statue of the god.

This is the first in a row of buildings by Pigage; alongside is one of his finest works, the **Bath House** (daily in summer 10am–12:30pm and 1–6pm). Its nine rooms are adorned with rosewood panelings, sculptures, landscape paintings, and Chinese tapestries and silks. The marble bath repeats the elliptical shape of the central drawing room; its water pipes are artistically decorated, and the chamber itself adorned with mirrors and jewels. Next to the Bath House is an arbor with a fountain of water-spouting birds; it's nicknamed "The End of the World" because of the trompe l'oeil perspective, which terminates in a painted diorama.

Crossing the moat and continuing northwards, you come to the **Temple of Botany**, supposedly representing the trunk of an oak tree, and the **Roman Waterway**, a spectacular fake of a fort and aqueduct, deliberately built as an ivy-covered ruin to enhance its illusory effect. Beyond here are the outer reaches of the park, laid out in the contrastingly untamed style of an English garden. By following the path traversing this section, you can return to the main part of the park via the humpbacked **Chinese Bridge**.

Pigage's remaining buildings are at the opposite end of the park. The **Temple of Mercury** is reached via either of the paths along the side of the artificial lake. Originally, this was intended to be redolent of ancient Egypt, but ended up as a pastiche of the clifftop ruin of a European Romanesque castle, anachronistically adorned with scenes of the life of Mercury. From here, there's a spectacular vista over a pond to the pink cupola and minarets of the **mosque** (daily in summer 10am–12:30pm and 1–6pm), the most original structure in the gardens, and the last to be built. It's a unique translation of Oriental forms into the language of eighteenth-century European architecture; down the years, Islamic visitors have continually been impressed by it, to the extent that nature has imitated art, with the building occasionally being used for worship. Inside are marble floors and walls covered with stucco, non-figurative paintings and quotations from the Koran. The rear view is no less impressive—a huge courtyard is surrounded by corridors for prayer, punctuated by washrooms and chambers for the use of the priests. Returning in the direction of the circular section of the garden, you come to the sixteen-columned **Temple of Minerva**, which derives from the favorite source of inspiration, classical Rome. The goddess of wisdom is seated inside; more significantly, she also appears in a frieze above the entrance, poring over a plan of the gardens of Schwetzingen, to which she gives her seal of approval.

Buses to and from Heidelberg stop at the Schlossplatz in front of the gardens; services run every half-hour for most of the day. The **tourist office** (Mon.–Fri. 9am–noon and 2–5pm, Sat. 9–11am; ☎06202 4933) is also on the square, in one of the few imposing buildings in the town itself, the eighteenth-century **Palais Hirsch**. This is also where you can book for performances in the Schlosstheater. The **Bahnhof**, on the main line between Mannheim and Karlsruhe, is five minutes' walk down Carl-Theodor-Strasse. There's no particular reason for staying in Schwetzingen, unless Heidelberg is booked solid; **rooms** at around DM30 per head are available at *Stadtschänke*, Carl-Theodor-Str. 31 (☎06202 25614), and *Silberner Anker*, Herzogstr. 31 (☎06202 15961), while *Seitz*, Zeyherstr. 3 (☎06202 26077) and *Jägerhaus*, Lindenstr. 20 (☎06202 26058), charge DM35 each.

Asparagus has been cultivated in Schwetzingen for more than three centuries; in season (April–June) it can be sampled in any of the town's restaurants, several of which are close to the Schloss. Each April and May, the Schlosstheater is the setting for an international **music festival**, often focusing on a regular guest, the composer Christoph Willibald Gluck, who was a key figure in bridging the transition from baroque to Viennese Classicism. Another festival in September is devoted solely to Mozart, who gave a recital here at the age of seven; there are also regular musical and theatrical performances of all kinds throughout the year.

Mannheim

MANNHEIM, 18km northwest of Heidelberg, was formerly considered one of the most beautiful cities in Germany. Writing in 1826, William Hazlitt called it "a splendid town, both from its admirable buildings and the glossy neatness of the houses. They are too fine to live in, and seem only made to looked at." A mere stripling among German cities, it was founded in 1606 as a fortress at the strategically important intersection of the rivers Rhine and Neckar. Its meteoric rise to prominence came with the return of the counts palatine to Catholicism; unable to establish a satisfactory relationship with the burghers of Heidelberg, Carl Philipp decided in 1720 to make Mannheim the main seat of his court. A daringly original **planned town** was laid out, which served as capital of the Palatinate for the next 57 years, becoming one of Europe's most celebrated centers of the performing arts. The nineteenth century saw heavy industrialization, centerd on the harbor trade and shipbuilding, though its most prestigious feature was the automobile factory established by Carl Benz, who demonstrated his first vehicle here in 1886.

Alas, the continued prominence of industry, coupled with heavy damage in the last war, means that the city's overall appearance is no longer pleasing. However, the highly-esteemed **grid plan**, based on a chessboard layout on the strip of land between the two great rivers, still survives. A simple system for naming and numbering the streets was adopted, which was used in a modified form throughout North America; this was later scrapped in favor of conventional designations, but has since been reinstated. The city is divided into 144 squares, each bearing a letter followed by a number. Streets to the west of the central axis are designated A to K, moving northwards; proceeding in the same direction, those to the east are L to U. The street number indicates proximity to the axis, so that D7, for example, is to the far west, whereas R7 is at the extreme east. Obviously, each house then bears a second number, which indicates its position on the square. At first the system can be confusing, particularly when you arrive at the **Hauptbahnhof**, which is at the extreme southwestern corner of the grid, at a point where the

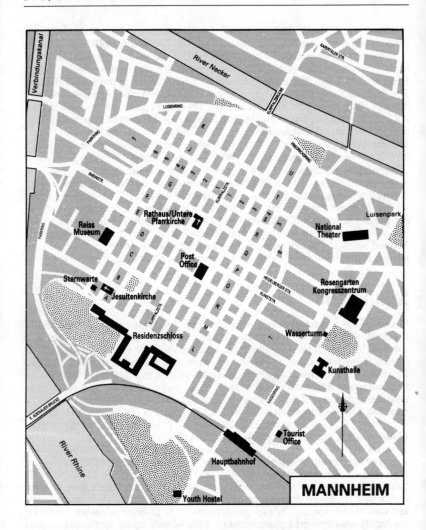

MANNHEIM

blocks are of widely varying sizes. However, once you get the hang of it, there's really no other European city which it's so simple to find your way around.

The pivot of the planned town is the horseshoe-shaped **Residenzschloss**, the most massive baroque palace ever built in Germany. Despite its regular appearance, it's a cooperative venture by several architects, begun by Johann Clemens Froimont, but only finished forty years afterwards by Nicolas de Pigage. Soon it became an expensive white elephant—the court transferred to Munich seventeen years later when Carl Theodor inherited the Bavarian electorate. The dignified exterior is heavily indebted to Palladianism; the interior was far more sumptuous, including rich stucco work and ceiling frescos by the Asam brothers. These were obliterated by wartime bombs; afterwards, the building was put to functional use to house the university, with only the outside restored in full.

However, as a real labor of love, the **chapel** (daily 9am–5pm) at the end of the western wing, plus the main **reception rooms** (guided tours April–Oct. Tues.–Sun. 10am–noon and 3–5pm, Nov.–March same times Sat. and Sun. only; DM1.50) were re-created from old photographs. The success of this project is highly debatable, but at least the *Rittersaal*, reached via a monumental staircase, provides an effective concert hall, which is particularly appropriate as the Mannheim court's greatest achievements were in the field of music. Its orchestra, which pioneered the mellow tones of the clarinet, was regarded during the eighteenth century as the best in the world, while the symphony (previously no more than a potboiler) was developed here into the chief form of instrumental music.

On A5, just to the west of the Residenzschloss, is the **Jesuitenkirche**, deliberately constructed as the largest church in town to symbolize the Palatinate court's return to Catholicism. It was designed by the Italian Alessandro Galli di Bibiena, who simultaneously worked on the palace; the grandiose facade and the central dome are the most striking features. Immediately to its rear is the **Sternwarte**, an observatory tower built for Christian Mayer, a Jesuit father who doubled as court astronomer; it's now subdivided for use as artists' studios.

Just to the north on C5 sits the **Zeughaus**, erected in the penultimate year of Mannheim's period as Palatine capital. It now houses the **Reiss Museum** (Tues. and Thurs.–Sun. 10am–1pm and 2–5pm, Weds. 10am–1pm and 2–8pm; free), with collections of Dutch and Flemish cabinet pictures, decorative arts, and local history—look for the old maps and prints which give an idea of the original dignified appearance of the grid plan streets, something hardly even hinted at now. On the square directly in front of the Zeughaus is a new building specially designed to house the most important section of the museum, the archaeology department. This originated as the elector's private cabinet of antiquities, and ranges from the Stone Age to the early medieval period. Also in the new museum are ethnological displays from Africa, the Islamic countries, India, China, and Japan.

The **Marktplatz**, which occupies the square G1, is the scene of markets on Tuesday, Thursday, and Saturday mornings; an enticingly varied picnic can be assembled at a bargain price by shopping here. In the center rises a large monument presented by Carl Theodor; originally representing the Four Elements, it was reworked into an allegorical composition in praise of Mannheim by the son of the original sculptor. On the south side of the square is a curious Siamese-twin of a building, erected just before Mannheim became the seat of the court. Sharing a central tower, the eastern part serves as the **Rathaus**, while the western is the **Untere Pfarrkirche**; their physical union is supposed to symbolize the concord between Justice and Piety, between secular and sacred authority.

The other main square, the Jugendstil **Friedrichsplatz**, is due east from here, just outside the central grid. It was laid out around the **Wasserturm**, which is some fifteen years older, and is the main example of a style which left a considerable mark all over the city. Another fine Jugendstil building is the **Kunsthalle** (Tues., Weds., and Fri.–Sun. 10am–5pm, Thurs. 10am–8pm; free) on Moltkestrasse, the next street to the south. This contains one of the best collections of nineteenth- and twentieth-century painting and sculpture in Germany, and is now the city's most obvious single draw. Highlight is one of the great masterpieces of Impressionism, **Manet**'s *Execution of Emperor Maximilian of Mexico*, the largest and most complete of the four versions he painted of this subject. Other notable works in the same room are **Cézanne**'s *Pipe Smoker*, and still lifes by Renoir and Van Gogh. The German section was brutally pruned in the Nazi purges against "degenerate art," but there's a room devoted to Romanticism, including several important examples of **Feuerbach**. *Portrait of the Writer Max Herrmann-Neisse* is one of **George Grosz's** best canvases, while there's an outstanding array of modern German sculpture, with **Barlach** and **Lehmbruck** strongly represented, along with a host of avant-garde works. Major temporary exhibitions are frequently held in the gallery.

At the northernmost end of the grid plan the central axis road continues over the Neckar by the Kurpfälzbrücke. Moored close to the bridge is the 1920s passenger steamer *Mainz*, which now houses a **Navigation Museum** (Tues.–Sat. 10am–1pm and 2–5pm, Sun. 10am–5pm; free). Nearby is the departure point for **harbor cruises** (June–Aug. Mon. and Thurs. 10am and 2:30pm; duration two hours; DM9). Eastwards along the river is the city's playground, the **Luisenpark** (May–Aug. 9am–9pm; rest of year 9am–dusk; DM3). This boasts various flower gardens, hot houses, an aquarium, a menagerie of farmyard animals and water fowl, an open-air stadium for concerts, a gondola course, and a watersports center. There's also a **Television Tower** (11am–dusk; DM3) offering the best overall view of the city. Just south of the park on Wilhelm-Varnholt-Platz is the **Planetarium** (showings Tues.–Sun. 3pm, also Mon. and Fri. 8pm, Sat. and Sun. 5pm and 7pm; DM6).

Practicalities and Nightlife

The **tourist office** (Mon.–Fri. 8:30am–6pm, Sat. 8:30am–noon; ☎0621 101011) is in a pavilion directly facing the Hauptbahnhof. For DM1 you can pick up their monthly program of events, *Mannheimer Veraltungsprogramm*, which includes limited listings for Heidelberg. This is also the place to book for Mannheim's most extravagant tourist attraction, a 15-minute **flight** over the city, which, if you're in the money, isn't too outrageously priced at DM75 for up to three people, DM25 for each additional passenger. **Exchange facilities** are available within the Hauptbahnhof (Mon.–Sat. 7am–8pm, Sun. 9am–1pm). **Mitfahrzentrale** have an office at N4, 19 (☎0621 21846).

The **youth hostel** is at Rheinpromenade 21 (☎0621 822718); take the underground passageway at the back entrance of the Hauptbahnhof, then turn left; it's only a couple of minutes' walk away. This convenient location means it's worth considering as a base for touring the surrounding area. **Camping** is possible (April–Sept. only) on the banks of either of the city's two great rivers. The larger and cheaper site is at NEUOSTHEIM (☎0621 412536) on the Neckar to the east; the other is to the south on Strandbad in NECKARAU (☎0621 856240); in spite of its name, it's located on a bend of the Rhine. **Hotels** are overwhelmingly geared to expense accounts, but two well-situated exceptions are *Arabella* at M2, 12 (☎0621 23050), with singles at DM30, doubles DM50; and *Rosenstock* at N3, 5 (☎0621 27343), whose singles cost DM35, doubles DM62. Otherwise, there's a clutch of places on Tattersallstrasse just to the north of the Hauptbahnhof; cheapest is *Goldene Gans* (☎0621 105277), with singles at DM38, doubles from DM58.

Mannheim has a vibrant **theater** tradition; the *Nationaltheater* on Goetheplatz is the successor to the now-destroyed building near the Schloss which was associated with Schiller's youthful *Sturm und Drang* phase. Performances of plays, opera, ballet and musicals are presented, along with special shows for kids; it has three auditoriums, at least two of which are in operation each evening. Other venues are *Klapsmühl" am Rathaus* at D6, 3 for cabaret and pantomime, and *Puppenspiele*, Collinistr. 26 for puppets, while **concerts** are held at *Kongresszentrum Rosengarten* on Friedrichsplatz.

Among a wide choice of places to **eat** and **drink**, *Elsässer* at N7, 8 serves some of the best food in town, while the brewery-owned *Andechser* at N2, 10 has a particularly lively atmosphere. The beer hall of Mannheim's main brewery, *Eichbaum*, is just north of the Neckar at Käfertalerstr. 168; its Weizen beers are renowned. Two vegetarian restaurants are *Heller's* at N7, 13 and *Redlich* at H1, 16, while a good Italian one is *Augusta*, Augustaanlage 40. Among many fine cafés is *Herrdegen*, in an eighteenth-century mansion at N2, 8. Look out for the local specialty, *Mannemer Dreck* ("Mannheim Mud"), invented during the last century at a time when there was an overreaction by the police to dogs fouling the pavement; a humorous baker retaliated by making a chocolate roll in a similar shape, and the recipe has remained popular ever since.

NORTH-WESTERN FRANCONIA

Like Swabia, **Franconia** (*Franken*) was one of the five great provinces of medieval Germany. Under Napoleon, nearly all of this was incorporated into Bavaria, but the northwestern part—consisting of the Hohenlohe plain and part of the valley of the Tauber River—was split off and used to beef up both the Grand Duchy of Baden and the Kingdom of Württemberg. For touring purposes, there's no particular need to pay much attention to these political divisions, particularly in the light of the fact that the famous Romantic Road cuts through both the Bavarian and Baden-Württemberg sections of Franconia.

The Hohenlohe

The **HOHENLOHE** is the name given to the plain between the Tauber Valley and the Swabian Forest, forming the northwestern part of the old province of Franconia. It's a quiet rural area, rich farming country interspersed with the inevitable stretches of woodland, cut by two contrasting rivers—the fast-flowing Jagst and the placid Kocher—which follow a remarkably parallel course. There's a stong feudal tradition here, which to some extent lingers on—the area is about as far removed from the thrusting, competitive nature of modern German society as it's possible to be. The House of Hohenlohe gradually spread out from its original base at Weikersheim, forming a series of collateral lines which each ruled a miniature territory. Unlike the Prussian *Junkers*, they were enlightened, paternalistic landlords, and it seems poetic justice that they've managed to hold on to their possessions while their counterparts found themselves dispossessed after World War II; there are still a round dozen historic castles in the family's possession. The area is almost entirely free of tourist hordes, and is ideal for quiet exploration. However, it's probably better visited on day-trips from a base in Schwäbisch Hall or the Neckar or Tauber Valleys, as there's nothing much to do come the evening. Hostels and campgrounds are practically nonexistent, though there are plenty of hotel rooms available at under DM30. It's really better to have your own car or bike; communications by public transportation are generally much better east–west (as the railroad lines follow the rivers) than north–south.

Neuenstein
NEUENSTEIN, on the scenic main railroad line from Schwäbisch Hall to Heilbronn some 25km northwest of the former, boasts the area's most

magnificent **Schloss** (guided tours, lasting 1 hr., mid-March–mid-Nov. 9am–noon and 1:30–6pm; DM5). Part of the original moated castle can still be seen in the keep and ring walls. However, when this came into the possession of the House of Hohenlohe in the sixteenth century, it was transformed into one of the most spectacular Renaissance palaces in Germany, a building fully worthy of comparison with the châteaux of the Loire. To see its resplendent exterior, bristling with elaborate scrollwork gables, to best effect, you have to walk along the main road leading westwards out of town; the vista from the square facing the entrance is consider-ably less impressive. Actually, this oversized Schloss was seen as a white elephant before the end of the seventeenth century, when the line of Hohenlohe-Neuenstein died out; the prince who inherited it converted it into an orphanage, old peoples' home, and workhouse, functions it served for nearly 200 years. Inside are several large halls, notably the *Kaisersaal* with its weapons and hunting trophies; there are also rooms furnished in various period styles, and collections of sacred art, furniture, and *objets d'art*. However, by far the most arresting room is the late Gothic **kitchen**, one of the best preserved in existence; the corner set aside for the slaughtering of game is guaranteed to turn the stomach of any vegetarian.

Öhringen

ÖHRINGEN, just 4km west of Neuenstein and the next stop on the train, was the seat of a different Hohenlohe scion. Their **Schloss**, facing the Marktplatz, is a horseshoe-shaped construction straddling the late Renaissance and baroque periods, and is now used as offices. It's rather eclipsed by the **Stiftskirche** opposite, the fifteenth-century rebuild of a collegiate church founded in 1037 at the request of Countess Adelheid, mother of the first Salian emperor, Conrad II; her sarcophagus, made two centuries after her death, can be seen in the crypt. Far more grandiose are the Renaissance funerary monuments in the chancel, which constitute the necropolis of the local princes. Look out in particular for the *Tomb of Philipp von Hohenlohe and Maria von Oranien* (daughter of William the Silent) adorned with reliefs illustrating episodes from the Netherlands' War of Independence against Spain. Also of note are the late Gothic carved retable of *Madonna and Child with Saints* at the high altar, and the elaborate keystones of the vaults which have portraits and coats-of-arms of various aristocratic families.

Half-timbered houses abound throughout the town center. In contrast, the *Karlsvorstadt*, to the east of Marktplatz down Poststrasse, is a piece of eighteenth-century town planning, separated from the old quarter by a neoclassical gateway. On this street is the **Weygang Museum** (Tues.–Sun. 10am–noon and 2–4pm; DM1), which concentrates on objects made of pewter, including a complete workshop. Another collection of specialist appeal is the **Motor Museum** on Stettiner Strasse (April–Oct. daily 1–5pm, Nov.–March Mon.–Fri. only 1–5pm; DM3), with classic sports and touring cars, along with over fifty historic motorbikes.

Jagsthausen

Some 20km due north of Öhringen is **JAGSTHAUSEN**, which lies on a different railroad line terminating at Heilbronn. Its heavily restored medieval **Burg**, now mostly converted into a hotel, is celebrated as the birthplace of Germany's answer to Robin Hood, **Götz von Berlichingen** (1480–1562), a more recent and historically substantiated figure than his English counterpart. A man who used the most unscrupulous of methods to achieve his lofty ideals of helping the poor and persecuted (see also p.260), part of Götz's aura derived from the fact that he was apparently impervious to physical pain. While storming the Burg in Landshut at the age of 23, his right hand was torn off, but so engrossed was he in the struggle that he failed to notice it. He had a replacement made out of iron, which he claimed was just as effective as its predecessor, and it lasted him for the rest of his life. Goethe used the folk hero's *Memoirs* as the basis for his first important work, a typical if disorganized product of the *Sturm und Drang* movement in its Shakespearian influences, its eulogy of the central character, its medieval setting, and its condemnation of a corrupt society. This play is invariably featured among the open-air drama performances held annually between June and August (☎07943 2295 for more information). Götz's famous iron hand is the star exhibit of a small **museum** (mid-March–Oct. 9am–noon and 1–6pm; DM1).

Schöntal

SCHÖNTAL is 6km up the Jagst River, in the precincts of a former Cistercian **Kloster** (guided tours April–Oct. daily at 11am, 3pm, and 4:30pm; DM2). This was founded in the twelfth century, but the present complex largely dates from its baroque rebuilding by Leonhard Dientzenhofer. The church has a particularly handsome facade, its twin towers crowned by bulbous domes. Inside are four outstanding alabaster altarpieces, among the finest German sculptures of the seventeenth century, a period when the country's internal political problems led to a devastating lull in artistic activity. The cloister contains the tomb of Götz von Berlichingen, complete with a carving of his emblem of the iron hand. Also included on the tour are the **Ordensaal**, which is covered with paintings showing the 300 religious and military orders which then existed, and the monumental staircase of the **Neue Abtei**, cleverly fitted into the smallest possible space.

Krautheim

Another 20km upstream is **KRAUTHEIM**, whose simple **youth hostel** at Brunnengasse 13 (☎06294 393), is the only one in the Hohenlohe. Unfortunately, opportunities for viewing the fortified medieval **Burg**, which includes an early Gothic chapel, a tower, and a partially preserved *Palas*, are very restricted (Sat. and Sun. only 2–4pm; DM2). The **Johanniterhaus** (Mon.–Thurs. 9–11am and 2–4pm; DM1) belonged to the Order of the Knights of St. John of Jerusalem, and now contains a small museum documenting their history.

Langenburg

The resort of **LANGENBURG** lies farther up the Jagst, but this stretch is awkward to cover by public transit, and it's easier to reach by bus from Schwäbisch Hall. Built high above a bend in the river, the town still clusters behind its walls, and preserves a fine collection of historic houses, particularly along Hauptstrasse. At the far end is the **Schloss** (Easter–mid-Oct. daily 8:30am–noon and 1:30–6pm; DM2.50), seat of yet another branch of the House of Hohenlohe. It clearly illustrates the gradual evolution from medieval fortress to pleasure palace. Three towers survive from the thirteenth-century castle, but the bulk of the building is Renaissance, though the eastern wing was remodeled in the seventeenth century to baroque taste. Particularly notable is the courtyard, which is richly embellished with an octagonal stair turret, three tiers of galleries, ornamental pediments, and scrollwork. The interiors are furnished in various period styles, up to and including the nineteenth century. A **Car Museum** (Easter–Oct. daily 8:30am–noon and 1:30–6pm, rest of year Sun. and holidays only 1:30–5pm; DM3), with seventy historic vehicles, occupies the former stables.

Creglingen and Weikersheim

The last leg of the famous tourist route known as the **Romantic Road**, with the exception of the terminus at Würzburg, is in Baden-Württemberg; it closely follows the course of the Tauber River on its northward journey towards its confluence with the Main. This is a lush, verdant landscape of gentle valleys and undulating hills, often dotted with vineyards, which stands in sharp contrast to the rugged contours of the neighboring Swabian Jura. Despite the inevitable summer influx of visitors to what the tourist board invariably dubs *Liebliches Taubertal* ("Lovely Tauber Valley"), it manages to preserve an agreeable atmosphere of rustic peace and quiet.

The Land boundary is crossed immediately after leaving the municipal area of ROTHENBURG OB DER TAUBER (see *Chapter One*). Some 18km north lies **CREGLINGEN**, an old-world village with half-timbered houses, some of which are built directly over the former ramparts. Creglingen's renown, however, is entirely based on the isolated **Herrgottskirche** (*Church of Our Lord*; April–Oct. daily 8am–6pm, Nov.–March Tues.–Sun. 10am–noon and 1–4pm; DM1.50), a Gothic pilgrimage chapel founded in the fourteenth century after a plowman had dug up a miraculous holy wafer in a nearby field. If you're traveling by *Europabus*, a stop is made here; otherwise the quickest and most pleasant way to come from Creglingen is via the path running alongside the brook named after the church.

The Herrgottskirche is architecturally unremarkable, but houses four large retables, including a polychromed *Passion Altar* from the school of Veit Stoss. This, however, is totally outclassed by the linden-wood *Altar of the Assumption* in the middle of the nave, which was carved by **Tilman Riemenschneider** in about 1510. Set in a filigree shrine specially constructed in order to catch the day's changing light effects, the main scene surpasses this sculptor's other masterpieces in Würzburg, Rothenburg, Bamberg, and Heidelberg, and would certainly be a candidate for the title of the greatest woodcarving ever made. The youthful beauty of the Virgin, and the rapt expressions of the Apostles, each carefully characterized in hairstyle and bone structure as well as expression, make for a truly moving effect. Around are four scenes in relief from the life of the Virgin; they are of markedly lower quality, and are presumably not the work of the master, who employed as many as twenty assistants in order to fulfil the flood of commissions which came his way. However, Riemenschneider certainly made the exquisite predella scenes of *Epiphany* and *Christ Among the Doctors*; the calm, pensive central figure in the group of scholars is almost certainly a self-portrait. A couple of decades after the retable was made, the chapel was given over to the Lutherans. Its extraordinary state of preservation is due to the fact that, as the main scene was anathema to Protestant doctrine, it was closed off—not to be re-opened until well into the nineteenth century.

Just below the church is a group of farm buildings, one of which now houses the **Finger Thimble Museum** (daily April–Oct. 9am–6pm, Nov.–March 1–4pm; DM1). Even by German standards this is an unlikely subject, but it's presented in a wholly serious manner, tracing the craft from antiquity to modern times.

The countryside around is described, without a trace of irony, as **Hergottsländle** (*The Lord God's Little Land*), as much through local belief that it resembles the Garden of Eden as from the name of the church. In the streams and lakes are good **fishing** possibilities, with abundant supplies of trout, eel, perch, pike, and carp. Beside the Münstersee some 3km away is a **campground** (☎07933 321), while there's a **youth hostel** on a hillside at the eastern end of

Creglingen itself at Erdbacherstr. 30 (☎07933 336). Otherwise, there are several **pensions** in town, where you should be able to find a room for DM30 or less; among these is *Króne*, Hauptstr. 12 (☎07933 558), which has a superb and inexpensive restaurant. There are also a number of **farmhouses** offering bargain deals; for more information about these, contact the **tourist office** in the Rathaus (Mon.–Fri. 9am–5pm; ☎07933 631).

WEIKERSHEIM, 13km down the Tauber from Creglingen and connected by regular local buses, is a good example of a seigneurial town. It's the ancestral seat of the **House of Hohenlohe**, who first came to local prominence during the twelfth century, and whose various branches ruled for centuries over tiny tracts of territory between the imperial cities of Schwäbisch Hall, Heilbronn and Rothenburg ob der Tauber).

The planned central **Marktplatz**, laid out at the beginning of the eighteenth century, was emphatically not designed for the use of the local inhabitants—it formed a processional way linking the Stadtkirche, which contains the Hohenlohe pantheon, to their **Schloss** (guided tours daily April–Oct. 8:30am–6pm, Nov.–March 10am–noon and 2–4pm; DM3). A particular touch of swagger was provided by the arcaded buildings immediately fronting the main entrance, shaped like embracing arms in the manner of the colonnades before St. Peter's in Rome. In 1586, when Count Ludwig II reestablished Weikersheim as the family's main residence, he decided to replace the old moated castle with a magnificent new Renaissance palace. The Dutch architect Georg Robin chose a daringly original floorplan based on an equilateral triangle. Only one wing of this, characterized by six magnificent scrollwork gables, was actually built, as the Hohenlohes turned their money and attention to supporting the Protestant cause in the Thirty Years' War. During the early eighteenth century the complex was finally completed in the baroque style, though still retaining some parts of the medieval fortress.

Unquestionably the highlight of the reception rooms is the **Rittersaal**, the most sumptuous banqueting hall ever built in Germany, whose decorations are a hymn of praise to the dynasty and its preoccupations. The huge coffered ceiling is painted with depictions of the glories of the hunt, the entrance doorway is carved with a scene of a battle against the Turks, and the colossal chimneypiece is adorned with a complicated allegory which appears to illustrate the family motto, "God gives Luck." Flanking the fireplace are the reclining stucco figures of Count Ludwig and his wife, sister of William the Silent of Oranien-Nassau, above which are their respective family trees. Even more eye-catching are the life-sized stuccos of deer parading along the main walls, joined by an elephant, a beast the craftsmen had clearly never seen. The baroque rooms of the palace are on a much smaller scale, but evocatively capture the flavor of courtly life of the time in their comprehensive array of furniture, tapestries, wallcoverings, porcelain, and objets d'art.

The **gardens**, which are contemporary with the later parts of the Schloss, are exceptionally well-preserved. They're bounded by chestnut trees, and are arranged symmetrically, with formal clipped hedges offset by the blazing color of the flower arrangements. The statues are particularly notable. On the terrace immediately behind the palace are a series of sixteen caricatures of members of the court, inspired by the engravings of the Lorraine artist Jacques Callot; this is the only set of what was once a very popular subject to have survived intact. In the central pond is a representation of *Hercules Fighting the Hydra*. Like many other petty German princes, the Hohenlohes fondly saw analogies between themselves and the great hero. Further evidence of their megalomania comes with the **Orangery** at the end of the garden, which provides a theatrical backdrop to the Tauber valley beyond. Among the figures represented are what they imagined to be their spiritual ancestors—the emperors of ancient Assyria, Persia, Greece and Rome, no less.

You can indulge in a bit of **wine-tasting** at the *Gutskellerei* (Mon.–Fri. 8am–5pm, Sat. 9am–5pm, Sun. 11am–5pm), just beside the entrance to the Schloss. In the Marktplatz is the **Tauberland Village Museum** (April–mid-Nov. 10am–noon and 2–5pm; DM1.50) which contains folklore displays on rural life throughout Franconia. Opposite is the **tourist office** (Mon.–Fri. 9am–noon and 2:30–5:30pm, also Sat. 2–4pm in summer; ☎07934 7272). The three **hotels** on the square cost upwards of DM30 per head, while *Krone* at Hauptstr. 14 (☎07934 8314) is marginally cheaper. Alternatively, there's a very superior **youth hostel** on the banks of the Tauber at Im Heiligen Wöhr (☎07934 7025). Weikersheim is the first town on the Romantic Road since DINKELSBÜHL to be on a railroad line, and for the rest of the journey down the Tauber there's a choice between trains and buses.

Bad Mergentheim

BAD MERGENTHEIM, the next stop on the Romantic Road some 11km due west of Weikersheim, is one of Germany's most celebrated spas. Judging from the evidence of excavations, which have led to the uncovering of a Celtic well, the presence of hot saline springs at this point was known to Bronze Age tribes. However, they lay forgotten for over two millennia, until their rediscovery during a dry spell in 1826 by a shepherd who noticed his flock crowding round a trickle of water close to the north bank of the Tauber. Three years later, the first hotel opened, and the town has never looked back.

The timing of the finding of the springs was fortuitous, as seventeen years before Mergentheim had lost the prestigious role it had held since 1525—as seat of the **Order of Teutonic Knights** (*Deutschritterorden*). It's the only place still on German soil offering important reminders of the Order, who so often played a crucial role in the nation's history. Even if you normally find spas a turn-off, it's worth coming to see the old part of town, on which the knights left a characteristic stamp. This is sharply differentiated from the cure facilities, and situated on the opposite side of the river.

Originally founded as a hospitaler community in Palestine in 1190, the order quickly took on a religious and military character. It increasingly turned its attention towards the Christianization of eastern Europe; by the early fourteenth century it controlled a powerful Baltic state from its Prussian headquarters at Marienburg, growing rich through the profitable grain trade, and repopulating the territories with German peasants.* Prosperity bred complacency, and successive defeats by the now-landlocked Kingdom of Poland meant that the knights had to cede half their lands and reestablish themselves at Königsberg in East Prussia. In 1525, the Grand Master Albrecht von Hohenzollern converted to Protestantism and transformed the territory into a secular duchy, initially under Polish control.

---

* The knights' policies now seem ominously anticipatory of Hitler's ideas on *Lebensraum* 600 years later—but they were, of course, far more successful in achieving their aims than he was.

Those of the order still loyal to Catholicism moved their base to Mergentheim, where they had owned land since the thirteenth century. They established themselves in the former Hohenlohe castle, which was expanded and rebuilt to form the **Deutschordensschloss**, which in turn was partly replaced during the early eighteenth century. This gargantuan complex of buildings takes up the whole of the eastern part of town; most of it is now used as offices, while the **Schlosspark** beyond, laid out in the English style, forms a south-bank counterpart to the *Kurpark*. In accordance with the tenets of the order, the architecture is severly ascetic, with only the occasional touch of liveliness, as in the bright orange **Torbau** which forms the main entrance. At the corner of the main courtyard is the handsome rococo **Schlosskirche**, in part the work of the two greatest German architects of the day—Balthasar Neumann designed the twin towers, and François Cuvilliés provided plans for the white stuccoed interior, whose vault is covered by a huge fresco glorifying the Holy Cross.

Opposite the facade of the church is the main range of the Schloss, approached by two Renaissance **staircases**, the northern one of which is of an ingenious corkscrew shape. Its more conventional counterpart leads to the **museum** (March–Oct. Tues.–Fri. 2:30–5:30pm, Sat. and Sun. 10am–noon and 2:30–5:30pm; Nov.–Feb. Sat. and Sun. only; DM3). The first room is the *Kapitelsaal*, the main reception hall, richly but coolly decorated with neoclassical stuccowork; nowadays it's often used as a concert hall. Notwithstanding some rococo ceilings by Cuvilliés, the other rooms are surprisingly unostentatious, and are used for displays on the history of the order, including valuable treasury items and portraits of all the Mergentheim grand masters. Though it played an important part in the Catholic League during the Thirty Years' War, the order was in irreversible decline throughout its period here. Nonetheless, its offices belonged to the highest rank of German nobility, and when the best-known grand master, the Elector Clemens August (see Brühl, *Chapter Five*), gained the title, he considered it the ultimate achievement in a career in which he had collected an archbishopric, four other bishoprics, and numerous secular titles. Napoleon finally disbanded the order in 1809, but it was reconstituted in Vienna 25 years later, where it's still active as a charitable body.

Mergentheim's spacious central Markt is divided in two by the step-gabled sixteenth century **Rathaus**; the arms of the grand master who built it are borne by the hero Roland in the fountain in front. The rest of the square is lined by a colorful array of houses of various dates erected by vassals of the order. One of the neoclassical pavilions on the north side contains the **tourist office** (Mon.–Fri. 9am–noon and 2:30–5pm, Sat. 9am–noon; ☎07931 57135). Tombs of some of the most illustrious of the knights are found in both the **Marienkirche** just off the southern side of the square, and the **Stadtkirche**, down an alley at the opposite end; the latter church, oddly enough, was originally founded by another order of crusaders, that of St. John of Jerusalem. Beside it stands the **Spital**, whose chapel is adorned with Gothic frescos. On Burgstrasse is the **Automobile Museum** (Tues.–Sun. 10am–6pm; DM3), a large collection of vintage cars, ranging from Bugatti to Rolls-Royce, and motorbikes.

The **Bahnhof** is conveniently situated between the medieval and spa parts of the town, on the same side of the Tauber as the former. There's a **youth hostel** at Erlenbachtalstr. 44 (☎07931 6373) in the outlying village of IGERSHEIM (which has its own Bahnhof) to the northeast. The **campground** is 2km south of town at Willinger Tal (☎07931 2177). Cheapest **pensions** are *Haus Ursula*, Lorenz-Fries-Str. 3 (☎07931 3309), with singles at DM19, doubles DM33, and the more central *Helen*, Mühlwehrstr. 31 (☎07931 8378), which charges upwards of

DM21 per head. *Zum Wilden Mann*, Reichengasse 6 (☎07931 7638), where room prices start at DM28, has what's arguably the best **restaurant** in town. At 9pm on Fridays in summer, a trumpeter plays from the Schloss" Bläserturm, while the main **festival** is the *Stadtfest* in June.

STUPPACH, a village 5km south of Bad Mergentheim (of which it's now officially a part) possesses one of the supreme masterpieces of German Renaissance painting, **Grünewald's** *St. Mary of the Snows*, in its otherwise unremarkable Pfarrkirche (daily April–Oct. 8:30am–5:30pm, Nov.–March 8:30am–noon and 1:30–5pm; DM1). This is part of a triptych, one wing of which also survives and can be seen in Freiburg. Be warned that the presentation here is marred by a compulsory lecture on the painting and the techniques used in its creation.

The Lower Tauber Valley: Tauberbischofsheim, and Wertheim

Just beyond Bad Mergentheim the Tauber makes a sharp bend, and thereafter follows a broadly northerly course. This point also marks the boundary of the rather artificial transition from Württemberg into Baden, decided in the Napoleonic carve-up of Franconia.

TAUBERBISCHOFSHEIM, some 25km north, is the last stop on the Romantic Road before its terminus at Würzburg. This picturesque little wine town, a mixture of half-timbered and sandstone buildings, nowadays claims for itself the title of world capital of fencing. At the 1976 Olympic Games, the team trained here scooped a bucketful of medals, six of them gold—then did even better at the next olympiad.

The town's other claim to fame is as the home of the first convent in the country. This was founded in 730 by the Devon-born Benedictine monk Saint Boniface, known as the "Apostle of the Germans"; the town's name derives from the fact that he became archbishop of Mainz. Subsequently, the convent became known as **St. Lioba** after its first abbess, who was a relation (perhaps even a sister) of Boniface. The name lives on in the restrained baroque church of a suppressed Franciscan successor to the original convent in the middle of town. A short walk down Klostergasse is a series of sixteenth-century almshouses, while the central **Marktplatz** is lined with a varied group of buildings, including the restored pharmacy and the early seventeenth-century post office, dating from the days of the Thurn and Taxis monopoly (see Regensburg, *Chapter One*).

However, Tauberbischofheim's dominant monument is the **Schloss**, with its stern cylindrical watchtower, at the southern end of town. Construction was begun during the thirteenth century by the archbishops of Mainz, soon after they had gained full control over the town. The interior, which includes a couple of Gothic halls, now houses the **Heimat Museum** (Easter–Oct. Tues.–Sat. 2:30–4:30pm, Sun. 10am–noon and 2:30–4:30pm; DM1). This features prehistoric finds from the area, colorful costumes, and furniture from Renaissance to Biedermeier.

The **youth hostel** sits on a hill to the northwest commanding a fine view over the town, at Schirrmannweg 2 (☎09341 3152); follow Wellenbergstrasse to the left of the Bahnhof's exit. **Pensions** charging DM25 or less per head are *Block*, Würzburger Str. 23 (☎09341 2410); *Hammel*, Hauptstr. 2 (☎09341 2276); and *Café Stein*, Hauptstr. 67 (☎09341 3204). *Badischer Hof*, Hauptstr. 70 (☎09341 2385), is only slightly more expensive, and boasts an excellent **restaurant**; other good places to eat are *Lamm*, also on Hauptstrasse, *Paradies* on Waldtorstrasse and *Pilsstube Ritter* on Bahnhofstrasse, while *Schlosscafé*, again on Hauptstrasse, is the best choice for coffee and cake. The **tourist office** is in the Rathaus on Marktplatz (Mon.–Fri. 9am–12:30pm and 2–5pm; ☎09341 80313).

From Tauberbischofsheim, you can travel along the last section of the Romantic Road by either bus or train to WÜRZBURG (see *Chapter One*), but a more enticing alternative is to follow the Tauber northwards, through what's arguably its finest stretch. **BRONNBACH**, on the railroad line 16km farther on, is built around its **Kloster** (guided tours, lasting 45 minutes, Easter–Oct. daily 9:30am–noon and 2–5pm; DM3). This former Cistercian monastery was a daughter foundation from Maulbronn, established just a few years later in 1151. The bulk of the architecture is in the severe Transitional style favored by the order, with just a nod towards the Gothic in the church, but rather more awareness of the new style in the later cloisters and chapter house. Whereas Maulbronn became Protestant at the Reformation, Bronnbach remained Catholic. This accounts for significant differences in their present appearances: during the early eighteenth century, the passion for baroque led to a desire to transform the face of the old monastery. The church was adorned with a cluster of ornate altarpieces; these are fine works in themselves but mar the architectural purity. A rather happier addition, on the other hand, was the *Josephsaal*, a sumptuous refectory for use during the summer months.

Bronnbach is now officially part of **WERTHEIM**, the most northerly town in Baden-Württemberg, situated 7km farther north at the point where the Tauber joins the westward-flowing Main. It's nicknamed "Little Heidelberg," and with some justification, as there are clear similarities between the two—the setting between the riverside and wooded slopes, the prevalence of superb and varied panoramic viewpoints, the twisting alleyways, the ruined castle looming high above. Wertheim's beauty silenced even the caustic pen of Kurt Tucholsky, the brilliant Berlin satirist in the cabaret heydays of the Weimar Republic: "Autumn unleashes its tints and the woods are ablaze . . . the Main flows here as a picture-book river," he drooled. The original town was situated on the northern bank of the Main for fear of flooding, but it moved in the twelfth century when the local counts, realizing the strategic importance of the spit of land between the two rivers, used it as the basis for building up a territory between the two ecclesiastical principalities of Mainz and Würzburg. A precarious independence was maintained down the centuries from the prying hands of the bishops, whose unwelcome advances were a major factor in Wertheim becoming one of the earliest bastions of Protestantism.

The town is an ideal place in which to simply wander at leisure. On the right bank of the Tauber, the quays are lined with old fishermen's houses; on the **Kittstein Tor** there's a scale recording the watermark of each flood since 1595. Farther up towards the Main is the **Spitzer Turm** (*Pointed Tower*), the original corner point of the fortifications erected around 1200. The streets immediately behind housed a large Jewish population right up until the days of the Third Reich. At the heart of Wertheim is the **Marktplatz**, lined with half-timbered houses, and scene of colorful markets on Wednesday and Saturday. At the far end is the Renaissance **Engelbrunnen**, made from the local red sandstone, which shows two angels bearing the town's coat-of-arms. Behind is the **Kilianskapelle**, an unusual fifteenth-century double chapel; the lower story served as an ossuary. Opposite is an earlier Gothic building, the **Stiftskirche**, in whose choir are a series of ornate Renaissance tombs, the pantheon of the House of Wertheim.

A short walk down Mühlenstrasse is a half-timbered house containing the **Glass Museum** (April–Oct. Tues.–Sun. 10am–noon and 2–4pm; DM1), a surprisingly comprehensive collection on three floors. Across the street is the **Historical Museum** (April–Dec. Mon.–Fri. 10am–noon and 2–4pm, Sat. and Sun. 2–4pm; free), with wide-ranging displays of Franconian sacred art, traditional costumes, ceramics and local history. There are also a number of paintings of Wertheim by Otto Modersohn, the leading light of the artistic community at Worpswede (see *Chapter Six*); these date from holiday visits in the 1920s, long after the death of his estranged spouse, the more talented Paula Modersohn-Becker. The building housing the museum is a baroque palace which was built to replace the **Schloss**, a casualty of the Thirty Years' War. From the twelfth-century fortress, the tall watchtower and part of the walls survive; later additions include the twin-towered barbican and the residential quarters. In spite of its condition, it's well worth climbing up for the outstanding view over the two rivers, with the vast stretch of the Odenwald to the west and the wooded Spessart hills to the north.

The **Bahnhof** is on the left bank of the Tauber, only a few minutes' walk from the center. There's a **youth hostel** in the hills at Alte Stiege 16 (☎09342 6451), and also a **campground** (☎09342 5719). Cheapest **hotels** in Wertheim itself are *Hofgarten*, Untere Heeg 1 (☎09342 6426), and *Waldhaus*, Bismarckstr. 51 (☎09342 1314), where you should be able to stay for DM30 or less. Lower rates are available in outlying villages; the **tourist office** (Mon.–Fri. 9am–12:30pm and 2–5pm, Sat. 9am–noon; ☎09342 1066) will find a room free of charge. Best **restaurant** for hearty traditional food is *Bach'sche Brauerei* on Marktplatz; alternatively, try *Zepfhahn* on Mammelgasse.

travel details

Trains

From Stuttgart to Freiburg (1 an hour; 45 min.), Karlsruhe (2; 1 hr. 10 min.), Ludwigsburg (frequent; 10 min.), Marbach (2; 25 min.), Esslingen (2; 10 min.), Tübingen (2; 1 hr.), Rottweil (1; 1½ hr.), Donaueschingen (1; 2 hr.), Konstanz (1; 2 hr. 40 min.), Ulm (3; 1 hr.), Schwäbisch Gmünd (2; 40 min.), Schwäbisch Hall (1; 1 hr.), Heilbronn (1; 45 min.), Heidelberg (2; 1 hr. 10 min.).

From Karlsruhe to Baden-Baden (3; 20 min.), Freiburg (2; 1 hr.), Freudenstadt (1; 2 hr.), Schwetzingen (2; 40 min.), Mannheim (frequent; 30 min.).

From Ulm to Blaubeuren (1; 10 min.), Heidenheim (1; 40 min.), Aalen (1; 1 hr.).

From Heidelberg to Bruchsal (2; 20 min.), Bad Wimpfen (1; 50 min.).

CHAPTER THREE

HESSEN

O ccupying the geographical center of the Federal Republic and mani-
festing elements of both north and south German culture, **HESSEN**
claims to be the very heart of Germany. Modern Hessen is a relatively
new creation, having been flung together by the Americans as an
administrative unit after World War II; and although Hessen had existed as a
geographical and cultural concept before the unification of Germany, until then it
was a fragmented region divided along political and religious lines. For centuries
various nobles struggled for supremacy in a series of petty feuds and wrangles
culminating in the general bloodletting of the Thirty Years' War, an upheaval
which resulted in the devastation of much of Hessen.

During the eighteenth century the region's main export was mercenary
soldiers, and a large, press-ganged contingent helped Britain lose the American
War of Independence. The nineteenth century was a period of more conventional
commercial activity, with the arrival of the industrial revolution and the founding
of big concerns like *Opel* (originally a sewing-machine factory) along the banks of
the Main. It was also a period of political wheeling and dealing as the local nobility attempted to play Prussia and Austria off against each other. Despite this,
most of Hessen was absorbed by the expanding Kingdom of Prussia in 1866
before eventually becoming part of the Greater German Reich five years later.

Today Hessen is one of the most prosperous of the German Länder, focused
on the American-style dynamism of **Frankfurt**. Although traditional heavy industry still exists around the confluence of the Rhine and the Main, it's the serious
money generated by banking and modern communications-related industries in
Frankfurt which provides the region's real economic base. The other mainstay of
the area's economy is the heavily industrial city of **Kassel**, at the northern end of
Hessen. Otherwise, apart from occasional light industrial pockets, most of
Hessen's inhabitants live from farming or tourism. The old university town of
Marburg is one of the region's most important historic centers and, in conjunction with the nearby **Lahn** valley, has a lot to offer the visitor. The same can be
said of the baroque city of **Fulda**, which also offers easy access to the
Vogelsberg and **Rhön** hills. **Darmstadt** is an underrated city which has been
home to several artistic movements, most notably Jugendstil, the German form of
art nouveau. Hessen's other main hot spot is the **Rheingau**, the scenic but
touristy stretch of the Rhine, west of the Land capital **Wiesbaden**, which is a
bland and money-oriented playground and gambling center.

Hessen is fairly accessible—Frankfurt has the busiest international airport in
Europe and is easily reached by rail and road from the rest of Germany. There
are good rail links between most of the major towns, although remoter areas like
the Vogelsberg are probably best explored by car.

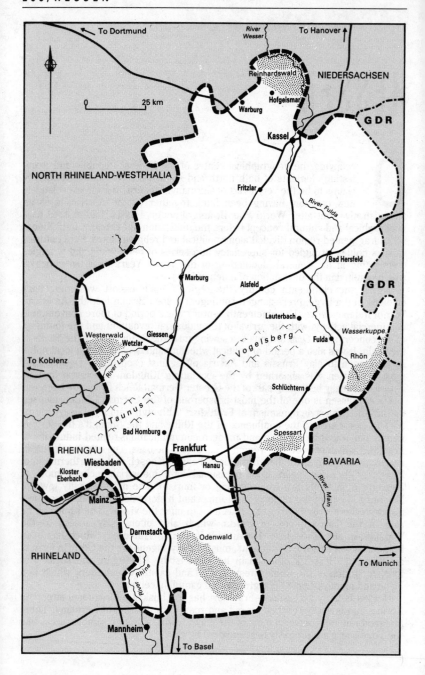

FRANKFURT

Straddled across the Main a few kilometers before it converges with the Rhine, **Frankfurt** is the spiritual and cultural (though not the political) capital of Hessen. It's a modern international city, a communications and transport center for the whole of West Germany, with a frenetic commercial and social life that sets it apart from the relatively sleepy hinterland. For many travelers Frankfurt will be their first taste of the country—it's a place with a surprising amount to offer and it's worth spending at least a couple of days here rather than treating it as a mere transit point.

The City

FRANKFURT is a city with two faces, both of which it's equally willing to show to visitors. On the one hand it's the cutthroat financial capital of West Germany, centered around the **Westend** district, a yuppie hellhole where bankers and media people cut their teeth before moving on to the real killing fields of Manhattan. On the other it's a surprisingly civilized city which spends more per year on the arts than any other city in Europe and whose inhabitants like nothing better than to spend an evening knocking back a few jugs of *Ebbelwei*, the local apple wine, in the open-air winetaverns of the **Sachsenhausen** suburb.

The city's commercial tradition (it boasts 388 banks) goes back to Roman times, when its importance as a river crossing point and junction between north and south Germany was first recognized. Modern Frankfurt owes its existence to Charlemagne who had a fortress built on the old Roman site during the eighth century. By the twelfth century Frankfurt was well established as a trading center, and merchants flocked to the **Römerberg** to sell their goods in the shadow of the royal palace built by Charlemagne's successors. This market evolved gradually into the Frankfurt fair, a tradition that still exists, albeit in new premises just outside the town center. The Frankfurt stock exchange was opened in 1585 and it was in Frankfurt that Meyer Amschel Rothschild founded both a banking house and a financial dynasty at the beginning of the nineteenth century.

Frankfurt was the main center of the postwar German economic recovery. It was here that the Americans set in motion the currency reform that put the shattered nation back on its feet—overnight, on June 20, 1948, they introduced DM10.7 billion worth of new currency, printed in the States and delivered to Frankfurt under armed guard, to replace the vastly inflated *Reichsmark*. Today banking and related jobs account for most of the city's employment and at times it seems to be one vast hive of commercial activity, an impression enhanced by its ultramodern high-rise architecture. Over half of the city, including almost all of the center, was destroyed during the war and the rebuilders decided to follow a policy of innovation rather than restoration. The result is a skyline that smacks more of Chicago than the Federal Republic—appropriate enough in a city that has the reputation of being one of the most Americanized in Europe.

Today the city has an energetic nightlife and is a thriving recreational center for the whole of Hessen, with a good selection of theaters and galleries, and an even better range of museums concentrated along the **Museumsufer** (the south bank of the river Main) in Sachsenhausen. Frankfurt comes across as a confident and tolerant city, and in the Bockenheim district there's a healthy "alternative" scene, not self-consciously institutionalized in the way that Berlin's has become.

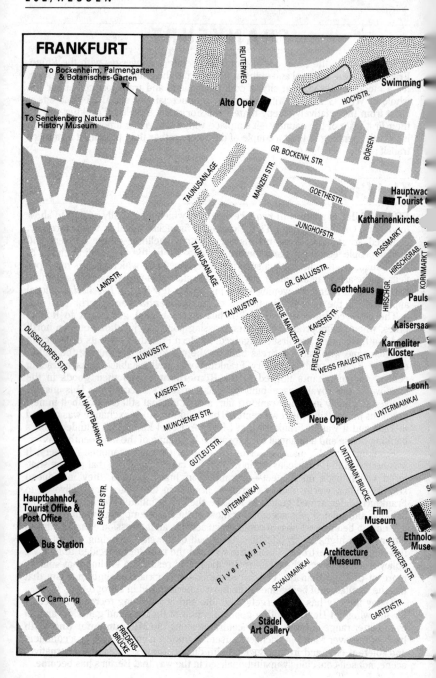

FRANKFURT

To Bockenheim, Palmengarten
& Botanisches-Garten

To Senckenberg Natural
History Museum

REUTERWEG

Alte Oper

Swimming

HOCHSTR.

BÖRSEN

GR. BOCKENH. STR.

MAINZER STR.

GOETHESTR.

Hauptwac
Tourist

Katharinenkirche

JUNGHOFSTR.

ROSSMARKT

HIRSCHGRAB.

KORNMARKT

TAUNUSANLAGE

LANDSTR.

GR. GALLUSSTR.

Goethehaus

Pauls

TAUNUSTOR

NEUE MAINZER STR.

KAISERSTR.

Kaisersaa

FRIEDENSSTR.

Karmeliter
Kloster

TAUNUSSTR.

WEISS FRAUENSTR.

Leonh

DÜSSELDORFER STR.

KAISERSTR.

Neue Oper

UNTERMAINKAI

AM HAUPTBAHNHOF

MUNCHENER STR.

UNTERMAIN BRÜCKE

GUTLEUTSTR.

BASELER STR.

Hauptbahnhof,
Tourist Office &
Post Office

Film
Museum

Ethnolo
Muse

Bus Station

UNTERMAINKAI

Architecture
Museum

SCHWEIZER STR.

To Camping

River Main

SCHAUMAINKAI

Städel
Art Gallery

GARTENSTR.

FRIEDENS-
BRÜCKE

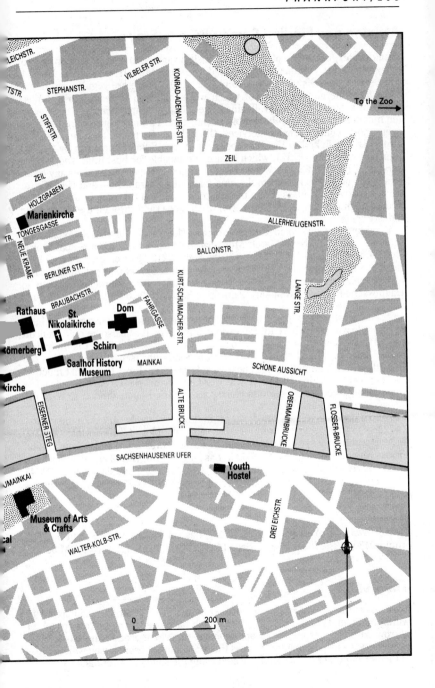

Arriving and Finding Somewhere to Stay

Frankfurt **airport** is one of the world's busiest (and best), and is a major point of entry into West Germany from abroad (**information** Arrival Hall B, Level 1; Mon.–Fri. 8am–4:30pm; ☎212 4000 or 212 4100). There are regular **rail** departures from the airport **Bahnhof** which will enable you to reach most of West Germany's cities fairly easily. Trains leave the airport approximately once every ten minutes for the **Hauptbahnhof** (journey time 11 min.) from where there are even more comprehensive services throughout Germany and beyond. The airport is also linked to the Hauptbahnhof by two S-Bahn lines, run by the city transport company (*FVV*), which is also responsible for bus, tram ,and U-Bahn services. There's a flat rate of DM1.70 for all journeys (which includes any transfers) and you buy tickets from the blue machines for trams, S- , and U-Bahns, or from the driver for buses. From the Hauptbahnhof you can walk to downtown in about fifteen minutes or take tram #11, which goes right through the heart of the old city center.

Frankfurt has two main **tourist offices**. There's one in the Hauptbahnhof, opposite Track 23 (Nov.–March Mon.–Sat. 8am–9pm, Sun. 9:30am–8pm; April–Oct. Mon.–Sat. 8am–10pm, Sun. 9:30am–8pm; ☎212 8849 or 212 8851), where they'll be able to give you general information about Frankfurt, book hotel rooms, and organize guided tours. There's also an office for general information in Hauptwache-Passage (Mon.–Fri. 9am–6pm, Sat. 9am–2:30 pm; the S-Bahn runs direct from the airport).

Accommodation is predictably pricey, thanks to the expense-account businesspeople who come here for the various trade fairs. It can also be quite difficult to find and it's best to try and sort out in advance. Best budget bet is the **youth hostel** at Deutschherrnufer 12 (☎619058), in Sachsenhausen, reached by bus #46 from the Hauptbahnhof. As for cheap **hotels** and **pensions**, there isn't much in the city center under DM50. If you don't mind the sleazy environs, the few reasonably priced hotels seem to cluster around the Hauptbahnhof, close to the Kaiser Strasse red-light district .

The following is a brief run-down of the low-cost hotels. *Atlas*, Zimmerweg 1 (☎723946), has singles from DM44 and doubles from DM65; *Backer*, Mendelssohnstr. 92 (☎747992), has singles from DM25 and doubles from DM40; *Bruns*, Mendelssohnstr. 42 (☎748896), has singles from DM42 and doubles from DM42; *Excelsior*, Mannheimerstr. 7–9 (☎256080/413061), has singles from DM45 and doubles from DM99; *Franken*, Frankenallee 183 (☎738 0041), has singles from DM48 and doubles from DM88; *Glockshuber*, Mainzer Landstr. 120 (☎742628), has singles from DM49 and doubles from DM85; *Pension Ilona*, Mainzer Landstr. 123 (☎236204), has singles from DM42 and doubles from DM68; *Wesereck*, Weserstr. 12 (☎231014), has singles from DM50 and doubles from DM80; *Westfälinger Hof*, Karlstr. 14 (☎234748), has singles from DM 50 and doubles from DM83.

The Center

Most of central Frankfurt can be covered on foot; almost all the main sights lie within the bounds of the old city walls, which have been turned into a stretch of narrow parkland describing an approximate semicircle around the city center. From here it's an easy matter to cross the Main into Sachsenhausen, where most of the museums are conveniently located along the southern river bank.

The Römerberg and Around

As good a point as any to begin your explorations is the **Römerberg**, the historical and, roughly speaking, geographical center of the city. Charlemagne built his fort on this low hill, on the site of earlier Roman and Alemannic settlements, to protect the ford which gave Frankfurt its name—*Frankonovurd* ("Ford of the Franks"). Throughout the Middle Ages the Römerberg was Frankfurt's focal point, serving as market place, fair ground, venue for every imaginable kind of *Volksfest* and, less frequently, for celebrating an imperial coronation.

At the start of this century the Römerberg was still the heart of the city, an essentially medieval quarter, ringed by half-timbered houses built by the rich merchants and bankers who had made Frankfurt one of Germany's richest centers—its "secret capital," according to Goethe. All this came to an end in March 1944 when two massive air raids flattened the Römerberg and with it the city's historic core .

Only a handful of the prewar buildings survived the raids. The most significant survivor was the thirteenth-century **St. Bartholomäus**, inaccurately referred to as the Dom (March–Oct. 9am–12:30pm and 3–6pm; Nov.–Feb. 9am–12:30pm and 3–5pm; Fri. 9–10:30am only), and even that emerged from the destruction with only its main walls intact. Today, after extensive restoration from old plans, the Dom stands more or less as it once did, a towering, red-sandstone Gothic structure at the eastern end of the Römerberg. Before the construction of the modern skyscrapers it was the tallest building in the city, as befitted the venue for the election and coronation of the Holy Roman emperors. The treasures of the spacious, light-filled interior include an intricately carved choir stall dating back to 1352, the fifteenth-century *Maria-Schlaf-Altar,* and the *Deposition from the Cross* by Van Dyck from 1628.

To the right of the choir is the relatively simple and unadorned **Wahlkapelle**, where the seven electors used to make their final choice as to who would become Emperor. The Dom's bells, the second largest of any church in Germany, have been tuned in with all the others in the city, and four times a year they all unite to form a deafening carillon. For a fabulous panorama, climb the 95-meter-high tower (April–Oct. 9am–12:30pm and 2:30pm–6pm; DM1). The unexceptional **Dommuseum** (Tues.–Fri. 10am–5pm, Sat. and Sun. 11am–5pm; DM2) contains a lot of ecclesiastical garments and an old altarpiece.

Slightly to the north, on Domstrasse, looms the newly-completed **Museum für Moderne Kunst**, looking like a high-tech slice of cake. Its large collection has work by the likes of Warhol, Beuys, and Lichtenstein.

Just in front of the Dom looms the **Historische Garten**, where the foundations of some of the Roman, Carolingian, and medieval buildings which occupied the Römerberg at various times have been laid bare to form a little park. Opposite the southern side of the Dom is the fourteenth-century **Leinwandhaus**, formerly a cloth hall which now contains three galleries, including the town photographic gallery (check with the tourist office for opening times).

At the opposite end of the Römerberg is the building that gave the area its name—the **Römer**, formerly the *Rathaus*. Its distinctive facade, with its three-stepped gables, fronts the **Römerplatz**, the market square on which the **Gerechtigkeitsbrunnen** (*Justice Fountain*) of 1611 stands. The facade of the Römer was more or less all that remained after the war but the building has been restored with consummate skill. The two upper stories house the **Kaisersaal**, a banqueting hall containing 52 rather effete-looking nineteenth-century portraits of the kaisers (Mon.–Sat. 9am–5pm, Sun. 10am–4pm; DM1, students DM0.25).

On the southern side of the Römerplatz stands the former court chapel, the **Nikolaikirche**, another red-sandstone Gothic affair, and the only one of seven Protestant churches in Frankfurt to survive the war. The interior is refreshingly restrained, a real refuge from the noise and rampant commercialism of the Römerplatz. Though the church was given a Gothic facelift in the fifteenth century, the lines of the original Romanesque structure are visible on the inside, where only the chancel underwent alteration. Opposite the Nikolaikirche is the **Steinerne Haus**, a postwar reconstruction of one of the few stone-built houses of the Frankfurt *Altstadt*; it now houses an art gallery (Tues. 11am–6pm, Weds. 11am–8pm, Thurs.–Sat. 11am–6pm; DM4, students DM2).

For a long time the area between the Römer and the Dom remained little more than an ugly hole in the middle of the city. By the mid-1970s the space had been partially filled by a stopgap concrete structure while debate raged about the eventual form of the reconstruction of the heart of the Römerberg. In 1978 it was decided to build replicas of some of the medieval buildings which had originally occupied the site, and to fill the remaining space with an ultramodern complex.

Opposite the Römer a row of seven half-timbered houses was built using original plans and traditional construction methods. The attention to detail is incredible, but somehow the net effect is slightly jarring and the buildings seem like filmset backdrops. Behind is a totally new development which in some ways works better, although many Frankfurters have mixed feelings about it. At its core is an ambitious building called the **Kultur-Schirn**, a general-purpose cultural center consisting of a glass tunnel for exhibitions and a rotunda with more display space and a cafeteria. The locals call the place the "Federal Bowling Alley," or, in their more fanciful moments "Murder at the Cathedral," due to its proximity to the Dom. Whether you like it or not will probably depend on how you feel about Post-Modernism, but in many ways it represents a brave attempt to recreate a sense of the Römerberg as the center of Frankfurt. Running roughly parallel with it, and bounded to the south by Saalgasse, is a row of gabled townhouses which, though essentially modern in design and construction, echo the medieval past of the Römerberg.

The **Saalhof**, an amalgamation of architecturally diverse imperial buildings now housing the **Historisches Museum**, is nearby on Mainkai, overlooking the river. Its twelfth-century chapel is all that remains of the old palace complex, which grew up around the Römerberg in the Middle Ages. The museum (Tues. 10am–5pm, Weds. 10am–8pm, Thurs.–Sat. 10am–5pm; free except for special exhibitions DM2) contains an extensive local history collection, highpoints of which are replicas of the crown jewels of the Holy Roman Empire (the originals are in Vienna) and a facsimile of the *Goldene Bulle* of 1356, which ratified Frankfurt's status as venue for Imperial coronations. There's a model of the city as it looked in 1912, and an eye-opening section on the devastation caused by the bombing. The **Rententurm**, which dates from 1456 and forms part of the building, is one of the few surviving towers from the old city defenses.

A short distance to the west, on Untermainkai, stands the **St. Leonhardskirche**, a thirteenth-century church embellished in the Gothic era. Surviving Romanesque features include the octagonal east towers and the carved doorways. Although the best feature of the church is its external appearance, the interior has a number of attractions, chiefly some intricate stained-glass work, and a magnificent gilded altar with skillfully carved scenes from the life of Christ.

A little farther along Untermainkai is the **Karmelitenkloster**, a late Gothic building most famous for Jerg Ratgeb's colossal fresco in its cloisters, depicting scenes from the life of Jesus. Painted between 1514 and 1523, the eighty-meter-long fresco was badly damaged during the war, but recent work has restored its exquisite coloring and vividness. The southern part of the building now houses the **Museum für Vor- und Frühgeschichte/Archäologisches Museum**, a collection devoted to early and pre-history and to the archaeological work carried out in Frankfurt.

Nearby at Untermainkai 14–15 is the **Jüdisches Museum** (Tues.–Sat. 10am–5pm, Weds. 10am–8pm), which recounts the history of Frankfurt's once-powerful and wealthy Jewish population. From the Karmelitenkloster go a few hundred meters north along Kurt-Schumacher-Strasse, then take a right, and you're in the **Zeil**, one of West Germany's most expensive and exclusive shopping streets.

Just past the Saalhof, a right turn up Buchtgasse will take you to the neoclassical **St. Paulskirche**, on the northern edge of the Römerberg. Now used as a meeting hall, its main claim to fame is that the first-ever German National Assembly was held here during the revolutionary upheavals of 1848–49. Unfortunately, the event turned out to be little more than a talking shop and nothing was achieved. On the northern wall of the church there's a monument to the victims of the Nazis.

Just west of the St. Paulskirche, at Grosser Hirschgraben 23, is the **Goethehaus und Museum** (April–Sept. Mon.–Sat. 9am–6pm, Sun. 10am–1pm; Oct.–Mar. Mon.–Sat. 9am–4pm, Sun. 10am–1pm; DM3, students DM2), the interior of which has been immaculately restored after being completely burned out during the war. This is where Goethe was born and raised, and not surprisingly it's become a popular tourist spot. To Germans, Goethe represents the pinnacle of their distinguished literary tradition, and he's accorded the same sort of reverence that's bestowed on Shakespeare in English-speaking countries. Immensely prolific over a creative career which spanned six decades, his output included poems, novels, and criticism, though he's chiefly renowned for his plays. Towering above all his other works is the epic drama *Faust*, which touches on all the main themes of European civilization; it was written at a leisurely pace throughout his life, and completed just before his death.

The guided tours tend to be pretty tedious—you'd be better off zipping around the place by yourself in about half an hour or so. The house has been made to look as much as possible like it did when Goethe lived here and there are even a few original objects which somehow survived the war. In the well-stocked library are some autographed examples of Goethe's writings, though nothing as impressive as the collection in Weimar in the GDR, where the writer spent most of the latter part of his life. The **Katharinen-Kirche**, a little further along on Kleiner Hirschgraben, is where Goethe was baptized and confirmed.

A couple of minutes away from here is the **Hauptwache**, an eighteenth-century baroque building which during the nineteenth century was Frankfurt's biggest (and aesthetically most pleasing) police station—these days it's a pricey downtown café. (The station of the same name is a junction on nearly all of Frankfurt's S- and U-Bahn lines.) Nearby on the Liebfrauenberg is the **Liebfrauenkirche**, a fifteenth-century church with a startling geometric design; look inside for the unusual altar, a huge alabaster-and-gilt affair which sits well in the dusky, pink-sandstone interior. Today eight Franciscan monks live in the church and spend a lot of time helping local down-and-outs, whom they allow to sleep in the pews. In the **Markthalle** just behind the church you can buy Turkish products and stock up on the best fresh fruit and vegetables in town. A little to the northwest of the Hauptwache is the **Börse**, Frankfurt's stock exchange. It's open to the public on weekdays from 11:30am to 1:30pm if you'd like a first-hand glimpse of where Frankfurt's conspicuous money comes from.

Appropriately enough two of the most expensive shopping streets in the city are just around the corner. **Goethestrasse** is Frankfurt's Wilshire Boulevard, all expensive jewelers and designer clothes shops, while **Grosse Bockenheimer Strasse**, known to the natives as *Fressgasse* ("Munch Lane") is home to upscale delicatessens and smarter restaurants. Look out for *Stefan Weiss*, a butcher's shop that's sometimes described as a "meat boutique," owing to its immaculate interior and high prices.

Both of these streets lead into Opernplatz, home of the grandiose neoclassical **Alte Oper**, built in 1880 in imitation of, and as a rival to, the opera houses of Paris and Dresden. The present structure is the result of years of work to restore the damage of 1945—the vestibule and first-floor café, all fake marble and colonnades, recapture something of the late nineteenth-century ambience. With its excellent acoustics, the Alte Oper is often used as a congress hall as well as playing host to classical musicians and the likes of Barbra Streisand and Liza Minelli. Oddly enough you won't see much opera here, apart from the occasional production which doesn't need elaborate staging.

It's worth taking a walk through the **Taunusanlage** and the **Gallusanlage**, two narrow stretches of parkland running into each other that begin south of Opernplatz and curve round to the Main, following the line of the old city wall. As you walk through it you get an excellent overview of Frankfurt old and new, with the Alte Oper to the north, the Hauptbahnhof to the west, the Römerberg to the southeast and all around you the ultramodern high-rise office buildings which give Frankfurt its distinctive skyline.

Another pleasant stroll from Opernplatz is in the opposite direction through the **Bockenheimer Anlage** and past a small lake to the **Nebbienische Gartenhäuschen**, a playful little villa built in 1810 by a local publisher to mark his third marriage. At the end of the Bockenheimer Anlage rises the fifteenth-century **Eschenheimer Turm**, the highest defensive tower in Germany. There were once 42 towers ringing the city and this is the most imposing of the survivors, looking like it was designed by some mad Gothic architect. Look out for the nine holes in the shape of a figure 9 on the weather vane which, according to legend, were shot into it by a local poacher.

Nearby in Stephanstrasse is the **Petersfriedhof**, which for years was Frankfurt's most fashionable cemetery; in the adjacent school courtyard is the grave of Goethe's mother, "Frau Aja." About ten minutes walk to the south, just off Fahrgasse, is a surviving stretch of the **Staufenmauer**, the twelfth-century city wall which was the granddaddy of all Frankfurt's subsequent defenses. Just beyond here, a left turn into Berliner Strasse will lead you to Battonstrasse and the **Jüdischer Friedhof**, in use from 1462 to 1828 and containing the Rothschild family vault.

Sachsenhausen and the Museumsufer

If you want to escape from the center of Frankfurt, or have a laid-back evening out, then head for **Sachsenhausen**, the city-within-a-city on the south bank of the Main. This part of town is known as the "apple wine quarter," in honor of its most famous produce, *Ebbelwei*, an apple wine served in practically every bar in the area. Sachsenhausen is the liveliest district of the city, and it's here that you'll find Frankfurt's most civilized nightlife.

Sachsenhausen has been part of the city since 1390, yet retains a distinctive atmosphere. In Schweizer Strasse there's every imaginable kind of specialty shop, while in the old *Schlachthaus* (slaughterhouse) on Deutschherrnufer (opposite the Flösserbrücke bridge) there's a *Flohmarkt* (flea market) every Saturday morning—it claims to be the largest in Europe.

The best way to approach Sachsenhausen is over the **Eiserner Steg**, an iron foot bridge which runs from the Römerberg. Otherwise take bus #46 from the Hauptbahnhof or, if you're feeling in the mood for a bit of tourist tackiness, take the *Ebbelwei-Express*, an old-time tram with on-board apple wine and pretzels (Sat. and Sun. afternoon; DM3 inclusive). However you decide to get there, you'll be doing a lot of walking when you arrive since most of Sachsenhausen is pedestrianized. You'll be able to dispense with the conventional sights fairly quickly. Just to the east of the Eiserner Steg is the **Dreikönigskirche**, an uninspiring nineteenth-century neo-Gothic church. A little farther along, just off Walter-Kolb-Strasse is the **Deutschordenshaus**, a three-winged, eighteenth-century building whose baroque facade cunningly hides a Gothic church. Last of all there's the **Kuhhirtenturm** (Cowherds Tower), built in 1490 as part of the Sachsenhausen fortifications, and which looks like an elongated fortified barn.

Most people go to Sachsenhausen to eat, drink, and be merry in the restaurants and bars of **Alt Sachsenhausen**, the network of streets around Affentorplatz. The main attractions are the apple-wine houses—recognized by the pine wreath or *Fichtekränzi* hanging outside—where drinkers sit at long wooden benches in an atmosphere that makes it easy to get into conversation. Made by the same process used in the production of ordinary wine, apple wine is bought in blue-grey stone jugs called *bembel* and drunk from a *schobbeglas*. There are four types: *Süsser*, sweet and fresh from the presses in autumn, and relatively weak; *Rauscher*, which will blow your head off if you don't treat it with respect; *Heller*, which is clear and smooth; and the hazy and golden *Alte*. Those in the know order *Handkäs mit Musik* (cheese served with onions and vinaigrette dressing) or *Rippchen mit Kraut* (smoked pork chop with sauerkraut) as a culinary accompaniment to their *Ebbelwei*.

The Museumsufer

There's entertainment of a different sort to be had on the **Museumsufer** (also known as Schaumainkai), which runs between the Eiserner Steg and the Friedensbrücke. Here you'll find the best museums in Frankfurt, seven in all, which you'll easily be able to spend the better part of a day exploring. With one exception, the museums are open from Tuesday to Sunday from 10am to 5pm (staying open until 8pm on Wednesday), and are closed on Monday. (The Deutsches Filmmuseum is open Tues.–Sun. 11am–6:30pm.) Entry is free to all except the Städel, which costs DM3.

The **Museum für Kunsthandwerk** (Schaumainkai 15) has a huge collection of applied art,, one of the best in the world, housed in a discreetly innovative building designed by the American architect Richard Meier—all sloping ramps in place of stairs and glassless internal windows framing objets d'art. The museum is divided into four sections: European, featuring a unique collection of furniture models, glassware, and ceramics; Islamic, with some fine carpets; Far Eastern, with lots of jade and lacquer work, plus a liberal sprinkling of porcelain and sculptures; and finally a section devoted to books and writing.

Housed in a nineteenth-century villa, the **Museum für Völkerkunde** (Schaumainkai 29) is a small ethnographical museum with an extensive collection of masks and totems from all over the world.

The new **Deutsches Filmmuseum** (Schaumainkai 41) is Germany's biggest and best film museum, and features a huge collection detailing the development of films and the film industry. A distinctly hands-on approach encourages visitors to get to grips with the various film-related items on display, which range from early bioscopes to modern movie cameras. On a larger scale, there's a reconstruction of the *Grand Café* in Paris where the Lumière brothers showed the first-ever public film, and of a Frankfurt movie theater from 1912. There's also a good collection of film posters and a very extensive section on film music. Not surprisingly the museum has its own movie theater (entry DM6), plus there's a good little café in the basement.

A passage leads from the Filmmuseum café to the **Deutsches Architektur-museum** (Schaumainkai 43), installed in a self-consciously avant-garde conversion of a nineteenth-century villa. The highpoint of the interior, which has been gutted and restyled in dazzling white, is the "house within a house," which dominates the museum like an oversized dollshouse. Somehow it doesn't quite work, and despite a glass roof and clever use of lighting, the building has a very claustrophobic feel which detracts from the actual exhibits themselves, the bulk of which are architectural drawings and models.

More conventional in layout is the **Reichspostmuseum** (Schaumainkai 53), basically a big collection of anything remotely connected with postal matters. Conceivably it might be of interest to a philatelist; there are lots of postage stamps, mailmen's uniforms, mail coaches, mailboxes, models of mail trains, and the like. The museum is also big on telephones, since Frankfurt calls itself the birthplace of the telephone, irrespective of the claims of Alexander Graham Bell.

The **Städel** ranks as one of the most comprehensive art galleries in Europe. Unlike the galleries of Munich and Berlin, it is not rooted in a royal collection—it was founded in the early nineteenth century by a local banker as an art college, with an assembly of old masters from which students could learn.

Chronologically, the layout begins on the top floor. The earliest German work is a mid-fourteenth century retable from the Middle Rhenish region; also from this area are a naive but surpassingly beautiful *Garden of Paradise* from the early fifteenth century, and *The Resurrection* by **Master of the Housebook**. **Dürer**'s *Job on his Dungheap* and two grisailles from a lost altarpiece by **Grünewald** are other works to seek out.

Holbein the Elder's large *Passion Altar*, painted for the city's Dominican monastery, is one of his finest works, with no quarter given in the representation of gruesome detail. **Cranach**'s *The Holy Kinship*, which incorporates portraits of some of the leading personalities of the day, is another major altarpiece from the eve of the Reformation. The idiosyncratic art of **Baldung** is represented by a *Baptism of Christ* triptych and *Two Weather Witches*, while in **Altdorfer**'s opulent *Adoration of the Magi* the artist typically indulges his love of rich and elaborate detail. The outstanding *Portrait of Simon George of Cornwall* by **Holbein the Younger** is particularly interesting for the fact that the subject was clean-shaven when the sittings began; the artist had to carry out a skillful modification in order to show the whiskers his patron subsequently grew.

One of the main strengths of the gallery is its wealth of paintings from the early Netherlandish School, dominated by the gem of the whole collection, **Van Eyck**'s *Lucca Madonna*, which shows his legendary precision at its finest. The first great painter of the School, now generally identified as **Robert Campin** but labeled here as the Master of Flémalle, is represented by several works, while his pupil **Roger van der Weyden** features with a magnificent *Virgin and Child with SS. Peter, John the Baptist, Cosmas and Damian*. Also in the room are superbly observed male portraits by Memling and Massys, and one of **Bosch**'s earliest known works, *Christ Presented to the People*; though restrained by his standards, it already shows his penchant for caricature and facial distortions.

The Madonna and Child, a frequent subject in the Netherlandish section, predominates in the Italian, where the outstanding treatment is the ethereal image by **Fra Angelico**. Versions by Verrocchio, Moretto da Brescia, Perugino, Bellini, Cima, and Carpaccio make fascinating comparisons. Other highlights here are an *Annunciation* by **Carlo Crivelli**, *St. Mark* by **Mantegna**, *Portrait of Simonetta Vespucci* by **Botticelli**, and **Pontormo**'s *Lady with Lap-Dog*.

Pride of place among seventeenth-century paintings goes to Frankfurt's own **Adam Elsheimer**. The largest work ever painted by this master of the small-scale is the *Altarpiece of the Cross*, the seven panels of which have been patiently accumulated over the years. Also here are *The Great Flood*—a miracle of compression—and *The Dream of Joseph*.

Poussin, Claude and Rubens, all admirers of Elsheimer, are on display in the next section, which also includes the most purely baroque work in **Rembrandt**'s entire output, the violent *Blinding of Samson*—a striking contrast with the quiet dignity of his very early *David Playing the Harp before Saul*. There's a gloriously luminous **Vermeer**, *The Geographer*, and examples of most of the lesser artists of seventeenth century Holland. Representation of the eighteenth century is sparser, but there are two scenes from a *Horrors of War* series by **Goya**, and examples of Tiepolo, Canaletto and Chardin. A recent acquisition is a newly-discovered **Watteau**, the marvelously frothy *Isle of Cythera*.

Paintings from the late eighteenth century onwards occupy the first floor. Of the big French names, **Courbet** (a *View of Frankfurt*), **Degas**, and **Monet** are the ones to look out for. However, German artists predominate. *Goethe in the Roman Campagna* by **Johann Heinrich Tischbein** is the most celebrated of the many Romantic portrayals of the writer. The Nazarene Brotherhood figures strongly, notably with a huge detached fresco of *The Introduction of the Arts into Germany*, painted by **Philip Veit**, once director of the Städel. If this isn't to your taste, you might prefer the realism of **Leibl**, whose *Unlikely Couple* is an update of a favorite Renaissance theme—mercenary love.

Until the days of the Third Reich, the Städel had perhaps the finest array of modern painting in Germany. However, over 500 paintings were removed in the measures against "degenerate art," and the collection has never recovered, although it now has the benefit of being able to display loans from local industrialists and financial institutions. German highlights include **Beckmann**'s *The Synagogue* (bought by public appeal as an atonement for past sins), **Dix**'s unflattering *The Artist's Family*, **Ernst**'s spooky *Nature in Morning Light* and **Kirchner**'s *Nude Wearing a Hat*; the most notable foreign paintings are **Matisse**'s *Still Life* and **Picasso**'s *Portrait of Fernance Olivier*.

Finally there's the **Liebighaus** (Schaumainkai 71), which is home to a big sculpture collection—the building can be identified by the bits and pieces of statuary on display in the garden, including *Ariadne on the Panther* by Johann Heinrich Dannecker. The collection is a sort of step-by-step guide to the history of sculpture—the earliest pieces date back to the third millenium B.C., followed by Sumerian, Egyptian, Greek, Roman and Coptic examples. There are more than enough Madonnas, and innumerable specimens of baroque altar art.

Westend— and Bockenheim

Frankfurt's financial district, the **Westend**, developed as home to the commercial class during the nineteenth century. Until the Nazis came to power many of the wealthier members of Frankfurt's Jewish community (the second largest in

Germany) lived here; for example, huge swathes of land between Bockenheimer Landstrasse and Reuterweg were owned by the Rothschild family until the city bought them out in 1938 for a "bargain" price. In the 1960s the property speculators moved in, forcing ordinary people out of their homes so the old buildings could be converted into offices, or the sites used for skyscrapers. Scant attention was paid to planning laws as the developers fell over themselves to grab every available inch of land, and from 1970 onwards there was a rash of house occupations and squattings in protest. Fierce clashes with the police ensued, but caused only temporary delays in the process of redevelopment.

Ugliest building in the area is undoubtedly the **Hochhaus am Park** on Fürstenberger Strasse, a totally incoherent structure designed by a succession of architects. The most impressive of the high rises is the sleek **Deutsche Bank**, a little to the west of the Alte Oper, which dominates the Frankfurt skyline; the bank has an art collection which can be viewed by prior arrangement (☎7150) or, should you so desire, you can just have a look around the foyer and watch the moneymakers going purposefully about their business in the shadow of a cascading fountain. At **Siesmayerstrasse 6** you can take a look at a piece of very recent history; this elegant upper-middle-class villa (now fallen on very hard times) was the last squatted house in the Westend to succumb.

Westend has its own stretch of greenery too. In the northwest of the area is the **Grüneburgpark**, a nineteenth-century, English-style park which these days is popular with joggers and weekend ballplayers. On the northeastern edge is the **Botanischer Gartern**, a good place to go for a walk, as it has a sort of cultivated wildness to it. Avoid the **Palmengarten** (entry DM4.50), which is full of old ladies and manicured lawns.

Bockenheim

Bockenheimer Landstrasse, once Frankfurt's millionaires' row, will take you from Westend to **Bockenheim**, a predominantly blue-collar district which since the 1960s has become the focus of Frankfurt's alternative scene following a big influx of "boho types" and students. The area also has a big *Gastarbeiter* population, and is best thought of as a Frankfurt version of Berlin's Kreuzberg, with the difference that the various groups who have made it their home are not as factionalized and stand-offish as in that city. Leipziger Strasse is the main shopping drag (on U-Bahn line #6) and there are a lot of good bars and restaurants around—the Italian ones are best from a culinary viewpoint, but the Greek places are usually better value for money.

The university complex lies at the southeastern edge of Bockenheim, which partly accounts for its popularity with students. In the vicinity is the **Senckenbergmuseum**, Senckenberganlage 25 (Mon.–Fri. 9am–5pm, Weds. 9am–8pm, Sat. and Sun. 9am–6pm), a massive natural history museum and worth a visit if you're into that sort of thing.

Höchst

It's worth taking a trip out to **Höchst** (S-Bahn line #1 from Hauptbahn or Hauptwache), home of the *Hoechst* chemical company. Although dominated by the chemical works, Höchst does have a small **Altstadt**, which rewards a quick look around. The **Balongaropalast** (Balongarostr. 109) is a slightly excessive baroque townhouse, in whose gardens open-air theater performances are occasionally held, and a little farther down the same street, in the **Dalberghaus** (no.

186), Höchst porcelain is once again being manufactured—replica eighteenth century shepherdess figurines and the like are for sale at unhealthy prices. On Schlossplatz there's a run-of-the-mill **Schloss** and in the old **Zollturm** (Customs Tower; Schlossplatz 13) there's a **Heimatsmuseum** which, having been sponsored by *Hoechst*, tends to dwell on the none too exciting history of that company. Bus #54 from the Altstadt it will take you down Höchster Farben Strasse and to your left you'll see the huge chemical complex stretching out down to the Main. The cathedral-like administrative offices of the factory were designed by the Jugendstil architect Peter Behrens and must be among the most aesthetically balanced factory buildings in the world. The bus then goes on to Zeilsheim, which in the immediate postwar years was *the* black market center of Germany and where, around **Coburger Strasse**, you can still see the little cottages of the **Arbeiter Kolonie Zeilsheim**, a turn-of-the-century model housing development for *Hoechst* workers.

Eating and Drinking

Not surprisingly, given its status as one of Germany's main urban centers, Frankfurt has a wealth of gastronomic possibilities catering to even the most esoteric tastes. Whether it's vegan breakfast or Japanese afternoon tea you're after, you'll be able to find it somewhere.

Café-Bars

Downtown
Lipizzaner-Bar, Frankfurter Hof, Bethmannstr. 33. An extremely elegant and expensive piano bar.

Café Schwille, Grosse Bockenheimer Str. 50. This traditional *Kaffee und Küchen* spot is also the place for an early breakfast (it opens at 7am). Good in the summer as there's a terrace. Also branches at Rossmarkt, and next door to the Katharinenkirche.

Rotlint-Café, Rotlintstr. 60. Recommended for breakfasts, this one is just outside the city center (tram #12 from Grosse Friedbergerstrasse) and is popular with a youngish alternative crowd. Open until 1am.

TAT-Café, Grosse Eschenheimer Str. 2. Café of the Theater am Turm, the food is indifferent but the black-clad *Szene* (i.e. "Scene") types and trendies don't seem to care.

Bockenheim and Westend
Café Laumer, Bockenheimer Landstr. 67. One of Frankfurt's oldest cafés, halfway up the Westend's main thoroughfare, now enjoying a new lease on life with a young, arty clientele.

Stattcafé, Grempstr. 21. Another place which does good breakfast. The emphasis is on healthy eating in an informal atmosphere—popular with the Bockenheim arty crowd; work from Frankfurt artists on the walls.

Sachsenhausen
Café Bar, Schweizerstr. 14. Despite an unimaginative name, this is the trendiest café in Sachsenhausen, all black-and-mirrored decor with a posy clientele.

Das Lesecafé, Diesterwegstr. 7. Popular with would-be intellectuals, the gimmick here is that you read as you eat and drink. Phone up to order your book in advance.

Pubs and Wine Cellars
Balalaika, Dreikönigstr. 30 (Sachsenhausen). Popular with Brits and Americans but don't let that put you off. Live music with a Slavic flavor.

Club Voltaire, Hochstr. 5. Good food with a Spanish bias, and an eclectic clientele: political activists, artists, musicians, Greens, gays—you'll find them all here in one of Frankfurt's best-established meeting places.

Der alte Hut, Deutschherrnufer 28 (Sachsenhausen). Fleamarket decor and river views make this a popular place to sink a few drinks. 8pm–1am.

Dominicus, Brückhofstr. 1. A vaulted cellar establishment with live music at weekends, whose good wines and free *Schmalzbrot* draw a young crowd.

Dünker, Bergerstr. 265 (U-Bahn line #4 to Bornheim Mitte). Originally a sampling house selling wine by the crate, you can now drink in the unpretentious cellar. Closes at 9pm.

Fidelio, Bockenheimer Landstr. 1. A favorite Westend wateringhole for the media and advertising types, with a wine-bar atmosphere. Normally open until 1am.

Haus Wertheym, Fahrtor 1. A medieval inn on the Römerberg with *Bockbier*, traditional food and a friendly atmosphere. Closed Tues.

Sachs, Darmstädter Landstr. 119 (Sachsenhausen). A huge old brewery cellar which has been fixed up and now attracts phenomenal numbers of people. Not bad for all that.

Apple-Wine Taverns

Apple wine or *Ebbelwei* is a specialty of this part of Germany, and Frankfurt has some of the best apple-wine taverns in the country. They are concentrated around Sachsenhausen and although they have become something of a tourist magnet, native Frankfurters patronize them too. If you're selective you should be able to have a congenial and alcoholic night out.

Aprikösie, Neuer Wall 3. Old-fashioned, with a secluded courtyard. Closed on weekends.

Buchscheer, Schwarzsteinkautweg 17/Gablonzerstr. 12. Set amidst the rose gardens on the southeastern edge of Sachsenhausen, and very popular with walkers. Good home cooking and home-produced apple wine. (To get there take tram #14 or bus #35 from downtown or tram #17 from the center of Sachsenhausen.)

Eichkatzerl, Dreieichstr. 29. A traditional Sachsenhausen apple-wine tavern with a very popular restaurant. Closed Weds. and first Thurs. of every month.

Klaane Sachsehäuser, Neuer Wall 11. A family place favored by native Sachsenhauseners.

Nagur, Schweizer Str. A little upmarket but worth dropping in.

Wagner, Schweizer Str. 71 Worth checking out; a lively clientele ranges from young to middle aged.

Zu den Drei Stuebern, Dreieichstr. 28/Klappergasse. Mainly locals with a small bar-room and pleasant terrace at the rear. Closed Sat.

Zum Gemalten Haus, Schweizer Str. 67. A bit on the "olde worlde side" with its oil-painted facade and stained-glass windows, yet quite lively, with long rows of tables outside.

Zum Grauen Bock, Rittergasse 30. There tend to be a lot of tourists at this one but it does stay open until 1am.

Apple-wine houses are not restricted to Sachsenhausen; there are a couple of recommended ones in other parts of the city.

Momberger, Alt-Heddernheim 13 (U-bahn lines #1, 2, and 3 to Weisser Stein). Very traditional and full of locals rather than tourists, due to its being out on the northern edge of the city. The apple wine comes straight from wooden vats on the premises and the food is cheap.

Scherer, Lindenau 9 (U-bahn lines #1, 2, and 3 to Weisser Stein). A cozy place in the suburb of Escherheim; serves real wine too.

Zur Eulenburg, Eulengasse 46 (U-bahn line #4 to Seckbacher Landstrasse). Unappealing middle-aged clientele, but the food and *Ebbelwei* are as good as any.

Restaurants

There is an incredible range of choice when it comes to eating out in Frankfurt, from the ultra-trendy joints of the Westend to the cheapo Italian restaurants of Bockenheim. The following are some of the better ones.

Downtown and Around

Alte Kanzlei, Neidenau 50. Alsatian specialties which means things like dandelion salad from DM28. Closed Sat.

Aubergine, Alte Gasse 14. Good food, good service, reasonable prices (by central Frankfurt standards)—lunch DM20, four courses DM45. Open until 11pm.

Bombay Place, Taunusstr. 17. A tandoori-and-chicken joint near the Hauptbahnhof.

Byblos, Vilbeler Str. 32. A bit extravagant—good Lebanese food, plenty of *arak*, and the added attraction of belly dancing from 10:30pm on Friday.

Casa del Pittore, Zeisselstr. 20). An expensive downtown Italian, but their fish is excellent—if you've got DM30-plus to spare.

Die Leiter, Kaiserhofstr. 11 (just off Grosse Bockenheimer Strasse). Classy yet not too expensive with pavement tables in the summer. DM15–25.

Divan, Elbestr. 9. Turkish restaurant with traditional music and belly dancing. Open 6am–1am.

Eden, Rahmhofstr. 4 . Real heavy-duty vegetarian place patronized by true adherents. Open until 8:30pm but closed Sun.

El Pacifico, Boulterrasse, Sandweg 79 (U-Bahn line #4 to Merianplatz). It's worth going out of the way for the enchiladas and tacos, which even attract jaded Americans.

Estragon, Jahnstr. 49. It's tarragon with everything in this reasonably priced restaurant (DM15–30), which attracts a lot of office workers.

Green Hill, Gutzkowstr. 43. Not particularly cheap but quite tasty vegetarian. Try their tofu stroganoff. Open until 11pm most nights but closed Mon.

Juchheim's, Am Salzhaus 1. An authentic Japanese tea house and restaurant. The tea house is open until 6:30pm and the restaurant until 10:30pm. Closed Sun.

Mikini, Fahrgasse 93. A Japanese restaurant which makes few concessions to the west.

Nibelungen-Scänke, Niblungenallee 55 (U-bahn line #55 to Niblungenallee). Typical Greek food at reasonable prices. The clientele is young and the place is usually open until 1am.

Niza, Untermainkai 17). A small Chinese restaurant overlooking the Main. The food's OK and it stays open all night on Sat.

Panda, Düsseldorfer Str. 10. The cheapest good Chinese restaurant in the Hauptbahnhof area where there are quite a few others.

Scarlet Pimpernel, Krögerstr. 7. Recommended Polish restaurant open Sat. and Sun. only 8pm–1am.

Tse-Yang, Kaiserstr. 67. Pricey but very good Chinese. In the middle of the red-light district. The Peking duck is excellent.

Westend

Erno's Bistro, Liebingstr. 15/Staufenstr. Westend French with an Alsatian accent and business clientele. It's not cheap, but if you've got some money to burn then you can get three courses for DM40. Open until 10pm; closed on weekends.

Golfo di Napoli, Leipziger Str. 16. Pricey Italian, popular with the Westend yuppies, but the food and atmosphere are good.

Jüdisches Restaurant, Savignystr. 66. Frankfurt's only Jewish restaurant, in the Jewish community center.

Knoblauch, Staufenstr. 39/Liebingstr. Friendly, intimate little place where everything seems to come liberally laced with garlic. DM15–25.

Rosa, Grüneburgweg 25. Good food for Westend types not so keen on conspicuous consumption. Closed weekends.

Bockenheim

Gargantua, Friesengasse 3. One of Bockenheim's best, with a three-course meal for DM38. If that's too meager you could always go for the seven-course one at DM98. Open until 9:30pm; closed Mon. and first Sun. of the month.

Union International Club, Am Leonhardsbrunn 12/Ditmarstr. This place is so chi-chi that it doesn't even have a sign on its wrought-iron gates to say it's a restaurant. You get a couple of courses for about DM35.

Sachsenhausen

Atschel, Wallstr. 7/Abstgäschen. One of the ubiquitous Alsatian specialty places. Fish dishes and apple wine. Closed Mon.

Flo, Textorstr. 89. A mixture of traditional cooking and absurdly decadent smoked salmon and caviar dishes. DM20–30.

St. Hubertus, Gartenstr. 175 (☎637266). A game and wildfowl specialty place with a garden; you should be able to come away with change from DM25.

Nightlife

Not surprisingly Frankfurt's nighlife is pretty eclectic, though in this money city quite a lot of what's going on is out of the reach of most pockets. The following is a selective run down of the more affordable venues. Worth knowing about is Kleine Bockenheimer Strasse, aka *Jazzgasse* ("Jazz Alley"), the center of Frankfurt's lively jazz scene. Many leading German jazzers cut their musical teeth playing in the bars around here and there's usually live music going on most nights.

Live Music Venues

Batschkapp, Maibachstr. 24. Open most days of the week 9pm–1am with live music or fairly up-to-the-minute DJ dance sounds.

Irish Pub, Kleine Rittergasse 11. Every big German city has its Irish pub; Frankfurt's is very popular, with good Irish music. Open until 1am.

Jazz Keller, Kleine Bockenheimer Str. 18a/Goethestrasse. This atmospheric cellar is Frankfurt's premier jazz venue. Open 9pm–3am. Closed Mon.

Music-Hall, Voltastr. 74. Big venue northwest of the Hauptbahnhof, with regular live music and discos. Open until 3am with food.

Schlachthof, Deutschherrnufer 36. Rough-and-ready rock-and-jazz joint, housed in Sachsenhausen's old slaughterhouse.

Sinnkasten, Brönnerstr. 5. This place has everything—pool room, cabaret stage, disco, and, most importantly, a concert hall where they put on everything from jazz to avant-garde and indie stuff. Open 9pm–2am. Entry DM7.

Discos

Amadeus, Kirchnerstr. 7. Very exclusive place with neurotic door policy. If you look right you might get in. Italian food, and open until 4am.

Club KIZ, Karlstr. 17. In the heart of the seedy Hauptbahnhof quarter, popular with rich pimps and their friends.

Dorian Gray, Airport C, level 0. Oddly located at airport, one of largest discos in Germany, and not always so easy to get into. Entry DM10; open until 6am. Closed Mon. and Tues.

Le Jardin, Kaiserhofstr. 6. Centrally located nightspot for smooth bankers and their well-dressed partners.

Maier-Gustl's, Münchener Str. 57. Another Hauptbahnhof joint—this time the emphasis is on recreating every cliché you've ever heard about Germany. All beer *Steins* and brass music, but the tourists like it.

Paradieshof, Paradiesstr. 23. Middle-aged crowd, reflected in the music. Closed Mon.

Vogue, Junghofstr. 14. Epitomizes Frankfurt at its affluent worst. Money and appearances are everything here. Open until 4am.

Gay Frankfurt

Blue Moon, Eckenheimer Landstrasse. Women's place, full of intense political lesbians.

Keller, Bleigstrasse. Extremely chic with a slightly intimidating atmosphere.

Madame, Alle Heiligen Strasse. Also for women; a little more laid back.

Schweig, Schäfergasse. Relaxed and unpretentious—a good way into the Frankfurt gay scene.

Culture

Frankfurt has a predictably lively **theater** and **classical music** scene, centered on the aforementioned *Alte Oper* on Opernplatz (☎13400) and the *Städtische Bühnen* on Theaterplatz (☎256 2335). The latter has one auditorium for opera (whose productions, with a strong bias in favor of twentieth-century music, are regarded as the most innovative in Germany) and two for drama. Among the city's orchestras, pride of place goes to the world-class *Radio-Sinfonie Orchester Frankfurt*. There are two **English-language theaters** in the city—*Café-Theater*, Hamburger Allee 45 (☎777466) and *Playhouse*, Hansaallee 152 (☎151 8326). Also worthy of special note is *Gallus-Theater*, Krifteler Str. 55 (☎738 0037), which has a fair claim to be regarded as the main contribution the *Gastarbeiter* have made to the national culture. Satirical cabaret can be seen at *Die Schmiere*, Im Karmeliterkloster (☎281066) and *Die Maininger*, Neue Rothofstr. (☎280227).

Listings

Airlines *Air Canada*, Friedensstr. 11 (☎250131); *Air New Zealand*, Rathenauplatz 1a. (☎291897); *British Airways*, Rossmarkt 23 (☎290371); *Lufthansa*, Am Hauptbahnhof 2 (☎25700); *TWA*, Hamburger Allee 2-10 (☎770601).

Area code (☎069).

Bike rental from *Per Pedale*, Falkstr. 28, in Bockenheim (☎707 2363).

Consulates *British*, Bockenheimer Landstr. 51-3 (☎720406); *American*, Siesmayerstr. 21 (☎753040); *Australian*, Grosse Gallusstr. 10-14 (☎20057).

Cultural institute *Amerika-Haus*, Staufenstr. 1 (☎722794).

Festivals Main folklore events are the *Waldchestag* on Pentecost weekend and the *Main Volksfest* in early August.

Mitfahrzentrale, Gutleutstr. 125 (☎2305113).

Post offices. The main post office is at Zeil 110 and there's also one with longer opening hours in the Hauptbahnhof.

Swimming. There's an open-air swimming pool on Mörfelder Landstrasse (bus #61, tram #15). There are also a couple of indoor pools—the *Stadtbad Mitte*, near the Eswchheimer Turm at Hochstr. 4-8, and the *Rebstockbad* at August-Euler-Str. 7.

What's happening. The tourist office publishes a free listings magazine, *Frankfurter Woche*.

Women's Frankfurt. There is a women's center at at Hamburger Allee 45 (☎772659). The women's *Mitfahrzentrale* at is at Konrad-Brosswitz-Str. 11, in Bockenheim (☎771777).

Around Frankfurt

From Frankfurt it's an easy rail journey to **BADHOMBURG**, a biggish spa town which lies at the foot of the Taunus mountains. There's not much to see, but if you feel in the mood go for a stroll in the **Kurpark**. From the entrance walk down the Brunnenallee to the fake Roman temple which houses the **Elizabeth-Brunnen**, the most famous of the eleven springs. The main bath-house is the **Kaiser-Wilhelm-Bad**—for DM18 you can wallow in the mineral baths for two-and-a-half hours and see if it deserves its reputation as a pickup joint. There's also a **Spielcasino** which the locals like to claim was the inspiration for the casino in Monte Carlo.

The town itself has a **Schloss** (Tues.–Sun. 10am–4pm; DM1), a fairly typical seventeenth-century residence with only the 55-meter high **Weisse Turm** as a reminder of its original defensive purpose. The Schloss was built by Friedrich II, Prince of Homburg, who was the model for Kleist's hero in the eponymous play; his wooden leg, displayed inside the Schloss, is known as the "Silver Leg" because of its silver joints. From 1866 to 1918 the building was the summer residence of the kings of Prussia, who from 1871 onward were also the emperors of Germany. From Bad Homburg it's worth taking a trip to **Saalburg**, a reconstructed Roman fort about 6km northeast of the town (open daily 8am–5pm; DM1.50)—it gives a good impression of how a fortified Roman frontier post must have looked. Bad Homburg has plenty of hotels, though they tend to be on the pricey side. One of the better bets is *Johannisberg*, Thomasstr. 5 (☎06172 21315), which starts at DM21. There's a **youth hostel** at Meiereiberg 1 (☎06172 23950) and the **tourist office** is in the *Kurhaus*, Louisenstr. 58 (06172 12130).

The thickly wooded slopes of the Taunus themselves are atmospheric and invigorating rather than breathtaking, and they can be explored in a single day, when traveling betwen Frankfurt and Wiesbaden. The highest peak, the **Grosser Feldberg** (880m), is the tallest mountain in any of the Rhineland schist massifs; from the tower at the summit there's a marvelous panorama of the surrounding area. In the nearby village of **OBERREIFENBERG** there's a **youth hostel** at Limesstr. 14 (☎06082 2440). The main Taunus town is **KÖNIGSTEIN IN TAUNUS** (buses from Frankfurt and Wiesbaden), which boasts a moderately exciting ruined castle from whose crumbling keep you can just about see Frankfurt. If you want to spend a little longer in the area there are a few **hotels** and **pensions**, one of the cheapest of which is *Zur schönen Aussicht*, Schneidhainer Str. 30 (☎06174 21525).

Another possible excursion from Frankfurt is to **GELNHAUSEN**, a small town perched on the slopes of the **Kinzig** valley on the fringes of the **Spessart**, an upland forest region which sprawls south into Bavaria. Gelnhausen calls itself *Barbarossa-Stadt*, a reference to its foundation by Barbarossa in the twelfth century. Parts of the defensive walls remain, and you can visit the ruins of Barbarossa's palace, the **Kaiserpfalz** (daily 10am–1pm and 2pm–5pm DM0.50.), standing on an island in the middle of the Kinzig River. The other attraction here is the **Marienkirche**, a Romanesque church with a fine decorative chancel—it's on the highest point of the town, overlooking the market place. The **tourist office** is at Am Obermarkt (☎06051 820054 or 82000). There's a **youth hostel** at Schützen-graben 5 (☎06051 44240) and the cheapest **hotel** is the *Scheim von Bergen*, Obermarkt 22 (☎06051 2755, rooms from DM25). About 10km to the north of Gelnhausen is **BÜDDINGEN**, a small town with an intact *Stadtmauer*—look out for the decorated Gothic gateways. There's also a still-inhabited **Schloss** which is worth a look (Mar.–Oct.; guided tours at 2pm, 3pm and 4pm; DM3).

SOUTHERN HESSEN

The southern part of Hessen offers a wide variety of scenery, ranging from the wooded heights of the Odenwald at the extreme tip of the province to the famous vineyard growing areas on the east bank of the Rhine. There are only two cities in this area: the staid spa of **Wiesbaden** and the former ducal residence of **Darmstadt**, which is a place with more than a few surprises in store.

Darmstadt

A cursory inspection of **DARMSTADT** is unlikely to leave you with much of an impression. The only way it differs from any other bombed-out, rebuilt German city—with featureless modern facades interspersed with the odd incongrous prewar structure—is in the survival of the planned neoclassical layout, with broad streets and spacious squares. Don't be discouraged, though—Darmstadt has a rich cultural heritage, traces of which have survived both the bombs and the planners.

During the second half of the eighteenth century the *Darmstädter Kreis'* (the "Darmstadt Circle") flourished under the protection of Countess Karoline of Hessen, numbering among its members Goethe, Martin Wieland and Johann Herder. The playwright Georg Büchner spent much of his short life in Darmstadt and wrote his great play *Danton's Death* here in 1834, while under police observation for suspected revolutionary activities. It was at the very end of the last century, however, that the arts flourished most freely in Darmstadt and it's from this period that the most lasting and visible symbol of the city's support for artistic innovation dates. The **Mathildenhöhe**, a unique artists' colony on the eastern edge of the city center established by Grand Duke Ernst Ludwig of Hessen (a grandson of Queen Victoria), is a living monument to Jugendstil, and if you only have time to see one thing in Darmstadt it should be this. The best way to reach the Mathildenhöhe is on foot, as it's only a fifteen-minute walk along Erich-Ollenhauer-Promenade from just behind the **Schloss**. Alternatively, take tram #4 from **Luisenplatz**, the broad square that stands more or less in the middle of the city center; get off at the lake known as **Grosser Woog**, and from there head up Eugen-Bracht-Weg to Europa Platz.

At the center of the Mathildenhöhe stands a building which fits in well with the Jugendstil buildings but didn't originally have anything to do with the colony itself—the **Russische Kapelle**, a heavily ornamented Russian Orthodox chapel crowned by two gilded domes. The chapel was built in 1898 at the behest of the last czar of Russia, Nicholas II, who often spent the summer in Darmstadt with his Hessen-born wife. You're asked to make a small offering before going into the opulent interior. Serbian Orthodox services are regularly held here for Darmstadt's Yugoslav community.

Work on the Mathildenhöhe colony began in 1901 with the construction of the **Ernst-Ludwig-Haus**, designed by the Viennese architect Joseph Maria Olbrich for the *Dokument Deutscher Kunst 1901*, an exhibition whose aim was to encapsulate all aspects of the Jugendstil movement. Approached via a broad flight of steps, the building has something of the mausoleum about it, with its imposing portal flanked by two monumental figures representing Adam and Eve. As well as being used as an exhibition hall the Ernst-Ludwig-Haus also contained studios for sculptors. Nowadays it's home to a design institute, though there are plans to

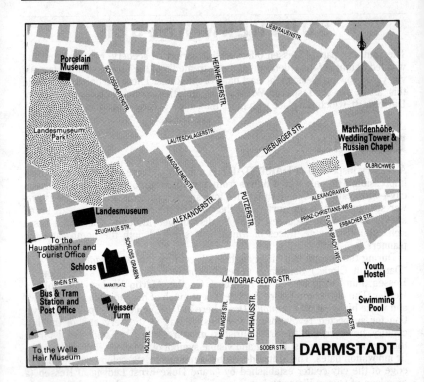

establish a Jugendstil museum here. To complement the Ernst-Ludwig-Haus, Olbrich built seven houses as artists' residences in the immediate vicinity, also in 1901. One was destroyed by a bomb during the war and has been replaced by a fountain, but six are still intact, though some of these were also damaged and inaccurately restored. They vary in style from the slightly subverted villa-look of the **Olbrich Haus** to the angular southern European appearance of the **Haus Habich** and the **Kleine Glückert-Haus**, and all have unique and intricate design features which differentiate them from each other. The ethos of the original project is best preserved in the **Grosse Glückert-Haus**, a building in which every internal and external detail has been invested with verve and style. This is the only house in which you're allowed to venture indoors; you can try ringing at the gate, but it's advisable to ask the tourist office to arrange a visit for you.

Next door to it is the **Behrens-Haus**, designed by the Hamburg architect Peter Behrens, also in 1901. Its brick-framed white facade and red-tiled roof inject an element of Hanseatic sobreity into the colony, in deliberate contrast with Olbrich's more playful Mediterranean efforts. Only the door, decorated with swirling bronze appliqué work and flanked by rippling turquoise columns, has much in common with the neighboring houses.

In 1908 work on the huge and gleaming **Austellungsgebäude** (*Exhibition Hall*) at the top of the Mathildenhöhe was completed. It's still in use, and the first-floor café is equipped with Jugendstil furnishings. Look out for the Olbrich-designed mosaic in the roof of the pavilion halfway up the entrance steps. Next to the Austellungsgebäude rises the **Hochzeitsturm**, a 48-meter high brick tower with a distinctive roof which, when seen head-on, looks like a hand facing palm outwards. The tower was presented to Grand Duke Ernst-Ludwig and his bride by the city of Darmstadt three years after their 1905 wedding. Adopted informally as a symbol of the city, it's now Darmstadt's official emblem. An elevator takes visitors to the top from Tuesday to Sunday (10am–6pm, DM1.50).

Today most of the Mathildenhöhe buildings are used by various design institutes and cultural organizations, while Darmstadt's practising artists have moved to the nearby **Rosenhöhe** area. This is reached in about ten minutes from the Olbrich-Haus by following Alexandra Weg, turning right into Fiedlerweg, left into Seitersweg, and then crossing the railroad bridge. During the late 1960s a new artists' colony was established here in the **Rosenhöhe Park**. At the entrance to the park is the **Löwentor**, a gate comprising six Jugendstil lions (brought here from the Platonenhain Park on the Mathildenhöhe) standing on top of decorative brick pillars. The original purpose of the park was to provide a last resting place for members of the Hessen royal family. Nearby is the **Ostbahnhof**, a station built in the style of a Russian country station at the request of Czar Nicholas II.

Compared to the stylized glories of the Mathildenhöhe, the city center looks very drab. Before the war Darmstadt was capital of part of Hessen, and had its fair share of grand buildings, mostly dating from the time of Count Ernst Ludwig (1678–1739), who transformed it from a hick town into a *Residenzstadt*. But on the night of September 11, 1944, 300,000 incendiary bombs and 700 high-explosive bombs were dropped on the city—the resulting fire storm, deliberately created following the tried-and-tested Hamburg pattern, killed 12,000 people and destroyed half of Darmstadt's buildings. Although it had to surrender its status as capital to the town of Wiesbaden, Darmstadt made a remarkably quick recovery, particularly in the cultural arena, but most of its historic quarter was gone forever. (For a fictionalized account of the raid, from the point of view of both sides, read *Bomber* by Len Deighton.)

At the center of modern Darmstadt sprawls **Luisenplatz**, a windswept shopping plaza crisscrossed by tram and bus lines and notable only for the **Ludwigsäule**, a memorial to Grand Duke Ludwig I. From Luisenplatz the Rheinstrasse leads to the **Schloss**, an extensive but unexceptional complex which developed gradually over 700 years. Reduced to a shell in the 1944 bombing raid, it has been diligently restored. The baroque *Neuschloss* (new castle) houses a library and the town archive, while the predominantly Renaissance *Altschloss* is home to a technical college and the **Schlossmuseum** (Mon.–Thurs. 10am–1pm and 2pm–5pm, Sat. and Sun. 10am–1pm; DM2.50). Basically this is another example of the dreaded German *Heimatmuseum*, but it's redeemed by **Hans Holbein the Younger**'s *Madonna of Jacob Meyer*, painted in 1526, one of the supreme masterpieces of Renaissance painting. It's particularly intriguing in being the last Catholic altarpiece by any of the great German masters of the period, all of whom (including Holbein himself) became Protestant. The picture shows the former burgomaster of Basel, accompanied by his living and deceased wives, asking the Virgin to intercede on behalf of his sickly baby son, whose features—bizarrely—duplicate those of the Christ child. Apart from the Holbein the museum is packed with routine stuff—a lot of furniture, a collection of eighteenth century and nineteenth century clothing and militaria, and a couple of rooms done out in eighteenth-century and nineteenth-century style.

Slightly to the north of the Schloss, however, is one of the best general museums in the country—the **Landesmuseum** (Tues.–Sun. 10am–5pm, Weds.

also 7–9pm; free). In the basement is a sparkling collection of **art nouveau** objets d d'art, in which German Jugendstil can be compared with its variants from elsewhere in Europe. There's an equally glittering array of medieval **stained glass**, the most notable being a cycle from the Ritterstiftskirche in Bad Wimpfen. On the ground floor are examples of decorative art from the Middle Ages, Renaissance and baroque periods including a *Crucifixion* group by **Riemenschneider**. The rooms on the first floor are devoted to **natural history**; an abandoned shale strip mine near Darmstadt has proved fruitful ground for excavations, and remains of prehistoric crocodiles, fish, and horses recently dug up there are now on view.

However, the Landesmuseum's main claim to fame is as a picture gallery. One wing of the ground floor contains one of the best collections of German Primitives, going back as far as a mid-thirteenth-century altar-table from Worms. **Lochner's** gorgeous *Presentation in the Temple* shows the Cologne School at its mid-fifteenth-century peak, while the **Master of Saint Bartholomew's** *Madonna and Child with Saints Adrian and Augustine* belongs to the final flowering of this movement a couple of generations later. Mid-Rhenish painters closely followed Cologne's lead, and one of the finest products of this region is the work from which the **Master of the Darmstadt Passion** derives his name.

Several pictures by **Cranach** dominate the Renaissance section, including one of his greatest canvases, *Cardinal Albrecht von Brandenburg as Saint Jerome*, an allegory which shows the Reformation period's most conciliatory member of the Catholic hierarchy in the traditional pose of Saint Jerome in this study.

Among the old masters on the second floor, the most important is the enigmatic *Magpie on the Gallows*, one of **Pieter Bruegel the Elder's** last works. The evil-looking contraption for public executions strikes a menacingly discordant note in the sunny landscape, which forms the backdrop to a peasant dance. Presumably, the magpie symbolizes the gossip, and thus serves as a warning of the consequences of talking too much—something particularly pertinent in the Spanish-occupied Netherlands of Bruegel's day, when the Inquisition was in full swing. Highlights from the seventeenth century include pieces by Rubens, Domenichino, and Domenico Fetti, and a touching *Lamentation over the Dead Christ* by **Louis Le Nain**.

A number of canvases by the Swiss **Arnold Böcklin** dominate the Romantic section, which also includes *Iphigenia*, one of **Feuerbach's** finest works. The German avant-garde gets precedence in the galleries of the new extension, though many of the country's best-known twentieth-century artists, such as Corinth, Kirchner, Beckmann, and Dix, are also represented. Focal point is the *Werkstatt* of the iconoclastic **Joseph Beuys**, of whom the museum has some 300 works.

Just behind the Landesmuseum is the **Herrngarten**, a spacious "English-style" park which contains the tomb of Countess Karoline and a monument to Goethe designed by Ludwig Habig, one of the Mathildenhöhe artists. At the north-eastern end of the Herrngarten, in the Rococo **Prinz-Georg-Palais**, is the **Porzellansammlung** (Mon.–Thurs. 10am–1pm and 2–5pm, Sat. and Sun. 10am–1pm; DM2.50), an extensive porcelain museum on two floors set up by Ernst Ludwig in 1907. On the ground floor there are examples from the local Kelsterbach factory and a whole room is devoted to the products of the imperial Russian porcelain factory. There are also some huge Chinese and Japanese porcelain vases. On the second floor there's a big collection of intricate German pieces and an English room which, as well as a few Davenport and Wedgwood pieces, features various horrendous British royal souvenirs.

There isn't much to write home about in the rest of the town center. In front of the Schloss lies the **Marktplatz**, with an uninspiring vintage-1780 fountain. A feature to look out for here is the **Weisse Turm**, a replica of a fifteenth-century defensive tower which was restyled in fashionable baroque in 1708. Nearby is the gabled Renaissance **Rathaus** and around the corner is the **Stadtkirche**. Repeated extensions of the fourteenth century core have created a rather staid but unobjectionable exterior; inside, the only saving grace is the immense sixteenth-century alabaster memorial to Count Georg I and his wife with which the modest nobleman replaced the church's original altar. This huge piece of self-aggrandisement features figures representing members of the count's family, reliefs of Darmstadt and Jerusalem, plus various coats of arms and inscriptions.

Darmstadt's most curious museum is the **Wella Museum**, at Berliner Allee 65, near the Hauptbahnhof. Founded by the *Wella* hair-care product company, the museum contains 2500 objects crammed into one claustrophobic room, covering and every conceivable aspect of hair and beauty care from ancient times to the present. A gruesome selection of surgical instruments is a reminder of the days when barbers doubled as surgeons, and there are some bizarre pictures woven in human hair by nineteenth-century apprentice hairdressers. Visits are by appointment only—ring ☎06151 342459 and ask for Frau Schwab, who provides a guided tour in English.

Another museum oddity is the **Jagdmuseum** in the suburb of Kranichstein (10am–noon and 2–4pm; DM2.50). Housed in the former hunting lodge of the counts and grand-Dukes of Hessen-Darmstadt, it's a museum devoted to their hunting exploits, and features paintings of hunting scenes, guns and trophies. To get there take bus #H from the town center.

Practical Details

The **tourist office** is in the Neues Rathaus, Luisenplatz 55 (Mon.–Fri. 9am–6pm, Sat. 9am–5pm; ☎06151 132071). There's another one at the **Hauptbahnhof** (☎06151 132783), where they will arrange hotel and pension rooms. **Hotels** are expensive, with little below DM40. The following are the only cheapish central possibilities: *Ernst-Ludwig*, Ernst-Ludwig Str. 14 (☎06151 26011), which has singles from DM36 and doubles from DM76; *Zentral-Hotel*, Schuchardstr. 6 (☎06151 26411), with singles from DM35 and doubles from DM70; and *Pension Wetzstein*, Landwehrstr. 8 (☎06151 20443), which has singles from DM28 and doubles from DM60. In the northern suburb of Ahrheiligen *Pension am Elsee*, Raiffeisenstr. 3 (☎06151 372613), starts at DM25. There's a **youth hostel** at "Am Grossen Woog," Landgraf-Georg-Str. 119 (☎06151 45293), which is very handy for the Mathildenhöhe and the nearby open-air swimming pool at the Grosser Woog lake. **Mitfahrzentrale**'s office is at Rheinstr, 40-42 (☎06151 33696).

Considering its size, Darmstadt has a fairly moribund **nightlife**. There is, however, a good cluster of **bars** and cheap **restaurants** just west of the Herrngarten, around Alicenstrasse, Kahlertstrasse, and Pallaswiesenstrasse. Recommended is *Las Palmas* in Pallaswiesenstrasse, a good, cheap Spanish restaurant which serves German food as well. Also in the neighborhood is *Sumpf*, a studenty pub which does fairly cheap snacks. Most of the *Apfelwein* places are to the east of the Herrngarten, around Mauerstrasse and Lauteschlagerstrasse—this is where many of Darmstadt's students live, and it makes a good starting point for a bar hop. Near the Mathildenhöhe, at Erbacher Str. 5-7, is *Worschtküsch*, an excellent jazz bar and cheap restaurant housed in a converted butcher's shop - it advertises itself as "a pub without standards." At the corner of

Landwehrstrasse and Viktoriastrasse you'll find *Oktave*, a more upscale jazz bar. Also worth checking out if the weather is good is the *Kronenbräugarten*, a beer garden at the corner of Dieburgerstrasse and Spessart Ring.

The Bergstrasse

Today the **Bergstrasse** (*Mountain Road*) is a tourist route running from Darmstadt to Heidelberg, but to the Romans—who called it the *Strata Montana*—it was an major military road. During the Middle Ages it developed as a trading route, and numerous castles sprang up along it to protect the merchants from outlaws lurking in the marshland around the Rhine. These days the area's known primarily for the fact that spring starts here earlier than anywhere else in Germany. The best time to explore the little towns and castles of the Bergstrasse is in late March or early April, when the fruit trees that line it suddenly blossom.

If you take bus #5504 south out of Darmstadt you'll hit a string of small towns which seem to merge into one another. First up is **SEEHEIM**, an innocuous little place with a red-brick, beamed **Rathaus** and not much else. Nearby there are a few castles: **Schloss Alsbach**, at the end of a long winding road, is little more than a circular pile of stones, while the nineteenth-century **Schloss Heiligenberg** is very much intact—it's owned by the Battenberg family, whose English cousins changed their name to Mountbatten, and Prince Charles and Princess Di are frequent visitors. At **Burg Frankenstein**, a ruined fortress standing on a 370 meter hill overlooking the Frankfurt suburb of Eberstadt, they've hit upon the idea of cashing in on a spurious connection with Mary Shelley's doctor and his monster, a ruse which seems to have fooled lots of young Americans. The first place of any real consequence you'll come to on the Bergstrasse is **ZWINGENBERG**, a romantic little half-timbered town which would make a good place to spend the night in. The unusual thirteenth-century **Bergkirche** towers over the market place from on top of a huge retaining wall. There's a **youth hostel** at Auf dem Berg 41 (☎06251 75938), and rooms at *Gasthof zur Traube*, Heidelberger Str. 23, start at DM25 per night.

Next stop is **BENSHEIM**, a biggish town with a typically half-timbered center incorporating all the usual features (*Hochzeitshaus*, *Pfarrkirche*, and so forth), focussed on the market place. In the **Lorscher Klosterhof** (Marktplatz 14) you can visit the **Bergstrasser Heimatsmuseum**, a predictably dull local museum devoted to the Bergstrasse. It's worth taking a trip to **AUERBACH**, a suburb of Bensheim, to take a look at the **Schloss** (Tues.–Sun. 10am–6pm), from where there's a great view out across to the Rhine. Bensheim's **tourist office** is on Beaunerplatz. Although there aren't really any cheap **hotels** in Bensheim, there are a couple of possibilities in Auerbach: *Gasthof Auerbacher Haus*, Darmstädter Str. 170 (☎06251 75689), has rooms from DM30, and *Pension Waldschlöschen*, Burgstr. 36 (☎06251 71324), starts at DM25 per person.

Just to the south-east of Bensheim is **LORSCH**, which is notable only for the **Lorscher Halle**, the gatehouse to what was once one of the most powerful medieval monasteries in Germany. It dates back to 774, and is the only building to have come down intact from this period of Carolingian architecture.

HEPPENHEIM, next down the line, has a few quaint half-timbered streets but the overall effect of the town center is ruined by an ugly department store. There is, however, a **youth hostel** in the grounds of the ruined **Schloss Starkenburg** (☎06252 77323), a couple of kilometers to the north-east of the town.

The Odenwald

Directly to the east of the Bergstrasse lies an upland region known as the **Odenwald**, which, like most of Hessen's mountain ranges, is pleasant but unspectacular, a region of gentle hills and small villages which makes a good day trip. Basically it's a steep version of the Bergstrasse, with the usual postcard-pretty array of castles and half-timbered houses. There are plenty of youth hostels and campgrounds if you'd like to spend a few healthy days outdoors here.

The towns to make for are **MICHELSTADT**, a smallish market town with a well-preserved medieval core, or **ERBACH**, with its **Schloss** (containing a more interesting than average local museum) and the **Deutsche Elfenbein-museum**, devoted to the art of ivory carving, which has flourished here since the eighteenth century. There's a **youth hostel** in Erbach at Eulbacherstr. 33 (☎06062 3515), and there are **camping** facilities at *Camping Safari* in the suburb of Bullau (☎06062 3159). Trains go to both towns roughly every hour from Darmstadt.

About 10km to the south is the town of **BEERFELDEN**, the center of which was rebuilt along neoclassical lines in 1810. Look out for the **Mumlingquelle**, where natural spring water is pumped into a huge trough from twelve outlets, and the **Galgen**, one of West Germany's last surviving gallows and in use until 1806. The **tourist office** is at Metzkeil 1 (☎06068 2071) and there are **camping** facilities at *Fischhäuselquelle*, (☎06068 20710). A reasonable local **hotel** is *Odenwald-Hotel*, Kräberger Weg 19 (☎06068 3784). Also worth a visit is **NECKARSTEINACH**, a little place straggling along the Neckar at the extreme south of Hessen, which has four substantial castles all to itself.

Wiesbaden

Strolling around the center of **WIESBADEN** it's not difficult to imagine how the city must have looked during its glory days as a nineteenth-century *Kurstadt*, when the aristocracy of Europe flocked here to take the waters at the numerous thermal spas and to gamble away their fortunes in the famous casino. Today the city trades on its past reputation, conjuring up the atmosphere of a bygone era to attract visitors. The Russian nobles who were once the main patrons have been replaced by wealthy Arabs and tanned, nouveau-riche Germans. It's worth stopping off in Wiesbaden for a couple of hours just to get a taste of the atmosphere, but the chances are it won't be long before the conspicuous wealth and overt snobbery of the place start to get to you.

At the heart of Wiesbaden is the **Kurhaus** (about 15 minutes from the **Hauptbahnhof** on foot, or take bus #1 or #8). Completed in 1906 in a neoclassical style which would have been fashionable a hundred years previously, the Kurhaus is the bland symbol of a city where appearances are everything. The extravagant decor of the halls has been the backdrop to many a glittering provincial night out, and the building also houses the **Spielbank** (casino), which is a handy source of extra revenue for the city. The Spielbank was opened in 1949, but gambling started in earnest in 1771 and Wiesbaden's original casino was the inspiration for "Roulettenburg" in Dostoyevsky's novel *The Gambler*. Gambling was suspended in Wiesbaden between 1872 and 1949 by Kaiser Wilhelm I, after his son the Crown Prince Friedrich III had formed an "unsuitable" attachment to a woman gambler. Behind the Kurhaus is the **Kurpark**, an English-style park, complete with weeping willows, a giant chess set, and duck ponds; from here you can walk up into the wooded slopes of the **Taunus**, which rise to the north of the city.

Wiesbaden city center, though pleasant enough to look at, doesn't really have much to offer. **Wilhelmstrasse**, the main shopping street, which runs past the Kurhaus into Friedrich-Ebert-Strasse, is full of expensive antique shops and glitzy designer stores. On Schlossplatz the **Altes Rathaus** is the oldest bulding in the city but none too inspiring for all that. Nearby stands the **Stadtschloss**, originally a palace for the dukes of Nassau and now the Hessen state parliament. In front of it, on the market place, there's a small fountain topped by a playful-looking lion, one of the symbols of the city. Halfway up Mauergasse there's a second-hand shop called *Junkyard* which has a fine selection of bric-a-brac and old clothes.

You can sample the famous waters at the **Kochbrunnen**, just off Taunus-strasse a few minutes walk from the Kurhaus; despite the much-vaunted healing

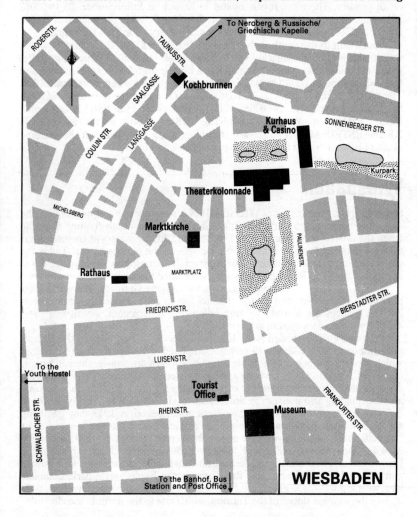

WIESBADEN

properties you are advised to restrict your intake to one liter per day. The neoclassical colonnades surrounding the fountains which dispense the water now house a café and crêperie, which slightly undermines the elegant atmosphere. That's really about it for downtown, apart from the **Städtische Museum**, in Friedrich-Ebert-Strasse (Thurs.–Mon. 10am–4pm, Tues. also 5pm–9pm); it possesses a few paintings by the Russian artist Alexei Jawlensky, a member of the Expressionist *Blaue Reiter* group, but is nonetheless a pedestrian collection .

If you have time, you might care to sample the delights of the thermal baths. The most atmospheric (and expensive) is the *Kaiser Friedrich Bad*, Langgasse 38-40 (bus #1 or #8), which features a pseudo-Roman pool; the modern *Thermalbad Wiesbaden*, Leibnizstr. 7 (bus #18), is cheaper but has more of a public-baths feel.

On the northern edge of Wiesbaden looms the **Neroberg**, a 245-meter Taunus foothill with an open-air swimming pool and good views of the city. To get there take bus #1 to Nerotal and from there take the water-powered funicular railroad. On the summit stands the **Russische Kapelle**, also known as the *Griechische Kapelle*, a nineteenth-century Russian-style chapel instantly recognizable by its five gilded cupolas; it was built as a mausoleum for the Russian-born princess Elisabeth of Nassau, who died in childbirth at the age of 19.

It's also worth taking a trip to the southern suburb of Biebrich, for the **Schloss Biebrich**, former residence of the dukes of Nassau (bus #3, 4, 13, A3 or A13 from the town center). The restrained elegance of this eighteenth-century baroque palace, facing out over the Rhine, puts the showy center of Wiesbaden to shame.

Accommodation and Entertainment

Hotels under DM40 are few and far between in Wiesbaden and you'll have more chance of finding something reasonable in Mainz. The cheapest possibility in Wiesbaden itself is *Ring*, Bleichstr. 29 (☎06121 400177) which has singles from DM35. Other possibilities exist in the suburb of Biebrich: try *Schützenhof*, Am Schlosspark 45 (☎06121 66920), which has singles from DM26 and doubles from DM65, or *Union-Bayer*, Friedensanlage 1 (☎06121 66233) which starts at DM33. The **youth hostel** is at Blücherstr. 66 (☎ 06121 48657) best reached by bus #14 from the Hauptbahnhof.

Eating and **drinking** in Wiesbaden can be an expensive affair too. There are plenty of fancy restaurants and bars, but the best value for money and atmosphere is at *Domizil*, in Moritzstrasse, an alternative bar which also serves cheap meals. They sometimes have live music on a Saturday. There's also a good take-out pizza place in Hermannstrasse, just one door away from the corner of Bismarckring. Wiesbaden's **tourist office** is at Rheinstr. 15 (☎06121 312847).

The Rheingau

The Hessen side of the Rhine, running from **Wiesbaden** to the border with Rhineland-Pfalz at Lorchhausen, is known as the **RHEINGAU**. Sheltered from the elements by the gentle slopes of the Taunus, the region has developed into one of West Germany's foremost wine-producing districts, and its vineyards, ruined castles, and drowsy little villages make it a favorite destination for motor-coach parties and package tourists. You can cover it fairly well by train from Wiesbaden, but to visit the out-of-the-way corners you'll need a car. Road B42, running from Wiesbaden to the Rheinland-Pfalz border and taking in all the little wine villages, has been designated the *Rheingauer-Riesling-Route*, a special-interest stretch for wine fans, enabling them to stop off and do a bit of tasting and buying. There's also a walking route, the *Rheingauer-Riesling-Pfad*, which runs through the lower slopes of the **Rheingau-Gebirge**—the part of the Taunus which rises from the banks of the Rhine.

First stop out of Wiesbaden is **ELTVILLE**, a town famous for its sparkling wines (it's on the main Frankfurt-Cologne railroad line and there are plenty of buses in all directions). This is where Thomas Mann's urbane conman Felix Krull spent his youth, but apart from Felix's fictional presence, the town's only cultural highlights are a lot of half-timbered houses and a very fresh-looking fifteenth-century fresco of the Last Judgment in the late Gothic *Pfarrkirche*. The **tourist office**, Schmittstr. 4 (Mon.–Fri. 8am–5pm; ☎06123 6891) will fill you in on Eltville and the surrounding area. One of the cheapest **hotels** is *Zur Post*, Rheingauer Str. 46 (☎06123 2231), with rooms from about DM30 per night.

From Eltville you can take a bus up to **KIEDRICH**, an improbably medieval-looking little place dominated by the ruins of **Scharfenstein** castle. The main tourist attraction is the **St. Valentinus-Kirche** (April–Oct. Tues.–Sun. 2:30–4:30pm), a fifteenth-century church which was once a pilgrimage destination for epilepsy sufferers. Inside, look out for the oldest (1500) working organ in Germany, the *Kiedricher Madonna* (1330), and the intricately carved pews with their vine motifs.

A few kilometers west of Kiedrich, set in the wooded slopes of the Rheingau-Gebirge, is **Kloster Eberbach** (April–Sept. 10am–6pm; Oct-March 10am–4pm; DM1.50), founded in 1135 by the Cistercian order, and one of the best-preserved medieval monasteries in Germany. A couple of tombs in one of the fourteenth-century chapels are all that detract from the austerely grandiose architecture.

Behind the church are the leafy cloisters and a ruined well-chapel, surrounded by the former living quarters of the monks. The monks' dormitory, an immense vaulted affair built in the 1240s, is one of the most impressive early Gothic rooms in Europe, and like the church is almost devoid of decoration. In the refectory the huge wine presses once used by the monks are on display; wine production continued after the dissolution of the monastery in 1803, and some of the monastery buildings are now used to press, ferment, and store the produce of the Eberbacher Steinberg, the former monastery vineyard. There are yearly wine auctions and some of the vintages are reckoned to be world-class.

The road back down to the bank of the Rhine brings you to **HATTENHEIM**, a conventional little Rhine village where there are **camping** facilities at *Zur Brückenschänke* make inquiries at Hauptstr. 4 (☎06723 2827). From here head west past **Schloss Reinhardshausen**, a castle of sorts turned *Weingut* (wine tavern), to **OESTRICH**, where there's a seventeenth century wooden river-crane once used to load wine barrels onto ships for conveyance down the Rhine and beyond. *Gasthaus Schwan*, built in 1628, is an atmospheric little watering-hole, and *Pension Schäferhof*, at Waldstr. 10 (☎06723 1234), is the most reasonable local hotel, with rooms from DM22 per night. A couple of kilometers down the road sits **WINKEL**, which officially belongs to Oestrich. Here you can visit the **Brentanohaus**, which belonged to the step-brother of the Romantic writer Clemens Brentano; Clemens himself spent his summers here, often entertaining the likes of Goethe and other prominent literary figures. Also of interest is the **Graues Haus**, the oldest intact stone house in Germany.

The main point of interest at the nearby half-timbered village of **GEISENHEIM** is the over-restored **Schloss Schönborn**, where Johann Philipp von Schönborn, elector and archbishop of Mainz, negotiated the provisional agreement of the Peace of Westphalia which ended the disastrous Thirty Years' War. Up in the Taunus, a few kilometers outside Geisenheim, there are a couple of worthwhile castles. The eighteenth-century **Schloss Johannisberg**, was restyled along fashionable neoclassical lines between 1826 and 1833 by the Metternich family, who are still in possession; there's an impressive panoramic view of the region from its southern terrace. **Schloss Vollrads**, with its moated fourteenth-century tower, is one of the best preserved castles in the Rheingau. There are **camping** facilities at Geisenheim; for details call ☎06722 8515.

RÜDESHEIM claims the dubious distinction of being the most visited town in the region, attracting over 3 million sightseers a year. It's a favorite stopping-off point for tour buses and Rhine cruisers, as it conforms pretty well to the general conception of what a typical Rhine town should look like—all crooked narrow streets, half-timbered houses and souvenir shops, sloping down gently from the wooded hills and terraced vineyards above. The big local attraction is the **Drosselgasse**, a street comprised entirely of pubs, and generally full of tourists being ripped off. The twelfth century **Brömserburg**, a squat and angular fortress, is worth visiting for the **Rheingau-und Weinmuseum** (May– Nov. 9am–noon and 2–6pm, closed Mon.; DM2.50); it contains 21 old presses and a vast collection of wine vessels, including some fine examples of vases, dating from Roman times through to the Middle Ages, used to store and transport wine. Rüdesheim also has a few reminders of an era when this stretch of the Rhine was a turbulent and contested area, in the shape of a twelfth-century defensive tower called the **Boosenburg** and the circular, late Gothic **Adlerturm**. Also of interest are two medieval nobles' houses: the **Brömserhof**, which has a half-timbered tower with the added attraction of a large collection of mechanical musical instruments, and the **Klunkardshof**, with a particularly well-preserved half-timbered facade.

A reminder of a later phase in the development of Germany is the **Niederwalddenkmal**, a bombastic remnant of the imperial German Reich. This immense monument 225m above the town can be reached either by foot or by chair lift over the vineyards which swarm up the slopes behind Rüdesheim. The monument itself was built to mark the unification of Germany in 1871 and features a huge allegorical statue of *Germania*, symbol of the emergent and ulti- mately doomed empire. Nearby are the undeniably romantic ruins of the thir- teenth-century **Burg Ehrenfels**, a one-time toll castle, which, in conjunction with the Mäuseturm, a tower on a mid-river island, was used by the archbishops of Mainz to control Rhine river traffic.

Rüdesheim's **tourist office** is at Rheinstr. 5 (☎ 06722 3041)—they'll provide information about the rest of the Rheingau and the Taunus hinterland. The local **youth hostel** is set amidst the vines at Am Kreuzberg (☎ 06722 2711). There are plenty of **hotels** but they tend to be on the expensive side and most of them will be full up during the summer. A couple of cheap possibilities are *Gasthof Winzerschänke*, Marktstr. 27 (☎06722 2733) and *Pension Bach*, Langstr. 13 (☎06722 2512), both from DM25. On the whole you're probably better off sticking to the smaller places nearby as they'll be cheaper and more likely to have vacan- cies. There are two **camp sites** in Rüdesheim, the *Campingplatz am Rhein* (☎06722 2528 or 2582) and the *Landgut Ebental* (☎06722 2518) near Niederwald. At the beginning of July there's a firework display and in mid-August Rüdesheim has its wine festival—during the latter it seems like all of those 3 million visitors have hit town at once.

Just out of town the Rhine suddenly bends through ninety degrees to flow more or less north–south, and there follows a treacherous stretch of river called the **Binger Loch**, where most of its barges normally take a pilot on board to negotiate the channel through the rapids and reefs. The first town you'll come to is **ASSMANNSHAUSEN**, a smaller and less touristy version of Rüdesheim. In the terraced vineyards surrounding some of Germany's best red wines are produced. For cheap accommodation head to the *Pension Milberg*, Am Rathaus 2 (☎06722 2945), with rooms from DM25. From Assmannshausen you can ride a chair lift up to *Schloss Niederwald*, an eighteenth century hunting lodge turned hotel, from where there are good views of Rhine and its sloping banks.

While you're in the area you might also care to visit AULSHAUSEN, a secluded little resort village lying in a sheltered side valley, or **PRESBERG**, a few kilometers into the Rheingau-Gebirge—famous for its clean air and as a base for exploring the **Naturpark Rhein-Taunus**, a national park established to protect the area's natural assets from overexploitation.

The final stretch of the *Rheingauer-Riesling-Route* takes you through to LORCH. Facing the Rhine is the **Hilchenhaus**, a sixteenth-century Renaissance mansion featuring a distictive stepped gable and ornate carvings. In the Gothic **St. Martinskirche** there's an ornately carved altar to Saint Martin with painted panels, and a late thirteenth-century choir decorated with fantastic animals. Look out for **Burg Nollig** , a fourteenth-century fortified dwelling tower which stands at the point where the river Wisper flows into the Rhine. Cheapest local **hotel** is *Gasthof Henninger Eck*, Rheinstr. 50 (☎06726 692). You can **camp** at *Suleika* (☎06726 9464)and the **youth hostel** is at Schwalbacher Str. 54 (☎ 06726 307).

NORTHERN HESSEN

Northern Hessen is, relatively speaking, off the beaten track. To the west there's the valley of the Lahn, a Rhine tributary, while the east of the province is characterized by forested highland. By far the biggest city is **Kassel,** whose center is one of the dullest in Germany, but is very much worth visiting on account of its art treasures. Far more congenial is **Fulda**, which has preserved its baroque character intact. The gem of the area, however, is the old university town of **Marburg**.

Marburg

One of West Germany's finest small cities, **MARBURG** clusters up the slopes of the **Lahn** valley in a maze of narrow streets and medieval buildings, crowned by an impressive castle. It's primarily a university town and the presence of 15,000 students gives it a relaxed and lively atmosphere. Marburg has good rail and road links with Frankfurt, Kassel, and Koblenz, and is one of the few Hessen towns worth going out of your way to visit.

The town's most important historic building is the **Elisabethkirche**, the first Gothic church to be built on German soil. It was erected in 1235 by the Knights of the Teutonic Order to house the remains of Saint Elisabeth, daughter of the king of Hungary and widow of Landgrave Ludwig of Thuringia. Elisabeth came to Marburg after the death of her husband and set up house next door to a hospital for the dying, which stood more or less where the present church does. A great follower of the teachings of Saint Francis of Assisi, she devoted the rest of her short life to caring for the sick. She died in 1231 at the age of 24, and canonization followed in 1235 at the behest of the city's ruler, Landgrave Conrad, who had been Elisabeth's mentor during the final years of her life. A year later her body was placed in the newly built church, which soon became a stopping-off point for Jerusalem-bound pilgrims.

The building itself is a handsome twin-towered structure, strongly influenced by the French cathedrals of Reims and Amiens, but with a pronounced German accent, thanks largely to having adopted a hall-church format. Inside, the church is like a museum of German religious art, full of statues and frescoes, mainly celebrating Elisabeth's piety. The first thing you'll see, on the right as you enter, is the **Elisabeth-Altar**, whose three panels depict scenes from her life: one shows Elisabeth looking suitably devout, another shows her husband setting off on the Crusades (where he was to die of plague), and a third the Landgrave Conrad giving her a beating, to discourage any lapse in her religious devotion. At the opposite end of the nave on the left is a curvaceous statue of Elisabeth dating from about 1470, past which is the Elisabeth-Chor, containing the saint's original grave and the tombs of the Kings of Prussia. The back of the church contains the **Hochaltar** (High Altar) in which Elisabeth is depicted in the exalted company of the Virgin Mary. A side chapel to the left of the Hochaltar houses the thirteenth-century golden shrine which contained the relics of Saint Elisabeth until her descendant, the Landgrave Philipp of Hessen, embraced the Protestant faith in 1539; he put an end to the veneration of Elisabeth's bones and had her re-interred in the pilgrim's cemetery in the Michaelskapelle.

The **Landgrafen-Chor**, opposite the Elisabeth-Chor, contains the tombs of the Landgraves of Hessen. In a side alcove just to the left of the entrance is the tomb of Hindenburg, the *Reichspresident* who appointed Hitler chancellor in 1933. Hindenburg's body was brought here after the war by the Americans and occasionally demonstrations are held outside the church to protest against old Nazis and their sympathizers, who have made the tomb a place of pilgrimage. Look out also for the old pews which are constructed so as to tip forward suddenly if you lean also far back in them—a medieval device to stop people coming into the church to sleep during the day.

Beneath the church and in the surrounding area are the **Kasermattenführungen**, a network of underground tunnels used by the military during the war. Tours are by appointment only—check with the tourist office for details.

From the Elisabethkirche the **Steinweg**, an old stepped street hemmed in by half-timbered buildings, leads up to the **Marktplatz**, the center of Marburg's **Altstadt**, with its Saint George fountain and lineup of golden half-timbered houses. During the school semester the square is the focal point of Marburg's nightlife, but out of term it's very peaceful. Here you might see older women in the traditional costumes which are still sometimes worn in the area, a holdover from times when Protestant and Catholic had to be able to tell each other apart—the Protestants wore black, dark brown, blue, or green, while the Catholics wore bright colors with plaited hair. The **Rathaus** is a sixteenth- century Gothic building with a gabled Renaissance staircase tower and a statue of Elisabeth, holding a heraldic figure said to be the arms of the count who financed the building's completion. The heraldic symbol is supposedly a lion, but the mason made it look like a monkey, suggesting that the count was not quite dealing with a full deck. At Marktplatz 4–8 is the **Emil von Behring Austellung**, a permanent exhibition about the life of Emil von Behring, a nineteenth-century immunology pioneer.

Nearby is the **St. Kiliankirche**, which has served variously as a church, school, and SS headquarters. It was also the final place to which Marburg's Jews were taken before deportation. Not far away is the **Aula**, the Romanesque university church these days used only for occasional public events or the inaugural lecture of a new professor. Inside the frescoes depict important events in the history of Marburg, but you'll have to contact the tourist office if you want to take a look.

From the Marktplatz head up Rittergasse to the thirteenth-century **Marienkirche**, from whose terrace there's a good view out over the town towards the Lahn. Just past here are the Ludwig-Bickell-Treppe which will lead you up to the **Schloss**, the residence of the Landgraves of Hessen, which towers over the town 102m above the Lahn River (April 16–Oct.15 Tues.–Sun. 10am–1pm and 2–6pm; Oct.16–April 15 Tues.–Sat. 10am–1pm and 2–5pm, Sun. 2–5pm). There was a castle in Marburg as far back as the twelfth century, but the present structure was begun by Sophie, the daughter of Saint Elisabeth. It was she who effectively founded Hessen in 1248 by proclaiming her four-year-old son "the child of Hessen," and naming him as future ruler before the populace on the Marktplatz. The bulk of what can be seen today dates from the fifteenth and sixteenth centuries. Look out for the **Schlosskapelle**, a high Gothic chapel built by the same craftsmen who constructed the Elisabethskirche; the lurid rose-colored interior is quite striking, and has a few badly faded and inexpertly restored murals. Also noteworthy is the *Rittersaal*, the largest secular Gothic hall in Germany. In October 1529 Landgrave Philipp the Magnanimous, who introduced the Reformation in Marburg, engineered a fruitless meeting between Martin Luther and Ulrich Zwingli to try to reconcile the differences between the two reformers—in the room where the talks took place hang portraits of the Landgrave and of Luther by Lucas Cranach the Elder. The castle also houses the **Museum für Kulturgeschichte** (Tues.–Sun. 10am–1pm and 2–5pm).

As well as attempting to do his part for religious harmony Philipp also founded the University of Marburg in 1527, whose roll call of illustrious professors includes characters as diverse as the Brothers Grimm and Boris Pasternak. Though the original enrollment of 88 students has now swollen to 15,000, today's university is still an elitist place. Most of its building are now concentrated on the eastern outskirts of the city, on the other side of the Lahn.

Attached to the university is the **Universitätsmuseum für bildende Kunst**, Bigenstr. 11 (Weds.–Mon. 10am–1pm and 3–5pm; free), which has a Lucas Cranach the Elder portrait of Luther, a Klee, a Kandinsky, and a Picasso, but features mainly local and German artists—none of whom, with the exception of Karl Bantzer from Marburg, is anything to write home about.

Practical Details

Marburg's **tourist office** is at the **Hauptbahnhof** (☎06421 201262 or 201249); it has lists of private rooms for rent and will be able to supply you detailed information about other forms of accommodation. There's a shortage of cheap **hotels** in Marburg. Cheapest in the center are *Reher*, Alte Kasseler Str. 66 (☎06421 65624), which has singles from DM28 per night and doubles from DM56, and *Haus Müller*, Deutschhausstr. 29 (☎06421 65659), which has singles from DM38 and doubles from DM72. Otherwise head for the suburbs;in Einhausen, for instance, *Gasthof Barth*, Einhäuser Str. 13 (☎06420 7440), has singles from DM28 and doubles from DM56. The **youth hostel** is at Jahnstr. 1 (☎06421 23461), a little to the south of the Altstadt, and **camping** facilities are at Am Trojedamm (☎06421 21331). **Boats** can be rented from *Bootsverleih*, Auf der Weide (☎06421 26864).

There's no shortage of places for **eating** and **drinking** in this student-dominated town. Quite a few little pubs are to be found in the half-timbered buildings on Hirschberg, the street leading off from the Marktplatz, and you could also try your luck on Untergasse. *Pizzeria Sardegna*, just off Rudolphsplatz, cooks pizzas in a wood oven, and the *Café Barfuss* on Langgasse does a good selection of tacos and pasta. Nearby is another pizza place called *Rustikale*, which does a good Italian-style breakfast. *Café Velo* on Augustinergasse is popular with students. Near the *Mensa Parkplatz*, just off Kurt-Schumacher-Strasse on the eastern side of the Lahn, is a recommended vegetarian place, *Kalimera,* and on the corner of Marktgasse and Marktplatz you'll find a good health food shop.

The Lahn Valley

The Lahn River runs south from Marburg into Rhineland-Palatinate, where it eventually flows into the Rhine just south of Koblenz. The Hessen stretch is well served by rail and road, and if you're traveling by car you could spend a pleasant day taking in the landscape and stopping off in one or two of the towns en route.

Giessen

Traveling south out of Marburg there isn't much to see until you reach **GIESSEN**, a biggish, light-industrial town about 30km away. The Giessen tourist office publishes a brochure in English called "Giessen in 100 Minutes" but "Giessen in 10 Minutes," would be more than enough. Before the war it was famous for its half-timbered houses, but now only a few examples remain and the town is a typically bland example of postwar reconstruction. Giessen has also suffered the added misfortune of being selected by the U.S. army to serve as a garrison town and supply center. The only real reason for staying here would be to use it as an overnight stopover or base for exploring surrounding the area.

There's not much to see in the sprawling, ugly town center. Best thing the tourist office can come up with is the **Burgmannenhaus** on Georg-Schlosser-Strasse, a pedestrian, fourteenth-century half-timbered affair which was restored in 1979 and now houses the town museum (Tues.–Sun. 10am–4pm; free). There are a few attractions around Brandplatz: the **Neues Schloss** is a late Gothic half-timbered residence, and next door to it is the **Zeughaus**, the fifteenth-century Renaissance-style town arsenal which now houses part of Giessen University. The **Altes Schloss** houses the **Oberhessisches Museum und Gail'sche Sammlung,** an uninspiring art collection (Tues.–Sun. 10am–4pm; free), behind which is the **Botanischer Garten**, the old university botanical garden; dating back to the seventeenth century, it's the town's most attractive feature. Apart from that there's only the **Liebig-Museum** at Liebigstr. 12 (Tues.–Sun. 10am–4pm; free), which is devoted to the life and work of the scientist Justus von Liebig.

Just to the southeast of Giessen is the **Schiffenbergkloster**, a ruined monastery in whose walled gardens students conduct "secret" fencing matches at the crack of dawn on Sunday. Concerts are held here on Saturday evenings and Sunday afternoons. You can walk from Giessen or take bus #6 from Berliner Platz (departures a couple of times an hour, but watch out on Sunday as the only buses from the monastery back to Giessen are at 1:06pm and 6:06pm).

The **tourist office** is at Berliner Platz 2 (Mon.–Fri. 9am–noon and 2–6pm, Sat. 9am–noon; ☎0641 3062489) and the **youth hostel** at Richard-Schirmann-Weg 53 (☎0641 65879). Cheapest local **hotel** is the *Frankfurter Hof*, Frankfurter Str. 205-207 (☎0641 22782), which starts at DM23 per night. If you happen to find yourself in Giessen at night, head for Ludwigstrasse, which is known as *Kneipenstrassee* by the locals because it's full of pubs. Also worth checking out for occasional live music is the *Eulenspiegel* in Seltersweg.

Wetzlar

Following the Lahn west from Giessen you come to **WETZLAR**, the town where Goethe fell in love with Lotte Buff while working as a legal clerk at the imperial court, an experience which inspired him to write *The Sorrows of Young Werther*. These days Wetzlar is another light industrial town, but the narrow streets of the **Altstadt**, with their half-timbered, gray-roofed houses (many of them only restored to their original state during the last few years), bear witness to a more prestigious past. The Altstadt is centered on three squares—the **Schillermarkt**, the **Eisenmarkt**, and the **Kornmarkt**—and crowned by the thirteenth-century **Dom**. Begun in 1235 around the nucleus of an earlier Romanesque church (whose basalt-and-limestone north tower still stands), the Dom evolved over the next century-and-a-half into a strange hybrid of Romanesque and Gothic. In 1370 work was suddenly halted, leaving the west side of the building incomplete. The south tower, the only Gothic part to be finished, was later surmounted with a bell tower and watchtower. Inside, look out for the figures of a supercilious-looking Madonna and Child—the infant looks more like a pig than a baby and the pair are surrounded by moronic angels.

The other main attraction in Wetzlar is the **Lottehaus**, the house where Lotte Buff lived with her parents, which stands in the **Hof des Deutschen Ritterordens** (The Court of the Teutonic Knights). A must for Goethe aficionados, the house has been turned into a small museum containing furniture, pictures, and books—lots of first editions and translations of *Werther*, not surprisingly. Also in the Hof des Deutschen Ritterordens is the **Städtische Museum**, which details Wetzlar's history as an imperial city from 1180 to 1830, and the development of its iron and optical industries (the town is home to *Leitz*, the camera manufacturers). Both the Lottehaus and the Städtisches Museum are open from 9am to noon and 2 to 5pm, except Monday and Sunday afternoons.

The **tourist office** is at Domplatz 8 (Mon.–Weds. and Fri. 8am–noon and 2–4:30pm Thurs. 8am–noon and 2–5pm, Sat. 9:30–11:30am; ☎06441 405338). Wetzlar has a **youth hostel** at Richard-Schirmann-Str. 3 (☎06441 71068), and **camping** facilities at *Dutenhofener See*, in the suburb of Dutenhofen (☎0641 212450). Cheapish **hotels** include *Gasthaus Bill*, Gabelsbergstr. 30 (☎06441 31617), for singles from DM28, and *Hotel-Restaurant Mayerle*, Kirchstr. 1 (☎06441 32197), with rooms at similar prices.

Weilburg

The road southwest from Wetzlar takes you through rolling countryside and along the banks of the Lahn to **WEILBURG**, a town which makes up in visual appeal what it lacks in size. The showpiece of the compact old quarter—which stands on a peninsula enclosed by the Lahn—is the elegant sixteenth-century **Schloss**, with its warm facade of orange stucco. Once the residence of the counts of Nassau, the Schloss is a sprawling affair, almost a little town in itself. Major additions were made during the early eighteenth century, when stables were added to the northern part of the building and the **Schlossgarten** was constructed in a series of terraces leading down to the Lahn. The Schloss is now a museum (March–Oct. 10am–noon and 1–4pm, with guided tours every half hour; Nov.–Feb. 10am–noon and 1–3pm, with guided tours every hour; DM2).

If you go for a walk through the town, don't miss the baroque **Schlosskirche**, one of the most outstanding Protestant churches in Hessen, which with its elaborate pillared altar, decorated with cherubs and sunbursts, has an almost rococo feel to it. Just in front of it, on the **Marktplatz**, splashes the heavily ornamented **Neptunbrunnen** fountain. Also worth a look are the five-arched **Steinerne**

Brücke , which spans the Lahn just north of the Schloss, and the **Schiffstunnel**, built during the nineteenth century to save ships having to sail right around the peninsula.

The **tourist office** is at Mauerstr. 8 (☎06471 31424), and there's a **youth hostel** at Am Steinbühl (☎06471 7116). Cheapest local **hotel** is the *Gasthof Felsenkeller*, Ahäuser Weg 4 (☎06471 30489), whose rooms start at DM27. Cheap possibilities exist also in some of the small towns and villages around Weilburg—the tourist office will tell you what's available.

Limburg

The last Lahn valley town in Hessen is **LIMBURG**, which is chiefly famous for a particularly pungent type of cheese. The town is dominated by its unusual **Dom**, which, built between 1212 and 1250, represents the last great phase of Romanesque architecture in Germany. Although it's basically a late Romanesque building, the Dom incorporates many tentative Gothic features, chiefly on the inside. The medieval orange-and-white color scheme is a bit jarring, but it's definitely worth a quick visit, as no other German church captures so well the spirit of the transition from Romanesque to Gothic.

Next to the Dom is the **Burg**, a fortification complex dating back to the nineth century when the Niederlahn counts chose this spot as the site for a defensive castle. In Domstrasse, within the compound of the Burg, is the **Diözesanmuseum**, a museum of religious art and artifacts—the big attraction here is the *Dernbacher Beweinung*, a sculpture depicting the Lamentation of Christ. The **Domschatz**, in the old bishop's palace (just off Rossmarkt), has a rich collection of treasure and plunder—search out the *Limburger Staurothek*, a tenth-century Byzantine reliquary in the form of the cross, which was brought back from the Crusades by a local knight. Below the Dom and Burg is the **Altstadt**, the substantially intact medieval district, which features some predictably fine and venerable half-timbered houses. There's a big cluster around Fischmarkt, including the **Historisches Rathaus**, an extremely well-preserved fourteenth-century Gothic building complete with great hall.

Limburg's **tourist office** is at Hospitalstr. 2 (☎06431 203222). There's a **youth hostel** at Auf dem Guckucksberg (☎06431 41493), and a few reasonable **hotels**, the cheapest of which are *Gasthof Schwedenhof*, Offheimer Weg 11 (☎06431 6848), which starts at DM25 per night, and *Gasthof Weisses Ross*, Westerwaldstr. 2 (☎06431 8776), which has rooms from DM30.

The rest of the Lahn valley, although actually in Rhineland-Palatinate, contains only a couple of major towns and is therefore included here for reasons of convenience. **DIEZ** clusters at the foot of its immensely tall castle which now houses a **youth hostel**. Also here is the gracious palace of **Oranienstein**, one-time residence of the House of Orange-Nassau, with its extensive collection of seventeenth and eighteenth-century art and furniture (9:30–11:30am and 2–4pm; DM1). A few kilometers down valley are **Schloss Balduinstein** and **Schloss Schaumberg**—the former built by one of the archbishops of Trier during the fourteenth century (and now ruined), the latter a nineteenth-century approximation of an earlier fortification built with more serious intent. **NASSAU**, about 10km to the west along the Lahn valley, doesn't really rate a visit despite its historical associations—William of Orange belonged to one branch of the House of Orange-Nassau. You're better off heading for **BADEMS**, a fashionable, elegant, and expensive spa town; it still retains much of the *Kurort* ambience that drew figures like Kaiser Wilhelm I to take the waters, and is an attractive place to break your journey for a coffee stop.

Fulda

Lying in a narrow river valley between the Vogelsberg and the Rhön, **FULDA** is best known to the outside world for two things: its immaculate baroque center and the "Fulda Gap"—the weak point in NATO's front line at which the massed tanks of the Warsaw Pact are supposedly most likely to break through into the heart of Western Europe. As you approach the town, little prepares you for the glories of the baroque quarter—developed gradually during the first half of the eighteenth century—but walk down Sturmiusstrasse from the **Hauptbahnhof** and it rises up on your right, a vision of golden turrets and crosses.

Despite the predominantly eighteenth-century atmosphere of the town center, Fulda has roots which go back to the eighth century, when a small town grew up around the abbey founded by Saint Boniface, a monk sent from England to convert the Germans. After Boniface's martyrdom in 754, Fulda became a pilgrimage site, and over the years its abbey grew into one of the most important monasteries in Germany. It was here that a couple of monks transcribed the *Lay of Hildebrand*, one of the first recorded pieces of German literature.

It wasn't until 1704 that Prince-Abbot Adalbert von Schleifras had the eighth century Romanesque basilica demolished to build the imposing **Dom**, designed by Johann Dientzenhofer. It's a classic early baroque structure, free of the excesses of later Bavarian baroque, but with an attention to detail and complexity of design which gives it a different feel from most German churches. The glory of the spacious and stuccoed interior is the high altar, depicting the Assumption of the Madonna in full-blown gilded splendor, and flanked by six marble columns. Behind lies a small and more austere chapel where the monks used to assemble for prayer. Saint Boniface's tomb is in the slightly oppressive crypt beneath the High Altar—it's incorporated into a sepulchral black marble altar with carved reliefs depicting the saint's martyrdom and his resurrection on Judgment Day. The **Dom Museum**, reached via the crypt, contains Boniface's relics, which include his sword, his head, and the book with which he vainly tried to fend off his murderers. (Guided tours April–Oct. 10am–5:30pm, Sat. 10am–2pm, Sun. 12:30–5pm; Dec.–March Mon.–Fri. 9:30am–noon and 1:30–4pm, Sat. 9:30am–2pm, Sun. 12:30–4pm; DM1.50.)

Next door to the Dom is the **St. Michaelskirche**, founded in 822, destroyed in 1000, and rebuilt in the shape of a Greek cross as a copy of the Church of the Holy Sepulcher in Jerusalem. It's the only building from that period to have survived the wholesale conversion of Fulda to the baroque. In comparison to the mighty Dom the St. Michaelskirche is quite inconspicuous, but in some ways its interior is more impressive than that of its larger rival, incorporating as it does the rotunda of the original church; although this structure has been much altered, two of its eight columns date back to 822.

After the Dom, the **Stadtschloss**—a creamy stone-and-stucco palace—is the main attraction in the center of Fulda. It's a huge building with several wings, parts of which now house the town hall, while other rooms are occupied by the **Vorderau Museum**, a collection covering history, anthropology and the fine and applied arts. The condition of the Schloss took a downward turn in 1945 when it was occupied by the U.S. army, who painted over the interior decorations for "hygienic" reasons—which meant lengthy and expensive repair work when they finally pulled out. Despite the sterling efforts of the restorers, the guided tour of the Schloss interior isn't as pleasurable as a stroll in the **Schlossgarten**, a geometrical ornamental park which leads to the **Orangerie**, the best-looking of

Fulda's secular baroque buildings. Inside, look out for the *Sauerkrautbild*, a ceiling painting showing Greek deities eating sausages.

As for the rest of Fulda town center, the **Hauptwache**, a baroque former police station across the road from the Schloss on Bonifatiusplatz, is worth a look in passing. From here Friedrichstrasse takes you to the **Stadtpfarrkirche**, which pretty much conforms to Fulda house style, and the **Altes Rathaus**, which breaks the mold by having a nonconformist half-timbered facade (a reconstruction of the sixteenth-century original).

The **Hessisches Landesbibliothek**, the state library on Heinrichstrasse (Mon.–Fri. 10am–noon and 2–4pm), features a Gutenberg Bible, various illuminated manuscripts,nd some unusual medieval satirical drawings. In the **Alte Stadtschule museum** there's a prehistoric collection which is as dry as the bones it contains, and on St. Laurentius-Strasse, on the western side of the river Fulda (bus #9 from the Hauptbahnhof), the **Deutsches Feuerwehrmuseum** is a collection of fire fighting appliances and equipment from the eighteenth-century to the present (Tues., Weds., and Fri.–Sun. 10am–5pm, Thurs. 2–9pm).

The **St. Andreaskirche**, in the western suburb of Neuenberg (a ten-minute walk from the Dom), is worth a visit for the more-or-less intact eleventh-century frescoes in its crypt. In the southern suburb of Johannisberg is the **Denkmalpflege Fortbildungszentrum** (☎0661 45081), one of the world's leading study centers for the restoration and maintenance of historic monuments. If you call them and make an appointment they'll be happy to show you around.

Further baroque delights await at the **Schloss Fasanerie**, about 6km southwest of Fulda, which is considered to be the finest baroque palace in Hessen (April–Oct. Tues.–Sun. 10am–4pm; guided tours in English are available—call ☎0661 41913 for details). Built at enormous expense during the eighteenth century by the prince-bishop Amand von Buseck, the place is so huge that simply wandering around it could take a couple of hours. If you get tired of the rococo opulence and the ranks of Fulda porcelain, go for a coffee in the elegant suroundings of the Schlosscafé, or take a walk through the magnificent park.

Another spot worth heading for just outside Fulda is the **Petersberg**, a 400-meter-high hill with good views of Fulda itself and across to the Vogelsberg and Rhön. The Petersberg is crowned by the **Peterskirche**—check out the eerie statues and paintings of the interior and the ninth-century frescoes in the crypt.

Practical Details

Fulda's **tourist office** is at Schloss Str. 1 (☎0661 102345) and there's a **youth hostel** at Neuenberger Str. 107 (☎0661 73389). Fulda isn't too bad as far as reasonable **hotels** go, and you should be able to find a single for less than DM30 per night. One of the most centrally located is the *Gasthof Grüne Au*, Abtstor 35 (☎0661 74283), in the shadow of the Dom, which has singles from DM25 and doubles from DM60. Another fairly central possibility is the *Pension Hodes*, Peterstor 14 (☎0661 72862), with singles from DM27, doubles from DM54. A little more remote is the *Gasthof Zum Nussknacker* Burgunderstr. 33 (☎0661 35937), with singles from DM25 and doubles from DM45—take the bus from the Hauptbahnhof to the *Städtische Kliniken*.

As for **eating** and **drinking**, upwardly mobile types gravitate towards the *Dachsbau Bistro*, Pfandhausstr. 7–9, where food and drink are good but a little on the pricey side. Fulda's "alternative" scene is centered on *Eisernes Kreuz*, Schlitzer Str. 81, and *Krokodil*, Karlstr. 31, a fairly ritzy café-bar which stays open until 1am. *Löhertor*, Gerberstr. 9, has just about everything including a disco upstairs and occasional film shows. *Zur Windmühle*, Karlstr. 17, is a traditional pub while *Schoppen-Keller*, Paulustor 6, is a *Weinkeller* with a very mixed clientele and relaxed atmosphere.

The Vogelsberg, Spessart, and Rhön

Within easy reach of Fulda is the **Vogelsberg**, a quiet region of gently rolling hills, forests, and small villages which has long been known to the weekend trippers of Hessen but remains relatively undiscovered by outsiders. A massive extinct volcano about 50km in diameter, the Vogelsberg rises to a maximum altitude of 774m at the **Taufstein**—not a dramatic landscape, but a good place for a bit of rustic recuperation. There are regular bus connections between the small towns and villages, and plenty of youth hostels and campgrounds. The area is roughly bounded by Alsfeld in the north, Giessen in the west, Hanau in the south, and Fulda in the east, and its heart is is the area known as the **Hoher Vogelsberg**, which has been designated a *Naturpark*.

If you're exploring the Vogelsberg from Fulda, head initially for **LAUTERBACH**, a run-of-the-mill little town with a half-timbered **Altstadt**, which more or less sets the tone for the rest of the region. There's a worthy but dull Renaissance **Schloss**, a small baroque residence called the **Hohhaus** (which looks like a provincial railroad station) and a tame rococo **Stadtkirche**. More importantly, there's a **youth hostel** at Schlitzer Str. 50 (☎06641 2181). A few kilometers south of Lauterbach is **Schloss Eisenach**, an extensive semifortified residence set amid the forest; there's no public access, as the place is still inhabited by the descendants of the nobles who built it. A little farther on is HERBSTEIN, pleasant enough from a distance with its baroque spires, but less impressive close up.

From Lauterbach make for **ALSFELD**, about 20km to the northeast, which is one of the largest Vogelsberg towns. It's conventionally attractive and very sleepy—even the punks hanging around the marketplace are well behaved. Alsfeld's buildings conform to the local half-timbered blueprint, and many of them are so old that they seem ready to pitch forward into the cobbled streets. The town's slightly sinister, sixteenth-century **Rathaus**, one of the finest in Germany according to the locals, stands on the minute **Marktplatz**, focal point of Alsfeld's historic quarter. There's also a Renaissance **Hochzeitshaus**, a rare stone building, originally built for the celebration of weddings and festivals. At Hersfelder Strasse 10–12 are two of the oldest half-timbered houses in Germany. Apart from these, the only other really notable building is the thirteenth-century **St. Walpurgiskirche**, a grey, geometrical church built onto the remains of an earlier structure. At Rittergasse 3–5 two gaudy baroque buildings have been combined to house the **Regionalmuseum** (Mon.–Fri. 9am–12:30pm and 2–4pm, Sat. and Sun. 10am–4pm) and local **tourist office** (☎06631 18224). The cheapest **hotel** is *Zur alten Schmiede*, Untergasse 12 (☎06631 2465). For cheap eats, and the closest you're likely to get to a lively atmosphere in Alsfeld, make for *Bistro Swing*, which is up a small alley just before the *China Restaurant* on the right hand side of Obergasse. Alsfeld's only passable café is *Venezia* at Obergasse 23.

SCHOTTEN lies in the middle of the Hoher Vogelsberg, and the route from Alsfeld takes you through the core of the *Naturpark*, along a stretch of the *Deutsche Ferienstrasse* (German Holiday Road), under the shadow of the Taufstein. It's a quiet little town which would make a good starting point for exploring the Taufstein's wooded slopes or the nearby **Nidda-Stausee**, a water-sports and fishing center with **camping** facilities. Schotten's **youth hostel** is at Lindenweg 17 (☎06044 2354), and the *Hotel Adler*, Vogelsbergstr. 160 (☎06044 2437), has rooms from DM26 per night. .

About 10km west of Schotten is **LAUBACH**; again there's not much to see, apart from a seventeenth-century **Schloss** which is closed to the public, but its relaxed atmosphere makes it a pleasant place to sit in the sun outside a café—try *Café Göbel* in Friedrichstrasse or *Café Venezia* in Wildemanngasse. There's a **youth hostel** at Am Ramsberg (☎06405 1376). Traveling southeast from Schotten along the B276 you come to GEDERN, where there are **camping** facilities at Gederner See (inquiries ☎06045 333).

About 25km southwest of Fulda lies SCHLÜCHTERN, notable only for the fact that it lies on the edge of the Hessen section of the **Spessart**, Germany's largest continuous upland forest area. A few kilometers southwest of here is **STEINAU**, a typical little half-timbered town, in whose **Hanauisches Amtshaus** the Brothers Grimm spent part of their youth; there's a memorial to them in the town's **Schloss**, as well as a puppet theater which performs their stories. Both these towns are served by road and rail links from Fulda.

Between Fulda and the border with East Germany stretches the **Rhön**, a volcanic region a little more wild and threatening than the Vogelsberg. These hills have become a big hang-gliding center and there are some good walking and bicycling routes (inquire in the Fulda tourist office for detailed information). The Rhön is split between Hessen, Bavaria, and Thuringia in East Germany, but Hessen has the **Wasserkuppe**, which at 950m is the highest peak in the range. There's been a gliding center on the Wasserkuppe since 1911 and its **Segelflugmuseum** is worth a quick visit.

For exploring the Rhön the best base is **GERSFELD**. It's a small tourist-oriented town with a baroque **Pfarrkirche** whose altar, pulpit, and organ are piled on top of one another to great dramatic effect. The baroque **Schloss** contains a museum which displays some fragile-looking examples of Fulda porcelain work. The **tourist office** is in the *Kurverwaltung*, Brückenstr. 1 (☎06654 7077), the **youth hostel** at Jahnstr. 6 (☎06654 340), and there's no shortage of reasonable **hotels** and **pensions**: *Pension Weinig*, Am Kreuzgarten 4 (☎06654 557), starts at DM22, and *Hotel-Pension Goldener Stern*, Rommerserstr. 8 (☎06654 267), has rooms from DM24 per person.

Kassel

Despite its aggressive attempts at self-promotion, **KASSEL** is a dull city. For any art lover, however, it certainly merits a detour, on account of the *documenta*, the huge modern art exhibition held there once every five years, and the wonderful Gemäldegalerie, one of the country's finest picture collections. Since its inception in 1955, as a retrospective of twentieth-century art, the *documenta* has become a multimedia event which embraces everything from painting to video art and whose venue is in effect the whole city. The *documenta 8* of 1987 featured the diverse talents of Joseph Beuys, Rainer Werner Fassbinder, Yoko Ono, and hundreds of others in one of the most significant avant-garde art events in the world. The late Joseph Beuys was responsible for some of the *documenta*'s zanier moments—one of his schemes entailed planting 7000 oak trees throughout the city, each one marked by a small basalt stone.

The *documenta* aside, Kassel is basically an industrial town. Its big armaments industry ensured eighty per cent destruction of its center during the war, and consequently most of the buildings in the core of the city date from the 1950s.As the city publicity brochures are only too keen to remind you, Kassel was the first town in West Germany to feature the now-obligatory pedestrian zone.

In non-*documenta* years the **Wilhelmshöhe**—a park, castle and associated bits and pieces at the western edge of town—is the best Kassel has to offer (fifteen mins. by tram #1 from Königsplatz). The eighteenth century **Schloss Wilhelmshöhe** houses the **Staatliche Kunstsammlung Kassel** (Tues-Sun. 10am–5pm; free), whose ground floor is devoted to Greek and Roman art—look out for the *Kassel Apollo*, a Roman copy of an archetypal Classical Greek bronze. Far more enthralling, though, is the **Gemäldegalerie** (Picture Gallery), a treasury of old masters which originated in the collection of an eighteenth-century land-grave of Hessen, Wilhelm VIII, whose spell as governor of Breda and Maastricht fueled a passion for the painting of the Dutch Golden Age. He accumulated what remains one of the world's finest collections of this period, supplemented by seven-teenth-century paintings from elsewhere in Europe.

Until recently, the gallery claimed to own seventeen canvases by **Rembrandt**, but current research has demoted six of these to the status of works by followers. Among the undisputed pieces, though, there are still some supreme master-pieces, most notably the profoundly touching *Jacob Blessing his Grandchildren*. This rarely depicted subject shows the patriach choosing to bless Joseph's second son Ephraim first, on the grounds he was destined for greater things—namely, to be the ancestor of the Gentiles. Rembrandt accordingly showed Eph-raim as a fair-haired Aryan type, in contrast to the dark features of the first-born, Manasseh. From the same period comes one of his greatest portraits, *Nicolaes Bruyning*, vividly conveying the sitter's animated personality. Two paintings from a decade earlier are unique in Rembrandt's oeuvre. *Winter Landscape* is his only nature study executed in bright colors, while the intimate *Holy Family with the Curtain* presents the scene in the manner of a tiny theater set. *Profile of Saskia* is a demonstration of the young artist's virtuosity, with his first wife, gorgeously decked out in velvet and jewelry, depicted as an icon of idealized womanhood.

Frans Hals's *Man in a Slouched Hat* is a late work, clearly showing the influ-ence of Rembrandt, married to his own talent for caricature, which can be seen more plainly in the earlier *Merry Toper*. Other pieces from seventeenth century Holland on show include paintings by Terbrugghen and Jan Steen, and more than twenty works by **Philips Wouwerman**.

In spite of Landgrave Wilhelm's strict Calvinism, which drew him to the Dutch School above all others, he assembled a magnificent group of Flemish paintings of the same period. There are some choice canvases by **Rubens**, notably *The Crowning of the Hero*, *The Madonna as a Refuge for Sinners*, the highly unflattering *Nicolas de Respaigne as a Pilgrim to Jerusalem* and a beautiful nocturnal *Flight into Egypt*. **Van Dyck** is represented by portraits drawn from all phases of his career, while the examples of **Jordaens** show his taste for the exotic on a large scale.

The seventeenth-century Dutch and Flemish collection takes up most of the first and second floors, but the end cabinets are devoted to small-scale fifteenth-and sixteenth-century paintings, mostly from Germany. **Cranach**'s early *Resurrection Triptych* is one of a number of highlights, others being **Dürer**'s *Elsbeth Tucher*, **Baldung**'s *Hercules and Antaeus* ,and an impassioned *Crucifixion*, set in a Danube landscape, by **Altdorfer**. On the top floor a group of Italian Renaissance pictures is dominated by a magnificent full-length *Portrait of a Nobleman* by **Titian**. However, once again it was the seventeenth-century masters who most appealed to the Hessian taste, and there are some spectacular examples of Italian baroque, finest of which is **Preti**'s *Feast of Herod*. From Spain come outstanding pieces by **Murillo** and **Ribera**, while **Poussin**'s *Cupid's Victory over Pan* represents French art of this same period. **Schönfeld**'s *The Great Flood* is one of the finest of all seventeenth-century German paintings, while there are a couple of examples of the brilliant but short-lived **Johann Liss**—the enigmatic *Scene with Soldiers and Courtesans* and the effervescent *Game of Morra*, a work anticipatory of the rococo style of a century later.

The *Weissensteinflügel* of the Schloss houses the predictable **Schlossmuseum** (March–Oct. Tues.–Sun. 10am–5pm; Nov.–Feb. Tues.–Sun. 10am–4pm), with its furniture, glassware, porcelain, and other standard stately home equipment.

Immediately to the north of the Schloss is the **Ballhaus**, a neat little neoclassical building which King Jerome, Napoleon's brother and king of the puppet state of Westphalia, had built as a theater in 1808. It was turned into a ball-room twenty years later and has the same role (intermittently) today. Not far away is the **Gewächshaus**, a greenhouse dating back to 1822 (Jan.–April daily 10am–5pm).

On the other side of the lake stands the **Löwenburg** (Tues.–Sun. 10am–4pm, with guided tours on the hour; DM2), a ruined castle which is not quite what it seems. It was in fact built as an medieval-style ruin, complete with artificial portcullis and drawbridge, in keeping with the romantic spirit of the late eighteenth century. It represented a whim on the part of Elector Wilhelm I who, peeved by the revolutionary upheavals of the era, wanted to recreate the atmosphere of feudal times when masters and servants knew their places and stayed in them. Inside the "ruin" is a museum full of medieval bits and pieces.

The Wilhelmshöhe is dominated by the **Bergpark**, an enormous baroque ornamental garden complete with a 250-meter-long, 885-tiered cascade which descends the slopes of the Habichtswald forest; it's overlooked by the famous **Herkules** statue, which may look like an eighteenth-century Michelin Man but is a source of great pride to the burghers of Kassel. The statue lounges on top of a bizarre-looking pyramidal structure, which is in turn set into a purely decorative castle called the **Oktogon**. Highpoint of the Wilhelmshöhe day is the ornamental fountain display at 2:30pm, when floodgates at the foot of Hercules are opened and water pours down the cascade and over a series of obstacles to the fountain in front of the Schloss.

At the foot of the Wilhelmshöhe, at Wilhelms Allee 361, there's a huge and slightly tacky modern spa complex complete with saunas, jacuzzis, movie theater and restaurant (Mon., Tues., Thurs. and Sun. 9am–11pm,Wed, Fri. and Sat. 9am–noon; DM13 for 90min or DM34 for the day).

The center of Kassel isn't really notable for very much apart from bad architecture, though it has a few museums which are just about worth bothering with if you're in town. The **Neue Gallerie**, at Schöne Aussicht 1 (Tues.–Sun. 10am–5pm; closed Dec.; free), takes up the history of art where the Schloss Wilhelmshöhe collection leaves off, covering the period from 1750 to the present, with emphasis on work by local artists and pieces produced at Willingshausen–Schwalm, Germany's oldest artists' colony; pieces from most major European artistic movements are also featured, with a few works by the omnipresent Joseph Beuys.

The **Museum Fredericianum**, in the eighteenth-century *Kulturhaus* at Ständeplatz 16 (the oldest museum building on the European mainland) houses the archives of the *documenta* (Mon., Tues., Thurs. 10am–4pm, Wed, Fri. 10am–2pm or by appointment); the same building also houses the **Stadtmuseum**, Kassel's local museum (Tues.–Fri. 10am–5pm, Sat. and Sun. 10am–1pm; free).

Just next door, at Steinweg 2, is the **Ottoneum**—built between 1603 and 1606, it was the first permanent theater in Germany. Today it houses the **Naturkunde-museum**, the natural history museum (Tues.-Fri. 10am-4:30pm, Sat. and Sun. 10am-1pm, free).

The **Brüder-Grimm-Museum** in **Schloss Bellevue** (Tues.-Fri. 10am-1pm and 2pm-5pm, Sat. and Sun. 10am-1pm; free), at Schöne Aussicht 2, will tell you everything you ever wanted to know and more about the famous fairy tale tellers and philologists, being full of Brothers Grimm ephemera and first editions. The brothers were born in Hanau, and studied in Marburg before becoming as court librarians in Kassel, where they compiled their anthologies of fairy-tales. They then took up academic posts in Göttingen but were expelled from that city for political reasons in in 1837; by 1841 both were members of the Academy of Sciences in Berlin, where they remained to compile the *Deutsche Wörterbuch*—the German equivalent of the Oxford English Dictionary.

The **Landmuseum**, Brüder-Grimm-Platz 5 (Tues.-Sun. 10am-5pm; free), is mainly given over to pre- and early history in Hessen. There's also a substantial astrophysics section, including a 1560 observatory and various clocks and astronomical instruments made by Tycho Brahe. The building also houses a branch of the **Staatliche Kunstsammlung**, which is mainly concerned with applied art, and the **Deutsches Tapetenmuseum** (*German Wallpaper Museum*). The latter is apparently the only wallpaper museum in the world and has exhibits from all eras and continents; it's only marginally more interesting than it sounds.

The only other thing worth knowing about in the city center is the **Karls-Aue** park; the **Orangerie**, a postwar restoration of an eighteenth-century palace, is now used as an exhibition hall and venue for *documenta* events.

One easy excursion from Kassel is to **Schloss Wilhelmstal** (March-Oct. Tues.-Sun. 10am-5pm, Nov.-Feb. Tues.-Sun. 10am-4pm; DM1), a Rococo palace about 13km north-east of the city. Designed by François Cuvilliés, architect of the Amalienburg in Munich (from which it's derived), it features an ornamental garden and sumptuously decorated interior.

Practical Details

The **tourist office** is at the **Hauptbahnhof** (Mon.-Fri. 9am-5:30pm, Sat. 9am-12:30pm; ☎0561 13443), and they'll be able to arrange a private room for you. There's a shortage of cheap **hotels** in the center, but there are a few possibilities towards the outskirts of town. Cheapest central place is *Gasthaus Hamburger Hof*, Werner-Hilpert-Str. 18 (☎0561 16002), near the Hauptbahnhof, which has singles from DM29.50 and doubles from DM49.50. *Autoreisehotel*, Mombachstr. 19 (☎0561 895947), to the north of the Hauptbahnhof (tram #1 or #5 from Königsplatz), has singles from DM30 and doubles from DM60. On the eastern edge of Kassel, *Gasthaus Bürgerhof*, Umbachsweg 53 (☎0561 522615), has singles from DM27 and doubles from DM54. Also in the east is *Gasthaus zum Sportplatz*, Lilienstr. 108 (☎0561 59060), which has singles from DM30 and doubles from DM60—it's best reached by bus #17 from Königsplatz. Other possibilities include *Zum Herkules*, Hüttenbergstr. 14 (☎0561 312400), near the Herkules monument, with singles from DM35 and doubles from DM70. There's a **youth hostel** at Schenkendorfstr. 18 (☎0561 776455), and **camping** facilities at Giesenallee 7 (☎0561 22433), on the northwestern edge of town.

The best **bars** and **cafés** in Kassel seem to be in the area around Goethestrasse, a studeny district on the western edge of the city center, where a few Jugendstil houses break up the general architectural monotony. *Wirtschaft* on the corner of Goethestrasse and Querallee is a recommended bar, while *Café Berger* opposite is a good *Kaffee und Kuchen* place. *Vis-a-Vis* on the corner of Goethestrasse and Lassallestrasse is an alternative-type café-bar, and at *Werkstatt*, a small café-bar on the corner of Friedrich-Ebert-Strasse and Diakonissenstrasse, they occasionally put on avant-gardish art exhibitions.

Around Kassel

North of Kassel is an area known as the **Reinhardswald**, an upland forest region which has been turned into a *Naturpark* and where it's still possible to encounter wild boar and bison. One of its centers is **HOFGEISMAR**, a small former *Kurort* about twenty minutes from Kassel by rail—there's little to see apart from the eighteenth-century *Kur* buildings, and the town has the atmosphere of a place bypassed by history. From Hofgeismar it's only about 10km to **Schloss Sababurg** (fairly frequent buses), which in a cunning move on the part of the local tourism people, has been designated Sleeping Beauty's castle. The domed towers are passably picturesque from a distance, but close up it's not much more than a glorified hotel and restaurant, with a shabby zoo attached to amuse the kids. It lies on the **Deutsche Märchenstrasse** (German Fairy Tale Route), which, cashing in on the Grimm connection, runs from Hanau to Bremen and attempts to inject a bit of interest into a lot of otherwise mainly dull towns and castles.

More interesting by far is **BAD KARLSHAFEN** (frequent buses from Kassel), a baroque town straddling the river Weser at the very northern tip of Hessen. Now a *Kurort* and a popular tourist destination, it was founded in 1699 by Landgrave Karl of Hessen, who planned to build a canal from here to Kassel which would enable Hessian merchant ships to avoid the Customs toll imposed at the Hanoverian town of Münden. Although his grandiose scheme never came to fruition, the town retains a unique ambience which it owes in part to the role originally intended for it—the harbor basin, surrounded by delicately colored gabled baroque houses, is particularly atmospheric. Karl brought in Huguenot refugees from France to run the new harbor town, and their part in the development of Bad Karlshafen is recorded in the **Hugenotten-Museum**, at Schützen Allee.

The **tourist office** is in the *Kurverwaltung* at Hafenplatz 8 and there's a **youth hostel** at Winnefelderstr. 7 (☎05672 3380). There are plenty of cheap **pensions**, the best bets being *Hotel-Pension Freise*, Mündener Str. 46 (☎05672 2551), which starts at DM20 per night, and *Pension Haus Weserblick*, Unter den Eichen 4 (☎05672 890), which starts at DM24 per night.

To the southeast of Kassel lies the sleepy **Kaufunger Wald** and the 106,000 acre *Naturpark Kaufunger Wald-Meissner*, as yet barely discovered by tourists. The regional center is the overgrown village of **KAUFUNGEN**, about fifteen minutes by rail from Kassel (get out in Ober-Kaufungen), whose sizable **Klosterkirche** once belonged to a Benedictine convent founded in 1017 by the future saint Kunigunde, wife of Emperor Henry II.

If you're looking for somewhere to stay in this area, you could do worse than to head for **NIESTE**, a slate-roofed little village just a few kilometers north of Kaufungen. The most reasonable **hotels** are *Gasthof zum Adler*, Witzenhäuser Str. 24 (☎05605 2642), which starts at DM22 per night, or *Gasthof zum Niestetal*, Kaufunger Str. 9 (☎05605 2490) which starts at DM18. From Kaufungen it's easy enough to reach **HESSISCH-LICHTENAU** by rail; here part of the medieval fortifications which once surrounded the town has survived, and there's a richly decorated Renaissance **Rathaus**. Cheapish **hotels** include: *Hotel zur Lichten Aue*, Desselerstr. 6 (☎05602 2087), with rooms from DM26, and *Hotel Ratskeller*, Landgrafenstr. 17 (☎05602 2772), which starts at DM29. Inexpensive accommodation can also be found in some of the surrounding villages—check with the local **tourist office** at Landgrafenstr. 52 (☎05602 2061). Here you'll also be able to get information about the various walking routes that exist on the **Hoher Meissner**, the highest peak in northern Hessen (754m), just to the east of Hessich Lichtenau.

From Hessische Lichtenau trains run regularly to **WITZENHAUSEN**, the so-called "Cherry Town" about 25km to the northeast. The cherry orchards contain some 200,000 trees and march right up into the old fashioned town itself; the place gets particularly busy during the *Kesperkirmes* ("Cherry Fair"), when the "Cherry Princess" is crowned. The **tourist office** is at Am Markt 1 (☎05542 2506); the cheapest local **pensions** are *Dovidat* Burgstr. 20 (☎05542 2506), with rooms from DM25, and *Hotze*, Kasseler Str. 29 (☎05542 3214), from DM20.

Twelve kilometers southeast of Witzenhausen is **BADSOODEN-ALLENDORF**, a double town cut in two by the Werra river . Bad Sooden is a salt-spring *Kurort*, while Allendorf is chiefly notable for its half-timbered houses and the fact that its hemmed in on three sides by the East German border. Affordable **hotels** and **pensions** are plentiful: try *Gasthof zum Stern*, Kirchstr. 71 (☎05652 2252), which has beds from DM25, or *Pension Haus Erika*, Am Haintor 22 (☎05652 2278), which starts at DM24. The **tourist office** in the *Kurverwaltung*, on Landgraf-Philipp-Platz, will be able to give you details of other possibilities.

Heading farther south you come to **ESCHWEGE**, the main town of the Werra valley region, with its half-timbered **Marktplatz** , Renaissance **Schloss** and two Gothic churches (one for the Altstadt and another for the Neustadt). The **tourist office** is at Hospitalplatz 16 (☎05651 304210), and there's a **youth hostel** at Fritz-Neuenroth-Weg 1 (☎05651 60099). In the town center cheap hotels are in short supply—check with the tourist office for details.

Another possible excursion from Kassel is to **BADHERSFELD** qually accessible from Fulda), which is famous chiefly for its July drama festival. Inaugurated in 1951, it takes in both classical drama (this is Germany's most celebrated Shakespeare stage) and modern works (material as diverse as Brecht and *Kiss Me Kate*), the plays being performed against the backdrop of the **Stiftsruine**, the remains of an eleventh-century basilica destroyed by French soldiers in the eighteenth century. As for the rest of the town, there's the familiar spectacle of a half-timbered **Altstadt** with a Renaissance **Rathaus**, but outside of the drama festival there's not that much to see. If you intend visiting Bad Hersfeld for the festival, try to arrange tickets and accommodation by the preceding February through the **tourist office** at Am Markt 1 (☎06621 201274). Bad Hersfeld's **youth hostel** is at Wehnebergestr. 29 (☎06621 2403), and reasonable local **hotels** include *Gasthof Jäger*, Homberger Str. 93 (☎06621 3810), which starts at DM23, and *Gasthof Café Eichhof*, Brelauerstr Str. 12 (☎06621 2682), with rooms from DM25.

travel details

Trains

From Frankfurt to Wiesbaden (2 hourly; 30 min.), Darmstadt (3 hourly; 15 min), Kassel (2 hourly ;2hr.), Marburg (2 hourly; 1hr) Fulda (2 hourly;1 hr).

From Wiesbaden to Rudesheim (1 hourly; 35 min.)

From Kassel to Marburg (1 hourly; 1 hr.)

CHAPTER FOUR

RHINELAND-PALATINATE AND SAARLAND

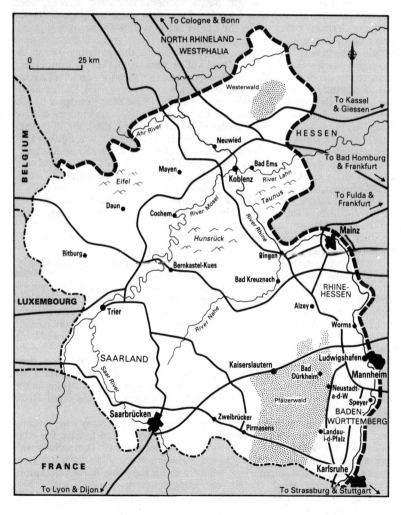

To Cologne & Bonn

NORTH RHINELAND –
WESTPHALIA

0   25 km

Westerwald

BELGIUM

Ahr River

HESSEN

To Kassel
& Giessen

Neuwied

Mayen

Bad Ems

Koblenz

River Lahn

To Bad Homburg
& Frankfurt

Eifel

Daun

River Mosel

Taunus

To Fulda &
Frankfurt

Cochem

Hunsrück

River Rhine

Mainz

Bingen

Bitburg

Bernkastel-Kues

Bad Kreuznach

RHINE-
HESSEN

LUXEMBOURG

Alzey

Trier

River Nahe

Worms

SAARLAND

Saar River

Kaiserslautern

Ludwigshafen

Bad
Dürkheim

Mannheim

Neustadt-
a-d-W

Speyer

Pfälzerwald

BADEN-
WÜRTTEMBERG

Saarbrücken

Zweibrücker

Pirmasens

Landau-
i-d-Pfalz

FRANCE

Karlsruhe

To Lyon & Dijon

To Strassburg & Stuttgart

Of all the German Länder, the **RHINELAND-PALATINATE** is the one most overlaid by legend. The **Rhine River** is seen here at its majestic best, and there's hardly a town, castle, or rock along this stretch which hasn't made a distinctive contribution to its mythology. This is the land of the national epic, the *Nibelungenlied*—an extraordinary tale of heroism, chicanery, dynastic rivalry, vengeance, and obsession—which bites deep into the German soul. It's also the land of the deceptively alluring Lorelei, of the robber barons who presided over tiny fiefs from lofty fortresses, and of the merchant traders who used the natural advantages of river to bring the country to the forefront of European prosperity.

Nowadays, the Rhine's once-treacherous waters have been tamed, enabling pleasure cruisers to run its length, past a wonderful landscape of rocks, vines, white-painted towns, and ruined castles. Everything conforms perfectly to the image of Germany promoted by the tourist office: visitors swarm in, and people living on the trade do very nicely. Although the Rhine gorge is the part most people want to write home about, the rest of the Land does rather well in the picture-postcard stakes too. The **Mosel valley**, running all the way from France to its confluence with the Rhine at **Koblenz**, scores highly for scenic beauty and has the advantage that it's not quite as oversubscribed and spoiled. Farther north, the valley of the **Ahr River**, which flows into the Rhine near **Remagen** (of *The Bridge at . . .* fame), manages to rival both of the larger rivers in terms of good looks and touristic allure. Only in the **Hunsrück** and the **Eifel**, the Rhineland-Palatinate's "mountain" ranges, do the otherwise ever-present vines give way to bare heathland and forest, creating landscapes that are at times almost desolate.

Industry exists only in isolated pockets, and **Mainz**, the state's capital and chief city, doesn't even rank among the thirty largest in West Germany. Its monuments, though, together with those of the two other Imperial cathedral cities of **Worms** (the font of Germany's once-rich Jewish culture) and **Speyer**, do their part for the historic side of things, the wealth of their architectural heritage equaling the natural beauty of the surrounding countryside. However, the number-one city from the point of view of sights is **Trier**, which preserves the finest buildings of classical antiquity this side of the Alps.

Trier's Roman survivals are a potent reminder of the area's illustrious **history**. The Rhine itself marked the effective limit of Roman power, and from that period onward the settlements along its western bank dominated national development. Throughout the duration of the Holy Roman Empire, the importance of this area within Germany can be gauged by the fact that two of the seven electors were the archbishops of Mainz and Trier, while another was the *Pfalzgraf*, or count palatine of the Rhine. (The last-named actually lived in what is now Baden-Württemberg, but his territories have provided the present-day Land with its name.) Like the Romans, the French have often regarded the Rhine as the natural limit of their power, and their designs on the region—ranging from the destructive War of the Palatinate Succession launched in 1689, via the Napoleonic grand design, to the ham-fisted attempts to foster an independent state there after World War I—have had a profound impact on European history.

As far as **getting around** is concerned, it's one part of Germany where having your own vehicle is a definite benefit. Otherwise, buses tend to have the edge over trains for seeing the best of the scenery. Despite their associations with over-organized tour groups, the pleasure steamers which glide down the great rivers throughout the summer are definitely worth sampling. **Accommodation**, whether in hotels, youth hostels, or campgrounds, is plentiful, but is best reserved in advance during the high season in the most popular areas.

Today, in contrast to the turbulence of the past, it's all quiet on the Rhineland front, with the economic base heavily sustained by tourism and wine. Predominantly Catholic and rural, it's a CDU stronghold, and the current federal chancellor, **Helmut Kohl**, first came to prominence as the Land's minister-president. This is in marked contrast to the miniature neighboring province of **Saarland**, a place of scant tourist interest, whose heavily industrialized valley has been a natural breeding ground for radical political leaders.

THE WESTERN RHINELAND

Spaced out along the western bank of the Rhine are three of Germany's most venerable cities—**Mainz**, **Worms**, and **Speyer**—which have all, at one time or another, played a key role in the country's history, the most potent reminder of their status being the mighty Romanesque Dom dominating each city. The distinctive size and shape of these three cathedrals reflects the curious power-sharing arrangement between civil and ecclesiastical power—with each having an unusually large say in the other's affairs—that sustained the fragile structure of the Holy Roman Empire for so long.

Farther west lies the hill and forest countryside of the **Pfalz** and **Hunsrück**. By German standards, it's little known, particularly to foreigners, and thus an ideal place to get away from it all. However, public transportation is comparatively sparse, making it a region best explored by car or bike.

Mainz

"The capital of our dear Fatherland" was how Goethe styled **MAINZ**. That's a position this 2000-year-old city, situated by the confluence of the Rhine and Main, has never officially held, though its influential role throughout German history certainly gave it a far stronger claim for nomination as the postwar seat of government of the Federal Republic than Bonn. Mainz's importance developed in the mid-eighth century, thanks to the Englishman Saint Boniface, who raised it to the rank of the main center of the church north of the Alps. Later, the local archbishop came to be one of the most powerful princes in the Holy Roman Empire, holding electoral status, and having the official title of archchancellor. Further kudos were gained courtesy of Mainz's greatest son, the inventor **Johannes Gutenberg**, whose revolutionary fifteenth-century developments in the art of printing made a colossal impact on European civilization. Since the Napoleonic period—which saw Mainz for a time become the French city of "Mayence"—it has never managed to recover its former status, while its strategic location inevitably made it a prime target for World War II bombers. Nonetheless, it's now Land capital of the Rhineland-Palatinate, and is an agreeable mixture of old and new. If you're flying in or out of Frankfurt, Mainz makes a good alternative place to stay, as the airport lies on the S-Bahn line between the two cities, with several services every hour, and a journey time of less than thirty minutes.

The City

Rearing high above all the other buildings in the center of Mainz are the six towers of the massive red sandstone **Dom** (or **Kaiserdom**), which still ranks,

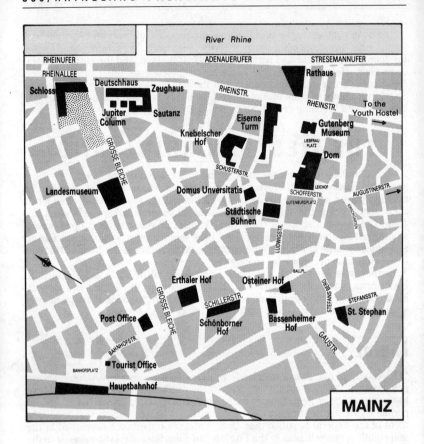

along with Cologne, as one of the two most important Roman Catholic cathedrals in the country. A few years ago it celebrated its 1000th anniversary, even though little remains from this epoch other than the floorplan, some of the lower masonry, and the bronze doors by the normal north entrance; most of what can be seen today is twelfth-century Romanesque.

One of the Dom's most singular features—which was a deliberate ploy to emphasize its mass—is that it's completely surrounded by buildings, stuck right up against its walls. The present picturesque group of houses dates from the eighteenth century, but the **St. Gothard Kapelle**, two stories high and of a contrasting grey stone, is from the first half of the twelfth century. Once the archbishop's own chapel, it's now the area set aside for private prayer and is entered from the north transept. The Dom's status as an imperial cathedral, with a special area required for the Emperor as well as the clergy, can be noticed at once in the **choirs** at both ends of the building, each flanked by one large and two small towers. What's perhaps less immediately obvious, but a further emphasis of its historical importance, is that it follows the precedent of St. Peter's in Rome in being oriented from east to west, the reverse of normal.

The solemn and spacious **interior** for the most part preserves its architectural purity. Above the nave's arcades is a cycle of murals of the life of Christ. Painted in the gentle Nazarene style—which aimed at recapturing the freshness and faith of medieval painting—they're a far more successful adornment than most such well-meaning nineteenth-century attempts at "improving" old churches. However, the interior is remarkable above all as a very superior cemetery for the archbishops. These men were no shrinking violets, commissioning grandiose monuments to themselves which adorn the piers of the nave, forming an unrivaled panorama of sculpture from the thirteenth century to nineteenth century. Not only is this a must for necrophiles; many of the **tombs** are artistically first-rate.

Among the finest is the poignant, late fifteenth century *Monument to Adalbert von Sachsen*, third from the end on the north side; its youthful subject died before his consecration and is thus not shown in ecclesiastical robes. The same sculptor made the touching *Holy Sepulcher* in the *Magnuskapelle*. From early in the following century are the most grandiose of all the tombs, carved by a local man, **Hans Backoffen**, one of the outstanding crop of German sculptors who bridged the late Gothic and early Renaissance. His masterpiece is the *Monument to Uriel von Gemmingen*, on the last but one pillar of the north side of the nave; two others by him are directly opposite.

The **Diocesan Museum** (Mon.–Wed and Fri. 9am–noon and 2–5pm, Thurs. and Sat. 9am–noon; free), laid out in rooms opening off the cloisters, houses the best sculptures of all. These are fragments from the demolished rood screen, created around 1240 by the anonymous mason—one of the supreme artistic geniuses of the Middle Ages—known as **Master of Naumburg** from his later work in the East German cathedral of that name. In his carvings here, such as the scenes of the Elect and the Damned, and above all in the *Head with Bandeau*, note his beautiful sense of modeling, and the uncanny realism and characterization which are far in advance of any other sculpture of the time.

The spacious **Markt** is the scene of markets on Tuesday, Friday, and Saturday mornings. Here also is the riotously colorful **Marktbrunnen**, the finest of Mainz's many fountains, a joyful Renaissance concoction adorned with putti and topped by a statue of the Virgin and Child.

Dominating the adjoining Liebfrauenplatz is the resplendent pink Renaissance facade of the **Haus zum Romischen Kaiser**, which houses the offices of the **Gutenberg Museum**, also known as the **World Museum of Printing** (Tues.–Sat. 10am–6pm, Sun. 10am–1pm; free); the actual displays are in a modern extension behind. It's a fitting tribute to one of the greatest inventors of all time, making amends for the abysmal treatment he received at the hands of the authorities of his own day. An illegitimate son of a canon of Mainz, Gutenberg dreamed of being able to reproduce manuscripts of the same beauty and quality as that achieved by copyists, but without the painstaking physical labor that was involved. Although it's a myth that he invented printing as such—the Chinese had been able to do it for centuries—it was only through his pioneering development of movable type that the mass-scale production of books became possible. His inventions were of tremendous significance, and were to survive without appreciable technological advancement right up to the present century. However, they led to Gutenberg's personal ruin; his short-sighted creditors, interested only in making a quick profit, wrested his inventions from him by means of a lawsuit. Totally destitute, he thereafter had to rely on charitable handouts to continue his researches.

Until 1978, Mainz had only the second volume of Gutenberg's most famous work, the **42-line Bible.** Made in the 1450s, it's a gravely beautiful production employing magisterial Gothic lettering. The city then managed to repatriate from America the last of the forty-odd surviving complete versions still in private hands. This has pride of place in the vault on the second floor, where it is exhibited alongside other productions of the time, notably an *Apocalypse*, printed by means of the painfully slow "block book" method. Most of the rest of the museum is given over to displays of printed books from all over the world, while the basement contains a mock-up of Gutenberg's workshop, and printing machines of later dates.

Despite war damage, the center of Mainz, especially around the Dom, contains many fine old streets and squares lined with examples of vernacular building ranging from half-timbered Gothic to rococo. North of the Dom, the magnificent **Knebelscher Hof** is reminiscent of the Weser Renaissance style of northern Germany, while Kirschgarten and Augustinerstrasse to the south are particularly well preserved. Just off the end of the latter is the sumptuous church of **St. Ignaz**, marking the transition from rococo to neoclassicism. Outside, a monumental *Crucifixion* group by Hans Backoffen stands over the sculptor's own tomb, which is even more imposing than those he had made for the archbishops. This marks the end of the historic quarter—beyond is a particularly sleazy red-light district, the largest vice center in the Frankfurt conurbation.

Across Schöfferstrasse from the Dom is Gutenbergplatz, with the municipal theater (*Städtische Bühnen*) and a statue to the inventor by the Danish neoclassical sculptor, Bertel Thorwaldsen; farther down the street is the whitewashed Renaissance frontage of the **Domus Universitatis**. Continuing down Ludwigstrasse, you shortly come to Schillerplatz and Schillerstrasse, which are lined with impressive Renaissance and baroque palaces, now used as offices. Here too you'll find the elaborate modern **Karnevalbrunnen**, honoring the annual Carnival festivities, whose celebration here ranks for spectacle second only to Cologne's.

Up the hill by Gaustrasse is the fourteenth-century Gothic church of **St. Stephan** (daily 10am–noon and 2–5pm). Although a pleasant enough building with a pretty cloister, it's now chiefly remarkable for possessing what must rank as the most impressive of all the many postwar embellishments found in German churches. In 1976, the parish priest persuaded **Marc Chagall**, the great Russian Jewish artist long resident in France, to make a series of stained glass windows. The theme chosen was reconciliation, symbolizing that between France and Germany, Christian and Jew. There are nine windows in all, luminously brilliant in their coloring and quite astonishingly vibrant for an artist in his nineties; they were finished in November 1984, just a few months before Chagall's death.

Most of Mainz's remaining monuments of interest are situated in close proximity to the Rhine. The quayside is dominated by the stark black-and-white lines of the 1970s **Rathaus**, designed by Arne Jacobsen and another impressive modern addition to the city's heritage. Across the road is the so-called **Eiserne Turm** (Iron Tower), once part of the medieval fortifications, now a commercial art gallery; the other surviving city gate, the **Holzturm** (Wooden Tower), is south down Rheinstrasse. Continuing northwards up the same street, you come to the baroque **Zeughaus** and **Deutschaus**; behind is the gabled Renaissance facade of the old arsenal, the **Sautanz**. Near here, a copy of the Jupitersäule—whose original is in the Landesmuseum (see below)—has been set up.

Farther on is the **Schloss**, the enormous former palace of the archbishop-electors, a superbly swaggering late Renaissance building with a baroque extension. The once-famous interiors were completely destroyed in the war; in their place is the **Roman-Germanic Museum** (Tues.–Sun. 10am–6pm; free), a rather confusing collection in which copies of famous antiquities are mingled with original pieces.

Far more worthwhile is the **Landesmuseum** (Tues.–Sun. 10am–5pm; free), occupying the old imperial stables directly down Grosse Bleiche. The outstanding **archaeology** department includes a hall full of Roman sculptural remains, dominated by the original **Jupitersäule**, the most important Roman triumphal column in Germany. Also here are important fragments from demolished medieval buildings, especially the fourteenth century **Kaufhaus**, one of only two German secular facades of the era to have survived. The most important paintings are at the very end of the ground-floor gallery. They include a series of nine canvases of the *Life of the Virgin* from the studio of the mysterious, highly original fifteenth-century Middle Rhenish draftsman known as **Master of the Housebook**; the two Nativity scenes are by the master himself. Also of note are copies of Dürer's celebrated *Adam* and *Eve* by his pupil **Baldung**, *Saint Jerome* by **Cranach**, and an altar wing by the **Master of Saint Bartholomew**, whose companion is in London's National Gallery. Upstairs are seventeenth-century Dutch cabinet pictures and a modern section whose main pull, an array of colorful drawings by Chagall, is unfortunately only occasionally on view. There's also a glittering collection of Jugendstil glass.

Practicalities and Entertainments

The **Hauptbahnhof** is situated northwest of the city center. A short way down Bahnhofstrasse is the **tourist office** (Mon.–Fri. 9am–6pm, Sat. 9am–1pm; ☎06131 233741). Many of the least expensive **hotels** are close by, though they hardly charge bargain-basement rates—expect to pay upwards of DM40 for a single, DM65 for a double. At Bahnhofstr. 15 is *Pfeil-Continental* (☎06131 232179), while there are two possibilities on Alicestrasse to the right—at no. 4 is *Terminus* (☎06131 2298760), at no. 6 *Richter's Eisenbahn* (☎06131 234077). Comparable in price but with a better location very near the Dom are *Stadt Coblenz*, at Rheinstr. 49 (☎06131 227602), and *Zum Schildknecht*, at Heliggrabgasse 6 (☎06131 225755). For markedly lower prices, you'll have to stay some distance out. The suburb of GONSENHEIM (reached by trams #10 and #11, buses #22 and #23) is the likeliest, with two hotels in the range of DM30 for a single, DM50 for a double—*Roseneck*, at An der Bruchspitze 3 (☎06131 680368), and *Zarewitsch*, at Kurt-Schumacher-Str. 20 (☎06131 42404). Alternatively, there's the **youth hostel** (☎06131 85332), situated in the wooded heights of Am Fort Weisenau; catch bus #1 or #22.

Mainz is unashamedly a **wine** rather than a beer city, boasting more vineyards within its boundaries than any other German city. If you fancy a wine-tasting session, you don't need to stray far from the vicinity of the Dom; there's an abundance of traditional **Weinstuben** on Liebfrauenplatz, Grebenstrasse, Augustinerstrasse, Kartäuserstrasse, and Jakobsbergstrasse. Most of these serve meals; some are open in the evenings only, such as the oldest, *Alt Deutsche Weinstube* in Liebfrauenplatz, which fills up with locals of varying ages, and does cheap daily dishes. There's even better food at *Weinhaus Schreiner*, just across Rheinstrasse.

In the annals of **beer**, Mainz's main claim to fame is as the home town of Adolphus Busch, who emigrated to America and founded what grew into the world's largest brewery. The city does, however, have a traditional beer hall in *Brauhaus Zur Sonne* on Stadthausstrasse, along with an excellent brewery-owned *Gastätte Zum Salvator* on Grosse Langgasse. *Calvados* on Steingasse is a recommendable crêperie, serving both sweet and savory varieties. By far the hottest

nightspot at the time of writing is *Terminus* on Rheinallee, a sparsely decorated former warehouse, which attracts clientele from miles around.

Other than Carnival, the principal **popular festivals** are: the *Johannisnacht* in mid-June, which includes fishermen's jousts and firework displays; the *Weinmarkt* jamboree on the last weekend in August and the first in September; and the *Nikolausfest* on the first Saturday in December, featuring a procession of children. Main **theater** venue is the *Städtische Bühnen* on Gutenbergplatz; "alternative" fare is offered at the *Forum Theater Unterhaus* on Münsterstrasse. On the **classical music** front, it's worth looking out for concerts by the *Mainzer Kammerorchester*, who are especially renowned for their performances of Mozart.

The stretch of the Rhine between Mainz and Koblenz is touristically the most popular. **Steamers** depart from in front of the Rathaus (March–Oct. only); also here are the *K-D Line* offices (☎06131 24511). **Mitfahrzentrale** is at Bonifatiusplatz 6 (☎06131 612828).

Rhein-Hessen

The hinterland of Mainz is an area called **Rhein-Hessen**, chiefly famous as a major wine-producing area. Look out for small *Trullos*, conical, white shelters for vineyard workers among the vines. These are of a type only normally found in Apulia in Italy, and are said to have been built by Italian immigrants 150 years ago.

Heading south by rail or road out of Mainz in the direction of Worms, you pass through a series of small towns, all within a stone's throw of the Rhine, which make ideal points at which to break your journey. First up are BODENHEIM and NACKENHEIM, run-of-the-mill places but pleasant enough on a sunny day. Then you hit **NIERSTEIN**, with its eighteenth-century baroque **St. Kilianskirche** and the **Schiffermuseum** (Sun. 9am–noon; free) in the Altes Rathaus on the **Marktplatz**, which concerns itself with the development of Rhine river traffic and the boatman's trade. For (fairly) reasonably priced food try *Alte Vater Rhein* at Grosse Fischergasse 4.

The next town is **OPPENHEIM**, full of half-timbered houses set in narrow little streets. Most vaunted local feature is the **Katharinenkirche**, one of the most significant Gothic churches between here and Strassburg. Inside, look out for the *Oppenheimer Rose*, a fourteenth-century stained glass window. The other local church is the **Bartholomäuskirche**, which, despite a dubious-looking exterior, has a spacious Gothic interior and a truly bizarre altar featuring assorted bishops and sundry others gathered around Christ, some of whom seem to be standing on their heads. The only other attraction worth mentioning is the **Deutsches Weinbaumuseum**, Wormser Str. 49 (Tues.–Sun. 1–5pm), which has a wide range of exhibits related to vine growing and wine production.

Worms

Charlemagne, Frederick Barbarossa, Luther—these are just three of the names which have made their mark on **WORMS**, a former imperial city about 40km south of Mainz. A rich web of fact and myth has also been spun around the city, which is the main backdrop for the greatest of all German epics, the *Nibelungenlied*. Originally settled by Celtic tribes and then by the Romans, Worms was, according to legend, heart of the fifth-century Burgundian kingdom.

This was brought down by the Huns as a result of the vengeance long planned by the Burgundian princess Kriemhild in retribution for the murder of her husband Siegfried, the famed dragon-slayer. Although it's debatable whether the Burgundians ever settled around Worms, the city did achieve immense fame and prosperity during the Middle Ages and for a while was a venue for sittings of the imperial parliament—the **Diet**.

Foremost among Worms' bygone glories are the seven city-center churches, not one of them built later than 1744. The jewel in the crown is the **Dom** (or **Kaiserdom**), a huge late Romanesque building which dominates the city skyline even from a distance, and is one of the three foremost imperial cathedrals in Germany. From outside it's highly distinctive in appearance, with its pair of domes and four corner towers. Restoration work has been carried out on the exterior, but it's those parts which have escaped the attention of the sand-blaster which best preserve the staid grandeur of the original.

These days the richly decorated Gothic **Südportal** is the main entrance to the Dom, but look out also for the **Kaiserportal**, on the north side of the building. According to the *Nibelungenlied*, this was the site where Kriemhild and her sister-

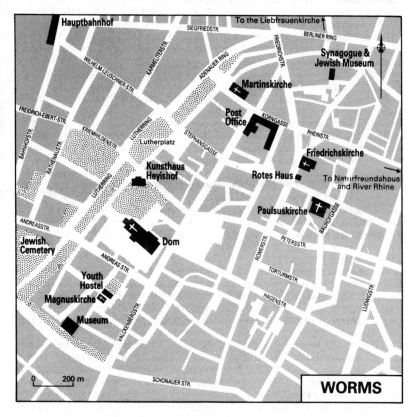

in-law Brunhild had words with each other about just who had the right to enter the building first. This petty quarrel led to the murder of Siegfried and the eventual collapse of the Burgundian nation. On the northern facade there's a inscription which recalls both the mythic and historic past of Worms: "Here is one of the most memorable places in the West, here the was the holy temple of the Romans, the royal fortress of the Nibelung, the palace of Charlemagne, the court of the prince-bishops of Worms . . .'

As you enter the Kaiserdom through the Südportal, the sight of Balthasar Neumann's huge baroque **high altar** provokes a gasp. It's a a real technicolor extravaganza in gold and marble, featuring four awe-inspired Apostles pointing at the Madonna and Child, who seem to be coming straight towards you. There's an austere stained glass window backdrop whose simplicity offsets the altar effectively. Otherwise the Dom is relatively spartan. The only other real point of interest is the dank and eerie vault, the last resting place to five generations of the Salier family, where eight sinister-looking sarcophagi sit in oppressive silence.

Just to the north of the Dom is the **Heylshofgarten**, occupying the site of the now-vanished imperial palace. In April 1521 this was the scene of the *Lutherreichstag*, a convocation of the Imperial Diet hastily set up by the newly-elected emperor Charles V in response to an antireformist bull from the Vatican. At the hearing Luther refused to renounce his views; he was forced to go into exile and the Reformation was set in motion. Within the park is the **Museum Kunsthaus Heylshof** (May–Sept. daily 10am–5pm, Oct.–April Tues.–Sat. 2–4pm, Sun. 10am–noon and 2–4pm; DM2, DM1 students), a private art museum with a collection of paintings, porcelain, glassware, and ceramics that's large but slightly dull, in an exquisite sort of way.

Just south of the Kaiserdom on Domplatz is the **Adlerapotheke**, a complacent-looking baroque town house and apothecary's shop from the early eighteenth century. From here cross Andreasstrasse and go down Dechaneigasse until you come to the **Magnuskirche**, the first church in southwest Germany to go over to Protestantism. This dates back to the Carolingian times but has been extended and altered so much since then that you could be forgiven for not realizing it.

About fifty meters away is the **Andreasstift**, comprising a Romanesque church and cloisters which now house the **Museum der Stadt Worms** (Tues.–Sun. 10am–noon and 2–5pm; DM2, DM1 students). The most significant exhibits are in the **Lutherzimmer**, which details the events of the *Lutherreichstag* and the beginning of the Reformation, and includes some of Luther's original writings. Otherwise it's just the usual selection of local bits and pieces from pre-Roman times to the present day. Just behind the Andreasstift is a surviving section of the old **Stadtmauer** (the city wall), with the still-intact **Andreastor**. Other sections of the Stadtmauaer have survived, including a section built on top of an earlier Roman city wall near the Heylshofgarten. In the northern part of the city center two of the medieval gateways to Worms can also be seen: the **Raschitor** and the **Friesenspitze**, also known as the **Judenpforte**. On the eastern side of the old city the **Bürgerturm** the **Torturm** (defensive towers) and the **Lutherpförtchen** have also survived.

A little to the northeast of the Dom stands the **Dreifaltigkeitskirche**, a fairly typical eighteenth-century baroque number, while around the corner is the Marktplatz, with an ugly modern Rathaus and the obligatory fountain. From here head straight down Stephansgasse and turn right onto Lutherplatz, where you'll find the 1868 **Lutherdenkmal**, commemorating Luther and his refusal to renounce his views. The memorial, a collection of no-nonsense bronze figures with Luther at the center, shows the great man making his terse declaration before the Imperial parliament: "Here I stand. I cannot do otherwise. God help me. Amen."

From Lutherplatz make your way down the pedestrian streets Hardtgasse and Am Römischen Kaiser until you come to Römerstrasse. An immediate right turn will bring you to the unexceptional eighteenth-century **Friedrichskirche** and to the **Rotes Haus**, the only surviving Renaissance town house in Worms. When you see its pink curlicued gables you might begin to suspect that the destruction of the others was no accident. A couple of minutes' walk to the southwest is the **St. Paulus-Kirche**, one of Worms's finest churches. This one is a rough hewn sandstone affair dating from about 1016, with an unusual triple tower construction and a classic Romanesque circular window. The other main downtown church, again Romanesque, is the **St. Martins-Kirche** on Ludwigsplatz, just off Korngasse. Somehow it doesn't look quite real, with its white facade and angular tower. Supposedly Saint Martin was once imprisoned in a dungeon underneath this church.

To the east of the center, fans of the *Nibelungenlied* may wish to take a look at the **Hagenstandbild**, a statue on the banks of the Rhine. This bronze depicts the scene from the epic in which the villainous Hagen hurls into the Rhine the cursed treasure of the Niblungen just after Siegfried's death. A little to the south is the **Torturm**, a massive medieval gateway which straddles the **Niblungbrücke** over the Rhine. If you're coming into town by the B46 road it gives you the impression that you're about to enter some mysterious medieval world.

Which just leaves the **Liebfrauenkirche**, an architecturally unremarkable Gothic church in the north of the city, whose **vineyards** (April–Oct. 9am–6pm, Nov–March 9am–5pm) produce *Liebfraumilch*, a bottle of which is invariably left on the kitchen table at the end of all bad parties. It's the kind of place that looks good on brochures but is best avoided in reality. The German version of *Liebfraumilch* isn't anything like the sickly syrup, specially sweetened for export, that finds its way on to North American supermarket shelves. On the contrary, it's a quality product which has to pass through a control center; *Blue Nun* and *Madonna* are the best-known labels.

Worms' Jewish Community

Until 1933 Worms was home to a large and long-established **Jewish community** and there are still many reminders of their presence in the city today. A visit to some of the Jewish sites in Worms brings home the reality of the Holocaust and the destruction it wrought in human and cultural terms. So strong and influential were the Jews of Worms, both locally and in the broader German context, that the city was long known as "Little Jerusalem." Worms had its own Talmudic school and it was here that Rabbi Salomo ben Isaak aka Raschi wrote his *Commentaries* to the Torah and Talmud, works still referred to by Hebrew scholars today. The Jews of Worms survived for 1000 years despite sporadic attacks on them over the centuries. In 1096 fanatical crusaders destroyed the synagogue and Jewish quarter; during the Great Plague of 1349 the Jews were attacked by their fellow townsfolk who accused them of having poisoned local wells; and in 1615 social unrest among the rest of the populace once again meant persecution. By the nineteenth century, however, things had started to improve. The ghetto to which the Jews had been restricted was opened up and from 1849 to 1852 Worms had a Jewish mayor, Friedrich Eberstadt. It wasn't until the Nazis came to power that Worms' ancient Jewish community was finally destroyed. In 1933 there were still 1100 Jews in Worms; by 1945 the Jews had ceased to exist here—all were either dead or had fled the country, never to return.

The most famous and poignant reminder of the community is the **Heiliger Sand**, the oldest Jewish cemetery in Europe. Despite its leafy and tranquil setting, the cemetery, located just off the Andreasring at the southwestern corner of the old city wall, has a sad and disturbing atmosphere. As you stroll amidst the crooked gravestones, some dating back as far back as 1076, you feel like a tres-passer. The most recent gravestone dates from 1940—after that the Jewish citi-zens of Worms found other less peaceful and more distant resting places.

The northern part of the city center, around Judengasse, is the site of the old Jewish quarter. Here you'll find the **Alte Synagoge**, Worms's Romanesque syna-gogue, originally constructed in 1034, rebuilt in 1174 and re-inaugurated in 1961 following its destruction on *Kristallnacht*. In the precincts of the synagogue you can also visit the Talmudic teaching room known as the **Raschi Kapelle**, and the underground **Tauchbad** or ritual bathhouse (daily tours May–Oct. 10am–noon and 2–5pm, Nov.–April 10am–noon and 2–4pm; inquire at Judengasse 22). In the **Raschi-Haus**, a former school and meeting house, is the **Judaica Museum** (Tues.–Sun. 10am–noon and 2–5pm; DM1), with an extensive collection detailing the history of the Jews of Worms.

Practical Details

Worms' **tourist office** is at Neumarkt 14 (Mon.–Fri. 9am–noon and 2–5pm, April–Oct. also Sat. 9am–noon; ☎06241 25045 or 853560). There's a **youth hostel** handily located between the Dom and the Andreasstift at Dechaneigasse 1 (☎06241 25780), and also a *Naturfreundehaus*, just to the east of the old city wall at Flosshafenstr. 7 (☎06241 23660). Among the **hotels** in the city center, try: *Wormser Eck*, Klosterstr. 80 (☎06241 6671), which has singles from DM30 and doubles from DM54; *Lortze-Eck*, Schlossergasse 10–12 (☎06241 24561), with singles DM28, doubles DM45; *City*, Siegfriedstr. 29 (☎06241 6284), with singles DM30, doubles DM60; and *Nordend*, Siegfriedstr. 2 (☎06241 45940), with singles DM30, doubles DM54. **Camping** facilities are on the eastern bank of the Rhine near the Niblungenbrücke.

There are plenty of reasonably priced places to **eat** and **drink** in the city center. For a cheapish sit-down Italian meal try *Etna*, Am Ziegelofen 14, or *Fischereck*, Rheinstr. 54, which does good chicken dishes; for typically hearty German fare head for *Neue Post* at Rheinstr. 2. There are also lively hangouts in and around Judengasse, such as the trendy *Café Jux*, and the bars *Kutscherschänke* and *Schwarzer Bär*. The city gets quite busy at the end of August and the beginning of September for the *Backfischfest*, a wine festival where fried fish is the culinary specialty.

Ludwigshafen

South of Worms is **LUDWIGSHAFEN**, home town of Federal Chancellor Helmut Kohl. It's a sprawling industrial mass, dominated by the *BASF* chemical works, and forms a virtual continuation of the ex-capital of the Palatinate, Mannheim (see *Chapter Two*), which lies directly across the Rhine. If you happen to find yourself here, your initial impulse will be to get out of town fast, a reaction you'd do well to heed. Ludwigshafen's only real positive point is the **Wilhelm-Hack-Museum** (Tues. and Thurs.–Sun. 9:30am–5pm, Wed 9:30am–9pm; free), a large art museum at Berliner Str. 23, which has an exciting collection of mainly modern art, including works by Kandinsky, Mondrian, and Malevich.

Speyer

In many ways **SPEYER** is like a slightly smaller version of Worms. It too lies on the Rhine, and is the final member of the triumvirate of imperial cathedral towns. Speyer was also a key town in the unfolding of the Reformation, and it was here that Lutherans protesting against the Edict of Worms first became known as Protestants. It's the kind of place worth visiting for an afternoon, taking in the major sights, and then perhaps using as overnight stop.

From the **Hauptbahnhof** head straight down Bahnhofstrasse and turn right onto Maximilianstrasse. You'll pass the **Altpörtel**, a rugged, thirteenth-century city gateway with an eighteenth-century pitched roof and belfry, which is one of the few medieval buildings in Speyer to have survived. Maximilianstrasse itself is lined by elegant gabled baroque houses and leads straight to the **Dom** (or **Kaiserdom**), which ranks as one of the largest and finest Romanesque buildings in Germany. It's a magnificent cathedral, austere and regal, and is one of only five buildings in the country to have made it onto the UNESCO list which singles out the world's most significant historic monuments.

The Dom was originally built during the mid-eleventh century and modified a generation later, in accordance with new architectural developments—the most significant alteration, the stone vault, was higher than any other in the world. Despite being badly damaged by French troops in 1689 and extensively rebuilt during the eighteenth century, the Dom still retains its clear Romanesque lines. The interior is basically a pillared basilica and the vaulting mentioned above helps give a tremendous impression of space. Even finer is the **crypt** (Mon.–Fri. 9am–5:30pm, Sat. 9am–4pm, Sun. 1:30–4:30pm; DM1), the largest in Germany. With its sandstone pillars and slabbed floor, this has an almost Middle Eastern flavor. The crypt has been divided into three connected spaces and contains eight royal tombs, a legacy of the 300 years after 1039 when the Dom was an imperial burial church.

In the **Domgarten** there's a sixteenth-century relief of *The Capture of Christ* which marks the center of the former cloisters. Also worth a quick look is the **Heidentürmchen**, a section of the old city wall on the site of the former Rhine bank (the river has since shifted a little to the east). Just to the north of the Dom are the fourteenth-century **Sonnenbrücke** and the **Wirtschaft zum Halbmond**, a seventeenth-century half-timbered inn with a strange polygonal window. Just to the north on the other side of Hasenpfuhlstrasse is the **Klosterkirche St. Magdalena**, an eighteenth-century convent church with an atmospheric baroque interior spoiled only by some ugly hanging spotlights. The Jewish-born philosopher and Carmelite nun Edith Stein, whom the Nazis gassed in Auschwitz, was a teacher in the convent school from 1923 to 1931.

If you head down Grosse Himmelgasse from the Dom you'll come to the baroque **Dreifaltigkeitskirche** (daily 1:30–4:30pm), built between 1701 and 1717 after the destruction of the War of the Palatinate Succession, which took a heavy toll on Speyer's churches. A competition was held to select the design and the winning effort, though presenting no surprises (stucco facade, ornamented gable, and dinky bell tower), is appealing enough. The interior is fairly extravagant but somehow subtly different from run-of-the-mill baroque; the most impressive features are the two-story wooden gallery with its painted side panels, and the fanciful painting on the wooden vaulting which adds to the extrovert character of the church. Beside the Dreifaltigkeitskirche are the **Retscherhof**, the ruined palace of a noble family, and the **Läutturm**, a tall late Gothic tower.

Nearby Geschirrplatz is a small square where crockery salesmen used to sell their wares. Directly opposite, the eighteenth-century **Rathaus** has internal decorative features which are worth a quick look (viewing is usually possible during working hours, but it's best to check with the tourist office for details). A few hundred meters away in Korngasse is the thirteenth to fourteenth-century **St. Ludwig-Kirche**, which contains the only surviving medieval altar front in the Palatinate and the winged, late Gothic *Bossweiler Altar*.

Just to the south of the Dom on Domplatz is the **Historisches Museum der Pfalz** (daily 9am–noon and 2–5pm; DM1.50), a palatial triple-towered building devoted to the history of the Palatinate. It includes objects found in the imperial graves in the Dom, but the most celebrated exhibit is the Bronze Age *Golden Hat of Schifferstadt*, found in that nearby town. The same building also houses the **Weinmuseum**, which details everything there is to know about wine. Every conceivable kind of wine-related object is featured, and the museum possesses what it claims to be the oldest bottle of wine in the world, dating from A.D. 300

Not far from the museum is the **Judenbad** (*Mikvah* in Hebrew), a twelfth-century Jewish ritual bathhouse (Mon.–Fri. 10am–noon and 2–4pm; DM0.50) which is the oldest and best preserved example in Germany—you reach it via *Hotel Trutzpfaff*, Webergasse 5. The baths themselves were constructed 10m below ground level and, like the Jewish remains in Worms, are a poignant reminder of a vanished culture. There are guided tours on Saturday at 2pm and Sunday at 11am. In Judengasse there's a memorial tablet which relates the history of the Jews in Speyer.

At Allerheiligenstr. 9, about ten minutes' walk west of the Judenbad, lies the **Feuerbachhaus** (Mon.–Fri. 4–6pm, Sun. 11am–1pm), the birthplace of the Romantic painter Anselm Feuerbach (1829–1880), who is chiefly remembered for his sweeping Italianate canvases of mythological scenes. The modest single-storey house is now a small museum which has regular changing exhibitions.

In Landauer Strasse, on the southwestern edge of the city center, is the **Gedächtniskirche der Reformation** (or **Retscherkirche**; Mon.–Fri. 9am–noon and 2–5pm, Sun. 1–5pm), a heavy neo-Gothic affair built between 1893 and 1904 in memory of the 1529 Reichstag, at which supporters of Luther made their formal protest against the Edict of Worms. Look out for the statue of Luther in the entrance hall and for the complex stained glass work.

Practical Details

Speyer's **tourist office** is at Maximilianstr. 11 (☎06232 14395). The **youth hostel** is at Leinpfad (☎06232 75380), a little south of the center between the town swimming pool and the Rhine. **Hotels** with a convenient location include *Haus Weidenberg*, St. Guido-Str. 29 (☎06232 75885), which has singles from DM15 and doubles from DM30; *Weisses Tor*, Herdstr. 21a (☎06232 71510), with singles from DM25 and doubles from DM50; and *Zum Deutschen Kaiser*, Allerheiligenstr. 37 (☎06232 75630), which has singles from DM28 and doubles from DM50. Also worth checking out is the *Gasthof Zur Grünen Au*, Grüner Winkel 28 (☎06232 72196), which has singles from DM35 and doubles from DM55.

Eating and **drinking** in Speyer won't be a problem. For *Kaffee und Kuchen* try *Café-Conditorei Schumacher* at Wormserstr. 23; for something a little more substantial, go to *Weisses Ross*, or the atmospheric old *Wirtschaft zum Alten Engel*, Gilgenstr. 27.

The Weinstrasse

The **Weinstrasse** (*Wine Road*), Germany's oldest designated tourist route, runs south for 80km from BOCKENHEIM, a small town about 14km west of Worms, to SCHWEIGEN-RECHTENBACH on the French border. In this area there are about 58,000 acres of vineyards and in some places the climate becomes almost subtropical, enabling farmers to grow lemons, figs, and tobacco as well as vines. As with most German tourist routes, it's meant for cars (look out for the bunch-of-grapes signposts), but with a little planning you could follow most of it by train and bus.

Head south as far as GRÜNSTADT and then make for the village of **NEULEININGEN**, just off the E50 expressway about 4km to the southwest. This is a medieval half-timbered place which it would be worth spending an hour or so strolling around. There's a romantic-looking ruined church whose sandstone walls have turned dusky pink with age, and an old vicarage which has been turned into an excellent upscale restaurant called *Die Alte Pfarrei*.

South from Grünstadt on the B271 is **BADDÜRKHEIM**, which hosts a gargantuan wine festival oddly named the **Wurstmarkt** (*Sausage Fair*) and boasts one of the largest wine casks in the world, but will be a little too touristy for most tastes. There are **camping** facilities here at *Azur-Knaus*, Am Badesee (☎06322 61356). Next stop is DEIDESHEIM, the richest town on the Weinstrasse, but rather sanitary and unenticing. A better choice of stop, if only for an hour or two, is **NEUSTADT**—it's another half-timbered town with a sixteenth-century **Rathaus**, at the foot of the **Haardt** hills (a branch of the Vosges).

Continuing south by rail or on the B38 brings you to **HAMBACH** with its disappointingly new-looking restored **Schloss** (March–Nov.9am–5pm) which you'll be able to see as you approach the town. The original was destroyed by French soldiers in 1688; nothing much has happened here since, though in 1832 German patriots, peeved at having to live in a country fragmented into dozens of principalities and duchies, raised the black, red and gold tricolor here for the first time. Hambach, which officially belongs to Neustadt, has a **youth hostel** at Hans-Geiger-Str. 27 (☎06321 2289). There are also a few reasonable **hotel** possibilities: try *Jägerstübchen*, Andergasse 84 (☎06321 86328), with singles from DM24 and doubles from DM47, or *Haus Weissgerber*, Käsgasse 80 (☎06321 84542), with doubles from DM32. More cheapish hotels can be found in nearby MAIKAMMER.

Buses run from Hambach to the **Kalmit** (673m), about 4km east, which commands incredible views out across the Rhine plain as far as Speyer and Ludwigshafen. From here head for **ST. MARTIN**, another small village, which, with its vine covered restaurants and narrow streets, makes a good place to break your journey. St. Martin is dominated by the ruined **Kropsburg**, a thirteenth-century fortress which suffered the usual fate at the hands of the French in the seventeenth century—much of the castle wall is still intact, though, as is part of the tower.

A couple of kilometers to the south is the village of **EDENKOBEN**. Signs direct you to **Schloss Villa Ludwigshöhe** (April-Sept. 9am–1pm and 2–6pm, Oct.–March 9am–1pm and 2–5pm), a nineteenth-century castle built for King Ludwig I of Bavaria, with some good wall and ceiling frescoes. These days the building houses a small museum, devoted mainly to the work of the German Impressionist painter Max Slevogt.

From Edenkoben bus #6807 runs to **RHODT**, a typical small wine town full of half-timbered *Winzerhäuser* (wineries). Look out for the arches of vines which grow on frames across some of the streets, notably Dieschirnerstrasse. *Café Wansganz* on the main street is a good place to stop for a drink on a hot summer afternoon. If you're traveling by car or bike you might care to leave the marked route of the Weinstrasse and head through a series of little vine-growing villages in the direction of the cobbled, half-timbered village of **LEINSWEILER**. The gently rolling landscape, with forested hills in the background, is a perfect backdrop, and this stretch is well off the beaten track. Just outside town is *Restaurant Slevogthof* (Sat.–Wed 11am–2pm and 5–9pm), a slightly expensive restaurant in the the painter Max Slevogt's old house, run by his granddaughter. Guided tours are run through the Slevogts' private rooms (Mon.–Wed at 11:15am and 1:30pm, Sat. and Sun. at 3:50pm and 5:30pm).

If you're traveling by public transit from Rhodt you'll probably end up in **LANDAU**, an unexceptional medium-sized town which has never really recovered from being burned down in 1689. The huge fourteenth-century Stiftskirche is the only monument of note. From here, **BADBERGZABERN** is reached by bus #6817. There's nothing remarkable about its Schloss, which is Renaissance with baroque additions. On the other hand, the **Gasthaus zum Engel**, the gabled former residence of the dukes of Zweibrücken, is undoubtedly one of the finest Renaissance buildings in the Palatinate. There's a **youth hostel**, at Altbergweg (☎06343 8383), and a few cheap **pensions**: try *Maxburg*, Weinstr. 92 (☎06343 2438), singles from DM19 and doubles from DM38, or *Haus Rita*, Petronellastr. 4 (☎06343 8202), with singles from DM20 and doubles from DM40.

South of Bad Bergzabern the vines thin out and forest takes over. Directly on the French border, 8km south and reached by bus #6817, is **SCHWEIGEN-RECHTENBACH**, which marks the terminus of the Weinstrasse—apart from the **Weintor**, a huge gateway, there isn't very much to see.

The Pfälzerwald

Stretching north from the French border as far as the large industrial town of KAISERSLAUTERN, and bounded to the east by the Weinstrasse and to the west by the border with Saarland, the **PFÄLZERWALD** is one of the most compelling and unspoiled parts of the province. A sparsely populated, heavily wooded stretch of countryside, it's dotted with castles and half-forgotten villages, and most of it is designated a *Naturpark*. It's popular with walkers and climbers; if you're in more of a hurry, the best way to get around is by car, as bus services are a little sparse. From Landau it's a twenty-minute train journey to **ANNWEILER** from where regular bus services run to **Schloss Trifels** (April–Sept. Wed–Sun. 9am–1pm and 2–6pm, Oct., Nov., and Jan.–March 9am–1pm and 2–6pm). Imperiously set on a jagged crag, this is a reconstruction of a typical Hohenstaufen palace. You have to walk up a steep hill, but it's well worth the trek. The Schloss dates from the eleventh century, and was supposedly one of Frederick Barbarossa's favorite haunts. In 1193 Richard the Lionheart was imprisoned here and only released on payment of an enormous ransom. It subsequently served as an imperial treasury, and then gradually fell into ruin after its abandonment in 1635; the rebuild (which is surprisingly effective) was carried out between 1938 and 1966. The chapel houses copies of the Imperial crown jewels, while from the **Kapellenturm** there's a tremendous panoramic view of the surrounding area, including the ruins of **Burg Anebos** and **Burg Scharfenberg** to the south. In Annweiler itself are a **youth hostel** at Turnerweg 60 (☎06346 8438) and a couple of cheap **pensions**: *Radke*, Am Flotz 17 (☎06346 2114), has singles from DM17 and doubles from DM32 and *Haus Schönblick*, Zum Hönigsack 30 (☎06346 7001), has singles from DM18 and doubles from DM32.

From Annweiler carry on to **ERLENBACH**, where the main attraction is **Schloss Berwartstein** (March–Nov. Mon.–Sat. 9am–6pm, Sun. 1–5pm, Dec.– Feb. Sun. only 1–5pm; DM3.50), a castle with a checkered past. It started life in 1152 when Frederick Barbarossa gave it to the bishop of Speyer. By 1314 it had become a hideout for local bandits, who caused so much trouble in the area that the authorities had the Schloss destroyed. It was then rebuilt, only to be burned down in 1591. At the end of the nineteenth century it was again reconstructed; looking like an archetypal fairy tale castle, it now houses a restaurant. You can still see some of the old rooms which were carved out of the rock on which the castle was built. Just to the north of Erlenbach is the ruined **Burg Drachenfels**, which suffered a similar fate to Schloss Berwartstein, but escaped the ignominy of being turned into a restaurant. It too has rooms hewn out of the rock and similarly constructed stone staircases.

Nearby FISCHBACH is notable only for the huge U.S. military facility housed there; it's one of the largest nerve-gas centers in Europe, which the locals are understandably none too happy about. Unless you're a Soviet spy, avoid Fischbach and head instead for **DAHN** (reached by bus #6840 from Erlenbach), where untold delights await. Above the town are the ruins of three castles within one outer wall, set on top of a long rocky ridge. The biggest and best-preserved is **Altdahn**, which features lookout posts, rooms cut out of the rock face, and some semi-intact towers. Only a few rock chambers and the remains of the walls are left of **Grafendahn** and practically nothing is left of **Tanstein** apart from a few broken stones. Just outside town are the **Braut und Brautigam** (*Bride and Groom*), two immensely tall pillars of limestone, one slightly higher than the other. Dahn has a **youth hostel** at Am Wachtfelsen 1 (☎06391 1769), while there are **camping** facilities at Im Büttelwoog (☎06391 5622). Cheapest **pensions** are *Frischmann*, An der Reichenbach 13a (☎06391 1535), which has singles from DM17, doubles from DM34, and *Haus Burgenland*, Am Griesböhl 13 (☎06391 5641), which charges DM22 per person.

PIRMASENS, a sizable town specializing in light industry, claims the dubious distinction of being the German shoe metropolis; here begins the **Deutsche Schuhstrasse** (*German Shoe Road*), the most laughable of Germany's tourist routes. You can get quality, cheap footwear here and there's a **Heimatmuseum** at Hauptstr. 26 (guided tours Thurs. 3–6pm, Sun. and hols. 10am–1pm; inquire at the Altes Rathaus, Hauptstr. 26; ☎06331 84208), which is big on shoes from all over the world. However, unless you're a foot fetishist, Pirmasens doesn't really have much to offer.

The Hunsrück

The **HUNSRÜCK**, which rises up between the rivers Mosel and Nahe, is one of the three huge volcanic and schist massifs (the others are the Eifel and the Vosges) to the west of the Rhine. It's not too well served by the rail network and bus services are meager in some places—once again this is a region best explored by car. Most of the Hunsrück is forested and dotted with small villages, with the occasional incongruous small industrial town rearing up out of the woods. In the past it was a big source of precious stones and metals, and even today quarrying and related industries are still important to the economic life of the area.

IDAR-OBERSTEIN, in the Nahe valley on the southern edge of the range, should definitely be on your itinerary. (It has good rail links with BINGEN and the Saarland towns.) Formerly a mining center for precious stones and minerals, Idar-Oberstein has remained, even with the exhaustion of most of the old lodes, a center for stonecutting and polishing, and for the manufacture of jewelry. In reality, it's two towns joined together: Oberstein, crammed into the steeply wooded Nahe valley, is the historic part, while Idar, sprawling northwards up the narrow Idarbach valley, is more commercial in character.

From Oberstein's Marktplatz, 214 steps lead up to the late fifteenth-century **Felsenkirche** (April 1–Oct. 15, 9am–6pm; DM2) set into the rocky northern face of the Nahe valley. Inside, look out for the graphic five-paneled altar painting, dating from 1410, of scenes from the life of Christ, and for the fine stained glass windows, some of which are as old as the church itself. Above the Felsenkirche are the **Schloss** ruins, the jagged remains of two medieval fortresses, from where there's a good view of Oberstein and the Nahe valley.

On Marktplatz itself is the **Heimatmuseum** (daily 9am–5:30pm; DM3), which details the development of the local precious stone and jewelry industry. It shows how stones were once cut and polished using *Schleifmühlen*, huge sandstone wheels powered by the waters of the Nahe River. Look out too for the translucent flakes of *Landschaftsachat*, fragments of agate on which patterns seem to take the form of ghostly landscapes.

In Idar an ugly 22-story office building in Schleiferplatz houses the **Diamant-und Edelsteinbörse**, Europe's only diamond and precious stone exchange. On the first floor of the same building is the **Deutsches Edelsteinmuseum** (May–Sept. 9am–6pm, Oct.–April 9am–5pm; DM5), which is full of every possible kind of precious stone with "before and after" examples of the stone-cutters art. On the outskirts of Idar in Tifensteinerstrasse is the **Weiherschleife** (Mon.–Fri. 10am–noon and 2–5pm, Sun. and hols. 10am–noon), the last surving water-powered jewel cutting shop—there used to be over a hundred in the area. Here craftsmen still finish stones in the traditional way, lying on wooden beams and pressing the stones against sandstone grinding wheels.

A little to the west of Idar itself, reached by bus #6435, is the **Edelsteinminen Steinkaulenberg**, Europe's only precious-stone mine, which is open to the public (check with the tourist office for details of opening times and guided tours). Not for the claustrophobic, this is a huge network of underground tunnels and chambers which have been mined since Roman times and are still a source for the agates you'll see in all the ritzy jewelry shops in town. Between FISCHBACH and BERSCHWEILER (reached by bus #6455), there's the **Kupfermine**, a similar type of complex, but this time a copper mine. Waxwork figures are used to show how copper ore was mined in days gone by (guided tours daily March 1– Nov. 15 10am–6pm, rest of year Sat., Sun. and hols. 10am–noon and 1–3pm; DM3.50).

The Idar-Oberstein **tourist office** is at Bahnhofstr. 13 (☎06781 27025) in Oberstein. Here you'll not only be able to find out about Idar-Oberstein but also about the rest of the Hunsrück. There's a **youth hostel** at Alte Treibe 23 (☎06781 24366) and quite a few reasonable **hotels** and **pensions** in Oberstein. *Hotel-Café Keller*, Hauptstr. 584 (☎06781 22138), has singles from DM25 and doubles from

DM50; *Pension Schlie*, Amtsstr. 2 (☎06781 25526), has singles from DM25 and doubles from DM46; while *Fremdenheim Trarbach*, Wüstlautenbachstr. 11 (☎06781 25677), has singles from DM22 and doubles from DM36. There are **camping** facilities in the suburb of TIEFENSTEIN (☎06781 35551; take bus #6443, #6445, or #6446). At the end of June the *Spiessbratenfest* takes place, with pork and steak cooked over an open fire, garnished according to a recipe brought back from South America by German agate miners during the last century.

The **Deutsche Edelsteinstrasse**, another of Germany's theme tourist routes, this time on the theme of precious stones, is centered on Idar-Oberstein. Follow it northwards through the village of KATZENLOCH towards ALLENBACH; the first right turn after Katzenloch, in the direction of the village of SENSWEILER leads to the **camping** facilities of *Oberes Idartal* (☎06786 309), which are between the main road and the lake. Next to the Idar-Bach river in Sensweiler there's an open-air geological museum in the form of a little park with signposted exhibits. In Allenbach you're not far from the **Erbeskopf**, at 816m the highest peak in the Hunsrück, where there are **skiing** facilities in winter.

From Allenbach, continue via MORBACH, where there's a **youth hostel** at Jugendherbergstr. 16 (☎06533 3389). Bus #6204 continues eastward along the **Hunsrück Höhenstrasse** (B327), taking you through the heart of the range. The countryside is dotted with grey slate-roofed villages and there are magnificent views of the wooded Hunsrück slopes. Look out for a ruined Roman watchtower, a few kilometers beyond Morbach on the right-hand side of the road. After this turn on to the B50. The first village of any consequence is KIRCHBERG, a half-timbered hill-top settlement, followed by **SIMMERN**, a few kilometers to the east, whose **Stephanskirche** contains the Renaissance tombs of some of the local aristocracy. Simmern has a **campground** (☎06761 6046), while *Gasthof Zum Rebstock*, Koblenzer Str. 71 (☎06761 2283), has singles from DM22 and doubles from DM40. There's a **tourist office** at Brülstr. 2–4 (☎06761 3880).

THE MOSEL VALLEY

The **Mosel River** (better known in English under its French name, *Moselle*), rises in the foothills of the Vosges in France. In its German stretch, it flows between the Eifel and Hunsrück massifs, entering the Rhine at Koblenz. Abroad, it's best known as a **wine**-producing area, and vineyards crowd the south-facing slopes, with more rugged terrain elsewhere. The lethal combination of wine and scenery, plus castles and history, attracts a lot of visitors—making it the kind of place that most Germans under the age of thirty wouldn't be seen dead in. That said, there's a great deal to recommend it—though not in high season, when hordes of tourists turn the most popular destinations such as **Cochem** into real hellholes.

There are still a few corners which have managed to fend off bus-tour attacks and retain some of the atmosphere which so impressed the **Romans**, on the edge of whose world the Mosel valley was. They've left their mark all along the valley, particularly in **Trier**, which has some of the best-preserved remains of classical antiquity in northern Europe. You'll be able to cover the ground described here in a rushed four to five days; reckon on at least twice as long to see it in detail.

Trier

"Trier existed 1300 years before Rome!" exclaims the inscription on one of Trier's historic buildings. In fact, this is a piece of hyperbole: although **TRIER** is the oldest city in Germany, it was actually founded by the Romans themselves. Once the capital of the Western Empire, and residence of the emperor Constantine, Trier became an important early center of Christianity. This helped give it political clout throughout the Middle Ages and beyond, its archbishop ranking as one of the seven electors.

Nowadays, it has the less exalted role as regional center for the upper Mosel valley, its relaxed air a world away from the status it formerly held. Despite a turbulent history, an amazing amount of the city's past has been preserved, in particular the most impressive group of **Roman monuments** north of the Alps. These alone would be enough to put Trier in the rank of "must-see" German cities, and it's one of the few places in the Rhineland-Palatinate which deserves an unqualified recommendation.

The City

The center of modern Trier corresponds roughly to what used to be the Roman city and can easily be covered on foot. From the **Hauptbahnhof**, it's just a few minutes' walk down Theodor-Heuss-Allee to the second-century **Porta Nigra** (*Black Gate*), the northern gateway to Roman Trier. By far the most imposing Roman building in northern Europe, it's also the biggest and best-preserved city gate of its period in the world. The massive sandstone blocks are held together by iron rods set in lead, and it has been weathered black by the passage of time (hence its name). Towering above the surrounding streets and buildings, it's an awesome symbol of Roman architectural skill and military might. Would-be attackers could be trapped between inner and outer gates, enabling defenders to pour boiling oil and molten lead down from above. The Porta Nigra served its purpose well and was never breached—when Trier was eventually captured, the besiegers had to break through elsewhere.

The Porta Nigra probably owes its post-Roman survival to the fact that during the eleventh-century Saint Simeon, a Sicilian hermit who was a friend of the powerful archbishop Poppo, chose the gloomy ground floor of the east tower as a refuge from the world. After his death in 1035 the Porta Nigra was made into a double **church** in his honor. Various additions were made to the original building, but in 1803 Napoleon ordered their removal, so that only the twelfth-century Romanesque choir and some slightly frivolous rococo carvings from 1750 remain from the post-Roman period.

(**Opening times** for the Porta Nigra and for the rest of Trier's Roman monuments are as follows: April–Sept. daily 9am–1pm and 2pm–6pm, Oct. daily 9am–1pm and 2pm–5pm, Nov. and Jan.–March Tues.–Sun. 9am–1pm and 2pm–5pm. Entry to individual Roman sites is DM2, DM1 students, or you can save by buying a ticket valid for all of them for DM6, DM3 students.)

Next door is the **Simeonstift**, a monastery built by Archbishop Poppo in 1037 as another memorial to his deceased friend. After dissolution in 1802 it was allowed to fall into disrepair and was only properly restored in the 1930s. Its **Brunnenhof** is the oldest monastery courtyard in Germany and unique in that the cloisters are on the first story and supported by the arcades below. Today the ground floor of the north wing houses a restaurant.

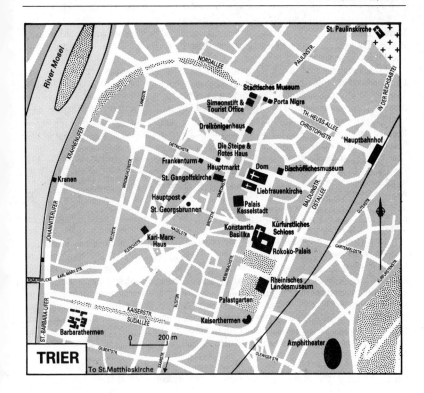

From the Porta Nigra, Simeonstrasse runs down to the Hauptmarkt, roughly following the route of an old Roman street. Today it's a busy pedestrian shopping area, but can boast some outstanding medieval monuments. The most important is the **Dreikönigshaus** (*House of the Magi*), which dates from the first half of the thirteenth century. An early Gothic dwelling tower of the kind found in Regensburg, this was once a secure home in uncertain times for a rich merchant family. Then, the ground floor would not have opened on to the street at all; the original front door can still be seen at the upper floor level, high above the street. It was probably reached by a wooden staircase which could easily be dismantled in times of trouble, or by a ladder which could be pulled up from the street.

Also worth a peep is the huge arched Gothic wine warehouse underneath the *Karstadt* department store. These days it houses the store's restaurant, the unimaginatively named *Historischer Keller*, which isn't particularly worth recommending in itself. The **Hauptmarkt** is a real focal point, especially in summer. There are always a few stalls selling fruit and flowers, and Trier's kids and punks like to sit around the **Petrusbrunnen**, with its ornate Renaissance sculptures of the four Virtues.

On the western side of the Marktplatz is the **Steipe**, a fairly convincing post-war replica of Trier's fifteenth-century Renaissance town hall, now housing a café and a pricey *Ratskeller*. Behind it in Dietrichstrasse is a reconstruction of the

Rotes Haus, which bears the inscription about Trier being much older than Rome. Though basically Renaissance in design, it has an ornate baroque gable and looks quite stately.

At the southern end of the Hauptmarkt a baroque portal leads to the Gothic **St. Gangolfskirche**, which was built by the burghers of Trier between 1410 and 1460 in an attempt to outdo the Dom and irritate the archbishops, whose political power they resented. The tower, added in 1507, actually made the St. Gangolfskirche higher than the Dom, which angered the archbishop so much that he had the southwestern tower of his cathedral specially extended to restore episcopal superiority.

If you go up Sternstrasse from the Hauptmarkt you come to the **Domfreihof**, the old cathedral quarter. Trier's magnificent Romanesque **Dom** has a history as illustrious as that of the city itself. Its origins go back to the days of Constantine, who had a huge church built on this site in 325. The *Domstein*, part of one of the granite pillars from the Roman original can be seen in front of the southern portal, and another pillar, 18m tall, now stands in the courtyard between the Dom and the Liebfrauenkirche.

The present building was started in 1030 on the orders of Archbishop Poppo, and the southern facade (which you see as you approach from the Hauptmarkt) has not changed significantly since the eleventh century. Apparently the curved front of the **west choir** was inspired by Trier's Roman baths; it's flanked by two solid, defensive-looking angular towers. Inside there's an incredible sense of space enhanced by the ribbed vaulting of the ceiling; the relative austerity of the construction is enlivened by devotional and decorative features which have been added through the centuries. Chief among these is the black Gothic **Sarcophagus of Archbishop Balduin,** which sits in brooding splendor in the west choir.

The Dom has an important relic in what purports to be the "Seamless Robe of Christ," kept in the eighteenth-century **Heiltumskammer** at the eastern end of the Dom. No one has actually seen it since 1792, but according to its keepers it's the real thing. The **Schatzkammer** (Mon.–Sat. 10am–noon and 2–4pm, Sun. 2–4pm; DM1, DM0.50 students) has many examples of the work of local goldsmiths, notably a tenth-century portable altar; also various illuminated manuscripts, the earliest of which comes from sixth-century Byzantium.

From the **cloisters** there's a good view of the ensemble of the Dom and the **Liebfrauenkirche** next door. This, one of Germany's first Gothic churches, was begun in 1235 on the site of the southern section of Constantine's double church. Its floorplan takes the form of a rotunda with a cross superimposed on it and the vaulted roof of the transept and choir is supported by twelve pillars representing each of the Apostles. The interior exudes a kind of gloomy majesty; its most significant feature is the black marble tomb of the warlike archbishop Karl von Metternich.

From the Liebfrauenkirche walk down Liebfrauenstrasse past the ritzy baroque Palais Kesselstadt to the **Konstantinbasilika** (April–Oct. daily 9am–1pm and 2–6pm, Nov.–March Tues.–Sun. 11am–noon and 3–4pm; free) on Konstantinplatz. This huge brick structure, once part of Constantine's palace, dates back to A.D. 300; after the Porta Nigra, it's the most impressive of Trier's Roman remains. Built as Constantine's *Aula Palatina* (*Throne Hall*), its dimensions are awe inspiring. As you enter and look down towards the apse where the emperor's throne once stood, you begin to appreciate the immense size of this great hall which, at 30m high and 75m long, has no pillars or buttresses and is completely self-supporting. Although now comparatively spartan, in Roman times it was richly decorated, in accordance with its role (albeit short-lived) as seat of the Roman Empire. Having served successively as royal fortress and archbishops' residence, in the mid-nineteenth century it became a church for the local Protestant community, a role it still has today.

Next door is the **Kurfürstliches Schloss**, dating from the early seventeenth century. Despite its grandiose appearance and venerable past as residence to the archbishop-electors of Trier, it now, more mundanely, houses a local government office.

More impressive is the rococo **Palais der Kurfürsten**, built in 1756 for an archbishop who felt that the old Schloss wasn't good enough for him. By 1794 rococo was out and the last elector moved to a more fashionable neoclassical residence in Koblenz. Although it took some knocks over the next 150 years, particularly during World War II, the facade survived and now sits in shocking-pink glory overlooking the **Palastgarten**, which is populated by replica rococo statues.

At the southern end of the Palastgarten are the **Kaiserthermen**, the imperial Roman baths, built by Constantine. Although they haven't survived intact, the scale of the enormous bath complex is still apparent. Today only the ruined *caldarium* (hot bath) is visible above ground. The extensive underground heating system has also survived, and you can walk around the service channels and passages. But bathtime was soon over for the Romans, and by the Middle Ages local lords had turned the baths into a castle, which was incorporated into the **Stadtmauer**, surviving sections of which can still be seen nearby. By the nineteenth century the ruins were gradually disappearing under a pile of rubble, and only the efforts of twentieth-century archaeologists saved them.

From the Kaiserthermen the route to the **Amphitheater** is well signposted. It was built into the slopes of the Petrisberg above the city around A.D. 100 and is the oldest of Trier's surviving Roman buildings. The structure has been exposed in most of its original glory, and you can still sense the grandeur of the original, which had a seating capacity of 20,000. You can see some of the arched cages were the animals were kept and take a look under the arena itself, which is partly supported by timber blocks and has an elaborate—and still functioning—drainage system cut into its slate base.

If you return to the town center down Olewiger Strasse and then head down Südallee, you'll eventually come to the **Barbarathermen**, Trier's second set of Roman baths. Built in the second century, they look more like Roman ruins should—piles of rock, vaguely defined foundations, and ruined walls. Only the subterranean sections retaining their original shape, a seemingly endless maze of passages, channels, and chambers.

Following Südallee down to the banks of the Mosel brings you to the **Römerbrücke**. In spite of its name, only the basalt supporting pillars are actually Roman, and it now looks just like any other regulation-issue bridge, with cars and trucks constantly pounding over it. A little way downstream are the **Kranen**, two old customs cranes which date from the days when the Mosel was the main route for incoming and outgoing goods. The first was built in 1774, while the next downriver dates from 1413. Old winding gear is still visible in both and the locals claim that they're still in working order.

Taking a right from Kranenufer, up Kalenfelstrasse, you come to the **Irminenstift**, a former monastery turned old peoples' home which has grown up on the site of the Roman warehouses. Beyond is the **Frankenturm** on Dietrichstrasse, a fourteenth-century fortified dwelling tower which has not been fixed up like the Dreikönigshaus, and still looks like a fortification. Again, it originally had no street level entrance and was reached via an elevated door. The **Flakturm**, just off Lorenz-Kellner Strasse, is similar in conception, but dates from a more recent architectural school—that of the Third Reich.

Outside the center, Trier has a couple of other important churches which are very much worth visiting. The **St. Matthiaskirche**, on the southern edge of town, claims to be the resting place of the head of the Apostle Matthew, a relic supposedly brought back from the Holy Land by crusaders in 1127. To accommodate the tomb and the large numbers of pilgrims who came to see it, an existing church, dating back to Roman times, was taken over, extended and reconsecrated. From the outside the church looks baroque, thanks to the addition of a gable and various decorative features to the facade during the seventeenth century, but in fact most of the building dates back to the twelfth century. The tomb of Saint Matthew along with those of Saints Eucharius and Valerius are at the intersection of the nave and transept. In the vault beneath the St. Quirinskapelle there's a well-preserved Roman sarcophagus.

At the other end of town is the **St. Paulinkirche**, designed by Balthasar Neumann in 1757 to a replace a building destroyed by the French sixty years earlier. From the outside the church looks quite restrained, sober even, but the interior is an all-singing, all-dancing, rococo extravaganza of color and light. The eye is assaulted by the ornate pillars—dripping with cherubs and alabaster scroll work—and the complex ceiling frescoes, and it's difficult to comprehend all the gilded finery and exquisite detail. The effect is otherworldly, particularly if you catch it when the sun's rays flood the building through the tall, narrow south-facing windows. It's all just as Neumann intended; his idea was that entering his church should be like entering heaven. Look out for the carvings on the high altar and the choir stalls by Jakob Tiez, which are some of the best examples of rococo decoration in the Rhineland-Palatinate.

Trier's Museums

Bischöfliches Museum, *Windstrasse. Mon.–Sat. 9am–1pm and 2–5pm, Sun. 1–5pm; DM1.*
Housed in an ultramodern complex, which has been inserted into the framework of an older building, this has a rich collection of religious art and early Christian gravestones. The most important exhibits are the frescoes: these include fourth-century portraits from the imperial palace, plus a ninth-century Carolingian cycle from the vanished church of St. Maximin.

Karl-Marx-Haus, *Brückenstr. 10. Tues.–Sun. 10am–1pm and 3–5pm, Mon. 3–5pm; DM2, DM1 students.*
The life and work of Trier's most influential son is the subject here and the detail verges on the excruciating. There's far too much political theory and not nearly enough human interest to make this really gripping.

Landesmuseum, *Ostallee 44. Mon.–Fri. 9:30am–4pm, Sat. 9:30am–2pm, Sun. 9am–1pm; free.*
This is easily the best of Trier's museums and has a fantastic collection of Roman relics which must rate as one of the best outside Italy. Prize exhibit is the famous **Neumagener Weinschiff**, a Roman sculpture of a wine ship, found at Neumagen-Dhron in the Mosel valley. There are some excellent mosaics, best of which is the third-century A.D. **Rennfahrer Mosaik** of the chariot driver Polydus and his four horses in action. A fine collection, bringing to life the sophistication and complexity of Roman civilization.

Städtisches Museum, *Simeonstift. April–Oct. daily 9am–5pm, Nov.–March Tues.–Sun. 9am–5pm; DM1.*
Trier's version of the inescapable Heimatmuseum isn't too bad, thanks to a slightly anarchic layout and some off-the-wall exhibits. There's a big selection of art from the fourteenth up until the twentieth century with the emphasis on devotional work. Also included are the obligatory examples of local craftsmanship and an ancient history section with Egyptian grave masks and paintings, hundreds of Roman lamps and a lot of Greco-Roman statuary.

Practical Details
Trier's **tourist office** is at An der Porta Nigra (May–Aug. Mon.–Sat. 9am–6pm, Sun. 9am–1pm, Sept.–Oct. Mon.–Sat. 9am–6pm, Nov.–April Mon.–Fri. 9am–5pm, Sat. 9am–1pm; ☎48071). For news of **events**, pick up their monthly news sheet, *Der fröhliche Steuermann*. The **youth hostel** is at Maarstr. 156 (☎29292) on the banks of the Mosel, about 25 minutes' walk from the Porta Nigra. There are **campgrounds** on the western bank of the Mosel at Luxemburger Str. 81 (☎86921) and in the grounds of the Schloss in the suburb of MONAISE (☎86210) on the same side of the Mosel. Additional facilities can be found in the nearby town of KONZ (easily reached by train) at *Saarmündung* (☎06501 3477), situated at the confluence of the Saar and Mosel.

If you want to stay in a **hotel**, *Kolpinghaus*, Warsberger Hof, Dietrichstr. 42 (☎75131), which is just a couple of minutes from the Hauptmarkt, charges upwards of DM26 per head, or DM20 in its *Jugendhotel*. Similarly central are *Zur Krone*, Bruchhausenstr. 4 (☎73890), whose rates begin at DM27, *Saarbrücker Hof*, Saarstr. 46 (☎75161), at DM28 per person, and *Zur Glocke*, Glockenstr. 12 (☎73109), which charges upwards of DM30. Over on the other side of the Mosel *Haus Magda*, Biewerer Str. 205–207 (☎66372), has rooms from DM22, while *Kappes*, Biewerer Str. 209 (☎61001) has singles from DM27 and doubles from DM52.

As far as **eating** is concerned, Trier has something to to suit every taste and pocket. Most importantly, there are plenty of places where you can get really good and inexpensive food, thanks to the presence of a large and hungry student population. The best bet for mountainous piles of cheap grub is *Astarix*, Karl-Marx-Str. 11, a big, relaxed student bar which stays open until 2am on weekends; DM10 should cover the tab here. Other student haunts are *In Flagrante*, Viehmarktplatz 13, and *Simplicissimus*, Neu Str. 27, which is a good choice for breakfast. There's a recommendable Chinese, *Hong Kong Haus*, near the youth hostel at Georg-Schmitt-Platz, Am Zurlaubener Ufer; for reasonably priced Italian food, check out *Restaurant da Paolo*, at the corner of Neu Strasse and Pfützenstrasse. For something slightly more upscale, try *Zum Christophel*, standing directly in the shadow of the Porta Nigra.

There's a similarly eclectic range of **drinking** choices. Best traditional pub is *Sutträng* on Jüdengasse. At *Mephisto*, Am Irminen Freihof, you can sit outside drinking Guinness in the summer; they also do cheap food. On Pferdemarkt are *Blaues Blut*, where the "punk's not dead" crew congregate, and *Zapotex*, hangout of Trier's fashion victims. *Rizz*, Dietrichstr. 3, is where the *Zapotex* crowd head for when they start to earn a bit more money, while *Zur Glocke*, Glockenstr. 12 is gayish. *Rubycon*, Roonstr. 1, is Trier's *Rock und Blues Kneipe*, and fine if you like that sort of thing. Also worth a mention are the cluster of riverside pubs near the youth hostel on Zurlaubener Ufer, where you can sit outside and soak up the riverside ambience in summer; best of these is *Bagatelle*.

Listings

Boat trips From Zurlauben in both directions.

Cable car From Zurlauben to Weisshaus on the west bank of the Mosel.

Festivals Main events are Carnival (variable date in Feb./March), plus a *Weinfest* on the first weekend in August.

Mitfahrzentrale Karl-Marx-Str. 15 (☎44322).

Poste restante right beside the Hauptbahnhof on Bahnhofsplatz.

Area code (☎0651).

Women's center Saarstr. 38 (☎40119).

Saarburg and the Lower Saar Valley

SAARBURG, although not actually in the river valley itself, is a kind of honorary Mosel town with that characteristic, slightly Gallic atmosphere which sets the area between the French border and the Rhine apart from the rest of the Federal Republic. For many years it was the ball in a long-running game of catch between France and Germany in which the result, more often than not, was the torching of the town by French soldiers. Parts of the old fortifications are still intact and there's a ruined **Schloss** with a tall and solid-looking tower looking out over the Saar valley. In the Altstadt the **Leukbach**, a tiny tributary of the Saar, drops twenty meters in a series of cascades between old houses with sickly pink-and-green facades, and the vines used to make *Saarburger Rausch* wine. One local curiosity is the **Glockengiesserei**, a foundry where bells are cast using methods which have hardly changed over the centuries. It can be visited by arrangement—check with the **tourist office** at Graf-Siegfried-Str. 32 (Mon.–Fri. 9am–5pm, Sat. 10am–5pm; ☎06581 81215) for details.

Saarburg has a **youth hostel** at Bottelter Str. 8 (☎06581 2555), while the cheapest **pension** is *Gasthof Zur Zentrale*, Merzkirchen, Hauptstr. 4 (☎06581 4055), which has single rooms from DM21 and doubles from DM40. There are **camping** facilities on a hill just to south of town at the *AEGON Ferienpark* (☎06581 2037).

To the south, reached by a regular train service, the village of **SERRIG** is famous for its *méthode champenoise* sparkling wines and for the remains of a Roman temple and settlement. There are more extensive Roman remains in the nearby village of **KASTEL-STAADT**, including parts of a road, the foundations of houses, and fragments of a fortress with water and sewage pipes still intact. High above the village are the **Klause**, hermits' cells set into the rocks that tower over the Saar valley. Next to them is the **Grabkapelle** (Tues.–Sun. 9am–1pm and 2–6pm; DM1), a funerary chapel designed by Karl Friedrich Schinkel in 1838 to house the remains of King John of Bohemia, who died in battle during the fourteenth century. The remains of the Luxembourg-born king, which had been shipped from pillar to post over the previous 400 years, were kept here until after the last war when, bizarrely, they were sent to back to Luxembourg as war reparations.

WINCHERINGEN, set in a very French-looking landscape of rolling green fields and light woodland about 6km west of Saarburg, is a town where there's a **Burgturm** without a Burg and a late Romanesque church without a tower.

The Mosel Weinstrasse

From Trier you can follow the **Mosel Weinstrasse** (*Mosel Wine Road*) by bus or car to where the Mosel flows into the Rhine at KOBLENZ. You can also do the stretch by rail as there are plenty of trains throughout the day—both express services, which will take you directly from Trier to Koblenz in about ninety minutes, and slower local services, which stop off at many of the small towns. The river meanders through innumerable wine villages and towns in a series of tortuous curves, the slopes of its valley lined with vineyards. If possible do this trip by road, since the railroad leaves the valley for substantial stretches and crosses relatively nondescript countryside. However, if you follow the B53 as it criss-crosses the Mosel you won't miss any of the splendid scenery which lines the route. An agreeable alternative is to travel by **boat**—see the end of this section for details.

Neumagen-Dhron and Around

Bus #6246 will take you from Trier to SCHWEICH and from here you can take bus #6230 as far as BULLAY. **NEUMAGEN-DHRON**, the first town you'll hit en route, is best known for its Roman remains and for being the oldest wine-producing town in Germany. These days it's a largish place with a lot of modern buildings, but during the fourth century Neumagen-Dhron was the summer residence of the emperor Constantine and you can still see the remains of his castle, which originally covered the size of a football pitch. Fronting the **Peterskapelle** is a replica of the *Neumagener Weinschiff*, a stone sculpture of a Roman wine-ship complete with miserable looking crew wielding matchstick-like oars, the original of which is now in the Trier Landesmuseum. The **Heimatsmuseum**, Römerstr. 137 (April 16–Oct. 31 10am–noon and 2:30–5pm, Nov. 1–April 15 2:30–5pm) is marginally more interesting than average, with finds from Constantine's castle and local wine-related exhibits, including a huge wooden press.

Also in the museum building is the **tourist office** (✆06507 2001) and through them you may be able to rent private rooms. There are **camping** facilities at Römerstr. 100 (✆06507 3212) and at *Zum alten Leienhaus* (✆06507 3212). For reasonable **accommodation** try *Pension Krebs*, Römerstr. 65 (✆06507 5377), at upwards of DM20 per head, or *Fröhlicher Steuermann*, Moselstr. 8 (✆06507 2240), charging from DM25.

Beyond PIESPORT the scenery becomes much more enthralling, with a succession of tiny wine-producing villages on each side of the river. On the southern bank you pass through half-timbered WINTRICH, backed by steep cliffs, and FILZEN with its *Franziskanerkloster*. It's worth taking a little diversion off the beaten track to **VELDENZ**, where a twelfth-century ruined Schloss towers over a village that was once center of a medieval dukedom. In the village an uninspiring modern church has been tagged onto a thirteenth-century bell tower, with slightly bizarre results. There's a *Weinfest* here on the last Sunday in July. Also meriting a detour is the little town of **MARING-NOVIAND**, in the Eifel foothills on the north side of the river. Just outside town, the **Klosterhofgut Siebenborn**, features a dank, vaulted wine cellar and Roman foundations. The local *Weinfest* is celebrated in the streets with much gusto over the fourth weekend in June.

A few kilometers downstream, the double town of **BERNKASTEL-KUES** straddles the river. (To get here by rail you'll have to change at WITTLICH-WENGEROHR.) This attracts its fair share of bus-touring tourists and can get

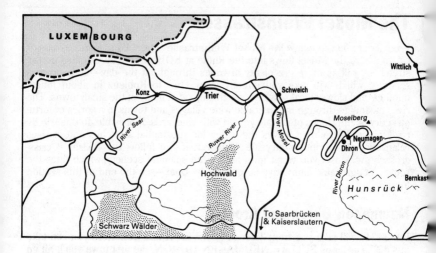

pretty oversubscribed in summer, but it's worth a visit, particularly out of season or if you just stop off for a couple of hours in the early morning.

In Bernkastel, on the south side of the Mosel, the main attraction is the half-timbered, gently sloping **Marktplatz**, which for once actually lives up to tourist brochure hyperbole. The coffee-and-cream-colored Renaissance **Rathaus** looks suitably stately, while next door the **Spitzhaüschen**, an absurdly narrow half-timbered building with a ridiculously steep grey slate pitched roof, now houses a *Weinstube* where there isn't even room to swing the proverbial cat. In the middle of the vineyards above Bernkastel is **Burg Landshut**, a thirteenth-century castle which went up in flames in 1693 and has been a ruin ever since, but from which you get panoramic views of the town and around.

In Kues, across the river, the bank is lined with the villas of nineteenth-century vineyard owners. Fronting the river is the **St. Nikolaus-Hospital**, also known as the **Cusanusstift**, a poorhouse founded by a local fifteenth-century theologican, Nikolaus von Kues. These days the Gothic riverside buildings are home to 33 destitute old men—a symbolic figure representing each year of Christ's life. In its heavily ornate **Kapelle** there's a vivid mid-fifteenth-century *Crucifixion* triptych by the Cologne narrative painter known as Master of the Life of the Virgin. The **Stiftsbibliothek** has a collection of manuscripts from the ninth to the fifteenth centuries which, unfortunately, can only be viewed by appointment. Also in Kues is the **Moselweinmuseum**, Cusanusstr. 1 (April 16–Oct. 31 Tues.–Sun. 10am–noon and 2:30–5pm, Nov. 1–April 15 Tues.–Sun. 2:30–5pm) with a large but badly laid out and labeled collection of wine presses, vessels and other related objects.

The **tourist office** is at Am Gestade 5 (☎06531 4023) and there's a **youth hostel** at Jugendherbergstr. 1 (☎06531 2395). Bernkastel-Kues isn't such a good bet for **hotels** because of the volume of summer traffic, but the following are the best budget possibilities. In Kues *Gästehaus Port*, Weingartenstr. 57 (☎06531 6744), charges upwards of DM20 per head, while *Pension Mertz*, Rausstr. 19 (☎06531 6394), starts at DM21 per person; in Bernkastel *Pension Esslinger*, Kirchhof 8 (☎06531 6617), has singles from DM22 and doubles from DM44. The local **camping** facilities are at Am Hafen 2 (☎06531 8200).

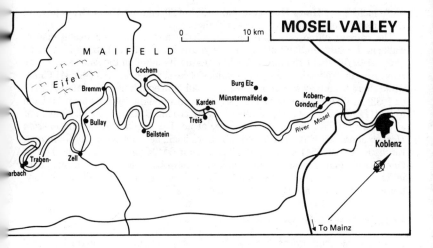

For reasonable **food** try *Huwer*, Römerstr. 35, where you'll be able to get a simple, cheap, and appetizing meal. Not surprisingly, there are dozens of cafés and restaurants in Bernkastel-Kues and the general rule is that the ones in the quieter streets are less likely to be full of tourists being ripped off. During the first weekend in September the biggest *Weinfest* on the Mosel takes place in Bernkastel-Kues, at which gallons of the most famous local vintage, *Bernkasteler Doctor*, bring plenty of life to the streets.

Kröv and Traben-Trarbach

From Bernkastel-Kues the Mosel snakes round to **KRÖV**. Here there's a vineyard called *Nacktarsch*—literally "Naked Ass"—which, according to local dialect experts, is a corruption of "nectar." Other things worth knowing about are the standard array of half-timbered houses, including the mid-seventeenth-century **Dreigiebelhaus** (*Three Gable House*), and the *Weinfest* which takes place in the first weekend of every October.

Round one more bend in the river is yet another double town, **TRABEN-TRARBACH**. In days of old Traben (on the northern bank) was a prime strategic site, which didn't go down too well with the locals, who soon tired of seeing their town destroyed every time one of the two fortresses above the town was besieged. Sighs of relief went up all around when **Schloss Grevenburg**, now reduced to a couple of pathetic walls, was blown up in 1697 in accordance with the terms of a recently signed peace treaty. In 1734 **Mont Royal**, built just 44 years previously by Louis XIV, suffered similar treatment, leaving the citizens free to get on with more peaceful pursuits like building half-timbered houses.

Most of these are actually in Trarbach on the opposite bank, where they rub shoulders with more substantial upper-middle-class villas from the nineteenth century. Also on the Trarbach side of the connecting bridge is the **Brückentor**, a hideous monumental gateway designed by the Jugendstil architect Bruno Möhring on what must have been an off day. Möhring created several other buildings in town in the same style, but only a few of them are worth seeking out;

these include the **Haus Huesgen**, Am Bahnhof 20, and the **Haus Breucker**, An der Mosel 7, both on the river bank in Traben.

The **tourist office** is at Bahnstr. 22 in Traben; pick up their useful map of walks in the surrounding hills. There's a **youth hostel** at Am Letzten Hirtenpfad (☎06541 9278) about 15 minutes' walk from the Bahnhof on the same side of the river. Also in Traben are **camping** facilities at Rissbacher Str. 165 (☎06541 6352), while there's another site 2km down the road at Wedenhofstr. 25 (☎06541 9174 or 1033) in WOLF. On Wildbadstrasse, the road wending upwards from Trabach to KAUTENBACH are three **hotels** charging around DM20 per head: *Haus Jutta* at no. 227 (☎06541 9544), *Pension Bartz* at no. 161 (☎06541 2349) and *Pension Härdter* at no. 194 (☎06541 6404). In the town itself, best bet is *Gasthof Germania*, Kirchstr. 101 (☎06541 9398), with singles from DM24 and doubles from DM48. One recommended local *Weinstube* is *Moselschlösschen* at Neue Rathausstr. 12–16 in Traben. Traben-Trarbach's *Weinfest* is held during the last weekend in July; there's another on the last Sunday in June in Wolf.

From Enkirch to Cochem

Following the southern bank of the Mosel eastward from Traben-Trarbach will bring you to the village of **ENKIRCH**. This was founded by the Romans, but there's nothing exceptional to see, apart possibly from the sixteenth-century **Drehkäfig**, a cell which was originally built to house young men who had been leading local girls astray. The *Weinfest* here is on the first Sunday in August and there are plenty of places where you can sample the product.

Farther north, on the opposite bank, is **ALF**. From here it's an easy ascent to the ruins of **Burg Arras**, a tenth-century castle with a semirenovated tower reached by rickety wooden stairs. There's a fine panoramic view from its restaurant. Nearby **SPRINGIERSBACH** has a slightly faded baroque **Klosterkirche** with a funereal ceiling fresco. There are **camping** facilities locally in BULLAY at Moselufer 1 (☎06542 22921); another can be found just outside the half-timbered village of **EDIGER-ELLER** (☎02675 701) on the way to COCHEM.

BEILSTEIN is a relatively undiscovered and sleepy little place crowded into a tributary valley on the south bank of the Mosel, with plenty of reasonable **accommodation** possibilities. Try *Burgfrieden*, Im Mühlental 62 (☎02673 1432), which has singles from DM26 and doubles from DM48, or *Gute Quelle*, Marktplatz 34 (☎02673 1437), with singles from DM20 and doubles from DM40. The best local food and drink can be had at the musty old cellar of *Weingut Joachim Lipmann* on Marktplatz, which is open on Monday when most of the competition tends to close. As far as actual sights go, there's only **Burg Beilstein**, a romantic ruin built between the thirteenth and fifteenth centuries and owned by the Metternich family until shortly before its destruction in 1689.

Next town of any size is **COCHEM**, on the northern bank of the river, a place which has sold its soul to tourism, and should be avoided like the plague in summer. The main attraction is the **Burg** (March 15–Oct. 31 9am–5pm; DM3), one of the Rhineland-Palatinate's more famous replica castles. If it weren't a complete fake (the eleventh-to-fourteenth-century original went up in smoke in 1689, assisted by enthusiastic French soldiers), the Burg, which dominates the town with its cluster of towers and implacable walls, would be quite impressive, but somehow the knowledge that it's only an *ersatz* castle makes it look a bit ridiculous. Inside, the Burg has been decorated in mock medieval style, though there are some fine pieces of Renaissance furniture.

As for the rest of Cochem, it's an averagely uninspiring town, the majority of whose inhabitants seem to live from from either the hotel trade or by selling beer *Steins* and funny hats to the bus trippers. There's a regulation issue half-timbered **Marktplatz** with a sober baroque **Rathaus**. Behind stands the **Martinskirche**, with a tower that looks like a rococo soldier's helmet. It's a postwar restoration of an original which dated back to the ninth century. Parts of the old city wall are also still intact, including three chunky city gates. From one of them, **Enderttor**, you can take a chair lift ride (daily 9am–6pm; DM5.50) to the top of the **Pinnerkreuz** hill, from where there's the best view of the town and its environs. Don't be fooled by local promptings to go and see the **Brauseley**, billed as the Mosel's answer to the Lorelei—it's utterly underwhelming.

Cochem's **tourist office** is on Endertplatz (☎02671 3971). There's a **youth hostel** at Klottener Str. 9 (☎02671 8633) on the south side of the Mosel. The town has four **campgrounds**, the most accessible of which are *Schausten*, Endertstr. 124 (☎02671 7528) and *Behrens*, south of the river on Stadionstrasse (☎02671 7762). Most of the numerous **hotels** are pricey and full. If you're stuck, try *Gästehaus Lenz*, Zehnthausstr. 37 (☎02671 7615), which has singles from DM18 and doubles from DM36, or the *Zur Weinhexe*, Hafenstr. 1 (☎02671 8482), with singles from DM25 and doubles from DM50.

Karden, Burg Eltz, and Around

From Cochem it's another 11km to **KARDEN**, which preserves houses dating back as far as the twelfth and thirteenth centuries. The **Stiftskirche St. Kastor** was under construction for over 300 years, marking the full transition from Romanesque to Gothic. Although small, its simple white lines make it one of the most visually appealing churches of the Mosel. Inside, there's a fine early seventeenth-century side altar of *The Martyrdom of Saint Stephen*, and a slightly faded wall painting of Christ which looks startlingly modern. Built into the cliffs behind the town on the south bank of the Mosel are two castles: the restored twelfth-century **Wildburg** and **Burg Treis**, an eleventh-century ruin.

Beyond Karden the Mosel valley starts to lose its specialness, but you might stop briefly in the riverside town of **HATZENPORT**, clustered around a pair of Romanesque stone churches and the old restored **Fährturm** (*Ferry Tower*). In **BRODENBACH** on the far shore there's a **youth hostel** at Moorkamp 7 (☎02605 3389) and a **campground** at Rhein-Mosel-Str. 63 (☎02605 1437).

In any event, make sure you don't miss **Burg Eltz** (April 1–Nov. 1 9am–5:30pm; DM4.50), one of only two intact medieval castles in the Rhineland-Palatinate (the other is the Marksburg—see below). To get there, catch bus #6039 from Hatzenport to MÜNSTERMAIFELD, from where you can take another bus to Burg Eltz. This castle really is something else: it seems to rise straight out of the woods of the Elzbach valley, and bristles with conical towers. It goes back at least as far as the twelfth century, developing over the next 400 years as a defensive home for the various branches of the Eltz family, who managed to live there peaceably for a couple of hundred years until a run-in with Balduin, the elector of Trier. This resulted in a two-year siege, during which **Burg Trutzeltz** was built by Balduin directly in front in order to lob rocks at the castle. After Burg Eltz fell the Eltz family was allowed to remain in possession as vassals of Balduin and peace returned. Most of what you see today was built during the fifteenth century; inside the walls are a number of residential towers crammed together around an inner courtyard, which escaped destruction by the

French in 1689 only because a member of the Eltz family happened to be an officer in the French army.

The **interior** of the castle, which you can see only by guided tour, is more or less as it was during medieval times, complete with original furnishings, wall hangings, and paintings. Particular impressive are the *Rübenach Untersaal*, with sixteenth-century Flemish tapestries of unlikely-looking exotic animals and plants, and the panel paintings, including Cranach's *Madonna with Grapes*. The **Schatzkammer** (DM2.50 supplement) is full of silver- and gold-ware, glass, porcelain, weapons, and armor, including a suit of armor which belonged to Emperor Maximilian I. There's also an exquisite jeweled traveling altar and a gold-and-silver drinking vessel topped by a clockwork-powered statuette of Diana.

Be warned that Burg Eltz is snarled up with tourists in summer; make sure you arrive early, or visit it out of season. Bring your own picnic—the snack bar is tacky and overpriced.

Kobern-Gondorf and Winningen

KOBERN-GONDORF is a double town trailing out along the Mosel bank 10km east of Hatzenport. The most unusual local attraction is the **Goloring**, a prehistoric circular tomb complex dating from between 1200 and 600 B.C. In Kirchstrasse (in Kobern) you can see the **Abteihof**, the oldest half-timbered house in the Rhineland-Palatinate; built in 1321, it looks in suspiciously good shape for its age. Also worth visiting is the castle; the **Niederburg** is an extensive pile of crumbling masonry with a more-or-less-intact tower, while the **Oberburg** has the almost perfectly symmetrical Romanesque **Matthiaskapelle**, which once housed what were said to be the remains of the Apostle Matthew (later transferred to the Matthiaskirche in Trier). In Gondorf there's also an **Oberburg**, but it's been cut in half by the road and railroad, which hasn't done a lot for it aesthetically.

The **tourist office** is on the Marktplatz (☎02607 1055). Cheapest **hotels** are *Gasthof Zur Fähre*, Marktplatz 12 (☎02607 571), and *Hähn*, Lennigstr. 1 (☎02607 246), both charging upwards of DM25 per head. For **eating** and **drinking**, try *Weingut Thomas Höreth* (☎02607 647), housed in an old mill, complete with wine museum. To get there, take the road up to the Matthiaskapelle, then turn down the road opposite the cemetery. Kobern-Gondorf is big on *Weinfeste*; there's one in late June and early July, another during the second weekend in September, and a third in the second weekend in October.

Weinfeste also figure in **WINNINGEN**, the last town of any interest before Koblenz, a half-timbered place which holds the oldest wine festival in Germany at the end of August and beginning of September. At this time, wine flows from the town fountain instead of water. A grisly attraction here is the **Hexenhugel**, (*Witches' Hill*) a popular picnic spot where, during the Thirty Years' War, 21 women were burned alive as witches. Just outside the town is the huge bridge which carries the E31 highway over the Mosel valley; fortunately, it hasn't destroyed the local atmosphere.

Boat Trips Along the Mosel

One way of getting from A to B along the Mosel is by boat. There are a number of lines operating routes along the river and it's possible to travel the length of the German Mosel from Trier to Koblenz, or just to make short local trips. *Rhein- und Moselschiffahrt Collee-Hölzenbein*, Rheinzollstr. 4, Koblenz (☎0261 37744) operates between Koblenz and Cochem (total journey time 2½ hr.) and will also undertake special trips for groups by arrangement. *K-D Line*, Frankenwerft 15, Cologne (☎0221 20880), operates a similar service and also does two- and three-day trips between Koblenz and Trier. *Gebrüder Kolb Personenschiffahrt* handles services between Cochem and Trier between May and October. It has local agents in Cochem (☎02671 7387), Zell (☎06542 5335), and Trier (☎0651 263170). The ship *Princesse Marie-Astrid* runs between Bernkastel-Kues and Luxembourg; details for this (as for all other services) are available from local tourist offices. *Bernkastel-Kueser Personenschiffahrt*, Goldbachstr. 52, Bernkastel-Kues (☎06531 8222 or 22257) operates between Bernkastel-Kues and Traben-Trarbach and *Mittelmosel-Personenschiffahrt Gerhard Voss*, Goethestr. 15, Bernkastel-Kues (☎06531 6316) sails between Bernkastel-Kues and Leiwen.

THE RHINE GORGE

Beyond Mainz, the **Rhine** bends westwards and continues its hitherto stately but unspectacular journey. Suddenly, there's a dramatic change—the river widens and swings back to a northerly course, threatening the low banks on either side, while long wooded islands block the view ahead.

This marks the entry to the spectacular eighty-kilometer-long **gorge**, which, though it's only a small part of the river's total length of 1320km, *is* the Rhine in popular imagination. The combination of the treacherous waters, whirlpools, and rocky banks lining the sharp twists of the river pose a severe test of navigational skill. Nowadays, this has been considerably eased by the digging of channels to control the movement of the river, but the river's natural state inevitably spawned legends of shipwrecks, sirens, and mermaids. The lure of the castles of the medieval robber barons, the raw elemental beauty of the landscape itself, and the famous wines made from the vines which somehow cling to the lower slopes, make this one of Europe's major tourist magnets. Yet the pleasure steamers are still greatly outnumbered by the long, narrow commercial barges, a reminder of the crucial role the river has played in the German economy down the centuries.

The Rhine from Bingen to Koblenz

The first stretch of the gorge, up to the confluence with the Mosel, is undoubtedly the finest, lined with cute half-timbered towns and an extensive range of castles in various states of repair. In high season, this means a flood of organized tour parties. If you must do this part of the Rhine in summer, try to avoid spending the night in the area, since **accommodation** under DM30 tends to be thin on the ground and heavily subscribed, often well in advance. Bearing in mind that the true identity of the region has been sacrificed to the hard-sell, you could do worse than take the **train** through this stretch and admire the best feature—the scenery—in comfort.

However, it's undeniably more fun to go by **boat**. The imperious white vessels of the *K-D* line (Frankenwerth 15, Cologne; ☎0221 20880) have several sailings each day in both directions. Fares aren't exactly cheap, with one-way tickets verging on the extortionate—Bingen to Koblenz costs DM43.80 single, DM49 return. However, both *EurRail* (though not *InterRail*) and *Deutsche Bundesbahn*'s own train passes are valid. Many smaller companies also offer sailings along shorter stretches. The high season runs from mid-June to mid-September; the services thereafter progressively run down, and stop altogether at the end of October, to resume in a skeleton format in April.

Spring and autumn are undoubtedly the best times to visit the area, and you could easily spend several days meandering around. Rail and road links lie on either side of the river and, although there are no bridges between Bingen and Koblenz, fairly frequent ferry links for passengers should enable you to hop from one side of the river to the other without too much difficulty.

Bingen, Bacharach, and Oberwesel

Poor relation of Rüdesheim on the other side of the Rhine, **BINGEN** doesn't really have much going for it, other than as the starting-point of the great gorge. Look out, however, for the **Mäuseturm**, a former customs tower in which, according to grisly legend, Archbishop Hatto of Mainz was devoured alive by mice after having burned all the local beggars alive during a famine. Also worth a look is **Burg Klopp**, a former castle of the electors of Mainz, which towers over the town, commanding a great view out over the Rhine to the Taunus. Even this is not what it seems; the original fortress was destroyed in 1689 and the ruins were blown up in 1711, so that what you see today is a nineteenth-century replica. Housed in its tower is the local **Heimatmuseum** (Tues.–Sun. 9am–noon and 2–5pm), whose prize exhibit is a brutal-looking set of Roman doctor's instruments.

The **tourist office** is at Rheinkai 1 (☎06721 14269). There's a **youth hostel** at Herter Str. 51 (☎06721 32163), in the suburb of BINGERBRÜCK—a place most famous for its railroad yards. Bingen itself isn't bad for cheap **hotels**, which could be good news if you want to spend the night in the area but can't really afford the tourist-inflated prices in Rüdesheim. *Krone*, Rheinkai 19–20 (☎06721 17016), and *Horst*, Fruchtmarkt 7 (☎06721 12111), both charge from DM25 per person, while *Gasthof Frambach*, Gerbhausstr. 25 (☎06721 14986), starts at DM26. There are **camping** facilities near the Hindenburgbrücke in the suburb of KEMPTEN.

The fun starts a few kilometers north of Bingen at **Burg Rheinstein** (9am–5/7pm according to season; DM3.50) which, you might think, looks like the turret of a Victorian Gothic railroad bridge. You wouldn't be far wrong—in fact Burg Rheinstein inspired the nineteenth-century trend for replica medieval castles when Prince Friedrich Ludwig of Prussia, influenced by then-fashionable romanticism, rebuilt a ruined thirteenth-century castle he had inherited in 1823 as a summer residence. The castle is now owned by an opera singer who, keeping faith with the tackiness of spirit which inspired the reconstruction, now hires the place out for "medieval" banquets. There are **camping** facilities in the nearby village of TRECHTINGHAUSEN at Am Morgenbach 1 (☎06721 6133).

BACHARACH, 10km downstream, was called *Baccaracum* by the Romans after an altar stone to Bacchus which once stood in the Rhine. This was blown up in 1850 to ease navigation of the river, but parts of the old town wall are still intact and there are plenty of half-timbered houses, particularly around Marktplatz and in Blücherstrasse. The **Peterskirche** on Marktplatz is early Gothic on the outside and late Romanesque on the inside, and **Burg Stahleck** is a chunky-looking castle which now houses the local **youth hostel** (☎06743 1266). From the overgrown and half-timbered Posthof square there's a good view of the **Wernerkapelle**, the red sandstone frame of a never-completed Gothic chapel.

The **tourist office** is at Oberstr. 1 (☎06743 1297). There's a dearth of cheap **hotels**; one of the few possibilities is *Kranenturm*, Langstr. 30 (☎06743 1308), which has singles from DM25 and doubles from DM50. The local **campground** is at Strandbadweg (☎06743 1752).

OBERWESEL, a few kilometers to the north, is overlooked by the huge **Schönburg** castle, now a ruin but, as you'll realize when you walk around its battlements, still impressive. In town, the Gothic **Liebfrauenkirche** is known to the locals as "the red church," after the huge red sandstone blocks used to build it. In the airy interior, look out for the *Niklausaltar*, on which the saint is shown helping three knights who have been sentenced to death for crimes they didn't commit, saving three sisters who have been forced into prostitution by their father, and protecting passengers on board a ship. There are **camping** facilities (☎06744 245) just off the B9 road to the north of town.

From Oberwesel passenger and car ferries run across the Rhine to **KAUB**. Here you get a great view of the **Pfalz** (April–Oct. 9am–noon and 1:30–5:15pm; DM1.50 plus DM1.80 for the boat trip), a white-walled fortress standing on a mid-river island which has become a famous Rhineland symbol. The five-cornered central tower was built in 1327 and the many-turretted outer wall added later. This stronghold enabled the lords of **Burg Gutenfels** above Kaub to extract a toll from passing ships until well into the nineteenth century. Burg Gutenfels as you see it today is a late nineteenth-century restoration of the thirteenth-century original, in which Gustav Adolphus lived during the Thirty Years' War.

It was at Kaub that Field Marshal Blücher, the Prussian general who saved the day at Waterloo, crossed the Rhine during an earlier campaign against Napoleon. He's commemorated in the **Blüchermuseum**, Metzgergasse 6 (daily April–Oct. 10am–noon and 2–4pm, Nov.–March 10am–noon), in the building he used as his headquarters. The rooms are done out in grand Empire style and are full of military bits and pieces from the Napoleonic Wars and old Prussia. There are **camping** facilities at *Am Elsleinband* on Blücherstrasse (☎06774 560).

The Lorelei, St. Goarshausen, and St. Goar

From Kaub head north towards **ST. GOARSHAUSEN**, which trails along the river bank for a couple of kilometers. On the way you'll pass the **Lorelei**, the famous outcrop of rock where, according to legend, a blonde woman used to sit combing her hair while luring passing sailors to watery graves with her eerily compelling song. There's a hokey statue at the water's edge to commemorate the legend. The rock itself has been over-hyped—it's impressive but not staggeringly so. However, there are outstanding views from the top (you reach it via St. Goarshausen itself on bus #6147 or by following the signs marked *Loreley Felsen* if you're traveling under your own steam). Apart from a viewing platform, the summit has a **campground** (☎06771 7519). Also up here is the *Loreley Freilichtbühne*, an open-air stage frequently used for rock concerts.

Above St. Goarshausen itself is **Burg Katz** (*Cat Castle*), the partially reconstructed fourteenth-century fortress of the counts of Katzenelnbogen, which can be visited by prior arrangement with the **tourist office** at Bahnhofstr. 8 (☎06771 427). Burg Katz was built to rival another castle a few kilometers downstream, which belonged to the archbishops of Trier and earned the inevitable nickname **Burg Maus** (*Mouse Castle*) because of its relative puniness. Today Burg Maus is an eagle and falcon station, giving daily displays of bird flight. The *Weinwoche* is during the second and third weeks in September, and there are other *Weinfeste* at the end of September and during the third weekend in October.

A ferry will take you back across to the west bank of the Rhine and the town of **ST. GOAR**, which is slightly prettier and more touristy than its counterpart. Looming above town is one of the best Rhine castles, the enormous **Burg Rheinfels** (daily April-Sept. 9am–6pm, Oct. 9am–5pm; DM2.50) which, until the French blew it up in 1797, was one of the most powerful fortresses on the Rhine. It was founded in 1245 by Count Dieter von Katzenelnbogen, who wanted to look after his Rhine toll-collecting racket, and just ten years later withstood a 9000 man siege by soldiers of the Alliance of Rhenish Towns. During the sixteenth and seventeenth centuries the dukes of Hessen extended what was already a formidable castle into an enormous fortification complex which was to prove virtually impregnable: it was the only Rhineland castle that the French were unable to take during the War of the Palatinate Succession. In 1796 the castle surrendered to the troops of Napoleon without a shot being fired, and over the next three years the French did their best to demolish it. Today, the medieval outline can still be seen and you can walk through the underground passages of the later battlements. Models in the **Heimatmuseum** (April–Sept. 9:30am–noon and 1–5pm), which is housed in a rebuilt section, show how the place looked before it was destroyed.

In town the main monument is the **Stiftskirche** on Oberstrasse (predominantly Gothic with a dash of Romanesque) which has some well-restored fifteenth-century religious paintings and sundry other artistic bits and pieces. The **tourist office** is at Heerstr. 120 (Mon.–Fri. 8am–12:30pm and 2–5pm; ☎06741 383). There's a **youth hostel** at Bismarckweg 17 (☎06741 388), just outside the town center, while **camping** facilities are at *Friedenau*, Gründelbachstr. 103 (☎06741 368), and *Loreleyblick*, An der Loreley 29–39 (☎06741 324), neither of which are too far out of town. As with most of the Rhine towns, it's probably better to avoid staying here in high season, but there are a few reasonable **hotel** possibilities: *Rhein-Hotel*, Heerstr. 71 (☎06741 485), has singles from DM20 and doubles from DM40, as does *Jost*, Gründelbachtal (☎06741 314).

Boppard

At **BOPPARD** the Rhine gorge gets shallower and the valley landscape becomes a gentler one of rounded, vine-covered slopes. It's a popular resort with the Rhine cruise brigade, since you can take round trips by boat as far as Rüdesheim, stopping off at all the little towns and castles described above.

The town has its own share of attractions, foremost of which is the **St. Severuskirche** on Marktplatz, yet another Romanesque-Gothic church, this time of cathedral-like dimensions. A twin-towered structure, brightly painted in white and orange, it was built during the twelfth century to house the remains of St. Severus, which had been brought here from Trier. Look out for the ceiling paintings, some of which date back to the thirteenth century, depicting *The Martyrdom of the Theban Legion* and *The Last Judgment*, and for the Gothic stained glass windows, which look almost Chagallesque.

The squat Gothic **Karmelitenkirche**, near the Rhine quay, has a couple of seventeenth-century altars and various tombs of local bigwigs. At the east entrance is a recess which houses the fourteenth-century *Traubenmadonna*. Traditionally, local vine growers place the first ripe bunch of grapes of the year by the statue and leave it there until it withers away.

At the end of Kirchgasse, which is just off Oberstrasse (Boppard's main street), are the remains of the Roman **Stadtmauer**, which has weathered the years remarkably well. Also here are a couple of watchtowers, the only two survivors of the 28 which the Romans built during the fourth century to fend off the locals. At the end of Bingergasse are the remains of more recent fortifications. The **Binger Tor** was built during the Middle Ages and has survived more or less intact, bar the random instance of crumbling here and there. Between Burgplatz and Rheinallee stands the **Alte Burg**, a castle and residence built by the archbishops of Trier to consolidate their grip in the area. The central keep, with its apertures for the pouring of boiling oil, molten lead, and the like, was built around 1327, while the more civilized-looking wings were added during the seventeenth century. These days the building houses Boppard's **Heimatmuseum** (April–Oct. Tues.–Fri. 10am–noon and 2–4pm, Sat. 10am–noon, Sun. 2–4pm). Part of this is devoted to the furniture of Michael Thonet, a son of Boppard, who, during the early nineteenth century perfected the technique of laminating wood and earned himself a fortune in the process.

Boppard's **tourist office** is at Karmeliterstr. 2 (Mon.–Fri. 8am–12:30pm and 1:30pm–5pm, Sat. 9:30am–noon; ☎06742 10319). **Camping** facilities are at *Sonneck*, just north of town on the B9 next to the Rhine (☎06742 2121 or 3225). Cheapest central **hotels** are *Gasthaus Sonnenhof*, Kirchgasse 8 (☎06742 3223), with singles from DM25 and doubles from DM46, and *Weinhaus Patt*, Steinstr. 30 (☎06742 2366), which has singles from DM26 and doubles from DM52.

From Boppard to Koblenz

From Boppard you can take a ferry across the Rhine to **KAMP-BORNHOFEN**, above which are two castles known as the **Feindlichen Brüder** (*The Rival Brothers*)—according to legend they were owned by two brothers who had fallen out. **Burg Liebenstein** is the better preserved of the two, with its Gothic dwelling tower and a keep set on top of a huge rock. The battlements seem to be partly directed at **Burg Sterrenberg**, which is set slightly lower on the other side of a small river valley. Both castles have small restaurants and you could spend a couple of pleasant hours exploring the pair.

About 10km north of Kamp-Bornhofen is **BRAUBACH**. Set in the hills about 25 minutes' walk above the town is the **Marksburg** (guided tours every hour March 15 Nov. 15, 9:30am–5pm, Nov. 16–March 14, 11am–4pm; DM4), the only medieval castle on this stretch of the Rhine to escape destruction by the French. The fact that this one is an original (showing a few signs of wear and tear) makes it a lot more impressive than the reconstructions you'll have already seen. Most of the building, including the turretted sandstone keep, was built between the twelfth and fourteenth centuries with a few additional defensive features added in the seventeenth century. Inside there's a big collection of weapons from the Middle Ages, including some extremely unpleasant instruments of torture. There are also displays about knightly life in the Middle Ages that throw a bit of light on the absurd way in which the Rhine Valley was ruled during medieval times—dozens of counts, often little more than glorified robbers, extracting tolls from Rhine traffic and lording it over their own little fiefs from their castle strongholds. Marksburg also has the only preserved medieval botanical garden in Germany, and in the souvenir shop they're very proud of the fact this is the only castle in Europe where you can buy authenticated medieval documents.

Next stop is **LAHNSTEIN**, where the Lahn River runs into the Rhine. Apart from the restored **Burg Lahneck** (Easter–Oct. 10am–5:30pm; DM3) above the town there's not much to see here. Lahnstein does, however, have a couple of **campgrounds**: *Rhein-Lahn-Eck*, Sandstr. 8 (☎02621 50916 or 8390), and *Burg*

Lahneck (☎02621 2765 or 2789), in the grounds of the castle. It's also not bad for **hotel** rooms: *Union*, Didierstr. 6 (☎02621 7355), and *Rheinischer Hof*, Hochstr. 47 (☎02621 2598), both have singles from DM25 and doubles from DM50.

From Lahnstein you can take the ferry (passengers only; if you're driving you'll have to go via the KOBLENZ road bridge) to **RHENS**, above which stands the momentous-sounding but rather pathetic-looking **Königsstuhl** (*Seat of Kings*). Resembling the base of some unfinished monument, this stone platform is where the German electors used to meet during the fourteenth and fifteenth centuries to choose their king. In fact, like so many of the Rhine's "medieval" monuments, it's a bit of a cheat. Although the original was put up around 1376, most of what can be seen today dates from as recently as 1842, a witness to the nineteenth-century mania for resurrecting Germany's medieval past. Rhens itself is a half-timbered kind of place with substantially intact medieval fortifications and a rather too pristine Rathaus.

Just to the north, practically in Koblenz itself, is **Schloss Stolzenfels** (April–Sept. Tues.–Sun. 9am–1pm and 2–6pm, Oct.–March 10am–1pm and 2–5pm), a Karl Friedrich Schinkel neo-Gothic version of a thirteenth-century Burg which went up in smoke in 1688. The interior is a bit extravagant, filled to saturation point with suits of armor and medieval weaponry. The most taste-affronting part is probably the *Rittersaal*, though the king's apartments come a close second.

Koblenz

KOBLENZ is always either thronged or deserted, according to the season. Its favorable geographical location at the confluence of the Rhine and Mosel first recommended it to the Romans, who established a settlement here in A.D. 14. Nearby, the Lahn flows in from the east, which means that the town lies close to the four distinct scenic regions separated by these rivers—the Eifel, Hunsrück, Westerwald, and Taunus, and thus makes an ideal touring base. The town itself polarizes opinion—some enjoy its relaxed, rather faded charm; others find it smug and boring. Its connection with tourism actually has deep roots, as it was in Koblenz in 1823 that **Karl Baedeker** began publishing his famous series of guidebooks which aimed at saving travelers from having to depend on unreliable and extortionate local tour guides for information. Old editions of these (the one on *The Rhineland* itself is a good example) are still worth seeking out; their sententious prose evokes a vanished epoch, and their pull-out maps are wonderful to handle.

The place to begin is the **Deutsches Eck**, where the Mosel flows into the Rhine—this is somewhat fancifully supposed to be the place where the Teutonic Knights first settled, so giving birth to the German nation. In 1897, a colossal equestrian monument in the heroic taste of the time was erected here to Kaiser Wilhelm I. It was destroyed in the last war, but the base, itself a pompous structure with over a hundred steps, was rebuilt and piously dedicated to the unification of Germany. Demolition would have been kinder, as it adds nothing of benefit to the view.

Close by is the finest building in the city, the Romanesque collegiate foundation of **St. Kastor**, largely twelfth-century, whose imposing facade has twin towers with characteristic "bishop's miter" roofs. A long-term restoration project of the interior is nearing completion, leaving it looking wonderfully fresh. See the elaborate **keystones** of the Gothic vault, especially the one showing the

Madonna and Child in a boat. There's a good view of the church from the floral garden of the adjacent **Deutschherrenhaus**.

The Rhine bank is today largely devoted to tourist facilities; the curious old **crane**, now converted into a pricey restaurant, is the only thing to catch the eye. Only a few monuments of medieval Koblenz's center, which bordered on the Mosel, remain; they're rather over-restored in the romantic image of old Germany, with the exterior walls painted in bright colors, but are undeniably picturesque. You come first of all to the **Deutscher Kaiser**, a sixteenth-century tower house which also is now a restaurant. Farther on is the Florinsmarkt, with the Romanesque-Gothic **St. Florin**, now a Protestant parish church; the **Schöffenhaus**, a pretty little orange building with corner turrets; and the **Altes Kaufhaus**. This last building now houses the **Mittelrhein Museum** (Tues.–Sat. 10am–1pm and 2–5:30pm, Sun. 10am–1pm; DM1.50), a fairly miscellaneous collection of paintings, sculptures and antiquities. The ground floor has a few German Primitives, including an *Adoration of Magi* by the Augsburg painter **Jörg Breu** which unashamedly plagiarizes a portrait by his fellow-citizen, Holbein the Elder, for the figure of one of the kings. Upstairs are many works by one of Germany's most accomplished rococo painters, **Januarius Zick**, who eventually settled in Koblenz.

Farther along the Mosel bank is the **Alte Burg**, transformed into a Renaissance palace, and now housing the municipal library, but originally constructed to defend the fourteenth-century **Balduinbrücke**. Turning away from the river, you come to **Münzplatz**, which still preserves the mint master's house. Also in the square is the mansion birthplace of the wily Habsburg states-man **Clemens von Metternich**, high priest of the theory (which was to dominate nineteenth-century politics) that the key to a peaceful Europe lay in maintaining a balance of power among the main states. His peak of influence came during his dominant hosting role at the Congress of Vienna in 1815, which laid down the structure of post-Napoleonic Europe; ironically, his native town was given to Prussia—arch-rival of his adopted Austria—as a result.

Down the pedestrian mall at the intersection of Löhrstrasse and Markstrasse there's a fine grouping of four houses, each with ornamental oriel windows. Left from here is another large square, Plan, lined with large eighteenth-century build-ings. Behind are the exotic, onion-shaped spires of the **Liebfrauenkirche**, a handsome if diffuse church with a galleried Romanesque nave and a Gothic chan-cel. Just beyond is the **Rathaus**, rather incongruously housed in a cavernous former Jesuit college.

During the late eighteenth century, Koblenz was expanded to the south in the form of a planned neoclassical town. The archbishop-electors of Trier moved their court here, centered on the huge **Schloss**; three years after its completion, the electors fled in the wake of Napoleon's advance, never to return. The build-ings were gutted during the last war, and now serve as offices. A more lasting memento of the period is the stately **theater** fronted by an obelisk on Deinhardplatz. Its programs of plays, opera, and other events put those of many larger cities to shame.

Across the Rhine lies **EHRENBREITSTEIN**, with the original **Residenz** of the electors, designed by Balthasar Neumann. Looming high above is the vast **Festung**—one of the largest fortresses in the world—with an impressive set of defenses which the Prussians painstakingly and quite needlessly rebuilt over a ten-year period after Koblenz passed into their hands. It now contains the youth hostel and the **Landesmuseum** (mid-March–Oct. daily 9am–5pm; DM1). Even if you don't want to stay here, it's well worth the climb for the sake of the memorable panoramas of the city and its two great rivers. Access is possible (but expensive) by chair lift in season; otherwise, follow the main road along the shore of the Rhine until you come to a path which snakes upwards.

Practical Details

The **Hauptbahnhof** and **bus station** are side by side, to the southwest of the historical part of the city. Immediately opposite is the main **tourist office** (May-Oct. Mon.–Fri. 8:30am–6pm, Sat. 9am–2am: additional hours in the summer, shorter hours in winter; ☎0261 31304). There's also a branch on the Rhine front at Konrad-Adenauer-Ufer (June–Sept. Tues.–Sat. 11:45am–6:15pm, Sun. 11:30am–6:30pm; ☎0261 129 2207). Pick up the large city map, which has exhaustive listings of hotels, restaurants, pubs, discos and leisure activities on the back.

The previously mentioned **youth hostel** (☎0261 73737)—buses #7, #8, #9, or #10 go closest—must rate as one of the best in Germany; not only is the view superb, it has recently been given a thorough modernization. Usually empty in winter, it's regularly full in summer. The **campground** is at Lützel, directly opposite Deutsches Eck (April to mid-Oct.; ☎0261 802489). A ferry crosses the Mosel here in summer, while another somewhat further south crosses the Rhine. **Hotel rooms** are remarkably reasonable—you can find them at around DM25 for a single, DM35 for a double. In the center, the best bargains are *Christ*, Schützenstr. 32 (☎0261 37702); *Weinand*, Weissernonnengasse 4-6 (☎0261 32492); and *Kroppenberg*, Clemensstr. 17 (☎0261 32973). There are also a number in Ehrenbreitstein—*Mäckler*, Helffensteinst. 63 (☎0261 73725); *Zur Kaul*, at no. 64 in the same street (☎0261 75256); and *Rehling*, Am Markt 219 (☎0261 73638). Some of the remoter suburbs, such as Arenberg in the woods, or the Mosel villages of GÜLS and LAY, are cheapest of all.

Food and Drink

For both **eating** and **drinking**, it's well-nigh impossible to escape the tourist syndrome. For sampling the local *Riesling* and *Müller-Thurgau* **wines**, the *Weindorf* near the Rheinbrücke (closed all Nov.) is the best-known center, grouping four taverns in the form of a village square. It was set up for the 1925 German Wine Exhibition and has been preserved ever since; its function as an attraction for visitors is a bit too obvious. Surprisingly, Koblenz is also a major **beer** center. The large *Königsbacher* brewery not only makes an excellent bitter-tasting Pils, but also has a subsidiary named *Richmodis* in Cologne, enabling it to produce its own very fruity *Kölsch*. There are plenty of bars and restaurants (including many international varieties) in the streets of the old town; those out of the center, such as in Ehrenbreitstein, have a more genuine local flavor. Numerous **discos** and **nightclubs** are on offer too, though this is hardly the place in which to look for anything very original.

For **river cruises**, go to the Rhine bank at Konrad-Adenauer-Ufer, where both the *K-D Line* (☎0261 31030) and the *Rhine-Mosel Line* (☎0261 37744) have booths. There's a **Mitfahrzentrale** office at Rheinstr. 34 (☎0261 18505). Anyone who shares the German passion for **forest trails** should pick up the tourist office leaflet *Unser Wald*, which details fifteen walks in the Stadtwald to the south of the city between the Rhine and Mosel, and in the various smaller woods to the east. The two main **festivals** are Carnival and *Der Rhein in Flammen*; the latter takes place on the second Saturday in August, and features fireworks and bonfires.

The Rhine from Andernach to Bonn

Soon after leaving Koblenz, the Rhine gorge opens out, cutting between the ranges of the Eifel and Westerwald. If this stretch doesn't quite match the grandeur of the immediately preceding section, it's impressive nonetheless, and well worth following by either boat or train. With exceptions, it's also less touristed, and hence **accommodation** prices are less of a rip-off.

Andernach

ANDERNACH, which lies 16km down the Rhine from Koblenz, can trace its history back farther than almost any other German town. It celebrated its 2000th anniversary in 1988, commemorating the foundation of a Roman base for the campaigns against the tribes on the eastern side of the Rhine. Subsequently Andernach became a Franconian royal seat, before passing to the control of the archbishop-electors of Cologne, serving as the southern border of their territory until the Napoleonic invasion. Nowadays, it's an odd hybrid, having a fair amount of industry, yet taking advantage of its situation and monuments to double as a holiday resort.

If you're traveling along the Rhine by boat, it's definitely worth alighting for a couple of hours in order to walk around the thirteenth-century **fortifications**, which were laid out on the Roman foundations. The walls survive largely intact, making a solid back for many later buildings, including a well-concealed row of houses. Extra defense on the southern stretch was provided by the **Burg**, the most important town castle in the Rhineland. Blown up by French troops in 1688, a fair amount has nevertheless survived, notably the later embellishments such as the **Pulverturm** and residential palace wing.

On the north, overlooking the river, is the **Rheintor**, whose inner gate has weather-worn statues illustrating the best-known local legend, that of the *Andernacher Bäckerjungen* "baker boys of Andernach", who saved the town from occupation by letting loose bees on the invading army. The most picturesque feature of Andernach's fortifications, however, is the fifteenth-century **Runder Turm** overlooking the Rhine on the northern side of town, whose octagonal upper storeys give it an exotic, oddly Moorish air. Thankfully, the French siege guns failed to penetrate its thick walls, but the enormous dent they made can still be seen clearly. Continuing down the river bank, you shortly come to a remarkable sixteenth century **crane** whose original wooden mechanism remained in service into the present century, and is still in full working order.

Just to the west of the Runder Turm, the tall twin facade towers of the **Pfarrkirche Maria Himmelfahrt** rise majestically above the rest of the skyline. For the most part, it's an archetypal late Romanesque basilica with a pronounced Rhenish accent, though the northeastern belfry, whose rough masonry stands in stark contrast to the super-smooth stonework of the rest of the building, is in fact a survivor of the previous church on the site.

Andernach's main axis, Hochstrasse, runs from here to the Burg; about halfway down is the **Altes Rathaus**, occupying the site of the former ghetto. A *Mikvah* (Jewish bath) was recently discovered underneath the session room; to see it, ask for the key at the **tourist office** (Mon.–Fri. 8am–12:30pm and 1:30–5pm, Sat. 9am–noon; ☎0263 406224) on the adjacent Läufstrasse. Directly opposite is the Gothic **Christuskirche**, a former Franciscan monastery with a curiously lopsided interior. A bit farther down the street the **Haus von der Leyen**, a Renaissance patrician mansion now houses the local **museum** (Tues.–Fri. 10am–noon and 2–5pm, Sat. and Sun. 2–4pm; DM2). Lack of space means only a small collection of antiquities is permanently on display, but the changing exhibitions (prominently featured on posters outside) are often surprisingly good.

Andernach hosts a number of **festivals**, including a medieval fair in the Burg (mid-July); *The Thousand Lights*, featuring fireworks and illuminations (first weekend in September); and, of course, Carnival. In summer, the town is a popular overnight stop with tour coach operators; hence there are plenty of **hotels**, but these are often fully booked and anyway charge independent travelers inflated prices. There's a clutch of cheaper options along Konrad-Adenauer-Allee overlooking the Rhine, and on Mauerstrasse directly behind; the going rate is upwards of DM35 per head. You should be able to stay for a bit less at *Alt Miesenheim*, Ringstr. 29 (☎0263 71840), *Hubertus*, Im Boden 13 (☎0263 45769), or in the few **private houses** (the tourist office has a list; single rooms are pretty well nonexistent). Beware of *Zum Stadtwappen* on Kirchstrasse; it's one of the cheapest options according to official listings, but the proprietress uses any old trick—from charging for breakfast twice to levying a supplement for proximity to a toilet—to bump up the bill. Most of what passes for **nightlife** goes on in Hochstrasse and the streets leading from it down to the Rhine. **Buses** leave from Am Stadtgraben, the western range of the old wall. The **Bahnhof** is on Kurfürstendamm; to reach the center, walk straight ahead, then turn right under the railroad bridge.

Beyond Andernach

Immediately beyond BROHL, the train's second stop, stands **Burg Rheineck**. This fortress, which was rebuilt during the nineteenth century, is no longer open to the public, but if you follow the path to the right, you come to a viewpoint commanding an impressive panorama. A farther 3km on is **BADBREISIG**, a popular spa and holiday resort, which makes the cheapest base for exploring this area; rooms can be found for as little as DM20 in private guest houses scattered all over the town, and there's also a **campground** (☎02633 95645).

From Bad Breisig, the railroad leaves the banks of the river for a spell, continuing to SINZIG, 6km away, which lies near the end of the valley of the Ahr. There's just one monument of note: the church of **St. Peter**, one of the smallest but most original of the Romanesque basilicas of the Rhineland. Even more than usual, the impression is of a dreamlike fantasy, an effect accentuated by the white and yellow paint covering the exterior walls. The lofty galleried interior, which uses differently colored stones for contrast, creates an impression of space all out of proportion to its modest length. On the south side of the chancel is a chapel adorned with noble though fragmentary frescoes which are contemporary with the building, while the high altar has a brightly colored, late fifteenth-century *Passion retable* from Cologne.

Remagen

Back on the Rhine, 4km north, is **REMAGEN**, a town famous for a **bridge** which no longer exists. This was built during World War I to aid the movement of troops and supplies to the Western Front. On March 7, 1945, an advance regiment of the U.S. Armored Division reached this point, to find that the bridge—

unlike all the others along the Rhine, Germany's most crucial natural defensive barrier—was still intact. The token Nazi force who had been left to guard it was quickly routed, enabling the Americans to establish a base on the opposite bank. Eisenhower declared the bridge to be "worth its weight in gold," while Hitler ordered the execution of four officers for their carelessness in failing to blow the bridge up. In retrospect, the importance of the Remagen episode seems exaggerated, as crossings were made by the Allies farther up the Rhine the following week. Moreover, the bridge itself collapsed ten days later due to overloading, killing 28 American soldiers in the process. However, it was symbolically a telling blow, and has remained a popular subject for books, the best of which is Ken Hechler's *The Bridge at Remagen*. The support towers on the Remagen side have been converted into a **Peace Museum** (March–Nov.daily 10am–5pm; DM2), which chronicles the story of the bridge by means of old photographs.

In the center of town, the dominant building is the curious church of **Saints Peter and Paul**. At the turn of the century, it was decided that the original Romanesque-Gothic church was no longer sufficiently big for the town's expanding population; accordingly, a new church, imitating the style of the old but on a much larger scale, was tacked at right angles directly on to it. More directly appealing is the enigmatic **Pfarrhoftor**, a double gateway forming the entrance to the parish courtyard. It's covered with carvings made by a Romanesque sculptor of limited technique but fertile imagination. Pregnant with symbolism, the subjects include water sprites, a male mermaid and Samson fighting the lion.

High above Remagen stands the mid-nineteenth-century **Apollinariskirche**, goal of a popular ten-day pilgrimage at the end of July. The church was built in tandem with the completion of the Dom in Cologne, and is a miniature version of it. Inside, the walls are covered with frescoes of the lives of Christ, the Virgin, and Saint Apollinaris. According to the old *Baedeker* guides, in its time this church was representative of the very best modern art and architecture. Though such a view was subsequently sneered at by more "enlightened" opinion, the building can by now be enjoyed for what it is—a true period piece.

With its central location, Remagen is undoubtedly the best base for this part of the Rhine, and there's a **campground** (☎02642 22222) right beside the river. The hotels beside the Bahnhof are geared to motor coach parties and are anyway best avoided as thundering freight trains pass through all night. Far better to go for a room in a **private house**—*Borsch-Genn*, Walburgstr. 23 (☎02642 23109), has singles at DM25, doubles at DM46, and also offer competitive full- or half-board rates, while *Fleschhut*, Birresdorfer Str. 26 (☎02642 22559), and *Flier*, at no. 69 on the same street (☎02642 23155), both have doubles (only) at DM40 or less.

Rolandseck

ROLANDSECK, another 6km north, has now been absorbed by Remagen. The train station building is now designated the **Künstlerbahnhof** (daily 10am–5pm; DM2.50), housing a notable collection of work by Hans Arp, along with changing exhibitions of contemporary art. More sculptures by Arp, and by Henry Moore, can be seen for free on the lawn outside.

One of the most famous Rhine legends is closely associated with the vicinity of Rolandseck. In the middle of the Rhine, just beyond the village, is the island of **Nonnenwerth**, occupied by a former convent. On hearing news of the death of Roland (Charlemagne's nephew) in an ambush in northern Spain, his betrothed is alleged to have come here, taking her final vows the moment before the hero, miraculously recovered from his wounds—which had killed him off in all alternative sagas—arrived to claim her. Stricken by grief, he built the **Rolandsbogen** fortress on the hill above, in order to catch occasional glimpses of her. Whatever the veracity of the story, it's well worth climbing up to the ruin, which commands one of the most extensive views of this part of the Rhine, with BONN and the SIEBENGEBIRGE (see *North Rhineland-Westphalia*) immediately to the north.

THE EIFEL

Strictly speaking, the mountains of the **Eifel** range—which are divided between the Rhineland-Palatinate and North Rhineland-Westphalia—are little more than big hills. On the whole, they aren't desperately exciting, which probably accounts for the lack of mass tourism. However, in the part of the Eifel which lies in the Rhineland-Palatinate you'll find a gentle landscape of wooded hills and bare heathland, dotted with volcanic lakes and intersected by quiet, unspoiled valleys. The area is used to visitors, but most of them are Germans who spend their summer vacations abroad and come here for a second break in late spring or early autumn. This means that it's a good place to escape the crowds, particularly if you're otherwise concentrating on a nearby tourist area, such as the Rhine or Mosel.

The only part of the region which has completely succumbed to tourism is the **Ahrtal** in the northeast where truly spectacular scenery brings hundreds of thousands of visitors during a season that lasts from May until late October. North of Trier, **Bitburg-Prüm**, is the region at its most unspoiled. The area known as the **Vulkaneifel**, where glassy circular lakes in the craters of extinct volcanoes and spectacular pillars of volcanic rock compete for attention, has some of the most unusual and spectacular scenery, with the added attractions of well-developed holiday and water sport activities. Best-looking town outside the Ahrtal is **Mayen**, with its restored medieval center and spectacular castles. Otherwise, much of the Eifel has a slightly sleepy air, its life revolving round the seasonal influxes of visitors and people coming to the various spa towns or *Luftkurorte* .

The Ahrtal

The **AHRTAL**, the valley of the Ahr River, rates as one of the most scenic corners of West Germany. The landscape and most of the towns in this valley, which cuts down through from the **Hohe Eifel** to join the Rhine just outside REMAGEN, are so postcard-pretty that at times you'll find yourself in a real Brothers Grimm landscape of ruined castles, forests, and vineyards. No effort has been spared when it comes to providing for mass tourism, and this is where the problems start. From May through to October all those idyllic little towns and villages are filled to overflowing with day-tripping German families, hikers, wine fans, and British motor coach parties, and the only people who really benefit are the owners of tacky souvenir shops and the hotel keepers who jack up their prices and rake the money in.

The best thing to do is to visit the area out of season when you can absorb the atmosphere of the place without the crowds. There really is a lot to take in: the countryside is magnificent once you hit the upper reaches of the valley (particularly around **Altenahr**), and many of the towns and villages look like they've hardly changed in centuries. The area is best explored by taking the train up from Remagen; at first the valley seems flat and nondescript but gradually vineyards start to hem in the railroad tracks and the sides of the valley become steeper.

Bad Neuenahr-Ahrweiler

First stop is **BAD NEUENAHR-AHRWEILER**, which threads its way along the Ahr for a few kilometers just before the valley becomes narrower and the spectacular stuff begins. It's really two towns which have grown into each other—Bad Neuenahr is fairly modern and commercially oriented while Ahrweiler is so impossibly old-fashioned that it looks like a film set.

From **Arweiler's Bahnhof** it's only a few minutes' walk to the center of town. One of the two **tourist offices** is at Wilhelmstr. 24 (Mon.–Fri. 8:30am–5:30pm, Sat. 9am–noon; ☎02641 5051). The walled kernel of the town dates back to the Middle Ages and seems wildly archaic with its narrow streets and half-timbered buildings. This impression is enhanced as you pass through the **Niedertor**, one of the four medieval city gates. Niederhutstrasse is the town center's main commercial street with plenty of tacky souvenir shops, along with delicatessens and wine merchants. There are also a few good, albeit slightly pricey, cafés and *Weinstuben*. *Café Sonntag* at no. 69 is fine in a touristy kind of way and *Zum Winzer Michel* at no. 65 is a good place to sample some of the red wines produced in the vineyards you'll have seen as you approached the town. Niederhutstrasse runs into the broad Marktplatz, where you'll find another recommendable restaurant, *Alte Post*, along with another branch of the tourist office.

On the northern side of the square stands the thirteenth-century **Pfarrkirche St. Laurentius**. Inside are fourteenth- and fifteenth-century frescoes and modern stained glass windows, some of which have an almost expressionist feel to them. At the other end of Marktplatz is the **Weisser Turm**, a defensive tower originally built around 1110 and then given a few baroque embellishments during the seventeenth century. This now houses the **Ahrgau Museum** (April–Oct. Fri. 10am–noon and 2pm–5pm, Sun. 10:30am–noon) which has a mainly uninspired collection of bits and pieces relating to the Ahrtal area with a emphasis on local wine production methods through the centuries.

The town center is ringed by the **Stadtmauer**, built between the thirteenth and fifteenth centuries and still more or less intact despite numerous attempts to breach it during the Thirty Years' War. It's straddled by four towers, of which the largest is the southern **Ahrtor**, overlooking the Ahr River. From here you get a good view across to the **Ursulinenkloster Kalvarienberg**, which sits on the edge of town surrounded by vineyards. This imposing building, resembling a French château, now houses a convent and girls' school.

There are plenty of **hotels**, although the budget end of the market is less well-catered for and obviously in summer it's advisable to check on room availability in advance. *Zum Ännchen*, Niederhutstr. 10 (☎02641 36021), has four singles from DM33 per night and doubles from DM54, while *Zum Stern*, Marktplatz 9 (☎02641 34738), has singles from DM36 and doubles from DM60. A little farther out of town, *Pension Kronen*, Alveradisstr. 17 (☎02641 34202) has doubles from DM56, and *Pension Vallender*, Goethestr. 3 (☎02641 34621), has a single room from DM22 and doubles from DM38. Ahrweiler's **youth hostel** is at Peter-Friedhofen-Str. 2 (☎02641 34924), a few minutes' walk from downtown and a stone's throw from the river. The **campground** is at Kalvarienbergstr. 1 (☎02641 36250), on the way out to the Ursulinenkloster.

Though less attractive than its sister town, Bad Neuenahr has a couple of things worth seeing: the **Willibrorduskirche** on Schweizerstrasse, with its Romanesque west tower and the usual melange of architectural details, and the **Beethovenhaus** on Beethovenstrasse, a baroque townhouse where the composer used to spend his holidays. Beethoven probably came to the town in order to benefit from its thermal springs and the healing properties of the locally bottled mineral water.

Today Bad Neuenahr is still a well-known *Kurort* and spa. The riverside **Kurgarten** (daily 7am–9:30pm; DM2.50) and the classically elegant **Thermal Badehaus** are survivors from an era when wealthy families from all over Europe came here to partake of the waters and hothouse social life. Another big attraction is the **Spielbank** in Casinostrasse, the largest casino in West Germany. The roulette wheels start rolling daily at 2pm and for DM5 admission you can gamble away your life's savings or, if you're more cautiously inclined, just watch the action. The **tourist office** is at Hauptstr. 60, next door to the Bahnhof.

The Upper Ahrtal and the Rotweinwanderweg

Heading west by rail out of Bad Neuenahr-Ahrweiler you pass through a string of little wine-producing villages. The railroad runs roughly parallel to the most interesting and scenic stretch of the **Rotweinwanderweg**, a walking route (look out for the distinctive red bunch-of-grapes signs) which starts at BAD BODENDORF and covers the 35km to ALTENAHR. The Ahrtal is at its most beautiful after Bad Neuenahr-Ahrweiler, where the valley narrows and its steep sides are terraced with vines in an effort to cultivate every available centimeter. Hundreds of years of viniculture have created a landscape as distinctive as the farming terraces of the Andes, and the way in which the slopes have been gradually altered gives a sense of the continuity of the local vine growing tradition.

First stop after Bad Neuenahr–Ahrweiler is **WALPORZHEIM**, which is actually an administrative part of the larger town. The local wine specialty is a late-Burgundy type which you can sample in the *Probierkeller* of the *Winzerverein Walporzheim*, Walporzheimerstr. 173 (☎02641 34763), the second oldest wine co-op in Germany. Also worth checking out is *Brogsitter's Sanct Peter*, Walporzheimerstr. 134 (☎02641 389911), a wine restaurant belonging to the famous *Weingut St. Peter*, a vineyard founded in 1246. During the second weekend in August the annual *Weinfest* takes place and the streets run with red wine.

Next along the line are the little wine villages of **DERNAU** and **RECH**. Dernau's *Hotel-Gasthaus Poppelreuther*, Friedenstr. 4, has one single from DM25 and doubles from DM52. Rech also has a good selection of pensions and it's worth bearing these villages in mind if you're in the area during high season when the hotels in the larger towns tend to fill up quickly.

MAYSCHOSS, a couple of kilometers up the line nestles in the Ahr valley and consequently attracts a lot of bus tours. Although the town boasts 500 hotel beds, few of them come cheap; best bets are *Gasthaus Fuhrmann*, Dorfstr. 45 (☎02643 7028) which has rooms from DM30 per person, and *Bacchus Keller*, Ahrrotweinstr. 20, whose rates begin at DM33 per person. The main non-wine-related local attractions are the ruined **Saffenburg**, which overlooks the village, and the black marble tomb in the **Pfarrkirche** containing the remains of Katherina Von der Mark-Schleiden, a serving girl-turned-countess who once ruled the area from the castle.

Altenahr

The next stop is **ALTENAHR**, a town which can only be described as picturesque and whose population seems to increase tenfold in the summer. It's horrendously clogged up then, but if you go off-season you could easily spend a few days here using the town as a base to explore the surrounding area. The landscape is magnificent; the valley is so narrow at this point it almost becomes a gorge, and the town is situated on a tortuous bend in the river. If you follow the river eastward out of town, precipitous rock faces soar from the northern bank, and on the southern side steep forested slopes lead up to the craggy peaks of the **Voreifel**. By night, the whole place has an almost unearthly atmosphere.

Altenahr's **tourist office** is housed in the Bahnhof building (Mon.–Fri. 10am–noon and 3–5pm, Sat. 10am–noon). There are plenty of suspiciously pristine half-timbered facades—and also plenty of souvenir shops and hotels. The best way to appreciate Altenahr's undeniable charms is to trek up to **Burg Are** from whose ruined heights you get a tremendous view of the surrounding area. Burg Are itself was was built around 1100 and the ruins have a romantic feel to them—you could easily imagine them as the setting for an illicit lovers' rendezvous in days gone by. Like most castles in this part of Germany it was destroyed by the French in 1690 after a nine-month siege, leaving only ruined walls. The whole town was once fortified but only a few remnants of the former wall and towers remain. There's also a Romanesque **Pfarrkirche** which, despite a few Gothic additions, retains very clear and simple lines.

In addition to the *Rotweinwanderweg*, there are fifteen signposted local **walking routes**. A number of paths lead up from the Bahnhof into the hills and to the nearby village of ALTENBURG. Look for the **Teufelsloch**, a famous local landmark and viewpoint, where the elements have eroded a giant hole into the rock. From up here you gain a good view of the **Langfigtal** *naturpark* and of the **Breite Ley**, a sheer volcanic rock formation rising from the Ahr valley just outside town. Another possibility is to take the chair lift which runs from the bottom of Seilbahnstrasse to the 330-meter-high **Ditschardhöhe**, with a café and good views.

The local **youth hostel** (☎02643 1880) is about thirty minutes' walk out of town down the unlit Langfigtal. **Camping** facilities are available just outside town near Altenburg (☎02643 8503). Biggest cluster of **hotels** is on Brückenstrasse, but you'd be well advised to shop around, using the tourist office's list. **Pensions**, for example *Maria Schäfer* at Rossberg 93, can cost as little as DM17 per person.

From Altenahr you can make a five-minute train journey to the end of the line at **KREUZBERG**; to go any farther, you're dependent on the buses. The **Burg** is an eighteenth-century reconstruction of an earlier one which was destroyed by the French. Near the Bahnhof is another **campground** (☎02643 8581).

The High Eifel

There are regular services (approximately one bus an hour) from Altenahr to **ADENAU** and the thirty-minute journey takes you through the upper reaches of the Ahr valley, via a succession of tiny villages, deep into the High Eifel (*Hohe Eifel*). Adenau is a pretty little tourist town straggling along the river valley, notable mainly for the fifteenth- and sixteenth-century half-timbered houses which surround its **Marktplatz**. These are actually the genuine article, as the occasional sagging roof or slightly buckled facade shows, but they have been prettified for the tourists and now house the usual range of cafés, bars, and shops. There's also a venerable church (eleventh- with thirteenth-century additions).

The **tourist office** is at Marktplatz 8 (☎02691 2015 or 2017). Reasonable local **hotels** include *Gasthaus-Restaurant Schmitz*, Trierer Str. 4 (☎02691 2957), with doubles from DM50, and *Gästehaus Kupper*, Hauptstr. 15 (☎02691 2156), whose doubles cost DM60.

From Adenau, regular buses run to the **Nürburg**, a ruined castle which stands on one a high peak (678m). The Nürburg was originally the site of a Roman fortress but the ruins you see today are of a twelfth-century fortress destroyed by French soldiers after a long siege in 1690. There are a few pensions and hotels in the eponymous nearby village, of which one of the cheapest is *Pension Hans Loosen*, Burgstr. 28 (☎02691 7418), with rooms from DM30 per person.

Easily reached from the village itself is the famous **Nürburgring** race track which, depending on your sensibilities, could well be worth a visit. No longer used for Formula One grand prix racing because of the dangers (it was here that Niki Lauda had a near-fatal crash in 1976), it's still used for minor motor races. The main entrance to the ring is just outside Nürburg itself and the track, built between 1925 and 1927, is a 28-kilometer-long figure-eight which winds its way through the forested Hoch Eifel. If you're traveling by car you can take a spin around the track yourself (DM15 for the whole run, DM12 for the 24-kilometer northern section or DM6 for a 4.5-kilometer short run). For DM75 a professional racing driver will chauffeur you round either of the tracks (☎02691 302154 Mon.–Fri. for more information about this; ☎02691 302156 for news of events).

If you're in the area you might also want to take a look in the **Rennsportmuseum** (daily 10am–6pm; DM8.50, DM5 students). This houses an extensive collection of thoroughbred cars and bikes of the kind that have raced on the Nürburgring for the last sixty years or so.

Mayen and Around

The first thing you should know about **MAYEN**, some 30km from Andernach on the main east–west Eifel railroad line, is that it was almost completely flattened by the RAF on January 2, 1945 to prevent the Germans from using it as a staging post for troops during the Ardennes offensive. This will save you from disappointment when you find out that all its quaint and charming buildings date from the last forty years or so. This rebuilding program has been carried out with a great deal of sensitivity and, apart from an ugly department store on the Marktplatz, no great architectural errors seem to have been made.

If you arrive by rail it's a five-minute bus ride from the **Westbahnhof** to the town center. The bus will drop you off at the **Brückentor**, which, along with the **Obertor** on Boemundring at the other side of town, is all that remains of the once 1600-meter-long city wall. Walking up Marktstrasse towards the Marktplatz you pass the **Pfarrkirche St. Clemens**, whose distinctive twisted steeple resulted from the tower on the original fourteenth-century building gradually becoming distorted owing to poor construction techniques and the influence of the weather. On Marktplatz itself is the baroque **Altes Rathaus**—the only town-center building to survive the war just about intact—which houses the **tourist office** (daily 8am–12:30pm and 1:30–5:30pm).

From the other end of the square the thirteenth-century **Genoveveburg** glowers over the town. Nowadays it houses the **Eifeler Landschaftsmuseum** (Feb.

16–Nov. 30, Mon.–Sat. 9am–noon and 2–5pm, Sun. and hols. 10am–1pm), where a range of Eifel-related exhibits takes you from the Stone Age to modern times. Look out for the before-and-after pictures showing the war damage inflicted on the town. About two-thirds of the **Herz-Jesu-Kirche**, which you can see from the battlements of the Genoveveburg, was destroyed, and a series of photographs records the destruction and reconstruction.

Close to Mayen is **Schloss Bürresheim** (April–Sept. 9am–1pm and 2–6pm, Oct., Nov. and Jan.–March 9am–1pm and 2pm–5pm; closed the first working day of every month; DM2), which is the epitome of the German fairy-tale castle. It rises out of the wooded valley of the river Nette and is only about five minutes out of town by bus (leaving from the stop between Im Möhren and Wittbende on the Habsburgring). Begun as a fortress in 1220, it was turned into a residential castle during the sixteenth century, a change clearly reflected in its appearance, the grim stone walls of the original fortress being topped by more fanciful Renaissance turrets.

Best **hotel** bets are *Zum Katzenburg*, Koblenzer Str. 174 (☎02651 43585), which is handy for the Westbahnhof and has rooms from DM20 per night, and the more central *Keupen*, Marktplatz 21–23 (☎02651 73077), which charges upwards of DM27. The **youth hostel** is some way out of the town center on Knüppchen (☎02651 2355); to get there walk down Göbelstrasse from Marktplatz, turn left on to Stehbachstrasse and then make an immediate right into Im Möhren and follow the road right up the steep hill. As far as **nightlife** goes, Mayen is a dead loss; the only place with any action is *Rote Rooster*, Töpferstr. 3, which attracts a vaguely "alternative" crowd.

Monreal

A few kilometers down the line from Mayen, **MONREAL** is an attractive place, but one that it's best to allow a wide berth during vacation time. Off season, its streets of half-timbered houses look as though they belong on a cookie box lid. Look out for the **Johannisbrücke**, which spans the Elz River (a stream really). It's also worth taking some time to explore the **Philippsburg** and **Löwenburg**, the two ruined castles which tower over the village. A number of *Wanderwege* start in Monreal; information about these can be obtained from Mayen tourist office.

Maria Laach

By far the most outstanding historical monument in the Eifel is the Benedictine monastery of **Maria Laach**, which lies in an isolated setting of forests, meadows, and fields roughly 15km northwest of Mayen. Its name is derived from the adjacent **Laacher See**, which was formed by a volcanic cave-in, and which still has a primeval feel to it. Bus #6032 links Maria Laach with the nearest railroad station (NIEDERMENDIG) and with Mayen, while bus #6031 runs there from Andernach.

The **church** is a visual stunner, ranking as the most beautiful of all the great Romanesque buildings of the Rhineland. Its sense of unity is all the more remarkable in that, although begun at the end of the eleventh century, it was not finished until well into the thirteenth century. One of its most distinctive features is its stonework—for the most part, it's constructed from the local yellow-brown tufa, but dark basalt was used for architectural highlighting. Each end of the church is girded with an arrangement of three towers, presenting as varied and striking a silhouette as the Middle Ages ever produced.

Even more remarkable is the last part to be built, the **Paradise**, a courtyard placed in front of the building to enclose the western choir. Apparently intended as a symbol of the innocence of the Garden of Eden, it's unique in Christian architecture, being suggestive of Islamic places of worship, an impression strengthened by the addition of the burbling Lions' Fountain in the middle. The capitals, showing a fabulous bestiary, are carved with a gossamer delicacy by a mason dubbed the Samson Master, who is also known to have worked at Andernach and Bonn.

After all this, the pure Romanesque sobriety of the interior comes as a surprise. However, the early Gothic **baldachin** at the high altar is again reminiscent of the art of Islam, and is quite unlike any other such object in Europe. There's also a fine polychrome **tomb** of the founder, Count Palatine Heinrich II, shown in an idealized youthful reclining pose, clutching a model of the church. To see the **crypt**, the earliest part of the building, you have to join one of the regular guided tours (offering expected) conducted by the monks. Their services employ the Gregorian chant; vespers, at 5:30pm, finishes in time to catch the last bus out. You can **eat** in style at the monastery's own hotel, or more simply in the cafeteria alongside.

The Vulkaneifel

The **VULKANEIFEL** (*Volcanic Eifel*) was the scene of explosive volcanic activity until about 10,000 years ago, which has done a lot to shape the physical and economic landscape of the region. Both the distinctive circular **crater lakes** (*Maare*) which dot the area so handily for windsurfers and water-skiers, and the natural springs that draw thousands of *Kurort* visitors and keep local mineral water-bottlers in business, owe their existence to these geologically recent upheavals.

Daun

DAUN, the middle of the Vulkaneifel, can be reached from Mayen by bus or train. Around here, the post-volcanic crater lakes have been turned into restrained resorts with facilities for sailing, fishing and other water sports. Daun itself makes a good base for exploring the area since there are plenty of cheap hotels. In the center of town, *Manderscheid*, Wirichstr. 23 (☎06592 2210), has rooms from DM25 per person. Similar rates are available at *Berghof*, Lieserstr. 20 (☎06592 2891), and *Zum Post*, Muhlenweg 7 (☎06592 2151), in GEMÜNDEN, near the town's cluster of crater lakes.

The three lakes **Gemündener Maar**, **Weinfelder Maar** (or **Totenmaar**), and **Schalkenmehrener Maar** are all easily reached from Daun town center either on foot or by bus. Weinfelder is easily the most compelling. Of the three lakes it's the only one where boating and fishing are forbidden, and it has a melancholy, almost threatening atmosphere, enhanced by the forlorn chapel on its bank and the still, dark surface of the water. A little farther afield near GILLENFELD sprawl the **Pulvermaar**, the largest of the lakes, with **camping** facilities on its bank (☎06573 523 or 311).

Going back to Celtic times, Daun's old town center sits on top of a chunk of volcanic rock—its name means "fortified heights." Though it looks impressive as you approach, closer up it turns out to be a slightly bland market town and *Kurort*. The **tourist office** is in the *Kurzentrum*, Leopold Str. 14 (Mon.–Fri. 8:30am–6pm,

Sat. 10am–noon; ☎06592 71477), but the town doesn't really have any sights to speak of. The only substantial surviving part of the old castle, (the **Höhenburg**), is now a hotel, and apart from that the only place worth a passing look is the **Pfarrkirche**, just off Wirichstrasse, which dates back to the tenth century.

Ulmen and Kelberg
ULMEN, on the edge of the **Ulmener Maar**, 10km east of Daun, can be reached by bus or train. It merits a call for its ruined castle and lakeside atmosphere, although the planners have rather thoughtlessly cut the town in two with an expressway. **KELBERG**, a tiny *Luftkurort* surrounded by rolling woodland, also rates a visit, but is a bit more difficult to get to, with only a couple of buses per day from Daun. The Romanesque-Gothic **Pfarrkirche** is pretty enough, if unjustifiably proud of its fifteenth-century wooden crucifix.

Gerolstein
West of Daun, at the junction of the railroad line from Andernach with that between Trier and Cologne, is **GEROLSTEIN**. Again, its main assets are natural ones: a couple of dolomite rock pillars which tower over the town in a most spectacular way, harboring the remains of a 300-million-year-old coral reef. In the north side of the one called **Munterley** is the **Buchenloch**, a cave which was once home to a band of Neanderthals.

Otherwise, Gerolstein hasn't got much going for it. The Roman **Villa Sarabodis** is interesting enough, but there's not much left. For a bit of light relief you can always visit the factory that produces *Gerolsteiner Sprudel*, one of Germany's favorite mineral waters. For details and opening times, check with the **tourist office** in the Rathaus (Mon.–Thurs. 7:45am–12:30pm and 1:30–5pm, Fri. 7:45am–12:30pm and 1:30–4pm).

Manderscheid
From Daun there are fairly frequent buses through the deep wooded valley of the Lieser River then up the alternating wood- and heathland of the Vulkaneifel, to **MANDERSCHEID**. It's yet another touristy little *Kurort*, clinging tightly to the banks of the river. Above the eastern bank of the Lieser are two castles: the **Oberburg** and the **Unterburg**. Together they once formed part of an extensive fortification system which, in the fifteenth century, was thought to be impregnable. It wasn't. Both castles were sacked during the Thirty Years' War and later the troops of Louis XIV finished the job. Fortunately the city authorities have done pretty good restoration work on both buildings.

It's also worth taking a trip to the **Meerfeldermaar**, about 5km east of Manderscheid, and to the **Hinkelmaar** on top of the **Moosenberg** just southeast of the town. The Hinkelmaar, although relatively small, looks much more like a former volcano crater than some of the other *Maare*, and at one point you can see where lava once broke through its sides in a sixty-meter-wide stream.

Another attraction in the Manderscheid area is the **Abtei Himmerod**, an eighteenth-century monastery with an impressively austere baroque church attached. This was was once one of the most important religious houses in the Eifel and was favored by monastically-inclined sons of the local nobility until the French dissolved it in 1802 and sold the buildings. It's been well restored, but bear in mind that the place is a day-trippers' destination in the summer.

Manderscheid's **tourist office** is in the *Kurverwaltung* building (Mon.–Fri. 8am–12:30pm and 2–5pm, May–Oct. Sat. 10am–noon; ☎06572 2377). The town's

youth hostel is at Mosenbergerstr. 17 (☎06572 557). Best **hotel** bets are *Kupferpfanne*, Wittlicher Str. 25 (☎06572 4936), from DM22 per person, and *Haus Elilzabeth*, Am Hohlen Weg 14 (☎06572 4402).

Wittlich

Buses run from Manderscheid south to **WITTLICH**, a conventionally attractive town situated at the point where the Eifel starts to level out and the Mosel valley proper begins. In summer, the town's bars and cafés spill out on to the streets, creating an atmosphere that makes you forget that you're in northern Europe. Wittlich's special climate enhances the illusion; it's so mild here that the usual vineyards keep company with a tobacco plantation.

The town's **tourist office** occupies the southeastern corner of the baroque Altes Rathaus on Burgstrasse (Mon.–Fri. 9am–noon and 1–6pm, Sat. 10am–noon and 2–5pm; ☎06571 4086). The rest of the building is home to the **Städtische Gallerie**, which puts on regular exhibitions. In the immediate vicinity, around **Marktplatz**, there are some baroque houses, which do a lot to help create the town center's un-self-consciously historic feel. Nearby is the **St. Markuskirche**, an early baroque church which would be unexceptional were it not for its impressively tall, steep-roofed bell tower. There's also a significant local Roman leftover in the shape of the **Römervilla**, just off Schloss Strasse on the way out of town.

The vibrant local street life gets excessive during the third weekend in August when the **Saubrennerkirmes** is celebrated. This fair is marked by the usual drinking-and-eating extravaganza, plus the roasting of over a hundred pigs in the market place. This commemorates the grudge held against all pigs by the people of Wittlich ever since it was captured after a long siege, thanks to a pig who ate the turnip being used to hold the town gate shut.

Centrally located hotels include *Schneck*, Trierer Str. 52 (☎06571 5692), with singles from DM25 and doubles from DM50, and *Wittlicher Hof*, Trierer Str. 29 (☎06571 772), with singles from DM35 and doubles from DM60. The town is full of cafés and bars and most of the centrally located ones aren't bad; *Journal*, Neustr. 8, is the trendiest hangout.

Bitburg-Prüm

North of Trier is the administrative region of **Bitburg-Prüm** which has a few relatively undiscovered corners. **BITBURG** itself is a bit of a dump. Apart from the famous **Bitburger Brauerei** at Romerstrasse 3 (Mon.–Thurs. 9:30am–1:30pm), which supplies beer to the whole Eifel and beyond, and the **Bierbrunnen**, a copper fountain in the town center which dispenses beer on festival days, there's not really much to see or do. The town achieved notoriety in 1985, when **President Reagan** laid a wreath at the town's war cemetery, the burial place of 49 SS officers. Coming immediately after his visit to Belsen concentration camp, this insensitve gesture deeply offended Germany's Jewish community.

Should you need to stay on, the **tourist office**, Bedastr. 11 (☎06561 8934), will supply further information on the town and its accommodation facilities. However, it's probably best to bypass Bitburg altogether and head straight for of **KYLLBURG**, about 11km to the north by road or rail and easily reached from Trier. This is a *Kurort*, the sort of place that could be the setting for a Thomas Mann novella with its lazy ambience, turn-of-the-century hotels, and sun terraces for convalescents. It makes a good base for exploring the surrounding area which, although unexceptional, is tranquil in a low-key way. Main sights are the **Stiftskirche**, with an intact sixteenth-century stained glass window, and the thirteenth-century defensive tower, which has a good vertigo-inducing view of the surrounding area (pick up the key from the market garden next door).

The **tourist office** is in the *Kurverwaltung*, Hochstr. 19 (daily 8am-6pm; ☎06563 2007). **Camping** facilities are available just outside town at Karl-Kaufmann-Weg 1 (☎06563 2570). The most central **hotel** is *Zur Post*, Bahnhofstr. 30 (☎06563 2216), with rooms from DM26 per person.

It's an easy walk of about 1km from Kyllburg to **Malberg**, a sixteenth-century castle which towers above the attached village in true fairy-tale fashion. A little to the east of Kyllburg is SEINSFELD, with a moated medieval castle. Halfway to Bitburg, just outside the village of NATTENHEIM, lies **Villa Otrang**, the best-preserved Roman monument in the area. You get a good impression of the original layout and there are some vivid animal mosaics.

From Kyllburg head for **PRÜM** by one of the three direct buses per day, or take the train to to Gerolstein and then a bus from there. This is a soporific little ex-market town (the Marktplatz is now a parking lot) and winter sports center. The **tourist office** is on Hahnplatz (☎06551 505) directly opposite the main tourist attraction, the baroque-fronted **Salvatorbasilica**, which was designed by Seitz and Neumann, the team responsible for the Matthiaskirche in Trier. Inside are the obligatory holy relic (a fragment of Christ's sandal) and tomb of local royal personage (Lothar I, grandson of Charlemagne).

In winter Prüm becomes a weekend skiers' mecca with a couple of good runs at the **Wolfschlucht** (just outside town) and on the **Schwarzer Mann**, the highest Eifel ridge, which is in a part of the range known as the **Schnee-Eifel** (or **Schneifel**), about 14km northwest of Prüm. For skiing information, contact the Prüm tourist office.

Prüm has plenty of central **hotels**; *Zum Goldenen Stern*, on Hahnplatz (☎06551 3075), has rooms from DM29 per person, while the less central *Haus Gertrud*, Reginostr. 42 (☎06551 3258), charges upwards of DM22 per head. There's a **youth hostel** (☎06551 2500) on the edge of town, at the top of an agonizingly steep hill.

For a real taste of the region's raw beauty head for **NEUERBERG** (four buses a day from Prüm), a picturesque little village in the remote Enztal, whose partially-ruined castle houses a privately-owned **youth hostel**. *Gasthof Balmes*, Kirchgasse 1 (☎06564 2314), is one of the cheaper **hotels**. There are **camping** facilities at Pestalozzistr. 7 (☎06564 2071), while the **tourist office** is at Herrenstr. 2 (☎06564 2017).

SAARLAND

The **Saarland**, taking its name from the river Saar which cuts through its length, is the poorest of the West German Länder, traditionally a big coal mining area which is now suffering from a bad case of postindustrial malaise. It's always been a bit of a political football; much of it belonged to France up until 1815, and a couple of times during this century they've tried to get their hands on it again. After World War I the Saarland passed onto League of Nations control, which effectively meant that the French took over, with the right to exploit local mines in compensation for damage done to their own mining industry during the war. In a January 1935 plebiscite ninety percent of Saarlanders voted for union with Nazi

Germany. After World War II the Saar once again found itself in limbo, nominally autonomous but with the French government, which was pushing for economic union, calling the shots. In November 1952 the population voted against reunion with Germany, but by January 1957 the increasing prosperity of the Federal Republic had convinced the the Saarlanders that their future lay there, and they thus rejoined the fold—much to the chagrin of the French government.

Most Germans see the Saarland only from the vantage point of one of the various expressways that criss-cross it; if you're driving through, it has to be said there aren't really any compelling reasons for getting out of your car. It's unlikely to be a place you'd want to go out of your way to visit, but if you happen to be in the area then there are one or two marginally interesting places and, away from the heavily industrialized areas, the gently rolling wooded landscape is relatively inoffensive. The French have left a small linguistic legacy in the shape of the greeting *Salü* which replaces the normal *Guten Tag* here. Of late there's also been a marked French influence on local **cuisine**, traditionally always a poor man's fare, based on a thousand-and-one potato variations like *Hooriche* (raw potato rissoles).

Politically, the Saarland has left a mark out of all proportion to its size. Erich Honecker, the veteran GDR head of state, was born in the town of Neunkirchen, where his sister—untempted by the regime he has been so prominent in molding—is still a Communist Party activist. Furthermore, the Land's current Minister-President, Oskar Lafontaine, is seen as the main future hope of the SPD, if the party is to recover from its long period in the doldrums at federal level.

Saarbrücken

The relative poverty of the Saarland is nowhere more apparent than in the capital **SAARBRÜCKEN**, which, despite the efforts of both the German and French governments over the years, remains a shabby industrial town. It's the kind of place that lists among its attractions the *Bergwerksdirektion* (Mining Administration Office), and apart from a few central historic buildings is almost unrelievedly modern.

The town (whose name means "Saar bridges"), has a vague harbor feel. What sights there are lie south of the river. There's a nondescript Schloss—which has seen better days—on the square of the same name, with a fifteenth-century **Schlosskirche** containing tombs of the princes of Nassau-Saarbrücken. (Some of these are replicas of the originals destroyed in the war.) About the most interesting feature of the Schloss is its park, and that suffers from its view over the autobahn.

The Schloss was designed during the eighteenth century by Friedrich Joachim Stengel, Saarbrücken's municipal architect, who also built the **Altes Rathaus** opposite. Today this houses the **Abenteuer Museum** (Tues. and Weds 9am–1pm, Thurs and Fri. 3–7pm, Sat. 10am–2pm; DM2), devoted in roughly equal parts to the lives and cultures of "primitive" peoples and to the ego of its founder Heinz Rox-Schulz, who has spent most of his life traveling to far-flung corners of the world collecting and filming. Bizarre items from the collection include a 2000-year-old Peruvian mummy and some shrunken heads.

From Schlossplatz head down Schlossstrasse and turn right into Eisenbahnstrasse. On the right you'll see the plain, white mid-eighteenth century **Friedenskirche** (*Peace Church*), which has a startlingly austere interior, with

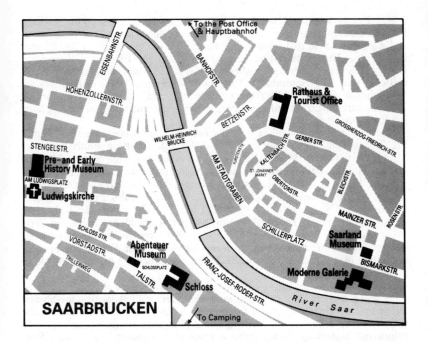

SAARBRUCKEN

just a single crucifix as decoration. Opposite in Ludwigsplatz is the baroque
Ludwigskirche, designed by Stengel and generally reckoned to be the best
church in the Saarland despite the fact that it was burned down in 1944 and has
been extensively restored. It's an odd building, quite low and severe, with a
strangely truncated octagonal tower. The interior, including the imposing pulpit,
is painted in brilliant white. At no. 15 on the square is the **Museum für Vor und
Früh Geschichte** (Tues.–Sat. 9am–4pm, Sun. 10am–5pm; free), an extensive but
dull archaeology collection.

The **Deutschherrenkapelle** in Moltkestrasse to the west of the city center is
Saarbrücken's oldest building, dating back to the thirteenth century, although
you wouldn't know it at first glance, because it has been frequently and radically
altered ever since. At the eastern end of town, on St. Arnualer Markt, is the
Stiftskirche St. Arnual, a solid early Gothic affair, topped by a baroque tower.
Inside there are a few tombs of members of the Nassau-Saarbrücken family; the
most spectacular are those of Count Johann III and Elizabeth von Lotharingen.

Crossing the **Alte Brücke** (originally sixteenth-century, but extensively redesigned a couple of hundred years later) brings you to the north bank of the Saar.
On the right is the **Staatstheater**, an angular, monumental building, nowadays
used for musicals and drama, and a good example of the kind of architectural
thinking that went on in the Third Reich. Head up Saarstrasse to St. Johanner
Markt, an old town square with some elegant eighteenth-century houses and a
baroque fountain, all designed by Stengel. Nearby stands the **Basilika St.
Johann**, a standard eighteenth-century baroque church also designed by Stengel
and financed by Louis XV of France.

St. Johanner Markt and Bahnhofstrasse to the northwest are supposedly where it's at in Saarbrücken—there are a few expensive shops, cafés, and restaurants, and a general sense that what money there is in the city tends to find its way here. In the **Altstadtgalerie** at St. Johanner-Markt 24 (Tues.–Sun. 10am–6pm; DM2) you'll find mainly eighteenth-century arts and crafts, while the **Moderne Gallerie und Alte Sammlung** (Tues.–Sun. 10am–6pm; DM2) at Bismarckstr. 11–15 has a passable collection of nineteenth- and twentieth-century art. It includes works by Raoul Dufy, Pissarro, Monet, and Franz Marc; on the first floor is a Rodin sculpture, *Despair*.

Saarbrücken's **tourist office** is in the *Info-Pavillon*, Trierer Strasse 2 (Mon.–Fri. 7:30am–8pm, Sat. 7:30–4pm; ☎0681 309 8222). There's a **youth hostel** at Meerwiesertalweg 31 (☎0681 33040), on the northeastern edge of town (bus #15, #16 or #4 from Bahnhofstrasse), and a *Naturfreundehaus* at Piesporter Weg (☎0681 74617). The cheapest central **hotels** are *St. Johanner Hof*, Mainzer Str. 3 (☎0681 34902), which has singles from DM30 and doubles from DM60, and *Bayrischer Hof*, St. Ingberter Str. 46 (☎0681 62545), with singles from DM28 and doubles from DM55. The local **camping** facilities are at Am Spicherer Berg (☎0681 51780), a few kilometers south of Saarbrücken on the Franco-German border. For non-EC citizens, who may require visas to visit France, the **French consulate** is at Johannisstr. 2 (☎0681 30626). Saarbrücken's **Mitfahrzentrale** is at Rosenstr. 31 (☎0681 67981).

Saarbrücken is a student town and you do get the feeling that there's something going on here, thanks in part to a strong arty contingent who are always trying to get various projects off the ground. A good way of finding out **what's happening** is to buy the *Stadtzeitung* (DM3), the local listings magazine which comes out bi-monthly. There's also a monthly information sheet called *Salü Saarbrücken*, which often has useful tips, available from the tourist office. One unusual event is the *Perspectives du Théâtre* **festival** of young French theater, held here every May, which usually features a few avant-garde offerings. Also worth knowing about is the *Max Ophüls-Preis* film festival held every January. Saarbrücken's **women's center** is at Türkenstr. 15 (Mon.–Fri. 8am–6pm, Sun. 2–6pm).

As for **eating** and **drinking** there are quite a few possibilities. The place to see and be seen in Saarbrücken is *Brasserie Fröschengasse* in Fröschengasse. For cheap Greek food, there's *Paros Gourmet* on Fass Strasse near the St. Johannermarkt; for reasonably priced local fare, try *Bastei*, Saaruferstr. 16, on the south bank of the Saar, while *Naturkost*, at the junction of Wilhelm-Heinrich-Strasse and Franz-Josef-Röder-Strasse, is the best bet for health food.

Worth mentioning is the *Kultur Café*, which forms part of the Stadtgalerie just off the St. Johanner Markt. Here, as well as being able to sit outside, you can also have art with your coffee as exhibitions are held on the second floor. The center of the local **gay** scene (men and women) is *Big Ben* in Försterstrasse, open most evenings. For **live jazz**, go to *Jazzkeller Giesskanne*, Am Steg 3.

Elsewhere in Saarland

At the eastern end of the Land, and easily reached by train from Saarbrücken, is **HOMBURG**. There's nothing much of interest in the town itself, but about ten minutes south by rail, just outside the village of SCHWARZENACKER, is the **Römisches Freilichtmuseum Schwarzenacker** (April–Nov.Mon.–Sat.

9:30am–noon and 1:15–5:30pm, Sun. 9:30am–noon and 1:15–6pm, Dec.–March Wed 9:30am–4:30pm, Sat. and Sun. noon–4:30pm, weather permitting), a big open-air museum on the site of an old Roman settlement which has been partly excavated and reconstructed. Also in the vicinity of Homburg are the **Schlossberghöhlen** (guided tours May–Sept. Mon.–Fri. at 4:30pm, Sat. 2–6pm, Sun. 10am–noon and 2–6pm, Oct.–April Sat. 3–6pm, Sun. 11am–noon and 2–6pm), a series of sandstone caves on twelve levels, covering 5km altogether. They were hollowed out over six centuries and at one time the sand from them was one of the area's main exports. During the seventeenth and eighteenth centuries, the caves were occupied by the French, who turned them into a frontier fortress, while in the last war they served as a massive communal air-raid shelter for the people of Homburg. Nearby there's a ruined **Schloss** set in gloomy wooded grounds.

Homburg **tourist office** is in the Rathaus, Am Forum (☎06841 2066) and there's a **youth hostel** at Sickingstr. 12 (☎06841 3679). The cheapest **hotels** are *Fasanerie Ursula Kiefer*, Kaiserslauterer Str. 21 (☎06841 65848), and *Haus Bergfrieden*, Steinbergstr. 16 (☎06841 244; in EINÖD), both of which have singles from DM30 and doubles from DM50.

About 15km by rail from Homburg (change at NEUNKIRCHEN) lies **ST. WENDEL**, a pleasant little market town whose main attraction is the Gothic **St. Wendelinuskirche**, with three towers and richly decorated interior. En route, you might want to break the journey at **OTTWEILER** which has a well-preserved medieval Altstadt. In the village of **OTZENHAUSEN**, just outside Nonnweiler, about 27km north of St. Wendel (train to TURKISMÜHL and then take bus #6430 to NONNWEILER), are the remains of a Celtic **Ringwall** or fortified hillside settlement.

Traveling west out of Saarbrücken you come to **SAARLOUIS**, a biggish town, originally built as a frontier fortress in 1680 by Louis XIV's architect, Sebastian Vauban. The town passed into Prussian hands in 1814 and although its fortress role was abandoned in 1889 much of the old Prussian fortification network, the **Kasematten**, is still intact—the buildings now house shops and bars rather than soldiers and cannons. Saarlouis has long since spilled out of its old confines but the center still retains a regularity that could only be the product of the military mind, and the town's main square, the **Grosser Markt**, is actually the former parade ground. Appropriately enough, the town's most famous son was a soldier—Marshal Ney, Napoleon's favorite general.

Heading northeast by road or rail will bring you to **METTLACH**, one of Saarland's prettier towns. The baroque **Abtei**, an eighteenth-century restoration of a much older structure, really stands out—but unfortunately it can't be visited as it's used as offices and a private museum by a ceramics firm. The more valuable treasures, including a triptych reliquary, can be seen in the **Pfarrkirche St. Liutwin**. In the woods of the nearby park, whose entrance is marked by a neat neoclassical fountain designed by Karl Friedrich Schinkel, stands the octagonal **Alter Turm**, a tenth-century Romanesque mausoleum. A couple of reasonable **hotels** in Mettlach are *Haus Becker*, at the corner of Steinbach and Saarschleife (☎06864 289), and *Kuhn*, Freiherr-vom-Stein-Str. 14 (☎06864 583), which both have singles from DM25 and doubles from DM50.

Take bus #6300 from Mettlach to the village of ORSHCOLZ, from where you can walk to **Cloef**, a viewpoint overlooking the Saar *Schleife*, a colossal loop in the river which has created a narrow wooded peninsula. There's a **youth hostel** in the village of DREISBACH (☎06868 270; bus #6300 from Mettlach). The same bus goes to **NENNIG**, in the Mosel valley very close to the Luxembourg border, where there's an old **Schloss** and, more significantly, the remains of the **Römischer Mosaikfussboden** (Tues.–Sun. April–Sept. 8:30am–noon and 1–6pm, Oct.–March 9am–noon and 1–4:30pm; DM1). Along with the huge villa to which it belonged, this Roman floor mosaic was unearthed by a farmer in 1852 on the southeastern edge of the village. The mosaic originally formed part of the villa entrance hall and includes vivid and detailed depictions of gladiatorial combat. There are **camping** facilities at Sinzer Strasse 1 (☎06866 322) in Nennig itself.

travel details

Trains
From Mainz to Koblenz (frequent; 50min), Worms (2 hourly; 40min).

From Koblenz to Trier (1; 90min).
From Saarbrücken to Mainz (1; 2½hr), Koblenz (1; 2½hr).

CHAPTER FIVE

NORTH RHINELAND-WESTPHALIA

NORTH RHINELAND-WESTPHALIA (*Nordrhein-Westfalen*) is only the fourth largest of the Länder in terms of area, but has, with 17 million inhabitants, by far the largest population. As its double-barreled name suggests, it's historically two distinct provinces, the North Rhineland having belonged to the Franks, while Westphalia marked the beginning of Saxon territory. During the industrialization process of the nineteenth century, the distinction between the two became hopelessly blurred by the mushroom growth of a vast built-up area around the mineral-rich valley of the river Ruhr. This formed a clearly recognizable unit, yet divided almost exactly in half by the traditional boundaries. After World War II, it was decided to preserve the economic integrity of the "Ruhrgebiet," as the area came to be known, by uniting the two provinces. In any event, both had lost a great deal of their former identities by internal migration, a factor subsequently compounded by high immigration from abroad.

Of the 31 West German cities registering a population of over 200,000, ten are in the North Rhineland, and a farther six in Westphalia. Many begin just as another ends, and the Ruhrgebiet is joined to a string of other cities stretching right to the southern border of Rhineland-Pfalz, making up the most densely populated area in Europe. In this conurbation, **Cologne** is by far the most outstanding city, managing to preserve much of the atmosphere and splendors of its long centuries as a free state, at times the most powerful in Germany. The Land's other city of first-class historical interest is **Aachen**, the original capital of the Holy Roman Empire. Next in line comes **Münster**, which would presumably be capital of Westphalia, if a separate province still existed. As it is, the Land government meets in self-consciously cosmopolitan **Düsseldorf**, which inspires admiration and revulsion in roughly equal measure. The federal capital, **Bonn**, sits at the southern end of the Land; as the years go by, it seems ever more unsuitable for the role it was so casually given in 1949. While the target of endless criticism, it's a place all too easily and unfairly maligned.

In spite of the stranglehold heavy industry has traditionally held over North Rhineland-Westphalia, much of the landscape is rural, with agriculture and forestry making key contributions to the economy. The **Eifel** in the Rhineland, and the **Sauerland**, **Siegerland** and **Teutoburger Wald** in Westphalia all offer varied scenery, and are popular holiday spots with the Germans themselves, being such obvious antidotes to urban life. In these areas some wonderful small towns—**Monschau**, **Bad Münstereifel**, **Soest** and **Lemgo**—can stand comparison with any in Germany. Their counterparts along the Rhine have been scarred by war, but **Brühl** and **Xanten** are still particularly worth visiting.

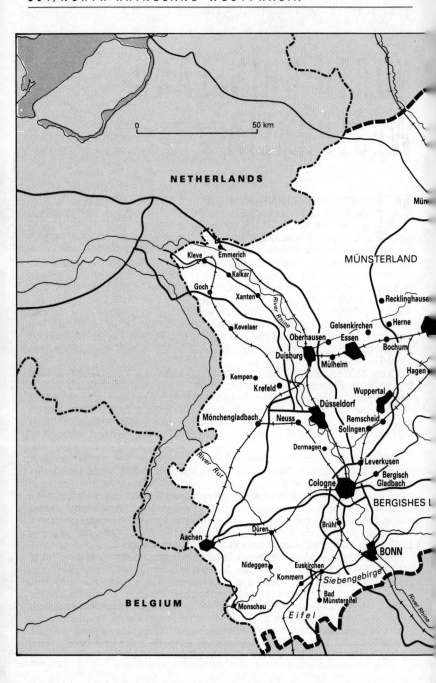

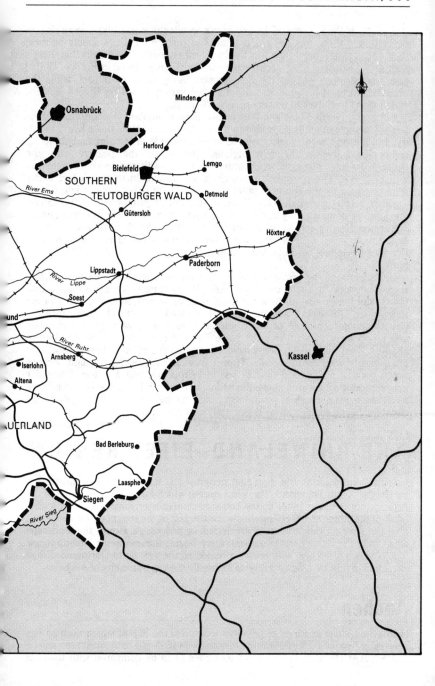

Sobriety is the keynote of the province's architecture; new styles were slow to develop, and there was far less readiness to replace buildings simply because they were old-fashioned than was the case farther south. This means that there's a legacy of **Romanesque architecture** which is unsurpassed in Europe. Gothic also took strong root, but the Renaissance barely made an impact, while the preferred form of baroque was the dignified variety based on Roman models, which didn't lend itself to flowery rococo offshoots.

Currently, North Rhineland-Westphalia faces a number of **economic problems**. Unemployment is high, due to the recent need to scale down heavy industry, and it hasn't been as successful as other Länder in developing and attracting companies active in the new high-tech fields. On the positive side, the *Gastarbeiter* have managed to integrate fairly well, with racism kept reasonably well in check. The province's main cities are now multicultural, a fact tacitly acknowledged by the common practice of translating public notices into Greek, Turkish, Serbo-Croat, Italian and Spanish—but not English or French. Politically, the Land is dominated by the Social Democrats; current Minister-President is **Johannes Rau**, a former candidate for the chancellorship, who, contrary to expectation, failed to develop into the party's much-needed successor to Willi Brandt and Helmut Schmidt, but who has now clearly found the right niche for himself.

Getting around the province couldn't be simpler. There's an extensive **public transit** network, including two integrated systems of main-line and S-Bahn trains, trams, and buses; one of these is based in Cologne and Bonn, the other in the Ruhrgebiet, Düsseldorf, and the Lower Rhineland. You can therefore turn the claustrophobic character of the conurbation to your advantage—it's certainly never necessary to wait long for some form of conveyance from one city to another. Even the country areas have a generous allocation of buses, which are often hardly used by the locals. Transit **freaks**, incidentally, will find oddities worth making a special detour to see in **Wuppertal** and **Minden**. Prices for **accommodation** are well above the national average in the cities, but there's the usual extensive network of youth hostels and campgrounds, while lodging in the countryside and smaller towns is generally excellent value.

THE RHINELAND–EIFEL REGION

Upland countryside is the dominant geographical feature of the southwestern part of the North Rhineland. The **Eifel range**, which forms a continuation of the Ardennes in Belgium, takes up the lion's share of this territory, while on the east bank of the Rhine the **Siebengebirge** are the last of the mountain ranges which give the river so much of its characteristic grandeur. At **Bonn**, the landscape adjacent to the Rhine flattens out, and there begins the enormous built-up megalopolis which stretches, with hardly a break, all the way up to Dortmund. Prime attraction of this area, however, is undoubtedly the venerable city of **Aachen**.

Aachen

"In Aachen I saw all kinds of priceless treasures, the like of which no man has seen rarer," wrote Dürer following a visit there in 1560. His enthusiasm can still be echoed; **AACHEN** possesses fabulous riches fit to be compared with those of

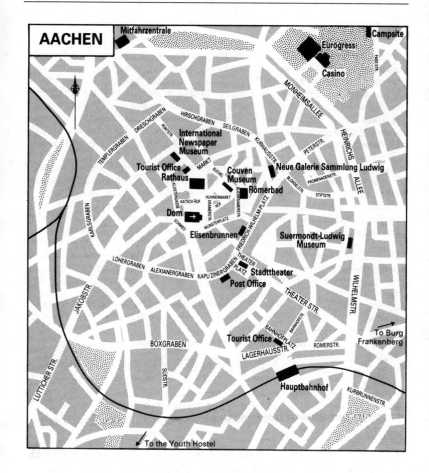

Istanbul or Venice, and it ranks, along with Cologne, as one of the two cities in North Rhineland-Westphalia which should on no account be missed. Now a frontier post—the municipal area includes stretches of border with both Belgium and the Netherlands, making it something of a smugglers' den—it has declined from a far grander role. In the late eighth and early ninth centuries the city was seen as the successor to ancient Rome, the hub of the great Frankish empire of **Charlemagne** which comprised pretty well all of present-day Germany, France, the Benelux, Austria, and Switzerland, as well as much of Italy and part of northern Spain. In 794, after 26 years of almost constant campaigning, Charlemagne established Aachen as the main seat of his court. The choice was made partly for strategic reasons, but also because of the presence of hot springs, over which the Romans had first built thermal baths. Exercising in these waters was one of the emperor's favorite pastimes, and his contemporaries rated him a swimmer without peer. The spa has continually given the city prestige and visitors, but its political power was short-lived, lasting only a generation after Charlemagne's death.

The Dom and Around

Modern Aachen's historical center—the interesting part—is reached from the **Hauptbahnhof** in about ten minutes by following Bahnhofstrasse and then turning right into Theaterstrasse. It's small and compact, and can comfortably be seen in a day, though you'll need longer to take in more than a few of the city's varied and excellent museums. Badly damaged in the last war, Aachen was also devastated by a terrible fire in 1656. This accounts for the unusually large number of baroque buildings by north German standards; their restrained, classically-derived style is a world away from the wild fantasies which were all the rage in Bavaria.

Thankfully, though the surviving architectural legacy of the Carolingian period is negligible, Aachen retains its crowning jewel in the former **Palace chapel**. Now forming the heart and soul of the present-day **Dom**, its presence is enshrined in the French name for the city, *Aix-la-Chapelle*. A ninth-century monk-chronicler, Notker the Stammerer, relates how skilled workmen were brought from many lands in order that this edifice should surpass any previously erected, and concludes that it was "built by human hands, yet with the inspiration of God." Charlemagne's courtier Einhard, who must have watched the building's construction, attributed its splendor to the Emperor's religious devotion, and fills in details of the decoration: "gold and silver, with lamps, and with lattices and doors of solid bronze." He also explained that marble columns were brought from as far as Ravenna, on whose basilica of San Vitale the chapel was largely modeled; indeed, the Pope's letter to Charlemagne authorizing the removal of marbles and mosaics from the palace there still exists.

Even after such descriptions, you can't help being overwhelmed by the Dom's extraordinary symmetry, height and grandeur. Designed by **Odo von Metz**, it's an eight-sided dome, surrounded by a sixteen-sided ambulatory, above which is a two-tiered gallery with eight arcades of columns; the number eight is significant, representing perfection and harmony. The circumference of the octagon is 144 Carolingian feet—the cardinal number of the heavenly Jerusalem—and that of the outer polygon exactly twice that: an impeccable concord and order which are intended to symbolize Heaven. As a result of the cult of Charlemagne (he was canonized by an antipope in 1165), and the possession of the so-called Great Aachen Relics (allegedly the swaddling clothes and loin cloth of Christ, the gown of the Virgin, and the garb of St. John the Baptist), pilgrims poured into the city in such numbers that there became a pressing need to expand the building. An airily high and narrow **Gothic chancel** was therefore added, again modeled on a great building from elsewhere in Europe, the Sainte Chapelle in Paris. Its original stained glass has been lost, but the modern replacements at least give the right effect. Also from this period is a series of two-story chapels encircling the octagon. The one specially endowed for the use of Hungarian pilgrims was later replaced by an Italianate baroque design, as successive epochs continued to leave their mark on the Dom; another important addition was the western tower, which was under construction for several centuries.

Some of the original furnishings survive: in the vestibule you can see the bronze doors with lions' heads mentioned by Einhard, along with a pine-cone which seems to have been a water-spout, and an antique she-wolf. These are rather overshadowed by the embellishments crafted from the costliest of materials with which Charlemagne's successors enhanced the Dom, making it positively drip with treasure. Adorning the main altar is the **Pala d'Oro**, an early eleventh-century antependium (altar front) with ten embossed scenes of the Passion. Behind, and of similar date, is the **ambo**, a pulpit like no other, fashioned from gold-plated copper adorned with precious stones, reliefs of the Evangelists, and ancient Egyptian ivories of profane subjects. Suspended from the dome by a mighty iron chain is the enormous twelfth-century **chandelier** given by Frederick Barbarossa, with 48 candles and sixteen towers. Regrettably, its weight quickly caused the mosaics to crack; those to be seen today are a nineteenth-century attempt at recreating the originals. The gilded **shrine of Charlemagne** has recently returned to its position at the end of the chancel, following a decade of restoration. Finished in 1215, after fifty years in the making, it contains the mortal remains of the saint, who is depicted on the front. It also serves as a glorification of the Holy Roman Empire he founded, with portraits of his successors along the sides, instead of the normal biblical personages. The lofty status accorded Charlemagne is emphasized by the early fifteenth-century statue of him on the pier behind, the only outsider in a cycle of the Virgin and Apostles.

In the gallery is the **imperial throne**, a marble chair with a wooden seat approached by six steps, in the manner of that in Solomon's temple; from here the emperor had a grandstand view of all that was happening below. Although popularly believed to have belonged to Charlemagne, it now seems certain that it's at least a century more recent, perhaps made for the coronation of Otto I, which initiated the tradition of emperors being crowned at Aachen, a practice which lasted until the sixteenth century. In order to see the throne (with the added bonus of a different perspective on the Dom and its furnishings) you've no choice but to join a **guided tour**. These cost DM2 and leave from the **Schatzkammer**, which has its own entrance on Klostergasse; there are at least a couple a day, rising to hourly departures at the height of the season.

The Schatzkammer itself (Tues.–Sat. 10am–5pm, Sun. 10:30am–5pm, Mon. 10am–2pm; in summer, open until 8pm on Thurs., 6pm on weekdays other than Mon.; DM3) is as much an essential sight as the Dom. It's the richest treasury in northern Europe, a dazzling feast for the eyes and an unashamed glorification of the wealth and power of the Church Triumphant. For maximum security, the most valuable pieces are kept in the basement. Prominent among them is the greatest of all processional crucifixes, the late tenth-century **Lothair cross**, studded with jewels and bearing an antique cameo of the Emperor Augustus; the Crucifixion is modestly engraved on the reverse. From the beginning of the following century come a **holy water vessel**, carved from an elephant's tusk, and a **golden book cover** with an ivory of the Madonna and Child, made as an accessory to the Pala d'Oro in the decoration of the altar. A damaged **ivory diptych** is the only item from the time of Charlemagne, while the large **Roman sarcophagus** carved with a scene of the rape of Proserpina served as the emperor's improbable coffin for 400 years. Finally, there's the thirteenth-century **shrine of the Virgin**, made to house the great Aachen relics, but not started until the companion piece dedicated to Charlemagne had at last been completed—another revealing illustration of how important his cult had become. On the ground floor, pride of place belongs to the **base plates** of the great chandelier, delicately engraved with angels and scenes from the life of Christ. Among many superb **reliquaries**, note the idealized portrait head of Charlemagne. Gifts from such devotees as Margaret of York and Louis of Hungary (who also endowed the chapel for his country's pilgrims) show the international extent of the Aachen cults. The astonishing vibrancy of the local goldsmith tradition through the centuries is proved by the sixteenth-century work of **Hans von Reutlingen**, which stands comparison with any of the older masterpieces.

Charlemagne's palace once extended across the Katsch Hof, now lined with ugly modern buildings, to the site of the present **Rathaus**. Facing the Markt, which boasts the finest of the medieval houses left in the city, its facade is lined with the figures of fifty Holy Roman Emperors—31 of them crowned in Aachen. Above the entrance, Charlemagne shares a niche with Christ and Pope Leo III, who conducted his coronation ceremony in Rome on Christmas Day 800. Built in the fourteenth century on the palace foundations, and incorporating two of its towers, the Rathaus is a mix of attempts to restore its original Gothic form with the inevitable baroque changes of later years. The glory of the interior (Mon.–Fri. 8am–1pm and 2–5pm, Sat. and Sun. 10am–1pm and 2–5pm, but liable to closure at any time for civic receptions; DM1) is the much-restored **Kaisersaal**. Here the Charlemagne Prize is awarded annually to the citizen deemed to have made the largest contribution to European unity, an ideal the city sees as having begun during its own imperial days. Five large frescos (by the Düsseldorf artist Alfred Rethel) give a romantic portrayal of scenes from Charlemagne's life, but your attention is more likely to be drawn by the crown jewels, dazzlingly displayed at one end. These are only reproductions, however; the originals have been kept in Vienna since the early nineteenth century, when they were commandeered by the Habsburgs (who had been hereditary holders of the title of Holy Roman Emperor for centuries) for their new role as Emperors of Austria. There's also a bronze statue of Charlemagne which was formerly part of the fountain in the Markt; it was replaced in 1969 after constant maltreatment.

This fountain is only one of seventeen which dot the streets of the spa city. Most popular is the **Puppenbrunnen** (*Dolls' Fountain*), reached down Krämerstrasse; each doll—a rider, a market woman, a harlequin, a canon, and a model—has moving limbs and represents a particular facet of Aachen life. In strong contrast is the stern neoclassical solemnity of the **Elisenbrunnen**, a rotunda with two pavilions designed by **Schinkel** as the public drinking fountain, which lies due east. Plaques on the walls list the names of illustrious visitors to the springs, liberally augmented by many graffiti artists making their bid for immortality. The pervading smell is sulphuric, and the taste of the water—if you find its heat palatable—is hardly more appetizing.

Aachen's Museums

Burg Frankenberg, *Bismarckstr. 68. Tues.–Fri. 10am–5pm, Sat. and Sun. 10am–1pm; DM1.*
This much-restored medieval moated castle southeast of the city center contains the local history museum. Though mainly of parochial appeal, it has interesting models which attempt to recreate the likely original form of Charlemagne's palace. Ceramic products from Aachen are displayed in the tower.

Couven Museum, *Hühner Markt. Tues.–Fri. 10am–5pm, Sat. and Sun. 10am–1pm; DM1.*
Named after a father and son team of architects who endowed Aachen with many baroque buildings, this elegant merchants' home has been embellished with period furnishings from the mid-eighteenth to mid-nineteenth centuries gathered from houses of the Aachen-Liège region, giving an idea of the stylish if frivolous priorities of the local bourgeoisie. Look out for the complete apothecary, a lavishly decorated first-floor living room with carved chimneypiece, and the huge Advent crib in the attic.

International Newspaper Museum, *Pontstr. 13. Tues.–Fri. 9:30am–1pm and 2:30–5pm, Sat. 9:30am–1pm; free.*

In 1850 **Paul Julius von Reuter** established his famous news agency, still a watchword in the world of the media, in another house in this street; carrier pigeons were initially used to circulate the reports. The museum, founded in his memory, boasts a collection of some 120,000 newspapers. An exhibition room has been set up to show by means of original editions how the press (German and English language examples dominate) reacted to the great stories of the day, from the 1848 revolutions to contemporary conflicts, by way of the two world wars. The obituaries of major figures prove that posterity's verdict is often very different from the instant response, while some curiosities are offered for light relief. If you're seriously interested, you can apply to see particular issues.

Neue Galerie Sammlung Ludwig, *Komphausbadstr. 19. Mon. and Tues. 10am–1pm and 3–7pm, Thurs. and Fri. 10am–1pm and 3–10pm, Sat. and Sun. 10am–2pm; DM1.*

Housed in the ornate setting of the Altes Kurhaus ("old spa rooms"), a late eighteenth-century building by the younger Couven, this gallery of modern art has changing loan displays as well as others drawn from its own holdings, which are too extensive to show all at once. What's on display at any one time is obviously luck of the draw, but American painting is well represented by **Roy Lichtenstein**, **Andy Warhol**, **Jasper Johns** and the realist school, among which is a portrait of Richard Serra by **Chuck Close** and sculptures by **Duane Hanson**, **John de Andrea** and **Nancy Graves**. Also worthy of note are **Claes Oldenburg**'s *Banana Splits and Ice Cream*, and a papier-mâché by a contemporary German sculptor, **Thomas Lanigan-Schmidt**, *A Rite of Passage—the Leprachaun*, which took eleven years to make. Soviet art is another strength—the star piece is **Dimitri Shilinsky**'s *Adam and Eve*, depicting the artist and his wife.

Suermondt-Ludwig Museum, *Wilhelmstr. 18. Tues.–Fri. 10am–5pm, Sat. and Sun. 10am–1pm; DM1.*

The ground floor of this museum has an excellent collection of northern European medieval sculpture, with a bewildering array of Pietà, Madonnas and Passions. These are almost exclusively anonymous and predominantly folksy in style, though some, such as the large Lower Rhenish *St. Peter Altar*, achieve a rather more developed artistic sense. In Room V are virtuoso baroque fancies, including a miniaturization of the Markt fountain, by **Dietrich von Rath**, the last important Aachen goldsmith. On the first floor, the collection of paintings ranges from Flemish and Cologne primitives through Dutch cabinet pictures, to twentieth-century German works; highlights are **Joos van Cleve**'s *Madonna of the Cherries*, **Cranach**'s *Judith*, **Ribera**'s *Holy Night*, **Zurbarán**'s *St. Francis* and a brilliant **Rubens** sketch, *The Fall of the Damned*. The top floor features a display of modern stained glass, including one by **Ewald Mataré**, an Aachen artist best known for his role in creating new works for German cathedrals and churches during postwar restoration. A number of his sculptures are also on view.

Practicalities and Entertainments

Aachen's main **tourist office** (Mon.–Fri. 9am–6:30pm, Sat. 9am–1pm; ☎180 2960) occupies Haus Löwenstein on the Markt, the oldest surviving house in the city; there's a branch immediately opposite the Hauptbahnhof (same times; ☎180 2965). **Camping** is possible just to the northeast of downtown at Pass Str. 85

(☎155495). The **youth hostel** is much farther away, situated on a little hill in a suburban park to the southwest, at Maria-Theresia-Allee 260 (☎71101; take bus #2 direction Preuswald from the Elisenbrunnen, and get down at Brüsseler Ring or Ronheide). Two of the cheaper **hotels** are near the Hauptbahnhof; on Bahnhofplatz itself *Kistermann* (☎32389) charges around DM35 for a single, DM70 a double, while a couple of blocks to the left *Hesse*, Friedlandstr. 20 (☎34047) has singles at DM32, doubles DM65. Also within walking distance is *Pension Göbbels*, Karlsburgweg 16 (☎21376); the four rooms cost DM23 for a single, DM40 a double. Other budget possibilities tend to be far out—*Göbel*, Trierer Str. 546 (☎523244) charges from DM25 per person; *Hansa Haus*, Von-Coels-Str. 42 (☎551380) has singles at DM28, doubles DM52; while *Neuenhof*, Vaalser Str. 387 (☎74518) costs from DM30 for a single, DM50 a double.

Many of the best places to **eat** and **drink** are found **in and around the Markt**. *Printen*, a spiced gingerbread, has the main claim to culinary peculiarity; *the* place to eat it is the old coffee house *Leo van den Daele* on Büchel. The only locally-produced beer is *Degraa*, available both in light and dark varieties. Unquestionably the most celebrated pub is the seventeenth-century *Postwagen*, built on to the end of the Rathaus, and a sight in itself, both for its cheerful baroque exterior and the cramped and irregular rooms within. For a livelier atmosphere, try *Goldener Schwan* or *Goldener Einhorn*, both occupying fine old houses on the Markt; the former has good-value lunches, while the latter offers an enormous menu with Italian and Greek cuisine as well as German, the specialty being thin fillets of veal with an ample choice of sauces. Also with an address on the Markt, but just off the square itself, is *Tomate*, which has regular live jazz sessions, while guitar music is sometimes featured at the busy *Domkeller* on Hof. For a sedate meal, try *Zum Schiffgen* or *Zum Goldenen Apfelbaum*, both on Hühner Markt.

The **student quarter** is centered on Pontstrasse, where *Tangente* turns from an elegant day-time café into a jumping, youthful watering hole at night. Its neighbor *Molkerei*, with which it shares a terrace, is bright and cheerful during the day, but lacks atmosphere come evening. *Café Kittel* is another student favorite, whereas *Labyrinth* is more in the nature of a traditional beer hall, with an older, more relaxed clientele. Further youthful hang-outs can be found in the streets south of the Markt: *Meisenfrei* on Boxgrabe is notable for the bewildering choice of games available, while *Bebop* and *Salsa*, both on Südstrasse, are haunts of the in-crowd.

Aachen's top **disco** is *Metropol* on Blondelstrasse to the eastern side of town, where the music bizarrely ranges from funk on top of heavy metal via Europop to the jazz and soul played at the café next to the dance floor; the place is best visited after midnight, when the schoolkids have cleared out. Nearby on Promenadenstrasse is *Hauptquartier*, the city's most eccentric bar, a living testimony to the enduring popularity in Germany of all things punk. Also in this area is *Club Voltaire* on Friedrichstrasse, the only all-night joint worth mentioning; it has a tiny dance floor, but music is kept at conversation level. Two discos in the traditional student quarter are the popular but cramped *Rotation* on Ponttor and the hard-rock *Make-Up* on Hirschgraben.

It would be a pity to leave Aachen without following Charlemagne's example and taking a **swim** in the warm waters. Conveniently located in the old city is the *Römerbad* at Buchkremerstr. 1 (Mon.–Fri. 7am–8pm, Sat. 7am–5pm, Sun. 7am–1pm). The temperature of these baths is kept at a constant heat (89°F) and there's no doubt that they're wonderfully refreshing. Three more pools are found in the parts of town most closely associated with the spa facilities: the suburb of **BURTSCHEID** and the streets around **Monheimsallee**. Both have extensive parks, while the former, located to the south of the Hauptbahnhof, has a distinctive skyline, thanks to a handsome pair of churches built on its heights by the elder Couven. Monheimsallee is best known for its **casino**, housed in a neoclassical building with a glitteringly modernized interior (3pm–2am, Fri. and Sat. until 3am; minimum stake is DM5 at the cheapest roulette table). The management want only the better class of visitor—"Jackets and ties for men are naturally obligatory, and ladies would definitely consider jeans and a T-shirt unsuitable for wear" state the regulations, with full evening dress being the normal attire. Unfortunately, you get the impression that sartorial stuffiness helps stifle enjoyment; the patrons all look glum and seem to be acting out a ritual. If you strike it lucky at the tables, the restaurant provides a tempting outlet for your winnings; it's one of the very best in Germany, glorying in two Michelin rosettes.

Next door to the casino, the new *Eurogress* center is where both rock and classical **concerts** are held. More highbrow culture is available at the *Stadttheater* on Theaterplatz just across from the Elisenbrunnen; there's a play or opera performing most evenings and standards are good—Herbert von Karajan first made his name as musical director there. *Grenzlandtheater* on Friedrich Wilhelm Platz offers modern drama, albeit with an emphasis on established playwrights.

Listings

Area code (☎0241).

Exchange facilities The only ones with extended hours are at the autobahn frontier crossing points; the one to the north of the city is open Mon.–Fri. 7:15am–7:45pm, Sat. and Sun. 8am–7:45pm, though these times are curtailed in winter.

Festivals The annual *Karlsfest* in honor of Charlemagne is held on January 31, while Carnival is celebrated with typical Rhenish enthusiasm.

Mitfahrzentrale Roermonder Str. 4 (☎155087).

Poste Restante Kapuzinergraben 19.

Sports Main event is an international equestrian competition in late June/early July.

The Northern Eifel

The German section of the **EIFEL** massif is divided by the Land boundary between North Rhineland-Westphalia and Rhineland-Pfalz; the former's share consists mainly of the **HOHES VENN**, an extensive plateau of impervious rocks which stretches into Belgium. Variation in the scenery is provided by the river Rur, which cuts a deep, winding valley, and by the vegetation of gorse, broom, and cotton grass. The area has been continuously inhabited since prehistoric times; its iron, lead and zinc were mined in the Middle Ages. However, it's poor in natural resources; no cities have ever developed, and the nineteenth century saw mass emigration, much of it to the U.S. Nowadays, the principal industry is the provision of **activity holidays**—skiing in winter, hiking, fishing, and sailing in summer—punctuated by dead periods between the seasons.

Monschau

The Northern Eifel's other main attraction is a series of well preserved small towns, at least two of which rank among the finest in Germany. One of these is **MONSCHAU**, some 30km south of Aachen. It's only accessible by bus, with slow but fairly frequent services; most of the Eifel railroads have closed because of the high cost of maintenance and low usage levels. Monschau dates from the twelfth century, but only received its Germanic name in 1918; previously it was known as *Montjoie* ("Mount of Joy"). The town's main characteristic is its dramatic setting deep in the Rur valley, with ruined fortresses—the **Burg** and the **Haller** (both with unrestricted access)—crowning two of the hills above. These offer some of the many superb **views** to be had in the area; others can be enjoyed from a belvedere just off the main road to Aachen, or from the commanding heights of the continuation of this road in the direction of Nideggen. The Burg, by far the larger of the ruins, is the building from which Monschau developed. Its keep and gateway are Romanesque originals; the ring wall and parapets date from a strengthening of the defenses in the fourteenth century, while the large *Eselsturm* ("Asses' Tower") was built a couple of hundred years later, as was the central *Palast* which has been restored to serve as a **youth hostel** (☎02472 2314).

The lower part of Monschau is an almost completely preserved townscape, dominated by the magnificent **multistory mansions** lining the Rur, with slate roofs sometimes pierced by two tiers of dormer windows. Though half-timbering is used extensively, these houses aren't as old as they might appear—they date from Monschau's main period of prosperity, engendered by cloth production, which followed the Thirty Years' War. The most ornate of all, the **Rotes Haus** (*Red House*), adds a rare splash of color to the town, which is otherwise so monochromatic that it seems to grow organically out of the landscape. Built by a merchant in the 1750s, the Rotes Haus remained in the hands of the original family for two centuries, until it was turned into a **museum** (guided tours Good Friday–mid-Nov. Tues.–Sun. at 10am, 11am, 2pm, 3pm, and 4pm; DM3). It features a rococo staircase with an elaborate iron railing, and is fully furnished in the same style. The nearby **Troistorff Haus** on Laufenstrasse, now used as municipal offices, is smaller, but has a fancier exterior and another fine stairway. On the same street is the the **Icon Museum** (mid-May–mid-Oct. Tues.–Thurs., Sat. and Sun. 10:30am–12:30pm and 1:30–5pm; DM3), with Russian works from the seventeenth century onwards; however, it can't hold a candle to the collection in Recklinghausen (see p.475). There's also a **Music Museum** (May–Sept. Sat.–Thurs. 10am–noon and 2–5pm; DM3) by the bus stop at the entrance to town.

The **tourist office** (April–Oct. Mon.–Fri. 9am–6pm, Sat. 9am–12:30pm, Nov.–April Mon.–Thurs. 9am–noon and 1:30–5pm, Fri. 9am–12:45pm; ☎02472 3300) is at Stadtstrasse 1 beside the main bridge. For DM2 you can arrange here to visit the **Senfmühle**, where mustard is still made using last century's equipment. The town has another historic workshop in the **Glashütte** (*glassworks*) at Burgau 14 (March–Oct. Mon.–Fri. 10am–5:30pm, Sat. and Sun. 10am–6pm; DM2.50). There are **campgrounds** at Perlenau (☎02472 636) and at Grünentalstr. 36 in the adjoining village of IMGENBROICH (☎02472 3931), while a second and more luxurious hostel is at Hargardgasse 5 in HARGARD (☎02472 2180), some 3km away. **Private houses** with rooms to let, generally at around DM35 a double, can be found on Kirchstrasse, Laufenstrasse, and Oberer Mühlenberg. **Hotels** charging DM30 per head or less include *Alt Montjoie*, Stadtstr. 18 (☎02472 3289); *Burgau*, St.-Vither-Str. 16 (☎02472 2120 or 2284); *Burghotel*, Laufenstr. 1 (☎02472 2332);

and *Haus Flora*, Laufenstr. 134 (☎02472 2289). The **cafés** and **restaurants** which dot the town center are mostly of a high standard. Try the products of the local *Felsenkeller* brewery; its specialty is *Monschauer Zwickelbier*, a dark, cloudy, bottom-fermented beer supposedly rich in vitamin B.

The Lake District

The area east of Monschau is known as the **Seven Lakes**, though all of these are artificial. As an alternative to reaching them by bus, there's the *Rurtalbahn*, a painfully slow but enormously scenic railroad which closely follows the course of the Rur. This begins at **DÜREN**, an industrial town midway between Aachen and Cologne; now totally modern, its main claim to fame is that it was where Holbein executed the ill-fated portrait of Anne of Cleves (see p.459). The other terminus is **HEIMBACH**, on the eastern bank of the **Rursee Schwammenauel**, the largest reservoir in West Germany, which attracts loads of tourists in summer with its possibilities for angling, water sports, and cruising. Heimbach is a spa town and in some ways resembles Monschau, its ruined Burg towering over streets of half-timbered dwellings; but in fact it's far less genuine—most of the houses are modern. If you want to stay, there are several **campgrounds** and plenty of cheap **rooms** to rent, but no hostel.

NIDEGGEN, some 11km north, is much more imposing, perched like an aerie high above the valley. The **Burg**, residence of the dukes of Jülich, dates partly from the twelfth century, but was transformed into a palace during the Renaissance; it survives as a ruin, and there's free access to the courtyard and tower, which commands an extensive view. Other sections have been heavily restored to house the local **museum** (Tues.–Sun. 10am–5pm; DM2). Within the precincts is the **Pfarrkirche**, a pure example of Romanesque architecture, adorned with frescos of the same period. A large section of the town **walls** has been preserved, including two fortified gateways; there are also a number of characteristic half-timbered houses. The **youth hostel** is at Rather Str. 27 (☎02427 226), while **rooms** at DM30 or less per head are available in numerous hotels and private houses. There's a **campground** in BRÜCK (☎02427 508), 2km below Nideggen, on the banks of the Rur near the Bahnhof. Also within the municipality is **SCHMIDT**, 10km southwest, an alternative resort to Heimbach, which scores points for having a more central location on the Rursee.

Euskirchen and Kommern

Communications in the eastern part of the North Eifel hub through the industrial town of **EUSKIRCHEN**, which lies on the railroad line between Cologne and Trier. At the opposite end of the town center from the Bahnhof are a couple of moderately interesting medieval monuments: the remains of the city wall and the church of **St. Martin**. The latter has a Romanesque tower and nave, a Gothic chancel, and several notable works of art, including a font from the Staufian epoch, carved with fantastic animals; a delicate fifteenth-century stone relief of *St. Peter Delivered from Prison*; an elaborate high altar from Antwerp; and a *Madonna and Child* attributed to Riemenschneider.

KOMMERN, 12km southwest and connected by regular buses, is a picturesque village of half-timbered houses. Just to the west, high above the main road, is the **Rhenish Open Air Museum** (April–Oct. daily 9am–6pm, Nov.–March daily 10am–4pm; DM4.50), with over fifty reassembled rural buildings from the two Rhineland provinces, a worthy counterpart to the larger West-phalian collections in Detmold and Hagen. The exhibits are grouped by region—Eifel, Westerwald, Lower Rhine, and Bergisches Land. Particularly impressive are a mid-fifteenth-century barn from Mönchengladbach (the oldest exhibit), a late eighteenth-century windmill, and the mansion from Remscheid of the Mannesmann family, Germany's leading machine manufacturers. At the southern end of Kommern is the **Hochwild Park** (daily 9am–6pm), in which various types of deer, plus elks, bison, and oxen are kept in as natural conditions as possible. If you wish to stay, *Ratskeller Eifeltrompeter* on the main Kölner Strasse (☎02443 5415) is about the only option, at upwards of DM30 per head.

Bad Münstereifel

BAD MÜNSTEREIFEL is located at the end of a branch railroad line 25km south of Euskirchen. For all its concealed position, deep in the valley of the Erft, it's a place of considerable character, rivaling Monschau; though not so homogeneous, nor so picturesquely sited, its monuments are superior. Prominent among these are the thirteenth- to fourteenth-century **walls**, which survive intact, and are as good an example as any in Germany of the sort of fortifications common to medieval towns. Straight ahead from the Bahnhof is the formidable northern gate, the **Werther Tor**; the corresponding position to the south is guarded by the **Orchheimer Tor**. To the east and west, the fortifications rise high into the hills, giving extra protection to the town huddled along the banks of the river. On the eastern side are the **Burg** (the only ruined feature) and the **Johannistor**; the western front now forms the boundary of the *Kurgarten* with its spa facilities, defended on its southern corner by the **Heisterbacher Tor**. You can walk freely along this stretch of rampart, which offers wonderful views over the town and the surrounding foothills of the **Ahrgebirge** range (see *Chapter Four*). For a wholly different perspective, it's worth following the footpath around the walls.

Münstereifel ("minster in the Eifel") derives its name from the town's having developed from a Benedictine monastery; founded in 830, this quickly became a popular place of pilgrimage through possession of the relics of the Roman martyr-saints Chrysanthus and Daria. The present **Stiftskirche** (named after these saints, whose graves are in the crypt) is a magnificently severe twelfth-century Romanesque church, which dominates the skyline of the lower town. Its main feature is a mighty westwork modeled on St. Pantaleon in Cologne, with a chunky square belfry flanked by a pair of tall towers whose structure curiously veers from the cylindrical to the octagonal. Across the Kirchplatz is the striking red facade of the **Rathaus**, a masterpiece of Gothic civil architecture, which began life in the mid-fourteenth century as a guild house, and was given an extension of similar size to the original building two centuries later. On Langenhecke to the rear of the church is the **Heimat Museum** (April–Oct. Tues.–Sun. 9am–noon, also Weds. 2–4pm; Nov.–March Sat. 10am–noon, Sun. 10am–noon and 2–4pm only; DM1). The building itself, which was the home of a lay brother of the monastery, is far more interesting than the local history displays inside—contemporary with the church, it's possibly the oldest intact house in Germany.

As well as these public buildings, Münstereifel offers one of the most satisfying townscapes in the region, enhanced by its rustic setting on the banks of the Erft, which is never more than a stream; almost every street within the walls merits inclusion in a gentle stroll. Finest of the half-timbered houses is the mid-seventeenth-century **Haus Windeck** on Orchheimerstrasse, the first floor of which is now a café. Also of interest is the seventeenth-century **Jesuitenkirche** facing the Markt; in common with this order's other churches in Germany, it's built in an anachronistic Gothic style.

The **tourist office** is at Langenhecke 2 (Mon.–Fri. 9am–5pm, Sat. 10am–noon and 2–4pm, Sun. 10:30am–12:30pm; ☎02253 505182). Private houses with **rooms** to rent at around DM20 per head can be found all over town, prominently displaying their *Zimmer frei* signs when they've vacancies. The **youth hostel** is high in the hills about 2km east of town at Herbergsweg 1–5 (☎02253 7438) just before the village of RODERT, while the **campground** is to the south on the banks of the Erft (☎02253 8282). There are plenty of reasonably priced places to **eat** and **drink**, particularly along the main Wertherstrasse. Look for lunchtime set menus, which are often tremendous bargains; this is particularly true of the *Burggaststätten* in the castle ruins, which specializes in *vom heissen stein* dishes (barbecued on a hot stone).

The surrounding countryside is good for **hiking**; pick up the free tourist board brochures which outline the best routes. Especially notable are the *Geologischer Lehrpfad* to the northwest of the town, and the *Naturkundlichen Lehrpfad* to the southwest. However, the most popular excursion in the vicinity is to the largest **radio-telescope** in the world, run by the Max Planck Institute, and situated just outside the hamlet of EFFELSBERG, 8km southeast. Visitors are admitted only in groups, but individuals can join these; as limits are placed on the numbers allowed on each guided tour, it's best to phone ahead (☎02257 30117; Tues.–Fri. 10am, 11am, 2pm, 3pm, and 4pm, Sat. 9am, 10am, 11am, and noon; DM2).

Bonn

The name of **BONN** is indivisibly associated with that of the Federal Republic, having served as the seat of government since the country was set up in 1949. Its choice as capital over many more appropriate candidates, especially Frankfurt, is explained by the fact that **Konrad Adenauer**, the overwhelmingly dominant figure in the postwar politics of the western zone, lived nearby and successfully championed its cause as a matter of personal convenience. General feeling was that German reunification would occur before long, and Berlin would then assume its obvious role; the nomination of a small provincial city symbolized the temporary nature of the new state. No ad hoc government quarter was designed; existing buildings around the banks of the Rhine to the south of the city center were converted to house parliament and the official residences. Four decades later, the issue of a united Germany has long since vanished from the political agenda, yet West German politicians feel duty-bound to keep the ideal alive. Thus Bonn continues in its fantasy role of "provisional capital," but is clearly set for an extended stint at the heart of affairs. Already, its character has changed markedly, having doubled in size with an influx of diplomats, officials, and hangers-on, and with the absorption of a number of neighboring towns. Even so, its population is still under 300,000 and Bonn remains the most unlikely and unloved of European capitals: *A Small Town in Germany*, according to the title of John le Carré's spy thriller, or "The Federal Village" in the condescending eyes of the inhabitants of grander German cities. Go there expecting a lively nightlife or the normal cultural trappings of a metropolis and you'll be disappointed, but Bonn is worth a visit of a day or two if taken on its own merits as an historic town given a new dimension as a result of being thrust in to the political limelight.

Around Town

Prior to its elevation to the role of capital, Bonn was chiefly famous as the birth-place of **Ludwig van Beethoven**. The house where he was born at Bonngasse 20 is one of the few old buildings downtown to have escaped wartime devastation; together with the more imposing building next door, it contains an unfussy and intelligently presented **museum** (April–Oct. Mon.–Sat. 9am–1pm and 3–6pm, Sun. 9am–1pm, Nov.–March Mon.–Sat. 9:30am–1pm and 3–5pm, Sun. 9:30am–1pm; DM2) dedicated to the great composer. Beethoven served his musical apprenticeship at the electoral court of his home town, but left for Vienna, then the musical capital of the world, at the age of 22. There he became successor to the tradition of Haydn and Mozart, developing the three great forms of the classical period—the symphony, the string quartet, and the piano sonata—to their ultimate limits. Though he never returned to Bonn, the city has zealously built up the best collection of memorabilia of its favorite son. There's a bunch of uncomfortable portraits of the tormented genius (who was a reluctant sitter) at various stages of his life, along with manuscripts and correspondence. The three instruments with which he was associated as a professional performer are represented in the form of the console of the organ (now destroyed) on which he played as a youth; his last piano, built for him in 1823 by Conrad Graf; and his viola. Most poignant of all are the ear-trumpets which a friend made especially in order to combat his advancing deafness. This affliction was partly responsible for endowing his late works with a menacing power so different from anything previously composed that many contemporaries were—literally—physically afraid of the sound.

At the end of Bonngasse is the **Markt**, one of two large squares in the midst of the pedestrian shopping mall. Here stands the pink rococo **Rathaus**; to its rear is the **Kunstmuseum** (Tues. and Thurs. 10am–9pm, Weds., Fri., Sat., and Sun. 10am–5pm; free) which houses a good collection of Expressionist paintings and drawings, many by the brilliant **August Macke** who spent part of his brief life in this city. Changing exhibits of avant-garde works are also featured. The other square is dominated by the huge Romanesque **Münster** whose central octagonal tower with its soaring spire is the city's most prominent landmark. Inside, it's airy and pleasing, the sensitive proportions reinforcing the feeling of massive space. Below the chancel is a fine crypt, while there's a large, severe cloister adjoining the southern side.

Bonn's other dominant building is the baroque **Schloss**, an enormously narrow structure that has been taken over by the University. It was formerly the seat of the archbishop-electors of Cologne, who had been forced to reside outside their city ever since a long-running dispute with the independent-minded burghers had been resolved in the latter's favor at the Battle of Worringen in 1288. Thereafter, Bonn was where they usually chose to live, though Godesburg and Brühl were preferred at other times. To the south, the Schloss is bounded by the open spaces of the Hofgarten, no more than an ordinary public park these days. At the far end is the **Academic Art Museum** (Mon.–Weds., Fri., and Sun. 10am–1pm, Thurs. 10am–1pm and 4–6pm; DM1) housed in a neoclassical pavilion designed by **Schinkel**. This has an eerie collection of casts of famous antique sculptures, originally made for the benefit of art students. All day Sunday, Tuesday, and Thursday afternoons also, the small and very basic collection of original antiquities is open as well.

Also branching out from the Schloss is the kilometer-long avenue of chestnut trees which leads to **POPPLESDORF**, where the Frenchman **Robert de Cotte**, who had undertaken modifications to the Schloss, was commissioned to build a

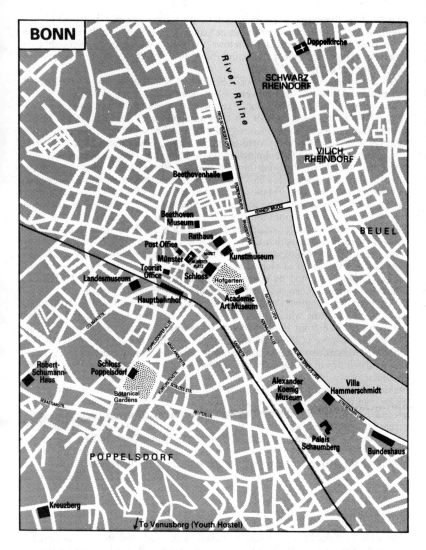

second electoral palace. He responded with an ingenious *trompe l'oeil* design, concealing the circular courtyard within a rectangular floorplan. Again, the palace is now occupied by university departments, the grounds serving as the **Botanical Gardens** (summer Mon.–Fri. 9am–7pm, Sun. 9am–1pm, winter Mon.–Fri. 9am–4:30pm). For a sociological as well as architectural stroll, wander in the streets immediately to the east, such as *Schloss Strasse, Kurfürstenstrasse, Argelanderstrasse,* and *Bismarckstrasse*—these represent a remarkably complete picture of turn-of-the-century town planning for the better-off sections of the middle class. Arranged in terraces, each house self-consciously tries a bit of one-upmanship on its neighbors, whether in gaudy color schemes, or by the richness of its door frames, ornamental windows, sculptural decoration or wrought-iron balconies. The overall effect shows the extent to which the competitive ethos had taken over the inhabitants' lives.

To the other side of Popplesdorf's Schloss at Sebastianstr. 182 is the **Robert Schumann House** (Mon. and Fri. 10am–noon and 4–7pm, Weds. and Thurs. 10am–noon and 3–6pm, Sun. 10am–1pm; free) containing a collection of memorabilia of the Romantic composer. In spite of a blissfully happy marriage to the pianist Clara Wieck, which inspired so many of his yearning, passionate song settings and so much of his virtuoso piano music, Schumann had a history of psychological instability, culminating in a complete mental breakdown and attempted suicide by throwing himself into the Rhine. At his own request, he spent the last two years of his life confined to the sanatorium adjoining the house.

Continuing south from Popplesdorf, a road leads uphill to the isolated pilgrimage church of **Kreuzberg**. The original seventeenth-century chapel was given the full rococo treatment a hundred years later, including the addition of the Holy Steps behind the altar, a lavishly ornate imitation by **Balthasar Neumann** of those now in Rome on which Christ allegedly ascended to receive Pilate's judgment. Penitents were once supposed to hobble up on their knees; nowadays railings bar any such acts of piety. Beyond, the city fans out into a number of old villages, often separated by open countryside. Among them is **VENUSBERG**, which has a game reserve with wild boar and both red and fallow deer.

As you might imagine, Bonn's **government quarter**, saddled with its "temporary" status, is on the whole rather humdrum. It can be reached either by following Reuterstrasse from Popplesdorf or by taking Adenauerallee from the Hofgarten; the distance is about the same. Both the **Villa Hammerschmidt** and the **Palais Schaumburg** are pompous Empire buildings from the last century, once private dwellings of the mega-rich, but now the official residences of the Federal President and Chancellor respectively. You aren't allowed near them, let alone inside. Farther south, the **Parliament buildings** are in the Bauhaus style of the 1930s, and were originally a college. This time admission is possible, but only for groups by written appointment, though you can try joining a party who have arranged to be shown around the Bundesrat (Upper House)—more trouble than it's worth, unless you're passionately keen on German politics. Indeed, the whole quarter offers even less than you'd expect, and the best reason for coming is the wonderful **view** over the Rhine and the Siebengebirge on the opposite bank.

The pick of Bonn's somewhat provincial museums is the **Landesmuseum** at Colmantstr. 14–16 behind the Hauptbahnhof (Tues., Thurs., and Fri. 9am–5pm, Weds. 9am–8pm, Sat. and Sun. 11am–5pm; DM3). Star piece is the **skull of Neanderthal Man**, found in a valley near Düsseldorf (see p.449), and calculated to be some 60,000 years old. Other important archaeological exhibits are a triumphal arch from Aachen, a mosaic dedicated to the sun, and an array of jewelry from both Roman and Frankish times. Among a generally mediocre collection of paintings on the first floor, look out for some lovely examples of the fifteenth-century Cologne school, particularly the delicate *Deposition* and *St. Sebastian* by an anonymous artist who has been named **Master of the Bonn Diptych** as a result, and five panels by the painter known as **Master of the St. Ursula Legend** after the dispersed series from which these came. There's also a rare work by **Elsheimer**, *Three Marys at the Sepulchre*. It's hardly worth climbing to the top floor, which has a dire display of modern art with not a single famous name represented. If you've a special interest in natural history, head for the

Alexander Koenig Museum at Adenauerallee 150–164 (Tues.–Fri. 9am–5pm, Sat. and Sun. 9am–12:30pm; DM1), four floors of stuffed animals from all around the world, presented with Germanic thoroughness.

The Outskirts

When Bonn was officially expanded in 1969, it gobbled up a string of small villages, giving it a foothold on the eastern bank of the Rhine for the first time. It also annexed the old spa town of **BAD GODESBERG** (reached by U-Bahn #16 or main-line train) to the south, stretching its boundaries to the Land border. Bad Godesberg's character had already made it a favored location for many of the diplomatic missions, who found its grandiose Empire-style villas just the sort of headquarters they were looking for. The town is also a famed conference center, and has hosted at least two fateful events: the series of meetings between Chamberlain and Hitler in 1938 which paved the way for the Munich Agreement in which "peace in our time" was bought at Czechoslovakia's expense; and the 1959 conference of the Social Democrats, when the party, bidding to end a period of three decades in opposition, disavowed its earlier connections with Marxism, class warfare, and anticlericalism, and became part of the postwar consensus rooted in acceptance of the idea of a "social market economy."

Rearing high over the town is the **Godesburg**, the most northerly of the great series of castles crowning promontories above the Rhine, built in the thirteenth and fourteenth centuries by the Archbishops of Cologne. It has been a ruin since 1583; that was the year the see's incumbent, **Gebhard Truchsess**, embraced Protestantism and married an aristocratic canoness, but refused to resign and tried to continue ruling from the Godesburg. He was excommunicated, and an army of the Bavarian Wittelsbach dynasty, who had now been given the archbishopric, was sent to crush him. They hired miners to tunnel through the hill and lay explosives, which were set off when the defenders refused to surrender. Various schemes for building a pleasure palace to replace the defensively useless castle came to nought; eventually a hotel was created utilizing what was left of the walls of the outer fortifications. The cylindrical keep is still intact and can be ascended (April–Sept. Tues.–Sun. 10am–6pm; 0:30DM) for an enormous panoramic **view**, including a distant glimpse of Cologne and the best of all the many perspectives of the Siebengebirge. Views, indeed, are Bad Godesberg's major attraction; you'll find plenty more if you saunter down the *Rheinufer*, the promenade along the river bank. Otherwise, there are two spa parks in the town center, separated by fashionable buildings, prominent among which is the late eighteenth-century **Redoute**, formerly the ballroom of the electors, now a renowned restaurant.

The only one of Bonn's outer villages worth making a special detour to see is **SCHWARZRHEINDORF**, on the right bank of the Rhine to the extreme north, reached by bus #540 or #550. It boasts a relatively little-known but outstanding monument in the form of the **Doppelkirche**, a former manorial church (Mon.–Fri. 9am–6:30pm in summer, 9am–5pm in winter; Sat. and Sun. 9am–5pm). Built in the mid-twelfth century by Arnold von Wied, later Archbishop of Cologne, it offers an intriguing insight into the social and religious preoccupations of the medieval world. The exterior cleverly disguises the fact that it encases two separate chapels, the upper reserved for the lord, the lower for the use of the laborers. Apart from its architectural idiosyncracies, the church has rare Romanesque **fresco** cycles. Turning on the light by the door reveals *The Vision of Ezekiel*, *The Transfiguration* and *The Crucifixion*, while upstairs the great visions of *The*

Apocalypse were painted for their lordships' contemplation. The upper chapel is only accessible on Saturdays and on Sunday afternoons, but its frescos can always be seen through an aperture. A short walk to the east is another old township, VILICH, with an abbey church and a rebuilt, moated Schloss.

Practical Details . . . and Nightlife

The **Hauptbahnhof** sits squarely in the middle of the city, the central pedestrian area opening out immediately before it. **Exchange facilities** are available here (Mon.–Sat. 7:30am–6:30pm, Sun. 9:15am–12:15pm). To the right is the **bus station**, whose local services, along with the trams (which become the U-Bahn in the city center), form part of a system integrated with that of Cologne. As the attractions are well spaced out, it's better to buy tickets in blocks of four, or a 24-hour pass which costs DM6.50 for Bonn alone, DM11.50 for the entire circuit. There's also a three-day pass available, at DM13 for Bonn only, DM18 for the whole circuit. Also shared with Cologne is the **airport** (☎02203 402222 or 402256 for flight information), which can be reached by means of a half-hourly bus service. The **tourist office** (Mon.–Sat. 8am–9pm, Sun. and holidays 9:30am–12:30pm; ☎773466) is at Münsterstr. 20 by the entrance to the shopping area. Make sure you pick up the handy *Bonn from A to Z*—not quite what it says, but with a good map and useful listings in English.

There's a choice of two **youth hostels**. The larger one is in Venusberg, at Haager Weg 42 (☎281200); take bus #520, #521 or #528. The alternative—one of the most luxurious in Germany—is at Horionstr. 60 in Bad Godesberg (☎317516); bus #515, leaving from the tram terminus beside the spa town's own Bahnhof, passes right in front. **Camping** is possible all year round at Im Frankenkeller 49 (☎344949) in MEHLEM on the banks of the Rhine south of Bad Godesberg. **Hotel rooms** downtown begin at around DM30 for a single, DM58 a double at *Zu den Stadtpatronen*, Berliner Platz 9–11 (☎633063), while *Weiland*, Breitestr. 98a (☎655057) charges DM33 per head. Bad Godesberg has a whole clutch of places at similar or lower rates; cheapest are *Wessel*, Bonner Str. 22 (☎351230); *Haus Erika*, Am Büchel 9 (☎352338); and *Gästehaus Scholz*, Annettenstr. 16 (☎379363).

Bonn's **nightlife** is largely dependent on the University; out of term and at weekends the center is little better than a ghost town come evening. In the Altstadt, three of the most popular places are situated together at the junction of Bornheimerstrasse and Berliner Platz—*Bla Bla*, the garishly-decorated meeting-place of punk diehards; the less outlandish *Namenlos*; and the disco *Novum*. *Jazz Galerie* on Oxfordstrasse features live sessions most evenings, while the brasserie *Köller* on Heerstrasse has a yuppie-ish appeal. To the west, *Aktuell* on Gerhard-von-Are-Strasse is a particular haunt of journalists. More youthful pubs are *Zebulon* on Stockenstrasse, patronized mainly by arts students, *Headline* on Sterntorbrücke, and *Mondrian* on Kasernenstrasse, which is particularly trendy and has the advantage of drinks being cheaper than usual. It's also worth traipsing south to Königstrasse, where you'll find the candlelit *Kerze*, bristling with alcoves and partitions; it's popular with a mixed age range, and serves excellent (if pricey) Italianate dishes. *Südstadt-Kneipe* on the same street offers a selection of reasonably priced cocktails and food to a background of good music.

To find out what's scheduled in the fields of **theater**, **concerts**, and **exhibitions**, consult the fortnightly *Kulturkalender* produced by the tourist office; a broader perspective is taken by the monthly *De Schnüss*, available from newsagents. The Bonn highbrow cultural scene is good but by no means outstanding: top international musicians sometimes appear at the *Beethovenhalle* overlooking the Rhine at Fritz-Schroeder-Ufer, while there's an *Opera House* (which also hosts ballet) at Am Boeslagerhof. Among the theaters are *Europatheater* at Mauspfad and *Kabarett* at Gaurheindorfer Str. 23. The main alternative cultural center is *Brotfabrik* at Kreuzstrasse in the right-bank suburb of BEUEL; it features exhibitions, film, readings, and feminist events. *Pantheon* at Am Bundeskanzlerplatz in the government quarter is on the same lines, and also holds a disco at weekends, while *Biskuit-Halle* on Wesselwerke is the main venue for visiting live bands.

Listings

Area code (☎0228).

Bookshops There's a wide selection in and around Am Hof (behind the Schloss).

Embassies *American* at Deichmanns Aue 29, Bad Godesberg (☎3391); *Canadian* at Friedrich-Wilhelm-Str. 18 (☎231061).

Festivals Every three years (1989, 1992 etc.) there's an international Beethoven festival in September. The main folklore event is the *Pützchensmarkt*, a colorful fair held annually on the first weekend of the same month in Beuel.

Markets Daily on the Markt; every third Saturday of the month, there's a flea market on Rheinaue.

Mitfahrzentrale Herwarthstr. 11a (☎693081).

Poste Restante Münsterplatz 17.

Rhine cruises These depart from Brassentufer just south of Kennedybrücke: *K-D Line* (☎632134), *Bonner Personnenschiffahrt* (☎636542).

The Siebengebirge

The **SIEBENGEBIRGE** (*Seven Mountains*), on the eastern bank of the Rhine just before the Land boundary with Rhineland-Pfalz, rank as one of the river's most suggestively grand stretches, steeped in the lore of legend and literature. According to one story, the mountains were created by seven giants clearing the dirt from their shovels; in size-wise contrast, they're often regarded as the site of the most famous of the Grimms' fairy tales, *Snow White and the Seven Dwarfs*. Poets and painters of the Romantic movement were inexorably drawn here, with the floweriest description being that by **Lord Byron** in *Childe Harold's Pilgrimage*:

> *The castled crag of Drachenfels*
> *Frowns o'er the wide and winding Rhine,*
> *Whose breast of waters broadly swells*
> *Between the banks which bear the vine;*
> *And hills all rich with blossom'd trees,*
> *And fields which promise corn and wine*
> *And scattered cities crowning these,*
> *Whose far white walls along them shine,*
> *Have strew'd a scene which I should see*
> *With double joy wert thou with me.*

Despite the name, there are about thirty summits in this extinct volcanic range, which stretches for about 15km north to south and 5km east to west. From Bonn, six of the main peaks can be seen; the number seven, with its traditional mystical significance, applies only to those visible from a point farther north. Of the group, **Drachenfels** (321m), **Wolkenburg** (325m) and **Lohrberg** (435m) are all of a mineral called trachyte; **Petersberg** (331m), **Nonnenstromberg** (336m) and **Grosser Ölberg** (461m) are of basalt, a later formation; while **Löwenburg** (455m) is of dolerite. For centuries, stone from these mountains was quarried to construct the great buildings of the Rhineland, most notably the Dom in Cologne; this activity was brought to an end in 1889, when the whole area was designated as Germany's first-ever national park. In accordance with the country's taste in such matters, the Siebengebirge are covered with thick woods, which means that views are very restricted most of the time, though all the more spectacular when you do reach a belvedere. This wasn't always so; old prints show the upper parts of the peaks free of trees, and generally crowned with a fortress.

"One day suffices to explore the most interesting points in this district, unless the visit be for geological purposes," intoned last century's *Baedeker Guide*. This piece of advice still holds good, and the Siebengebirge make an easy outing from Bonn, to which they're connected by U-Bahn #64 and #66. Alternatively, base yourself at either **KÖNIGSWINTER** or **BAD HONNEF-RHÖNDORF**. These two holiday resorts have avoided the fate of Bad Godesberg on the opposite bank of being swallowed up by the new capital. Königswinter is about the nearest Germany comes to a Sun Belt retirement community with its relaxed, rather dated air, awash with amusement arcades and Tin Pan Alley dance halls. As befits a spa, Bad Honnef is more upscale, preserving its *Kurhaus* in a fine park. It was the chosen residence of **Konrad Adenauer**, first chancellor of the Federal Republic, whose home at no. 8c in the street named after him is now a memorial **museum** (Tues.–Sun. 10am–4:30pm; free). A local government stalwart of the Catholic Center Party during the Weimar Republic, Adenauer seemed to be merely a stopgap leader when he finally entered the national stage at the age of 73. As it turned out, his impeccable record as an anti-Nazi and his moderate right-wing politics happened to be exactly in tune with the country's mood in the post-war period, and he remained in power for fourteen years, only retiring when his coalition partners made this a condition of their continued support. Adenauer's high reputation rests on his twin achievements of the "Economic Miracle" and the international rehabilitation of Germany, though there's little doubt that his inflexible attitude towards the Russians was a contributory factor in cementing the division of the nation into two hostile states.

Hotel rooms in both towns are plentiful and, being geared to vacationing families, are generally good value; they're certainly worth considering as an alternative to Bonn's inflated prices. In Königswinter, Hauptstrasse and Grabenstrasse have the main concentration of cheap places; those on Rheinallee are a discernable notch higher in class. *Im Alten Rathaus* at Hauptstr. 473 (☎02223 22163) has the lowest prices of all, provided you're sharing, at upwards of DM18 per head. Bad Honnef has a **youth hostel** at Selhofer Str. 106 (☎02224 71300) at the very southern end of town, and a couple of **campgrounds**. The cheapest hotels are both on Aegidiusplatz: *Zur Ewigen Lampe* (☎02224 8843) charges from DM22 per person, and *Zur Dorfshänke* (☎02224 8889) has singles at DM26, doubles at DM42. It's worth trying to coincide your visit with one of the numerous **festivals**, the most spectacular of which is *Der Rhein in Flammen*, a display of fireworks and illuminations held on the first Saturday in May; a week later, the cutting of the first crop of asparagus is celebrated. Bad Honnef's *Weinfest* is held on the first weekend in September; exactly a month later comes Königswinter's *Winzerfest*.

Although the lowest of the mountains, **DRACHENFELS**, situated immediately behind Königswinter, is by far the most interesting; unfortunately, it's heavily touristed and even more heavily exploited. Don't be tempted by the rack-and-pinion railroad, built in 1883 using a system pioneered in Switzerland; it may be an ingenious piece of engineering, but the fare is a rip-off, the more so as the footpath is paved and makes for a steep but easy ascent. Beware also of the many cafés lining this path; some charge fair prices, others certainly don't, so check carefully before ordering. About a third of the way up is the **dragon's cave**, traditionally supposed to be the home (the location isn't actually specified in *The Nibelungenlied*) of the fearsome monster slain by the hero **Siegfried**; by immediately immersing himself in its warm blood he gained a horny skin which would have rendered him invincible had a falling leaf not left a spot as vulnerable as Achilles' heel. From this legend comes the name of the wine, *Drachenblut* ("dragon's blood"), made from the grapes cultivated on these slopes, the most northerly vineyard in Germany. Pass on the cave, featuring a kitsch presentation of live reptiles and a model of the dragon, for which a stinging DM4 entrance fee is asked. Your money is better spent on **Schloss Drachenburg** (guided tours Tues.–Sun. 10am–6pm; DM2), which may not be too wonderful aesthetically speaking, but is a good example of the nineteenth-century German love of macabre Gothic fantasy. From the terrace is a spectacular **view**, which more than makes up for the ghastly tribulations en route. There's an even wider panorama from what's left of the Romanesque **Burg**, a ruin since the Thirty Years' War, at the summit of the mountain. Apart from being able to trace the Rhine's path both upstream and down, you can see over the Eifel to the west, and get an alternative perspective on the Siebengebirge to the familiar one from across the river; on even a half-decent day, the spires of Cologne can also be distinguished.

Thankfully gimmicks are wholly absent on the remaining mountains in the range, and a series of well-marked hiking trails enables you to choose your own route around. **PETERSBERG** is probably the best known; its summit is occupied by a grandiose luxury hotel often used for state visits; it was Chamberlain's base for his ill-fated talks with Hitler in Bad Godesberg. This has been under restoration for some time now; until such time as the work is completed, you'd be better off omitting it, as most of the area is fenced off. **LÖWENBURG** is allegedly haunted by a wild huntsman, doomed to an eternal chase as punishment for his cruelty when alive; **GROSSER ÖLBERG** is the most enticing after Drachenfels, commanding the next best views. Although farthest from the Rhine of all the peaks, it has the advantage of being the highest, and of including panoramas over the Taunus to the east.

From here, it's only a short descent to the area's sole great monument, the ruins of the early thirteenth-century Cistercian monastery of **Heisterbach**, built, like so many of this order's foundations, in the Transitional style between Romanesque and Gothic. One of the first priors, Caesarius, was a chronicler of legends, which he collected in the *Dialogus Miraculorum*. The most famous of these—which was retold by Henry Longfellow and must have inspired Washington Irving's *Rip van Winkle*—concerns a monk who, while out for his daily walk, was meditating disbelievingly on the text of Psalm 90, "a thousand years in thy sight are but as yesterday"; on returning for vespers, he found that a whole century had elapsed since his departure. Heisterbach was demolished at the beginning of the nineteenth century following the Napoleonic suppression, but the apse and its ambulatory were spared when the explosives failed to ignite. This tiny fragment had an impact on the Romantic imagination out of all proportion to its size; depictions of lonely, overgrown and crumbling abbeys set in wooded valleys, often illuminated by moonlight, became one of the favorite subjects of the movement's painters, most notably in the work of Caspar David Friedrich. Nowadays, the eighteenth-century monastic buildings are occupied by a convent of Augustinian nuns, who have built a modern church. They also run a café-restaurant, specializing in a huge choice of home-made *gateaux* which are wholly irresistible to all but slaves of the calorie count.

Brühl

Midway between Bonn and Cologne, set inland from the Rhine, lies **BRÜHL**, a town which developed from a castle founded by the archbishop-electors in the thirteenth century. The eighteenth-century successor to this is the most sumptuous palace in the Rhineland, seemingly a little piece of Bavaria wafted mysteriously northwards. It makes the town one of the most interesting in the province, but isn't the reason 2 million people swarm here each summer, nor why **kids** are likely to rate Brühl as the highlight of a holiday in Germany.

The main attraction nowadays is **Phantasialand** (April–Oct. daily 9am–sunset; adults DM18, kids DM16), the first amusement park in Europe to rival Disneyland, and a clear example of how strong North American influence has become in West Germany. It occupies the former site of a strip mine, at the extreme southern end of town, and can be reached by regular **bus** services from Brühl's Bahnhof. Provided you find the place palatable (not everybody does), and are prepared to enter into the spirit of fun and silliness, there are enough attractions to last a full day. These range from recreations of prewar Berlin, a Wild West town, and China of a thousand years ago, through rides on a Viking ship, an overhead monorail, a 1300-meter waterfall, and the world's largest roller coaster (in the *Space Center*), to *Cine 2000*, equipped with a 180° screen enabling you to drive the car or pilot the helicopter in a zany adventure movie. Be warned that even the park's owners admit that there are an uncomfortably large number of visitors on Sundays, and throughout July and August.

In its heyday Brühl's heart and soul, the **Schloss Augustusburg** (guided tours lasting 1 hr., Feb.–Nov. Tues.–Sun. 9am–noon and 1:30–4pm; DM1.50), must have seemed as much of an extravaganza as Phantasialand does now. Such is its splendor that it's *the* favorite venue for state visits and the Federal President's official binges; unfortunately, this means it's liable to unexpected periods of closure for up to three weeks at a time. It's very much a personal creation of the eighteenth century archbishop-elector **Clemens August**, a member of the Bavarian Wittelsbach dynasty. From an early age, he had been earmarked for an ecclesiastical career in order to advance the family's power base. In this, he was brilliantly successful, though he showed no piety whatsoever, living a life of unashamedly pampered luxury and gaining a reputation as a womaniser. He was summoned to Rome by the pope to explain the presence of two particularly beautiful singers at his court, and his death came after he had danced the night away rather too energetically. He favored Brühl as the seat of his court because of its ideal situation for his favorite hobby, falconry, and was determined to rebuild the medieval moated Schloss which had been destroyed by French troops in 1689.

Initially, the Westphalian **Johann Conrad Schlaun** was commissioned to design a dignified baroque *Wasserschloss*. The outer walls survive from this building phase, but there was then an abrupt change of plan as Clemens August came under the spell of the new light and airy rococo style which had taken root in his native Munich. Continuation of the project was entrusted to **François Cuvilliés**, who eliminated all features reminiscent of a fortress and transformed the complex into a pleasure palace facing a formal French-style **garden** of fountains, box hedges, clipped yews, and avenues of palisaded trees. This was designed by **Dominique Girard**, who had studied under the doyen of landscape gardeners, André Le Nôtre. As the final *pièce de resistance*, the greatest architect of the day, **Balthasar Neumann**, was recruited to draw up plans for the ceremonial **staircase**—a riveting fricassee of marble and stucco, crowned by a fresco glorifying the Virtues by the Italian Carlo Carlone. The decorative scheme of this and the following **Hall of Guards** and **Music Room**, which are almost equally sumptuous, is a complicated series of allegories in honor of the Wittelsbach dynasty.

Adjoining the west front of the Schloss is the **Orangery**; now housing a café and an exhibition room, it forms a processional way to **St. Maria zu den Engeln**. Built as a Franciscan monastery in the simplest form of Gothic, the church's interior was greatly pepped up for its new function as court chapel by the insertion of a lavish **high altar**—taking up the entire chancel—designed by Neumann.

Within the former monastic buildings are the Rathaus and **tourist office** (Mon.–Weds. 8am–noon and 2–4pm, Thurs. 8am–noon and 2–6pm, Fri. 8am-noon; ☎02232 79345). They keep a list of over twenty houses with **rooms** to let, costing from DM25 to DM30 per head. Most centrally placed is *Harth*, Wallstr. 103 (☎02232 47227); if you prefer a location near Phantasialand, try *Maeder*, Akazienweg 14 (☎02232 32314) or *Schmidt*, Akazienweg 19 (☎02232 32295). Alternatively, the following **hotels**, all close to the Schloss, charge between DM30 and DM35: *Kürfurst*, Kölnstr. 40 (☎02232 42239); *Clemens-August-Stube*, Römerstr. 86 (☎02232 27364); and *Brühler Hof*, Uhlstr. 30 (☎02232 42711). Brühl's prices are generally so much lower than those in both Cologne and Bonn that it's worth considering as an alternative base—both cities can be reached quickly either by tram (from the town center) or train (on the opposite side of the Schloss). **Concerts** by top international musicians in the Schloss *Galerie* are the main cultural attraction, while October sees a **festival** of international puppet theater. There are two **beers** to try: Brühl is sufficiently close enough to Cologne to be allowed to brew its own *Kölsch* (see p.432), named *Giesler*, while the local Pils is predictably called *Clemens August*. The town's other eminent citizen, the dadaist and surrealist painter **Max Ernst**, is commemorated by a small **museum** (Mon.–Thurs. 10am–noon and 2–4pm, Fri. 10am–noon; free) housed in his birthplace, a villa facing the northern wing of the Schloss. It has a few early oil paintings, but the bulk of the material is graphic work, displayed in a changing series of exhibitions.

Walking 2km eastwards through the Schloss grounds takes you to the **Jagdschloss Falkenlust** (Tues.–Sun. 9am–noon and 2–4pm; 1.50DM), Clemens August's base for his falconry adventures, designed once again by Cuvilliés. It's intimate in scale, and this time you're allowed to explore it at your leisure; there's also little chance of it being closed for state visits, unless it's intended to register official disapproval of the guest's policies by denying access to the main Schloss (as was the case with the hated Romanian President Ceausescu). In the oval main *Salon* is a series of portraits of the Wittelsbachs in their hunting attire, but the most impressive rooms are the smallest: the *Lacquer Cabinet*, reflecting the contemporary taste for chinoiserie, and the *Cabinet of Mirrors* directly above. Outside is a tiny **chapel**, a folly in imitation of a hermitage.

Lignite was formerly mined to the west of Brühl; this area has since been transformed into the northern section of the **Naturpark Kottenforst-Ville**, which stretches along the foot of the Eifel range all the way down to Bonn. Alongside the inevitable stretches of forest are numerous small lakes. The nearest of these to Brühl, the Heider Bergsee, offers fishing, swimming, yachting, and canoeing; it also has a **campground**.

COLOGNE

Although now in the political shadow of the neighboring upstarts of Bonn and Düsseldorf, **COLOGNE** (*KÖLN*) stands as a colossus in the vast urban sprawl of the Rhine-Ruhr conurbation, being unquestionably one of the great German cities, and currently the fourth largest with a population of just under one million. The huge Gothic **Dom** is the country's most visited monument, while its ensemble of Roman remains and medieval buildings is unsurpassed, and the museums bettered only by those in Berlin and Munich. If you time it right, the annual **Carnival** in the early spring is one of Europe's major popular celebrations. The city also ranks high as a **beer** center: there are 24 breweries (the highest total in Germany), all producing the distinctive *Kölsch*.

Originally founded in 33 B.C., Cologne quickly gained importance. It was the birthplace of Julia Agrippa, wife of the Emperor Claudius, who in A.D. 50 raised it to the status of a colony (hence its name) with full rights as a Roman city. Subsequent development owed much to ecclesiastical affairs—a bishopric was founded in the fourth century, and Saints Severin, Gereon, and Ursula were all martyred in the city; churches were soon dedicated to each and built over their graves. The cult of St. Ursula was especially popular, being associated with the alleged death of her 11,000 virgin companions, though the true figure was probably a more realistic eleven. In the twelfth century, Cologne acquired by force the relics of the Three Magi from Milan, thus increasing its standing as one of the greatest focuses of pilgrimage in northern Europe.

Medieval Cologne, a city of 150 churches, became enormously prosperous because of its strategic situation on the Rhine at the intersection of trade routes. The largest city in Germany, it was one of the great European centers of learning, and boasted a distinctive school of painters. Decline inevitably set in, but something of a comeback was made in the eighteenth century with a recipe imported from Italy for extracting flower-blossom essence with almost pure alcohol. Originally, this was meant as an aphrodisiac but was to achieve world-wide fame as a toilet water under the euphemism by which customers ordered it—*eau de Cologne*, water from Cologne.

Arrival and practicalities

The **Hauptbahnhof** is right downtown, immediately below the Dom. Moving on is never a problem, as some 1000 trains per day stop there. **Exchange facilities** are available from 7am to 9pm, including Sundays and holidays. The **bus station** is directly behind, with international services on the lower tier. For the **airport** (☎402222 or 402256 for flight information) take bus #170; there are departures approximately every 20 minutes, with a journey time of less than half an hour.

The **tourist office** is at Unter Fettenhennen 19, directly in front of the Dom (May–Oct. Mon.–Sat. 8am–10:30pm, Sun. and holidays 9am–10:30pm, Nov.–April

Mon.–Sat. 8am–9pm, Sun. and holidays 9:30am–7pm; ☎221 3345). Apart from the usual maps, there's an excellent array of free leaflets and brochures on every aspect of the city. For a **hotel room**, don't hesitate to shell out the DM2 they charge to find you a place. Accommodation is plentiful, but it's scattered all over the city and is mainly geared to the expense-account brigade attending the numerous trade fairs. This does mean, however, that some of the better hotels offer discount rates at slack times; an example is *Gülich*, Ursulaplatz 13–19 (☎120015), which halves its prices. If you prefer to look yourself, the following are centrally placed and charge in the region of DM30–40 for a single, DM50–60 for a double: *Stapelhäuschen*, Fischmarkt 1–3 (☎212193); *Im Kupferkessel*, Probsteigasse 6 (☎135338); *Schmidt*, Elisenstr. 16 (☎211706); *Einig*, Johanisstr. 71 (☎122128); *Henn*, Norbertstr. 6 (☎134445). You can obviously pay less if you're prepared to stay out in the suburbs.

There are two **youth hostels**: the more central is at Siegesstr. 5a in DEUTZ (☎814711), about 15 minutes' walk from the city center over the Hohenzollernbrücke, or just two blocks south of Deutz Bahnhof. It's rather dingy and claustrophobic; much more enticing is the youth guest house in the northern suburb of RIEHL (☎767081; take U-Bahn #5, #16 or #18 from Dom/Hauptbahnhof, and get down at Boltensternstrasse). This has modern spacious rooms with lockers, a bar, and (unsurprisingly) much higher prices. As far as **campgrounds** are concerned, the only one open all year is located at Peter-Baum-Weg in the extreme northeastern suburb of DÜNNWALD. There are two more in POLL (south of Deutz): that on Weidenweg (☎831966) is open from May to September and is intended for families; the other, on Alfred-Schutte-Allee (☎832337) is for schoolchildren, and only opens during vacation periods. Immediately south, but this time on the right bank, is the final grounds at Uferstr. 53a in RODENKIRCHEN (☎392421), open from March to October.

Cologne's **public transit** network uses a mixture of buses and trams; the latter become the U-Bahn around the center. The system is shared with Bonn, and it's possible to take a non-express tram between the two cities—useful if you intend to leave from or arrive at somewhere which isn't central. Ticket prices are high, making it better to invest in strips of four, or those valid for 24 hours (DM6.50 Cologne only, DM11.50 the whole circuit) or three days (DM13 Cologne only, DM18 the whole circuit).

The City

You don't need to walk very far to see the main attractions of Cologne; the Dom and the main museums are grouped together, with some of the traditional beer halls close by. Although most visitors venture no farther, it would be a pity not to see something of the medieval city (or Altstadt), which occupied an enormous area; among the surviving buildings are twelve Romanesque churches, much the finest collection anywhere. Don't expect to get more than a superficial impression in under two days, and a considerably longer period is needed to see everything. The best way to start your tour is to cross over to the right-bank suburb of Deutz—or at least to go some distance across either the Hohenzollernbrücke or the Deutzer Brücke—for the classic **view**, with the tall houses of the burghers lining the banks of the Rhine (crossed by no less than eight bridges within the city boundaries), and the chunky Romanesque tower of Gross St. Martin providing an ideal counterfoil to the soaring openwork steeples of the Dom.

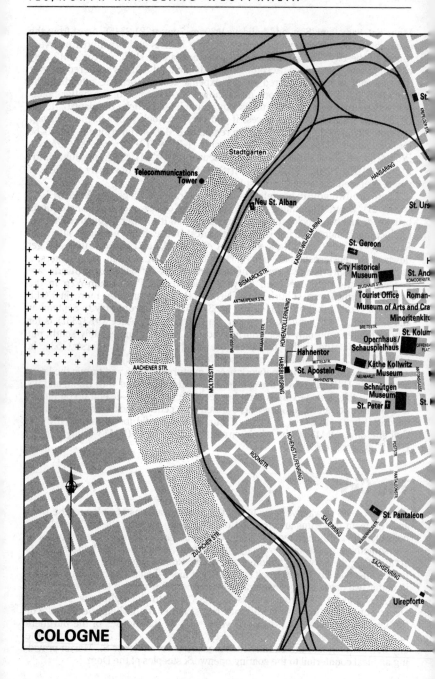

Stadtgarten

Telecommunications Tower ●

Neu St. Alban

KAISER-WILHELM-RING

St. Gereon

City Historical Museum

St. And

HANSARING

St. Urs

St.

KREFELDER STR.

COMODIENSTR.

ZEUGHAUS STR.

Tourist Office

Roman-

Museum of Arts and Cra

Minoritenkirc

BISMARCKSTR.

ANTWERPENER STR.

HOHENZOLLERNRING

BREITESTR.

St. Kolu

Opernhaus/
Schauspielhaus

Hahnentor

OFFENBA
PLAT.

BRUSSELER STR.

BRABANTER STR.

HABSBURGRING

St. Aposteln

Käthe Kollwitz Museum

HAHNENSTR.

NEUMARKT

ANTONSGASSE

AACHENER STR.

MOLTKESTR.

MITTELSTR.

Schnütgen Museum

St. Peter

St.

HOHENSTAUFENRING

ROONSTR.

POSTSTR.

PANTALEONSTR.

St. Pantaleon

SALIERRING

VOLKSHOFSTR.

SACHSENRING

ZÜLPICHER STR.

Ulrepforte

COLOGNE

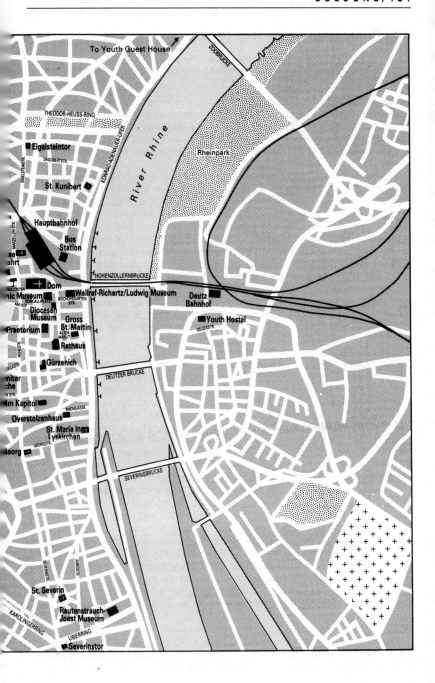

To Youth Guest House

ZOOBRÜCKE

THEODOR-HEUSS-RING

River Rhine

Rheinpark

Eigelsteintor

DAGOBERTSTR.

St. Kunibert

KONRAD-ADENAUER-UFER

EIGELSTEINTOR

MARZELLEN STR.

Hauptbahnhof

Bus Station

ahrt

HOHENZOLLERNBRÜCKE

Dom

Wallraf-Richartz/Ludwig Museum

Deutz Bahnhof

nic Museum

BISCHOFSGARTEN STR.

AM HOF

BONGALLPLATZ

Diocesan Museum

Gross St. Martin

ALTER MARKT

Youth Hostel

SIEGESSTR.

Praetorium

HOHESTR.

Rathaus

Gürzenich

nter che

IN STR.

im Kapitol

DEUTZER BRÜCKE

RHEINGASSE

Overstolzenhaus

St. Maria im Lyskirchen

GEORGSTR.

eorg

SEVERINSBRÜCKE

SEVERINSTR.

MARIENTL

St. Severin

Rautenstrauch-Joest Museum

KAROLINGERRING

UBIERRING

Severinstor

The Dom

". . . it was the most beautiful of all the churches I have ever seen, or can imagine. If one could imagine the spirit of devotion embodied in any material form, it would be in such a building."

Lewis Carroll's gushing tribute is typical of the extravagant praise which has been heaped upon Cologne's **Dom**. One of the most massive Gothic buildings ever constructed, it dominates the city in every sense, its size reflecting its power. The archbishop was one of the seven electors of the Holy Roman Empire, and, as "queen and mother of all German churches," it remains the seat of the Primate of Germany.

The history of the present building is an odd one, for although the foundation stone was laid in 1248, it was only finally completed in 1880; most of what can be seen today was put up in two concentrated periods of activity separated by five centuries, yet in an almost identical architectural style. Impetus for the creation of a new cathedral came with the arrival of the alleged relics of the Magi and the subsequent increase in pilgrims. A spectacular **shrine** was commissioned to house the relics, begun in 1181 by **Nicholas of Verdun**, the greatest goldsmith of the day, and finished in 1220 by local craftsmen. What was now needed was a fitting palace to house this memorial to the kings, whose relics were deemed important for symbolical reasons—they were the first earthly monarchs to be acknowledged by the King of Heaven, therefore whoever guarded them must hold a special place in the Kingdom of Christ on earth. It was decided to adopt the ethereal new Gothic style of architecture for the cathedral, rather than the late Romanesque style still in vogue in the Rhineland, but to surpass earlier French models in size and splendor.

The chancel, designed by **Master Gerhard**, was completed in 1322, but thereafter the sheer ambitiousness of the plans began to take its toll. In 1560, the project was abandoned, with a crane poised over the unfinished south tower, which, with the lower parts of the nave and facade, was all that had subsequently been built. That might have been the end of the story, had it not been for the impact of the Romantic movement in the early nineteenth century, which led to a campaign for the completion of the cathedral, boosted by the discovery of two pieces of parchment which showed the medieval builders' designs for the facade. From 1842, in a remarkable act of homage to another age, the work was carried out in a style that would have been completely familiar to the original masons.

It's seldom mentioned nowadays that there was a counter-movement which disapproved of this project, feeling that the building would lose its uniqueness and that the modern part would fail to match the old. Yet, looking with an unprejudiced eye, there's little doubt that the right decision was taken. Pollution has made it hard to distinguish the two sections, and there's every reason to be grateful for the crushing power of the finished facade, of which you get a great uninterrupted view from the square in front. There's none of the one-upmanship that disfigures most derivative architecture, and the only miscalculation was in going ahead with a full imitative sculptural program for the eight new portals; the figures are often feeble and would never have passed the scrutiny of a medieval workshop. Originally, the **spires** were, at 157 meters, the tallest structures in the world, but they were soon dwarfed by the Eiffel Tower and are no longer even the highest in Cologne. All the same, you need a fair bit of energy to climb up the south tower to the base of the steeple for a fine **panorama** over the city and the Rhine (daily 9am–4/5/6pm according to season; DM2).

Enter by the west door and your eye is immediately drawn down the great length of the building to the **high altar** with the shrine to the Magi, which illustrates the history of the world as described in the Bible, with Epiphany given due prominence. It's one of three artistic masterpieces to be found here; the others are in the chapels at the entrance to the ambulatory. On the north side is the ninth-century **Gero crucifix**, the most important monumental sculpture of its period. The corresponding chapel to the south contains the greatest achievement of the fifteenth-century Cologne school of painters, the *Adoration of the Magi* triptych by **Stefan Lochner**. His refined, idealized and otherworldly style finds a perfect outlet in this truly gorgeous scene; the wings feature two of the Cologne martyrs, Saints Ursula and Gereon, with their companions. Look out also for an elaborate sixteenth-century carved retable from Antwerp in the south transept, a colossal wooden figure of St. Christopher nearby, and (at the intersection of the north transept and the nave aisle) the fourteenth-century Clares altar. The whole **chancel** is outstanding, preserving an unparalleled set of furnishings contemporary with the architecture—choir stalls; painted wooden panels; vibrant statues of Christ, the Virgin and the Apostles; and a delicate altar front. To penetrate beyond the barrier for a marginally better view of these, you have to take one of the free **guided tours** (German only) which leave from below the organ in the north transept. Times of departures on any given day are prominently displayed on various boards—normally they're at 10am, 11am, 2pm, and 3pm except Sunday mornings.

Stained glass windows are an essential component of a Gothic cathedral, and Cologne has a marvelously varied assemblage. The oldest, dating from 1260, is in the axis chapel of the ambulatory and is a "Bible" window, pairing New Testament scenes with a parallel from the Old Testament; another is two chapels to the south. In a wholly different, far more monumental style is the late Gothic glass on the north side of the nave, designed by some of the leading local painters. These in turn contrast well with the brilliantly colored nineteenth-century Bavarian windows opposite, a gift from King Ludwig I towards the Dom's completion.

The **Schatzkammer** (daily 9am–4/5pm; DM2) has a few exquisite Ottonian manuscripts, but is far less interesting than the **Diocesan Museum** just outside in Roncalliplatz (Mon.–Weds., Fri,. and Sat. 10am–5pm, Sun. 10am–1pm; DM1). Another beautiful **Lochner**, *Madonna of the Violets*, forms the centerpiece; in a glass case, and easily missed, is his little *Nativity*. Also displayed here are most of the sculptures which adorned the portal of the south tower, the only one dating from the medieval building period. Carved in the workshop of **Michael Parler**, a member of the famous dynasty of masons (see Schwäbisch Gmünd, *Chapter Two*), they've been replaced in situ by faithful copies. Other highlights include an eleventh-century crucifix which bizarrely uses an antique lapis lazuli of a woman as the head; the *St. Severin medallion* with a portrait of the saint; and two priceless textiles—a sixth-century Syrian silk illustrating a hunt, discovered in the shrine of St. Kunibert, and a Byzantine cloth embroidered with lions.

Museums Around the Dom

Cologne's two most important museums are housed in ultramodern buildings right beside the Dom; neither should be missed. Unless you've a student card (which allows half-price admission), it makes sense to invest in the DM6 Museums Pass, which allows continued entry to these and to all the other municipal collections on any three days (not necessarily consecutive) in a week.

Wallraf-Richartz/Ludwig Museum, *Bischofgartenstr. 1. Tues.–Thurs. 10am–8pm, Fri.–Sun. 10am–6pm; DM3.*
This houses the city's collection of paintings. On the first floor is the Wallraf-Richartz Museum of old masters, centered on the unique holdings of the fifteenth-century **Cologne school** (see *Contexts*). Look out for the backdrop depictions of the medieval city, often featuring the unfinished Dom with its hanging crane, along with other church towers which have survived to the present day. **Stefan Lochner** is the most admired artist of the school, and his *Last Judgment* is a major work, enormously inventive in detail, gentle and fantastic in its view; an apocalyptic vision would have been quite out of character. *Madonna in a Rose Garden* and the portable triptych *Madonna in a Walled Garden* show his treatment of what must have been far more congenial subjects. From the preceding generation, the **Master of St. Veronica** is the most accomplished painter, with two contrasting versions of the *Crucifixion*, one as delicately refined as an illuminated manuscript, the other with monumental figures. The gems of the whole display, however, are the two large triptychs made for the Carthusians by the **Master of St. Bartholomew**, who represented the final flowering of the school at the beginning of the sixteenth century. His figures are executed as if in imitation of sculpture, and have a haunting, mystical quality.

Displayed alongside the Cologne masters are other German paintings, including a small **Dürer** *Fifer and Drummer* (in fact, the musicians who entertained Job on his dung heap—the companion scene is in Frankfurt); and several typical examples of **Cranach**. There are a number of Flemish panels, notably a *Nativity* by **Memling**, and Italian primitives, among which a *Madonna and Child* by **Simone Martini** stands out. Grouped around the staircase are the largest works, including two canvases by **Rubens**, *Juno and Argus* and *Stigmatization of St. Francis*. The latter was painted for the Capuchins of Cologne and is now hung back to back with *St. Francis in the Porzincula Chapel* by **Murillo**, offering a fascinating comparison of treatment by two of the great masters of the Counter-Reformation. Another comparative exercise can be made of the *Entombment* by the key figures in sixteenth-century Venetian painting, **Titian** and **Tintoretto**.

The corridor and galleries beyond have a rich representation of seventeenth-century Dutch artists, including what is probably the very last of **Rembrandt**'s great series of self-portraits, in which he depicted himself in the guise of a laughing philosopher from ancient Greece. (The two other works labeled as his are probably not originals.) There's a comprehensive array of French painting from the seventeenth century to Impressionism, while the nineteenth-century German school is dominated by a large collection of the local artist **Wilhelm Leibl**, leader of the realist movement.

The Ludwig Museum of Twentieth-Century Art occupies the remainder of the galleries, including all of the second floor. It's a shock to go up from the fifteenth century altarpieces and be confronted by Brillo boxes, Pepsi-Cola and Campbell's Tomato Juice, the favorite subjects of **Andy Warhol**, which are the centerpiece of a notable display of pop art which also includes examples of Tom Wesselmann and Roy Lichtenstein. The Swedish-American experimental sculptor **Claes Oldenburg** is represented by *The Street,* which occupies a whole room. Many other eye-catching pieces of sculpture, including the uncanny fibre-glass creations of the realists and **Ed Kienholz**'s *Portable War Memorial* (a devastating satire on his country's cultural values), are housed in the basement.

Among German works, there's a fine group of **Kirchner**s, notably a group portrait of *Die Brücke* (see *Contexts*); around it hang examples of these very painters. **Max Ernst** provided a similar memento of the surrealists, including posthumously included members, Raphael and Dostoyevsky. The same artist iconoclastically sets the theme of the *Madonna and Child* on its ear; the furious mother administers a sound thrashing on the infant's buttocks while Ernst and friends look on. **Beckmann** is given a room to himself, while **Nolde** and **Kokoschka** share one; by the latter is a *View of Cologne*. There are three superb portraits by **Dix**, including one of himself, and a number of sculptures in various media by **Barlach**. Two rooms are devoted to **Picasso**, who is represented by sculptures and ceramics as well as paintings from most phases of his career. In contrast, there's only a single spectacular **Dalí**, *Perpignan Station*, the elaborate symbolism of which is explained in a descriptive label. Beside it hangs one of the most famous surrealist canvases, *Presence of Mind* by **Magritte**, on loan from a private collection. An impressive array of Russian paintings includes a large **Chagall**, *Moses Destroying the Tablets of the Law.*

The third museum in the premises, the **Agfa-Foto-Historama**, shows old photographic equipment and a changing selection of prints from the vast holdings of the famous company, whose headquarters are in nearby Leverkusen; regrettably, it has only been allocated two galleries.

Roman-Germanic Museum, *Roncalliplatz 4. Tues. and Fri.–Sun. 10am–5pm, Weds. and Thurs. 10am–8pm; DM3.*
This is West Germany's most important archaeological museum, specially constructed around the star exhibit, the **Dionysos Mosaic**, excavated here in 1941. The finest work of its kind in northern Europe, it adorned the dining room of a patrician villa of about A.D. 200, and is made from over a million pieces of limestones, ceramics and glass, covering an area of some seventy square meters. In the middle is the inebriated Bacchus, leaning on his companion, his tankard on the floor. Around are bacchanalian dancers, satyrs, Cupid riding on a lion, Pan with his goat, and vignettes of the delights of the table. Its astonishing state of preservation is due to the protective covering it received from the burnt-out remains of the building falling on it when sacked by a Germanic tribe in the fourth century.

The other main item is the **tomb of Poblicius**, a veteran who served in the Fifth Legion. Dating from about A.D. 200, this is an even more recent discovery. It stands about 15 meters high, and has been reerected beside the mosaic, although considerably more restoration has been necessary. If you're broke, you don't need to pay to see these two objects—there's a good view to be had by peering in from the square.

Otherwise, the museum is arranged thematically. The collection of **glass** is reckoned to be unsurpassed anywhere in the world; it includes a tiny, idealized portrait of Augustus Caesar made in 27 B.C. From the second century on, the Cologne workshops developed their own distinctive forms, with colored serpentine threads used for decorative effects. This style culminated around A.D. 330 in the *diatreta* glass, decorated with a delicate network design. Perhaps of more general appeal is the dazzling array of **jewelry** on the first floor, which mostly dates from the so-called Dark Ages after the Romans had been driven out, and was found in Frankish graves. Also worthy of mention are the fragments of the city's North Gate, the Philosophers Mosaic of 260 A.D., a reconstruction of a Roman carriage, and an eye-straining display of over 1000 terra-cotta lamps.

The Altstadt and the Romanesque Churches

The vast area that was medieval Cologne suffered grievous damage in the last war. Much of what you now see is modern, due to the need to rebuild the city as quickly as possible to render it economically viable. Where there wasn't a pressing need for buildings to be reconstructed, as in the case of the churches, time was allowed in order to undertake faithful restoration projects, and these are still going on. What has been achieved is most impressive—you only need to look at the photographs displayed in each church showing its state at the end of the war—although there's no denying that much has been irretrievably lost and that the city has been altered for the worse. With that proviso, there's a lot to enjoy, and the twelve **Romanesque churches**, which range in date from the tenth to the thirteenth centuries, form one of the most coherent groups in a single architectural style to be found in any European city. Each has interesting features, but if you blanch at the prospect of seeing them all, the extraordinary **St. Gereon** is the one that shouldn't be missed for its architecture, while **St. Maria im Kapitol** has the finest furnishings, and **Gross St. Martin** and **St. Aposteln** have justifiably famous exteriors. Where there are standard times for visiting the churches, these are given in parentheses; outside of these hours the vestibule may still be kept open, allowing at least a restricted view inside. To avoid cultural indigestion, it's best to spread your exploration of the Altstadt over two or three days.

For nearly 600 years, **Gross St. Martin's** tower, surrounded by four turrets, was the dominant feature of the Cologne skyline, not being usurped by the Dom's spires until last century. The rest of the church (formerly a monastery occupied by Benedictines from Scotland and Ireland) seems rather truncated for such a splendid adornment, although the interior (daily 10am–6pm) has been returned to its simple original form. Such old houses as remain are in the streets nearby; seen at close quarters, it's rather obvious that many are recent reproductions. A short distance beyond is the Alter Markt, one of three large squares in the heart of the city. From here, you can see the irregular octagonal tower of the **Rathaus**, a building which is a real fricassee of styles, yet with marvelous features. Its core is fourteenth-century Gothic; the following century the tower was added in a more flamboyant idiom, while in the 1570s a graceful loggia, a rare example of Renaissance architecture in the Rhineland, was provided as a frontispiece. To see the historic parts of the interior—the *Hansa Saal* from the first building period and the tower rooms with doorways of inlaid woods—you have to take an hour-long guided tour (Mon., Weds., and Fri. at 3pm; free). Although in German only, you can pick up a leaflet in English which explains everything. Just in front of the entrance to the Rathaus is an unprepossessing door which leads down into the **Mikwe**, a Jewish ritual bath house dating from about 1160, the only remnant of the ghetto which was razed soon after the expulsion order of 1424. It's officially open on Sundays from 11am to 1pm, but from Monday to Friday you can ask for the key during office hours at the porter's desk in the Rathaus. More subterranean sights can be seen a short distance away in the form of the **Praetorium**, the foundations of the Roman governor's palace, and the **Roman sewer**, a surprisingly elegant vaulted passageway some 100 meters long. The entrance to both of these is at Kleine Budengasse (Tues.–Sun. 10am–5pm; DM2; but included on the Museums Pass).

Proceding southwards, you pass the burned-out **Alt St. Alban**, left as a war memorial; the **Gürzenich**, best known as the home of the Carnival balls; and the tower which is all that survives of **Klein St. Martin**. Behind is **St. Maria im**

Kapitol, not seen to advantage from outside as it was built in a severe convent style and is now hemmed in by modern houses, but with a majestic interior (daily 10am–6pm) complete with a full circuit for processions around the aisles. Originally constructed in the eleventh century, it pioneered the trefoil or clover-leaf chancel which was to be imitated throughout the Rhineland in the two succeeding centuries. Look out for the **wooden doors**, contemporary with the architecture and among the most precious works of their kind, depicting Christ's Nativity, Teachings, and Passion in a restrained, loving way. During recent restorations, the elaborate Renaissance rood screen was returned to its original position. You can also visit the spacious crypt, while the cloisters, unusually placed adjoining the facade, are the only ones left in Cologne.

Continuing in a southerly direction, go down Rheingasse to see **Overstolzenhaus**, the finest mansion in the city, a step-gabled patrician home contemporary with the later Romanesque churches. A short walk from here is the sailors' church of **St. Maria in Lyskirchen** (daily 10am–12:30pm and 3–5pm); their *Schöne Madonna* of about 1420 is one of several fine works of art. The vaults are covered with thirteenth-century frescos of scenes from the Old and New Testaments and lives of saints; they're seen to best effect if you climb the stairs to the gallery. From here, head up Grosse Witschgasse and Georgstrasse to **St. Georg** (daily 8am–6pm), an eleventh-century pillared basilica which resembles early Christian churches. The westwork, added the following century, looks squat and stumpy from without, but is impressively spacious when you're inside.

It's then a walk of some fifteen minutes due south to the **St. Severin** quarter. Although the church here (daily 7:30am–noon and 3–6:45pm) is classed as Romanesque, only the twin-towered apse and part of the transept remain from that time, the rest being late Gothic. Now it's of more interest to archaeology buffs, on account of the **Roman-Frankish graveyard** which has been found directly underneath; it can be visited on guided tours (Mon. and Fri. 4:30pm; free). Just beyond the church is the Severinstor, part of the medieval fortifications which were largely demolished last century when the Ring was built.

Following this road in a northwesterly direction, you pass the **Ulrepforte**, another turreted gateway. Farther along, turn right at Waisenhausgasse and you arrive at **St. Pantaleon** (daily 9am–5pm), the oldest surviving church in the city, dating from the end of the tenth century. It's chiefly notable for its massive westwork with vestibule; this was disrupted in the baroque period, before being returned to its original shape in a pioneering archaeological reconstruction last century. Inside, there's an airy Flamboyant Gothic rood screen, crowned by a seventeenth-century organ in a rococo case. North up Poststrasse and Peterstrasse is **St. Peter**, a Gothic church with gleaming stained glass windows. The magnificent *Crucifixion of St. Peter*, painted by **Rubens** (whose childhood was spent in Cologne) for the high altar, is now displayed in a chapel by the entrance. Next door is **St. Cäcilien**, the Romanesque church which now houses the **Schnütgen Museum** (see p.430 for details).

Across the road and down Antongasse is the tiny Gothic **Antoniterkirche**, now a Protestant parish church, best known for housing one of the most famous of twentieth-century sculptures, **Barlach's** *Memorial Angel*. This is a cast made from the plaster of the original, which was created for the 700th anniversary of the Dom in Güstrow (now in East Germany) but destroyed in the perverse Nazi measures against "degenerate art." Around the church is the main shopping center; the streets follow the same plan as their Roman predecessors, but almost all the buildings are modern. Up Herzogstrasse are the ruins of the Gothic **St.**

Kolumba, which wasn't restored after the war; instead **Gottfried Böhm** inserted a minute chapel in a wholly modern idiom within the shell in 1950. Farther down the same street is another Gothic church, the severe **Minoritenkirche**. It contains the tomb of John Duns Scotus, the Scots-born theologian who was the leading intellectual in early fourteenth-century Cologne. Ironically, he's the origin of the word "dunce"; his defenses of traditional religious orthodoxies so enraged his radical fellow-countrymen at the time of the Reformation that they used his name as a personification of stupidity.

A short distance west of the Antoniterkirche lies Neumarkt, dominated at the far end by the superb early thirteenth-century apse of St. **Aposteln** (*Holy Apostles*—a most unusual dedication outside the Orthodox world). This is an archetypal Rhenish basilica with all the characteristic features: clover-leaf chancel with dwarf gallery, central octagon with turrets and, above all, the great western tower with its "bishop's mitre" roof. Despite its apparently homogeneous design, building began in the eleventh century; the interior (Weds.–Mon. 10am–1pm and 2–6pm) is surprisingly plain. Nearby is another of the city gates, the **Hahnentor**, which resembles a castle's barbican. Due north of St. Aposteln is St. **Gereon**, most idiosyncratic of the twelve Romanesque churches, and a truly great building. Its kernel was an oval-shaped fourth-century chapel; in the eleventh and twelfth centuries a crypt, chancel and twin towers were added. Then, in the early thirteenth century, the Roman masonry was harnessed to form the basis of a magnificent four-story decagon with ribbed dome vault, a work which has no parallel in European architecture. At this time, the adjoining baptistery was also built and adorned with frescos. Make sure you come here when the whole of the church is open (daily 10am–noon and 3–5pm) to see the decagon's interior, which seems more graceful and less massive than from outside; the modern stained glass is a controversial addition. In the crypt, the original mosaic floor with Old Testament scenes is preserved.

From here, you can return towards the Dom, passing a fragment of Roman wall and the Arsenal en route to St. **Andreas**, which has a stately Romanesque nave preceded by a mighty westwork, an octagonal lantern tower and a Gothic chancel. Various frescos are preserved inside, along with the **Maccabeus shrine**, a notable piece of early sixteenth-century craftsmanship, doubtless inspired by the Dom's shrine to the Magi. Another casket contains the relics of St. **Albertus Magnus**, the thirteenth-century scholar who was the star teacher at Cologne's famous Dominican College; his pupils there included St. Thomas Aquinas, later to develop into the greatest philosopher of his time, and arguably of the entire medieval period. A short way along Marzellenstrasse is the pink exterior of St. **Mariae Himmelfahrt**, a seventeenth-century Jesuit foundation and Cologne's only baroque building of note. Its galleried interior, which surprisingly employs the out-of-favor Gothic pointed arch, is lavishly decorated—most unusual for the Rhineland, where Bavarian excesses never caught on.

A bit farther down the same street, turn left into Ursulaplatz, where St. **Ursula** (daily 9:30am–noon and 1–4:30pm), with its prominent sturdy tower, still retains some Romanesque features, along with Gothic and baroque accretions. Unless you're squeamish, try to get hold of the sacristan, who will show you the **Goldene Kammer**, an ornate baroque chamber lined with gruesome reliquaries. He can be elusive, but should be available at the fixed times (Mon. and Thurs. 11am–noon, Weds. and Fri. 3–4pm, Sat. 4–5pm). From here, the **Eigelsteintor**, another impressive survival of the medieval fortifications, is reached via the street of the same name. Dagobertstrasse then leads east to St. **Kunibert**, the final fling of Romanesque in the early thirteenth century, completed just as work began on the Dom. It's also the last church to be restored following war damage, with the nave and massive westwork not yet joined up. Inside (daily 7am–noon and 3–6pm), note the stained glass windows in the apse, which are contemporary with the architecture. On the piers of the transept are the two dramatic poly-chromed figures of an *Annunciation*, an important piece of Gothic carving by Conrad Kuyn, master mason at the Dom in the early fifteenth century.

Cologne's Other Museums

City Historical Museum, *Zeughausstr. 1–3. Tues., Weds., and Fri.–Sun. 10am–5pm, Thurs. 10am–8pm; DM2.*
Housed in the former Arsenal, this illustrates the history of Cologne, focusing on its trade and industry, along with sections on Carnival and eau de Cologne. Some good models show the building development of the city.

Engine Museum of Klockner-Humboldt-Deutz AG, *Deutz-Mülheimer Str. 111. Mon.–Fri. 9am–4pm; free.*
This is within the organization's headquarters, and focuses on the internal combustion engine which so transformed technological history. Among the displays are the first four-stroke test engine, pioneered by this company, and many subsequent versions. Regrettably, the only vehicles on show are a few early tractors; only four-stroke freaks need make the long trek here.

Käthe Kollwitz Museum, *Neumarkt 18–24. Mon.–Weds. 9am–4:30pm, Thurs. 9am–6:30pm, Fri. 9am–3:30pm; free.*
The odd opening times are explained by the fact that this museum is within a bank. It has a large display of graphics and a few sculptures by Käthe Kollwitz, one of the leading female artists of this century. Her preference for black-and-white media helps give her work an enormous pathos, evident in her variation on the *Mother and Child* theme, and her denunciations of the follies and sufferings of war. (See also Berlin, *Chapter Eight*).

Museum of Arts and Crafts, *An der Rechtschule.*
By now, this museum should have opened in the premises vacated by the Wallraf-Richartz Museum. Previously, the city's impressive holdings of European arts and crafts from the Middle Ages onwards had never been properly displayed.

Museum of East Asian Art, *Universitätstr. 100. Tues.–Sun. 10am–5pm, first Fri. in month 10am–8pm; DM2.*
Devoted to the arts of China, Japan, and Korea, this is yet another of Cologne's collections which has been given specially designed modern premises, appropri-ately enough by a Japanese architect, and with a traditional Japanese garden. It's arranged thematically—Buddhas; Chinese painting on scrolls, fans and album leaves; bronzes; ceramics; lacquer work; Japanese screens and sliding doors. Free leaflets in English are available on each topic.

Rautenstrauch-Joest Museum, *Ubierring 45. Tues.–Sun. 10am–5pm, first Weds. in month 10am–8pm; DM2.*
This large ethnological museum's particular strengths are Indochina and pre-Columbian America; West Africa, the Pacific and Indonesia are also well repre-sented. There are often special exhibitions; when these occur, the Museums Pass isn't valid for even the permanent displays.

Schnütgen Museum, *Cäcilienstr. 29. Tues.–Sun. 10am–5pm, first Weds. in month 10am–8pm; DM2.*
The Romanesque convent church of St. Cäcilien has been adapted to house the collection of religious art (except paintings) of the Rhineland. This setting greatly enhances the objects, although no medieval church would have been quite so packed with treasures. It's an ideal place to wander around at leisure and while away an hour or so. There are some wonderful ivories, notably a diptych which belonged to Charlemagne and the comb of St. Heribert. Major pieces of Romanesque sculpture include the church's own tympanum, carved in a heavily antique style; the wooden crucifix from St. Georg; and the mysterious *Siegburg Madonna*. From the Gothic period are many of the original carvings from the Dom's altar front (those in situ are mostly copies), and the museum's most famous possession, the polychromed console bust of a woman; this was carved by one of the Parler family, and is thought to be a portrait of a relative. Bridging the transition to the Renaissance is a highly elaborate Passion retable from Kalkar. In the former sacristy, stained glass windows can be seen at close quarters, and there's a collection of old embroideries on pull-out display racks.

Outside the Center

If you want to stray beyond the confines of the Altstadt, Cologne's suburbs offer a wide choice of **parks**, along with some of the most exciting **modern architecture** in Germany.

In every way, the dominant building is the **Telecommunications Tower** (daily 9am–11pm; DM4, including ascent by elevator to the viewing platform), completed in 1980; at 243 meters it's considerably higher than the Dom. In spite of the pricey admission, it's definitely worth going up for the breathtaking views over the city and the Rhine. Very close by, and actually within the Stadtgarden, is **Neu St. Alban**, one of several highly praised modern churches in Cologne. The city has taken the European lead in championing unashamedly contemporary designs in ecclesiastical architecture, which elsewhere has become something of a lost art this century. This one is austere, with only one side pierced by windows, and these only tiny ones designed to admit very little light in an attempt to give the interior a mystical quality reminiscent of early Christian churches. Also near the Ring, but to the north, is **St. Gertrud** on Krefelder Strasse, with an amazing tapering tower. It's the work of **Gottfried Böhm**, whose father **Dominikus** was a pioneer of radical church design between the world wars. An example of the latter's 1930s expressionism is **St. Engelbert**, a centrally planned building of eight identical concrete shells, located very near the youth guest house on Riehler Gürtel. From the penultimate year of his life in 1954 is **St. Maria Königin** in the southern suburb of MARIENBURG, one of the most accomplished of a new generation of churches built to serve the needs of the residential quarters then being built. It takes a directly opposite stance to Neu St. Alban in the matter of light, having one wall consisting of almost nothing but window, and a circular baptistery resembling an enormous drinking glass.

Although there are few areas of green downtown, about a quarter of Cologne is given over to open space. Most popular is the **Rheinpark** in Deutz, a legacy of large garden shows, with the *Tanzbrunnen*, around which are showbiz concerts in summer. It's linked by cable car (April–Oct. Sat.–Thurs. 10am–7pm; DM4) over the Rhine to the **Botanical Gardens** (daily 8am–dusk), near the **Zoo** and **Aquarium** (daily 8:30am–6pm in summer, 9am–5pm in winter; DM6). Other parks are in the far suburbs. To the southwest are the recreational *Volksgarten* and a forestry reserve at **RODENKIRCHEN** (daily 9am–4/6/8pm according to season) with trees, plants, and shrubs from around the world. The right bank has nature reserves at **DÜNNWALD**, **BRÜCK** and **PORZ**, the last featuring birds of prey (daily April–Sept. 9am–7pm, Oct.–March 9am–5pm).

There's one more important Roman monument, a second-century **Burial Chamber** (Tues.–Thurs. 10am–1pm, Fri. 10am–5pm, Sat. and Sun. 1–5pm; DM2) located to the west of the city center at Aachener Strasse in **WEIDEN**. It contains marble busts of a couple and a young woman which are contemporary with the building, and a sarcophagus from the following century with carvings of the seasons.

Weiden lies about halfway along the route to the village of **BRAUWEILER**, which is separated from Cologne by just a couple of kilometers of open country-side, and reached by regular bus services. It clusters around the **Abteikirche**, built as a Benedictine monastery in the twelfth and early thirteenth centuries in an exuberant late Romanesque style. There are no less than six towers: the western group belongs to the early part of the building period, whereas the two at the east end plus the central octagon, though originally planned, were not built until the Romantic revival last century. The crypt is sombre and architecturally pure, but the pillars of the nave are capped by sensual figurative capitals. A wooden *St. Nicholas* at the end of the north apse and a serene stone retable in the corresponding position to the south are contemporary with the architecture. The latter is one of the masterpieces of German Romanesque sculpture, in which the same saint, the church's patron, turns up in a gathering around the *Madonna and Child*.

Kölsch, Beer Halls, and Restaurants

Cologne crams over 3000 pubs, bars, and cafés into a relatively small area. The most ubiquitous feature is the city's own beer, *Kölsch;* it's as much a piece of local life as the Dom or Carnival and may only be produced in the breweries located in and around Cologne. It's clear, light, highly fermented, and aromatically bitter, with a strong hint of hops. Invariably, it's served with a substantial head in a tall, thin glass (*Stange*) which holds only a fifth of a liter. This gives it a rather effete image among macho beer drinkers from elsewhere in Germany, who tend to revile it, in contrast to the religious reverence it's accorded in Cologne. The denigratory view seems rather jaundiced, and there's no doubt that the modest capacity of the glasses ensures that the beer is always fresh. It's the staple drink of a multitude of *Eckkneipen* or corner pubs which pop up everywhere and, being of a uniform drabness, are generally worth avoiding.

Much more promising are the *Brauhäuser*, brewery-owned beer halls which largely date from the turn of the century, though claiming a much longer pedigree. Whilst smaller than their Munich counterparts, they have similarly cavernous interiors with sparse decor. They're staffed by horribly familiar *Köbes*, who all year round keep up the the Carnival tradition of making insulting and corny jokes. Inevitably, these pubs are often overrun with visiting businessmen and Dom-gaping tourists, but they're definitely worth sampling, as they offer some of the cheapest **eating** possibilities in the city, specializing in the local cuisine. Don't be misled by the dialect, however—*Halve Hahn* is not the half a chicken you'd expect but a rye roll with cheese, while *Kölsche Kaviar* is less of a bargain than it appears when you realise it's a black pudding, again with rye bread.

Three of the *Brauhäuser* are very close to the Dom; consequently they're the most prone to be packed with visitors. *Alt Köln* at Trankgasse 7–9 has a quite different interior from the others, a picturesque folly with wooden alcoves and galleries representing a recreation of a series of old German taverns. *Früh am Dom*, Am Hof 12–14 and *Brauhaus Sion* round the corner at Unter Taschenmacher 5 are archetypal. For a more authentic atmosphere and arguably better food, you'd be better trying those a bit farther away: the two called *Päffgen*, at Heumarkt 62 and Friesenstr. 64; *Haus Töller* at Weyerstr. 96; and *Zur Malzmühle* at Heumarkt 6.

If you've a really serious interest in the city's liquid culture, head out southwards to the *Küppers Kölsch Brauhaus* beyond the Südstadt at Altenburgerstr. 157, where a **museum** has been set up, including the re-creation of an old brewery (guided tours Sat. only, leaving every hour 11am–3pm; ignore the sign outside and the tourist office leaflets which say it's open until 4pm). Afterwards you can have a drink in the beer garden, or in the tavern reconstructed to resemble those downtown.

Most of Cologne's **ethnic restaurants** are either expensive or mediocre, but the following are exceptions: *Tchang*, Grosse Sandkaul 19 (Chinese); *Maharani*, Hohenzollernring 53 (Indian); *Bali*, Brüsseler Platz 2 (Indonesian); *Yakitori*, Friesenplatz 7 (Japanese); *Café-Especial*, Deutz-Neuhöffer Str. 32 (Mexican).

Nightlife

There are four distinct quarters of Cologne with a recommendable concentration of nightspots. The most obvious is the area around Gross St. Martin in the **Altstadt**; this tends to catch visiting tourists and businessmen, but the best places do manage to create their own atmosphere. Down the road from the University (in the southwestern part of the city), the **Quartier Lateng** is more like the real thing as far as mingling with locals is concerned, even if it has lost its trendy edge. The **Südstadt**, or St. Severin quarter, now has the most stylish bars and cafés, and the biggest crowds. For once, it pays to follow them—it's their sheer exuberance that make the place. The more relaxed **Belgisches Viertel** (the streets around the Ring, just to the west of the center) is nowhere near as packed or self-consciously trendy. Currently dominated by arty types, it's also hub of the **gay scene**, has the most original **discos**, and could yet become the in place. Here's a selection of the best establishments listed by street within each quarter. Also included are recommendations for **breakfast**, often available until the afternoon, although on Sundays it's a popular finish for late-night revelers.

Altstadt

Papa Joe's Klimperkasten, Alter Markt 50. The deservedly popular place to go for traditional live jazz which is belted out to an appreciative audience from 8pm onwards. Very expensive drinks but young clientele at weekends, more businessmen at other times.

Papa Joe's Em Streckstrumpf, Buttermarkt 37. A cozier, smaller, equally good version of the above; invariably standing room only, with music beginning at 8:30pm and special Sunday sessions at 11am.

Biermuseum, Buttermarkt 39. A favorite haunt with tourists and correspondingly pricey; there are eighteen kinds of beer on tap.

Künsterklause Timp, Heumarkt 73. Mainly noted for a fairly tacky transvestite cabaret, but is very lively and packed out on Saturday nights; can be touchy about letting women in.

Zum Gir, Lintgasse 14. Huge arched cellar decked out with medieval paraphernalia; features live classical or folk (especially South American) music on Thursdays at 7:30pm.

Kännchen, Am Bollwerck 13. Tiny traditional pub.

Kauri, Auf dem Rothenberg 11. Conveniently sited disco with good selection of funk and blues; free admission but drinks extortionate.

Alter Wartesaal, Am Hauptbahnhof. A die-hard of the disco scene which has lost some of its freshness; music a mixture of Europop and Gothic.

Quartier Lateng

Vanille, Zülpicher Str. 25. Appealing café with kitsch decor, good for food (especially breakfast) and cocktails; keeps a selection of newspapers and has occasional disco evenings.

Filmdose, Zülpicher Str. 39. One of the most original, fun pubs in Cologne when busy (at weekends); otherwise a bit depressing. It has a tiny stage for cabaret and also shows films in English.

Palä, Palanterstr. 12a. Backstreet café with a wide selection of ice creams and breakfasts.

Café Orlando, Engelbertstr. 9. Quiet café just off Zülpicherstrasse, offering breakfast and health food; 1950s decor with old juke box.

Gilberts Pinte, Englebertstr. 1. Notorious student dive, home to a thousand *Stammtische*, but with plenty of atmosphere.

Peppermint Lounge, Hochenstauffenring 23. One of the most popular late-nighters, springing into action around midnight; also good for a late breakfast.

Café Central, Jülicher Str. 1. Stylish café which is one of the best places for breakfast; good selection of newspapers.

Weinhaus Kyffhäuser Keller, Kyffhäuser Str. 47. As recommendable a place as any in Cologne for a glass of wine, with over forty varieties to choose from.

Luxor, Luxemburger Str. 40. Disco with a healthy mixture of black dance music and chart stuff; also a popular live venue. Free entry after 11pm.

Juke Box, Luxemburger Str. 83. Best place to come to hear local live bands; free entrance, but jammed solid at weekends.

Südstadt

Linus New Pub, Ubierring 22. In the forefront of the Südstadt scene with good music under subdued lights; beware of being short-changed on beer measures.

Climux, Ublerring 18. A place to spot the in-crowd; very dark with ear-splitting music.

Spielplatz, Ubierring 58. More in the style of a beer hall, with a lot more character than some of its newer counterparts.

Schröders, Altenburgerstr. 11. Very chic; rather like a French brasserie with bright lights and mirrors.

Opera, Altenburgerstr. 1. Huge, overlit barn of a place with a very young clientele lining to get in at the weekends; good music and plenty of atmosphere.

Chlodwig-Eck, Annostr. 1. On a backstreet off the Ring; very "in."

Lichtblick, Kurfürstenstr. 8. Easygoing café away from the crowds; good breakfasts.

Bi Pis Bistro, Rolandstr. 61. In the unlikely setting of the Boy Scouts' offices; older, left-wing clientele and regular poetry readings.

Belgisches Viertel

Schulz, Bismarckstr. 17. Right at the heart of the gay scene; very reasonably priced bar and café.

Café Limelight, Bismarckstr. 44. Small and cozy artists' pub, totally unpretentious, yet with poetry readings, plays, cabaret, and live music.

Alcazar, Bismarckstr. 39a. Snug and candlelit, with tasty if overpriced menu; somewhat older clientele.

E.W.G., Aachener Str. 59. Chaotic pub packed out with students.

Hammersteins, Antwerpener Str. 34. The place to meet Cologne's yuppies; best known for an excellent but exorbitantly-priced restaurant.

Café Klön, Brüsseler Platz 16. If you pine for a cup of tea, this is where to go—there's a huge range, all served with egg timer in quiet, pleasant surroundings.

Broadway Café, Ehrenstr. 11. At the entrance to the *Broadway* movie theater; good breakfast from late morning onwards.

Neuschwanstein Diskothek, Mittelstr. 12. At time of writing the best disco in Cologne, with an excellent mix of music.

Zorba the Buddha, Hohenzollernring 40. Disco with good selection of mainstream music. Dance floor sometimes clears at midnight so that the Rajneeshi owners, decked from head to toe in red, can let rip with percussion instruments.

Zorba the Buddha die Kleine, Brabanter Str. 15. Smaller and quieter than the above, with older customers.

Zorba the Buddha, Brüsseler Str. 54. Spacious café-restaurant with good quality vegetarian food; breakfast served 10am–3:30pm.

Stadtgarten, Venloer Str. 40. Home of the *Kölner Jazzhaus Initiative*, so most of the jazz is modern and experimental; there's also a good restaurant.

Carnival—the facts

While there's no doubt that Cologne is worth visiting at any season, by far the best time to come is during **Carnival**. It's celebrated here with a verve normally associated with Mediterranean countries, and is a useful corrective to the common misapprehension that the Germans are an excessively serious and respectful people. For the *drei tollen Tage* ("three crazy days"), the normal life of the city comes to a complete stop and everyone, from punks to grannies, dons make-up and costume, taking to the streets as clown, fool, harlequin or historical personality.

The present highly-organized festival (here always known as *Karneval*, as opposed to *Fasching* in southern Germany) dates back to 1823, but its true origins are lost in the mists of time. In part it derives from a pagan exorcism of evil spirits in the transition from one season to another, and in part from a Christian tradition of periods of fasting, which were invariably preceded by counterbalancing periods of merriment. This latter factor governs the timetable of the festival, which has movable dates; the climax occurs in the week preceding Ash Wednesday, immediately before the stringencies of Lent. However, the Carnival season actually begins as early as "the 11th of the 11th," i.e. November 11, a date which was seen as having a foolish significance. From then on, Cologne holds both costume balls and *Sitzungen* (sessions); at the latter, speeches are made in rhyming couplets in the local *Kölsch* dialect (incomprehensible to outsiders, but fairly close to Dutch).

The real business begins with **Weiberfastnacht** on the Thursday prior to the seventh Sunday before Easter. A ceremony in the Alter Markt, starting at 10am, leads to the official inauguration of the festival with the handing over of the keys of the city by the Mayor at 11:11am precisely to *Prinz Claus III*, who assumes command for the "three crazy days." Whereas in other cities he's aided by a "princess," in Cologne he has two companions—the peasant *Bauer Knut* and the virgin *Jungfrau Karla*, played by a man and is emphatically not his betrothed. The fun can then begin in earnest; in repentance for the chauvinism of earlier centuries, this particular day is now dedicated to the supremacy of women, who are allowed to take the liberties of their choice. At 3pm there's the first of the great **processions**, beginning at Severinstor, based on the **legend of Jan. and Griet**. The former was Jan. von Werth, a seventeenth-century cavalry officer who saved the city from ruin in the Thirty Years' War. Griet was the Cologne girl who spurned him, prompting him to assume a military career; they were not to meet again until she, as an ageing spinster, saw him enter the city as a general at the head of his troops. In the evening, the great series of **costume balls** begins, the most prestigious being those in the Gürzenich. However, there are plenty of spontaneous bouts of singing, dancing, and boisterous conviviality in the streets and taverns as an authentic alternative.

For the next two days, the city returns to relative normality during daylight hours, although fancy dress is still much in evidence, and on Saturday morning there's the **Funkenbiwack**, featuring the *Rote und Blaue Funken* (Red and Blue "Sparks"), men dressd up in eighteenth-century military outfits; they disobey every order—a symbol of Cologne's long tradition of anti-militarism. The celebrations climax in two big costumed processions with floats; on Sunday the **Schullun Veedleszög**, largely featuring children, forms a prelude to the more spectacular **Rosenmontagzug** (Rose Monday Parade). The latter is unquestionably the highlight of the celebrations, a riot of color featuring over 7,000 people (half of them musicians), and 300 horses, costing some DM1 million to mount. This is only partly due to the costumes; a ·dominant feature is the fact that forty tons of sweets, 100,000 chocolates, 100,000 packets of popcorn and innumerable bunches of flowers and containers of eau de Cologne are hurled into the crowd. The first part of the procession is a pageant on the history of the city; then comes the satirical section in which local, national and international politicians appear in effigy; finally there's the gala in honor of the Cologne Carnival, with the spectacular retinues of the peasant, the virgin and the prince bringing up the rear. It's all done with a proper sense of Germanic thoroughness, taking no less than four hours to pass by. After this, the festival winds down; there are numerous smaller parades in the suburbs on Shrove Tuesday, while the restaurants offer special fish menus on Ash Wednesday.

As for **practicalities**: although the city gets jam-packed with visitors, many are day-trippers, and there's no problem finding accommodation, but bear in mind that both youth hostels are likely to be full at the weekend. A greater difficulty comes in deciding where to stand during the processions; if you want the backdrop of the Dom, make sure you come several hours before they start (12:30pm on Sun., noon on Mon.) and choose a position on the elevated terrace. Alternatively, go somewhere towards the beginning or end of the route (the tourist office provides free maps), where the crowds are thinner. You could consider hiring one of the grandstand seats, positioned all along the course of the route; these are expensive for the Rose Monday parade, but definitely good value at DM5 on the Sunday. Remember to keep well wrapped up; even when the weather is sunny, it's likely to be cold. Don't expect to do anything else during the "three crazy days"; all the museums and most of the shops are closed, and even the Dom's doors are firmly locked except for the occasional service. Above all, join in the fun: it isn't essential to get dressed up (though it helps), and don't hesitate to follow the crowds, usually congregated around a big drum—it's the impromptu events as much as the set pieces which make this such a great festival. There's also a special deal allowing unlimited travel on the public transit network between Weiberfastnacht and Shrove Tuesday. For advance **tickets**, write to *Festkomitee des Kölner Karnevals*, Antwerpener Str. 55. **Dates** of forthcoming Rose Mondays are as follows: February 26, 1990; February 11, 1991; March 2, 1992.

Cologne and its Carnival form the setting for several novels and short stories by the local writer **Heinrich Böll**, notably *The Clown* and *The Lost Honor of Katharina Blum*, works which offer a trenchant examination of contemporary West German society. Böll's earlier books, such as *And Where Were You, Adam?* and *The Train Was on Time*, give an equally penetrating analysis of the national psyche during World War II. His simple, direct style, refreshingly different to the intellectualization so often found in German literature, and the fearless way he bared the soul of his nation, brought him an international reputation as Germany's leading postwar writer—a status reflected in the award of the Nobel Prize for literature in 1972. However, his work makes many Germans feel uncomfortable and even now, some years after his death, he has not yet been honored with a memorial museum.

Culture

For listings of what's currently playing in the fields of music, theater and film, consult the billboards (which are found all over the city); the posters are changed weekly for the movie theaters, every ten days for other entertainments.

Classical music performed to the highest international standards can be heard at the brand-new *Philharmonie* (☎240 2100) in the same building as the Wallraf-Richartz/Ludwig Museum on Bischofsgartenstrasse. There are two local symphony orchestras—the *Gürzenich* and the *Westdeutsche Rundfunk*, the latter being attached to the national radio, whose headquarters are in Cologne. The radio studios were one of the pioneer centers of electronic music, being particularly associated with the work of Karlheinz Stockhausen (probably the world's most controversial living composer), who is still a Cologne resident. As a contrast, look out for performances by *Musica Antiqua Köln*, Germany's leading specialist ensemble for baroque music played on period instruments. The *Opera House* at Offenbachplatz (☎212581) has a strong Anglo-Saxon connection, with the American James Conlon taking over the musical direction from Sir John Pritchard in 1989. This square's name, incidentally, commemorates the fact that Jaques Offenbach, who conquered Paris with his frothy operettas, and who wrote the ultimate can-can, was a native of Cologne. There are any number of free concerts in the churches; these are all listed in a monthly program which you can usually pick up in any of the churches themselves. Performances are of a good amateur standard at least, and often considerably more than that. One regular series, featuring a seasonally appropriate Bach cantata, takes place at the Antoniterkirche on the first Sunday evening of each month. Check at the *Musikhochschule* (near St. Kunibert) for more free recitals, sometimes by top professionals. **Pop concerts** and other spectaculars which attract large audiences tend to be held at the *Sporthalle* in Deutz. Best places to hear **jazz** are the *Stadtgarten* and the two pubs called *Papa Joe's* (see above).

The leading straight **theater** is the *Schauspielhaus* on Offenbachplatz (☎212651); *Schlosserei* is part of the same complex, but with a more experimental program. Alternatively, there are *Kammerspiele*, Ubierring 45 (☎212651) and the tiny *Theater der Keller*, Kleingedankstrasse (☎318059), both of which offer classical and contemporary works. For mime and cabaret, try *Atelier Theater*, Roonstr. 78 (☎561591). Productions suitable for **kids** are at *Comedia Colonia*, Löwengasse 7–9 (☎247670) and *Kleine Komödie*, Turiner Str. 3 (☎122552), while *Kefka* on Albertusstrasse (☎2401688) is Europe's only theater devoted solely to pantomime. *Puppenspiele*, Eisenmarkt 2–4 (☎212095) has celebrated marionettes, but be warned that the unintelligible Kölsch dialect is used.

The most ambitious **film** programs are those of *Die Cinemathek* (☎21136), which is actually part of the Museum Ludwig. Otherwise, try the following: *Kino in Stadtgarten*, Venloer Str. 40; *Broadway*, Ehrenstr. 11; *Off Broadway*, Zülpicher Str. 24; *Lupe 2*, Mauritiussteinweg 102; *Metropolis*, Ebertplatz; *Odeon*, Severinstr. 81; *Weisshaus*, Luxemburger Str. 255.

Listings

Airlines *British Airways*, Marzellenstr. 1 (☎135081); *Lufthansa*, Bechergasse 2–8 (☎8264); *Olympic Airways*, Minoritenstr. 7 (☎236138).

Area code (☎0221).

Bookshops The streets circling Neumarkt have a dense concentration of general bookshops; try also around the Dom, or on Komodienstrasse. Especially recommended is *Büchermarkt*, Ehrenstr. 4, which stocks a huge range of cut-price titles on the arts, including many in English. The area around the university, particularly the junction of Universitätstrasse and Zülpicher Strasse, has both academic and alternative bookstores.

Car rental *Avis*, Clemensstr. 29 (☎234333); *Hertz*, Bismarckstr. 19–21 (☎515084/5/6/7); *Europ-Car*, Schaafenstr. 2–6 (☎236633/4); *InterRent*, Christophstr. 2 (☎132071); *Europa Service*, Am Malzbüchel 1–3 (☎219797); *Condor*, Wilhelm-Mauser-Str. 53 (☎581055); also a number of offices at the airport.

Car repair *Colonia*, Matthias-Brüggen-Strasse (☎591009) and *Mauritius Garage*, Mauritiuswall 11–13 (☎219608) both offer 24-hour service. Gasoline is available around the clock from *BV Aral*, Augustinerplatz (☎210363).

Consulates See under BONN (p.413) or DÜSSELDORF (p.449); there are none for North Americans in Cologne.

Cultural institutes *British Council* at Hahnenstr. 6 (☎236677); *Amerikahaus* at Apostelnkloster 13–15 (☎209010/241367).

Eau de Cologne (*Kölnerwasser*) Obviously the most popular souvenir of a visit to the city, this can be bought in innumerable stores. About twenty different companies make the product. *Farina*, founded in 1709 and still in business today, is one of the original manufacturers; *Mülhens* is another firm with a long pedigree.

Exhibitions World-class displays are often held at the *Joseph Haubrich Kunsthalle*, Joseph-Haubrich-Hof 1 (☎2212335).

Festivals Everything else inevitably stands in the shade of Carnival (see above). However, the Corpus Christi celebrations (variable date in May or June) are also impressive, featuring a barge procession along the Rhine.

Kids *Phantasialand* in nearby BRÜHL (see p.416) is the biggest attraction; see also the theater listings above.

Language schools *Benedict School*, Gürzenichstr. 17 (☎212203), offering quick courses from DM250; *Berlitz*, Schildergasse 72–76 (☎230619).

Markets The large squares in the Altstadt provide a fitting setting for frequent markets; there's a weekly one all day Friday in Alter Markt, and a *flea market* in the same location every third Saturday. Special occasions are—the *flower market* in Alter Markt on weekends in late April and early May; the *junk market* in

Neumarkt in mid-May and again in mid-September; the *Wine Week* (actually more like two) in Neumarkt in late May/early June; and the *Weihnachtsmarkt* in both locations throughout Advent.

Mitfahrzentrale Saarstr. 22 (☎233464); there's a women-only branch (along with a feminist bookshop) at Moltkestr. 66 (☎523152).

Post office The main office with poste restante is on An den Dominikanern, and has a 24-hour service, except for parcels, which must be sent from the depot on Marzellenstrasse. A branch in the Hauptbahnhof is open daily 7am–10pm.

Rhine cruises *K-D Line* at Frankenwerft 15 (☎2088288); *Rhine-Mosel* at Konrad-Adenauer-Ufer (☎121600); *Colonia* at Lintgasse 18–20 (☎211325).

Sports The main outdoor stadium is at Aachener Strasse in the western suburb of MÜNGERSDORF; *FC Köln*, one of Germany's most successful soccer teams, plays here, and there's an international athletics meeting in August. An ice rink and swimming stadium are at Lentstr. 30 in Riehl, and a huge *Sporthalle* for indoor events is at Deutz-Mülheimer Strasse.

Travel agencies Many are to be be found in the vicinity of the Dom, including *Thomas Cook* at Domkloster 2 (☎202080).

24-hour chemist (☎11500).

24-hour doctor (☎720772).

What's scheduled The tourist office publishes a comprehensive monthly program, along with important forthcoming events, called *Köln-Monatsvorschau*, (DM1.50). Two weekly publications are *Stadt Revue* and *Kölner Illustrierte* (the latter somewhat yuppier), available from newsagents at DM5 each.

THE LOWER RHINELAND

The **Lower Rhineland** (*Niederrhein*) is the name given to the predominantly flat area north of Cologne; the great river thereafter offers no more dramatic scenery. Industrialization, though significant, is held in check most of the way up to **Düsseldorf**. Immediately beyond, however, begins the most developed industrial region in the world, consisting of the Ruhrgebiet (whose westernmost cities, such as Duisburg and Essen, overlap with this area) and the corresponding towns across the river, such as **Krefeld** and **Mönchengladbach**. After this, there's a dramatic change to a countryside very close in spirit to nearby Holland. There are no more cities, but a number of small historic towns, notably **Xanten** and **Kalkar**.

Zons and Knechtsteden

The curious village of **ZONS**, sometimes designated *Feste Zons* in honor of its original function as a fortified customs post on the Rhine, lies 25km downstream from Cologne. It's now part of the municipality of DORMAGEN, an industrial town of no interest in itself, and is some 3km east of the latter's Bahnhof, to which it's connected by regular bus services.

In 1372 the Archbishop of Cologne, Friedrich von Saarwerden, decided to levy taxes on the profitable shipping route through his domain, and began the building of a walled town on the site of his predecessors' long-destroyed castle. Despite Zons' history of bad luck—it's repeatedly been ravaged by fires and floods down the centuries—the original **fortifications** remain largely intact. They rank as one of the most important surviving examples of a medieval defensive system in Germany, though it now requires a bit of imagination to visualise their original setting, as silting means they're now some way back from the Rhine.

Zons is the sort of place you'd expect to be overrun by tour buses, but on weekdays at least it's remarkably quiet. The best views are obtained by walking around the outside of the circuit. Beginning at the bus stop, turn right and you shortly come to the **Mühlenturm**, the upper section of which was converted into a windmill early in its history. From here, you continue along the south side of the town, which has a double wall, the outer having been added for protection against flooding. At the corner are the ruins of **Schloss Friedestrom**, including the gateway, the chunky keep, and a courtyard which provides an apt setting for open-air theater and pageants (every Sunday afternoon mid-June to mid-Sept.; also other random days). The eastern wall has two cylindrical defensive towers, along with an octagonal watchtower; at its far corner is the **Rheinturm**, the medieval entrance to the town, and the place where customs dues were collected. Three sentry posts pierce the northern wall, which terminates in the battlemented **Krötschenturm**. In the town center there's one more tower, the round **Juddeturm**, which served as both prison and look-out. Around the Rheinturm are the few old houses which have survived the natural disasters; everything else is baroque or later. The handsome **Herrenhaus** contains the local museum (Tues.–Fri. 2–7pm, Sat. and Sun. 10am–12:30pm and 2–6pm; free) which mounts temporary exhibitions alongside its own collection of Jugendstil art.

Zons' **tourist office** (Mon.–Fri. 8:30am–noon, also Tues. 2:15–4:15pm, Thurs. 2:15–5:15pm; ☎02106 3772) is housed in the modern building behind the Juddeturm. By far the best **restaurant** in town is *Altes Zollhaus* on Rheinstrasse by the Rheinturm; unfortunately it's also the most expensive. Plenty of cheaper alternatives can be found on Schloss Strasse; some of these have **rooms** to rent, but the prices asked tend to be well above normal. The only reasonable rates, at DM28 per head, whether in singles or doubles, are at *Café-Restaurant Olligs* on Grünwaldstrasse (☎02106 42388). Otherwise, there are two **campgrounds** at STÜRZELBERG 1km to the north: *Strandterrasse* (☎02106 71717) and *Pitt-Jupp* (☎02106 42210). Throughout the summer, regular daily **boat trips** (☎02106 42149 or 42349) run to BENRATH; there are very occasional sailings to Cologne.

Also within the municipality of Dormagen is the Romanesque monastery of **Knechtsteden**, built in the austere style favored by its Premonstratensian founders, but enlivened by a central octagon flanked by twin towers. It stands in an isolated setting 3km west of the Bahnhof, reachable by a frequent bus service. As in the great imperial cathedrals, there's a choir at both ends of the building; the eastern one is a late Gothic replacement, while that to the west is adorned with mid-twelfth-century **frescos** showing *Christ as Pantocrator*, surrounded by angels and the evangelical symbols, with portraits of the Apostles below. Sadly, the effect of this imposing composition has been somewhat spoiled by the attentions of overzealous nineteenth-century restorers. The extensive baroque monastery buildings are nowadays the headquarters of the missionaries of the Congregation of the Holy Ghost, which operates in Africa and South America. If you's like a quiet night away from the cities, the *Klosterhof* (☎02106 80745) just outside the monastery gate has singles at DM40, doubles at DM74, along with a bar-restaurant.

The Bergisches Land

The green countryside on the right bank of the Rhine east and north of Cologne is known as the **BERGISCHES LAND**; it was formerly the Duchy of Berg, whose capital was Düsseldorf. In the nineteenth century this pastoral landscape (much of which is now designated a *Naturpark*) became punctuated by the series of bleak manufacturing towns responsible for putting Germany at the forefront of industrial development. Prominent among them is **LEVERKUSEN**, a northern continuation of Cologne, which is virtually a fiefdom of one of the country's largest companies, the *Bayer* chemical conglomerate. Here aspirin was invented in 1899, and polyurethane products first introduced to the world in 1937. In the past decade it has swallowed up the town's other famous company, the *Agfa* photographic plant. Adjoining Leverkusen to the east is **BERGISCH GLADBACH**, best known for its paper products.

Set in isolation in a wooded valley of the river Dhün just a few kilometers north is **ALTENBERG**, and the area's only outstanding monument, the so-called **Bergischer Dom**. In spite of this name, it isn't actually a cathedral—nor could it be, given its location—but a monastery built by the Cistercians, whose rule prescribed secluded settings of this kind. In 1133 the Count of Berg moved his seat and donated his ancestral home, set on the hill above, to this reforming order of monks, who used the stones to construct their first church. What makes the present building, begun in 1255, particularly interesting is that it's contemporary with, and of similar stature to, the Dom in Cologne, only this time it was completed in just over a hundred years. In accordance with the austere Cistercian tradition there's no tower and little in the way of decoration. Nevertheless, it's still enormously photogenic, seeming to blend effortlessly into the landscape; the best view is from the hill to the east, where you see the choir with its corona of chapels (the earliest and finest feature) to best advantage. Few buildings so perfectly encompass the basic tenets of the Gothic style: there are no grand gestures; everything is spacious, bright, and harmonious, a visible manifestation of the order's quest for spiritual tranquillity. The chancel has wonderful original silvery-grey **stained glass** windows which—in common with the decoration found in Arab buildings—employ geometric motifs only. This same type of glass, now with floral shapes, fills the big lights of the north transept, beaming down on the tombs of the counts (later dukes) of Berg. Relaxation of the normal Cistercian rejection of representational subjects is confined to the giant facade window, the largest in Germany: it depicts *The Heavenly Jerusalem* in predominantly golden tones, a particularly memorable sight when illuminated by the setting sun.

Buses run regularly between Altenberg and Bergisch Gladbach, or the monastery can be reached in an hour from downtown Cologne, if you luck out with connections: take U-Bahn #5 to the terminus at HOHENHAUS, from where there are up to a dozen buses per day. If you want to sample the atmosphere of rural peace, make sure to come on a weekday. On Sundays, Altenberg acts as a magnet for urban dwellers on their weekly retreat; a curiosity is that both Catholic and Protestant services are held. This condition was laid down last century by the Prussian King Friedrich Wilhelm IV when he arranged for the church's repair and return to worship, after a period of disuse and decay following the Napoleonic suppression. The baroque monastic quarters are now the home of the main German Catholic youth organization. Ask at *Küchenhof* (one of three bar-restaurants currently occupying the outbuildings) for the key to the early thirteenth-century **Markuskapelle**, the oldest surviving part of the complex.

Some 20km north lies **SOLINGEN**, which has gained an international reputation for its swords, knives, and scissors; the inevitable **Blade Museum** is at Wuppertaler Str. 160 in the northern suburb of GRÄFRATH (Tues., Weds., and Fri.–Sun. 10am–1pm and 3–5pm; DM1.50). Precision tools, needed to manufacture these and other products, are the specialty of the adjacent town of **REMSCHEID**.

Wuppertal

WUPPERTAL stands at the northernmost end of the Bergisches Land group of industrial towns, some 30km east of Düsseldorf. The overriding justification for a detour is to see its public transitation system—little recommendation, you would think, but the **Schwebebahn** ("hanging railroad"), a monorail suspension system without wheels, is genuinely unique. What even the local tourist office admits would otherwise be just another dull industrial town is given a freakish character—sonic as well as visual—by this creaking railroad, suspended on high by a steel structure supported by 472 triangular girders, and hailed by Jean Cocteau as the "flying angel." Wuppertal didn't exist as such when the line was built between 1898 and 1900 to link the various towns strung along the valley of the Wupper River—**BARMEN** and **ELBERFELD** being the largest. These communities united in 1929, yet still preserve distinct identities; Wuppertal hasn't evolved a recognizable city center.

The brainchild of **Carl Eugen Langen**, who failed to interest Berlin and Munich in his idea, the *Schwebebahn* runs directly above the river between fifteen of its nineteen stations. It then passes over the main thoroughfares of SONNBORN and OBERWINKEL to the west, leaving them permanently in the shade. The sleek orange-and-blue cars are fourth-generation; at weekends in summer, one of the original models is run. This is the only gimmick associated with a genuine local facility which is both fast (it's immune from delays) and efficient (services run every few minutes). Above all, it has proved to be the safest public transit system ever devised, never having had a serious accident in its lifetime. Travel along the whole route for a complete picture of the town, and look out for the *Werther Brücke* station, preserving its original Jugendstil decoration.

Almost incidental to the delights of the *Schwebebahn*, Wuppertal has a decent collection of nineteenth- and twentieth-century art in the **Von der Heydt Museum** at Turmhof 8 (Tues. 10am–9pm, Weds.–Sun. 10am–5pm; DM1), not far from Elberfeld Bahnhof. Highlights include a study for **Manet's** masterpiece, *Déjeuner sur l'Herbe*, and works by Delacroix, Daumier, Van Gogh, and Seurat; there's also a good display on a local man, **Hans von Marées**, who is now rated one of the last century's most important German artists. Currently, the paintings are doing a world tour; reopening of the building following renovation will not occur before autumn 1989. Nearby, on Poststrasse, is the **Clock Museum** (Mon.–Fri. 10am–noon and 4–6pm, Sat. 10am–1pm; DM3), a private collection in the basement of a jeweler's shop. Here you can see over 1000 weird and wonderful timepieces of all shapes and sizes, ranging from the earliest watch made in Germany to an eighteenth-century London whimsical clock with vase-bearing elephant and a rotating Chinese Emperor's court.

Of more marginal interest is the **Museum of Early Industry** (Tues.–Sun. 10am–1pm and 3–5pm; free) at Engelsstrasse in Barmen. In front stands the **Engels House** (same times; free), an elegant, late eighteenth-century building which belonged to a family of textile entrepreneurs. It's now a memorial to their celebrated black sheep **Friedrich Engels**, who was born in a nearby house which no longer exists. As a young man, he was sent to England to work at the sister factory of *Ermen & Engels* in Manchester; there he became fascinated by the plight of the urban proletariat, and on his return to Barmen in 1845 wrote his celebrated *The Condition of the Working Class in England*. Soon after, he began collaborating with Karl Marx, returning to work as a capitalist in Manchester in order to provide funds for their joint revolutionary writings. Though very much the junior partner in these, Engels always had a large input on matters concerning nationalities, diplomacy, the military, and business practices—even in the books such as *Das Kapital* in which Marx appears as sole author.

Barmen really seems to relish its reputation as an anti-establishment town, as it was also the scene of the 1934 Synod of the "Confessing Church," Protestant opponents of Hitler. At this meeting, the church declared its independence from state control, proclaiming itself the only true heir of the Lutheran tradition, in contrast to the bogus Reich Church most clergymen had been forced into joining. Their guiding force, **Pastor Martin Niemöller**, was later incarcerated in a concentration camp, but gained a reputation outside Germany as one of the most effective anti-Nazis, and survived to become a leading pacifist and international churchman after the war.

Wuppertal's **tourist office** (Mon.–Fri. 9am–5:30pm, Sat. 9am–12:30pm; ☎0202 563 2270) is just across from Elberfeld Bahnhof, beside the bus terminus. The *Schauspielhaus* on nearby Bundeallee presents plays and operas, but is best known for Pina Bausch's *Tanztheater,* by some way Germany's leading **modern dance** company. Her erotic, expressionistic programs make free use of mime and circus techniques. If you want to spend the night in town, the **youth hostel** is at Obere Lichtenplatzer Str. 70 (☎0202 552372), a few minutes' walk to the south of Barmen's Bahnhof; hotels tend to be on the expensive side. Reasonably priced places to **eat** and **drink**, on the other hand, can be found all over the city, especially in the large pedestrian mall in the center of Elberfeld; try the local *Wicküler* beer. There's a **Mitfahrzentrale** office at Luisenstr. 46 (☎0202 450316).

Düsseldorf

DÜSSELDORF is Germany's richest city, and in many ways the paragon of the new face of the Federal Republic—orderly, prosperous, and self-confident. Few places can have a name so inappropriate to their present status, since the "village on the Düssel," which celebrated the 700th anniversary of its city rights in 1988, and is now a thriving Land capital of 600,000 inhabitants on both banks of the Rhine, crossed here by no less than six bridges. Since the war, it has developed a cosmopolitan and strangely un-European character, consciously modeling itself on the thrusting "get up and go" American approach to life, and acting as the main foreign outpost of Japanese commerce's quest for world market supremacy.

Never as industrialized as its neighbors in the Ruhr, Düsseldorf has concentrated on its role as the region's financial and administrative center, and from this it derives its prosperity, in accordance with the inevitable pattern of the money manipulators skimming a disproportionate share of the profits. Along with one of the country's largest stock exchanges are the headquarters and offices of innumerable multinational giants. At least two of these, the **Thyssen Haus** in the heart of the city and the **Mannesmann Haus** on the banks of the Rhine, are dominant landmarks, in the way that churche steeples and town halls were in medieval cityscapes—an analogy both significant and disturbing.

The extent to which you'll like or loathe Düsseldorf depends very much on your reaction to the way it has sold its soul to the corporate dream. If luxury shops are your scene, there are none more stylish between Paris and Berlin. The city likes to think of itself as Germany's leading fashion outlet, with sartorial elegance and other ostentatious displays of wealth serving as indicators of individual standing in its fiercely competitive high society. Even for a short visit, it's an expensive option, but there's no doubt that the **nightlife**, at least, is one of the most varied and enjoyable in the country.

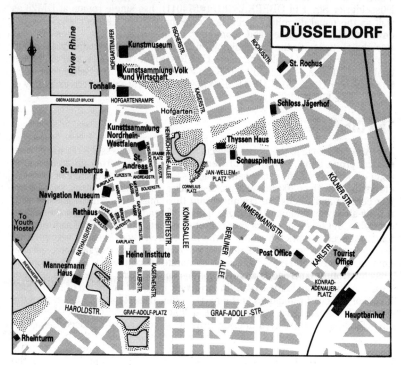

Arrival and Practicalities

The **Hauptbahnhof** is situated in the southeast part of downtown; from here, the shopping streets begin to fan out. **Exchange facilities** are available every day from 7:30am to 8pm. S-Bahn trains leave at twenty-minute intervals for the **airport** to the north (☎421223 for flight information). Unlike neighboring cities, most of Düsseldorf's attractions are within walking distance of each other, so the 24-hour ticket on the public transit network, costing DM8.50, is really only of use if you specifically want to see the outlying suburbs described on p.449. The **tour-**

ist office (Mon.–Fri. 8am–6pm, Sat. 9am–1pm; ☎350505) is on Konrad-Adenauer-Platz, directly facing the Hauptbahnhof; it has free maps and monthly programs of events. To reserve a **hotel room**, head for the separate booth within the station (Mon.–Sat. 8am–10pm, Sun. 4–10pm). Best check here for any good deals available, as accommodation is overwhelmingly geared to the business traveler, and prices are far above the national average, even in the suburbs. Those in the vicinity of the Hauptbahnhof are as cheap as any, especially *Manhattan*, Graf-Adolph-Str. 39 (☎370244), which has some singles at DM35 and doubles from DM65. More realistically, expect to have to pay at least DM45 per head to stay in a hotel. Faced with such prices, it's worth remembering that the **youth hostel**, Düsseldorfer Str. 1 in OBERKASSEL (☎574041), has single rooms at DM28 as well as the usual dormitory facilities. From the station, take bus #835 or walk down Graf-Adolf-Strasse and continue in a straight line, crossing the Rheinkniebrücke; it's the first building on the other side. Alternatively, there are two **campgrounds** (April–Sept. only). OBERLÖRICK (☎591401), also on the left bank of the Rhine, is reached by U-Bahn #76, #705, or #717 to Belsenplatz, then bus #828. For UNTERBACHER SEE (☎899 2038), out at the eastern extremity of the city, take bus #781.

The City

The **Altstadt**, close to the Rhine, reflects the meaning of Düsseldorf's name in its modest proportions. Never one of Germany's great cities from an architectural point of view, it's chiefly renowned nowadays for its remarkable range of places of entertainment. Over 200 restaurants, beer halls, wine cellars, bistros, snack bars, jazz centers and discos are crammed into this small area, which pulsates with activity all day and much of the night. This facet tends to overshadow the historical sights, but two very contrasting churches do catch the eye. St. **Lambertus**, a fourteenth-century brick building in the hall church style, is easily recognisable because of its tall twisted spire, now ousted from its former physical and spiritual dominance over the city by the huge corporate office towers. Inside, there's a graceful Gothic tabernacle, and a fifteenth-century *Pietà* housed in a modern shrine. A short walk to the east is St. **Andreas**, a Jesuit foundation of 1629 which is one of the chief reminders of the period when Düsseldorf was the seat of the electors Palatinate, who succeeded the defunct line of the dukes of Berg, the city's founders. Its galleried interior, ornately decorated with stucco, served as their mausoleum. The most famous and genuinely popular of the electors was Johann Wilhelm II, better known as **Jan. Wellem**, who ruled from 1679 to 1716. He's commemorated in the huge open area named after him in the heart of the city, and by a masterly equestrian statue (the work of his Italian court sculptor Gabriel de Grupello), erected during his own lifetime outside the Renaissance **Rathaus**. In the square immediately to the north is the **Schlossturm**, the only remnant of the old fortifications; it has been restored to house a small **Navigation Museum** (Tues.–Sun. 10am–5pm; DM2).

Wellem's successors employed French landscape gardeners to transform their seat into a city of parks, ponds and canals. This culminated in the creation of the main thoroughfare, the **Königsallee**, at the beginning of the nineteenth century. It's one of Germany's most famous streets, but is chic rather than beautiful; down one side are banks and offices, with expensive stores representing all the trendiest names in international designer-made goods lining the other. People shop here with an incredibly self-conscious air; in antithesis to the intended effect, the prevailing hallmark is one of vulgarity, and it's appropriate that the architectural setting is so mediocre. Only the late Jugendstil **Kaufhaus** by the Viennese Joseph Maria Olbrich has any merits as a building, though it has suffered from interior modernization. Diagonally opposite its rear entrance is **Wilhelm-Marx-Haus**, the earliest visible expression of Düsseldorf's infatuation with the New World, hailed as the first skyscraper in Germany when it was erected in the 1920s.

The largest of the parks is the **Hofgarten**, shaped like a great stiletto-heeled shoe, and now incongruously cut in several places by busy streets. At its far end is **Schloss Jägerhof**, a baroque palace which sustained severe damage in the last war. Its interior decorations have been almost entirely lost, but it has recently been been refitted as the **Goethe Museum** (Tues.–Fri. and Sun. 10am–5pm, Sat. 1–5pm; DM3) reckoned to be the best collection of memorabilia of the great poet and playwright (see Frankfurt, *Chapter Three*) after those in Frankfurt and Weimar. Unless you're an avid fan of this writer, the contents will seem fairly mundane, though it's worth glancing over the section on works of art inspired by his most celebrated drama, *Faust*.

Düsseldorf's own favorite son is another of Germany's most famous men of letters, **Heinrich Heine** (1797–1856), in whose honor a research institute and museum have been set up at Bilkerstr. 14 (Tues.–Sun. 10am–5pm; DM2). Heine's work, in which traditional Romantic themes are modified by a biting sense of irony, often uses the image of the *Doppelgänger*, reflecting his lifelong feeling of isolation—as a poet in a family of merchants, a Jew among Catholics, a Francophile who eventually settled in Paris yet remained German at heart, and as a revolutionary familiar with Marxism who kept faith with the bourgeois liberal tradition. His early *Buch der Lieder* provided the dying Schubert with the texts for his last songs, and was to be a similar source of inspiration for subsequent composers, notably Schumann, Brahms, and Hugo Wolf. Later, his *Reisebilder*, combining factual descriptions, poems, and political comment, initiated a new and much-imitated form of travel writing.

The two large **art museums** each warrant a couple of hours of gentle browsing. Housed in an ultramodern gallery in Grabbeplatz is the **Kunstsammlung Nordrhein-Westfalen** (Tues.–Sun. 10am–6pm; DM5). The genesis of this collection was a remarkable act of postwar contrition by the authorities. **Paul Klee**, the abstract painter, was a professor at the Düsseldorf Academy from 1930 until dismissed in the Nazi purges of 1933. In atonement for this, around ninety of his works were purchased from a private American source in 1960. Shortly afterwards, a rapid acquisitions policy of twentieth-century art only, was adopted. The Klee collection remains the obvious draw, although only about two-thirds of the works are on show at any one time. Even if you aren't attracted to this painter, there are many other highlights, such as one of **Picasso**'s most famous representational works, *Two Sitting Women*; **Léger**'s large *Adam and Eve*; **Kirchner**'s *Negro Dance*; **Modigliani**'s *Diego Rivera* (a portrait of the Mexican artist); and self-portraits by **Kokoschka** and **Chagall**. Already the collection resembles a who's who of modern art, and it continues to grow.

The **Kunstmuseum** (Tues.–Sun. 10am–5pm; DM5), directly north of the Altstadt at Ehrenhof 5, has extensive displays on three floors. This could very nearly have been one of Europe's finest art galleries, as the electors owned a marvelous array of paintings which followed the court to Munich in 1806, where they soon formed one of the bases of the Alte Pinakothek. A great **Rubens** masterpiece, an altarpiece of *The Assumption*, never made the journey because of its size; it now puts almost all the other old masters on the first floor completely in the shade. Among the few paintings not wholly outclassed are *Venus and Adonis* by the same artist, a *St. Jerome* attributed to **Ribera**, and *St. Francis in Meditation* by **Zurbarán**. Also on this floor is a series of powerful lithographs by **Otto Pankok** called *The Passion*, though in fact Christ's whole life is depicted. Their gloomy, highly charged emotionalism, with hateful mobs and angst-ridden victims, directly reflects the contemporary horrors of the Holocaust. Upstairs, there's a modern section which complements that in the Kunstsammlung, along with an extensive show of the nineteenth-century historical painters of the **Düsseldorf Academy**. In their day, these artists were lionized, and the old Baedeker Guides deemed their work to be the city's great glory. Now long out of fashion, they suffer from a lack of inspiration to match their undoubted technical skill. More pleasing is the sparkling **glass** section on the ground floor, dominated by art nouveau and art deco pieces from Germany, France, and America.

Directly in front of the Kunstmuseum is the **Landesmuseum Volk und Wirtschaft** (Mon., Tues., Thurs., and Fri. 9am–5pm, Weds. 9am–8pm, Sun. 10am–6pm; DM1), displaying economic and social facts about the world by means of charts and graphs. Primarily an educational institution, its presentation is sound but dry. The **Hetjens Museum** at Schulstr. 4 (Tues.–Sun. 10am–5pm; DM3) boasts of being the only one in Germany entirely devoted to the art of ceramics. It's a tidy collection, albeit one mainly for aficionados. The final specialist museum of note is the spanking new **Löbbecke Museum and Aquazoo** (daily 10am–6pm; DM6) at Kaiserwerther Str. 380, north of downtown; take U-Bahn #78 or #79. Combining an aquarium with serious scientific displays, it's an ideal outing if you have kids.

Some of Düsseldorf's **modern architecture** is worthy of mention, although reactions to it are inevitably varied. Just north of the Schloss Jägerhof is **St. Rochus**, the replacement for a pretentious neo-Romanesque church which was destroyed, except for its tower, in the last war. Outside, it resembles a giant beehive; the interior is deliberately dark, in an attempt to recreate the old mysteries of religion. Of the two dominant corporate structures which so altered the skyline in the late 1950s, **Thyssen Haus** is much the more arresting, offering a fascinating play of light on its three huge silvery-green slabs. Beside it, the daring white curves of the **Schauspielhaus**, built in 1970, provide an effective counterpoint, as well as a reminder that, in this city, the public structures stand very much in the shadow of big business. Nonetheless, the radio tower, the **Rheinturm**, built between 1979 and 1982, has now taken over as the city's highest building. You can ascend by high-speed lift to its observation platform (daily 10am–midnight; DM4), though it's doubtful if the view is sufficiently inspiring to justify the price.

Eating, Drinking, and Nightlife

Walking through the **Altstadt**, "the longest bar in Europe" according to the tourist office, is an enjoyable activity in itself, especially on summer days when it's even more crowded than usual and virtually every pub and restaurant offers the opportunity for imbibing alfresco. The heart of the quarter—the parallel *Kurzestrasse/Andreasstrasse* and *Bolkerstrasse*, and the streets perpendicular to them, *Mertensgasse*, *Hunsrückenstrasse*, and *Neustrasse*—is almost entirely given over to diverse places of entertainment. **Eating** is one of the few things it's possible to do cheaply in Düsseldorf, thanks to the various ethnic communities—one of many points of similarity with America. The way is led by the ubiquitous

pizzerias; those which make to order are almost uniformly good. Especially recommended is the little takeaway *Aldo-Snack*, situated at the corner where Mertensgasse divides Kurzestrasse from Andreasstrasse; it scores over rivals in providing oils and spices for you to add yourself. Other cuisines include Balkan, Hungarian, Spanish, Argentinian, various forms of Oriental, and fish specialties. For local fare, *Hühner-Max* on Mertensgasse has the air of a truck stop but serves tasty dishes (main courses only) at very low prices. If cost isn't the main factor, the Hungarian *Csicos* on Andreasstrasse has a high reputation; a little farther down the street is one of the city's top restaurants, *Tante Anna*, a historic wine bar with 150 vintages to choose from as an accompaniment to your meal.

However, Düsseldorf's favorite drink is the local **Alt** beer, dark in color and tending towards sweetness in some varieties, caused by the higher quantity of malt used than in lagers. There are plenty of traditional watering holes to choose from, particularly along Bolkerstrasse where *Zum Schlüssel*, the beer hall of *Gatzweilers* brewery, has a cavernous and well patronized interior. On the same street, *Im Goldenen Kessel*, the flagship of the *Schumacher* brewery, is equally renowned for its food, as is *Im Goldenen Ring* on Burgplatz. Just round the corner on Mühlenstrasse is *Schlossturm*, particularly enjoyable on fine days, offering a sheltered view over the Rhine from the cobbled square outside. *Marktwirtschaft* on Marktplatz is an excellent place to spend a quiet evening among the well-heeled youth of Düsseldorf, many of them students. For a livelier atmosphere, try along Kurzestrasse, where you'll find *V.I.P.* (with a beer garden), *Engelchen* and *Schaukelstühlchen*, along with the perenially crowded *Weisser Bar*, home to a curious mixture of young Düsseldorfer and young tourists, and staffed by relics of the '68 generation who've managed to avoid selling out to the city's corporations. On Hunsrückenstrasse is a surprisingly genuine *Irish Pub*, owned and staffed by expatriates; here *Alt* has to take second place to *Guinness*.

The northern boundary of the Altstadt is formed by Ratingerstrasse, which has several more good taverns, including *Im Füchschen*, another brewery-owned beer hall, and *Zum Goldenen Einhorn*, an enduringly popular spot with the youth of the city, especially in summer when it opens its leafy little beer garden. This street gained national notoriety because of *Ratinger Hof*, the first **punk** bar in Germany; although the premises look ready to collapse, its reputation lives on, still popular with cult die-hards, and blasting out ear-splitting music to match.

The opposite end of the Altstadt, in contrast, is more off the beaten track and correspondingly laid back. It's the best area if you're looking for **live jazz**. *Miles Smiles* on Akademiestasse plays a variety of styles, and has decently priced snacks and cocktails; round the corner on Rheinstrasse is *Dr. Jazz*, with different bands each evening. Farther south on Bäckerstrasse is *Front Page*, a cosy piano bar. Also in this area is *Zum Schiffchen* on Hafenstrasse, another traditional beer hall serving excellent food, and *Zum Uerige* on Bergerstrasse, a real drinking man's pub which is the only place you can sample the products of the adjoining house brewery, the smallest in the city. Tourists seldom penetrate the bars tucked away in the shopping area between the Altstadt and the Hauptbahnhof. One genuine local is *Café Bernstein* on Oststrasse, a stylish place for a nightcap, largely frequented by an endemic Düsseldorf group—monied student couples.

On the left bank of the Rhine, *ZAKK* (*Zentrum für Alternative Kunst und Kultur*) at Fichtenstr. 40 is, as its name suggests, a bar with a difference, drawing visitors from neighboring cities to its exhibitions, video showings, and other arty events. Also recommended on this side of the river are *Nachtcafé* on Collenbachstrasse, one of the few places in Düsseldorf open all night; and

Sassafrass on Düsseldorfer Strasse, whose young clientele are a lot less pretentious and concerned with looking cool than their counterparts in the prissier parts of the city.

There are some two dozen **discos** in the Altstadt, generally small in size. Most play standard modern fare, but *Big Apple* on Kurzestrasse specializes in golden oldies, while there's a *Soul Center* on Bolkerstrasse. Outside this quarter, *Relax* on Jahnstrasse is predominantly gay, although this is less true on Saturday nights, when about a quarter of the crowd are women. *Atmosphere* at the Hauptbahnhof, open Saturday only, is a safe bet, if rather conservative in terms of both clientele and music. Far more exciting is the city's leading disco, *Tor 3*, south of the center at Ronsdorfer Str. 143 in the suburb of BILK. A huge barn of a place, it has few concessions to high-tech comfort, but its customers are young, friendly, and out to enjoy themselves with a vengeance.

Music, Theater, and Festivals

Pop concerts and large-scale spectaculars are staged at the *Philipshalle*, Siegburger Str. 15 (☎899 7744/55) in the southern suburb of OVERBILK. There's also a strong local tradition in **classical music**. Both *Deutsche Oper am Rhein*, Heinrich-Heine-Allee 16a (☎370981/2) and the *Düsseldorfer Symphoniker* enjoy good provincial standing, even if present standards are short of the heydays last century when both Mendelssohn and Schumann did stints in charge of the city's musical affairs. The normal venue for concerts is the *Tonhalle*, Hofgartenufer (☎8996123), a circular building which began life as a planetarium.

Choice in **theater** is wide, with straight drama offered at the *Schauspielhaus*, Gustav-Grundgens-Platz 1 (☎363011), *Kammerspiele*, Jahnstr. 3 (☎378353) and *Theater an der Luegallee*, Luegallee 4 (☎572222). Cabaret and satire feature at the bizarrely spelt *Kom(m)ödchen* on Hunstückenstrasse. (☎325428), with comedy programs at *Komödie*, Steinstr. 23 (☎325151). For **kids**, there are the *Puppentheater*, Heimholtzstr. 48 (☎371368) and the *Marionettentheater*, Bilkerstr. 7 (☎328432). Offbeat fare is presented by two youth companies based in a wing of Wilhlem-Marx-Haus at Kasernenstr. 6—*Junges Theater in der Altstadt* (☎327210/37) and *Junge Aktionsbühne* (☎899 5465). Also in these premises is *Filminstitut Black Box* (☎8992490), most adventurous of the city's many **movie houses**.

It's worth trying to coincide with one of Düsseldorf's three main **popular festivals**. The **Carnival** celebrations (seven weeks before Easter) are ranked third in Germany, although those in nearby Cologne are the best of all. These are supposed to signify the end of winter; its beginning is heralded by St. **Martin's Eve** on 10 November, marked by an enormous procession of lantern-bearing children. In late July, the **Grosse Schützenfest** (riflemen's meeting) is a *kermis* along the banks of the Rhine lasting for eight days. Simultaneously, there's a huge amusement park (claimed to be the largest of its type in the world) offering gut-churning rides on a Ferris wheel, a Big Dipper, and other awesome machines. The most celebrated local tradition is **cartwheeling** by local lads in the streets of the Altstadt. This is in honor of an urchin who saved the day when a wheel became loose on Jan. Wellem's wedding coach, but the reason it survives is the less romantic one of extorting money from tourists. In spite of serving as an unofficial symbol of the city, you're unlikely to see any demonstrations out of season.

Listings

Airlines *British Airways*, Berliner Allee 26 (☎80021); *Aer Lingus*, Berliner Allee 47 (☎80231); *Air Canada*, Königsallee 30 (☎80451); *Olympic Airways*, Graf-Adolf-Str. 12 (☎84941); *TWA*, Berliner Allee 22 (☎84814/5).

Area code (☎0211).

Consulates *American*, Cecilienstr. 5 (☎490081); *Canadian*, Immermannstr. 3 (☎353471).

Mitfahrzentrale Kölner Str. 212 (☎774011).

Poste restante Immermannstr. 1.

Women's bookshop Becherstr. 2.

Women's center Kölner Str. 216 (☎782479).

Düsseldorf's Environs

It's easy enough to escape the cosmopolitan atmosphere of central Düsseldorf, and a few tranquil spots within and just outside the city boundaries make for good day trips. Top of the list is **BENRATH** to the south, best reached by S-Bahn. This pleasure palace and park was commissioned by the elector Carl Theodor in the mid-eighteenth century; the unusual harmony of the whole complex is due to the fact that the architect, the French-born **Nicholas de Pigage**, was also a landscape gardener. The central building, in a style hovering between rococo and neoclassical, represents a very clever piece of *trompe l'oeil* construction—for all its seemingly small size, it contains eighty rooms. Guided tours (Tues.–Sun. 10am–4pm, leaving at half-hourly intervals; DM2), take in the sumptuous reception and garden rooms on the ground floor, as well as some of the private apartments upstairs. Afterwards, you can stroll in the formal gardens and see the surviving block of the old palace.

At the exact opposite end of the city, beyond the airport, lies **KAISERSWERTH**, to all intents and purposes still an old village on the banks of the Rhine. Overlooking the river are the scanty remains of a twelfth century fortress, the **Kaiserpfalz**; there's also the Romanesque basilica of **St. Suitbertus**, containing a beautiful Gothic shrine dedicated to the saint, an Anglo-Saxon monk who founded a monastery here at the beginning of the eighth century. Adjoining Kaiserswerth is another old village, **KALKUM**, built around an enormous moated Schloss.

One of the slowest trains in West Germany wends its way up the river Düssel to METTMANN, stopping at **NEANDERTHAL** en route. This valley is named after the seventeenth-century Protestant poet **Joachim Neander**, who liked to meditate there. Though he only lived to the age of thirty, he became rector of the Latin School in Düsseldorf, and wrote a number of hymns which have crossed the barriers of language and denomination, most notably *Lobet den Herren* ("Praise to the Lord, the Almighty, the King of Creation"). During his lifetime, the valley was a rugged canyon, not easily accessible; subsequently, the landscape was changed completely by limestone mining, and it was this that led to a sensational discovery which made Neanderthal famous. In 1856, workers dug up bones from the bottom of a cave; these were later identified as belonging to an earlier form of mankind than *homo sapiens*, one still bearing a slight facial resemblance to the ape. The term **Neanderthal man** has since come to signify the tribes of humans who were wiped out by the last Ice Age. A small **museum**

(Tues.–Sun. 10am–5pm; DM1) explains the living conditions of these hunting peoples; there are also a few prehistoric bones (though the original discovery is now in Bonn—see p.410), and hypothetical reconstructions of what the race looked like, including a model of Neanderthal man wearing the clothes of a 1980s city gent. The valley has a game reserve, including animals such as bison which haven't evolved much since prehistoric times, but the landscape around is now irretrievably ruined, and the Düssel—little more than a ditch in the city—is still nothing grander than a stream here.

On the west bank of the Rhine, Düsseldorf's suburbs merge imperceptibly into **NEUSS**, officially a separate large industrial town with extensive dockyards; it's best reached by train, as the fare is the same as for the trams. From the **Hauptbahnhof**, turn left, and then left again into Krefelder Strasse, the start of the central shopping axis, which subsequently changes its name to Büchel, then Oberstrasse. About halfway down is the Markt, where you'll find the town's sole outstanding monument, the **Münster** or **St. Quirinus**. It represents the apotheosis of the Rhineland Romanesque style, built in the early thirteenth century at a time when Gothic was established elsewhere. There's all the exuberance characteristic of the end of an era—blind arcades are employed in playful patterns, and the clover-leaf shape favored by Rhenish architects is used in the design of the windows as well as in the plan of the chancel. The dome provides a touch of almost Oriental exoticism; together with its four turrets and the facade's belfry, it makes a memorable silhouette. In complete contrast is the early twentieth-century **Dreikönigekirche** to the south of the town center. Following war damage, it was embellished with a wacky hanging vault by the father-and-son team of Dominikus and Gottfried Böhm. The church also has a complete set of stained glass windows by the Dutch artist **Johan Thorn-Prikker**, one of the Jugendstil community based in Hagen; those in the chancel and transept are figurative and glow like jewels; the later geometric ones in the nave show his move to an abstract style. Neuss' only other building worth seeing is the **Obertor** (part of the thirteenth-century fortifications), situated at the far end of the main shopping street. Along with a modern extension, it now houses the **Clemens Sels Museum** (Tues.–Sun. 10am–5pm; DM2), an average local collection with some surprises, such as paintings by the Pre-Raphaelites and French symbolists.

Hotels in Neuss are a fallback if Düsseldorf seems too expensive, though none is an outstanding bargain. There's also a **youth hostel**, close to the Rhine at Macherscheider Str. 113 (☎02101 39273) in the suburb of UEDESHEIM. For a cheap and filling lunch, try the seventeenth-century tavern *Em Schwatte Päd*, at the point where Büchel changes to Krefelder Strasse; on the same street nearer the Hauptbahnhof is a good brewery pub-restaurant, *Im Kessel*.

Mönchengladbach

MÖNCHENGLADBACH, 30km west of Düsseldorf, is, like Bonn, an average-sized provincial town which has been catapulted to prominence since World War II. The new role for this old textile- and machine-manufacturing community is the rather less enviable one of serving as NATO's operations base for northern and central Europe, and as the headquarters of the British Army on the Rhine. An ad hoc suburb has been created at **RHEINDAHLEN** to the west; it's best described as "Little Britain." Not only does English reign supreme as the language; everything, bar the local buses and the use of the Deutschmark as currency, breathes of the British way of life, as the colony does its utmost to forget that it's living on German soil. There are cricket and rugby pitches, halls for Scout and Brownie packs, Anglican and Presbyterian churches; the main thoroughfare is styled *Queens Avenue,* while the side streets tend to commemorate trees rather than deceased political leaders.

Though not the most obvious destination unless you're visiting a friend or relative, Mönchengladbach does have some notable attractions, including the most audacious publicly owned art gallery in Germany, the **Museum Abteiberg** (Tues.–Sun. 10am–6pm; DM3), an ultramodern building right in the heart of the old part of the town, which is reached in about fifteen minutes from the **Hauptbahnhof** by turning left on exit and going straight up Hindenburgstrasse, the main shopping street. Inaugurated in 1982, it was intended from its conception a decade earlier to be a major piece of modern architecture. The twin aims were to make it a distinctive yet harmonious feature of the cityscape, and an integral part of the modern art collection displayed within. An architect who is also an artist, the Viennese **Hans Hollein**, was chosen to see the entire project through, and some of his own paintings are on exhibit. There's no doubt that the museum building is an eye-catching design, rising in terraces, with wavy curves, a stumpy tower and clusters of leaded windows juxtaposed with long stretches of unadorned wall. The acquisitions policy has eschewed nearly all the century's best-known artists, and supported the avant-garde in a big way. **Joseph Beuys**, who first sprang to fame following an exhibition in Mönchengladbach, is copiously represented; other artists similarly honored are Lucio Fontana, Giulio Paolini, Cy Twombly, Richard Sella, Sigmar Polke, Marcel Broodthaers and Arman Fernandez. If you're keen on the iconoclastic and experimental nature of modern art, this museum warrants a special trip, but if you've even a suspicion of allergy to it, best keep well away.

Directly behind is the **Münster**, successor to the tenth-century Benedictine abbey from which the town which subsequently developed derives its name (*Mönchen*=monks). The present building was erected throughout the thirteenth century, straddling the late Romanesque and early Gothic periods, culminating in the chancel by **Master Gerhard**, who was also master mason at the Dom in Cologne. Its central "Bible" window, pairing fourteen New Testament scenes with episodes from the Old Testament which were believed to anticipate them, is the only surviving piece of original glass. Notwithstanding the fact that three of the bottom panes have had to be replaced, it ranks as one of the loveliest in Germany. The **Schatzkammer** (Tues.–Sat. 2–6pm, Sun. noon–6pm; DM2) displays the church's treasures, the most valuable of which is a twelfth-century portable altar from Cologne. You may have to ask to see the crypt and the sacristy; the former, unusually large for its time, is the oldest part of the church. In keeping with the town's reputation for commissioning significant modern art, it was recently fitted with tiny gem-like stained glass windows interpreting biblical stories in a style veering between the representational and the abstract. The sacristy is a handsome Gothic room with delicately carved capitals and an amazingly well-preserved stone pavement. On the Münster's north side is the heavy baroque mass of its former conventual buildings, now the **Rathaus**. In front of this, facing the Alter Markt, is the late Gothic **Oberpfarrkirche**; the few surviving old houses are close by.

Schloss Rheydt, set in its own quiet grounds to the east of the city, is a handsome moated castle which contains most of the municipal museum collections (March–Oct. Tues.–Sun. 10am–6pm, Nov.–Feb. Wed, Sat., and Sun. only 11am–5pm; DM2). Unfortunately, there's a major snag—the *Hauptburg*, housing the works of art, is likely to be closed until 1995 for repairs, meaning you can only visit the rather parochial archaeology, local history, and weaving displays in the *Vorburg*. The restaurant, though not the cheapest, serves excellent food. At the southernmost end of town is **Schloss Wickrath**, a baroque building by the Aachen architect **J.J. Couven**; it houses an ornithological museum, but is only open on Sunday (10am–noon and 3–5pm).

Nightlife and Practicalities

Mönchengladbach has quite a swinging **nightlife**, much of it self-evidently geared to its foreign residents. On the Alter Markt itself is *Nostalgia-Pub Cannape*, while some of the bars around the corner on Aachener Strasse have live jazz. However, most of the action, in the evenings at least, takes place on the steeply plunging Waldhausener Strasse, which is almost entirely taken up by an enormous variety of ethnic restaurants, steak houses, snack bars, taverns, cafés, ice-cream parlours, and discos ranging from *Soul Center* to those playing the latest heavy metal. *Dicker Turm* has snug little bars on three floors of a rebuilt tower which was once part of the fortifications. The favorite **beer** is the dark **Alt**, particularly that made by *Hannen*, which has a large brewery here.

Unfortunately, the central **hotels** are mostly on the pricey side; try *Steffens*, Waldhausener Str. 160 (☎02161 32386) or *Gerohof*, Speicker Str. 82b (☎02161 32586), both at DM30 per head, whether in singles or doubles. If they're full, you'll probably have to pay a lot more, or else stay farther out. *Faassen*, Vorster Str. 233 (☎02161 559182) and *Kasteel*, Vorster Str. 529 (☎02161 559694), in the suburb of HARDT (bus #13 or #23) both charge around DM25 to DM28 per person and have restaurants, the latter's being particularly good. Also in Hardt, but a farther 1km south in the woods, is the **youth hostel** at Gritzkesweg 125 (☎02161 559512); continuing in a straight line from here, you come before long to the Rheindahlen garrison, so its location is less isolated than it might appear. Full lists of other accommodation possibilities are available from the **tourist office** at Bismarckstr. 23–27, between the Hauptbahnhof and Alter Markt (Mon.–Fri. 9am–6pm, Sat. 9am–1pm; ☎02161 22001), which also publishes a free monthly program of events.

Borussia Mönchengladbach gave the city additional claim to fame in the 1970s when, most improbably, it supplanted Bayern München as Germany's leading **soccer** team for several seasons; their tussle with Liverpool in the European Cup final of 1977 was rated by cognoscenti as one of the matches of the decade. They've now faded a bit, but if you want to see them in action their stadium is at *Bökelberg*, north of the center. Surprisingly, the most popular spectator sport is not soccer but horse-drawn wagon racing, a modern version of the Roman chariots, held at the *Trabrennbahn* stadium. The list of **festivals** is headed by Carnival, which is unusual in featuring its main parade on Shrove Tuesday, meaning you can move on to it after the main celebrations have finished elsewhere. As a farther show of acceptance of the presence of foreign troops, an international festival of military music is held in early July.

Krefeld

KREFELD, some 20km northeast of Mönchengladbach, has long been a by-word in the world of fashion, thanks to its standing as Germany's leading textile town. Although the industry originally developed by Huguenot refugees was centered on linen, and rayon is now the basis of much of the output, Krefeld is renowned above all for its luxury silk and velvet products, forming the principal European rival to the great French centre, Lyon. The town is also a Rhine port, thanks to the absorption of adjacent **UERDINGEN**, now overrun by the belching chimneys of the giant *Bayer* chemical works. As at downstream Leverkusen, this company's dominance even extends to owning the eponymous local football team, again one of the best in the country.

It would be idle to pretend that Krefeld is anything other than a typical industrial conglomeration, but its fine museums provide justification for a visit. The main concentration of these is in the suburb of **LINN**, reached from downtown by tram #44, or from any other town by S-Bahn. Formerly a separate community, it manages to preserve something of its old character, above all in the streets round Andreasmarkt, where a new building houses the long-established **German Textile Museum** (April–Oct. Tues.–Sun. 10am–6pm, Nov.–March Tues.–Sun. 10am–1pm and 2–5pm; DM3; same price and times apply to everything else in Linn). With some 20,000 items this is the leading collection in the country, with works from all countries and periods. For conservation reasons, these can only be displayed in rotation in the form of small temporary exhibitions. You can see any other object on request; if you've a serious interest in the subject, best write ahead. At the end of the square is the entrance to **Burg Linn**, a moated castle founded in the twelfth century by the Counts of Kleve, but remodeled in the fifteenth century by the archbishops of Cologne, who added Renaissance embellishments later. Left in ruins in 1702 following fighting in the War of the Spanish Succession, it has been partly restored and furnished in period style. The **Butterturm**, formerly the prison, can be climbed for an extensive view. In front of the moat is the **Jagdschloss**, once part of the outer bailey, but revamped in the 1730s as a hunting lodge, once it had been decided that the main castle was redundant. Its rooms have been fitted out with original objects from the homes of leading local families of the eighteenth and nineteenth centuries, while there's a display of old mechanical musical instruments on the ground floor (demonstrated mornings only). Finally, a modern building houses the **Niederrhein Museum**, which has important archaeology collections. Particularly outstanding are those excavated in nearby GELLEP, whose sandy soil ensured a remarkable state of preservation. They include pieces of Roman glass, notably lead-glazed earthenware vessels peculiar to this site. Even more spectacular are the contents of an intact sixth-century Frankish prince's grave—a gleaming gold helmet, a sword, a signet ring and other jewelry. On the second floor are wooden models of all the Lower Rhenish towns as they looked in the mid-seventeenth century.

In the middle of Krefeld proper, a shopping area of startling anonymity, is the **Kaiser Wilhelm Museum** (Tues.–Fri. 10am–5pm, Sat. and Sun. 11am–5pm; DM2) on Karlsplatz. Its ponderous architecture from the last years of the nineteenth century stands in sharp contrast to the modern art which occupies the lion's share of the space within. **Joseph Beuys** and **Yves Klein** are both extensively featured, and there are examples of all the main pop artists in a strong American representation. Graphic work takes up a large part of the display, and includes **Matisse**'s *Jazz*, a luxuriantly colored set of twenty stenciled cut-outs, and **Miró**'s *Makemono*, a folding lithograph on silk, which has equally brilliant kaleidoscopic effects. There's a good **Monet**, *Sunset over Westminster*; sculptures by **Rodin**, **Barlach**, and **Lehmbruck**, and a display of Jugendstil glass, ceramics, and metalwork, the last-named of local manufacture. More surprisingly, there's a decent representation of the Italian Renaissance, including sculptures by **Jacopo Sansovino**, **Nanni di Bartolo**, and the **della Robbia** family.

Open for temporary exhibitions only, when the same schedules are in force, are **Haus Lange** and **Haus Esters** at 91–97 Wilhelmshofallee, northeast of the center and reached by bus #91 or #97. Built between 1928 and 1930 by **Mies van der Rohe**—now firmly enshrined as the patron saint of property developers—they're among the earliest examples of the International Modern movement in architecture. This style, which reduced buildings to asymmetrical groupings of simple cubic shapes with large windows and unrelievedly plain wall surfaces, was soon to sweep across Europe and North America, conquering everything but public opinion, which was almost unanimously hostile. There's a fascinating contrast with the antithetical approach of the pompously grand but aesthetically far more pleasing villas all around, built by architects whose names have passed into oblivion.

All of Krefeld's sights can be covered in a day, so there's no particular reason to stay overnight, the more so as there's no hostel or indeed much in the way of cheap **accommodation**, the many hotels downtown all catering to the business traveler. Check with the **tourist office** on Theaterplatz (Mon.–Fri. 8am–6:30pm, Sat. 8am–1pm; ☎02151 29290/3) for any good deals; from the **Hauptbahnhof** go straight ahead along Ostwall. There are innumerable places to **eat** and **drink** in the main streets; *Et Bröckske* on Marktstrasse is a pub renowned for good food at reasonable prices. **Mitfahrzentrale** has an office at Rheinstr. 95 (☎02151 802081).

Kempen, Kevelaer, and Goch

Beyond Krefeld and the adjoining manufacturing town of MOERS immediately to the north, the Lower Rhineland loses its urban nature and increasingly resembles the neighboring Netherlands in character. This is true not only of the flat land-scape and predominantly brick architecture, but also of the local dialect, which is the original Low German from which the Dutch language is derived.

KEMPEN, a railroad junction just 10km northwest of Krefeld, is the presumed birthplace of one of the best-selling writers of all time—not that **Thomas à Kempis** ever enjoyed fame or fortune during his life, or would have wanted to. A modest, retiring man, he spent seventy of his ninety years in the same Dutch Augustinian monastery, where he wrote *The Imitation of Christ*, a book whose influence on the Christian world is surpassed only by the Bible itself. There's none of the deep intellectualization common in theological tracts, nor the ecstatic mysticism which limits the appeal of so many religious writings. Instead, the author deliberately addressed the common reader, using simple yet poetic prose to stress the importance of a spiritual and aesthetic lifestyle. An exhibition on Thomas à Kempis—including an example of the first Latin edition of his master-piece, published in 1487, sixteen years after his death—forms one of the main features of the **Niederrhein Museum of Sacred Art** (Tues., Weds., and Fri.–Sun. 11am–5pm, Thurs. 11am–7pm; DM2) which occupies the old Franciscan Paterskirche and its monastic buildings in the town center.

Nearby is the **Propsteikirche**, a bulky fourteenth-century Gothic church with a striking pink Romanesque tower. It's richly adorned with works of art collected during the town's heyday in the fifteenth and early sixteenth centuries: the three large altarpieces came from Antwerp, while the superb tabernacle and Renaissance organ were made in Cologne. The streets of Kempen barely fit the description of photogenic; there remain a number of old houses, parts of the forti-fications, and the medieval Burg, which was completely rebuilt last century in the Romantic manner. If you want to stay, the cheapest **hotel** in town is *Haus Becker*, Thomasstr. 9 (☎02152 519269), with singles for DM35, doubles DM60.

KEVELAER, some 30km north on the main railroad line to KLEVE, is Germany's premier **place of pilgrimage**, drawing some 500,000 believers each year in a "season" lasting from May to October. Just before Christmas 1641, a local peddler, Hendrick Busman, heard voices charging him to build a chapel on the site. Shortly after, his wife had a vision of the chapel containing the image of *The Blessed Virgin of Luxembourg* which she had seen carried by two soldiers; this picture had been attributed with healing properties during a plague in Luxembourg. Within six months, Busman had built a simple shrine with his own hands, in which the miraculous icon was placed; the cult quickly grew, and three years later the far more substantial **Kerzenkapelle** (*Chapel of the Candles*) was built in an archaic Gothic style to house the pilgrims. A decade later, Busman's construction was replaced by the elaborate hexagonal **Gnadenkapelle** (*Chapel of the Favors*), in which the image was displayed facing the square outside.

The fame of the pilgrimage spread so much in the nineteenth century that a vast neo-Gothic **Basilica** had to be built to accommodate the crowds who flocked from all over the country. Credit for the increased popularity must go to a poem composed by **Heinrich Heine**, who explained the miracle-working as follows:

The sick and ailing come there
And bring, as offering,
Limbs molded out of waxwork,
Wax feet and hands they bring.
Whoever brings a wax hand,
His hand is healed that day,
And he who brings a wax foot,
Walks well and sound away.

It's a wonderful irony—something the poet (a Jew and Protestant convert) doubt-less appreciated—that Heine's apparently mellifluous tone is in fact a mocking one. He based the ballad directly on the true story of a friend who went to Kevelaer with a wax heart, hoping to be cured of an unhappy love affair, only to find that the remedy didn't work at all.

No doubt it's a reflection of the Germanic nature that Kevelaer lacks the sheer, unadulterated bad taste that's the hallmark of other leading Marian shrines in Europe, such as Lourdes, Fátima, and Knock. Unlike them, it can't really be recommended as worth seeing just for shock value, which means you're unlikely to want to stay for long—unless you're intent on waiting for a miracle. Apart from the pilgrimage churches already mentioned, the only other attraction is the **Niederrhein Museum of Folklore** (daily 10am–5pm, Nov.–April closed Mon.; DM2). There's a **youth hostel** at Schravelen 50 (☎02832 8267); **hotels** are scat-tered all over town and, being geared to the pilgrim market, seldom ask for more than DM30 per person.

Another 10km north lies **GOCH**, ominously described in Patrick Leigh Fermor's *A Time of Gifts*; the town was his introduction not only to Germany, but also to the newly established Third Reich. His descriptions of an outfitter's shop, a tavern, and an SA parade vividly convey the Nazi regime's obsessiveness, regi-mentation, and above all, double-think; he found it impossible to square the delightful renditions of the folk songs commandeered for Party use with the thug-gery and philistinism practiced by those who sang them.

Only the **Steintor** survives of the 28 towers and gates which once defended Goch; it houses the local **museum** (Tues.–Sun. 10am–noon and 3–5pm; DM1), which features archaeological finds and sacred art. Round the corner on Steinstrasse is the resplendent brick facade of one of the finest patrician mansions in the Lower Rhineland, the sixteenth-century **House of the Five Gables**, now the Rathaus. From the square beyond, you can see the tower of the only other interesting monument in town, **St. Maria Magdalena**, a large Gothic church, also of brick, which is closely related to those in nearby Kalkar and Kleve; when locked, ask for the key at the parish offices in front of the facade. If you want to spend the night, the most convenient **hotel** is *Gocher Hof* on Bahnhofsplatz (☎02823 1460), which charges DM30 a head.

Xanten

XANTEN, set just back from the Rhine some 45km north of Krefeld, is one of the oldest settlements in Germany. In about 100 A.D. *Colonia Ulpia Traiana* was founded as a residential town (the only one in the Rhineland other than Cologne) in succession to the nearby garrison of Vetera, base of operations for the campaign to subdue the eastern Germanic tribes, which had come to grief in the Teutoburger Wald. It in turn was abandoned with the collapse of the empire, and followed by a new community built immediately to the south around the graves of Christians martyred in 363 during the last wave of purges. These were popularly but implausibly believed to be St. Victor and members of the Thebian Legion; the name given to the town is a contraction of the Latin *Ad Sanctos Martyres* ("To the Holy Martyrs"). Writing at the end of the twelfth century, the anonymous poet of *The Nibelungenlied*, describing semi-mythical events centuries earlier, characterizes Xanten as "great," "splendid" and "far-famed," the birthplace and court of the invincible hero Siegfried, Lord of the Netherlands, Norway, and the mysterious Nibelungland, home of the fantastic gold treasure of the Rhine which was to form the basis of the very different version of the legend unfolded in Wagner's epic *Ring* cycle some 700 years later.

Xanten is something of a Peter Pan, its current population of 16,000 little more than the probable size of the Roman town. It kept its medieval aspect until the last war, when it was badly bombed. Modern Xanten has successfully risen from the debris to appear once more as one of Germany's neatest country towns (the recipient of several prestigious conservation prizes), if one which is sometimes rather too crammed with day-trippers from the industrial hotbed to the south for its own good. The **fortifications** survive in part, still defining the town's perimeter on the north and east sides. They're pierced by several towers, many of which have been converted into luxury apartments, including the grandest of the group, the **Klever Tor**, whose double gateway formed the northwest entrance to the town. Just up Nordwall, the next tower underwent a rather more radical conversion in the eighteenth century, being re-shaped to form a windmill. Immediately facing it is Brückstrasse, best preserved of the old streets.

Between here and the Markt, the **Dom** lies cocooned in its own courtyard or "Immunity," so named from its status as a haven from external laws and taxes. An atmosphere of otherworldly peace still reigns in this confined space—but only at certain times of the day, since it now doubles as a school playground. From afar, the massive facade dominates the town; it was the only part of the Romanesque cathedral spared when a sober Gothic replacement was put up in the late thirteenth century. Subsequent builders tampered with it right up until 1525, by which time the towers had been considerably heightened. If you go around to the rear, you'll see a polychromed fifteenth-century statue to the Dom's patron saint, St. Victor; whether one of the ancient tombs discovered in the crypt excavations earlier this century is really his burial place is a matter resolved more by faith than cold logic. The five-aisled **interior** (10am–noon and 2–5/6pm according to season) gives a rare opportunity of sampling the genuine, cluttered feel of a medieval cathedral, thanks to the extraordinary range of objects it has preserved: expressive pier statues of saints, a rood screen, choir stalls, a hanging *Double Madonna*, stained glass windows and a crowd of altars. Particularly noteworthy are the four carved and painted late Gothic winged retables in the aisles, one from Antwerp and three from nearby Kalkar; finest is that on the south side, with scenes from the life of the Virgin springing from a superb *Tree of Jesse* by Henrik Douverman. The same sculptor made the reliquary busts for the high altar, which also incorporates the twelfth-century shrine of St. Victor and panels by Barthel Bruyn. In the southwest corner of the courtyard is the **Regional Museum** (Tues., Thurs., and Fri. 10am–5pm, Weds. 10am–8pm, Sat. and Sun. 11am–6pm; DM3), which serves as a repository for the Dom, with the treasury kept in the basement, and works of art no longer required for display on the ground floor. It also has extensive archaeology and local history collections, but be warned that these are presented in an extremely didactic fashion, and that the most important local finds are housed in its parent museum in Bonn.

From here you can pass out into the **Markt**, something of a hodgepodge of styles, with houses ranging from Gothic to rococo. At the far end, turn left down Karthaus, named after the former Charterhouse whose baroque facade is the dominant feature of the street, then continue along Rheinstrasse; across the main road is the site of Colonia Ulpia Traiana, now the **Archaeological Park** (daily 9am–6pm; DM3). This was the only Roman town in northern Europe which was never built over; that it subsequently disappeared is due to the fact that its stones were ideal building materials for later constructions, including the Dom. In the 1970s there was a proposal to develop the area into a recreation zone, but in return for sparing the site the authorities insisted that the excavations be given populist appeal. Thus, instead of merely uncovering ground plans, full-blooded conjectural reproductions of the main buildings of the town were attempted. The result is controversial to say the least, and purists will be horrified by the Disneyland touches. However, if you normally find archaeological sites hamstrung by scholarly timidity, this will come as a revelation, giving a graphic picture of the true size and scale of a Roman town. Eventually, the aim is to go as far as recreating the original riverside setting, which has now completely disappeared; at the moment, the **walls** with their massive fortifications, notably the **Harbor Gate** at the very far end of the park, form the most impressive feature. Just inside the main entrance, an **inn** has been reconstructed; here the presentation gets outrageously out of hand with toga-clad waiters serving the sort of meals it's alleged the Romans would have eaten. The **amphitheater**, which is partly original, now serves as a successful venue for open-air theatrical performances; the **temple**, on the other hand, has been rebuilt only as a ruin.

From the **Bahnhof**, the center is only a few minutes' walk via either Hagenbuschstrasse or Bahnhofstrasse. Services on the line northwards to KLEVE are often replaced by buses, which leave from the forecourt. The **tourist office** (mid-March–mid-Oct. Mon.–Fri. 10am–5pm, Sat. and Sun. 10am–4pm; rest of year 11:30am–4pm daily; ☎02801 37238) is located in the Rathaus at the corner of the Markt and Karthaus. Helpfully displayed in their window is a list of more than a score of private houses with **rooms** to rent; these are the cheapest option, as there's no hostel. Nearly all cost DM25 per head, although a few charge only DM22; you can choose a central location, or there are many in a more rural setting which are still within walking distance. The least expensive hotels, both just off the Markt, are *Van Bebber*, Klever Str. 16–18 (☎02801 1401), from DM34 per person, and *Galerie an de Marspoort*, Marsstr. 78 (☎02801 1057) with doubles at DM66. There are plenty of places to eat and drink downtown, though Xanten doesn't score highly for either gastronomy or nightlife. To the east of town, towards the Rhine, are peaceful **nature trails** in protected countryside, while to the north is the **Xantener Nordsee**, a watersports center, with a range of boats for rent (summer only).

Kalkar

KALKAR (or *CALCAR*) was built on a sandbank completely surrounded by an arm of the Rhine, but heavy silting has meant that it's now well inland. It lies on the least busy of the three railroad lines linking the Ruhrgebiet with Holland, midway between Xanten and Kleve; thanks to possessing one of Germany's most remarkable churches, it rivals the former as the most interesting of the Lower Rhenish towns.

The central **Markt** square lost much of its character to wartime bombs, but some old houses have been restored to provide fitting company for the **Rathaus**, a brick building with a prominent octagonal turret. Behind, a step-gabled merchant's residence, connected by a modern extension to the oldest house in the town, contains the **Stadtmuseum** (Tues.–Sun. 10am–1pm and 2–5pm; DM1). This has an excellent collection of manuscripts and charters, along with the work of painters, most notably the expressionist **Heinrich Nauen**, who lived in the town. Off the opposite end of the Markt is the well-restored facade of the **Beginenhof**, the former almshouse.

None of this prepares you for the splendors of **St. Nicolai**, built beside the Markt at the same time as the Rathaus. From the outside, it looks quite ordinary—a plain fifteenth-century brick building, enlivened only by its tall tower. The gleaming white interior (April–Oct. Mon.–Fri. 10am–noon and 2–6pm, Sat. 10am–noon and 2–5pm, Sun. 2–5pm, Nov.–March daily 2–5pm; DM1) is another matter altogether, bristling with such an astonishing array of **works of art** that it's now designated a "church-museum." It seems odd that what has never been more than a parish church in a town which has never been very large could have garnered such riches, but medieval Kalkar became wealthy through a cloth industry that used locally produced wool. The rich burghers showed their appreciation for this natural bounty by funding a school of woodcarving which flourished continuously for about a century from 1450, producing one great altarpiece after another, whose purpose was to illustrate the lives of Christ and the saints for the enlightenment of a largely illiterate congregation. Fifteen large retables and numerous other statues and paintings originally embellished the church; some were sold last century, but all the important pieces remain in situ.

It's worth taking time to examine the myriad details to be found in the big showpieces; all display an amazing level of technical virtuosity. **Henrik Douverman**, who made the *Altar of the Seven Sorrows of the Virgin* in the south apse, the *Double Madonna Candelabrium* in the middle of the nave and the superbly expressive *St. Mary Magdalene* in the north aisle, has long been recognized as a highly individual artist, who proved the continuing vitality of late Gothic forms well into the sixteenth century. However, many of his little-known predecessors, who were forced to submerge their artistic personalities in cooperative ventures, showed equal skill, especially in the crowded main *Passion Altar*, begun by the founder of the school, **Master Arnt**, and continued by **Ludwig Jupan**; these carvers were also responsible respectively for the *St. George Altar* and the *Altar to the Virgin* fronting the entrance to the chancel. Painted panels were added to many of the retables to fill out the story; particularly fine are the colorful scenes on the *Passion Altar* by **Jan. Joest**; the setting of *The Raising of Lazarus* is, incidentally, Kalkar's Markt.

From the **Bahnhof**, St. Nicolai's tower is clearly visible and is only a few minutes' walk away, but you're more likely to arrive by one of the far more extensive **bus** services, which conveniently stop in the Markt. The **tourist office** (Mon.–Fri. 9am–noon and 2–5pm; ☎02824 13138) is hidden away down Grabenstrasse at the back of the Rathaus; they have a list of the few private houses with **rooms** to let. There's an unofficial **youth hostel** in a quaint windmill setting just past the museum down Hanselaer Strasse, but it's only randomly open. Otherwise, there are two **hotels** on the Markt—*Seydlitz* (☎02824 2411) is perfectly adequate at DM30 per head; *Markt-Klause* (☎02824 2252), in a historic building, has singles at DM40, doubles from DM70. The latter also has the second-best restaurant in town, with eminently reasonable prices; it's only surpassed by the much more expensive *Ratskeller* directly opposite. Just north of Kalkar is the **Wisseler See**, a natural lake which is a watersports center; it also has a **campground** (☎02824 6613).

Kleve and Emmerich

KLEVE (*CLEVES* in its anglicized form) was obliterated during the war, its status as a frontier town making it a prime target for aerial bombardment. All that remains of the old city are the main public buildings, now heavily restored and, it could be argued, stripped of their soul in the process.

Unusually for the area, Kleve is built on hills, dominated by a cliff (which gives the town its name) crowned by the **Schwanenburg** (*Swan Castle*), which is closely associated with the legend of Lohengrin, Knight of the Holy Grail. It was the seat of the once-powerful local dukes, whose dynastic aspirations reached a climax in 1539, only to end in humiliation the following year. The English king, Henry VIII, was on the lookout for a new queen following the death of his third wife, Jane Seymour. He sent his painter, Hans Holbein the Younger, to a number of European courts to make likenesses of prospective brides, one of whom was Anne, daughter of the Duke of Cleves. It seems the artist—normally anything but a flatterer—was placed in an impossible position by having to execute the portrait quickly, and to the approval of his hosts. Henry was sufficiently pleased with the result (which can be seen in the Louvre in Paris) to contract a marriage, but disliked the "Flanders mare" from the moment he set eyes on her, and sent her back home in ignominy six months later; the unfortunate Holbein was dismissed from royal service for his part in the debacle. The present castle dates from the fifteenth century, but has had so many subsequent alterations it's impossible to categorise its style. Nowadays, it serves as law courts and local government offices, but you can ascend the **tower** (April–Sept. daily 11am–5pm, Nov.–March Sat. and Sun. only same times; DM2) for an extensive view.

Immediately opposite, the former stables house the town library, while behind is **St. Mariae Himmelfahrt**, a large brick church similar to Kalkar's St. Nicolai. In terms of artistic treasures, however, it's very much a poor relation, though its **high altar** was made by the star member of the neighboring town's school of woodcarving, Henrik Douverman. There's also a special burial chapel for the dukes, housing some fine tombs with recumbent figures. Little else remains of the old city, which has been transformed into a bland modern shopping center.

West of downtown, and reached via the street named after it, is the **Tiergarten**, a terraced garden in the Italian style, laid out in 1656 by order of Prince Johann Moritz von Nassau, who retired to run Kleve following a spectacular career in the service of the Dutch empire at its peak, which included an eight-year stint as governor of Brazil. The garden features a rotunda, an amphitheater, a canal and, as the centerpiece, a statue of Pallas Athenae by the Amsterdam baroque sculptor Artus Quellin. This is a copy, the original having been moved for preservation reasons to the municipal museum, **Haus Koekkoek** on Kavarinerstrasse in the middle of town (Tues.–Sun. 10am–1pm and 2–5pm; free). Also on display in the museum is a Book of Hours made in the workshop of the **Master of the Hours of Catherine of Cleves**, one of the most important illuminators of the late Middle Ages; the wonderful manuscript after which he's named became part of the transatlantic drain of works of art, and is now in the Pierpoint Morgan Library in New York. The town's other great artist was **Joos van Cleve**, who settled in Antwerp, developing a style heavily indebted to the Italian Renaissance, but tempered by a northern European brittleness. A *Male Portrait* by him has recently been placed on loan here by the Federal government in order that his work can once more be seen in the place of his birth. Also here are a large number of paintings by the Koekkoeks, a Dutch family of landscape painters who lived in the house last century, but the museum's most absorbing item is the hilarious carving of *A Pair of Lovers* by **Arnt van Tricht**, the last important member of the Kalkar school; this was made—believe it or not—as a holder for the towels used to wipe Communion cups.

Kleve's **tourist office** (Mon.–Fri. 9am–5pm; ☎02821 84254) is in the Rathaus farther down Kavarinerstrasse. The **youth hostel** makes an inexpensive base for touring the Lower Rhineland, being the only one (apart from Kevelaer) in the area. It's a fair distance out, at the top of a hill at St. Annaberg 2 (☎02821 23671); take bus #57. Most convenient of the cheaper **hotels** is *Koperpöttchen*, Hafenstr. 32 (☎02821 26396), at around DM35 per person; the nearest **campground** is at Wisseler See to the south (see p:459).

Whereas the towns on the left bank of the lower stretch of the Rhine are set back from the river, those on the opposite side tend to be commercial ports. **EMMERICH** is the most interesting of these; it's just 9km from Kleve, to which it's linked by the longest **suspension bridge** in Germany, an effortless structure spanning some 1300 meters. The town was very badly damaged in the war, but the restoration has been highly successful; the center once again has a spick-and-span appearance, its confident brick buildings making it seem even more Dutch than the other Lower Rhenish towns. Two hundred thousand vessels use the port annually; the importance of river trade to local life is celebrated in the **Rhine Museum** at Martinikirchgang just off the main square (Mon.–Weds. 10am–noon and 2–4pm, Thurs. 2–6pm, Fri. and Sun. 10am–noon; free); the **tourist office** (same times; ☎02828 2470) is also here. Cheapest hotel in Emmerich itself is *Zur Grenze*, s'Heerenberger Str. 298 (☎02828 2367) at DM30 per person; there are several similarly priced alternatives in the suburb of ELTEN.

Towards the river, the former monastery of **St. Martini** looks at first sight to be one of the Gothic brick hall churches so typical of the region. In fact, it's a real oddity: two quite distinct and fragmentary buildings, the newer section erected at right angles to the remains of its Romanesque predecessor, whose architecturally pure crypt survives intact. Housed in a reinforced room is the **Schatzkammer**, a treasury fully worthy of a great cathedral (no set opening times; if closed, ask at the priest's house behind the church; DM1). The most valuable item is the *Ark of St. Willibrord*, an elaborately embossed eleventh-century chest-reliquary remodeled four centuries later, but there are many other wonderful pieces. Note in particular some incredibly ornate buckles for choir mantles, and a fourteenth-century reliquary in the shape of a fish with spindly legs. Its humor is matched by the imaginative carvings adorning the fifteenth-century stalls in the church itself, such as a portrayal of two dogs fighting over a bone.

THE RUHRGEBIET

The **RUHRGEBIET** is the most heavily industrialized region in Europe, a continuously built-up area stretching unbroken for some 65km east to west, and up to 30km north to south, in the middle of which is the traditional boundary between the Northern Rhineland and Westphalia. It takes its name from the Ruhr River, which flows right through the region to its confluence with the Rhine, and owes its extraordinary development to fabulously rich mineral deposits, often located close to the surface. The constituent towns, most of which were little more than villages until last century, do their best to preserve some kind of identity, but, apart from the fact that it's hard to determine where one ends and the other begins, they're mostly very similar in feel. Though certain cities are associated with a particular product or service (**Essen** and **Mülheim** with steel, **Gelsenkirchen** with coal, **Duisburg** with its docks, **Dortmund** with beer, **Bochum** with cars), each has a broad economic base with heavy industry providing the lead.

The region has generally been glossed over in previous English-language guidebooks and, initially, it might seem you'd be out of your mind to want to come here. Yet once allowances are made for their less salubrious aspects, Dortmund and Essen, at least, can be enjoyed just like any other historic city. There's also no doubt that although recent years have brought many problems to the Ruhrgebiet, caused by the worldwide need to scale down old industries, they've led to a vast improvement in the region's physical appearance. Only a fraction of the mines and factories which formerly blotted the landscape now survive; the redundant plants have been removed, often to be replaced by parkland. Moreover, the prosperity brought by industry has funded a **vibrant cultural scene**—Bochum is one of Germany's leading centers for theater, while there are important and highly diverse art museums in many of the cities.

The Ruhrgebiet has played a crucial role in modern German (and hence, world) history. Industrialization occurred for the most part after the area had fallen under the control of Prussia, the great predatory power of the nineteenth century. It followed hard on the heels of the British lead, but avoided many of the pioneering country's mistakes. Weapons manufactured in the Ruhr helped win the battles which led to German unification; they also featured strongly in the arms race which led to World War I. Most ominously of all, it's doubtful if Hitler would ever have gained a truly national foothold, let alone come to power, had he not received the financial backing of many of the area's captains of industry.

Duisburg

With **DUISBURG**, separated from Düsseldorf by just a few kilometers of open countyside, the Ruhrgebiet begins with a vengeance. Until the early nineteenth century, this was a small walled town of about 5000 inhabitants which had changed little since the great geographer Gerhard Mercator worked there in the sixteenth century. The industrial revolution then saw it expand beyond recognition with the production of coal, iron, and steel; above all, it developed as a harbor for cargo, thanks to its key location at the point where the Ruhr River enters the Rhine. It still ranks as the world's largest inland port, although recent years have seen a movement towards a postindustrial economy, with the closure of all but one of the seven mines, and steel production extensively modernized. The city center has been tidied up and largely dedicated to pedestrian use, a green belt has been created, and the population has decreased by about 70,000 to its present level of 54,000 as people have been able to afford more congenial accommodation outside the conurbation. Alas, it's a case of too little too late; in spite of glossy brochures presenting the city in the most favorable light, there's no escaping that it has extraordinarily little in the way of general attractions. Medieval Duisburg has almost completely disappeared; the **Salvatorkirche**, a rather ordinary, large Gothic church where Mercator is buried, is virtually the only reminder of times past. It's not a city you're likely to want to stay in for long, and the only reason for coming at all is if any of its sights (which boil down to the river port and the museums) are in your field of interest.

One of the oddball attractions of Duisburg is a **harbor cruise**; these run from April to October, last a couple of hours and cost DM10. Be warned that the views are a world away from the legendary landscapes farther up the Rhine: coal tips, scrap heaps, gaunt warehouses, and belching chimneys are the order of the day. The two main departure points are the Schwanentor near the Salvatorkirche downtown (3pm daily, with an additional cruise at 10am on Sunday), and the Schifferbörse in the heart of the docklands at RUHRORT (2pm daily, also 11am on Sunday). Each has an extra departure at 5pm and 4pm respectively on Sundays between May and August, and on weekdays during the schools' summer vacation. Reservations can be made at the offices on Mülheimer Str. 72–74 (☎0203 3950). As a supplement, visit the **Inland Navigation Museum** housed in the former Rathaus in Ruhrort (Tues. and Fri.–Sun. 10am–5pm, Weds. and Thurs. 10am–4pm; DM1). This has a large collection of ship models, although the most interesting exhibit is a medieval dug-out canoe of indeterminate date. Included in the entry ticket is admittance to *Oscar Huber*, a paddle-wheel steam tug built in 1922, which is moored outside.

The other museums are in Immanuel-Kant-Park downtown. Modern art freaks should overlook Duisburg's shortcomings in order to visit the **Wilhelm Lehmbruck Museum**, Germany's premier collection of twentieth-century sculpture (Tues. 11am–8pm, Weds.–Sun. 11am–5pm; DM3). Its highlight is the legacy of the sculptor **Lehmbruck** himself, born to a Duisburg mining family, who committed suicide in 1919 at the age of 38. There are many examples here of his classically beautiful portrait busts, but it's his more ambitious compositions of elongated, writhing figures, such as *The Fallen One* (*Der Gestürzte*), *Mother and Child*, *Kneeling Woman* (*Kniende*), and *The Brooder* (*Sinnende*) which make a more lasting impression. The city took 45 years to get around to building a home for these; appropriately enough, the architect chosen for the project was one of Lehmbruck's sons. Since then, a glittering array of works by the most prestigious international sculptors of the century—Rodin, Barlach, Giacometti, Henry Moore, Archipenko, Marini, Lipchitz, Arp, Naum Gabo, Andy Warhol—has formed a fitting complement. An attractive feature is the way artists chiefly famous as painters are represented by their much rarer sculptures—the Fauvist **Derain** abandons his usual bright palette in *The Twin*; the surrealists **Dalí** and **Magritte** provide two of the most memorable pieces in *Head of Dante* and *L'Avenir des Statues*; while their colleague **Max Ernst**'s *Un Ami Empressé* and *Object Mobile* are shown alongside two of his canvases. In the entrance hall are the most spectacular exhibits, **Joseph Beuys' End of the Twentieth Century** and **Duane Hanson**'s *Vietnam War Piece*, a devastating attack on the folly of the conflict, with a horrifyingly real depiction of five American soldiers dead or dying in the mud. The gallery above has a light-hearted recent acquisition in *Das Märchenrelief* by **Jean Tinguely**, which needs to be set in motion for full effect; ask an attendant.

The modestly-sized **Niederrhein Museum** (Tues. and Thurs.–Sat. 10am–5pm, Weds. 10am–4pm, Sun. 11am–5pm; DM2) is for the most part of average interest only, with the usual archaeology and local history exhibits, including a series of models on how the city has developed. These are completely outclassed by the (German only) display on the work of **Gerhard Mercator**, born in Flanders of German stock, who settled in Duisburg in 1552 and remained there until his death 42 years later. His most enduring legacy is the Mercator projection, still in use in a modified form today in both sea and air transport; this enabled maps to be drawn accurately on a flat surface, and meant sailors could steer a course by plotting straight lines, instead of continually resorting to the compass. He was a prolific cartographer—several examples of his maps are shown—and it's from one of his collections that the term "atlas' has passed into linguistic currency. However, the most conspicuous items here are the terrestrial globe of 1541 and its celestial counterpart of ten years later, works of art as much as science whose beauty can be attributed to Mercator's early training in Antwerp as an engraver. Surprisingly, he doesn't seem to have drawn his adopted city, but a lovely and, as you'd expect, topographically accurate depiction of how it looked in 1566 is on view, the work of his pupil Johann Corputius.

The **Hauptbahnhof** is on the eastern side of the city center, reached from Immanuel-Kant-Park by Friedrich-Wilhelm-Stasse. Turning right from here is the beginning of Königstrasse, where you'll find the **tourist office** (Mon.–Fri. 8:30am–6pm, Sat. 8:30am–12:30pm; ☎0203 283 2025); pick up the free monthly program of events *Heute in Duisburg*. The city presents high-class performances at the *Theater der Stadt* (opera and drama) and the *Mercatorhalle* (concerts of all kinds), both of which are just around the corner. This part of the city is also the best place to look for other entertainments—*Kino Hollywood* at Königstr. 63–65 is rather trendy, and there are plenty of places to **eat** and **drink**. The obvious beer to sample is the locally produced *König* Pils, made at the largest German brewery still in private hands. Should you wish to stay, the **youth hostel**, Kalkweg 148 (☎0203 724164), is in the suburb of Wedau, near the main recreation parks; take bus #934, #936 or #944. **Hotel rooms** in the center tend to be expensive; check with the tourist office for any good deals, or be prepared to stay farther out.

East of Duisburg: Mülheim and Oberhausen

Adjoining Duisburg to the east is **MÜLHEIM**, where the Ruhr River is crossed by seven bridges. The town is dominated by **Schloss Broich** (Mon., Tues., Thurs., and Fri. 9:30am–1pm, Weds. and Sat. 9:30am–7pm, Sun. 9:30am–1pm and

3–7pm; DM2). Heavily restored, it's a melange of many styles—the circular ring wall is Romanesque, and encloses the foundations of a previous Carolingian building; the main *Palas* is Gothic with neoclassical modifications, while the central *Hochschloss* is Renaissance.

Mülheim's growth was tied so closely to the spectacular success of the steel mills founded by **August Thyssen** (1842–1926) that it became a virtual family fiefdom. Thyssen's eldest son Fritz was the first prominent industrialist to see Hitler as the man the upper classes were looking for: someone who would stamp out democracy and trade unionism at home, and restore military glory abroad. He helped fund the Nazi Party from 1925, and was later instrumental in persuading other magnates to follow his example, although he was soon to repent of his actions. His brother Heinrich, on the other hand, left Germany at an early age in favor of a succession of other European countries. He became well known as an art collector, establishing what will probably be the last ever private collection of old masters to rival those of the world's great museums. This was broken up after his death, but was reassembled and expanded by his son, who put the paintings on public display at his Swiss mansion in Lugano. Recently, German bids to provide a new home for the gallery (accompanied by special pleading on the grounds that the paintings had been acquired as a result of wealth created in the country) were rejected in favor of an offer from the Spanish government.

Immediately north of Mülheim is **OBERHAUSEN**, a dreary town of 250,000 inhabitants founded as recently as the mid-nineteenth century. Along with BOTTROP and GLADBECK, the northerly continuation of the conurbation, it forms an area singularly lacking in any attractions likely to detain you.

Essen

ESSEN is the largest city of the Ruhrgebiet, and the fifth in West Germany, a sprawling urban area of some 700,000 people. For centuries it was a small town under the control of its convent's abbesses, but it sprang to prominence as the steel metropolis in the industrialization process last century, being effectively run by the most powerful of all Germany's commercial dynasties, the **Krupp** family, whose real-life story of wealth, influence, and intrigue makes the fictional heroes of American soap operas seem trite in comparison. Essen is proud of its heritage, boasting northern Europe's earliest free-standing statue of the Madonna and Child, oldest parish church, largest synagogue and tallest town hall; indeed, the city's publicity manages to make it sound a very enticing destination. While that's something of an overstatement, Essen does nevertheless have a handful of worthwhile attractions—it's one Ruhr city that definitely merits a day or more of anybody's time.

The City

The center of Essen consists largely of an enormous shopping mall. At the northern end are two dominant features of which the tourist office is wildly proud, though in truth neither is an asset: the domed **Synagogue** is a horrendously ugly monstrosity from the early years of this century (remarkable mainly for having outlasted the Third Reich), while the **Rathaus**, a 1970s skyscraper, doesn't rate as one of the gems of modern architecture either. In this setting, the **Münster** (or **Dom**) seems rather incongruous. A ninth-century foundation, it functioned as a collegiate church for aristocratic women until the Reformation; since 1958, it has been the cathedral of a new diocese centered on the Ruhr. The west end is an eccentric tripartite eleventh-century structure apparently modeled on the Dom at Aachen; the rest of what must have been a magnificent building was destroyed by fire, and was replaced by an unexceptional Gothic hall church.

A stupendous collection of **treasures** by Ottonian craftsmen nonetheless makes the Münster a place of outstanding interest. Most prominent of these is the **Golden Madonna** of 965, the first known work of its kind. Housed in its own locked chapel beside the entrance to the crypt, it's highly venerated—at least as many people come to see it for devotional as for aesthetic reasons. The simplicity of form (in contrast to material) makes for a highly charged emotional impact similar to that found in the art of primitive tribes. Also in the church is a large, seven-branched candelabrum dating from about 1000, but the other star pieces are all in the **Schatzkammer**, housed in rooms off the south transept (Tues.–Sun. 10am–4pm; DM1), which should on no account be missed. Here are four dazzling **processional crosses** of the tenth and eleventh centuries; an evangelistary cover with scenes carved in ivory; the crown of Otto III; and many other priceless items. Joined to the front of the Münster by means of an atrium is the **Johanniskirche**, a miniature Gothic baptismal church containing a double-sided altarpiece by Barthel Bruyn; whether you see the Christmas or Easter scenes depends on the time of year.

Between the Münster and the Hauptbahnhof, in a multistoried building on Rathenaustrasse, is the **Deutsches Plakat Museum**, the largest collection of posters in the country (Tues.–Sun. noon–8pm; DM2), which shows its wares in changing thematic exhibitions. The main museum complex, however, is located well to the south of downtown at Goethestr. 41; to reach it, take Kruppstrasse westwards at the back of the Hauptbahnhof, turn left at Bismarckplatz into Bismarckstrasse, and continue straight ahead. Here are two separate collections—the **Ruhrland Museum** and the **Folkwang Museum** (Tues.–Sun. 10am–6pm; combined ticket DM3). The former has the usual local displays, with geology on the ground floor, customs, folklore, and industries upstairs. Far more enticing is the Folkwang Museum, one of Germany's top galleries of nineteenth- and twentieth-century art. Two rooms are devoted to the French Impressionists and their followers, including versions of Monet's favorite subjects, *Rouen Cathedral* and *Water Lilies*; an outstanding **Manet** *Fauré as Hamlet* (which in fact depicts a baritone singing in an opera based on Shakespeare's play); and four good examples each of **Gauguin** and **Van Gogh**. In the German section, two works by **Friedrich** stand out among the Romantics, while there are examples of all the main figures of the present century, with **Nolde**, **Rohlfs**, and **Kirchner** being particularly well represented; Kirchner's *Three Women in the Street* ranks as one of the key paintings in the development of the Expressionist movement.

The southern part of Essen has a surprising green belt. This begins with the **Gruga Park** (April–Sept. 8am–midnight, Oct.–March 9am–dusk; DM3), which incorporates the Botanical Gardens and large recreation areas. Beyond are extensive forests on both sides of the **Baldeneysee**, a long, narrow reservoir formed out of the Ruhr River. It's a popular recreation area in summer, with watersports and walking trails. In this area are the grounds of the **Villa Hügel**, built for the **Krupp** family between 1868 and 1872, and serving as their home until 1945. You have to buy a ticket at the entrance to the park, just behind the S-Bahn station; it covers admission to both houses (Tues.–Sun. 10am–6pm; DM1.50). This idyllic setting gives little clue to the significance of the family, who personify many of the tragedies of modern German history, their genius for both engineering and organization being channeled into the most destructive of ends. Alfred Krupp

(1812–87) brought the dynasty to national prominence 250 years after his ancestors had established themselves as Essen's foremost family. He was in some respects a model employer, pioneering sick pay, free medical treatment, pensions, and retirement homes for his workers. On the other hand, he also had a paranoid obsession for inventing ever more deadly weapons; he has appropriately been dubbed "the father of modern warfare" and his field guns were largely responsible for Prussia's victory over France in 1871 which sealed the unity of Germany. His son Fritz gave a hard business edge to this policy, developing an unrelenting cycle of inventing new offensive weapons, followed by defenses against them, only to make these superfluous by the creation of even more powerful means of attack. These were sold to all and sundry in the arms race which reached its inevitable conclusion in World War I, and ensured international honors and fabulous riches for the family despite the disappointment of German defeat. The next head of the clan, Gustav Krupp von Bohlen, provided Hitler with essential funding; he and his son Alfried were also enthusiastic participators in the Holocaust, making extensive use of concentration camp labor in producing new weapons for the Nazi onslaught on world civilization. Both were sentenced as war criminals at Nürnberg, but the Americans later took pity, and Alfried once more assumed command of an organization which continued to grow spectacularly, with his own personal fortune estimated at one thousand million dollars. Eventually he stretched his interests too far; the family lost control of their empire in 1967, but their name lives on in the corporation which succeeded it. The smaller of the houses has a technicolor PR-type presentation of the achievements of the corporation; upstairs, the family history of the Krupps is described, with the darker episodes carefully glossed over. In the large house, to which it's linked by a pavilion, you can wander at leisure around some of the forbidding, high-ceilinged, wood-paneled rooms, hung with tapestries and portraits of the leading personalities of the day, including the Kaisers, who were close friends. Every so often (generally June–Oct. in even-numbered years) there's a blockbuster international **loan exhibition** of old masters.

South of Hügel lies **WERDEN**, officially a suburb of Essen but still preserving its small-town atmosphere. It's built around the **Abteikirche St. Liudger**, one of the last of the great series of Romanesque basilicas in the Rhineland, dating from the end of the twelfth century, and the successor to a church founded by the saint himself, who is buried in the crypt. The exterior is especially impressive, with its massive westwork and central octagon, while the crypt is unusually an extension of the chancel, rather than its lower story. There's little in the way of furnishing any more; the former high altar is now in London's National Gallery. In a building behind the church is the **Schatzkammer** (Tues.–Sun. 10am–noon and 3–5pm; DM1) which contains many precious items, such as a fifth-century pyx, a ninth-century chalice, a bronze Romanesque crucifix and fragments of the saint's sarcophagus. Along Heckstrasse is the **Luciuskirche**, a daughter church of the abbey, but an even older building which is claimed as the earliest, still-existing parish church in northern Europe. It's been restored to its original and simple tenth-century form.

Some Practical Details

The **Hauptbahnhof** is situated right downtown, only a couple of blocks south of the Münster. **Exchange facilities** are available there (Mon.–Fri. 7:30am–7pm, Sat. 7:30am–5pm, Sun. 10am–1pm). The **tourist office** (Mon.–Fri. 9am–8pm, Sat. 10am–8pm, Sun. 10am–noon; ☎0201 235427) is also within the station, but it's easy to miss, being at the extreme southwest side—i.e. in the opposite direction to the city center. Availability of **hotel rooms** tends to depend on whether or not there's a trade fair on: Essen's prices are a bit lower than in many of the nearby large cities, ranging from about DM30 for a single, DM50 for a double. In the middle of town, *Lindenhof* at Logenstr. 18 (☎0201 233031) has the best location among the cheaper places. A little farther out are: *Roter Hahn* at Kurfürstenstr. 35 (☎0201 270203); *Hermannseck* at Eltingstr. 30 (☎0201 314937); and *Nordstern* at Stoppenberger Str. 30 (☎0201 31721). The **youth hostel** (☎0201 491163) is in WERDEN, a long way from the center, but in a delightful location in the woods, and this suburb is worth seeing anyway. To reach it, take the road passing uphill directly in front of the abbey, and continue straight; it lies well above the houses. Also in Werden, but on the opposite side of the river near the S-Bahn station, is one of the three **campgrounds** (☎0201 492978). The others aren't far away, being situated side by side on the south shore of the Baldeneysee in FISCHLAKEN. Most of the city's **restaurants** seem to have their eyes on the business market. However, *Kleiner Adler* at the corner of Akazienallee and Schwarze Meer, between the Münster and the Hauptbahnhof, offers hearty helpings of traditional cuisine at very reasonable prices, as well as a separate menu of game dishes—more expensive but superb. To mix with a younger clientele, try the cosy and crowded *Franziskus Keller* at I. Weber-Str. 6 just beyond the market square; it has cheap daily specials.

Listings of events, film, theater, exhibitions, and all kinds of music are found in *Live Essen*, available from newsstands, or you can sometimes pick up a free copy at venues. **Pop concerts**, musicals, and other large-scale shows are held at the *Grugahalle*, at the northern end of the eponymous park. **Classical music** is performed in both the *Villa Hügel* and the *Saalbau*, south of the Hauptbahnhof down Huyssenallee; the *Opernhaus* behind hosts opera, theater and dance. Alternative dramatic programs are presented at *Studio Theater am Rathaus*. Essen's **public transit** system is comprehensive, embracing buses, trams (some of which become the U-Bahn for part of their route), and the S-Bahn. Given the size of the place, a 24-hour ticket can be a good investment since it doesn't take many journeys to equal the DM8.50 price. Buying tickets in batches of four is also worthwhile if you're planning on spending more than a day in the city. **Mitfahrzentrale's** office is at Heinickestr. 33 (☎0201 221031).

Bochum

BOCHUM sits right at the heart of the Ruhrgebiet, sandwiched between the two giants of Essen and Dortmund; it marks the transition to the part of the area which is traditionally Westphalian. Appropriately enough it's the place to come to learn about the achievements of Germany industry, boasting as it does two of the best specialist technical museums in the country; if these don't appeal, to be honest there's little else to justify a visit here, other than the remarkably vibrant **theaters**, which manage an improbable rivalry to the likes of Berlin and Munich. A pleasant if anonymous shopping area forms the core of the town, devoid of any sense of history bar the rather ghostly reminder provided by the **Propsteikirche**, a Gothic hall church now standing forlornly in its own grounds. Even more than usual, Bochum seems a loose federation of disparate built-up areas, the green spaces between them (often the sites of abandoned mines) all the more necessary for the locals because of the complete lack of access to open countryside. In spite of the traditional emphasis on heavy industry, the leading employer is now the *Opel* assembly line, General Motors' European subsidiary.

Arriving at the **Hauptbahnhof**, the **tourist office** (Mon.–Fri. 8:30am–6pm, Sat. 8:30am–noon; ☎0234 13031) is found in the front part of the building. The center is straight ahead from here, but it's best to turn right and follow the inner ring road all the way to the **German Mining Museum** (*Deutsches Bergbaumuseum*; Tues.–Fri. 8:30am–5:30pm, Sat. and Sun. 9am–1pm; DM5); you can't miss it, as its sixty-meter-high winching tower is a dominant feature of the skyline. Established in 1930, this legitimately claims to be the most important collection of its kind in the world. It's both exhaustive and inventive in scope, with sections on the history, geography, geology, and economics of mining, along with displays on machinery, equipment, extraction, transport, and safety, while there's even a gallery on its appearances in art. Budget at least two hours for a visit, as the ticket includes a 45-minute conducted tour (German only, hourly departures) around the demonstration pit in the bowels of the earth immediately below. Less frequently, there are opportunities to ascend the tower.

Bochum's other main attraction is the **Railroad Museum** (*Eisenbahn Museum*), run by the national preservation society (Weds. and Fri. 10am–5pm, Sun. 10am–1pm; DM4). Take the S-Bahn to Dalhausen, and turn left at the exit; it's then about 1.5km ahead. Some of the trains are in open yards, but most are grouped in two sheds. The first contains the locomotives themselves, with some real beauties, especially the oldest item, an imperious black and red monster from the 1920s. In the second hall are the passenger carriages, the creature comforts of the first class contrasting strongly with the hard benches in the third. Also here is an example of Deutsche Bundesbahn's most singular contribution to transport history, the *Schiene-Strasse-Bus*, a bizarre hybrid which looks like a motorcoach but is also equipped with wheels for traveling along rails; it was widely used in forest areas until the late 1960s.

Still on a scientific theme, Bochum has a **Planetarium** on Castroper Strasse just north of the Hauptbahnhof (shows on Weds. and Fri. at 7:30pm, Sat. and Sun. at 2pm and 4pm). The **Museum Bochum** (Tues.–Fri. noon–8pm, Sat. and Sun. 10am–6pm; free) is just around the corner from the Mining Museum on Kortumstrasse; the displays here, mounted in a series of changing exhibitions, are devoted to post-1945 art only. There's a branch at **Wasserburg Kemnade**, a moated castle at the southeastern extremity of the city (Tues. 9am–3pm, Weds.–Fri. 1–7pm, Sat. and Sun. 11am–6pm; free). Although heavily restored, a couple of ornate chimneypieces remain, and a large collection of historical musical instruments has been installed, including such rarities as a pedal piano and a gusli. Adjacent is a **Farmhouse Museum** (same times, but May–Oct. only).

Between here and downtown are the eye-catching, futuristic buildings of the **Ruhr-Universität**, the main institution for technical education in the region, and a good place to meet people, although weekends are best avoided, as the campus tends to be deserted. Specific reasons for coming include the **Botanical Gardens** on the southern side (daily April–Sept. 9am–6pm, Oct.–March 9am–4pm), and the **University Museum** (housed under the library; Tues.–Fri. noon–3pm, Sat. and Sun. 10am–6pm; DM1) with a collection of antiques, notably glass and sculptures, and some modern art.

For listings of **events**, pick up the tourist office's free monthly *Wann, Wo, Was*. Bochum has a high reputation for **theater**; the repertory company based at the *Schauspielhaus* on Königsallee ranks as one of the top four in the country. Puppet shows and concerts by the *Bochumer Symphoniker*, a body of good provincial standing, also feature at this venue. The *Ruhrlandhalle* on Stadionring hosts large-scale spectaculars; next to it, the *Starlighthalle* was completed in 1988 specifically to cater for a run of Andrew Lloyd Webber's *Starlight Express*, a venture marking Bochum's bid for national leadership in Broadway-type productions—a lost art in Germany since the war. For **live jazz**, the place to go is *Bahnhof Langendreer*, at the extreme east end of town; this also hosts a festival each March.

There are abundant places to **eat** and **drink** downtown. Two local beers to try are *Vest* and *Fiege*; the *Stammhaus* of the latter brewery is at Bongardstr. 23, and is equally renowned for its food. Somewhat cheaper, but just as good, is the *Bochumer Brauhaus* on Rathausplatz. If you're out at the Railroad Museum, *Central Hof* is one of several places around Dalhausen Bahnhof offering inexpensive, homely cooking. Bochum has no youth hostel, but those in ESSEN and HAGEN are both within easy commuting range. The nearest **campground** is by the banks of the Ruhr in the adjacent town of HATTINGEN. Cheapest **hotels** with a central location are *Wiesmann*, Castroper Str. 191 (☎0234 591065), at DM26 per person and *Sandkühler*, Flurstr. 1 (☎0234 581588), which charges DM28. The **Mitfahrzentrale** office is at Ferdinandstr. 20 (☎0234 37794).

North and west of Bochum lies **GELSENKIRCHEN**, the most notorious of the Ruhr towns. Historically, it was the region's main coal mining center, and heavy industry still reigns supreme here, with all the attendant visual and other pollution. Even the tourist board is wary of trying to entice visitors. To the east is **HERNE**, a large canal port and another town definitely worth avoiding.

Dortmund

The name of **DORTMUND** immediately brings **beer** to mind—it was first granted brewing rights in 1293, and even jealous rivals are forced to admit it's the national drink's number-one city. Six top breweries are based here: *Kronen*, *Union*, *Ritter*, *Thier*, *Stifts*, and *Actien* (*DAB*). Their chimneys form a distinctive feature of the skyline; those of *Union* are right downtown, and about the first landmark you see on arrival at the Hauptbahnhof. In all, 600 million liters are produced annually, a total surpassed in world terms only by Milwaukee. Much of it is for export, which has led to the word being used to categorize certain types of beer.

Alone among Ruhr cities, Dortmund, now with a population of over 600,000, was important in the Middle Ages when it was an active member of the Hanseatic League; this helps give it a rounded and distinctive character which all its neighbors somehow lack. Provided you're prepared to overlook the obvious limitations of a place where wartime bombs wreaked horrendous damage and where heavy industry is still prominent, it's a surprisingly interesting and enjoyable city in which to spend a day or two.

The City

The inner ring road, whose sections all bear the suffix "wall," follows the line of the vanished thirteenth-century fortifications and thus defines the perimeter of the medieval city. Only a fraction of this area was left standing after the blitz, and not a single secular building from the Hansa days remains. The four civic churches, however, survived the onslaught in a battered condition, and a painstaking restoration program which lasted into the 1980s has returned them to their former state. Although they're now marooned in a modern shopping center,

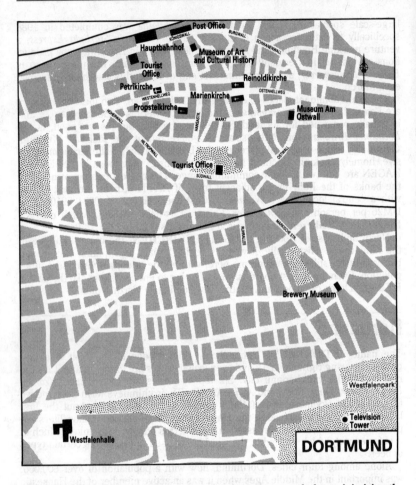

the layout of the old streets and squares has been preserved, thus minimizing the visual loss. None of the churches is architecturally outstanding, but their assemblage of Gothic art treasures justifies a visit to the city—if the beer isn't a sufficient attraction. Directly facing the Hauptbahnhof is the **Petrikirche** (Weds. 3–6pm, Fri. 9am–2pm, irregularly open on other weekday afternoons), boasting a colossal **Antwerp altar** from around 1520, which opens out to show expressively carved scenes of the Passion and Legend of the Cross, featuring no less than 633 separate figures. These can be seen between autumn and Pentecost; during the summer they're hidden behind the more modest painted section narrating the earlier part of Christ's life. A short walk down the central axis of Westenhellweg is the **Propsteikirche**, the one church retained by the Catholics when Dortmund embraced the Reformation. On the high altar is a colorful and crowded triptych from about 1490 by the Westphalian painter **Derick Baegert**, aided by his son **Jan**. Straddling the scenes of *The Holy Kinship*, *The Crucifixion* and *The*

Adoration of the Magi is a view of a medieval town proudly girt with numerous towers and spires—the earliest known depiction of Dortmund, and a poignant memorial to its long-lost splendors.

Continuing across Hansastrasse, Ostenhellweg leads to a large square overshadowed by the **Reinoldikirche**, named after the city's patron saint, who was stoned to death in Cologne. His coffin is supposed to have rolled all the way to Dortmund under its own steam—perhaps just as well for the preservation of his memory, given that Cologne was already well endowed with holy martyrs. He's depicted as a young knight in a superb fourteenth-century wooden statue guarding the entrance to the chancel; the corresponding but later figure of a richly attired emperor is almost certainly Charlemagne. Unfortunately the choir area is fenced off, so you can only admire its furnishings—an early fifteenth-century carved and painted Netherlandish retable, a tabernacle, a set of stalls, and statues of the Apostles—at a respectful distance.

Immediately opposite is the **Marienkirche**, the oldest of the churches, with a nave which is still largely Romanesque (Tues.–Fri. 10am–noon and 2–4pm, Sat. 10am–1pm). Its two masterpieces of International Gothic painting are the city's finest works of art. The high altar triptych dates from around 1420 and is by **Conrad von Soest**, a Dortmund citizen in spite of his name, and as endearing a painter as Germany ever produced. These panels of *The Nativity*, *The Dormition of the Virgin*, and *The Adoration of the Magi* show the uniquely graceful and delicate "Soft Style" (see *Contexts*) at its greatest, even though all were truncated in order to fit into a baroque altar, with the central panel shorn of subsidiary figures to reduce it to the same size as the others. The inner wings of *The Annunciation* and *The Coronation of the Virgin* have suffered such heavy paint loss that they're generally kept under cover, although the caretaker will open them if you express an interest. In the nave, the *Berswordt Altar*, a Crucifixion triptych, is about 25 years earlier, but has survived in much better shape. Named after its donor, the artist is unknown; he is robuster in treatment and more melancholy in feeling than Conrad von Soest, but otherwise similar enough in style to suggest that he must have been his teacher, and most likely his father or uncle. Look also at the late Gothic stalls—their irreverent carvings include, appropriately enough, a man downing a mug of beer.

The **Museum of Art and Cultural History** (Tues.–Sun. 10am–6pm; free), very near the Hauptbahnhof at the beginning of Hansastrasse, occupies a rather wonderful art deco building of the 1920s which was formerly a bank. Its highlight is a series of reassembled **interiors**—an eighteenth-century Westphalian pharmacy, the *Fliesensaal* ("tiled room") with hunting scenes in Delft tiles, and a paneled music room from a bourgeois residence in Bremen. Most notable of all is *Der Raum als Gesamtkunstwerk* ("The Room as a Complete Work of Art") by the Jugendstil architect-interior designer **Joseph Maria Olbrich**, in which every trivial detail has been thought out in relation to its effect on the whole. There's more, too, from the artists whose works adorn Dortmund's churches—two little versions of *Madonna and Child* are attributed to Conrad von Soest, and there are devotional canvases by both the Baegerts. Also of note are the tiny house altars, *St. George Triptych* by the Dutchman **Cornelis Engelbrechtsz** and *Life of the Virgin* by the Ulm artist **Daniel Mauch**. The Romantic section includes a stunning, sombre **Friedrich**, *Night on the Sea*, along with a couple of smaller works, and *Rocky Landscape* by **Andreas Achenbach**, another haunting evocation of wild nature. In the basement the archaeology display is dominated by the *Dortmunder Goldschatz*, a hoard of fourth- and fifth-century gold coins found locally.

On the inner ring road is the **Museum am Ostwall** (same times; free), devoted to the municipal collection of modern art, with changing exhibitions on the ground floor. Upstairs is a comprehensive display of Expressionism, dominated by what's arguably **August Macke**'s masterpiece, *Grosser Zoologischer Garten*, which experiments with the new cubist forms in an anachronistic triptych format. **Christian Rohlfs** is represented by some fifteen canvases, including a pointillist landscape; other highlights are a noble *Annunciation* by **Kokoschka**, and *Self-Portrait*s by **Beckmann** and **Paula Modersohn-Becker**. Experimental sculpture includes several works by **Joseph Beuys**, but the most eye-catching item is **Wolf Vostell**'s *Thermo-Elektronischer Kaugummi* of 1970. Occupying a whole gallery, this has 13,000 forks and spoons grouped behind two barbed wire fences, and—believe it or not—features 5000 pieces of chewing gum.

From here, continue along Ostwall, and turn left into Märkischestrasse; you eventually come to the *Kronen Brauerei*. In 1982, Dortmund's long-felt need for a **Brewery Museum** was at last satisfied by a display set up in the premises here (same hours as the other museums; free). After seeing the old equipment, you can end your visit in perfect style by buying a glass of *Classic* at the bar. A little farther south the city's large green belt begins; it would be attractive were it not marred by the uncomfortable proximity of some of the most satanic-looking mills still in operation. You have to pay to enter the **Westfalenpark**; buy the DM3 ticket which includes admission to the **Television Tower** at the entrance gate, as it costs more if you decide you'd like to go up later on. It's 212 meters high, an older and simpler structure than those in Cologne and Düsseldorf. There's a high-speed lift which whisks you up to the platform with its extensive and starkly contrasting panorama over the industries of the Ruhr and rolling landscape of its playground, the Sauerland. Also within the park is the *Deutsches Rosarium*, featuring thousands of roses from all over the world.

Nightlife and Practicalities

Inevitably, the **taverns** must head the list of entertainments, and downtown is ideal for a bar hop; there's no need to move very far to sample the products of all the different breweries. The **Markt** is the obvious place to begin; here *Krone* claim to have had an uninterrupted presence since 1430, an even longer pedigree than the Hofbräuhaus in Munich. It's therefore disappointing that what's there today isn't even a sham re-creation, but a modern interior with plastic decor and elaborate swinging chairs, whose main line of business is an expensive rotisserie (which admittedly has a high reputation). Next door, *Wenker's*, named after the most eccentric of Dortmund brewers, is much more animated, being a great favorite with the youth of the city. The drink to order is *Utrüb*, a blonde ale top-fermented with plenty of yeast sediment left in. Two watering holes in a more traditional vein on the same square are *Kiepenkerl*, which serves *Union*, and *Zum Alten Markt*, whose allegiance is to *Thier*, and which also has reasonably priced food cooked in the old Westphalian style. Another *Thier* pub, *Gänse Markt*, is just around in the corner beside the Marienkirche in what was once the goose market. Facing the Reinoldikirche, *Zum Ritter (Restaurant Marché)* is a good value self-service restaurant, using fresh market ingredients and extremely popular at lunchtimes.

The **Ostwall** has another concentration of places to eat and drink, beginning with *Café Knüppel* at the corner with Ostenhellweg, a genteel salon in which to have coffee and cake. In contrast, some noisy taverns and discos are directly opposite, while a *Victorian Pub* features among the more staid ale houses down the road. Farther west along the ring, you come to Hoherwall, with *Hövels*

Hausbrauerei, offering a beer garden and some of the best food in town. Hansastrasse also has promising possibilities, notably *Schwarzer Rabe*, arguably Dortmund's top restaurant.

For the most decadent nightspot, you have to head to the old village of **SYBURG**, now the most southerly suburb. On the heights between a ruined Romanesque Burg and its restored parish church stands the vast modern palace of glass that is the **casino** (slot machines open from 1pm, the real stuff from 3pm). During gaming hours regular bus services run from the Hauptbahnhofs of both Dortmund (#444) and Hagen (#544). Even if you don't want to play, it's a good place to do a bit of people-watching, particularly at weekends. It's possible to wander around the building without hassle; the top floor has historic American one-armed bandits, a vintage GFG car and old British telephone booths. If you're a gambler, entry to the slot machines is DM1; formal registration is necessary for the tables, where minimum stakes are DM2 at roulette, DM10 for black jack, and DM40 for baccarat. To find out about **events**, consult either *Blick in die Stadt* or *Dortmunder Bakanntmachungen*; both cost a nominal amount at newsstands. **Theaters** include the *Schauspielhaus* and its *Studio* on Hiltropwall, and the *Theater am Ostwall*, while the *Opera House* is on Hansastrasse. There are plenty of **movie houses** downtown, again on Hansastrasse and the parallel Brückstrasse. The huge *Westfalenhalle* southwest of the center is used for **sports** and other blockbuster shows such as **jazz** and **pop concerts**.

In front of the Stadtgarten at Südwall 6 is the main **tourist office** (Mon.–Fri. 8am–4pm; ☎0231 542 25666). More convenient, but with fewer leaflets, is the branch opposite the Hauptbahnhof (Mon.–Fri. 9am–6pm, Sat. 9am–1pm; ☎0231 542 22174). There's a **campground** at Syburger-Dorfstr. 69 (☎0231 774374), not far from the casino. The youth hostel closed a few years ago, but those in HAGEN and CAPPENBERGER SEE are near enough to make commuting cost-effective. For **hotel rooms**, most of the best bargains are in outlying suburbs; an exception is *Pension Fritz*, Reinoldistr. 6 (☎0231 571523) which could hardly have a better location; singles are DM31, doubles DM60. Other centrally sited places are *Carlton*, Lütge Brückstr. 5–7 (☎0231 528030/9) with singles at DM35, doubles at DM70; *Sport-Hotel*, Mallinckrodtstr. 212–4 (☎0231 821047/8), with singles DM39, doubles DM62; and *Atlanta* (☎0231 579518/9), Ostenhellweg 51, at DM38 per person. **Mitfahrzentrale's** office is at Grunestr. 3 (☎0231 822067).

Hagen

Like nearby Wuppertal, **HAGEN** would be a characterless large town were it not for an imaginative and rather brilliant act of initiative around the turn of the present century. **Karl Ernst Osthaus**, a local industrialist and patron of the arts, was instrumental in persuading a group of talented international designers in the art nouveau style to come to Hagen. Prominent among them were the architects Peter Behrens of Hamburg, Henry van de Velde from Belgium and Mathiew Lauweriks from Holland, along with another Dutchman, the decorator Johan Thorn-Prikker. The artists' colony thus founded was a fitting successor to the one in Darmstadt, Germany's other main center of what was always called Jugendstil, to which Behrens had also belonged. Nor were other styles shunned; the Expressionist painter Christian Rohlfs was summoned and stayed until he died in 1938, seventeen years after Osthaus' own premature death put an end to his ambitious plans for a complete garden city.

Your first glimpse of this legacy comes at the **Hauptbahnhof**; illuminating the exit is a large stained glass window by Thorn-Prikker, an allegory entitled *The Obeisance of the Crafts before the Artist*. From the square in front, turn right and then follow Elberfelder Strasse straight ahead, eventually taking any of the small side streets into the parallel Hochstrasse, where you'll find the **Karl Ernst Osthaus Museum** (Tues., Weds., Fri., and Sat. 11am–6pm, Thurs. 11am–10pm, Sun. 11am–4pm; free). The exterior is in the stolid end-of-century Wilhelmine style, but the interior, created a few years later by van de Velde, has all the sense of fantasy and romance characteristic of the best art nouveau. Originally this contained Osthaus' private art collection, the Folkwang Museum, which was hung in an unconventional thematic manner. After his death, it was sold *en bloc* by his heirs to the city of Essen, where it can still be seen. Since the acquisition of the building by the Hagen authorities in 1945, belated attempts have been made to re-create the original effect by acquiring works in line with Osthaus' tastes. There's a good representation of Expressionism and other twentieth-century German art, with several examples of **Rohlfs**, whose studio was housed here, along with works by **Macke** (*Women in Front of a Hat Shop*), **Dix** (the erotic *Artist and Muse*), **Kokoschka** (*The Actor Sommarunga*), Kirchner, Pechstein, Heckel, Nolde, Beckmann, and Schmidt-Rottluf.

To the east of the center, reached by bus #502, is the projected garden suburb of **Hohenhagen**, of which only an incomplete crescent known as **Stirnband** was built. The nearer side of this consists of a row of houses by Lauweriks, homogeneous in style but each given its own identity. Still in private ownership, they are undoubtedly the ultimate in desirable residences within the Ruhrgebiet. Fronting the other entrance to the crescent is **Haus Cuno** by Behrens, now an academy of music; on weekdays it's worth sticking your head in the door to see the impressive stairwell. The rest of this street really forms a processional way to the vast **Hohenhof**, designed as Osthaus' own residence by van de Velde. This is one of the great achievements of the art nouveau movement, a dream home if ever there was one, and a building which seems to change dramatically from every angle of vision. Now owned by the city, it's a cultural center, but the interior is generally only accessible on Saturdays between 2pm and 6pm. Try to come then to see the intricacies of its decorations, which include furniture designed by its architect, stained glass windows by Thorn-Prikker, and a huge canvas, *The Elect*, by the Swiss **Ferdinand Hodler**.

If you've a serious interest in this style of architecture, there are other examples dotted round Hagen. South from Stirnband, in the suburb of DELSTERN, Behrens built an appropriately severe **Crematorium** with a gaunt unpierced belfry. You're dependent on the presence of a mourning party for the opportunity to peek inside; adopt the proper respectful attitude and follow along. Closer to town, **Haus Springman** at the highest point on Christian-Rohlfs-Strasse is another van de Velde commission from a wealthy industrialist; outside it looks like a miniature cut-price version of the Hohenhof. Farther west, on Berliner Strasse, there's a stark contrast with the luxuriant self-indulgence of the city's other Jugendstil buildings in the functional red-brick offices of the **Lehnkering** transport company.

To the east, Hagen has swallowed up the old town of **HOHENLIMBURG**, which has a few streets with elaborate terraces of houses built just before the Jugendstil era. The main attraction, however, is the **Burg** of the counts of Limburg, set on the heights above (April–Sept. Tues.–Sun. 10am–6pm; times reduce variably in winter as far as 1–4pm; DM2). Although preserving the external appearance of a medieval fortress, it was gutted by fire in the seventeenth century, so that the modest apartments to be seen today are actually in late baroque style.

Hagen's only other attraction is the **Open-Air Museum** (April–Oct. Tues.– Sun. 9am–6pm; DM3) south of the city in SELBECKE; take bus #507. Laid out in the valley of the Mäckingerbach, this marks the point where the industrial Ruhr-gebiet gives way to the rural Sauerland. There are some 65 traditional buildings, but it differs from other museums of the same type in that the emphasis is techni-cal, rather than social or architectural. Horny-handed old sons of toil demonstrate all kinds of historical equipment, ranging from machinery for producing iron and steel, through printing and papermaking, spinning, weaving and dyeing, to baking and mustard production; it's possible to buy many of the products made here. There's also a windmill near the entrance; as it's some distance from the other buildings, check first for the times when it's going to be put into action. Just to walk around the site takes quite a while, and you need to budget at least three hours for a visit—longer if you want to see all the crafts demonstrated.

Practicalities

The **tourist office** (Mon.–Fri. 9am–6pm, Sat. 9am–1pm; ☎02331 13573) occupies a pavilion in Mittelstrasse, the continuation of Elberfelder Strasse. Most of the nightlife gets going in the streets around here. The *Stadttheater* and the two main **movie theater** centers are both on Elberfelder Strasse, while **concerts** are held at the *Stadthalle* on Wasserloses Tal. For **live jazz**, go to *Tuba Keller* on Hohenzollernstrasse; the pub above has a beer garden, while that behind, *Loüster*, swarms with young locals and is the best choice if you want an animated atmosphere with blaring rock. Traditional beer halls serving hearty food are *Andreas am Museum* (named after Hagen's own beer) on Hochstrasse, *Alt Nürnberg* on Elbersufer, and *Stadtschänke* on Friedrich-Ebert-Platz.

The **youth hostel** is at Eppenhauser Str. 65a (☎02331 50254; bus #502 or #503), just a few minutes from Stirnband. Although there's no **campground** in the city boundaries, that at SYBURG (see p.473) is only a few kilometers away, reached by bus #544. **Hotel rooms** are cheaper than in most other Ruhr cities; in the center, *Gasthof Bürgerkrug*, Werdestr. 2–4 (☎02331 26779) has singles from DM25, doubles at DM50; *Haus Toimann*, Eppenhauser Str. 195 (☎02331 53504) charges from DM28 per head; while *Danne*, Hochstr. 76–78 (☎02331 32626) and *Targan*, Hugo-Preuss-Str. 5 (☎02331 16863) both cost around DM30 for a single, DM60 for a double. Given the fact that the places you'll want to see are so far apart, a day ticket on the **public transit** system, costing DM8.50, is worth consid-ering; it allows you to go as far afield as HOHENLIMBURG and SYBURG. There's a **Mitfahrzentrale** office at Södingstr. 3 (☎02331 337555).

Recklinghausen

The northern part of the Ruhrgebiet, before the vast built-up area gives way to the open spaces of Münsterland, is known as the district of RECKLINGHAUSEN, after its principal town; the other main communities— none of them with much to offer—are MARL, CASTROP-RAUXEL, and HALTERN. Recklinghausen itself, though small-scale compared to the cities to the south, does its best to appear distinctive. Originally founded as a royal seat by Charlemagne, it was a Hanseatic city in the Middle Ages, dominated by black-smiths and cloth merchants. Nothing major in the way of surviving monuments, but you still get something of the feel of the old town amidst all the usual later accretions—there's certainly more of a sense of continuous history here than is to be found anywhere else in the Ruhr. Streets downtown still follow the old twisting and turning pattern, there are a number of half-timbered houses, some fragments of the city wall, and, as centerpiece, the **Petruskirche**, predominantly Gothic, but incorporating parts of its Romanesque predecessor as well as sundry modifications by subsequent builders. From the baroque period, the **Engelsburg** on Augustinessenstrasse is a handsome mansion built around a courtyard; it's now the best hotel in town. Around the corner on Geiststrasse is the **Gastkirche**, formerly an almshouse chapel, containing several striking altarpieces.

Recklinghausen's pride and joy, however, is its **Icon Museum** (Tues.–Fri. 10am–6pm, Sat. and Sun. 11am–5pm; DM2) at Am Kirchplatz beside the Petruskirche. This isn't just another example of the seemingly inexhaustible German capacity for creating museums on the most obscure subjects, but genuinely is the finest collection of this simple yet haunting and powerful art form outside the Orthodox world. The star piece is the huge late sixteenth-century Russian *Calendar Icon of the Year*, a tour de force illustrating the main stories of the Bible, as well as portraying hundreds of saints, arranged according to their feast day. From the following century comes *The Credo*, executed using techniques reminiscent of Western manuscript illuminators, and a masterly *Enthroned Christ*, a signed work by the Cretan **Elias Moskos**. The earliest works, from the fifteenth-century Moscow and Novgorod schools, have perhaps the most overtly emotional appeal; among the finest are the symbolic *Christ the Unsleeping Eye* and *St. Nicholas with Scenes from his Life*. In addition to over 400 icons, there are extensive collections on the decorative arts of the Orthodox churches. Repair work to the building means the museum is likely to be closed until late 1989; until then, the most important icons can be seen as one of the temporary displays featured at the **Kunsthalle** (same times) on Grosse Perdekampstrasse, just east of the historic part of town, directly facing the **Hauptbahnhof**.

Cultural life in Recklinghausen revolves around the *Ruhrfestspiele*, a **festival** of concerts, plays, exhibitions, and discussions held annually in May and June. Run in conjunction with the nationwide Federation of Trade Unions, it's an indication of how events regarded as highbrow in other countries appeal to all sectors of German society. The *Festspielhaus*, in the Stadtgarten west of the city center, was opened in 1965 as the specially designed home for the festival. For the rest of the year, the normal **concert** hall is the *Saalbau* on Dorstener Strasse, while the main venue for **drama** is *Theater im Depot* on Castroper Strasse.

Recklinghausen has no **tourist office** as such, but you can pick up maps and leaflets at the Rathaus during working hours; the museums also keep a stock. The cheapest **hotels**, charging around DM30 per head, are *Haus Korte*, Castroper Str. 365 (☎02361 43201) and *Kolping-Haus*, Herzogswall 38 (☎02361 22640). Nearest **campgrounds** are at HALTERN to the north—*Dülmener See*, (☎02594 2125), *Hoher Niemen* (☎02364 2511) and *Seegesellschaft Haltern* (☎02364 3360); the first two are open all year, the last from April to September only. For an animated **pub**, try *Boente* on Augustinessenstrasse, where you can sample the products of the local *Kornbrennerei* brewery in a large Bavarian-style beer garden. Note that maps of the Rhine–Ruhr transport network make Recklinghausen seem far less accessible than is actually the case. It's on the main railroad line between ESSEN and MÜNSTER; to reach it from other Ruhr cities, you may have to change at CASTROP-RAUXEL, but connections are frequent.

WESTPHALIA

WESTPHALIA is named after one of the three main Saxon tribes; by the early Middle Ages, the term came to be used for all of Saxony west of the Weser River. Despite this long tradition as a definable part of Germany, it's never really been governed as a unit, and the boundaries have often been changed dramatically—the short-lived Kingdom of Westphalia, established by Napoleon for his brother Jerome, consisted mostly of Hessen, while the present political division of the country has seen parts of the historic province transferred to Lower Saxony. Apart from the cities in the Ruhrgebiet which are traditionally Westphalian (Dortmund, Recklinghausen, Gelsenkirchen, Hagen, and Bochum), there are three distinct constituent parts: the fertile **Münsterland** plain to the north; the predominantly rural **Sauerland** and **Siegerland** to the south; and the depression to the east bounded by the vast stretch of the **Teutoburger Wald**. The last-named now incorporates what was formerly one of the smallest states of the German Reich, the **Principality of Lippe**. Of the cities, the two largest, **Bielefeld** and **Münster**, could hardly be more different: the former is predominantly industrial whereas the latter is the epitome of modern middle-class prosperity. **Paderborn**, like Münster, is an important episcopal center. However, many of the most memorable towns in the area—**Soest**, **Lemgo**, and **Höxter**—are modest in size.

According to its own tourist board, Westphalia is associated with "the solid and substantial things in life." In architecture, the characteristic features are moated castles, lofty hall churches and half-timbered farm buildings. Gastronomically, it's famous for hams, spit roasts, beer, schnapps, and (above all) rye bread—"Bread which might make the dinner of a king," according to a poem James Boswell wrote in its honor. Westphalia is an archetypal German province and a favorite vacation destination with the Germans themselves. In spite of a fair number of Britons visiting friends and family in the military bases, there's no more than a trickle of tourists from abroad—a definite plus from the viewpoint of authenticity.

Münster

Northern Westphalia is dominated by the province's former capital, **MÜNSTER**, one of the most varied and enticing of the cities spread across the flat German plain. It has an unusually rich architectural heritage, including examples of all the main styles from Romanesque to baroque. Industry has been confined to the peripheries, and the chic shops crowding the center are an unabashed celebration of the affluent consumerism enjoyed by a population which is overwhelmingly middle class. The university is the third largest in Germany; one consequence of this is that the city has come firmly under the rule of the bicycle. However, the dominant influence on Münster has been the Catholic church, its very name—the equivalent of the English word "minster"—deriving from the evangelizing monastery of **St. Liudger** who was consecrated bishop in 805 as part of Charlemagne's policy of converting the Saxon tribes to Christianity. Apart from the years 1534–5 when it was taken over by the fanatical Anabaptist sect, it has remained intensely loyal to Roman Catholicism, even during the Third Reich, when the city's bishop, **Clemens August von Galen**, was one of the regime's most courageous and persistent opponents. In 1936, he organized a popular revolt which succeeded in overturning an edict to remove crucifixes from school buildings—an apparently trivial incident, but one of the few occasions the Nazis gave in to domestic opponents. This defiance counted for nothing with the Allied bombing missions, who administered particularly brutal treatment on Münster, but the city recovered well, thanks to a much praised rebuilding program.

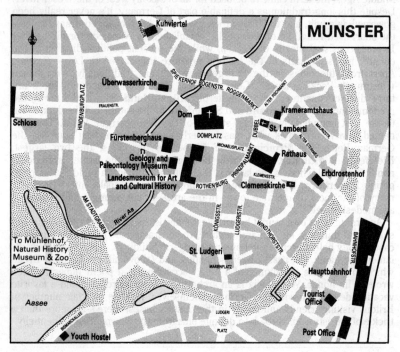

Arrival and Practicalities

The **Hauptbahnhof** is directly east of downtown, and reached by heading straight down Windthorststrasse. **Bus services** both within the city and to other places in the province leave from the string of stops on both sides of Bahnhofstrasse. Directly opposite is the main **tourist office** (Mon.–Fri. 9am–8pm, Sat. 9am–1pm, first Sat. in month 9am–6pm, Sun. 10:30am–12:30pm; ☎0251 510180); there's also a branch within the Rathaus (Mon.–Fri. 9am–5pm, Sat. 9am–4pm, Sun. 10am–1pm; ☎0251 492 2745). The **youth hostel** is at Bismarck Allee 31 (☎0251 43765) in a good location by the right bank of the Aasee; bus #13 goes closest. **Camping** is possible from mid-March to mid-October at Dorbaumstr. 35 (☎0251 329312) in the northeastern suburb of HANDORF. **Hotel rooms** definitely don't come cheap. Most convenient among the better buys is *Zum Schwan*, Schillerstr. 27 (☎0251 661166) facing the back of the station, at DM38 for a single, DM72 for a double; the pub downstairs offers *vom heissen Stein* dishes at a very reasonable cost. A centrally sited alternative is *Zur Krone*, Hammerstr. 67 (☎0251 73868) at DM35 per person; unless you're prepared to pay a bit more, you'll have to stay farther out. At the extreme southwest of the city proper are *Lohmann*, Mecklenbeckerstr. 345 (☎0251 71525) which charges

DM29 per head, and *Haselmann*, Flasskamp 41 (☎0251 717055) at DM25 and up. There's also a concentration of hotels in the outlying town of HILTRUP directly to the south, which are generally cheaper than in the city. **Mitfahrzentrale** is at Papenburger Str. 6 (☎0251 661006).

The City

Münster's population is swollen by the British and American soldiers whose bases ring the suburbs. They may be unpopular with the locals, but their justification for being there—the maintenance of the peace and balance of power in Europe—happens to be the historical role of which Münster is most proud. In the center of the main street, the **Prinzipalmarkt**, stands the magnificent Gothic **Rathaus**, scene of the signing in 1648 of the **Peace of Westphalia** , which brought to an end the multitude of religious, constitutional, and dynastic conflicts known as the Thirty Years' War. For the previous five years, the Catholic parties had been in congress at Münster; the highly complex negotiations which took place represent the beginnings of modern diplomacy as still practised. In honor of the treaty, the room where it was signed was renamed the **Friedensaal** (*Peace Hall*); it's the one part of the Rathaus generally open to the public (Mon.–Fri. 9am–5pm, Sat. 9am–4pm, Sun. and holidays 10am–1pm; DM1). The elaborate chimneypiece, installed only a few years before the delegations arrived in the city, appropriately features a figure of Justice lording it over the room. Other walls are covered with superb woodwork in a style hovering between late Gothic and Renaissance. Best are the lusty moralizing carvings at the far end which face the doors to archive cases; the backs of the councillors' seats feature Christ and the Apostles, while portrait heads of prominent burghers crane out above. This assemblage survived an air raid which completely sliced off the top half of the Rathaus' ornate facade, one of the supreme masterpieces of German civic architecture. So loving was the restoration, however, that the wartime photographs can scarcely be believed.

Next door, the **Stadtweinhaus**, a Renaissance building with an abutting Italianate portico, has also been returned to its former splendor. The rest of what must once have been one of the handsomest main thoroughfares in Europe, lined with the grand arcaded houses of the self-confident merchant class of the sixteenth and seventeenth centuries, is rather more of a compromise; alongside faithfully rebuilt houses are some which are mere approximations, while others are deliberately modern reinterpretations using the old motifs.

At the end of Prinzipalmarkt is **St. Lamberti**, a good example of the spacious hall church style characteristic of Westphalia. Its elegant openwork spire, one of the chief landmarks of the city, reflects the nineteenth-century German obsession for embellishing Gothic buildings. High up on the older part of the tower hang three wrought-iron cages; in them were displayed the bodies of the Anabaptist leader **Jan. van Leyden** and his two principal lieutenants, following the crushing of their "Reich" (which, like Hitler, they believed would endure for a millennium) by the prince-bishop's army. Apart from insisting on adult baptism, this sect believed in the common ownership of property, and in heeding the biblical injunction to be fruitful and multiply—the leader himself took no less than sixteen wives. Had he established his capital in what is now the GDR, he would doubtless be fêted there as a great revolutionary hero; but such ideas gained little support in such a bastion of traditionalism as Münster. The iconoclastic tendencies of the Anabaptists led them to destroy the beautiful sculptural decoration which was a key feature of the city's medieval churches; one of the rare examples left in situ is the elaborate *Tree of Jesse* over St. Lamberti's south doorway. Facing the church's apse on Alter Steinweg is the **Krameramtshaus**, a late sixteenth-century brick building in the Dutch style which is the oldest guild hall to have survived; nowadays it serves as the main public library.

The vast **Domplatz**, on which markets are held on Wednesday and Saturday, is reached in just a few strides from Prinzipalmarkt down either Domgasse or Michaelisplatz. Almost any point on the square offers a superb view of the huge thirteenth-century **Dom**, built in less than forty years in a style bridging the transition from Romanesque to Gothic. The only entrance is via the porch (or "Paradise"), adorned on the inside with statues of Christ and the Apostles which date from the very beginning of the building period. The pier figure of St. Paul, the Dom's patron, dates from 300 years later, the first of several subsequent additions worthy of a Gate of Heaven, to which such doorways aspired.

The Dom's **interior** is highly unusual, the nave having just two bays of massive span. It's jam-packed with sculptural memorials and other works of art; look out for the the tiny fourteenth-century gilded relic statues adorning the modern high altar, and the powerful Romanesque triumphal cross suspended above. What really catches your eye, however, is the **astronomical clock**, made in the 1530s, in the southern arm of the ambulatory. Based on the most precise mathematical calculations available at the time, it shows the orbit of the planets and the movement of the fixed stars, as well as fulfilling the normal function of charting the course of the sun and the moon; the lowest section is a calendar. The leading Münster painter of the day, **Ludger tom Ring the Elder**, decorated the clock with the Evangelical symbols, delicate scenes of the Labors of the Months and a gallery of entranced spectators. If you brave the crowds at noon, you can hear the carillon and see the Magi emerge to pay tribute to the infant Christ.

From the northern side of the transept, the plain fourteenth-century cloisters are entered; the garden was, at the time of writing, the object of extensive archaeological excavations. At the far end, an uncompromisingly modern building entitled the **Domkammer** (Tues.–Sat. 10am–noon and 2–6pm, Sun. 2–6pm; DM1) houses the treasury. The basement displays liturgical vestments and the upper story illustrates the building history of the Dom, but most of the star items are on the ground floor. Pride of place goes to the eleventh-century gold reliquary of St. Paul, studded with jewels a couple of hundred years later; other outstanding pieces are the thirteenth-century processional cross and fourteen bust-reliquaries of the prophets. Also shown are works of art commissioned at various times for the decoration of the chancel, but in time rejected as surplus: the fourteen portraits of prophets and sibyls by Hermann tom Ring, the figures of Apostles from the Renaissance rood screen by Johann Brabender, and the six monumental baroque reliefs by Johann Mauritz Gröninger of scenes from the life of Christ and the four saints especially venerated in the Dom.

A short distance to the west of the Dom stands the **Liebfrauenkirche**, usually known as the **Überwasserkirche** (*Church by the Water*) since it stands beside the Aa, Münster's tiny river. Like St. Lamberti, it's a fourteenth-century hall church, with a floridly decorated tower. Its superb sculptures proved particularly repugnant to the Anabaptists, who smashed and buried them; some 350 years later, they were dramatically rediscovered, but were considered too fragile to return to their original location. From here, Frauenstrasse leads to Schlossplatz with the resplendent eighteenth-century **Schloss** of the prince-bishops, its two side wings reaching out like embracing arms. The front facing the **Botanical Gardens** (daily 7:30am–5pm) is quite different, but the interior was completely destroyed in the war, and has been modernized for use by the university. Its architect, **Johann Conrad Schlaun**, was almost single-handedly responsible for making Münster the capital of north German baroque, which was far more restrained as well as considerably less ubiquitous than its southern counterpart. A couple of other buildings by him can be seen at the opposite end of the city center; they can be reached from the Rathaus by following Klemensstrasse. The **Erbdrostenhof**, a nobleman's mansion, again shows his talent for the grand manner; it has survived in better shape than the Schloss and is currently being restored to house a museum. Immediately opposite, the **Clemenskirche**, a former hospital church, presents a clever solution to the problem of building in a restricted space: a circular design was chosen and the interior richly decorated with a huge ceiling fresco glorifying the patron saint.

The Domplatz, which also contains several baroque mansions, serves as the city's museum focus. The **Landesmuseum for Art and Cultural History** (Tues.–Sun. 10am–6pm; free) houses works of art of mostly Westphalian origin, but is of far more than parochial significance. On the ground floor is a really outstanding collection of **medieval sculpture**, including the original statues from the Überwasserkirche, some of which have survived their long entombment remarkably well. From the Dom are some of the original decorations of the Paradise, and the massive group of *Christ's Entry into Jerusalem*, which adorned the upper part of the facade destroyed in the war. The latter is the work of **Heinrich Brabender**, a long-forgotten name who now appears as one of the most individual of the remarkable group of late Gothic German sculptors. Also by him is a series of Passion scenes made for the Domplatz; despite their weary appearance—the Anabaptists smashed them only a few years after they were made—the wonderful dignity and characterization of the figures can still be appreciated. Also on display are examples of the quite different art of his son **Johann Brabender**, who was fully Renaissance in style and happiest on a small scale, as in sensitive and delicate works such as *Calvary* from the Dom's rood screen and *Adam and Eve* from the Paradise. A dimmed room is devoted to **stained glass**, which can be examined in far more favorable conditions than in a church.

Upstairs, the history of Westphalian painting is traced, beginning with the "Soft Style" of **Conrad von Soest** and the **Master of Warendorf** in the early fifteenth century. From the next generation is **Johann Koerbecke**, whose masterpiece, the *Marienfeld Altar*, contains background depictions of Münster. Later in the century, the tougher approach of **Derick Baegert** makes an interesting contrast with the various anonymous masters who were at their best in crowded Passion scenes. The Renaissance section is dominated by the diverse interests of the **tom Ring** family; apart from the portraits by which they are best known, there are religious works by Hermann and pioneering still lifes by Ludger the Younger. On the second floor are two rooms of Expressionist paintings, with a good cross-section of the work of **Macke**, notably a large *Paradise* he painted jointly with **Marc** for his own studio. The **Westphalian Archaeology Museum** (same times; free) in the interconnected building is also extensively laid out on three floors. However, it has to be said that it's chiefly documentary; there's a notable lack of objects likely to give much aesthetic pleasure. If you've a serious interest in the subject, the University's archaeological collections are housed across the road in the **Fürstenberghaus** (Weds. 4–6pm, Sun. 11am–noon and 2–3pm; free). Next door is another specialist academic collection, the **Geology and Palaeontology Museum** (Mon.–Sat. 9am–12:30pm and 1–5pm, Sun. 10:30am–12:30pm; free).

Heading southwest from the center, the sausage-shaped **Aasee**, some 6km in circumference, is the most popular recreation area in the city, particularly on weekends when the yachts and motorboats of prosperous locals speckle the water. At the lower end of the left bank is the **Mühlenhof**; though small, it's one of Germany's longest-established open-air museums (mid-March–Nov. daily 9am–5pm, rest of year Mon.–Sat. 1:30–4:30pm, Sun. 11am–4:30pm; DM3; take bus #14). On a fine day, it's worth a stroll around the twenty or so agricultural buildings from the province which have been reerected here, the centerpiece being a tressel windmill of 1748. Even more atmospheric is an early seventeenth-century millhouse, completely fitted out with authentic furnishings, including, over the fireplace, what's known as a "Heaven" for the smoking of hams. A little farther south is the **Natural History Museum** (Tues.–Sun. 9am–6pm; free), with a **Planetarium** (showings Tues.–Thurs. at 10am, 11am, and 3pm, Fri.–Sun. 3pm only). Beside it are the **Zoo** and **Dolphinarium** (daily 9am–4/5/6pm according to season; DM5).

Eating, Drinking, and Nightlife

Not the least of Münster's attractions is the wonderful choice of **bars**, **cafés**, and **restaurants**. The most obvious place to begin is around the Prinzipalmarkt. Next door to the Stadtweinhaus is *Stuhlmacher*, the city's most celebrated pub; it has a wide selection of beers and is ideal for people-watching, particularly in the early evening. Its restaurant is expensive, however, and you can eat better elsewhere. Across the road is the leading café, *Otto Schucan*, which is pricey but serves delicious coffee and has an irresistible display of cakes; again it attracts a varied clientele—students, businessmen, and elderly women. Just down the road, *Café Kleimann*, occupying one of the finest of the old guild houses, makes a good alternative. Continuing into Roggenmarkt, you'll find two of the best **discos**: *Club Leo*, in the basement of a clothes shop, is popular with people in their early twenties; *Der Elephant*, down an arcade, appeals to an older age range. Where the street becomes Bogenstrasse there are more pubs, notably *Altes Brauhaus Kiepenkerl*, named after the statue of the peddler outside; it has a ground-floor beer hall and an upstairs café to provide elegant competition to those already mentioned. If you prefer tea, the best selection in town is available at *Palmen Café* at the end of Rothenburg, the opposite extension of the Prinzipalmarkt.

An equally notable nightlife area is the **Kuhviertel** just beyond the Überwasserkirche. It's usually described as the Latin quarter, but students no longer predominate. Most of the best hangouts are to be found on Kreuzstrasse; *Pinkus Müller*, which is now Münster's only brewery, has two places here—the main pub-restaurant and the *Bier Galerie*. The former is decked out in traditional style; it fills up heavily from mid-evening and is extremely popular with the American community. Although not the cheapest, it's the best place in Münster for a traditional Westphalian meal. You should also sample some of the amazing range of beers produced by what is only a small (albeit highly regarded) brewery—they make Pils, Alt, Weizen, Malz and their own *Special*. Alt, whether from Pinkus or imported from that other snobbish city, Düsseldorf, is the most popular drink in this quarter; it's generally mixed with syrup (*mit Schuss*) or with a punch of fresh raspberries and peaches (*Altbierbowle*). Also on this street are two very similar youthful pubs, *Cavete* and *Das Blaue Haus*, which offer loud music and inexpensive pastas and puddings. Nearby on Schlaunstrasse is a long-established fish restaurant, *Fischbrathalle*, but note that it closes around 5pm.

Other good night-spots are scattered around the city center. On Alter Steinweg are a number of old-fashioned beer halls, among which *Altes Gasthaus Leve* serves the best food, along with the trendier *Der Bunte Vogel*. At the corner of this street and Mauritzstrasse is *Hardies*, one of the main student pubs, with a large but not exclusively **gay** clientele. Just to the north, Hörsterstrasse has what the army contingent calls the "Bermuda Triangle," with the student café *Scala*, the Italian *Bier-Café Roma, Pasadena Piano Bar,* and *Byblos Discotheque*, which has an American night on Saturdays. For cheap eating, there are a couple of recommendable places at the junction of Königstrasse and Marienplatz in the shadow of the remarkable octagonal tower of **St. Ludgeri**. *Gambrinus*, besides being a lively pub, does good-value schnitzels cooked in a score of different ways, while *Cadaqués'* bistro cooking is best sampled as the freshly cooked lunchtime specials—though it's not a place to come to if you're in a hurry. When the weather is fine, try *Kruse Baimken* at Am Staatgraben by the north bank of the Aasee; you may find close to a thousand people, including many of the beautiful set, relaxing in its beer garden. As a less self-conscious alternative, there's *Treibhaus* at Steinfurter Strasse to the north, which also does low-priced meals.

The main **popular festival**, known as *Send*, is a five-day fair held three times annually (March, June, and October) in the Hindenburgplatz in front of the Schloss. Carnival is also celebrated, if not with the same gusto as in the Rhineland, while the *Lambertusfest*, beginning on 17 September, is a festival for children. Surprisingly, Münster isn't especially renowned for its highbrow culture, although there's a modern *Stadttheater* at Neubrückenstrasse, and the *Halle Münsterland* on Albertsloher Weg south of downtown hosts large-scale events.

Münsterland

MÜNSTERLAND is the name given to the large tract of Westphalia stretching from the Rhine to the Teutoburger Wald, bounded by the Netherlands and Lower Saxony to the north, and by the Ruhrgebiet to the south. Its rich soils are agriculturally highly productive, and it remains predominantly rural, with no large towns other than the capital. Being almost unrelievedly flat, it's emphatically not a province you visit for scenery, but it boasts over fifty **historic castles**, quite the densest concentration to be found in Germany, and the nearest the country comes to rivaling the chateaus of the French Loire. They're known as *Wasserburgen*, since their most characteristic feature is a surrounding tract of water. This form, developed in the sixteenth century by local landlords wanting strongholds to protect their fiefdoms, was necessitated by the lack of natural strategic points which more undulating countryside would provide; it superseded the earlier technique of building on artificial mounds, which had been rendered highly vulnerable by advances in gunpowder and firearms. A couple of centuries later, in more peaceful times, baroque country houses were built in this countryside—some of them as replacements for their redundant predecessors, others completely new. These generally still included a moat, although now for aesthetic reasons only. **Voltaire** set the opening of his great satire *Candide* in one of these estates, lampooning the degenerate lifestyle of Baron Thunder-ten-tronckh and his 350-pound wife, and the intellectually bankrupt philosophy of the complacent tutor Dr. Pangloss, who convinced everyone they were living "in the most beautiful and delightful of all possible mansions, in this best of all possible worlds."

The local tourist offices are keen to promote these castles, whose virtues they flaunt by means of utterly irresistible photographic posters. However, there are pitfalls which you should be aware of, as it's easy to end up frustrated and disappointed. Firstly, the vast majority of the castles remain private dwellings, generally still in the hands of old aristocratic families, who are alive, well, and managing very nicely without the need of extra cash from prying outsiders. Few show much enthusiasm for the tourist board's initiatives; many castles can be seen from the outside only, and in some cases even that is kept out of bounds by the erection of large hedges and impenetrable gates. Secondly, the alluring posters are nearly all aerial views, and for good reason—from above the castles invariably look far more arresting than they do from the ground, where it's never possible to see the complete layout of the complex, and where your own photos often have to be made from very narrow angles. Thirdly, the interiors of those castles which are open for visits never measure up to the exteriors, where the amniotic relationship of the water to the buildings plays such a poetic and essential role.

Offputting as all this sounds, it should be stressed that the best of the castles, which are described below, are very much worth visiting, and have the easiest access. It definitely pays to be well organized; that way you can hope to see several in a day, as it's unlikely you'll need more than a couple of hours at any single one. Although there's a comprehensive local bus service, the timetabling isn't ideal for castle-crawling. If you haven't a car, consider **hiring a bicycle**, available almost everywhere and at competitive prices. The most convenient place to go is the *Gepäckabfertigung* at Münster Hauptbahnhof, which charges DM10 per day; this is halved if you're initially taking the bike on a train. Many

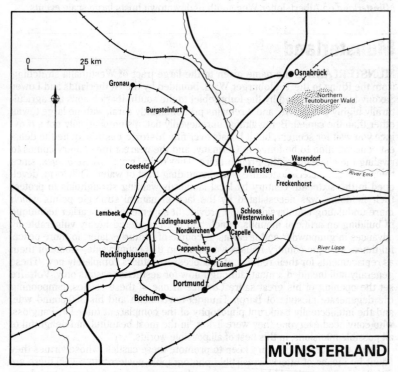

other stations in the province offer the same deal, and there are plenty of private firms with daily rates of DM8 or less. A full list is published in the tourist office's *Gastgeberverzeichnis—Münsterland* brochure, a handy companion for touring the province. If you develop a really serious interest in the castles, this lists them all, and tells you when and where you must write or phone in advance for an appointment. Münster itself is the obvious base to choose; you should be able to find a **room** for no more than DM35 per head in any of the smaller towns, but they're uniformly dull places come evening. Youth hostels are unusually thin on the ground, and, like the more numerous campgrounds, are not in the best locations.

Around Münster

You don't need to venture far out of Münster for your first taste of these chateaus, as **Haus Rüschhaus** (guided tours every half-hour April–mid-Dec. Tues.–Sun. 9am–12:30pm and 2:30–5pm; DM2) stands just beyond the end of the built-up area, and can be reached by bus #5. The present building was designed and built from 1745 to 1748 by **Johann Conrad Schlaun** as a summer house for himself. It's quite an eccentric little construction, mostly homely in feel, but with touches of baroque swagger, as in the sloping roofline, and the sweeping facade which in fact fronts a fully practical barn, integrated into the house as was the norm in traditional local farmsteads. The *Italian Room*, named after the capriccio scenes on the hand-made wallpaper from Paris, provides the only decorative note in the house. Originally Schlaun's bedroom, it was transformed to its present state by later owners, the family of Germany's leading nineteenth-century authoress, **Annette von Droste-Hülshoff**, who lived here for 20 years from 1826, during which time she produced much of her finest work. Best known for her charming poetic vignettes of nature, she spent the first three decades of her life in the original seat of her aristocratic family, **Haus Hülshoff** (March–Oct. daily 9:30am–6pm; DM2 for park, DM2 for house). Bus #563/4 goes there from Münster, or you can walk from Rüschhaus in about half an hour by continuing straight ahead, and turning left down the footpath just past the highway junction; don't follow the road, which adds a considerable distance to the journey. This castle is a classic example of the Renaissance *Wasserburg* design, the outer barrier (*Vorburg*) being a severe, low-lying building with square corner towers, the inner building (*Hauptburg*) an airy L-shaped dwelling in the Dutch style, to which a neo-Gothic chapel was added last century. There's also an attractive park, recently re-created after old designs. Whether or not it's worth the extra to see inside the *Hauptburg* is debatable; you're only allowed to visit a suite of six rooms, authentically furnished in the early nineteenth-century style familiar to the poetess.

Burgsteinfurt

The most varied castle in Münsterland is found in the town of **BURGSTEINFURT**, some 35km northwest of Münster, on the main railroad line to GRONAU. It's still the home of the dukes of Bentheim, who introduced the Calvinist faith to northern Germany; although the present incumbent is more generous with access than most private owners in the area, the organization of visits has been left in the hands of a particularly feckless **tourist office** based at the former Rathaus. This bunch don't seem at all interested in individual visitors, and you must hope to be able to latch on to one of the many tour groups who are escorted around in the summer months. Obviously, it's best to phone ahead (☎02551 1231) to find out when these are, but be warned that the staff are uncooperative and that, without an appointment, all you can see is part of the exterior. That said, it's a fascinating building, with all manner of fragments from diverse periods surviving in a ramshackle way, the courtyard alone serving as an encyclopedia of European architectural history. From the twelfth century comes a Romanesque double chapel, the lower of which remains in its simple original state, while the upper has been adapted according to Protestant tenets. The *Rittersaal*, a Gothic hall, is now successfully used for chamber concerts. On the left-hand side, a Renaissance wing was built, centered on a superb two-story oriel window, carved by the Münster mason Johann Brabender. The tall *Treppenturm* ("stair turret"), on the opposite side, also Renaissance in origin, was modified in baroque times, as buildings continued to be added right up to the nineteenth century. To the south is the **Bagno**, a spacious public park laid out in the English manner, offering good distant views of the castle.

Lembeck

LEMBECK, about 50km southwest of Burgsteinfurt, can be reached by train from there or Münster via COESFELD. The castle, set back from the village, is also still in private hands, but the fact that part of it is now a hotel means that access is easier than normal (guided tours daily mid-March to mid-Nov. every hour 9am–5pm; DM3). Construction began in 1670 on the site of an earlier building. In spite of the impressive severity of the exterior, conforming to the old *Wasserburg* design, it seems to be the first in the province to have been built more for pleasure than defence, a fact suggested by the exuberant helmets on the towers and by the very obvious vulnerability of the rear, connected by a small causeway to the gardens. The interior, on a surprisingly intimate scale, has a rather modest *Great Hall* built by the young J.C. Schlaun. Just to the east of Lembeck is the **Naturpark Hohe Mark**, a protected area of gently sloping forests, a veritable oasis in the midst of so much flatness.

Lüdinghausen

There's a choice of bus or train from Münster to **LÜDINGHAUSEN**, 30km south; the buses are better, as the railroad is circuitous, and the Bahnhof a long way out. The moated castle named after the town itself has been too messed about down the years to be of much interest, but **Burg Vischering** at the northern boundary is the archetypal *Wasserburg*, and the only one wholly devoted to tourism, as the **Münsterland Museum** (March–Oct. Tues.–Sun. 8:30am–12:30pm and 2–5:30pm, Nov.–Feb. Tues.–Sun. 10am–12:30pm and 2–3:30pm; DM2). Its *Hauptburg*, horseshoe in shape, with a singular octagonal tower in the center of the courtyard, was beautified around 1620 by the addition of the *Erker*, the abutting Renaissance section with an elegant oriel window. Directly facing this are the spreading branches of a trumpet tree, the most remarkable of several rare species planted in the grounds. As usual, the interiors are plain by comparison, but the *Rittersaal* with wooden beamed ceiling has been restored to good effect. There's an exhibition on life in the medieval castles of the region; other folklore displays, on the farms and towns, are to be found in the *Vorburg*.

Nordkirchen

If you've only a day to spare on the castles, the best way to spend it is to combine visits to Lüdinghausen and **NORDKIRCHEN**, 8km southeast. This red-brick giant is by far the largest and most spectacular of the group, a manifestation of the fantastic wealth of the **Plettenberg** dynasty of prince-bishops who decided to replace their old fortress with a palace in the French manner. Begun in 1703 to plans by the court architect Gottfried Lorenz Pictorius, it was finished three decades later under the direction of J.C. Schlaun. Every tourist brochure refers to it as the "Westphalian Versailles," a nickname it has had since its conception, when it referred to the older and much smaller palace at Versailles, on which Nordkirchen was directly modeled. Now, the comparison actually smacks of false modesty, as it's aesthetically far superior to the Sun King's overblown, megalomaniacal monstrosity. The complex is on one island only (instead of the two normally required for a *Wasserburg*), and exhibits all the sense of order characteristic of the Age of Reason. It's almost completely symmetrical, and is designed to produce a spectacular main vista, an effect achieved by breaking up the main block into sections, and preceding them with long, narrow pavilions. Behind, there's a formal garden with baroque sculptures; the rest of the grounds have been left in a more natural state, although you can also see the **Oranienburg**, a two-story garden house itself of palatial dimensions. Nowadays, Nordkirchen belongs to the Land government, which has adapted it as a college for financial studies; consequently there's free access at all times, and what you can see from outside definitely justifies a visit. Official opportunities for viewing the **interior** aren't generous (guided tours Sat. and Sun. 2–5pm, usually on the hour; DM2, leaflet in English available). However, there are many private visits on weekdays throughout the summer, to which you're allowed to tag on; consult the list posted in the porter's office or, better still, phone ahead (☎02596 1001). The rooms are less grandiose than you might imagine from outside, but have the full pomp of the baroque in their rich stucco work, ceiling paintings, wood paneling and plentiful furnishings, with the chapel and the entrance hall being particularly fine.

Beware that there are no buses out of Nordkirchen on Sundays, and only one on Saturday afternoons (to Lüdinghausen), which entails taking the 2pm tour. The nearest station, on a line with a very restricted weekend service, is at CAPPEL, 5km east. If you travel this way, you can also visit **Schloss Westerwinkel** (April–Oct. Tues.–Fri. 2–5pm, Sat. and Sun. 2–6pm; DM3), situated a farther 2km east. Although only a few years older than Lembeck, it's still Renaissance and strongly fortified, with a *Hauptburg* built on a square groundplan; the interiors, however, reflect the tastes of the nineteenth-century owners.

Cappenberg

CAPPENBERG, 12km south of Nordkirchen, stands just outside the industrial town of LÜNEN, which marks the beginning of the Ruhrgebiet. There's been a **Schloss** here since the ninth century; the present building is baroque, and for many years it was home to the art treasures of Dortmund. With the creation of a new museum in the city, it has been freed to host temporary exhibitions of various kinds (Tues.–Sun. 10am–5pm; free). Far more significant is the **Stiftskirche** directly in front, founded by the brothers **Gottfried** and **Otto von Cappenberg** in atonement for the part they had played in helping Lothair of Saxony sack the city of Münster in 1121, destroying most of the Dom in the process. Their confessor, Norbert von Xanten, suggested that a fit form of repentance would be the establishment of German headquarters for the Premonstratensian order he had recently founded in France. The plain architecture favored by these monks, Romanesque with later Gothic additions, gives no hint of the riches within, which include two of the supreme masterpieces of German medieval art. Displayed in a safe in the south transept is the stunning **head-reliquary of Frederick Barbarossa**, the oldest surviving portrait of a German emperor made from life. Actually intended to contain a relic of St. John the Evangelist, it's probably the work of an Aachen goldsmith of about 1160. In the choir is the early fourteenth-century **founders' memorial**, depicting them as rather jolly youths with virtually identical features clasping a model of the church. At around the same time, a tomb was made for the now-canonized Gottfried; it's kept in the south transept. Other important works of art are the polychrome Romanesque triumphal cross, the elaborately carved Gothic stalls (every one of the misericords is worth looking at), a fourteenth-century *Madonna and Child* on the west wall, a triptych by Jan. Baegert in the north transept, and an original baroque organ. Below the castle complex is a privately owned **Wildpark** offering various nature trails. A farther 2km on, actually within Lünen, is the artificial boating lake named **Cappenberger See**; there's a **youth hostel** (☎02306 53546) at Richard-Schirrmann-Weg on its northern shore.

Freckenhorst and Warendorf

FRECKENHORST, 25km east of Münster, also has an important Romanesque **Stiftskirche**. This time, it's the architecture that's most striking, though ruggedly impressive rather than beautiful. The massive solemn facade is particularly memorable, with two cylindrical corner towers huddling up against the great belfry. At the east end, a pair of square towers form a perfect counterpoint. In the crypt is the thirteenth-century **tomb of Geva**, a memorial to the woman who founded the original convent in the ninth century. The most important work of art is the **baptismal font**, dating from the present church's dedication in 1129; the upper register is adorned with masterly carvings of scenes from the life of Christ, with fantastic animals below. On the walls around are paintings from a dismembered "Soft Style" retable of about 1430 by the **Master of Waren-dorf**. Others from the series can be seen in the Landesmuseum in Münster, but the central panel, a brilliantly colorful *Calvary* surrounded by four other Passion scenes, remains in its original location, **St. Laurentius** in **WARENDORF**, 3km north. This is a typical Westphalian hall church, which also has some fine sculptures, notably the three figures from the portal who have been moved inside for protection, and the group of *St. Peter, St.Paul, and a Canon* by Heinrich Brabender at the end of the north aisle. The adjacent Markt is lined with old buildings, including the **Rathaus**, whose upper floors are open as a museum (Tues.–Fri. 3–5pm, Sat. 10:30am–12:30pm, Sun. 10:30am–12:30pm and 3–5pm; free).

Soest

About thirty minutes from Dortmund by train, **SOEST** was a city of similar importance at the time of the Hanseatic League. Nowadays it's a whole world away in spirit, never having expanded much beyond its walls, which survive minus their battlements, and it preserves a medieval air and layout. It ranks as one of Germany's most delightful towns, yet it could so easily have been incorporated into the Ruhr megalopolis. This proximity to the industrial heartland resulted in Soest being heavily bombed during the war, but restoration has been so deft that the scars have healed completely, and there's scarcely a street within the fortifications which doesn't live up to the tourist board image of Romantic Germany. All the main buildings were constructed from a local sandstone whose deep lime greens bestow a distinctive character on the town and are well offset against the many red-roofed and whitewashed half-timbered houses. The play of light on these surfaces produces such magical effects it's little wonder that Soest has nurtured more than its fair share of German artists.

Both the **Hauptbahnhof** and the **bus station** are located just outside the northern stretch of the city walls. Turn left from either along Bahnhofstrasse and then right into Wiesenstrasse; the twin spires of the Gothic **Wiesenkirche** (*Our Lady of the Meadows*) rise straight ahead (summer 10am–12:30pm and 2:30–6pm ; winter 10am–noon and 2–4pm). This is a key building in German architectural history, when the favored but problematic hall church design finally acquired an elegance to match any other style of building. Although only a parish church, it's a cathedral in miniature, with an interior nothing short of stupendous. Slender unadorned piers thrust effortlessly up to the lofty vault, and the walls seem to be made of nothing but dazzlingly brilliant stained glass. These were inserted over a period ranging from just after the church's construction in the fourteenth century to the early sixteenth century, when money ran out before the south side could be glazed. The masterpiece of this assemblage, placed over the north portal, is from the final period, showing *The Last Supper* with a Westphalian menu of beer, ham, and rye bread. As a bonus, the church houses a richly varied collection of works of art, including three large triptychs. The most important of these is in the right-hand apse chapel; its wings were painted by Heinrich Aldegraver, a follower of Dürer and resident of Soest.

On higher ground to the rear stands the **Hohnekirche** (*Our Lady on the Hill*; summer 9:30am–noon and 1–5pm; winter 1–4pm only). The same Protestant congregation owns both this and the Wiesenkirche, taking refuge in the cozier surroundings of this squat, box-like structure for the winter months. It's a Romanesque attempt of about a century earlier at creating a hall church; the rather plain result was, however, greatly enlivened by a sumptuous fresco decoration, much of which has survived. Also here are a couple of fine works of art: the *Passion Altar* by the late fifteenth-century Westphalian painter known as the Master of Liesborn, and the remarkable *Scheibenkreuz*, a four-meter-high triumphal cross from about 1200, adorned with delicate reliefs of the life of Christ.

The center is soon reached from here by returning to Wiesenstrasse, and continuing via an old water mill up Am Seel, where you'll find the **tourist office** (Mon. and Weds.–Fri. 8:30am–12:30pm and 2:30–4:30pm, Tues. 8:30am–12:30pm and 2:30–5:30pm, Sat. 9:30am–noon; ☎02921 103323). Dominating the skyline here is the noble tower of **St. Patrokli**, generally (if inaccurately) referred to as the **Dom**. This forms part of a resplendent Romanesque westwork, which is so inspiringly grandiose a frontage that the rest of the building comes as an anticlimax, despite its spaciousness and homogeneous construction. The upper gallery houses the **Dom Museum** (Sat. 10:30am–12:30pm and 2–4pm, Sun. 11:30am–12:30pm and 2–4pm; DM1.50), with the church treasure and some lovely stained glass, including precious twelfth-century examples.

Only a few yards in front stands the **Petrikirche** (Mon.–Fri. 9:30am–12:30pm and 2:30–6:30pm, Sat. 10am–2pm), towering over the square of the same name which also contains the **Rathaus**, the only significant baroque addition to the city. Again with a westwork as its most notable feature, the Petrikirche is Romanesque with the addition of a Gothic chancel. On the third piers of the nave are two *Crucifixion* frescos attributed to **Conrad von Soest**, a major figure of the fifteenth century, and one of the few early German masters known by name. An important painting definitely by this artist, *St. Nicholas Enthroned with Saints Catherine, Barbara, and the two St. Johns*, occupies the altar of the tiny Romanesque **Nicolaikapelle**, situated behind the east end of St. Patrokli. In spite of an unprepossessing exterior, the inside of the chapel is a real gem, another variation on the hall church theme, with rounded column shafts dividing the space into two equal aisles. It's generally locked (officially open 11am–noon on Tues., Weds., Fri., and Sun., but not always adhered to); if so, ask for the key at the **Wilhelm Morgner Haus**, the local cultural center housed in a modern building directly in front (Mon.–Sat. 10am–noon and 2–5pm, Sun. 10:30am–12:30pm; free). This is named after Soest's own Expressionist painter, whose short career overlapped with the presence in the city of two of the movement's leading lights, Christian Rohlfs and Emil Nolde. A number of Morgner's canvases can be seen on the first floor, revealing a versatile talent which was to end at the age of 26 on a Flanders battlefield. Also on view is a selection of Aldegraver's engravings, his favorite and most effective medium.

From here, follow Ulricher Strasse southwards, turning left into Burghofstrasse. You shortly come to a complex of buildings, including a rare Romanesque house and the **Burghof**, a sixteenth-century mansion now housing the local history museum (Tues.–Sat. 10am–noon and 3–5pm, Sun. 11am–1pm; DM1). The main feature is the *Festsaal* on the ground floor, whose walls are covered with white stuccowork; the Biblical subjects are original, the battle scenes and emperors skillful modern pastiches. Another small museum is housed in the **Osthof-entor** (Tues.–Fri. 2–4pm, Sat. 11am–1pm, Sun. 11am–1pm and 3–5pm; DM1), a stately Renaissance gateway which once formed the north-east entrance to the town, and a rare surviving adornment of the walls. The display here is mostly concerned with medieval warfare; what looks like a spectacular modern sculpture in the attic turns out to be a fancy arrangement of 25,000 crossbow bolts.

Practical Points

Although Soest has been spared the ruthless commercial exploitation of so many picturesque old German towns, it's not immune from tourism, particularly on weekends, when day-trippers from the Ruhr stream in. One consequence of this is that there's a bewildering choice of **restaurants**—over a hundred in all, few of them especially cheap. For budget eating, the pizzerias offer good value; you'll find a couple on Brüderstrasse not far from the Hauptbahnhof. At the opposite end of the scale, *Pilgrim Haus* on Jacobistrasse is Westphalia's oldest inn, with an uninterrupted tradition from the early fourteenth century; though expensive, the food could hardly be bettered. Otherwise, many old-world **cafés** provide a relaxed atmosphere for coffee and cake; a good choice would be *Sauerland* on Filzenstrasse, which has been run by the same family for two centuries. However, the food you should on no account miss is Soest's own contribution to culinary history, the famed **pumpernickel**, a strongly-flavored black rye bread popular throughout Germany at breakfast time. It's made by leavening the dough for 24 hours, then baking it for as long again, until the sugars in the rye turn dark. For the genuine article, go to *Wilhelm Haverland*; their factory on the Markt has been in operation since 1799, and you can choose from several different recipes in their side-street shop behind. There's no local beer, but you can't go wrong with the wide range of Dortmund and Sauerland brews on offer in the taverns. Soest's main **festival** is a colorful market held on All Saints' Day (1 Nov.).

The **youth hostel**, Kaiser-Friedrich-Platz 2 (☎02921 16283), is just outside the southern section of the city wall. There's no **campground**, but those around MÖHNESEE (see p.495) are just a few kilometers away, and connected by regular bus services. **Hotel rooms** are almost invariably reasonable in price. Lowest rates are at *Lindenhof*, Niederbergheimer Str. 74 (☎02921 73551), southeast of the old city, at DM25 for a single, DM45 for a double, and *Zum Schwarzen Raben*, just south of the Dom at Ulricher Str. 15 (☎02921 16309), upwards of DM25 per head.

Lippstadt

About 25km northeast of Soest is **LIPPSTADT**, another historic city which has remained modest in size. The main reason for coming here is the **food**; the town's restaurants are reputed to be the best in Westphalia. If you aren't willing to splash out on these, a stay of a few hours is sufficient to take in everything of interest. On arrival at the **Hauptbahnhof**, turn left and follow Langestrasse all the way to the Markt. En route is **Haus Köppelmann**, one of several fine baroque palaces; it served as a hotel for most of the last two centuries, but has now been split up internally, with the prize room, the first-floor *Rokokosaal*, a rather seedy café. The Markt is dominated by the **Grosse Marienkirche**, a craggy weather-beaten giant of a church, mostly thirteenth-century in date, but with a late Gothic chancel. Its interior (Mon.–Fri. 3–5pm, Sat. 10am–noon) is far more pleasing, with frescos of various dates. Facing this is the **Heimat Museum** (Tues.–Sat. 10am–noon and 3–6pm, Sun. 10am–1pm; free), which has a large childhood section on the top floor, though the main interest is in the building itself with its rococo blandishments, particularly the many ornate ceilings. At the opposite end of the square are two bold baroque public buildings, the **Rathaus** and the **Stadtpalais**, at the southeast and northeast corners respectively; the former contains the **tourist office** (Mon.–Fri. 8:30am–12:30pm and 1:30–5:30pm; also Sat. in summer 10am–noon). Most of the classy **restaurants** are in this area; two which are in wonderful Renaissance buildings are *Goldener Hahn* on the northern continuation of Langestrasse, and *Altes Brauhaus* directly opposite the Heimat Museum. Westwards along Marktstrasse is a park with the evocative ruins of the **Kleine Marienkirche**, saved from total demolition last century by the personal intervention of King Friedrich Wilhelm IV of Prussia. The church is a roofless shell whose main body is pure early Gothic, although the first part to be built, the nuns' choir at the west end, is Romanesque. Grouped around are the still-intact former conventual buildings; against one of them, the ghostly silhouette of the cloister can be made out.

The river Lippe and its tributaries, which virtually encircle the town center, are also the setting for a series of moated castles in the environs. Far more interesting than these, however, is another convent, the twelfth-century **Stift Cappel** of the austere Premonstratensian order, which lies to the west; take Cappelstrasse northwards, cross two bridges, and turn left into Beckumerstrasse; it's then a thirty-minute walk (or there's an irregular bus service). Although suppressed at the Reformation, this has remained in female hands, first as a charitable foundation, then a boarding school. The whitewashed, twin-towered church is predictably solemn and plain; it may have been the first German building to be given a stone vault. Inside, you can see the original nuns' gallery, Gothic and Renaissance furnishings and a large number of elaborate tombstones. Get the key from the offices near the entrance (Mon.–Thurs. 9am–noon and 3–5pm, Fri. 9am–noon).

The Sauerland

The **SAUERLAND** forms an extensive part of eastern Westphalia, stretching from the edge of the Ruhrgebiet across to the border with Lower Saxony. Literally translated, the name means "Bitter Land," though it's unclear whether this comes from the fierce Saxon tribes who once inhabited the region and put up a doughty resistance to Charlemagne, or from the poor soils and hostile, rugged terrain; there's also the possibility that the name is simply a corruption of "South

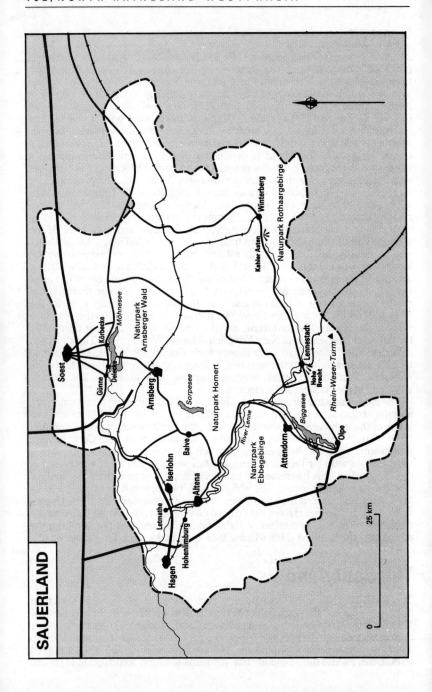

SAUERLAND

Winterberg

Naturpark Rothaargebirge

Kahler Asten

Naturpark Arnsberger Wald

Möhnesee

Korbecke

Soest

Gunne

Delecke

Lennestadt

Hohe Bracht

Rhein-Weser-Turm

Arnsberg

Sorpesee

Naturpark Homert

Biggesee

Olpe

Balve

River Lenne

Attendorn

Iserlohn

Naturpark Ebbegebirge

Altena

Letmathe

Hohenlimburg

Hagen

25 km

0

Land." It's rural, upland country, supposedly containing a thousand mountains; nowadays it serves as an obvious vacation and recreation area for the teeming millions who live in the nearby cities of the Rhine-Ruhr conurbation. The Sauerland's attractions are quintessentially German: above all, it's good **hiking** country, with nearly 12,000km of marked footpaths, and four national parks fall wholly or largely within its boundaries. Dotted with rivers and artificial lakes, it's also one of the country's main meccas for **fishing** (trout above all, but also carp, pike, perch, and eel) and more strenuous **activities**, such as surfing, rowing, canoeing, sailing, and hang-gliding, while riding in covered wagons Wild-West style has also been made into a regional specialty. Much of the Sauerland is of a surprisingly Alpine character for a place so far north, and **winter sports** help to bring in tourist trade all year round.

On the surface, the Sauerland is the mirror opposite of the Ruhrgebiet. However, while there are no major cities, there are many medium-sized industrial towns. **Beer** is a leading product—the soft local spring water is a crucial ingredient; as a result, many aficionados rate Sauerland brews superior even to those of nearby Dortmund. *Warsteiner*, dubbed "the queen of beers" for its delicate taste, is currently being heavily promoted abroad; *Veltins* is popular throughout Germany, while *Iserlohner* and *Hirsch* are also very fine. Sauerland water, moreover, plays a key role in the economy of the Ruhrgebiet, and the great **dams** of the region are key features of the German inland waterway system. Their importance to the economy was highlighted by the famous **"Dambusters'** episode of World War II (told in Paul Brickhill's book, and in the popular film which, however, wasn't shot on location). At the time, these massive concrete structures would hardly have been grazed by conventional explosives. In order to penetrate them, the British inventor Barnes Wallis developed enormous, super-accurate ten-ton bombs which were dropped by the Lancasters of 617 Squadron on May 17, 1943 with devastating effect. Such havoc was caused by the ensuing flooding, which destroyed 123 factories, 25 bridges and 7500 acres of arable land, that it was estimated to have taken the equivalent of several months' work by 100,000 men to repair the damage—a telling blow to the Nazi war effort and a major propaganda coup. This, at any rate, is how the evidence has traditionally been presented: more recent research suggests that the claims were exaggerated.

The Germans have kept the Sauerland largely to themselves, and it's fairly easy to see why. Such towns that exist are by no means outstanding, and they're all short on major sights. The scenery may be consistently impressive, but it lacks the legendary associations of the Rhine, the grandeur of the Bavarian Alps or the distinctiveness of the Black Forest. Nonetheless, the area makes a good choice if you want to escape the obvious destinations for a while. It's also easy on the budget, as you don't need to look far for cheap **accommodation**—campgrounds and youth hostels pepper the entire district, while private houses with rooms to rent at around DM20 are legion; there are also many farmhouses offering inclusive deals at bargain rates. If you're attracted to the region, get hold of the free annual tourist board publication *Gastgeberverzeichnis—Sauerland* which has exhaustive listings on all forms of lodging, plus full details of sports and activities.

Märkisches Sauerland

There are four constituent parts to the Sauerland. Farthest west is the **MÄRKISCHES SAUERLAND**, corresponding to the old Duchy of Mark. This is sometimes taken to include Hagen itself; more logically, it begins with

Hohenlimburg, where the continuously built-up land of the Ruhrgebiet first gives way to open countryside. A scenic railroad line follows the course of the Lenne River, and continues all the way south to Siegen. On the east bank is the Lennegebirge range, which forms part of the **Naturpark Homert**; to the west begins the **Naturpark Ebbegebirge**.

ALTENA, which is reached in about thirty minutes from Hagen, is the obvious star of the Sauerland towns, thanks to its superb setting deep in the valley, high above which is its massive **Burg**, one of the largest medieval castles in Germany. Begun in the twelfth century, the buildings were erected at intervals up to the sixteenth century; the central keep is strongly protected by an outer bailey and no less than three consecutive gateways. The complex inevitably crumbled with disuse, and there were plans last century to rebuild it in a phony Romantic style. These were fortunately never carried out, and the present condition of the castle is due to a drastic restoration in the early years of the present century, which has the merit of being reasonably authentic. In 1909, a teacher named Richard Schirrmann (1874–1961) established the **world's first-ever permanent youth hostel** in the Burg, having previously operated from a schoolroom in town. Inspired by the simple idea of the need to provide low-cost accommodation for young travelers, Schirrmann's choice of Altena is explained by the fact that the countryside around is particularly good for hiking. In time, hundreds of hostels sprang up all over Germany, and became an established and important feature of national life. The idea was slow in catching on elsewhere (more than two decades elapsed before an international federation was set up), but eventually spread right around the world, to the gratitude of millions of travelers, not all of them young. Schirrmann's reward has been to have a plethora of streets named after him (usually the ones leading to the local hostel)—indeed, he's commemorated just as prolifically in this way in the Federal Republic as Marx and Lenin are in the GDR.

This being Germany, the original hostel has been ossified as one of several **museums** in the castle (Tues.–Sun. 9:30am–5pm; inclusive ticket DM3). The day room is in the style of a traditional Westphalian farmstead; adjoining it is the area for groups, while downstairs is the spartan main dorm, its solid wooden bunks standing in triple-tiers, and looking as if they could yet withstand many more years of service. Several of the rooms in the Burg have been restored in period style and equipped with impressive furniture. Highlights include the *Stadthalle* by the entrance, with its carved Renaissance chimneypiece; the Great Hall, with a notable collection of pewter; and the chapel, adorned with retables from Antwerp and Cologne, a Romanesque font, and a graceful fifteenth-century *Madonna and Child* made from Bamberg sandstone. Scattered throughout the rooms are important examples of **arms and armor**, reflecting the fact that the Sauerland was a major center for their production. Altena itself was for long the world's leading wiremaking town; so prestigious was this that the craftsmen were granted exemption from Prussian military service—a rare privilege indeed. This tradition is celebrated in the **German Wire Museum** in the former commander's house by the ticket office; to be frank neither this nor the **Smithy Museum**, honoring the fact that iron smelting has been carried out in the Altena area since the ninth century, offers very exciting subject matter. In the outer bailey there's what's rather cheatingly called the world's oldest functioning **youth hostel** (☎02352 23522); its location makes it the most attractive place to stay in town, but there are only forty beds and it's regularly full. Another, much larger hostel is at Linscheider Bach 2 (☎02352 22815) at the extreme northern end of town, but note that there's no campground and hotels are, by regional standards, relatively expensive.

ISERLOHN, the Sauerland's largest town, can be reached circuitously from Altena by either bus or train, but it's more fun to take the direct 9km path over the hills. (If you want to do serious walking in the Sauerland, it makes sense to invest in decent **maps**, which can be bought from any newsstand, as signposting of the paths is by no means as frequent as it could be.) Still a focus of the iron industry, Iserlohn has a couple of moderately interesting churches, both with carved altars—Gothic St. **Marien**, dominating the town from its hill, and the Romanesque **Bauernkirche**. Beside the latter is the **Heimat Museum** (Tues., Weds., and Fri.–Sun. 10am–5pm, Thur 10am–7pm; DM1), housed in a ritzy baroque mansion. The main attraction, however, is the **Dechenhöhle** in the outlying village of LETHMATHE, arguably the most outstanding of several **stalactite caves** in the Sauerland (daily guided tours lasting 45 minutes, April–Oct. 9am–5pm, Nov.–March 10am–4pm; DM3). Discovered last century when the railroad was being constructed, the geological formations are reckoned to be anything from 300 to 350 million years old. Inevitably, the chambers have been given nicknames according to the shapes they supposedly resemble; particularly impressive are the *Palm Tree Grotto*, with its single, tapering stem, and the *Kronleuchter*, so called for looking like an abstract version of the famous Romanesque crown-shaped chandeliers in Aachen, Hildesheim, and Comburg.

Two more caves can be found near **BALVE**, which can be reached by bus or train via MENDEN. Within the town boundaries is the **Balver Höhle** (April–Oct. Tues.–Thurs. 10am–4pm, Sat. 10am–3pm, Sun. 11am–4pm; DM3); the more impressive **Reckenhöhle** is in VOLKRINGHAUSEN just to the north (March–Nov. daily 9am–4pm; DM3). The area's most singular sight, however, is the **Luisenhütte Wocklum** (May–Oct. Tues.–Sat. 10am–6pm, Sun. 11:30am–6pm; DM1.50) just to the east. Dating from 1732, this is the oldest surviving blast furnace in Germany, and one of the most important pieces of industrial heritage in the country. It's still in perfect working order but, needless to say, is no longer kept ablaze.

Nordsauerland

Soest and Lippstadt are sometimes counted as part of the **NORDSAUERLAND**, an area dominated by a 10km-long artificial lake, the **Möhnesee**. The north bank has been developed as a holiday resort area for fishing and water sports, and there are **campgrounds** all along this shore. **Cruises** depart from GÜNNE, DELECKE, and KÖRBECKE from April to October. Between these first two villages is the famous **dam** which, though not the largest, was the prime target of the "Dambusters," due to its proximity to the industrial cities. Controlling the flow of the river Heve into the river Ruhr, it's 650m long and 40m high; when it was breached, 134 million tons of water gushed out into the countryside. Now long repaired, it's one of four causeways or footbridges interspersed at fairly regular intervals allowing you to cross over to the opposite bank of the lake. This has been left in its natural state, and a southerly arm, the **Hevesee**, is a protected area for birdlife. The **youth hostel** (☎02924 305) lies directly across from Körbecke. Immediately beyond is the beginning of the **Naturpark Arnsberger Wald**, an upland forest of beech, birch, and larch, which stretches for some 30km east to west, and up to 15km north to south. Within its boundaries, on the road between HIRSCHBERG and WARSTEIN, is another fine cave, the **Bilsteinhöhle** (April–Nov. daily 9am–5pm, Dec.–March Mon.–Sat. 10am–noon and 2–4pm, Sun. 9am–4pm; DM3).

Hochsauerland

The **HOCHSAUERLAND** is by far the largest of the four districts, beginning immediately beyond the Arnsberger Wald, and continuing east to the boundary with Lower Saxony, and south to the Siegerland. **ARNSBERG** itself is traditionally considered the "capital" of the Sauerland, and is the administrative center for the whole region. It's built on a spur of land on a bend of the Ruhr River, rising neatly upwards in tiers. To the north are the ruins of the **Schlossberg**, scene of a two-day festival in late May or early June. The southern part of the old town is dominated by the **Propsteikirche**, a Gothic church with rich baroque furnishings, beside which stands the ornate **Hirschberger Tor**, a rare example of north German rococo. Numerous half-timbered houses line the streets of the town, while the **Sauerland Museum** (Mon.–Fri. 9am–5pm, Sun. 9am–1pm; DM1) occupies the Renaissance **Landberger Hof**. There's a **youth hostel** at Rumbecker Höhe 1 (☎02931 10627) on the east side of town, by the Arnsberger Wald.

The **Sorpesee**, another artificial lake, lies 10km to the south. Again, it's a center for fishing and water sports; cruises run from May to September, departing from LANGSCHEID on the northern shore. There are a string of **campgrounds** and a **youth hostel** (☎02935 1776) on the western bank, which is actually very close to Balve in Märkisches Sauerland. To the east and south of here is the bulk of the aforementioned **Naturpark Homert**; apart from its numerous trails, it's a good area for birdwatching, being inhabited by some 450 species.

Farther south is the **Naturpark Rothaargebirge** (*Red-Haired Mountains*), a range covered with conifers and deciduous woods, which separates the Sauerland from the Siegerland to the south. It's best known as winter sports country; the main resort, **WINTERBERG**, can be reached by train from Arnsberg via a branch line from BESTWIG. As well as the *pistes*, Winterberg has an indoor skating rink, and bobsled and toboggan runs, while international dogsled races are held each January. The town stands at the foot of the **Kahler Asten**, which at 841m is the highest peak in the Sauerland; it's covered with snow for about a third of the year, and the average winter temperature is freezing point. You can ascend to a belvedere for a huge, if not particularly inspiring, panorama of the district. There's a **youth hostel** not far from the mountain in ASTENBERG (☎02981 2289); Winterberg itself has an abundant choice of **rooms** in private houses at only marginally higher rates.

Südsauerland

The heart of the **SÜDSAUERLAND** is the largest of the reservoirs, the appropriately named **Biggesee**, which lies below the Ebbegebirge range. A branch of the main Hagen–Siegen railroad runs from FINNETROP down the western bank of the lake. **ATTENDORN**, on the northern shore, is an old Hanseatic town. Its fourteenth-century **Rathaus**, apart from being the only secular structure of its period in the entire region, is a striking building, with elaborate gables on both its short ends, and an open lower story which was intended to serve as a market hall. The upstairs rooms now house the **Heimatmuseum** (Tues.–Fri. 9am–1pm and 3–5pm, Sat. 9am–1pm, Sun. 11am–1pm; DM1), which includes a notable collection of pewter figures. **St. Johannes** is a fourteenth-century Gothic hall church incorporating the tower of its Romanesque predecessor. It's nicknamed the "cathedral of the Sauerland" due to its preeminence among the region's churches. Just to the north of town is the **Attahöhle** (daily April–Oct. 9am–5pm, Nov.–March 10am–4pm; DM4), a particularly impressive stalactite cave. To the east is **Burg Schnellenberg**, the largest of the few surviving hilltop castles in Westphalia. Part of it has been rebuilt as a luxury hotel, but a section has been preserved as a **museum** with a collection of weapons (April–Oct. Tues.–Sun. 10am–5pm; DM1). There are two **campgrounds** just outside town, and there's a **youth hostel** at Heldener Str. 5 (☎02722 2455). **Festivals** include the best Carnival celebrations in the Sauerland, and various parades during Holy Week, while the first Saturday in August sees *Der Biggesee in Flammen*, with fireworks and illuminations. **Cruises** are run on the lake between Easter and mid-October from both Attendorn and **OLPE**, the highly developed water sports resort on the southern bank. There are three **campgrounds** in the latter's surrounding area, plus a **youth hostel** in nearby STADE (☎02761 6775).

LENNESTADT, on the main Hagen–Siegen line almost due east of Attendorn, straddles the junction of the *Naturparks* Homert, Ebbegebirge, and Rothaargebirge. South of the town, a minor road leads shortly to the **Hohe Bracht**, at 584m the finest vantage-point in the Südsauerland, commanding a sweeping view from its belvedere tower over the three ranges as far as Kahler Asten. An alternative for a broadly similar panoramic view is the **Rhein-Weser Turm**, some 12km southeast of Lennestadt.

Siegen and the Siegerland

The Rothaargebirge range provides a horizontal dividing line separating the Sauerland from the **SIEGERLAND** to the south. This region is a somewhat bizarre mixture of a heavily industrialized valley and a holiday resort area which, even more than the Sauerland, the Germans have reserved for themselves. It's a land of hills and mountains, cut right across the middle by the Sieg River, which flows due westwards, entering the Rhine just north of Bonn.

SIEGEN, the geographical center of the Federal Republic, is the capital of this district, and the only place within a radius of about 100km which can properly be called a city. Iron and steel production were the reasons for its development last century; relative isolation meant that its growth was checked, and even now its population is barely over 100,000. One of Siegen's main assets is its setting, rising from the banks of the river high into the hills above; this has recently been enhanced by the construction of a spectacular **viaduct** (the biggest in the country) which carries the A45 autobahn—linking the Ruhrgebiet with Hessen—104m above the Sieg.

Before industrialization, the town was chiefly associated with the fortunes of the **House of Nassau-Siegen**, a line founded in the late thirteenth century by the local count, Otto I. In 1530, the name was changed to **Oranien-Nassau**, following intermarriage with an aristocratic family from Orange in Provence. Subsequently, this dynasty had a profound impact on the course of northern European history, thanks to the acquisition of land in the Low Countries. **William the Silent** (1533–84), born in nearby Dillenberg, was the creator of the modern Dutch state, driving out the occupying Spanish forces and establishing a new Protestant and mercantile power. Later luminaries included Johann Moritz (see p.460) and another William (1650–1702), who became king of Britain and was to play such a prominent part in Irish history that he continues to inflame folk memories to this day.

A curiosity of Siegen are the two castles originally belonging to this family: one at the top of the town, the other a few hundred meters below. This is due to the fact that the line split in 1623 over continued support for the Reformation; thereafter, the Catholic branch lived in the **Upper Schloss**. The original fortified Burg has been much modified over the centuries and isn't particularly picturesque, but its ramparts command the best views over the town, while the gardens, in honor of the Dutch connection, are planted with 60,000 tulips. Part of the building has been adapted to house the **Siegerland Museum** (Tues.–Sun. 10am–12:30pm and 2–5pm; DM3). This contains varied collections, including a realistic model of a mine 14m under the courtyard. Several rooms are devoted to the Oranien-Nassau family, whose likenesses are preserved in a host of portraits, often of a decent artistic standard. There's also a display of memorabilia on the **Busch** brothers, a remarkable twentieth-century Siegen family whose anti-Nazism gave further impetus to their international careers. Adolf and Hermann founded the Busch Quartet with two friends; their 78rpm recordings, particularly of Beethoven, have never been surpassed in terms of interpretation, and many can still be bought in modern remasterings. They also blazed a pioneering trail by championing the playing of baroque music by authentic-sized chamber groups, instead of in the souped-up arrangements which had been the norm for the previous century. Fritz Busch was a leading conductor who was prominent in the establishment of opera at Glyndebourne—which has become a key feature of the summer season for London high society—while Willi was one of Germany's best actors.

However, the museum's main attraction is its display on the art of **Peter Paul Rubens** who, by a sheer fluke, can be counted a native of Siegen, though he was in no sense a German. His father Jan., a Calvinist sympathizer, was forced to flee his native Antwerp, settling in Cologne, where he entered the service of Princess Anna of Saxony, second wife of William the Silent. Eventually he graduated from being her adviser and diplomatic agent to sharing her bed when her husband was at war. An untimely pregnancy led to his unmasking; lucky to escape with his life, he was banished to Siegen, where the great painter was born in 1577. A year later, the family was allowed to return to Cologne; after Jan. Rubens' death, they went back to Antwerp. Not only was the young artist quickly reconciled with Roman Catholicism, he was later one of the most ardent propagandists of the Counter-Reformation; he further defied his background by becoming a faithful diplomatic servant of the Spanish imperial power. A man who was almost indecently successful (he ran the equivalent of a picture factory, which churned out canvases by the hundred, all bearing the master's characteristic stamp, even when he had contributed little to their actual execution), Rubens was an incorrigible social climber, a groveling toady to all political and religious authority. This stance is clearly imbued in his paintings, as is his chauvinistic attitude toward women, whom he eyed lustfully as fodder for his insatiable sexual appetite. Yet it's a measure of his greatness as an artist that these off-putting opinions don't seem to matter—his works can be enjoyed for their phenomenal technical skill, carefully planned design, glorious colors, and unabashed *joie de vivre*. These qualities are all present in a late masterpiece here: somewhat pompously named *The Victorious Hero Seizes the Opportunity for Peace*, it's an allegory featuring Perseus with the head of Medusa, Minerva, Abundance, Opportunity, and Time. From a decade earlier, *Roman Charity* illustrates the legend of Cimon, who was saved from starving to death in prison by being breast-fed by his daughter Pero. There's also a haughty *Self-Portrait* from about the same time, and five more original works.

The **Lower Schloss**, the seat of the Protestant line, originally occupied an abandoned Franciscan monastery. This was destroyed by fire in 1695, and replaced by the present extensive baroque complex. It's now largely occupied by offices, but the royal crypt has survived. Between the two castles is the Markt, with the eighteenth-century Rathaus and the **Nikolaikirche**, one of the most distinctive of the extravagant series of late Romanesque churches founded in the Rhineland and around. The kernel of the building is a thirteenth-century galleried hexagon, the only example of this design in northern Europe. The handsome red and white tower was added two centuries later. Inside is a baptismal plate made in Peru, a legacy of the time when the Oranien-Nassau family, who used the Nikolaikirche as their court chapel, played an important role in the colonization of South America. Lower down the hill is the **Martinikirche**, the unremarkable late Gothic successor to one of the most important Ottonian churches in Germany, from which the mosaic pavement has been preserved.

The **tourist office** (Mon.–Fri. 9am–1pm and 2–6pm, Sat. 9am–noon; ☎0271 593517) is located immediately in front of the **Hauptbahnhof**. To reach the Altstadt from here, walk right through the pedestrian precinct and turn left uphill at the end. **Mitfahrzentrale** has an office at Freudenberger Str. 15 (☎0271 54083). There's a **youth hostel** at Am Alten Friedhof 1 (☎0271 52215) within the grounds of the upper Schloss. Cheapest **hotel**, charging DM25 per head, is *Schäfer*, Rosterstr. 111 (☎0271 334222), while DM28 is the going rate at the following: *Gasthof Rörig*, Eintrachtstr. 9 (☎0271 332484); *Gasthof Meier*, St.-Johann-Str. 3 (☎0271 332609); and *Laterne*, Löhrstr. 37 (☎0271 57034). The last named, occupying one of the few surviving half-timbered houses in Siegen, has one of the best **restaurants** in town; there are several more inexpensive places to eat and drink on the same street, which dips downwards from the Markt. Local **beers** have the advantage of using the clear, pure mountain water of the Siegerland; *Krombacher* is well known throughout Germany, whereas consumption of *Irle*, no less fine, is confined mainly to this district. In the lower part of town, on Koblenzerstrasse, is the *Siegerlanderhalle*, the venue for **concerts** of all kinds. There are two **theaters**—*Siegener Theater* on Spandauer Strasse, and the minute *Kleine Theater Lohkasten* at Löhrtor.

The Siegerland

FREUDENBERG, 11km northwest of Siegen—to which it's linked by regular bus services—is an archetypal picture-postcard town which seems to feature on just about every German calendar. In 1540 the town, then less than a century old, was destroyed by fire; the streets built thereafter as replacements have survived almost intact: row upon row of black-and-white half-timbered houses, whose steeply pitched slate roofs bear witness to the harsh winter climate. It's a popular recreation resort all year round, and there are plenty of pensions where it's possible to stay for as little as DM20 per head—try along Oranienstrasse, the most impressive street of all.

There's also a string of vacation complexes on the slow but scenic railroad line skirting the Rothaargebirge, linking Siegen with **FRANKENBERG** in Hessen. Snow can fall early in the winter—often before it arrives in the Alps—whereupon the towns are besieged by skiers. **BAD BERLEBURG** is the best-known resort, its spa facilities giving it a balancing pull in summer; it also has a baroque Schloss, one of the few large-scale historical monuments in the region. Closer to Siegen are HILCHENBACH and ERNDTEBRÜCK; from the latter a different railroad line leads to **LAASPHE**, another spa with half-timbered buildings reminiscent of Freudenberg. All resorts have good hiking possibilities, while accommodation is both plentiful and cheap.

Paderborn

The cathedral and market city of **PADERBORN** lies some 30km east of Lippstadt, just before the north German plain gives way to the Teutoburger Wald. It's a characterful place with a variety of archaeological and artistic attractions to add to the geological curiosity from which it derives its name, meaning "source of the Pader." This, the country's shortest river at a mere four kilometers in length, rises in a park in the heart of the city. It's formed by the surfacing of more than 200 warm springs, which pour out over 5000 liters of water per second. These originate as subterranean streams in the **Eggegebirge** range to the east; they're suddenly forced out into the open at this point by the abrupt change in topography from the plateau to a lowland whose soil contains an impermeable layer of marl. Although the visual impact is less startling than might be supposed, the park is an idyllic spot, and makes the obvious place to begin your tour, offering as it does the best view of the city's two main churches—the twin-towered former **Abdinghof** monastery in the foreground, with the massive single steeple of the **Dom** rearing up behind.

Paderborn was first brought to prominence in the eighth century by that great lover of hot springs, **Charlemagne**. He established a royal seat, which became a base both for his first parliaments and for his campaigns against the Saxons. In 799, Pope Leo III, having narrowly escaped an assassination attempt, visited the emperor here; the alliance subsequently forged led to the foundation of the Holy Roman Empire, and Charlemagne's coronation in Rome the following year. This was to prove an event of the utmost significance in European history, giving the papacy a new, less overtly political role, and defining the basic power structure for German internal affairs which was to last for the next millennium. During postwar rebuilding of the city, the foundations of the **Carolingian Palace**, the site of these momentous meetings, were discovered just to the north of the Dom; they had been hidden from view since a fire destroyed the building in the year 1000. Soon it became the most exciting archaeological site in the country, and was excavated in the 1960s, revealing the ground plan of a sizable complex which included a king's hall, a church, a monastery, and courtyards. Also unearthed was an open-air throne, now under cover beneath the Dom's north portal; you can see it by peering in through the protective glass.

Behind was found the replacement **Ottonian Palace**, dating from immediately after the disaster, and itself desecrated by another fire in 1165. This time the controversial decision was taken to go beyond a routine excavation, and to try and recreate its original form in as scholarly a manner as possible. The task was entrusted to **Gottfried Böhm**, an architect of international reputation who had made his name designing unashamedly modern churches in Cologne, and in 1976 the palace made its belated reappearance, its pristine stonework making an odd contrast with the venerable status of the design. It now houses the regional **Archaeology Museum** (Tues.–Sun. 10am–5pm; DM1), but interest centers on the structure itself, as no original palaces from this epoch survive. You pass through a subsidiary building to the vestibule; to the right is the two-story **Ikenbergkapelle**, while to the left is the **Great Hall**, which takes up the lion's share of the complex. Standing on its own near the entrance is the only authentic remnant of the palaces, the tiny **Bartholomäuskapelle**. Surviving documents relate that it was built in 1017 by Greek workmen, although it is more likely that these visitors were Byzantine masons from Italy. As the very first hall church erected in Germany, it can claim to be the precedent of what became the preeminent national architectural form. Despite a glum exterior, it's very dapper inside, a classically inspired design of three aisles of rounded pillars crowned with flowery Corinthian capitals.

In preparation for the Pope's visit, Charlemagne ordered the construction of a no-expense-spared church which was almost immediately raised to the status of a cathedral; ever since, the city's history has been dominated by its ecclesiastical role. The present **Dom** is a cavernous and monotonous thirteenth-century Gothic hall church whose tower, slit by innumerable little windows, incorporates its Romanesque predecessor. It's entered by the southern porch (or "Paradise") whose portal is adorned with French-style figures. More refined carvings from a now vanished doorway can be seen on either side of the transept window; look for the cartoon-like fables—a boar blowing a horn, a hare playing the fiddle, a crane removing a bone from a wolf's throat, and a fox dressed as a scholar to receive his diploma. Inside, the Dom resembles a museum of seventeenth-century heroic sculpture to the glory of the prince-bishops, much of it by one of Germany's few Mannerists, **Heinrich Gröninger**. His masterpiece, almost facing you on entry, is the grandiose *Monument to Dietrich von Fürstenberg*, complete with depictions of the buildings this bishop commissioned to transform the city. The Dom's most enduring attraction varies the animal theme, and comes in the form of a puzzle, which you should try to work out in advance. Follow the signs marked *Hasenfenster* into the cloister garden; the tracery of one of the windows is the emblem of Paderborn, and a mason's trick which was celebrated in its day. This shows three hares running around in a circle, but although each clearly has two ears of his own, it has only been necessary to carve one per creature.

The south side of the Dom faces the open space of the vast Markt, lined with tall baroque houses and the Romanesque **Gaukirche**. In this setting, the lead-plated glass palace which houses a couple of shops, a café, and the **Diocesan Museum** creates a strident impact, the more so as it masks some of the wonderful views of the Dom. This brash modernist intrusion into the old city clearly had its supporters, as its architect was none other than the same Gottfried Böhm who immediately afterwards was asked to rebuild the Ottonian Palace. The interior, rising abruptly in tiers, is a cleverly thought-out design to provide a majestic setting for the museum (Tues.–Sun. 10am–5pm; DM1). In the basement, the **Schatzkammer**'s most valuable pieces are two inlaid reliquary cabinets, made for the Dom and the Abinghof in about 1100 by a local monk, **Roger von Helmarshausen** and, in contrast, the baroque shrine and bust of Paderborn's patron saint, St. Liborius. The Dom's old bells are invitingly displayed with hammers, allowing you to indulge in a bit of instant campanology. Most of the collection exhibited upstairs is junk, but pride of place at the summit is rightly given to a masterpiece, the *Imad Madonna*, a hierarchic mid-eleventh-century wooden statue named after its bishop donor.

The remaining sights can be covered by means of a short circular walk. Following Schildern at the southwest corner of the Markt, you come to the city's most handsome building, the **Rathaus**, adorned with arcades, gables, and oriel windows, and fronted by a striking facade of highly original design which obsessively explores the possibilities of a triangular motif. Erected in the early seventeenth century in the Weser Renaissance style, it was modeled on the patrician **Heisingsches Haus** just down the street. The top story contains a small **Natural History Museum** (Tues.–Sat. 10am–6pm, Sun. 10am–1pm; free), focusing principally on the region's ornithology. Up the hill from here is the **Jesuit College** from the end of the same century, whose church, like the one in Cologne, has a vast galleried interior with anachronistic Gothic pointed arches. Farther along

Kamp is the sober **Dalheimer Hof** by the Westphalian baroque architect, Johann Conrad Schlaun. Going back downhill along Kesselerstrasse, you see the Romanesque **Busdorfkirche**, whose main joy is a tiny cloister. A couple of minutes' walk down Heierstrasse, then left into Thisaut, stands the oldest remaining half-timbered house, **Adam-und-Eva-Haus**, now the local museum (Tues.–Sat. 10am–6pm, Sun. 10am–1pm; free). The most arresting exhibits are a couple of exquisite drawings of the city by Schlaun, and a display of engravings by **Heinrich Aldegraver**, a native of Paderborn and one of Dürer's most faithful followers. From here, the Dom is back in view and only a few minutes' walk away.

Practicalities

The **Hauptbahnhof** is southwest of downtown; turn right at the exit and keep going straight. En route to the Markt you'll pass the **tourist office** on Marienplatz (Mon.–Fri. 9am–6pm, Sat. 9am–1pm; ☎05251 26461). For once, the **youth hostel** is conveniently sited just a few minutes' walk from the main attractions at Meinwerkstr. 16 (☎05251 22055), the continuation of Heierstrasse. The two **campgrounds** are both in the northern fringes of the city—*Am Waldsee* at Husarenstr. 130 (☎05251 7372) and *Stauterrassen* at Auf der Thune 14 (☎05251 4504). Most **hotel rooms** are reasonably priced; among the cheapest are *Hubertushof*, Hubertusweg 51 (☎05251 4463) at DM25 for a single, DM40 for a double, and *Bürgerkrug*, Detmolder Str. 394 (☎05251 4254) with singles DM28, doubles DM45. The tourist office publishes a free monthly program of **events**, *Paderborn von Tag zu Tag*. Pubs offering **live music** are *Tuba*, Kasseler Str. 26, *Das Treibhaus*, Detmolder Str. 21, and *Kukoz*, Tegelweg 3–5. Concerts, musicals, dance, opera, and jazz make up the varied fare at the ultramodern *PaderHalle* on Maspernplatz. Pick of the **movie theaters** is *Studio*, Westernstr. 34, which frequently features films in English. The main **popular festivals** occur in July, including a *Schützenfest* on the second weekend. There's also a beer week in October.

Bielefeld

BIELEFELD, some 35km north of Paderborn, clusters around the narrow middle strip of the Teutoburger Wald. It's strongly reminiscent of the cities of the Ruhrgebiet in both history and appearance, and is the overwhelmingly dominant economic center of eastern Westphalia. Founded in the thirteenth century by the counts of Ravensburg, the town gained prosperity in the late Middle Ages through the linen trade. The nineteenth century saw mushrooming growth, due to the increased importance of this traditional industry, plus various new engineering products associated with it. Development was facilitated by the fact that nearby Minden, with a far more favorable geographical location, was hampered by its role as a garrison.

The **Hauptbahnhof** is to the north of downtown; directly opposite is the **tourist office** (Mon.–Fri. 9am–6pm, Sat. 9am–1pm; ☎0521 178844). From here, continue straight ahead down Bahnhofstrasse to Jahnplatz; this takes you on to the ring road, which encloses the modestly-sized Altstadt. Continuing down Niederwall, you come to the **Rathaus**, an ugly imitative monstrosity from the beginning of this century, which contains another tourist office (same times Mon.–Fri. only; ☎0521 178899); next door, and built simultaneously, is the luxuriant Jugendstil **Stadttheater**, the city's main venue for opera and drama.

At the end of this road, Spiegelstrasse leads up towards the **Sparrenburg**, built between 1240 and 1250 as the seat of the counts of Ravensberg. It's on the edge of the Teutoburger Wald, which runs right through the modern built-up area. Heavily restored, the castle has the twin attractions of a round tower which can be ascended for a panoramic view, and some 300 meters of underground passageways and dungeons (March–Nov. Tues.–Sun. 9am–1pm and 2–6pm; combined ticket DM2). In the courtyard is a statue to Margrave Friedrich Wilhelm of Brandenburg, the man who established Bielefeld's prosperity by introducing the *Leinenlegge*, a quality control edict concerning linen.

Below the Sparrenburg to the north is the so-called "new town," grouped around the **Neustädter Marienkirche**, a handsome Gothic church built during the late thirteenth and early fourteenth centuries, and now standing, much in the manner of an English cathedral, in splendid isolation on a green. Its tall twin towers are crowned by unusually long and sharply pointed lead steeples; they look so venerable it's hard to believe they were devastated in an air raid and had to be rebuilt almost from scratch. The church, which contains outstanding **works of art**, is unfortunately kept locked; ring at the door of the halls directly in front for the sacristan. On the high altar is a masterpiece by the same Westphalian "Soft Style" artist who painted the *Berswordt Altar* in Dortmund. This *Madonna and Child with Saints* is surrounded by a dozen small panels, mostly of scenes from Christ's life; the wings were cut up and sold last century, and are now in museums all over the world. A major but nameless fourteenth-century sculptor (whose works can also be seen in Cappenberg and Marburg) carved the frieze of apostles above the altar, which belonged to the former rood screen. He also created the magnificent *tomb of Otto III von Ravensberg and Hedwig von Lippe*, featuring a touching yet unsentimental portrayal of their previously deceased son. The other elaborate Ravensberg family monument is clearly modeled on this tomb, even though it was made over a century later.

On nearby Artur-Ladebeck-Strasse is the smooth red sandstone pile of the **Kunsthalle** (Tues., Weds., Fri., and Sun. 11am–6pm, Thurs. 11am–9pm, Sat. 10am–6pm; DM2, Fri. free). The building itself, erected in the 1960s, was intended to be a significant addition to the city's heritage; it was designed by **Philip Johnson**, Mies van der Rohe's principal American follower, who was himself one of the leading lights in propagating the International Style in architecture. This implantation of an overtly New World building has been greeted with a fair amount of critical derision, but the authorities are convinced of the long-term wisdom of their choice. The collections, worth seeing if you're in town but not special enough to justify a detour, are typical of current German taste. Most of the Expressionists are represented, with good examples of Beckmann, Kirchner, Nolde, and Macke; there are sculptures by Rodin, Barlach, Archipenko, Lipchitz, Caro, and Moore (some inside, others in the garden); and several rooms of European and American abstract painting. Most of Bielefeld's other museums tend to be of fairly parochial interest; an exception is the **Farmhouse Museum** (April–Oct. Tues.–Sun. 10am–1pm and 3–6pm, Nov.–March Tues.–Sun. 10am–1pm and 2–5pm; DM1.50), set on the edge of the Teutoburger Wald to the west of the center, and reached from the Kunsthalle by following Dornberger Strasse straight ahead. Several traditional agricultural buildings from the surrounding region have been re-erected here, including a seventeenth-century windmill.

What remains of the Altstadt is a short walk from the Kunsthalle—turn right into Obernstrasse at the end of Artur-Ladebeck-Strasse. The Markt is lined by patrician houses built by prosperous linen merchants. Oldest is the late Gothic **Crüwell House** of 1530; the others are in the cheerful Weser Renaissance style of the following century. Around the corner on Postgang is the Gothic **Altstädter Nicolaikirche**, which contains a spectacular sixteenth-century altar from Antwerp, featuring some 250 figures in the carved depictions of the Passion. Behind the church is the *Leineweber* ("linen weaver") statue; he is depicted with the traditional characteristics of a long pipe and walking stick.

Festivals and Practicalities

If Bielefeld is thin on historic monuments, its **popular festivals** compensate. Best is the *Leineweber Markt* on the last weekend in May, which includes street theater, jazz, and rock concerts, plus folklore displays. Open-air music of all kinds is played throughout the city during the summer, while every third Saturday from May to October sees a flea market; the location varies, but the Markt itself is a regular venue. In mid-July, the *Sparrenburgfest* in the castle features tournaments and a medieval fair, and there's a week-long *Weinfest* in mid-September.

For a full list of the month's **events**, pick up the tourist office's free program. Apart from the Stadttheater already mentioned, drama is also performed at the *Theater am Alten Markt*, while there's a *Puppenspiele* ("puppet theater") at Ravensberger Str. 12. Concerts are given at *Oetkerhalle* on Stapenhorststrasse. Bielefeld's most original venue, however, is the **Alten Ravensberger Spinnerei**, east of Jahnplatz on Heeper Strasse, a grandiose nineteenth-century linen mill, well worth seeing in its own right as a rare survivor of the sort of factory which once dotted large German industrial towns. Lovingly restored, it's now a cultural center, featuring exhibitions, film shows and musical recitals.

The **youth hostel**, Oetzer Weg 25 (☎0521 22227), is 4km south of the center in an isolated location within the Teutoburger Wald; take tram #2 to its terminus, then bus #121, but note that the latter stops running soon after the evening rush hour. There are two **campgrounds**, both on the edge of the forest, at Vogelweide 9 (☎0521 450336) and Beckendorfstrasse (☎0521 3335). Centrally located **hotels** are almost entirely geared to business visitors; *Kaiser*, Schildescher Str. 47 (☎0521 81275), just to the north of the Hauptbahnhof, is the one exception, charging DM25 per head. The tourist office can supply lists of alternatives in the suburbs (there's a whole clutch in BRACKWEDE to the south), but you'd be better off looking for a room in a more congenial small town nearby, such as Lemgo or Detmold. One of the city's best **restaurants** is *Sparrenburg* within the castle; another good choice is *Im Bültmannshof*, Kurt-Schumacher-Str. 17a. The **Mitfahrzentrale** office is at Helmholtzstr. 26 (☎0521 68978).

Around Bielefeld

Almost adjoining Bielefeld to the southwest is **GÜTERSLOH**. This market town, with a population of 50,000, would hardly be worth mentioning were it not for the fact that it's the improbable headquarters of *Bertelsmann*, now firmly established as the largest publishing empire in the world, having overtaken its giant American rivals by means of a hawkish policy of acquiring other companies. There's a **youth hostel** here at Wiesenstr. 30 (☎05241 822362).

ENGER, 15km north of Bielefeld, to which it's connected by bus, is associated with the memory of **Widukind**, leader of the Saxon resistance to Charlemagne. After seven years of struggle, he was defeated in 785 and subsequently baptized, after which he's said to have founded the predecessor of the present **Stiftskirche**. His Renaissance sarcophagus, kept behind the church's carved high altar, is covered by a masterly late eleventh-century portrait slab. Copies of the valuable church treasures are on display in a small museum; the originals are in the Museum of Decorative Arts in the Schloss Charlottenburg, Berlin.

Just to the east of Enger is the old Hanseatic town of **HERFORD**. Though now best known for its excellent *Herforder* Pils, in the Middle Ages it was dubbed "Holy Herford" on account of the large number of monasteries and churches. Among these are the late Romanesque **Münster**, reckoned to be the earliest full-scale example of the characteristic Westphalian hall church style, and the Gothic **Johanneskirche** on Neuer Markt, with a glittering array of stained glass windows, and (as a necessary adjunct when the town embraced the Reformation) a full set of painted seventeenth-century woodwork—pulpit, galleries and pews—adorned with the emblems of the guilds who donated them. The town also possesses a number of old houses, the most notable of which are the **Riemenschneiderhaus** at Brüderstr. 6 and the **Bürgermeisterhaus** at Höckerstr. 4. In the latter the great architect Matthäus Daniel Pöpplemann, creator of many of the splendors of baroque Dresden, was born in 1662.

Minden

Minden is a mighty fortress,
A strong weapon and protection.
With Prussian fortresses, however, I'd
Prefer to have no connection.

So scoffed the libertarian Heinrich Heine, savagely parodying Luther's great Reformation hymn *Ein' feste Burg ist unser Gott*. **MINDEN**'s strategic importance, at an easily fordable point of the river Weser, has meant that military affairs have dominated its history. The old ramparts were converted into a full-scale fortress by the Swedes during the Thirty Years' War; it was the scene of a decisive battle in 1759 in which the British and Prussians defeated the French; and, during the Napoleonic Wars, it was equipped with the very latest defensive systems as a leading Prussian frontier town, a role it retained until this became superfluous with the unification of Germany in 1871. The city kept its historic appearance until the last war, when its strategic importance inevitably led to severe aerial bombardment.

Minden's role as a fortress meant it could not expand and industrialize, but its favorable geographical position led to its development as the hub of the German inland water transport system, and it's from this function that its main present-day attraction derives. In the northern part of the city, you'll find the **Wasserstrassenkreuz** (*Waterway Junction*) which is unique in Europe. Most riveting feature is the surrealistic **Kanalbrücke** (*Canal Bridge*), a 375-meter long aquatic overpass built between 1911 and 1914; it allows the *Mittellandkanal*—which stretches right across northern Germany, linking the Rhine with the Elbe—to pass directly over the Weser. The heart of the system is the fortress-like **Schachtschleuse** (*Great Lock*) which shifts 12,000 cubic meters of water while transferring ships from canal to river or vice versa in just seven minutes. It's under restoration until the end of 1989, with no access until then, but you can visit the exhibition hall alongside (Mon.–Sat. 9am–5pm, Sun. 9am–6pm; DM1.50) which explains the layout and working of the *Wasserstrassenkreuz* by means of models and diagrams. A series of paths enable you to explore the area on foot, but it's far more fun to take a **cruise**. Run by the *Mindener Fahrgastschiffahrt* (☎0571 41046; Weds., Thurs., Fri. 3pm, May–Sept. Sun. and holidays 10:15am, duration 90 min.; DM8), these leave from the jetty immediately opposite the Great Lock. Check locally for shorter trips; it's possible to combine a trip around Minden's waterways with a cruise down the Weser—see Hameln, *Chapter Six*.

The **Hauptbahnhof** is on the east side of the river; its situation, a good twenty minutes' walk from town, is explained by the fact that it was built as part of the Prussian fortifications. Along with the three small forts grouped in a semicircle around, it's one of the few survivors of that period, as the citizens had no more love for their citadel than did Heine, and dismantled it as soon as it was declared redundant. **Steam trains** run every second Sunday in summer to NAMMEN and HILLE. Each journey lasts about 45 minutes, and costs DM8 return (☎0521 58300 for farther information).

The Altstadt is dominated by the **Dom**, whose massive westwork, with two subsidiary towers glued like afterthoughts to the main belfry, is in the severest form of Romanesque. The main body of the building, however, is a hall church, erected in the late thirteenth century in a pure early Gothic style; this has a light and airy feel, thanks to the huge windows decorated with highly elaborate tracery. On the south transept wall is a frieze of Apostles, the remnant of a former Romanesque rood screen; from the same period is the bronze *Minden Crucifix*, the Dom's most important work of art. However, the one currently displayed here is a copy; the original is in the **Domschatz** in the *Haus am Dom* opposite (Tues., Thurs., Sat., and Sun. 10am–noon; Weds. and Fri. 3–5pm; free). Among many other valuable items, note three contrasting reliquaries to St. Peter, the Dom's patron saint: an eleventh-century gilded shrine, a fourteenth-century bust, and a sixteenth-century statuette of him attired as Pope.

Just beyond lies the Markt, whose north side is taken up by the **Rathaus**. Its lower story, featuring an arcaded passageway, is contemporary with the Dom; the upper part is late Renaissance. Continuing up the steps from here takes you to the best preserved part of the Altstadt, centered on Martinikirchhof. On this square are two survivors of the Prussian garrison buildings—the **Körnermagazin**, where weapons were stored, and the **Martinihaus**, which served as the bakery. Also here is the **Schwedenschänke**, used by the Swedish troops as their refectory during the Thirty Years' War. **St. Martini** itself is the pick of Minden's gaunt and blackened parish churches, with a dignified interior housing notable furnishings—late Gothic stalls, Renaissance pulpit, and wrought-iron font—and a magnificent organ, partly dating back to the sixteenth century.

Just off the square on Brüderstrasse is the **Alte Münze**, formerly the house of the master of the mint; today, less suitably, it's a Greek restaurant. A rare example of Romanesque civil architecture, it owes its survival to the fact that it was subsequently embellished according to the tastes of the time (with a stepped gable during the Gothic period, and an oriel window during the Renaissance). Mansions in the characteristic Weser Renaissance style are dotted all over the quarter—the finest are on Bäckerstrasse, Am Scharn, and Papenmarkt. The densest concentration, however, is on Ritterstrasse, where five houses have been adapted to contain the **Minden Museum** (Tues., Weds., and Fri. 10am–1pm and 2:30–5pm, Thurs. 10am–1pm and 2:30–6pm, Sat. 2:30–5pm, Sun. 11am–6pm; free). Displayed in two courtyards are fragments of sculptural decoration from buildings such as these; see in particular a wonderful *Story of Samson*. Upstairs, along with the usual folklore displays, there's a room devoted to the **Battle of Minden**. A turning point in the Seven Years' War, its outcome was to a large extent decided by a successful assault by the British infantry on the French cavalry, the first time such a rash reversal of roles had ever been attempted, even if it only happened through a misunderstanding of orders.

The **tourist office** is at Grosser Domhof 3 (Mon.–Weds. and Fri. 8am–1pm and 2–5pm, Thurs. 8am–1pm and 2–6pm, Sat. 9am–1pm; ☎0571 89385). Among the best places to **eat** and **drink** are *Domschänke* on Kleiner Domhof, and *Laterne* on Hahlerstrasse. Look out also for *Zum Fischbäcker* on Obermarktstrasse, which fries fish, and offers bargain lunchtime menus. If you want to spend the night in town, *Marienhöhe*, Marienglacis 45 (☎0571 22854) is by far the cheapest **hotel** in the center at DM30 per head. Other options tend to be farther out—an example is *Grashoff*, Bremer Str. 83 (☎0571 41834), charging DM26 for singles, DM48 for doubles; it's in the suburb of TODTENHAUSEN, where the Battle of Minden was fought.

Around Minden

There's a much wider choice of accommodation possibilities in **PORTA WESTFALICA** (*The Westphalian Gap*), a scattered holiday resort and spa 8km downstream, just one stop away on the train. Across the river from the Bahnhof is the **campground** (☎0571 72743; April–Oct. only). The **youth hostel** is at Kirchsiek 30 (☎0571 70250); turn right on leaving the Bahnhof, then first left, and continue straight ahead. There are also numerous **rooms** available in private houses for DM20 or less; a full list is available from the *Haus des Gastes* in the *Kurpark*. Porta Westfalica lies between the two ranges of the **Wiehengebirge** to the west and the **Wesergebirge** to the east. The former is crowned by the stolidly grandiose **monument to Kaiser Wilhelm I**, whose view is rivaled by the **Portakanzel** directly opposite. Higher up on the right bank side, you get the best view of all from the **television tower** on the Jakobsberg. Plenty of marked **nature trails** pass through both ranges.

The countryside to the **north and west of Minden**, on the other hand, is flat and ideal cycling country (bike rental available at the city's Hauptbahnhof). It's peppered with **windmills**—37 historic examples survive. Get hold of the glossy tourist-board brochure *Die Westfälische Mühlenstrasse* (English insert available), and the separate leaflet detailing when the mills are operating—this is done in rotation on weekend afternoons from April to October. Various **farms** in the area offer lodging from as little as DM19, or DM29 full board.

Lemgo

LEMGO, 12km north of Detmold and 25km east of Bielefeld, would be a strong contender in any competition to find the prettiest town in northern Germany. It scores heavily on two points—it's never been bombed, nor has it suffered from mass tourism. Many of the buildings from its sixteenth-century Hanseatic heyday survive, and are now immaculately cared for, with the merchant class which built them from the profits of foreign trade now replaced by a mixture of retailers, wealthy commuters (over half the population works elsewhere), and public entities. With its surprising vistas and architectural groupings, and the myriad of delicate decorative details on the buildings, it's as if the town had been specially made for the benefit of photographers.

The **Bahnhof**, on a small branch line from Bielefeld, is just to the south of the historic kernel of the city; most **buses** leave from the bays in front, but not the services to and from Detmold, which stop a couple of minutes' walk to the right along Paulinenstrasse. At the end of this road, turn right into Breitestrasse and you're immediately in one of Lemgo's finest thoroughfares, soon arriving at the spectacular **Hexenbürgermeisterhaus** (*Witches' Burgomaster House*) on the left hand side. The facade, with its elegantly tapering gables, its *Fall of Man* over the doorway, and its two quite different oriel windows (something of a Lemgo specialty) adorned with the Seven Cardinal Virtues, ranks as one of the supreme masterpieces of the joyous Weser Renaissance style. It was built in 1571, three years after the completion of the rest of the house, by a local man, **Hermann Wulf**, who was an uncommonly fine architect to judge from this and his other buildings in the town, but whose provinciality has denied him lasting fame. Originally commissioned by a merchant family, the house's present curious name derives from an occupant in a later, more morbid period, the notorious **Hermann Cothmann**. He was burgomaster of Lemgo at the height of the hysterical campaign against supposed witches between 1666 and 1681, apparently sentencing some ninety women to death. Inside, an above-average **local museum** (Tues.–Fri. and Sun. 10am–12:30pm and 1:30–5pm, Sat. 10am–1pm; DM1.50) appropriately includes a room devoted to gruesome instruments of torture, from the inquisition stool with its seat of protruding nails, through thumb and leg screws, to less brutal items such as the barrel which formed a moveable version of the stocks. However ridiculous these now seem, it's worth reflecting just how much suffering they caused, and in an age still basking in the glow of the Renaissance. On a happier note, there are rooms furnished in period style, and an exhibition on a considerably more enlightened Lemgo citizen of the same period, **Engelbert Kämpfer**. A pioneering traveler in Russia, Persia, Java, and Japan, Kämpfer had deluxe accounts of his journeys printed and published in his native town, which was then a leading center of book production.

Just off Breitestrasse, down Stiftstrasse, is the **Marienkirche**, the Gothic hall church of a convent which was suppressed when Lemgo went over to the Reformation. It has one of the richest musical traditions in Germany, so any concert will be worth hearing—there's a small international festival in the first week of June. The choir is celebrated, the **swallow's nest organ** even more so. Built between 1587 and 1613, initially by a Dutchman, and then by two brothers from Hamburg, it's rated among the sweetest-sounding instruments in Europe. If you aren't lucky enough to hear it, the woodwork is still an artistic treasure in its own right, although sadly stripped of its original bright polychromy. Also from the Renaissance is the **font**, the work of a local sculptor, **Georg Crossmann**, with unashamedly sensual figures of the Four Christian Virtues. Behind it are statues of the nobleman Otto Zur Lippe and his wife, masterpieces of late fourteenth-century funerary art.

Beyond the end of Breitestrasse, past the so-called **Squires' Houses**, you reach the **Wippermannsches Haus**, the only one of the great merchant buildings in the extravagant late Gothic style, which must have been due to the archaic tastes of its owner, as it's a few years younger than the Hexenbürgermeisterhaus. Nowadays it houses the **tourist office** (Mon.–Fri. 9am–5:30pm, Sat. 9am–noon; ☎05261 213347); pick up their brochure in English which has a map and good photographs. It's then just a few paces to the **Markt**, one of Germany's finest squares, lined by a wealth of superb structures from the fourteenth century onwards. The **Rathaus** complex on the east side represents the changing building fashions in its photogenic jumble of arcades, pinnacles, and gables. Its northern corner, the old **Apothecary**, is still used as a pharmacy, and has a magnificent oriel window. The gossamer carvings, again the work of Crossmann, include a frieze of ten famous scientists with their engraved words of wisdom, while the columns of the upper windows show the Five Senses. Around the corner, the same artist had previously adorned Hermann Wulf's elegant loggia with a frieze of the Seven Liberal Arts. The south side of the square is fronted by the early seventeenth-century **Ball House**; beside it is the sixteenth-century **Zeughaus**, its rear wall painted in psychedelic zigzags. You won't find photographs of the west side of the Markt in tourist brochures, and for good reason—the effect of its stately Renaissance edifices was long spoiled by two unworthy later buildings. In the 1970s, it was decided to demolish the latter and replace them with structures in a style that was modernist, yet imbued with motifs from Lemgo's past. The result won a prestigious architectural prize, though something less stridently obtrusive might have fitted in better. There can be no complaints, however, about the northern frontage of the square, which also forms part of Lemgo's central axis, Mittelstrasse. Appropriately, this is the street most evocative of the Hansa; half-timbering was used extensively, and some of the mansions have nicknames deriving from their decoration, such as **House of the Planets** and **Sundial House**. The buildings on the right also have handsome backs, forming part of the court of the Gothic **Nicolaikirche**, whose twin towers were later varied by the addition of contrasting lead spires. Its interior, a characteristic hall design, has an assortment of artworks in different styles, including another font by Crossmann.

To see a house like no other in Lemgo (or anywhere else), continue to the end of Mittelstrasse, then straight ahead down Bismarckstrasse to Hamelner Strasse, where you'll find the **Junkerhaus** (Tues.–Fri. and Sun. 10am–5pm, Sat. 10am–1pm; DM1.50). It's the obsessive single-handed creation of a totally eccentric local architect, painter, and sculptor, **Karl Junker** (1850–1912), who was determined to bequeath his own vision of a dream house as a modern counterpart to the sixteenth century mansions he knew so well. From the outside, it looks like the witch's cottage from *Hansel and Gretel*, while the interior is spookier than anything Hammer House of Horror ever produced. The sinuous and virtuoso monochrome woodcarvings are indeed the stuff of dreams, albeit nightmarish fantasies, produced by a man who was a surrealist before such a movement existed. Returning down Hamelner Strasse, go sharp left into Pagenhelle before the start of Bismarckstrasse; you shortly come to **Schloss Brake**, a moated Renaissance castle partly built by Wulf, scheduled to open soon as a museum.

From here, the **campground** (April–Nov. only; ☎05261 14858 or 12206) can be reached by following the path of the river back towards the town. There's no hostel; the tourist office has a list of **rooms** in private houses from about DM20 per head, although these are all situated in the outskirts. The cheapest **hotels** with a central location are *Bahnhofswaage*, Am Bahnhof (☎05261 3525) at DM28 for a single, DM44 a double; *Zum Landsknecht*, Herforder Str. 177 (☎05261 68264) from DM25 per head, whose restaurant does French-style cuisine; *Stadt Lemgo*, Paulinenstr. 29 (☎05261 4695) and *Hansa Hotel*, Breitestr. 14 (☎05261 4889) which both charge upwards of DM30 per person. **Cafés** and **restaurants**, including all the usual ethnic varieties, abound throughout the town center.

Detmold and the Southern Teutoburger Wald

DETMOLD, capital of the former Lippe Principality, makes an obvious base for seeing the varied attractions of the **SOUTHERN TEUTOBURGER WALD**. If you're understandably baffled by the competing claims of Germany's innumerable forests, most of which seem to offer much the same as any other, then this is truly one with a difference, adding extra natural, historical, and artistic delights to the usual fare of wooded trails, for which there's such a national penchant. An old jingle, quoted ad infinitum in tourist brochures and on billboards all over town, describes Detmold as *eine wunderschöne Stadt*. That ranks as something of an exaggeration, but it's an agreeable place nonetheless, with a far more laid-back approach to life than is normal in Germany. Arriving at either the **Bahnhof** (on the line between Bielefeld and the important junction of Altenbeken) or the **bus station** alongside, turn left along Bahnhofstrasse, then right into Paulinenstrasse; the largely pedestrianized historic area lies a short walk down to the left. The **tourist office** (Mon.–Thurs. 9am–noon and 1–5pm, Fri. 9am–5pm, Sat. 9am–noon; ☎05231 767328) is located in the Rathaus just off the Markt on Langestrasse. They have lists of the extensive choice of **private rooms** available all over the surrounding area, which cost from as little as DM15. Most of these are only practical if you've got your own transportation; the solitary one in Detmold itself is *Pillath* at Nachtigallenweg 21 (☎05231 25709), still a good bargain at DM25 per person. The cheapest **hotels** are *Hermann*, Woldemarstr. 17 (☎05231 22527) at DM30 for a single, DM56 a double, and *Meier*, Bahnhofstr. 9a (☎05231 33007 or 23026) at DM30 per head. There's a **youth hostel** at Schirrmannstr. 49 (☎05231 24739) right on the edge of town; from Paulinenstrasse, turn right into Freilingrathstrasse, then left into Brahmsstrasse, and follow its continuation, Schützenberg, to the end.

Langestrasse and the streets around, such as Bruchstrasse, Scülerstrasse, Krummestrasse and Exterstrasse, are lined with large half-timbered **old houses**, many now containing the most obvious places to **eat** and **drink**, interspersed with imposing stone buildings of the Wilhelmine epoch. Easily the most attractive street is the venerable and smaller-scale Adolfstrasse, running parallel to and east of Langestrasse. North of the Markt is a green space centered on the **Residenzschloss** (guided tours daily April–Oct. every half-hour 9:30am–noon and 2–5pm, Nov.–March at 10am, 11am, 2pm and 3pm; DM4; leaflet in English available), which is surrounded by water on three sides. The keep of the medieval fortress was incorporated into the present Renaissance structure, which was progressively shorn of its defensive features over the years. It remains in the possession of the descendants of the counts (later princes) of Lippe who built it; unfortunately, their attitude to visitors is extremely high-handed. Not only are you shunted around as quickly as possible and treated in a condescending way by the lackeys, you're also subjected to ludicrous restrictions such as being forbidden to photograph the courtyard from ground level (though you can later do so from an upstairs window. The interior is not what you'd expect from outside; its rooms were transformed in the eighteenth and nineteenth centuries according to the tastes of the time, but their most valuable adornment is a superb set of seventeenth-century Brussels tapestries of *The Life of Alexander the Great*, woven from cartoons made by the great French designer Charles Le Brun. From here, the **Landesmuseum** (Tues.–Fri. 9am–12:30pm and 2–5:30pm, Sat. 9am–12:30pm, Sun. 10am–5:30pm; DM2) is reached down Ameide, to the rear of the Schloss. It's housed in two buildings, with natural history in one, archaeology, local history, and folklore in the other. The last-named includes a number of reconstituted period rooms, and comprehensive displays on the history of fashion and on local agriculture, incorporating a rebuilt tithe-barn and granary.

This makes a good prelude to the spectacular **Open-Air Museum** (April–Oct. Tues.–Sun. 9am–6pm; DM3), the most important in Germany, which is being laid out at the southern side of the town; to reach it, go in a straight line down the Allee, the continuation of Langestrasse. When complete (which will not be for several years) it will comprise 168 redundant original buildings from rural Westphalia; currently over ninety are in place. These are grouped together according to region, thus giving a clear picture of the different construction styles. As a highlight, there will be three complete simulated villages, although only that from the Paderborn area exists as yet; other parts of the province are represented by a more modest selection, generally constructed round a large manor house. Apart from farmsteads and workshops of diverse kinds, you can see watermills and windmills, humble privys, wayside chapels and a complete school. The whole way of life associated with these buildings is preserved as well—thus the traditional crafts of weaving, spinning, pottery, milling, and forging are demonstrated, farmyard animals are reared, and the gardens are planted to give a practical yield of vegetables. Several hours are needed to do justice to the museum; reasonably priced lunches are available at the eighteenth-century inn *Zum Wilden Mann* on the main street of the Paderborn village, less substantial fare at *Tiergartenkrug* near the Tecklenburg and Minden group of houses. If you're attracted by this sort of presentation, catch a bus to **OERLINGHAUSEN**, some 15km west, which has an **Archaeological Open-Air Museum** (April–Oct. Tues.–Sun. 9am–noon and 1:30–6pm, Nov.–March Tues.–Sun. 9am–noon and 1:30–5pm; DM3). Here the exhibits aren't original buildings, but plausible reconstructions of the type of dwellings inhabited from the Stone Age until early medieval times.

Four of the **Teutoburger Wald**'s top sights are within 10km of Detmold; in a crunch, it's possible to see all in a day, following a southerly route. Firstly, there's what might be regarded as Germany's nearest equivalent of the Statue of Liberty, the **Hermannsdenkmal** (daily April–Oct. 9am–6:30pm, Nov.–March 9am–4:30pm; DM1), situated on the **Grotenburg** to the southwest of the town; two buses go out daily, or it can be reached on foot by gently ascending paths from the suburb of HIDDESEN. The monument commemorates **Arminius** (*Hermann*), a warrior prince of the Cherusci tribe, originally allies of the Romans. Having served for three years in the imperial army, he became wise to the fact that, by stealthy means, the Germanic peoples were in danger of being subjugated in the same way as the Gauls. In A.D. 9 he inflicted a crushing defeat on the Roman army in the Teutoburger Wald, using techniques akin to modern guerilla warfare. He then tried to forge an alliance with the southern Germanic tribes, which might have spelt real disaster for the Empire, but was frustrated by their quisling leadership. Nevertheless, two more Roman campaigns to subdue Germania were repelled, leading them to abandon the attempt. The hero was murdered by his own in-laws in A.D. 21 and was forgotten for centuries, only to be rediscovered and eulogized by the Romantic movement, who saw him not only as a great liberator, but also (rather fancifully) as the first man with the vision of a united Germany, which was at long last to be achieved. It was decided to erect a huge monument to him as near as possible to the scene of his great victory, although the completion of the project was entirely due to the single-minded dedication of the architect–sculptor **Ernst von Bandel**, who worked at it on and off from 1838 to 1875, according to the availability of funds. Resting on a colonnaded base, the monument is crowned with an idealized vision in copper of the hero brandishing his sword on high; the total height to the tip of the sword is 53.44 meters, and the figure weighs a measly 169,681lb. From the platform there's a superb **view** over the whole range of the Teutoburger Wald.

Following Denkmalstrasse you descend in less than 2km to the first of two ornithological treats, the **Vogelpark** (*Bird Park*; variable date in March/April–Oct. 9am–6pm daily; DM4) with over 2000 varieties from all over the world, from miniature hens hardly bigger than insects to the large South American nandu. Particularly impressive is the collection of parrots and cockatoos, showing off a kaleidoscopic range of colors, and sufficiently domesticated to be left uncaged. From here, you can follow the footpath to the right and continue in a straight line to the **Adlerwarte** (*Eagle Watch*; daily 8:30am–6pm, or until dusk in winter; DM3) in BERLEBECK. This aerie, commanding a fine panorama over the forest, serves as a breeding station and clinic for birds of prey, with around ninety of these magnificent creatures kept here permanently. Displayed on chains or in cages are all kinds of eagles—imperial, golden, prairie, sea, bald, martial, and the enormous and rare harpy—as well as falcons, hawks, kites, buzzards, vultures, condors, griffons, and various breeds of owls. The site was specially chosen because of its suitability for **free flight**, and the demonstrations of this (April–Oct. 11am and 3pm, Nov.–March 11am and 2:30pm) are a memorable experience not to be missed. There are three directions the bird can choose to ascend; it then glides out of sight for a while before returning to make a flawless swoop on the bait on the hand of the falconer, whose every movement it can follow from as far as 2km away. The flight of several different breeds is demonstrated, but only one eagle is sent up at a time, as this bird guards its airspace so jealously that it attacks any rival.

The **Externsteine**, another 3km south just before the town of HORN-BAD MEINBERG, are a jagged clump of sandstone rocks set by an artificial lake, a striking contrast to the wooded landscape to be found all around. It's one of Germany's most evocative sites, with origins lost in the twilight world. The pregnant sense of mystery is increased by the enigmatic mixture of natural and man-made features, whose precise meaning and significance has teased and baffled generations of scholars. Adorning the bulky rock at the far right is a magnificent, large **twelfth-century relief** of *The Descent from the Cross*, which was carved on the spot, making it quite unlike any other known sculpture of the period. Although Romanesque in style, it's imbued with the hierarchical Byzantine spirit, one of the few German works of art, illuminated manuscripts apart, so influenced. Some limbs have been lost, but its state of preservation is otherwise remarkable. Directly below is a worn carving, probably representing Adam and Eve entwined around the serpent. To the side is a series of caves, now closed off; one of these bears an inscription saying it was consecrated as a chapel in 1115. There's also a stairway leading up to a viewing platform at the top. The next rock, fronted by an open-air pulpit, retains its natural peak, below which is a roofless chapel with a circular window exactly aligned to catch the sunrise on the summer solstice. It's too upright to accommodate a staircase, but you can ascend from the top of the stumpy rock to the left by means of a little bridge bent like a bow; from the ground it looks precarious, but is totally secure. The fourth rock, bearing a plaque depicting the coat of arms of the counts of Lippe, is again crowned with apparent danger, in this case a large stone which seems ready to fall down, but which is actually fastened with iron hooks, following repeated unsuccessful attempts to dislodge it.

Many pundits are convinced that the Externsteine served as a focus of pagan worship (although the dates proposed vary enormously); others maintain that the site's religious origins go back no farther than the twelfth century, and that it's a re-creation of the holy places of Jerusalem, inspired by Crusaders' tales. Part of the charm of the place is that firm evidence for such theories remains tantalizingly elusive. What's known for sure is that it was an anchorite hermitage throughout medieval times; it then passed to the local counts, serving successively as a fortress, a pleasure palace, and a prison, undergoing many alterations in the process, before being restored to its present form (assumed to be the original) early last century.

Höxter

HÖXTER, about 45km southeast of Detmold, is the easternmost town in Westphalia. Lower Saxony is soon entered if you follow the course of the Weser River, whether downstream to Hameln or upstream to Münden, two places which are far closer to it in feel than anywhere in its own province.

The main claim on your attention is the once-powerful monastery of **Corvey**, just over 1km from the town center, and reached by either following the river eastward, or going in a straight line down Corbiestrasse. A ninth-century Carolingian foundation, it was a famous center of scholarship, with its greatest legacy being *The History of the Saxons*, written around 975 by the monk-chronicler **Widukind** (not to be confused with Charlemagne's long-standing opponent of the same name). He gave the newly conquered barbarian race an appropriately grand origin as veterans of Alexander the Great's army, and vividly related their story right up to his own day. The **Abteikirche** (daily 9:30am–1pm and 2–6pm; DM0.70) actually retains the great westwork of the original building, one of the few pieces of architecture of this period to have survived anywhere in Europe. The towers and the gallery between them are twelfth-century modifications, but inside you can see the solemn entrance hall with the *Kaisersaal* above, surviving much as the early emperors would have known them, except that the organ now blocks the view downstairs. In any case, the church they looked down on was so badly ravaged in the Thirty Years' War that it had to be replaced by a completely new building, which dates from 1667–71. Although normally described as baroque, the architecture is Gothic in every respect, although this style was by then a total anachronism. In contrast, the complete set of painted wood furnishings are so much of their own day, with no later intrusions in evidence, that it's easy to feel transported three centuries back in time.

To the side of the church is the extensive complex of monastic buildings, built a generation later in the plain baroque favored in northern Germany. After the Napoleonic secularization it became a ducal **Schloss**, and is now a museum (April–Sept. daily 9am–6pm; DM3). Temporary exhibitions are featured, and there are displays on folklore and local history, but you're likely to derive most pleasure simply from being allowed to roam loose through umpteen rooms. On the upper floor, the *Festsaal* forms an elegant setting for classical concerts by star international artists in May and June; in the adjacent rooms are displayed some of the 80,000 volumes from the abbey's famous library. From 1860 until his death fourteen years later, the poet **Heinrich August Hoffmann von Fallersleben** served as their custodian, and there's an exhibition on his work. He's best known for what soon became the national anthem of a united Germany, *Das Lied der Deutschen*, as set to the finest piece of music ever used for such purposes, Haydn's stately and spacious *Emperor's Hymn.** The *Schloss Restaurant* offers some of the best food in town, and is reasonably priced, provided you stick to the set menus.

---

* Its opening line *Deutschland, Deutschland über alles* became notorious under the Nazis, who were unaware that the melody was based on a Croatian folksong, and was thus part of the hated and "inferior" Slav culture. In reality, there's nothing sinister about the words, which are liberal in sentiment; what might seem to be an assertion of national superiority is actually a clarion call to abandon the petty feuding of the old states in favor of German unity. The third stanza remains the national anthem of the Federal Republic, and recently there were moves to reinstate the first verse in pious anticipation of the reunification of the country. Alas, the frontiers delineated—"from the Maas to the Memel"—are very out of date: the latter is now in the Soviet Union.

The center of Höxter itself is dominated by the twin towers of the red sandstone **Kilianikirche**, a Romanesque building clearly modeled on Corvey; inside is a Renaissance pulpit adorned with fine alabaster reliefs. Otherwise, the town is notable for the prevalence of **half-timbered houses**, which include the mid-sixteenth-century **Küsterhaus** facing the church, in which the **tourist office** (Mon.–Fri. 8am–1pm, 2–5:30pm, Sat. 9am–noon; ☎05271 63244) is now situated. Beyond is the **Rathaus**, a late Renaissance structure from the following century, adorned with octagonal turret and an oriel. It's rivaled in splendor by the earlier **Dechanei** (*Deanery*), an asymmetrical double house reached down Marktstrasse. Although it's the busiest street, Westerbachstrasse is astonishingly well preserved, offering a complete panorama of half-timbering down the centuries, from late Gothic (e.g. no. 43, *Haus Ohrmann*) to neoclassical (eg no. 40). There's little doubt that the Renaissance buildings steal the show, particularly *Tilly Haus* (no. 33–37), *Corveyer Hof* (no. 29) and *Altes Brauhaus* (no. 28). The last-named remains Höxter's most famous **beer hall**, specializing in *vom heissen Stein* dishes. Other old-world pubs include *Adam-und-Eva-Haus* on Stummrigenstrasse, originally a Renaissance mansion, and *Strullenkrug* on Hennekenstrasse. The latter building is early nineteenth-century, but the site, with the largest beer garden in town, has a much longer tradition. Facing it is Rodiewerkstrasse, with another varied collection of old houses of various dates.

The **Bahnhof** is surnamed Rathaus with good reason; it's just a stone's throw from the center, right beside the Weser River. Services on this branchline are slow; a pleasant alternative (May–early Oct. only) is to travel to HAMELN or MÜNDEN by **boat**; there's a departure point near the Bahnhof and another at Corvey. The **campground** (☎05271 2589) has a good location on the right bank of the Weser opposite the town. Alternatively, there's a **youth hostel** at An der Wilhelmshöhe 59 (☎05271 2233): from the far end of Westerbachstrasse, cross over to Gartenstrasse; after a couple of minutes' walk, turn left and follow the road to the end. **Hotel rooms** are all reasonably priced; even the aforementioned *Corveyer Hof* (☎05271 2272), the classiest option, need cost no more than DM36 per head. *Braunschweiger Hof*, Corbiestr. 5 (☎05271 2236), *Zum Landsknecht*, Stummrigestr. 17 (☎05271 2477) and *Zum Weserstrand*, Stummrigestr. 38 (☎05271 2477) all charge around DM28 per person. A room in a private house may cost as little as DM16; the tourist office has a complete list. The main **festival**, as in many other towns in the area, is the *Schützenfest* in early July.

travel details

Trains

From Cologne to Aachen (3 an hour; 45 min.), Bonn (4; 20 min.), Düsseldorf (frequent; 25 min)., Siegen (1; 1hr 35 min.), Wuppertal (1; 30 min.), Hagen (2; 50 min.).

From Düsseldorf to Mönchengladbach (frequent; 30 min.), Wuppertal (2; 40 min.), Duisburg (frequent; 15 min.), Kleve (1; 1 hr. 25 min.), Dortmund (frequent; 1 hr.).

From Kleve to Xanten (1; 40 min.), Kalkar (1; 10 min.).

From Dortmund to Essen (frequent; 25 min.), Bochum (frequent; 10 min.), Hagen (2; 30 min.), Münster (2; 30 min.).

From Bielefeld to Lemgo (1; 1 hr.), Detmold (1; 1 hr. 15 min.).

From Münster to Düsseldorf (2; 1 hr. 20 min.), Hagen (1; 1 hr. 5 min.), Wuppertal (1; 1 hr. 25 min.).

CHAPTER SIX

BREMEN AND LOWER SAXONY

The Land of **LOWER SAXONY** (*NIEDERSACHSEN*) only came into being in 1946, courtesy of the British military authorities. In forging this new province, the former **Kingdom of Hannover**—which had shared its ruler with Britain between 1714 and 1837, but which had later been subsumed into Prussia—was used as a basis. To it were added the two separate **Duchies of Braunschweig and Oldenburg**, plus the minute but hitherto seemingly indestructible **Principality of Schaumburg-Lippe**.

In spite of this diverse patchwork, and some anomalies (**Ostfriesland** is very much an area apart, while **Osnabrück** properly belongs in Westphalia), the Land actually has strong historical antecedents. It forms the approximate area inhabited by the Saxon tribes, other than the Westphalians, at the time of the Roman Empire and the succeeding Dark Ages. Thus, it more accurately bears the name "Saxony" than the large chunk of eastern Germany (all now within the GDR) which was so designated from the Middle Ages right up to the post-World War II settlement. In accordance with the general north-south divide, the Reformation took strong root in most of Lower Saxony. **Politically**, however, it's very finely balanced, and is something of a national barometer, with the CDU (just as is the case at federal level) holding a very precarious grip on power at the moment.

Geographically, Lower Saxony is highly diverse. It contains much of West Germany's sparse provision of **coastline**, behind which stretches a flat landscape, often below sea-level. Further south is the monotonous stretch of the North German Plain, but this gives way to the heathland known as the **Lüneburger Heide** to the east, and to highland countryside farther south, in the shape of the hilly region around the **River Weser** and the gentle wooded slopes of the **Harz** mountains.

That Lower Saxony is probably one of the least known parts of Germany to English-speaking visitors is in some ways surprising. Apart from the Hanoverian connection, there are long-standing trading and dynastic bonds with Britain, while the island of **Helgoland** was actually once part of the United Kingdom. Furthermore, one of literature's great comic characters, Baron Munchausen of **Bodenwerder**, was originally introduced to the world through a book written in English. Other semi-historical figures from Lower Saxony are if anything even more familiar, especially the rat-catching Pied Piper, and the jester Till Eulenspiegel. The province is also associated with another famous (and very German) legend—the witches' sabbath of *Walpurgisnacht*.

Lower Saxony is the second most extensive Land after Bavaria, but only fourth most populous, with the lowest population density of all. None of its cities is as large as the old Hanseatic port of **Bremen**, an enclave within the province, but a Land in its own right, in continuation of its age-long tradition as a free state. Otherwise, there are just two cities with a population of over 200,000. Much the larger of these is the state capital, **Hannover**, which only really came to promi-

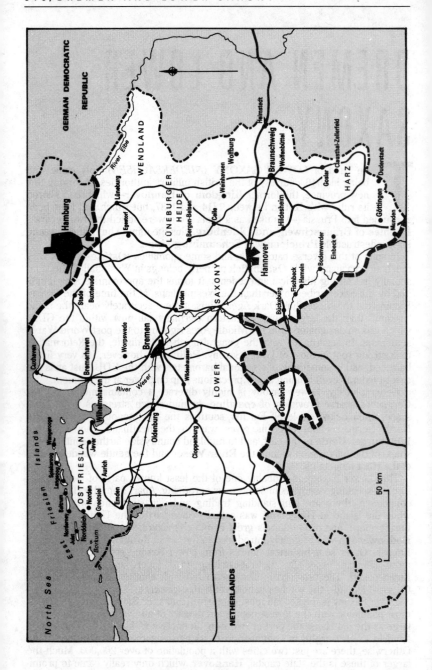

nence in the seventeenth century, and which is to be visited more for its museums and magnificent gardens than for its monuments. **Braunschweig** is altogether more venerable, and still preserves considerable reminders of its halcyon period at the end of the twelfth century.

The province's smaller towns and cities present a fascinating contrast. **Hildesheim**, with its grandiloquent Romanesque architecture (revolutionary in its day, and of enormous influence throughout Europe) is the most outstanding from an artistic point of view. **Wolfenbüttel** is an early example of a planned town, and, with **Celle** and **Bückeburg**, is among the few places in Germany to be strongly marked by Italian-inspired Renaissance and Mannerist styles. Very different is the exuberantly ornate architecture of the archaic Weser Renaissance style, which reached its peak in and around the Pied Piper's stamping ground of **Hameln**. A mining town quite unlike any other in the world can be seen at **Goslar**, while **Göttingen** boasts one of Germany's most famous universities, and thus the liveliest nightlife in the province. **Einbeck**, home of *Bockbier*, is a reminder of the strength of the brewing tradition in these parts, and beer aficionados will generally find themselves spoilt for choice.

Getting around is seldom a problem, thanks to the usual efficient network of buses and trains. The only possible exceptions to this rule are in the Lüneburger Heide (in much of which there's a ban on fuelled transit) and in traveling to and from the islands off the coast, where ferry prices are relatively expensive.

BREMEN AND NORTHERN LOWER SAXONY

Throughout much of its past **Bremen** was governed not by the nobility, but by its merchants, as a free city state—a sharp contrast to most of the three hundred or so German principalities, some quite tiny, that were run by feudal barons right into the nineteenth century. Those centuries of self-government and economic power have marked the character of the city and its inhabitants. There's a certain air of self-assuredness, superiority even, and pride in their political independence that marks out the Bremen people—a hangover that's inextricably linked to the town's **Hanseatic** past. Bremen still governs itself (and its deep-water harbor of **Bremerhaven**, 60km north), as the **smallest state in the Federal Republic**. It's the country's oldest and second largest port too, safe from the North Sea on the banks of the River Weser. Imports of exotic commodities from far-flung destinations—cotton, coffee, tobacco, tropical fruits, and cereals—coupled with the export trade in wool and wood have been the foundation of Bremen's status (still maintained today) as one of Germany's most prosperous cities. The hinterland is entirely within Lower Saxony, and the city makes the obvious base for exploring the northern part of this province.

Bremen

Of the cluster of North German cities—Hamburg, Hannover, and Bremen—it's **BREMEN** which is the most manageable. Though a city, it has an atmosphere reminiscent of a small country town, lacking the commercial buzz of Hamburg, and the ugly redevelopment of Hannover. In one or two days you can get a good impression of the place: the former fortifications where a windmill still stands, almost in the center of town; the Schnoorviertel, crammed with former fisher-family houses; the bold, mural-painted backs of houses near the river; the elegant villas of the last century. Right in the center of town, the darkened, beautiful interior of the Dom and the sumptuous Rathaus shouldn't be missed.

Some History

It was in the eighth century that the Holy Roman Emperor Charlemagne dispatched the Anglo-Saxon Willehad to the Weser to convert the Saxons there to Christianity; seven years later a bishop of Bremen was appointed, and in 789 the first church was built where the Dom stands today. Another two hundred years on, the city was granted free market rights, giving independent merchants the same **trading rights** as those working on behalf of the crown, a vital step for Bremen's economic expansion. The city was an important center for the church in the eleventh century, and over the centuries saw considerable conflict between civic and ecclesiastical interests. In 1358 Bremen joined the Hanseatic League and, having survived a virtual cessation of trade during the Thirty Years' War, was granted free city status in 1646.

This was renewed in 1949 when Bremen, together with Bremerhaven, was declared a Land of the Federal Republic of Germany. Since then, it's had a reputation for being the most politically radical part of the country, with the SPD having held power without a break. One of their most significant acts was the establishment of a university, which has set up an alternative, multi-disciplinary curriculum in opposition to the normal conservative, highly specialized bent of the country's higher educational system. In 1979, Bremen was the scene of the key breakthrough by the Green Party—for the first time, they achieved a large enough share of the vote to enter a regional parliament, and successfully used this as a springboard towards becoming a major force in national politics.

Getting Around and Finding Somewhere to Stay

The **Hauptbahnhof** is just to the north of the city center; immediately outside stands the **tourist office** (Mon.–Thurs. 8am–8pm, Fri. 8am–10pm, Sat. 8am–6pm, Sun. 9:30am–3:30pm; ☎36361), best source of information for what's on in town, and with a room booking service. Pivotal **tramline** is the #5, which starts from the airport, heads close to the Rathaus and Hauptbahnhof, and runs northwards parallel to the Bürgerpark. A **24-hour go-anywhere ticket** is available for DM6; this and other tickets may be bought at the booth outside the Hauptbahnhof.

Bremen's **youth hostel** is very well located in the western part of the old town at Kalkstr. 6 (☎171369), and there's a good central **campground**, *Internationale Campingplatz Freie Hansestadt Bremen*, Am Stadtwaldsee 1 (☎212002), on the north side of the Bürgerpark close to the university; buses #28 to Stadtwaldsee or #23 to the university go in the right direction. Another budget option is the *Seemannsheim* at Jippen 1 (☎18361); sailors are given priority, but there's seldom any problem getting a room. Women are accommodated in more salubrious and slightly more expensive quarters than men. The densest and most convenient cluster of **hotels** downtown is near the Hauptbahnhof; not suprisingly these are expensive, with prices ranging from DM45 upwards per person. Less costly but still fairly close to the center is *Heinisch*, Wachmannstr. 26 (☎342925; on #5 tramline, or 10 minutes' walk from Hauptbahnhof), singles DM29, doubles DM64. Just east of the Ostertor are: *Weidmann*, Am Schwarzen Meer 35 (☎494055), singles from DM29, doubles DM50; *Kosch*, Celler Str. 4 (☎447101), singles from DM35, doubles DM65. Across the Weser, but not too remote, is *Haus Hohenlohe*, Buntentorsteinweg 86/88 (☎554743), with singles from DM35, doubles DM55.

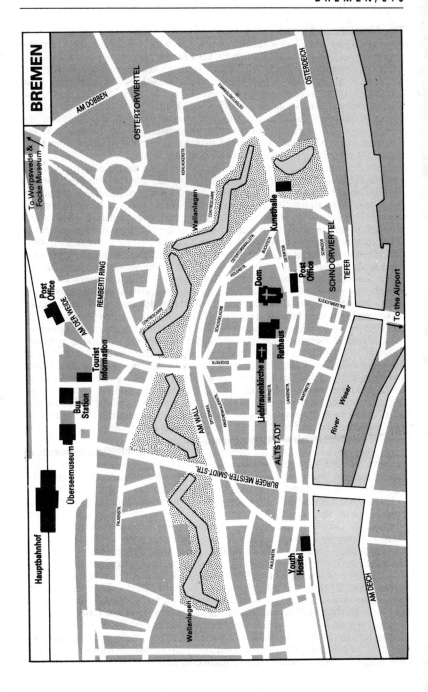

BREMEN

To Worpswede &
Focke Museum

AM DOBBEN

OSTERTORVIERTEL

OSTERTORSTEINWEG

OSTERDEICH

Wallanlagen

KOHLHOKERSTR.

CONTRESCARPE

Kunsthalle

SCHNOORVIERTEL

OSTERTORSWALLSTR.

BUCHTSTR.

OSTERTOR

Post
Office

REMBERTI RING

AM DER WEIDE

Post
Office

CONTRESCARPE

VIOLENSTR.

Dom

TIEFER

SCHNOOR

BALGEBRÜCKSTR.

To the Airport

Hauptbahnhof

Übersemuseum

Bus
Station

Tourist
Information

SCHÜSSELKORB

Rathaus

Liebfrauenkirche

OBERNSTR.

SODERSTR.

AM WALL

SPIETENWEG

KNOCHENHAUERSTR.

LANGENSTR.

MARTINISTR.

ALTSTADT

River Weser

FALKENSTR.

BÜRGER MEISTER-SMIDT-STR.

Wallanlagen

FALKENSTR.

Youth
Hostel

AM DEICH

The Altstadt and Around

Although more than half a million people live here, Bremen doesn't give the impression of being a large city—partly because the main area of historical interest is the **Altstadt**, on the Weser's northeast bank. The former fortification that surrounded it, the **Wall**, is now an area of green park, with a zigzagging moat forming a curve around the perimeter of the old city. To the north, the **Ostertorviertel** (known as *das Viertel*—"the Quarter") was the first part of the city to be built outside those city walls, and is today the liveliest part of town, the area to head for at night. North of the Hauptbahnhof, the **Burgerpark** and **Schwachhausen** areas are worthy of a stroll for their many streets of villas, each discreetly advertising Bremen's turn-of-the-century wealth.

From the Hauptbahnhof, getting to the old town is a simple matter of walking straight ahead, and crossing the bridge over the Wall into the pedestrian zone. A life-size bronze of some pigs, a swineherd, and his dog marks the beginning of the Sögestrasse ("Sow Street"), along which swine used to be driven to the market. This is Bremen's main shopping street, and, as a standard Euro-shopping precinct, it's not particularly inspiring—many of the old shops have given way to the ubiquitous chains. The single place worth stopping off for is Bremen's bastion of *Kaffee und Kuchen*, the *Café Knigge*, up on the right-hand side. Left at the top is the **Liebfrauenkirche**, a lovely hall church with contrasting Romanesque and Gothic towers that's swathed by the flower market, with a number of booths around its walls—the flashy built-in sausage stand is the most incongruous.

The **Marktplatz** ahead is relatively small, and is dominated by the **Rathaus**, whose highly ornate **facade**—rich in moldings, life-size figures and bas-reliefs, and with the undersides of its large rounded arches set with enormous "jewels'—is in Weser Renaissance style. It was added to the original Gothic structure between 1609 and 1612, two hundred years after the latter was first built. One of the most splendid of north Germany's buildings, it fortunately survived World War II unscathed. You can only visit the interior as part of a guided tour—usually at 10am, 11am, and noon daily except winter weekends, and it's worth it to see the extremes of Bremen's civic pride: rooms awash with gilded wallpaper and busy, ornate carving. Downstairs the Ratskeller is as usual pricey, but wine buffs can buy a glass or two from the cellar's collection of 600 vintages, some stored in the eighteenth-century barrels which double as partitions.

On the left as you face the Rathaus is a ten-meter-high stone **statue of Roland**, nephew of Charlemagne, who brandishes the sword of justice and carries a shield bearing the inscription (in the *Plattdeutsch* dialect): "Freedom do I give you openly." Erected by the burghers in 1404 as a symbol of Bremen's independence from its archbishop, he's the city's traditional protector; as long as Roland stands, they say, Bremen will remain free. In 1989 he was de-Nazified, when a lead casket containing Nazi documents, a Hitler-era time-capsule placed there in 1938, was removed. Poor Roland now spends his time staring at the much-disputed modern facade of the *Haus der Bürgerschaft* (Parliament Building), one of the ugliest edifices ever to disgrace a German town center.

A happier postwar addition to the square is the bronze group of the **Bremen Town Band** by the leading local sculptor, Gerhard Marcks. Rising like a pyramid, it shows a cock standing on a cat standing on a dog standing on a donkey, and is an illustration of an old folk tale retold by the **Brothers Grimm**. In fact, this is the town band that never was: en route to the city, the animals arranged themselves in the way depicted and started to make music. In so doing, they frightened a group of robbers away from their hideout, and took over the comfortable house for themselves, remaining there ever after.

On a small rise beyond the Rathaus stands the twin-towered **Dom**, formerly the seat of one of medieval Germany's five archbishops, but now a Protestant church. Any youngish men you see sweeping the steps are doing it because they have reached their thirtieth birthday without finding themselves a wife—this is the traditional penance (or, perhaps, a way of advertising their availability). The cathedral itself has been restored recently, its brooding interior beautiful in architectural styles ranging from eleventh-century Romanesque to late Gothic. There are crypts at both ends of the building (one for the use of the emperor, the other for the archbishop), though that to the west had to be truncated when the huge twin-towered facade was erected in the thirteenth century. Just above the entrance is the early sixteenth-century **organ gallery**, adorned with statues, including Charlemagne and Willehad, by the Münster sculptor Heinrich Brabender. In the eastern crypt are more fine works of art, notably an eleventh-century *Enthroned Christ* and a magnificent thirteenth-century bronze **font**, which is supported by men riding on lions. Off the southeast corner is the **Bleikeller**, where lead for the roofing was stored; it was opened up a while ago, and some bodies, perfectly preserved due to the lack of air, were discovered. Unusually, it's open to visitors, the "mummies' providing a popular—if macabre—attraction.

Off the south side of Marktplatz is a strange street which seems to combine elements of Gothic, art nouveau and fantasy: the **Böttcherstrasse** or Coopers' Street. Once a humble alleyway in which barrel makers lived and worked, it was transformed in the 1920s by the Bremen magnate **Ludwig Roselius**, who made much of his fortune from *Kaffee Haag*, the first-ever decaffeinated coffee. He commissioned local avant-garde artists (notably Bernhard Hoetger, whose characteristic plump figures are reminiscent of Chinese laughing Buddhas) to effect the change. In among the bronze reliefs, the arches, and turrets are a number of craftspeoples' workshops and booths, and a musical clock depicting the history of transatlantic crossings. The only old house in the Böttcherstrasse is no. 6, a fourteenth-century step-gabled building with a sixteenth-century facade, that's now known as the **Roselius Haus**. Roselius bought the property at the turn of the century, and converted it into a **museum** (Mon.–Thurs. 10am–4pm, Sat. and Sun. 11am–4 pm; DM2.50, students DM1.50). Though it gives an interesting opportunity to see the interior of a Hanseatic merchant's house, its collection of medieval art and furniture is not especially well displayed; the best works are paintings by Cranach the Elder and the Younger and an alabaster statue of *Saint Barbara* by Riemenschneider. Adjoining is the **Paula-Modersohn-Becker-Haus** (Mon.–Fri. 10:30am–12:30pm and 3–7pm, Sat. and Sun. 10am–2pm), which contains a number of paintings by that artist, who lived and worked at an artists' colony in the nearby village of Worpswede.

Tucked away between the Dom and the river is a small, extraordinarily well-preserved area of medieval fisherfolks' houses known as the **Schnoorviertel**. It's worth a wander through the small streets, far too narrow for modern traffic to pass, to see the variety of buildings and to get a feeling for the city's past.

Just east of the Schnoorviertel at Am Wall 207 is the **Kunsthalle** (Tues. 10am–9pm, Wed.–Sun. 10am–5pm; DM6), one of the oldest municipal art galleries in Germany. The ground floor is mostly given over to changing displays of modern art, but also contains a Jugendstil room containing valuable collections of graphic art. Sadly, most of the outstanding group of watercolors by **Dürer** were destroyed in the war, but a small panel of *Saint Onofrio* by this artist can be seen in the first room upstairs, along with **Altdorfer**'s earliest surviving work, *The Nativity*, and several examples of **Cranach**. The adjacent galleries contain Dutch and Flemish paintings: *Noli me Tangere* is a successful co-operative composition between **Rubens** (who painted the figures) and **Jan. Brueghel** (who did everything else); there's also the striking full-length *Portrait of Duke Wolfgang Wilhelm of Pfalz-Neuburg* by **Van Dyck**, and the *Portrait of a Man* attributed to **Rembrandt**. In the small cabinet rooms to the side are works by earlier European masters, notably Italians, of which the most important are *Madonna and Child* by **Masolino** (one of very few works by this artist to have left Italy), and *A Doctor* by **Moroni**.

However, the gallery's main draw is its superb array of nineteenth- and early twentieth-century painting. Among the French School, there are five canvases by **Delacroix**, including *King Rodrigo*, which was painted for a costume festival organized by Alexandre Dumas. A room is devoted to the Nabis; the most impressive works here are *Homage to Cézanne* by **Maurice Denis**, and **Vuillard's** designs for the decoration of the former Champs Elysées Théâtre. Other highlights are an important early **Monet**, *Camille*, and **Manet's** *Portrait of the Poet Zacharie Astruc*. Pick of the German works are **Beckmann's** *Apache Dance* and *Self-Portrait with Saxophone*, **Kirchner's** *Street Scene by Night* and a comprehensive representation of the Worpswede colony, with some forty examples of **Paula Modersohn-Becker** on view around the landing.

Next door to the Kunsthalle is the **Gerhard-Marcks-Haus** (Weds.–Sun. 10am–6pm; DM2) which contains sculptures, drawings, and watercolors by the artist. Apart from the monument to the Bremen Town Band, Marcks is best known for the bronze doors and other works of art he made for a number of German cathedrals and churches to replace those lost in the war. Another collection of specialized appeal is the **Überseemuseum** (Tues.–Sun. 10am–6pm; DM3), right beside the Hauptbahnhof, which has a large range of ethnological exhibits drawn from all over the Third World.

Of more general interest is the **Focke Museum** (Tues.–Sun. 10am–6pm; DM3), unfortunately rather a long way from the center of town at Schwachhauser-Heerstr. 240. Laid out in an imaginative and informative manner, this traces the history of Bremen and its port, and has a collection of decorative arts. Among the most important exhibits are the original statues of Charlemagne and the seven Electors from the Rathaus facade. If you're out this way, it's well worth continuing to the nearby **Botanical Gardens** which, in season, are ablaze with some 800 different species of rhododendrons and azaleas.

Eating, Drinking, and Entertainment

Given the number of good **café-bars** in Bremen, it's hard to single out individual ones. The *Café Am Wall* at Am Wall 164 has a lively atmosphere and vegetarian food, as does the *Tee Haus* in the middle of the Schnoorviertel; the *Café Caruso* at Friesenstr. 6–7 is also good. In Schwachhausen the *Vivaldi Café* at Schwachhauser-Heerstr. 4 is highly popular, and on the same street, no. 281 is the *Sowieso Bistro*, with the *Cartoon Café* nearby. Both are relaxed and handy for light meals. For pizza, try the *Restaurant Souterrain* at Sielwall 50, and for a tropical, all-night atmosphere *Bistro Brasil* in the Ostertorviertel at Ostertorsteinweg 83.

Bremen is one of Germany's most famous **beer** cities; the brewers' guild, founded in 1489, is the oldest in the country. It's the home of the internationally famous *Beck's*, one of the most heavily exported brews in the country, though it's a comparative newcomer, having existed for just over a century. *St. Pauli Girl* is another brand well-known abroad, but the products of *Haake-Beck* are the ones to go for in the city itself. They make both a filtered and an unfiltered Pils (the latter known as *Kräusen*), as well as the refreshing *Bremer Weisse*, which is usually sweetened with fruit syrup. Best choice of beers is at *Kleiner Ratskeller* on Hinter dem Schütting. The *Ratskeller* itself (see above), according to an old statute, can serve only **wine**—but offers an astonishing choice.

Best source of **nightlife info** is the tourist office, which has pamphlets listing events, and is the city's main ticket-booking agency. The monthly **listings magazines** *Bremer Blatt* and *Kursbuch* are both around DM3, but a free magazine *Lokal Spezial* can be picked up in restaurants/cafés—useful for addresses rather than actual events. German-speakers staying longer might be interested in *Bremen bei Nacht* (DM5). Excellent concerts of **classical music**, mainly of chamber music and appearances by international guest orchestras, are arranged by the *Philharmonische Gesellschaft*. Tickets (between DM15–30) from *Praeger and Meier*, Böttcherstr. 7 (☎325173), are usually in short supply, but it's worth a try, especially as a limited number are available at half-price for students. The *Jazz Club Bremen* in the Tivoli building by the Hauptbahnhof has live concerts, mainly of traditional styles, on Fridays and Saturdays. Main **theaters** are *Theater am Goetheplatz*, which offers standard traditional fare, and *Concordia*, Schwachhauser-Heerstr. 17, which specializes in modern and experimental works.

Listings

Festivals Leading folklore events are the *Eiswette* on 6 Jan. (Epiphany), and the *Freimarkt*, starting with a procession in mid-Oct., and continuing for a fortnight.

Gay line (☎704170).

Harbor cruises Departures April–Oct. at 10am, 11:30am, 1:30pm, 3:15pm, and 4.40pm from Martini–Anleger.

Mitfahrzentralen *Bremer Mitfahrzentrale* (in the Ostertorviertel), Humboldstr. 6 (☎72011). *Mitfahrladen und Reiseladen*, Weberstr. 44 (☎72022/72167). For women, the *Mitfahrzentrale für Frauen* is run from the women's bookshop at Friesenstr. 12 (Fesenfeld) (☎74033).

Poste Restante At junction of An der Weide and Löningstrasse, beside the Hauptbahnhof.

Sports *SV Werder Bremen* have been one of the most successful football teams in the country in recent seasons. Indoor sporting events are held in the *Stadthalle*, just behind the Hauptbahnhof.

Taxis (☎14141).

Telephone code (☎0421).

Womens' center (☎349573).

Bremerhaven

BREMERHAVEN is the Federal Republic's busiest fishing port, founded in 1827 as Bremen's deep-water harbor. Unless you're a naval buff, it has nothing that can't be seen better, and more conveniently, elsewhere.

Pride of the town is the **National Museum of Navigation** (*Deutsches Schiffahrtsmuseum*) in Von-Ronzelen-Strasse (Tues.–Sun. 10am–6pm; DM3), tracing German sailing from prehistoric times to the present; star exhibit is a fourteenth-century Hanseatic cog which was dredged up from the port of Bremen. Outside in the harbor, several historic vessels are moored, including *Seute Deern*, the last German wooden sailing ship, and the Arctic explorer *Grönland*.

If you're waiting for a boat, there's a **Museum of Twentieth Century Art** at Karlsburg 4 (Tues.–Sat. 3–6pm, Sun. 11am–1pm); and if you need to stay, the **tourist office** at Friedrich-Ebert-Str. 58, can advise on rooms.

Around Bremen

If you're staying in Bremen and want a trip out, the most obvious places to head for are the coast and area around **Stade**, and the former artists' colony of **Worpswede**. **Verden** is a worthwhile stop-off if you're heading towards Hannover or the Lüneburg Heath.

Verden

Between Bremen and Hannover—or Bremen and the Lüneburger Heide—the small city of **VERDEN** on the River Aller is at first sight not particularly interesting. But hidden away at the end of a tedious shopping center is North Germany's oldest brick-built church, and a Dom that dates back to the twelfth century.

However you approach it, the **Dom** is very impressive indeed. The interior has a feeling of great space; it was one of the first full-scale churches in Germany to be built in the hall style, with nave, aisles, and choir all the same height. Its lightness is increased by the apparent slenderness of the columns, your eye drawn up their vertical moldings. Just outside and opposite the Dom is a rather good café, *Das Andere Café*. The **St. Johanniskirche** on Ritterstrasse, built during the twelfth century and gothicized in the fifteenth century, isn't as impressive, but has a homely feel, and a few medieval frescos.

Verden has always been an equestrian center, with major horse auctions taking place here in spring and autumn. Horsey types from all over the country are drawn to the **German Equestrian Museum** here (Andreasstr. 7; Tues.–Sun. 9am–4pm)—a rather serious institution with a huge collection of equine artifacts, and a valuable library in the Hippological Institute.

The **tourist office**, straight ahead and right from the Hauptbahnhof, sells cycle touring maps (DM7 each) of places within easy reach on a few days' tour. One tour leads to the **Vogelpark Walsrode** (daily mid-March–Oct. 9am–7pm; DM10), a large park around 30km southeast of the town, where about 5000 indigenous and exotic birds are on view in large birdhouses. Here the countryside begins to take on the heathland characteristics of the Lüneburger Heide.

Verden is very small, and nowhere is more than ten minutes' walk from the Bahnhof. There are plenty of **places to stay**: a modern youth hostel is at Saumurplatz (☎04231 61163), and at the inexpensive end of hotels is *Der Oelkenhof*, Im Dicken Ort 17 (☎04231 62963).

Worpswede

About 25km outside Bremen in the **Teufelsmoor** (the forbiddingly-named "Devil's peat bog") is the intriguing village of **WORPSWEDE**. Back in the 1880s this was a simple farming village, where the inhabitants scraped together a living. The artists Fritz Mackensen and Otto Modersohn came here then, and over the next ten or so years Worpswede developed into an artists' colony, a movement run on roughly similar lines to the pre-Raphaelites. The famous poet Rainer Maria Rilke was closely associated with them, as was his wife, Clara Westhoff.

It was **Paula Becker**, who subsequently married Modersohn, who became the most significant of the set—her powerful, depressing pictures depicting the grim realities of peasant life, poverty, and death stand out from the pretty, though comparatively facile, impressionistic scenes of the others. The exhibition hall in the center of town that sometimes shows her work was built in 1927 in a flamboyant style, reminiscent almost of a Thai temple.

If you make a trip to Worpswede you're not limited to the exhibitions by the original artists—many craftspeople are based here and have studios, and although the town is quiet it has various restaurants and cafés—and a **youth hostel** (☎04792 1360). You can reach Worpswede by bus #140 from Bremen Hauptbahnhof; a **trolley** runs from BREMERVÖRDE, and it's possible to come from Bremen by (infrequent) **boat** in summer. Ask at the tourist office in Bremen for exact times of both services.

The Altes Land

The blunt stump of land between the Elbe and the Weser is not easy to explore without your own transportation—it's gentle countryside, though, scattered with interesting villages whose charm partly lies in being off the beaten track.

The area closest to Hamburg, the so-called **Altes Land** (*Old Country*), sees most visitors. Traditionally the Altes Land is Hamburg's garden—fruit and vegetables are the main crops of a sheltered, cultivated area that's picturesque and pleasant to meander through by bike or car on a sunny day, with plenty of places to stop off for a hearty German lunch. Such a trip is easily combined with a visit to the small town of **BUXTEHUDE**, though the town itself is of slender interest, with but a few restored houses from its Hanseatic past.

About 26km north and west of Buxtehude, the little port of **STADE** used to be in Swedish hands back in the seventeenth century, and the **museum** (Tues.–Sun. 10am–5pm) in the *Schwedenspeicher* ("Swedish Warehouse") in the harbor records that history. One or two surprisingly grand house facades indicate that Stade was once relatively affluent—as it is today, thanks to industry on its outskirts. There's a strange atmosphere to the town, though; the old harbor (the **Westwasser**) and houses there that form the heart of the town were under threat of demolition back in the 1960s, and, following a successful protest that stopped the area being turned into a parking lot, a lot of renovation was carried out. The job was done so well, so thoroughly, that Stade now has an odd, artificial, almost toytown feel to it. The large **Cosmaekirche** dates from the thirteenth century and is topped by an onion-shaped spire, and may be open for a look inside. Also by the old harbor is the **Goebenhaus** (birthplace of Prussian Field Marshal von Goeben) which has a reasonably priced café with home-made snacks and cakes.

WESTERN LOWER SAXONY

This area takes in points west of Bremen, as far as the border with the Netherlands—much of it is agricultural land, and the main area of interest is **Ostfriesland**, or East Friesia. Over the centuries the Friesians have resolutely avoided complete absorption by their German neighbors, retaining their own language and cultural identity. They inhabit a low-lying, fertile province that was prey to constant inundation by the sea; it was a miserable sort of existence, as **Pliny** observed around A.D. 50:

> *Here a wretched race is found, inhabiting either the more elevated spots or artificial mounds where they pitch their cabins. When the waves cover the surrounding area they are like so many mariners on board a ship, and when again the tide recedes their condition is that of so many ship-wrecked men.*

Not surprisingly, the Friesians got pretty fed up with this sort of life and, as soon as the technology arrived, began to build the dikes that have culminated in the sea-barrier that extends right around the coast from **Emden** to **Wilhelmshaven**.

Ostfriesland may have poor weather and interminably flat countryside, but it has spawned an ingenious tourist sub-culture taking advantage of the "bracing maritime climate . . . that regenerates the blood and nerves" while "a walk along the foreshore will provide natural inhalation treatment." If you want more, you can pay for the privilege of being submerged in genuine North Sea mud in a number of large health spas, or join organized walks across the mudflats (the *Watt*) that encircle the coast.

There are less esoteric alternatives: several **towns**, such as **Norden**, merit a visit; great stretches of land are designated **nature reserves** and there are two long-distance **footpaths** connecting Emden with Wilhelmshaven. The first follows the Ems-Jade canal, the second the coastline taking the name of Klaus Störtebeker, a fifteenth-century Friesian pirate and Robin Hood type character whose name is much lauded locally. Further information from *Wiehengebirgsversand d.v.*, Bierstrasse 25, 4500 Osnabrück.

The **East Friesian islands**, with their long sandy beaches, lie just off the coast, and are immensely popular holiday resorts. Each island has a full range of tourist facilities, and trains connect the ferries to most major German cities. With the possible exceptions of **Norderney** and **Juist**, this popularity has more to do with West Germany's truncated coastline than any special charm.

Oldenburg, on the eastern edge of Western Lower Saxony, has eighteenth-century buildings worth seeing in passing, while to the south the main town is the old episcopal center of **Osnabrück**, a major railroad junction.

Most inland **travel** can be done by bus, though it's worth noting that services can be sparse on Sundays; **ferry** details are listed in the text.

Emden

EMDEN is West Germany's fourth largest seaport and the principal town of Ostfriesland, with a population of some 50,000. A trading center from the time of Charlemagne, Emden was becalmed when the river Ems changed its course during the seventeenth century, and only revived some 300 years later with the digging of the Dortmund-Ems canal, and the building of a new harbor. Heavily bombed in World War II, there's precious little left of the old town; what remains marks Emden as a pleasant but unremarkable place. The **Bahnhof** and **bus station** are five minutes from the center—turn right after the water tower down Ringstrasse and first left—where you can find the **tourist office** (Mon.–Fri. 9am–1pm and 3–5:30pm, Sat. 10am–1pm) moored in an old light-ship. They will help with **accommodation** or you can try the cheapest place in the center of town: *Pension Ewald*, Neutorsgang 7, charging DM30 per person. The **youth hostel** is at An der Kesselschleuse 5 (☎04921 23797) on the eastern outskirts, and **Camping** *Knock* is 8km west along the coast road.

The center of Emden has one or two minor attractions. There are the remains of the medieval church of Cosmas and Damian; a rather incongruous Renaissance gate stuck by the water-side and a **Museum of Modern Art** on Hinter dem Rahmen 13 (Tues.–Fri. 10am–5pm, Sat. and Sun. 11am–5pm) that concentrates on Expressionism. The **Ostfriesisches Landesmuseum** (Mon.–Fri. 10am–1pm and 3–5pm, Sat. and Sun. 11am–1pm; closed Mon. Oct.–April) right in the middle of town has a selection of local items, and one of the largest collections of **armor** in Europe. Finally, the tourist office will provide details of **boat trips** around the waterways that once protected Emden—a pleasant way to spend an afternoon.

The strip of agricultural land to the west of Emden, known as the **Krummhörn**, was reclaimed from the sea between the wars; at its northern tip is the picturesque fishing village of **GREETSIEL.**

All roads lead to Rome, and all tourist buses in Ostfriesland probably lead to Greetsiel, a shrimp-fishing village since the fourteenth century, with cobbled streets, hump-backed bridges, windmills, and teashops, but—in season—definitely not for those with a low tour bus tolerance. There's plenty of accommodation for visitors, mainly in bed and breakfast arrangements, and the **tourist office** at Sielstr. 17 (☎04926 1331) can arrange places to stay, though it gets difficult if you leave it too late in the day. The **youth hostel** is at Kleinbahnstr. 15 (☎04926 550) and **camping** fairly close by at Loquard (☎04927 595). Don't miss *Is Teetied* opposite the church in Greetsiel, an East Friesian style olde tea shoppe with many good things to eat. Friesians may account for only two percent of the population, but they drink thirty percent of the tea; they like it strong, poured over special giant sugar crystals (*klöntjes*), and topped up with cream. **Buses** connect Greetsiel with Norden and Emden, though Sunday services are poor.

Just down the road, FREEPSUM is Germany's lowest point, 2.3m below sea level. From nearby **DIEKSKIEL** you can go out on the Watt with a *Wattführer*, an experienced guide who will lead you through the treacherous mudflats; emphatically not something you should try on your own.

Borkum

The island of **BORKUM** is the largest and most westerly of the East Friesian islands. A popular holiday spot, it has all the facilities of a resort including a casino, an indoor swimming pool with sea water and artificial waves, a marina, and long sandy beaches. **Ferries** for Borkum leave from the harbor (*Aussenhafen*) just south of EMDEN four times daily in summer, twice daily in winter (journey takes 2hr 30min). There are onward connections from the ferry terminal to Emden and other major German cities. Frankly, Borkum has nothing special to offer, and does not warrant the long and expensive trip—other islands are more appealing, and more easily reached.

Aurich, Norden, and Norddeich

AURICH is the administrative center of Ostfriesland, and an easy bus ride from Emden. Once the seat of the East Friesian nobility, the town is quite grand, in spite of its small size, with a large, pink Schloss and some impressive baroque buildings to its credit. The old part of town is still surrounded on two sides by a **moat**, and in the town center is the enormous **Marktplatz**, created in the early sixteenth century by Count Edzard. You have to go the **Historical Museum** at Burgstr. 25 (Tues.–Sat. 10am–noon and 3–5pm, Sun. 3–5pm) to see a reconstruction of the houses that used to edge the square. Their graceful lines are marred these days by several incongruous postwar additions, notably the grey lump of the savings bank that still makes local hackles rise. Close to the museum are some of the town's best **Renaissance facades**, and the **Lambertikirche**, with the solid, square tower typical of this region (though in this case topped by a spire) has an altar carved in Antwerp around 1500.

It's easy to walk across town, and although the **youth hostel** (Am Ellernfeld, ☎04941 2827), for example, is on virtually the other side of town from the Bahnhof, it doesn't take any more than twenty minutes on foot. In yet another corner is the **Pferdemarkt**, the original site of Aurich's market from the thirteenth century until the creation of the new square, but now a parking lot and the main place for **bus** arrivals and departures. The **tourist office** is here, too, and has accommodation lists. Along the Oldersumer Strasse is an **old windmill**, the Stiftsmühle, built in 1858 and now open to visitors (May–Sept. Tues.–Sat. 10am–noon and 2–5pm, Sun. 2–5pm).

About 5km west of Aurich, in the peat-bog (*Moor* in German) of the Südbrookmerland, is the **Moormuseum Moordorf**, (Victoburer Moor 7a, Südbrookmerland-Moordorf; May–Oct. Tues.–Sun. 10am–5:30pm; DM2), dedicated to 200 years of history of the **Moordorf colony**. The museum records the tough life in the colony, whose inhabitants depended on peat fires for heating and cooking. The museum is housed in an old cottage and other small buildings; peat-digging and traditional crafts are often demonstrated.

At the center of **NORDEN** stands the medieval **Ludgerikirche**, built between the thirteenth and fifteenth centuries. Its **organ**, made in the 1680s and housed in an elaborate baroque case, is one of the most beguiling instruments in the world, ranking as the masterpiece of northern Germany's greatest exponent of the craft, Arp Schnitger. The tall, narrow building near the church is its freestanding bell-tower. Together they stand in the huge **Marktplatz**, half of which is grassed over and dominated by shady, mature trees, forming an odd, or at least unfamiliar, picture in this part of the world. Along the paved part of the market place are two Renaissance houses, and several other facades of similar age. Up the Osterstrasse is perhaps the best of the town's Renaissance buildings, a late sixteenth-century **burgher's house**, which today contains an excellent and reasonably priced Italian restaurant, *Vesuvio*. Also near the church are the **Heimatmuseum** (Weds. and Fri. 3–5pm, Sat. 10am–noon) and the **tourist office** (June–Aug. Mon.–Fri. 8am–5pm, Sat. 10am–5pm, Sept.–May Mon.–Fri. 8am–2:30pm), who can help with accommodation.

Perhaps because of the large square, perhaps because it has escaped the standard German pedestrian zone, Norden has an individual, if a little sleepy, atmosphere. It's a far more pleasant place to be based than its seaside neighbor Norddeich, especially if you stay at the *Hotel zur Post*, a sort of alternative hotel rescued from a dilapidated state by the two women who now run it. The downstairs adjoining **café-bar** appears to be the center of Norden life (and is next to the post office on the market place).

Ten minutes by bus from the Marktplatz is **NORDDEICH**. **Ferries** run from here to the islands of Juist and Nordeney, and the train, timed to coincide with the boats, goes right up to the jetty (**Norddeich-Mole**). If you are going to Baltrum, a bus meets appropriate trains to take passengers to the ferry at Nessmersiel. Alternatively, you could stop off in Norddeich itself, though it's an ugly rambling town with precious little to recommend it. Almost every house takes **bed and breakfast** visitors—just look out for *"Zimmer frei"* signs. The **youth hostel**, at Strandstr. 1 (☎04931 8064) is signposted, and has camping facilities. From Norddeich-Mole there are trains to a range of German cities, and even direct services to Amsterdam and Copenhagen.

The Islands: Juist and Norderney

Depending on the tides, between one and three ferries leave Norddeich Mole for the island of **JUIST** every day; the trip takes eighty minutes, and costs DM22 for a day return, DM36 for a period return. One of the most attractive and popular of the East Friesian islands, Juist is a narrow strip of land 17km long and a few hundred yards wide. A sandy, dune-fringed beach extends the entire length of its northern shore, and even on hot summer days privacy is not hard to find. The only **settlement** is halfway along the island near the ferry terminal. It's a rather drab suburban affair, but at least it's not dominated by high-rise hotels, and, best of all, there are no cars. Criss-crossed by foot and cycle paths, Juist has the full range of tourist facilities with dozens of bars and restaurants, a large covered swimming pool, and a nature reserve (the "Bill"). **Accommodation** can be a little tricky in summer, but the **tourist office** (*"Kurverwaltung,"* April–Sept. Mon.–Sat. 8am–noon and 3–5:30pm, Oct.–March Mon.–Sat. 8am–noon; ☎04935 491) in the Rathaus is more than willing to help. Reckon on about DM30 per person. The **youth hostel** (March–Oct. only) at Loogster Pad 20 (☎04935 1094) has 400 beds and family rooms. There are no campgrounds.

The most popular and distinctive of the East Friesian islands, **NORDERNEY** is also the most accessible. Depending on the season, **ferries** make the fifty-minute journey from Norddeich Mole to Norderney between nine and thirteen times a day; a period return costs DM14. Norderney **town** is at the western end of the island, a short bus ride or a fifteen-minute walk from the ferry terminal. The **tourist office** (Mon.–Fri. 8am–noon and 2–6pm, also May–Sept. Sat. 10am–noon and 2–4pm, Sun. 10am–noon; ☎04932 8910), just off the main square at Bülow Allee 5, will arrange **accommodation**—though things get tight in high season. There are two **youth hostels** (open March–Oct.), one at Südstr. 1 (☎04932 2451), and the other to the east of the town at Am Dünensender 3 (☎04932 2574) with attached **camping** facilities. There are two farther **campgrounds**, one of them on the eastern edge of town, and the other several kilometers farther on.

Slightly self-conscious, Norderney is the oldest spa on the German North Sea coast, and was once a favorite royal vacation residence. The central square with its manicured gardens, elegant cafés, and classical buildings has retained a certain nineteenth-century grace, though most of the town is a dull mixture of modern architectures. Its only surprise is a huge **pyramid of stones** piled up in the middle of an ordinary suburban side-street. Crass in the extreme, this is in fact a monument to Kaiser Wilhelm and his efforts to unify Germany; sixty-one stones marked with their state of origin.

Norderney tries hard to cater to all tastes. In summer the bars are packed with serious drinkers, vast middle-aged couples tuck into apple strudels, and gamblers fill the casino with no time to eat or drink. Meanwhile, earnest joggers trot round the myriad footpaths, families sunbathe on the long sandy beach, pensioners take the cures, and cyclists tour the nature reserve. If that's not enough, there are innumerable gourmet restaurants, a couple of small museums, and the first-ever covered swimming-pool to have sea water and artificial waves. For an account of the very different lifestyle of the islanders in the first half of the last century, read the second part of Heinrich Heine's *Reisebilder*. Norderney also inspired *The North Sea,* a cycle of poems by the same author.

More Islands: Baltrum, Langeoog, Spiekeroog, Wangerooge

With none of the polished sophistication of their westerly neighbors, these four islands have five things in common: sandy beaches to the north, and mud-flats to the south; drab modern settlements with a suburban air; nature reserves, and **bus/ferry** connections from Norden's Bahnhof.

BALTRUM is the smallest and least remarkable with two or three buses from Norden station to the ferry point at Nessmersiel per day. The **tourist office** supplies an **accommodation** list, there's a **campground** on the edge of the nature reserve, and a quiet atmosphere not found at the busier resorts.

Buses leave Norden Bahnhof for **Bensersiel**, the ferry port for **LANGEOOG** between three and five times daily. The ferry costs DM9 each way, takes fifty minutes and connects with the island's toytown railroad to the main settlement. The best place to stay must be the **youth hostel** (April–Sept.) some 3km to the east, pleasantly sited behind the Melkhörn sand dunes—ring ahead in high season (☎04972 276). The village is particularly dull, and Langeoog's only claim to fame is its enormous colony of seabirds found in the **nature reserve** at the east end of the island.

The same bus from Norden continues along the coast to **Neuharlingersiel** for **SPIEKEROOG**—two to four ferries per day, fifty minutes. Attractions here include an island railroad and a seventeenth-century church containing fragments of a wrecked galleon from the Spanish Armada. There's also a youth hostel (15 March–30 Oct.; ☎04976 329).

The bus continues to **Harlesiel** for **WANGEROOGE**. **Ferries** make the seventy-minute trip two or three times daily in summer and once in winter; return tickets cost 41DM. The **tourist office** (*Kurverwaltung* April–Sept. Mon.–Sat. 9am–noon and 3–4:30pm, Oct.–March 9am–noon; ☎04469 890) will help with **accommodation**—reckon on about DM35 per person—and there's also a **campground** (☎04469 307). The main settlement is in the middle of the island, connected by rail to the ferry terminal; a branch-line goes to the western tip where you can find the **youth hostel** (May–Sept.; ☎04469 439). Founded in 1804, high tides swept the old resort away some fifty years later, and precious little has survived from its Victorian past. One of the more attractive islands, Wangerooge has all the usual tourist facilities, a small museum in the old lighthouse, and several **bird sanctuaries**.

Along the Coast

Other villages along the coast vary in character—the fishing villages with their old-fashioned boats, such as DORNUMERSIEL and the inland harbor of CAROLINENSIEL, are inevitably more picturesque than the newly built resorts such as BENSERSIEL. The **bus services** to all these places are fairly good, but tend to dovetail with island ferry sailing times, so it's best to pick up a local bus timetable. Carolinensiel has a **Sielhafenmuseum**, devoted to boat building, fishing, dike building, and other activities on the Lower Saxony North Sea coast. It's in an old corn warehouse, right on the harborside, open mid–June to mid-October. More or less opposite is a rather imposing hotel with strange staff, but there's a **youth hostel** at Herbergsmense 13 (☎04464 252).

Jever

Strictly speaking, **JEVER** is not part of East Friesia but belongs to its rival Friesia, or the Jeverland. The town's heroine is Fräulein Maria, an energetic and gifted sixteenth-century countess who gave Jever city rights, had the fortifications built, founded a school, and commissioned several works of art. Subsequently, through marriage and conquest, Jever came under Russian, Dutch, and French rule. The rather magnificent pink **Schloss**, which was begun in the sixteenth century and subsequently extended, is now a very good **museum** (March–Dec. Tues.–Sat. 10am–1pm and 3–5pm, Sun. 11am–1pm and 3–5pm). Look out, if you go, for the carved oak ceiling of the audience room, which Fraülein Maria had made by an Antwerp artist. Otherwise, exhibitions of crafts and reconstructed rooms are the museum's main features. It might be possible to go up the tower for a **view** of the town and across the castle gardens, planted with some beautiful trees.

On the way through narrow streets towards the center of the old town and the church, you pass the sixteenth-century **Rathaus**. The **Stadtkirche** has been burned down and rebuilt at least nine times in its 900-year history. It last had a fire in 1959, when over half of the church was completely destroyed and replaced, for better or worse, with a contemporary design. The enormous monument that Fraülein Maria had erected for her father somehow survived, and can be seen in the remains of the baroque church, now integrated into the new building. A work of architecture as much as sculpture (its creator, Cornelis Floris of Antwerp, was equally brilliant in both arts), it's particularly remarkable for the extraordinary mixture of materials used—wood, marble, sandstone, and clay. From May to September there are weekday tours of the **Jever brewery**; turn up by 10:30am at the brewery in Elizabethufer 17. The Pils is celebrated as the most bitter-tasting beer made anywhere in Germany.

Halfway between Jever and Wilhelmshaven is the village of **SILLENSTEDE**, and if you have your own transport you might want to stop off to look at the **St. Floriankirche**, a twelfth-century Romanesque church made of granite blocks—its organ is quite famous, too, and there are concerts here on Saturday evenings.

Wilhelmshaven

As German reunification gathered momentum, Wilhelm I of Prussia coveted British naval supremacy, and decided to build a westward naval base and dock-yard on the North Sea coast. This purpose-built military town was to be the epitome of efficiency with an integrated rail, canal, and dock system. The result was **WILHELMSHAVEN**, founded in 1853 and a key determinant in German naval planning by the end of the century. Heavily bombed in World War II, the center was rebuilt as an ugly, concrete shopping center, and there are few reminders of Wilhelmshaven's imperial past. The dockyards are still the main employers, but the naval base is no longer of any great strategic significance, and the town has a rather desolate, insular atmosphere.

The **Hauptbahnhof** and adjoining **bus station** are in the middle of town, ten minutes from the **tourist office** (Mon.–Fri. 9am–6pm, Sat. 9am–1pm) at Börsenstr. 55b—left out of the station, immediately left up Virchowstrasse, and then the third left. They will phone for **accommodation**, and provide town maps.

Alternatively, you can try the convenient *Hotel Flacke* at Virchowstr. 30 (DM35 per person) or the **youth hostel** at Freiligrathstr. 131 (☎04421 60048), a couple of kilometers north of the city center; the nearest **campground** is about 4km farther on by the sea. In emergencies there's a large, wooded park at the far end of Virchowstrasse where you could try to bed down—though this is illegal.

The town has a number of curiosities within easy walking distance—the high Victorian elegance of the houses on Kielerstrasse, south of Peterstrasse; the old harbor; the naval base, and the Kaiser Wilhelm bridge with its symmetrical Prussian sentry-boxes. The nearest **"beach"** is at Südstrand, though it's really a mole with a few inches of sand. Finally, Wilhelmshaven has a flourishing punk scene, attracting surprisingly good bands like the *Mekons* and *Shock Therapy*.

Most tourists bypass Wilhelmshaven. Vacationers heading for the islands of Langeoog, Spiekeroog, and Wangerooge go through the railroad junction of SANDE a few miles to the west, whilst those traveling to HELGOLAND go straight through the town to the ferry terminal. There are **railroad** connections from Wilhelmshaven to a wide range of German cities via Sande and **bus** services to the surrounding small towns. Services are, once again, poor on Sundays.

Helgoland

Ferries leave Wilhelmshaven once a day between April and September for the three-hour trip to **HELGOLAND** (or *HELIGOLAND*). A single fare costs DM52. Alternative sailings depart from BREMERHAVEN, NORDDEICH/NORDERNEY (once weekly), and CUXHAVEN. The red limestone island of Helgoland stands on its own seventy kilometers from the mouth of the Elbe, and was once an important naval base and coaling station. Occupied by the British, it only came into German hands in 1890, when it was swapped for Zanzibar. Bombarded during World War II, the inhabitants were forcibly evacuated in 1947, and the remaining fortifications blown up. For five years it served as a bombing target for the RAF, until finally returned to Germany in 1952. Reconstruction began immediately, and Helgoland has become a popular holiday resort with all the usual facilities—and duty-free status. The craggy cliffs are dramatic, but frankly Helgoland is not special enough to warrant the time and expense of getting there—other more accessible islands are just as enjoyable. If you do make it here the **tourist office** (☎04725 80860) will help with **accommodation**—ring ahead in high season—and there's a **youth hostel** (☎04725 341) open from April to October.

Oldenburg

South of Wilhelmshaven, **OLDENBURG** is a pleasant enough place to change trains, but unlikely to qualify as a major stopping-off point otherwise. A former ducal residence town, it's now mostly modernised and criss-crossed with large shopping streets, busy with people on shopping trips from the surrounding countryside. As the town has a student population, there's plenty going on in the evenings. Oldenburg keeps busy with various festivals throughout the year, the **Kramermarkt** in October being the annual high point.

Arriving by train it's soon obvious that Oldenburg is not expecting visitors—no signposts to the town center, no hint of where you might spend the night or find a map of the town. Turning immediately right out of the station, along the Mosle Strasse, leads to the northernmost part of the moated Aldtstadt. (**Tourist information** is at Lange Str. 3 in the **Lappan**, the fifteenth-century tower of the medieval Heiligen-Geist-Hospital.) Alternatively, heading straight out of the station takes you to the end of the harbor, a busy inland port linked to the North Sea and, by canal, to the Netherlands. You can then turn right, follow the old moat to the left, crossing it at some point into the southern part of the Aldtstadt, thereby dodging the shoppers and arriving in the area of Schlossplatz, Markt, and Berg Strasse, the "cultural" end of town.

In the Schlossplatz, the seventeenth- and eighteenth-century **Schloss** houses the **Landesmuseum of Art and Cultural History** (Tues.–Fri. 9am–5pm Sat. and Sun. 9am–1pm; free) whose lure is a large collection of paintings, interiors and ceramics—and, most celebrated of all, the **Tischbein room**. The name of Tischbein is often associated with that of Goethe, who was apparently inspired by the painter's idyllic scenes. Duke Peter Friedrich Ludwig of Oldenburg was a patron of Tischebein, hence the large collection here. Modern art is housed in the **Augusteum** (same times; free), a separate building on the corner of Elisabeth Strasse and the Damm.

Up in the market place is the thirteenth-century **Lambertikirche**, whose Gothic exterior has been built round and over, and is today scarcely visible. The interior was completely reworked by Peter Friedrich Ludwig in the 1790s into a classical round shape based on the Pantheon in Rome. It's rather like a Wedgewood vase turned inside out—quite astonishing.

The area around Berg Strasse is good to look at; Berg Strasse itself has a few crafts shops, and runs down to the Theaterwall. The present **Staatstheater** was built at the end of the last century, and was extensively renovated in 1974 as a venue for concerts, ballet, and opera performances, as well as drama. To the south of the old town is the **Schlossgarten**, which used to be the source of vegetables, eggs, and milk for consumption in the Schloss. It was subsequently laid out as an English-style (that is, informal) garden, and is a good place to relax and picnic.

Practical Details

The **youth hostel** is at Alexander Strasse 65 (☎0441 87135), north of the Pferdemarkt, and summer **camping** facilities exist by the Flötenteich lake, up in the northeast part of town, by bus from the town center to Nadorst.

The least expensive **hotels** are well out of town, except for *Hotel Mandel* (DM30) at 91er Str. 2 whose proximity to the railroad may lead to sleepless nights, and *Hotel Sprenz* (DM30) at Heiligengeist Str. 15, which is by the Pferdemarkt. Two private addresses offer bed and breakfast. *Frau Bundkiel*, Friedrich-Rüder-Str. 30 (☎0441 12340), is about ten minutes' walk south of the Schloss, and east of the Schlossgarten; *Frau Kretz*, Cäcilien Str. 2 (☎0441 77520) is across the moat by the theater—Roon Strasse—and then right. Both of these cost DM25. Other than this, the tourist office has the usual reservation service.

For **eating**, the café in the Schlossplatz has salads, and Lange Strasse and Achtern Strasse have several good places: *Campino* at Achtern Str. 57 for pizza, sandwiches, and salads; *Laterne*, at Heiligengeist Str. 19; *Le Journal*, Wallstr. 13, and *Kartoffelkiste* at Artillerie Weg 56. For **drinking**, head for Kurwick Strasse; there's also *Ulenspegel* (open late) at Burg Str. 12 and *Hannenfass*, Baumgarten Str. 3, whose specialty is Altbier, and features music on Wednesdays. At the same address is *Sunup's* (a disco-café-bar), or there's *Bebob*, next to the station.

Best way to get around town is on foot, but you can **hire bikes** at *Fahrrad Bonke* in the Haupt Strasse, or *Die Speiche* in Donnerschweer Strasse. The tourist office sells a cycle map, and the cycle paths are extensive and good. Lastly, the *Mitfahrzentrale* is at Nadorster Str. 38 (☎0441 885656).

Around Oldenburg

A relaxed 20km bike ride, or a twenty-minute train trip east leads to **HUDE**, where remains of a natty thirteenth-century Cistercian **monastery** stand by a water mill. There's a **youth hostel** at Linteler Str. 3 (☎04408 414).

From Hude, you could then cycle, stopping at the thatched village of DÖTLINGEN (there's also a direct bus that takes just over an hour from Oldenburg) to **WILDESHAUSEN**. The small settlements dotted around here make up a so-called "square mile of prehistory" consisting of Bronze Age graves (at PESTRUP), burial chamber and stones at KLEINKNETEN, and more stones at RECKUM. The Alexanderkirche, Wildeshausen's medieval church, has thirteenth- and fifteenth-century frescos, and the town hall is Gothic, too. The **youth hostel** is at Am Filleberg 9 (☎04431 2223).

CLOPPENBURG, some 15km west, is worth making for, to see the **Open Air Museum** (March–Oct. Mon.–Sat. 8am–6pm, Sun. 9am–6pm, Nov.–Feb. Mon.–Sat. 9am–5pm, Sun. 10am–5pm; DM3.50). This has a collection of about 100 historic rural buildings from all over Lower Saxony re-erected on one site, with craftspeople using old techniques. A little farther south, you might want to stop off to see the *Schloss Dinklage*, which still has its moat.

Osnabrück

OSNABRÜCK stands somewhat apart from the rest of Lower Saxony, at its extreme western end. Geographically and historically, it really belongs to Westphalia, and it has many parallels with Münster, which is just 55km to the south. Each city is now home to a large British army base, and has a sizeable student population. Both owe their foundation to Charlemagne; in the Middle Ages, both were ruled by a prince-bishop, and were important trading centers. Subsequently, they shared the hosting of the long negotiations—regarded as the birth of modern diplomatic practices—which led to the signing of the **Peace of Westphalia** in 1648, bringing the Thirty Years' War to an end. One curious agreement resulting from these talks was that Osnabrück was to be ruled in future by a Catholic and a Protestant bishop in turn. The Welfs provided the latter incumbent; the ambitious Duke Ernst August of Hannover was one holder of the see, and his son, the future King George I of Britain, was born in the city. When the bishopric was secularized under Napoleon, the Hanoverians annexed its territories. After World War II, Osnabrück therefore joined the rest of Hannover in the new province of Lower Saxony, though the fact that the city's publicity is handled by the Westphalian tourist office is an indication of where loyalties lie.

As a railroad junction on major north–south and east–west lines (a legacy of the old trading routes), Osnabrück is very easily accessible. From the **Hauptbahnhof**, the center is best reached by following Möserstrasse straight ahead. You'll quickly see that much of the city is modern; heavy damage was caused by bombing in the last war, and restoration has been less successful than in Münster. Some highly characterful streets and squares do remain, but it's a pity that more thought wasn't given to the planning of the bland shopping areas with which they're now intermingled.

After crossing the River Hase, you arrive at the **Dom**, which has a spacious setting in the middle of its own square. If, as is often claimed, cathedrals should represent the character of the city around them, Osnabrück's readily fits the bill. Built in fits and starts between the twelfth and sixteenth centuries, it's something of a curate's egg. The facade **towers** are a fascinatingly unlikely combination—the late Gothic one on the southern side is almost twice the width of its Romanesque neighbor—but they are outclassed by the dignified octagon (the oldest part of the present building) over the transept crossing.

Inside, the Dom has a pleasingly sober, predominantly Gothic appearance. Among a number of notable **works of art**, the early thirteenth-century bronze font and the exactly contemporary polychromed wood *Triumphal Cross* are outstanding. The latter's name is something of a misnomer, as Christ is here depicted as a pathetic, suffering, all-too-human figure. In the south transept is a monument to a provost, made by the north German baroque architect, J.C. Schlaun. Wonderful gilded wrought-iron gates guard the ambulatory, at the end of which is the *Margarethenaltar*, a limewood retable by the same sculptor of the *Madonna of the Rosary* in the north transept. The identity of this emotional artist, who was still working in the late Gothic style well into the sixteenth century, remains elusive: he's known simply as the Master of Osnabrück.

Further works by him can be seen in the **Diocesan Museum** (Tues.–Fri. 10am–1pm and 3–5pm, Sat. and Sun. 10am–1pm; DM1.50), housed in rooms above the cloister. The most eye-catching item here, however, is the gilded *Kapitelkreuz*, made in the early eleventh century and studded with two pontifical rings, a couple of Roman cameos, and a variety of colored gems. The early seventeenth-century confessional, from a nearby convent, was made in the wake of the Tridentine reforms and is the earliest example in northern Europe of what was to become a very familiar structure. Other highlights of the museum are a tenth-century ivory comb, a number of pieces by the local fifteenth-century silversmith Johannes Dalhoff, and the figures from the demolished rood screen.

Just beyond the Dom is the other main square, the triangular **Markt**. Its colorful step-gabled mansions are modeled on the merchant houses of the Hanseatic ports, while in the center there's a fountain which is supposed to gush with beer whenever there's a festival on. On the northern side of the square is the Gothic **Marienkirche**, which takes the hall church design to its logical conclusion by omitting the transept. Inside are a fourteenth-century *Triumphal Cross*, a sixteenth-century *Passion Altar* from Antwerp and numerous tombs—including that of Justus Möser, whose researches into Westphalian folklore in the eighteenth century were to serve as a trail-blazer for the Romantic movement.

Closing the end of the Markt is the early sixteenth-century **Rathaus**, from whose steps the Peace of Westphalia was proclaimed. However, the present stairway dates from the nineteenth century, as do the large statues of German Emperors, in which Kaiser Wilhelm I is lined up alongside his medieval predecessors. During normal working hours, you can go inside to see the wood-paneled *Friedensaal*, and its generally glum portraits of the representatives of Sweden and the Protestant German principalities, who deliberated here while their Catholic counterparts met in Münster. Ask at the porter's desk to see the *Schatzkammer*, which contains valuable documents and treasury items. Star piece is the magnificent fourteenth-century *Kaiserpokal*, a goblet adorned with colored glass and figurines. Also notable is the late sixteenth-century *Schützenkette*, a trophy awarded to the winner of the annual marksmen's festival.

Facing the rear of the Rathaus on Bierstrasse is the half-timbered frontage of Osnabrück's most famous inn, *Walhalla*. It features extensively in Erich Maria Remarque's *The Black Obelisk*, a novel describing the traumatic hyper-inflation of 1923. Neither this nor any of his subsequent books ever matched the spectacular success of his first novel, *All Quiet on the Western Front*, which was the one German book to match the eloquence of the British literature of World War I.

Most of Osnabrück's surviving **old houses** are nearby—on Marienstrasse, Hegerstrasse, Grosser Gildewartare, Krahnstrasse, and Bierstrasse itself. The first three form a yuppified pedestrian precinct, where antique shops and bistros vie with each other for prominence. At the end of Bierstrasse is the former **Dominikanerkirche**, now a cultural center which often features exhibitions of contemporary art. It also contains a weather-worn late Gothic statue of Charlemagne, the only survivor of the original cycle from the Rathaus facade. Beyond here, several fragments of the city wall can be seen round the ring road, including the neoclassical **Heger Tor**, celebrating the victory at Waterloo.

Diagonally opposite is the **Museum of Cultural History** (Tues.–Fri. 9am– 5pm, Sat. 10am–1pm, Sun. 10am–5pm; DM1.50). On the ground floor, the local history collections are of interest for such fragments as the original medieval sculptures from the *Brautportal* of the Marienkirche. Upstairs there's a large collection of works by the local Jewish artist **Felix Nussbaum**, a member of the *Neue Sachlichkeit* art movement, which rejected Expressionism in favor of a starkly realistic form of representation. Nussbaum died in Auschwitz, aged 40, in 1944.

Continuing southwards along Heger-Tor-Wall, you soon see on the left the tall tower of the **Katharinenkirche**, a church broader than it is long. In the big square behind is Osnabrück's most original building, the **Leidenhof**. The sixteenth-century merchant owners converted their original fourteenth-century stone house into a miniature palace by the addition of a staircase tower and a new wing, whose facade resembles a gigantic cardboard cut-out. What really catches the attention, however, are the zigzags painted on the two Renaissance additions, making them look strangely modernistic.

South of here, Neuer Graben and Neumarkt mark the boundaries of the Altstadt, though the "new town" beyond (which had its own set of fortifications) was founded as early as the beginning of the eleventh century. Across from the Leidenhof is the yellow **Schloss** of the prince-bishops, built in an Italianate baroque style. The interior has been modernized to house part of the new University. Down Johannisstrasse is the twin-towered **Johanniskirche**, another thirteenth-century Gothic hall church, whose chancel contains a fine fifteenth-century cycle of sandstone figures of the Apostles. From here, it's just a short walk due east back to the Hauptbahnhof.

Practical Details

The **tourist office** (Mon.–Fri. 8:30am–6pm, Sat. 8:30am–1pm; ☎0541 323 2202) is at no. 22 on the Markt. There's a brand new **youth hostel** to the south of town at Iburger Str. 183a (☎0541 54284); take bus #23 or #25 from Neumarkt, and alight at Kinderhospital. In addition, there are two **campgrounds** in the environs— *Niedersachsenhof* (☎0541 77226) and *Attersee* (☎0541 124147). Cheapest centrally-placed **hotels** are *Vennemann*, Johanisstr. 144 (☎0541 572589), with singles DM26, doubles DM50 and *Nord-Hotel*, Hansastr. 31 (☎0541 64133). Plenty more with similar rates can be found a bit farther out.

Many of the best places to **eat** and **drink** (there's a fine *Osnabrücker* Pils) are in the old streets to the rear of the Rathaus. A couple of more traditional places, each offering Westphalian cuisine at reasonable prices, are *Der Landgraf* on Domhof and *Dom-Restaurant* on Kleine Domfreiheit. The *Lagerhalle* on Rolandsmauer is the most popular **nightspot** in town, featuring live rock, jazz and folk music, along with regular disco evenings. Main **theater** venue is the Jugendstil *Städtische Bühnen* opposite the Dom, while the modern *Stadthalle* on Schlosswall is used for **concerts**.

EASTERN LOWER SAXONY

Almost immediately south of the River Elbe the landscape transforms itself from coastal plain to the rolling heathland of the **Lüneburger Heide**, which contains the contrasting towns of **Lüneburg** and **Celle**, as well as several nature reserves. This extends eastwards to an area known as the **Wendland** that juts into the GDR, and south towards the state capital of **Hannover** and the province's second city, **Braunschweig**. Continuing in a southerly direction, you soon come to more elevated land; **Hildesheim** stands in the foothills leading to the Harz, while there are fine rolling landscapes around **Hameln** in the valley of the River Weser farther west.

The Lüneburger Heide

Between Hamburg and Hannover the undulating landscape of the **LÜNEBURGER HEIDE** provides the first welcome relief from North Germany's otherwise relentless flatness. Part wooded, but mainly uncultivated open heathland, the Heide is grazed by large flocks of *Heidschnucken*, goaty-sheep descended from the Corsican *mouflon*. It's the grazing by these large, long-haired and curly-horned creatures that maintains the heath by keeping down the seedlings. In late August the heather erupts in deep purple swathes, adding a mass of color to the heath's otherwise subtle palette.

The main towns of Lüneburg, in the north of the heath, and Celle, to its south, are detailed below. Picturesque villages, with timber-and-brick houses and churches, are also dotted around, forming an idyllic backdrop for festivals, the annual coronation of the queen of the heath, and shepherds who still wear their traditional green outfits. The only blots on the pastoral horizon are the large British troop **exercise areas and gunning ranges**, a legacy of the fact that it was here, on 4 May 1945, that Field Marshal Montgomery received the German surrender.

One of these bases is right on the edge of the **Naturpark Lüneburger Heide**, the main, and most central, of four large nature reserves in the northwest of the Heath, where the heathland and villages are least changed. Motor traffic is forbidden in this park (apart from a road from Egestorf–Undeloh–Welle), but there are networks of footpaths and cycle paths (hiring a bike is usually easy) and it's lovely cycling country. Riding is available, too (most tourist offices have details). Bees buzz over the heather, and the local honey is renowned—as are the potatoes, oddly enough. Places to stay abound, and it's well worth picking up the annual (free) *Lüneburger Heide Gastgeberverzeichnis* which lists hotels, guesthouses and pensions in all the villages throughout the region. Depending on the time of year, you can probably rely on finding accommodation as you go; most towns have a tourist office for visitors. Many places would make a good base—**BISPINGEN** is one, a pretty village with a fourteenth-century church and a youth hostel. **UNDELOH** is another attractive village, with a timbered church going back to the twelfth century, and close by is the village of Wilsede. At **WILSEDE**, which is reached by walking 4km from Undeloh, an old Heide farmhouse, *Dat Ole Huss*, preserves the ways of the past. You can also climb up northern Germany's highest hill, the Wilseder Berg, for all-round views of the heath.

Public transit in this area is fiddly; there are a number of railroad lines crisscrossing the area, but you can get involved in countless changes. The Lüneburg–

Uelzen–Celle line, for instance (don't get off at Uelzen unless you really have to see its thirteenth-century church, as its industrial chimneys are too depressing) does not run via the Naturpark Lüneburger Heide, but the Lüneburg–Undeloh bus runs in the right sort of direction, every couple of hours. You could change from the Lüneburg–Celle train at Uelzen, though, and go west to Soltau, and then take to bicycles. (Soltau has a youth hostel and camping.)

The **Südheide**, another nature reserve down towards Celle, has more forest than farther northwest; the Unterlüss forest is an extensive area of natural woodland, and footpaths lead through it for "Wandern." The youth hostel in this area is at Müden. Close by, just south of Bergen, is **BERGEN-BELSEN**, site of **Belsen concentration camp**. It's a monument and museum now, run by the state office for political education, but nevertheless still horrific. The buildings were destroyed at the end of the war, but the mass graves remain, and a visit to the site of such horror is deeply disturbing. Just down the road is a British army base, and the sound of their heavy guns going off makes events of 45 years ago seem eerily close. In Bergen itself there's a small **open-air museum** of old farm buildings (Am Friedenplatz 7; Mon.–Thur 9:30am–noon and 3–5pm, Fri. 9:30am–noon). It's very hard to find—follow the sign near the church.

Lüneburg

In medieval times salt was a rare and essential commodity, almost worth its weight in gold—and the magnificent old brick houses of **LÜNEBURG** demonstrate the wealth and power that city gained from the salt it extracted and sold, from the tenth century onwards, to Scandinavia, Burgundy, Poland and Russia. Gabled facades, from Gothic to baroque, line many streets, in spite of subsidence caused by disused mines. (The salt deposits haven't been worked since 1980.)

Coming by train, you arrive at Bahnhof West, Bahnhof Ost, or Bahnhof Süd, which together form the **Hauptbahnhof**. You can then go north along Lünertor Strasse into the center, or south along Altenbrückertor Strasse—catching a glimpse from the bridge of one of the water mills, the *Ratsmühle*, on the left.

Altenbrückertor Strasse leads past the impressively large brick church of **St. Johannis**. This was begun in the thirteenth century, but the tall tower, which leans a couple of meters out of true, was only erected in the early fifteenth century. The church's organ is celebrated—the case and some of the pipework are early eighteenth-century, but it incorporates much of its mid sixteenth-century predecessor, one of the oldest instruments in the country. Almost equally precious is the high altar retable, a co-operative work by several fifteenth-century artists from Hamburg and Lübeck.

Am Sande, whose name reflects the fact that it was laid out on a sandy marsh, is Lüneburg's elongated main square, lined with historic frontages marred occasionally by modern shops. Peek in the Bäckerstrasse for the old **pharmacy**, the 1598 *Rathsapotheke*—they don't mind you going in just for a glimpse at the interior. Further west, on J.S.-Bach-Platz, is another brick Gothic church, **St. Michael**. Its *Goldene Tafel* treasures are now in the Kestner Museum and Landesgalerie in Hannover; nowadays the building is chiefly remarkable for the tottering appearance it presents because of its insecure foundations.

Tuesdays, Wednesdays and Saturdays are market days in the square in front of the **Rathaus** (reached along Auf der Meere), whose baroque facade masks a medieval structure begun around 1230. (Guided tours Tues.–Sun. 10am, 11am, 2pm and 3pm; DM4, DM2 students.) The *Gerichtslaube*, the old council chamber, with its powerful and beautifully painted pillars and arches, is the most impressive and famous part, but equally striking is the *Grosse Ratsstube*—adorned with carvings by Albert von Soest, it's one of Germany's most important Renaissance halls. In addition, you get to see the silver collection. Under the Rathaus' front arches is the **tourist office** (May–Sept. Mon.–Fri. 9am–1pm and 2–6pm, Sat. and Sun. 9am–1pm, Oct.–April Mon.–Fri. only; ☎04131 24593) which has various maps and pamphlets in English. They also keep the *Lüneburger Heide Gastgeberverzeichnis* accommodation list (handy if you are going into the Heide), and bus and train timetables.

There's a lovely walk along the Lüner Strasse to the old **port** (*Wasserviertel*) past one of the city's oldest houses, formerly the town house of the Kloster Lüne. The imperious buildings, peaceful riverside setting, trees, bridges, mills and 200-year-old crane create a picture far more pleasant than any modern-day harbor could ever be. Formerly a herring warehouse, the **Altes Kaufhaus** had to be rebuilt after a fire in 1959, but still has its cheery baroque facade. Opposite is the **Bräuhaus**, a gabled Renaissance building which was once the town's brewery.

Kloster Lüne itself (guided tours April–Oct. Mon.–Sat. 9am–noon and 3–6pm, Sun. 11:30am–1pm and 2–6pm; DM3) lies 2km north of town. The present complex dates largely from the late fourteenth and early fifteenth centuries, though the half-timbered outbuildings were added later. It became a Protestant convent at the Reformation, but has served as a plush retirement home since the early eighteenth century. You might want to hire a bicycle to get there—*Laden 25* at Am Werder 25 near the Altes Kaufhaus rents them out (closed lunchtime Wed, Sat. afternoon and all day Sun.).

Among the best places to **eat** and **drink** are *Kronen* on Heiligengeiststrasse (the westward continuation of Am Sand), which has a beer garden, and *Scheffler*, in an old half-timbered house on Bardowicker Strasse. For a relaxed *al fresco* summer atmsophere, when tables are put out on the street, try along Stintmarkt, on the western side of the Wasserviertel. Lüneburg's long tradition of making **beer** is maintained with the very dry *Moravia Pils*. If you want to stay, there's a **youth hostel** at Saltauer Str. 133 (☎04131 41864) well to the south of town, best reached by bus #1. The **campground** (☎04131 791500) is by the banks of the River Ilmenau even farther south; catch a bus towards DEUTSHEVERN.

Wendland and the Elbufer

If you look at a map of this area, two things might strike you about its eastern part (which, strictly speaking, is no longer the Lüneburger Heide): first, that the border with the GDR follows the River Elbe southwards but then cuts right back in, leaving a V-shaped wedge of West Germany jutting into the East; second, that many place names have a curiously Slavic character—for example Lüchow, Gartow, Meetschow. The area is known as **Wendland** after a Slavic tribe called the Wends, who left their mark on the landscape in the form of the distinctive round villages called *Rundlingdörfer*. Basically, a cluster of about ten thatched, timbered houses are arranged close together in a circle, all facing inwards so the village could be better defended. The *Rundlingsdörfer* are tucked away in the trees, off the main roads—look out for signposts indicating "Rundlingsdorf." Most of them are still lived in, but the inhabitants are used to being peered at by visitors. Some offer **pension accommodation**—in **GÖTTIEN** for instance (near Küsten, just west of Lüchow) you can stay at *Der Eichenhof* (☎05841 3156).

Most of the area along and near the banks of the Elbe, known as the **Elbufer**, belongs to the nature park Elbufer-Drawehn, an arm of which reaches down to Clenze. Much of the park is wooded, including the large forest at Göhrde and the Gartower Forst, but there are wetland areas along the banks of the Elbe. It's an unspoilt and picturesque stretch, much less visited than nearby Lüneburger Heide, though its isolation is rather spoiled by the border lookout posts and by **GORLEBEN**. Back in the 1970s the government decreed the salt mines at Gorleben a suitable storage place for nuclear waste. There was massive public resistance, not only for ecological and safety reasons, but because of the provocative location—virtually at the furthest point of this "intrusion" into the East. An "independent" state—*Freies Wendland*—was even established as part of the protest, and the alternative/green influence still has a high profile. Test drilling is now going on, and the conflict is not yet over, so Gorleben still hits the headlines from time to time.

Most of the towns have some historic church or tower to see: tiny **SCHNACKENBURG** qualifies officially as a town, because it used to be a toll point for Elbe shipping; **DANNENBERG** (trains and buses from Lüneburg) is all timbered houses and has a twelfth-century tower; **HITZACKER** is lovely, built on an island where the river Jeetzel joins the Elbe (it has the area's **youth hostel** and is again connected to Lüneburg by bus and train).

If you are cycling, especially, you could follow the Elbuferstrasse along the bank of the Elbe up to Hamburg—cycle tracks near the city avoid the busy roads.

Celle

Somewhere between Lüneburg and **CELLE** (pronounced "tseller") is an invisible line—as you go south you leave behind the magnificent brickwork of the Hanseatic towns and flatland, and enter the domain of timbered buildings that stretches to Germany's southern borders and beyond. So while Lüneburg and Celle are the northern and southern hubs of the Lüneburger Heide, these two old and beautiful towns seem to have come from different worlds. Which in fact they did, for while Lüneburg resembles the Baltic merchant towns it had such close contact with, the ducal town of Celle was centered much more on castle and military life. Celle's abundance of sixteenth- to eighteenth-century timbered buildings has been impressively preserved, and whole streets are intact.

The **Schloss** dominates the old town, and the main streets run towards it with a gesture of subservience. Originally built in the late thirteenth century, it became the main residence of the Dukes of Lüneburg in 1378, when the independently-minded burghers of Lüneburg flexed their collective muscle and chucked out their feudal overlords. In 1530, the building was completely rebuilt in the Renaissance style; the present whitewashed exterior, with its idiosyncratic corner towers, decorative gables, and lofty, confined courtyard, dates almost entirely from this period.

Sole survivor of the medieval castle is the **Schlosskapelle**, which was cleverly incorporated into the southeastern tower facing the town, its pointed Gothic windows being the only giveaway as to its presence there. The highlight of the **guided tour** of the Schloss (daily at 9am, 10am, 11am, noon, 2pm, 3pm and 4pm; DM1) is the chapel, whose architectural simplicity was obscured in the second half of the sixteenth century by an integrated program of Mannerist decoration that is still stunningly fresh and vibrant. The cycle of 76 paintings, commissioned from the Antwerp artist **Marten de Vos** (once an assistant to Tintoretto in Venice), forms a complete illustrated Bible, in accordance with the new Protestant doctrines. The two galleries are adorned with portrait sculptures of Old and New Testament figures, and wacky pendants of varying shapes and sizes hang from the vault. Both the pulpit, with reliefs of the Passion, and the organ, resplendent with painted shutters, are intrinsic parts of the scheme, and are beautiful works of art in their own right.

Early in the eighteenth century the Duchy of Lüneburg was reunited with Hannover (which had split off the previous century) when Sophie Dorothea, daughter of the last Duke of Lüneburg, married the future George I of Britain. Thereafter, Celle was no more than the second-string German residence of the Hanoverian dynasty, and a place where those who had fallen from grace could readily be dumped. Sophie Dorothea, mother of George II of Britain and grandmother of Frederick the Great of Prussia, was banished there for life following an alleged indiscretion with a courtier. In the 1770s the Schloss became home for a few years to another exiled queen, Caroline Mathilde of Denmark, and her **suite of rooms** can be visited independently (Mon.–Sat. 10am–4:30pm, Sun. 10:30am–12:30pm; DM1).

An especially pleasant way to sneak a look inside other parts of the Schloss is to go to a performance at its **theater**—dating back to 1674, it's the oldest one in Germany to have a resident company. Concerts and plays are performed throughout the year, except during July and August. Tickets and information are available (mornings only) from the box office at Schlossplatz 13. Unfortunately, the powers-that-be don't allow you near the handsome baroque auditorium unless you're attending a performance.

Celle's other outstanding feature is its sheer quantity of original **half-timbered buildings**—480 in all. The town is trying to resolve the problem of how to protect them, yet keep the center alive. Unless businesses are given the chance to modernize property, the council believes, an alternative commercial center would soon be set up in a different part of town, and the Altstadt would become a museum-piece. A careful check is supposedly made on modifications that are carried out, but it's still jarring when you see a beautiful seventeenth-century building fitted with a chain-store's shop front, or a concrete structure faced with mock timber (as with the *C&A* building).

All this notwithstanding, every street in the Altstadt is a visual treat, and well worth including in a gentle stroll. The place to begin is Stechbahn (formerly a yard used for tournaments) which runs from the center of Schlossplatz; here you see a Renaissance house with oriels and the early sixteenth-century court pharmacy, the **Löwenapothek**. Opposite the latter is the **Stadtkirche**, whose tower (Tues.–Sat. 3–6pm; DM 0.50) commands the best view of the town—and a trumpeter plays a chorale from here at 6:30am and 6:30pm every day. The church itself, originally Gothic, has a baroque interior and serves as the pantheon of the local dukes. Behind is the **Rathaus**, whose fourteenth-century *Ratskeller* is the oldest pub in northern Germany. Most of the building, however, is in the carefree Weser Renaissance style, and is distinguished by two beautifully contrasted oriel windows: one at street level, the other an extension of a gable.

The most outstanding half-timbered house in Celle is the **Hoppener Haus** at the corner of Rundestrasse and Poststrasse. Built for a courtier in 1532, it's richly carved with allegorical figures, monsters, scrollwork and scenes of rural life. In front stands a lion fountain, known as the *Piepenposten*. Oldest dated house is at Am Heiligen Kreu 26, which states that it was built in 1526, though Neue Str. 32

(originally fifteenth-century but with a Renaissance oriel) has the best claim to be regarded as the most venerable house in town. Look out for the corner of Nordwall and Bergstrasse, where someone built their home on top of a piece of the original city wall. Among later baroque stone buildings is the **Stechinellihaus** on Grosser Plan, named after an influential Italian architect and courtier who lived in a house on this site.

The **Bomann museum** (Mon.–Sat. 10am–5pm, Sun. 10am–1pm; DM1), in a grandiose Jugendstil building at the corner of Schlossplatz and Stechbahn, is above average for a local collection. The displays on regional trades, history and folklore feature several reconstructed farmhouses and (in the courtyard) a half-timbered house fully furnished in the Biedermeier style.

Just outside the eastern edge of the Altstadt is the old ghetto, though the colorful baroque half-timbered houses themselves hardly offer any clue as to the area's former status. Within one of these houses, Im Kreise 24, is the **Synagogue** (Mon.–Fri. 3–5pm; free). Its decoration was destroyed on *Kristallnacht*, but, most unusually, it wasn't burned down. After the war it was well restored, and it stands today as one of the very few historic Jewish temples left in Germany.

Not far from here, bounding the southern side of the Altstadt, is the **Französischer Garten** (*French Garden*), which was laid out in the seventeenth century and later adapted in the informal English manner. Within the park is the **Bieneninstitut** (Mon.–Fri. 9am–noon and 2–4pm; free), the main bee-keeping station in Lower Saxony. Beyond is the **Ludwigskirche**, the only neoclassical church in northern Germany, designed by the great Berlin architect, Karl Friedrich Schinkel. Its exterior is marred by the later addition of a pair of towers, but the interior is a gem—a miniature, updated version of the columned basilicas of the Romans.

West of the Schloss, on the road between the town and the **Hauptbahnhof**, are more half-timbered houses, plus a number of baroque palaces in the French style. The most impressive of these, complete with gate-house, courtyard and a handsome facade bearing the ducal coat of arms, is the **Justizvollzugsanstalt**. This, strange to say, served as the local prison and workhouse.

South of here, reached down Breite Strasse, is the **Niedersächsische Landgestüt** (*Lower Saxon Stud Farm*), which was founded by King George II in 1735. It can be visited outside the season, when the 250 or so stallions are put out to stud (mid-July to mid-Feb. Mon.–Fri. 8:30–11:30am and 3–4:30pm; free), but the time to come is during the big autumn **festival**, the highlight of Celle's social calendar. Held on the last Sunday in September and the first in October (or, on occasions, the last two in September), plus the Wednesday preceding these, each program lasts for three hours, and features a parade of the stallions, as well as a quadrille performed by coaches-and-ten.

The **tourist office** (mid-May–mid-Oct. Mon.–Fri. 8am–6pm, Sat. 9am–1pm and 2–5pm, Sun. 10am–noon, rest of year Mon.–Fri. 8am–5pm, Sat. 10am–noon; ☎05141 23031) on Schlossplatz will find a **room** for you free of charge. Hotels within the Altstadt are uniformly expensive, and you'll have to stay some way outside to save money. Cheapest option is *Sohneman*, Reite 1 (☎05141 51170) at DM27 per head; DM30 is the going rate at *Gudehus*, Celler Str. 11 (☎05141 51528); *Rastätte Davy*, Celler Str. 43a (☎05141 51765) and *Urban*, Waldschmiede 6 (☎05141 41962). Alternatively, there's a **youth hostel** at Weghausstr. 2 (☎05141 53208); turn left on leaving the Hauptbahnhof and continue straight ahead for about 2km, or take bus #3 to Dorfstrasse. The **campground** is at *Silbersee* (☎05141 31223) in VORWERK, a suburb at the northern end of town.

Among places to **eat** and **drink**, pride of place goes to the *Ratskeller*. It's on the expensive side, but worth it in view of the superb food and historical setting. Almost as good are *Union* on Thaerplatz and *Schwarzwaldstube* on Bergstrasse. After a long gap, the town is once more a center of **beer** production. You can sample *Celler Urtrüb* and the powerful *Cellenser Bock* at the brewery's own *Gaststätte Urtrüb-Klause* at Nordwall 56. For a beergarden atmosphere, there's *Bier-Akademie* on Am Weissen Wall; for a wine bar, try *Utspann* on Im Kreise.

Wienhausen
WIENHAUSEN, a village of half-timbered houses 10km southeast of Celle, clusters around a remarkable **Kloster** (guided tours April–Sept. Mon.–Sat. at 10am, 11am, 2pm, 3pm, 4pm and 5pm, Sun. at 11:30am, 1pm, 2pm, 3pm, 4pm and 5pm, Oct. same times except Mon.–Sat. at 4pm and 5pm; DM5). Founded in 1231 by Agnes von Meissen, daughter-in-law of Henry the Lion, the convent became Protestant at the Reformation, and is still in use today. The superb brick buildings are something of an anomaly this far south. Their severity stands in contrast to the brightness of the nuns' chancel, whose walls are covered with a well-preserved cycle of fourteenth-century frescos illustrating the life of Christ and legend of the Holy Cross, along with secular subjects. In the center of the choir is a wooden *Holy Sepulchre*, complete with a figure of the dead Christ, which dates from the late thirteenth century.

The Kloster's most valuable treasures are its **tapestries**. Woven by the nuns in the fourteenth and fifteenth centuries, they rank among the greatest ever made. Unfortunately, they're only put on display for eleven days around Pentecost each year; check with the tourist office in Celle for the exact dates.

Hannover

At first, for some reason or other, Hanover strikes you as an uninteresting town, but it grows upon you. It is in reality two towns: a place of broad, modern, handsome streets and tasteful gardens, side by side with a sixteenth-century town, where old timbered houses overhang the narrow lanes; where through low arches one catches glimpses of cobbled courtyards, once often thronged, no doubt, with troops of horse, or blocked with lumbering coach and six, waiting its rich merchant owner and his fat placid frau . . .

Though written at the turn of the century, this description of **HANNOVER** (one of the "n"s is dropped in the anglicized form) by Jerome K. Jerome is still apposite. Initial impressions of this city are unlikely to be very promising, and, despite having had the benefit of a long special relationship with Britain, and having played an important part in European cultural history to boot, it hasn't generally been given a good press in guidebooks.

Hannover was something of a late developer, only really coming to the fore in the second half of the seventeenth century, and much of its best architecture belongs to the nineteenth and early twentieth centuries. An even bigger handicap is the fact that Hannover's great showpiece is not a great cathedral (it's never had one), palace or town hall, but a **series of gardens**. However, these are no ordinary gardens—they're by far the most impressive in Germany (arguably, in Europe), preserving their spectacular original baroque features almost intact. Add this to a number of first-class **museums** and a vibrant cultural scene, and there's plenty in Hannover to keep you occupied for a couple of days.

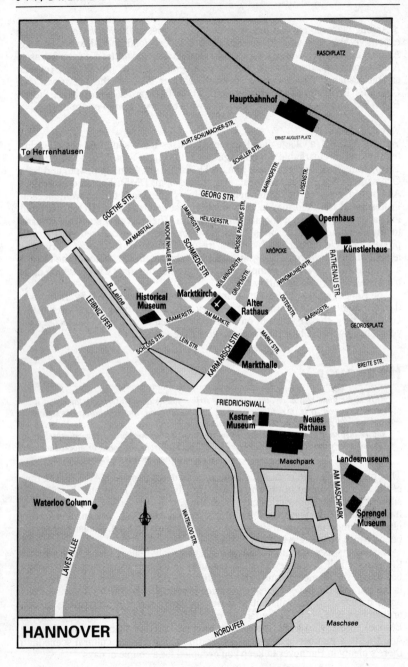

RASCHPLATZ

Hauptbahnhof

KURT-SCHUMACHER-STR.

ERNST-AUGUST-PLATZ

To Herrenhausen

SCHILLER STR.

BAHNHOFSTR.

LUISENSTR.

GEORG STR.

GOETHE STR.

LIMBURGSTR.

HEILIGERSTR.

GROSSE PACKHOF STR.

Opernhaus

Künstlerhaus

AM MARSTALL

KNOCHENHAUER STR.

SCHMIEDE STR.

SELWINDERSTR.

GRUPENSTR.

KRÖPCKE

WINDMÜHENSTR.

RATHENAU STR.

OSTERSTR.

R. Leine

LEIBNIZ UFER

Historical Museum

Marktkirche

Alter Rathaus

KRAMERSTR.

AM MARKTE

BARINGSTR.

GEORGSPLATZ

SCHLOSS STR.

LEIN STR.

KÄRMARSCH STR.

MARKT STR.

Markthalle

BREITE STR.

FRIEDRICHSWALL

Kestner Museum

Neues Rathaus

Maschpark

Landesmuseum

AM MASCHPARK

Sprengel Museum

Waterloo Column

WATERLOO STR.

LAVES ALLEE

NORDUFER

Maschsee

HANNOVER

Arriving and Getting Around

The **Hauptbahnhof** is right in the center of town; **exchange facilities** are available there Mon.–Fri. 8am–8pm, Sat. 8am–5pm, Sun. 10am–2pm. To the rear is the **bus station** for long-distance routes. The **tourist office** (Mon.–Fri. 8:30am–6pm, Sat. 8:30am–noon; ☎168 2319)) is on Ernst-August-Platz, the square facing the Hauptbahnhof. Here you can pick up maps, lists of what's on (and book tickets for main events), and *The Red Thread*. This is a horribly chatty but very useful free booklet to Hannover's sights, guiding visitors along the Red Thread—a painted red line running along the sidewalks, across roads and down subways, and not a bad way of acquainting yourself with the city.

For DM3 the tourist office will book you a **hotel**. As a flourishing center of the lucrative trade fair industry (the April *Messe* is the largest in Europe), Hannover hoteliers can afford to charge fancy prices. Provided there isn't a fair on, it's probably best to check with the tourist office first to see if there are any bargains going. Normally the lowest rates, at around DM40–47 per head, are at *Hospiz am Bahnhof*, Joachimstr. 2 (☎324297); *Flora*, Heinrichstr. 36 (☎342334); *Knuth*, Marienstr. 7 (☎17577); *Reverey*, Aegidiendamm 8 (☎883711); and *Gildehof*, Joachimstr. 6 (☎15742/4). All are centrally located; there are plenty of more distant alternatives, but they're no cheaper.

Otherwise, there's a **youth hostel** at Ferdinand-Wilhelm-Fricke-Weg 1 (☎322941); take U-Bahn #3 or #7 direction Mühlenberg, and alight at Fischerhof, from where it's a five-minute walk to the left over the bridge. Alongside is a **campground**. More expensive than these, but still a bit cheaper than any hotel, is the *Naturfreundehaus* on the edge of the wooded Eilriede park at Hermann-Bahlsen-Allee 8 (☎691493); take U-Bahn #3 direction Lahe or #7 direction Fasanenkrug to Spannhagenstrasse.

There are only two fares on the entire **public transit** network; it's well worth buying tickets in strips of six, for DM10, or investing in a DM6 24-hour pass. Some trams stop on Ernst-August-Platz, while others go underground to form the U-Bahn in the city center, with stops at the Hauptbahnhof and Kröpcke.

Hanoverian History . . . and the British Connection

In the seventeenth century, the territories of the Welf House of Braunschweig-Lüneberg were split up, and a new duchy, clumsily named Braunschweig-Calenberg-Göttingen, came into being. This was commonly known as Hannover, after the old Hanseatic market and brewing town which was its principal city. A new summer residence for the court was slowly laid out at the village of HÖRINGEHUSEN, a couple of kilometers from Hannover's Altstadt.

Ernst August, who acceded to the duchy in 1679, was a man of high ambition. He charged Gottfried Wilhelm Leibnitz, the great philosopher and scientist who served as librarian and historian to the Welfs for forty years, with the task of proving that the House was descended from the Italian Este family. The successful conclusion of this entitled the duke to claim a new Electorate in the Holy Roman Empire, which was formally bestowed in 1692. Even more significant was Ernst August's marriage to **Sophie von der Pfalz**, daughter of Elizabeth Stuart, the "Winter Queen" (see Heidelberg, *Chapter Two*). In 1710, the newly united Parliament of Great Britain passed the Act of Settlement, in order to cut off the Catholic "Old Pretender" and his heirs and ensure the continuation of a Protestant monarchy. This named Sophie as next in line to the throne after Princess (later Queen) Anne. In the event, Sophie died just before Anne in 1714, and her son **Georg Ludwig** became King George I of the United Kingdom.

As well as a monarch, Britain gained one of the greatest composers of all time. Anticipating the accession, the court director of music, **Georg Friedrich Händel**, was already well established in London by the time his employer had taken up residence. Hitherto a footloose wanderer, the composer at last found his spiritual home there, anglicizing his name, and taking British nationality. His output came to center on oratorios set to English texts, the most famous of which, the sublime *Messiah*, has become a setpiece of Protestant culture.

Until 1837, Britain and Hannover shared the same ruler. At first, monarchs divided their residency between the territories (George I understandably so, as he never learned to speak English), but gradually they neglected their original seat. When William IV died without issue, however, the union came to an end. The exclusion of women from the succession in Hannover meant that another Ernst August ascended to its throne (it was by now a kingdom in its own right) whereas his niece Victoria became the British Queen.

This led to another bright period in Hannover's history, during which the city was transformed in neoclassical style by the court architect, **Georg Ludwig Friedrich Laves**. In the event, this turned out to be a false dawn. During the Seven Weeks' War of 1866, the blind King Georg V opted to back neither Prussia nor Austria; the rampaging Prussian victors responded by driving him into exile, and annexing his kingdom. Hannover thereafter remained part of Prussia until 1946, when the old duchy became the main component of the newly created Land of Lower Saxony, with the city itself reinstated as a provincial capital.

The City Center

Hannover has had to reconstruct itself after being almost totally demolished by World War II bombing, and the view on arrival at the Hauptbahnhof isn't exactly prepossessing, with a bland pedestrian precinct stretching ahead. Underneath runs the **Passarelle**; mostly under cover, but with sections in the open-air, it's meant to be a sort of subterranean bazaar-cum-piazza. While the prime sites at the flashy end are occupied by expensive shops, towards the station it predictably becomes seedier; many shop-sites are empty, and walking through at night is a little disconcerting.

Standing at Hannover's most popular rendezvous, the Café Kröpcke, the most imposing building in view is the **Opernhaus**, a proud neoclassical design which is arguably the finest of the city's Laves-designed showpieces. Nearby are other self-confident public buildings from later in the century, close in style to British architecture of the time. On Sophienstrasse, the yellow and red brick **Künstlerhaus**, originally a museum, is now a lively arts center, while the neo-Renaissance **Ständehaus**, built as a guild hall, now houses the state treasury department. The **Bourse** on Rathenaustrasse actually imitates the Tudor style—proof that British influence continued long after the end of the monarchical link.

Southwards, across the Friedrichswall (once a city wall but now a wide road with subways) is the **Neues Rathaus** (open during working hours), a gargantuan early twentieth-century art-deco-cum-neo-Gothic fantasy, which is held into its marshy foundations by over 6000 beechwood piles. It's definitely worth a peek inside; there are occasional guided tours but no-one seems to mind if you just wander round, up and down the spiral staircases. Between April and October (9:30am–noon and 2–5pm; DM2) you can ascend to the dome for what are the best views of the city. However, the main attraction is the elevator which takes you up—it follows an inclined path and is apparently one of only two in Europe like this. Look out for the models of Hannover at various stages of its history; the one of the bombed wartime city is a shocking record of the damage it suffered.

Directly behind the Neues Rathaus is the **Maschpark**, with a small artificial lake. Farther on is a much larger man-made lake, the **Maschsee**, which serves as the locals' main playground. You can saunter down its tree-lined promenades; take a cruise on a pleasure steamer, or else hire a rowing boat or canoe. The city's three most important museums (see below) are all in the vicinity.

Across Friedrichswall is the **Laves Haus**, which the architect designed as his own home. He also erected the **Wagenheim Palais** next door, and completely transformed the **Leineschloss** (now the Land parliament) down the street, whose dignified porticos are modeled on the temples of ancient Greece. Down Lavesallee is yet another of his works, the **Waterloo Column**, commemorating the part played by the Hanoverian troops in the final defeat of Napoleon. It was mainly thanks to them that Wellington's central line held long enough for Blücher's Prussian forces to reach Waterloo and turn the tide in favor of the beleaguered British. A short walk to the north is the former priory church of **St. Clement**, built in the early eighteenth century by one of Laves' predecessors as court architect, the Venetian Tommaso Giusti.

To the rear of the Leineschloss are a few streets of rebuilt **half-timbered buildings**, conveying something of the impression of the medieval town, which had already been much altered before the devastation of the last war; its form is easier to imagine if you've seen nearby **CELLE**, which is preserved almost intact. The main buildings, however, have been well restored, notably the high-gabled fifteenth-century **Altes Rathaus**, whose elaborate brickwork is enlivened with colorful glazed tiles.

Alongside is the fourteenth-century **Marktkirche**, the most southerly of the series of brick hall churches characteristic of the Baltic lands. Its bulky tower, terminating in a spire of unusual design, has long been the emblem of the city. Originally it was meant to be much higher, but an old chronicle reports that it was finished off quickly because "the masons had become tired and sick in the purse." The unadorned interior walls are now closer to how the building origi-nally looked than has been the case for some 300 years. There's a noble carved *Retable of the Passion*, made around 1500, at the high altar; miraculously, the four teenth- to fifteenth-century stained glass in the east windows has survived, and has recently been cleaned and restored.

A couple of streets north is the **Ballhof**, a seventeenth-century half-timbered sports hall which is now the main repertory theater. On nearby Holzmarkt (not its original location) the **Leibnitz Haus** has been re-erected following its total destruction in the war. This magnificent Renaissance mansion was the home of **Gottfried Wilhelm Leibnitz**. A historian by profession, Leibnitz was active in a vast range of intellectual fields: he developed Pascal's calculating machine, arrived independently at the theory of differential calculus at the same time as Newton, charted the origins and migrations of mankind, and made enormous contributions to the disciplines of jurisprudence, philosophy, theology, geology and linguistics.

Finally, if you're keen on modern architecture, make sure you see the **Anzeigerhochhaus**, just a short walk from the Hauptbahnhof on Goseriede. This newspaper office, made of brick-clad reinforced concrete and topped with a green copper dome, is an example of the 1920s Expressionism of Fritz Höger. Even if it's hardly the skyscraper it purports to be, and is less dramatic than the same architect's Chilehaus in Hamburg, it's nonetheless an arresting, balanced, and well-thought-out design.

Herrenhausen

The royal gardens of **HERRENHAUSEN** (as Höringehusen came to be known) can be reached from the center by U-Bahn #1 or #2. However, it's advisable to walk either there or back, as the route goes through two of the four gardens which make up the set; before venturing out, make sure you pick up the free tourist office leaflet which has an excellent plan of the complex. Proceeding north from town along Nienburger Strasse, the least remarkable of the gardens—the **Welfengarten**—lies to the right, dominated by the huge neo-Gothic pile of the **Welfenpalais**, now occupied by the university. To the left, the dead straight avenue of lime trees named Herrenhäuser Allee cuts through the **Georgengarten**. This is a *jardin anglais* of the type beloved by the Romantics, featuring trees arranged in an apparently natural setting, and an artificial lake, crossed by two graceful little bridges designed by Laves. Also within this park is the neoclassical **Georgenpalais**, home of the Wilhelm Busch Museum (see below).

The Georgengarten was created as a foil to the magnificence of the formal **Grosser Garten** (daily 8am–8pm in summer, 8am–4:30pm in winter; free), which is justifiably the city's pride and joy. It's best to time your visit to coincide with the playing of the **fountains** (May–Sept. Mon.–Fri. 11am–noon and 3–4pm, Sat. and Sun. 10am–noon and 3–5pm) or when the **illuminations** are switched on (May–Sept. Wed, Fri. and Sat. at dusk). Credit for the splendor of the layout goes to the Electress Sophie, who called them "my life," and her gardener, the Frenchman Martin Charbonnier, who completely transformed the initially modest garden into a spectacular showpiece which drew on elements of the French, Italian and Dutch traditions. Sadly the original palace was totally destroyed by Allied bombing in the war, but the **Galerie**, a festive hall adorned with frothy frescos of Virgil's *Aeneid*, and the **Orangery** have survived.

Just inside the entrance gate is one of the most striking features, the **Hedge Theater**. Temporary structures for music and drama were commonplace within royal gardens, but this one was permanent, featuring an auditorium in the form of an amphitheater. The hornbeam hedges cleverly doubled as scenery and changing rooms, while a series of gilded statues on pedestals served as stage props. Plays by Molière and Racine, and music by Händel, formed the staple repertoire of this theater in its early days, and are still performed during the summer season. Immediately to the east is the **Grande Parterre**, whose eight sections are planted with geometric arrangements of flowers and shrubs. In front stands the Italianate **Great Cascade**, belonging to the original garden, plus a sundial and grotto, while the maze is at the far end.

Behind the Grande Parterre is a modern embellishment: eight small plots have been laid out to illustrate different styles of landscape gardening down the centuries. Particularly notable is the **Renaissance Garden**, which reproduces a section of the now-vanished *Hortus Palatinus* in Heidelberg; others include a north German "Garden of Love" and an English "bowling green." West of here is the secluded **Bosquet Garden**, used by courtiers for intrigues and romantic encounters.

The rear section of the Grosser Garten consists of a series of radiating avenues bounded by hedges and trees, each ending at a fountain. As a centerpiece, there's the **Grosse Fontäne**, which spurts Europe's highest jet of water. Its operation has been a continued technological challenge: after many teething problems, the eighteenth-century engineers managed to get it to rise to 36 meters; using the same nozzle, it now reaches 82 meters. Remarkably little water is needed for its operation—its spectacular effect is achieved by sheer speed, with the water traveling through a narrow slit at 140 kilometers per hour.

Across Herrenhäuser Strasse to the north of the Grosser Garten is the **Berggarten**, set up to tend rare and exotic plants. Its collection of orchids was considered the finest in Europe, and many are still cultivated in its hothouses. Behind these are a rock garden, a pergola garden and an iris garden; the last-named is in full bloom in April and May. Even more glorious is the central "Paradise" of rhododendrons. At the far end of the Berggarten is the **Mausoleum** of the House of Hannover, a late work by Laves in the sternest neoclassical manner. A graphic illustration of how the architect's style had developed is provided by the domed **Library** at the entrance, which he designed thirty years earlier in a carefree idiom still showing echoes of the baroque.

Some compensation for the loss of the palace is provided by a number of courtly buildings to be found to the west along Herrenhäuser Strasse. The so-called **Fürstenhaus** (daily April–Sept. 10am–6pm, Oct.–March 10am–5pm; DM3.50) has been adapted as a sort of museum of the House of Hannover; whether it's worth paying the steep entrance fee depends on what value you place on royal mementoes. There's one striking room entirely covered by a panorama of a hunt, and some fine portraits, including likenesses of King George III and Queen Sophie Charlotte as seen by both Thomas Gainsborough and Johann Zoffany.

Hannover's Museums

Historical Museum, *Pferdestr. 6. Tues. 10am–8pm, Wed–Fri. 10am–4pm, Sat. and Sun. 10am–6pm; free.*

Housed in a modern building which incorporates the fourteenth-century *Beginenturm* (the last surviving remnant of the city walls), the displays here are far more imaginative and enjoyable than is usual in a local history museum. On the ground floor to the left are the four **state coaches** of the House of Hannover. Though they can't be much use to them, these are still family property—even the gold carriage, adorned with rococo paintings and carvings, which was made in London in 1783, and used for state openings of the Westminster Parliament. Upstairs, there's a telling contrast to these limousines in the form of the *Hanomag*, a tiny two-seater convertible developed in 1928, which was a sort of trial run for the *Volkswagen* as a family car. A series of pictures, town plans and models illustrates the changing face of Hannover, while several reconstructed **interiors** from farmhouses in the province give an insight into rural life.

Kestner Museum, *Trammplatz 3. Tues., Thurs. and Fri. 10am–4pm, Wed 10am–8pm, Sat. and Sun. 10am–6pm; free.*

This compact decorative arts museum is named after its founder August Kestner, a Hanoverian diplomat in Rome. He was the son of Charlotte Buff, Goethe's first love and a central character in his novella *The Sorrows of Young Werther.*

On the first floor, the medieval collection features treasures and textiles from Lower Saxon convents; outstanding are surviving items from the *Goldene Tafel* of Saint Michael in Lüneburg, and the magnificent gilded bronze head-reliquary of an unknown saint, made around 1200 for Stift Fischbeck. The remaining galleries have an eclectic array of exhibits, ranging from Renaissance bronzes through eighteenth-century porcelain to a luxuriant selection of art nouveau *objets d'art* from America as well as Europe. Upstairs are examples of the ancient Greek,

Etruscan, Roman and Cypriot civilizations, along with a more comprehensive Egyptian collection, among whose highlights are the *Head of the Pharaoh Akhenaten* from about 1350 B.C. and a painted limestone of *The Priest Kinebu and his Wife Isis*, made a couple of centuries later.

Landesmuseum, *Am Maschpark 5. Tues., Wed and Fri.–Sun. 10am–5pm, Thurs. 10am–7pm; free.*

The Landesgalerie on the second floor is the main draw here, with an excellent collection of paintings from the Middle Ages to the early twentieth century. On the left are two rooms of Primitives, of which the most notable is a *Passion Altar* by the first German artist known by name, **Master Bertram**. Most of the other works are by his anonymous Saxon contemporaries; particularly striking are *Two Scenes from the Life of St. Paul* by a Hildesheim artist dubbed **Master of the Lambertikirche**, and the retables from which the **Master of the Golden Table** and the **Master of the Barfüsser Altar** get their names.

In the following rooms, the star painting is an exquisite *Portrait of Philipp Melanchton* by **Hans Holbein the Younger**, displayed alongside its lid, which is one of the few surviving examples of Holbein's skill as a decorative artist. Hanging beside it is a lurid *Luther on his Deathbed* by **Cranach**, and a small *Christ Carrying the Cross* attributed to **Dürer**. A decent display of Italian Renaissance work includes pictures by Botticelli, Raphael, Pontormo and Bronzino.

The large *Bacchus and Venus* by the Antwerp Mannerist **Bartholomäus Spranger** is an allegory illustrating an old proverb: "Wine and women bring two sorrows to life." It's one of the most imposing paintings created in the erotic style cultivated at the turn of the seventeenth century at the court of the Emperor Rudolf II in Prague (and at nearby Bückeburg—see p.553). In the same room is *Solomon in the Temple* by another weird seventeenth-century artist, the Frenchman **François da Nomé**, whose images invariably show, as here, the heavens ablaze while death and destruction reign below. As a total contrast, the peaceful classical world is evoked in **Poussin's** *Inspiration of Anacreon* and **Claude's** *River Landscape with Goatherd*.

Pick of the seventeenth-century Flemish paintings are **Rubens'** *Madonna and Child*, **Van Dyck's** *A Gentleman of Santander, the Governor of Antwerp*, and *Men Bathing by Moonlight* by **Michael Sweerts**; the last, characteristically for this artist, is a highly original subject, with wonderful luminous effects. There's a good cross-section of the Dutch school, including one of **Rembrandt's** rare excursions into nature painting, *Landscape with the Baptism of the Eunuch*, another masterly exposition of contrasts of light and shade. Also of special note is *A Woman in Profile* by his most talented pupil, the short-lived **Carel Fabritius**.

A comprehensive array of the varied styles practised in nineteenth-century Germany includes a set of four small canvases illustrating *The Times of Day* by **Friedrich**; several humorous paintings by Spitzweg, **Leibl's** haunting *Peasant Girl*, and numerous examples of the Impressionists Liebermann, Corinth and Slevogt. A specially dimmed room shows the giant cartoons made by the members of the **Nazarene Brotherhood** for the decoration of the Casa Bartholdy in Rome.

On the first floor of the museum, the **archaeology** department has as its show-piece the bodies of prehistoric men preserved naturally in the peat bogs of Lower Saxony. The varied contents of several excavated graves are another highlight, along with an array of Bronze Age jewelry. On the same floor is a **natural history** section with a wide variety of stuffed animals and a full-scale reconstruction of a dinosaur, while downstairs there's an **aquarium** with live fish from all round the world.

Sprengel Museum, *Kurt-Schwitters-Platz. Tues. 10am–10pm, Wed–Sun. 10am–6pm; DM2.*
Named after the chocolate magnate Bernhard Sprengel, whose gift of his private collection formed the basis of the museum, this ranks as one of the most exciting places in Germany in which to see modern art. An unusually high proportion of the display space is given over to changing exhibitions of photography, graphics, and various experimental art forms, but there's also a first-rate permanent display of twentieth-century painting and sculpture.

Centerpiece of the museum is a huge range of the work of one of this century's most controversial and influential artists, Hannover's own **Kurt Schwitters**. His pleasing early landscapes and still lifes come as a surprise if you're only familiar with the famous Dadaist collages, which, in an attempt to create art out of non-art, tack all kinds of junk on to the canvas. The artist coined the term *Merz* to describe these, and set himself the target of creating a *Merzbau*, a work of art which would fill a house. Both completed versions of these were destroyed in the Nazi measures against "degenerate art," but an accurate reconstruction can be seen here.

Other highlights of the museum include a cross-section of **Picasso**'s work; complete rooms devoted to **Klee** and **Arp**; sculptures by Barlach and Henri Laurens; an updated *Prodigal Son* by **Beckmann**, along with self-portraits painted forty years apart; Surrealist paintings by Magritte, Tanguy and Ernst; and the usual range of Expressionist canvases, with Munch, Nolde, Kirchner and Kokoschka all well represented.

Wilhelm Busch Museum, *Georgengarten 1. Tues.–Sun. 10am–5pm, closes at 4pm Nov.–Feb.; DM2.*
A handsome neoclassical palace serves as the home for the German Museum of Caricature and Critical Drawing, named after the nineteenth-century father of the comic-strip cartoon, **Wilhelm Busch**, who lived and worked in Hannover. Local people flock to the temporary exhibitions on the ground floor, which generally center on the work of an artist who has made a significant contribution to satirical expression—Daumier, Doré, and Cruickshank have all been featured in recent years, as well as contemporary cartoonists.

Upstairs, there's a permanent display on Busch himself, who was a capable painter of landscapes and genre scenes, but who gained world-wide popularity through his illustrated books, notably *Max and Moritz*. In these, he invented what has become a stock vocabulary for cartoonists, using patterns of oscillation to express movement, and conventional signs to depict each emotion. Like Edward Lear, Busch was a poet as well as an artist, and the comic verses he wrote to accompany the illustrations are an integral part of his books, though they also stand up well in their own right. The museum has almost equally extensive holdings of the Berlin cartoonist, Heinrich Zille, but these are not always on view.

Eating, Drinking, and Nightlife

Hannover's major find for **snacks** is the *Markthalle*, where German, Italian, Spanish and Turkish stallholders sell not only provisions to take home but terrific examples of their cooking. It has a cheap and cheerful atmosphere, and seems to be the stallholders' own spontaneous idea. As an alternative, there's the self-service *Mövenpick* in the shopping arcade behind the tourist office.

For wholly **vegetarian** fare, try *Klatschmohn* at Lange Laube 20, or the Vietnamese *Hoa Binh* at Strangriede. Two of the best Chinese restaurants in Germany are in Hannover—*Mandarin-Pavillon* in an arcade at Marktstr. 45, and *Tai-Pai*, a short way south of the center at Hildesheimer Str. 73. Best choices for traditional German **pub-restaurants** are *Altdeutsche Bierstube*, Lärchenstr. 4, and the somewhat cheaper *Härke-Klause* at Ständehausstr. 4.

Hannover's best-known **brewery** is *Lindener Gilde*, which has operately uninterruptedly since 1546; its main product is *Broyhan-Alt*, which is named after the sixteenth-century Hannover man who allegedly invented export beer. The Pils of the rival *Herrenhausen* brewery is also worth seeking out. Good **cafés** include *Klatsch*, Limmerstr. 58 and the celebrated *Kröpcke* on the square of the same name. *Leine Domizil* opposite the Markthalle makes a good choice for breakfast or a snack, and has live music most evenings.

Main venue for **pop concerts** is the *Pavilion* on Raschplatz. Many of the best **classical music** performances are to be heard in the Protestant churches; these are listed in a bi-monthly leaflet. The *Knabenchor Hannover* is currently at least as good as its famous Viennese counterpart; in spite of the name it generally performs with adult male voices as well as boys. Concerts by the *Staatsorchester* alternate with operas at the *Opernhaus*. The best place for **theater** is the *Ballhof*; other venues include *Theater am Aegi* on Aegidientorplatz and *Landesbühne* on Bultstrasse. More experimental dramatic fare is offered at the *Künstlerhaus*, which also has the most adventurous **film** programs in town.

Listings

Cultural institute *Amerika Haus*, Prinzenstr. 9 (☎327284).

Exhibitions As well as the venues listed in the text, worthwhile shows are held at *Forum des Landesmuseums*, Am Markt 8; *Kestner-Gesellschaft*, Warmbüchenstr. 16; *Kubus*, Theodor-Lessing-Platz 2.

Festivals Hannover's *Schützenfest* (marksmen's festival) for ten days in late June/early July is the most spectacular of the many held in northern Germany. It features processions with floats, fireworks, and a considerable intake of alcohol, notably the *Lüttje-Lage*, in which you drink simultaneously from two glasses—one containing beer, the other schnapps—placed one inside the other.

Markets As well as the general markets on and around Am Markt, there's a flea market each Saturday morning on Hohen Ufer.

Mitfahrzentrale Weisse-Kreuz-Str. 18 (☎312021).

Poste Restante Beside the Hauptbahnhof on Ernst-August-Platz.

Sports There's a huge *Sportpark* with indoor and outdoor stadia and swimming pool on the west bank of the Maschsee.

Telephone code (☎0511).

Bückeburg

The tiny principality of Schaumburg-Lippe (formerly Holstein-Schaumburg) was one of the great survivors of imperial Germany. By skilful diplomacy it managed to avoid being swallowed up by unwelcome suitors, and kept its place on the map until 1946, when it became a part of Lower Saxony. At the very end of the sixteenth century, the then hamlet of **BÜCKEBURG**, which lies just 8km east of the Westphalian border town of Minden, was chosen as the state capital, and adorned with a series of Mannerist buildings which rank among the most important of their kind in Germany. Now reduced to the status of a quiet country town, it still encapsulates something of the feel of its former role, and makes a convenient stopping-off point (even if only for a few hours), on a journey across northern Germany. Also worth bearing in mind is that its main sights can be visited on Mondays—one of very few places in the country where this is so.

The Bahnhof is at the northern end of town; from here follow Bahnhofstrasse in a straight line, and you arrive at the Rathaus, beyond which are the entrance gates of the **Schloss**. The bridge over the moat bears two superb bronzes of *Venus and Adonis* and *The Rape of Prosperine* by the Dutchman **Adrian de Vries**, one of the leading lights in the idiosyncratic group of artists associated with the court of Emperor Rudolf II in Prague. From here, you can cross over into the courtyard. The wing facing you was rebuilt after a fire in the eighteenth century—walk round to the right to catch a glimpse of the resplendent Renaissance sections of the exterior, which were added to the original fourteenth-century tower-house in the mid-sixteenth-century. Continuing onwards, you come to the sombre neo-Romanesque **Mausoleum** (April–Oct. daily 9am–noon and 1–6pm; DM2) whose dome has what's apparently the largest mosaic in Germany.

A far better investment is to take a **guided tour** (daily 9am–noon and 1–6pm; DM6) of the Schloss itself; this takes in the photogenic inner courtyard and the most imposing apartments. These are eclectic, to say the least—you pass in quick succession from a grandiose Wilhelmine banqueting chamber with a huge Venetian-style fresco, through an intimate rococo smoking room, to a Renaissance hall hung with a superb set of Brussels tapestries. The **chapel** is a real eye-grabber: originally Gothic, it was adapted in the Mannerist period for Protestant worship. As if to give the lie to the belief that the new faith was inimical to wordly beauty, it was decorated in the most extravagant manner possible: every inch of the walls is covered with frescoes, and there's a complete set of gilded and carved furnishings. In the same period, the even more sumptuous **Golden Hall** was built as a secular counterpart. Its doorway, rising to the full height of the room, is flanked by huge statues of Mars and Flora, with Mercury floating above in the company of cherubs and goddesses. Luxuriant pine cones hang from the coffered and painted ceiling.

The brothers Hans and Ebbert Wulf of Hildesheim, who had carried out the decoration of the chapel and Golden Hall, were afterwards commissioned to build Bückeburg's other focal building, the **Stadtkirche**, which lies at the top of the main Lange Strasse. This contends with Wolfenbüttel (see p.571) the title of first full-scale Protestant church ever to be built. It's much the more unified building of the two, and is a real masterpiece of design, notwithstanding the Latin inscription running across the facade which declares that it is: "An Example of Piety, not of Architecture." Apart from its facade the exterior is a glum affair, but the **interior** is stunning (May–Sept. Mon.–Fri. 10:30am–noon, Oct.–April Wed 2–4pm only). Massive Corinthian pillars shoot right up to the vault, and your eye is drawn to the gleaming gold case of the massive organ at the far end, at which Johann Christoph Friedrich Bach, son of J.S., presided for 45 years. In adapting the old hall church formula to the Protestant emphasis on preaching, brightly painted galleries were added all round, and the **pulpit** placed in the center; the latter is one of the most beautiful in the country, its base lined with gold-plated reliefs of the life of Christ. The fiery figures of Moses and Saint Paul keep the preacher company during his sermon, whereas the cherubs on the sounding board serve as an antidote to any overly-serious discourse. Even more impressive is Adrian de Vries' **font**, where the Holy Ghost, hooked up by wires, hovers above the Baptism of Christ.

Outside the church is a monument to its most famous pastor, **Johann Gottfried Herder**, who served there from 1771 to 1776. As a collector of German folksongs and folk-poetry, and an ardent admirer of Shakespeare, he was something of a mentor to Goethe as well as an inspiration to later Romantics such as Armin, Brentano and the Grimms. At Goethe's suggestion, he left Bückeburg for a church position in Weimar (now in the GDR), and played a prominent part in the extraordinarily rich cultural life of its court.

Between the Schloss and the Stadtkirche, the **Heimat Museum** (Tues.–Sun. 11am–5pm; DM2.50) occupies the handsomest house in the street, a half-timbered building with an oriel window dating from c.1600. The vaulted cellars of its fourteenth-century predecessor can be seen inside, along with a display of historic costumes. Also in a historic house (albeit with a jarring modern extension) is the fascinating **Helicopter Museum** (*Hubsch-raubermuseum*; daily 9am–5pm; DM4) on Sablé Platz, the pedestrian area between Lange Strasse and Bahnhof Strasse. A reminder of the proximity of the German and British military bases, it incorporates an educational display on vertical flight technique, and is well labeled in English. Following a section on the history of man's attempts to fly, there are machines from all the famous names in helicopter design.

Opposite the Helicopter Museum is the **tourist office** (Mon.–Fri. 8am–12:30pm and 2–5pm, Sat. 9–11am; ☎05722 20624). Best **restaurant** in town is the *Ratskeller*; otherwise try *Zur Falle*, *Brauhaus* or *Le Bistro*, all on Lange Strasse. The last two also offer **rooms**. Nearest youth hostel is at Porta Westfalica (see *Chapter Five*), two stops away on the train; there are campgrounds there and at Doktorsee (☎05751 2611) near RINTELN, some 10km south of Bückeburg.

Hameln

"A pleasanter spot you never spied" was how Robert Browning characterized the venerable town of **HAMELN** (anglicized as *HAMELIN*), situated on the River Weser 45km southwest of Hannover. His verse rendition of the **legend of the Pied Piper** has made the place one of the best-known towns in Germany as far as English-speaking people are concerned—and earned him the eternal gratitude of the local tourist board.

Inevitably, the Pied Piper legend—arguably the most enduringly fascinating of Germany's rich store of folk-tales—always looms large, which makes Hameln an ideal outing if you have **kids**. The story is enacted in a **historical costume play** held in the town center at noon every Sunday from mid-May to mid-September; performances last thirty minutes, and are free. There are various versions of the legend; it was first chronicled in 1384, the exact centenary of when the event allegedly took place. A mysterious stranger dressed in a multicolored coat appeared in Hameln, and offered to rid the town of its plague of rats and mice. Upon promise of payment, he played on his pipe and lured the vermin to the Weser, where they all drowned. The ungrateful burghers reneged on the reward and sent the ratcatcher packing. He returned one Sunday morning when the adults were at church, dressed in a weird yellow-and-red huntsman's costume. This time it was the town's 130 children who answered the magnetic strains of his pipe, and they followed the stranger out of town and out of sight, apparently disappearing into a cavern, never to be seen again. The only children who were saved were a cripple and a deaf-mute.

Many **interpretations**, none of them conclusive, have been placed on this story. It may symbolize the plague epidemics that were a fact of life in medieval Europe—the term "children" of a town was often used in old chronicles as a synonym for "citizens." It's possible the piper was actually a land agent charged with finding settlers—the Count of Schaumburg had a plantation in Moravia, while there are communities in Transylvania which claim descent from the children of Hameln. Another plausible theory is that the events were linked to the disastrous Children's Crusade of 1212, when youngsters from all over Europe joined in an attempt to conquer the Holy Land from the Infidel by peace—something their seniors had failed to do by force. One of the two main leaders was a boy from Cologne by name of Nicolas, and it's quite likely that there were recruits to the cause from Hameln.

During the 1960s a comprehensive restoration program was started, which has left Hameln looking in immaculate shape. Along with nearby Lemgo (see *Chapter Five*), it's the best place to see the distinctive **Weser Renaissance** style, a form of civil architecture which typically features large projecting bay windows, richly decorated gables ornamented with pyramids and scrollwork, ornamental fillets with coats of arms and inscriptions, and lavish grotesque carvings, many of which are appropriately dubbed *Neidköpfe*—envious "neighbors' heads."

From the **Bahnhof**, situated well to the east of the old town, turn right into Bahnhofstrasse; at the end go left along Deisterstrasse. The **tourist office** (May–Sept. Mon.–Fri. 9am–1pm and 2–6pm, Sat. 9:30am–12:30pm and 3–5pm, Sun. 9:30am–12:30pm; Oct.–April Mon.–Fri. 9am–1pm and 2–5pm; ☎05151 202517/8/9) is situated in the Bürgergarten to the right. They keep plenty of brochures in English, but the most useful is an index-folder in German with all sorts of helpful tips, even including the best times of day for photographing the main buildings.

Until this point, there's little to suggest the architectural beauties in store. This is because Hameln was for centuries no more than a small milling and market town, which lay within a heavily fortified circular town wall. In the wake of the Thirty Years' War, its potential for growth was stunted by the strengthening of its defences by the Hanoverians, to the extent that it acquired the nickname of "the Gibraltar of the North." Napoleon ordered the demolition of the fortress in order that the town could expand. The only surviving sections of the fortress are two isolated medieval towers at the north end of town (the **Pulverturm** and the **Haspelmathsturm**) and the **Garnisonkirche**, just over the ring road from the tourist office. The last was built in the Lutheran baroque style for the use of the Hanoverian troops; it now houses a savings bank.

Ahead lies **Osterstrasse**, one of Germany's finest streets and now a pedestrian precinct. Facing the Garnisonkirche on the left is the **Rattenfängerhaus** (*Rat Catcher's House*). Built for a local councillor at the beginning of the seventeenth century, its name is due solely to an inscription on the side wall documenting the legend. Its facade is one of the most original in Hameln, the delicacy of its ornamental details (which include plenty of jealous neighbors) standing in deliberate contrast to the massiveness of the overall design. The interior is only marginally less impressive; it now houses what's probably the best **restaurant** in town. Though not cheap, it's excellent value, and there's a wide selection of ice-cream-based dishes if you don't want to splash out on a full meal.

Further up the street to the right is the **Leisthaus**, built about fifteen years earlier for a merchant by the local mason Cord Tönnies. The statue of Lucretia in a niche above the oriel window offers a profane contrast to the figures of the Seven Christian Virtues on the frieze below, a juxtaposition of sacred and secular that is typical of the German Renaissance. In this case inspiration was obviously provided by the carvings on the timber supports of the sixteenth-century **Stiftsherrnhaus** next door, which feature the planetary deities along with the Apostles and other biblical personages; its ground floor is now one of the best of the many fine **cafés** found along the street.

The rest of the Stiftsherrnhaus, along with all of the Leisthaus, is given over to the **Museum Hameln** (Tues.–Fri. 10am–4:30pm, Sat. and Sun. 10am–12:30pm, May–Sept. stays open until 4:30pm on Sun.; DM1). Among the collection of religious art on the first floor, the most striking items are a set of Apostles which formerly stood on the rood screen of the Münster, and the *Siebenlingsstein*. The latter commemorates another Hameln legend, that of the birth of septuplets to a local family in 1600; though the parents and elder siblings are shown praying at the foot of a crucifix, there was again no happy ending, as all the babies died soon afterwards. Elsewhere, you can see a number of period interiors, documentation on the history of the town and, of course, a display on the Pied Piper story.

At the end of Osterstrasse is the huge **Hochzeithaus** (*Wedding House*), a festival hall erected in the early seventeenth century, whose main features are its high end gables and its elaborate dormer windows, under each of which there is an doorway, which formerly led into a shop. Nowadays, a branch of the tourist office is housed here during the summer. On the side facing the Markt, a **carillion** has been installed. At 1.05pm, 3.35pm and 5.35pm each day, its figures enact the Piper's two visits to Hameln. Opposite is the **Dempterhaus**, built a few years earlier for the burgomaster after whom it's named. The **Marktkirche** rather detracts from the scene; it was Hameln's only major loss to wartime air raids, and has been poorly rebuilt with smooth stones which clash with the remains of the original masonry.

Among many fine buildings on Bäckerstrasse, which begins off the left hand side of the Markt, two stand out. The Gothic **Löwenapotheke**, still in use as a drugstore, illustrates that the Weser Renaissance style sprang from quite plain origins—the basic form is similar, but there's almost no decoration, apart from the hexagonal star on the gable, which was intended to ward off evil spirits. Further along is the **Rattenkrug**, which was built by Cord Tönnies a couple of decades before the broadly similar Leisthaus. Originally the home of a burgomaster, it has long served as an inn.

Halfway down Wendenstrasse, a fine narrow street opposite the Löwenapotheke, is the **Lückingsche Haus**, whose profuse carvings mark it out as the best example of the revival of half-timbering which occurred in the mid-seventeenth century. Also worth seeing is Alte Marktstrasse, which joins Bäckerstrasse by the Rattenkrug. Its most notable building is **Kurie Jerusalem**, a large half-timbered store from about 1500 which was long derelict, but has been magnificently restored as a play-center (where kids can be left if you want to go sightseeing without them in tow). Further down is the **Redenhof**, the only remaining nobleman's mansion in Hameln. Dating from the mid-sixteenth century, it's surprisingly plain in comparison with the contemporary houses of the prosperous burgher families. Old buildings of more conventional design can be found on Hummerstrasse and Neue Marktstrasse.

At the end of Bäckerstrasse, overlooking the Weser, is the **Münster**, successor to a Benedictine monastery founded around 800. It's something of a mix of styles—the eleventh-century crypt and the squat octagonal lantern tower survive from a Romanesque basilica which was converted into a Gothic hall church from the thirteenth century onwards, the austere belfry only being added some 200 years later. Inside, the raised chancel is the most striking feature.

Practical Points

In summer, it's a good idea to spend the night in Hameln; that way you can see the town before or after the daytrippers have come and gone. The **youth hostel** is well placed about five minutes' walk north of the old town at Fischbecker Str. 33 (☎05151 3425), at the point where the Hamel (no more than a stream) flows into the Weser. On the latter's western bank is the **campground** (☎05151 61157), which is open all year round. There are surprisingly few **hotels**, and they're not particularly cheap; lowest rates are at *Kretschmer*, Süntelstr. 35 (☎05151 24271), with singles DM38, doubles DM58, and *Altstadtwiege*, Neue Marktstr. 10 (☎05151 27854), at around DM40 per head. However, there are some dozen **private houses**, some in the heart of the old town, with rooms to let at around DM25 per person; the tourist office has a full list. Many of the best places to **eat** and **drink** occupy historic buildings mentioned in the text. Another good choice is *Pfannenkuchen* on Hummenstrasse, which offers a huge choice of delicious pancakes, while there's a top-class Chinese restaurant, *Peking*, at 164er Ring 5.

Cruises on the Weser (bear in mind that strong currents mean the upstream journeys are painfully slow) are run by *Weisse Flotte* and *Oberweser Dampfschiffahrt*, with departures from the jetty by the Münster. Each Thursday in summer, the former company runs a special service to HANNOVER via the *Wasserstrassenkreuz* in MINDEN (see *Chapter Five*).

The Weser Country Around Hameln

As a supplement to a visit to Hameln, it's well worth taking in some of the nearby sights. Three destinations in particular stand out; all are easy to reach, and needn't take up too much time.

Fischbeck

Situated 8km north of Hameln and connected by regular bus services (passenger trains no longer stop there), **FISCHBECK** is dominated by its **Stift**. This women's collegiate church was founded in 955, and has preserved an unbroken tradition ever since, thanks to turning Protestant in the mid-sixteenth century. Today, five elderly canonesses keep up its charitable work, only taking their vows once they have retired from a professional career. One of their tasks is to show visitors round the complex; admission is by **guided tour** only (Easter–mid-Oct. Tues. and Fri. 9am–11am, Weds., Thurs., Sat. and Sun. 2–4pm, duration 1hr; DM4). It's best to phone ahead (☎05152 8603), or check at Hameln's tourist office, to ensure admission; one of the guides provides tours in English.

The present church was built in the twelfth and early thirteenth centuries as a columned basilica in the manner of the churches of the early Christians, but was ravaged by fire soon after it was built. A drastic restoration at the turn of the century removed most of the baroque accretions, but some additions remain— such as the wooden balconies from where the canonesses, in true aristocratic manner, observe the services. Architecturally the finest part of the Stift is the **crypt**, whose capitals are all carved in a different manner. The **cloister** is a Gothic structure, with the houses of the canonesses on its upper story.

Fischbeck has several outstanding **works of art**, but there's only a copy of the most famous, a gilded head-reliquary of a saint; the original is now in Hannover (see p.549). Earlier this century, the long-lost polychromed wood *Statue of the Foundress Helmburg* was discovered and placed in the chancel. Made around

1300, it's an imaginary, idealized portrait, showing her as a young woman, instead of the elderly widow she was when she founded the Stift, a story illustrated in a late sixteenth-century tapestry in the south transept. On a wooden beam high above the end of the nave is a thirteenth-century *Triumphal Cross*, while beside the pulpit there's an extraordinary wooden *Seated Man of Sorrows*—carved around 1500, it radiates an enormous sense of pathos. According to legend, it was made for the Stift by an itinerant craftsman in gratitude for having been cured there of the plague.

Schloss Hämelschenburg

If Hameln has given you a taste for the Weser Renaissance style, it's worth taking a bus to **Schloss Hämelschenburg** (guided tours, lasting 40min, April–Oct. Tues.–Sun. at 10am, 11am, noon, 2pm, 3pm, 4pm and 5pm; DM4), some 12km south of town near the village of EMMERN. A sort of enlarged version of the burghers' mansion, and almost certainly designed by Cord Tönnies, it was built between 1588 and 1610 for the Klencke family, in whose possession it still remains. The exterior is particularly impressive, thanks to its moat and distinctive horseshoe shape. Inside, there are some splendid doorways and chimneypieces, along with a varied array of furniture, trophies, weapons and portraits. At the entrance to the complex is the former **Schlosskirche**, now a parish church, which has a memorial tablet to the Schloss's original owner, along with a late Gothic limewood *Madonna and Child in the Garden of Paradise*.

Bodenwerder

BODENWERDER, 25km downstream from Hameln, is a good choice of destination if you want to take a short cruise on the Weser. Its name is synonymous with **Baron Munchausen**, the King of Liars, who is one of Germany's most famous literary characters. He's been rather a forgotten figure elsewhere, though that has changed with the release of Terry Gilliam's lavish cinematic version of the Baron's tall tales.

The real-life Karl Friedrich Hieronymous Munchausen was an eighteenth-century soldier of fortune who fought for the Russians against the Turks, before retiring to his ancestral seat, where he regaled credulous listeners with monstrously boastful tales of his adventures. One of his audience was **Rudolph Erich Raspe**, himself a real rogue, who embroidered the stories further and published them under the Baron's name in Britain. For all his failings, Raspe was highly talented—he had been a protegé of Leibnitz in his native Hannover—and the book is stylishly written, capturing the understated manner of a boring old raconteur launching every few minutes into yet another implausible anecdote.

Munchausen's mansion, now the Rathaus, contains a small **museum** (daily 10am–noon and 2–5pm; DM1) in his honor. Outside is a fountain illustrating one of his most famous exploits (which consistently defeats the film-makers)—stopping to water his prize Lithuanian horse, he found that the liquid was pouring outof its body, the rear end having been shot off in battle. (Needless to say, the two parts of the steed were later successfully reunited.) The Baron's numerous adventures included stranger travels than even Gulliver's—he made two trips to the moon (one of them unintentional), a journey all the way through the earth's crust, and a voyage through a sea of milk to an island of cheese. In less far-flung parts, he shot a stag with a full-sized cherry tree between its antlers (thus obtaining haunch and sauce at the same time), served as a human cannonball in the war against the Turks, and single-handedly saved Gibraltar from falling into Spanish hands by tossing the enemy's 300 pieces of artillery into the sea.

If you want to stay in Bodenwerder, there's a **youth hostel** in the hills to the east of town on Richard-Schirrmann-Weg (☎05533 2685) and a **campground** at Schünemann (☎05533 4938), along with several hotels.

Hildesheim

HILDESHEIM, which lies 30km southeast of Hannover, stands unrivaled as Lower Saxony's premier city of art. Some of the finest buildings in all of Germany are to be found there, and its importance to European culture can hardly be exaggerated. During the eleventh century Ottonian period, the **Romanesque style**—emerging hesitantly elsewhere—achieved a state of perfection here, not only in architecture, but in sculpture and painting as well. But even if you've no deep fascination for art and architecture, it's a city that has an intense and immediate visual appeal—with the sunlight streaming through the streeets of painstakingly crafted half-timbered houses, it's easy to imagine the Germany of centuries ago. To see a good cross-section of Hildesheim's buildings, and soak up its atmosphere, allow a long day.

The City

In old guides, Hildesheim was rightly considered one of the "must" cities of Germany. Looking at more modern books, the usual impression given is of a place of moderate interest only. Needless to say, the reason for this slump in reputation was war damage. Hildesheim was bombed just a month before the German surrender in 1945, and the consequent fire, fuelled by the wooden buildings, caused damage which even some exemplary restoration cannot disguise.

The 1980s have seen Hildesheim make an astonishing comeback. Fortified by post war prosperity, the city council made the bold decision to recreate what had hitherto been regarded as irretrievably lost. They were given a fillip by UNESCO's decision to list the two main churches, both of which had been shattered in the war, among the monuments of the world which must be protected at all costs.

In 1983 work began on resurrecting the picturesque jumble of buildings around the central **Marktplatz**. The fifteenth-century **Templarhaus** at the southeast corner of Marktplatz is the one absolutely genuine building left on the square, having somehow remained intact while all its neighbors collapsed. The most likely explanation for its puzzling name and distinctive shape is that it was inspired by a Crusader's description of buildings he had seen in the Holy Land. Some softening of the rather spare, flat textures occurred with the addition of a late sixteenth-century oriel window bearing carvings of the Prodigal Son. Nowadays, the building houses a bookshop and the offices of the *Hildesheimer Allgemeine Zeitung*, the longest continually-running daily newspaper in Germany. The sixteenth-century **Wedekind Haus** next door, the baroque **Lüntzel Haus** and the part-Gothic, part-baroque **Rolandstift** (formerly a home for poor girls), were restored by the local savings bank to serve as its headquarters. Directly opposite, *Trusthouse Forte* have rebuilt the mid-seventeenth-century inn known as the **Stadtschänke**, along with the aptly-named **Rokokohaus** and the early sixteenth-century **Wollenwebergildehaus** (*Wool Weavers' Guild House*) to serve as their second hotel in Germany. The council themselves have paid for a copy of the Renaissance **Marktbrunnen**, which is topped by a figure of a knight, and has

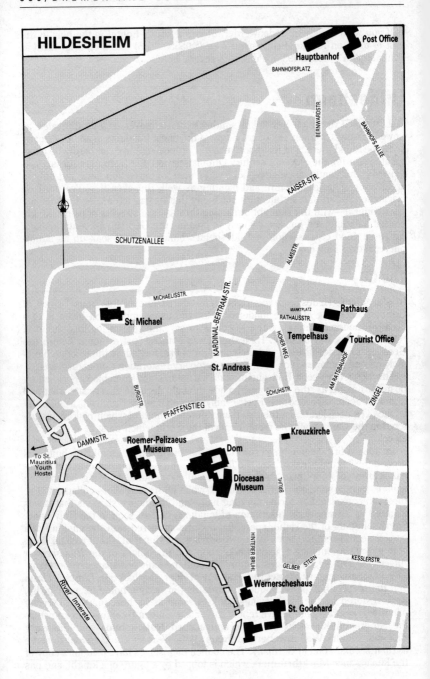

HILDESHEIM

Post Office

Hauptbanhof

BAHNHOFSPLATZ

BERNWARDSTR.

BAHNHOFS ALLEE

KAISER-STR.

ALMSSTR.

SCHUTZENALLEE

MICHAELISSTR.

St. Michael

KARDINAL-BERTRAM-STR.

MARKTPLATZ

RATHAUSSTR.

Rathaus

Tempelhaus

Tourist Office

HOHER WEG

St. Andreas

AM RATSBAUHOF

ZINGEL

BURGSTR.

PFAFFENSTIEG

SCHUHSTR.

Kreuzkirche

DAMMSTR.

Roemer-Pelizaeus
Museum

Dom

To St.
Mauritius
Youth
Hostel

Diocesan
Museum

BRUHL

HINTERER BRUHL

GELBER STERN

KESSLERSTR.

River Innerste

Wernerscheshaus

St. Godehard

the municipal arms depicted on the basin. On the west side, the colossal early sixteenth-century **Knochenhaueramtshaus** (*Butchers' Guildhall*) and the much smaller **Bäckeramtshaus** (*Bakers' Guildhall*) of 1800 have been the last to be rebuilt. The former was described in the old Baedekers as "probably the finest timber building in Germany"—which, given the amount of competition, gives some idea of its quality. All this leaves the Gothic **Rathaus** at the eastern end of the square, which was hurriedly reconstructed after the war, looking very much a poor, forlorn outsider.

Hildesheim's supreme building, the mold-breaking church of **St. Michael**, is about ten minutes' walk west of the Marktplatz, reached via Michaelisstrasse. Perched on a little hill and girded with six towers, it's not too fanciful to see it as a depiction of the heavenly Jerusalem. Originally a Benedictine monastery, Saint Michael's was very much a personal creation of **Bishop Bernward**, who ruled the see of Hildesheim between 993 and 1022. Confidant of Emperor Otto II and tutor to Otto III, Bernward was an well-traveled and erudite man who is known to have taken a direct part in the art and architecture he fostered in Hildesheim.

The nave forms the centerpiece of St. Michael's meticulously thought-out design. An important innovation was the move away from the columned basilica of the Romans to a new system, subsequently known as the Lower Saxon style, whereby each bay is demarcated by a hefty square pillar, between which are placed two columns. These are topped by another new device, the cubiform capital, from which spring the arches, colored in alternate white and red to impart a sense of rhythmic movement. The height of the roof is exactly twice the length of each bay of the nave, a marriage of art and mathematics which is the key to the serenity of the church.

Shortly after Bernward was canonized in 1192, substantial embellishments were made in order to make it a worthy resting-place for his relics. Seven elaborately carved capitals were made for the nave, and in the west transept a **choir screen** was erected; only part of this remains, yet its stucco carvings rank among the masterpieces of German sculpture.

An even more spectacular addition was the **ceiling**, which is one of only two Romanesque painted wooden ceilings to have survived. Fortunately, it had been removed for safety during World War II, and its fresh state of preservation is remarkable—three quarters of its 1300 separate oak panels are original. Executed in the style of contemporary illuminated manuscripts, its program is based on the imagery of the tree, a decision prompted by the fact that the church's most sacred relic was a piece of the Holy Cross. In the first main scene, Adam and Eve are shown beside the Tree of Knowledge. Next comes the sleeping Jesse, from whose loins springs the rod which passes through descendants such as David and Solomon before arriving at the Virgin Mary (shown here as the humble "handmaiden of the Lord") and Christ himself.

St. Bernward's body is interred in a stone sarcophagus in the ground-level **crypt** at the western end of the building; this necessitated a rebuilding to accommodate a raised chancel, which impaired the previously perfect architectural unity of the church. The Catholics were allowed to retain the crypt when St. Michael became Protestant at the Reformation; it's only open for mass, but you can peek in by opening the door to the left of the choir screen. Another later addition was the Gothic **cloister** to the north of the church, of which only one wing survives.

As a building, the **Dom**, which is set in its own close and reached via Burgstrasse, is very much the poor relation of St. Michael's, but its hauntingly romantic cloister and superb art treasures convinced the UNESCO inspectors that it was an equally important piece of cultural heritage. The exterior is largely a fake, with prominent Gothic side-chapels and a Romanesque facade and towers that are a modern guess at how the building might have looked before it was completely transformed in the baroque epoch. Inside, the architecture has been restored to its original eleventh-century layout, a close adaptation of the forms pioneered at the great monastery fifty years before.

One of St. Bernward's particular enthusiasms was the art of bronze-casting, and he established a foundry which was to flourish for centuries. Its first major product was a pair of **processional doors**, originally made for St. Michael's, but moved a few years later to the Dom's main entrance, where they were installed on the inside. They tell the story of Adam and Eve on the left-hand side, and of Christ on the right, each episode unfolding with a lively attention to anecdotal details. Soon afterwards, the craftsmen made the **triumphal column**, now in the southern transept. Rather more obviously inspired by Roman victory monuments, this illustrates the lives of Jesus and Saint John the Baptist in a manner akin to strip cartoons.

Around 1065, the huge **wheel-shaped chandelier** was suspended from the vault of the nave. Mantled with alternate towers and gateways, it's yet another representation of the heavenly Jerusalem, and was to serve as the prototype for the even more ornate candelabra in Aachen and Gross Comburg. In the baptismal chapel is the **font**; made in 1225, it rests on personifications of the four sacred rivers, while the basin and lid illustrate various Biblical stories, mostly with a watery theme.

The **cloister** (Mon.–Sat. 9:30am–5pm, Sun. noon–5pm; DM1) most unusually is built onto the transepts, forming a protective shield round the apse, on which grows the **thousand-year-old rosebush**, to which the legend of Hildesheim's foundation is inextricably tied. In 815, Ludwig the Pious, a son of Charlemagne, hung the royal chapel's relics of the Virgin on the tree while he was out hunting near *Hildwins Heim* (the home of a farmer named Hildwin). When he tried to remove them, they would not budge; taking this to be divine instruction, he decided to endow the mother church of a new diocese on the very spot. Whether this is really the original bush is disputed, but it's certainly many centuries old, and does seem to lead a charmed life—it burst into flower not long after the air raid which had flattened most of the Dom itself, and has blossomed every year since. In the center of the cloister garden is the **St. Annen Kapelle**, a beautiful fourteenth-century miniaturization of a Gothic cathedral, with an arresting set of gargoyles spouting from its walls. The sumptuous Renaissance **rood screen**, which fenced off the Dom's chancel until 1945, can be seen in the Antoniuskapelle off the cloister's southern walk.

Hildesheim's **Diocesan Museum** (Tues.–Sat. 10am–5pm, Sun. noon–5pm; DM2) contains the second richest ecclesiastical treasury in Germany. Among the highlights are several works dating from the time of Saint Bernward—the *Golden Madonna* (actually wooden but covered with gold-leaf), a pair of candlesticks, and two crucifixes named after the bishop himself. Equally imposing are various twelfth-century pieces—the *Cross of Henry the Lion*, three shield-shaped crucifixes, and a set of enamel plates. The eagle-lectern was made around the same time as the font, while the *Chalice of Saint Bernward*, though it has no real connection with the bishop, is an outstanding piece of goldsmith's work from around 1400.

Adjoining the north side of the Dom's close is the old Franciscan monastery, which now contains the **Roemer-Pelizaeus Museum** (Tues.–Sun. 10am–

4:30pm; DM3). Refreshingly different from the standard provincial museum, this hosts an international loan exhibition on a major archaeological topic each summer, when the opening times are extended. What's on display is subject to change, but you're sure to be able to see part of the collection of **Egyptian antiquities**, which is one of the best in Europe, and in itself enough to justify a visit to Hildesheim. The most famous exhibit is the white limestone funerary monument of Hem-iuni from 2530 B.C. Other outstanding sculptures include statuettes of Amenophis III and Teje (parents of Akhenaton), a statue of the fearsome half-man, half-jackal Anubis (the god of death) and the reliefs from the tomb of Seschem-nefer IV. The museum's other main strengths include a comprehensive collection of Chinese porcelain, and a varied array of exhibits from the Peru of the Incas.

Proceeding eastwards along Pfaffenstieg and Schuhstrasse, you see the tall tower of **St. Andreas** on the left. Within its exhilaratingly lofty Gothic interior, Luther's friend Johannes Bugenhagen converted the city to the Reformation. The church itself actually gained from the air raids—it was rebuilt according to the ambitious schemes of the original masons, which had never previously been fully put into effect. On the other hand, this hardly makes up for the almost complete loss of the square round the church, formerly regarded as a worthy rival to Marktplatz.

The southern part of Hildesheim was largely spared from war damage, and presents several streets of half-timbered houses as a reminder of what the whole of the old city once looked like. At the top end of Brühl, the nearest of these streets to the center, the one surviving secular building from the time of St. Bernward can be seen. Originally a fortified reception hall-cum-law court, it was converted into a collegiate foundation known as the **Kreuzkirche** in the late eleventh century, and now forms part of the otherwise baroque parish church of the same name, making a truly odd combination. To the west of the southern section of Brühl runs the parallel Hinterer Brühl, an almost completely preserved old street. Look out for the early seventeenth-century **Wernesches Haus**, with its allegorical depictions of the Virtues and Vices, and representations of historical personalities.

At the end of the street is **St. Godehard**, a former Benedictine monastery church built in the mid-twelfth century to commemorate the recent canonization of the man who had succeeded St. Bernward as Bishop of Hildesheim. Unusually well preserved, it boasts a pair of round towers on its facade, with a larger version of these over the transept. There's a delicate stucco relief over the north doorway showing Christ between St. Godehard (holding a model of the church) and St. Epiphanus. The interior proves the durability of the style pioneered at St. Michael's, the only advance being the rich carvings on the capitals. Star piece of the church's rich treasury is a magnificent early twelfth-century psalter illuminated at the sister English monastery of St. Albans; it's periodically kept here, but is sometimes shown at the Diocesan Museum.

East of St. Godehard is another fine old street, Gelber Stern, among whose buildings is the mid-sixteenth-century **Haus des Waffenschieds**, the guild house of the armorers, decorated with carvings of the tools of the trade. At the end of the road is Lappenberg, which runs perpendicular to the south; it has a complete row of craftsmen's homes. Nearby stands the **Kehrwiederturm**, the only surviving example of the gates which once surrounded the inner city. To the east is Kesslerstrasse, arguably the most imposing of the old streets, lined with impressive Renaissance and baroque mansions. The largest and finest of these is the **Dompropstei** (*Deanery*) at no. 57, set in its own spacious yard. Just north of here is the **Lambertikirche**, which contains a lovely early fifteenth-century "Soft-Style" retable painted by an unknown local master.

Another well-preserved old quarter is the *Moritzberg*, on a hill to the west of the city center, and reached along Dammstrasse, Bergsteinweg, and Bergstrasse. It's grouped round yet another Romanesque church, **St. Mauritius**. Although dating from the second half of the eleventh century, this favored the traditional format of a columned basilica still evident despite the fact the interior now being cloaked with baroque decoration. The crypt and cloister, however, have been preserved in their original state. Unfortunately, there isn't much of a view from these heights; for that, go to the **Galgenberg**, at the opposite end of the city.

Practicalities and Entertainment

The **Hauptbahnhof** is at the northern end of the city; best way to reach the center is to follow Bernwardstrasse then Almstrasse, but be warned that these characterless shopping precincts make rather an inauspicious introduction. Tucked away behind the Marktplatz on Am Ratsbauhof is the **tourist office** (Mon.–Fri. 9am–6pm, Sat. 9am–1pm; ☎05121 15995/6). If you want to find out more about the city and its wealth of monuments, invest DM1 in the *Hildesheimer Rosenroute*, a detailed guide along the tourist trail traced on the streets by a trail of white roses. **Mitfahrzentrale** have an office at Annenstr. 15 (☎05121 39051).

The nearest **campground** is way to the east of town at DERNEBURG (☎05062 565). Unfortunately, the **youth hostel** isn't much more convenient; it occupies a rustic location high in the wooded hills above Moritzberg at Schirrmannweg 4 (☎05121 42717), and is a good hour's walk from the center. No bus goes anywhere near, though #1 or #4 will take you part of the way. Cheapest **hotel** with a decent location is *Kurth*, Küsthardtstr. 4 (☎05121 32817), at DM30 per head. *Zum Klee*, Renatastr. 4 (☎05121 83685) and *Weisser Schwan*, Schuhstr. 29 (☎05121 12053/4) both charge DM34 per person, while rates at *Dittmann's*, Almsstr. 15 (☎05121 35566) start at DM35.

Pride of place among places to **eat** and **drink** must go to the *Ratskeller*, which is far less expensive than its counterparts in most other cities (there are cheap daily specials at lunchtimes), yet can rival any of them in quality. A good alternative is the *Bürgermeisterkapelle* on Rathausstrasse, directly behind. The cosy little *Schlegels Weinstube*, in a half-timbered sixteenth-century building on Am Steine (directly opposite the Roemer-Pelizaeus Museum), is as renowned for its superb food as for its wine list, but note that it's open only on weekday evenings. Bohemian-style cooking is offered at *Schweik* on Osterstrasse, while a good Italian restaurant occupies the *Alte Münze*, one of the few historic buildings left on Andreasplatz. The nearby *Hive's Fass* on Andreas Passage is a bistro with an adjoining beergarden. If you really want to splash out, go 5km south of town to the Steinberg Wald, where you'll find *Kupferschmiede*. One of the most famous restaurants in northern Germany, offering both *nouvelle cuisine* and hearty Germany fare, it serves a four-course gourmet dinner for DM42.50, though you can run up a somewhat larger bill without too much trouble.

Jazz fans should head for Hildesheim at Whit weekend, when the *Jazz-Time* festival presents the whole gamut of styles, both in formal concerts and impromptu open-air events. All kinds of **music** are featured along with **drama** in the varied programs of the *Stadttheater* on Theaterstrasse; it's also worth checking on the regular recitals and concerts in the Protestant churches. Main **popular festivals** are the *Frühlingsfest* for nine days in March, the *Weinfest* for a week in mid-May, and the ubiquitous *Schützenfest* in mid-June.

Braunschweig

BRAUNSCHWEIG (known as *BRUNSWICK* in English) must have been magnificent in the Middle Ages. During the twelfth century it was the chosen residence of **Henry the Lion** (*Heinrich der Löwe*), one of the most powerful princes in Europe. Duke of both Saxony and Bavaria, founder of the city of Munich and the port of Lübeck, Henry devoted his energies to building up a powerful Baltic state, commissioning innumerable works of art to grace its capital. Over the next few centuries Braunschweig became increasingly important as a commercial center; its trade connections stretched into Russia, Scandinavia, Flanders and England, and the consequent wealth was put to use creating buildings worthy of the city's power and status. In the mid-eighteenth century Braunschweig had yet another brilliant period. The first technical university in the world, the *Collegium Carolinum*, was established there in 1745. When the local dukes took up residence again the following decade, having been absent for over 300 years, their superb art treasures were put on public display, and the city became a flourishing cultural center.

The City

Arriving at the **Hauptbahnhof**, you may well wonder where the magnificence has gone—don't worry, the station is some distance to the southeast of the center. It's quite a walk, so best take one of the many buses to the "island" which forms the historic heart of the city. This is still completely surrounded by water— a man-made system based on the two arms of the River Oker—and contains several distinct medieval districts, which were formerly governed separately. Each of these quarters was centered on a market square and usually had its own parish church. Severe bomb damage in the last war means that the old buildings are now interspersed with plenty of ugly modern shops and offices, but it's still possible to visualize the medieval layout.

To look at the city in chronological order, the **Burgplatz** in the middle of the "island" is the place to start. It's full of memories of Henry the Lion, whose early career brought one spectacular success after another. By allying himself with Emperor Frederick Barbarossa, he quickly regained the two duchies of which his father, Henry the Proud, had been divested. This seemed to take the heat out of the dynastic feud between Henry's family, the Welfs, and the ruling Hohenstaufens. However, "The Lion" became too powerful for his own good, posing a threat to the feudal structure of the Holy Roman Empire. He fell out with Frederick over the price of support for the Crusades, and consequently was stripped of his titles and confined to his ancestral lands of Braunschweig-Lüneburg. The Welfs' feuding with the Hohenstaufens thereafter continued to bedevil medieval Germany, but the family retained control over at least part of their heartland right up to the present century.

At the time Burgplatz was laid out, Henry was at the peak of his power. In 1166, he commissioned the **Lion Monument** to form the centerpiece of the square. Perched high on a pedestal, this bronze statue, originally gilded, was the first freestanding sculptural monument to be made since the days of the Romans.

Seven years later the **Dom** was begun, and was substantially complete before the end of the century. Its craggy exterior appearance is the prototype of a distinctive Braunschweig style, which was followed in all the other medieval churches of the city. This fortress-like appearance seems as much a symbol of the power of the Welfs as the Lion Monument. Another feature copied throughout the city was the later insertion of a Gothic bell-gable between the two towers, which further increases the sense of the facade's massiveness.

The interior is far lighter in feel. This is partly due to the well-preserved Romanesque **frescos**, dating from around 1220, which were hidden behind plaster for centuries. The portraits of saints in the nave, executed with the finesse of manuscript miniatures, are particularly fine. More crucial was the opening out of the north side of the Dom in the mid-fifteenth century by masons who seem to have been familiar with English Tudor architecture; the two new aisles are separated by a row of writhing columns which twist in alternate directions.

On the end wall is the sole survivor of the previous cathedral on this site, a Byzantine-inspired wooden *Crucifixion* signed by a certain Master Imerward. At the entrance to the choir a seven-branched candelabrum, donated by the founder, springs from a base of four crouching lions. In front is the limestone **tomb** of

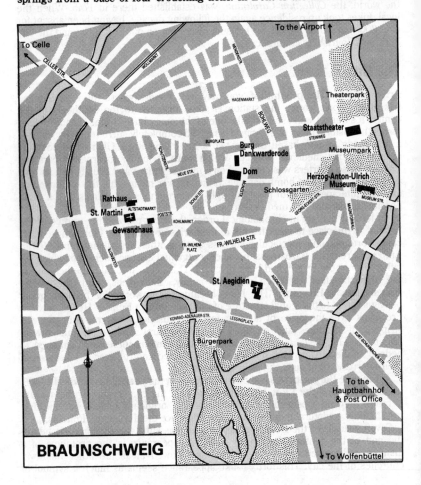

BRAUNSCHWEIG

Henry the Lion and his wife Matilda, daughter of Henry II of England. The beautifully carved reclining figures, made a good generation after their deaths, impart a sense of peaceful repose which is in contrast to the turbulence of their lives. Memorials to other members of the Welf dynasty are housed in the crypt.

Facing the Dom is the castle, **Burg Dankwarderode** (Tues.–Sun. 10am–5pm; free). Named in honor of the semi-mythical ninth-century founder of the city, it was constructed at the same time as the Dom. Its unusually complete appearance is mainly due to a nineteenth-century restoration, which follows the original form far more faithfully than most projects inspired by the Romantic reverence for the Middle Ages. Appropriately, it now houses a museum of medieval art and artifacts. Highlights include an eighth- or ninth-century walrus-tooth casket, the eleventh-century arm-reliquary of Saint Blasius (patron of the Dom), the cloak of Emperor Otto IV and a number of exquisite book covers. However, the gem is a delicate late fifteenth-century altar for private devotion known as the *Braunschweig Diptych*. The egg-shaped heads, subtle colors and extreme delicacy of execution mark it out as the work of the Dutch artist Jacob Jansz.

The Burgplatz used to be a courtyard in its truest sense—the houses that used to stand around its edge belonged to the courtiers. Two half-timbered sixteenth-century successors to these survive—the **Guildehaus** and the **Minsterialhof**, the latter now the seat of the local chamber of commerce. The neoclassical mansion in the opposite corner of the square was originally a publishing house, but now houses the **Landesmuseum** (daily 10am–5pm; free). Make sure you go in, if only to see the original of the Lion Monument, which was recently replaced outside by a copy for conservation reasons. The museum also contains sculptural fragments and folklore displays, and often features special exhibitions.

North of Burgplatz, reached via Casparistrasse or Bohlweg, is the old district of Hagen, centered on Hagenmarkt. Its fountain bears a nineteenth-century statue of Henry the Lion carrying a model of the church of **St. Katharinen**, which he also founded. Closely modeled on the Dom, St. Katharinen's interior was later transformed into a spacious Gothic hall church. The same is true of **St. Andreas** farther to the west, which was the parish of the Neustadt district. Across from this church is the **Liberei**, a fifteenth-century library building which is the only example of Gothic brick architecture in the city.

A more significant cluster of the past is found at the **Altstadtmarkt**. A corner of this is taken up by the former **Rathaus**, which ranks as one of the most beautiful and original secular buildings in Germany. Consisting of two wings arranged in an L-shape, its present form dates back to the early fifteenth-century, when the open upper arcades were added. The graceful lead **Marienbrunnen** in the middle of the square was made around the same time; it's topped by a shrine-like structure with the Virgin and Child and the four Evangelists.

Opposite stands the **Gewandhaus** (*Drapers' Hall*), its grandeur reflecting the importance of the medieval tailors. The facade is a Dutch-influenced Renaissance composition of extraordinary elaborateness, whose triangular gable is crowned by a figure of Justice. Alongside is the half-timbered seventeenth-century **Zollhaus**, once used by customs officials and the military. Also on the square is the baroque **Stechinellihaus**, designed by the Italian court architect after whom it's named, who was also responsible for many buildings in Celle.

St. Martini, originally a twelfth-century basilica, stands at the far end of Altstadtmarkt. The finest and earliest of Braunschweig's parish churches, it follows the usual pattern of being modeled on the Dom, but altered inside to form a spacious hall. It also gained some fine sculptures in the fourteenth-century, notably the group of the Wise and Foolish Virgins on the north doorway. Another addition is the Gothic chapel dedicated to St. Anne, housing a Renaissance pulpit that shows Saint Martin dividing his coat in order to clothe a beggar.

Raised above the old city on a slight hillock at its southern edge is the former Benedictine monastery of **St. Aegidien**, the only pure-Gothic church in Braunschweig. The original late Gothic reliefs on its handsome pulpit were carved by Hans Witten, a sculptor who was the equal of the more famous Riemenschneider and Stoss, but whose reputation suffers from the fact that most of his work is in remote East German towns. The monastic buildings now house part of the **Landesmuseum** (daily 10am–5pm; free). Adjacent is the **Jewish Museum** (same times; free), which contains part of a synagogue dismantled earlier this century. Unusually, it provides useful information in English on the exhibits.

Braunschweig's other significant district is the Altewiek a few blocks farther north. This is now usually known as the *Magniviertel* after the church of **St. Magni** which forms its core. The few half-timbered streets to have completely escaped destruction in the air raids are found around here; the semicircular group immediately behind the church, and the blind-alley called Herrendorftwerte, just to the east, are particularly evocative.

Further north, on Museumstrasse, is the **Herzog Anton Ulrich Museum** (Tues. and Thurs.–Sun. 10am–5pm, Weds. 10am–8pm; free). Of outstanding quality for a regional museum, it's particularly intriguing in that it reflects the personal artistic tastes of the duke after whom it's named, who was responsible for building it up some 300 years ago. The collection was opened to the public in 1754, thus making it the first museum in Germany.

On the first floor is the print room, which sometimes features important exhibitions of graphic work. Next floor up is the picture gallery, where pride of place goes to the Dutch school, and in particular to one of **Rembrandt's** most psychologically acute works, *A Family Group*. It was painted at the very end of his life, and shows his style at its most advanced and daring, with its loose brushwork supplemented by extensive use of the palette knife, its heavy chiaroscuro effects, and the informal arrangement of its subjects. Rembrandt's very personal vision of Biblical stories is represented here by a tender nocturne of *The Risen Christ Appearing to Mary Magdalene*. The dramatic *Landscape with Thunderstorm*, bathed in warm golden hues, shows yet another side of his diverse genius.

Vermeer's *Girl with the Wineglass* displays a level of technical virtuosity fully equal to, but very different from, Rembrandt's. Probably executed with the help of a *camera obscura*, it captures the three-dimensional space of the interior to uncanny effect. Other highlights of the Dutch collection include a sharply-observed *Self-Portrait* by the country's leading sixteenth-century artist, **Lucas van Leyden**, and the brilliantly contrasted *Democritus and Heraclitus* (the laughing and crying philosophers of ancient Greece) by the Mannerist **Cornelis van Haarlem**. Most of the specialist painters of the seventeenth century are represented; *The Marriage of Tobias and Sara* by **Jan. Steen** and three landscapes by **Jacob van Ruisdael** are particularly notable. Among Flemish works of the same period are several pieces by **Rubens**, a fine **Van Dyck** and a particularly fetching **Teniers**, *The Alchemist's Workshop*.

The most important German work in the gallery is *Portrait of Cyriacus Kale* by **Holbein the Younger**; it was painted in London, where the Braunschweig-born sitter worked at the Hansa trading headquarters. A strong representation of **Cranach** includes a lively workshop cycle of *The Labors of Hercules*, and a *Hercules and Omphale*. The latter is by Cranach's hand alone, as is the *Portrait of Albrecht von Brandeburg-Ansbach*, which depicts the cross-eyed Hohenzollern who had been Grand Master of the Teutonic Knights. By the time this picture was painted, Albrecht had converted to Protestantism, secularized his Order's holdings, and become Duke of Prussia—events which were crucial in his family's ultimately successful drive to win leadership of the German nation. A delicate *Morning Landscape* by the short-lived **Elsheimer** rounds off this section.

Duke Anton Ulrich's taste in Italian painting seems to have been confined to the sixteenth century Venetians and the bombastic artists of the baroque. The most important work is what's labeled as a *Self-Portrait* by the mysterious father-figure of Venice's Renaissance, **Giorgione**. One of the few surviving paintings widely accepted as genuine, it's probably a cut-down version of a *David with the Head of Goliath*. Important examples of the later Venetian Renaissance include works by Veronese, Tintoretto and Palma il Vecchio.

In the decorative arts section on the top floor Italy features rather more extensively, with a notable array of bronzes and porcelain, plus a valuable onyx vase from Mantua. Other particular strengths are Chinese lacquerwork, Limoges enamels, and jewelry, ceramics and furniture from all over Europe.

Practical Details

The **tourist office** (Mon.–Fri. 9am–6pm, Sat. 9am–12:30pm; ☎0531 470 2757) is in a pavilion on Bohlweg. Check here for information about the **youth hostel**, which has moved around in recent years; an unofficial hostel is at Salzdalumer Str. 170 (0531 62268) to the south of the city, reached by bus #11 or #19. Otherwise, there are two cheap central **hotels**: *Gästehaus Kohlmarkt* is cozy and friendly, charging DM35 for singles, DM65 for doubles; *Hotel am Wollmarkt* has similar prices, but is YMCA-run and has an institutional feel. The best **restaurants** in town are *Haus zur Hanse* on Güldenstrasse and the previously-mentioned *Gewandhauskeller;* both are pricey, but worth it. Even if you aren't normally a **beer** drinker, try the local *Mumme*; dark, low in alcohol and very sweet. A specialty of the **bakeries** is bread in the shape of owls and monkeys. This is in celebration of a prank perpetrated by the mischievous Till Eulenspiegel (see p.574), who served as a baker's apprentice in the city.

Braunschweig has a strong **theater** tradition; in the now-demolished building on Hagenmarkt the first part of Goethe's *Faust* received its premiere in 1829. The building was replaced a few decades later by the *Staatstheater* on Am Theater (between Museumpark and Theaterpark), which remains the leading venue for highbrow performances. Shows with an alternative slant are presented at *FreiBiZe* in the Bürgerpark. This community center occupies the old waterworks, which are themselves of note as an early example of industrial architecture. **Concerts** of all kinds are held at the modern *Stadthalle* on Leonhardplatz, not far from the Hauptbahnhof. There's a **festival** of modern chamber music each November, while the main annual folklore event is a medieval market held in Burgplatz in mid-May. Though the city center is compact enough for walking, it's worth noting that a 24-hour **public transit** ticket costs DM5. **Mitfahrzentrale** have an office at Bohlweg 42–43 (☎0531 14041).

Königslutter Am Elm

Some 20km east of Braunschweig is **KÖNIGSLUTTER AM ELM**, lying in the shadow of the beech forest of Elm. The one monument worth seeing here is the former **Abtei**, set at the opposite end of town from the Bahnhof. Founded by Emperor Lothar III in 1135, its earliest and finest parts were built by Romanesque masons from Lombardy. Their small scale and infinitely varied sculpture is an outstanding illustration of the thoughts and obsessions of the medieval mind. It can be seen on the exterior of the apse, adorned with grotesque human masks, imaginary beasts, and hunting scenes, and on the north doorway, whose twisted columns are guarded by menacing lions. It's also present in the north walk of the cloister, each of whose columns is of a different shape and design from any other. The interior of the church is covered with frescoes—an over-enthusiastic nineteenth-century attempt, admittedly using some rather ghostly traces as a starting-point, to recreate the original appearance.

The Border Crossing-Points

HELMSTEDT, which lies a farther 20km east of Königslutter am Elm, is the crossing point on the most heavily-used railroad line into the GDR—that which forms the corridor to West Berlin. Unless timetables dictate otherwise, it's not really worth stopping off at this grim town, whose only redeeming factor is the russet-colored, late Renaissance **Juleum**. Built by Paul Francke, who later laid out much of Wolfenbüttel, it served as a Protestant university between the sixteenth and early nineteenth centuries. Nowadays, its basement houses the local history museum (Mon.–Fri. 9–11am and 3–5pm, Sat. 3–5pm, Sun. 11am–12:30pm).

If you're forced to spend the night, the tiny **youth hostel** is at Am Bötschenberg 4 (☎05351 41021), not far from the *Gasthaus Autobahnraststätte Helmstedt*. Alternatively, try for a private **room** at *Rasiak*, Vorsfelder Str. 157 (the next road on the right leading off the town's central ring road when approaching from the Autobahn; ☎05351 33339), or at *Paesler*, Bötticherstr. 14 (☎05351 33365), on the road leading directly up to the Juleum.

The alternative point for entering or leaving the GDR is **WOLFSBURG**, 30km farther north. Note that trains from here do not go to Berlin, hence you'll need to obtain a visa or accommodation vouchers beforehand if you're intending to cross the frontier.

Wolfsburg is the archetypal company town. As late as the 1930s, it was a hamlet of 150 souls, clustered round a part-Gothic, part-Renaissance moated Schloss. Nowadays 130,000 people live there, no less than half of them employees of the giant *Volkswagenwerk*. The impetus for this company (which was initially wholly state-owned)* came directly from Hitler, who wanted a small, reliable car that anyone could afford to buy and run. It was Ferdinand Porsche—a name indelibly associated with vehicles aimed at the very opposite end of the market—who in 1936 provided the design for the distinctive little machine whose hallmarks were its sloping bonnet and its starting crank, and which popularly came to be known as the *Beetle*. Two years later, the factory was built; it was destroyed during the war, whereupon the story might well have ended.

In the event, *Volkswagen* became a fairy-tale postwar success, and one of the linchpins of West Germany's "economic miracle." The Beetle's cheapness and durability made it a huge export hit, and up to 20 million models were produced in any given year. However, the company ran into serious difficulties in the 1970s: no attempt had been made at diversification, and the *Beetle*'s sales plummeted as increased general affluence led to a demand for more luxurious cars. To halt the

---

* In 1961, the majority shareholding was sold to 1.5 million small investors. The present CDU government, which has otherwise been far less besotted by privatization schemes than its Conservative counterpart in Britain, has decided to dispose of the remaining publicly-owned shares by 1990.

decline, the drastic decision was taken to scrap the old faithful altogether (though it's still made under licence in Mexico), and to develop a new range of models, based on the more upmarket but still modest *Rabbit*. It was also decided to make extensive use of robots in the construction process. This has by and large been successful, even if the Midas-touch formula of the past is now accepted as having been lost for ever.

Guided tours of the *Volkswagenwerk* are offered every weekday afternoon, generally at 1:30pm. Obviously it would be best to reserve in advance or check the times with a tourist office before setting out. Other than this, the town boasts significant examples of **modern architecture** which have, inevitably, attracted widely diverging opinions from the critics. The most important are the **Kulturzentrum** in the heart of town and the **Heilig-Geist-Kirche** 1km south, both by the internationally acclaimed Finnish architect Alvar Aalto, and the **Stadttheater**, a late work by one of Germany's leading twentieth-century designers, Hans Scharoun.

Wolfenbüttel

Reached in just a few minutes from Braunschweig via what was, when it opened in 1838, the first state-owned railroad line in Germany, **WOLFENBÜTTEL** is a place which deserves to be far better known. The House of Braunschweig-Lüneburg had its seat there from 1432 to 1754, and even today it preserves much of the layout and atmosphere of a ducal *Residenzstadt*. Indeed, it offers the most evocative example of the petty courts which once dotted the politically-fragmented map of the Holy Roman Empire. When the local dukes moved back to Braunschweig, Wolfenbüttel seems to have fallen into a deep slumber; it came through World War II unscathed, and no less than 600 historic half-timbered houses survive, as well as plenty of large public buildings. It's also the earliest example in Germany of a **planned town**—in fact, it evolved from several consecutive plans, all of whose outlines are still visible. This subsequently became a favorite idea with German princes—Freudenstadt, Mannheim, Ludwigsburg and Karlsruhe were all built in this way—but none is anywhere near as intact as Wolfenbüttel.

From the Bahnhof, cross over the River Oker, then turn left along Schuwall, coming to the spacious **Schlossplatz**, whose eastern side is lined with the plain timber-framed buildings characteristic of the town. Directly opposite is the huge, dazzlingly white **Schloss**. Apart from the moat and some re-used masonry, nothing remains of the medieval moated fortress, whose present form is a conflation of Renaissance and baroque rebuilding. The most distinguished feature is the Renaissance **tower**, whose unusual design includes a gabled clock-face on each side; it was built in the early seventeenth century by **Paul Francke**, who was responsible for many of the buildings in the first phases of the planning of Wolfenbüttel. This apart, the exterior of the Schloss dates from a century later, and was designed by the highly inventive **Hermann Korb**.

The upper arcades of the Palladian-style inner **courtyard** were originally open, following normal Italian practice; however, they were filled in soon after, when the incompatibility of open arcades and northern weather became apparent. Round the back of the Schloss, a troupe of English actors under Thomas Sackville established themselves as the first permanent theater company in Germany in 1590. This ushered in a golden era for the performing arts in

Wolfenbüttel, but the opera house built there the following century has unfortunately not survived. The surprisingly modest **state apartments** (Tues., Thurs. and Sun. 10am–1pm, Wed 3–5pm, Fri. and Sat. 10am–1pm and 3–6pm; free) are worth a quick look to get an impression of how the dukes lived.

On the north side of Schlossplatz is the **Zeughaus**, again by Francke. Its cheerful crimson exterior, decorated with richly carved gables, hardly suggests its original function as an arsenal, whose cavernous lower story once housed the biggest and most powerful cannons in Germany. Immediately behind is the grandest of Wolfenbüttel's half-timbered buildings, a huge mid-seventeenth-century storehouse.

Nowadays, the Zeughaus hosts temporary exhibitions from the pride of the town, the **Herzog August Bibliothek** (daily 10am–5pm; combined ticket DM3), whose headquarters are in the nineteenth-century pseudo-*palazzo* diagonally opposite. The Dukes of Braunschweig were true bibliophiles; by the mid-seventeenth century the scholarly August the Younger had built up the largest library in Europe, consisting of 130,000 volumes, all catalogued by himself. When the philosopher Leibnitz (see p.545) served as custodian of the Welf family collections, he collaborated with Hermann Korb in designing a magnificent wooden rotunda to house the books, but this was demolished last century when larger premises became necessary.

Four rooms of the main library have been laid out as a **museum**. Among the rare books on display in the first hall are a first edition of Luther's *New Testament* with colored woodcuts, and a copy of the *Psalter* with his own annotations. The dimmed **Schatzkammer** has precious medieval illuminated manscripts; outstanding are the eleventh-century *Perikopenbuch* from Reichenau, a thirteenth-century *Calendar* from Hildesheim, and two beautiful northern French books—the twelfth-century *Liber Florius* and the fifteenth-century *Miroir des Dames*. To the left is a room with Renaissance maps and globes, while a comprehensive display of twentieth-century artists' sketchbooks is mounted in the corresponding chamber to the right.

At the time of writing the library's greatest treasure, the **Evangelistary of Henry the Lion**, had yet to be put on display, though this should by now be rectified. Perhaps the most sumptuous manuscript produced in the Romanesque period, it was commissioned around 1180 for use in the Dom in Braunschweig. Among its 24 beautifully colored full-page miniatures is a scene showing Christ crowning Henry and his English wife Matilda—the saints in paradise include Thomas à Becket, recently murdered as a result of a misunderstood remark made by his friend Henry II, Matilda's father. Last century, the Welf family reacquired this heirloom, but sold it after the last war to a secretive private collector. In 1983, it was auctioned by Sotheby's in London; desperate to gain this key piece of their heritage, the Land government of Lower Saxony headed a consortium which splashed out £10 million, setting a world record price for a work of art. It remains the most expensive book in the world.

The **Lessing Haus** (same times and tickets) in front of the Bibliothek was the official residence of the librarian. A triple-winged summer house, it was finished just three years before the dukes decided to abandon Wolfenbüttel as a residence. Its present name comes from the second famous holder of the librarian's post, the hugely influential playwright **Gotthold Ephraim Lessing**, who spent the last eleven years of his life there; a collection of memorabilia pays tribute to him. The main work from his Wolfenbüttel years is *Nathan the Wise*, a piece particularly interesting in the light of subsequent German history—its wholly admirable hero is a Jew.

East of Schlossplatz is the original late sixteenth-century planned town, the *Alte Heinrichstadt*. One of its focal points is the **Stadtmarkt**, a square lined with half-timbered buildings, in the center of which is a bronze statue of Duke August the Younger, depicted leading his horse rather than riding it. On one of the houses is a plaque to Justus Georg Schottelius, father of German grammar, who lived there in the mid-seventeenth century. He's the man accredited with introducing the **semi-colon** into linguistic practice.

Off the north side of the square, on the street named after it, is the **Kanzlei** (*Chancellery*). Though somewhat messed about, it's notable as being the only surviving building by the Dutchman Hans Vredeman de Vries, the leading architectural theoretician of the Northern European Renaissance. The Kanzlei now houses the moderately interesting **Archaeology Museum** (Tues.–Sat. 10am–5pm, Sun. 10–1pm) of the Braunschweig region. Almost all the other streets around here are worth walking along; look out for *Klein Venedig* (Little Venice), so named because it fronts a canal.

As a climax to the *Alte Heinrichstadt*, the **Hauptkirche** was begun in 1608 by Paul Francke; after two decades of restoration, it's now looking in pristine shape. Notwithstanding the dedication to *Beatae Mariae Virginis*, it was not only Lutheran from the outset, but was the first parish church to be built specifically for the Protestant faith (although Bückeburg's Stadkirche, started three years later, was actually finished first). It's an extraordinary confection, mixing late Gothic, Renaissance and Mannerism, while the main portal—designed like a triumphal arch with statues of two of the dukes ensconced between Moses and Aaron below, and Christ at the summit—has all the swagger of the emergent baroque style. On the long sides of the building are a series of profusely decorated gables, while on the facade and in the vestibule are hundreds of delicately carved reliefs of animals and demons.

The church's **interior** (Tues.–Fri. 10am–1pm and 3–6pm, Sat. 10am–1pm and 2–4pm), which doubles as the ducal pantheon, is airily light and spacious. In accordance with Protestant needs, the nave takes up the lion's share of the space, the short chancel being reserved for the administration of the two central sacraments—baptism and the Eucharist. Regular recitals are held on the magnificent early baroque organ, first presided over by the composer Michael Praetorius, who is buried below. He's best known for his beguiling arrangements of over 300 foot-tapping dance melodies, collectively known as *Terpsichore*; many of these have again become familiar, having done service as television signature tunes to period plays.

East of the Hauptkirche is the *Neue Heinrichstadt*, centered on the Holzmarkt; for the most part, its buildings faithfully follow the style of the earlier part of town. In the early eighteenth century, Hermann Korb finished off the square in an ingenious fashion by inserting the oval **Trinitiaskirche** between the two redundant gateways at the far end, transforming the latter into a pair of towers for the church in the process.

Further east, across the Oker, a huge new town of manufacturing workshops called the *Juliusstadt* was once planned. However, it never got beyond a couple of streets. Instead, the far more modest craftsmen's suburb of *Auguststadt* was laid out at the opposite end of Wolfenbüttel, to the west of the Schloss. Its houses are remarkably similar to those in the "better" part of town, and the half-timbered **Johanniskirche**, set beside its detached belfry in a shady green, brings a touch of rusticity to the quarter.

Wolfenbüttel's **tourist office**, which publishes a useful free English-language walking tour of the town, is down an alley off the south side of Stadtmarkt (Tues.,

Thurs. and Fri. 9:30am–1pm and 2–4pm, Wed 9:30am–1pm; ☎05331 27593). Most enticing place to stay is the **youth hostel**, which occupies a wing of the Schloss (☎05331 1031). Cheapest **hotels** are *Augustädter Schänke*, Dr.-Heinrich-Jasper-Str. 32 (☎05331 26873), with singles DM28, doubles DM50; and *Kaltes Tal*, Goslarsche Str. 56 (☎05331 43828), charging upwards of DM27.50 per head. Places to **eat** and **drink** include *Alt Wolfenbüttel*, an old inn on Kramerbuden, just off the Stadtmarkt, and *Karlsberg* on the site of the old bastion overlooking Lange Strasse at the eastern end of town.

Some 12km east of Wolfenbüttel is **SCHÖPPENSTEDT**. On Nordstrasse there's a **museum** (Mon.–Fri. 2–5pm, Sat. and Sun. 10am–noon and 2–5pm) in honor of one of Germany's legendary characters, the jester **Till Eulenspiegel**, who was born just outside the town around 1300. Of peasant stock, he lived by his native wit, consistently putting points over on pompous aristocrats, merchants, churchmen and scholars with his practical jokes and punning sense of humor. Anecdotes about him were popular all over medieval Europe, and were first published in book form in the early sixteenth century. His name has since been enshrined in the German word for tomfoolery (*Eulenspiegelei*) and the French name for a rogue or scoundrel (*espiègle*). He has also inspired two major works of art—a brilliant orchestral showpiece by Richard Strauss, and an epic poem by a winner of the Nobel Prize for Literature, Gerhart Hauptmann.

SOUTHERN LOWER SAXONY

South of Wolfenbüttel, Lower Saxony's landscape soon makes yet another significant change, this time to the gentle wooded slopes of the **Harz** mountain range. This was long a famous mining area, thanks to rich deposits of gold, silver, and other less precious minerals, but these have, in the present century, become exhausted. At the edge of the mountains, the old imperial city of **Goslar** is the area's main draw, a place as evocative of medieval Germany as any you'll find. Nothing else within the West German section of the Harz is of comparable quality, but just beyond the range are a number of impressive old half-timbered towns, such as **Einbeck**, the home of *Bockbier*, **Duderstadt** and **Münden**. As a complete contrast to these, there's the university city of **Göttingen**, which isn't particularly notable for its monuments, but boasts the most exciting atmosphere of any town between Hannover and Frankfurt.

Goslar

The stereotype of a mining town immediately conjures up images of rows of grim identikit terraced houses paying obeisance to the gargantuan, satanic-looking machinery in whose shadow they lie. **GOSLAR**, which stands in a superb location at the northern edge of the Harz, could not be more different. Admittedly, the mining here was always of a very superior nature—silver was discovered in the nearby 600-meter-high **Rammelsberg** in the tenth century, and the town immediately prospered, soon becoming the "treasure chest of the Holy Roman Empire," and a favorite royal seat. As a Free Imperial City in the later Middle Ages, Goslar, though never very large, ranked as one of the most prosperous communities in Europe, with lead and zinc now added to the list of ready-to-hand mineral deposits.

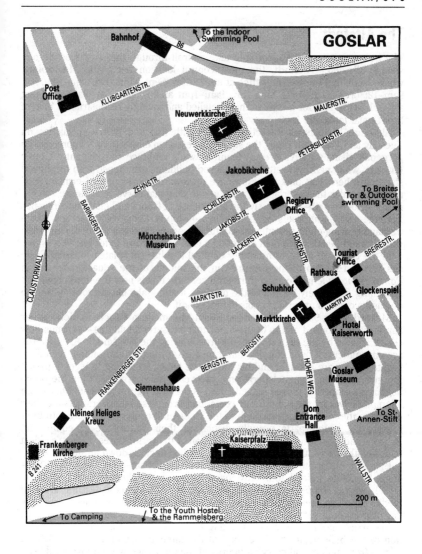

GOSLAR

Bahnhof
To the Indoor Swimming Pool
B6
Post Office
KLUBGARTENSTR.
MAUERSTR.
Neuwerkkirche
PETERSILIENSTR.
ZEHNSTR.
Jakobikirche
To Breites Tor & Outdoor swimming Pool
BARINGERSTR.
SCHILDERSTR.
JAKOBISTR.
Registry Office
BACKERSTR.
HOKENSTR.
BREITESTR.
Mönchehaus Museum
CLAUSTORWALL
Tourist Office
Rathaus
MARKTSTR.
Schuhhof
Glockenspiel
MARKTPLATZ
Marktkirche
Hotel Kaiserworth
FRANKENBERGER STR.
BERGSTR.
BERGSTR.
HOHER WEG
Goslar Museum
Siemenshaus
Kleines Heliges Kreuz
Dom Entrance Hall
To St. Annen-Stift
Frankenberger Kirche
B 241
Kaiserpfalz
WALLSTR.
0   200 m
To Camping
To the Youth Hostel & the Rammelsberg

Despite two fires sweeping through the streets in 1800, much survives as a reminder of this heady epoch. The presence of a POW hospital during World War II spared it from Allied bombing, ensuring that the entire town now enjoys the status of being *unter Denkmalschutz* (a protected monument). With just cause too, as Goslar claims to have more **old houses** (over 1500, with 168 pre-1550) than any other town in Germany. Though there's a great deal to see, you may find Goslar's magic fading after a while—one day, and certainly no more than two, should be enough to cover the main sights.

The Altstadt

The best way to see the town is to take a stroll through the streets of the one square kilometer **Altstadt**, the most central location being the **Marktplatz**, where you'll find the **tourist office** at no. 7 (May–Sept. Mon.–Fri. 9am–5pm, Sat. 9am–12:30pm, Oct.–April Mon.–Fri. 9am–1pm and 2–5pm, Sat. 9am–12:30pm; ☎05321 2846). Ask for a copy of their detailed and lovingly reconstructed map of how Goslar looked in 1500.

Although it hosts an attractive market with fish and pastry specialties on Tuesday and Friday morning, the square is best seen empty to fully appreciate its gorgeous visual variety. Creamy-textured walls embrace the elegantly Gothic Rathaus, while nearby, pretty half-timbered buildings are topped with bright red slate; on others, soft pink flowers weave up towards classic gray German roofs, the rectangular tiles overlapping on a gentle diagonal curve. Across the square, **Hotel Kaiserworth**—previously the guildhouse of tailors and cloth-makers—has Baroque and Gothic roofs tumbling down on top of Romanesque arches, and a frontage bearing eight seventeenth-century wooden statues of German emperors, with a naked Renaissance man excreting a gold coin thrown in for good measure.

In the center of all this, the rather comical looking gold-plated Imperial Eagle sits perched on top of the **fountain** in the middle of the square. Sculpted in Romanesque style in the early thirteenth century, this is now the third copy, but, remaining completely faithful to the original, it still looks like a cross between a dog and a chicken uncertainly poised for take-off.

Meanwhile, at 9am, noon, 3pm and 6pm, the modern **Glockenspiel**—rather appropriately housed on top of the municipal treasurer's building—explains how Goslar rose to be the richest town in Europe during the late Middle Ages. To the accompaniment of bells chiming out a medley of hunting and mining melodies, first to appear are a knight and his horse; the latter, according to legend, pawed the ground of the Rammelsberg, and uncovered silver traces. When the boom began, the emperors moved in, and Otto I is the next figure, presented here with a lump of silver by the knight. The remaining groups show miners hacking their way from the Middle Ages through to the nineteenth century, finishing with their present-day counterparts proudly displaying their state-of-the-art equipment. Rather a sad twist, then, that due to depletion of the various ores, Europe's oldest mine—with nearly 3000 employees—recently had to close down for good.

Cross the square to the **Rathaus** (daily June–Sept. 9am–5pm, Oct.–May 10am–4pm; 15-minute guided tour only, on the hour and half-hour; DM2, students DM1), whose *Huldigungssaal* ("Hall of Homage") contains a dazzling array of medieval wall and ceiling paintings. The name is misleading, as homage was actually paid in the great hall where the admission desk is now situated. The superb gold-starred marine blue paneled ceiling here dates from the original construction of the building in the latter half of the fifteenth century; the chandeliers, carved from antlers and carrying figures of the emperors, were transported from the Dom a few decades later. The *Huldigungssaal* itself was the former assembly hall of the city council from 1500 onwards and later used for the town's archives. Its richly decorated panels contain portraits of Christ and various citizens of Goslar painted by an unknown artist over 400 years ago. Only slightly retouched, they still retain their original delicate translucence. Several valuable relics are hidden in altar niches and closets behind the paneling, among them, a precious gold and silver tankard from the fifteenth century, elaborately embellished with mining and hunting scenes and the *Goslarer Evangeliar*, a thirteenth-century manuscript with exquisite Byzantine-inspired Romanesque miniature paintings.

Just behind the Rathaus, the **Marktkirche**, dedicated to Saints Cosmas and Damian, recalls a different expression of spirituality. Now the patron saints of the medical profession, these twin brothers were doctors who lived in Goslar during the third century A.D., healing people and animals, not for financial gain but for the simple glory of God. Surviving numerous attempts on their lives, they were finally beheaded during the Diocletian prosecution in 303, but not before their fame had spread out as far as Rome, where a church in the *Forum Romanum* was consecrated to them a few centuries later. The architecture of the present day church, a mix of Romanesque and Gothic, does little to honor their noble calling, but it is worth popping into for its unusually fashioned and grandiose bronze baptismal **font**, the creation of a local artist, Magnus Karsten, in 1573: just about every major Bibical event is represented on it in magnificent detail.

Goslar's **half-timbered** beauty begins in earnest in the streets behind the Marktkirche. The styles to look out for are Gothic, Renaissance, and Baroque, many homes having two and sometimes all of these: Gothic pointed arches are transformed into three-stepped inlays, usually dull red, gold, and olive green in color, resulting in a curious resemblance to art nouveau; sombrely brilliant rosettes cartwheel across the rafters of the Renaissance houses, while gaudily colored Baroque devils lie like flattened gargoyles bereft of their power in their **prisons of beam.**

The oldest houses lie in the Bergstrasse and Schreiberstrasse areas; the **Siemenshaus** is conveniently situated on the corner of both. Built by a forefather of what is today one of Germany's largest suppliers of medical equipment, electrical appliances and armaments parts, it's now a museum (Mon., Tues., Thurs. and Fri. 9am–12:30pm) detailing the rise and rise of the Siemens empire. Half timber, half stone, the baroque exterior has some of the best examples in Goslar of the criss-crossing diagonal beams depicting the "wild man," a symbol of sexuality normally more common in southern Germany. Further down Schreiberstrasse, classic Gothic bower brick houses abound, the style typical of the early sixteenth century embodied at no. 10, with its lavishly decorated chimney passing through the two single-roomed stories.

Back past the Siemens house, turning right into Bergstrasse, wind your way up to the roughly-hewn **Frankenberger Kirche**, situated in tranquil solitude on the boundaries of the Altstadt. (From November to April you'll need to get the key from the *Küsterin*, at the door of the courtyard.) Built during the twelfth century as a Romanesque basilica, the later Gothic additions form part of the town's western ramparts. The miners used to get married here; the church's pastel red and blue beams and pinkish gold altar serve now to give the dream-like quality of a hot summer's afternoon, making it an ideal spot to rest for a while if you're footsore from tramping round the town. The gigantic baroque wooden carved Passion altar verges on pastiche and could easily dominate the place until you begin to take in a few other details: towards the back of the church, two fierce lions stand facing each other to absorb the evil believed to have come from the west; some faint thirteenth-century frescoes compete in vain for attention against an over-charged baroque pulpit, and then there's the strange *Triumphal Cross* nearby, doing its best to belie its own name with four powerful-looking symbols of the Evangelists firmly surrounding a deathly-white and particularly ineffectual Christ (macabrely topped with a wig of the artist's own hair). This design was used frequently in the Harz area, but whether the final effect of the cross having triumphed over Jesus—rather than the other way round—is intentional, or a merely subconscious aberration of faith, is anybody's guess.

A little to the left of the church, guarded by the tangled thread design of the wrought-iron Gothic archway, the **Kleines Heiliges Kreuz** old people's home is set in spacious gardens with the occasional oriental tree, where the old folk—and dozens of chickens—can amble about at their leisure. You can too, but only if you take the guided tour on Tuesdays at 2pm. This costs DM3, and departs from the Grosses Heiliges Kreuz on Hoher Weg.

Down Peterstrasse, past the **Cow House** at no. 27 (named after its previous function) and the **Pumpkin House** at no. 23 (named after its shape), past the **Klaus Kapelle** on your right and the **Blacksmith's House** opposite (where the miners would pray, then and collect their sharpened tools before beginning their daily trek up to the Rammelsberg), past all these minor, but charming attractions, lies what has to be Goslar's biggest let-down, the highly overrated and over-restored **Kaiserpfalz** (*Imperial Palace*). It's certainly of some interest, not least for the impressive exterior and imposing position overlooking the town, but you wouldn't miss out on so very much if you took a cue from the punks lolling around on the steep hill below, enjoyed the view, and waited for the Hungarian artist Christo to come and fulfil his desire to wrap the whole building up.

Built at the beginning of the eleventh century to be home to a succession of greedy emperors enticed by the riches hidden in the Rammelsberg behind it, the Kaiserpfalz continued to flourish for the next 300 years, hosting important Imperial Diets and benefitting from Goslar's proximity to the crossroads of the two major trade routes of the Middle Ages (from Flanders to Magdeburg, and from Lübeck to Venice). A fire which gutted the palace in 1289 and a decline of interest around the same time by the emperors kept the building in a state of disrepair over the next few centuries, humbling it even to the point of being used as a barn and stables during the seventeenth century. Kaiser Wilhelm I came to the rescue in 1868, paying for the palace to be reconstructed to its former status.

In the **interior** (May–Sept. 9:30am–5pm, March, April and Oct. 10am–4pm, Nov.–Feb. 10am–3pm; DM2.50, students and under 18s DM1.25) enormous arched window openings that must have given birth to many a draughty Diet during the palace's heyday line the equally vast *Reichssaal*, which was covered, floor to ceiling, with late nineteenth-century romantic paintings during the restoration period. Various emperors are depicted being valiant (in battle), pious (distributing riches to the poor), conquering earth whilst being blessed by heaven, and so on. The 47m by 16m hall covers most of the Kaiserpfalz, with the early twelfth century **St. Ulrichskapelle** on its southern side. Here lies Heinrich III's heart, in the tomb in the center of the Greek cross shaped ground floor. The rest of his body lies somewhere in Speyer.

Behind the palace (where, if you face it directly, the irregular shaped stones to the left are the only ones remaining of the originals), the *Goslar Warrior* by Henry Moore lies reclining with his shield on his toe. Carry on past him, and a pretty semi-walled rose garden, dotted about with firs and shady spreading trees, leads down to a small bridge, a stream, and a stone-walled tower. Formerly used to defend the town from invaders, it can now be lived in only by those families with the money and inclination to defend it from the attacks of time.

On the opposite side of the Kaiserpfalz, the enormous parking lot stretching below you was once the site of the eleventh-century **Dom**, pulled down in 1822 due to lack of funds for restoration. Only the entrance hall with its facade of eighteenth-century statues survived (June–Sept. Mon.–Sat. 10am–1pm and 2:30–5pm, Sun. 10am–1pm, Oct.–May 10:30am–noon; 60pf; inquire at the Kaiserpfalz reception for entrance). The original part bronze **imperial throne** from the eleventh century is inside; it was used symbolically at the opening assembly of the Second

Reich in Berlin in 1871. Other relics from the cathedral, including the altar, are housed in the Goslar Museum (see below). The Dom's stones are now embedded in any number of houses, having been sold at the time of demolition to townsfolk who subsequently built their homes with them.

Directly in front of the Dom entrance hall, **Hoher Weg** leads down to the **Grosses Heiliges Kreuz** at no. 7, one of the oldest hospices in Germany. Built in 1254, it's currently undergoing badly needed repair, although there's still one resident. What will become of her when the planned art restoration center is completed, nobody knows. In the meantime, a tasteful but uninspired ceramics and trinkets shop downstairs and a rather good photo montage of the town upstairs provide a pleasant enough diversion. If you have a penchant for rare and beautiful dolls, the **Museum für Musikinstrumente mit Puppenmuseum** a little farther down the road from the Grosses Heiliges Kreuz, might briefly quench your thirst. Briefly, because it's more akin to a large private collection than a museum proper, and contains a fair proportion of junk. A *Bébé Jumeau* in excellent condition and a *Bru* are the highlights; other than that there's an Italian *Lenci* circa 1925 in Florentine carnival costume thrown in among the teddies.

Goslar's most famous house, the sixteenth-century **Brusttuch**, lies at the bottom of Hoher Weg, almost opposite the Marktkirche. The beams of the top story are crammed with satirical carvings of figures from medieval life, folklore, religion and mythology: mischievous cherubs firing arrows at angels, dignified ladies perched on top of goats and a carelessly suggestive dairymaid churning the butter and squeezing her buttocks at the same time.

A ten minute walk along Marktstrasse and the streets behind the Marktplatz is the **Mönchehaus Museum** on the corner of Mönchestrasse and Jakobistrasse (Tues.–Fri. 10am–1pm and 3–5pm, Sun. 10am–1pm; DM2.50, kids DM1). A black and white half-timbered building over 450 years old, it's the curious home to Goslar's permanent modern art exhibition. The contrast works rather well indoors, with de Koonings, Tinguelys and Vasarelys hanging amidst the oak beams. Outside, however, the huge mobiles and metal sculptures grate against their lush surroundings and your eyes begin to long for a classical line or two. Nevertheless, it's nice to see something in Goslar with an experimental touch.

Keep an eye out for no. 15 as you head down Jakobistrasse before turning right into Münzstrasse. Originally a craftsman's house, the work on the Renaissance frontage has a superb finish and is probably one of the most polished and professional pieces of restoration of all the houses in Goslar.

Münzstrasse itself contains more architectural beauties, including a seventeenth-century coaching inn, the **Weisser Schwan** at no. 11, where a tin figure museum (daily 10am–1pm and 2–5pm, Thurs. until 9pm, closed Mon. in winter) depicts the history of Goslar à la Lilliput. A step farther and you're in the **Schuhhof**, the site of the former market square and shoe-maker's Guildhall. Fires over the centuries have ravaged one part of the square, but the surviving side has three and four story half-timbered houses from the seventeenth century, their uneven roof heights bobbing up and down in a sea of sky and their window boxes laden down with so many brightly colored flowers that they threaten to tip over the heads of the customers of the clothes shops below. The combination of an Italian ice cream parlour and shady linden tree in the heart of the square makes this a good place to take a brief rest, or alternatively, there's a wonderful enclosed garden with a sort of wild cultivation about it, just over on the other side of Münzstrasse (daily 7am–7pm).

Skirting the huge modern shopping precinct to the east of the Schuhhof, cross straight over the Marktplatz and down Worthstrasse, where a fairly successful attempt at an artists' quarter has been constructed along the **banks of the Abzucht**, the tiny stream that passes through southern Goslar. Never mind the limp-looking contents of the crafts shops and galleries, the atmosphere is there. The Abzucht bubbles along the cobbles, occasionally to bump into one of the four or five rickety water mills remaining of an original twenty-five; follow the red stones in the middle of the pathways here and in the upper part of town (where the Abzucht turns into the Gose) to find the sites of the former mills, now replaced by houses. Look for the **St.-Annen-Stift**; dating from 1488, this hospice is the oldest half-timbered building in Goslar. There are seventeenth-century wall paintings and medieval furniture inside—knock at the front door for entrance.

On the corner of Abzuchtstrasse and Königstrasse, the **Goslar Museum** (June–Sept. Mon.–Fri. 10am–5pm, Sun. 10am–1pm, Oct.–May Mon.–Fri. 10am–1pm and 3–5pm, Sun. 10am–1pm; DM2.50, students DM1) contains the exotic *Krodo* altar from the Dom—looking more as if it were fashioned deep in the heart of Africa than in eleventh-century Europe—and a section on mining in the Rammelsberg.

Taking Rosentorstrasse northwards from the Markt, you pass the **registry office** with its fire engine red portal and flourishing embellishments, before reaching the **Jakobikirche**. Only the west wing remains from the original Romanesque structure, which was rebuilt in Gothic style. Inside, there's a moving *Pietà* by the great but elusive early sixteenth-century sculptor, Hans Witten. Further down the street, the **Neuwerkkirche** stands in a peaceful garden. Built as a Cistercian convent during the late twelfth and early thirteenth centuries, the church's main features are its two polygonal towers, and the delicate late Romanesque carvings on the exterior of the apse. Inside, there are works of art dating back to the period of construction, notably the choir screen and some rather clumsily retouched frescoes.

A two-hour walk round the **city ramparts** will take you along sections of the original walls, through stretches of greenery and by the various towers and gateways of the old town. Best preserved is the **Breites Tor**, a bulky ensemble, the sight of which alone must have been enough to scare off any would-be invaders.

Entertainment and Practicalities

Goslar isn't exactly *the* place to go and swing, but if you feel like a bop and aren't too choosy, there's *Charleston*, Marktstr. 15, a little more upmarket than *Merlyn* in Bergstrasse, whose clientele tends towards people from a 1960s time-warp. For **restaurants**, try the Worthstrasse and An der Abzucht area: *Eno's Taverne*, Abzuchtstrasse 5, has good value full meals; *Kontrast*, Worthstr. 10, does more health foods stuff; the somewhat more pricey bistro next door serves crêpes and light French dishes; *Worthmühle*, on the same street, is good for hot provincial cooking at very low prices. All of the above are also the best bets if you're just looking for a place to have a **drink**. On the other side of town, *Zebra*, Bäckerstr. 18, is a cheap and cheerful new wave hang-out (no meals); *Christall*, also on Bäckerstrasse and *Filou*, Marktstrasse (often packed out) do very cheap lunches. *W*, on Petersilienstrasse (to the east of the Jakobikirche), would be a good venue for a more relaxed lunch: the best salads in Goslar in a friendly West-Coast-of-America style décor. Without a doubt, best place for **tea and cakes** is *Barock-Café Anders*, Hoher Weg 4; walk straight to the back of the restaurant to sit outside, where there's a leafy vista of the hills of the Harz.

The tourist office has a comprehensive list of **hotels**, **pensions** and **private rooms**. Expect to pay between DM25 and DM35 per person for a double room in a hotel or pension and around DM20 each for a double room in a private house.

Most of the accommodation is in period buildings; the early eighteenth-century *Hotel Zur Börse*, Bergstr. 53 (opposite the Siemenshaus) is one of the prettiest. If you're in a group—or if your budget can run to it—it might be worth seeing if they will give you a room for just the night at the *Burg im Zwinger*, Thomasstr. 2 (☎05321 41088/85135). These are apartments (for two people, one room only) set in the six-meter-thick walls of the ivy-covered tower once used by the town's artillery (approx. DM70 for a twin-bedded room and DM100 for a four-bedded apartment). The **youth hostel**, Rammelsbergerstrasse 25 (☎05321 22240), is at the foot of the mine, not too far from the center, but a bit of a trek (30-min. walk) from the **Bahnhof**, which is at the northern end of town. Nearest **camping** is the well-equipped *Sennhütte*, Clausthalerstr. 28 (☎05321 22498/22502), in the Gose Valley, several kilometers along the B241 in the direction of Clausthal-Zellerfeld.

Outside Goslar

The tourist office can supply information on **walks** in the countryside around; the most interesting are a geological trail around the Rammelsberg, and another through the Oker valley. Best **winter sports** facilities are at the neighboring resort of **HAHNENKLEE**, which has both cross-country and downhill skiing, ice-skating, plus all the usual subsidiary activities: inquire at *Sporthaus Deckert*, Fischemäkerstr. 1A. This town has arguably the best of the several **festivals** celebrating *Walpurgisnacht* (see p.582).

Four kilometers north of Goslar, **Klosterkirche Grauhof** has some fine displays of baroque opulence inside its rather plain exterior, including an enormous organ. Occasional **concerts** are given during the summer; ask at the tourist office in Goslar for details. The **Riechenberg** crypt northwest of Goslar (take the B6 and then the B82 if you're driving; ask at the tourist office for bus times) is all that's left of a once splendid Romanesque building. It's worth going if you've got time, for the richly ornamented pillars and intricately fashioned birds and animals on the capitals. Finally, there's talk of a museum being erected at the **Rammelsberg** silver mine in the next few years, but in the meantime, you can visit the oldest part by arrangement with the tourist office.

The Harz Mountains

Nowhere, other than in Berlin itself, is the reality of the post-war division of Germany more evident than in the **HARZ** mountains, the first barrier encountered by the icy winds which sweep across the North German Plain. A popular holiday area since the idea of a vacation away from home took off in the course of the nineteenth century, the Harz are now divided right through the middle by the notorious barbed-wire frontier. Most roads now come to a dead end, and adjacent villages are now completely cut off from each other, often to the ruination of local economies. A fascinating social contrast is presented by the two sides, though there's no doubt that East Germany inherited the more enticing bit—the legendary Brocken (scene of the witches' sabbath on *Walpurgisnacht*), some gorgeous unspoiled old towns and a network of mountain steam railroads.

The range has a climate which is euphemistically described as "bracing." This means that there's lots of rain and fog, with heavy snowfall in winter; but for some reason this does not deter hordes of mainly elderly holidaymakers who have earned the region the derisive sobriquet *Rentnergebirge* ("pensioners' mountains"). Perhaps the old folk are drawn by the relatively gentle slopes of the mountains ("the skiing here is for babies," according to another insult) which make the Harz ideal for healthy but undemanding **walking** holidays. In 1962 the author Rudolf Hagelstange wrote: "The little mountains are rich in history, myths and poetry," thereby accounting for the region's popularity with various literati. Today a re-wording to ". . . rich in tacky tourism, spas and senior citizens," might be more appropriate, at least on the West German side of the border. (The GDR part, aside from being intrinsically more inviting, also avoids such excesses.) All the towns cater enthusiastically to tourist tastes. Goethe, the Harz's most illustrious literary wanderer, would be shocked if he were to follow the walking route named after him today.

The best thing that can be said for the Harz is that if you avoid the obvious tourist traps then the range has a certain romantic, if not dramatic, appeal. It's not really an area to spend a lot of time in, but if you happen to be passing through then there are a few places where it's worth stopping off for a short while. The Harz tries hard but no amount of tourist office PR can make up for the fact that it's just a little uninspiring, and although a big deal is made of local walking and skiing possibilities, quite frankly you can do both a lot better elsewhere. For detailed information about walking in the Harz, check with any of the local tourist offices or buy the *Wegweiser Naturpark Harz* which is available in most local bookshops. Skiing information is also available from tourist offices; the best slopes are on the **Wurmberg** near Braunlage.

Clausthal-Zellerfeld

The most direct route into the Harz from Goslar will take you to **CLAUSTHAL-ZELLERFELD** (hourly buses, journey time about 30min). The best thing about this town is the journey to it from Goslar along the B241 which winds and climbs its way through dense forest flanked by a number of small, hidden lakes. If you're **camping** there's a site just off the main road about 5km out of Goslar which is better than either of those in Clausthal-Zellerfeld. Despite the atmospheric approach road, both sites overlook a very depressing-looking ex-mining town.

Two old towns merged into one, Clausthal-Zellerfeld was dominated by mining until the last pit shut down in 1931. Even today it looks like it never really got over the demise of its main industry and the **Bergwerks- und Heimatmuseum**, Bornhardtstr. 16 in Zellerfeld (9am–1pm and 2–5pm, Tues.–Sun., DM2.50), a museum all about the mining methods employed in the Harz, is one of the two main attractions: hardly the highspot of anyone's holidays. The other thing worth seeing is the **Marktkirche**, the largest wooden church in Central Europe and around which the town of Clausthal clusters. Built in the first half of the seventeenth century, its main body is of spruce, while the tower is made of oak. Inside are notable furnishings, of which many, including the double gallery and pulpit, are also fashioned from wood.

The **tourist office** is in the old railroad station building between the towns, Im alten Bahnhof, Bahnhofstr. 5a (☎05323 7024), and quite difficult to find. Should you wish to linger they'll organize rooms and, in winter, ski and sled hire. There's also a **youth hostel** at Altenauer Str. 55 (☎05323 2293).

Torfhaus

From Clausthal-Zellerfeld strike out southeastwards towards Braunlage; the road takes you through scenery similar to that on the route from Goslar. At the **Oder-Teich**, a small wayside lake, you can stop and have a swim; watch out, too, for the stalls selling locally produced honey.

TORFHAUS, which lies 5km north, is nothing special in itself, but offers the best views of the celebrated **Brocken** (1142m), rendezvous of the witches on *Walpurgisnacht* (30 April), an event vividly described in Goethe's *Faust*. Sadly, it's currently inaccessible—not only is it over the boundary in the GDR, it's also a restricted military area. The legend seems to have arisen at least partly as a result of the so-called "spectre of Brocken"—when the sun is low, it casts magnified silhouettes from the peak on to clouds hanging around the lower neighboring mountains. *Walpurgisnacht* is somewhat oddly named after St. Walburga, the English-born eighth-century missionary saint whose name is invoked as protection against evil spirits; however, it seems she gained this role through her name having been confused with that of Waldborg, the pagan goddess of fertility. If you want to stay, Torfhaus has a **youth hostel** (☎05320 242), which serves as a good hiking base. The path northwards in the direction of BAD HARZBURG follows the frontier and presents a chilling picture of the reality of the division of Germany.

Braunlage

BRAUNLAGE, which lies 8km south of the Oder-Teiche, has gone overboard on tourism. There are dozens of souvenir shops and scores of pseudo-Alpine hotels and pensions. If you're in the area, the town would probably make a good place for an overnight stop because, if nothing else, it's not lacking in facilities. It's a *Kurort* and popular destination not only with the senior citizen crowd but also with young families who come here for the skiing (five pistes, served by cable car) on the **Wurmberg** which at 965m is one of the highest peaks in West Germany and an attraction in itself. You can ride a cable car to the top and back for DM10, students DM7.50.

The **tourist office** is in the *Kurverwaltung*, Elbingeröder Str. 17 (☎05520 1054). A couple of reasonably priced hotels are *Tannerhof*, Tanner Str. 23 (☎05520 582) which starts at DM25 per person and *Haus Hamburg*, Bodestr. 4 (☎05520 1806) also from DM25 per person. There are, however, plenty more possibilities and the tourist office will be able to fill you in more comprehensively. The **youth hostel** is at Von-Langen-Str. 63 (05520 2238). Braunlage has a number of walking routes: again information from the tourist office.

St. Andreasberg and Herzberg

Just to the west of Braunlage is **ST. ANDREASBERG**, 400 years old and the highest town in the Harz. It's not particularly thrilling, but if you're passing through, stop off at the old silver mine known as **Bergwerkmuseum Grube Samson** (guided tours, lasting an hour, daily at 11am and 2pm; DM2.50). The **tourist office** is in the *Kurverwaltung*, Am Glockenberg 12 (☎05582 1012) from where you'll be able to get information about cheap hotels and pensions. There's also a **youth hostel** at Am Gesehr 37 (☎05582 269).

From St. Andreasberg head for **HERZBERG**, a spectacular journey of corkscrew curves along the steep, wooded slopes of the **Sieber** valley. Herzberg is slightly less tourist-oriented—which comes as a relief after the frantic attention-seeking of Braunlage. It's overlooked by the **Welfenschloss**, a half-timbered seventeenth-century castle built in the "Wild Man" style seen in Goslar. A biggish lake in the town center itself gives the place a distinctive atmosphere.

Altenau and Osterode

Of the remaining Harz towns, only a couple are really worth mentioning—the others are little more than villages. **ALTENAU** is quite inoffensive and home to

Germany's second largest wooden baroque church. The **tourist office** is in the *Kurgeschäftstelle*, Schultal 5 (☎05328 8020). There are plenty of cheap hotels, including *Pension Haus Thomas*, Stettiner Str. 43 (☎05328 612) where beds start at DM18 per person, and there's a **youth hostel** at Auf der Rose 11 (☎05328 361).

OSTERODE, on the edge of the Harz, is quite pleasant in a bland sort of way. Self-consciously striving to live up to its status as the birthplace of the great sculptor Tilman Riemenschneider, and to a few lines of praise bestowed on it by Heinrich Heine in 1824, it boasts a lot of over-restored half-timbered houses and a few historic municipal buildings. Look out for the shark's rib above the entrance to the **Rathaus** which is supposed to ensure protection against flooding. The **tourist office** is at Dörgestr. 40 (☎05522 6855). Cheapest place to stay is the *Gästehaus Inge Neumann*, Hengstrücken 88 (☎05522 3693) which has beds from DM16 per person.

Einbeck

EINBECK, which lies just to the west of the Harz, is something of a mecca for **beer** lovers. In the Middle Ages the town boasted no less than 700 breweries (virtually all of which were tiny part-time operations run within the household), which produced *Einpöckisches Bier*. Made from wheat and top-fermented, this strong brew was designed for export, and fermentation took place in the course of the journey to the customer. This developed in time into *Bockbier* (so-called after a corruption of the town's name), which has long been as popular in Bavaria as in Lower Saxony; two crucial differences from the earlier version are that it's made from barley, and bottom-fermented. Nowadays, the *Einbeckerbrauerei* is the only brewery left in the home town of this headily potent beer, a few glasses of which can turn even the most hardened of boozers into a legless drunk. It produces both light (*Hell*) and dark (*Dunkel*) varieties, as well as the special brown *Maibock*, available only in springtime. All of these have a smooth, dry, and highly satisfying flavor.

Einbeck is now equally celebrated for its medieval center (even the local *Woolworths* is half-timbered). Centerpiece of it all is the **Marktplatz** which is surrounded by well-kept and obviously genuine sixteenth-century houses. Look out for the **Brodhaus** and the **Ratsapotheke,** which stand next door to each other like two superannuated old men opposite the vaguely sinister-looking **Rathaus**. The Rathaus could well have served as a model for the witch's house in the Hansel and Gretel story thanks to three low conical spires which seem to have sprouted out of the ground directly in front of it. It's rather dwarfed by the baroque **St. Jakobskirche**, which is pleasing enough but unexceptional. In **Marktstrasse**, house no. 13 is particularly unusual as its whole facade is covered with intricate allegorical carvings, drawing on Christian and classical themes. Many of the figures are remarkably expressive and you get the impression that the artist used local characters as models.

There are a couple more passable churches: the **Stiftskirche St. Alexandri** proudly boasts the oldest choir stall in Germany (1288), while the thirteenth-century **Kapelle St. Bartholemäi** on Altendorfer Strasse contains some slightly faded late Gothic frescoes. The only interesting museum is the **Einbecker Fahrad-Museum**, Papenstr. 1–3 (Tues. 3–5pm, Weds. 10am–noon, Thurs. 4–6pm, Fri. 10am–12pm, Sat. 10am–noon; free), a collection of bikes which has everything from the wooden wheeled boneshakers of 1817 to the very latest racers. It's also worth taking a walk round the surviving sections of the old city wall, the **Stadtmauer**. Much of the fortification network is intact and you can stroll along the massive earthworks which were constructed to increase the protection afforded by the wall itself.

The **tourist office** is in the Rathaus (☎05561 316121; May–Sept. Mon.–Fri. 9am–1pm and 2:30–6pm; Sat. 9:30am–noon, Oct.–April Mon.–Thur 9am–1pm and 2:30–5pm; Fri. 9am–1pm). Of the **hotels** with a central location, the most reasonably priced are *Gästehaus Herkur*, Bismarckstr. 4 (☎05561 2300), which starts at DM20 per person, and *Stadt Hannover*, Möncheplatz 10 (☎05561 5496), which charges upwards of DM28 per person.

Roughly halfway between Einbeck and Göttingen is **NORTHEIM**. It's historic in a run-of-the-mill kind of way but by the time you reach it you'll probably be feeling a bit jaded by half-timbered houses. In many ways Northeim is like a smaller, less impressive version of Einbeck with a few ugly, modern buildings upsetting the architectural balance of the town center. The **tourist office** is at Am Münster 30 (☎05551 63650) and there's a **youth hostel**, named for some reason after World War II *Luftwaffe* ace Adolf Galland, at In der Fluth 1 (☎05551 8672). There are also **camping** facilities at Sultmer Berg (☎05551 51559).

Göttingen

It's worth spending at least a day and a night in **GÖTTINGEN**, a city which seems positively metropolitan in contrast to the surrounding area. Göttingen owes its exciting, buzzing atmosphere to its large student population (30,000 students out of a total populace of 130,000), who have made sure that the nightlife here almost has a big-city feel to it. In fact, a lot of students come to Göttingen after studying in Berlin, and they seem to have brought some of the latter's pace with them.

The **University** was founded in 1737 by King George II of Great Britain in his capacity as Elector of Hannover, and ranks as one of the most prestigious in Germany. It immediately promoted a free-thinking, liberal atmosphere in contrast to the authoritarianism of the country's other seats of learning. In its early days, it was associated with poets, such as the group known as the *Göttinger Hain-Bund*, early Romantics who wrote on folklore, nature, and homely themes, and the balladeer Gottfried August Bürger, whose *Leonore*, (with its vivid image of Death), was enormously influential. The University's literary reputation continued in the nineteenth century with the appointment of the Brothers Grimm to professorships—Jacob wrote an exhaustive study, *Teutonic Mythology*, while there, which inspired similar studies of national folklore all over Europe. Unfortunately, this tradition, along with Göttingen's liberal standing, was severely tarnished by the dismissal of the brothers and five colleagues in 1837 for failing to kow-tow to the reactionary new constitution introduced into the Kingdom of Hannover.

Mathematics and science have, if anything, been even stronger academic specialties in Göttingen. In the eighteenth century, the leading figure was Georg Christoph Lichtenberg, who invented the prototype of the Xerox copying machine; he was also a brilliant satirical writer, relentlessly sending up the excesses of both the Romantic movement and the world of academe. Throughout the first half of the last century, Karl-Friedrich Gauss, whose name is given to a unit of the field of magnetic intensity, dominated the University's intellectual life. Since World War II, Göttingen has been the headquarters of the fifty separate high-powered scientific research units of the **Max-Planck-Institut**, named in honor of the discoverer of quantum theory, who passed his last years in the town.

Göttingen's students flirted briefly with the spirit of '68 but today they're more interested in patronizing the town's *Musikkneipen* and jazz clubs by night while studying for well-paid, secure careers during the day. Things quieten down a little outside term time, but there's usually something going on. To make the most of the place, arrive in the evening (perhaps after traveling down through the Harz from Goslar in the afternoon), check out the bars and restaurants that night and then spend the following day absorbing the half-timbered city center.

From the **Hauptbahnhof**, follow Goethe-Allee straight ahead, and you shortly come to the pedestrianized town center. On the Markt is the **Altes Rathaus**, with Göttingen's main **tourist office**, the *Fremdenverkehrsverein* on the first floor (Mon.–Fri. 9am–6pm, Sat. and Sun. 10am–4pm; ☎0551 54000). In the same building is the *Fremdenverkehrsamt* (☎0551 40023) which deals with hotel bookings and individual guided tours. The Altes Rathaus itself is a massive sandstone structure which has an almost Venetian feel to it, quite at odds with the half-timbered buildings nearby. Most of what you can see today dates back to 1369–1444 but the building was never completely finished, as resources had to be diverted to fortifying the city, which may well account for its relatively uncomplicated appearance. There are guided tours of the building but it would be advisable to check with the tourist office about times, which seem to be a bit erratic. Look out for the medieval-looking wall frescoes and coats-of-arms painted on the inner walls. These turn out to be little over 100 years old, having been commissioned by the city authorities during the restoration of the building during the 1880s. When the weather is good the *Ratskeller* takes over part of the market place and you can have a drink or a meal while looking at the **Gänseliesel**, "the most kissed girl in the world," a bronze statue of a goosegirl to whom, according to tradition, the students must give a few smackers when they pass their finals.

Next door to the Altes Rathaus is the **Johanniskirche**, a twin-towered, fourteenth-century Gothic church which has a certain decrepit elegance. It's an imposing building but some of its impact is diminished by the shops that crowd in around it. Theological students are allowed free accommodation in one of the towers but they have to endure the sound of the bells from the other tower and miserable living conditions (no running water). In the old days the tower was part of a medieval early warning system from where a watch was kept for fire and enemy attack. Behind the church is the medieval **Johannesviertel**, more or less a slum district until the 1970s, when the city hit upon the bright idea of tarting it up for the tourists. At the point where Johanniskirchhof runs into Paulinerstrasse is the former **Paulinerkirche**, originally built by Dominican monks in 1331, which in 1529 was the scene of the first Lutheran church service in Göttingen. Used as the provisional home of the University when it first opened, the building now houses part of its library.

The **St. Marienkirche** stands on what used to be the boundary between Göttingen and the so-called **Neustadt** which was built as a rival town outside the city walls by a local nobleman in an attempt to challenge the increasingly powerful burghers. The citizens' response to this threat was an astute one. They waited until the nobleman went bankrupt and then bought the Neustadt from him, incorporating it into Göttingen itself. The St. Marienkirche looks quite unecclesiastical, which probably has something to do with the fact that its bell tower used to be one of the gateways to the Neustadt (the street still passes underneath it).

Anybody who knows anything about German history won't be able to resist the **Bismarckhäuschen**, a small tower on the southern edge of the town center which is part of the old **Stadtmauer** or city wall. In 1833 this was home to the seventeen-year-old Otto von Bismarck, then a student in the city. The man who later became the "Iron Chancellor" and who finally realized, by a mixture of brute force and astute politicking, the long-established ideal of a united Germany, was forced to live here, having been banned from the city center for drunkenness and "misbehavior of various kinds." Apart from such obvious sights, the town offers plenty of curiosities, hidden away in nooks and crannies—just take a wander around the streets and see what you find.

Göttingen is a bit low on museums and the ones that do exist are the sort you'll probably only want to visit if it's pouring with rain when you hit town. The **Städtishes Museum**, Ritterplan 7–8 (Tues.–Fri. 10am–1pm and 3–5pm, Sat. and Sun. 10am–1pm) has a Göttingen bias, with a big collection of religious art and plenty of examples of locally produced glass and porcelain. The **Museum am Thie**, Am Geismar Thie 2 (Thurs. 8–10pm and first and third Sun. in month 10am–noon) is a not terribly exciting collection of farm tools and domestic bits and pieces. Otherwise there are the university collections which tend to be open to the public only a couple of days a week (usually at the weekend). There are zoology, archaeology, chemistry, geology and music related collections which the tourist office will be able to supply details about. Of more general interest is the **Kunstsammlung** Auditorium, Weender Landstr. 2 (Weds. 3–5pm, Sun. 10am–1pm) which has an extensive collection of engravings plus about 300 seventeenth-century Dutch paintings. There's also the **Völkerkundliche Sammlung**, Theaterplatz 15 (Sun. 10am–1pm or by prior arrangement), a collection of ethnographic bits and pieces from all over the world which includes a slightly bizarre, 400-exhibit collection of fertility symbols and mother-god effigies.

Nightlife and Practicalities

Above all, Göttingen is a city where you can enjoy yourself. There are dozens of **cafés**, **bars** and **restaurants** which, thanks to the heavy student presence, tend to be high on atmosphere and low in cost. *Zum Altdeutschen*, Prinzenstr. 16, is Göttingen's most famous student pub but these days its clientele is more likely to be tourists than students, who prefer hang-outs like *Havana Moon*, Rote Str. 18, a trendy Texan style bar. Nearby is *Can Cun*, Kornmarkt 9, a chrome decor basement café, which, thanks to its cheap baguettes and live music in an animated atmosphere, is also popular with undergraduates. *Blue Note* in Wilhelmplatz is a slightly upmarket jazz/blues bar which seems to be favored by medical and law students drawn by its snob appeal. A recommended pizzeria is *Taormina*, Groner-Tor-Str. 28, which stays open until 1:30am; there's a good but pricey Turkish restaurant next door. Also worth knowing about is *Naturell*, a vegetarian restaurant at Lange-Geismar-Str. 40 (Mon.–Fri. 11am–7pm, Sat. 11am–2:30pm). Just next door is a wholefood supermarket if you feel like stocking up.

Most of Göttingen's **hotels** tend to be on the pricey side. The cheapest with a central location is *Hotel-Gaststätte zur Rose*, Kurze Geismarstr. 37 (☎0551 57050), with singles from DM33 and doubles from DM66. *Pension am Theater*, Planckstr. 12 (☎0551 59362) has three singles from DM30 and two doubles at DM70. In the eastern suburb of Herberhausen (bus #10 from the town center), *Landgasthaus Lockmann*, Im Beeke 1 (☎0551 21582) has singles at DM26.50 and doubles from DM45. At the northern end of town *Weender Hof*, Hannoversche Str. 150 (☎0551 36048) charges DM30 for singles, DM50 for doubles. On the way out of town, just off the B27 heading for Braunlage, is the *Gasthaus zum Drakenburg*, Lange Str. 43 (☎0551 24613) which has singles at DM28 and doubles at DM55. Göttingen's

youth hostel is at Habichtsweg 2 (☎0551 57622; bus #18 from the town center) and there's also a 31-bed *Naturfreundehaus* at An der Springmühle 30 (bus #23 from town center).

Each June, Göttingen celebrates the **Handel festival**, one of Europe's best and most adventurous celebrations of the work of a single composer; many long-forgotten masterpieces have successfully been dusted off here, and brought back into the repertoire. **Mitfahrzentrale's** office is at Obere-Masch-Str. 18 (☎0551 44004).

Duderstadt

DUDERSTADT lies just a few kilometers from the East German border and is easily reached by road from Göttingen. The journey is depressing, through a landscape of uniform, bare green fields traversed by stark, modern road bridges and interspersed with municipal refuse dumps—but it's worth the effort. Despite yet more half-timbered houses Duderstadt has a unique subtlety which somehow makes it stand out from all the other towns in the area. Before the Thirty Years' War Duderstadt owed allegiance to the Archbishops of Mainz and the town likes to claim that it's the northernmost part of south Germany. Some of the timber-frame houses (there are over 500 in all) are really impressive and many are decorated with carvings and inscriptions, messages from the past which still have an uncanny vitality. The best examples are in **Hinterstrasse**, where there's a rich mix of architectural styles reflecting phases in the town's history of partial destruction followed by intense reconstruction. This can also be seen in the **Rathaus** which seems to have started off Gothic and then turned Renaissance halfway through.

Duderstadt's other main sight is the **Westertorturm**, a gatetower whose high, narrow roof has, over the years, gradually turned on its own axis and taken on a characteristic spiral appearance. There are also a couple of notable churches: the Gothic **St. Cyriakus** has an opulent baroque interior, while **St. Servatiuskirche** was redecorated on the inside in art noveau style after being burned out in 1915. Also worth a glance is the **Mariensäule** on the Gropenmarkt, a sandstone statue of the Virgin Mary set on top of a tall pillar whose base is flanked by palm trees, creating an incongruously Mediterranean atmosphere.

The **tourist office** is in the Rathaus (April–Oct. Mon. 8am–1pm, Thurs. 2–5pm, Fri. 8:30am–1pm and 2–5pm, Sat. and Sun. 9:30am–12:30pm and 2:30–4:30pm, Nov.–March Mon., Thurs. and Fri. am only; ☎05527 841200). A couple of cheap, central **hotel** recommendations are *Zum halben Mond*, Haberstr. 17 (☎05527 2698), charging from DM28 per person and *Schutzenhaus*, August-Werner-Allee 28 (☎05527 5506), at upwards of DM25 per person. The **youth hostel** is at Schutzenring 6 (☎05527 3833). **Camping** facilities are available at *Campingplatz Forsthaus Nesselröder Warten* (☎05508 364) in NESSELRÖDE, which lies on the Duderstadt–Göttingen road.

Since border crossing restrictions were eased in 1973 Duderstadt has become a stopping off point for travelers journeying east. The town used to be the center of the **EICHSFELD** region, a remote land that time forgot, which was by-passed by the Reformation and whose inhabitants were, according to popular prejudice, a little slow on their feet because of centuries of in-breeding. Most of this area now lies in East Germany, and these days Duderstadt calls itself center of *Die Goldene Mark* ("The Golden Borderland"), an expression used to denote that part of the

Eichsfeld which was lucky enough to find itself in the western sector when Germany was divided. If you fancy a Cold War thrill, the road back to Göttingen skirts the border itself before passing through NESSELRÖDEN.

Münden

Playing the time-honored game of listing the Seven Wonders of the World, the great German traveler-scholar Alexander von Humboldt—who had seen a fair bit of the globe for himself—listed **MÜNDEN** (formerly *HANNOVERSCHE MÜNDEN*) as ranking among the seven most beautifully-sited towns. This was doubtless due to the fact that the **River Weser** is formed here by the merging of the **Fulda** and **Werra**; the actual point of convergence is marked by a stone which bears a predictably trite inscription.

Münden has even more **half-timbered houses** than Duderstadt—over 700 in all. Separated by some six centuries of history, they completely dominate the face of the town. The plain white **Rathaus**, however, is of a more solid stone construction. It's in the early seventeenth-century Weser Renaissance style, with ornate gables and the obligatory oriel window. Next door is the **St. Blasiuskirche**, an unusual-looking Gothic hall church with a hexagonal tower and a very steeply pitched roof of red slate. The only other major set-piece is the **Welfenschloss**, a rather tame-looking Renaissance château affair overlooking the Werra. It now houses an uninspiring local history museum, but also boasts several fresco cycles from soon after the time of the building's construction, among the few in Germany from this period. Behind the Schloss is the **Werrabrücke**, an old bridge which dates back at least as far as the fourteenth century.

The **tourist office** is in the Rathaus (May–Sept. Mon.–Fri. 8:30am–5pm, Sat. 8:30am–12:30pm, Oct.–April Mon.–Thurs. 8:30am–12:30pm and 1–4pm, Fri. 8:30am–12:30pm; ☎05541 75313). There are a couple of cheapish hotels: *Gasthaus Zur Hafenbahn*, Blume 54 (☎05541 4094), which starts at DM23 per person, or *Gasthaus im Anker*, Bremer Schlagd 18 (☎05541 4923) whose prices begin at DM23. The **youth hostel** is way to the north of town at Prof.-Oelkers-Str. 10 (☎05541 8853), while the **campground** has a handier location on an island in the River Fulda named Oberer Tanzwerder (☎05541 122257). However, whether it's worth staying the night is questionable—Münden has little to offer in the way of nightlife, and the young just seem to hang around, waiting for something to happen.

Each Sunday between mid-May and the end of August sees the enactment of an open-air **costume play** on the life of Münden's most celebrated citizen, Johann Andreas Eisenbart, an eighteenth-century doctor who built up a reputation as a miracle-worker. His house can be seen at Lange Str. 34, outside which is a commemorative statue. Another possible diversion is to take a **river cruise**—there are several daily departures in summer to HÖXTER and HAMELN.

From Münden you might want to visit the **Europäisches Brotmuseum** (Mon.–Sat. 10am–4:30pm, Sun. 10am–5:30pm; guided tours only), a slightly eccentric museum devoted (appropriately enough in Germany) to the history of bread. You'll only really be able to reach it if you're traveling by car as it's not very easy to get to. From Münden head for HEDEMÜNDEN and then for GERTENBACH. From here take the road to MOLLENFELDE which winds through a lush green and gold landscape of rolling arable land. From there, follow the signs. The museum is worth visiting for a laugh alone. There are

30,000 bread-related exhibits detailing the history of bread from Ancient Egyptian times until today. There's also a droll section devoted entirely to bread in art.

Also in the area, but probably best avoided unless you're traveling with kids or harbor a passionate interest in vintage cars, is the **Erlebnispark Ziegenhagen** (signposted from GERTENBACH), a horrendous amusement park (March–Oct., 10am–5pm, DM7.50, kids DM6). The complex incorporates a car and motor-cycle museum which is a little more civilized.

travel details

Trains

From Bremen to Bremerhaven (1 an hour; 50min), Oldenburg (2; 35min), Wilhelmshaven (2; 1hr 40min), Emden (1; 2hr), Norddeich (1; 2hr 50min), Osnabrück (1; 2hr), Hannover (2; 1hr).

From Hannover to Einbeck (1; 1hr), Hildesheim (3; 25min), Göttingen (3; 1hr), Braunschweig (2; 50min), Celle (3; 25min), Lüneburg (2; 1hr 20min), Wolfenbüttel (2; 1hr 10min), Münden (1; 2hr), Hameln (1; 50min), Goslar (1;1hr 20min).

Ferries

From Emden to Borkum (winter 2 daily, summer 4; 2½hr).

From Norddeich Mole to Juist (1–3; 1hr 20min), Norderney (9–13; 50min).

From Bensersiel to Langeoog (3–5; 50min).

From Neuharlingersiel to Spiekeroog (2–4; 50min).

From Harle to Wangerooge (2–3 summer, 1 winter; 1hr 10min).

From Wilhelmshaven to Helgoland (1 summer only; 3hr).

CHAPTER SEVEN

HAMBURG AND SCHLESWIG-HOLSTEIN

J utting up between the North and Baltic seas, and stretching as far as the Danish border, **SCHLESWIG-HOLSTEIN** is the most northerly of Germany's Länder. One of the Federal Republic's few coastal regions, it's not surprising that maritime influences have defined the Land: in the Dark Ages the town of **Schleswig** thrived as a Viking trading center, and now records that era in an excellent museum. During the medieval period the port of **Lübeck** was one of the main pivots of the Hanseatic League, and today it's the region's most impressive town, the architectural heritage of its former mercantile glory revealed in the houses of patrician families, the warehouses in which their goods were stored, and the churches they built with the wealth they accrued. **Flensburg** too has similar trading connections, and shows the influence of Danish occupation—throughout its history, control of Schleswig-Holstein has shifted back and forth between Germany and Denmark.

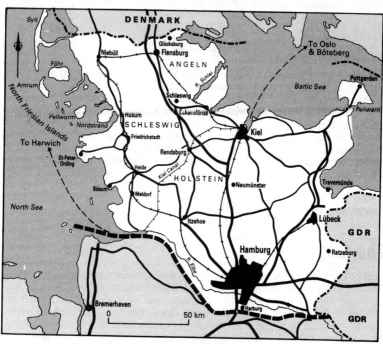

Inland Schleswig-Holstein is a mix of dike-protected marsh, peat bog and rich alluvial farmland. No mountains or fairytale castles here, nor jovial thigh-slapping dances: northernmost Germany contrasts starkly with the south, and a Bavarian would feel less at home than someone from England. Areas like **Angeln** in the northeast are dotted with half-timbered houses and ancient villages, and though there's little else in the way of specific "sights," and public transit is at best erratic, it's an area easily explored by bike.

Both the coastal region east of Angeln and the western North Friesian coast have miles of sandy beaches and a surprising amount of sunshine. The **North Friesian Islands**, scattered along the west coast, are also popular in summer for sun and sand; venture here in winter and you'll be rewarded with bracing sea air and what the brochures kindly term "health-promoting walks." The **coastal towns** are more than just a springboard for the islands: **Niebüll** has two surprisingly fine collections of art, and **Husum** has charm tempered by its working fishing harbor.

Hamburg, a Land in its own right, exists like an island in the south of the state, a city infamous for the prostitution and sleaze of the Reeperbahn. That's about as much as most people care to know about the place, but Hamburg has plenty to offer: not least a sparkling nightlife and a city center that's made up of enjoyably contrasting and easily explorable neighborhoods.

It's possible to travel to Hamburg **by ferry** from Hull in the U.K. or Harwich, the latter also having ferry connections to ESJBERG in Denmark. Arriving at one port and leaving from the other, ten days to a fortnight would allow you to travel through Schleswig-Holstein, taking in the best of each coast and the major towns. For more details on ferries, see _Basics_.

HAMBURG

The Elbe River marks the southern border of Schleswig-Holstein, and 90km inland stands the port of **Hamburg**. Exhilaratingly different from any other German city, Hamburg has always been a city-state, free to trade as it pleased, unencumbered by dukes and princes. Even now it officially bears the title of _Freie und Hansestadt:_ "Free and Hanseatic City." Its contemporary reputation is tainted by tales of the red-light area, but that's only a small part of what the city is about—it's a stylish media center, a huge modern seaport, a scene of radical protest, and home of the latest generation of a long-standing merchant class. Unless you arrive at one of the coastal ports, Hamburg is also where you're likely to begin your travels around Schleswig-Holstein; allow two or three days to explore downtown and the suburbs, and as many nights as your pocket (and constitution) will stand to soak up its nightlife.

The City

Each of Germany's cities somehow reflects the intrinsic character of its region. **HAMBURG** has none of the sentimental folklore tradition of the Rhineland and the south; instead it has a certain coolness, solidity, openness, and sense of excitement. If that is a reflection of regional characteristics, then Hamburg represents not only northernness but something of its lost hinterland along and east of the Elbe, now in the GDR. To get Hamburg in perspective, it's best not to see the city as just a port in West Germany's northeastern corner, but to remember its position in the old context.

A vital port for centuries, and a self-governing city, Hamburg has learned to look outwards, to horizons that have become more distant over the centuries. The Elbe is deep, and navigable by the largest ships as far as Hamburg's docks. The ships are a constant reminder of what Hamburg is about, and even away from the docks there's more water—at the very heart of the city are the Alster lakes. The small **Binnenalster** is half encircled by graceful frontages, while the much bigger **Aussenalster** (the largest lake to be found in the center of any city in Europe), with its sailing boats and windsurfers, its grassy banks busy with joggers, strollers, and sunbathers, brings life to the middle of town. You can stand beside it and look back towards Hamburg's skyline, dominated by the pale green of its copper spires and domes. Much of the postwar rebuilding (bombing destroyed over half the housing) may not be especially beautiful, but has conformed to policies that have kept the city on a human scale.

Scarcely anything remains of old Hamburg, which must have looked much as Lübeck or, to an extent, Amsterdam does today. The few houses along the Deichstrasse, the Krameramtswohnungen, and the churches are just about all that's left from before the nineteenth century. The Great Fire of May 1842 was a main cause of this loss, followed by demolition to make way for the Speicherstadt, the warehouse area of the free port. These two events, however, did generate some very fine nineteenth-century architecture, especially in the elegant residential areas, which fortunately suffered little during the war.

Arriving—and Finding Somewhere to Stay

Ferries from Harwich and Hull in Britain arrive at the **St. Pauli Landungsbrücken**, close to the city center, and it's an easy hop via the U-Bahn to anywhere in town. **Buses** run from the **airport** to the **Hauptbahnhof** every twenty minutes, though it's a little cheaper to take the *HVV* (Hamburg City Transit) airport express bus to the U- and S-Bahn stop at Ohlsdorf, and then catch a train into town. **Exchange facilities** are available at the bank within the Hauptbahnhof from 7:30am to 10pm daily, including Sundays and holidays. Immediately opposite is the **tourist office** (daily 7am–11pm; ☎2487 0230), which has a full room-finding service. If you need more leaflets, go to the head office in the *Bieberhaus* in nearby Hachmannplatz (Mon.–Fri. 7:30am–6pm, Sat. 8am–3pm; ☎2487 0245); another branch is in the shopping arcade Hanse-Viertel on Poststrasse. (Mon.–Fri. 9am–6:30pm, Sat. 9am–3pm, Sun. 11am–3pm; ☎2487 0220). **Orientation** from the Hauptbahnhof is easy, provided you know which of the four exits to take. Two lead out to the eastern (Kirchenallee) side, which is best for hotels and the St. Georg district; the other two exit on the western side, for the Binnenalster and the city center. The integrated **public transit** network comprises buses, the U-Bahn, and S-Bahn. A day pass makes a good investment at DM6; a family ticket is even better value at DM10.50.

Accommodation of all types is easy to find but rarely cheap; the budget option is the large **youth hostel** called *Auf dem Stintfang* near the St. Pauli Landungsbrücke (Alfred-Wegener-Weg 5; ☎313488), which has beds for DM17 and can sell you a youth hostel pass. Another hostel is *Hamburg-Horn* (Rennbahnstr. 70; ☎651 1671), out of town in the suburb of Horn. Alternatively, there are a couple of others: MUI, Budapester Str. 45 (☎431169) charges from DM25 per head (singles available), while *Kolpinghaus St. Georg*, Schmilinskystr.

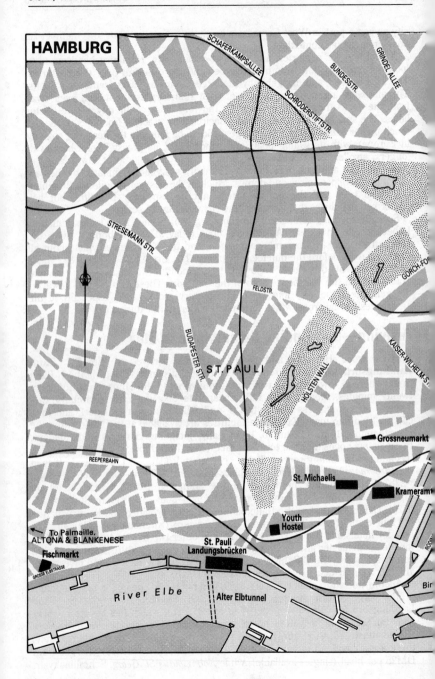

HAMBURG

SCHAFERKAMPSALLEE

BUNDESSTR.

GRINDEL ALLEE

SCHRODERSTIFTSTR.

STRESEMANN STR.

GORCH-FO

FELDSTR.

BUDAPESTER STR.

ST. PAULI

HOLSTEN WALL

KAISER-WILHELM-ST.

Grossneumarkt

REEPERBAHN

St. Michaelis

Krameram

Youth
Hostel

To Palmaille,
ALTONA & BLANKENESE

St. Pauli
Landungsbrücken

Fischmarkt

GROSSE ELBSTRASSE

Bir

River Elbe   Alter Elbtunnel

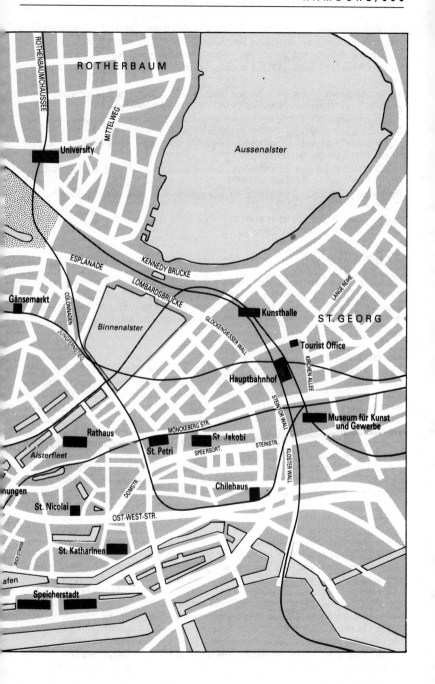

ROTHERBAUM

Aussenalster

University

MITTELWEG

ROTHENBAUMCHAUSSEE

ESPLANADE

KENNEDY BRUCKE

LOMBARDSBRUCKE

Gänsemarkt

COLONNADEN

JUNGFERNSTIEG

Binnenalster

GLOCKENGIESSER WALL

Kunsthalle

ST. GEORG

LANGE REIHE

Tourist Office

KIRCHEN ALLEE

Hauptbahnhof

STEINTOR WALL

Museum für Kunst
und Gewerbe

Rathaus

MONCKEBERG STR.

St. Jakobi

STEINSTR.

St. Petri

SPEERSORT.

Alsterfleet

DOMSTR.

KLOSTER WALL

nungen

Chilehaus

St. Nicolai

OST-WEST-STR.

DEICHSTRASSE

St. Katharinen

afen

Speicherstadt

78 (☎246609), has singles from DM32, doubles from DM54. The **campground** (June–Sept. only) is at Kieler Str. 374 (☎540 4532); nearest S-Bahn stop is Stellingren. Other than these, you need to look long and hard to find **pensions** under DM55 for a single, DM75 double. The following are the cheapest and most central.

Bei der Esplanade, Colonnaden 45, 2nd floor (☎342961). Small fairly comfortable hotel/pension close to shopping center. Singles DM50–77, doubles DM79–84.

Alameda, Colonnaden 45 (☎344290). In the same building as *Bei der Esplanade*, rather more basic, though not noticeably cheaper: singles DM56 and up, doubles DM80–120.

Basler Hospiz, Esplanade 11 (☎341921). Large, slightly austere, but conveniently situated. Singles DM63–93, doubles DM100–145.

Steen's Hotel, Holzdamm 43 (☎244642). Delightful small hotel near the Hauptbahnhof. Singles DM63 and up, doubles from DM75.

Hotel Royal, Holzdamm 5 (☎243753). Simple, old-fashioned hotel near the Hauptbahnhof. Singles DM50–77, doubles DM80–135.

Hotel Wedina, Gürlitt Str. 23 (☎243011). Rather stuffy small hotel in the St. Georg area, handy for the lakes and the Kunsthalle.

Around Town

Hamburg has no obvious core to start your explorations, and it's best to begin in the city's oldest and liveliest area, the port. From here, you're within easy walking distance of the Fischmarkt and Altona. The commercial center of the city is a bus or U-Bahn ride away—as are the suburbs of Övelgönne and the area around the lakes.

The Harbor Area

If you come to Hamburg by ship, this will be where you dock. The journey up the Elbe takes a good couple of hours, a frustratingly long time when you're eager to arrive. Eventually, though, the city is in sight—the clock tower and green dome tell you you're approaching the **St. Pauli Landungsbrücken**. Even if you have arrived by ship, you might still want to go on a **Hafenrundfahrt**, a trip around the harbor. Boats leave regularly from the St. Pauli Landungsbrücken, and many have an English commentary. (There are also **Alternative Hafenrundfahrten**, which aim to point out environmental problems.) Hamburg is Europe's third largest port, and container ships from China, the Soviet Union, and India attest to its importance. Its **800-year history** has taken a different course since the loss of Hamburg's traditional hinterland along the Elbe; today, for most of the cities in the Federal Republic, Rotterdam has become more convenient. Hamburg competes by offering high-speed handling of containerized cargo; this, though, has been achieved only by greater mechanization—which means a smaller workforce. The shipbuilding industry here is on the decline, too, and the main shipbuilder has had to diversify into other areas to survive.

Hamburg's port and shipbuilding workforce has been organized and powerful ever since industrialization—their first strike action occurred during the 1840s, when unionized as the *Bund der Gerechten* (League of the Righteous). The first copies of Karl Marx's *Das Kapital* were printed in Hamburg, and the socialist movement grew, in spite of being forbidden by Bismarck, Germany's military unifier. In the 1880s Hamburg became a free port, and a massive restructuring of the city took place to create the warehouse area, the Speicherstadt; some 170,000 people—merchants and workers—lost their homes to make way for it. The wealthy inhabitants left their elegant Baroque houses and moved to the Alster's banks, where they created the villas of Pöseldorf and Eppendorf; their dock-worker neighbors eventually settled in the new working-class areas of St. Pauli Nord, Eimsbüttel, and Barmbek. There was a ten-week strike by 18,000 dock workers in the process (during the winter of 1886–87) when *Red Hamburg* was declared. In the turmoil immediately following World War I there was more action: a sailors' revolt in November 1918, two days after the one in Kiel. In 1923 came the **Hamburg uprising**, with fighting on the streets at the height of the postwar crisis of inflation and hunger.

East of the harbor, away from the ships and mighty cranes, is the late nine-teenth-century **Speicherstadt**. The tall, ornate warehouses belong to a bygone era of port life, but are still very much in use. You can see bundles of oriental carpets being hoisted up to top stories of the grand, red-brick warehouses, and smell spices and coffee wafting on the breeze, which comes as a surprise in these containerized times. The Speicherstadt is within the **Freihafen** (duty-free zone), which you can walk into unrestricted (though it's a different matter if you're trying to drive or transport anything—the zone is somewhat like an airport transit lounge, as goods here are not technically within the Federal Republic). It is a magical place to stroll around, criss-crossing the bridges, more numerous than in either Venice or Amsterdam.

Just to the north of the St. Pauli Landungsbrücken is **St. Pauli** itself—the nightlife center, with erotica to suit all tastes, and visited these days rather more by outsiders than by Hamburgers themselves. Wary tourists are even offered quite respectable "Hamburg by night" trips from the main station. The **Reeperbahn** is the best-known street, quite ugly and unassuming by day, but sizzling with neon at night. The Grosse Freiheit and Kleine Freiheit streets (Big Freedom and Little Freedom) sound aptly named, but their names have nothing to do with sexual mores; they signify the freedom of craftsmen to practice their trades here since medieval times. As a craftsmens' quarter St. Pauli has a long history, and there must have been scope for sailors to keep amused for a long time, too. But St. Pauli's role as *Vergnügungsviertel* (pleasure quarter) really only got going once transatlantic liners started running, and shipfuls of people awaited departure—Hamburg was a major emigration port for the U.S., first from Germany and subse-quently Eastern Europe and Russia. Music halls, cabarets, bars, and cafés have slowly been ousted by the sex industry, and although it isn't seedy in the manner of Times Square, and free-thinking Hamburgers wouldn't dream of condemning it, today's St. Pauli is not the one they used to be so proud of.

The main road running along the waterfront on St. Pauli's edge is the **Hafenstrasse**, whose main feature for the last couple of years has been its squat-ted houses. They stand on a prime redevelopment site, with amazing views right out across the Elbe. This may be a reason why the authorities are so keen to evict the occupants, who have set up an alternative community. During 1987, in partic-ular, there was an ongoing legal and sometimes physical battle with the city authorities, who were unwilling to provide tenancy agreements. For a while the Hafenstrasse residents barricaded their doors and unrolled barbed wire on the roofs to defend themselves against police or army attempts to move them. The clash polarized opinion in the city and was in and out of national news. Tension was relieved by a form of agreement late in 1987. If they are still there, you could visit the easily-spotted *Volksküche*—the collective kitchen—to find out the latest news. Heading westwards along the Hafenstrasse you come to the suburb of Altona and the fish market.

The Fischmarkt and Altona

ALTONA is completely integrated into Hamburg now, but used to be a city in its own right, ruled by the Holstein dukes. Its reputation for racial tolerance, notably towards Jews and Portuguese, is one of the reasons it grew—this part of the harbor still has a large Portuguese population, and good, very cheap, Portuguese restaurants. Directly on Altona's waterfront one of Hamburg's main weekly events—the **Fischmarkt**—takes place. Squeeze yourself out of bed at five or six on a Sunday morning, or make Saturday night last, and you will find yourself in an amazing hubbub. If you want to buy bananas by the box, or an eight-foot potted palm, this is the place to do it, for the market by no means sells only fish. The bars and restaurants are in full swing by six, strains of accordion music and jollity drifting into the street, Saturday-nighters in their dishevelled outfits chowing down. By ten, in accordance with an old bylaw forbidding competition with church services, trading must cease; by eleven it's all over, and the atmosphere gone.

Plod up the hill into Altona proper, and you can take a look at the street of grand patricians' houses along the **Palmaille**. Altona's museum, mentioned later, is worth a look, too, as are its own Rathaus and Christianskirche. The latter contains the tomb of the great eighteenth-century poet Friedrich Gottlieb Klopstock, a Hamburg citizen by adoption. A man who felt he had been divinely called to be a Christian Homer, Klopstock took 25 years to write *Messias*, a huge epic poem on the life of Christ. Outside Germany his fame chiefly rests on the verses used by Mahler for the overwhelming finale of the *Resurrection* symphony.

Övelgönne

Just downriver from Altona is **Övelgönne**, where the main thing to see is the collection of old boats, mainly sailing freighters, at the **museum harbor**. Some of the boats can be boarded and visited, and the collection is often supplemented by visiting ships. You can get down there by bus #183 or by boat from St. Pauli using the *HADAG Niederelbedienst* (the Lower Elbe boat service run by *HADAG* shipping), which charges half-fare for bicycles, making this a good starting point for a bike ride down river. Övelgönne is a good lookout point for surveying the shipping traffic on the Elbe, either from the café terraces or from farther along the waterside. If you feel like a treat, there are a couple of expensive fish restaurants near the museum harbor.

Downtown

To most intents and purposes Hamburg's center is the commercial and shopping district around the **Binnenalster** and **Rathaus**. Strolling by, sitting by, having a boat ride on (or, in winter, skating on) the **Alster lakes** is an obvious occupation while you're in the middle of town. The imposing **Rathaus** is nineteenth-century neo-Renaissance, built to replace the one burned down in the 1842 fire. It's the seat of Hamburg government, but when sessions aren't taking place you can go on a guided tour around the interior (times are displayed just inside the front door). It's sumptuously decorated, the walls partly hung with tooled and gilded leather: a magnificent, if pompous, demonstration of the city's power and wealth in that era.

The Rathaus has one of the six distinctive towers, all well over 100 meters in height, whose green copper spires form a key feature of the Hamburg skyline, as well as a necessary reminder, among the overwhelmingly modern face of the city, of its historic past. All the other five towers belong to churches, two of which are a short walk to the east along Rathausstrasse. **St. Petri** is the oldest surviving building downtown, and the tower itself, like the lion's head door-knocker, dates back to the mid-fourteenth-century, though the bulk of the structure was rebuilt in neo-Gothic style. Far more impressive is neighboring **St. Jakobi**, in the late Gothic hall style typical of the Baltic regions. It has three original altarpieces and a superb organ by the seventeenth-century master Arp Schnitger, frequently used for recitals.

Southeast of here is a district of office buildings, built as a result of a municipally-led planning operation in the 1920s. At the junction of Burchardstrasse and Pumpen is Hamburg's most original building, the **Chilehaus**, designed by the Expressionist architect Fritz Höger. It's named after the country where its owner made his fortune, but the building is really a celebration of Hamburg's role as a great port. Rising like the prow of a huge ocean liner, the end of the Chilehaus still seems a daringly unorthodox conception. Though built on what's just a normal blunt corner, it gives the effect of terminating in a sharp point. The two small pavilions flanking the entrance are crucial factors in creating the illusion; they also serve to symbolize the sea breaking against the ship. Across Buchardstrasse is the huge **Sprinkenhof**, which Höger began immediately after completing the Chilehaus.

From here continue along Dovenfleet to the Gothic church of **St. Katharinen**, whose Baroque tower rises high above the waterfront. Farther to the west is **Deichstrasse**, one of the few surviving streets of old Hamburg. The gabled houses here have stone frontages facing the street, whereas half-timbering is used for the backs overlooking the Nicolaifleet canal. Just to the north is the tallest of the six towers, that of **St. Nicolai**. The church was built as a result of a competition following the fire of 1842; this was won by—of all people—Sir George Gilbert Scott. In some ways, the building looks as though it has escaped from England, but the tapering tower is consciously modeled on those of Ulm and Cologne, which were then at last being built to centuries-old plans. Ironically, British bombers destroyed this unexpected part of their heritage in the last war, and the body of the church has been left in ruins as a war memorial.

Farther along Ost-West-Strasse is **St. Michaelis**, with the last and most imposing of the towers. This time you can ascend (April–Oct. Mon.–Sat. 9am–5:30pm, Sun. 11:30am–5:30pm, Nov.–March Mon.–Sat. 10am–4pm, Sun. 11:30am–4pm; DM3 by lift, DM1.80 on foot) for a grandstand view of the city center and the port. As outstanding a piece of architecture as the Chilehaus, the church is a dignified example of the classically-inspired Lutheran Baroque style. Behind the church on Kreyenkamp are the **Krameramtswohnungen**, late seventeenth-century half-timbered houses built for widows by the Guild of Mercers.

Just up the Poststrasse is a building with a Florentine touch—the old post office (**Alte Post**). This marks the heart of Hamburg's shopping area, where a number of classy arcades have been opened in the last few years. Architecturally they're stunning, and the exclusive shops they house put *Neiman Marcus* in the shade: *Galleria* and the *Hanseviertel* are the ones to look out for.

Along the southwestern edge of the Binnenalster runs the **Jungfernstieg** or maidens' walk, so named because of its nineteenth-century popularity as a Sunday afternoon promenade for young women. Today it's still a refreshing stroll, one worth rounding off with afternoon coffee in the *Hotel Vier Jahreszeiten*, farther down the Neue Jungfernstieg. The hotel itself is of interest, as each accessory and item of furniture is made by the hotel's own craftspeople. The **Lombardbrücke** crosses to the Alster's southern bank. Opposite is the **Kunsthalle** (see *Museums and Galleries*) and to the south and east the blue-collar neighborhood of **St. Georg**. It's virtually a village of its own—safely "alternative" now, with a population of (mainly Turkish) immigrant workers whose shops add a tinge of the exotic. There's a good assortment of bars and cafés, and it's quite likely you'll end up sleeping in this area too, though many of the hotel rooms are rented on an hourly basis to local prostitutes—you only find out which by judging the clientele or by a sour-faced proprietors' refusal of a room.

Pöseldorf

This area directly northwest of the Aussenalster is made up of quiet, tree-lined streets of beautiful nineteenth-century villas, some of which are wonderful examples of Jugendstil. This is where the wealthy made their new homes when the Freihafen was created; today you'll find professionals and media people. Shops and restaurants cater to the "Schickeria" who frequent the area, and prices are correspondingly high.

Museums and Galleries

Hamburg's one unmissable collection is the **Kunsthalle** (Tues.–Sun. 10am–5pm; DM4), handily close to the Hauptbahnhof at Glockengiesserwall 1. The collection of paintings and sculpture ranges from medieval to contemporary, and is often augmented by major special exhibitions, in which case there's a compulsory supplement to the entrance fee. Upstairs to the right are the earliest works; the layout continues in a broadly chronological manner.

A room is devoted to three retables by **Master Bertram**: an important figure in German art, the country's first painter identifiable by name, and the first to challenge the artistic dominance held within the Holy Roman Empire by Bohemia. He worked for most of his life in Hamburg; his masterpiece is the huge folding altar, mixing paintings and sculpture, which was made for St. Petri. The panel showing *The Creation of the Birds and Beasts* is outstanding; the characterization of each creature grouped around the benevolent Almighty is delightfully fresh, but a prophetic warning note is struck—already the polecat has attacked a sheep. In the next room are parts of the dismembered *St. Thomas à Becket Altar* by Bertram's successor, **Master Francke**. Painted for the league of merchants who traded with England, it shows a very different style—the figures are more monumental, the structure tauter, the mood more emotional. The most interesting work here from the Renaissance period is **Cranach's** *The Three Electors of Saxony*. This uses the religious format of the triptych, with a continuous landscape background, in order to show the deceased dukes, Frederic the Wise and John the Fearless, alongside the then-ruler, John Frederic the Magnanimous.

The Flemish section begins with a tiny *House Altar* by **Isenbrandt** and the coolly beautiful *Mary Magdalene Playing the Lute* by the mysterious Antwerp painter dubbed **Master of the Female Half-Lengths** because of his preferred way of depicting his subjects. Also on view is a mature religious masterpiece by **Van Dyck**, *The Adoration of the Shepherds*. Most of the specialist painters of seventeenth-century Holland are represented, but they're rather overshadowed by two examples of **Rembrandt**. *The Presentation in the Temple* is one of his earliest surviving works: he was only 21 when he painted it, yet there's no sign of immaturity or lack of confidence. Light falls diffusely over the scene, in which the aged Simeon and Hannah are brilliantly contrasted with the youthful Virgin, while Joseph is daringly shown from behind, and in shadow. From five years later, when Rembrandt was established as a fashionable society portraitist, comes *Maurits Huyghens*.

Highlights among the display of seventeenth- to eighteenth-century European painting are: **Claude**'s *Dido and Aeneas at Carthage*; a pair of **Tiepolos**, *The Agony in the Garden* and *The Crowning with Thorns*; **Canaletto**'s *Capriccio with a View of Padua*; **Bellotto**'s *Ideal View with Palace Steps*; **Goya**'s *Don Tomás Pérez Estaha*; and *The Creation of Eve* by the eccentric Swiss artist **Heinrich Füssli**, whose sensationalism makes a fascinating contrast with the work of Bertram four centuries before. There's one outstanding sculpture from this period: a bust of a cardinal by **Bernini**.

The nineteenth-century German section is one of the museum's main strengths. Of a dozen works by **Caspar David Friedrich**, three rank among his most haunting and original creations. *Wanderer above the Mists* shows an isolated figure with his back to the viewer, contemplating an eternity of sky and clouds; overpowering and intimate at the same time, it stresses the awesome, unfathomable power of the natural world. This same theme is present to even greater effect in *Eismeer*. Inspired by the voyages of polar exploration which were then beginning, it depicts a ship half-submerged against a cracked iceberg, and has a menacing aura of timelessness. In contrast, *The First Snow of Winter* imparts a dimension of grandeur to a quite ordinary landscape scene.

Another German artist with a distinctive vision of the world was the short-lived **Philipp Otto Runge**, most of whose best work can be seen here. His most arresting images are portraits of children, usually using his own offspring as models. Chubby-cheeked, over life-size and bursting with energy, they're placed at eye-level to face the viewer head-on; the painter's intention was to show them not as mere young innocents, but as embryonic adults, already with minds and souls of their own. Very different, but equally effective, is the realist approach of **Wilhelm Leibl**, the German equivalent of Courbet. *Three Women at Church*, with its phenomenal detail, super-smooth texture, and uncanny evocation of the rapt concentration of the subjects, is rightly considered his masterpiece.

The German Impressionists, **Max Liebermann** and **Lovis Corinth**, are each allocated a room, close to a choice collection of their French counterparts, including a version of **Manet**'s *Fauré as Hamlet* which is less finished but livelier than the one in Essen. Among the Expressionists, look out for two masterpieces by **Munch**: *Girls at the Seaside* and *Girls on the Bridge*. Pick of the usual range of twentieth-century paintings are **Otto Dix**'s *Der Kriog* triptych, a powerful antiwar statement: and **Paul Klee**'s translucent *Goldfish*, an abstract composition with a rare sense of poetry. The **Kunstverein** next door (Tues.–Sun. 10am–6pm) has exhibitions of (usually) modern art.

The **Museum für Kunst und Gewerbe** (Arts and Crafts Museum, Steintorplatz 1; Tues.–Sun. 10am–5pm) just across the road—or rather, through the subway—from the Hauptbahnhof, has excellent and well-displayed collections of art ranging from ancient Egypt, Greece, and Rome through this century. The art nouveau/Jugendstil collection is very extensive and well known; also impressive are the sections dedicated to Chinese and Japanese art. Traditional Japanese tea ceremonies are held in an authentically outfitted room; advance reservations are best for these.

The **Hamburg Historical Museum** (Tues.–Sun. 10am–5pm; DM3, DM5 family ticket) at Holstenwall 24 has extensive displays on the history of the city and its port. Contained within the museum is the **Historic Emigration Office** (closed 1–2pm Mon.–Sat. and all day Sun.), which has the most extensive archive in existence of German and Eastern European emigration to North America; for the period 1850–1914 there are complete records of the name, age, sex, occupation, and place of origin of each and every passenger.

Away from downtown the **Museum der Arbeit** (Museum of Labor, Maurienstr. 19; check opening times with tourist office) is served by the U- and S-Bahn stations at Barmbek. It's housed in an old factory used between 1873 and 1953 by the New York-Hamburg Gummi-Waren Company, and presents a picture of working life over the last century, with many old machines on display.

Buses continuing down the Elbe from Övelgönne to Blankenese, or S-Bahn to Klein-Flottbek, take you to **Ernst Barlach House** (Tues.–Sun. 11am–5pm) and **Jenisch House** (Tues.–Sat. 1–5pm), both of which stand in the Jenisch Park. Ernst Barlach House exhibits the work of twentieth-century sculptor Barlach, whose deceptively simple, rounded figures can be surprisingly moving. A few yards away, through the trees, Jenisch House is also open to visitors, its furnishings reflecting a grand lifestyle from the sixteenth to the nineteenth centuries.

Hamburg's Outskirts: Blankenese and Neuengamme

Expeditions to the edge of Hamburg take you to opposite ends of the spectrum: Blankenese, an extremely pleasant "village" of fine houses, built on the steep banks of the Elbe by the city's merchant families, with beautiful wooded parks and walks; and Neuengamme, on the eastern edge of the city, the site of one of Hamburg's wartime concentration camps and now a sobering museum.

Blankenese is easy to reach by S-Bahn or buses that continue on down the **Elbchaussee**, an appealing tree-lined road, from Övelgönne. Blankenese used to be the site of an Elbe ferry, and before the patrician mansions were built was home to fisher-families and seagoing people. Today the houses cling to the banks, explorable by clambering up the steep stone staircases. In the nearby **Hirschpark** (deer park) there are footpaths to stroll along, and from the river banks themselves wide views across the Elbe. The woods conceal many cafés, notoriously hard to find. The *Witte Hüs*, for example, has music, many sorts of tea, and wonderful, wholesome cakes; its address is Elbchaussee 499a, but you'll need to ask directions.

Access to the **KZ-Gedenkstätte Neuengamme** is via S-Bahn to Bergedorf and then the #227 or #327 bus. It's open from 10am to 5pm every day but Monday and has no entrance fee, as it's a political education center. Nothing remains of the old buildings; it's the exhibition of photos and documents that recreates the horrors of the past, recording the story of resistance and opposition, as much as it could exist. Hamburg's other concentration camp was at Fühlsbüttel (now the airport), and 50,000 people died in these two camps. At the end of the war, after internees had been moved from the camps to two ships anchored near Lübeck, unknowing British pilots bombed the ships and another 7000 lives were lost.

While in Bergedorf, which is otherwise not interesting, you could look at its lovely **thirteenth-century Burg**, close to the S-Bahn. Inside is a local museum (Tues., Thurs., and Sun. 10am–4pm).

Eating and Drinking

Café-Bars

Most **café-bars** (Café-Kneipen) have food—which can be very good indeed—as well as drinks and sometimes music. They're great places for breakfast and lunchtime snacks (expect to pay around DM8–12). Each reflects the area it's in: Pöseldorf ones are mainly chic, pricey, and full of Hamburg yuppies; in the

Karolinenviertel/Schanzenviertel (especially around the Neue Pferdemarkt) they're likely to be more studenty/alternative; the same goes for St. Georg and the Uni-Viertel, the area around the university. Specific places are innumerable— the following are good starting points.

Karolinenviertel/Schanzenviertel

Frank und Frei, Schanzenstr. 93. A big, slow-paced Kneipe. Long a favorite bar with students.

Unter den Linden, Julius Str. 16. The place where the arty avant-garde meet over their coffee and cakes.

Zarbitter, Neue Pferdemarkt. Cheap and cheerful student Kneipe, usually pretty busy.

St. Georg

Café Gnosa. Lovely 1930s café with good food. Popular with the gay community.

Café Urlaub, Lange Reihe 63. Breakfast from 7am, and billiards.

Geel Haus, Koppel 76. One of the better places for lunch in this area. Try also the daytime café in the *Galerie Koppel* at Koppel 66.

Max und Consorten, on the main square in St. Georg at Spadenteich 7. More bar than café, this can get crowded and smoky—but the food is good, and comes in large portions.

Uni-Viertel

The Grindelallee has the best concentration of café-bars: try *Klett* at 146; *Ele-Dil* at 1; *Schweinske II* at 117; *Café Backwahn* at 148. The *Café Wintergarten* on the corner of Rothenbaumchaussee and Hartungstrasse is the watering-hole of the city's rich and glamorous.

For *Kaffee und Kuchen*, try the *Café Oertel* above the Konditorei of the same name at Esplanade 29; the *Condi* in the Hotel Vierjahrzeiten on Neuer Jungfernstieg (bring large amounts of money); the *Alsterpavillion* on the Jungfernstieg, at the edge of the Alster, which is a bit geriatric but pleasant if you can sit outside; and the *Hotel Reichshof*, opposite the Hauptbahnhof on the Kirchenallee side—a wonderful place to have coffee and cakes while waiting for a train.

Restaurants

If you want to eat at a proper restaurant, the choice is endless. The following are a few favorites, but you shouldn't have any problem augmenting the list with the cuisine of your choice.

There are two local specialties to try. *Aalsuppe*, generally made with plums and mixed vegetables as well as eels, is one of the most outstanding soups you'll ever encounter in Germany. *Labskaus*, a traditional sailor's dish, is more controversial, not to say indigestible; it's a hash which typically contains pickled corned beef, herring, beetroot, mashed potato, onions and gherkins, all topped with a fried egg.

Ahlberg, Strandweg 33. Down by the river in Blankenese, this is one of the city's best German/fish places, with carp a specialty. Main dishes at DM25–45 mean it's best kept for a splurge.

At Nali, Rutschbahn 11. Turkish restaurant with a large menu and friendly atmosphere. Main dishes for around DM 14.

Avacado, Kanalstr. 9 ☎220 4599. At DM30 for a set, four-course menu, or DM50 for six, this isn't cheap, but the food (basically French) is delicious. Reservations recommended, no smoking.

Gansemarkt Passage, off Poststrasse. Self-service cafeteria with a wide selection of dishes. Handy for lunches.

Medded, Bahrenfelder Chaussee 140. Reasonable Egyptian restaurant.

The Old Spaghetti House, Gänsemarkt-Passage, Poststrasse. Cheap and cheerful pasta place, with pasta dishes for DM13, salads DM10.

Sagres, Vorsetzen 42. Busy, homely Portuguese restaurant popular with Portuguese dock workers—which means giant portions. Try the swordfish and paella.

Tre Fontane, Mundsburger Damm 45. Closed Tues. Fairly-priced and intimate Italian.

Vegetarian Gastatte, Rathausmarkt. Closed Sun. Yummy veggie fodder for DM10–17.

Nightlife

Hamburg's nightlife is among the best the country has to offer. The scene is ever-changing, so you can expect some variations from the list of venues that follows. For up-to-the-minute listings, get hold of a copy of *Szene* magazine, which has full details of what's scheduled and where, and includes a survey of the classical music scene.

Live Music Venues

Grosse Freiheit, Grosse Freiheit 36, St. Pauli. The city's main outlet for rock/contemporary live music, with big-name bands mostly playing at weekends. Admission charge depends on who's on.

Knopf's Music Hall, Spielbudenplatz 19–20. Worth checking, but the acoustics here are poor, and it can get very stuffy.

Logo, Grindelallee 5. Mainly English and American underground bands.

Markthalle, Klosterwall 9–12. Along with *Fabrik*, Barnerstr. 36 in Altona, venue for better-known European bands.

Werkstatt 3, Altona. This center for alternative projects often acts as a stage for Third World bands. Friday and Saturday evenings are tropical dance nights.

Bars with Music

Bei Tante Hermine, *Onkel Max* and *Ahoi*. Three reliable beer-and-music joints around Hafenstrasse.

Café Kaput, Gertigstr. 32. Mostly golden oldies and blues.

Café Schöne Aussichten, Gorch-Fock-Wall. Mainly German bands.

Mitternacht, Gerhardstr. 16. German, UK, and US new wave/underground.

Tropical Brasil, Spielbudenplatz 14a. Salsa daily.

Jazz

Hamburgers' tastes tend toward traditional rather than modern jazz. The places to go are *Dennis Swing Club*, Papenhuder Str. 25 and *Cotton Club*, Grossneumarkt 50.

Discos

Kaiserkeller, Grosse Freiheit 36. Part of the *Grosse Freiheit* building, and one of the city's largest discos. DM4 admission includes a drink, open daily 9pm–4am, until 6am at weekends.

Bendula, Spielbudenplatz 6. Situated among the fleshpots of the Reeperbahn, Bendula has Afro-Caribbean music from 10pm Weds.—Sat.; DM10 at weekends, cheaper weeknights.

Fun Club, Elbchaussee 14, Altona. Dancing to new wave/punk in the back room of a bar called *Im Eimer*.

Gala, Mittelweg 22. Popular with trendy media types and a place to be seen. Tues.–Sun. 10pm onwards.

Grünspan, Grosse Freiheit 58. Long-established, late-closing hard-rock disco. Fri. 9pm–7am, Sat. 9pm–8am.

Mambo Jambo, Marktstr. 140 Karolinenviertel. The place to go for African music. Tues.–Fri. 10pm–4am, Sat. 10pm–6am.

Top Ten Club, Reeperbahn 136. Holds the distinction of being the city's longest-hours disco: 10pm–9am, 10pm–noon on Fri. and Sat.

Music

Hamburg's musical tradition can match that of any city in the world. The present *Staatsoper* at Dammtorstr. 28 (☎351555), not far from the famous but now vanished old building on Gänse Markt once run by Telemann, is one of the top half-dozen **opera** houses in the world, with Munich as its only German rival. In recent years, it has benefited from the inspired management of Rolf Liebermann. The **ballet** company attached to the house, run by the American John Neumeier, is also considered to be the best in the country at the moment.

There are three **orchestras**: the *Hamburger Philharmoniker*, the *Hamburger Symphoniker*, and the *Nord-Deutscher-Rundfunk* (the house orchestra of the local radio station); the main concert hall is the *Musikhalle* on Karl-Muck-Platz (☎346920). The *Monteverdi-Chor*, which excells in music of the Renaissance and Baroque eras, keeps up the city's choral tradition. It's also worth looking out for what's being performed in the churches, especially St. Jakobi.

Theater

The *Deutsches Schauspielhaus* at Kirchenallee 39 (☎248710) is one of the country's leading theaters. It's the successor to the *Nationaltheater*, one of whose first employees was the great eighteenth-century playwright and critic Gotthold Ephraim Lessing. Current director is the innovative Peter Zadik, one of the few leading Jews to return to Germany after the war; his productions of even the most venerable of the classics deliberately employ shock tactics when necessary.

Other venues for drama include *Thaliatheater*, Raboisen 67 (☎328140), *Kammerspiele*, Hartungstr. 9 (☎445620) and *Theater im Zimmer*, Alsterschaussee 30 (☎446539). For kids, there's a *Kinder Theater* at Max-Brauer-Allee 76 (☎382538), while plays in English are performed at the *Englisch Theater*, Lerchenfel 14 (☎225543). In contrast, the local dialect is used at *Ohnsorg Theater*, Grosser Bleichen 22 (☎354574) and at *Hansa Theater*, Steindamn 17 (☎241414); the latter presents circus-type variety shows.

Gay Hamburg

Not surprisingly, Hamburg has a lively **gay scene**. Other than talking to people in bars and cafés, the best way to find out what's on is to study the city's two gay publications, the magazine *Du und Ich* and the free sheet *Gay Express*, both available in most gay bars. Good starting points are the *Café Gnosa* (see "Café-Bars" above); *Adagio*, Max-Brauer-Allee 14 (closed 2–5pm); *Image*, Poststr. 39; and *Café Spund*, Mohlenhof Str. 3.

Women's Hamburg

Two **women-only cafés**: *Café Meg Donna*, Grindelallee 43, and the café in the women's bookshop *Frauenbuchladen*, at Bismarck Str. 98. *Café Lilith*, in Alsterdorfer Str. 46, is not exclusively for women, but has a lively atmosphere and a summer garden; closed Monday.

Listings

American Express Rathaus Markt 5 (☎331141).

Area code (☎040).

Bike rental Either from the tourist office or *Fahrrad Richter*, Barmbeker Str. 60. Cycle paths through the city make this a relaxing way of getting about.

Boat rental There are booths for renting craft (approximately DM20 per hour) to sail on the Aussenalster at An der Alster, beside Kennedybrücke.

Brewery tours The famous *Holstenbrauerei*, Holstenstr. 224 has regular free tours (Mon.–Fri. except in Aug.) round the premises, concluding with a chance to sample the products.

Consulates *American* at Alsterufer 27 (☎441061); *Canadian* at Esplande 41–47 (☎351805).

The Dom Not a cathedral but an amusement park on the Heiligengeistfeld, close to the St. Pauli U-Bahn station, that's open in spring, summer, and autumn sessions.

Festivals are by no means a Hamburg specialty, but the *Übersee Tag* on May 7 celebrates the founding of the port in 1189.

Mitfahrzentrale Högerdamm 26a, (☎234123). There's also a women's *Mitfahrzentrale* at Grindelallee 43, (☎450556).

Poste Restante Kirchenallee exit out of Hauptbahnhof.

Sports *Hamburger SV* are one of Germany's best soccer teams; sailing regattas are frequently held on the Aussenalster; there are various international events, such as a tennis championship in late May, and an equestrian event in early June.

Swimming The beautiful baths at Bismarckbad in Altona are the city's most luxurious, and have women-only days. For outdoor swimming the smaller lakes around Hamburg (such as the Grossensee, Mönchsteich and Bredenbeker Teich) are the best: getting to them is however tricky, so ask at the tourist office for details.

Views The **television tower** on Lagerstrasse (daily in summer 9am–11pm, in winter 10am–10pm; DM4 including ascent by lift) is now the highest building in Hamburg; an alternative is the tower of St. Michael (see above).

SCHLESWIG-HOLSTEIN

A land between two seas, **Schleswig-Holstein** is Germany's northernmost province, and almost belongs more naturally to Scandinavia and the lands around the Baltic than to Germany. It's an agricultural region chiefly, with large areas of forest and moorland: there's practically no heavy industry, and only three major cities. **Kiel**, destroyed in the war and now drably rebuilt, is the capital of the Land; this is where the government sits, and is the only university town. It's a newcomer though—**Schleswig**, former capital of Denmark, and **Lübeck**, once one of Northern Europe's most important merchant centers, have longer pedigrees, and consequently the most historical interest.

Long, dark winters here are cold and depressing. In summer, though, the landscape vibrates with blues and greens, the corn dotted with poppies and cornflowers, the fields burning with the bright yellow of rapeseed. It's beautiful countryside to meander through by any means, ideally on a bicycle: along the coast, frequent local boat services provide enjoyable alternatives.

Schleswig-Holstein has two remarkably contrasting coastlines; the flat, battered **North Sea coast**, protected by enormous dikes, and the gently-lapped and more undulating **Baltic shore**. The **North Friesian Islands** offer a relaxing, if uneventful, break from the mainland.

The most obvious **route to take**, assuming that you are coming from and returning to Hamburg, is up the North Sea coast and down the Baltic—though with so many ferries heading off to Scandinavia, it's tempting to move on.

Lübeck

In medieval times, **LÜBECK** was one of Europe's most important mercantile cities and ports—now it is dwarfed by the North Sea ports of Hamburg and Bremen, which replaced it as international seaports. But the city proudly retains the magnificent architectural wealth of its trading days: Germany's oldest town hall still in use, beautiful merchants' houses reminiscent of Amsterdam, fine Gothic brick churches—and, not the least of its attractions it boasts a wonderful marzipan shop.

Lübeck is just over half an hour from Hamburg by train, and certainly worth a visit of a day or two. Since many north- and southbound trains depart from here it's not necessary to return to Hamburg in order to continue your tour. Scandinavia-bound ships leave from nearby Travemünde. And although there are no private rooms, basic accommodation is cheaper here than in Hamburg, making it a handy base for the area.

Some Hanseatic History

A trading town was first established here in the mid-twelfth century, in the harbor where the Trave is joined by the Wakenitz. This move was none too popular with Henry the Lion, Duke of Saxony, whose own trading was affected by the success of this new Baltic port. Henry forced the Count of Holstein to hand over Lübeck, and gave it city rights—a precedent for over a hundred other Baltic towns who adopted so-called "**statutes of Lübeck.**" This free Saxon community was governed by the merchants themselves, had its own magistrate, and grew quickly in wealth and trading power; such scope for self-government and individual wealth contrasted with the feudal system outside the city. Northern Europe's first canal link was built to join the Trave with the Elbe (and thus the Baltic with the North Sea). Lübeck soon united with Hamburg and Bruges to afford one another protection against pirates, and was the natural source of counselors to settle disputes and squabbles among the vast and powerful merchant league that developed from this: the **Hanseatic League**, which came to have its own fleet of ships and a network of trading posts abroad—in London and Bergen, for example. Throughout the sixteenth century the Hanseatic League declined, as the balance of power in Europe shifted, valuable herring stocks in the Baltic diminished, trading routes changed due to the discovery of the Americas and new shipping routes to the East and, finally, the Thirty Years' War drained energy and resources. It met for the last time in Lübeck in 1630.

Lübeck remained a significant trading city and port, and it was only in 1937 that it lost its free-city status and became part of Schleswig-Holstein.

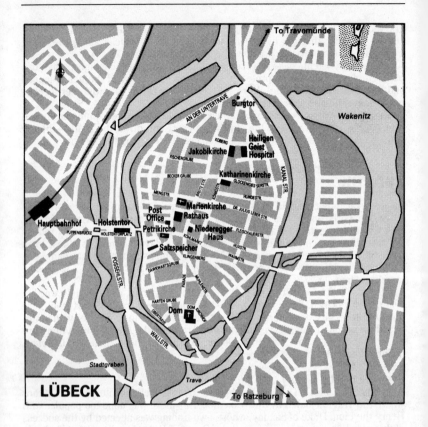

LÜBECK

Arriving and Finding Somewhere to Stay

The **tourist office** (Mon.–Sat. 9am–1pm and 3–8pm, Sun. 10am–noon) in the **Hauptbahnhof** has good maps and brochures, and can reserve hotel rooms for the usual fee. There's a second, smaller office on the Markt. Lübeck is unfortunate in having no accommodation in private houses. However, the YMCA has an **InterRail-Point-Sleep-In**—a hostel with ten-bed dorms in a renovated 800-year-old house in the middle of the old town, at Grosse Petersgrube 11 (☎78982). It costs DM11 per night, DM15 including breakfast, and sleeping bags can be hired for DM3. Reception is open from 9 to 11am, and 5pm to midnight, and reservations, or at least arriving early, is strongly recommended in summer. Failing that, there's a **youth hostel** at Gertruden Kirchhof 4 (☎33433)—leave the old town through the Burgtor, bear left, and walk about 200m. The best **hotel bargains** in or near the center are *Zur Burgtreppe* at Hinter der Burg 15 (between the Jakobikirche and Burgtor; ☎73479)—singles from DM35, doubles DM60, triples DM90 including breakfast. *Bahnhofshotel*, Am Bahnhof 21 (☎83883), has singles from DM35, doubles DM65, triples DM85, four-bed rooms DM105. *Gästehaus Lentz* has singles without shower from DM26, from DM35 with, doubles DM40–70. It's managed by the *Hotel Alter Speicher*, Beckergrube 93 (☎75533).

The City

Most things of interest to see in Lübeck are in the **Altstadt**, an egg-shaped island still surrounded by the aquatic defenses of the Trave and the city moat. Heading left out of the Hauptbahnhof, it's only five-minutes' walk to the old town, passing the **Holstentor** (recognizable from the DM50 note) and the Salzspeicher on the right. Just keep going over the bridges—it's very easy to find your way around.

Entry to the town was once through, but is now along the side of, the **Holstentor** (*Holstein Gate*), whose two sturdy circular towers with turret roofs, joined by a gabled center section, form the city's emblem. Built in 1477, it leans rather alarmingly these days but that shouldn't put you off visiting its small **Historical Museum** (April–Sept. Mon.–Sat. 10am–5pm, Oct.–March 10am–4pm)—a useful introduction to the city and Hanseatic history. On the waterfront to the right of the Holstentor is a row of lovely old gabled buildings—the **Salzspeicher** (salt warehouses). They were built in the sixteenth and seventeenth centuries to store precious salt, destined for Scandinavia, that had been brought up the old salt road from the Lüneburg salt mines.

Going straight ahead over the bridge and up Holstenstrasse, the first church on the right (just down a side street) is the Gothic **Petrikirche**, one of the many buildings to suffer during the massive Allied bombing of March 1942. An elevator goes to the top of the spire (closed winter; DM0.60), and Lübeck's center is small enough for this vantage point to be very useful for getting the layout of the town. Back across Holstenstrasse is the **Markt** and soaring above it the imposing **Rathaus** (tours hourly Mon.–Fri. 10am–4pm, Sat. and Sun. 11am and noon). The front of the north wing has a high fifteenth-century facade with holes to lessen wind resistance. The adjacent east wing, with an arcade leading to Breitestrasse behind, was added around 1300 and its extension around 1440. The best view of the original thirteenth-century building is from beside the Marienkirche, around the back of the north wing. All sections of the town hall have Lübeck's **characteristic brickwork**—alternating rows of red unglazed and black glazed bricks. The variety of the style, with its enormous wind openings, open and bricked-in arches, and gilded coats of arms set into the brickwork, is tremendous. At the back of the east wing, on Breitestrasse, is a Dutch **Renaissance stone staircase**. While splendid in itself, the staircase clashes horribly with the main building.

You can get a particularly fine view of the staircase from the first floor café of the **Niederegger Haus** opposite. Doing this means struggling through the **vast display of marzipan**. As a hub of European trade in former eras, Lübeck had access to fine Italian almonds, and began producing marzipan in the Middle Ages. A certain Herr Niederegger perfected the art in 1806, and this mind-boggling variety is the result. The **café**, one of the old-fashioned opulent variety, is renowned and parts of its menu are surprisingly affordable: breakfast from DM6, various lunch possibilities from DM6–12.

Behind the north wing of the town hall is the **Marienkirche** (daily 9am–4pm, closed during services). Built between 1200 and 1440 on the site of an earlier church, it's a soaring building in the French Gothic style—but in brick, rather than stone. The Marienkirche is thought to be the earliest brick-built Gothic church in the country, a style that became characteristic of north Germany. Its twin square towers are topped by spires to a height of 185m, while the nave is supported by flying buttresses that rise from the verdigris roofs of the side aisles. Though the outline is Gothic, the brickwork gives it a slightly sensible look that stone would not have. In the **1942 bombings** the Marienkirche was severely damaged and burnt out—an exhibition inside shows dramatic photographs of the devastation and also of the restoration, completed in 1959. War damage was a mixed blessing: the roof timbers and spires were destroyed, threatening the whole structure; both organs and many other items, including the chancel screen and much other fine woodwork, were lost. On the other hand, original Gothic wall paintings which had been covered for centuries were revealed and restored—indeed the entire interior was laid bare for a restoration to its original simplicity. Today it's very light, with a feeling of loftiness. The atmosphere, though, is like a museum, characteristic of so many German churches that have shared the fate of the Marienkirche. Detail of the fine ribbing and vaulting is picked out against the pale gray chalk wash in the old terracotta and gray-green colors. It makes a good backdrop for the church's treasures: a magnificent 1518 carved altar in gilded wood, depicting the life and death of Mary; a life-size carving of John the Evangelist dating from 1505 (unfortunately only partly restorable after 1942 damage); a beautiful Gothic gilded tabernacle, 9.5m high, made in Lübeck and consecrated in 1479, and the early fourteenth century murals. In the south chapel lie the bells that smashed as they fell during the bombing. If you'd like to know more about the church, pick up the English booklet (DM2).

Nearby, **Jakobikirche** provides quite a contrast to the Marienkirche. A sailors' church built during the thirteenth and fourteenth centuries, it is small, dark, and intimate, its only similarity with the Marienkirche being Gothic wall paintings on its square pillows. The carved oak organ lofts (sixteenth and seventeenth centuries) are particularly impressive, and a beautifully crafted spiral staircase leads up to the west gallery. Sadly, the original Gothic winged altar was replaced by another, presumably thought to be bigger and better—a monstrous Baroque concoction of dark wood, marble and gilding. The chapel at the west end is dedicated to all Lübeck sailors lost at sea, and contains a lifeboat from a ship sunk off the coast in 1957 with great loss of life.

On the other side of the Breite Strasse stands a step-gabled Renaissance house that used to belong to the fishermens' guild: the **Haus der Fischergesellschaft**. It has been a restaurant/tavern since 1535, and is decked out inside with all sorts of seagoing paraphernalia; predictably, it's on the agenda of every tour group.

Back past the Jakobikirche, on the other side of the Königstrasse, sits the thirteenth-century **Heiligen-Geist-Hospital** (*Hospice of the Holy Spirit*; summer Tues.–Sun. 10am–5pm; winter 10am–4pm), one of the earliest and best-preserved hospices from this period. Characterized outside by its gables and octagonal turrets, the hospice has a thirteenth-century vaulted chapel with wall paintings and a Gothic altar screen. The tiny chambers leading off the main hall were built in the nineteenth century as an improvement on communal space; today the hospice is still used as a home for the elderly.

Down the Königstrasse, on the isthmus joining the old town peninsula to the surrounding land, you reach the **Burgtor**, a lovely square tower topped by a bell-shaped roof. The side buildings of the gateway were originally used for stabling the horses of people arriving in the city at this point. The vast building on the left, in black and red Lübeck neo-Gothic style, is the **Versorgungsamt**—a town administration office of the 1890s.

Returning south from here, there is a good chance to look into some of the **courtyards**, whose small houses were built by seventeenth-century benefactors for homeless widows and old people. Often you can step through what appears to be just a door in a wall into a pretty "Hof." The *Haasenhof* in Dr. Julius-Leber-Strasse is an attractive one; also the *Rosengang* at Rosen Str. 19, or the *Füchtingshof* at Glockengiesser Str. 25. These Höfe are the exact parallel of the *Hofjes* of Amsterdam, and houses such as Grosse Grotselgasse 4, with tidy step-gables and large windows, or those of the Mengstrasse, are a reminder that two and three centuries ago the ports of the North Sea and Baltic had more in common with one another than with their national hinterlands.

The **Behnhaus** and the **Drägerhaus** are two patricians' houses, now museums, sharing an entrance in the Breite Strasse (just north of the Glockengiesser Strasse; Tues.–Sun. 10am–5pm; DM2). It's surprising to see how large these houses are inside, compared with the narrow street frontage; tax was once paid on a building's width rather than than its overall size, which led to houses being built long and narrow. The Drägerhaus is part of the **Museum for Art and Cultural History**, and has impressive interiors with original nineteenth-century furniture, paintings, clocks, porcelain, and so forth, and a room documenting the lives of the two important literary figures of Lübeck, Thomas Mann and his brother Heinrich. A great European literary figure, **Thomas Mann**'s greatest achievement is probably *Der Zauberberg* ("The Magic Mountain"), a story that symbolically examines the morbid state of early twentieth-century Europe. He also wrote *Der Tod in Venedig* ("Death in Venice") and, most pertinent to Lübeck, *Buddenbrooks*, the chronicle of a Lübeck merchant family—a sort of Germanic "Forsyth Saga." Heinrich, more prone to social and political comment than his soul-searching brother, gave us *Professor Unrat* (filmed as the Marlene Dietrich classic, *Der Blaue Engel*—"The Blue Angel"). The museum has a model of the house in which *Buddenbrooks* was set and the house itself, which belonged to the Mann family from 1841 to 1891, can be visited at Mengstrasse 4. The *Behnhaus*, on the other hand, has a good collection of paintings: works by the Romantics, the Expressionist painter Kirchner, and Edvard Munch.

No need to go inside, but take a look at the facade of the **Katharinenkirche** on the corner of Königstrasse and Glockengiesser Strasse. In the niches of the west (street side) facade, are nine twentieth-century life-size figures. The first three on the left (*Woman in the Wind, The Beggar* and *The Singer* are by the sculptor **Ernst Barlach**: he was commissioned to make a series of nine in the early 1930s, but had completed only three by 1932, when his work was banned by the Nazis. The other six are by Gerhard Marcks (1947–48). A closer look at the Marcks works is possible in the Schloss Gottorf in Schleswig, where another set of terracotta castings from the same molds is exhibited. The church, a former Franciscan priory, is now a church museum—and about as interesting as it sounds. (April–Sept. Tues.–Sun. 10am–1pm and 2–5pm; DM2, students DM1.)

In the southern corner of the Aldtstadt are the **St. Annen Museum** and the Dom. The museum (daily 10am–5pm, Oct.–March 10am–4pm; DM2, student reductions) is housed in the late Gothic St. Annen Kloster and has a first-rate collection reflecting domestic, civic and church art/history from the thirteenth to eighteenth centuries. Most attractive of all is the magnificent *Passion* triptych by Memling. The large, brick-built **Dom**, with its two 120-meter towers, was founded in 1173 by Henry the Lion and completed, as a Romanesque building, in 1226. A huge Gothic chancel was added in the fourteenth century, and the enormous triumphal cross by Bernt Notke survived the war. Notke, a native of Lübeck, was a celebrity throughout the Baltic lands of his day. Probably a painter as well as a sculptor, he specialized in the grandiose, making spectacular works of art to adorn churches in Denmark, Sweden, and Estonia.

Eating, Drinking, and Entertainment

As a student town, Lübeck has a good choice of cafés and eating places—*Tipasa*, at Schlumacher Str. 14 has a large, ever-changing menu of very reasonable **Afghani** dishes, served by a roaring open fire in winter. The innovative Lübeck

Ratskeller has introduced a very good selection of **vegetarian** dishes from DM10–14. Especially worth shelling out for is their vegetarian Sunday brunch buffet (noon–2pm)—eat as much as you like for DM20: fruit and vegetable juices, salads, soups, hot and cold vegetarian entrees. *Schmidt's*, Dr. Julius-Leber-Str. 60–62 is a café-restaurant with a wide choice, good for **breakfast** (served until 5pm). *Casablanca*, corner of Fleischhauer Strasse and Bei St. Johannes, has Indian snacks and cheap dishes. *Café Amadeus*, across from the Marienkirche, is good for rolls and salads. Opposite the station, *Belmondo*, a pleasant café with snacks, is a better place to wait for a train than the Hauptbahnhof. The Engelsgrube is the best street to try for **bars**, though the most enjoyable is probably the old, atmospheric *Zum alten Zolln*, in the mall behind *C&A*.

Lübeck's **entertainment** includes frequent organ concerts in many of the churches; the composer Diderik Buxtehude lived and worked here, so his music is often performed. Originally from Denmark, Buxtehude was one of the first ever musicians to achieve fame as a virtuoso solo instrumentalist, drawing huge crowds to his improvisatory recitals at the Marienkirche. Such was his fame that it's said that the young J.S. Bach made the 350-kilometer trek on foot from his home in Thuringia in order to hear the maestro perform.

A monthly program of concerts is available from the tourist office. **Music and dancing** happen at *Galaxis* (a converted factory); *Body and Soul* (Wall Strasse); *Tiffany* (near central bus station); and *Das Riverboot* (large barge moored next to the Puppenbrücke). All are free during the week, and cost DM2–3 at weekends, when they can be very full. *Café Amadeus*, mentioned earlier, is a good place to find out what's on in town.

Listings

Area code (☎0451).

Bike rental Schwartauer Allee 39 (DM5 per day; ☎42660). No bicycle rental at the Hauptbahnhof at the time of writing, but check in case it has been introduced.

Car rental is available at the station (*Autohansa*) but *Miera* (office in the *Lysia Hotel* near the station) is considerably cheaper.

Exchange facilities at the Hauptbahnhof (same office as tourist office).

Festivals Main events are: *Markt Anno Dazumal*, an old-time fair held in the Rathausmarkt for ten days in early May; a two-week *Volksfest* in mid-July; and the *Altstadtfest* on the second weekend in September.

Mitfahrzentrale Grosse Gröpelgrube 11 (☎77825).

Post offices near the Hauptbahnhof (on the left as you come out) and in the Marktplatz by the Rathaus (with Poste Restante).

Around Lübeck: Ratzeburg and Travemünde

The main outing south of Lübeck is to **RATZEBURG**, reachable from Lübeck by train or by occasional boat trips in summer—check with the tourist office. Ratzeburg, only just in the Federal Republic, sits on an island (joined to the shore by a couple of bridges) in the Ratzeburg Lake. Part of the east bank forms the border with East Germany; consequently if you head off in your paddle boat you can find yourself very close to the fence that marks the border. Apart from its position, which is both picturesque and rather vulnerable looking, Ratzeburg's charms include the twelfth-century **Dom**, a triple-naved basilica founded by

Henry the Lion which survived a major fire in the seventeenth century that destroyed virtually the whole of the town.

Its other main sight is the **Ernst Barlach Museum** (Tues.–Sun. 10am–noon and 3–6pm), dedicated to the sculptor who created the figures on the facade of Lübeck's Katharinenkirche. As time goes on, it seems more evident that Barlach, who lived in Ratzeburg before moving to Güstrow (now in the GDR), ranks among the most significant artists of the twentieth century. His bronzes and woodcarvings, using themes borrowed from the medieval and Renaissance German masters, show a warm humanity and convey a haunting sense of pathos. Barlach carried his Expressionism into other media—he was a fine graphic artist, and also an accomplished playwright, being particularly concerned with the awesome theme of the cosmic relationship between God and humankind.

Just to the north of Lübeck is **TRAVEMÜNDE**, Lübeck's rather glamorous seaside resort. Go there in winter and you might find the odd playful seal on the fine sandy beach. In summer, though, Travemünde is hardly the place to go to get away from it all. The beach is packed full of busy *Strandkörbe*, (hooded basket-seats rented out like deck chairs to keep off the breeze), sail-boats and windsurfers ply the water, and the fashionable **casino** makes fat profits (not least on its terrace, *the* place to sit for cool drinks and ice cream). The town itself is still quite attractive, but it is dominated by the shipping and fishing quays; this is the main port for ferries to and from Scandinavia. From the beach it's odd to watch large ships apparently sailing right onto land, whereas they are actually entering the mouth of the Trave. If you walk northwards up the beach, it eventually peters out and is replaced by cliffs, the Brodtemer Ufer. This is where everybody goes to get a rare view of the Baltic from above sea level.

Each year in late July/early August, there's a major yachting event. The centenary of this was celebrated between July 28 and 31 1989 with a race featuring the Cutty Sark Tall Ships.

The Coast: Travemünde to Kiel

Along the coast north of Travemünde are several resorts where the beaches are good, with fine sand, and camping facilities abound. **TIMMENDORFER STRAND** is fairly elegant, in the manner of Travemünde, but others, such as HAFFKRUG, are more like fishing villages still. By and large the beaches are narrow, and backed by thick pine forest—especially around **KELLENHUSEN** (just inland from here lies the thirteenth-century monastery of CISMAR). The railroad runs over a bridge to the island of **FEHMARN**, where ferries from PUTTGARDEN go over to Scandinavia. The island would be worth a small trip for its own sake: it has plenty of beaches and camping. West of Fehmarn you are in the Kieler Bucht—Kiel Bay. **LÜTJENBURG** makes a good stopover; it's very small but pretty, and you can visit the ancient burial ground (*Hünengrab*) nearby.

Kiel

KIEL had to be almost completely rebuilt following wartime bombing; consequently, there's not much point in looking for charm amongst its sober 1950s three- and four-story buildings. A member of the Hanseatic League from 1284 to 1518, Kiel was always overshadowed by Lübeck during that era. However, once the **Kiel Canal** was opened up in 1895 to provide a shipping link between the Baltic and the North Sea, the town's importance as a strategic naval harbor was confirmed. The canal is now the world's biggest shipping lane. It was the sailors of Kiel who, late in 1918, mutinied and started a march on Berlin, an intrinsic part of the German revolution. That's more or less forgotten these days, and the face Kiel now presents to the world is that of a modern port and university town. Twice host to the Olympic Games watersports (1936 and 1972), it stages a major **annual regatta** (the *Kieler Woche*, last week in June). The town is also known for a tasty species of smoked sprats—known as *Kieler Sprotten*.

Virtually all buildings of historical or architectural interest that do remain have been rebuilt following wartime damage—the Gothic and neo-Gothic Nikolaikirche, the Jugendstil Petruskirche and the renowned Jugendstil **Rathaus** with its 106-meter-high tower and tremendous views. (Guided tours May–Oct. 10:30 and 11:30am.) Other than this, you'll have to content yourself with one of several museums. Housed in a rare surviving example of nobleman's timbered town house at Dänische Str. 19 is the **Museum of City History**. More relevant to Kiel's seagoing connections are the **Schiffahrtsmuseum** (Nautical Museum) in the old fish market hall at Wall 65, and the **Institut für Meereskunde Kiel** (Oceanography Museum) at Düsternbrooker Weg 20, where there are large **aquariums**, and seals. The **Art Gallery** at Düsternbrooker Weg 1 has a large collection of works from all over northern Europe (Thurs.–Sat. and Tues. 10am–6pm, Sun. 10am–5pm, Wed 10am–8pm).

Kiel's most interesting museum is perhaps the **Schleswig-Holstein Open Air Museum** (April 1–Nov. 15 9am–5pm, Sun. 10–6pm; rest of the year Sun. only, 10am till dusk; closed Mon. except July 1–Sept. 15; DM3) just southwest of town at MOLFSEE. Here thirty or so beautiful old sixteenth- to nineteenth-century farmhouses and barns from around the Land have been reassembled piece by piece in regional groups to give a picture of 500 years of Schleswig-Holstein rural life. A pottery, bakery, four mills, a forge and a dairy are all worked in the old ways by craftspeople, and their produce is on sale. Many of the houses, incidentally, have tiny cabin beds that used to be slept in by the whole family; in winter they slept sitting up and huddled together against the cold.

Like Flensburg, Kiel is situated on a fjord (though "inlet" is a more realistic term as this is nothing like as dramatic as the Norwegian variety) and has some good nearby **beaches** that can be reached from the city by boat. LABOE, HEIKENDORF and MÖLYENORT are the main beach resorts: at Laboe a 75-meter-high monument stands in memory of sailors lost in the two world wars, and a 1943 U-Boat is open in the summer months as a **museum**.

Practical Details

The **bus station** and the **tourist office** (at Auguste-Viktoria-Str. 16; ☎0431 62230) are both opposite the **Hauptbahnhof**. The tourist office can arrange hotel, pension, or private bed and breakfast. **Hotel and pension** prices in Kiel start at around DM55 for a double. In Kiel-Gaarden (slightly southeast of town) the *Friesenhof* (Kaiserstr. 63a; ☎0431 731789) has singles from DM17 and doubles from DM30. During the Kieler Woche accommodation is extremely difficult to come by. The **youth hostel** is at Johannesstr. 1, Kiel 14 (☎0431 731488). There's also **camping** at the *Falkenstein* grounds—ask at tourist office.

Being Schleswig-Holstein's only university town, Kiel is fairly lively. The place to go for music and to find out what else is going on is *Die Pumpe* at Hass Str. 22. In the Bergstrasse is a multistory **disco**, with different music on each floor, live music at weekends.

From Kiel's Bahnhofsbrücke, the quay right by the station, **harbor trips** run from July to September, and daily trips go up the Kiel Canal during the second half of August.

The Holsteinische Schweiz

The **HOLSTEINISCHE SCHWEIZ**, the so-called Switzerland of Holstein, just southeast of Kiel, has nothing resembling the Alps, so presumably gets its name on account of its **lakes**. **The Grosser Plöner See** is the biggest of over a dozen lakes in this area of forest and water. The main towns are Plön, Eutin, and Malente, all of which are designated *Kurorte*, centers for health-orientated holidays, and offering their many visitors all sorts of sports and leisure facilities. Round about, though, are many smaller and quieter places, linked by waterways, trails, and bike paths. Yet again, the bicycle is an ideal way to get around. **PLÖN** is dominated by its grand, late Renaissance **Schloss**, open to visitors and usually holding art exhibitions. Likewise **EUTIN** has a Schloss, and hosts jazz and opera festivals in the summer season. Though **NEUMÜNSTER** is a sizeable place, it's one of Schleswig-Holstein's few industrial towns, and not somewhere to aim for. It does have a "free-range" zoo on its northwest outskirts, where indigenous animals such as wild boar roam at liberty.

Rendsburg and the Dänischer Wohld

Thirty kilometers inland from Kiel, **RENDSBURG** has a history as a fortified town and trading post dating back to the eleventh or twelfth century. Its historic buildings are clustered around the **Altstädter Markt**; the sixteenth-century timbered **Rathaus** is interesting because of its archway, beneath which the street runs. It now houses a small **local museum** (Tues.–Sun. 10am–5pm), supervised by a curious pair of elderly citizens. The twelfth-century **Marienkirche** is close by and has as the highlight of its ornate interior a seventeenth-century Baroque altar; its chancel is of the same vintage.

But it's not so much Rendsburg's old buildings that impress as much as three extraordinary feats of transportation engineering—the Kiel Canal, the tunnel beneath it, and the railroad bridge above. Bizarrely, one of the best views of Rendsburg is the aerial one from the train. The Lübeck–Flensburg railroad line performs some intriguing gymnastics to cope with crossing the Kiel Canal high enough for shipping to pass beneath, yet getting back to ground level for the Rendsburg railroad station a couple of kilometers farther on; a large, gently sloping railroad loop is the solution. A four-lane tunnel takes traffic beneath the canal, and the **longest escalator in Europe** runs down to the tunnel for pedestrians.

It's fascinating to watch the enormous ships, often from the USSR and Poland, gliding past weirdly out of scale with the landscape. Even before seagoing ships had access to Rendsburg, however, the town was on an important meeting of ways, as the Eider canal passed through here. This joined the Kiel fjord with the Eider river, providing a North Sea-Baltic link, but for small vessels only. It was completed in the late eighteenth century and Rendsburg grew significantly as a result.

Towards the coast from Rendsburg is the **DÄNISCHER WOHLD**, the area between Eckernförde and Kiel. The Kiel canal runs right through it, and the train stops at GETTORF, best base for exploring the villages nearby. There are cliffs (quite high in places) along the coast here, and the villages are not as developed for tourists as in the Kieler Bucht. Try DÄNISCH-NIENHOF (buses from Kiel) for a stopover.

Schleswig

It's quite astonishing just how different **SCHLESWIG** is from neighboring Flensburg. An administrative center, it has a sleepy, civil-servant pace and lacks Flensburg's commercial bustle. Dozing gently at the water's edge on the beautiful Schlei, Schleswig could almost trick you into thinking nothing had ever happened there. Things did, though—in the eighth and ninth centuries the **Vikings**, whose trade routes stretched from the Black Sea to Greenland, had their main north European trading center here, at a settlement called **Haithabu**. Following the demise of the Vikings around 1000, a new town was founded which became the seat of the dukes of Gottorf and of Schleswig, and was for a time the seat of the government of Denmark.

What is now Schleswig's **Altstadt** nestles around the twelfth-century Romanesque and Gothic **Dom**, which has an eleventh-century granite basilica as its foundations, and towers from the nineteenth century. (There's an excellent pamphlet in English that provides full details on the interior.) What immediately demands your attention is the **Bordesholm Altar** by Hans Brüggemann, one of Europe's most astonishing pieces of woodcarving. Commissioned by the Duke of Gottorf and carved from oak between 1514 and 1521, it shows nearly 400 figures on a background so intricate it resembles filigree, and it's seriously worth taking binoculars to get a closer look. Legend has it that the duke had the unfortunate artist blinded after completion of the work, so that he would never again create anything so beautiful. The altar originally stood in the church in the village of Bordesholm, close to Kiel; the enormous carving of **St. Christopher** by the door is also Brüggemann's work.

Other specific sights in the Altstadt are few. The oddly ecclesiastical **Rathaus** was built as a Franciscan monastery on the site of the eleventh-century royal court; the ground floor is open daily. Down by the waterside a cluster of tiny houses makes up the **Holm**, an old fishing village. There's another monastery in the Johanniskloster; phone first to arrange a visit, which costs DM1 (☎04621 26263).

Schleswig's unmissable target in the west of town is **Schloss Gottorf**, a white castle with three fortress-like wings from the sixteenth century and a later, more graceful château-style wing from the seventeenth century. (Open daily from April to the end of October, 9am–5pm, though on Mondays only the Nydamhalle and medieval art sections are open. November to March opening is Tues.–Sun., 9:30am–4pm.) It stands on an island in the Burgsee, a small lake created by damming off an arm of the Schlei. Today it's home to the **Schleswig-Holstein State Museum**, whose collections are divided around the Schloss itself. The **Nydamhalle** is a separate new building to the left of the castle, housing the pre- and early history sections. Its major treasure is a huge **Nydam boat**, an oak rowing boat from around 350 A.D., and there are also two giant oak gods, male and female, from around this period, as well as many other artifacts. Another, rather grisly display is of the *Moorleichen*, **peat-bog corpses** over 2000 years old. The skin and hair of the corpses have been preserved by the peat and tanned like leather. Most shocking are the facial expressions, ranging from the beatific look of someone who was presumably dead before burial, to the utter anguish of another, whose fate can only be imagined.

In another building on the other side of the Schloss is a surprisingly good collection of **twentieth-century art**, which includes work by Munch, Kokoschka, Macke, Nolde, Marcks and others. The main museum in the Schloss itself

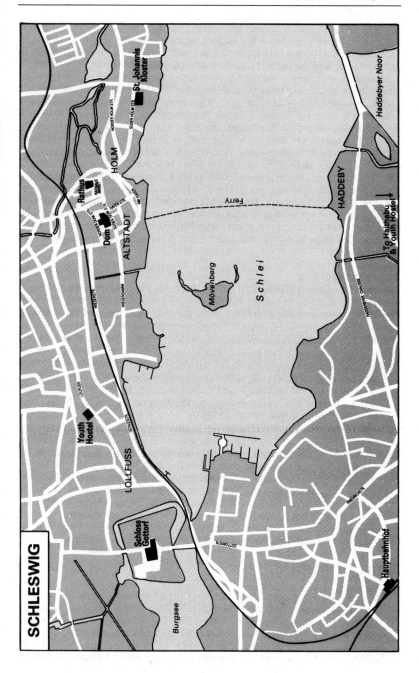

SCHLESWIG

St. Johannis Kloster

NORDER HOLM STR.

SODER HOLM STR.

HOLM

Haddebyer Noor

Rathus

HAFEN STR.

ALTSTADT

AM HOLM

Dom

SODER STR.

RATHAUS

HINTER DOM STR.

HADDEBY

Ferry

To Haithabu & Youth Hostel

MOORWEG CHAUSSE

Schlei

Mövenberg

WESEN STR.

WESEN STR.

LÖLFUSS

Youth Hostel

LÖLFUSS

SCHLESTR.

FRIEDRICHST.

Burgsee

Schloss Gottorf

GOTTORFSTR.

Hauptbahnhof

contains art and crafts from the seventeenth through the nineteenth centuries, somewhat tediously displayed but quite a treasure trove if you feel up to it. You have to go round by a set route, but try to see the private chapel, the Gothic hall (medieval art), and the painted *Bauernstube*, a room in rustic style.

More ancient history is on hand at the Haithabu site, which has recently been turned into a fascinating **Viking museum**. (April–end Oct. daily 9am–6pm, Nov.–March Tues.–Fri. 9am–5pm Sat.–Sun. 10am–6pm; DM3, student reduction; the ticket is also valid for Schloss Gottorf).You can get there in summer by boat (a 20-minute ride) from the Stadthafen, the town quay that's directly south of the Dom, with a ten-minute walk at the other end, or by bus (in the direction of Kiel). (April–end Oct. daily 9am–6pm, Nov.–March Tues.–Fri. 9am–5pm Sat.–Sun. 10am–6pm; DM3, student reduction; the ticket is also valid for Schloss Gottorf.) The impetus for excavations at Haithabu was the discovery of a Viking longboat, whose retrieval took several years. The ship is now displayed, with models showing how it was constructed, along with a multitude of subsequently unearthed artifacts that give some idea of what life was like in a major Viking center. The settlement was protected by a ten-meter-high semicircular rampart, and the museum buildings that now stand there are constructed, Viking-fashion, like upturned boats.

Some Practicalities

The **tourist office** at Plessenstr. 7 (May–Sept. Mon.–Fri. 9am–6pm, Sat. 9am–noon, closed at lunch in winter; ☎04621 814226) has details of private **bed and breakfast**. Some of these addresses are in the Holm, but are probably snapped up fast. You could try Frau Tesmer, Süderholmer Str. 48 (☎04621 26388) or Frau Stammberger, Am St. Johanniskloster 4 (☎04621 25195). For small **hotels**, try *Zum Stadtfeld*, Stadfeld 2a (☎04621 23947) or the *Wikinger*, Michaelis Str. 54 (☎04621 25514). Both are just north of the old town and cost around DM30 per person. **Camping** in Schleswig is 3km out in the village of Haddeby, near the Viking Museum (☎04621 32450), and there's a **youth hostel** at Spielkoppel 1 (bus #1 or #2 from the station to opposite the theater, then walk up the steps known as the Lollfusstreppe (☎04621 23893).

For **food**, the Rathausmarkt has places to sit out when it's warm, and there are several good eating places here. The *Senatorkroog* is a bit on the expensive side, but has a good atmosphere and excellent cooking—especially fish. Between the Holm and the Dom, on Fischbrückstrasse is the *Ringelnatz* café—a little house, each room with its own character, serving reasonable food, teas, beer and so on.

Bikes can be rented from the Bahnhof or the Stadthafen. **Boat rental** is also available at the Stadthafen (Plessenstr. 1), or from the sailing school, Segelschule Schlei. In summer, **boat trips** run up and down the Schlei, but not every day; get the latest timetable from the tourist office. LINDAUNIS is one popular destination, and has a beautiful sixteenth-century thatched house, the **Lindauhof**.

Around Schleswig

From Schleswig you might follow the River Schlei by boat or bus through the countryside to the sea, through LINDAU, LINDAUNIS, and ARNIS (claiming to be Germany's smallest town) to KAPPELN. The coast between there and Eckernförde has **swimming beaches**. DAMP 2000 is a modernistic resort built in the early Seventies, but the rest is much more natural, until you get to **ECKERNFÖRDE**, which has a Kurzentrum (modern resort facilities) tacked on to the **Altstadt** and port. The old part of town is pretty enough, and the **Nikolaikirche** is worth looking into for its carved and beautifully painted oak choir ceiling and altar. A new **local museum** (Tues.–Sun. 10am–5pm; irregular hours Oct.–March) has just been opened up in the old Rathaus, mainly with collections to demonstrate life earlier this century. One room is a typical *Flüchtlingszimmer* or refugee-room, with a collection of simple belongings and mementos brought on a long trek from the east. It is a reminder that, just after the war, Schleswig-Holstein became the new home of many **refugees** who left behind virtually all their worldly goods and trekked for weeks or months to avoid living in the Soviet sector. **Eating** in Eckernförde seems to focus on Frau-Clara-Strasse. The **youth hostel**, at the southern end of town (Sehestedter Str. 27; ☎04351 2154), has views over the sea. The **tourist office** has lists of bed and breakfast accommodation, and is situated in the entrance to the seawater swimming pool in Preusserstrasse.

Flensburg and Glücksburg

German today, though only a few kilometers from the Danish border, **FLENSBURG** was once Denmark's richest merchant city, with 200 ships plying the Baltic Sea. With boats coming and going, Denmark so close, and the former trade with the West Indies, Flensburg, small as it may be, is not the parochial town its size may suggest. It stands at the head of the gentle Flensburger Fjord, originally just along the waterfront, though later building has crept slowly up the surrounding hillsides. Ten years ago Flensburg was rather shabby, but renovation programs have rescued many of the **merchants' houses**, yards, and **old warehouses**. The only pity is that the town is now separated from the water, and effectively cut in half by wide, fast roads which ensure that traffic dominates outside the pedestrian zones.

Most of the interesting buildings are either on the **Holm** (called, farther up, the Grosse Strasse and the Norder Strasse), which together make up a two-kilometer-long **pedestrian zone** running roughly from the Südermarkt (South Market) to the Nordertor (northern Gate), or between this road and the water. Buses to Flensburg, or into town from the Hauptbahnhof, will deliver you at the bus station, from which a footbridge leads over the road and straight towards the Holm. If you plan to see everything at once, turn left and go down to the Südermarkt with its fourteenth-century **Nikolaikirche** and nearby twelfth-century **St. Johannis Kirche**. If you then head back up the Holm you come to no. 19/21 on the corner of the Nikolaistrasse, a sixteenth-century merchant's house and courtyard and, a little higher up on the opposite side at no. 10, another impressive facade. At the back of no. 24 is the seven-story **West Indies Warehouse**, dating from the eighteenth century but extensively restored.

It was the West Indies sugar trade, combined with Flensburg's pure spring water, that got the Flensburg **rum business** underway; at last count there were 58 varieties being produced here—try to benefit from them, if you're around in the winter. Apart from the distillery trade, Flensburg's commercial base has been its port, shipbuilding, whaling and oyster fishing. At the Nordermarkt, Neptune's Fountain pumps out the famous rum-making **springwater**.

The Marienkirche that also stands here was begun in the thirteenth century, and between it and the square are **covered arcades**, the *Schrangen*, where traders' stalls stood, starting in the sixteenth century. The Kompagnie Strasse goes down to the right, to the Kompagnie-tor, where a plaque reveals something of the Northern mercantile philosophy that behaving justly will, with the help of God, always reap large profits.

Back on the main street, at Nordertor 6, the helpful **tourist office** is situated in a gabled house (open 9am–5pm June–Sept.; rest of year Mon.–Fri. 9am–1pm Sat. 10am–1pm; ☎0461 25901). Farther along on the left is a flight of stone steps known as the Marientreppe, and if you climb up you can get a good view across the harbor to the other side of town, traditionally the preserve of working people rather than the rich merchants who lived on this side of the water.

The recently-opened **Nautical Museum** (Schiffbrücke 39; Tues.–Sat. 10am–5pm, Sun. 10am–1pm), in the old customs house, shows the history of the port and its trade, along with fetching model ships made by sailors. On up past the sixteenth-century **Kaufmannshaus** you come to the Nordertor, the so-called "gateway to the North," a step-gabled building constructed in 1595. If you still have some energy, there's the **Städtisches Museum** at Lutherplatz 1 (Tues.–Sat. 10am–5pm, Sun. 10am–1pm; free) recording town history and everyday life.

Somewhere to Stay

The **youth hostel** is at Fichte Str. 16 (☎0461 37742) which is quite a way out of town in the suburb of Kielseng, near the stadium. Any long-distance bus towards Glücksburg will take you there. **Hotels** in town, all with prices of around DM30–35 per person, are the *Hotel am Stadtpark*, Nordergraben 70 (parallel with the Holm; ☎0461 24900); *Hotel Zoega*, Norderstrasse 33 (☎0461 23508); *Flensborg-Hus*, Norderstr. 76. There is no **campground**; there is, however, a **Mitfahrzentrale** at Jürgensplatz 1 (Mon.–Fri. 9am–noon and 3–7pm, Sat. and Sun. 10am–1pm; ☎0461 17961).

Eating and Entertainment

The pedestrian zone, especially around the Nordermarkt, has plenty of eating places—*Das Kleine Restaurant* at Grosse Str. 73 has good salads, and there are snacks at the *Eis und Milch Bar* on the corner of Grosse Strasse and Kompagniestrasse.

To find out what's going on, you can pick up the monthly *Flensburger Programm* from the tourist office, or the alternative magazine called *Hallimasch* which also has listings. Both will probably mention the *Galerie Musikkneipe* at Holm 66, which has live music—quite well-known names—and food. There are also concerts at the *Lagerhaus*, Segelmacher Str. 10; the very fine **café** here seems in danger of closing. *Kunstwerk*, Norderstr. 107–109, is a café-Kneipe that does **breakfasts** until well into the afternoon.

Glücksburg

A little farther down the Flensburg fjord towards the sea is **GLÜCKSBURG**, a fairly typical spa town with beaches, forest walks, a first-rate seawater swimming pool, and a 400-year-old **Schloss** that's a little austere, but actually rather impressive, especially when floodlit, because it stands in a lake; you may recognize it from the ten-Pfennig postage stamp. Visits are by guided tour only (daily summer 10am–4:30pm; winter 10am–noon and 2–4pm: tours in German, but you might find someone to speak English). The Schloss has a large collection of tapestries, leather wallcoverings, and paintings. **Classical music concerts** are held there during the summer.

Angeln

The land to the east of the rail line between Flensburg and Schleswig is **ANGELN**, home of the Angles who came to Britain in the fifth century. They must have felt at home there: Angeln's slightly hilly landscape, with clusters of woodland and fields divided by hedgerows and pocked with marshes, is far more reminiscent of England than of most of Germany. Many of the place names around this area are Danish in origin: names ending in *by* are familiar to English speakers (Grimsby, for example), but in German it's not pronounced *bee*, but rather as in the last syllable of de*but*. The larger villages here have some unimpressive modern buildings, but in the smaller hamlets and along the lanes, you come across plenty of **traditional farmhouses**. Unique to Angeln are the **early churches** built of enormous blocks of granite—the oldest, with a thirteenth-century font, is in **SÖRUP**, roughly 20km south and east of Flensburg: HUSBY, NORDERBRARUP, EGGEBEK, MUNKBRARUP, OEVERSEE, and STRUXDORF all have thirteenth-century Romanesque churches too. Many small areas are designated nature reserves, such as the peat bog of **Satrupholmer Moor**. The **Torsberger Moor** is the site of major archaeological finds of early Germanic settlements, though the best place to find out more and actually see anything of this is in the Schloss Gottorf museum in Schleswig.

Getting around this area is not exactly straightforward; trains will take you from Flensburg to Sörup and onward either to Schleswig or via Süderbrarup to Eckernförde. Buses, however, are notoriously rare. The best way to explore the countryside is under your own steam—hire a bike in Flensburg or Schleswig and you can explore the coastline (beaches and campgrounds all the way along) as well as the villages with their Danish-sounding names. The Flensburg tourist office has a cycle map called *Rad und Wanderwege*, indicating touring routes in this area. Most of the roads are pretty quiet, and there are some special routes, such as the old railroad line from Tarp to Süderbrarup.

South of the Schlei and thus not really in Angeln, is the **Hüttener Berge nature reserve** (birdlife and deer). Again, a bicycle would be the ideal way to explore here.

North Friesland and the North Friesian Islands

NORTH FRIESLAND, East Friesland, and Dutch Friesland are closely linked culturally and linguistically. They share a history of battling to preserve their precious, flat land and islands from the sea's stormy threats, their trees are bent by the constant onshore wind, while indoors hot tea and stiff alcohol help the winter pass. This part of mainland Germany is little visited, and for obvious reasons: towns are few, the landscape bleak, and the coastline not a prime choice for summer bathing. But a few days here can be well spent: given time, North Friesland's rugged individuality becomes more and more likable, and its flora and fauna (bird-watching especially) are hard to beat. The towns of Niebüll and Husum have enough to detain you for a morning at least, Niebüll being the jumping-off point for Sylt, the largest and most developed of the North Friesian Islands.

Niebüll

A one-horse town in Schleswig-Holstein's farthest-flung north-west corner isn't top of anyone's list of places to visit, but **NIEBÜLL** has one or two surprises. First, it's from here that the train runs across a narrow causeway to the island of SYLT; secondly, there are two terrific museums each dedicated to artists who fell afoul of the Third Reich—Emil Nolde, and less famously, Richard Haizmann.

The **Richard Haizmann Museum** (April–Oct. Tues.–Sun. 10am–noon and 2–5pm) in the Rathaus is dedicated to the artist's sculpture, pottery and pictures. Haizmann was exiled to Schleswig-Holstein in what was termed "inner emigration" following the banning of his work by the Nazis. Some of his work had been displayed in the famous 1930s Berlin exhibition of so-called degenerate art, and was subsequently destroyed. Haizmann's work bears the influence of oriental and African art, and is beautifully displayed in a museum created by the curator and the artist's widow, who struggled for many years to open a museum, achieving her ambition only days before her death.

The **Nolde Museum** (similar opening hours; DM4) stands alone in the countryside at SEEBÜLL (about 5km from Niebüll) in the house and gallery that Nolde built in the 1950s. These were the years that Nolde could be acknowledged again after his work had been condemned by the Nazis. A novel by postwar author Siegfried Lenz, *Die Deutschstunde* (The German Lesson), has as a main character an artist, painting in secret during the war, who was based on Nolde. The museum—marred by its unhelpful staff—can be very full in summer, but if you are there on a quiet day you may have the luxury of enjoying Nolde's vibrant colors on your own. His expressionistic paintings have some themes that are quite brutal, and hard to take—the brilliant flower and landscape series are simpler, but powerful, nonetheless. In accordance with Nolde's wishes, the shop sells books and postcards, but no reproductions. A bus runs out to the museum from Niebüll, and the way is clearly signposted if you are traveling by car or bike.

Niebüll itself has little else to see: there's a small **Friesian museum** at Osterweg 76 (open only by arrangement with Frau Scheck; ☎04661 3656) and a small natural history museum open from May to mid-September, at Hauptstr. 108. You can stay at the **youth hostel** at Deezbülldeich (☎04661 8762) or try the *Insel-Pension*, close to the station at Gotteskoogstr. 4 (☎04661 2145).

INTO DENMARK

From both Flensburg and Niebüll it's very easy to get across the border into Denmark. Boats run regularly from Flensburg to SØNDERBURG, and there are regular bus connections. It's definitely worth making a **short trip** by bus from either Flensburg or Niebüll to TØNDER, the **oldest market town** in Denmark, first mentioned in the twelfth century. The semicircular old town has at its heart the lovely **Kristikirk**, with **small gabled houses** round about. Some, such as in the Uldgade, are so tiny you can touch the roof. On the last weekend of August Tønder hosts a large international **jazz and blues festival**, but all through the summer there are music performances in the market place. The extremely helpful **tourist office** (they speak excellent English—proof that you're in Scandinavia) is at Ostergade 2A (☎721220), right in the center of the old town. For further information and advice, see the forthcoming *Real Guide: Scandinavia*.

Husum

HUSUM's small **harbor** is virtually in the middle of town, and must have given welcome shelter to generations of fishermen returning from the stormy North Sea. As a town, it's a mixture of small-scale grandeur and workaday simplicity, filled with fishy smells from the port, and with a sufficient scattering of interesting buildings to catch the attention.

Husum is perhaps best known in association with the name of **Theodor Storm**, a nineteenth-century novelist, poet and civil figure (it was Storm who gave the town its rather unfair title "die graue Stadt am Meer"—the gray town by the sea), who was especially active in Schleswig-Holstein's struggle to remain independent of the expanding Prussian empire. It says much about the town that the three most lauded sights are Theodor Storm's birthplace, his later home (now the Theodor Storm museum), and the Theodor Storm memorial in the Schlosspark—you may even find yourself staying at the Theodor Storm youth hostel.

One of Husum's busiest times of the year for tourism is the spring, when the **Schlosspark** turns into a great sea of mauve crocuses; they were originally planted in the Middle Ages by monks who had a monastery on this site, possibly as a source of saffron. Other visitors pass through Husum on their way to HELGOLAND (a ferry runs from here) or on trips to the Hallig islands. Especially in winter, Husum, small as it is, provides a welcome change from the blustery bleakness of the Friesian landscape— it's when you think of the isolated houses out on the dike or on the islands that Husum's importance suddenly becomes clear.

Both bus station and Hauptbahnhof are within easy walking distance (up the Herzog-Adolf-Strasse and then left) of the center of town, the area south of the castle and north of the harbor, marked by the broad Grosse Strasse which opens out into the **Markt**. Both are lined with large houses, mainly eighteenth- and nineteenth-century (though there are one or two beautiful seventeenth-century gabled buildings reminiscent of Lübeck), most of which now have shops on their ground floors. Here too is the step-gabled fourteenth-century **manor house**, supposed to be the oldest building in the town, though its sandstone pillars and doorway were added in the seventeenth and eighteenth centuries. On the north side stands the seventeenth-century **Rathaus**, with the **tourist office** (☎04841 666133) on its ground floor. They have a lot of local information (including a good, free English pamphlet, *A Stroll Through the Town*), and provide hotel and pension lists, though not a reservation service.

If you turn northwards by the town hall you come into the **Schlossgang** (castle walk), a narrow walkway leading up past small houses, a couple of cafés and craft/gift shops to the **Schloss**. The small house over on the left, the former **gatehouse**, is actually more attractive than the Schloss at a distance—it has retained its ornate Renaissance features, whereas the Schloss itself, built at the same time, underwent extensive modification in the eighteenth century, giving it a **Baroque interior** with fine sandstone and alabaster fireplaces. There's now a **museum** here too, with collections of furniture and everyday objects from North Friesland.

Back past the Gross Strasse and a hundred meters or so farther south lies the **Schiffbrücke**, an inner anchorage busy with fishing boats; it's also the place where the ferry takes shelter in winter. One famous catch landed here is *Husumer Krabben*—not crabs, confusingly, but very tasty little brown shrimps.

(They are found in abundance on local menus, especially in the form of *Husumer Krabbensuppe*, a soup that often comes topped with whipped cream.) In summer a **shrimp stall** is open on the quayside, selling the freshly boiled catch. The port is lined on three sides by eighteenth- and nineteenth-century houses, amongst which the *Hotel zur Grauen Stadt am Meer* stands out. It has a very good restaurant serving **local fish**—rather *bürgerlich*, but better value than the touristy fish restaurant on the corner nearby. Another good place for food and drink near here is the *Café Schöneck* on the corner, with steps leading up to its door. All the rooms inside are crammed with ancient Friesian furniture, and masses of old pictures (which are for sale). It has very good soups, a vast array of warming alcoholic hot drinks, and Danish pastries far above the usual standard to be found south of the Danish border.

Up the small street beside this (the Wasserreihe) on the right is the **Theodor Storm museum** (generally Tues.–Sat. 10am–4pm; DM1.50), in the house he owned from 1866 to 1880 when at the height of his career. With many original documents and manuscripts, and as the base of the Theodor Storm society, it's chiefly of interest to Storm fans. However, the house is worth catching as an example of the nineteenth-century middle-class lifestyle in this area, as the rooms still have their original furnishings. Storms's wood-paneled study, where he produced about twenty of his novels, has a display of documents, such as correspondence with the Russian novelist Turgenev and other literary figures. The Wasserreihe itself is a narrow and characterful street, with several typical **fisher-family houses**.

Another of Husum's museums, closed for restoration at the time of writing, is the **Ostenfelder Bauernhaus Farm Museum** in Nordhusumer Strasse. Also situated here is the **North Friesian Museum** in the Nissenhaus (Herzog-Adolf-Str. 25; April–Oct. Mon.–Sat. 10am–noon and 2–5pm, Sun. 10am–5pm; closes at 4pm Nov.–April). It was founded in the early 1930s by local-boy-made-good Ludwig Nissen, who made his fortune in the United States, and is especially interesting on the geological background of the area, flood control and town history. It also houses a valuable collection of American paintings, unfortunately hidden away.

Practicalities

Most of the **hotels** work out at DM30–35 per person, and the *Hotel zur grauen Stadt am Meer*, mentioned above (☎04841 2236) is good if it fits your budget. *Gästehaus Fischer*, Brinkmann Str. 41 (☎04841 2686) is cheaper at DM28. Many private houses offer bed and breakfast at DM15–20 per person—these often fill in summer, so it's best not to turn up late in the day. The **youth hostel** is at Schobüller Str. 34 (☎04841 2714), in the northeast corner of the town. There are two **campgrounds** near Husum; a bus runs hourly in summer to the one at Dockkoog, right by the beach.

As well as the restaurants already mentioned, there's no lack of traditional **places to eat**. *Dragseth's Gasthof* at Zingel 11 is a sixteenth-century house with a small gallery, tea shop and a good selection of food, including vegetarian dishes. The *Husumer Speicher* is a converted warehouse at Hafen Str. 17, and this is where live music and entertainment happen in Husum. You'll find a **laundromat** at Norderstr. 12 and **bicycle rental** at *Peter Schurr*, Schulstr. 4 (☎04841 4465). **Ferries** to Helgoland and the Halligen islands leave from the Aussenhafen (outer harbor). There's a regular bus service from the station to the island of Nordstrand.

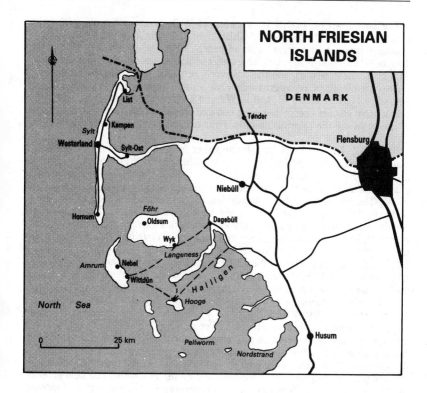

NORTH FRIESIAN ISLANDS

The North Friesian Islands

The **NORTH FRIESIAN ISLANDS** lie scattered off the coast, storm-battered for centuries and until recently the home of a small population of fisherpeople and farmers eking out a fragile existence: today tourism is by far the biggest source of income. The land is so flat directly offshore that the sea retreats to reveal large areas of mudflat—the **Watt**—which have their own sensitive ecosystem, including masses of birdlife. The main islands are Amrum, Föhr and Sylt, which although little more than a strip of land running north–south, is touristically the most developed and sophisticated. They are all family holiday centers, with holiday homes and riding, tennis and windsurfing facilities. In season, all are likely to be very busy.

PELLWORM in the south (ferry from Nordstrand) has an eleventh-to-thirteenth-century church and a seventeenth-century one bearing witness to its history. The future may be anticipated by Pellworm's huge **solar collector** (this is Germany's sunniest place, which bodes well for visitors), generating 280,000 kilowatt hours per year. A small **Watt museum** holds the former local postman's lifetime collection of finds from the Watt. Tourist information (*Kurverwaltung*; ☎04844 544) is right by the harbor.

The only town on **FÖHR** is peaceful old WYK (thirteenth-century church), which is connected by ferry to DAGEBÜLL on the mainland. Ferries continue to a smaller island with a great swath of beach, **AMRUM**, where they land at the town of WITTDÜN. Walks, beaches, seabirds, and sports are the order of the day on both of these islands, and the bracing breeze becomes enjoyable in the end. There are plenty of **campgrounds and youth hostels** in Wyk auf Föhr at Fehrstieg 41 (☎04682 2010), and in Wittdün auf Amrum at Mittelstr. 1 (☎04681 2355). Most visitors occupy hotels or bed and breakfasts for a week or more, so it is easiest to ask the information offices about vacancies in season—they may be hard to come by.

SYLT is a different kettle of fish altogether from the other homey islands. Its main town, WESTERLAND, is considered rather chic and glamorous: a place to dress up for an evening in the **casino** rather than stomp around in foul-weather gear. Outside of Westerland the island is quieter (though again full of vacation villas). There's plenty of **fine, sandy beach**; the island is shaped rather like a reclining "T", with Westerland on the stalk (east side) and the cross-stroke running north-to-south for about forty kilometers in a narrow strip, under a kilometer wide, lined with beaches, dunes and some small cliffs (the *Rote Klippen*). The main settlements apart from Westerland are KAMPEN, WENNINGSTEDT, and LIST, and buses run between them. Sylt is joined to the mainland at Niebüll by a narrow causeway which trains monopolize—if you want to take a car, it has to be loaded onto the train first. Again, accommodation is best found through the tourist office in Westerland (☎04682 861). The only **youth hostel** is in List (Mövenberg hostel; ☎04652 397).

The **Halligen** constitute another, smaller group of islands, south of Pellworm and scarcely above sea level; as you approach them by ship all you see are a few houses apparently sitting on the waves. Once you set foot on dry land you discover that these houses are built on specially constructed hummocks that stay dry when the rest of the land is washed over by winter storms. The land is really only good for grazing sheep, and bed-and-breakfast is a major source of income for the Hallig inhabitants nowadays. Even more so than on the mainland, few young people are interested in staying on to maintain old ways of life, and the Halligen seem set for a slow but sure period of decline.

The main Halligen are inhabited, but the tiny HALLIG HABEL is a nature reserve, with just one family present in summer; the even smaller NORDEROOG is a **bird-nesting sanctuary**, and also just has a summertime warden. The main islands, NORDSTRAND and Pellworm (together with Hamburger Hallig, and Nordstrandischmoor) used to form a far larger island known as **Alt-Nordstrand**, or just Strand, which had five quays and some 59 churches and chapels—a major settlement in its time. A tidal wave in 1634 drowned most of the island (and, presumably, its unfortunate inhabitants), creating today's geography. Nordstrand is now connected to the mainland by a narrow causeway, as are Nordstrandischmoor and Hamburger Hallig; in fact the latter has become a virtual peninsula because of silting up on both sides of its link with the mainland.

HALLIG LANGENESS is similarly connected to HALLIG OLAND, which in turn has a mainland connection, but Föhr, Amrum and Pellworm, plus Hallig Hooge, are reached by **ferries** running from Dagebüll and Schlüttsiel (run by *WDR* lines) and from Nordstrand (*Kurt Paulsen*). All the tourist offices and some railroad stations have leaflets and posters with details of ferries. It doesn't take long to look around a Hallig, so unless you feel like communing with wind and water, the few hours between boats may be all the time you want to spend there.

Eiderstedt and Friedrichstadt

Directly north of the Eider estuary is the *Halbinsel* (peninsula) of Eiderstedt, where **TÖNNING** and **ST. PETER ORDING** are to be found. These are both little port towns, not spectacular, but possible bases for exploring the country-side. Tönning, for instance, is right by the Katinger Watt, while St. Peter Ording has twelve kilometers of beaches, backed by forest and dunes.

FRIEDRICHSTADT, a small corner of Holland apparently transported to North Friesland, is certainly worth a look. It was built in the 1620s by Dutch settlers (part religious exiles, part merchants) with the encouragement of Duke Friedrich III, who hoped it would develop into a major commercial town. It didn't, but the town, complete with its canals and bridges, remains a small gem of Dutch Renaissance architecture in an unlikely setting.

Between the Eider and Hamburg

Between the Elbe and the Eider is the area of **Dithmarschen**, with **Heide** at its center. Coming here from the west, incidentally, you can bypass Hamburg by crossing the Elbe by ferry from Wischhafen (north of Stade) to Glückstadt.

The railroad line between Friedrichstadt and Hamburg travels via Heide to **Meldorf**, then **Itzehoe**, providing a good exploratory route. With your own transportation it's possible to stop off and explore the area around **Marne** (the art nouveau town hall is worth a look if you go) and the "KOOG" area near the coast—**Friedrichskoog**, for example, is a small, pretty shrimp-fishing town with beaches.

Dithmarschen

The region encircled by the waters of the North Sea, the Eider, the Kiel Canal, and the Elbe is **DITHMARSCHEN**. Though Heide is the market town today, nearby Meldorf was originally more important. The **diking** of Dithmarschen began around the fifth century A.D. Maybe the struggle to preserve the land they worked from the ravages of the sea made the Dithmarschen peasants especially defensive of their property—In the thirteenth century they expelled the nobility from Dithmarschen and founded an independent peasants' republic. The nobility never returned, and Dithmarschen gained a reputation for being an individualistic stronghold.

West of Heide lies the seaside town of **BÜSUM**, which has good beaches, but is a fairly staid, family resort. Better are the far less busy **beaches** that run north of Büsum as far as the Eider. Boats run daily from Büsum to Helgoland in the summer. This whole coast is diked and the mouth of the Eider barred against tidal floods (which used to rush 100km inland) by the *Eidersperrwerk*. (You can cross this barrier by road, towards Tönning and St. Peter Ording, but not by rail.)

Dithmarschen is covered by a network of some 1500 kilometers of signposted **bike paths**, so you can tour away from the traffic, which is in any case light. Detailed **cycling maps** are available from the tourist offices and bookshops; three maps, DM9.80 each, cover the area.

HEIDE itself is little more than a blip on the horizon, distinguished only by its vast market square and the ancient stones that mark a burial ground from 2600 B.C. These stones and the small **museum** (prehistory and local history) are close to the unusual water tower. **Hotels** start at around DM35 per person (such as *Hotel zur Markthalle* on the market place), but there are plenty of private bed and breakfast possibilities for about DM15. Ask at the **tourist office** in the Rathaus (signposted from the market place; ☎0481 991) for addresses.

MELDORF was once the capital of the Dithmarschen peasants' republic, and was the first town in the area to have a church, in 810. On the site of that church now stands the St. Johanniskirke—thirteenth-century but modified in the nineteenth. Finally, at the **Dithmarscher Landesmuseum** you can be enthralled by models showing how the diking and drainage process works.

travel details

Trains

From Hamburg to Lübeck (2 an hour; 40 min.), Kiel (2; 1½ hr.), Rendsburg (2; 1 hr. 35 min.), Schleswig (2; 1hr. 50 min.), Flensburg (2; 2¼ hr.), Husum (2; 2 hr.).

From Kiel to Lübeck (1 an hour; 1 hr. 25 min.), Flensburg (1; 1 hr. 10 min.), Rendsburg (10 daily; 30 min.), Schleswig (9 daily; 50 min.), Husum (9 daily; 1 hr. 25 min.).

Ferries

From Nordstrand to Pellworm (winter 3 daily, summer 5 daily; 45–60 min.).

From Dagebüll to Föhr (winter 7, summer 10; 45 min.), Amrum (winter 5, summer 8; 2 hr.).

From Schlüttsiel to Hallig Hooge (1; 1¼ hr.), Hallig Langeness (1; 1¾ hr.), Amrum (1; 2¾ hr.).

From Hamburg to Harwich (1 every other day; 20½ hr.).

CHAPTER EIGHT

BERLIN

B ERLIN is like no other city in Germany, or, indeed, the world. For over a century, its political climate has either mirrored or determined what has happened in the rest of Europe. As heart of the Prussian kingdom, economic and cultural center of the Weimar Republic, and, in its final days as a united city, the headquarters of Hitler's Third Reich, it is a weather vane

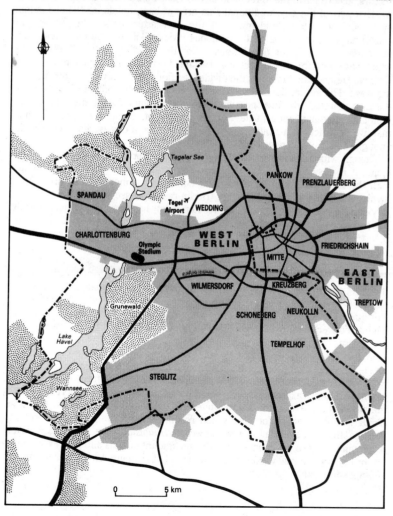

of European history. Today, the world's two most powerful military systems stand face to face here, sharing the spoils of a city split by that most tangible object of the East-West divide, the Berlin Wall. Whichever side of that Wall you're standing, it's the weight of history, the sense of living in a hothouse where all the dilemmas of contemporary Europe are nurtured, that gives Berlin its excitement and troubling fascination.

It was, of course, **World War II** that defined the shape of today's city. A seventh of all the buildings destroyed in Germany were in Berlin; Allied and Soviet bombing razing 92 percent of all the shops, houses, and industry here. At the end of the war, the city was split into French, American, British and Soviet sectors, according to the agreement at the Yalta Conference: the Allies took the western part of the city, traditionally an area of bars, hotels, and shops fanning out from the Kurfürstendamm and the Tiergarten park. The Soviet zone contained what remained of the pompous civic buildings, churches, and grand museums around Unter den Linden. After the building of **the Wall** in 1961, which sealed off the Soviet sector and enabled it to became capital of the young German Democratic Republic, the divided sections of the city developed in differing ways. The authorities in the West had a policy of demolition and rebuilding; the East restored wherever possible, preserving some of the nineteenth-century buildings that had once made Berlin magnificent. Even now, after so much massive destruction, it's indicative of just how great a city Berlin once was that enough remains to fill pages of a guidebook.

Though without some knowledge of its history Berlin is impossible to understand, it is easy to enjoy. **West Berlin**'s pressure-cooker mentality, combined with the fact that a large and youthful contingent comes here to drop out or involve itself in alternative lifestyles (Berlin residents are exempt from the military service compulsory in the Federal Republic), has created a vivacious **nightlife** and a continuous sense of excitement on the streets. And even if you try and ignore them, the constant reminders of the war years add spice to your wanderings.

To get an idea of the city as an entity, and to understand the schizophrenia that now mars it, it's essential to escape the bright lights and rampant consumerism of the West and make a few day-trips to **East Berlin**. On first glance, it seems little different. Preconceptions about drab lifestyles, food lines, and numbing militarism quickly evaporate; it's only when you scratch below the glossy surface and fall into conversation with locals that you realize how far apart these two sections of the same city really are.

In the final analysis, both East and West are now products of the deeply divided systems that prop them up. Although never officially a part of the Federal Republic, West Berlin received DM12 billion in direct aid from Bonn in 1987, along with huge tax concessions. The amount Bonn gave to support the arts in the city was more than the entire United States federal art budget for that year. Similarly, the diversion of money and resources from the rest of the country ensures that East Berlin is the showcase *Hauptstadt der DDR*, expensively disproving western misconceptions. But no amount of facts and figures, economics, or history can really explain the place; only by seeing it for yourself can you attempt some understanding.

WEST BERLIN

West Berlin is an island, surrounded by the barbed wire and watch towers of the Wall, and existing deep inside the GDR. You're closer to Poland here than you are to the Federal Republic, and you're constantly reminded of the fact that this is occupied territory: NATO troops are everywhere, American accents twang out on the radio, and British Airways planes swoop over the Reichstag on their way to the airport. No one in their right mind comes for light-hearted sightseeing. West Berlin is a profoundly scarred city, and even in the flashiest sections of its new center, around the **Memorial Church**, it still seems half-built, the modern buildings somehow making it less finished and more ugly. Unlike Paris, Amsterdam, or Munich, this isn't a city where you can simply stroll and absorb the atmosphere. You need to target your points of interest, using the city transit system to cover what can be longish distances. Those points of interest are, almost without exception, somber: the **Reichstag**, looming symbol of the war years; the garishly decorated **Wall**, facet of its aftermath; and several **museums** which openly and intelligently try and make sense of twentieth-century German history.

On the bright side, this isn't the only face of modern Berlin. By night the city changes, awakening into a **nightlife** that's among the best in Europe. The bars here are by turn raucous, shady, stylish, promiscuous, the discos and clubs blasting their stuff well into the earliest hours; restaurants are excellent, cheap, and of unequaled variety.

Culturally, the city has the advantage of massive subsidies from Bonn, and a legacy of great art collections. By far the finest of these is in the suburb of **Dahlem**, where a complex of museums holds everything from medieval painting to Polynesian huts. Elsewhere, something is bound to catch your taste. About a third of Berlin is either **parkland or forest**, and some of these green stretches are surprisingly beautiful: in the center, **Schloss Charlottenburg** and its gardens are a great place to loll away a summer afternoon, and on the city's western outskirts, the **Havel lakes** and the **Grunewald forest** have a lush, relaxed attraction that's the perfect antidote to the city's excesses.

The downside of all this is that Berlin is by no stretch of the imagination a cheap city. Transit, drink, and nightlife are costly, and though many museums are free, and others soften their charges for those with student ID, expenses can quickly mount up. Combine this with the fact that you'll be paying at least DM25 a night for accommodation and it's easy to see that you're going to need a little extra cash during your time here.

Getting There from the Federal Republic

By Train

Trains connect Berlin with most West German cities, and the rest of Europe.
Border crossing points are, from north to south:

- BÜCHEN (journey time to Berlin approximately 3 hr. 15 min.)

- HELMSTEDT (2 hr. 40 min.)

- BEBRA (5 hr. 40 min.)

- LUDWIGSTADT (5 hr.)

- HOF (5 hr. 20 min.)

Tickets from these towns cost between DM45 and DM75, less if you book a youth/student ticket: *DB Tourist Cards* and the *DB Junior Tourist Card* (see *Basics*) reduce the fare to around DM50 return; *InterRail* passes are not valid. **Transit visas** for the Democratic Republic are issued, without charge, on the train. From the border, trains are run by *Deutsche Reichsbahn*, the GDR rail company; it's a good idea to bring your own **food** for the journey.

By Bus

Connecting over 170 West German cities to Berlin (see "Travel Details" at the end of the chapter), buses are a slightly cheaper option than the trains. Certain operators offer a **student discount** on return tickets; inquire when buying, either at any DER agency, many travel agents, or the central bus station in Berlin (see below).

By Car

In order to take your car to Berlin you'll need an international driving licence, vehicle registration document and an insurance coverage extension. These should be presented at one of four **border crossing points**, each of which is open day and night:

GUDOW–ZARRENTIN (on the Hamburg Autobahn)

HELMSTEDT–MARIENBORN (Hannover Autobahn, and the fastest route, taking 2–3 hr.)

HERLESHAUSEN–WARTHA (Frankfurt Autobahn)

RUDOLPHSTEIN–HIRSCHBURG (Nürnberg Autobahn)

At the border crossing each passenger will need to buy a **transit visa** (DM5). Once on the transit roads, **rules** are strict and strictly adhered to:

● Do not leave the transit road at any time.

● Stop only at designated turnouts or *Intertank* service stations. Gas and food here must be paid for in West German marks.

● Do not pick up hitchhikers when in the GDR.

● Speed limits are 100kmh (62mph) on autobahns, 80kmh (50mph) on major roads. Seatbelts are compulsory.

● You do not need to return on the same route by which you entered.

From any of the border points (*before* entering the GDR) it's also quite feasible to **hitch**—just make sure your ride is going all the way to Berlin.

Arriving

All scheduled and charter flights arrive at **Tegel airport** (☎41011), from where frequent #9 buses run directly to the Zoo Station in the city center (journey time 35min; DM2.70). Taxis cover the distance in half the time and cost DM15–DM25. At the airport you'll find exchange facilities but scant duty-free shopping. The Zoo Station is also where you'll arrive if coming by **train**. International **buses** mostly stop at the central bus station, west of the center near the Funkturm; regular #94 buses or the U-Bahn from Kaiserdamm station link it to the city center.

Finding Somewhere to Stay

Berlin has a plethora of accommodation, from youth hostels to five-star hotels. But **easily the best way** of finding somewhere to stay is by contacting one of several **Mitwohnzentrale** organizations. These are agencies that can find just about any type of room, and for any length of time—from a weekend stay in a shared bedroom in a family flat to an entire luxury apartment for six months. Even in the summer, your chances of their being able to find you something immediately are high, but where the *Mitwohnzentrale* come into their own is for arranging **longer-term stays**. Monthly charges for a self-contained apartment range from DM400 to DM600, about half to two-thirds that if you're prepared to share; agency fees are usually 1% of the annual rent per month. For **shorter stays**, expect to pay DM23 per night for a single, central room with shared use of bathroom and kitchen. Almost all *Mitwohnzentrale* will take advance reservations by phone, and vary only in the number of places they have on their books.

Mitwohnzentrale, 3rd floor, Ku'damm Eck, Kurfürstendamm 227–8 (☎882 6694). Mon.–Fri. 10am–8pm, Sat. and Sun. 11am–5pm. Biggest and best of the *Mitwohnzentrale*, and an easy walk from the Zoo Station. Also has rooms for women in women-only apartments; there's a separate phone number for these—☎882 6284.

Mitwohnzentrale, Holsteinischestr. 55 (☎861 8222). Mon.–Fri. 10am–7pm, Sat. 10am–2pm, Sun. 11am–1pm. Fairly central and friendly, specializing in inner city rooms. They also have women-only apartments on their lists.

Mitwohnzentrale Kreuzberg, Mehringdamm 72 (☎786 6002). As the name suggests, their rooms tend to be in the Kreuzberg/eastern part of the city only, and therefore cheaper.

Compared to the *Mitwohnzentrale*, most other forms of accommodation seem overpriced or inconvenient. The **tourist office**, *Verkehrsamt Berlin*, Europa Center, 1000 Berlin 30 (daily 8am–11pm; ☎21234) with an additional office in the Zoo Station, offers the standard hotel and pension booking service for DM3, though their options, especially in the high season, are limited to midrange and luxury places. However, you may strike lucky and get something for around DM40 single, DM70 double, or be offered a cheap private room. The *Verkehrsamt* also offers a booking service; write at least two weeks in advance, stating the length of your stay and how much you're prepared to spend.

Otherwise, your chances of finding somewhere directly are good, if you're prepared to phone around and wear out some shoe leather. Summer weekends are the most problematic periods, and if you're arriving on a Friday night from June to August it makes sense to have at least the first few days' accommodation reserved—even if you intend to utilize the *Mitwohnzentrale* subsequently. The *Verkehrsamt*'s leaflets *Tips für Jungendliche* and *Berlin Hotelverzeichnis* (also available from German National Tourist Offices; see *Basics*) have useful lists of hotels and pensions.

Youth Hostels

Berlin's youth hostels are used extensively by school and athletic parties from the rest of Germany, and rooms tend to be booked well in advance; hence it's essential to phone first. The **Informationszentrum Berlin**, Hardenbergstr. 20 (☎310040; see also "Information and listings Magazines' below) can reserve rooms in most hostels free of charge.

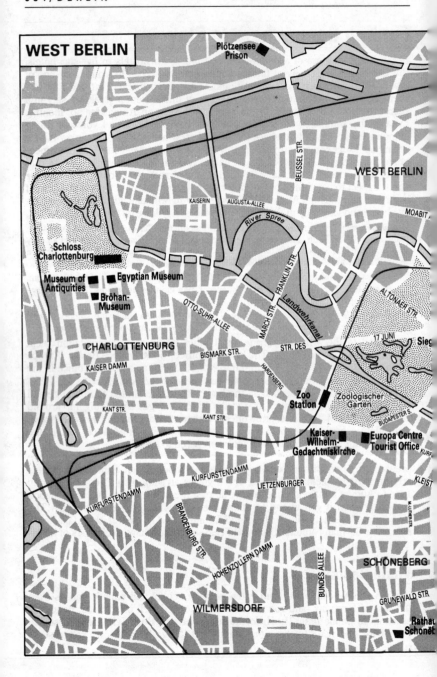

WEST BERLIN

Plötzensee Prison

WEST BERLIN

MOABIT

KAISERIN

AUGUSTA-ALLEE

River Spree

BEUSSEL STR.

ALTONAER STR.

Schloss Charlottenburg

Museum of Antiquities

Egyptian Museum

Bröhan-Museum

OTTO-SUHR-ALLEE

FRANKLIN STR.

MARCH STR.

Landwehrkanal

17 JUNI

Sieg

CHARLOTTENBURG

BISMARK STR.

STR. DES

KAISER DAMM

HARDENBERG

KANT STR.

KANT STR.

Zoo Station

Zoologischer Garten

BUDAPESTER S.

Kaiser-Wilhelm-Gedachtniskirche

Europa Centre Tourist Office

KURF

KURFURSTENDAMM

LIETZENBURGER

KLEIST

KURFURSTENDAMM

M.LUTHER STR.

BRANDENBURG STR.

SCHÖNEBERG

HOHENZOLLERN DAMM

BUNDES ALLEE

GRUNEWALD STR

WILMERSDORF

Rathau Schönel

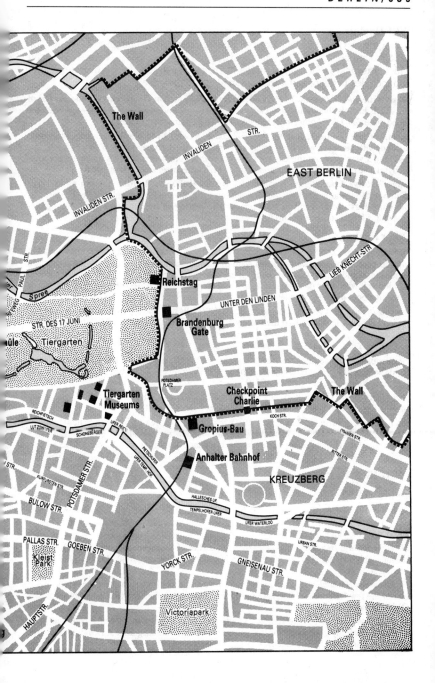

The Wall

INVALIDEN STR.

STR.

EAST BERLIN

INVALIDEN STR.

PAUL STR.

WEG

Spree

Reichstag

LIEB KNECHT STR.

STR. DES 17 JUNI

UNTER DEN LINDEN

üle

Tiergarten

Brandenburg
Gate

POTSDAMER
PLATZ

Tiergarten
Museums

REICHPIETSCH

LUTZOW PLTZ

SCHONEBERGER

UFER REICH

Checkpoint
Charlie

The Wall

KOCH STR.

MANN STR.

Gropius-Bau

RITTER STR.

POTSDAMER STR.

UFER TEMPHOF

PIETSCHER

Anhalter Bahnhof

KREUZBERG

KUPFGRABEN STR.

BULOW STR.

HALLESCHES UF.

TEMPELHOFER-UFER

UFER WATERLOO

URBAN STR.

PALLAS STR.

GOEBEN STR.

Kleist
Park

YORCK STR.

GNEISENAU STR.

HAUPTSTR.

Victoriapark

IYHF Hostels

All require a YHA card (see *Basics*), although this can be bought from the organization's offices in Templehofer Ufer 32 (☎362 3024; nearest U-Bahn Möckernbrücke). Each has a midnight curfew (frustrating in this insomniac city) and includes bedding and a spartan breakfast in the price.

Jugendgästehaus, Kluckstr. 3 (☎261 1097). Bus #29, direction Oranienplatz. Most central of the IYHF hostels, handy for the Tiergarten museums, and very solidly booked. DM20 for those under 25, DM23 otherwise, key deposit DM10. 9am–noon lockout.

Jugendherberge Wannsee, Badweg 1 (☎803 2034). S-Bahn #3 to Nikolassee. Very pleasantly located, with plenty of woodland walks on hand near the beaches of the Wannsee lakes, but it's quite a way out from the city center—and with a curfew that renders it useless if you're enjoying the nightlife. DM20 for under 25s, DM23 otherwise, key deposit DM20.

Jugendherberge Ernst Reuter, Hermsdorfer Damm 48–50 (☎404 1610). U-Bahn #6 to Tegel then bus #15 towards Frohnau. So far from town that it's the least popular of the hostels and therefore least likely to fill in summer—worth bearing in mind as an emergency option. Under 25s DM17, otherwise DM20; key deposit DM10.

Other Hostels

Bahnhofsmission, Zoo Station (☎313 8088). Church-run mission with limited accommodation for one night only. No risk that you'd want to stay for any longer, mind, since the rooms are windowless and dingy and the atmosphere starchily puritan. DM15 per person for a 4-bedded cell with a meager breakfast; rise and shine by 6am. A desperate option, but worth knowing about if you're penniless or arrive in town very late.

Jugendgästehaus am Zoo, Hardenbergstr. 9a (☎312 9410). Zoologischer Garten U- and S-Bahn. Excellent location, extremely popular. Singles DM30, doubles DM50, triples DM70. No curfew.

Jugendgästehaus Genthiner Strasse, Genthiner Str. 48 (☎261 1481). #29 bus direction Oranienplatz. Located near the grimmer section of the city's canal, but just ten minutes' away from the nightlife of Winterfeldtplatz. Singles DM35, doubles DM66, triples DM90, breakfast included. No curfew, key deposit DM20.

Jugendhotel International, Bernburger Str. 27–8 (☎262 3081). #29 bus direction Oranienplatz. Interesting position near the Wall. Singles DM38, doubles DM70.

Studentenhotel Berlin, Meiningerstr. 10 (☎784 6720). #73 bus to Rathaus Schöneberg, or Eisenacherstrasse U-Bahn. Dormitory accommodation at the relaxed edge of the city's action. Doubles DM29 per person, including breakfast. No curfew, key deposit DM25.

Hotels and Pensions

Below DM50

Centrum Pension Berlin, Kantstr. 31 (☎316153). Great location, two minutes' walk from Savignyplatz and just five minutes' bus ride from Zoo Station. Renovated with style, and great value at DM30 single, DM49 double.

Hotelpension am Bundesplatz, Bundesallee 56, corner of Hildegard Str. (☎853 5770). Central position only five minutes by U-Bahn from Zoo Station. Singles DM40, doubles DM80, with breakfast.

Hotelpension Hansablick, Flotowstr. 6 (☎391 7007). A short hop from the Tiergarten, this is one of the few "alternative" hotels in town, being run by a collective. Singles DM45, doubles DM80, breakfast included.

Hotelpension Lietensee, Neue Kantstr. 14 (☎321 5982). Near to an attractive lake and park, this is surprisingly good value for the quietly chic Charlottenburg area at DM45 for a single, DM86 double, breakfast included.

Pension am Savignyplatz, Grolmanstr. 52 (☎313 8392). Slightly seedy, but in the midst of Savignyplatz's nightlife. Singles DM37, doubles DM60.

Pension Kreuzberg, Grossbeerenstr. 64 (☎251 1362). Close to Kreuzberg hill at the smarter end of that neighborhood. Singles DM39, doubles DM65.

Pension Niebuhr, Niebuhrstr. 74 (☎324 9595). Clean and fresh pension in a quiet backstreet location that's within spitting distance of the Ku'damm and Kantstrasse. Singles DM35, doubles DM55.

DM50 and Up

The following all include breakfast in the price.

Alpenland Hotel, Carmerstr. 8 (☎312 9370 or 312 4898). Well situated and an excellent choice at this price. Singles DM60, doubles DM90.

Hotel Bogota, Schlüterstr. 45 (☎881 5001). Pleasant luxury at sensible prices. Singles DM50, doubles DM88.

Hotel Früling am Zoo, Kurfürstendamm 17 (☎881 8083). As central as you can get. Modern and spacious, but little more than that. Singles DM65, doubles DM100.

Hotel Heidelberg, Knesebeck Str. 15 (☎310103). Central hotel in an area good for bars and a street noted for its bookshops. Singles DM100, doubles DM135.

Hotel Meineke, Meineke Str. 10 (☎882 8111). Old fashioned, typical Berlin hotel, with an amiable atmosphere and about a minute's walk from the Kurfürstendamm. Singles DM105–129, doubles DM160.

Hotel Schweizerhof Berlin, Budapesterstr. 21–31 (☎26960). Excellent food, service, and style. And so it should be at DM195 for a single, DM245 double. One for a splurge . . .

Hotelpension Adria, Knesebeckstr. 74 (☎881 6550). Convenient location (between Savignyplatz and the Ku'damm). Singles DM55, doubles DM85.

Hotelpension Haus Trinitatis, Imchenallee 62 (☎365 4262). Way over to the west of the city, near the Havel lakes, and worth considering if you have your own transportation. Sumptuous food, lovely rooms, and a view over the lake. Singles DM50, doubles DM90.

Campgrounds

None of Berlin's three **campgrounds** is close to the center, each requires time and effort to reach, and, unlike many other European cities, there's no specifically youth-designated grounds. However they're all inexpensive (prices are a uniform DM5 per tent plus DM6 per person), well run and, with one exception, open year-round. If you are looking to cut costs, and intend to stay for a while, bear in mind that a *Mitwohnzentrale* flat may work out almost as cheaply.

Camping Dreilinden, Albrechts Teerofen (☎805 1201). From Oskar-Helene-Heim U-Bahn, take #18 bus in the direction of Kohlhasenbrück. Open April 1–Sept. 30. Close to the border in the southwest of the city, the site is a 2½-km walk from the nearest bus stop, and therefore unadvisable unless you have wheels. Free showers and a small restaurant.

Camping Haselhorst, Pulvermühlenweg (☎334 5955). #10 bus in the direction of Haselhorst. The most accessible campground, but the least picturesque. A few minutes' walk from the Havel lakes, and not far from Spandau Citadel. Facilities include a restaurant, bar, showers (DM0.50), and a small shop. Four-week maximum stay.

Camping Kladow, Krampnitzer Weg 111–117 (☎365 2797). Bus #34 in the direction of Gatow or #35 direction Kladow, then change at Ritterfeld Damm for the #35E. Friendly ground with the best facilities of all the three sites, including a free nursery, bar, restaurant, shops, and showers (DM0.50). Six-week maximum stay.

Getting Around and Information

Berlin is a large city, and sooner or later you'll need to use its efficient if expensive transport system. The **U-Bahn**, running both under-and over ground, covers much of the center and stretches into the suburbs: trains run from 4am to between midnight and 1am, an hour later on Friday and Saturday. Sections of the system run under the wall into East Berlin, and back out to the West: even if you don't want to get off and enter the GDR at Friedrichstrasse station, you can use these lines without fear of official hassle. It's also possible to get off at Friedrichstrasse U-Bahn and stock up on cheap East German duty-free goods without going through passport control. The **S-Bahn** system was largely destroyed during World War II, and has never fully recovered. These days it's far less frequent than the U-Bahn system, but better for covering long distances fast—say for heading out to the Wannsee lakes. You never seem to have to wait long for a **bus**, the timetables at the stops are uncannily accurate, and the city network covers most of the gaps in the U-Bahn system.

Single tickets (*Einzelfahrschein Normaltarif*) common to all the systems cost DM2.70 irrespective of how far you want to travel; they're valid for two hours, enabling you to transfer across the three networks to continue your journey, and to return within that time too. An *Einzelfahrschein Kurzstreckentarif* or short-trip ticket costs DM1.70 and allows you to travel up to 3 train or 6 bus stops. On U- and S-Bahn you're supposed to punch your ticket before traveling; on the bus the driver checks. It's possible to save a little money by buying a *Sammelkarte* of five tickets for DM11.50, but if you're intending to use the system frequently, it's a much better idea to buy a **day ticket** (*Tageskarte*) from any U-Bahn station or the *BVG* office on Grunewaldestrasse, next to Kleistpark U-Bahn station (Mon.–Fri. 8am–6pm, Sat. 7am–2pm). These cost DM9 per day for as many days as you wish, (though longer-duration tickets are only available from the *BVG* office), and allow unlimited travel on the entire system.

Taxis are plentiful, and though expensive (DM3.40 + DM1.58 per kilometer), hardly more so than public transit, especially if you're traveling in small groups. They cruise the city day and night and congregate at useful locations, such as Savignyplatz and the Zoo Station. To summon one, phone ☎6902 or ☎240202. **Bike rental** is available from several shops, though not at the Zoo Station. Try *Fahrradbüro Berlin*, Hauptstr. 146 (near Kleistpark U-Bahn; ☎784 5562), which charges around DM10 per day, DM50 per week; DM50 deposit and passport needed.

For more information, and a large-scale U-Bahn map, it's worth getting the *BVG Liniennetz* leaflet (DM2), either from their cubicle outside Zoo Station or from the tourist office. Most U-Bahn stations also have simple free maps.

Information and Listings Magazines

Though the **tourist office** has the usual selection of glossy promo, including listings of the higher-brow cultural events, the best starting point for gathering info is the **Informationszentrum** at Hardenbergstr. 20 (Mon.–Fri. 8am–7pm, Sat. 8am–4pm; ☎310040). As well as a host of English leaflets on the city's history and sights (including material on East Berlin), they also give away the handy booklet *Berlin for Young People*. If your German's up to it the parallel version *Berlin für junge Leute* is more detailed and up-to-date.

Berlin has two essential **listings magazines**, which come out on alternate weeks. *Zitty* (DM3.40) is marginally the better of the two, with day-by-day details of gigs, concerts, events, TV and radio, theater and film, alongside intelligent articles on politics, style, and the Berlin in-crowd, and useful classified ads. *Tip* (DM3.40) doesn't quite match it for conciseness or flair. Both magazines also have brief listings on East Berlin. The monthly *Berlin Programm* (DM2.50) has more condensed listings alongside info on opening times, and national and international train, bus, and plane timetables. There's also a flimsy giveaway English-language rag, *The Edge*.

The City

The results of wartime damage have left Berlin with the appearance of a badly patched-up skeleton: beneath the surface the former street plan survives, but in haphazard fashion and severed with cool illogicality by the Wall. The city center is marked by the **Zoologischer Garten**, or more properly the combined U-Bahn, S-Bahn and train **Zoo Station** adjacent. A stone's throw from here is downtown's single notable landmark, the rotting tusk of the **Kaiser-Wilhelm-Gedächtniskirche** (*Kaiser Wilhelm Memorial Church*); the **Kurfürstendamm**, or "Ku'damm" as it is universally known, an expensive shopping boulevard, homes in on the church from the west. North and east of the Zoo is the **Tiergarten** park, ending in the east with the old **Reichstag** building and the most chilling sections of the **Wall**. Near the **Tiergarten Museum district** the Wall cuts east to run above **Kreuzberg**, Berlin's enclave of immigrant workers, "alternative" living, and the most vibrant area at night. West of the center are the **Havel and Wannsee** lakes with good (if packed) beaches and thick woodland; southwest is the superb museum complex at **Dahlem**. In between, the city is mostly residential and suburban, and unless you've opted for a pricey central hotel, is where you're likely to end up finding **accommodation**.

Zoo Station, the Kurfürstendamm, and the Tiergarten

Chances are you'll arrive at Bahnhof Zoologischer Garten or **Zoo Station**. Perched high above the street, and with views across to the Zoo, it's an exciting place to end a journey, conjuring memories of prewar steam trains under its glassy roof. At street level, though, it's an unkempt and conspicuously lavatorial-smelling place that until recently was run by the East Berlin authorities. By day, but chiefly by night, it's the meeting place for the city's drunks and dope pushers, but has been much cleaned up since its role a few years back as a market for heroin-dealing and child prostitution.

Step out of the station and you're in the center of the city's maelstrom, a seemingly senseless mess of bright lights, traffic, and high-rise buildings. A short walk south and you're at the eastern end of the **Kurfürstendamm**, a 3.5-kilometer strip of ritzy shops, movie theaters, bars, and cafés that zeros in on the geographical center like the spoke of a broken wheel. The great landmark here, the one that's on all the postcards, is the **Kaiser-Wilhelm-Gedächtniskirche**, built at the end of the nineteenth century and destroyed in 1943. Purposefully left as a reminder of wartime damage, the church is a strangely effective memorial, the crumbling tower a hint of the old city. Adjacent, a new **chapel** (daily 9am–7:30pm) contains the tender, sad *Stalingrad Madonna*, while at the back the blue glass tower of the new church has gained the local nickname of the "Soul-Silo." The area around the church acts as a focal point for Berlin's punks and down-and-

The U & S Bahn

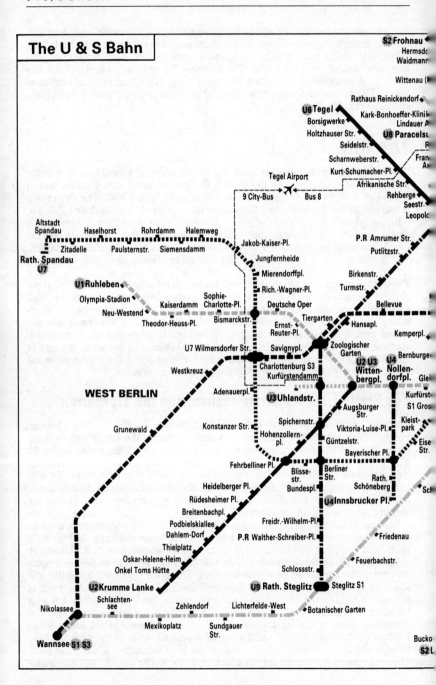

S2 Frohnau
Hermsd
Waidmann

Wittenau (

Rathaus Reinickendorf

U6 Tegel
Borsigwerke
Holtzhauser Str.
Seidelstr.
Scharnweberstr.
Kurt-Schumacher-Pl.
Afrikanische Str.
Rehberge
Seestr.
Leopold

Kark-Bonhoeffer-Klinik
Lindauer A
U8 Paracelsu
F
Fran
A

Tegel Airport
9 City-Bus   Bus 8

Altstadt
Spandau   Haselhorst   Rohrdamm   Halemweg
Zitadelle   Paulsternstr.   Siemensdamm
Rath. Spandau
U7

Jakob-Kaiser-Pl.
Jungfernheide
Mierendorffpl.
Rich.-Wagner-Pl.
Deutsche Oper

P.R Amrumer Str.
Putlitzstr.

Birkenstr.
Turmstr.

U1 Ruhleben
Olympia-Stadion
Neu-Westend
Theodor-Heuss-Pl.
Kaiserdamm
Sophie-
Charlotte-Pl.
Bismarckstr.

Bellevue
Tiergarten   Hansapl.
Ernst-
Reuter-Pl.
Zoologischer
Garten

Kemperpl.

U7 Wilmersdorfer Str.
Savignypl.
Charlottenburg S3
Kurfürstendamm

U2 U3
Witten-
bergpl.
U4
Nollen-
dorfpl.
Bernburge
Glei

WEST BERLIN

Adenauerpl.
U3 Uhlandstr.
Augsburger
Str.
Viktoria-Luise-Pl.
Güntzelstr.
Bayerischer Pl.

Kurfürst
S1 Gros
Kleist-
park
Eise
Str.

Grunewald

Konstanzer Str.
Spichernstr.
Hohenzollern-
pl.

Westkreuz

Fehrbelliner Pl.
Heidelberger Pl.
Rüdesheimer Pl.
Breitenbachpl.
Podbielskiallee
Dahlem-Dorf
Thielplatz
Oskar-Helene-Heim
Onkel Toms Hütte

Blisse-
str.
Bundespl.
Berliner
Str.
Rath.
Schöneberg
U4 Innsbrucker Pl.

Freidr.-Wilhelm-Pl.
P.R Walther-Schreiber-Pl.

Sch

Friedenau

Feuerbachstr.

U2 Krumme Lanke
Schlachten-
see
Nikolassee
Zehlendorf
Mexikoplatz
Sundgauer
Str.
Lichterfelde-West
Schlossstr.
U9 Rath. Steglitz   Steglitz S1

Botanischer Garten

Bucko
S2 L

Wannsee S1 S3

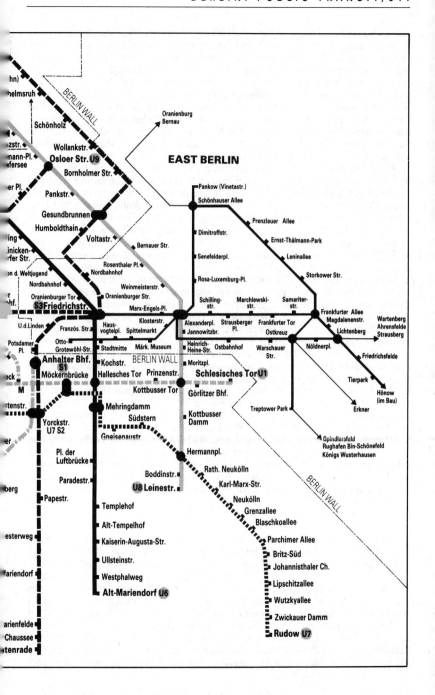

outs, who threaten the well-heeled Ku'damm shoppers with demands for cash. It's a menacing, unfriendly, spot, and the square behind isn't much better, a tatty concrete slab usually filled with skateboarders and street musicians. This area marks the beginning of Tauentzienstrasse, with the **Europa Center**, a huge shopping mall that contains the *Verkehrsamt* (tourist office) at its head. It's worth a climb to the **observation platform** (daily 9am–11pm; DM2) under the rotating Mercedes symbol for a preliminary reconnaissance of the center, the dazzling lights of the Ku'damm sharply contrasted with the darkened memorial church. Farther down Tauentzienstrasse is the *Ka-De-We*, an abbreviation of the German for "the Largest Store of the West"; this it isn't, though it's still an impressive statement of the city's standard of living.

If you'd turned west along the Ku'damm you'd have been at the beginning of its stretch of shops and cafés, which (roughly) get cheaper the farther west you go, blazing a trail at night in a dazzle of bright neon. The Ku'damm was built under Bismarck in the nineteenth century, and Thomas Wolfe called it "the largest coffee-house in Europe" when hanging out here in the 1920s; these days there's little left from either man's time. If the shops are beyond your means, some of the street stalls selling clothes and jewelry are fun places to pick up trinkets. By the time you reach **Adenauerplatz** the slick showrooms have died out, and the bars become affordable: a good starting point for an evening's drinking. Better still for nightlife is **Kantstrasse**, the street running north of the Ku'damm. After a few hundred meters it crosses **Savignyplatz**, a neat broad square that's the hub for some of the city's most enjoyable bars and restaurants.

Back in the center, the **Zoologischer Garten** (daily 9am–sunset; DM6.50) forms the beginning of the **Tiergarten**, a restful expanse of woodland and lakes originally laid out under Elector Friedrich III as a hunting ground and destroyed during the Battle of Berlin in 1945—though so successful has its replanting been that these days it's hard to tell. The zoo itself is much like any the world over, and expensive to boot; preferably wander through the Tiergarten tracing the course of the **Landwehrkanal**, an inland waterway off the Spree River. Near the Corneliusbrücke a small, odd sculpture commemorates the radical leader **Rosa Luxemburg**. In 1918, along with fellow revolutionary Karl Liebknecht, she reacted against the newly formed Weimar Republic and especially the terms of the Treaty of Versailles, declaring a new Socialist Republic in Berlin along the lines of Soviet Russia (she had played an important part in the abortive 1905 revolution). The pair were kidnapped by members of the elite First Cavalry Guards: Liebknecht was shot while "attempting to escape;" Luxemburg was knocked unconscious and shot, her body dumped in the Landwehrkanal at this point.

The broad avenue that cuts through the Tiergarten is the **Strasse des 17 Juni**, its name commemorating the day in 1953 when workers in the East rose in revolt against the occupying Soviet powers, demanding free elections, the removal of all borders separating the two Germanys, and freedom for political prisoners. Soviet forces quickly mobilized, and between 200 and 400 people died; the authorities also ordered the execution of 21 East Berliners and eighteen Soviet soldiers—for "moral capitulation to the demonstrators." At the center of the avenue is the **Siegessäule**, the victory column celebrating Prussia's victories over France in 1871. Though the boulevard approaches exaggerate its size, it's still an eye-catching city monument: 67m high, and topped with a gilded winged victory that symbolically faces France. The view from the top is one of Berlin's best—the Brandenburg Gate and the East seem tantalizingly close, the Wall barely visible, and the Reichstag standing like a gnarled protector at the edge of the park. Have a look too at the mosaics at the column's base, which show incidents and notables from the Franco-Prussian War: they were removed after 1945 and taken to Paris, only to be returned when the lust for war spoils had subsided. (April–Nov. Tues.–Sun. 9am–6pm, Mon. 1pm–6pm, last entrance 5:45pm; DM1.20, DM0.70 students).

From the Siegessaüle it's possible to walk down to the Brandenburg Gate and Reichstag, but it's a tiring hike and most visitors take the #83 or #69 bus that runs from downtown. If you do come this way it's worth looking out for **Schloss Bellevue**, an eighteenth-century building that's the Berlin home of the Federal President and only visitable when he's not around. On the southeast side of the park the **Tiergarten Museum Complex** offers a variety of cultural delights (see p.648).

The Wall: From the Reichstag to Checkpoint Charlie

Strasse des 17 Juni comes to an end at the Brandenburg Gate, but it's better to start a little farther north—at the **Reichstag**.

Built in the late nineteenth century to house the German parliament, familiar from flickering newsreels as it burned in 1933*, and the scene of Hitler's wresting of control of Germany in the same year, the Reichstag today seems lost in a sea of irony. Inscribed with the words *Dem Deutschen Volke*, what was once the symbol of national unity today stands hard by the Wall; in front, on the broad green square, Turkish workers picnic and occupying troops play football. But it's not difficult to imagine scenes the building has witnessed: in November 1918 the German Republic was declared from a balcony here, while Karl Liebknecht was busy proclaiming a Socialist Republic down the road—and cementing his and Rosa Luxemburg's fates. Nowadays the Reichstag, restored following a wartime gutting, contains the fascinating exhibition "Questions on German History" (Tues.–Sun. 10am–5pm; free), which chronicles the alliances and divisions, the war and rebuilding that led to Berlin's insular existence. Inevitably the best sections are those concerning the Third Reich: photos of the Olympic Games, anti-Jewish propaganda, horrific pictures of the Plötzensee executions, and much documentary evidence of the war years that's not often seen. Most of the commentary is in German, so it's well worth shelling out DM6 for the written English guide, or DM2 for an audio tape.

Immediately behind the Reichstag runs the **Wall** that divides the city, and just to the left of the entrance, a series of plaques marks the names (where known) of some of those killed trying to swim to the West across the nearby river Spree. The memorial is a poignant one, and indeed this stretch of the Wall running south of the Reichstag is one of the most interesting and evocative. Erected over-night on August 13 1961 to cordon off the Soviet sector and corral the British, American, and French sectors of the city some 200km inside the GDR, the Wall underlines the city's schizophrenia and frenzy and marks (as Berliners are fond of telling you) the city's *raison d'être*—the "stabilization of the impossible." Today, with the thawing of East-West relations and Gorbachev's *perestroika*, it's

---

* Debate as to who actually started the fire has resumed in recent years. In a show trial, Göring, as Minister of the Interior for the State of Prussia, successfully accused a subnormal half-blind Communist Dutch bricklayer, **Marius van der Lubbe**, of arson; he was executed the following year. It's equally likely that members of the SA, the precursors of the SS, set the fire to allow draconian measures to be brought in against the Nazi's enemies. By an emergency decree on the day after the fire, the basic civil rights guaranteed by the Weimar constitution were suspended, and the death penalty introduced for various political offenses.

THE CENTER

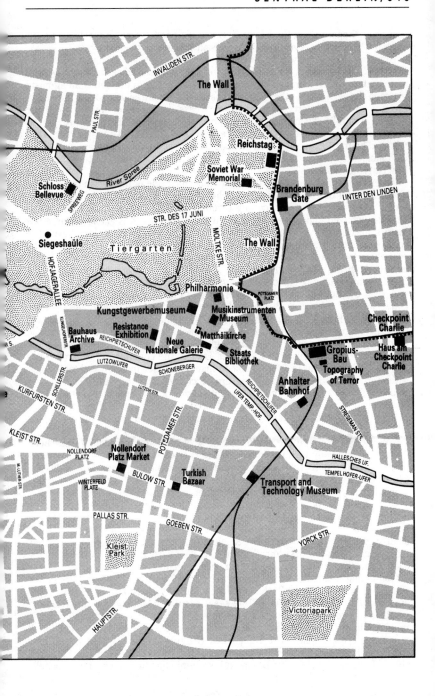

INVALIDEN STR.

The Wall

PAUL STR.

Reichstag

River Spree

Soviet War
Memorial

Schloss
Bellevue

SPREEWEG

Brandenburg
Gate

UNTER DEN LINDEN

STR. DES 17 JUNI

MOLTKE STR.

Siegeshaüle

HOFJAGERALLEE

Tiergarten

The Wall

Philharmonie

POTSDAMER
PLATZ

Kungstgewerbemuseum

Musikinstrumenten
Museum

Checkpoint
Charlie

Bauhaus
Archive

Resistance
Exhibition

LINDENUFERSTR.

REICHPIETSCHUFER

Matthäikirche

Neue
Nationale Galerie

Gropius-
Bau

Haus am
Checkpoint
Charlie

SCHILLERSTR.

LUTZOWUFER

Staats
Bibliothek

Topography
of Terror

STRESEMAN STR.

SCHONEBERGER

LUTZOW STR.

REICHPIETSCHUFER

Anhalter
Bahnhof

KURFURSTEN STR.

UFER TEMP-HOF.

KLEIST STR.

POTSDAMER STR.

M. LUTHER STR.

NOLLENDORF
PLATZ

Nollendorf
Platz Market

HALLESCHES UF.

BULOW STR.

Turkish
Bazaar

TEMPELHOFER-UFER

WINTERFELD
PLATZ

Transport and
Technology Museum

PALLAS STR.

GOEBEN STR.

YORCK STR.

Kleist
Park

HAUPTSTR.

Victoriapark

easy to be flippant about the border between the two Germanys; a walk along this stretch forces you to revise a few opinions and review a little history.

After the war, Berlin was split between its conquerors, as Stalin, Roosevelt, and Churchill had agreed at Yalta. Each sector was supposed to exist peacefully with its neighbor, under a unified city council, but almost from the outset antagonism between the Soviet and other sectors was high. Only three years after the end of the war the Soviet forces closed down access corridors to the city from the Federal Republic, forming what was known as the **Berlin Blockade**; it was successfully overcome by a massive Western airlift that lasted nearly a year. This, followed by the 1953 uprising, large-scale cross-border emigration, and innumerable "incidents," led to the building of what is known in the GDR as the "anti-Fascist protection wall."

When the four powers were deciding on sectors, one of the parish maps of the Greater Berlin of 1920 was used to delineate them: the Wall follows the Soviet sector boundary implacably, cutting through houses, across squares and rivers with its own wild logic. One oddity about the wall is that it is actually built a few meters inside GDR territory: the West Berlin authorities therefore have little control over the **graffiti** that covers it like a static New York subway car. It's an ever-changing mixture of colors and slogans, with the occasional burst of bitterness (*"My friends are dying behind you,"*), humor (*"Er . . . Does this belong to Pink Floyd?"*), and stupidity (*"We shoulda nuked 'em in '45"*).

A walk by the Wall reveals some of this, and takes you to the **Brandenburg Gate**, another of those Berlin buildings dense with meaning and history. Originally built as a combination city gate/triumphal arch in 1791 and modeled after the Propylaea, the entrance to the Acropolis in Athens, it became, like the Reichstag later, a symbol of German unity, looking out to the Siegessäule and guarding the leafy passage of Unter den Linden, the continuation of Strasse des 17 Juni in East Berlin. In 1806 Napoleon marched under the arch and took home with him the **Quadriga**, the horse-drawn chariot that tops the Gate. It was returned a few years later, and the revolutionaries of 1848 and 1918 met under its gilded shape. Later the gate became a favored rallying point for the Nazi's torch-lit marches: it's still a well-enough known image to give a frisson of unease.

Today the Gate lies in East Berlin, though you can actually get closer to it from the Western sector. To the south, one of several **observation posts** has been erected, presumably with the idea of giving curious tourists a view of the "other side"; what they don't realize is that most of the people they gaze at pityingly are Western tourists on day-trips to the East. Nevertheless, the view was apparently emotive enough to reduce Margaret Thatcher to tears on a recent visit here.

From the Gate the wall cuts directly south but before following it, cross to the north side of Strasse des 17 Juni for a look at the **Soviet War Memorial** to the troops who died in the Battle for Berlin. Built from the marble of Hitlers's destroyed Berlin headquarters, the Reichs Chancellery, and flanked by two tanks that were among the first to reach the city, it's guarded by two Soviet soldiers, each under the "protection" of a British enlisted man.

Continuing south the wall reaches a farther observation post at **Potsdamer Platz**, the heart of prewar Berlin and once a hub of the city's transport and nightlife. The old trolley lines can still be seen, running headlong into the Wall and continuing into the almost-featureless no-man's land that's occupied only by rabbits. Climb the observation post and look to the left of the Platz, and a small hummock of land marks the remains of **Hitler's bunker**, where the Führer spent his last days, issuing meaningless orders as the Battle of Berlin raged above. Here he married Eva Braun and wrote his final testament: he personally was responsible for nothing; he had been betrayed by the German people, who had proved unequal to his leadership, and deserved the future he could now see ahead of them. On April 30, 1945 he shot himself, his body hurriedly burned by loyal officers. In the wrangles after the war to prove his death, the Soviet Army apparently came up with Hitler's teeth, which they had managed to retrieve from the charred remains and have verified by the Führer's dentist. The latest on this apocryphal tale is that the teeth are now stored away in a museum in East Berlin.

Just below Potsdamer Platz the Wall swings east, and the drab buildings on the Eastern side of the Wall are those of Göring's **Air Ministry**. Göring promised the people that not a single bomb would fall on Berlin during the war; ironically, the Air Ministry was one of the few buildings to remain unscathed.

Below Potsdamer Platz the woodland of the Tiergarten falls away and you enter a semi-desolate area that's never really recovered from 1945 devastation. A magnificently restored exception is the **Martin-Gropius-Bau**, which today contains the Museum for Design (see p.663), and is the venue for the city's most important exhibitions. Its small café is a useful stopping point and needed pick-me-up before tackling an adjacent exhibition, "**The Topography of Terror**" (daily 10am–6pm; free). This is housed in a newly built structure a little way from the Gropius-Bau, for nothing is left of the buildings that once stood here. Formerly known as Prinz-Albrecht-Strasse, Niederkirchenstrasse was the base of the Gestapo, the SS, and Reich Security offices: in buildings along here Himmler planned the Final Solution—the deportation and genocide of European Jews—and organized the Gestapo, the feared secret police. The exhibition is housed in the former cellars of the Gestapo building, where important prisoners were inter-rogated and tortured. Though the photos here tell their own story, you'll need the English translation (DM2) for the main text of the exhibits.

The land behind the Gropius-Bau is more wasteland, the place where Berlin's student drivers come to practice. From here it's a ten-minute walk (or #29 bus ride) down Wilhelmstrasse and Kochstrasse to **Friedrichstrasse**, once one of the city's great streets, packed with cafés and shops, now a dusty avenue heavily pockmarked by wartime shell damage. At its northern end is **Checkpoint Charlie**, the transit point for non-West Germans on foot or with car and one of Berlin's more celebrated landmarks. With the dramatic signs "YOU ARE NOW LEAVING THE AMERICAN SECTOR" and the unsmiling teenage East Berlin border guards who frisk you over, it's easy to feel part of a Len Deighton thriller. The reality is rather more mundane: Checkpoint Charlie is a much slower entrance to the East than Friedrichstrasse U-Bahn station, and the American troops who mope around here seem thoroughly bored. In the Cold War years it was the scene of repeated border incidents, with sporadic standoffs between Soviet and American troops which usually culminated in tanks from both sides growling at each other for a few days.

More tangible evidence of the trauma the Wall has caused is on hand at the **Haus am Checkpoint Charlie** (daily 9am–10pm; DM3.50, students DM2.50; nearest U-Bahn Kochstrasse), which tells the history of the Wall in photos of escape tunnels, the (actual) converted cars and home-made aircraft by which people have tried and often tragically failed to break through the border. Films document the stories of some of the 75 people murdered by the East German border guards, and there's a section on human rights behind the Iron Curtain, but it's a scruffy, rather dated collection, and not quite the harrowing experience that some American visitors seem to expect. For more details, pick up a copy of *It Happened at the Wall* or *Berlin—from Frontline Town to the Bridge of Europe*, both on sale here.

The Tiergarten Museum Complex

To the west of Potsdamer Platz, the Tiergarten complex is a recently built mixture of museums and cultural forums that could easily fill a day of your time. Far and away the finest building is the **Neue Nationalgalerie**, Potsdamer Str. 50 (Tues.–Fri. 9am–5pm; main collection free), a black-rimmed glass box that seems almost suspended above the ground, its clarity of line and detail having all the intelligent simplicity of the Parthenon. Designed by Mies van der Rohe in 1965, the upper section is used for temporary exhibits, often of contemporary art, while the underground galleries contain paintings from the late eighteenth century on. Many, though by no means all, of the works are German: **Menzel** begins the collection with portraits, interiors, and landscapes, followed by the more recognizable works of **Courbet**. The paintings of **Feurbach** seem thoroughly nineteenth-century and thoroughly German, and are followed by those of **Böcklin**—most typically the *Landscape with Ruined Castle*. After the bright splotches of **Lovis Corinth** and a clutch of **Monet**s the galleries move on to the portraits and Berlin cityscapes of **Grosz** and **Dix**, notably Grosz's *Gray Day* and Dix's *Maler Family*. **Kirchner** spent time in Berlin before World War I, and his *Potsdamer Platz* dates from 1914, though it might as well be another country as just down the road. There's also work by Miró (*Little Blonde in an Attraction Park*), Klee, Karel Appel, Jasper Johns, and Francis Bacon: a fine, easily assimilated collection.

North of the Nationalgalerie the **Matthäikirche** stands in lonely isolation on a blitzed landscape that now forms a parking lot for the **Philharmonie**, home of the Berlin Philharmonic and, until he was at last booted out into "retirement" in 1989, their renowned conductor Herbert von Karajan. Looking at the gold-clad ugliness of the building, designed in the 1960s by Hans Scharoun, it's easy to see how it got its nickname among Berliners of "Karajani's circus." Should you wish to reserve a ticket the office is open Monday to Friday from 3:30 to 6pm, Saturday and Sunday 11am to 2pm (☎261 4843); chances of a seat for major concerts are slim unless you've reserved months in advance, but the acoustics are so good that it's worth trying your luck for other performances under guest conductors.

Continuing the musical theme, the **Musikinstrumenten Museum** (Tues.–Sun. 9am–5pm; free) just below the Philharmonie comes as something of a disappointment. Its collection of (mostly European) keyboards, wind, and string instruments from the fifteenth century to present day is comprehensive and impressively laid out; but it's all strictly look-don't-touch stuff, with guards vigilant for the slightest tinkle—the antithesis of what such a collection should be. Content yourself with the prerecorded tapes that give a taste of the weird and wonderful sounds the instruments make.

Much better is the **Kunstgewerbemuseum** (Tues.–Sun. 9am–5pm; free), an encyclopedic but seldom dull collection of European arts and crafts. The top floor contains the Renaissance, baroque, and rococo pieces (wonderful silver and ceramics), along with Jugendstil and art deco objects, particularly furniture. The ground floor holds the Middle Ages–Early Renaissance collections, with some sumptuous gold pieces. The highlight, though, is the basement: a small but great assembly of Bauhaus furniture, glittering contemporary jewelry, and a display of the evolution of product design.

Lastly, the **Staatsbibliothek** (Mon.–Fri. 9am–9pm, Sat. 9am–5pm; free access) across Potsdamer Strasse from the other buildings has over 3 million books, occasional exhibitions, a cheapish café, and a wide selection of British newspapers. Its other claim to fame is to be the last building designed by Hans Scharoun, and the most popular of his works among his fans.

Kreuzberg

East of the Gropius-Bau the Wall runs from west to east, and the area directly below it forms **Kreuzberg**, famed for its large immigrant community and self-styled "alternative" inhabitants, nightlife, and goings-on. Effectively there are two Kreuzbergs: that to the west, the area bounded by Friedrichstrasse, the Viktoriapark and the Südstern, which is a richer, smarter, more sedate neighbor to that in the east, which is sometimes refered to as SO 36 after its postal code. This is Berlin's happening quarter, the place to hang out and nightclub, and where the youth of the Federal Republic come to get involved in alternative politics, drop out, or simply avoid the draft. Though there's precious little in the way of things to see, it is, in many ways, the city's most exciting strip.

West Kreuzberg

First **the west**. It's only a short walk south, cutting down Stresemann Strasse, from the Gropius-Bau to the remains of the **Anhalter Bahnhof**, a sad reminder of misguided civic action that some would term civic vandalism. The Anhalter Bahnhof was once one of the city's (and Europe's) great rail termini, forming Berlin's gateway to the south. Completed in 1870, it received only mild damage during the war and was left roofless but substantial in 1945. Despite attempts to preserve it as a future museum building, it was blown up in 1952—essentially because someone had put in a good bid for the bricks. Now only a fragment of the facade stands, giving a hint at past glories. The patch of land that the station once covered is today a wasteland, and though there's nothing to see save a mock-up skeleton of its exit, and the paths of the old railtracks, it's an oddly atmospheric spot. The blunt and featureless building to one side, incidentally, is a fortified bunker-storehouse from the war years.

An alternative and easier approach to the area is to catch the U-Bahn to Möckernbrücke station on line #1, an enjoyable above-ground ride through old warehouses and towering postwar redevelopment. Crossing south over the Landwehrkanal and turning right along Templehofer Ufer you pass one of the decaying but still ornate **public toilets** erected in the early years of this century; gents can pop in for a Bismarckian moment of relief. A little farther on at Trebbiner Str. 9 is the **Museum für Verkehr und Technik** (*Museum of Transport and Technology*; Tues.–Fri. 9am–6pm, Sat. and Sun. 10am–6pm; DM3.5, students/children DM1.5). This is one of the city's most enjoyable museums, a button-pushers' and kids' delight. The technology section has plenty of experiments, antiquated machinery, and computers to play with, alongside some elegant old cars and planes. The transportation museum, a collection of ancient steam trains and carriages, is even more impressive, the great machines brought to rest in what was once a workshop of the old Anhalter Bahnhof.

Reaching the **Viktoriapark** from here means a half-hour's walk, retracing your steps to the U-Bahn, and heading south down Grossbeeren Strasse. On the slopes of a hill, the park is one of the city's most likable, a relaxed ramble of trees and green space with a pretty brook running down the middle. The streets that flank it have a scattering of cafés, and on summer afternoons there's no better place to stretch out and relax. Atop the hill is the **Cross** (though it's more of a neoclassical spire) from which Kreuzberg gets its name, designed by Schinkel to commemorate the Napoleonic Wars. The view is a good one too, made all the more pleasant by the wafting aromas from the Schultheiss brewery on the southern slopes.

South and east of the Viktoriapark, the housing fades away to the flatlands that contain **Tempelhof Military Airport**. Built by the Nazis and now used mainly by the U.S. Air Force, it was here that the Allies flew in supplies to beat the Berlin Blockade of 1948–49—an act that was to strengthen anti-Soviet feeling among West Berliners and increase the popularity of the occupying forces. At the height of the airlift a plane was landing every minute, and the **Luftbrückendenkmal**, a memorial at the entrance to the airport symbolizing the three air corridors used, commemorates the seventy airmen and eight groundcrew who died in crashes while attempting to land.

East Kreuzberg: SO 36

In the 1830s, Berlin's industries started recruiting peasants from the outlying countryside to work in their factories and machine shops. It was to the small village of Kreuzberg that many came, to work in the east of the city and live in buildings that were thrown up by speculators as low-rent accommodation. Kreuzberg became established as a solidly working-class area and, in time, a suburb of Greater Berlin. **Siemens**, the electrical engineering giant, began life in one of Kreuzberg's rear courtyards. In the 1930s, local unionists and workers fought street battles with the Nazis, and during the war it was one of very few areas to avoid total destruction, and among the quickest to revive in the 1950s. When the Wall was built in 1961, things changed: Kreuzberg became an isolated outpost of the city, severed from its natural hinterland in the East. Families moved out, houses were boarded up, and Kreuzberg began to die. At the same time, the city, deprived of cheap East Berlin labor to work in its factories, began to look farther afield, for the migrant workers who have come to be known as *Gastarbeiter*. Turks began to move to the city in large numbers, in time bringing their families and Islamic customs; few landlords welcomed the new workers, and gradually they began to found a community in the area with the cheapest rentable property—Kreuzberg.

Throughout the 1960s and 1970s, Kreuzberg developed as Berlin's Turkish enclave, with other *Gastarbeiter* from Yugoslavia, Spain, and Italy joining them. Along too came the radicals, students and dropouts of the 1968 generation—often attracted to the city because it was a method of avoiding national service, and to Kreuzberg because it offered vast potential for **squatting**. In the 1980s Kreuzberg became the focus and point of reference for squatters throughout the Federal Republic, and the Social Democratic city government adopted a liberal approach to them, offering subsidies to well-organized squats and giving them some security of tenure. Projects like the **Mehringhof** (actually over the "border" in west Kreuzberg), a center for alternative industries and arts, flourished.

All went well until the Christian Democrats took over the city. Using arguments over the role of city property—many of the buildings here are owned by the government—and the growing problems of crime and drug-dealing, the right-wing Minister of the Interior ordered the riot police to enter Kreuzberg and forcibly close down the squats. There were riots in the streets, demonstrations all over the city, and intense political protest, which reached its peak when a 15-year-old boy was killed by a bus during a demonstration. Activists called a strike and the city government was forced to back down.

Which is how things have remained. The Turks and other immigrant communites are thriving, an uneasy truce exists between the radical squatters and the new civic authorities, and slowly, though perhaps inevitably, the odd signs of gentrification are there, as astute Berliners (with an eye to their political profiles)

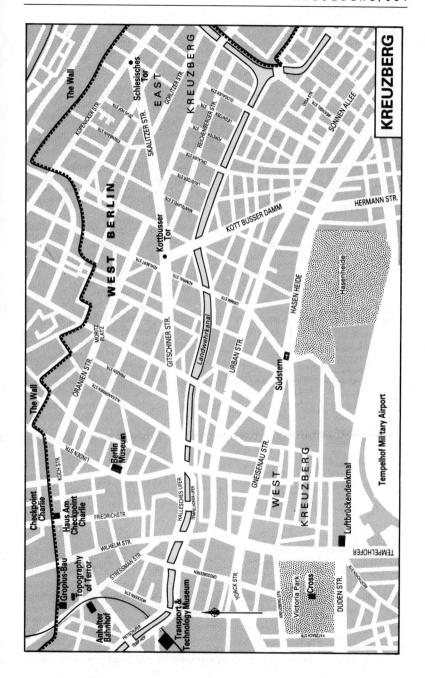

KREUZBERG

The Wall

Schlesisches
Tor

EAST

KREUZBERG

KOPENICKER STR.

GORLITZER STR.

ZEUG HOF STR.

EISENBAHN ALLE

WRANGEL STR.

SKALITZER STR.

SONNEN ALLEE

WEICHSEL STR.

OSSO STR.

FORSTER STR.

REICHENBERGER STR.

LAUSITZER STR.

GLOGAUER STR.

OHLAUER STR.

WEST BERLIN

LAUSITZER STR.

MANTEUFFEL STR.

HERMANN STR.

KOTT BUSSER DAMM

Kottbusser
Tor

ADALBERT STR.

ADMIRAL STR.

GRIMM STR.

URBAN STR.

HASEN HEIDE

Hasenheide

MORITZ
PLATZ

GITSCHINER STR.

Landwehrkanal

Südstern

The Wall

ORANIEN STR.

PRINZEN STR.

ALEXANDRINEN STR.

Berlin
Museum

LINDEN STR.

GNEISENAU STR.

WEST

KREUZBERG

Tempelhof Military Airport

KOCH STR.

Checkpoint
Charlie

Haus Am
Checkpoint
Charlie

HALLESCHES UFER

TEMPELHOF UFER

FRIEDRICHSTR.

Luftbrückendenkmal

TEMPELHOFER

Groplus-Bau

Topography
of Terror

WILHELM STR.

STRESSMAN STR.

YORCK STR.

GROSSBEEREN

Victoria Park

Cross

MOCKERN STR.

Anhalter
Bahnhof

TEMP HOF

BELLE ALLIANCE

Transport &
Technology Museum

KREUZBERG STR.

KATZBACH STR.

DUDEN STR.

MONUMEN STR.

move to the area. For to say you live in Kreuzberg is to make a statement. If you want to gauge the political temperature of Berlin, you have only to see what's happening on the streets here. During the meeting of the IMF in Berlin in 1988, the authorities briefly sealed off Kreuzberg, even closing down the U-Bahn network; perhaps surprisingly, things remained fairly calm.

You don't, however, need any interest in revolution or city machinations to enjoy Kreuzberg. The **nightlife** here is the city's best, and it's an enjoyable area to wander through by day, stopping off at the innumerable Turkish snack bars for a kebab, breakfasting on a 9am vodka-and-beer special at a café, or just taking in the feel of the place—which is much like an Istanbul market in an Eastern European housing development.

Catching U-Bahn line #1 (unkindly dubbed the "Istanbul Express" in this stretch) to **Kottbusser Tor** or **Schlesisches Tor** stations up against the Wall is a good introduction to Kreuzberg. The area around Kottbusser Tor is typical, a scruffy, earthy shambles of Turkish street vendors and cafés, the air filled with the aromas of southern European cooking. Cutting through Dresdener Strasse, past the Turkish movie theater, takes you on to Kreuzberg's main strip, **Orianienstrasse**, which from Moritzplatz east is lined with café-bars, art galleries, and clothes shops, and in a way forms an "alternative" Kurfürstendamm. Stop off at *Cazzo* at no. 187 for a taste of what the locals call a *Szene* place—somewhere that's in and happening. Around the Schlesisches Tor things are more residential, the nearness of the Wall heightening the atmosphere. If you read German, there's some interesting graffiti on the Wall and walls here, reflecting the tone of the neighborhood: "GERMAN AND TURKISH WOMEN UNITE AND FIGHT THE REAL ENEMY—PATRIARCHY" is just one example. At night both areas seem a little sharper, darkness giving them an edge of danger and a sense of concealed, forbidden pleasures.

The Landwehrkanal runs south of Oranienstrasse, and below that the broad path of Hasenheide-Gneisenaustrasse marks the transition from east to west Kreuzberg. Around the Südstern (which has a convenient U-Bahn station) are another cluster of café-bars (the *Wunderbar* opposite the U-Bahn is a favorite) and Gneisenaustrasse has some good restaurants, but the flavor of east Kreuzberg has gone, and things feel (and are) a lot tamer.

Schöneberg

Like Kreuzberg, **Schöneberg** was once a separate suburb, one that was swallowed up by Greater Berlin as the city expanded in the late eighteenth and the nineteenth century. Blown to pieces during the war, it's now a mostly middle-class residential area, stretching below the Tiergarten and sandwiched between Kreuzberg to the east and Wilmersdorf to the east. Things to see are few, but what is here is both fascinating and moving.

To the north, almost in Tiergarten, Reichpietsch Ufer follows the leafy course of the Landwehrkanal to the west of the Neue Nationalgalerie. **Stauffenbergstrasse**, a right turn off the Ufer, takes its name from one of the instigators of the plot to assassinate Hitler that came closest to success. **Claus Graf Schenk von Stauffenberg**, chief of staff to the German Army Office that once stood on this street, organized the bomb plot of July 20 1944. During a conference at Hitler's East Prussian headquarters in Rastenburg, von Stauffenberg placed his briefcase packed with explosives no more than four meters from the Führer, slipped out of the meeting and headed back to Berlin, where he and fellow conspirators had made extensive contacts among high ranking army officers with anti-Nazi sentiments. By some fluke Hitler escaped unscathed, and von Stauffenberg and the rest of the conspirators were quickly arreste;, taken to the courtyard of the army office, and shot. Throughout Berlin anyone even vaguely connected with the plot was also arrested, many meeting their fates at Plötzensee Prison (see p.659). Today the site of the building where von Stauffenberg worked and died is occupied by the permanent exhibition **Resistance to National Socialism** (at Stauffenbergstr. 14; Mon.–Fri. 9am–6pm, Sat. and Sun. 9am–1pm; free; bus #29), a well-mounted collection of photos and documents covering the suprisingly wide range of groups opposed to the Third Reich. This is one exhibition rarely highlighted to visitors, and there's little translation of material; but if you have any interest in the war years, it's deeply absorbing.

Potsdamer Strasse leads south into Schöneberg, quickly becoming a broad, untidy strip of Turkish cafés, restaurants, and wholesalers, with the **Turkish Bazaar**, a market place of tacky Taiwanese junk, parked in an old U-Bahn station. A little farther south, the **Kleist Park**, fronted by the **Köningskolonnaden**, a colonnade dating from 1780 (summer 7am–8pm; winter 7am–4pm), gives this stretch a touch of dignity; on a misty morning you might be fooled into thinking you were in Paris. The building behind the park, incidentally, was once the Supreme Court of Justice, where the Nazi courts under the infamous Judge Freisler held show trials of their political opponents.

It's worth detouring off Potsdamer Strasse west to **Nollendorf Platz** for a couple of offbeat attractions. On the western side the **flea market** (Weds.–Mon. 11am–7pm) is one of the best in the city; housed in a group of old carriages on a disused U-Bahn station, it sells more antiques than junk, though most of the stuff here is reasonably priced. There's a bar here too, which often has live jazz and adds to the sense of fun. Crossing back onto Nollendorfplatz, past the proto-deco **Metropol disco** (for details, see p.665), Massenstrasse leads on to Nollendorfstrasse, where at no. 17 stands the building in which **Christopher Isherwood** lived during his years in prewar Berlin, a time that was to be elegantly recounted in perhaps the most famous collection of stories about the city ever written— *Goodbye to Berlin*:

> *From my window, the deep solemn massive street. Cellar shops where lamps burn all day, under the shadow of top-heavy balconied facades, dirty plaster frontages embossed with scroll work and heraldic devices. The whole district is this: street leading into street of houses like shabby monumental safes crammed with the tarnished valuables and second hand furniture of a bankrupt middle class.*

These days, Schöneberg has cleaned up its act to be reborn as a smart, even chic neighborhood; the would-be Isherwoods of the moment hang out in SO 36 or Prenzlauer Berg—on the other side of the Wall. At night, this part of Schöneberg, especially the area around **Winterfeldplatz**, is a good one for eating and especially drinking: tidily bohemian, far less sniffy than Savignyplatz, and much more middle-of-the-road than SO 36.

Schöneberg's most famous attraction actually has the least to see: the **Rathaus Schöneberg** on Martin-Luther-Strasse, next to the last stop on U-Bahn line #4. Built just before World War I, the Rathaus became the seat of the West Berlin Parliament and Senate after the last war, and it was outside here in 1963 that **John F. Kennedy** made his celebrated statement on the Cold War political situation, just a few months after the Cuban missile crisis :

There are many people in the world who really don't understand, or say they don't, what is the great issue between the free world and the Communist world. Let them come to Berlin. There are some who say that Communism is the wave of the future. Let them come to Berlin. And there are some who say in Europe and elsewhere we can work with the Communists. Let them come to Berlin. And there are even a few who say it is true that Communism is an evil system, but it permits us to make economic progress. Lässt sie nach Berlin kommen. Let them come to Berlin . . . All free men, wherever they may live, are citizens of Berlin, and, therefore, as a free man, I take pride in the words "Ich bin ein Berliner."

Rousing stuff. But what the president hadn't realized as he read from his phonetically written text was that he had actually said "I am a small jam-filled doughnut," since *Berliner* is the name given locally to those cakes. So popular has this subtext become that it's possible to buy little plastic doughnuts, bearing the historic words. The day after Kennedy was assassinated, the square in front of the Rathaus was given his name—a move apparently instigated by the city's students, among whom the President was highly popular.

If you've time and interest it's possible to climb the Rathaus tower, and see the replica **Liberty Bell** donated to the city by the USA in 1950, though it's more pleasant, and certainly less strenuous, to take a stroll in the small **Volkspark** that runs west from here.

Charlottenburg—the Schloss and Museums

The district of **Charlottenburg** stretches north and west of the center of town, reaching as far as the forests of the Grunewald. To the west it contains a number of attractions (dealt with under "The Suburbs"), but far and away the most significant target, one that needs a day at least to cover, is the **Schloss Charlottenburg and Museum Complex** on Spandauer Damm. The Schloss is magnificent, and something of a surprise after the unrelieved modernity of the city streets. Commissioned as a country house by the future Queen Sophie Charlotte in 1695 (she also gave her name to the district) the Schloss was expanded throughout the eighteenth and early nineteenth century, the master builder Karl Friedrich Schinkel adding the final touches. Approaching the sandy elaborateness of the Schloss at the main courtyard, you're confronted with Andreas Schlüter's **statue** of Friedrich Wilhelm, the Great Elector, cast as a single piece in 1700. Immediately behind is the entrance to the Schloss (Tues.–Sun. 9am–5pm; DM6, DM3 students, including entrance to all other Schloss buildings; nearest buses #54 or #74). To see this, the central section of the Schloss, you're obliged to go on a conducted tour, in German only, which makes it worth buying the (English) guide book before you start. The tour is a traipse through increasingly sumptuous chambers and bedrooms, filled with gilt and carving. Most eye-catching are the **porcelain room** packed to the ceiling with china, and the **chapel**, including a portrait of Sophie Charlotte as the Virgin ascending to heaven.

It's as well to remember that much of the Schloss is in fact a fake, a reconstruction of the former buildings following wartime damage. This is most apparent in the **Knobelsdorff Wing** to the right of the Schloss entrance as you face it; the upper rooms such as the rococo "Golden Gallery" are too breathlessly perfect, the result of intensive restoration. Better is the adjacent "White Hall," whose destroyed eighteenth-century ceiling painting has been replaced by a witty contemporary paraphrase.

Downstairs, the Knobelsdorff Wing contains the **Galerie der Romantik** (Tues.–Sun. 9am–5pm; free), a collection of nineteenth-century painting from the

the German Romantic masters. Most dramatic are the works of **Caspar David Friedrich**. All of these express a powerful, elemental, and religious approach to landscape, most evident in *Morgen im Riesengebirge* and *Der Watzmann*, where it seems as if some massive, primeval force is about to leap out of the landscape. Typical of the brooding and drama of his Romantic sensibility is the *Cloister among Oak Trees* of 1809, perhaps the most famous of his works. **Karl Friedrich Schinkel** was the architect reponsible for the war memorial in Kreuzberg, and more notably, the neoclassical designs of the Altes Museum and many other buildings today in East Berlin. His paintings are meticulously drawn Gothic fantasies, often with sea settings; *Gothic Church on a Seaside Bluff* is perhaps the most broodily dramatic. Elsewhere in the galleries a superb collection of works by **Watteau** includes two of his greatest paintings, *The Embarcation for Cythera* and *The Shop Sign*—delicate rococo fripperies tinged with sympathy and sadness. Look for the topographical paintings of **Eduard Gaertner**, which show the Berlin of the early nineteenth century—and reveal just how good a restoration job the East Berlin authorities have made of Unter den Linden.

The western wing of the Schloss once adjoined the Orangerie (much depleted after the war) and the **gallery** there now houses major exhibitions. If what's on isn't to your taste, there are few better ways to idle away a morning in Berlin than to explore the **Gardens** (open daily until 9pm in summer) of the Schloss. Laid out in the French style in 1697, they were transformed into an English-style landscaped park in the early nineteenth century; after severe damage in the war, they were mostly restored to their Baroque form. Though it's possible to buy a map in the Schloss, it's easy enough to wander, heading through the garden to the lake and on to the grounds behind, which do indeed have the feel of an English park. Places to head for are the **Schinkel Pavillion**, on the far eastern side of the Schloss (Tues.–Sun. 9am–5pm), built by the architect for Friedrich Wilhelm III, and where he preferred to live away from the excesses of the Schloss. Square and simple, it today houses Schinkel's drawings and plans. On the western side, a long, tree-lined avenue leads to the atmospheric **Mausoleum** (April–Oct. Tues.–Sun. 9am–noon and 1–5pm; DM0.50) where Friedrich Wilhelm III lies buried, his sarcophagus making him seem a good deal younger than his seventy years. Later burials here include Kaiser Wilhelm I, looking every inch a Prussian king.

Though you could spend an idle day wandering the Schloss, just across the way a group of excellent museums beckons. Best of these is the **Ägyptisches Museum** (Schloss Strasse 70; Tues.–Fri. 9am–5pm; free), the result of innumerable German excavations in Egypt from the early part of the century. The museum's pride and joy is the *Bust of Nefertiti* on the first floor, a treasure that has become a symbol for the city as a cultural capital. There's no questioning its beauty—the queen has a perfect bone structure and gracefully sculpted lips—and the history of the piece is equally interesting. Created around 1350 B.C., the bust probably never left the studio in which it was housed, acting as a model for other portraits of the queen. (Its use as a model explains why the left eye was never drawn in.) When the studio was deserted, the bust was left there, to be discovered some 3000 years later in 1912. In the last few days of the war, the bust was "removed" from the Soviet sector of Berlin; the authorities there would still like it back. Elsewhere in the museum, atmospheric lighting focuses attention on the exhibits, which are of a uniformly high standard. Look out for the expressionistic, almost futuristic *Berlin Green Head* of the Ptolomeic period, and the *Kalbasha Monumental Gate*, given to the museum by the Egyptian government in 1973.

Across Schlosstrasse is the **Antikenmuseum** (same times); pretty standard Greek and Roman collections, not excitingly housed and nowhere near as impressive as the Pergamon Museum in East Berlin. Highlights include the Corinthian helmets, jewelry (both on the ground floor), and a collection of Greek vases, considered by those in the know to be the finest in the world. A little down from the Antikenmuseum, the **Bröhan-Museum** (Tues.–Sun. 10am–6pm; DM3, students DM1.50) houses a great collection of art deco and Jugendstil ceramics and furniture, laid out in period rooms dedicated to a particular designer and hung with contemporary paintings. Small, compact, and easily taken in, it forms a likable alternative to the Egyptian Museum or the Schloss collections.

Continuing westward, Charlottenburg breaks out into open country and forest, with the Olympic stadium and tower the main draws (see "The Suburbs").

Dahlem: the Museum Complex

The suburb of Dahlem lies south-west of central Berlin, a neat villagey enclave that feels a world away from the technoflash city center. Mostly residential, it's home to the Free University, the better-off bourgeoisie, and a group of museums that's the most important in the city—and among the best in Europe.

Housed in a large new building, the **Dahlem Museum** can be overpowering if you try and do too much too quickly; preferably make a couple of trips here, taking time out to visit the Botanical Gardens nearby (detailed below). If you are pushed for time, the musts are the Picture Gallery and South Seas Ethnographic Collection. To reach the museums, take U-Bahn line #2 to Dahlem-Dorf and follow the signs; the main block is on Arnimalle, and open from Tuesday to Sunday 9am to 5pm. Admission to all the collections is free.

The Picture Gallery

The **Picture Gallery** is the highlight of the trip to Dahlem. Arranged in chronological order, it covers the early medieval to late eighteenth-century periods, the section of early **Netherlandish Painting** being the most authoritative. This begins in Room 143 with the artist credited with the creation of European realism, **Jan van Eyck**; his beautifully lit *Madonna in the Church* is crammed with architectural detail, the Virgin lifted in the perspective for gentle emphasis. Nearby, his *Portrait of Giovanni Arnolfini* shows a character more famous from the wedding portrait in London's National Gallery. **Petrus Christus** may have been a pupil of van Eyck, and certainly knew his work, as *The Virgin and Child with Saint Barbara and a Carthusian Monk* reveals; in the background are tiny Flemish houses and street scenes, the artist carefully locating the scene in his native Bruges. His *Last Judgement*, on the other hand, is full of medieval nightmares. **Dieric Bouts'** figures tend to be stiff and rather formalized, but his *Christ in the House of Simon the Pharisee* is filled with gesture, expression, and carefully drawn detail—especially in the food and shoes. Much of the next room is given over to the work of **Rogier van der Weyden**, which shows the development of the Eyckian technician to a warmer, much more emotional treatment of religious subjects. Like the St. Columba altarpiece in Munich's Alte Pinakothek, the figures in the *Bladelin Altarpiece* here reveal a delicacy of poise and approachable humanity that was greatly to influence German painting in the fifteenth century. **Aelbert van Outwater** was also a major influence on his contemporaries and followers, although his *Raising of Lazarus* is the only complete work to have survived; it's a daring picture, the richly dressed merchants on the right contrasting strongly with the simplicity of the Holy Family on the left. **Geertgen tot Sint Jans** was Outwater's pupil, though his *Saint John the Baptist* is quite different from his master's painting—the saint sits almost comically impassive against a rich backdrop of intricately constructed landscape. The two other major paintings in this room (146) are both by **Hugo van der Goes**. The *Adoration of the Shepherds* (painted when the artist was in the first throes of madness) has the scene unveiled by two characters representing the prophets and with the shepherds stumbling into the frame. His *Adoration of the Magi* (also known as the *Monforte Altarpiece*) has a superbly drawn realism that marks a new development in Netherlandish art, carrying precision over into a large-scale work with a deftly executed, complex perspective. The small altarpiece *Triptych with the Adoration of the Magi* by **Joos van Cleve** reveals how these themes were absorbed by Goes's successors. Room 148 moves into the sixteenth century and the works of Jan Gossaert, Quentin Massys, and **Pieter Bruegel the Elder** whose *Netherlandish Proverbs* is an amusing, if hard-to-grasp, illustration of over a hundred sixteenth-century proverbs and maxims. As a fascinating contrast to the fifteenth-century Netherlandish works, look out for a rare French panel painting of the same period, **Jehan Fouquet**'s *Etienne Chevalier and Saint Stephen*, which shows the treasurer of France accompanied by his patron saint.

Following the Netherlandish sections are the **German Medieval and Renaissance** rooms, revealing the contrast between German and Netherlandish treatments of religious subjects; almost always, the German treatments are darker and more crudely drawn. Crudest of all is the large *Passion Altar* of 1437, made in the workshop of the great Ulm sculptor, **Hans Multscher**; its exaggerated gestures and facial distortions mark it out as an ancient precursor of Expressionist painting. There's an interesting contrast with *Solomon before the Queen of Sheba*, painted in the same year by **Conrad Witz**, who was far more subtle in his aim of developing German painting away from its hitherto idealized forms. The exquisite *Nativity* by **Schongauer** is the most important surviving panel by the father-figure of the German Renaissance.

Otherwise, the best works here are by **Altdorfer**, one of the first fully realized German landscape painters (in his *Nativity* the figures of Christ and the Holy Family seem less important than the depiction of the ruined stables), and **Dürer**—a marvelous group of portraits. Dürer's eccentric pupil **Baldung** is represented by an impressive group of works, notably an exotic *Adoration of the Magi* triptych. By **Holbein the Younger** are five superbly observed portraits, most celebrated of which is *The Danzig Merchant Georg Gisze*, featuring a still-life background which is a real tour de force of artistic virtuosity. Pick of the many examples of **Cranach** is *The Fountain of Youth*, whose tongue-in-cheek humor is adroitly achieved: old women emerge from the miraculous bath as fresh young girls, whereas the men are rejuvenated merely by association.

To the right of these rooms is the collection of **French and German** painting of the sixteenth, seventeenth, and eighteenth centuries (which includes work by Holbein and Watteau), but to continue in chronological order, carry straight on to the **Italian Renaissance** section. The collection is particularly strong on works from the Florentine Renaissance; **Fra Filippo Lippi**'s *The Adoration in the Forest* is a mystical image of unusual grace and beauty, rightly among one of the most admired of all the paintings of the period. Another much-prized work is the gorgeously colorful *Adoration of the Magi* by the rarely seen **Domenico Veneziano**, which perfectly captures the full regal splendor of the subject. **Correggio**'s wonderfully suggestive *Leda with the Swan* is a good example of the classical preoccupations of the period; its subject so offended an eighteenth-century religious fanatic that he hacked it to pieces. There's work here too by Giotto, Verrocchio, Masaccio, Mantegna, Raphael, and Titian, and most importantly by another Florentine, **Sandro Botticelli**, whose *Virgin and Child with the Two Saint Johns*, *Portrait of a Young Woman* and *Saint Sebastian* are among the highlights of a comprehensive account of works from Renaissance Italy.

On the next floor the museum reveals its second strength in the **Dutch and Flemish** collection. This begins with the large portraits of Van Dyck and the fleshy canvases of Rubens, and continues with a fine group of **Dutch interiors**, hung together and inviting comparison. The work of **Vermeer** is the most easily identifiable—even if his *Woman with a Pearl Necklace* is not one of his greater works. Better is *Man and Woman Drinking Wine*, which uses his usual technique of placing furniture obliquely in the center of the canvas, the scene lit by window light. **De Hooch** used a similar technique in *Woman Weighing Gold*, though more complex, both compositionally and morally, is his *The Mother*, a masterly example of Dutch interior painting at its finest.

The subsequent rooms trace the development of Dutch art through the works of Maes, Terborch, Dou, Jan Steen and Frans Hals, and, in perhaps the largest collection anywhere in the world, the paintings of **Rembrandt**. Recently, his most famous picture here, *The Man in the Golden Helmet*, has been proved not to be his work but that of his studio, though this does little to detract from the elegance and power of the portrait, its reflective sorrow relieved by the bright helmet. Other verified works include a *Self-Portrait* of 1634, at the height of the artist's wealth and fame; a *Portrait of Saskia*, Rembrandt's wife, painted in the year of her death; a beautifully warm and loving *Portrait of Hendrickje Stoffels*, the artist's later, common-law wife; and numerous other religious works.

Continuing through the painting galleries, there's work by Goya, Caravaggio (*Cupid Victorious*, heavy with symbolism and homoeroticism), Poussin, and Claude, and concluding with a clutch of Canalettos.

Other Collections and Sights

If you've just spent the morning wandering the picture gallery, this could be the moment to adjourn to the museum's basement **café**. Alternatively, the **Sculpture Court** adjoining the Picture Gallery on the upper floor forms a good complement to the paintings: it's more specifically German and best in its sections detailing the Middle Ages—everything from simple religious artifacts to complex polychrome carvings, including work by Tilman Riemenschneider and Hans Multscher. Also included is an excellent Byzantine and early Christian section, plus works from the Italian Renaissance, notably by Donatello.

The **Ethnographic Sections** of the Dahlem Museum are worth a visit in their own right: rich and comprehensive collections from Asia, the Pacific and South Seas, imaginatively and strikingly laid out. In particular, look out for the group of sailing boats from the South Seas, dramatically lit and eminently touchable. Other collections within the museum include Islamic, Asian, East Asian, and Indian art, to dip into according to your tastes.

At Im Winkel 6, a short, signposted walk from the main complex, is the **Museum of German Ethnology** (*Museum für Deutsche Volkskunde*; Tues.–Sun. 9am–5pm; free) a rather dull collection of furniture, tools, and costumes from the sixteenth century onwards. In the other direction (turn left out of the U-Bahn and continue to Königin-Luise-Strasse) is the **St. Annenkirche**, a pretty little brick-built church that dates back to 1220. If it's open (officially Mon., Sat., and Weds., 2–5pm, but seemingly random hours), pop in for a glimpse of the Baroque pulpit and gallery and carved wooden altar. Alternatively, as an escape from cultural overload, catch a #1 or #68 bus north-east to the **Botanical Gardens** (Königin-Luise-Str. 6–8; daily 9am–sunset; DM2.50, students DM1.20), where you'll find palatial, sticky hothouses sprouting every plant you've ever wondered about, some enticingly laid-out gardens, and an uninspiring **Botanical Museum** (Tues. and Thurs.–Sun. 10am–5pm, Weds. 10am–7pm; free).

The Suburbs

While there's more than enough to detain you in Berlin's center, the western **suburbs** hold a disparate group of attractions of considerable historical interest; and once you're out of the urban claustrophobia, the verdant countryside and lakes come as a surprise, a reminder of Berlin's position in *Mittel-Europa*—and of the fact that one-third of the city is greenery and parkland. Thanks to the efficient U- and S-Bahn system it's possible to reach the farthest limits of West Berlin in under three-quarters of an hour, making the contrast between inner city excitement and rural relaxation all the stronger.

The Plötzensee Memorial

Berlin sometimes has the feel of a city that has tried, unsuccessfully, to sweep its past under the carpet of the present. When concrete reminders of the Third Reich can be seen, their presence in the occupied, postwar city becomes all the more powerful. Nowhere is this more true than in the buildings where the Nazi powers brought dissidents and political opponents for imprisonment and execution—the **Plötzensee Prison**.

Plötzensee stands in the northwest of the city, on the border between the boroughs of Charlottenburg and Wedding. To get there, take the #23 bus from Zoo Station to the beginning of Saatwinkler Damm and walk away from the canal along the wall-sided path of Hüttigpfad.

The former prison buildings are now refurbished as a juvenile detention center, and the memorial consists of the buildings where the executions took place. Over 2500 people were hanged or guillotined here between 1933 and 1945, usually those sentenced in the Supreme Court of Justice in the city. Following the July bomb plot (see "Schöneberg"), 89 of the 200 people condemned were executed here in the space of a few days; Hitler ordered the hangings to be carried out with piano wire, to prolong the agony, and spent evenings watching movie footage of the executions. Many of those murdered were only vaguely connected to the conspirators; several died simply because they were relatives. Today the execution chamber has been restored to its wartime condition; on occasion victims were hanged eight at a time, and the hanging beam, complete with hooks, still stands. Though decked with wreaths and flowers, the atmosphere in the chamber is chilling, and as a further reminder of Nazi atrocities an urn in the courtyard contains soil from each of the concentration camps. Perhaps more than at any other wartime site in Berlin, it is at Plötzensee that the horror of senseless, brutal murder is most clearly felt. (The memorial is open March–Sept. 8am–8pm, Oct. 8:30am–5:30pm, Nov. 8:30am–4:30pm, Dec. 8:30am–4pm, Jan. 8:30am–4:30pm, Feb. 8:30am–5:30pm.)

Points Westward: the Funkturm, Olympic Stadium, and Beyond

Reaching the **Funkturm**, the skeletal radio and televsion transmission mast that lies to the west of Charlottenburg, is an easy matter of catching U-Bahn line #1 to Kaiserdamm, or bus #66, #92, or #94 from Zoo Station. Since being built in 1928 it's been popular with Berliners for the toe-curling views from its 138-meter-high observation platform (daily 10am–11pm; DM4, students DM2). With the aluminium-clad monolith of the **International Congress Center** immediately below, it's possible to look out across deserted, overgrown S-Bahn tracks to the gleaming city in the distance—a sight equally mesmerizing at night.

You may have to line up to catch the elevator up to the observation platform; the **Museum of Radio and Broadcasting** (Tues.–Sat. 10am–6pm, Sun. 10am–4pm; free), housed in a former studio to one side of the tower, is much less popular. An assembly of old wirelesses and Rube Goldberg radio equipment, some of the shiny Bakelite contraptions are rather wonderful; the sort of thing your grandmother keeps on her sideboard. Tracing the development of radios, record players, and televisions from the beginning of broadcasting in Germany in 1923 until World War II, it's as much a history of design as technology, made all the better by a scattering of period rooms and a mock-up of the first-ever German radio studio.

To reach the **Olympic Stadium** from here, jump back on the #1 U-Bahn and travel the three stops westward to the station of the same name, whence it's a fifteen-minute signposted walk to the stadium itself (8am–sunset; DM2). Built for the 1936 Olympic Games, the stadium is one of the few Fascist buildings left in the city, and still very much in use. Whatever your feelings about it, it's still impressive, the huge neoclassical space a deliberate rejection of the Modernist architecture then prevalent elsewhere. Hitler used the international attention the games attracted to show the "New Order" in Germany in the best possible light. Anti-Semitic propaganda and posters were supressed, German half-Jewish competitors were allowed to compete, and when (for the first time) the Olympic flame was relayed from Athens, the newsreels and the world saw the road lined with thousands wearing swastikas and waving Nazi flags. To the outside world, it seemed that the new Germany was rich, content, and firmly behind the Führer.

Though the games themselves were stage-managed with considerable brilliance (a fact recorded in Leni Riefenstahl's poetic and frighteningly beautiful film of the events, *Olympia*), not everything went according to the National Socialist ideology. Black American athletes did supremely well in the games, **Jesse Owens** alone winning four gold medals, disproving the Nazi theory that blacks were "subhuman" and the Aryan race all-powerful. But eventually Germany won the most gold, silver, and bronze (there's a memorial at the western end of the Stadium), and the games were judged a great success.

The area in which the stadium stands is under the control of the British, and the fields around are used for drilling teenage recruits into shape. This means that much of the stadium's environs are out of bounds, and probably explains its survival—the British being less prone to demolish interesting structures than the other Allies. If you cut south and west around the Stadium, down the road named after Jesse Owens, and take a right onto Passenheimer Strasse, you reach the **Glockenturm** or bell tower (April–Oct. daily 10am–5:30pm; DM2.50). Rebuilt after wartime damage, it's chiefly interesting for the stupendous **view** it gives, not only over the stadium but also across the beginnings of the Grunewald to the south. Central here is **Teufelsberg** (*Devil's mountain*), a massive mound that's topped with a faintly terrifying fairy-tale castle that is a U.S. signals and radar base. The mountain itself is artificial; at the end of the war Berlin was reduced to a mass of rubble, which was carted to several sites around the city. Beneath the poplars, maples, and ski-runs lies the old Berlin, about 25 million cubic meters of it, presumably awaiting the attention of some future archaeologist. To the north, a natural amphitheater forms the **Waldbühne**, an open-air concert venue (see "Music and Nightlife").

Spandau

The name **Spandau** immediately brings to mind the name of its jail's most famous—indeed in later years only—prisoner, **Rudolf Hess**. Hess, for a time the deputy leader of the Nazi party, flew to Scotland in 1941 in an attempt to sue for peace with King George VI and ally Great Britain with Germany against the Soviet Union. This, at least, is the official version, though the whole Hess story has a hollow ring to it. There seems no sane reason why Hess, arrested immediately and held until the Nürnberg trials, should have attempted his flight; and in recent years, evidence has come to light that the man held in the jail until his suicide in 1987 was not actually Hess (the doctor who examined the corpse could find no trace of serious wounds Hess had suffered in World War I). Perhaps in the next few years the truth will be uncovered . . . .

However there's little connection between Hess and Spandau itself. The jail, 4km away on Wilhelmstrasse, has subsequently been demolished, and the reason to come here today is to escape the city center, wander Spandau's village-like streets, and to visit the **Citadel** (Tues.–Fri. 9am–5pm, Sat. and Sun. 10am–5pm; DM1.50, students DM0.50), a fort established in the twelfth century to defend the town. Surprisingly pretty from the outside, with its moat and russet walls built during the Renaissance by an Italian architect, it is explorable, if not totally engrossing. There's a small museum, a pricey *burgerlich* restaurant, and the **Juliusturm**, from which there's a good view over the ramshackle citadel interior and the surrounding countryside. Other than this, Spandau town (a ten-minute walk from here) is of minor interest, best around its church (where there's a good *Konditorei*), in the playful sculptures of its modern marketplace, and in the recently restored street called Kolk (turn right off Am Juiliusturm opposite Breite Strasse). Quickest way of getting here is to take U-Bahn line #7 to the Zitadelle station—or to Altstadt Spandau and doubling back to the Citadel.

Woodlands and Lakes: the Grunewald, Havel, and Wannsee

Few people associate Berlin with walks through dense woodland and swimming from crowded beaches, though that's just what the **Grunewald** forests and beaches on the **Havel** lakes have to offer. The Grunewald is 32 square kilometers of mixed woodland that lies between the suburbs of Dahlem and Wilmersdorf and the lakes to the east; it's popular with Berliners for its refreshing air and walks. Seventy percent of the Grunewald was cut down in the postwar years for badly-needed fuel, and subsequent replanting has replaced the original pine and birch with oak and ash, making it all the more popular. One possible starting point is the **Jagdschloss Grunewald** (Tues. and Sun. April–Sept. 10am–6pm, March and Oct. 10am–5pm, Nov.–Feb. 10am–4pm; DM2.50, students DM1.50), a royal hunting lodge built in the sixteenth century and enlarged by Friedrichs I and II. Today it's a museum, housing old furniture and Dutch and German painting, including works by Cranach the Elder and Rubens. It's refreshing to walk by the nearby lake, the Grunewaldsee, and concerts are held here on summer evenings (usually starting at 6pm; see *Zitty* magazine for details). To reach the Jagdschloss, take bus #60 from Tauentzienstrasse in the center to the stop at Pücklerstrasse (where you'll find the Brücke Museum—see "Berlin's Other Museums," below), and head down that street into the forest.

An alternative approach to the Grunewald, with the added attraction of beginning at a strip of beaches, is to take the #1 or #3 S-Bahn to Wannsee station and to catch one of the frequent buses to **Strandbad Wannsee**, a kilometer-long strip of pale sand that's packed as soon as the sun comes out. From here it's easy to wander into the forests, or, more adventurously, catch one of several **ferries** that leave a little way from the S-Bahn station (ask there for directions). It's possible to sail to Spandau (DM6), to Kladow, across the lake (DM2.50) or to the **Pfaueninsel** (*Peacock Island*; daily April and Sept. 8am–6pm, May–Aug. 8am–8pm, March and Oct. 9am–5pm, Nov.–Feb. 10am–4pm; ferry DM2), whose attractions include a mini-Schloss, built as a folly by Friedrich Wilhelm II for his mistress, and today containing a small **museum** (Tues.–Sun. April–Sept. 10am–5pm, Oct. 10am–4pm). Most enjoyable though are the gardens, landscaped by Peter Lenneé, the original designer of the Tiergarten. No cars are allowed on the island, which has been designated a conservation zone.

Berlin's Other Museums

It's quite possible you'll be surfeited on Culture after working your way around the Charlottenburg, Tiergarten, and Dahlem museum complexes, the city's big three. But scattered around town are some excellent and offbeat collections, most of which repay a visit.

Bauhaus Archive, *Klingelhöferstr. 13–14. Bus #29 to Lützowplatz. Weds.–Mon. 11am–5pm; DM3, students DM1.*
The Bauhaus school of design, crafts and architecture was founded in 1919 in Weimar by Walter Gropius. It moved to Dessau in 1925 and then to Berlin, to be closed by the Nazis in 1933. The influence of Bauhaus has been tremendous, and you get some idea of this in the small collection here. Marcel Breuer's seminal **chair** is still (with minor variations) in production today, and former Bauhaus director Mies van der Rohe's designs and models for buildings show how Bauhaus style has changed the face of modern cities. There's work too by Kandinsky, Moholy-Nagy, Schlemmer, and Klee, each of whom worked at the Bauhaus. The building, incidentally, was designed by Gropius himself.

Berlin Museum, *Lindenstr. 14. Buses #41, #29 and #24. Tues.–Sun. 11am–6pm; DM3.50.*
This attempts to show the history and development of the city through paintings, prints, and crafts. The earlier sections are reasonably successful but best are the exhibits from this century, particularly the collections of wartime posters and kids' toys, and Klaus Richter's portraits of Hitler and Göring. One unmissable attraction is the **Kaiserpanorama**, a large stereoscope from the last century designed to allow several viewers to see its rotating slides simultaneously. Usually it's loaded with pictures of prewar Berlin, giving a vivid portrait of the lost city.

Until a permanent venue can be found, the museum also holds part of the **Jewish Museum**, a small but moving collection of Judaica chronicling the history and tragedy of Berlin's Jewish community. The remainder of the collection is in the Martin-Gropius-Bau (see below). More whimsically (and the reason most people come here), there's a mock-up of an old Berlin bar, the *Alt-Berliner Weissbierstube* (closes at 4pm at weekends, often crowded) which serves a traditional Berlin buffet (very heavy on pork).

Brücke Museum, *Bussardsteig 9. Bus #68. Weds.–Mon. 11am–5pm; DM3.50, students DM1.50.*
A collection of works by the group known as *de Brücke* (The Bridge) who worked in Dresden and Berlin from 1905 to 1913. The big names are **Kirchner**, **Heckel**, and **Schmidt-Rottluff**, who painted Expressionist cityscapes and had considerable influence over later artists.

Hamburger Bahnhof, *Invalidenstr. 50/51. S-Bahn line #3 to Lehrter Stadtbahnhof or bus #83. Opening times and prices vary.*
Like the Anhalter Bahnhof to the south, the Hamburger station was damaged in the war, though it had ceased working as a station as early as 1906. Fortunately it didn't suffer its twin's fate in postwar redevelopment, and is today an important forum for changing art exhibitions, usually contemporary in feel. It's an exciting and innovative venue, with a good café and bookshop.

Käthe Kollwitz Museum, *Fassanstr. 24 (off Ku'damm). Weds.–Mon. 11am–6pm; DM6, students DM3.*
The drawings and prints of **Käthe Kollwitz** are among the most moving to be found in the first half of this century. Born in 1867, she lived for almost all her life in Prenzlauer Berg in Berlin, where her work evolved a radical left-wing perspective. Following the death of her son in World War I, her woodcuts and prints became explicitly pacifist, often dwelling on the theme of mother and child. When her grandson was killed in World War II her work became even sadder and more poignant. The museum's comprehensive collection of her work makes it possible to trace its development, culminating in the tense, tragic sculptures of the top floor.

Martin-Gropius-Bau, *Stresemann Str. 110. Buses #24 and 29. Tues.–Sun. 10am–6pm; main collections free, times and prices for temporary exhibitions vary.*
Designed in 1877 by Martin Gropius, the uncle of Bauhaus guru Walter and a pupil of Schinkel, the Gropius-Bau was, until its destruction in the war, home of the museum of applied art. In recent years it has been rebuilt, and is now the city's main venue for large, prestigious exhibitions. Also contained in the building are the main sections of the **Jewish Museum**, with a frightening section on the war years, and large collections of German **applied and fine art**. If you do visit, the adjacent "The Topography of Terrors' is one of the city's essential exhibitions (see "The Wall: from the Reichstag to Checkpoint Charlie," above).

Drinking and Eating

Nowhere is more than a stone's throw from a **bar** in Berlin. Just about every street corner has a small *Kneipe*, ranging from lugubrious beer-swilling holes to slick upscale hangouts for the city's night people. You'll find that most places—especially those found in the clusters of drinking spots grouped below—stay open later than anywhere in West Germany; it's quite feasible to drink around the clock here, the result of a law that requires bars only to close for an hour a day for cleaning. Berlin specialties include *Berliner Weisse*, a watery top-fermented beer that's traditionally pepped up by adding a shot of fruity syrup or *Schuss*. Ask for it *mit grün* and you get a dash of woodruff, creating a greenish brew that tastes like liquid silage; *mit rot* is a raspberry-flavored kiddie drink that works wonders at breakfast time.

The city's compressed, cosmopolitan nature means that the range of **restaurants** is wider than in any other German city; indeed the national cuisine takes a back seat to Greek, Turkish, Balkan, Indian, and Italian food, and plenty of places exist where a meal costs under DM15. Almost all the better bars serve food too, and this can be good value—though beware the chic-est places, where that interesting-looking item on the menu turns out to be a plate of asparagus tips for DM25. For cheap, on-your-feet **snacks**, hit an *Imbiss* kiosk—a few marks for a *Wurst* or burger.

Drinking

Though it's fun enough just to dive into any bar that takes your fancy, Berlin has three focal points for drinking, each with enough bars to tackle through the course of an evening, and each with a subtly differing character. Those **around Savignyplatz** are the haunt of the city's conspicuous good-timers; the area **around Nollendorfplatz and Winterfeldtplatz** is the territory of blitzed all-nighters and the pushing-forty crew. **Kreuzberg** drinkers include political activists, punks, and the Turkish community, in a mix that forms this area's appeal. Unless you're into brawling soldiers and sloshed businessmen, avoid the Ku'damm and the rip-off joints around the Europa Center.

Savignyplatz and Around

Airport Lounge, Schlüterstr. 72. What in America would be called a "theme bar," this is decked out with old aircraft seats, plastic planes, and international tack. A bit like JFK International on acid, and great fun.

Café Bleibtreu, Bleibtreustr. 45. One of Savignyplatz's more disreputable cafés. Pleasantly down-at-heel, and cheap.

Café Savigny, Grolmannstr. 53. Bright, sharp café on the edge of Savignyplatz catering to an arty/media crowd. Mildly gay.

Dicke Wirtin, Carmerstr. 9. Noisy, boozy, and popular place, more for the 1970s rock crew than anyone else. Excellent bowls of filling stew for DM3.50 are the main attraction.

Dralles, Schlüterstr. 59. At least twice as expensive as most other bars, *Dralles* is *the* place to see and be seen: the 1950s decor is chic and understated, the clientele aspire likewise. Go beautiful and loaded, or not at all . . .

Filmbühne, corner of Hardenbergstrasse and Steinplatz. One of the least pretentious and more original cafés in Berlin, with friendly service to boot.

Grolman's, Grolmanstr. 21. Swish bar/restaurant with slick sitting area and a 30-ish business crowd with a scattering of monied punks. Food at DM15–30.

Hegel, Savignyplatz 2. Tiny café on the southeastern side of Savignyplatz that attracts an older crowd. Can be gregarious fun when someone starts up on the piano.

Mimikry, Kantstr. 29. Ultra-hip hangout—though it's hard to figure out why.

Paris Bar, Kantstr. 152. Once the local of the city's actors and film crowd, the *Paris* today seems to live on a long-dead reputation. Middle-aged, sedate, and very expensive.

Schwarzes Café, Kantstr. 148. Open 24 hours, closes 8pm Mon. and Tues. Kantstrasse's best hangout for the young and chic, with a relaxed atmosphere, good music , and food (including breakfast day and night). One to dust off your leathers for . . .

Shell, Knesebeckstr. 52. The archetypal Berlin posing parlor, the air thick with the sipping of Perrier and the rustle of carefully organized datebooks. Slick, starchy, and self-consciously superior.

Zillemarkt, Bleibtreustr. 48. Wonderful, if tatty, old-fashioned bar. Unpretentious and fun, and a good place to start Savignyplatz explorations—it's by the S-bahn. Serves breakfast until 6pm.

Zwiebelfisch, Savignyplatz 7. Corner bar for would-be arty/intellectual types. Lots of jazz and earnest debate. Good cheap grub.

Around Nollendorfplatz and Winterfeldtplatz

Café am Arsenal, Fuggerstr. 35. New Italian-style coffee house furnishings, usefully near the *Arsenal* movie theater (which often shows films in English).

Café Einstein, Kurfürstenstr. 58. Housed in a seemingly ancient mansion, this is about as close as you'll get to the ambience of the prewar Berlin *Kaffeehaus*, with international newpapers and breakfast served until 2pm. Literary readings and other activities, and a good garden. Expensive and a little snooty.

Café M, Goltzstr. 34. Littered with modern art and video monitors, *M* is Berlin's most favored rendezvous for creative types and the conventionally unconventional. The cool thing to drink is Flensburger Pils, from the bottle. Usually packed, even for its famous breakfasts.

Café Sidney, corner of Maasenstrasse and Winterfeldtstrasse. Big and brash modern meeting place, especially for breakfast on Saturday mornings. Good snacks.

Café Swing, Corner of Kleistrasse and Motzstrasse. Plasticy modern café which is a little way from *Metropol*. Convivial new-wave atmosphere, and featuring live music, especially on Monday.

Café Winterfeldt, Winterfeldtstr. 37. Sparsely decorated with a narrow drinking area, but a relaxing alternative to other places around this area—when it's not full.

Metropol, Nollendorfplatz 5. Warehouse-sized art deco dance hall (for which see "Music and Nightlife" below), with a downstairs bar fine for vegging out in front of the enormous TV screen. Popular with all-nighters and transvestites.

Sexton, Winterfeldtstr. 35. Dimlylit hell-hole of hard rock and denims. Low on the trendiness scale, but always full.

Slumberland, Goltzstr. 24. The gimmicks here are sand on the floor and a tropical theme. Laid back, likable, and one of the better bars of this area.

Kreuzberg

The lifespan of bars and cafés in Kreuzberg is notoriously unreliable, with places opening and closing almost weekly. Use these listings as a base for your explorations, but don't be suprised if characters have changed, or addresses disappeared.

Café am Ufer, Paul-Linke-Ufer 43. Good views of the Landwehrkanal if you sit outside and of the frequent fights if you stay inside. Nevertheless a fun place, and with all-you-can-eat breakfasts for DM10 at weekends.

Café Anfall, Gneisenaustr. 64. Sharp, punk-filled bar that looks as if it were thrown together from local junkshops. Music at maximum distortion level.

Cazzo, Orianienstr. 187. Trendy *Szene* bar, and a good place to sample the austere cosiness of contemporary Kreuzberg. Gay-ish.

Golgatha, Viktoriapark. Enormous open-air café perched near the top of Kreuzberg's hill. Enormously popular with everybody.

Homo-Bar (aka *Oranienbar*), Oranienstr. 168. Famed Kreuzberg watering hole, which despite a recent name change is by no means solely a gay bar. The interior is half-plastered (as are most of the clientele), giving it a sort of post-nuclear chic. At the time of writing, its future looked uncertain.

Max und Moritz, Oranienstr. 162. Old fashioned bar-restaurant that's a world away from the *Szene* places down the street.

Pinox, Oranienstr. 45. Typical Kreuzberg drinking spot, popular with locals and open late.

Tango Baerwaldstr. 52. Likable bar-restaurant in a scruffy street. Homely and welcoming with good, straightforward food at around DM10.

Wunderbar, Körtestr. 38. New, large, and lively bar with pool room and youthful, varied customers. Essential for the first drink of the evening when arriving at Südstern U-Bahn, just across the street.

Zum Alten, Dresdener Str. 17. Once a haunt of Kreuzberg's smackheads, now much cleaned up but still fairly stoned. The spirit of 1976 lives on . . .

Elsewhere

Blisse 14, Blissestr. 14. Café-bar designed especially, but not exclusively, for disabled people. A good meeting place.

Café Hardenberg, Hardenbergstr. 10. Old fashioned café with excellent and cheap food. Recommended.

Café New York, Olivaer Platz 15. Clean-cut, pop-loving teenagers' hang-out.

Café Voltaire, Stuttgarter Platz 14. Modern bar-restaurant whose chief claim to fame is the fact that it never closes. Reasonably priced food, good value breakfasts.

DA DA DA, Kurfürstendamm 73. Bright 'n' brash 'n' loud with constant videos blaring over the pool tables and a clientele that's a mix of Berlin wide-boys, local pool sharks and ocupation recruits. Open 11pm–8am.

Kastanie, Schlosstr. 22. Amiable bar near Schloss Charlottenburg that's best on summer evenings for its small beer garden.

Kronenbourg Café, Pfalzburgerstr. 11. Friendly, classy café in Schöneburg serving German nouvelle cuisine at the usual inflated prices.

Loretta im Garten, Lietzenburger Str. 89. Though it's slanted mainly toward tourists, this large beer garden can be fun if you're in the mood.

Luise, Königin-Luise-Str. 40. A smaller and more convivial beer garden, just a stone's throw from the Dahlem museums.

Saftladen 2, Wegenerstr. 1. When the booze gets too much for you this could be the place: it specializes in alcohol-free drinks, some of which are quite inventive.

Wintergarten, Fasanenstr. 23. Part of the *Literaturhaus*, an institution devoted to poetry readings and other bookish events, this has a beautifully renovated interior and a small garden that's a welcome break from nearby Ku'damm. Moderate prices.

Gay Men's Bars

The most concentrated area of gay men's bars is between Wittenbergplatz and Nollendorfplatz, south of Kleiststrasse. For the full picture on the Berlin gay scene, pick up a copy of Berlin von Hinten *(DM13), the city's most useful gay guide.*

Anderes Ufer, Hauptstr. 157. Quiet Schöneberg café-bar favored by students and "alternative" types. Serves breakfasts.

Andreas' Kneipe, Ansbacher Str. 29. A good place to begin wanderings in the Wittenbergplatz area.

Blue Boy Bar, Eisenacher Str. 3. Small, convivial, and relaxed bar, far less raucous than many that surround it.

Fingerhut, Damaschkestr. 12. Popular with media types, and a little upscale.

Flip-Flop, Kulmerstr. 20. Imaginatively decorated bar-cocktail lounge that attracts a diverse clientele.

Kleine Philharmonie, Schaperstr. 14. Shoebox-sized place packed with antiques. Unavoidably intimate.

Tom's Bar, Motzstr. 19. Dark, sweaty, and wicked cruising bar with a large back room.

Women's Bars

Begine, Potsdamer Str. 139. Stylishly decorated café-bar and cultural center for women only. Highly recommended.

Dinelo, Vorbergstr. 10. Plush women-only bar, traditional and comfortable. Open from 6pm.

Paramount, Hauptstr. 120. Small, recently renovated feminist bar for women only. 7pm–3am daily.

Swingtime, Furbringerstr. 29. Lesbian bar with live music.

Eating

You can spend as much or as little as you like on **food** in Berlin; it's the one item that won't break the bank. The following listings detail budget options and sit-down restaurants, and the prices quoted are for main courses, exclusive of starters, drink, or tips. Don't forget that many of the **bars** listed above can be excellent (and inexpensive) choices for food, especially breakfast.

Snacks

Cheapest way of warding off hunger pangs is to use the small **Imbiss** snack stands found on many street corners, where for a few marks you can fill up on *Currywurst* and french fries. Many butchers' shops sell meaty snacks at low prices, and around Zoo Station are any number of cut-rate burger bars and pizzerias.

For something a bit more substantial but not that much more expensive, try any one of four sit-down **Imbiss restaurants**, which charge between DM5 and DM12 a meal, or, at lunch time, either of the city's **mensas**, offically for German students only but usually open to any one who fits that description, and always for those with ISIC cards.

Ashoka-Imbiss, Grolmanstr. 51 (off Savignyplatz). Daily 11am–midnight. About the best of the bunch, dishing up good portions of tremendous value Indian food. Vegetarian options.

Fuji-Imbiss, Goethestr. 6 (near Knesbeckstrasse). Mon.–Sat. noon–11pm. Japanese snacks and light meals.

Guru, Ku'damm 156. Tues.–Sun. noon–3am. Indian fast-food place with snacks and meals.

Mensa of the Free University, Habelschwerdter Allee, at the junction with Thiel Allee (nearest U-Bahn #2 to Dahlem-Dorf). Mon.–Fri. noon–2pm. Only worth considering if you're spending the day at the Dahlem museums. Around DM3, ISIC advisable.

Rani Indischer Imbiss, Goltzstr. 34. Noon–midnight. Another budget-priced Indian, ideal for cheap eats when exploring the bars of Winterfeldtplatz.

TU Mensa, Hardenbergstr. 34. Mon.–Fri. 11:15–2:30. Meals around DM4, buy your meal ticket before getting your food.

Restaurants

French, Italian, Spanish, and Greek

Akropolis, Wielandstr. 28. Taped Greek communist songs accompany the moussaka in a tranquil locale. More expensive than the average Greek place: DM12–20.

Café Einstein, Kurfürstenstr. 58. Elegant literary café (see "Drinking") with pricey French-style food served in a lovely tree-filled garden.

Chapeau Klack, Pfalzburgerstr. 55. Discreet and elegant French restaurant. Upmarket menu with prices to match. DM20 and up.

Cour Carrée, Savignyplatz 5. Deservedly popular French restaurant with fin-de-siècle decor and garden seating. DM15–DM25.

Dionysos, Schöneberger Ufer 47. Slightly more expensive than most Greek restaurants, but miles better value than any of the cafés in the surrounding Tiergarten museums. DM8–20.

La Cascina, Delbnickstr. 28. Quality Italian restaurant beloved of Berlin's film crowd. Pricey.

Osteria No.1, Kreuzbergstr. 71. Classy Italian restaurant run by a collective. DM10–20.

To Steki, Kantstr. 22. Mountains of inexpensive (DM7–15) Greek food, boisterous live music.

German and Austrian

Ax-Bax, Leibnizstr. 34. Limited menu of Viennese dishes, with yummy cakes and desserts. Favorite stomping ground for arts and film people. DM10–25.

Exil, Paul-Lincke-Ufer 44. Popular with the Kreuzberg arts crowd for its attractive site next to the canal and its moderate-to-expensive Viennese food. Something of a boho meeting place.

Florian, Grolmanstr. 52. Leading light of the new German cuisine movement in Berlin, this is as much a place to be seen in as to eat. The food, similar to French *nouvelle cuisine*, is light, flavorful—and expensive. DM20 and up.

Gusto, Mehringdamm 80. (South of Kreuzbergstrasse). Large corner restaurant with outdoor seating. Mixed menu; German cuisine along with pizzas, steaks, and breakfasts. DM9–25.

Haus Trinitas, Inchenallee 62. Glorious views over the Havel River and fresh fish in a villa far removed from the hustle of downtown. DM20 and up.

Paris Bar, Kantstr. 152. This was once the city's most famous meeting place for artists, writers, and intellectuals. Now high prices (DM30 plus) mean that it's wholly the preserve of the monied middle classes. The food is Viennese in style and the service immaculate.

Weissbierstube, in the Berlin Museum, Lindenstr. 14. Recreation of a traditional German buffet-restaurant, serving local specialties and very heavy on pork. Often packed; closed Monday. Complete meals for under DM15.

Egyptian, Indian, and Southeast Asian

Der Ägypter, Kantstr. 26. Egyptian falafel-type meals. Spicy, filling, and an adventurous alternative to the safe bets around Savignyplatz. Good vegetarian selections. DM10–15.

Ho Lin Wah, Kurfürstendamm 218. The former Chinese embassy transformed into a Chinese restaurant. An oddity.

Kalkutta, Bleibtreustr. 17. First and arguably the finest Indian restaurant in Berlin. DM20 and up.

Tuk-Tuk, Grossgörschenstr. 2. Amiable Indonesian near Kleistpark U-Bahn. Inquire about the heat of your dish before ordering. DM10–20.

Restaurant am Nil, Kaiserdamm 114 (near Sophie-Charlotte-Platz). Moderately priced Egyptian, easy-going service. DM10–30.

Vietnam, Suarezstr. 61. One of the city's most favored Vietnamese restaurants, quietly situated in a street of junk shops. DM10–30.

Mexican and Latin American

La Batea, Krummer Str. 42. Latin American food in a convivial atmosphere with frequent live music. DM7–15.

Patio, Görlitzer Str. 32. Good Mexican cooking in an attractive restaurant incongruously decorated with Italian cartoons. A stone's throw from the wall.

Som Tropical, Kaiser-Friedrich-Str. 40. Small South American restaurant with live music at weekends. DM7–20

Vegetarian and Other

Café Voltaire, Stuttgarterplatz 14. Primarily an all-night bar, but serving hot, inexpensive meals (pasta, quiche) until 5am. DM10 and up.

Jewish Community Center Restaurant, Fasanenstr. 79. Wonderful kosher delights in a good atmosphere.

La Maskera Koburger Str. 5 (just south and east of Rathaus Schöneberg). Among the best vegetarians in town, with an Italian slant adding color to the food and atmosphere. DM8–20

Litfass, Sybelstr. 49. Don't be put off by the bunker-like exterior: great portions of Portugese food, with particularly tasty seafood dishes. DM10–20.

Pik-As, a boat: from Kottbusser Tor U-Bahn, head along Plan-Ufer. Eat as you rock on a floating restaurant, with Kreuzberg's alternative crowd above deck, and their ideological opposites, the corner-*Kneipe*-crowd, below. Varied menu, dancing on Friday and Sunday.

Thurnagel, Gneisenaustr. 57. Small, smart, friendly vegetarian in west Kreuzberg. DM10–20.

Music and Nightlife

Since the time of the Weimar Republic, and even through the lean postwar years, Berlin has had a reputation for having the some of the best—and steamiest—nightlife in Europe, an image fueled by the cartoons of George Grosz and films like *Cabaret*. Today, it's still a city that wakes up when others are going to sleep. **Musically** there's much of appeal here: venues cover the range of tastes, and are rarely expensive. **Clubs and discos** range from slick hangouts for the trendy to dingy, uninviting punk hangouts; as ever, it's the tension the city seems to generate that gives the nightlife its color.

Berlin's reputation as a leader of the avant-garde is reflected in the number of small, often experimental **theater groups** working here. The scene is an active one, though it's worth remembering that many theater companies take a break in July and August. **Classical music** has long been dominated by the world-class Berlin Philharmonic, though other orchestras play in the city, and several museums and historic buildings often host chamber concerts and recitals.

Two of the city's venues are unclassifiable: the *Waldebühne* is a large outdoor amphitheater on the Hollywood Bowl model, just west of the Olympic Stadium. It presents everything from opera to movies to hard rock—unbeatable in summer. The *Tempodrom*, two tents in the Tiergarten, hosts concerts and circuses in the larger tent, cabaret and more intimate performances in the smaller.

Discos and Clubs

Berlin's discos are smaller, cheaper and less exclusive than their counterparts in London or New York. You don't need much savvy to work out that the places along the Ku'damm are tourist rip-offs: the real all-night sweats take place in Kreuzberg, where glitz is out and post-punk cool in. Admission is often free to discos—when you do pay, it shouldn't be much more than DM15. Like most cities, Berlin's turnover in nightspots is rapid; expect the following listings to have changed at least slightly by the time you arrive.

Abraxas, Kantstr. 134. Tues.–Sun. 10pm–5am. Hot and sweaty dance floor, specializing in salsa and Latin American sounds. Entrance fee at weekends.

Basement, Mehringdamm 107. Daily 10pm–6pm. Competitively trendy atmosphere, occasional performance happenings. No entrance fee.

Bronx, Wiener Str. 34. Daily, 10pm onward. Chic and popular hip-hop disco, done out in bomb-damage decor.

Blue Note, Courbierestr. 13. Daily, 10pm–5am. Eclectic mix of rock, Latin, but chiefly jazz sounds. Small dance floor.

Cha-Cha, Nürnberger Str. 50. 11pm onwards, closed Mon. Currently the number one *Szene* spot in the city, ouoting even *Dschungel*, next door.

Dschungel, Nürnberger Str. 53. 11pm–3am, closed Tues. The Berlin nightclub scene how you always imagined it. Mixed crowd of nightpeople, all heavily into style, posing, and dancing to the excellent music. Not cheap, but essential.

Havana Club, Winterfeldtstr. 50. 11pm onwards. Rock 'n' roll bar for youthful and aging rockers. Good sweaty fun.

Kumpelnest 3000, Lützostr. 23. Quirky kitsch decor, noisy friendly atmosphere. Average prices, open all night long.

Lipstick, Richard-Wagner-Platz 5. Biggest and best of the gay nightclubs. Women only Mon., Fri. and Sat.; mixed on Sun., Tues. and Thurs.; closed Weds. Good music.

Madow, Pariser Str. 23. 10pm onwards, Weds.–Sun. Big unpretentious disco, ideal for a no-nonsense boogie in a friendly atmosphere.

Metropol, Nollendorfplatz 5. The city's largest though rather ordinary disco and lightshow in a marvelous art deco building.

Pool, Motzstrasse; adjacent to *Tom's Bar* at no.19. Gay men's disco.

Sox, Oranienstr. 39. 11pm onwards, closed Tues. Punk lives on in this small but lively disco.

Trash, Oranienstr. 40. 11pm onward, closed Mon. Current home of Berlin youth's weirder elements. Black walls, black clothes, and U.V. lights.

Turbine Rosenheim, Eisenacher Str. 40. Daily 11pm–6am. Spartan, rough-and-ready disco-bar for night zombies.

Wu-Wu, Kleiststr. 6. Gay mens' disco, popular at weekends.

Live Music Venues

As ever, the way to find out exactly what's on and where is in the listings magazines or on the innumerable fly posters about town.

Contemporary

Blockshock, Körtestr. 15. In the heart of the Kreuzberg underground movement, though
thanks to action by its complaining neighbors, no longer as lively as it was.

Café Swing, corner of Motzstrasse and Kleiststrasse, off Nollendorfplatz. A tiny venue, but
one offering free concerts on Monday and Thursday at around midnight or 1am. Anything is
possible, from avant-garde performance art to straight rock and roll.

Ecstasy, Hauptstr. 30. Hardcore underground bands from Germany and around the world.
Wild, manic, and fun.

K.O.B., Potsdamer Str. 157. A pub in a (now legally) squatted house which on weekdays
hosts interesting groups at low prices (DM5). R&B, jazz, and psychedelia sounds play here,
but the favorites are local anarcho- and fun-punk bands.

The Loft, part of the *Metropol*, Nollendorfplatz 5. Features a whole range of independent
artists, with a view to innovation and introducing new music. Also organizes larger concerts
in the *Metropol* itself.

Quartier Latin, Potsdamer Str. 96. Seated club-venue that often hosts middle-league touring
bands. Consistently good and varying selections of contemporary groups.

Jazz, Folk and Blues

Badenscher Hof, Badensche Str. 29. (open from 6pm, 8pm on Sat.). Lively café-restaurant that
draws in the Schöneberg crowd for its frequent jazz concerts, the best of which are at
weekends.

Blues Café, Körnerstr. 11. Hidden away in a small street off Potsdamer Strasse, this low-
profile café is the place to head for if you like your blues pure and original.

Flöz, Nassauische Str. 37. Basement venue that's the meeting point for Berlin's jazz musicians, and a testing ground for the city's new bands. Also offers occasional salsa and cabaret.

Go-In, Bleibtreustr. 17. The place for folk music, with musicians from the Philippines to the
Pyrenees, from India to Scotland. But despite the cosmopolitan acts, the *Go-In* still doesn't
seem to have discovered the full potential of world music.

The Irish Inn, Damaschkestr. 28. Sing-along Irish folk music, washed down with plenty of
booze.

Jazz for Fun, Kurfürstenstr. 10. A place to bring your own instrument and join in the jam
session. Informal and free.

Quasimodo, Kantstr. 12a. Berlin's best jazz venue, with daily programs starting at 10pm. A
high quality mix of international stars and up-and-coming names.

Classical

For years classical music in Berlin meant one man and one orchestra: Herbert
von Karajan and the Berlin Philharmonic. Since his resignation in 1989 the
orchestra has retained its popularity, and tickets for their near-acoustically
perfect home, the *Philharmonie*, are still extremely difficult to get. Try calling in
at the box office (Mon.–Fri. 3:30pm–6pm, Sat.–Sun. 11am–2pm; ☎254880) as far
in advance as possible.

Thankfully, the *Philharmonie* is by no means the only option. As well as opera
and ballet, the *Deutsche Oper*, Bismarckstr. 34 (☎341 0249) has good classical
concerts and student standby tickets, which can reduce the price of a seat in the
peanut gallery to as little as DM10. The *Urania*, An der Urania 17 (249091), has a
wide-ranging program and reasonably priced seats.

Theater, Dance, and Cabaret

Berlin's reputation as Germany's *Theaterstadt* still holds firm for the thousands of eager young West Germans who flock to the city every year, rent a space, and stage their work. In recent years, however, many professional people have left the birthplace of experimental theater and returned to Munich and the lure of the film business. Nevertheless, Berlin is still a major venue for experimental work, and if your German is up to it a number of groups are worth the DM3-to-30 ticket price; check in *Tip* or *Zitty* for up-to-the-minute listings. *Theaterkasse Centrum*, Meinekestr. 25 (☎882 7611), is an agency from which to buy tickets.

Venues and Theater Groups

BELT, Stierstr. 5 (offices ☎801 3467). The Berlin English Language Theater group. No permanent home but occasionally plays in cafés and smaller venues. Check *Zitty*, *Tip* or phone for further information.

Berlin Play Actors (offices ☎784 7362). Another English-speaking group playing in various venues about town.

Berliner Figurentheater Yorkstr. 59 (☎786 9815). Experimental puppet theater group dealing with topical issues; constantly innovative. Superbly crafted dolls.

Freie Volksbühne, Schaperstr. 24 (☎881 3742). Not as radical as it once was, but with a reputation for excellent stage designs.

Grips, Altonaerstr. 22 (☎391 4004). First-class children's/young people's theater; usually all improvized.

Rote Grütze, Mehringdamm 51 (offices ☎692 2618). The only children's theater with audience participation. Often touches on sensitive subjects. No fixed abode; phone or check the listings mags for more details.

Schaubühne am Lehniner Platz, Kurfürstendamm 153 (☎890023). State-of-the-art equipped theater, that holds performances of the classics, and some progressive pieces.

Schiller Theater, Bismarckstr. 110 (☎319 5236). The best state-run theater in West Berlin. Three stages and as experimental as can be.

UFA-Fabrik, Victoriastr. 13 (☎752 8085). The most famous, and most efficiently run, cultural factory, with just about every aspect of the performing arts available.

Dance

Deutsche Oper, Bismarckstr. 34 (☎341 0249). Performances of classical ballet and, to a lesser extent, contemporary work, both rather lacking in flair and inspiration.

Phantoms-Mimentheater, Pfalzburgerstr. 72 (☎881 8103). Mime group which brings myths and fables into a contemporary setting.

Tanzfabrik Berlin, Möckernstr. 68 (☎786 5861). Experimental and contemporary works, usually fresh and exciting.

Tanz Tangente, Kuhligkshofstr. 4 (☎792 9124). Highly praised modern dance company that works closely with jazz musicians. Often has visiting international groups.

Cabaret

In the 1920s and 1930s, Berlin had a rich and intense cabaret scene. Hundreds of small venues presented acts that were often deeply satirical and political; when the Nazis came to power these quickly disappeared, to be replaced with anodyne entertainments in line with party views. Sadly the cabaret scene has never recovered; most of what's on view today is either semi-clad titillation for tourists, or that most German of predilections, the drag show. However a couple of places are worth trying: *CaDeWe*, Gneisenaustr. 2A (☎691 5099), and *Die Drie Tornados*, Möckernstr. 79. Your German will need to be pretty good to appreciate the gags.

Listings

Airline offices *Air France*, Europa Center (☎261051); *British Airways*, Europa Center (☎691 1021);*Pan Am*, Europa Center (☎881011); *TWA*, Kurfürstendamm 14 (☎882 4066).

Area Telephone code (☎030)

Bookshops Best selection of Penguins, English paperbacks, and books on the city can be found at *Kiepert*, Hardenbergstr. 4–5.

Car rental Least expensive firms are Allround, Kaiser-Friedrich-Str. 86 (☎342 5092); *First & Second Hand Rent*, Lohmeyerstr. 7 (☎341 7076); and *Mini-bus Service*, Zietenstr. 1 (☎261 1456). International firms have offices at Tegel airport and are listed in the phone book.

Consulates *USA*, Clayallee 170 (☎832 4087); *Canada*, Europa Center 12th floor (☎261 1161).

Cultural centers *Amerika Haus*, Hardenbergstr. 22–24 (Sept.–June Mon., Weds. and Fri. 11:30am–5:30pm, Tues. and Thurs. 11:30am–8pm, July–Aug. Mon.–Fri. 1–5:30pm). U.S. newspapers, magazines, and a well-stocked library. Regular movies and cultural events.

Emergency doctor (☎310031).

Emergency dentist (☎1141).

Laundromats Dahlmannstr. 17 (Mon.–Fri. 9am–1pm, 3–6pm); Uhlandstr. 53 (6:30am–10:30pm); Hauptstr. 151 (7:30am–10:30pm).

Luggage consignment Lockers at Zoo Station. DM2 or DM3 for 24 hours. Left luggage at Zoo Station (Mon.–Fri. 6am–midnight, Sat.–Sun. 6am–5.40pm and 6pm–midnight); does not accept backpacks.

Mitfahrzentralen Südstern 14 (☎693 6095); Kurfürstendamm 227 (☎882 7606). *Frauenmitfahrzentrale* Potsdamer Str. 139 (☎215 3165). Many more listings can be found in *Tip* and *Zitty* magazines.

Money Outside of normal banking hours the most useful place to change money and traveler's checks is the exchange at the main entrance to the Zoo Station (Mon.–Sat. 8am–9pm. Sun. 10am–6pm). This will also give cash advances on major credit cards, subject to a DM200 minimum.

Pharmacies Prescriptions can be filled at any *Apotheke*: outside normal hours a notice on the door of any *Apotheke* indicates the nearest one open. Otherwise try *Europa-Apotheke*, Tauentzienstr. 9 (☎261 4142); 9am–9pm daily.

Post office Handiest is at Zoo Station (Mon.–Fri. 8am–6pm, Sat. 8am–noon), with a counter open 24 hours. This is also the place for **Poste Restante** facilities: Postampt Bahnhof Zoo, 1000 Berlin 12.

Supermarket *Ullrich* on Hardenbergstrasse, under the rail bridge near Zoo Station. Enormous selection of food and drink.

Women's bookshops *Lillith Buchladen*, Knesebeckstr. 86. *Labrys*, Hohenstaufenstr. 64.

Women's center Stresemannstr. 40 (☎251 0912).

EAST BERLIN

Ever since the Berlin Wall went up on August 13 1961 **EAST BERLIN** has been relegated to the communist hinterland beyond the capitalist confines of island West Berlin. Visitors to West Berlin often forget about the "other Berlin," or at best take a quick glimpse over the Wall from one of the observation platforms, in between admiring the graffiti and a visit to the museum at Checkpoint Charlie. A lot of West Berliners too, seem to have banished East Berlin from their minds, regarding the Wall as some kind of insurmountable barrier beyond which lies a wasteland without culture or consumer durables.

But East Berlin is no wasteland. Neither is it a cut-price shadow of a city, a second-best imitation of West Berlin. In many ways East Berlin *is* Berlin, home of the city's historic heart, unlike West Berlin which really amounts to little more than a collection of suburbs without a real center. Division left East Berlin with the lion's share of the city's treasures, including Karl Friedrich Schinkel's neoclassical architectural legacy and most of the old museums.

However, there's more to East Berlin than past glories. It's a modern city, but one which has developed very differently to its western counterpart. After the war, as American aid flooded into West Berlin, the East Berliners watched the Russians dismantle and ship east practically everything that was still working. Despite this they managed to rebuild their totally destroyed city and preserve much of its historic identity with no help from outside, a feat of which many East Berliners are justifiably proud.

When you visit East Berlin try and avoid the usual day-visa trap of just wandering around the city center wondering how to spend your money. Take in the old imperial thoroughfare of **Unter den Linden** and the museums, and go up the huge **Fernsehturm** (TV tower) for the view if you want, but then get away from the center and head out for **Prenzlauer Berg** or one of the other suburbs and try and get to meet people—the only real way to get to know East Berlin.

Getting In

Unlike the West Berlin authorities the East German government treats the Wall as an international frontier and entering East Berlin involves full passport and customs control. For non-German visitors there are two possible points of entry: **Checkpoint Charlie** for vehicles and pedestrians, and the much faster **Bahnhof Friedrichstrasse** for pedestrians only. A day visa costs DM5 and there's a compulsory hard currency exchange of DM25 for which you get 25 Ost Marks (M). Car drivers must pay an additional DM10 "tax." All these sums are demanded in Deutschmarks and although other hard currencies will be accepted, having the necessary Deutschmarks will save time. Customs controls have relaxed over the last few years; you're only likely to face problems if you try to bring in porn or neo-Nazi political material (obviously drugs and firearms don't go down too well either). You are required to fill in a customs form (*Zollerklärung*) declaring hard currency (not travelers' cheques) and items like personal stereos and cameras. Although you probably won't be checked on the way out you may have to show that you still have everything you brought in with you, and haven't changed money or sold goods on the black market. In East Berlin Deutschmarks are usually accepted in lieu of East German Marks but make sure you get a *Bestätigungschein* (receipt) in case you're asked to account for it at the border. The same applies if you change money in the bank—always get a receipt (but see "Money" below).

Both Checkpoint Charlie and Friedrichstrasse crossing points are open 7am–midnight (last admission at 8pm). It's best to try and cross as early as possible before the crowds start to build up; plan on it taking about 45 minutes to get through, although you may have to wait longer on public holidays and at weekends when a lot of people go to visit relatives. You have to go out the same way you came in and you must be back at the border by midnight at the latest. The prospect of going through the Wall can be a daunting one, but don't be put off—it's very rare for any problems to arise. It's really not much more nerve-wracking than going through a normal border or passing through departure formalities at an international airport; the biggest headache you're likely to encounter will be seemingly interminable lines if it's busy. Make sure you join the right one—non-Germans can wait in any line marked "Andere Staaten." It's also worth knowing that punks and other sartorial nonconformists are frequently denied entry.

Longer Visits

Arranging a longer stay in East Berlin can be tricky. *Berolina Travel*, 22a, Conduit St., London, England W1R 9TB (☎01 629 1664), the GDR state travel bureau, should be able to help you out here. They will arrange package holidays, but it's quite difficult to set up an independent visit. Best bet (in summer) is **camping**, although the campgrounds designated for western tourists are a long way from the city center. The **hotels** in which western tourists can stay are all prohibitively expensive (100M and upward) and the only other way to arrange a long stay in the country is to visit friends or relatives. A visa application for this kind of private visit can be made via *Berolina*, but this must be done six to eight weeks in advance (four to six weeks with an additional "express" payment).

Money

You might as well do everything you can to spend your 25M when you're in East Berlin because, when you leave, you can't take it with you. If you have any GDR money left you're supposed to declare it and in exchange you will get a receipt which is redeemable for the amount of money in question at East Berlin banks for exactly one year after your visit. With your 25M you should be able to eat and drink very well (a couple of times even), and failing that you can usually find Cuban cigars, Russian vodka, and other Comecon delicacies on sale relatively cheaply. For German speakers it's worth having a look around some of the bookshops as books in the GDR are usually very cheap (non-German speakers might appreciate some of the art books that occasionally appear in the shops).

In the GDR it's against the law to **change money** except through authorized channels, i.e. banks or in the big tourist offices where DM1 will get you one Ost Mark. If your nerve's up to it you can buy Ost Marks in a West Berlin bank for about seven times the official rate and then take them through the border—although it's *totally illegal* to import Ost Marks into the GDR. The domestic **black market rate** is from four to seven times the official rate. If you do want to take the risk, avoid street transactions as hard currency hustlers can turn out to be plain-clothes policemen and if you're caught you can, at the very least, expect to be thrown out of the country after a suitably unpleasant grilling. For an "honest" deal waiters and taxi drivers are often a good bet, but you'll still be breaking the law.

Information and Getting Around

For general information about East Berlin head for the **tourist office** in the *Reisebüro-Hochhaus*, Alexanderplatz 5 (ground floor) (☎215 4410) (Mon., Tues., Thurs., Fri. 8:30am–7pm, Weds. 10am–7pm, Sat. 10am–2pm). Here you should be able to get hold of German guidebooks, brochures, street plans and tickets for theaters or public transit. On the first floor of the same building there's an office dealing specifically with foreign visitors (☎215 4402) (Mon.–Fri. 8am–8pm, Sat. and Sun. 9am–6pm) which has some English-language information. There's also a smaller tourist office at Charlottenstr. 45 (Mon., Tues., Thurs., and Fri. 9:30am–5pm, Weds. 10am–5pm).

The city center has a good **bus, trolley,** and **U-Bahn** network which extends out to most of the suburbs and routes are usually shown on street maps. Downtown trolley termini are at **Am Kupfergraben** near Friedrichstrasse and **Hackescher Markt** near Marx-Engels-Platz, and a lot of bus routes converge in the Alexanderplatz area. The standard fare on buses, trolleys, and the U-Bahn is 0.20M. On buses and trolleys passengers pay into a sort of "honor box" rather than, as is possible, simply taking a ticket from the dispenser without paying. Tickets must be validated using one of the on-board hole-punchers. The East Berlin S-Bahn network is also very comprehensive and good for longer suburban trips, with fares from 0.20M to 1.30M depending on length of journey. For S- and U-Bahn trains, tickets are available from entrance hall machines or from ticket offices and must be validated before boarding. Twenty-four-hour passes are available at 1M for S-bahn services only and 2M for the whole city public transit network. These can be bought at station ticket offices. Services run from 4am until about midnight and from then on there are less frequent night services on bus and tram routes. The **Service Städtischer Nahverkehr** (☎246 2255) at the S-Bahnhof Alexanderplatz will be able to fill you in on transit details.

The city also has a fairly good **taxi** service which, by western standards, is relatively cheap. There's a basic charge of 0.50M and it's 0.80M per km until 10pm and 1M per km thereafter. Quite a few car owners earn a bit on the side as unofficial taxi-drivers, so if you're out late and want to get somewhere in a hurry it's always worth sticking your thumb out on the off-chance. There are taxi ranks at the *Centrum* department store and *Einrichtungshaus* entrances to the Alexanderplatz S-Bahnhof, at the *Hotel Stadt Berlin* nearby, at the northern entrance to Bahnhof Friedrichstrasse, and at the *Palasthotel* on Unter den Linden.

The City Center

When you finally step out of the arrival hall and into Bahnhof Friedrichstrasse itself you realize immediately that the world you have just entered is very different from the one you have left behind in Zoo Station. The first thing that hits you is the distinctive East Berlin street smell: a cloying mixture of two-stroke engine fuel, unfiltered heavy industry emissions, and the lignite which fuels the city's central heating systems. You're now on **Friedrichstrasse**, one of East Berlin's main streets, but compared to the frenetic, crowded streets of West Berlin the pace of life seems slow. The cars are mainly Eastern Bloc models, foremost among them the puny-looking GDR people's car, the fiberglass-bodied Trabant, and they seem to be outnumbered by heavy trucks, buses, and trams. The people

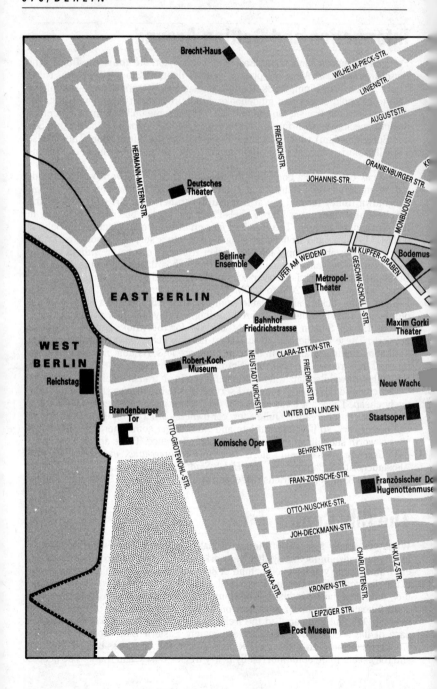

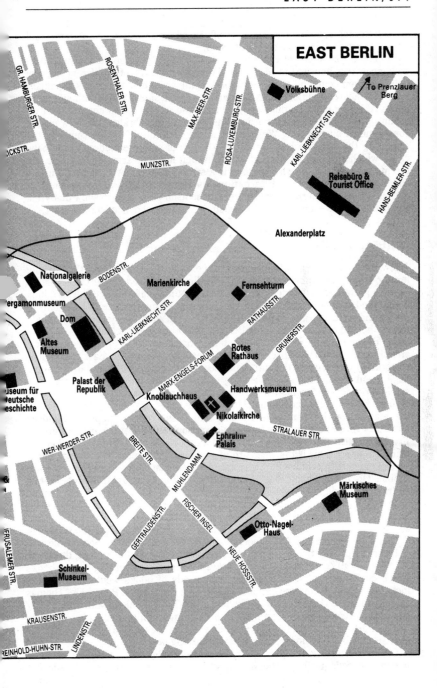

EAST BERLIN

GR. HAMBURGER STR.

ROSENTHALER STR.

MAX-BEER-STR.

ROSA-LUXEMBURG-STR.

KARL-LIEBKNECHT-STR.

ICKSTR.

MUNZSTR.

Volksbühne

To Prenzlauer Berg

HANS-BEIMLER-STR.

Reisebüro & Tourist Office

Alexanderplatz

Nationalgalerie

BODENSTR.

Marienkirche

Fernsehturm

RATHAUSSTR.

ergamonmuseum

Dom

KARL-LIEBKNECHT-STR.

GRUNERSTR.

Altes Museum

MARX-ENGELS-FORUM

Rotes Rathaus

useum für
eutsche
eschichte

Palast der Republik

Knoblauchhaus

Handwerksmuseum

Nikolaikirche

WER-WERDER-STR.

BREITE STR.

Ephraim Palais

STRALAUER STR.

MÜHLENDAMM

GERTRAUDENSTR.

FISCHER INSEL

Märkisches Museum

Otto-Nagel-Haus

NEUE HOSSSTR.

ERUSALEMER STR.

Schinkel-Museum

KRAUSENSTR.

LINDENSTR.

REINHOLD-HUHN-STR.

are still Berliners, but not as obviously affluent as their western counterparts, and the shops are smaller and less well-stocked.

Directly opposite you at Friedrichstr. 101 is the **Admiralspalast**, a Jugendstil building which houses the **Metropol Theater**, purveyor of indifferent musical light entertainment, and **Die Distel** theater, the sorry heir to Berlin's legendary inter-war cabaret tradition. Here they put on satirical shows which, although lacking in real bite, often go quite far politically and give people a chance to let off steam. Turn right under the Friedrichstrasse railroad bridge, where a plaque commemorates two young Wehrmacht soldiers executed for "desertion" by the SS during the last hopeless days of WWII, one of many reminders of the cataclysm which shaped this city and which has left indelible scars on its fabric. On the northern side of Friedrichstrasse is a symbol of the new East Berlin in the shape of the Japanese-built **Internationales Handelszentrum**, a giant piece of self-consciously modernist architecture whose main purpose is to show that West Berlin doesn't have a monopoly on thrusting commercial dynamism.

Unter den Linden

A few hundred meters farther along you come to the **Unter den Linden**, the former main thoroughfare of imperial Berlin which used to be connected to Berlin's prewar entertainment strip by the street now called Strasse des 17 Juni. Today the Unter den Linden is a broad boulevard going nowhere. It leads only to the **Brandenburg Gate**, the huge triumphal arch, (backed by the Wall), which marks the end of the city for East Berliners, and no longer actually accessible to them. Beyond it is the Wall itself, which here has none of the enraged or satirical artwork and graffiti which decorate the western side. In the East the Wall is remarkably unobtrusive; the authorities seem to have done all they can to camouflage it and most of the streets leading to it are empty and half-abandoned, with semi-barricades of stanchions, or trees set in concrete tubs.

From here turn around and head back up the Unter den Linden. On the right is the massive **Soviet Embassy** building and farther up (a couple of hundred meters beyond the Friedrichstrasse intersection) an equestrian **monument to Frederick the Great**, the enlightened despot who laid the foundations of Prussian power. This is the vanguard of a whole host of historic buildings, survivors of nineteenth-century Berlin, restored over the last forty years from post-war rubble. On the left-hand side of the street is the **Humboldt Universität**, a restrained and dignified neoclassical building from 1748, and originally intended as a royal palace. The Philologist, writer and diplomat, Wilhelm Humboldt founded a school here in 1809 which was later to become the University of Berlin, and be re-named in his honor in 1946. Flanking the entrance gate are statues of Wilhelm and his brother Alexander, famous for his exploration of South America.

Directly opposite the university is **Bebelplatz**, formerly Opernplatz, the scene on May 11, 1933 of the infamous *Buchverbrennung*, the burning of the books which conflicted with Nazi ideology. Thousands of books went up in smoke, including the works of "un-German" authors like Erich Maria Remarque, Thomas Mann, Heinrich Mann, Stefan Zweig, and Erich Kästner, along with volumes by countless foreign writers. The most fitting comment on this episode was made with accidental foresight by Heinrich Heine during the previous century: "Where they start by burning books, they'll end by burning people.'

On the western side of Bebelplatz is the **Alte Bibliothek**, an old library building known colloquially as the **Kommode**, whose curved Baroque facade has been immaculately restored and where Lenin spent some time poring over dusty tomes while waiting for the Russian Revolution. On the north side of the square is the **Deutsche Staatsoper**, another flawless eighteenth-century neoclassical building by the architect Georg von Knobbelsdorff which, like everything else around here, has been almost totally reconstructed since 1945. Today it's the venue for excellent operatic productions, particularly of the *Ring Cycle*, and occasional classical concerts (box office ☎207 1362; tickets 3–15M). Behind here is **St. Hedwigs-Kathedrale** which is still in use and was built for the city's Catholic minority in 1747. It's thought to have been designed by Knobelsdorff, with "advice" from Frederick the Great himself, which was bad news for the Catholics who had to pay for it, since the resulting pantheon-like structure isn't really suited to the demands of the liturgy. Next door to the Deutsche Staatsoper is the **Palais Unter den Linden** which was built in 1663 and given a Baroque facelift in 1732. One wing of this palace now houses the **Operncafé**, one of East Berlin's tackier bar/restaurant/disco complexes.

Just behind the Palais Unter den Linden in the shadow of the huge Foreign Ministry is the **Schinkel Museum**, Am Werderschen Markt, a museum about the life and work of Karl Friedrich Schinkel, the architect who gave nineteenth-century Berlin its distinctive neoclassical stamp. Appropriately enough, it's housed in one of his own buildings, the **Friedrichwerderschen Kirche**, a stolid affair, much more sober than some of his other efforts. A permanent exhibition in the church's upper gallery gives a full rundown of Schinkel's achievements, setting them in the context of the times. Directly opposite the Operncafé is one of Schinkel's most famous buildings, the **Neue Wache**, built between 1816 and 1818 as a sort of neoclassical police station to house the royal watch.

Today the building, which looks like a stylized Roman temple, houses the "Memorial to the Victims of Fascism and Militarism." It's here that one of East Berlin's better-known ironies is played out when the guard of honor is changed; as one detachment goose-steps out, another goose-steps in.

Next door, housed in one of East Berlin's finest Baroque buildings, the old Prussian Arsenal, is the **Museum für Deutsche Geschichte** (*Museum of German History*) (Mon.–Thurs. 9am–6pm, Sat. and Sun. 10am–5pm; 1.05M, 0.80M students as in all East Berlin museums) Although for non-German speakers it can be a bit inpenetrable, most of it is quite interesting, particularly the later sections which deal with aspects of German history like the inter-war worker's movement and Communist-inspired resistance to the Nazis, which tend not to be so well documented in western museums. The section on the development of the GDR throws some light on the social and economic patterns that have emerged here over the last forty years or so. In the **Schlüterhof**, the museum's inner courtyard, look out for for the 22 contorted faces of dying warriors by the eighteenth-century sculptor Andreas Schlüter which adorn the walls. In the summer there are classical concerts here every Thursday at 7:30pm. Just behind the Museum für Deutsche Geschichte is the **Maxim Gorki Theater** (box office ☎207 1790 Mon.–Fri. noon–2pm and 2:30–6pm; 1–10M) which puts on consistently good productions, including a lot of Soviet works. Not surprisingly Gorki figures highly.

Just to the south of the Unter den Linden sprawls the **Platz der Akademie**, a historic cluster of restored buildings, which was once considered one of the most beautiful squares in Europe. Here you'll find the **Französische Dom** which was built for Berlin's influential Hugenot community at the very beginning of the eighteenth century. It's a dignified, classically influenced building which has now been completely restored, after having been all-but-destroyed during the war. In the tower of the church there's a smart restaurant (see "Eating and Drinking") and there's a great view from the balcony which runs around the outside near the top. On the ground floor is the **Hugenottenmuseum** (Mon.–Fri. 10am–5pm) which details the flight of the Hugenots from France and the establishment of the Hugenot community in Berlin. Nearby is **Deutsche Dom** which was built around the same time for the city's Lutheran community, and is the stylistic twin of the Französischer Dom. Between the two is Schinkel's neoclassical **Schauspielhaus**, a former theater which fits in well with the two churches, making this one of the most striking and architecturally balanced corners of the city.

A little farther to the south is **Leipziger Strasse**, a showpiece housing and commercial development which dates from the 1970s "big is beautiful" phase of East Berlin town planning. On June 17, 1953 this street was the focal point of a city-wide antigovernment and anti-Soviet demonstration. Several hundred people died when Soviet tanks moved in to restore order, and afterwards Bertolt Brecht sardonically suggested that the GDR government should "dissolve the people, and elect another." Today bland and functional high-rise buildings are set on either side of a six-lane boulevard and the whole street has a desolate feel, almost as if it was built to prove some bombastic architectural point rather than to provide homes and shops for real people.

The Museum Island

From the Unter den Linden the **Marx-Engels-Brücke** leads onto Marx-Engels-Platz, former site of the old Imperial Palace, the remains of which were demolished after the war. Only the balcony from which Karl Liebknecht proclaimed the German revolution in 1918 was preserved and has since been incorporated into the **Staatsrat** (State Council) building on the south side of the square. Marx-Engels-Platz now forms the midpoint of a large island in the river Spree. The northwestern part of the island, extending peninsula-like from Marx-Engels-Platz, is known as the **Museumsinsel** (*Museum Island*) and it's here that you'll find East Berlin's best-known museums. Some **words of warning**: often whole sections of the museums are closed for vaguely defined "technical reasons," and remember that all except the Pergamon are closed on Monday.

The Museumsinsel contains the best of what was left of prewar Berlin's collections after the ravages of war and occupation. Directly to the north of Marx-Engels-Platz is the **Altes Museum** (Weds.–Sun. 9am–6pm, Fri. 10am–6pm), another heavily neoclassical Schinkel building which now houses an art museum. The post-war and GDR section is basically a large collection of state-sponsored and state-promoted artists brought together in an attempt to create a sense that there is such a thing as homegrown GDR art. Only Albert Eberd's quasireligious scenes seem to break away from the pedestrian conformity or, at best, conventional experimentalism of the other artists represented. With luck you may also be able to see the **Kupferstichkabinett** (*Print Collection*), a large collection of engravings and prints, including 57 exquisite drawings by **Botticelli** for Dante's *Divine Comedy*. Also included are works by Rembrandt, Dürer, and Lucas Cranach. In the nineteenth- and twentieth-century German graphic art section of this collection there are works by Käthe Kollwitz and Max Slevogt, and another section contains prints by Daumier, Manet, Degas, Rodin, Renoir, Munch, and Toulouse-Lautrec.

Just behind the Altes Museum is the **Neues Museum**, one of East Berlin's few remaining war ruins, which is now being gradually restored to house overspill from other museums. Next door is the **Nationalgalerie** (Weds.–Sun. 9am–6pm, Fri. 10am–6pm), a slightly extravagant example of post-Schinkel neoclassicism, which now houses East Berlin's largest art collections. The ground-floor, nineteenth-century section is full of dull portraiture and landscapes, a legacy of the conservatism of Kaiser Wilhelm II, who vetoed a decision to buy more adventurous works. Apart from a couple of Cezannes, and, thanks to the Kaiser, a very small Impressionist section it's all pretty uninspiring. The twentieth-century section is good on the Expressionist, Bauhaus, and *Neue Sachlichkeit* (New Objectivity) movements and includes work by the Dresden and Munich Expressionist collectives *Die Brücke* and *Der Blaue Reiter*. Also worth checking out are works by Otto Dix, John Heartfield's highly political 1920s and 1930s photomontages, and the expressive realism of the Ernst Barlach sculptures.

To the north of the Neues Museum is the **Pergamonmuseum** (Sat.–Thurs. 9am–6pm, Fri. 10am-6pm), which is reached from Kupfergraben on the south bank of the Spree. It's a massive structure built in the early part of this century to house the treasure trove of the German archaelogists who were busy plundering the ancient world. The museum is divided up into four sections, the most important of which is the Department of Antiquities containing the **Pergamon Altar**; this huge structure, dedicated to Zeus and Athena, dating from 180–160B.C., was unearthed in Turkey and brought to Berlin in 1903. This section also contains other pieces of Hellenistic architecture (albeit on a smaller scale), including a market gate from the town of Miletus and various examples of Greek sculpture. The Western Asian Section has items going back almost 4000 years to Babylonian times, including the enormous Ishtar Gate, the Processional Way, and the facade of the Throne Room, all of which date back to the reign of Nebuchadnezzar II in the sixth century B.C. The museum's Islamic section contains the facade of a Jordanian castle presented to Kaiser Wilhelm II by the Sultan of Turkey as well as a host of smaller but no less impressive exhibits from Arabia and Persia. Finally the East Asian collection has a large collection of ceramics, lacquerwork, and jade spanning 4000 years.

At the northeastern tip of the Museumsinsel is the **Bodemuseum**, housed in an impressive, not to say intimidating, neo-Baroque building which was put up at the turn of the century. The collection itself is very traditional and divided up into museums within a museum. The **Egyptian Museum/Papyrus Collection** contains art and papyri from 5000 B.C. to the third century A.D. plus mummies, grave artifacts, wall friezes, weapons, and jewelry. The **Early Christian and Byzantine Section** has an extensive range of objects, mainly religious in nature, from the pre-medieval eastern Mediterranean. Worth checking out are the sixth-century mosaic from the church of San Michele in Ravenna, the Eastern Orthodox icons, and the Coptic art exhibits. In the **Picture Gallery** there's an extensive, albeit unremarkable, collection of German, Italian, Dutch, and Flemish old masters. More interesting is the **Museum for Ancient and Early History** which has archaeological material from all over Europe right up to the eleventh and twelfth centuries, including the Heinrich Schliemann Collection, which consists of items unearthed by the great German archaelogist on the site of ancient Troy during the nineteenth century. Tragically the best of the Schliemann Collection was destroyed during the war, crushed in the rubble of the supposedly impregnable Tiergarten flak tower. The **Sculpture Gallery** has twelfth-to-eighteenth-century pieces with a few interesting late Gothic German and early Renaissance Italian examples.

From the Bodemuseum head back to Marx-Engels-Platz. Adjacent to the Altes Museum is the **Berliner Dom**, built at the behest of Kaiser Wilhelm II between

1894 and 1905 on the site of an eighteenth-century cathedral. With its distinctive dome and towers it was intended to serve the House of Hohenzollern as a family church and its vault contains the remains of various members of the family. The building was badly damaged during the war but has undergone a long period of re-construction which might just about be finished by now. Opposite the Dom stands the **Palast der Republik** which houses the *Volkskammer*, the GDR's parliament, and an entertainment complex including restaurants, cafés, a theater, and a bowling alley (none recommended). This huge angular building with its bronzed, reflecting windows was completed in less than 1000 days and is a source of great pride to the authorities here. At the southern end of the mid-Spree island is an area known as the **Fischerinsel** (*Fisherman's Island*), home to yet another 1970s high-rise development which, considering its showpiece status, is spectacularly shoddy when seen at close range.

Alexanderplatz

Alexanderplatz is the commercial hub of East Berlin. If the Unter den Linden represents the glories of Berlin past, then Alexanderplatz and the area around it definitely represent the glories of East Berlin present—although only time will tell whether the concrete giganticism of the new capital will wear as well as the neoclassical efforts of Schinkel and Co. To get to "Alex" from the Palast der Republik head up the big shopping street of Karl-Liebknecht-Strasse. On the other side of the street is the **Marienkirche**, a thirteenth-century Gothic church overshadowed by the gigantic **Fernsehturm** or TV tower (daily May–Sept. 8am–11pm; Oct.–April. 9am–11pm, 2nd and 4th Tues. in month 1–11pm; 3M) that dominates the East Berlin skyline and looks like a displaced satellite stuck on the end of a factory chimney. The tower does have a couple of positive features: it makes a good orientation point if you get lost and there's a tremendous view (40km on a rare clear day, although the top is so often so shrouded in cloud that you don't get to see anything) from its observation platform, showing you just how cruelly the city has been divided. Above the observation platform is the **Tele-Café**, a café whose main attraction is that it turns on its own axis once every hour. When the sun shines on the globe of the tower, the reflected light forms a cross visible even in West Berlin, much to the reported chagrin of the authorities and amusement of the Berliners who call it the "Pope's revenge." At the foot of the tower there's a jumble of cafés, restaurants, and glass-fronted exhibition halls, all welded together by a series of walkways. Occasionally interesting exhibitions are staged, and the **Espresso** café is where the city's youth head after a hard day's skateboarding on the nearby concrete surfaces.

In front of the TV tower is the **Neptunbrunnen**, a fountain incorporating statues of Neptune and friends, built in 1891. This stands directly in front of the **Rotes Rathaus** (tours Sat. 11:15, 11:30am, noon, and 12:30pm from the main entrance)—the "Red Town Hall," so called because of its bricks rather than its politics. It's a grandiose, almost Venetian-looking building which has lost some of its impact now that it's been hemmed in by new buildings to the southwest. From the Rathaus follow the pedestrianized section of Rathaus Strasse, past what passes for a luxury shopping complex, as far as **S-Bahnhof Alexanderplatz**. After passing under the railroad bridge go through the gap between the **Alexanderhaus** and the **Berolinahaus**, two buildings designed at the beginning of the 1930s by the architect Peter Behrens, whose ideas influenced the founders of the Bauhaus. These two buildings, which now house a bookshop and the

Central Berlin District Council, are the only two Alexanderplatz buildings to have survived the war. **Alexanderplatz** itself, made famous by Alfred Döblin's novel of life in the Weimar era, *Berlin Alexanderplatz* (subsequently filmed by Fassbinder), is a huge, windswept pedestrianized plaza surrounded by high rises. Behrens' buildings, once the tallest in the area, have long since been put in the shade by the ugly **Hotel Stadt Berlin**, from whose 39th-floor *Panorama-Restaurant* there's a fairly stupendous view (make a reservation or bribe the head waiter—it's popular and the food is okay), and the huge and even uglier **Reisebüro der DDR**. In the center of Alexanderplatz stands the sorry-looking **Brunnen der Völkerfreundschaft** (*Friendship of the Peoples Fountain*) but a more famous monument is the **Weltzeituhr** (*World Clock*) in front of the Alexanderhaus which tells you what time it is in different world cities and looks like a product of the same architectural school responsible for the Fernsehturm.

Before the war Alexanderplatz was one of the city's main shopping meccas; commercial life on Alexanderplatz now centers around the **Centrum** department store. By GDR standards it's very well stocked and compares favorably with western department stores, which will come as a surprise if you've brought your notions of shortages and lines with you. On closer inspection, though, some of the stuff on sale turns out to be a bit shoddy, particularly the 100%-synthetic garments made on-site in Romanian oil refineries, modeled by deformed-looking mannequins in the windows. However the place is always packed with happy shoppers, including large numbers of American GIs and their families who come over to buy cheap glassware, crockery, and bedding. Other good buys include stationery and, if you like trendily arcane souveniers, GDR flags.

The Nikolaiviertel

Slightly to the southwest of the Rotes Rathaus lies the **Nikolaiviertel**, a recent development which attempts to re-create the old prewar heart of Berlin. This compact network of streets is a radical architectural departure for the GDR. No longer, it seems, do the city planners feel compelled to build enormous monuments to the concrete pourer's art; most of the Nikolaiviertel buildings are no more than four or five stories high and a concerted effort has been made to inject a bit of vernacular individuality into the designs. The Nikolaiviertel consists partly of exact replicas of historic Berlin buildings which didn't make it through to the postwar era, such as the *Zum Nussbaum* pub (see "Eating and Drinking"), and partly of stylized buildings not based on anything in particular but with a distinct "old Berlin" feel to them, or at least an approximation thereof. Sometimes it doesn't quite come off, and the use of obviously prefabricated pillars and gables isn't always too convincing, but all in all the Nikolaiviertel represents a commendable attempt to get away from the monumentalism of most earlier post-war construction projects. It also represents an attempt to attract big-spending tourists, with a series of fancy and expensive shops, restaurants, cafés, and Gaststätten (again see "Eating and Drinking" for details).

At the center of it all is the Gothic **Nikolaikirche,** which has been restored to its twin-towered pre-war glory and now houses a museum about the development of medieval Berlin. Nearby is the **Knoblauchhaus**, built in 1759 and a rare survivor of the war. Inside is a museum about the eighteenth-century German Enlightenment and some of the figures associated with it. On Mühlendamm the rebuilt rococo **Ephraim-Palais** is home to another museum, this time recording the city's development from "electoral residence to great bourgeois city of the nineteenth century." At Mühlendamm 5 the **Handwerksmuseum** (Mon. 10am–5pm, Tues., Weds. 9am-5pm, Sat., Sun. 10am–6pm) takes a slightly more-interesting-than-average look at the various trades of old Berlin.

On the southern side of the Spree (reached on foot via the Fischerinsel) at Am Köllnischen Park is the **Märkisches Museum** (Weds., Sun. 9am–6pm, Thurs., Sat. 9am–5pm, Fri. 9am–4pm), full of material relating to the history of Berlin and the surrounding province of Brandenburg. The oldest exhibit is the **Berlin-Biesdorf** deer mask, which dates from the seventh century B.C. and is the earliest relic of human settlement in the Berlin area. There's also material about the life and work of **Heinrich Zille**, the Berlin artist who produced critical/satirical drawings of the city's Weimar-era life, drawing attention to the privations suffered by its working class.

Not far away, at Märkisches Ufer 16–18, the **Otto-Nagel-Haus** is billed as a collection of proletarian, revolutionary, and antifascist art, based around the life of **Otto Nagel**, a biggish wheel in revolutionary/artistic circles in pre-Nazi Berlin who painted gloomy indictments of the hardship of life for ordinary people. Also featured here is work by other artists, including Ernst Barlach, Käthe Kollwitz, Otto Dix, Conrad Felixmüller, and Kurt Querner.

Around Downtown

If, instead of turning right out of Bahnhof Friedrichstrasse, you had turned left, you would have crossed the wrought-iron **Weidendammbrücke**. Immediately to the left on Bertolt-Brecht-Platz is the **Berliner Ensemble** theater (box office Mon. 11am–5pm, Tues.–Fri. 11am–1:30pm, 2–6pm, Sat. 5–6pm; tickets 2–10M: ☎282 3160 or 288 8155). This is the official Brecht theater, although now only the invocation of Brecht's name bears witness to the greatness of the man who was once the main driving force behind modern German drama, since the diet consists mainly of staple Brecht fare served up without much panache to audiences of school kids and tourists. A few streets away at Schumannstr. 13a is the **Deutsches Theater** (box office ☎287 1225, or 287 1226). In 1905 Max Reinhardt, who was to dominate Berlin theater for nearly three decades, took over as director and in 1922 a young and unknown Marlene Dietrich made her stage debut here. Until recently this was the best theater in East Berlin, thanks to the inspired direction of Alexander Lang, but he's now in the west and the productions have fallen off slightly.

Make your way back to Friedrichstrasse via Reinhardtstrasse, and then into Chauseestrasse via Oranienburger Tor. Here, on the left is the **Dorotheen-städtische Friedhof**, East Berlin's VIP cemetery, which contains the graves of Bertolt Brecht and his wife Helene Weigel, the author Heinrich Mann, John Heartfield the Dada luminary and inter-war photomontage exponent, the philosopher Georg Hegel whose ideas influenced Marx, and Berlin's great nineteenth-century neoclassical architect Karl Friedrich Schinkel. Just beyond the cemetery at Chauseestr. 125 is the **Brecht-Haus**, Brecht's last home and workplace. It now houses a Bertolt Brecht archive and there are guided tours of the rooms where the playwright worked and lived every half hour (Tues., Weds., and Fri. 10am-noon and 5–7pm, Sat. 9:30–11:30am and 12:30–2pm).

Head back to Oranienburger Tor and turn down into Oranienburger Strasse, where, a few hundred meters along on the right-hand side, you come to the old **Synagoge**, once Berlin's central one, which was burned out on *Kristallnacht* (the night of 9/10 November 1938), when the Nazis launched an all-out assault on Germany's Jewish community. *Kristallnacht*, so called after the sound of breaking glass as Jewish businesses and institutions were wrecked, marked an intensification of Nazi attacks on the Jews, preparing the ground for the horror of the Final Solution. Apart from additional wartime damage, the Oranienburg Strasse synagogue has not been touched since that violent night in 1938, and remains a desolate reminder of the savagery of Nazi rule. A little farther to the east on Grosse Hamburger Strasse is the site of Berlin's oldest Jewish cemetery (established in 1672) and the first Jewish old people's home to be founded in the city. In 1943 the Nazis dug a trench through the cemetery, using gravestones to shore it up, and turned the old people's home into a detention center into which Berlin's Jews were rounded up before they were shipped off to concentration camps.

Just off Grosse Hamburger Strasse is the **Sophienkirche**, dating back to 1734 and one of the city's finest Baroque churches. A little farther along a sharp turn to the right takes you into **Sophienstrasse**, a restored nineteenth century street which now houses a number of arts and crafts workshops. In places the restoration is only skin-deep and the pastel facades of the old apartment houses conceal squalid, crumbling courtyards.

The Suburbs

Behind the scenes in East Berlin is another city—a real one where people live, work, and play, and which has nothing to do with the tourist attractions of downtown. Most of this is located in the **suburbs** which are all as different in character as those in any western city. They're all easily reached by S- and U-Bahn, trolley or bus, and if you don't make an effort to get out to them you'll only see a minute part of what East Berlin is all about.

Prenzlauer Berg

The one place you should definitely head for when you're in the city is **Prenzlauer Berg**. This run-down, blue-collar district fans out from the northeastern edge of the city center and is East Berlin's hidden heart. During the war it was fought over but not flattened, and most of the tenement blocks put up during the late nineteenth century and early twentieth century to house the city's rapidly expanding factory worker population are still standing. Many of the blackened buildings with their overgrown *Hinterhöfe* (courtyards) look as if they haven't been renovated since the war and still bear the scars of small-arms fire from the Battle of Berlin.

To get to Prenzlauer Berg head for either Dmitroffstrasse or Schönhauser Allee U-Bahn stations. In the maze of run-down streets bounded by Schönhauser Allee in the west, Prenzlauer Allee in the east, Dmitroff Strasse in the south and Wisbyer Strasse in the north you'll find some of the best cafés and bars in the whole city (see "Eating and Drinking"). Prenzlauer Berg, just like Kreuzberg in West Berlin, has had a big influx of alternative lifestyle adherents and artists who have chosen this district to live on the edge of established GDR society, which, given the all-embracing nature of the state here, is by no means as easy to do as it is in "alternative" West Berlin. It's no coincidence that you'll see more cars here with white ribbons flying from their radio aerials, indicating that the owners have applied to emigrate to the west, than anywhere else in the city. There are even squats here, although in the GDR there's a different approach to the idea. Here, rather than merely occupying illegally (although this also happens) it's often a case of moving in to an empty flat, finding out the rent account number and then paying the rent. However, this too is illegal and there have been clashes with the police, although the housing crisis here is so bad that the authorities sometimes allow squatters to become legal tenants after fining them.

Over the last few years the authorities have also wised up to the potential appeal of the Prenzlauer Berg, and although they don't exactly encourage tourists to go into the seedier parts, they have started to include the more accessible and presentable streets on the tourist itinerary. Foremost among these is **Husemannstrasse**, an old nineteenth-century tenement street which has been restored to its former glory and turned into a kind of living museum in a unique and encouraging attempt to preserve the grandeur of old Berlin. Husemann-strasse features shops and cafés with appropriate nineteenth-century decor—but the prices and goods are modern. There's also an expensive antique shop and a livery stables from which you can rent a horse and cart if you really want to get into the turn-of-the-century swing of things. To get here take the U-Bahn to Dmitroffstrasse or walk from Rosa-Luxemburg-Platz (about 20–25 min.).

The street also has a couple of East Berlin's better museums. The **Museum Berliner Arbeiterleben um 1900** (*Museum of Working-Class Life*) (Tues. and Thurs.–Sun. 11am–6pm, Weds. 10am–8pm) at no. 12 concentrates on the living conditions of Berlin's working class population at the turn of the century, and re-created apartment house rooms filled with period artifacts conjure up the over-crowded atmosphere of Berlin tenement life. There's also a section devoted to the kitchen allotments which for many Berliners, trapped in factory jobs, represented a weekend escape back to their village roots, and a chance to augment their diets with home-produced fruit and vegetables. When times turned tough during and after World War I these plots saved many Berliners from starvation, and some families actually lived in their allotment sheds during the housing crises of the era. Although the museum has a turn-of-the century bias, there's also a section about Nazi attacks on the workers' movement during the 1920s and 1930s.

A couple of doors down at Husemannstr. 8 is the **Friseurmuseum**, (*Hairdressing Museum*), interesting and, for a change in the austere world of East Berlin museums, fun. It's privately run and the curator is a real enthusiast who will give you a personal guided tour if you're interested. The opening times are a bit erratic, but knock on the door and if there's anyone in you'll usually be able to take a look around.

One word of warning about Prenzlauer Berg: Some of the more run-down streets can get dangerous after dark. All that stuff about there being no crime in East Berlin is a myth—there *are* muggings and if you look in any way unconventional or if you're non-European there are a lot of skinheads around who can be just as violent and racist as skinheads anywhere else.

Karlshorst

If you take a walk through the streets of **Karlshorst** (S-Bahn from Alexanderplatz, change at Ostkreuz) you're more likely to hear Russian spoken than German, as the area has in effect become East Berlin's Russian quarter. The Russians have been here since the end of the war when they accepted the unconditional surrender of the German armed forces on May 8, 1945. A former *Wehrmacht* barracks now serves as the headquarters of the Soviet garrison in East Berlin, and the streets of Karlshorst are full of Russian soldiers and their families who have taken over the local apartment blocks. There are shops where you can buy Russian food, books, newspapers, and *papirosi* cigarettes (which have cardboard filters and will turn your lungs inside out).

At the end of Fritz-Schmenkel-Strasse, the building where the German surrender was signed, contains the **Berlin-Karlshorst Museum** (Tues.–Fri. 9am–1pm and 3–6pm, Sat. 9am–2pm but closed last Sat. in month, Sun. 9am–4pm), run by matronly-looking Russian women on behalf of the Soviet army and telling the story of World War II from the Soviet point of view. Fourteen rooms of exhibits, battlefield reconstructions, and dioramas open up a new perspective on the war to westerners who are inclined to forget the colossal losses suffered by both sides on the eastern front. There's also a section about German internal resistance to the Nazis.

Köpenick

Köpenick is one of East Berlin's pleasanter suburbs, located on the banks of the Spree towards the southeast edge of the city and easily reached by S-Bahn from Alexanderplatz (change at Ostkreuz). It's a sleepy kind of place, but good to head for if you want to escape the downtown griminess. From a sightseeing point of view the best thing about Köpenick is the **Kunstgewerbemuseum** (Weds.–Sat. 9am–5pm, Sun. 10am–6pm) in Köpenick's **Schloss**. (trolley #84, #86 or bus #27 from Köpenick S-Bahn). This applied-art museum includes porcelain, glass, textiles, leather, jewelry, tin, iron, gold, and silver from the Middle Ages through to the present day. The treasury has an opulent hoard of gold and silver, highpoint of which is the eleventh-century *Giselaschmuck* collection. Also impressive is the huge seventeenth-century *Berliner Silberbuffet*, a set of silver table ware made for the Brandenburg prince who was to become King Friedrich I of Prussia. There's also a disappointingly small *Jugendstil* section and a collection of contemporary GDR applied art.

From the Dammbrücke near the Rathaus you can rent boats and from Luisenhain it's possible to travel by a *Weisse Flotte* ship to the nearby **Grosser Müggelsee** lake and the **Müggelbergen**, the gentle hills which surround it. Head for the *Müggelturm* observation tower with its café, bar and restaurant from where there's a great view of the lake and woods round about.

Treptow

Treptow is worth visiting to see the huge and sobering **Sowjetisches Ehrenmal** in the Treptower Park, erected to commemorate the Soviet soldiers killed during the Battle of Berlin in April–May 1945 and the burial place of 5000 of them. If you approach it via the Am Treptower park entrance, you pass first through a triumphal arch, then you see a sculpture of a grieving mother; a quick right turn and you're suddenly face to face with a vast symbolic statue. Over 11m high, it shows a stylized Russian soldier clutching a saved child and resting his sword on a shattered swastika. This isn't exactly a cheerful place, with busloads of Soviet tourists coming here to pay their respects to their war dead, but it's one you should visit just to appreciate why things are the way they are in Berlin today.

Eating and Drinking

Geographically there are two main clusters of places to **eat** and **drink** in East Berlin: downtown and Prenzlauer Berg. Unless otherwise indicated the bars, cafés, and restaurants listed below are in these two areas. Bars are often a better bet than restaurants for food, both economically and gastronomically, and the best of everything tends to be in Prenzlauer Berg. Tipping (about ten percent) is expected, and if you're a vegetarian then bring your own food or be prepared to live on cheese while you're here.

Bars

There are basically two kinds of bar in East Berlin: the traditional German *Kneipe*, where the main business is beer-drinking, and the *Speisegaststätte* where you can usually have a full sit-down meal. Both are generally open from late morning to around midnight and offer a cheap and unpretentious environment in which to eat and/or drink. Half a liter of beer will cost between 0.98M and 1.26M and in *Speisegaststätten* food will range from 2M to 11M. Most places are fairly civilized although some get a bit wild—avoid the ones where there are people lying in the street outside.

Downtown

Die Bärenschänke, Friedrichstr. 124. This cheap *Speisegaststätte* makes a good starting (or ending) point for an East Berlin bar-hop. It's usually full of workers letting off steam at the end of the day and tourists blowing their last Ost Marks before going west via the nearby Friedrichstrasse border crossing. Food 5–10M. Closed every second Mon. of the month.

Zur Letzten Instanz, Waisenstr. 14-16. Near the old city wall this is one of the oldest and best city bars, the kind of place where you end up getting into heated political discussions with complete strangers. It's popular with people from the nearby youth arts and drama center. Wine upstairs, beer downstairs, and in summer there's a beer garden. Food 3.60–11M.

Zum Nussbaum, Propstrasse/Am Nussbaum. In the heart of the Nikolaiviertel, overshadowed by the red-brick Nikolaikirche, this is an exact replica of a prewar pub destroyed in a war-time air raid. It verges on the expensive and is rather kitsch.

Zum Paddenwirt, Nikolaikirchplatz 6. Pseudo-old Berlin *Speisegaststätte* but not too bad. On Sunday morning you can enjoy the old German tradition of *Fruhschoppen*—Sunday-morning drinking, while indulging in a game of cards or dice.

Probierstube, Sophienstrasse 11. On a recently restored street, which has some fine nineteenth-century facades, this is East Berlin's only tasting house. It's privately owned and you can try out the wines and spirits with the option of buying more of the same to take out.

Tante Olga, Linienstr. 71. An old Berlin pub that's for real. A back street spit 'n' sawdust establishment not much bigger than someone's front room with just a few sit-down tables and a *Stehtisch*, a circular counter around which you can stand. The cheapest beer in town at 0.48M for a quarter liter.

Wernersgrünerbierstuben, Karl-Liebknecht-Strasse 11. A city center cellar *Speisegaststätte* opposite the TV tower. A lot of locals come here but it's equally popular with tourists who like the rustic decor and cheap food and beer. For 3–8M you'll be able to shock a rumbling stomach into submission. No smoking from 11am–3pm.

The Suburbs

Alt Berliner Bierstube, Saarbrückerstr. 18. A gay pub, although not exclusively so, as by day it's often invaded by busloads of Polish and Hungarian tourists. At night there's a definite cruising atmosphere in the front bar. Food 3–9M. Closed every fourth Mon. of the month.

Budike Nr 15, Husemannstrasse/Sredzkistrasse. Ersatz old Berlin bar but recommended. Turn-of-the-century decor but up-to-date prices. 11–15.30M for food.

Metzer Eck, Metzer Str. 33. Founded in 1913, this one is popular with the Prenzlauer Berg *Szene* denizens. It's also a favorite with actors (including some from West Germany) whose signed photos adorn the walls.

Offenbachstuben, Senefelderstrasse/Stubbenkammerstrasse. Highly recommended for both food and drink; a young, eclectic crowd make this one of the best places to head for in Prenzlauer Berg. Also popular with gays. Closed Sun. and Mon.

Panke Eck, Wolfshagenerstrasse/Eintrachtsstrsasse (Pankow). An atmospheric little place down a turn-of-the-century side street. It's frequented by the local arty/intellectual crowd and the interior was designed by a Pankow artist. A good place to strike up a conversation with people who like to talk, and, more importantly, actually have something to say.

Cafés

In East Berlin people tend to go to pubs to drink beer, eat, and then drink more beer but they meet in cafés to talk and exchange ideas. At the moment the cafés seem to be the real focal point of Berlin social and cultural life—and for that reason you should make a point of visiting at least one.

Downtown

Bar Espresso Vis-a-vis, Friedrichstr. 130. Don't be put off by the dreadful mid-1970s decor; this is actually one of the city's better cafés, permanently packed with students from the nearby Humboldt Universitat. Close to Bahnhof Friedrichstrasse, it's a good place to head after the rigors of the border crossing.

Café 130 Radke, Chauseestr. 130. Another favorite student hangout, with an incredible selection of ice cream (made on the premises) and milk shakes—try their strawberry milk shake with egg liqueur. Closed every first Mon. of the month.

Café Arkade, Französische Strasse (opposite the Platz der Akademie). An affluent and arty bunch come here, drawn by the sinfully good ice cream and coffee specialties. Snack-type dishes are available too.

Café Jugendmode, Karl-Marx-Allee 77–85. Newly opened and very stylish—the designer disease hits East Berlin. It's part of the *Berliner Jugendmode* store and looks set to become *the* rendezvous for the hip young dudes of East Berlin.

Cufé im Palais, Poststrasse 16. Part of the Ephraim-Palais Museum, this café has a very prewar feel (pre-World War I that is) and is full of extremely well-spoken and correct ladies who come here for gossip and nostalgia over *Kaffee und Kuchen,* to the strains of an ancient violin and piano duo.

Sophieneck, Grosse Hamburgerstrasse/Sophienstrasse. At the end of the recently renovated Sophienstrasse this one attracts both the local arty/trendy contingent and the elderly *Kaffee und Kuchen* crowd. There's a beer garden at the back in summer.

The Suburbs

Café Flair, Stargarderstr. 72. Also known as *Café Lila,* this is one of the best in the city, owned by an eccentric, music-loving couple who have made a valiant attempt to re-create a nineteenth -century Parisian café in the heart of Prenzlauer Berg.

Café Lotos, Schönhauser Allee 45. The decor would have been very up-to-date in 1975 but it somehow suits the *Schickey Mickey* (money, smart clothes, and minds uncluttered by thought) crowd here. Expensive by East Berlin standards.

Café Mozaik, Stubenkammerstrasse/Prenzlauer Allee. A *Szene* café which, until the authorities closed it down for "renovation" a few years ago, was an *Ausreisler* (people who have applied to emigrate to the West) hangout, and it seems to be going that way again. Food 3–10M. Closed every third Mon. in the month.

Café Papillon, Greifenhagenerstr. 16. Another East Berlin "must," with a great atmosphere and a young crowd. There's a garden at the back which is part of a tenement *Hinterhof* (courtyard). Closed Fri.

Wiener Café, Schönhauser Allee 68. Formerly the *Café Schröder*, this one attempts to re-create the atmosphere of old Vienna for its arty clientele, some of whom belong to the unofficial *Ausreisler* club.

Restaurants

In East Berlin **eating out** tends to revolve around a basic steak-and-fries theme, particularly in the bland and expensive downtown hotel restaurants. However there are exceptions, and in the places listed below you have a good chance of avoiding the city's endemic lack of culinary verve. If you find yourself paying over 20M then you're being ripped off; in fact, it should be possible for two people to have a decent meal with drinks for less than this.

At the very bottom of the price scale are the ubiquitous *Imbiss* and *Grilletta* stands where you can buy a *Bockwurst* and roll with mustard or a *Grilletta*, East Berlin's answer to the hamburger. Some stands also sell a kind of hot-dog called *Ketwurst*, or pancakes with sweet fillings called *Pallatschinken*. Prices range from 0.90M to 1.50M and most stands sell soft drinks and beer. Also worth investigating are the *Goldbroiler* restaurants which sell anything remotely connected with chicken. The chicken is sold by weight (about 5M for a whole one) and you can get alcoholic and soft drinks too. There are also plenty of canteen-style places where you can eat solid, if basic, meals for a minimum outlay.

The Center

Ermeler Haus, Am Märkischen Ufer 10. Inside this Spree-side building check out the *Raabediele*, an unpretentious restaurant where you can get fair-priced traditional German dishes in slightly folksy surroundings. The cheapish, no-nonsense approach ensures that it gets crowded.

Gerichtslaube, Poststr. 28. Three possibilities here; the *Bierschänke* and *Weinschänke* are basically gussied-up tourist restaurants with prices to match. The food in both is okay, although not exactly imaginative (4–15.80M). Best value for money is the pizzeria above these two which does a passable, if slightly esoteric, interpretation of pizza at 5.80–8.95M.

Haus Budapest Berlin, Karl-Marx-Allee 91. In this supposedly Hungarian restaurant most of the dishes are German, but with paprika. It's quite classy in an old-fashioned sort of way and not *too* pricey (5–30M).

Keller Restaurant Brecht Haus, Chausseestrasse 125 (☎282 3848). This atmospheric basement restaurant, decorated with Brecht memorabilia, is in the basement of Brecht's old house. It's one of the few good ones in the area, and gets crowded—reserve in advance if at all possible.

Neubrandenburger Hof, Wilhelm-Pieck-Strasse/Borsigstrasse. Good food, good value for money, and easily reached from the Bahnhof Friedrichstrasse area. One of the few restaurants in central Berlin deserving an unqualified recommendation; 5–12M.

Turmstuben, Französischer Dom, Platz der Akademie (☎229 3463). In the tower of the Französischer Dom, this classy restaurant is the flagship of the new-look East Berlin the authorities are trying to create. Reserve if you can; it gets crowded in the evenings. Food 5.90–17.50M.

The Suburbs

Krusta Stube, Stargarderstr. 3. Prenzlauer Berg's only full-scale pizza house, although the pizzas might raise a few eyebrows in Italy. No smoking. Food 2.50–5.75M.

Park Idyll, Schulstr. 27 (Pankow). Claims to be a Swiss and farmhouse specialty restaurant, and for once this doesn't mean the usual range of German dishes with fancy names.

Pfeffermühle, Gaudystr. 6. Everything comes heavily sprinkled with pepper (the name means "Pepper Mill") but it's prepared to a high standard. One of the best in Prenzlauer Berg.

Restaurant Aphrodite, Schönhauser Allee 61. A really good restaurant with a vaguely Mediterranean accent. Not over-priced at 4–20M. Closed Sun.

Nightlife

East Berlin's **nightlife** takes some finding, and unless you know where to go you're likely to come away with the impression that this city shuts down at 11pm. Avoid the downtown tourist hotel discos, which serve mainly as pick-up joints bringing prostitutes into contact with hard-currency-rich foreigners. There are a few discos in Prenzlauer Berg and Pankow which are just about bearable, with taped western chart music and lots of polite boys and girls trying to pick each other up. Most of these have dress restrictions, so try and avoid ripped jeans and battered leather jackets. If you do encounter any problems in this department, letting slip that you're a westerner often has a magical door-opening effect (either that or they'll knock your teeth out). Admission will be between 4M and 6.50M and drinks will be a little more expensive than normal.

As for vaguely "alternative" nightlife the best bet is, surprisingly enough, the discos run in some of the clubhouses of the FDJ (the party youth organization, or in some of the *Kreiskulturhäuser* (arts centers) which are to be found in different East Berlin districts. Bear in mind, though, that much of the **really good music and the arts** in East Berlin tends to happen behind the scenes in private flats and tenement-building courtyards, with addresses circulated only by word of mouth. These kind of private initiatives take place on the very fringes of legality and the only way to find out about them is to go to the bars and cafés listed in the "Eating and Drinking" section and meet the East Berliners. The following listings give a cross section of nightlife possibilities in East Berlin.

Discos and Clubs

Alibi, Saarbrückerstr. 14 (Prenzlauer Berg). One of the area's smarter discos. Open until 2am most nights, closed Tues.

Café Nord, Schönhauser Allee (Prenzlauer Berg). Retro in an unstylish sort of way, this is pretty much typical of the okay end of East Berlin nightlife. Admission 6M.

Nachtbar Pinguin, Rosa-Luxemburg-Str. 39. An uninspiring corridor-like venue in the city center which is nevertheless usually packed. Popular with East Berlin gays.

Party Thek, Arkonastrasse/Borkumstrasse (Pankow). A friendly and, by East Berlin standards, quite trendy nightclub which attracts a slightly older sort of crowd. Bizarre point of reference: it's opposite the remand jail for political prisoners. Weds.–Sat. until 6am. Admission 4.60M.

Schoppenstuben, Schönhauser Allee (Prenzlauer Berg). More of a gay wine-bar but the atmosphere approaches that of a western nightclub. It's a small, crowded, and intimate place, but although it's overtly gay you shouldn't feel intimidated if you're straight. Wine costs 11–26M per bottle.

Live Music

There's a good **music scene** in East Berlin and people here are quick to pick up on what's going on in the West. This means that there are dreadful bands churning out bastardized western pop pap, but also plenty of bands who pick up on elements that interest them, and fuse them with their own ideas to create a specifically East Berlin musical identity. Tickets for big stadium gigs cost about 15M and upward depending on who's playing, while smaller FDJ clubhouse and *Kreiskulturhaus* gigs cost 4M to 6M. For information about gigs (and other less mainstream cultural events—film, theater, art exhibitions, etc.) check the poster-covered pillars called *Litfasssäule* which can be found on most East Berlin main streets. Another source of information is a tourist office handout called *Wohin in Berlin* (Where to Go in Berlin) available from the Alexanderplatz tourist office.

The following FDJ club-houses and *Kreiskulturhäuser* can usually be relied on to stage worthwhile gigs (and arts events in general), so check their notice boards for forthcoming events:

Erich-Franz-Club, Schönhauser Allee 36–39 (Prenzlauer Berg)

FDJ Jugendclub, Sophienstrasse

Haus der jungen Talente, Klosterstr. 68–70

Kreiskulturhaus "Erich Weinert," Johannes-R.-Becher-Strasse (Pankow)

Kreiskulturhaus "Prater," Kastanienallee 7–9 (Prenzlauer Berg)

Kreiskulturhaus Treptow, Puschkin Allee 8 (Treptow)

Jazz and Folk

Few specific venues, so it's a question of using the available information sources to check out who is playing the various *Kresikulturhäuser*. There are regular jazz evenings in the *Haus der jungen Talente*, at the *Deutsche Theater*, in the *Erich-Franz-Club*, and in the *Haus der Freundschaft*, Puschkin Allee, Treptow.

Gay East Berlin

The GDR is the most liberal country in the Eastern Bloc when it comes to **gay rights**, and the population as a whole is no more tolerant or intolerant than in West Germany. The age of consent for men is eighteen and there are a number of gay groups (mostly set up under the auspices of the Protestant church). On the whole East Berlin gays are eager to meet gays from the west and there a couple of gay or semi-gay bars and nightspots, which are included in the listings sections (best of these is the *Schoppenstuben)*. One other place worth checking out is the *Mehrzweckgebäude*, Buschallee 87, Weissensee (trolley #70 from the Kupfergraben in the city center) where there are discos (Weds. 7pm–midnight, Fri., Sat. 8:30pm–3am, Sun. 7pm–1am) in a big canteen building. It's hugely popular and always packed with a youngish gay crowd of both sexes.

Listings

Airline Interflug, Alexanderplatz, (☎555 7222).

Area Code From West Berlin to East Berlin ☎0372; from West Germany to East Berlin ☎00372; from East Berlin to West Berlin ☎849.

Embassies The *British Embassy* at Unter den Linden 32–34, (☎220 2431) also handles the interests of Canadian travelers. *American Embassy*, Neustädische Kirchstr. 4–5. (☎220 2741).

Emergencies police ☎ 110; ambulance ☎115.

Intertank gas stations Chauseestr. 98; Prenzlauer Allee 1–4; Holzmarktstr. 36–42, Friedrichshain (24 hr.).

Lost and found, Wilhelm-Pieck-Str. 164 (☎282 613 or 282 3472).

Pharmacies *Dorotheenstädtische Apotheke*, Friedrichstr. 154; *Kronen Apotheke*, Friedrichstr. 165; *Robert-Koch-Apotheke*, Karl-Marx-Allee 101.

Post Offices Rathausstr. 5 (Mon.–Fri. 7am–8pm, Sat. 8am–1pm); Bahnhof Friedrichstrasse (Mon.–Fri. 7am–8pm, Sat. 8–11:30am).

travel details

The following listings are from West Berlin only

By train

To Büchen (4 daily, 3 hr. 15 min.); Helmstedt (8, 2 h.r 40 min.); Bebra (2, 5 hr. 40 min.); Ludwigstadt (2, 5hr.) and thence to other German towns. Hook of Holland (1 weekly, 10 hr.)

By bus

To Bremen (daily, 6hr 45min), Düsseldorf (4 weekly; 9hr 30min), Frankfurt (daily, 10hr 30min), Braunschweig (daily, 3hr 35min), Hannover (daily, 4hr 25min), Hamburg (daily, 4hr 20min), Goslar (daily, 5hr), Lübeck (6 weekly, 4hr 35min), Munich (daily, 9hr 15min).

PART THREE

THE
CONTEXTS

THE HISTORICAL FRAMEWORK

To think of a continuous German history is impossible, since there was no single nation called Germany until 1871, and even then it was not strictly speaking a country, but an empire made up of a number of sovereign states. Nevertheless, a recognizable German culture can be traced through the history of a large and disparate group of territories and traditions.

THE BEGINNINGS

The **earliest trace** of human habitation in Germany is a jawbone found near Heidelberg and therefore dubbed *Homo heidelibergiensis*; this is one of the oldest human remains ever found, thought to date back 500,000 years. Rather more can be surmised about *Homo neandertaliensis* of 400,000 years later, whose name derives from Neanderthal near Düsseldorf. This group of hunters and cave-dwellers survived for some 65,000 years, before dying out in the last Ice Age.

From around the eighth century B.C., the bulk of present-day Germany was inhabited by **Celtic peoples**, who established the first permanent settlements. Warlike, nomadic Germanic tribes gradually appeared farther north, and began pushing their way into the Celtic lands. Their loose structure later made them awkward opponents of the expanding **Roman Empire**, which decided to use the natural boundaries of the rivers Rhine and Danube as the limit of their territory attempts to push eastward were finally abandoned after a crushing defeat at the hands of the Cherusci tribe in the Teutoburger Wald in A.D. 9. The strongly fortified Limes Wall was then erected to protect the empire from barbarian attacks. A number of towns founded by the Romans—Trier, Regensburg, Augsburg, Mainz, and Cologne—were to be the main bases of urban settlement for the next millennium. Christianity was introduced under Emperor Constantine, and a bishopric (the first north of the Alps) was established in Trier, where he had begun his reign, in 314.

The Roman Empire, which had been under siege from various barbarian tribes since the third century, finally succumbed at the beginning of the fifth century. Germany was overrun by the Huns, an action which precipitated the indigenous Saxons to invade England. Gradually the **Franks**, who had been based in what is now Belgium, began to assert themselves over the other Germanic peoples, particularly towards the end of the fifth century under King Clovis, who established the **Merovingian** dynasty and built up a powerful Rhenish state. This depended on a strong administrative structure, resting on the twin pillars of the nobility and the church. In time, the Merovingians were supplanted by their former henchmen, the **Carolingians**, with the help of papal support. The new dynasty was bent on expansionism, and saw the benefits of involving the church in its plans. Missionaries—the most influential of whom was the English-born Saint Boniface—were recruited to undertake mass conversion campaigns among rival tribes.

Under **Charlemagne**, who succeeded to the throne in 768, the fortunes of the Franks went from strength to strength. A series of campaigns saw them stretch their power base from the North Sea to Rome, and from the Pyrenees to the Elbe River. In the context of western Europe, only Britain plus the southern parts of Spain and Italy lay beyond their control. This was buttressed by a tightening of the administration, which had been decentralized, with considerable powers invested in hereditary nobles. The support of the papacy was gained for measures to repulse heathen peoples, such as the Saxons in Germany and the Longobards in Italy. As a logical consequence of this, a power-sharing structure for Europe, in which the pope and the king of the Germans would be the dominant forces, was agreed. On Christmas Day 800, Charlemagne was anointed emperor in Rome, giving him the official status as heir to the Caesars. Though the name was only coined much later, this brought into existence the concept of the **Holy Roman Empire**, which was to last for the next thousand years. This gave the German king considerable power over Italian internal affairs, while the church's influence in matters of state was similarly assured.

Once Charlemagne died, however, this second of the great European empires began to crack under its very weight. In 843, by the **Treaty of Verdun**, it was split into a Germanic eastern Europe and a Latin western Europe, thus sharply delineating the French and Germans for the first time. The first king of the newly formed German eastern empire was **Ludwig the German**. Under his rule the Germanic people became more closely defined, with a specific culture of their own—still scattered over many disparate regions but recognizably made up of the same peoples. When the last of Charlemagne's descendants died in 911, rulership passed to the Saxon King Henry, bringing the Carolingian era to an end.

THE BUILDING OF AN EMPIRE

Under the second Saxon monarch, **Otto the Great**, there was a serious threat to western Europe in the form of the rampaging Magyars, who forced their way deep into German territory. Otto's army, however, repulsed the invaders at the Battle of Lechfeld in 955. Internally, Otto was faced with a problem of similar dimensions in the growing power of the hereditary duchies which posed a threat to the unity of the empire. In order to curb this, he strengthened his alliance with the papacy. The church was given grants of land, coupled with temporal powers of jurisdiction over them, thus creating the basis for subsequent ecclesiastical dominance over much of the country by a series of prince-bishoprics. In 962, he was crowned Holy Roman Emperor, firmly establishing

himself as the main ruler in the Christian world. In many respects, this marks a second foundation of the curious dichotomy that characterized the Holy Roman Empire; from then on, only kings of Germany could gain the title of Roman Emperor, and it was only the Pope who could grant this title.

In time, however, the putting into practice of Otto's policies led to a series of bitter **power struggles** between the papacy and the emperors, who, in exchange for the grants of land, now had the right to make many top ecclesiastical appointments. The crunch eventually came in 1076, when Emperor Henry IV appointed an archbishop to Milan whom Pope Gregory VII found unacceptable. When the pope, a passionate reformer, began to flex his political muscles, the emperor removed him from office, finding in turn that he had been excommunicated. This battle of the titans was eventually won by the pope, with the emperor forced to go on a humiliating pilgrimage of penance. Not only was imperial interference in church affairs from then on severely curtailed, so was the centralized power of the emperor, as the nobility were released by the pope from their vows of allegiance to any secular authority. They soon made their own demands, the most important of which was that emperors should no longer be hereditary rulers, but elected by a council of princes.

By the twelfth century, most of the powerful **dynasties** which were to dominate German politics at both local and national level for hundreds of years had appeared. These were the Wittelsbachs in Bavaria and the Palatinate, the Hohenstaufens, Hohenzollerns, and Württembergs in Swabia, the Zähringens in Baden, and the Welfs and Wettins in Saxony. There was an intense feud between the two most powerful, the **Hohenstaufens** and **Welfs**, which was to continue for centuries, particularly in Italy. The former, until they died out, managed to hold the upper hand, holding on to the office of Holy Roman Emperor for well over a century. **Frederick Barbarossa**, best known as an enthusiastic crusader in the Holy Land, was their most successful ruler. He quelled the pretensions of his Welf rival, Henry the Lion, duke of both Bavaria and Saxony, who tried to establish a powerful Baltic state which would seriously have disrupted the feudal balance of the empire.

However, it became increasingly impossible to keep ambitious princes in check, and by the mid-thirteenth century, there was no real central authority left in Germany; the identity of the legal king was even at times a matter of dispute. Around this period, the nation's boundaries began to be pushed increasingly eastward, following a policy begun by Otto the Great. Impetus for this came from many sources; it's particularly associated with the **Knights of the Teutonic Order**, originally a hospitaller community founded in Palestine, but one which turned its attentions towards the Christianization of eastern Europe. By the early fourteenth century, they had conquered much of Poland (notably the area known as Prussia) and repopulated the land with German peasants. Subsequently, they grew rich on their control of the highly profitable grain trade.

THE MIDDLE AGES

During the fourteenth century, a number of significant changes were made to the structure of the Holy Roman Empire. The **Golden Bull** of 1356 finally established the method for choosing the monarch. This fixed the electoral college at the traditional number of seven, with three **electors** drawn from the ecclesiastical sphere (the archbishops of Cologne, Mainz, and Trier) and four from different ranks of the nobility (the king of Bohemia, the duke of Saxony, the margrave of Brandenburg and the count palatine of the Rhine).

From then on, these seven princes were tremendously powerful grandees—they had the right to construct castles, mint their own coinage, impose tolls, and act as judges in all disputes, with no right of appeal. Oddly enough, the title of emperor almost invariably went to a candidate outside this group. Increasingly, this was conferred on a member of the **Hapsburg** dynasty. This family had first held hereditary lands in Switzerland, but from the thirteenth century onward were indelibly associated with Austria, building it up into the most powerful of the German states.

Such a clear-cut electoral system had the benefit of putting a halt to papal intervention in the elections. In any event, the church's power over internal German affairs was killed off for good by the **Great Schism** of 1378–1417, in which rival popes held court in Rome and Avignon. This also gave the emperors the

opportunity to reestablish their right to make ecclesiastical appointments within their domains; there were by now over a hundred German bishops and abbots with temporal powers.

By this time, the social structure was undergoing changes that had far-reaching effects. The most important was the growth of **towns** at strategic points, and along important trading routes. Initially, these were under patrician domination. However, merchants and craftsmen organized themselves into guilds which gradually wrested control of civic life, and laid the foundations for a capitalist economy.

The most prosperous families, for example the Fuggers in Augsburg, took over former royal and religious functions, such as patronage of the arts and the establishment of charitable foundations. They formed an elite group within the towns—although government in each community was in the hands of a council, this by no means constituted democratic rule. Most of the towns gained the status of **free imperial city**, which meant they were independent city-states, responsible only to the emperor. Their prosperity was greatly enhanced by the ruinous Hundred Years' War between France and England, which enabled them to snap up diverted trade to and from the Mediterranean. Though in many ways in competition with each other, the leadership of the towns realized they also had common cause.

This led to the foundation of various trading and defense leagues. Of particular importance was the north German **Hanseatic League**, founded in Lübeck, which successfully combated piracy, and led not only to German economic domination of the Baltic and North Sea, but to increased political power as well, with the establishment of German communities in Scandanavia and all along the opposite coast as far as Estonia.

The **bubonic plague** swept across Europe in the fourteenth century, finding easy breeding ground in the filthy medieval towns and unhygienic rural settlements. Over a quarter of the German population was wiped out by the Black Death, spreading fear and bringing vast areas to a virtual standstill.

In all probability, the plague was introduced by merchants returning from Asia, but a different scapegoat had to be found, and the **Jews**, who lived in segregated settlements around the towns, readily fitted the bill. Jews had lived in northern Europe since the tenth century, but their place had never been an easy one, with their close-knit and separate communities giving rise to popular suspicion and prejudice. Segregation from Christian communities was enforced by papal decree rather than by choice, and even went to the extent of their having to wear distinctive uniforms. Excluded from guilds and trades, they took up the only occupation forbidden to Christians: money-lending—a necessary but hated service that did nothing to endear them to the locals. **Pogroms** therefore frequently occurred.

Meanwhile the great stretches of rural countryside depopulated by the plague were gathered up into **large landholdings** by the nobility, and formerly independent farmers and peasants were soon swallowed up in a system of enforced labor in return for exemption from financial levies and military service. This practice rapidly transformed itself into established serfdom for the majority of the rural inhabitants, who still accounted for 85 percent of the country's total population. Thus at the end of the medieval period there was a vast gulf between the affluent and the destitute, with only a minority in between.

The fifteenth century saw the Hapsburgs firmly establish themselves as the driving force in high politics, holding on to the office of Holy Roman Emperor from 1432 until its abolition nearly four hundred years later. **Maximilian I**, "the last of the German knights," acceded to the title in 1493, and proceded on a policy of making his family the most powerful not just in Germany, but in all of Europe. His own wedding to Mary of Burgundy gained him the Netherlands; a series of astute dynastic marriages involving his relatives led to Spain, Hungary, and Bohemia all coming under Habsburg control. However, he antagonized the members of the Swiss Confederation, which broke away from the empire to become a separate state in 1499.

THE REFORMATION AND AFTER

The Catholic church enjoyed absolute spiritual authority throughout the Middle Ages, with faith being the only comfort for the majority of people, who clung to the idea that "the meek will inherit the earth." The underside, however,

was blind zeal and widespread superstition; witch-hunting and religious persecution were common, with torture and burning at the stake standard procedure for dealing with suspects.

In order to cash in on popular fear, the church demanded money from the faithful to ensure salvation of their souls, and a lucrative trade in **indulgences** was established, whereby people could buy absolution of their sins. These were rather like modern-day shares, to be bought in whole or part by as many people as wished to participate. Bishops across the land acted as agents, and meanwhile the papal coffers filled up to finance the building of St. Peter's and many other great sacred buildings.

Discontent with the church was particularly rife within Germany, given the church's dual role within society, and the fact that territories under the control of religious officeholders tended to be particularly harshly run. Thus it was hardly surprising that it was here that the full-frontal assault on the church's traditional powers began.

The attack was led by a man of burning religious convictions, the Augustinian monk **Martin Luther**, who had been appointed to the influential position of professor of theology at the University of Wittenberg (now in the GDR). Believing that the church was corrupt and had totally lost its way, Luther focused his attentions on the problem of **salvation**, finding support in the Bible for the tenet that man justifies himself by faith alone. This meant that he could play no part in his own salvation; therefore the trade in indulgences was a total fraud. On the eve of All Saints' Day 1517, he nailed his **95 Theses** to the door of the court church in Wittenberg. This was in fact the normal way of inviting academic discussion, but it was seen as a deliberately provocative act, and is now considered the official **beginning of the Reformation**.

Luther in time widened his attack, denouncing the centralized power of the pope, the privileged position of priests as intercessors between God and the faithful, and the doctrine of transubstantiation, which maintained that the bread and wine used in the sacrament of the Eucharist physically turned into Christ's body and blood.

However, Luther's arguments might have had as little impact as any other scholarly dispute, or led to his immediate execution as a heretic, had not the curious power structure in Germany dealt him an amazing piece of good fortune. The death of Maximilian I in 1519 led to a bizarre **European-wide power struggle** for the crown of the Holy Roman Empire. Francis I of France decided to stake a claim for the title, in order to stop the unhealthy concentration of power in Europe which would ensue if victory went to the Habsburg candidate, Charles I of Spain; for a time, England's Henry VIII was also in the running. In order to stop this interference from abroad, the pope had to keep the electors sweet, even suggesting one of their number, Luther's patron Duke Frederick the Wise of Saxony, as a compromise candidate.

After much bribery by the two main contenders, the Spanish king duly won the election unanimously and took office as Emperor Charles V. However, he immediately became embroiled in a war with France. As a result, the powerful princes of the Holy Roman Empire seized this golden chance to establish a far greater degree of independence. Many of them saw the religious struggle as a convenient cloak for their ambitions. Luther was excommunicated in 1520, but still had the right, as a citizen of the empire, to have a hearing before an imperial Diet. This was hastily convened at Worms the following year, and, though Luther was branded an outlaw and his books were ordered to be burned, he was given a safe haven at the Wartburg castle in Thuringia (now in the GDR), under the protection of Duke Frederick. There he made his **translation of the Bible**, thus making it accessible to the common man for the first time; this work is also seen as the foundation stone of the modern German language.

Luther's ideas spread like wildfire throughout society, greatly aided by the fact that books could now be produced cheaply and quickly, thanks to the printing revolution launched by the German inventor Johannes Gutenberg during the previous century. They found a ready market among the oppressed classes, who took the attacks on church authority as invitations to attack authority in general.

This led to the **Peasants' Revolt** of 1524–25, which brought wholescale destructions of monasteries and castles. Poorly armed, organized, and led, the rebellion was brutally crushed by the princely armies. To the dismay of the rebels, Luther aligned himself on the side of worldly authority, arguing that it was God's will that there should be different strata in society; equality was only for the hereafter. Thus, the Reformation progressed as a revolution controlled from above, setting the tone for German history for centuries to come.

In 1529, the representatives of six principalities and fourteen free imperial cities which supported Luther met at Speyer, where the name **Protestant** came to be used for the first time. The following year, Charles V convened a Diet at Augsburg in an attempt to defuse the growing crisis. However, he was confronted by a closely argued definition of the Reformers' position, thereafter known as the **Confession of Augsburg**, which was drawn up by Luther's indispensible sidekick, the brilliant scholar Philipp Melanchton. This set the seal not only on the division of the Western church, but also on the effective division of Germany into a plethora of small states.

Another year on, the Schmalkaldic League was formed as an armed alliance to protect Protestantism. Despite a number of setbacks, so many states had joined the Protestant cause by 1555 that Charles V had to admit defeat, abdicating in order to retire to a Spanish monastery. He was succeeded by his brother Ferdinand, who almost immediately signed the **Peace of Augsburg**, a historic agreement that institutionalized religious tolerance, leaving the decision as to the form of religion practiced in each state firmly in the hands of its secular rulers. Though a measure of considerable significance, it was in effect a power-sharing between the Catholics and Lutherans at the expense of more radical Protestant groups.

THE STRUGGLE FOR RELIGIOUS SUPREMACY

After Luther's death in 1546, the Catholics began to make something of a comeback via the reforms thrashed out at the Council of Trent. This launched the **Counter-Reformation**, which met the Protestants head-on by reaffirming as unshakable truths many of the cherished dogmas that had been savaged by the reformers. Radical Protestantism was also given a boost by Melanchton's shift away from central Lutheran doctrines to more extreme solutions, and the creed known as **Pietism** gained a particular hold in Swabia and central Germany.

Inevitably, one of the political goals of Protestantism was to gain control of the imperial electoral college, and oust the Catholic Hapsburgs from their long tradition of preeminence. In 1583, the difficulty of usurping the built-in Catholic advantage was unexpectedly eased by the decision of the archbishop of Cologne to switch to the Protestant side, and continue ruling his territories as normal. However, that ploy swiftly came to nought when he was excommunicated and defeated in battle; from then on, it was necessary to capture all four of the secular electorates.

A Catholic attack on the Protestant Bavarian town of Donauwörth in 1608 led to the formation of the **Protestant Union**, an armed alliance under the leadership of the Palatinate. The **Catholic League** was set up in opposition by the Bavarians the following year, meaning that there was now a straight division of the country into two hostile camps. Meanwhile, the manner in which central authority in Germany had collapsed was cruelly exposed by the weak 36-year reign of Rudolph II, who chose to govern from the very fringe of the empire. His court in Prague is chiefly remembered for its bizarre erotic practices, and he himself eventually became insane.

As it happened, this same city was to see the beginning of the great trial of strength between the two faiths. In 1618, the youthful Count Palatine Friedrich V usurped the crown of Bohemia, which itself was an elected office, thus seemingly ensuring a Protestant majority in the next imperial election. Unfortunately for him, he lost both his titles a year later, and had by then set in train the complicated series of religious and dynastic conflicts commonly known as the **Thirty Years' War**.

Eventually all Europe became involved in the war, except Russia and Britain, but the battles were fought almost exclusively on German territory. Much of the countryside was laid waste, towns were pillaged, and there was mass rape and slaughter, at the end of which the population of the country may have been reduced by up to a third. Initially, the Catholic League, commanded by the brutal Johann Tilly, held the upper hand, but first Denmark, then Sweden intervened, fearing for both their independence and their Protestant faith. The Swedes, led by King Gustavus II Adolphus, had their greatest moment of triumph on the European stage, defeating Tilly and overrunning the country, thus briefly rising to the rank of a major power. Spain intervened on behalf of her Habsburg cousins, while Catholic France supported the Protestants, on the grounds that their faith was a lesser evil than the threatened Habsburg hegemony over Europe.

From 1643, concerted attempts were made to end the war, with the Catholics meeting in Münster, the Protestants in Osnabrück. The negotiations are generally seen as the beginnings of modern diplomacy; they culminated five years later in the signing of the **Peace of Westphalia**. While the ending of the messy conflicts was a major achievement in itself, for Germany the peace treaty was as disastrous as the war itself. The Holy Roman Empire was killed off in all but name, with the emperor reduced to a figurehead, who could only raise taxes and make laws with the assent of the "perpetual" imperial Diet (itself a toothless monster) established at Regensburg.

Real power was concentrated in a **plethora of states**, numbering some 300 principalities, plus over 1000 other territories, some of them minute—a system which could hardly have been better designed to waste resources and stunt economic development. Each two-bit state had its own currency, which was worthless abroad, while there were complicated customs controls, and absurd restrictions in the movement of goods and labor. Political development was similarly stunted: there was a lack of fertile ground for progressive ideas to grow, any sense of national consciousness disappeared, and the way was set for a multiplicity of petty tyrants to reestablish a feudalistic social system. Moreover, Germany ceased to be a factor of importance on the European stage.

THE RISE OF PRUSSIA

In the course of the late seventeenth century and eighteenth century, almost all the petty German princes adopted an **absolutist** system of government, based on the divine right of rulers. They spent a vast amount of their revenue building palaces on a scale out of all proportion to their needs, in order that there could be at least the visual pretense that they were mighty monarchs. Only a few managed to rise above the general level of mediocrity; one of these was the House of Welf, which made an astonishing comeback after centuries of confinement to their Lower Saxon heartlands. As a result of clever politicking, the **Hanoverian** branch of the family gained the British crown in 1714, and maintained a royal union until 1837.

Within the Holy Roman Empire itself, **Austria** at first maintained her dominance, with the Hapsburgs holding on to the imperial title, for what it was worth. The country received a severe jolt when the rampaging Turks reached the gates of Vienna in 1683, but after the enemy was beaten back, the way was cleared for Austria to build up an empire in the Balkans, which gradually came to act as a consolation for the loss of influence over the German states. As German-speaking influence spread eastward, the western flank become vulnerable. The **French**, like the Romans before them, saw the Rhine as the natural limit of their territory. They formally annexed Alsace and Strasbourg in 1681, then laid claim to the Palatinate in a series of bloody campaigns between 1688 and 1697.

By then, a new power had arisen in north-eastern Germany in the shape of **Branden-burg-Prussia**. In 1415, the old frontier district of Brandenburg had been given to the ambitious **Hohenzollern** family, whose attempts to gain power at the heart of the empire had met with no success. Though it carried the status of an electorate, it was a decidedly unpromising piece of land, and it remained one of the most backward parts of Germany. Since 1525, the family had also held the Baltic territory known as Prussia, gained when Albrecht von Hohenzollern, Grand Master of the Knights of the Teutonic Order, had converted to Protestantism and secularized the order's holdings as a duchy under the Polish crown. In 1660, this was wrested from Polish control and amalgamated with their own lands, which thereafter generally became known as "Prussia."

There was a convincing reason for the adoption of this name. Prussia proper lay outside the Holy Roman Empire, and thus was not subject to any of its rules. One of these forbade princes from promoting themselves to royal titles; in 1701, Friedrich III defied this with impunity by having himself crowned as king of Prussia. The Hapsburgs duly turned a blind eye to this in order to gain Hohenzollern support in the **War of the Spanish Succession**, which broke out as a result of rival Austrian and French claimants for the throne of Spain.

Thoughout the eighteenth century, Prussia was built up as a strongly centralized state, based on Berlin. There was a tight administrative structure, but it became associated above all with **militarism**. It was a second Sparta, described with some justification as not a state with an army, but an army with a state; at times, an amazing two-thirds of national revenue was spent on the military. The other dominant force in society was the **Junker** class, landowners who ran huge estates, in which the laborers were treated as little more than serfs. A tradition of unquestioning obedience was inculcated in the lower orders, while the upper class was driven by an insatiable lust for power and conquest.

Prussia's rise to the rank of a major European power was achieved under **Frederick the Great**, who came to the throne in 1740. A Francophile and epitome of the enlightened despot, Frederick softened his country's rough-hewn image by introducing a few liberal reforms at home, and developed a cultured courtly life. However, his main concern was expansion by military force, and he used an old Prussian claim on Silesia to extract that territory from Austria. In revenge, the Hapsburgs launched the Seven Years' War in 1756, thereby hoping to annihilate Prussia as a potential rival; in this, they had the full military backing of the two other great continental powers, France and Russia, whereas Frederick had only the tacit support of Britain and Hannover to fall back on.

Within three years, the highly rated Prussian troops seemed to be on the brink of defeat, having paid the penalty for overextending themselves. They were given an unexpected reprieve when the Austrians and Russians fell out; new recruits were thrown into the conflict, eventually achieving an incredible turnaround in fortunes, and in the process establishing Prussia as a force of the first rank. By annexing much of Poland in the partition of 1772, Frederick achieved his aim of establishing a north German version of Austria; this policy was continued by his immediate successors.

THE NAPOLEONIC PERIOD AND ITS AFTERMATH

Ironically, the first steps towards the unity of Germany came as a result of the expansionist aims of revolutionary France. By the War of the First Coalition of 1792–97, the left bank of the Rhine fell—quite happily, it would seem—under French control. However, it was only with the advent of the dictator **Napoleon Bonaparte** that radical changes were made. Following the defeat of Austria in 1802 in the War of the Second Coalition (in which Prussia tactfully remained aloof), he decided to completely reorder the German map, which he rightly saw as anachronistic. All but a handful of the free cities, and every single one of the ecclesiastical territories, were stripped of their independence, which in many cases went back five or six centuries.

In their place, a chain of buffer states was created. Bavaria, Württemberg, and Saxony were raised to the rank of kingdoms, while Baden and Hessen-Darmstadt became grand duchies. In 1806, during the War of the Third Coalition, the Holy Roman Empire was officially abolished, with the Hapsburgs consoling themselves for suffering yet another defeat by promoting themselves from archdukes to emperors of Austria, deciding thereafter to concentrate their energies on preserving their Balkan lands. Gradually, the German satellite states began to remove economic, religious, and servile restrictions, developing into societies which were liberal by German standards of the past.

The same year, Prussia suffered a series of humiliating defeats; Berlin was occupied and the country forced to sign away half its territory and population. Thereafter, it was forced to mend its ways: serfdom was abolished, and its cities were allowed to develop their own municipal government. In the event, Prussia's humiliation was short-lived, and it soared in international prestige as a result of its key role at the **Battle of Waterloo** in 1815, when Napoleon's overambitious plans for the total subjugation of Europe were finally put to rest. By delaying his attack, and thus failing to press home his numerical superiority over the combined army of Britain and Hannover, the French dictator allowed the Prussians, who had been defeated and cut off from their allies just two days before, just enough time to make a heroic quick-march to the scene of battle, where they decisively swung the result.

The **Congress of Vienna**, which met the same year to determine the structure of post-Napoleonic Europe, established Prussian dominance in German affairs. Westphalia and the Rhineland were added to its territories, meaning that it now stretched all the way from the French border to the river Memel, interrupted only by a few enclaves. Otherwise, much of the Napoleonic reorganization of the Holy Roman Empire was ratified, leaving 39 independent states: still far too many, but a major step forward nonetheless. A German Confederation was established, with each state represented in the Frankfurt-based Diet, which, however, had no effective power.

TOWARDS GERMAN UNIFICATION

Whereas the main political forces in German society in the aftermath of the Congress of Vienna were still staunchly conservative, the accelerating **Industrial Revolution** was resulting in radical economic and social changes. The German Confederation closely followed the British lead, but profited by learning from the pioneering country's mistakes. The first German railroad was established in 1835, and industrial production advanced in leaps and bounds. Thanks to its rich mineral deposits, the dominant center for industry was the Rhine-Ruhr area, which had recently been allocated to Prussia. In 1834, Prussia's increasingly dominant role within the German nation was underlined by the establishment of a customs union, known as the **Zollverein**. Austria opted out of this, on the ground that the tariff rates were too low to suit her protectionism; the northwestern states were the only others not to join—for precisely the opposite reason.

The Industrial Revolution led to a whole **new social order**, with wage-earning workers and an emergent bourgeoisie. Both groups were quick to agitate for their vested interests: the workers for better working conditions and the bourgeoisie for political representation. Meanwhile most of the peasantry was still living in abject poverty and under almost feudal conditions, which worsened during the failed harvests of the late 1840s. Social unrest was inevitable, and violence erupted both in the countryside and the cities, causing ever more reactionary policies from the land-owning elite with the political power.

In 1848, there were uprisings all over Europe. This forced the Prussian king to allow elections to the **National Assembly** in Frankfurt, thereby hoping to nip republican and socialist aspirations in the bud. For the first time, an opportunity was presented to found a liberal tradition in the country, but it was completely muffed. The bourgeois members of the assembly were much too eager to establish the new-found status of their own social groups to attempt any far-reaching political reforms, and they certainly posed no threat to the existing order. If anything, the bourgeoisie was prone to blend in with the privileged upper classes rather than agitate with either workers or peasants. Valuable time was wasted in trying to bring the Habsburg and Hohenzollern monarchs around to the idea of a federal union under a hereditary emperor; neither was remotely interested in such a restricted role. Thus, when armed rebellions broke out in 1849, the National Assembly was exposed as an ineffective talking shop, easily disbanded in the face of the revolutionary emergency. Any other steps towards constitutional rule were wiped out by the combined forces of the Prussian army and battalions from other German kingdoms and principalities.

The 1850s saw political stagnation, but the increasing success of the Industrial Revolution meant that the creation of a single internal German market, preferably accompanied by a political union, was of paramount importance. By now, Prussia had maneuvered herself into a position of such power that she was the only possible agent for enforcing such a change. For **King Wilhelm I**, ordering this from above had the additional benefit that conservative forces would prevail against the troublesome parliamentary liberal opposition.

In 1862, he chose as chancellor the career diplomat **Otto von Bismarck**, a member of the Junker class who had aleady gained a reputation as an operator of a rare sharpness. From the word go, Bismarck was candid about the methods he intended to use: "The great questions of the day will not be settled by resolutions and majority votes—that was the mistake of the men of 1848 and 1849—but by blood and iron," he declared. He was as good

as his word, ruthlessly manipulating and destroying his opponents, whether at home or abroad. A policy of force also made sense in the light of the fact that the weapons produced by the Krupp factory in Essen were always a step ahead of anything else being manufactured in other countries.

In order to win over the Prussian liberals, Bismarck backed the concept of universal men's suffrage. He also played the nationalist card immediately: seeing that the chancellor was bent on creating a united Germany, the liberals muted their opposition and backed his plans for a thorough modernization of the army. The Germany that would emerge, Bismarck realized, would have to exclude Austria altogether, but at the same time, he astutely recognized that the Habsburg Empire would have to be kept as a strong force in European affairs, in order to counterbalance France and Russia.

In 1864, Bismarck lured Austria into supporting him in a war against Denmark to recapture the lost duchies of Schleswig and Holstein. Having achieved an easy victory, he then provoked a disagreement over the spoils; the result was the **Seven Weeks' War** of 1866, in which the superior Prussian weapons and organization achieved a crushing victory. Not only was Austria forced out of Germany's affairs, but those states which had remained neutral, including Hannover and Hessen, were forcibly incorporated into Prussia. The German Confederation was dissolved, to be replaced by one covering the north of the country only, and was totally under Prussian domination.

To complete the "crazy quilt," Bismarck still needed to woo the southern states; in this, he was greatly helped by the fact that national feelings were running strong. His tactic was a decidedly original one: to provoke a war against the old enemy, France. In 1870, having carefully prepared the diplomatic ground to ensure that no other power would intervene to support the French, he goaded them by proposing that a Hohenzollern should succeed to the vacant throne of Spain. The French Emperor, Napoleon III, managed to force the Prussians to withdraw, but foolishly sent a telegram asking for an apology. Bismarck doctored this to make it seem worse than it was, giving the excuse to begin the **Franco-Prussian War**.

By January 1871, the Prussian field guns had helped chalk up yet another easy victory. A united German Empire, which once more included the long-disputed provinces of Alsace and Lorraine, was proclaimed in Versailles. King Wilhelm I of Prussia was the inevitable choice as kaiser; four other monarchs were among the rulers who were henceforth subjugated to him. The new empire became known as the Second Reich, in honor of the fact that it had revived the German imperial tradition after a gap of 65 years.

THE SECOND REICH

In his domestic policy for the united Germany (which in reality was no more than Prussia writ large), Bismarck indulged in a series of **liberal reforms**. Uniform systems of law, administration, and currency were introduced, an imperial bank was set up, restrictions on trade and movement of labor were lifted, and cities were given municipal autonomy.

By such measures, Bismarck aimed to control the opposition parties in the Reichstag, and to keep power in the hands of the elite. The darker side of his nature came out in the *Kulturkampf*, which aimed at curbing the power of the Catholic church, whose power and influence was anathema to the Protestant aristocracy of Prussia. However, this met with spirited opposition, which led to Bismarck making a rare retreat, though not until he had exacted his price: the Catholics were forced to support protectionist agricultural measures, designed to subsidize the large, outdated Junker estates. By then, a formidable new opposition had arisen in the shape of the **Social Democratic Party** (SPD), founded in 1875. In order to take the wind out its sails, Bismarck introduced a system of welfare benefits for workers, a system belatedly copied in many other industrialized countries.

Bismarck's **foreign policy** involved a complicated set of jugglings. He set up the *Dreikaiserbund*, an alliance of the three great imperial powers of Germany, Austria, and Russia; indulged in a Mediterranean naval alliance with Britain in order to check Russian designs on the Balkans; but initiated a bit of colonial rivalry with the British.

Bismarck's awesome reputation for political surefootedness meant that Germany's internal and external stability seemed completely safe in his hands. However, Friedrich III, who succeeded his father Wilhelm I in 1888, died after only a few months on the throne. His son, **Wilhelm II**, was a firm believer in the divine right of kings. He was of a generation which did not feel beholden to Bismarck, and strongly disliked the veteran politician. Two years later, he removed the chancellor from office—a move comparable to dropping the pilot from a ship—and thereafter relied on a series of ineffective kowtowers to lead his government.

Britain, which had hitherto been a natural ally of Germany as a result of dynastic ties and mutual suspicion of France, was increasingly seen as the main rival. There was a great deal of jealousy about the number of colonies held by the British, and finding Germany "a place in the sun" became an obsession. By the time the Germans got in on the imperialist act, however, there were only the crumbs left from a previously rich table. A notorious telegram sent by the kaiser in support of the Boers in 1896 signaled the beginning of a severe deterioration in relations between the two countries.

This was fueled by an **arms race**, affecting all of Europe, in which the Krupp factory once more played a crucial role. It deliberately developed a cycle of making offensive weapons, then successful defenses against it, followed by a more sophisticated attack which rendered the defenses useless, and so on; these were sold all over the world. Nowhere was the attempt to establish supremacy more evident than in the naval sphere, in which the Germans set out to usurp Britain's long period of hegemony, achieving parity by 1909.

By this time, the major powers of Europe were divided into **two nervous alliances**. Bismarck's successors failed to maintain his two-faced foreign policy. As a result, Germany was bound up once more with Austria, whose eastern empire was tottering under the nationalist aspirations of the many ethnic groups contained within it; Italy was a somewhat reluctant partner. Ranged against them were France and Russia, drawn together by mutual fear of the ever-increasing power of the German-speaking countries; the latter were also implacable foes of Austria with regard to policy in the Balkans. Britain, maintaining her time-honored policy of trying to preserve an effective balance of power in Europe, was increasingly drawn towards the latter alliance.

WORLD WAR I

Everybody expected that war would come sooner or later, and master strategies were carefully planned. The Germans developed the **first-strike theory**, which envisaged a quick knockout blow against both France and Russia, as a prelude to a more protracted struggle against the more formidable British. Public opinion in the country was easily won over by the bogus theory that the Fatherland was under threat from the "iron ring" which surrounded it. Even the social democrats were persuaded of the necessity and desirability of a war.

The spark which lit the inferno happened to emerge from **Austria's unwieldy empire**. In 1914, the crown prince, Archduke Franz Ferdinand, was assassinated in Sarajevo by a Bosnian nationalist. A military force was sent to crush the independent neighboring state of Serbia, although no connection between its government and the conspirators who planned the assassination was ever proved. This inevitably provoked the Russians, who, as "Big Brother Slav," had an agreement to protect them from any threat. The German generals, who had been itching for a war, saw this as a golden opportunity to put their first-strike theory into operation. As soon as the Russians mobilized, German troops were sent to attack France. The quickest route was through Belgium, thus violating its neutrality, which was guaranteed by Britain. So fast did events move that the kaiser sent a telegram ordering withdrawal, but this was ignored. **World War I** was thus underway.

The German High Command believed the French would capitulate within six weeks, the Russians within six months. They were soon proved hopelessly wrong, and found themselves with what they had been most anxious to avoid—a war on two fronts. Even then, they could hardly have anticipated the Armageddon which was unleashed. After the first Battle of the Marne in September, they were forced to retreat and dig **trenches** all across northern France and Belgium, which led to a wholly new form of warfare, with casualties quite unlike any that had previously been known. In 1916, an attempt to exhaust the French at the four-month-long Battle of Verdun proved to be self-defeating, while the same year saw the British prove their continued mastery of the seas at the Battle of Jutland.

As a result of these setbacks, the kaiser handed over effective military and political power to the dual leadership of Field Marshal **Paul von Hindenburg**, and Quartermaster-General **Erich Ludendorff**; though the latter was nominally the junior partner, he effectively became the dictator of the country. In January 1917, it was decided to capitalize on Germany's U-boat strength by introducing unrestricted submarine warfare. This was a complete disaster—not only did the British defeat it by adopting the convoy system, but its barbarity prompted the United States to enter the war. Later the same year, an all-out offensive on the western front was routed. A reprieve was gained as a result of the revolution in Russia that autumn; this not only closed the eastern front, but allowed the Germans to impose a draconian peace settlement with the Treaty of Brest-Litovsk, which included vast annexations of territory. However, the euphoria of this triumph was tempered by the knowledge that defeat in the west was now seemingly inevitable.

THE END OF WORLD WAR I AND THE FAILURE OF THE GERMAN REVOLUTION

The Allied penetration of the German lines on 8 August 1918 finally convinced Ludendorff that the war was irretrievably lost. Unwilling to countenance the likelihood of a humiliating military defeat and foreign occupation, he looked for ways to minimize the High Command's loss of face. Although the idea of democracy was anathema, he seized on the idea of letting a parliamentary government handle the peace negotiations; it would be likely to secure more lenient terms, and would also be a useful scapegoat in the event of a harsh treaty. Furthermore, it would act as a powerful counteractive against the far more horrifying alternative of a Bolshevik-style revolution, an only-too-likely prospect once the German people realized the extent to which their leaders had been deceiving them.

Accordingly, he persuaded the kaiser to appoint the liberal monarchist **Prince Max von Baden** as chancellor. A fully parliamentary democracy was proclaimed, with universal suffrage and secret ballots; the cabinet was drawn from the ranks of the Reichstag, with social democrats included for the first time; censorship was abolished; and the kaiser was stripped of his overall political and military supremacy.

On October 3, Prince Max sued for peace on the basis of the Fourteen Point Plan drawn up earlier in the year by the American president, Woodrow Wilson. Ludendorff, sensing that the Allies were going to drive a hard bargain, subsequently resigned; Hindenburg offered to do likewise, but was allowed to remain at his post.

Towards the end of the month, Admiral Scheer decided to mount a futile last-ditch offensive; his crews mutinied, refusing to lay down their lives so unnecessarily. This revolt spread throughout northern Germany, and might well have developed into the full-scale revolution Ludendorff had been conniving to avert, had it not been for the bitter **division of the political left wing** into three factions.

The SPD had previously split into two separate parties over the matter of continued support for the war; the pacifist group, the USPD, were now frustrated by the tepid nature of their erstwhile colleagues' socialism, which embraced constitutional monarchy and a bourgeois social order. In turn, their politics were seen as too tame by the Spartacist League, a Marxist group which aimed to follow the example of their Russian mentors by seizing power in Berlin. **Friedrich Ebert**, leader of the SPD, decided to forestall them by calling a general strike to demand the kaiser's abdication. Prince Max took matters into his own hands by announcing this without the monarch's consent, and then himself resigned in favor of Ebert. Matters were still more delicately poised with the news that **Karl Liebknecht** of the Spartacists intended to proclaim the establishment of a socialist republic on November.

In order to wrest the initiative, Ebert's lieutenant **Philipp Scheidemann** made an impromptu declaration of a free German Republic from the Reichstag balcony, thus bringing the regime of the kaisers to an abrupt end. Two days later, an armistice was signed, as Ebert realized that either a collapse of military discipline, or the spread of Bolshevism, would lead to an Allied invasion. As part of his plans, he made a pact with the High Command, which provided him with an army to protect the state against internal left-wing opponents, but at the price of allowing it almost complete autonomy.

This policy paid immediate dividends for him, as the military was used to crush an attempted revolution by the Spartacists in January, a last-ditch attempt at a Communist seizure of power before the elections for the new National Assembly later in the month. The brutal behavior of the army—Liebknecht and his coleader Rosa Luxemburg were among those murdered—exacerbated the already deep divisions on the left. However, it did not signal military acceptance of the democratic ideal; indeed, the unholy alliance into which Ebert had entered was to have disastrous long-term consequences for the fledgling republic, which should have made a purging of the anti-democratic and war-crazed officer class one of its most urgent priorities.

THE WEIMAR REPUBLIC

Elections confirmed the SPD as the new political leaders of the country, with 38 percent of the vote; as a result, Ebert was made president, with Scheidemann as chancellor. Weimar, the small country town which had seen the most glorious flowering of the German Enlightenment, was chosen as the seat of government in preference to Berlin, which was tinged by its monarchical and militaristic associations.

A **new constitution** was drawn up, hailed as the most liberal and progressive in the world. It aimed at a comprehensive system of checks and balances to ensure that power could not become too concentrated. Authority was formally vested in the people, and the state was given a quasifederal structure to limit excessive Prussian domination. Executive authority was shared between a president (who could rule by emergency decree if necessary) and the Reich government in a highly complex arrangement. Reichstag deputies were elected by proportional representation from party lists.

While on the surface an admirable document, this constitution was hopelessly idealistic for a people so unfamiliar with democratic practice and responsibilities. No attempt was made to outlaw parties hostile to the system; this opened the way for savage attacks on the republic by extremists at both ends of the political spectrum. The use of proportional representation, without any qualifying minimum percentage of the total vote, favored a plethora of parties promoting sectional interests. This meant that the Weimar governments were all unwieldy coalitions, whose average life was about eight months, and which often pursued contradictory policies in different ministries.

Two months before the constitution was ratified in July 1919, Germany had been forced to accede to the **Treaty of Versailles**. In contrast to the Habsburg Empire, which was broken up into a series of successor states, German territorial integrity was largely preserved, but the losses were painful ones—the industrially productive Saarland and Alsace-Lorraine went to France, while the resurrected country of Poland was given Upper Silesia plus a corridor to the sea, which left East Prussia cut off from the rest of the country. All overseas colonies were confiscated, the Rhineland was declared a demilitarized zone, the navy limited to six light battleships, and the army to 100,000 men with conscription prohibited. Germany and her allies were found guilty of having started the war, and, as a result, were saddled with an enormous **reparations bill**, which would have taken over half a century to pay.

In all, this amounted to a pretty stiff settlement, albeit one considerably less harsh than the Germans had recently foisted on the Russians at Brest-Litovsk. So incensed were the military leaders with this humiliating diktat that they toyed with the idea of resuming hostilities. As this was not a feasible option, they contented themselves with inventing the **"stab in the back" legend**, maintaining that the army, undefeated in the field, had been betrayed by unscrupulous politicians—a preposterous distortion accepted all too easily by gullible sections of the public.

The treaty spelled the beginning of the end for the social democratic republic. Scheidemann immediately resigned as chancellor, and, following gains by the two political extremes in the 1920 elections under the new constitution, the party, though still the largest in the Reichstag, withdrew from government altogether, leaving power in the hands of minority administrations drawn from liberal and moderate conservative parties. Right-wing extremism flourished in a series of political murders and

attempted putsches, which were barely punished by a judiciary which rivaled the army in its contempt for the republic.

The reparations bill crippled the economy, to the extent that payments began to be withheld. This gave the French the excuse to occupy the Ruhr in 1923; they were met by a policy of passive resistance. As no work was done, galloping **inflation**—the most catastrophic ever known in world history—quickly ensued, causing the ruin of the entire middle class as the currency became utterly worthless. The Weimar Republic seemed irretrievably doomed, but it made an astonishing comeback, largely due to the political skills of the new chancellor, **Gustav Stresemann**. He was an unlikely saviour, an old-fashioned conservative who had begun his career as Ludendorff's mouthpiece in the Reichstag, and whose precise commitment to the republic is still disputed. A supreme pragmatist, he realized the danger of economic collapse and the futility of confrontation with the Allies. Therefore he ended passive resistance, and negotiated huge American loans to rebuild the economy; this was so successful that by October 1924 money had regained its former value; (nearly) full employment and general prosperity soon followed.

Although Stresemann's government broke up long before these effects were felt, he subsequently served as foreign minister for six years in a variety of coalitions, achieving **Germany's rehabilitation on the world stage**. By the 1925 Locarno Pact, he gained rapprochement with France, and guarantees that there could be no further threat of foreign occupation. The following year, Germany's essential role in international affairs was confirmed by her admission to the League of Nations, the forum for world peace established after the war. Reparation payments were scaled down, and more American aid given, making Germany a net gainer from these transactions. It seemed that the republic was set for a secure future, even if the political immaturity of the German people was still apparent, most notably in the presidential election of 1925. This was won by the 78-year-old Hindenburg, a wily operator basking in an undeserved military reputation, vocal exponent of the "stab in the back" legend, and an embarrassing reminder of times past.

THE RISE OF NAZISM

The **National Socialist German Workers' Party** was founded in 1918 by a locksmith by the name of Anton Drexler, but only gained momentum when he was ousted three years later by **Adolf Hitler**, a failed artist and ex-corporal from Austria. It was a ragbag group of fanatics and misfits whose views, as the party name suggests, were an odd mixture of the extreme right and left. They modeled their organization on the Communists and the Italian *Fascisti*, adopting their own uniform and slogans, and developing a private army, the brown-shirted **SA** (*Sturmabteilung*, or "Storm Troopers"). Such limited success as the party enjoyed was at first confined to Bavaria, where a botched attempt at a putsch was made in 1923; following this, Hitler was arrested and convicted of high treason.

The leniency shown by the judiciary to right-wing opponents of the republic—aided by the fact that he had involved Ludendorff in the plot—meant that Hitler only served nine months in prison, during which time he set out his ideology and political program in his autobiography, *Mein Kampf*. This consists of verbose rantings and ravings over an enormous range of topics; it's stunningly unoriginal, drawing freely from all the nastiest and most reactionary theories of the day, but is an important source, as it sets out unequivocally what Hitler genuinely believed, and was to serve as his blueprint for power.

Racism forms the keynote: the so-called Aryans were the earth's rightful masters, while inferior peoples such as the Slavs were fit only to serve them. All ills could ultimately be laid at the door of the Jews, who were stealthily conspiring for world dominance, using every conceivable method from Bolshevism to control of big business. The German *Volk* had been betrayed by socialism, democracy, and the traitors who had signed the Versailles Treaty. A new German Reich must be created under the direction of an all-powerful *Führer*, uniting with Austria and gaining living space (*Lebensraum*) to the east; to this end, France had to be subdued and Russia crushed.

This prognosis fooled few people at first; sales of the book—in spite of its ready captive market in the ranks of the party faithful—failed to reach 10,000 in the first year, and declined

steadily over the next five. Nazi representation in the Reichstag also decreased from 25 in 1924 to just twelve after the 1928 elections, making it the ninth and smallest party, and one widely regarded as something of a joke. Only the extraordinarily mesmeric personality of Hitler held it together; having learnt from past mistakes, he was now determined to gain power by strictly legal means.

Stresemann died in October 1929, exhausted by overwork and by persecution from his former right-wing allies. Three weeks later came the **Wall Street crash** in America, whose repercussions swiftly destroyed the new German order he had created. Wholesale withdrawal of credit—on which the economy was totally dependent—led to another bout of escalating employment and inflation, to which there was no ready-made solution, as there had been in 1923. The coalition partners quarreled over what measures to take; as a result, the SPD, which had only recently returned to government following eight years voluntarily out of office, once more abdicated the responsibility of leadership. A minority government was set up under the centrist **Heinrich Brüning**; frustrated by having to rely on rule by presidential decree, he took a gamble by asking Hindenburg to dissolve the Reichstag.

The elections, held in September 1930, offered a golden opportunity for the political extremes, with their formulas for righting all wrongs. Despite increasing their support, the Communists once more failed to make a significant impact; their overobvious subservience to Moscow meant they were held in deep distrust by the bulk of the population. In contrast, the Nazi rise was meteoric, taking even Hitler by surprise—they gained 6.4 million votes and became the second largest party. This support was overwhelmingly from the disaffected ranks of the unemployed (particularly the young) and the ruined petty bourgeoisie.

Though a significant breakthrough, it was far from being a decisive one, and there was still no inevitability about the Nazi triumph, which was only achieved because of the **short-sightedness and greed of the traditional right wing**. The sort of people who would have formed the backbone of a strong and stabilizing conservative party in most other advanced societies had consistently shown a quite irrational hatred of the republic. This had actually treated them far too benevolently, leaving the army, judiciary, and universities unpurged, allowing banks and big business to make enormous profits, and subsidizing the uneconomic Junker estates.

Not content with their wealth, power, and privileges, the upper classes were imbued with a feudalistic mentality, hankering for a return to the days when there was no democracy and no trade unionism. In Hitler, they at last found their kaiser-substitute, a man who could give them the broad mass of support they could not otherwise muster, and who would return Germany to its traditions of hierarchical authoritarian rule at home, and military glory abroad. Leading figures in industry and politics latched on to Hitler and gave him respectability; by acting as his financiers and power brokers, they believed they would be able to control his excesses. Nazi coffers were swelled by contributions from many of the giant corporations, following a lead given some years before by the steel magnate Fritz Thyssen. The army began to abandon its role above party politics, overlooking its earlier aversion to the paramilitary SA.

Hitler exposed the naiveté of these hopes by standing against the revered Hindenburg in the 1932 presidential election, only just managing to secure German citizenship in time to be eligible. The desperate straits into which the republic had fallen was shown by the fact that the ancient soldier, teetering on the verge of senility, was supported by the SPD and all the other democratic parties, who abstained from fielding a candidate of their own in the belief there was no other way of beating Hitler.

In the event, Hindenburg only just failed to obtain an outright majority on the first ballot, and comfortably won the second, with the Communists trailing a very poor third. Fresh hope was provided by the remarkable success of Chancellor Brüning, still dependent on presidential decree, who was developing into a worthy successor to Stresemann. His sensible economic program alleviated the worst hardships, and he was on the verge of pulling off a tremendous double success in foreign affairs, with the end of reparations and Germany's right to equality of armaments in sight. An attempt at reforming the outdated pattern of land ownership proved to be Brüning's undoing; the aristocracy howled with rage at this alleged crypto-Bolshevism, and Hindenburg was left with no alternative but to ditch him.

That marked the last attempt to make the republic work; power passed to **a small coterie of traditional conservatives** close to the president, who bear the final responsibility for Hitler's assumption of power. The next two chancellors—the bumbling intriguer **Franz von Papen** and the far more astute fixer **General Kurt von Schleicher**, who had elaborate plans for using Hitler and then destroying him—had no taste for democracy, and were content to play courtier-style politics.

Nonetheless, attempts still had to be made to obtain a working majority in the Reichstag. There were two inconclusive elections in 1932; in the first, after a campaign of mass terror by the SA, the Nazis won nearly 14 million votes and became the largest party, though still well short of a majority. As Hindenburg's hand-picked cabinet failed to secure the Reichstag's support, new elections were called; these saw the Nazis lose 2 million votes, as their true aims and methods became clearer. However, having been toppled by von Schleicher, it was von Papen—a figure seemingly escaped from a comic opera, now at center-stage in one of the world's greatest-ever tragedies—who entered into a disastrous plot with Hitler which brought the end of the republic.

Von Papen persuaded Hindenburg to make Hitler chancellor, with himself as deputy, of a coalition able to command a Reichstag majority. As the Nazis would only be given two other cabinet seats, von Papen assumed that he would retain the real control for himself. Hitler was therefore sworn in on 30 January 1933, having achieved with incredible ease his objective of coming to power by constitutional means.

THE THIRD REICH

The underestimation of Hitler by the traditional right is as puzzling as their hatred of the republic. Once in power, **Hitler acted swiftly to make his position absolute**; he had no intention of being beholden to anyone, least of all a fool and political amateur such as Papen. New elections were arranged for March; this time, the Nazis had the advantage of being able to use the full apparatus of the state to back up their campaign of terror. In this, they were greatly aided by the fact that **Hermann**

Göring, one of the Nazis in the cabinet, was Prussian Minister of the Interior, and thus in control of the police.

On the night of February 27, the **Reichstag** was burned down; a simple-minded Dutch Communist was arrested for this, though the fire was almost certainly the work of the Nazis themselves. At any rate, it gave them the excuse to force Hindenburg to declare a state of emergency; opponents could now legally be gagged, and Communists persecuted. The Nazis were duly elected with over 17 million votes, just short of an absolute majority.

An **Enabling Bill** was laid before the Reichstag, which was effectively asked to vote itself out of existence. By the arrest of the Communist deputies and some of the SPD, plus the support of the traditional right, Hitler was only just short of the two-thirds majority he needed to abolish the Weimar Republic quite legally. The SPD salvaged some self-respect by refusing to accede to this, but the Catholic centrists failed to repeat their act of defiance against Bismarck, meekly supporting the measure in return for minor concessions.

Now officially the country's dictator, Hitler immediately put into effect the remainder of his **policy of coordination** (*Gleichshaltung*), by which society was completely Nazified. With breathtaking speed, every institution surrendered. The Länder were stripped of their powers, making Germany a centralized state for the first time. All political parties except the Nazis were forced to dissolve, and free trade unions were banned. Purges were carried out in the police, judiciary, and professions, to ensure that each was in the control of party loyalists.

The entire media was subordinated to **Joseph Goebbels'** Ministry of Popular Enlightenment, relentlessly churning out monotonous propaganda designed to produce a hypnotic effect on the public. Protestants were organized into a Reich Church which was an integral part of the state, while Catholic independence was bought at the price of a concordat with the Vatican legitimizing the regime.

Many of the vicious features for which Nazism became notorious soon made their appearance. **Jews were ostracized and persecuted**: their businesses were boycotted and they were banned from the professions; two years later, they were stripped of citizenship and forbidden to marry Germans. Many found their way into the fifty or so **concentration camps** set up for political opponents, who were sadistically tortured and often coldbloodedly murdered. Conformity was ensured by networks of informers under the control of the secret police, the **Gestapo**. The educational system was perverted in order to indoctrinate the great "truths" of Nazi ideology.

Recognizing the importance of controlling young minds at all times, recreational activities were also placed under party control, with membership of the Hitler Youth and League of Young German Women made compulsory. Cultural life virtually collapsed, as "degenerate" forms of expression were suppressed. These ranged from virtually all modern art to books and plays with a liberal or socialist slant; it even affected music, as the performance of works by composers with Jewish blood was outlawed.

But the main threat to the regime lay within the Nazi Party itself, with the original socialist wing, backed by the SA, pressing for a second revolution. On 30 June 1934, the **"Night of the Long Knives,"** hundreds of potential Nazi opponents were assassinated, notably the leading left-winger Gregor Strasser and the SA chief Ernst Röhm. The SA was stripped of its powers and put under the control of **Heinrich Himmler**'s black-shirted **SS** (*Schutzstaffel*), originally no more than Hitler's bodyguard. This measure also had the benefit of laying to rest the one remaining threat, that of intervention by the army; with their potential usurpers out of the way, they quickly came to terms with Nazism. When Hindenburg died a few weeks later, Hitler combined the offices of president and chancellor into that of an all-powerful *Führer*, a measure he had ratified by a plebiscite in which he was endorsed by ninety percent of those eligible to vote.

The genuine **popular support** Hitler enjoyed is one of the most striking and disturbing features of what became known as the Third Reich, the successor to the empires of Charlemagne and Bismarck. Although many of the most talented people, especially in the arts and sciences, fled the country, and many others tenaciously defied it from within, the level of opposition was negligible.

A clear indication of this is provided by the fact that, unlike in most other totalitarian regimes, few restrictions were initially placed on travel in either direction. Such people as defected were the sort Hitler wanted to lose, while he was perfectly happy to encourage foreigners to come and see the revival of Germany that was occurring under his leadership.

In part this acquiescence was a simple continuation of the German authoritarian tradition. However, there's no doubt that the economic policies Hitler pursued were popular on both sides of industry. Full employment was restored, and, although industrial and agricultural workers were reduced to the status of serfs, there was no question of starvation or total financial ruin. Business leaders were pleased for a different reason—when it came to profits, the totalitarian state stopped short of its normal all-embracing function.

Hitler actually understood and cared little about economics; this sector was left in the hands of a financial wizard, the banker **Hjalmar Schacht**, who had previously been responsible for overseeing the return of the Weimar mark to stability following the Ruhr crisis. This time, the economy Schacht created was one designed for war, thus tying in with **Hitler's foreign policy**, conducted in tones of sweet reason using demands on the installment plan, which deceived the leaders of other countries with the same ease with which he had outmaneuvered his domestic opponents in his rise to power.

One by one, the terms of Versailles were breached. Reparations payments were stopped; the formerly secret rearmament was stepped up and made open, with conscription reintroduced; the Rhineland was reoccupied; and Austria was forced into becoming part of the Reich. The German-speaking people in the Sudetenland part of Czechoslovakia, who had never previously been a source of discontent, were used as an excuse to begin the policy of *Lebensraum*; the matter escalated into an international crisis in 1938, in which the British and French backed down humiliatingly with an agreement signed at Munich, in which they sacrificed Czech territorial integrity—a despicable and self-interested act—for what they believed would be world peace.

Hitler was encouraged by this show of weakness to act on one of his most cherished ambitions the following year—the elimination of Poland. It's probable he believed there would be a similar collapse of will by the west-

ern powers, the more so as he first pulled off the spectacular coup of signing a non-aggression pact with his ultimate enemy, the Soviet Union, thus ensuring there would not be a war on two fronts. However, this was a miscalculation; two days after the invasion began on September 1, 1939, Britain and France, realizing that the earlier promises of an end to German expansion in eastern Europe were a sham, decided to honor their treaty obligations; thus **World War II** began.

WORLD WAR II

At first, the war went well for the Nazis, aided by the fact that Germany was the only country properly prepared. Not only was Poland routed, but the Low Countries soon fell, leading to the British evacuation at Dunkirk in May 1940. Within a month, France had signed an armistice, and a puppet government was installed. A quick invasion might then have accounted for Britain, but Hitler delayed in favor of an aerial bombardment in which the *Luftwaffe* was repulsed by the RAF. Rather than prolong this approach, German sights turned eastward again. The Balkans were subdued, and in June 1941 plans were hatched for the largest military operation in history—the invasion of the Soviet Union.

This period also marks the beginnings of the worst **concentration camps**, in which Hitler's racial theories were put fully into practice. Inmates from the conquered territories were used as slave labor, and horrendous experiments in the name of Nazi "science" were carried out, followed by an attempt at the "final solution" of the Jewish "problem." Over 6 million (about a third of the population of world Jewry) perished, mostly between 1942 and 1945, as a result; a similar number of other "undesirable" peoples were massacred in addition.

Perhaps beginning to believe he was invincible, Hitler's thoughts moved to the time when he would be unchallenged master of Europe; the USA would then be the main enemy. In order to ensure that the Americans would remain neutral in the European war, and to gain an ally for the great future showdown, he **began courting Japan**. The hope was that the Japanese would attack the USSR from the east; the crushing of the world's first Communist state would meet with at least tacit

American approval, while Japan would be rewarded with Britain's Asian colonies. However, the Japanese (whose strength had anyway been much overrated) proved to be fickle partners, who were just as prepared as the Germans to make use of the new alliance for their own ends. They repeatedly stalled on the plans for invading the Soviet Union, and instead turned their attentions to their real enemy—the American Pacific fleet.

On 7 December 1941, they attacked Pearl Harbor, an action which almost immediately **brought the USA into the war**, the very reverse of Hitler's intentions. In any event, Nazi Germany had hopelessly overreached itself; defeats in North Africa in 1942 were followed by **the turning point at Stalingrad** the following year, when the Russian winter and the vast size of the country combined, not for the first time, to repulse a foreign invader. German losses rivalled those sustained in World War I, and a crushing blow was dealt to morale, as this ranked as the most disastrous defeat in the country's military history.

From then onwards, the story is one of Nazi retreat on all fronts. A **German resistance movement** sprang up under the leadership of senior army officers, who realized that the continuation of the war would only lead to more unnecessary loss of life. Furthermore, total military defeat would be followed by a severe peace treaty; there was also the likelihood that Bolshevism would ensue if the Russians occupied the country. Various attempts were made to assassinate Hitler, and he had several extraordinary escapes, most notably in the carefully hatched plot of July 20 1944, when a bomb killed several people sitting alongside him. Yet, bad luck apart, the conspiratorial groups were handicapped by their excessive concern to secure in advance lenient terms for a defeated but democratic Germany; they also had no firm base of popular support, nor a detailed plan of campaign of what to do once Hitler had been killed.

As it turned out, the country's ultimate collapse was drawn out, and did not occur before all major German cities and innumerable small towns had been ruthlessly bombed. Eventually, the Allies occupied the entire country; on April 30 1945, marooned in his Berlin bunker, Hitler committed suicide, so bringing the "thousand year Reich" to an inglorious end.

THE DIVISION OF GERMANY

The Allied powers, determined not to repeat the mistakes of Versailles, now had to decide **what to do with Germany**. Drastic measures were necessary to root out Nazism, and ensure that the country would never again provoke a global conflict. At Potsdam in August, the country was partitioned into four zones of occupation, corresponding to an agreement made earlier in the year at Yalta when the war was still in progress; Berlin was similarly divided. The eastern frontier of Germany was redrawn at the Oder-Neisse line, meaning that East Prussia and most of Pomerania passed to Poland, in compensation for territory now formally annexed by the Soviet Union.

There was, however, no consensus as to what should be done as a final settlement; some of the solutions bandied about were draconian, such as the dismantlement of all German industry, or a return to the days of a multiplicity of independent states. Initially, there was a great deal of cooperation among the Allies. All the leading Nazis who had survived were brought to **trial in Nürnberg** for war crimes or crimes against humanity, and the civil service was purged of the movement's sympathizers. Relief measures were taken against the terrible famine sweeping the country, refugees from the former Eastern Territories were helped to begin new lives, and the first steps were made towards rebuilding destroyed cities and the shattered economy.

Germany's internal **political life** was relaunched under the leadership of prominent anti-Nazis. The right of the spectrum was occupied by a new and moderate party, the **Christian Democrats** (CDU), formed as a union of the Catholic centrists and Protestants who shared similar social ideas. Left-wing politics were still marred by the legacy of bad blood between the SPD and the Communists. In the Russian zone, the SPD took the lead in forming a new group, the **Socialist Unity Party** (SED); the Communists only tagged along under Russian pressure after the poor showing of the party in the Austrian elections.

This new grouping was not repeated in the other zones. Inevitably, **strains developed among the Allies**; after all, they represented two conflicting ideologies thrown into an ad hoc alliance by the Nazi threat. The Americans came increasingly around to the view that the best way forward was to build Germany up as a responsible nation; the Russians believed some harsh punishment was necessary first. Simultaneously, the zones began to develop in different ways, mirroring the societies of their conquerors. Frustrated by Russian stalling, the western powers began a currency reform in their zones in 1948, soon extended to West Berlin. This gesture was regarded as highly provocative by the Soviets, who retaliated by cutting off western access to the divided city. Another world war could have ensued, but the beleaguered western zones were saved by the success of **airlifts** bringing essential supplies, forcing the Russians to abandon the blockade within a year.

By this time, two different societies were emerging on German soil: the Russians enforced massive nationalization and collectivization; in contrast, the western powers allowed even those industrialists most associated with the Nazis, such as Thyssen and the Krupps, to return to their businesses with minimal punishment. Rocked by the independent line taken by Tito in Yugoslavia, the Russians transformed the SED into a Soviet-style party led by a politburo, while a parliamentary council was set up in the west to draft a new constitution. The logical conclusion of these events—the creation of two rival states—soon followed. In May 1949, the three western zones amalgamated to form the **German Federal Republic**; four months later, the Russians launched their territory as the **German Democratic Republic**.

THE FEDERAL REPUBLIC

Like the Weimar Republic, the new West German state was founded on **liberal democratic principles**, only this time the constitution was much tighter. The power of the president was sharply reduced, giving him a role not unlike that of the British monarch. A true federal structure was created, in which the Länder were given considerable powers over all areas of policy except defense, foreign affairs and currency control. Proportional representation was retained, but with a five-percent qualifying minimum, and quadrennial elections were established. A constitutional court was established to guarantee civil and political liberties, and antidemocratic parties were outlawed.

Konrad Adenauer became the first chancellor following elections in which his Christian Democrats emerged as the largest party, though far short of a majority. Aged 73 and with no experience of national politics—he had been mayor of Cologne until removed by the Nazis—he bore the looks of a temporary leader, though as an elder statesman with an untainted past he fitted the precise needs of the time exactly.

In the event, the evening of his career was a prolonged one; he remained in power for fourteen years, in which time he developed an aura of indispensability at home, and appeared as a figure of substance abroad. Much of this success was due to the **"Economic Miracle"** masterminded by **Ludwig Erhard**, in which the wrecked economy made a spectacular recovery, with high-quality products fueling an export boom. An annual growth rate of eight percent was achieved; within a decade West Germany ranked as the most prosperous major European country.

In many ways, this was due simply to disciplined hard work by the bulk of the population, but it was also aided by the fact that a fresh start had to be made. Hence industry was relaunched with the most modern equipment, and in a sensible atmosphere of partnership between management and just seventeen large trade unions, which eliminated the class-based fear and interunion rivalry which continued to plague other countries. Erhard also promoted the concept of the "social-market economy," giving due emphasis to the development of a welfare state.

In foreign affairs, priority was given to **ending the long era of enmity with France**; the two countries formed the European Coal and Steel Pact in 1951, serving as a prelude to the creation of the European Economic Community six years later. The Federal Republic's integration into the western alliance was cemented by admission to **NATO**, and the adoption of a hard-nosed attitude towards the Soviet Union and her satellites. Adenauer believed that the only answer to these countries was to rival them in the military sphere, and outdistance them economically. In the case of the GDR, the latter wasn't a problem—it was poor in natural resources, lacked a heavy industrial base, was exploited by the Soviet Union, and hamstrung by the application of out-of-date ideological doctrines.

By the **Hallstein Doctrine**, the Federal Republic claimed to be the legitimate voice of all Germany, arguing that it was the only part properly constituted. Not only did it fail to recognize the GDR, it successfully ostracized its neighbor by refusing to establish diplomatic relations with any country which did. As a way to the country's reunification—West Germany has always officially been only a provisional state—this policy clearly misfired, driving the two new countries even farther apart.

THE BERLIN WALL

The late 1950s saw the beginning of a period of **unprecedented West German prosperity and expansion**. A shortage of labor meant that workers had to be imported; the unskilled laborers (**Gastarbeiter**) tended to come from Turkey, Greece, Yugoslavia, Italy, and Spain. For the better-qualified positions, industry looked to East Germany, and a flood of **emigration** started.

Quickly realizing that he could not afford to lose so many professionals, engineers, intellectuals, and craftsmen, the GDR leader Walter Ulbricht was forced into drastic action. The loophole was the western sector of Berlin; if it could be sealed off, the problem would disappear. Having failed at a second attempt to make the allies evacuate the city, Ulbricht persuaded the Soviets of the necessity of constructing the **Berlin Wall**, erected on August 13, 1961. It was immediately patrolled by armed guards under instructions to shoot to kill, and the main boundaries of the country were also greatly strengthened.

This was the first time in history that fortifications had been put up not to repel an invader, but to keep the inhabitants inside. A visual and moral affront to humanity, it was justified as the "Antifascist Protection Wall," a label it retains to this day. The official mythology of its construction—again still adhered to, even in literature for foreign consumption—is that plans had been hatched in NATO for an invasion of the GDR, and that it was only by sealing its frontiers in this way that another world war was averted. Even Ulbricht admitted in private, however, that the Wall was an admission of the regime's failure to attract sufficient loyalty.

The West was too numbed by this to offer any kind of effective response to what, in some respects, was a more dramatic change than the earlier division of the country. Yet, paradoxically, the Wall did much to bring **inter-German relations on to a more regulated footing**. It became increasingly clear that the Federal Republic would have to adopt a more positive attitude to its neighbor in order to minimize the hardship and suffering of the many families divided by the Wall, who had so suddenly been cut off from each other completely. However, these developments had to wait several years to bear fruit.

Adenauer was finally forced into retirement in 1963, to be succeeded by Erhard, who proved far less successful as the country's leader than he had been as economic guru. The liberal Free Democrats (FDP) who had served as the CDU's junior coalition partners for all but a short period of the Federal Republic's history, went into opposition in 1966. A **"Grand Coalition"** was established with the SPD, who thus returned to government for the first time since 1930. To rid itself of its tarnished image, the party had undergone a substantial reform (or sellout, according to many) at its 1959 conference, disavowing its roots in Marxism and class conflict and its traditional anticlericalism, embracing instead the CDU's "social market economy," but with a stronger emphasis on the social side of the equation.

The chancellor, the CDU's Kurt Georg Kiesinger, was remarkable mainly for being a reformed Nazi—a rather uncomfortable indicator of how far West Germans were prepared to forget the past. It was hardly surprising that the period of the Grand Coalition saw the first simmerings of disenchantment with the cosy form of consensus politics which had dominated the country's postwar history, with the Communists reformed as a counterweight to the neo-Nazi NPD; neither party, however, has gained much of a following.

More serious were the beginnings of what has since become a persistent feature of West German life, **extraparliamentary opposition**. This first came to the fore with the 1968 student revolt under Rudi Dutschke. Grievances initially centered on unsatisfactory conditions in the universities—then, as now, one of the worst-run sectors in the Federal Republic—but spread to wider discontent with society and the new materialistic culture.

OSTPOLITIK

A more positive feature of the Grand Coalition was the rise of **Willi Brandt**, the dynamic leader of the SPD, who assumed the foreign affairs portfolio. A former Resistance journalist, he had been mayor of West Berlin throughout the period of crisis leading up to the building of the Wall, and was determined to take a new tack on the problem. His **Ostpolitik** began in earnest, helped by a general thawing of the Cold War, when he became chancellor in 1969, at the head of a SPD-FDP coalition, itself something of a mold-breaker. Treaties were signed with the Soviet Union and Poland in 1970, recognizing the validity of the Oder-Neisse line; West Berlin's special status was guaranteed by the Four Power Agreement the following year; and in 1972 a Basic Treaty was signed between the two Germanys which at last normalized relations.

This stopped short of full diplomatic recognition of the GDR, but the Federal Republic recognized its frontiers and separate existence, abandoning the Hallstein Doctrine. In return, West Germans were given access to visit family and friends over the border, though movement the other way was confined to pensioners and the disabled. One consequence of *Ostpolitik* was the fall of Ulbricht, who wanted to drive a harder bargain than suited the Soviets, in 1971. His successor was Erich Honecker, who had a compelling personal reason for favoring inter-German détente—he was a native of the Saarland, where his family continued to live.

Boosted by the success of both his *Ostpolitik* and his welfare programs, Brandt led his coalition to victory in 1972, with the SPD winning more votes than the CDU for the first (and, as yet, only) time. In view of the reconciliatory nature of his approach to the GDR, it was ironic that Brandt's downfall occurred two years later as a result of the unmasking of one of his closest aides as an East German spy.

Staying on in the influential role as SPD chairman (until 1987, when another scandal, this time over a bizarre choice of a young CDU-sympathizing Greek woman as party spokesman, caused his retirement), Brandt was succeeded by **Helmut Schmidt**, an able pragmatist who increasingly came to be seen as something of a right-winger, though this was in part due to the nature of the problems he faced. The quadrupling of OPEC oil prices in 1974, and the stagnation in world trade which ensued, posed particular difficulties for the export-led and growth-geared German economy. These were tackled more successfully than in most countries, but **unemployment** became an issue for the first time since Hitler, even if it was mostly transitional in nature, caused by the need to scale down heavy industry.

Extraparliamentary opposition had by now taken on a fearsome and anarchic character. In the early 1970s, there had been a spate of kidnappings and armed bank robberies by the Baader-Meinhof gang. These had no sooner been quelled when there arose a far more organized and ruthless offshoot, the **Red Army Faction**, who assassinated a number of public figures. The turning point in the government's campaign against them came with the hijacking of a *Lufthansa* plane in 1977 with a threat to kill the hostages if the remaining members of the gang were not released from prison. On personal instructions from Schmidt—on which he was prepared to stake his chancellorship—the aircraft was successfully stormed; within three years, most of the terrorist leaders had been arrested and imprisoned.

Peaceful extraparliamentary opposition proved to have a far more potent significance. This was inspired above all by fears that divided Germany would serve as the stage for a future nuclear war. NATO's 1979 decision to install medium-range American nuclear missiles in West Germany was a particular source of protest, but there was also **increased general concern about the environment**, especially pollution of the beloved forests.

These issues then served as a focus for the many who were dissatisfied with a society which had become overcompetitive and too obsessed with consumerism, and out of an amorphous collection of pressure groups active in these areas the **Green Party** was born. Schmidt's backing of the bases alienated the SPD's left wing, but he was still able to lead his coalition to victory in 1980. In this he was aided by the CDU's recurrent leadership problem, which reached its nadir at this point with the fielding of **Franz Josef Strauss**—who had last held federal office under Adenauer—as chancellor-candidate. Long-standing leader of the CSU, the separate and exclusively Bavarian counterpart of the CDU, this blatant careerist and strident right-winger unsurprisingly proved to be a major electoral liability.

THE 1980s

Despite this lifeline, the long period of SPD domination was coming to an end. Schmidt's tough economic policies under the influence of another round of drastic oil price increases further widened the party's divisions, leading the FDP to lose confidence and withdraw from the government in September 1982. The CDU, now revived under **Helmut Kohl**, gambled on a "constructive vote of no confidence"—the only way around the fixed-term parliaments enshrined in the constitution. Having won this, they formed a new government with the FDP and called for fresh elections. Fears that the FDP would fail to surmount the five-percent threshold (having damaged themselves by their rather dubious stance) proved unfounded, and Kohl was able to continue as before.

However, there was now a significant new factor, as the Greens also passed the five-percent hurdle and brought another dimension to parliamentary life, with their collective leadership and rotating system of deputies. Kohl himself was something of a departure, the first German leader drawn from a generation too young to have Nazi associations of any kind.

He has remained in power ever since, winning another term of office in 1987, in spite of his government having been rocked by a **series of scandals**, the most damaging being the Flick affair. This brought to light widespread tax evasion by the political parties on donations from large corporations, which were often given in exchange for fairly direct favors. The chancellor himself was directly involved in some of these highly dubious dealings, but was eventually exonerated, helped by the fact that all of the three main parties were implicated. This gave a boost to the clean image of the Greens, as did the horrendous consequences of the Chernobyl disaster, and meant the party improved its showing in 1987, confounding the many pundits who had predicted it would quickly run out of steam.

However, the Green party found itself in several quandries, being indecisive about whether or not to enter coalitions in local government, and finding disadvantages in the rotating leadership system. Splits in the SPD multiplied over defense policy; eventually the party came out against deployment of nuclear missiles, a decision which caused Schmidt to retire from politics. The SPD fought a poor election, and continues to be bedeviled by leadership problems.

Kohl, meanwhile, has led a rather unexciting government which has cut back on the state's very modest role in economic intervention. There have, however, been **further strides in Ostpolitik**. Since Brandt, this had become low-key, and depended very much on the climate of superpower relations. The new developments are in many cases cynical—massive **interest-free loans** have been given to the GDR in return for allowing greater numbers of its citizens to emigrate, and huge "ransoms" have been paid for its political prisoners. Nevertheless, such measures have helped to relieve a great deal of individual heartbreak on both sides of the frontier, and there are signs at last of the thawing of restrictions on travel to the west by East Germans of working age.

To some extent, the seal of legitimacy was bestowed on to the GDR when Honecker, whose previous attempts to visit the Federal Republic had been vetoed by the Russians, finally made it in September 1987. Amid much publicity, he was received at a level just below that normally accorded to a head of state. More recently, every overture by Soviet President Mikhail Gorbachev—whose sweeping impact on the world stage has kindled hopes that German reunification may come back on the political agenda before too long—has been greeted with an enthusiasm bordering on the euphoric, much to the consternation of other members of the western alliance.

THE CURRENT POLITICAL SCENE

Following a period of uncertainty caused by the breakup of the postwar consensus, the **political map of the Federal Republic** seems to have crystalized into a new form in which parliamentary methods are again overwhelmingly predominant. On both economics and the twin defense/environmental issue, there's now a straight left–right division, with the CDU and FDP lined up against the SPD and Greens.

The current ruling coalition partnership seems fairly well entrenched, but the unpredictable factor is the **staying power of the Green Party**. Despite being generally more radical on most issues than the SPD, it attracts support from across the political spectrum. A new generation of SPD leaders—most notably its rising star, Oskar Lafontaine of the Saarland—see the creation of an effective red-green alliance as being the left's only way forward. As yet, coalitions between the two have been confined to a local level; unless this develops further, the CDU and FDP must be favorites to remain in office for some time to come.

However, the ruling parties have been rocked by a **succession of defeats at the polls** over the last couple of years in the staggered system of local and regional elections. Most humiliating of all was the loss of Frankfurt, the showpiece of German capitalism, leaving Stuttgart as the only major city under CDU control. In these same elections, a new far-right group, the Republicans, has made worrying advances, notably in West Berlin. Evidence suggest this is more than a flash in the pan, though its hardly represents a neo-Nazi revival. If kept within reasonable limits, it could be taken as a further sign of the health of West German democracy that such a party can exist without being proscribed, and yet remain harmless.

The end of the postwar consensus is by no means a phenomenon unique to the country, but the patterns it has taken are quite different from elsewhere. Nowhere else is the **nuclear issue** so fiercely contested—appropriately enough, given the prime strategic location of Germany in the Cold-War division of Europe. And it's not merely alternative groups who are reacting against the emphasis on hard work and intense competition which has been the country's ethic for so long. There's a general desire to relax more, to have a shorter working-week and more vacations, and the average German now puts in fewer hours than his counterpart in almost any other major industrialized country.

Yet this is occurring at a time of much tougher international competition, above all from Japan, which poses a particular threat to West Germany's traditionally strong showing in the export field. Another indicator of desire for a more self-indulgent lifestyle is the birthrate, the lowest in the world; this poses potential long-term difficulties, but initially is not of concern, as it will help to overcome the **unemployment problem**. Although allegedly transitional in nature, this has been getting steadily worse, with no more signs of a permanent solution than are evident in Britain, or North America.

German society does, however, seem well integrated; the country has learned its lessons from the debacle of the Third Reich, and there's little taste for extremism. The *Gastarbeiter* have not developed into a major issue, even if the fact that their number is approximately equal to that of the ranks of the unemployed has drawn many facile comparisons. They have inspired only crank racism; many have integrated well, and they play valuable roles in what, despite the lack of much of a colonial tradition, is now a multicultural society in the same way as the USA.

It's to be hoped that the improved climate in international affairs, and the increase in the number of East Germans traveling to the west, will eventually lead to the dismantling of the **Berlin Wall**. Such a measure would be unlikely to destabilize East German society to the extent that is sometimes imagined; ties of family and friendship are inevitably less strong than they were when the Wall was built, and the problems of the west, above all the unemployment rate, mean that it's no longer seen as a utopia, particularly to the large percentage of the population who have grown up in such a cosseted society.

Although the division of Germany has long been a firmly established fact, recognized as part of the price for the abominations of the Third Reich, the issue of **political reunification** refuses to die completely. Until very recently, even the most optimistic could not, in their heart of hearts, regard it as a feasible option in the foreseeable future, for all the lipservice paid to the ideal. While the opposite prognosis—that reunification had become an impossible pipedream—was also always an overdramatic simplification, the fact was that it could only take place as a result of actions **beyond German control**, under vastly different conditions in the world balance of power. Among the plausible scenarios which were touted were: a retreat into isolationism by the Soviet Union; the same country's economic collapse, leading to withdrawal from the satellites; a general convergence of capitalist and socialist societies; or a significant change in the dominance of the two superpowers, perhaps caused by the rise of China or Japan.

Mikhail Gorbachev's explosive impact on the world scene, and continuing ability to outfox his domestic opponents, has suddenly given **fresh impetus to reunification hopes**. As things stand at the moment, the western powers are officially committed to supporting a united German state, and have gained much political capital by presenting the Russians as the only obstacle. However, the oft-quoted solution of a neutralized united Germany—which, freed of high defense spending, would have awesome economic power—has never held any more appeal to them than to the Soviets. Furthermore, there's no doubt that West Germany's allies would consider the loss of the larger, more prosperous, and prestigious part of the nation from their alliance to far outbalance any gains which would ensue.

It remains to be seen whether Gorbachev will at some point try to trip up the West by proposing this very solution. Hitherto, it has been assumed that the Soviets would never allow the precedent of a country being able to vote a Communist system out of existence, but that has all been changed by the retreat from Afghanistan. On the other side of the equation, it remains something of a moot point as to whether the West German people would really want to make the sacrifices which would be necessary to bring their counterparts' social and economic structure up to a level of parity with their own.

MONUMENTAL CHRONOLOGY

1st c. First surviving Roman monuments: Tomb of Poblicius in Cologne, Amphitheater at Trier.

2nd–4th c. Other Roman monuments in Trier: Porta Nigra, Konstantinbasilika, Kaiserthermen. Jupitersäule, Mainz; remains of Colonia Ulpa Traiana, Xanten, and Arae Flaviae, Rottweil.

8th c. Carolingian gateway at Lorsch, Marienkapeel, Marienburg, Würzburg.

9th c. Charlemagne's Palace chapel at Aachen (now part of the Dom). Other Carolingian churches: St. Georg, Reichenau, westwork of Corvey.

10th c. Beginnings of Romanesque style with St. Pantaleon, Cologne.

early 11th c. Romanesque architecture perfected at Hildesheim, with introduction of Lower Saxon method of alternating pillars and columns: St. Michael is best example of this.

11th c. Imperial cathedrals of Speyer and Mainz, with choirs at both ends of the building; Kaiserpfalz at Goslar (surviving as a rebuild) is the secular counterpart. Distinctive style of church building in Cologne with trefoil plan begun with St, Maria in Kapitol. Hall church style, subsequently a favorite German form, introduced with Bartholomäuskapelle in Paderborn.

late 11th c. Abbeys of Cluniac reform at Hirsau and Alpirsbach.

12th c. Great period of monastic building: Königslutter, Fischbeck, Eberbach, Maria Laach. Imperial cathedral at Worms; imperial palaces at Gelnhausen and Bad Wimpfen.

early 13th c. Last phase of highly picturesque Rhenish late Romanesque style in Cologne (notably St. Gereon), Bonn, and Andernach.

early 13th c. Introduction of pointed arch and ribbed vault with the Transitional style at Bamberg Dom; St. Georg, Limburg; Sebalduskirche, Nürnberg; and Kloster Maulbronn.

ca.1235 Fully-fledged Gothic style, already well developed in France, appears at Elizabethkirche, Marburg, and Liebfrauenkirche, Trier.

mid 13th c. on-wards Beginning of great period of Gothic cathedral building with east end of Dom in Cologne. Work here and at Altenberg and Regensburg follows French models. Huge Münster at Freiburg, with single tower and open-work spire introduces a distinctive German accent. In the north, notably at Lübeck, churches are constructed of brick.
Major period of defensive architecture: town walls at Rothenburg; castles at Marksburg and Eltz are best surviving examples.

14th c. Hall church style becomes increasingly refined and lofty; best examples are the Wieskirche, Soest, and the Heiligkreuzmünster, Schwäbisch Gmünd. The latter initiates the style of the Parler dynasty, who also work at Augsburg, Nürnberg, Cologne, and Freiburg.
Resplendent town halls are built as a sign of the power and status of the new merchant class: Lübeck, Lüneburg, Münster, and Aachen. Römer in Frankfurt is an example of the patrician house of the time.

15th c. Brick churches are built in the Lower Rhineland: Kalkar, Kleve, and Goch. In southern Germany, the hall church style becomes even more spectacular at Landshut, Nördlingen, Dinkelsbühl, and Munich. Many outstanding pieces of civil architecture: town halls of Ulm and Braunschweig; Alte Hofhaltung, Bamberg; Tempelhaus, Hildesheim.

early 16th c.	Introduction of the Italian Renaissance style with the Fuggerkapelle in Augsburg.
mid 16th c.	Construction of Italianate palaces at Landshut and Stuttgart; the latter includes the first-ever church designed for Protestant worship. The Ottheinrichsbau in Heidelberg introduces a more original German Renaissance style of architecture. Rothenburg's Rathaus is the finest of the municipal structures in this style. Highly ornamented and colorful town houses characterise the Weser Renaissance style, notably in Lemgo and Hameln, which continues for nearly a century.
late 16th c./ early 17th c.	St. Michael, Munich introduces the Counter-Reformation style of the Jesuits to Germany. Wolfenbüttel becomes the first planned town in the country, followed closely by Freudenstadt. The Mannerist style appears at the Friedrichsbau in Heidelberg Schloss, and at the Schloss and Stadtkirche of Bückeburg; the latter, along with its exact contemporary in Wolfenbüttel, ranks as the first full-scale Protestant church. Sumptuous late Renaissance palaces are built in the Hohenlohe region. Elias Holl creates the most refined and original German Renaissance buildings in Augsburg.
late 17th c.	After long lull in building activity caused by the Thirty Years' War, Italianate Baroque style introduced with Theatinerkirche, Munich; Passau also adopts this. More distinctively German are the works of the Voralberg School (e.g. Obermarchtal), and the first buildings of the Dientzenhofer dynasty (e.g. Waldsassen). These mark the beginning of a long era of south German monastic building.
early 18th c.	Beginning of Berlin Baroque, under Andreas Schlüter. Johann Dientzenhofer builds at Fulda, Banz, and Pommersfelden. Joseph Effner expands Residenz in Munich, and builds pavilions at Nymphenburg. Laying out of planned towns of Mannheim and Ludwigsburg. Johann Conrad Schlaun begins building in a sober Baroque style in and around Münster, continuing for the next three decades.
1720– 1760	Brilliant period of rococo, especially in southern Germany. Balthasar Neumann is the most ingenious architect of the period; his masterpieces are Würzburg Residenz, Vierzehnheiligen pilgrimage church, and the staircases of Bruchsal and Brühl. Other outstanding builders are François Cuvilliés (Amalienburg and Residenztheater, Munich), Cosmas Damian and Egid Quirin Asam (Asamkirche, Munich), Johann Michael Fischer (abbeys of Zwiefalten and Ottobeuren), and Dominikus Zimmermann (Wieskirche). Georg von Knobelsdorff builds in a less ornate version of this style in Berlin. Luxuriant Italianate Baroque buildings were also erected in this period, eg the Opernhaus in Bayreuth and the Jesuitenkirche in Mannheim. In contrast is the restrained Lutheran Baroque of Ansbach and St. Michaelis, Hamburg.
late 18th c.	Transition from rococo to neoclassicism with buildings of Nicolas de Pigage (palace at Benrath, theater and pavilions at Schwetzingen), and Pierre Louis Philippe de La Guêpière (Schloss Solitude, Stuttgart). Another Frenchman, Michel d'Inxard, introduces full-blooded neoclassicism to Germany with abbey at St. Blasien.
early 19th c.	Karlsruhe is made into a planned neoclassical city by Friedrich Weinbrenner. Subsequently, the royal capitals of Berlin, Munich, and Hannover are transformed by the extensive provision of neoclassical public buildings; the dominant architects were respectively Karl Friedrich Schinkel, Leo von Klenze, and Georg Friedrich Laves.

mid to late 19th c.
Romantic movement inspires a passion for mock-medieval castles, the most spectacular of which are associated with King Ludwig II of Bavaria – Hohenschwangau, Neuschwanstein, Linderhof, and Herrenchiemsee. Others include Sigmaringen, Hohenzollern, and Lichtenstein. The same spirit is behind the projects for completing the cathedral in Cologne, and the tower of Ulm. Solid Wilhelmine style of architecture is seen at its best in town villas, notably in Bonn.

1900–1914
Jugendstil has brief flowering in the artistic communities established at Darmstadt and Hagen.

1918–1933
Expressionism becomes the dominant form of architecture, with churches in Cologne by Dominikus Böhm, factories by Peter Behrens (notably at Höchst near Frankfurt), and offices by Fritz Höger in Hamburg and Hannover.
Bauhaus style of plain, geometrical architecture is born in what is now the GDR. Among West German examples are Mies van der Rohe's houses in Krefeld and the Weissenhofsiedlung, Stuttgart.

1933–45
The Nazis build in a grandiose, debased classical style, e.g. the Olympic Stadium, Munich, and the Nürnberg Parade Grounds.

Post-1945
Building of avant-garde churches (notably in Cologne) to replace those lost in World War II. Television towers erected in many German cities, beginning with Stuttgart. Planned town of Wolfsburg laid out. Major showpiece public buildings designed for West Berlin, including Hans Scharoun's Philharmonie and Mies van der Rohe's Neue Nationalgalerie. Among many new museum buildings, the most important are those by Hans Hollein in Mönchengladbach and James Stirling in Stuttgart.

PAINTING AND GRAPHICS

Germany's artistic history is marked more by solid and sustained achievement than by the more usual pattern of preeminence followed by decline. As in Italy, the fragmentation of the nation into a multitude of tiny states led to the development of many important centers of art, often of a very distinctive character.

The country's geographical position means it has served as a melting pot for influences from Italy, France, and the Low Countries, although, with several notable exceptions, the work of German painters never managed to gain the same international esteem. This, however, is mainly because the vast majority of German paintings have remained within the German-speaking countries, a consequence of the fact that many of the petty princes were great art collectors, and to the influence of the Romantic movement, which fostered a sense of awareness of the national heritage. As a result, important museums existed all over the country by the mid-nineteenth century.

German graphic work, being by its nature for dissemination, is perhaps more immediately familiar; the stark contrasts enforced by the media of woodcut, engraving, and etching obviously proved temperamentally ideal for the country's artists, whose legacy in these fields far surpasses that of anywhere else in Europe.

BEGINNINGS

German painting has its roots in the ninth-century Carolingian epoch. **Illuminated manuscripts** were created in the scriptoria of the court and the monasteries; these typically featured vibrant figures in flowing draperies, charged with movement, and set in elaborate architectural surroundings. This art form was refined and developed in the subsequent Ottonian period, most notably in Trier, which during the late tenth century boasted the first great German artist in an illuminator now dubbed **Master of the Registrum Gregorii**. A number of manuscripts by him have been identified; they show a new, more plastic style based on an understanding of classical antiquity which solved the problems of space and form which baffled all the other illuminators of the time. He built up a highly influential fund of forms which was imitated in the other great places of book production—Fulda, Hildesheim, and Bavaria—although there were also more conservative centers, particularly those on the island of the Reichenau, which favored an expressive linear form.

Fresco cycles were the other chief form of painting, and were often more closely related to the art of the book than might be supposed from the contrasting nature of the two forms. One of the best early examples to have survived is again from Trier; probably dating from the end of the ninth century, it originally adorned the crypt of St. Maximin, but has been removed to the museum. From the following century, there is an important cycle still in situ at St. Georg in Oberzell on the Reichenau, along with one in the Andreaskirche am Neuenberg, just outside Fulda. Belonging more obviously to international Romanesque currents are the later fresco cycles of the Lower Rhineland and Regensburg. The former—St. Gereon in Cologne, Schwarzrheindorf, and Knechtsteden—are all influenced by Byzantine concepts of form, style, and iconography; regrettably, their quality has been impaired by overenthusiastic nineteenth-century restorers who indulged in far too much speculative retouching.

Later Romanesque illuminated manuscripts tend to follow rather than develop the Ottonian forms, although there was something of a revival in the late twelfth century, with such deluxe products as the *Gospels of Henry the Lion*, now in Wolfenbüttel. Roughly contemporary is a survival which is unique of its kind, the painted **wooden ceiling** illustrating the Tree of Jesse which adorns the vault of St. Michael in Hildesheim.

THE EARLY GOTHIC PERIOD

The earliest Gothic panel paintings to have survived in Germany date from around 1300. Throughout the fourteenth century, religious themes retained their monopoly, and the most active workshops were in Cologne and Westphalia. The former was the dominant city of medieval Germany, and maintained its own strong and characteristic traditions right up until the early sixteenth century, assimilating varied foreign influences yet remaining rooted in tradition. Painting there was based on a strict guild system, which imposed stiff tests of skill on would-be applicants, and even stipulated the quality of materials which had to be employed. Among the most important productions of this school in the fourteenth century are the monumental paintings on the backs of the stalls and the *Clares Altar* in the Dom, and some very ruinous frescos for the Rathaus which have been attributed to a somewhat legendary figure named **Master Wilhelm**.

The first German artist about whom much information has survived is **Master Bertram** (ca.1345–1415), a Westphalian who worked in Hamburg. He seems to have been influenced by the art of Bohemia, which was part of the Holy Roman Empire, and was far in advance of fourteenth-century Germany in terms of the achievements of its painters. Bertram favored narrative cycles of little panels grouped around pieces of sculpture; his major work is the *Grabow Altar* of 1379 in Hamburg, which displays prodigious and original imaginative powers, particularly in the charming scenes of the Creation. From about a decade later is the *Passion Altar* in Hannover, while the *Buxtehude Altar*, again in Hamburg, is from ten years later; both are remarkably consistent in style.

Another Westphalian was **Master of the Berswordt Altar** (active late fourteenth century), named after a triptych still in situ in the Marienkirche in Dortmund; he also painted a polyptych for the Neustädterkirche in Bielefeld. The influence of French and Burgundian manuscripts is apparent, and he

was an early representative of the courtly and idealized International Gothic style which was to spread all over Europe. In Germany, this is usually referred to as the "**Soft Style**," and is found in sculpture as well as painting. Its greatest exponent was **Conrad von Soest** (active ca.1394–1422), one of the most immediately appealing of all German painters, who may even have been the son of the previous artist. His panels are refined and beautiful, executed in glowing colors, and including a fair amount of amusing anecdotal detail. The late high altar triptych of the Marienkirche in his native Dortmund shows his art at its peak, but is sadly truncated. Another major painter in this style was **Master Francke** (active ca.1405–25), who succeeded Bertram in Hamburg, and could conceivably have been his pupil; his reputation rests largely on the *Saint Thomas à Becket Altar* which was commissioned by the local merchants who traded with England. Also active at this time were **Master of the Virgin of Benediktbeuern** in Bavaria and various artists in Lower Saxony, most of whose works are now in Hannover.

THE 15TH C. COLOGNE SCHOOL

The entire fifteenth century was an outstandingly brilliant artistic period for Cologne. Although the artists still mostly remain anonymous, their styles became far more contrasted than in former times, and art historians have been able to group bodies of work under pseudonyms based on the names of their major masterpieces, which are now mostly housed in the city's Wallraf-Richartz Museum, or in the Alte Pinakothek in Munich. As well as large-scale commissions to adorn the plethora of churches and monasteries, there's increasing evidence of the burgeoning of the merchant class in the number of small altarpieces (obviously intended for private devotion) which have survived. The symbolical depiction of the Madonna and Child in the Garden of Paradise was enduringly popular; another vogue subject (the two were sometimes combined) was the Holy Kinship, depicting the extended family of Christ. First to develop a distinctive style was **Master of Saint Veronica** (active ca.1400–20), named after *Saint Veronica with the Sudarium*, now in Munich. The monumental faces in this work, mirrored elsewhere in his output, give evidence of influence from Bohemia, but that he had also understood the lessons of Burgundian miniatures is proved by the crowded *Calvary* in Cologne. His workshop may have been taken over after his death by **Master of Saint Lawrence** (active ca.1415–30), whose main work is a retable made for the demolished church of St. Lorenz, parts of which survive in the museums of Cologne and Nürnberg.

These artists were surpassed by **Stefan Lochner** (ca.1400–51), a Swabian who settled in the city and perfectly assimilated its traditions, along with innovations from Flanders. His soft, gentle, and painstakingly detailed panels are among the peaks of the entire International Gothic movement, and he appears to have been something of a celebrity, which accounts for his name surviving the oblivion into which his colleagues' have plunged. His masterpiece is the *Epiphany* triptych now in Cologne's Dom, originally painted for the Rathaus, a far more monumental work than was usual in Cologne. It has been criticized for a failure to characterize the figures, but that is to miss the point—Lochner's art is quite consciously ethereal in spirit. If anything, the later *Presentation in the Temple*, now in Darmstadt, is even more sumptuous, while his last work, *Madonna of the Rose Bower* in Cologne, takes the art of the small altar to a level beyond which it could not progress. Even with gruesome subjects, such as *Last Judgment* in Cologne and its reverse, *Martyrdoms of the Apostles*, now in Frankfurt, Lochner did not depart from his essential gentleness, always drawing the optimistic lesson from the subject; if that can be counted as a failing, his extraordinary inventive powers amply compensate.

The following generation moved away from static and decorative effects to a lively narrative style, clearly modeled on the great contemporary Netherlanders. Rogier van der Weyden's late *Saint Columba* triptych (now in Munich) was painted for a church in Cologne, and must have made an enormous impact, although the more rounded and less emotional style of Dieric Bouts is the obvious source for the leading artist of the group, **Master of the Life of the Virgin** (active ca.1460–85), so named from a cycle of eight panels, seven of which are also now in Munich. He displays all the qualities of a great storyteller, his figures strongly drawn

and richly clad, standing out in sharp relief from the background, with plenty of subsidiary anecdotal detail including exquisite still lifes. This artist's later work includes portraits of merchants, which mark the end of the ecclesiastical monopoly over art. Three other painters closely associated with him are **Master of the Lyversberg Passion**, **Master of the Saint George Legend** and **Master of the Bonn Diptych**; they may even have shared the same studio. Slightly later is **Master of the Glorification of the Virgin** (active ca.1475–95) who is less overtly Flemish in spirit; his backgrounds include accurate depictions of Cologne and its surrounding countryside.

Among the final generation of Cologne painters, **Master of the Holy Kinship** (ca.1450–1515) takes his name from the most spectacular version ever painted of the favorite Cologne subject, which shows acquaintance with the very latest Flemish innovations; otherwise, he seems to have been more adept on a smaller scale, his larger canvases betraying the use of inexperienced assistants. His contemporary, **Master of the Saint Ursula Legend** (active ca.1490–1505), developed the narrative tradition in a now-dispersed series, partly preserved in the museums of Cologne, Bonn, and Nürnberg. This artist displays far more interest in integrating the backgrounds with the action, and his handling of space and perspective show a sizable advance, while his technique of rapid brushstrokes is quite different from the smooth layered approach of his predecessors. He strongly influenced **Master of Saint Severin** (active ca.1490–1510) a prolific and uneven painter, with whom he probably shared a studio.

Ultimately, the Cologne School simply burned itself out, but it did come to a fitting climax with **Master of the Saint Bartholomew Altar** (active ca.1470–1510), whose highly idiosyncratic compositions display all the sense of freedom and mannerism which so often characterize the final fling of an artistic style. He was trained in Utrecht and may have been Dutch; at first he worked as a manuscript illuminator. His earlier panels are rather hesitant, but by about 1495 he was painting with ever-increasing confidence, using bright, enamel-type colors. Invariably his figures are executed as if in imitation of sculpture, and some of his paintings, such as the eponymous work in Munich and the *Crucifixion* triptych in Cologne, appear as trompe l'oeil versions of carved retables. Even more bizarre are canvases such as the *Saint Thomas Altar* in Cologne, where the highly realistic figures are made to float quite illogically in space.

GOTHIC ELSEWHERE IN GERMANY

During the early fifteenth century, Cologne unquestionably held the artistic lead in Germany; a gorgeous *Garden of Paradise* preserved in Frankfurt by an unknown Upper Rhenish master from about 1420 is a clear case of the hegemony this style enjoyed. As the century wore on, however, it was Swabian painters who pioneered moves towards more realistic forms, and thus paved the way for the Renaissance. First of these was **Lucas Moser**, probably a stained glass designer by training, whose sole known work is the outside of the triptych still in situ in Tiefenbronn, dated 1431. Although the execution is still very soft and beautiful, an attempt is made at diminishing perspectives, while the water in the sea has both ripples and reflections. Very different is the *Wurzach Altar* of six years later, now in Berlin, which was made in the workshop of the great Ulm sculptor **Hans Multscher** (ca.1400–67), though it's unresolved as to whether it was executed by the master himself, or an unknown assistant who specialized in the painting side of the business. The figures in these Passion scenes are made deliberately crude, with exaggerated theatrical gestures, and seem to have been modeled on real-life peasants; they are about as far away from the contemporary work of Lochner as it is possible to get.

A far more refined painter of the realist tendency was **Conrad Witz** (ca.1400–46) of Rottweil, who spent all his working life in Switzerland. His surviving legacy consists of about twenty panels taken from three separate retables; Basel and Geneva have the best examples, but others are in Berlin and Nürnberg. In them, he successfully resolved the new realism with traditional forms, and grappled with such problems as perspective and movement. His figures have a sculptural quality, and are treated as masses, not as means of portrayal; the rich and luminous colors employed are also an important feature. Most enduring of all was his contribution to land-scape painting, being the first to introduce topographically accurate views of scenery, as opposed to cities, into his pictures. Witz's influence is discernible in the few surviving works of **Master of the Darmstadt Passion**, who was active mid-century in the Middle Rhine region. **Friedrich Herlin** (ca.1435–1499) of Nördlingen, who painted grave, severe figures, was another to follow his example; he in turn was succeeded by **Bartholomäus Zeitblom** (ca.1455–1520) of Ulm.

Among Bavarian painters of this period, **Master of the Tegernsee Altar** (active ca.1430–50) was somewhat archaic in style but capable of highly dramatic effects, notably the curious *Crucifixion* in his native Munich, which is set within elaborate Gothic architecture. Also working in this city was **Master of the Polling Panels** (active ca.1434–50) who retained the International Gothic style, while injecting it with a dose of realism. In the same period, Nürnberg boasted **Master of the Imhoff Altar** and **Master of the Tucher Altar**; the latter's work is characterized by strongly-drawn thick-set figures, prominent still lifes, and attempts at perspective. They were succeeded by **Hans Pleydenwurff** (ca.1420–72), who showed a thorough knowledge of Netherlandish artists such as Bouts in color, figure modeling, and background cityscapes, often with small subsidiary scenes; he was also a notable portraitist. After his death, his workshop was taken over by **Michael Wolgemut** (1434–1519). **Rueland Frueauf** (ca.1440–1507) founded the Danube School of painting in Passau and Salzburg; although few works by him survive, the *Man of Sorrows* in Munich is an arresting masterpiece, achieved by great economy of means. His son of the same name (ca.1470–1545) carried on his style.

The late Gothic period also saw something of a revival in Westphalia. In Münster, **Johann Koerbecke** (active 1446–90) gave a more forceful treatment to facial expression than his Cologne contemporaries. A delicate, sensitive touch is revealed in the work of **Master of Liesborn** (active late fifteenth century); in contrast, **Derick Baegert** (ca.1440–1515) imbued his paintings with a rugged, dramatic quality.

Jan Joest of Kalkar (ca.1455–1519) submerged himself in the art of the nearby Netherlands; he appears to have had a remarkable career, traveling as far afield as Spain, where he painted a retable for Palencia Cathedral which remains in situ. Lübeck's **Hermen Rode** (active 1485–1504) was another practitioner of the new realism.

THE RISE OF THE GRAPHIC ARTS

Gutenberg's printing revolution sounded the death knell for illuminated manuscripts and gave an enormous stimulus to the black-and-white arts, with the traditional woodcut being followed by the new techniques of line engraving and drypoint, which appeared in the 1440s. At first, the forms were dominated by obscure figures from the Mainz area—the two pioneers were the so-called **Master of the Playing Cards**, whose reputation rests on an elaborate card deck, and **Master ES**, among whose creations is a fantastic alphabet. Another engraver known only by his initials is **Master LCZ** of Bamberg, by whom some expressive panels also survive.

A more versatile personality appears in **Master of the Housebook** (active ca.1470–1500), around whom a sizable body of work has been gathered; many attempts have been made to equate him with **Erhard Reuwich**, who executed a series of woodcuts for a book on a journey to the Holy Land. His pseudonym derives from an extraordinary book of drawings in a private collection; it was the manual of a master of munitions at a princely court, and contains elaborate astrological groupings as well as scenes of warfare. Even finer are his delicate drypoints, which depict with both humanity and humor the everyday life of the time, from the fashions and fantasies of the small courts to the earthy pastimes of the peasantry. The draftsman's technique is also evident in the linear form of his few paintings, which include two retables, one in Mainz, the other dispersed in the museums of Freiburg, Berlin, and Frankfurt.

An equally great but very different graphic artist was **Martin Schongauer** (ca.1450–91) of Colmar, which was then very much a German city. He has always been a revered figure, as he marks the transition from the late Gothic to the Renaissance, and is thus the founding father of the short but glorious period when the German visual arts reached the highest pinnacle of their achievement. Over a hundred surviving engravings show his successful assimilation of realism and expressionism from northern artists with the exotic interests and technical innovations of space, form and perspective which characterize the Italian Renaissance. They were to serve as a model and an inspiration to the succeeding generation, who increasingly came to realize that the print was an important new democratic art form closely in tune with the spirit of the age, with potential for reaching a far wider public than had ever been possible before. Schongauer's surviving paintings are tantalizingly few but always of very high quality—they include the large *Madonna of the Rose Bush* in his native city, some damaged frescos of *The Last Judgment* in nearby Breisach, and several highly finished little panels of *The Nativity*, the finest of which is in Berlin.

THE TRIUMPH OF THE RENAISSANCE

The most dominant personality in the history of German art was **Albrecht Dürer** (1471–1528), who trained under Wolgemut in his native Nürnberg. Dürer was a true man of the Renaissance, gaining a broad range of experiences in antithesis to the painstaking workshop traditions which were the lot of the medieval artist. He undertook travels to Italy, Switzerland, Alsace, and the Low Countries, assimilating their traditions and gained mastery in all artistic media, yet also found time to write and engage in mathematical and scientific research as well as be involved in the Reformation, ending up excommunicated for Lutheran sympathies.

Surprisingly, canvas painting does not always show Dürer at his best—he was at times rather conservative in his earlier religious panels, but increased in confidence with time, as can be seen in his valedictory *Four Apostles* in Munich. His portraits from life, however, are almost uniformly superb, laying bare the soul of the subject in penetrating psychological observations. as in *Jacob Muffel* and *Hieronymus Holzschuher*, both now in Berlin. With the woodcut, Dürer was in a class of his own; while still in his twenties he created an *Apocalypse* series of quite menacing power and profound imagination, which he printed and published himself. This was followed by two *Passion* series, a lovely *Life of the Virgin* and the stupendous *Triumphal Arch* commissioned by the Emperor Maximilian; he also made many memorable engravings, often deeply overlaid with symbolic meaning. Dürer was also the first artist to realize the possibilities of watercolor, making beautiful landscape, plant, and animal studies for his own edification. The originals of these are now rarely exhibited for conservation reasons, yet such works as *Young Hare* and *Blade of Grass* rank among the most familiar images in Renaissance art.

In Munich, the Polish-born **Jan Polack** (active ca.1480–1519) painted mannered altarpieces featuring emotional figures clad in swirling draperies, along with portraits more obviously imbued with the new Renaissance outlook. A far more significant artistic center was Augsburg, seat of the Habsburg court. **Hans Holbein the Elder** (ca.1465–1524) showed increasing Renaissance influence in his prolific output of retables, although the was never entirely able to free himself from the old forms. His brother-in-law **Hans Burgkmair** was more successful, benefiting from a spell as Schongauer's assistant; he seems to have particularly delighted in the most luxuriant Italianate features, which he skillfully synthesized into his altars. This decorative talent was given full rein by Emperor Maximilian I, who commissioned him to supervize the overall program of the huge series of woodcuts of his *Triumphal Procession*; many of the leading German artists, including Dürer, contributed, although the success of the project was due to the relish shown by Burgkmair. **Jörg Breu** (ca.1475–1537) was another fine retable painter resident in the city, while **Bernhard Strigel** (ca.1460–1528) served as court portraitist. The latter's linear approach is distinctive, and he developed family groups as an independent art form.

By far the greatest painter Augsburg produced was **Hans Holbein the Younger** (1497?–1543), but he left while still in his teens, and spent the rest of his career in Switzerland and England. He first settled in Basel (which retains by far the best collection of his art), where he was enormously productive in all kinds of media—portraits, altarpieces, decorative schemes of many types (now mostly lost), and woodcuts, including the celebrated *Dance of Death*. One of his master-

pieces from this period, and one of few works by him actually in Germany, is the *Madonna of Burgomaster Mayer* in Darmstadt Schloss, which combines sharply characterized portraits and a devotional theme. He subsequently concentrated almost exclusively on portraiture, developing a cool, detached style based on absolute technical mastery, and frequently incorporating amazingly precise still lifes based on the paraphernalia of the sitter's occupation; *The Danzig Merchant Georg Gisze*, now in Berlin, is an outstanding example. On his second visit to England, he became court painter to Henry VIII, and left a haunting series of drawings of that magnificent but tragic circle, though sadly few of the finished paintings have been preserved.

Lucas Cranach the Elder (1472–1553) was the first great Saxon painter. The first thirty years of his life are obscure; he is first known as a mature artist playing a dominant role in the Danube School, painting portraits and religious scenes set in lush and suggestively beautiful verdant landscapes. His masterpiece of this period is *The Three Crosses* in Munich, which uses a blatantly eccentric vantage point in order to emphasize the artist's technical control. Whereas these works have consistently been admired, Cranach's long second phase at Wittenberg (now in the GDR) in the service of the electors of Saxony is far more controversial. He ran the equivalent of a picture factory, often repeating the same subjects *ad infinitum* with only minor variations, the style is mannered with imperfections in drawing and subjects placed in wholly unrealistic relationships. Yet these were surely deliberate traits by a great humorist and individualist, whose sinuous nudes and erotic mythological scenes added a dimension to German painting which had previously been lacking. He seems to have invented the full-length portrait as a genre, and excelled at characterization. As a personal friend of Luther and Melanchton, he created the definitive images of the leaders of the Reformation, and made propaganda woodcuts on their behalf, but was not averse to accepting traditional commissions from the Catholics as well. His son **Lucas Cranach the Younger** (1515–86) took over the workshop and continued its tradition very faithfully, although at times he was prone to overdo the bucolic effect.

Albrecht Altdorfer (ca.1480–1538) of Regensburg became the leading master of the Danube School; his luxuriant landscape backgrounds assume even greater significance than with Cranach, and at times the the ostensible subject is quite unimportant, as with *Saint George and the Dragon* in Munich. Fantastic buildings also feature in several of his works, reflecting the fact that he was also a practicing architect. When the figures do matter, they are integrated with their surroundings and given highly expressive tendencies, achieved by deliberate anatomical imprecisions and exaggerated gestures. Light is often an important feature, with unnaturally colorful effects; unorthodox aerial perspectives further distinguish his paintings. The largest group of Altdorfer's work, in which all these features appear, is still mostly in situ in the Austrian monastery of St. Florian. However, his masterpiece is the *Battle of Darius and Alexander* in Munich; commissioned as part of a war series, each by different artists, it makes all the others look like the work of bumbling amateurs. The actual battle is depicted with all of the skill of a miniaturist, yet it is set within a spectacular cosmic perspective in what ranks as one of the most formidable displays of sheer pyrotechnics in the history of painting. His chief follower was **Wolf Huber** (ca.1490–1553) of Passau, who was rather more restrained in his effects.

The extreme tendency towards expression in German painting is found in the work of the painter known as **Grünewald**, although his real name was **Mathis Gothardt-Neithardt** (ca.1470?–1528), who is almost a direct opposite of Dürer. Fully proficient in the new Renaissance developments of space and perspective, he used them as mere adjuncts to his sense of drama; he was also the only great German artist of his time who seems to have had no interest in the print. Even in an early work such as *The Mocking of Christ* in Munich, Grünewald's emotional power is evident. No artist ever painted Passion scenes with anything like the same harrowing intensity; in the words of the nineteenth-century French novelist Huysmans, "he promptly strikes you dumb with the fearsome nightmare of a Calvary." His huge folding polyptych, the *Isenheim Altar*, represents the majority of his surviving work. Though its panels are of uneven quality, its moods—ranging from a tender

Madonna and Child to the blazing triumphant glory of *The Resurrection*—are of such variety that it deserves its reputation as the ultimate masterpiece of German painting; ironically, its Colmar home is now French territory. Its *Crucifixion* manages to radiate hope through the darkness, whereas the later version in Karlsruhe is of a forbidding bleakness.

Grünewald's art is so individual and overpowering that it had no successors. However, **Jerg Ratgeb** (ca.1480–1526) must have come under his influence as his few works—fresco cycles in Frankfurt and Maulbronn, and the *Herrenberg Altar* in Stuttgart—have an even rawer expressiveness, which might have developed further had he not been executed for his leading role in the Peasants' Revolt.

Of the younger generation of Renaissance artists, by far the most interesting is **Hans Baldung Grien** (1484?–1545), a flawed genius who studied under Dürer and eventually settled in Strasbourg. Colour and volume play a large part in his pictures, but his fascination with the bizarre is the most obvious recurring element, with moralistic fantasies being among his finest works. Baldung's main religious works are two altars for the Freiburg Münster, but there is no concentration of his output, which is now spread among many museums. The late engravings such as *Wild Horses* and *Bewitched Stable Boy* are quite unlike the work of any other artist, and arguably rank as his greatest achievements.

Hans Süss von Kulmbach (ca.1480–1522) and **Hans Leonard Schäuffelein** (ca.1483–1539?) were loyal followers of Dürer's example, but their productions ultimately lack his inspired touch; the specialist engravers, the brothers **Hans Sebald Beham** (1500–50) and **Barthel Beham** (1502–40), and the Westphalian **Heinrich Aldegraver** (1502–60) were arguably more successful at capturing his spirit. **Master of Messkirch** (active ca.1430–45) added a personal expressive sense to the Düreresque idiom.

The early sixteenth century also saw a mushrooming of talented provincial portraitists who were able to satisfy the ever-increasing demand from the rising middle classes; they often painted religious and mythological subjects as well, but with less success. In Nürnberg, **Georg Pencz** (ca.1500–50), possibly another pupil of Dürer, was strongly influenced by Venetian models. Augsburg at this time had **Cristoph Amberger** (ca.1500–61?), who was more associated with the court, and **Ulrich Apt** (ca.1460–1532). The works of Frankfurt's **Conrad Faber von Creuznach** (ca.1500–53) are particularly felicitous, with the sitters placed against landscapes reminiscent of the Danube School; he also executed a magnificent woodcut of the siege of his home city. **Barthel Bruyn** (1492?–1555) was the first Cologne painter to break away from two centuries of tradition; in spite of several diverse influences, the city's great heritage seems to have made little impression on his art. In Münster, **Ludger tom Ring the Elder** (1496–1547) founded a dynasty which specialized in slightly crude portraits and altars for both Protestant and Catholic use. His style was continued by his sons **Hermann tom Ring** (1521–96) and **Ludger tom Ring the Younger** (1522–84); the latter seems to have been the first German artist to treat still life as an independent form.

MANNERISM AND BAROQUE

Mannerism is already evident in the work of the generation after Dürer, but only appears in a full-blooded way with **Hans von Aachen** (1552–1616), who particularly excelled at sensual mythological subjects, and who played a leading role in the highly distinctive erotic style fostered at the court of Emperor Rudolph II in Prague. **Johann Rottenhammer** (1564–1625) traveled extensively in Italy, before returning to his native Augsburg. He came under the spell of Paolo Veronese's huge decorative works filled with figures; his response was to reduce such compositions to little copper panels, adding an extra degree of luminosity into the landscapes.

This highly skilled technique was developed by his pupil, **Adam Elsheimer** (1578–1610), who settled in Rome and achieved a remarkable synthesis of diverse influences which gives his works a stature that belies their small size. Elsheimer drew on Altdorfer's heritage in creating a union between the subjects and nature, which Rottenhammer left as rather disparate features. He also seemed to share the earlier master's genius for light effects, and was particularly adept at night scenes and at strong contrasts of brightness and shadow derived from Caravaggio. A slow and deliberate

worker, his early death meant that his legacy is numerically modest, but it was to influence such contrasting great successors as Rubens, Rembrandt, and Claude. The largest assemblage of his work is *Altar of the Holy Cross* whose panels have been painstakingly reassembled over the years in his native Frankfurt; many of his best paintings are in Britain, due to the esteem in which he was held by the aristocrats of the Grand Tour. Unfortunately, there was no great German successor, although his style was continued with varying success long after his death by **Johann König** (1586–1642).

The other main German painter of the early seventeenth century, **Johann Liss** (1597–1629), was constantly on the move, leaving his native Holstein for the Low Countries and then Italy, absorbing their diverse traditions. One vein of his work, the small arcadian landscapes, reveals the impact of Elsheimer or at least his Roman followers, but his best canvases are far more monumental in scale, swaggering in the full pomp characteristic of the new Baroque age. These religious and mythological scenes, sometimes featuring sumptuous banquets, are executed with fluid brushwork in luminous and daringly unorthodox colors.

Liss was also to destined for a premature grave, and it seems as if German painting in the seventeenth century was to be jinxed, in contrast to its richness and diversity in this period over the rest of Europe. The Thirty Years' War, which so exhausted and preoccupied the country, acted as a massive restraint on artistic activity at the time, but was to fuel a long-standing vogue for depictions of battles and genre scenes of military life evidenced in the work of **Matthias Scheits** (ca.1630–1700) and **Georg Philip Rugendas** (1666–1742), though these tend to follow the decorative Dutch manner, rather than convey the true horrors the country suffered. An increased religious fervor as a result of the war is mirrored in the emotional cycles of canvases and frescos by the Catholic convert **Michael Willmann** (1630–1706).

Specialist painters of the period include **Wolfgang Heimbach** (ca.1613–78), a deaf-mute who created small scenes of middle-class life and used nocturnal lighting to good effect; the animal artist **Karl Andreas Ruthard** (ca.1630–1703); and **Abraham Mignon**

(1640–79), whose cool and precise still lifes typically show ripe fruit and flowers in full bloom. Far more versatile than any of these was **Johann Friedrich Schönfeld** (1609–84), whose output is rather uneven due to an excessive number of changes of style in repsonse to the diversity he encountered on his Italian travels. His best paintings are colorful history scenes with elaborate backgrounds, painted under the influence of the classically derived compositions of Poussin which held sway in Rome, but tempered by the more light-hearted Neapolitan approach.

However, the most significant art works produced in mid-seventeenth- century Germany were the detailed engravings of towns, known as *Topographia Germaniae*, started by **Matthäus Merian** (1593–1650) and continued by his sons. In due course, the appearances of some 2000 German communities—a unique pictorial record—were preserved for posterity.

LATE BAROQUE, ROCOCO AND NEOCLASSICISM

The best late baroque German painting is not to be found in any museum, but on the walls of the ornate pilgrimage churches of Bavaria and Baden-Württemberg. These buildings, which aimed at fusing all the visual arts into a coherent synthesis, are among the most original creations in the country. Their rich interior decoration formed an intrinsic part of the architecture from the outset, and was often the work of the same masters.

One of the most accomplished of these was **Cosmas Damian Asam** (1686–1739), who formed a team with his sculptor brother, Egid Quirin Asam. At first they decorated existing churches, such as the Dom in Freizing, but later moved on to the logical conclusion of undertaking the entire program themselves. They trained in Rome, and remained loyal to its dignified High Baroque, rather than to the more frivolous rococo derivatives favored by their fellow countrymen. C.D. Asam's ceiling frescoes fall into two separate categories—the trick device of diminishing perspective in the manner of the Italian Jesuit Andrea Pozzo, and a more conventional spatial format of open heavens. **Johann Baptist Zimmerman** (1680–1758), in contrast, is fully rococo; he did not design buildings himself, but enjoyed a particularly close relationship with two of the leading architects of the time: François Cuvilliés, with whom he collaborated on the Munich Residenz and Schloss Nymphenburg; and his own younger brother Dominikus, most notably at the Wieskirche.

By this time, Prussia had arisen as a major power in European affairs, and was by far the dominant German state. Frederick the Great was a major patron of the arts, but he was also a Francophile whose court painter was the Parisian-born **Antoine Pesne** (1683–1757). This artist was commissioned to paint allegorical and mythological decorative schemes for the royal palaces, but his realistic portraits, very much in the French manner of the time with rich colors and subtle lighting effects, were more successful and ultimately highly influential, serving as the model for later Berlin artists. His most important pupil was **Bernhard Rode** (1725–97), who was also involved in the work on the palaces, but who is seen at his best in quietly observed genre scenes. For the last period of his life, he directed the Berlin Academy, one of several founded in the major cities in order to foster a theoretical approach to painting. Another of this circle was **Daniel Nikolaus Chodowiecki** (1726–1801), although his talent was best suited to vignette etchings, mostly to illustrated books. A later Berlin artist, the Danish-born **Asmus Jakob Carstens** (1754–98), was also at his finest in black-and-white media, executing large chalk cartoons of classically inspired subjects.

A strict neoclassical style was adopted at the Kassel Academy under **Johann Heinrich Tischbein** (1722–89). This was modified by his nephews **Johann Friedrich August Tischbein** (1750–1812) and **Johann Heinrich Wilhelm Tischbein** (1751–1829), who introduced the greater warmth found in English and French works of the time, though both remained loyal academicians. The latter's *Goethe in the Campagna* in Frankfurt is the most celebrated work of the dynasty.

Another family of painters had as by far its most accomplished member **Januarius Zick** (1730–97), who turned his back on the academic training he had received. He was a theatrical but effective fresco-ist in the grand manner, as can be seen in the cycles in Wiblingen and Bruchsal. In contrast, his canvases are often of modest size, achieving an original synthesis of the light effects often found in Rembrandt's deeply intimate small-scale works with the airy rococo grace of Watteau.

ROMANTICISM

The Romantic movement, a reaction against the rigidity of neoclassicism but with the same Roman roots, was particularly strong in Germany; the rich outpourings of music and literature make it one of the supreme high-points in the country's cultural history. Although there was not the same depth of talent in painting, the haunting and highly original landscapes of **Caspar David Friedrich** (1774–1840) form a fitting visual counterpart to the works of the great poets and composers of the time. Friedrich created a new spiritual way of looking at scenery; it was always the immensity and majesty of nature that he sought to convey, often using the technique of enormously long perspectives. Unlike his great predecessor Altdorfer, he did not stress the unity of man and landscape, but rather the unconquerable power of the latter. Where figures are introduced, they are typically seen from the back, contemplating the wonders before them; in the more common absence of humans, the evidence of man's presence tends to stress his fragility and ephemeral status— as in the famous *Eismeer* in Hamburg, or the many scenes with classical temples and Gothic abbeys—in comparison with the omnipotent changelessness of the surroundings.

The influence of Friedrich's way of looking can sometimes be detected in the canvases of architect **Karl Friedrich Schinkel** (1781–1841), who was forced by financial considerations to turn to painting, where he abandoned the neoclassicism of his buildings in favor of vast panoramas, architectural fantasies, and theatrical spectaculars. **Philip Otto Runge** (1777–1810) might have developed into Friedrich's figurative counterpart had he lived longer. He had enormously grandiose ideas, aiming to recover the lost harmony of the universe through the symbolism of colors and numbers, and began a project called *The Times of Day*, of four panels over eight meters in height, which he aimed to install in a specially-designed building in which poetry and music would be performed. That he managed to

persuade no less than Goethe to cooperate in this suggests that there was genuine substance to this apparently utopian dream, but it was never executed, and only studies survive, leaving Runge's reputation to rest largely on his portraits, particularly oversized ones of children.

Johann Friedrich Overbeck (1789–1869) was another Romantic with original convictions, settling in Rome where he founded the **Nazarene Brotherhood** of painters who lived like monks in a deconsecrated monastery. He produced two large cooperative fresco cycles: *The Story of Joseph*, which has been removed to the Bode Museum in East Berlin, and another, still in situ, of scenes taken from Italian Renaissance literature. These very detailed works emphasized theme and content at the expense of form. The figures are ideal types, not taken from nature, the aim being to return to the soft otherworldly beauty found in Quattrocento painting, an ideal followed soon afterwards by the English Pre-Raphaelites.

Whereas Overbeck remained in Italy, his collaborators **Peter Cornelius** (1783–1867), **Julius Schnorr von Carolsfeld** (1794–1872), and **Wilhelm Schadow** (1788–1862) returned to Germany where they pursued careers in the academies. Cornelius spent time in charge of the two most dominant, Düsseldorf and Munich, and aimed to establish a tradition of monumental historical painting to rival the great frescoes of Italy. Although both influential and genuinely popular in its day, this style of painting has, since the turn of the present century, attracted nothing but critical scorn, appearing as an empty display of bombastics. It can still be seen all over the country, often desecrating the walls of great medieval buildings; among the better efforts are the cycles by **Alfred Rethel** (1816–59) in the Aachen Rathaus and by the Austrian-born **Moritz von Schwind** (1804–71) in Karlsruhe's Kunsthalle. **Ferdinand Olivier** (1785–1841) painted narrative canvases in the Nazarene style, as well as more conventional Romantic landscapes. Standing somewhat apart are the expansive, open-ended fresco views painted in Munich by Ludwig I's court artist **Carl Rottmann** (1797–1850).

Romanticism in one form or another flourished throughout the nineteenth century. The brothers **Andreas Achenbach** (1815–1910) and **Oswald Achenbach** (1827–1905) continued in Friedrich's manner; the former was particularly successful at evocative northern scenery, whereas the latter added popular scenes to his pictures. **Karl Blechen** (1798–1840) also began in this style, but his later works, following a visit to Paris, became more consciously realist. **Anselm Feuerbach** (1829–80) pursued a heavily Italianate form of Romanticism in his portraits and densely crowded mythological scenes. There is a highly personal mixure of the neoclassical and Romantic in **Hans von Marées** (1837–87), who achieved his masterpiece in his one commission for monumental frescos, the Aquarium in Naples. For long out of critical favor, his canvases have recently begun to attract a great deal of interest, even if the technical execution falls short of the artist's challenging intellect. The inconsistent **Hans Thoma** (1839–1924) tried many styles in his time; the Romantic views of the Black Forest are by far the most successful.

OTHER 19TH C. STYLES

Although many different trends were current in nineteenth century German painting, none of them can match the vitality of the best Romantic work. A style which was largely confined to the country and its immediate neighbors from about 1815 to 1848 was Biedermeier, a bourgeois-inspired classicism which drew on the pleasant aspects of living. **Carl Spitzweg** (1808–85) was its principal exponent; his homely pictures of the middle-classes are injected with a touch of humor mocking the complacency that was all too apparent. **Franz Krüger** (1797–1857) chronicled Berlin life of the time in a more straightlaced vein, particularly in his ceremonial scenes and architectural views; **Eduard Gärtner** (1801–77) is another painter of this type. Though he sometimes worked in the Düsseldorf academic manner, **Georg Friedrich Kersting** (1785–1847) was at his best in small-scale interiors, in which he showed his interest in everyday objects and activities as matters of beauty in their own right. Another Düsseldorf painter was **Ludwig Richter** (1804–83), but again his true metier lay in a quite different field, in this case illustrations of legends for children's books.

In contrast to this movement, there was a continued demand for official portraitists; one of the most accomplished was **Franz von Lenbach** (1836–1904), who painted Bismarck no less than eighty times. **Franz Xaver Winterhalter** (1805–73) had the most dazzling career of all, progressing around all the main European courts, leaving behind unremittingly flattering portrayals of smug monarchs and their pampered retinue whose psychological penetration is nonexistent and artistic value small.

In the Realist tradition, Germany lagged some way behind France, although the versatile **Adolph von Menzel** (1815–1905), who also executed portraits and history scenes in the grand manner, was one of the first painters to portray the Industrial Revolution and its effects. **Wilhelm Trübner** (1851–1917) was another to undertake this mix of subjects. The best examples of this style were to follow from **Wilhelm Leibl** (1844–1900), who aimed to recreate the technical skill of the old masters. To this end he conducted such experiments as reviving tempera to create an enamel-like surface, and painting with the attention to detail of a miniaturist, as in *Three Women in Church* in Hamburg. Much of his finest work was done in the 1870s, when he lived in rural Bavaria, and used peasants as real-life models.

Impressionism was very slow to catch on, and never seems to have suited the German temperament, but three artists who adopted it at some point in their careers were **Max Liebermann** (1847–1935), who originally favored the somber colors of the French Barbizon School and the Realists; **Lovis Corinth** (1858–1925), whose best works are the late landscapes executed in cold colors; and **Max Slevogt** (1868–1932), who was also a book illustrator and, late in life, a painter of monumental frescos. Liebermann was the leading figure in the Berlin section of the **Secession movement** which began in the 1890s; this was a reaction by the avant-garde against the stultifying power wielded by the academies. The earlier Munich group was dominated by **Franz von Stuck** (1863–1928), an artist of violent mythological scenes, humorous drawings, and large-scale decorative work.

EXPRESSIONISM

Much as the early part of the nineteenth century saw the dominance of Romanticism in German painting, so the first decades of this century came under the sway of Expressionism, a new and largely indigenous style, which aimed to root modern painting firmly in the tradition of the old German masters, and to establish it on an equal footing with France, for some time the dominant force in world art. Because of the entrenched power of existing interests, artists found they had to bind themselves into **groups** in order to make an impact; the early history of Expressionism is particularly associated with two of these.

Although its members were younger, *Die Brücke* (The Bridge) was first to be founded, in 1905. Its initial personnel, **Ernst Ludwig Kirchner** (1880–1938), **Erich Heckel** (1883–1970), and **Karl Schmidt-Rottluf** (1884–1976) were architectural students in Dresden who felt constrained by the inability of their field to capture the immediate freshness of inspiration. Consequently, they turned to painting, in which none had much experience; they were shortly joined by **Max Pechstein** (1881–1955) and **Otto Mueller** (1874–1930). They valued color as a component in its own right, and later strove to enhance its surface effect as well. Their devotion to the country's artistic heritage was shown in the emphasis they placed on feeling, and on their revival of the woodcut as a valid alternative to oils.

The group moved to Berlin, where they turned away from their original preoccupation with landscapes to the depiction of city life. Kirchner developed into the leader and best artist of the group. *Three Women in the Street*, now in Essen, is a key work; its strong sense of line shows the impact made by the arts of primitive peoples, then being appreciated in Europe for the first time. The group broke up in 1913, and thereafter each artist pursued an independent career. Kirchner turned to decorative design in the 1920s, working on embroideries and tapestries; his later paintings show a stronger sense of abstraction. Heckel's work is closest to Kirchner, though he was later to add a greater sense of realism to his pictures. Pechstein, at the time regarded as the most important Expressionist of all, has since suffered a slump in reputation; he was the most loyal to naturalistic representation, and

thus stands furthest removed from the path followed by Schmidt-Rottluf. Gypsy culture features strongly in Mueller's work; he seems to have felt a genuine affinity with it, and spent much of the 1920s traveling among their Balkan communities.

The second group of artists was *Der Blaue Reiter* (The Blue Rider), a strongly intellectual movement originating in Munich which aimed at uniting all the arts. Its name is taken from its magazine, which appeared only once (in 1912); it was very loosely structured, and far more diverse than *Dei Brücke*, with the lead being taken by two contrasting artistic personalities. The Russian-born **Wassily Kandinsky** (1866–1944) was a pioneer of pure abstraction, using fluid and soft forms, but strong and vibrant colors; he was also a noted writer, and used words as the starting points for his images. **Franz Marc** (1880–1916), on the other hand, always retained at least a partial form of representation in his compositions. He was devoted to nature, and animals are a recurrent theme in his art; he regarded them as noble and uncorrupted, the complete antithesis to Man. At first they appear detached in the foreground; from 1913, when he adopted more abstract methods, they are more closely integrated with their surroundings. Geometry was always important to Marc, and he favored prismatic colors, to which he attached a mystical significance. His development was cut short by the outbreak of war, and he was to die in combat.

This fate also befell an even younger member of the group, **August Macke** (1887–1914). Although Macke was clearly influenced by the new cubist movement, his works are always representational, and he ranks as the most poetic and gentle of all the Expressionists. The figures are unmistakable; slim and column-like, as though from a medieval cathedral, they glide across the picture surface, taking their Sunday stroll in the park, or indulging in a bit of window-shopping. More often than not, they wear a hat, which serves to distinguish them, as their facial features are never included. Strong colors are used, but they are never strident; they rather add to the happy and relaxed atmosphere.

Paul Klee (1879–1940), born in Switzerland but having German nationality as well, was the fourth main member of the group. He never concerned himself with any of the social, political, or psychological problems of the age, but preferred to construct his own abstract language in which he aimed to recapture the mystery and magic of the universe. To this end, he developed a series of fractured and fragmented forms—arcs, forks, and bars—which were usually painted black against a colored background. In the 1920s, when they worked at the Bauhaus, he and Kandinsky formed *Die Blauen Vier* (The Blue Four) as a successor to *Der Blaue Reiter*.

The other members were **Alexej Jawlensky** (1864–1941), also of Russian birth, who specialized in characterful portrait heads; and **Lyonel Feininger** (1871–1956), who was born and died in New York, but who can be regarded as the most loyal German cubist, being most notable for his architectural and marine scenes. Russian influence is apparent in the paintings of **Heinrich Campendonk** (1889–1957), the youngest member of *Der Blaue Reiter*, although his preferred medium was the woodcut.

A number of Expressionists unattached to either group were active in the Rhine-Ruhr area, where Macke also spent much of his life. Throughout a very long career, **Christian Rohlfs** (1849–1938) tried many different styles; he clearly came under the influence of the Impressionists, but never fully adopted their manner. His true artistic personality did not emerge until his Expressionist phase, particularly the architecural paintings he made in Soest and Erfurt, and the very late flower pieces. Rohlfs clearly inspired **Wilhelm Morgner** (1891–1917), another war casualty. **Heinrich Nauen** (1880–1940) was one of several Expressionists who were quite overt about following French leads, in his case Matisse and the Fauves, whose bright colors form an important feature of his hybrid style.

Fauvism, particularly the classically-inspired works of Derain, was also important to **Carl Hofer** (1878–1955). Primitive art as filtered through Gauguin made a strong impression on **Paula Modersohn-Becker** (1876–1907), the most talented artist of the colony at Worpswede near Bremen. Whether or not she is really an Expressionist is debatable, as she did not concern herself with drama or emotions, though her favorite *Mother and Child* theme has achieved a certain poignancy given that she was to die during childbirth.

The most individualistic Expressionist of all, even though he had a spell as a member of *Die Brücke*, was **Emil Hansen** (1867–1956), generally called **Nolde** after his birthplace. In his depictions of the rugged Baltic coastline that was his home, he can be regarded as the successor to Friedrich. However, there's no sense of romance in Nolde's landscapes, which convey the harsh and forbidding nature of the terrain and its climate, emphasized in the way he captured its special colors and light effects by means of rich, strong and violently contrasting tones. Flowers and garden scenes provide a lighter note, but he also revived the somewhat lost art of religious painting, in which he aimed to recreate something of the intensity of Grünewald, along with the simple devotion he found in primitive art.

Ludwig Meidner (1884–1966) was dubbed the most expressionist of the Expressionists, as a result of the powerful apocalyptic visions he painted before the war, which stand at the opposite extreme to the primitive trends in the movement. The union of all the arts sought by so many found its best individual manifestation in the work of **Ernst Barlach** (1870–1938). Primarily a sculptor, he was also a talented graphic artist, illustrating his own plays and travel writings. Another sculptor, **Käthe Kollwitz** (1867–1945) achieved great emotional power in her pacifist woodcuts, engravings, and lithographs of wartime horrors.

OTHER 20TH C. MOVEMENTS

Expressionism, in spite of its dominance, does not by any means cover the entire richness of German art in the early part of this century. The nihilistic dada movement, which grew up during the war, included **Kurt Schwitters** (1887–1948), who took the concept of non-art to its extreme, experimenting with collages incorporating pieces of torn-up paper before moving on to using rubbish as his basic component. He dubbed his art *Merz* after the letters from one of the pieces of paper he used, and intended his life's work to be a huge composition which would fill a house, but the first two completed versions were destroyed, and his last attempt, in exile in England, was unfinished at his death. **Hannah Höch** (1889–1978) and the Austrian-born **Raoul Hausmann** (1886–1944) were two rather milder dadaists.

Georg Grosz (1893–1959) also began in this style, but his later works were more representational. A committed Communist, he was a savage satirist, particularly in his humorous drawings, ruthlessly attacking the corrupt and decadent vested interests of the Weimar Republic. Ironically, he was entranced by America, and emigrated there just before the Nazi accession to power.

Inevitably, there grew a tendency which stood in polar opposition to Expressionism: *Neue Sachlichkeit* (New Objectivity), a term first used in 1923 to describe trends already apparent. This can be thought of as an updated form of realism, which aimed at depicting subjects in a straightforward and detailed way. Some of Grosz's work belongs to this style, but its finest practitioner was **Otto Dix** (1891–1969), who had been profoundly affected by the war, which thereafter formed a persistent subject of his work, although he used it to depict Man's suffering as opposed to any directly political overtone. He aimed to recapture the actual technique of the old masters, and his portraits show larger-than-life characters under a rich sheen of paint. In spite of the overt eroticism of many of his canvases, he was also drawn to the Passion, on which he placed a humanitarian and allegorical interpretation. The former dadaist **Christian Schad** (1894–1982) represents a more extreme form of Dix's style, with many explicit scenes drawn from the bohemian world he himself inhabited; **Rudolf Schlichter** (1890–1955) had similar preoccupations. In contrast, there was a romantically-inclined wing of this movement, exemplified by **Georg Schrimpf** (1898–1938).

Max Beckmann (1884–1950) defies classification, lying somewhere between Expressionism and *Neue Sachlichkeit*. He believed it was the artist's duty to express man's spiritual condition. To this end, he used the self-portrait as a means of expressing his changing action to world events, making himself appear in different guises, whether as clown, convict, king, or hero. The symbolism associated with Carnival and the circus is a recurring theme in his work, as are the use of gesture to reveal character, and the manipulation of space. To express opposition to the Nazis, he took to the anachronistic format of the triptych.

Max Ernst (1891–1976) was another who began as a dadaist, producing first collages and then frottages. However, he is best known as one of the leading surrealist painters, a style he turned to at its foundation in 1924, and for which his early interest in psychology and the creative works of the mentally ill made him most suitable. His scenes are less suggestive than those of Dalí and Magritte, but at their best they present a gnawingly haunting imagery. To what extent he can be considered a German artist is debatable, as he left his native country in 1922, taking first American then French nationality.

Oskar Schlemmer (1888–1943) was one of the most varied German painters of the century, touched by seemingly every style; he also practised both decorative and functional art. Among the practitioners of abstraction following Kandinsky and Klee, **Willi Baumeister** (1889–1955), **Ernst Wilhelm Nay** (1902–68), and **Alfred Wolfgang Schulze** (1913–51), better known as **Wols**, acquired the largest reputations.

POSTSCRIPT – THE PRESENT DAY

In the postwar Federal Republic, avant-garde artistic activity has flourished, thanks to generous subsidy levels by all tiers of government. How many of the painters whose work currently lines the walls of the country's many museums of modern art will prove to be of lasting significance remains a moot point. Among those who have gained international standing, **Georg Baselitz** (b.1940) paints figuratively, but groups the different components of his works in a deliberately arbitrary way. **Sigmar Polke** (b.1941) can be seen as something of a disciple of dadaism in the objects he tacks on to his canvases, mirroring his interest in West German society's obsession with kitsch. **Anselm Kiefer** (b.1945) has been concerned with the German psyche in its historical context, focusing on gestures, symbols, and myths. **Jörg Immendorff** (b.1945) and **Bernd Koberling** (b.1938) have taken an overtly left-wing political stance in their work, with ecological themes also being associated with the latter.

BOOKS

TRAVEL

Mark Twain A Tramp Abroad (Running Heads, $12.95). The early, German-based part of this book, particularly the descriptions of Heidelberg, show Twain on top form, by turns humorous and evocative. There's an hilariously extravagant appendix entitled "The Awful German Language," which mercilessly pillories the overcomplexity of "this fearsome tongue."

Patrick Leigh Fermor A Time of Gifts (Penguin, $6.95). The author set out to walk from Rotterdam to Constantinople in 1933, traveling along the Rhine and Danube valleys en route. Written up forty years later in luscious, hyper-refined prose, it presents the fresh sense of youthful discovery distilled through considerable subsequent learning and reflection. Prewar Germany is shown suffering from all the schizophrenic influences of the era, yet the country's enduring beauty is also captured.

Anthony Bailey Along the Edge of the Forest: An Iron Curtain Journey (Random House, O/P). Describing a trip along the notorious border dividing the two Germanies, the idea behind this book is more inspired than either the experiences or their narration.

HISTORY

Einhard and Notker the Stammerer Two Lives of Charlemagne (Penguin, $4.95). Einhard was a leading courtier in the service of the founder of the Holy Roman Empire, and provided a beautifully written, all-too-short biography of his master. Written a century later, Notker's book is a series of monkish anecdotes, many no doubt apocryphal, which help flesh out the overall portrait of Charlemagne.

Geoffrey Barraclough Origins of Modern Germany (Norton, $12.95). The most easily digestible general introduction to the country's history, tackling the medieval period better than any more specialized book.

Ronald Bainton Here I Stand : A Life of Martin Luther (NAL, $3.95). The best and liveliest biography of Martin Luther, one of the undisputed titans of European history.

Owen Chadwick The Reformation (Pelican, $5.95). Traces the German origins of the biggest-ever rupture in the fabric of the Church, and follows their impact on the rest of Europe.

Veronica (C.V.) Wedgwood The Thirty Years' War (Routledge Chapman and Hall, $13.95). Easily the most accomplished book on the series of conflicts which devastated the country and divided the continent in the first half of the seventeenth century.

Walter Hubatsch Frederick the Great: Absolutism and Administration (O/P); **Christopher Duffy** Frederick the Great: A Military Life (Routledge Chapman and Hall, $17.95). Two contrasting biographies on different aspects of the man who brought Prussia to the forefront of German affairs, and to a place among the great powers of Europe.

Golo Mann The History of Germany Since 1787 (Praeger, O/P). Written by the son of Thomas Mann, this comprehensive study traces not only the politics, but also the intellectual and cultural currents of the period. Another recommendable general study, this time by a British author, is **William Carr** A History of Germany 1815–1985 (St. Martin's Press, $25.00).

A.J.P. Taylor Bismarck: The Man and the Statesman (David and Charles, $11.95). Britain's most controversial historian here provides a typically stirring portrait of the ruthless schemer who forged (reluctantly, in the author's view) the nineteenth-century unification of Germany.

Volker Berghahn Germany and the Approach of War in 1914 (St Martin's Press). Fundamentally a history book, but also presenting an instructive general picture of Germany before World War I. It chronicles the political, economic, and social pressures of the time, and succeeds in giving plausible explanations for the apparently inevitable.

Ebehard Kolb *The Weimar Republic* (Unwin & Hyman). The most recent study of the endlessly fascinating but fundamentally flawed state—as yet the only experiment at a united and democratic German nation—which survived for just fourteen years. Though not currently available in a U.S. edition look for the British edition by Unwin & Hyman.

John Willett *Weimar Years :A Culture Cut Short* (Abbeville Press, $19.95); *Art and Politics in the Weimar Period: The New Sobriety* (Pantheon, $14.95) In these two works, the man who has brilliantly translated Brecht's works into English here turns his attentions to the wider culture and politics of art of the Weimar Republic.

NAZISM AND WORLD WAR II

Alan Bullock *Hitler: A Study in Tyranny* (Harper & Row, $13.95). Ever since it was published, this scholarly yet highly readable tome has ranked as the classic biography of the failed Austrian artist and discharged army corporal whose evil genius fooled a nation and caused the deaths of millions.

William Shirer *The Rise and Fall of the Third Reich* (Simon & Schuster, $14.95). This makes a perfect compliment to Bullock's book: Shirer was an American journalist stationed in Germany during the Nazi period. Notwithstanding the inordinate length and excessive journalese, this book is full of insights, and is ideal for dipping into, with the help of its exhaustive index.

Hugh Trevor-Roper *The Last Days of Hitler* (Macmillan, $7.95). A brilliant reconstruction of the closing chapter of the Third Reich, set in the Berlin Bunker. Trevor-Roper subsequently marred his reputation as the doyen of British historians by authenticating the forged *Hitler Diaries*, which have themselves been the subject of several books.

Joachim Fest *The Face of the Third Reich* (Pantheon, $7.95). Mainly of interest for its biographies of the men surrounding the Führer—Göring, Goebbels, Hess, Himmler, Speer, et al.

The Speeches of Adolf Hitler (Gordon Press, $250.00) Hitler in his own words; an exhaustive collection which, because of its price, you'll want to find in your local library.

Rebecca West *A Train of Powder* (Viking, O/P) The author's celebrated writings on the Nürnberg Trials, which she covered on behalf of the *Daily Telegraph*, as well as a number of other inspired articles on postwar Germany.

SOCIETY AND POLITICS

John Ardagh *Germany and the Germans* (Harper & Row, $10.95). The latest and most up-to-date English-language characterization of the country and its people, taking into account its history, politics, and psyche, and covering almost every aspect of national life. Its approach is always lively, yet remains scrupulously unbiased. If you buy only one other book on Germany, this should be it.

Günther Wallraff *Lowest of the Low* (Freundlich, $16.95). In 1983, Wallraff put an ad in the papers saying: "Foreigner, strong, seeks work of any kind, including heavy and dirty jobs, even for little money." Then he spent two years laboring among Turkish and other immigrant workers, finding out about the underside of German affluence. The book was a political bombshell when it came out, painting a picture of exploitation and malpractice rarely discussed in Germany. Unfortunately, it now seems that the author was guilty of fabricating some of the evidence, thus diminishing its long-term impact.

Werner Hülsberg *The German Greens* (not available in U.S. edition; available in British edition by Verso) An in-depth analysis of Germany's most exciting political phenomenon, this book traces the movement's intellectual and political origins, chronicles the internal disputes, introduces the main characters, and analyzes its shortcomings.

W. A. Coupe *Germany Through the Looking Glass* (St Martin's Press, $14.95). The author presents the period 1945–1986 via a collection of German political cartoons, adding his own analysis of the issues in each case. Opinionated and subjective, the book introduces German humor and a German view of the country's postwar development.

Julia Becker *Hitler's Children* (not available in US edition). An analysis by a British writer of the political terrorism that rocked the complacent society of 1970s Germany to its very foundations. Available in a British edition that is currently out of print.

Ralf Dahrendorf *Society and Democracy in Germany* (Norton, $9.95). An in-depth sociological analysis of the German psyche, prompted by the awful question, "How was Auschwitz possible?"

Gordon Smith *Democracy in Western Germany : Parties and Politics in the Federal Republic* (Holmes and Meier, $16.95). The most up-to-date guide to West Germany's political setup.

GERMANY IN ENGLISH FICTION

Rudolph Erich Raspe *The Adventures of Baron Munchausen* (Hippocerne Books, $8.95). The outrageously exaggerated humorous exploits of the real-life Baron Munchausen were embroidered yet farther by Raspe and first published in English. This edition is illustrated with cartoons by Ronald Searle; copies with the classic nineteenth-century engravings of Gustav Doré can often be found in remainder and second-hand shops.

Jerome K. Jerome *Three Men on the Bummel* (Penguin, $3.95). Sequel to the (deservedly) more famous *Three Men in a Boat*, this features the same trio of feckless English travelers taking a bicycling holiday through Germany at the turn of the century. The second half of the book features plenty of entertaining anecdotes, with opinions bandied about on every conceivable subject.

Katherine Mansfield *The Short Stories of Katherine Mansfield* (Knopf, $22.95). Contains a collection of short stories, first published in *In a German Pension*, set in early twentieth-century Bavaria. Funny but often acerbic too.

CLASSIC PROSE

Johann Jacob Christoffel von Grimmelshausen *Simplicius Simplicissimus* (University Press of America, $26.00). This massive semi-autobiographical novel is one of the highpoints of seventeenth century European literature. Set against the uncertainties of the Thirty Years' War, it charts the story of its hero from boyhood to middle-age.

Johann Wolfgang von Goethe *The Sorrows of Young Werther* (Random House, $3.95). An early epistolary novella, treating the theme of suicide for the first time ever. *Wilhelm Meister: The Years of Apprenticeship* (Riverrun Press, 3 vols, $7.95 each) and *Wilhelm Meister: The Years of Travel* (Riverrun Press, 3 vols, $7.95 each) is a huge, episodic and partly autobiographical cycle of novels. *Tales for Transformation* (City Lights, $5.95) is a wide-ranging series of short stories, showing Goethe's interest in alchemy and the supernatural.

Heinrich von Kleist *The Marquise of O and Other Stories* (Penguin; $4.95). Like Hoffmann, who was only one year older, Kleist was one of the all-time greats of short story writing. His eight tales range in length from three to over a hundred pages, but they're all equally compelling.

Joseph von Eichendorff *Memoirs of a Good-For-Nothing* (Ungar, $5.95). A beautifully poetic little novel in the most optimistic Romantic vein.

Annette von Droste-Hülshoff *The Jew's Beech* (Basil Blackwell, $15.95). An English/German text of the great nineteenth-century poet's exquisite prose idyll in which the mastery of small-scale descriptions of nature is blended with a sense of the supernatural.

Theodor Storm *Immensee* (Irvington, $7.95). Storm's Romantic tale about an old man reminiscing about his lost youth is here found in an anthology which also includes **Georg Büchner**'s only prose work, *Lenz*.

Theodor Fontane *Before the Storm* (Oxford University Press, $6.95). Set in Prussia during the period of the Napoleonic Wars, this is by some way the greatest German novel of the second half of the nineteenth century, dealing with the conflict between patriotism and liberty. The much shorter *Effi Briest* (Penguin, $7.95) focuses on adultery in the context of the social mores of the age.

20TH C. NOVELS

Thomas Mann *The Magic Mountain* (Random House, $6.95). Generally considered the author's masterpiece, this is a weighty novel of ideas discussing love, death, politics and war through a collection of characters in a Swiss sanatorium, whose sickness mirrors that of European society as a whole. The earlier *Buddenbrooks* (Random House, $5.95) is the story of a merchant dynasty in the author's native Lübeck, while *Doctor Faustus* (Random House, $6.95) updates the Faust legend via the story of a twentieth-century German composer.

Heinrich Mann *Man of Straw* (Penguin, $6.95). The best book by Thomas Mann's more politically committed elder brother, here analyzing the authoritarian nature of life under the Second Reich.

Hermann Hesse *Narziss and Goldmund* (Bantam Books, $4.50). A beautifully polished novel, set in medieval Germany and narrated in the picaresque vein, about two monks, one a dedicated scholar, the other a wanderer, artist and lover. *Steppenwolf* (Bantam Books, $3.95) is a bizarre fantasy about schizophrenia, while *Magister Ludi:The Glass Bead Game* (Bantam Books, $4.95) is a monumental utopian novel, set in a future where an elite group develops a game which resolves the world's conflicts into a state of order.

Erich Maria Remarque *All Quiet on the Western Front* (Fawcett, $3.95). The classic German novel of World War I, focusing on the traumatic impact of the conflict on the life of an ordinary soldier.

Bertolt Brecht *The Threepenny Novel* (Available in British edition by Penguin). Brecht's only novel, a much-expanded version of the "Opera," is a disaster. The joke underpinning the book has worn thin after about three chapters, but the author plows on relentlessly through another 300 pages.

Alfred Döblin *Berlin-Alexanderplatz* (Ungar, $11.95). A prominent socialist intellectual during the Weimar period, Döblin went into exile shortly after the banning of his books in 1933. *Berlin-Alexanderplatz* is his weightiest and most durable achievement, an unrelenting epic of the city's proletariat.

Günther Grass *Dog Years* (Harcourt Brace, $6.95); *The Flounder* (Harcourt Brace, $12.00); *The Tin Drum* (Random House, $7.95). Grass is one of Germany's best-known postwar novelists, concerned to analyze and come to terms with his country's awful recent heritage. His highly political novels are all studies of the German character, concentrating on how Nazism found a foothold among ordinary Germans, and on postwar feelings of guilt, but also examining postwar materialism and spiritual poverty.

Heinrich Böll *The Lost Honor of Katharina Blum* (McGraw Hill, $6.95). Winner of the Nobel Prize for Literature in 1972, Heinrich Böll is the most popular postwar German novelist— at least with non-Germans. Certainly his books are accessible, though always treating contentious topics; this is the harrowing story of a young woman whose life is ruined by the combined effects of a gutter press campaign and her accidental involvement with a wanted terrorist. *The Clown* (McGraw Hill, $6.95) again uses the backdrop of the city of Cologne for a more detailed critique of modern German society.

Peter Handke *The Goalie's Anxiety at the Penalty Kick* (in *Three by Handke*, Avon, $3.95). Existentialist novella, dealing with the theme of paranoia. This collection also contains *Short Letter, Long Farewell* and Handke's memoir of his mother's suicide, *A Sorrow Beyond Dreams*. Two additional novels by Handke, acclaimed by some as the best writer of his generation, are collected in *Two Novels by Peter Handke* (Avon, $2.95) - *A Moment of True Feeling* and *The Left-Handed Woman*.

Gisela Elsner *Offside* (Available in British edition by Virago). Feminist novel about women's lives in middle-class postwar Germany.

H.M Waidson *The Modern German Novel* (Oxford University Press; O/P in US). Concentrating on the period 1945–65, this is one of the very few books that can introduce you to recent German writers whose work is not yet available in English translation. It also includes an excellent bibliography for further reading.

POETRY

Leonard Forster (ed.) *The Penguin Book of German Verse* (Penguin, $6.95). Best of the anthologies, representing all the big names (and many more) from the eighth century to the present day, with folksongs, ballads, and chorales added for good measure.

Anonymous *Carmina Burana* (Focus Information Group, $12.25). A wonderful collection of (originally) dog-Latin songs and poems from thirteenth-century Bavaria; in spite of their monastic origin, the texts are often bawdy and erotic. Many were used by Carl Orff in his choral showpiece named after the manuscript.

Johann Wolfgang von Goethe *Poems of Goethe* (AMS Press, $18.50), *The Poems of Goethe* (Richard West, $45.00), *Roman Elegies and Other Poems* (Black Swan, $7.95). Varied anthologies drawn from Goethe's prodigious output.

Heinrich Heine *Poems of Heinrich Heine* (Gordon Press, $75.00), *Selected Verse* (Penguin, $7.95). The favorite poet of the great nineteenth-century Romantic composers, Heine's works, with their strong rhythms and dramatic, acerbic thrusts, translate far better into English than those of any of his contemporaries.

Friedrich Hölderlin *Selected Poems of Freiderich Hölderlin and Eduard Moricke* (University of Chicago Press, $3.95). Hölderlin's poetry, with its classical meters and vivid imagery, is notoriously difficult to translate, but this anthology makes a successful stab at the thankless task. Also includes some of the very different lyric poetry of **Eduard Mörike**.

Bertolt Brecht *Poems* (Routledge Chapman and Hall, $14.95). Brecht's poems sound even more inspired when heard in the musical settings provided by Kurt Weill and the more ideologically-inspired Paul Dessau and Hans Eisler; plenty of recordings are available of these.

DRAMA

Johann Wolfgang von Goethe *Faust Parts One and Two* (Oxford University Press, $8.95). Goethe made the completion of this vast drama—which examines the entire gamut of preoccupations of European civilization—the major task of his life, and he duly finished it just before his death, having worked at it for around sixty years. Other Goethe plays include the historical dramas *Egmont* (Ungar, $5.95) and *Torquato Tasso* (Ungar, $5.95).

Friedrich Schiller *The Robbers, Wallenstein* (Penguin, $6.95). This pairs an early *Sturm und Drang* drama (which established him as the leader of that movement) with one of his later historical plays, set against the background of the Thirty Years' War. *William Tell* (University of Chicago Press, $8.95), is the playwright's last work. For those interested, there is now a pricey ($350.00) eight-volume set of all his works by Darby Books, *Complete Works in English*.

Gotthold Ephraim Lessing *Minna von Barnhelm* (University of Chicago Press, $10.00). One of German theater's earliest examples of middle-class comedy, using contemporary eighteenth-century events as a backdrop.

Georg Büchner *George Büchner: Complete Plays and Prose* (Hill & Wang, $7.95). Büchner died in 1837 at the age of 23. Two of his three plays are masterpieces—*Danton's Death* is a political statement about the French Revolution, while the astonishing unfinished *Woyzeck*, a tragedy based on the life of an insignificant soldier, must be the tersest drama ever written, with not a word wasted in the telling.

Gerhart Hauptmann *The Weavers* (in *Three Plays: The Weavers, Hannele, The Beaver Coat*, Ungar, $7.95). Focusing on the miseries of the early industrial world, and the common helplessness of the expoiters and expoited, this play succeeds in spite of its lack of a hero—or even much of a plot.

Bertolt Brecht *Collected Plays, Vols. 1–2, 5, 6–7, 9* (Random House, $3.95 to $7.95). Brecht's short but fruitful collaboration during the Weimar Republic with the composer Kurt Weill—*The Threepenny Opera, The Rise and Fall of the City of Mahogany* and *The Seven Deadly Sins*—show him on top form, though the music is an essential component in these works. Of his other plays, the "parables"—*The Caucasian Chalk Circle* and *The Good Woman of Sezuan*—are generally more successful than those with a more overtly political tone.

LEGENDS AND FOLKLORE

Jacob and Wilhelm Grimm *Complete Grimm's Tales* (Pantheon, $9.95). The world's most famous collection of folktales, meticulously researched by the Brothers Grimm, has stories to appeal to all age ranges.

Anonymous *The Nibelungenlied* (Penguin, $4.95). Germany's greatest epic was written around 1200 by an unknown Danubian poet; the story varies greatly from Wagner's *Ring*, which draws equally heavily on Nordic sources of the legend. It's here given a highly entertaining prose translation.

Gottfried von Strassburg *Tristan* (Penguin, $4.95), **Wolfram von Eschenbach** *Parzifal* (Random House, $6.95) are two more epic masterpieces from early thirteenth-century Germany, both based on the Holy Grail and associated legends.

Jennifer Russ *German Festivals and Customs* (Ungar, $12.95). A pity it's not a bit longer, but this book provides useful background information on all the main annual folklore celebrations.

THE ARTS

Amazingly, there's no good general book in English specifically on Germany's art and architecture. Standard academic monographs are, of course, available on the work of most of the great German painters, though these are usually very expensive, and prone to go out of print quickly. Many of the Pelican *History of Art* series are partly devoted to Germany; coverage is always very sound, with good black and white photographs, but the coverage is essentially scholarly and very dry.

Albrecht Dürer *The Complete Woodcuts* (Dover, $9.95), *The Complete Etchings, Engravings and Drypoints* (Dover, $8.95). These two books enable you to own, at minimal cost, a complete set of the graphic work of one of the world's greatest-ever masters of the art. The book of wooducts is particularly recommended.

Jost Amman *The Book of Trades* (Dover, $4.95). As much a work of history and literature as of art, the 114 woodcuts illustrate the trades and crafts practiced in early sixteenth century Germany; each is accompanied by a poem by the most famous of the *Meistersinger*, Hans Sachs.

Michael Baxendall *The Limewood Sculptors of Renaissance Germany* (Yale University Press, $18.95). One of the best art history books published in recent years, this examines the work of Tilman Riemenschneider, Veit Stoss, and many other lesser-known artists, in their social and political context. A lavish series of photographs accompanies the text.

William Vaughan *German Romantic Painting* (Yale University Press, $22.50). A good introduction to many of Germany's best nineteenth century artists, though the price is high for a book mostly illustrated in black and white.

Wolf-Dieter Dube *The Expressionists* (Thames & Hudson, $11.95). A good general introduction to Germany's most distinctive contribution to twentieth-century art.

Julius Baum *German Cathedrals* (Vanguard, O/P), **Ernst Gall** *Cathedrals and Abbeys of the Rhineland* (Abrams, O/P). It's well worth seeking these out in a library, particularly for their outstanding black-and-white photographs of architectural and sculptural details.

John Sandford *The New German Cinema* (Da Capo Press, $13.95). Now somewhat out-of-date, but gives good coverage for the period up to 1980.

GUIDE BOOKS

Karl Baedeker *The Rhineland, Northern Germany, Southern Germany, Berlin* (all O/P, but staple fare at second-hand bookshops). The old Baedekers are still indispensible classics. They covered a Germany which was considerably more extensive than it is today, stretching well into what is now the Soviet Union. Look out for the editions dating from the early years of the present century, immensely learned, and full of now-untenable opinions. The glossy successors to these (published in North America by Prentice Hall) are not in the same class.

Bob Larson *Your Swabian Neighbors* (available only in Germany). Written by a U.S. Army liaison officer and long-time resident of the semimythical part of Southern Germany known as Swabia, this book is very American and error-prone in places, but is nonetheless a highly entertaining and remarkably candid account of a fascinating part of the country.

George Wood *The Black Forest* (Hunter Publishing, New York $8.95). The only specific guide for hiking or driving around one of Germany's most beautiful—and touristed—areas; unfortunately, a bit short on detail.

LANGUAGE

German is a very complex language and you can't hope to master it in a short time. As English is a compulsory subject in the Federal Republic's school curriculum, most people who have grown up since the war have some familiarity with it, which eases communication a great deal. Nonetheless, a smattering of German does help, especially in out-of-the-way rural areas. Also, given that the country is occupied by American and British forces who make little effort to integrate into local communities or learn German, people are particularly sensitive to presumptious English-speakers. On the other hand, most will be delighted to practise their English on you once you've stumbled through your German introduction. Should you be interested in studying the language during your stay, the best places to enrol in are the *Goethe-Instituten*, which can be found in most major cities. The German Tourist Board or local information offices have all relevant addresses.

The most useful dictionary is the pocket-sized *German-English Dictionary* (Langenscheidt, $4.95), while the best phrase book for your trip is *Berlitz German for Travelers* (Macmillan, $4.95).

PRONUNCIATION

English speakers find the complexities of German grammar hard to handle, but pronunciation isn't as daunting as it might first appear. Individual syllables are generally pronounced as they're printed – the trick is learning how to place the stresses in the notoriously lengthy German words.

VOWELS AND UMLAUTS

a as in f**a**ther, but can also be used as in h**u**t

e as in d**a**y

i as in l**ee**k

o as in b**o**ttom

u as in b**oo**t

ä is a combination of a and e, sometimes pronounced like **e** in b**e**t (e.g. Länder) and sometimes like **ai** in p**ai**d (e.g. spät).

ö is a combination of o and e, like the French *eu*

ü is a combination of u and e, like tr**ue**

VOWEL COMBINATIONS

ai as in l**ie**

au as in h**ou**se

ie as in fr**ee**

ei as in tr**ia**l

eu as in **oi**l

CONSONANTS

Consonants are pronounced as they are written, with no silent letters. The differences from English are:

r is given a dry throaty sound, similar to French

s pronounced similar to, but slightly softer than an English z

v pronounced somewhere between f and v

w pronounced same way as English v

z pronounced ts

GENDER

German words can be one of three genders: masculine, feminine or neuter. Each has its own ending and corresponding ending for adjectives attached. If you don't know any German grammar, it's safest to use either neuter or male forms.

The German letter ß, the *Scharfes S*, occasionally replaces *ss* in a word: pronunciation is identical.

BASIC WORDS AND PHRASES

Ja, Nein	Yes, No	*Dieses*	This one
Bitte	Please/ You're welcome	*Jenes*	That one
Bitte Schön	A more polite form of *Bitte*	*Gross, Klein*	Large, Small
Danke, Danke Schön	Thank you, Thank you very much	*Mehr, Weniger*	More, less
Wo, Wann, Warum	Where, When, Why	*Wenig*	A little
		Viel	A lot
Wieviel	How much	*Billig, Teuer*	Cheap, expensive
Hier, Da	Here, There	*Gut, Schlecht*	Good, Bad
Jetzt, Später	Now, Later	*Heiss, Kalt*	Hot, Cold
Geöffnet, offen, auf	All mean 'open'	*Mit, Ohne*	With, Without
		Wo ist . . . ?	Where is . . . ?
Geschlossen, zu	Both mean 'closed'	*Wie komme ich nach . . . ?*	How do I get to (a town)?
Früher	Earlier	*Wie komme ich zur/ zum . . . ?*	How do I get to (a building, place)?
Da drüben	Over there		

GREETINGS AND TIMES

Guten Morgen	Good morning	*Vorgestern*	The day before yesterday
Guten Abend	Good evening		
Guten Tag	Good day	*Übermorgen*	The day after tomorrow
Grüss Gott	Good day (in southern Germany)	*Tag*	Day
		Nacht	Night
Wie geht es Ihnen ?	How are you? (polite)	*Woche*	Week
Wie geht es Dir ?	How are you? (informal)	*Monat*	Month
Lass mich in Ruhe	Leave me alone	*Jahr*	Year
Hau ab	Get lost	*Am Vormittag/ vormittags*	In the morning
Geh weg	Go away		
Heute	Today	*Am Nachmittag/ nachmittags*	In the afternoon
Gestern	Yesterday		
Morgen	Tomorrow	*Am Abend*	In the evening

DAYS, MONTHS AND DATES

Montag	Monday	*Januar*	January	*Frühling*	Spring
Dienstag	Tuesday	*Februar*	February	*Sommer*	Summer
Mittwoch	Wednesday	*März*	March	*Herbst*	Autumn
Donnerstag	Thursday	*April*	April	*Winter*	Winter
Freitag	Friday	*Mai*	May		
Samstag	Saturday	*Juni*	June	*Ferien*	Holidays
Sonnabend	Saturday (in northern Germany)	*Juli*	July	*Feiertag*	Legal holiday
		August	August	*Montag, der erste April*	Monday, the first of April
Sonntag	Sunday	*September*	September	*Der zweite April*	the second of April
		Oktober	October		
		November	November	*Der dritte April*	the third of April
		Dezember	December		

QUESTIONS AND REQUESTS

All inquiries should be prefaced with the phrase *Entschuldigen Sie bitte* (excuse me, please). Note that *Sie* is the polite form of address to be used with everyone except close friends, though young people and students often don't bother with it. The older generation will certainly be offended if you address them with the personal *Du*, as will all officials.

Sprechen Sie Englisch ?	Do you speak English ?	*Die Rechnung bitte*	The bill please
Ich spreche kein Deutsch	I don't speak German	*Die Speisekarte bitte*	The menu please
		Fräulein . . . !	Waitress . . . ! (for attention)
Sprechen sie bitte langsamer	Please speak more slowly	*Herr Ober . . . !*	Waiter . . . ! (for attention)
Ich verstehe nicht	I don't understand		
Ich verstehe	I understand	*Haben Sie etwas billigeres ?*	Have you got something cheaper ?
Wie sagt mann das auf Deutsch ?	How do you say that in German ?	*Haben Sie Zimmer frei ?*	Are there rooms available ?
Können Sie mir sagen wo . . . ist ?	Can you tell me where . . . is ?	*Wo sind die Toiletten bitte ?*	Where are the toilets ?
Wieviel kostet das ?	How much does that cost ?	*Ich hätte gern dieses*	I'd like that one
Wann fährt der nächste Zug ?	When does the next train leave ?	*Ich hätte gern ein Zimmer für zwei*	I'd like a room for two
Um wieviel Uhr ?	At what time ?	*Ich hätte gern ein Einzelzimmer*	I'd like a single room
Wieviel Uhr ist es ?	What time is it ?		
Ist der Tisch frei ?	Is that table free?	*Hat es Dusche, Bad, Toilette . . . ?*	Does it have a shower, bath, toilet . . . ?

NUMBERS

1	*eins*	12	*zwölf*	30	*dreissig*
2	*zwei*	13	*dreizehn*	40	*vierzig*
3	*drei*	14	*vierzehn*	50	*fünfzig*
4	*vier*	15	*fünfzehn*	60	*sechzig*
5	*fünf*	16	*sechszehn*	70	*siebzig*
6	*sechs*	17	*siebzehn*	80	*achtzig*
7	*sieben*	18	*achtzehn*	90	*neunzig*
8	*acht*	19	*neunzehn*	100	*hundert*
9	*neun*	20	*zwanzig*	1989	*neunzehn-hundert-neun-und-achtzig*
10	*zehn*	21	*ein-und-zwanzig*		
11	*elf*	22	*zwei-und-zwanzig*		

SOME SIGNS

Damen/Frauen	Women's toilets	*Geschwindigkeitsbegrenzung*	Speed limit
Herren/Männer	Men's toilets		
Eingang	Entrance	*Baustelle*	Building works
Ausgang	Exit	*Ampel*	Traffic light
Ankunft	Arrival	*Krankenhaus*	Hospital
Abfahrt	Departure	*Polizei*	Police
Ausstellung	Exhibition	*Nicht rauchen*	No smoking
Auffahrt	Motorway entrance	*Kein Eingang*	No entrance
Ausfahrt	Motorway exit	*Verboten*	Prohibited
Umleitung	Diversion	*Zoll*	Customs
Vorsicht !	Attention	*Grenzübergang*	Border crossing

GLOSSARIES

ART AND ARCHITECTURE

AISLE part of church to the side of the nave.

AMBULATORY passage around the back of the altar, in continuation of the aisles.

APSE vaulted termination of the east (altar) end of a church.

ART DECO geometrical style of art and architecture prevalent in 1920s and 1930s.

ART NOUVEAU sinuous, highly stylized form of architecture and interior design; in Germany, mostly dates from period 1900–15, and is known as *Jugendstil*.

BALDACHIN canopy over an altar or tomb.

BAROQUE expansive, exuberant architectural style of seventeenth and early eighteentth centuries, characterized by ornate decoration, complex spatial arrangements and grand vistas. The term is also applied to the sumptuous style of painting of the same period.

BASILICA church in which nave is higher than the aisles.

BAUHAUS plain, functional style of architecure and design, originating in early twentieth-century Germany.

BIEDERMEIER simple, bourgeois style of painting and decoration practiced throughout first half of nineteenth century.

CAPITAL top of a column, usually sculpted.

CHANCEL part of the church in which altar is placed; normally at east end, though some German churches also have one at west end.

CHOIR part of church in which service is sung, usually beside the altar.

CRYPT underground part of a church.

EXPRESSIONISM emotional style of painting, concentrating on line and color, extensively practised in early twentieth-century Germany; term is also used for related architecture of the same period.

FRESCO mural painting applied to wet plaster, so that colors immediately soak into the wall.

GOTHIC architectural style with an emphasis on verticality, characterized by pointed arch, ribbed vault and flying buttress; introduced to Germany around 1235, surviving in an increasingly decorative form until well into the sixteenth century. The term is also used for paintings of this period.

GRISAILLE painting executed entirely in monochrome.

HALF-TIMBERED, TIMBER-FRAMED style of building in which walls have a framework of timber interspersed with bricks or plaster.

HALL CHURCH (*Hallenkirche*) church design much favored in Germany, in which all vaults are of approximately equal height.

LAVABO well-house in a cloister.

MANNERISM deliberately mannered style of late Renaissance art and architecture.

MODELLO small version of a large picture, usually painted for the patron's approval.

NAVE main body of a church, generally forming the western part.

NEOCLASSICAL late eighteenth- and early nineteenth-century style of art and architecture returning to classical models as a reaction against baroque and rococo excesses.

ORIEL projecting bay window.

POLYPTYCH carved or painted altarpiece on several joined panels.

PREDELLA lowest part of an altarpiece, with scenes much smaller than in main sections.

RENAISSANCE Italian-originated movement in art and architecture, inspired by the rediscovery of classical ideals.

RETABLE altarpiece.

ROCOCO highly florid, light and graceful eighteenth-century style of architecture, painting and interior design; the last phase of baroque.

ROMANESQUE solid architectural style of late tenth- to mid-thirteenth-century, characterized by round-headed arches and a penchant for horizontality and geometrical precision. The term is also used for paintings of this period.

ROMANTICISM late eighteenth- and nineteenth-century movement, particularly strong in Germany, rooted in adulation of the natural world and rediscovery of the achievements of the Middle Ages.

ROOD SCREEN screen dividing nave from chancel (thus separating laity and clergy), originally bearing a rood (crucifix).

SOFT STYLE (*Weicher Stil*) delicate style of painting and sculpture pioneered in fourteenth century Bohemia, which dominated German art to the mid-fifteenth century.

STUCCO plaster used for decorative effects.

TABERNACLE a free-standing canopy or ornamental recess designed to contain the Holy Sacrament.

TRANSEPT arms of a cross-shaped church, placed at ninety degrees to nave and chancel.

TRANSITIONAL architectural style between Romanesque and Gothic in which the basic shapes of the older style were modified by the use of such new forms as the pointed arch and ribbed vault.

TRIPTYCH carved or painted altarpiece on three panels.

TROMPE L'OEIL painting designed to fool the viewer into believing its flat surface is three-dimensional.

TYMPANUM sculptured panel above a doorway.

WESER RENAISSANCE archaic, highly elaborate style of secular Renaissance architecture cultivated in and around the Weser valley in Hessen, Lower Saxony and Westphalia.

WESTWORK (*Westwerk*) grandiose frontage found on many German medieval churches, traditionally reserved for the use of the emperor and his retinue.

GERMAN TERMS

ABTEI abbey

ALTSTADT old part of a city

AUSKUNFT information

AUSSTELLUNG exhibition

BAD spa (before the name of a town), bath

BAHNHOF station

BAU building

BERG mountain, hill

BERGBAHN funicular

BIBLIOTHEK library

BRÜCKE bridge

BRUNNEN fountain, well

BUNDESKANZLER Federal Chancellor (prime minister)

BUNDESRAT Upper house of West German parliament

BUNDESTAG Lower house of West German parliament

BURG castle, fortress

BURGERMEISTER mayor

CAROLINGIAN dynasty founded by Charles Martel in early eighth century which ruled Germany until last quarter of ninth century. The term is particularly associated with the reign of Charlemagne (768–814).

DENKMAL memorial

DIET parliament of Holy Roman Empire

DOM cathedral

DONAU Danube River

DORF village

EASTERN TERRITORIES lands to the east of the Oder-Neisse line, occupied by German-speaking peoples since the Middle Ages, but forcibly evacuated, and allocated to Poland and the Soviet Union after the Second World War.

EINBAHNSTRASSE one-way street

ELECTOR (*Kurfürst*) sacred or secular prince with a vote in the elections to choose the Holy Roman Emperor. There were seven during most of the medieval period, with three more added later.

EVANGELISCHE KIRCHE federation of Protestant churches, both Lutheran and Reformed

FACHWERKHAUS half-timbered house

FASCHING name given to Carnival, especially in Bavaria

FASTNET name given to Carnival, especially in Baden-Württemberg

FEIERTAG legal holiday

FEST festival

FESTUNG fortress

FLUGHAFEN airport

FLUSS river

FRANCONIA (*Franken*) historical province of central Germany, stretching as far west as Mainz; name later became associated only with the eastern portion of this territory, most of which is now in Northern Bavaria.

FREE IMPERIAL CITY (*Freiereichstadt*) independent city state within the Holy Roman Empire

FREMDENZIMMER room for short-term rental

FÜRST Prince

FUSSGÄNGERZONE pedestrian area

GASSE alley

GASTARBEITER ('guest worker') anyone who comes to West Germany to do menial work

GASTHAUS, GASTHOF guest house, inn

GEMÄLDE painting

GRAF Count

GRÜNEN, DIE ('The Greens') West German party formed from environmental and anti-nuclear groups.

HAPSBURG the most powerful family in medieval Germany, operating from a power base in Austria. They held the office of Holy Roman Emperor from 1452 to 1806, and by marriage, war and diplomacy acquired territories all over Europe.

HAFEN harbor, port

HANSEATIC LEAGUE medieval trading alliance of Baltic and Rhineland cities, numbering about 100 at its fifteenth-century peak. Slowly died out in seventeenth century with competition from Baltic nation-states, and rise of Brandenburg-Prussia.

HAUPTBAHNHOF main railway station in a city

HAUPTBURG central, residential part of a castle

HAUPTSTRASSE main street

HEIDE heath

HEIMAT homeland; often given a mystical significance and used emotively in connection with Germans displaced from the Eastern Territories.

HERZOG Duke

HÖHLE cave

HOF court, courtyard, mansion

HOHENSTAUFEN Swabian dynasty who held office of Holy Roman Emperor from1138 to1254

HOHENZOLLERN dynasty of Swabian origin, who became margrave-electors of Brandenburg in 1415, and slowly built up their territorial base. In nineteenth century, they ousted the Hapsburgs from preeminent place in German affairs, forging the Second Reich in 1871, and serving as its Emperors until 1918.

HOLY ROMAN EMPIRE title used to describe the First German Reich, established in 800. Despite its weak structure, it survived until 1806, when the ruling Hapsburgs, in response to the Napoleonic threat, began building up a more solid empire from their Austrian base.

INSEL island

JAGDSCHLOSS hunting lodge

JUGENDHERBERGE youth hostel

JUGENDSTIL German version of art nouveau

JUNKER Prussian landowning class

KAISER Emperor

KAMMER room, chamber

KAPELLE chapel

KARNEVAL term used for Carnival, especially in Rhineland

KAUFHAUS department store

KIRCHE church

KLOSTER monastery, convent

KÖNIG King

KRANKENHAUS hospital

KREUZGANG cloister

KUNST art

KURHAUS assembly rooms (in a spa)

KURORT health resort

LAND (pl. **LÄNDER**) name given to the constituent states of the Federal Republic; first introduced in Weimar Republic

LANDGRAVE (*Landgraf*) count in charge of a large province

MARGRAVE (*Markgraf*) count in charge of a *Mark* ("March"; later "Margraviate", a frontier district first established at the time of Charlemagne

MARKT market, market square

MEER sea

MEROVINGIAN Frankish dynasty established by Clovis in 481; ruled until early eighth century

MIKWE Jewish ritual bath

MÜNSTER minster, large church

NATURPARK area of protected countyside

ODER-NEISSE LINE eastern limit of German territory set by victorious Allies in 1945

OSTPOLITIK West German policy of detente towards the GDR

OTTONIAN epoch of Otto I and his two eponymous sucessors. Term is used in connection with the early Romanesque art forms pioneered in this and the subsequent Salian epoch (mid-tenth to mid-eleventh century).

PALAS, PALAST residential part of a castle

PALATINATE (*Pfalz*) territory ruled by the countpalatine, a high-ranking imperial official. The present Land is only the western part of the historical province, whose original center is now part of Baden-Württemberg.

PFARRKIRCHE parish church

PLATZ square

PRINZ prince; since 1918, used in a less grandiose way as a courtesy title for aristocrats in place of the plethora of now-defunct titles.

PROPSTEIKIRCHE former monastic church transferred to parish use

PRUSSIA originally, an Eastern Baltic territory (now divided between Poland and the Soviet Union). It was acquired in 1525 by the Hohenzollerns who merged it with their own possessions to form Brandenburg-Prussia (later shortened to Prussia); this took the lead in forging the unity of Germany, and was thereafter its overwhelmingly dominant province. The name was abolished after the World War II because of its monarchical and militaristic connotations.

RASTPLATZ picnic area

RATHAUS town hall

RATSKELLER cellars below the Rathaus, invariably used as a restaurant serving *burgerlich* cuisine.

REICH empire

REISEBEÜRO travel agency

RESIDENZ palace

RITTER knight

ROMANTISCHE STRASSE ('Romantic Road') scenic road in Bavaria and Baden-Württemberg, running between Würzburg and Füssen.

RUNDGANG detour

SAAL hall

SALIAN dynasty of Holy Roman Emperors 1024–1125

SAMMLUNG collection

SAXONY (*Sachsen*) historic province, originally associated with the area now known as Lower Saxony, but reaching the height of its power when centered on the March of Lusatia, now the central and southern part of the GDR.

S-BAHN commuter railway network operating in and around conurbations

SCHATZKAMMER treasury

SCHICKIE yuppie

SCHLOSS castle, palace (equivalent of French *château*)

SEE lake

SEILBAHN cable car

SESSELBAHN chair lift

STADT town, city

STAMMTISCH table in a pub or restaurant reserved for regular customers

STAUFIAN pertaining to the epoch of th Hohenstaufen

STIFT collegiate church

STIFTUNG foundation

STRAND beach

STRASSENBAHN tram

SWABIA (*Schwaben*) name used for the southwestern part of Germany from eleventh century onwards; after the ruling Hohenstaufen dynasty died out, became politically fragmented

TAL valley

TALSPERRE reservoir, artificial lake

TANKSTELLE petrol station

TOR gate, gateway

TURM tower

U-BAHN network of underground trains or trams

VERKEHRSAMT, **VERKEHRSVEREIN** tourist office

VIERTEL quarter, district

VOLK people, folk; given mystical associations by Hitler

VORBURG outer, defensive part of a castle

WALD forest

WALDSTERBEN ('dying forest syndrome') term used to describe the environmental pollution which has decimated Germany's forests.

WALLFAHRT pilgrimage

WASSERBURG castle surrounded by a moat

WECHSEL exchange

WEIMAR REPUBLIC Parliamentary democracy established in 1918 which collapsed with Hitler's assumption of power in 1933.

WELF dynastic rivals of Hohenstaufens in Germany and Italy. Descendants became Electors of Hannover, and subsequently kings of Great Britain.

WIES field, meadow

WILHELMINE pertaining to the epoch of the Second Reich (1871–1918)

WITTELSBACH dynasty which ruled Bavaria from 1180 to 1918; a branch held the Palatinate electorate, while the family often held several bishoprics, notably the archbishopric-electorate of Cologne.

ZEUGHAUS arsenal

ZIMMER room

ACRONYMS

BRD (*Bundesrepublik Deutschlands*) official name of West Germany

CDU (*Christlich Demokratische Union*) ruling Christian Democratic (Conservative) Party

CSU (*Christlich Soziale Union*) Bavarian-only counterpart of CDU, generally more right-wing in outlook.

DB (*Deutsche Bundesbahn*) national railway company

DDR (*Deutsche Demokratische Republik*) official name of East Germany

GDR ('German Democratic Republic') English version of DDR

FDP (*Freie Demokratische Partei*) Free Democratic (Liberal) Party

NSDAP (*National Sozialistische Deutsche Abrbeiterpartei*, 'National Socialist German Workers' Party') official name for the Nazis, totalitarian rulers of Germany in the Third Reich of 1933–45.

SPD (*Sozialdemokratische Partei Deutschlands*) Social Democratic (Labor) Party

INDEX

HELP US UPDATE

We've gone to considerable effort to ensure that this first edition of the Real Guide: Germany is completely up-to-date and accurate. However, things do change – new restaurants and clubs appear, old favorites disappear, opening hours can be fickle—and any suggestions, comments, or corrections would be much appreciated. We'll credit all contributions, and send a copy of the next edition (or any other Real Guide if you prefer) for the best letters. Send them along to: The Real Guides, Prentice Hall, 1 Gulf + Western Plaza, New York, NY 10023.